The SAGE
Handbook of

Organizational
Research Methods

International Editorial Board

The SAGE
Handbook of

Organizational
Research Methods

Edited by
David A. Buchanan
and Alan Bryman

Los Angeles | London | New Delhi
Singapore | Washington DC

SAGE Publications Ltd
1 Oliver's Yard
55 City Road
London EC1Y 1SP

SAGE Publications Inc.
2455 Teller Road
Thousand Oaks, California 91320

SAGE Publications India Pvt Ltd
B 1/I 1 Mohan Cooperative Industrial Area
Mathura Road, Post Bag 7
New Delhi 110 044

SAGE Publications Asia-Pacific Pte Ltd
33 Pekin Street #02-01
Far East Square
Singapore 048763

Library of Congress Control Number: 2008935008

British Library Cataloguing in Publication data

A catalogue record for this book is available from the British Library

ISBN 978-1-4129-3118-2

Typeset by CEPHA Imaging Pvt. Ltd., Bangalore, India
Printed in Great Britain by MPG Books Group, Bodmin, Cornwall
Printed on paper from sustainable resources

Contents

**PART IV   METHODS: DATA COLLECTION IN
            ORGANIZATIONAL RESEARCH   449**

*Focusing on methods of data collection in organizational research, demonstrating the
inventiveness and innovation that now characterizes this field, and the widening range
of possibilities concerning the development of data collection tools.*

Acknowledgements

We would like to thank, first of all, the many contributors for the time, experience, effort, and insights that they have devoted to this project. Most chapters went through a number of drafts, in response to the reviews which some contributors had arranged on their own behalf, in addition to editorial commentary and feedback from members of our editorial board. This process was inevitably protracted, and we are extremely grateful to our contributors for their patience and their perseverance. We would like to thank in particular Emma Bell, Tim Hinkin, Tom Keenoy, and Michael Moss for their additional services in commenting on draft chapters. We must also thank, of course, the editorial board members who have played a major role in shaping the overall content of this *Handbook* as well as providing constructive reviews of chapters. Some editorial board members are also contributors in their own right, for which we are, naturally, doubly grateful.

We also owe a considerable debt to Patrick Brindle at Sage Publications for initiating and commissioning this project. Patrick's enthusiasm, encouragement, patience, and support have been instrumental throughout. Patrick's assistant, Claire Lipscomb, has also played a valuable role in dealing with the contractual and other administrative components of this project, and we are very grateful for her assistance and support, too.

About the contributors

Stephen Ackroyd is Professor of Organizational Analysis in the Lancaster University Management School, Lancaster, UK. He has published in some of the major journals in the organization studies and management fields, and is a member of the editorial board of many, including *Journal of Management Studies*, *Organization Studies*, and *Work, Employment and Society*. His books include: *Realist Perspectives on Management and Organization* (2000) and *Critical Realist Applications in Organization and Management Studies* (2004; both written and edited with S. Fleetwood), *The Organization of Business* (2002), and *The New Managerialism and the Public Service Professions* (2005, with Ian Kirkpatrick). Recently, he has co-edited and co-authored, with R. Batt and others, *The Oxford Handbook of Work and Organizations* (2006) and, with D. Muzio and J-F Chanlat, *Redirections in the Study of Expert Labour* (2007). His current research is concerned with the activities and strategies of the largest British companies still involved in manufacturing, and the current transformation of British and American capitalism.

Mats Alvesson is Professor at the Department of Business Administration, Lund University, Sweden, and University of Queensland Business School, Australia. He is author/co-author of numerous articles and books, including *Reflexive Methodology* (Sage, 2009, second edition with Kaj Sköldberg), *Postmodernism and Social Research* (Open University Press, 2002), *Knowledge Work and Knowledge-Intensive Firms* (Oxford University Press, 2004) and *Changing Organizational Culture* (Routledge, 2008, with Stefan Sveningsson). Research interests include methodology, leadership, identity, and organizational analysis.

Alison L. Antes is a doctoral student in the Industrial and Organizational Psychology program at the University of Oklahoma, USA. Her research interests include ethics and leadership.

Karen Lee Ashcraft is an Associate Professor at the University of Utah Department of Communication, USA. Her work addresses organizational forms and occupational identity and has appeared in such forums as *Administrative Science Quarterly, Academy of Management Journal,* and *Communication Theory*. Her book with Dennis Mumby, *Reworking Gender*, examines the complex relationship between critical organization studies and gender and feminist scholarship. Her current research investigates the role of gender, race, and the body in the evolution of commercial airline flying as a profession.

Emma Bell is Senior Lecturer in Organization Studies at the University of Bath, UK. She is the co-author of *Business Research Methods* (with Alan Bryman, revised edition, 2007) and has published articles and chapters on research ethics, ethnography, and visual methods. A substantial aspect of her work at the moment explores the relationship between religion, spirituality and organization, and also considers notions of organizational death and loss. Her research has consistently focused on the critical study of management and organization, and has been published in *Human Relations, Journal of Management Studies* and *Organization*. Her most recent book, *Reading Management and Organization in Film* (2008) is published by Palgrave Macmillan.

Alex B. Bitektine is Assistant Professor of Strategy at the Department of Management, HEC-Montreal, in Quebec, Canada. He is an author of several articles and papers exploring the use of innovative research methods in organization theory research (*Organizational Research Methods, 2008; Corporate Reputation Review, 2008*). Research interests include institutional theory, non-market strategies, and research methods. Current projects include studies of regulation-seeking behaviour in emergent industries, the institutional aspects of industry emergence, and global isomorphic pressures on MNCs from developing countries.

Maree Boyle is Senior Lecturer at Griffith Business School in Brisbane, Australia. Her research interests involve gender, organization and consumption, emotionalized workplaces, critical approaches to work-life balance, autobiographical and reflexive accounts of organizational experience, and organizational geographies.

Michael T. Brannick is Professor of Psychology at the University of South Florida, USA. He is author/co-author of numerous articles and books, including *Job and Work Analysis: Methods, Research and Applications for Human Resource Management* (second edition, with Edward Levine and Fred Morgeson, 2007), and *Team Performance Assessment and Measurement* (with Eduardo Salas and Carolyn Prince, 1997). His current research interests include research methods, particularly methods of meta-analysis, measuring individual and team performance, and work simulations in healthcare.

Alan Bryman is Professor of Organizational and Social Research, School of Management, University of Leicester, UK. He is author/co-author of numerous articles and books, including *Social Research Methods* (third edition, 2008) and *Business Research Methods* (with Emma Bell, revised edition, 2007). He is co-editor of *The SAGE Encyclopedia of Social Science Research Methods* (Sage, 2004) and *Handbook of Data Analysis* (Sage, 2004). Research interests include methodology, leadership, and organizational analysis. His current research interests include mixed methods research and leadership in higher education.

David A. Buchanan is Professor of Organizational Behaviour at Cranfield University, School of Management, UK. He is author/co-author of numerous articles and books, including *The Sustainability and Spread of Organizational Change* (with Louise Fitzgerald and Diane Ketley, 2007), *Organizational Behaviour* (2007, with Andrzej Huczynski) and *Power, Politics, and Organizational Change* (with Richard Badham, 2008). Research interests include change management and organization politics; current projects include a study of the realities of middle and front line management work in healthcare, and managing change in extreme contexts.

Marta B. Calás (PhD University of Massachusetts) is Professor of Organization Studies and International Management at the Isenberg School of Management of the University of Massachusetts, Amherst, USA, and adjunct faculty in this university's Women's Studies Program. She teaches undergraduate courses in International Management and doctoral courses in Conceptual Foundations of Organization Studies, Research and Theory in International Organization Studies, and Interdisciplinary Organization Theory and Research. Her work over the years continues to pursue the development of critical and socially engaged organization and management studies. Her research, in collaboration with Linda Smircich, applies insights from cultural studies and feminist theorizing to organizational topics such as business ethics, globalization, and issues of work and family. In 2006 Marta and Linda received the Sage Award for scholarly contributions from the Gender, Diversity and Organization division of the Academy of Management. Marta is part of the founding editorial team of *Organization: The critical journal of organization, theory and society*.

Glenn R. Carroll is Laurence W. Lane Professor of Organizations at Stanford University's Graduate School of Business and (by courtesy) Professor of Sociology, USA. He is also Chair (part-time), Durham Business School, Durham University, UK and Professor II, Department of Sociology and Human Geography, University of Oslo, Norway. His most recent books include *The Logics of Organization Theory: Audiences, Codes and Ecologies* (with M.T. Hannan and L. Pólos, Princeton University Press, 2007), and *Culture and Demography in Organizations* (with J.R. Harrison, Princeton University Press, 2006).

Catherine Cassell is Professor of Occupational Psychology at Manchester Business School, UK, where she is also Director of the School's postgraduate research programmes. Her research interests are in the area of organizational change, learning, and development and she has a particular interest in the uses of qualitative research in the organization and management field. Together with Gillian Symon from Birkbeck she has edited three books for Sage about qualitative research methods, the most recent being *Essential Guide to Qualitative Methods in Organizational Research*. She is joint editor of *Qualitative Research in Organizations and Management: An International Journal*, and an associate editor of the *British Journal of Management*.

Jay J. Caughron is a doctoral student in the Industrial and Organizational Psychology program at the University of Oklahoma, USA. His research interests include planning, creativity, and ethics.

Stewart Clegg is Research Professor and Director of CMOS Research at the University of Technology, Sydney, Australia. He is also a Visiting Professor at Copenhagen Business School and EM-Lyon. He is a prolific publisher in leading academic journals in management and organization theory, as well as the author of many books, including *A Very Short, Fairly Interesting, Reasonably Cheap Book about Studying Strategy* (with Chris Carter and Martin Kornberger, London, Sage, 2008), *Managing and Organizations: An Introduction to Theory and Practice* (with Martin Kornberger and Tyrone Pitsis, London, Sage, 2008), *The International Encyclopaedia of Organization Studies* (co-edited with James Bailey, Thousand Oaks, CA, Sage, 2008), and *Power and Organizations* (with David Courpasson and Nelson Phillips, Thousand Oaks, CA, Sage, 2006, Foundations of Organization Science series).

Robert J. David (PhD Cornell University) is Associate Professor of Strategy & Organization and Cleghorn Faculty Scholar at the Desautels Faculty of Management of McGill University, Canada. He is also Director of the Center for Strategy Studies in Organization at McGill. He studies the evolution of practices, organizations, and industries from an institutional perspective. Robert has published articles in *Research Policy*, *Strategic Management Journal*, *Academy of Management Journal*, and *Organization Science*.

Stanley Deetz, PhD, is Professor of Communication and Director of Peace and Conflict Studies at the University of Colorado, USA. He is author/co-author of numerous articles and books, including *Leading Organizations through Transitions* (2000, with Tracy and Simpson), *Doing Critical Management Research* (2000, with Mats Alvesson), and *Democracy in an Age of Corporate Colonization* (1992). His research focuses on corporate governance and communication processes in relation to democracy, micropractices of power, and collaborative decision making.

Jean-Louis Denis is Director of the Interdisciplinary Health Research Group, Professor at the Health Administration Department, and holds a CHSRF/CIHR Chair on the transformation and governance of health care organizations at the Université de Montréal, Canada. He is author/co-author of numerous publications, including *Governance and Management of Change in Canada's Health System* (2004), *A Knowledge Utilization Perspective on Fine-Tuning Dissemination and Contextualizing Knowledge* (with Pascale Lehoux and François Champagne, 2004), and 'Strategizing in pluralistic contexts: rethinking theoretical frames', in *Human Relations* (with Ann Langley and Linda Rouleau, 2007). Research interests include strategic change and leadership in pluralistic organizations, governance of health organizations, and the role of scientific evidence in the management of health care organizations.

David Denyer is a Senior Lecturer in Organization Studies at Cranfield School of Management. His research interests include evidence-based management, the analysis of social and organizational networks, safety leadership and managing change in extreme contexts. He has successfully completed two research council funded projects and numerous industry funded research projects. He teaches on various executive development programmes and speaks frequently at international academic and management conferences. He runs a novel part time masters programme which is targeted at busy practitioners who are interested in leadership, learning and development and change management.

MariaLaura Di Domenico is Lecturer in Organizational Behaviour at the Open University Business School, UK. Her research interests include discourse analysis, ethnography, organizational and individual identity, poststructural theory, social entrepreneurship, social and community enterprises, small and medium sized enterprises (SMEs), and home-work boundaries. Her research is published in journals such as *Human Relations, Organization Studies* and *Gender, Work and Organization*, as well as in books and monographs.

Sue Dopson is the Rhodes Trust Professor of Organizational Behaviour at the Said Business School, University of Oxford, UK. Her research interests include the changing nature of management work, the value and impact of case study research, workforce issues in health care, leadership in the public sector, and the management of innovation and change in health care. Current research includes the study of networks in health care, and exploring the role of support workers in the National Health Servive. She is author/co-author of numerous articles and books on these topics.

Mi Feng is a PhD candidate in Organizational Behavior at the Stanford Graduate School of Business, USA. His research interests include market competition in multiple geographic markets, technology management, and technology change in uncertain environments. Mi's dissertation focuses on the interaction between local embeddedness and geographic scope advantage that shapes the competitiveness of multi-location organizations.

Gary Alan Fine is the John Evans Professor of Sociology at Northwestern University, USA. He received his PhD in social psychology from Harvard University. For the past thirty years, he has published a set of ethnographies on topics of work and leisure, particularly examining the role of small group culture in the development of organizational affiliation. Among the research sites he has studied are Little League Baseball teams, fantasy role-play gaming groups, restaurant kitchens, mushroom collecting clubs, and meteorological offices. His current research is on the domains of competitive chess.

Louise Fitzgerald is Professor of Organization Development, Department of Human Resource Management, De Montfort University, UK. Her research centres on the management of innovation and change in professional, complex organizations, and the restructuring of professional roles. She is currently working on a major empirical project on the management of organizational networks in healthcare. She has published in a range of journals, such as *Academy of Management Journal* and *Human Relations*, and has co-authored a number of books, such as *Knowledge to Action? Evidence based health care in context* (Oxford University Press, 2005) and *The Sustainability and Spread of Organizational Change*, (Routledge, 2007). She has previously worked at City University, Warwick University, and Salford University.

Tamara L. Friedrich is a doctoral student in the Industrial and Organizational Psychology program at the University of Oklahoma, USA. Her research interests include creativity and leadership.

Christina Goulding is Professor of Consumer Research at The University of Wolverhampton, Wolverhampton Business School, UK. She has published a number of articles on qualitative research and consumer behaviour. She is author of *Grounded Theory: A Practical Guide for Management, Business and Market Researchers* (London, Sage, 2002) and joint editor of *Critical Marketing: Defining the Field* (London, Butterworth Heinemann, 2007). Her research interests include qualitative methodologies, consumer culture, identity and consumption, subcultures of consumption, and transgressive consumer behaviour.

David Greatbatch is Visiting Professor of Organizational Communication, Durham Business School, University of Durham, UK. He is author/co-author of numerous articles and books, including *Management Speak: Why We Listen to What Management Gurus Tell Us* (2005, with Timothy Clark). His research focuses on public speaking and interpersonal communication in organizational contexts. Current projects include studies of organizational storytelling, and the use of oratory by organizational leaders.

Royston Greenwood is the Telus Professor of Strategic Management and Associate Dean (Research) at the School of Business, University of Alberta, and Visiting Professor, Said Business School, University of Oxford. His current research focuses upon institutional processes and organizational change at the community level of analysis, with special interest in the role of the professions. His work has appeared in the *Administrative Science Quarterly*, *Academy of Management Journal*, *Academy of Management Review*, *Organization Science*, and *Organization Studies*. He serves on several editorial boards, is co-editor of *Strategic Organization*, and is a co-editor of the recently published *Sage Handbook on Organizational Institutionalism*.

Mark Griffin is Professor of Work Psychology in the Institute of Work Psychology at the University of Sheffield, UK. He received his PhD in Industrial/Organizational psychology from The Pennsylvania State University and has published his research in journals such as *Academy of Management Journal*, *Journal of Applied Psychology*, *Journal of Management*, and *Personnel Psychology*. He has managed large-scale organizational studies in areas such as leadership, safety, work performance, organizational climate, and work stress. His research seeks to understand the multilevel relationship between performance and well-being for individuals, teams, and organizations.

John S. Hassard is Professor of Organizational Analysis at Manchester Business School (Manchester University) and Senior Research Associate in Management Learning at the Judge Business School (Cambridge University), UK. His research interests are in organization theory, research methods, and comparative studies of management. Professor Hassard has published 13 books, and over 100 research articles, and has received a large number of awards from UK research councils. He is currently a Council Member of the Society for the Advancement of Management Studies.

Timothy R. Hinkin is Professor of Management at the School of Hotel Administration, Cornell University. He was founding co-editor of *Journal of Quality Assurance in Hospitality & Tourism*, and is associate editor of *Organizational Research Methods*. He is author of *Cases in Hospitality: A Critical Incident Approach* (second edition, 2006), and has published over 50 articles, as well as many book chapters. His research focuses primarily on leadership, managing service quality, employee turnover, and research methods.

Brooks C. Holtom is an assistant professor of management in the McDonough School of Business at Georgetown University in Washington DC, USA. In his dissertation he developed job embeddedness theory and has since reported a number of studies exploring and expanding the construct. These studies have appeared in the *Academy of Management Journal, Journal of Applied Psychology, Human Resource Management*, and *International Journal of Human Resource Management*. This research relied heavily on survey methodology and consequently stimulated interest in understanding how to improve it.

Ann Langley is Professor of Management at HEC Montréal, Canada and Canada research chair in strategic management in pluralistic settings. She is the author/co-author of numerous articles and two books, including *Strategy as Practice: Research Directions and Resources* (with Gerry Johnson, Leif Melin and Richard Whittington; Cambridge University Press, 2007). Her research deals with strategic management processes and practices in pluralistic organizations, notably health care. She has a particular interest in qualitative research methods, and is involved in studies of the dynamics of top management teams, strategic change, the diffusion of innovation, and the use of formalized strategic management tools such as strategic plans.

Mark Learmonth is an Associate Professor at Nottingham University Business School, UK. He is author/co-author of numerous articles and books, including *Leadership as Identity* (Palgrave, 2008), a co-edited volume, *Unmasking Health Management* (Nova Science, 2004), with another co-edited volume, *Public Sector Management: A Critical Approach*, forthcoming with Routledge in 2009. Qualitative studies of organizational issues in health remain a major focus for research, although forays into other areas are becoming increasingly regular. Particular interests include critical management education, and the different ways in which evidence can inform organizational life. Among current projects are a hospital ethnography, an exploration of the contribution of post-colonialism to empirical work, and the impact that reflections on personal mortality might have on our working life.

Pascale Lehoux is Full Professor with the Department of Health Administration, and Researcher with the *Groupe de Recherche Interdisciplinaire en Santé* (GRIS) at University of Montreal, Canada. She holds a Canada Research Chair on Innovation in Health and is the Canadian Director of an International Master's Program in Health Technology Assessment and Management, a project involving four universities in Canada and Europe. She has published more than 60 papers examining the use of computerized medical records, telemedicine, scientific knowledge, home care equipment, and mobile and satellite dialysis units. Her book, *The Problem of Health Technology*, was published in 2006 by Routledge. Her current research program examines the design process of health technology.

David G. McKendrick is Chair of Strategy at Durham University's Business School, UK. His research focuses on industrial and organizational evolution, strategic management, international competition, and the emergence of organizational forms. He is coauthor of *From Silicon Valley to Singapore: Location and Competitive Advantage in the Hard Disk Drive Industry* (Stanford University Press, 2000).

Adam W. Meade is an Associate Professor in the Department of Psychology at North Carolina State University, USA. He is the author of numerous published articles in peer-reviewed journals and serves on the editorial board of *Organizational Research Methods*. His research interests are related to psychological and organizational measurement issues.

Gaël Le Mens is a PhD candidate in Organizational Behavior at the Stanford Graduate School of Business, USA. His research interests include organizational theory and the psychology of learning, judgment and decision-making. Currently, Gaël develops a research program with Jerker Denrell that focuses on the role of information acquisition patterns on belief and attitude formation. A first theoretical paper has appeared in *Psychological Review* ('Interdependent sampling and social influence', 2007). Recent developments include results about the role of foregone payoffs on belief formation, as well as how attributes of multi-attributes alternatives interact in shaping learning.

Calvin Morrill is Professor of Sociology, Business, and Criminology, Law & Society at the University of California, Irvine, USA, where he has taught since 2001, and was former chair of the Sociology Department. His research interests span a wide variety of topics: law and society, organizational and institutional change, culture, qualitative field methods, sociology of youth and education, and social networks. His books include: *The Executive Way: Conflict Management in Corporations* (Chicago, 1995), with David A. Snow and Cindy White, *Together Alone: Personal Relationships in Public Places* (California, 2005) and, with Michael Musheno, *Makin' It Work: Youth Conflict and Control in a Multiethnic Suburban High School* (Chicago, forthcoming). His current research focuses on law and conflict in schools, and the role of social movements in organizational change.

Michael Moss is Research Professor in Archival Studies at the University of Glasgow, UK, where he directs the MSc programme in Information Management and Preservation. He is a non-executive director of the National Archives of Scotland and the National Trust for Scotland, and a member of the Lord Chancellor's Advisory Committee on National Archives and Records. He has a wide range of research interests. His recent books include *The Building of Europe's Largest Mutual Life Company – Standard Life 1825–2000* (Mainstream, 2000), *The Magnificent Castle of Culzean and the Kennedy Family* (Edinburgh, 2003), with Laurence Brockliss as co-editor, *Advancing with the Army: Medicine, the Professions and Social Mobility in the British Isles 1790–1850*, (Oxford, 2006), and with Alistair Tough as co-editor, *Record Keeping in a Hybrid Environment – Managing the Creation, Use and Disposal of Unpublished Information Objects in Context* (Chandos, 2006).

Michael D. Mumford is the George Lynn Cross Distinguished Research Professor of Psychology, and Director of the Center for Applied Social Research at the University of Oklahoma, USA. He serves as senior editor of *The Leadership Quarterly* and sits on the editorial boards of seven journals, including *Creativity Research Journal*, *Journal of Creative Behavior*, *IEEE Transactions on Engineering Management*, and *Journal of Business Ethics*. His recent books include *Innovation in Organizations* and *Pathways to Outstanding Leadership*. His current research is focused on leadership, creativity, ethics, and planning.

Ken Parry is Professor of Leadership and Director of the Centre for Leadership Studies at Bond University, on Australia's Gold Coast. He is author or editor of several books, most recently *A Short, Interesting and Reasonably Cheap Book about Studying Leadership* (with Brad Jackson, Sage, 2008). He was founding editor of the *Journal of Management & Organization*, the journal of the Australian and New Zealand Academy of Management. Ken is former founding director of the Centre for the Study of Leadership, in New Zealand. His current research interests involve corporate governance and leadership, critical realist approaches to grounded theory, autoethnography, and the aesthetics of leadership and management.

Mark F. Peterson is Professor of Management and International Business at Florida Atlantic University, USA and holds a part time position supported by the Hofstede Chair in Cultural Diversity as Professor at Maastricht University in The Netherlands. In addition to over 100 articles and book chapters, his recent books include the *Handbook of Cross Cultural Management Research* (Sage, 2008), co-edited with Peter B. Smith and David C. Thomas, and *Foundations of Cross Cultural Management* (Sage, 2008), co-edited with Mikael Soendergaard. His principal interests are in questions of how culture and international relations affect the way organizations are managed. Specific topics include cultural variability in the use of roles, rules, and norms in decision making in organizations throughout the world, and the links between the values of individuals, the cultural characteristics of within-nation regions, and national differences in cultures and institutions.

Nelson Phillips is Professor of Strategy and Organizational Behaviour at Tanaka Business School, Imperial College London, UK. His research interests include knowledge management, technology strategy, institutional theory, discourse analysis, and entrepreneurship. He has published over 60 academic articles and book chapters, including articles in the *Academy of Management Journal, Academy of Management Review, Management Science, Sloan Management Review, Organization Science, Journal of Management Studies, Journal of Business Ethics,* and *Organization Studies*. He has also written two books: *Discourse Analysis,* with Cynthia Hardy (2002), and *Power and Organizations,* with Stewart Clegg and David Courpasson (2006).

Anshuman Prasad is Professor of Management and University Research Scholar at the College of Business, University of New Haven, Connecticut, USA, and has a PhD from University of Massachusets at Amherst. He brings an interdisciplinary orientation in his research, which deals with such themes as globalization, postcolonialism, workplace diversity, resistance and empowerment in organizations, and epistemology. He is the editor of *Postcolonial Theory and Organizational Analysis: A Critical Engagement* (2003), and a co-editor of *Managing the Organizational Melting Pot: Dilemmas of Workplace Diversity* (1997). His articles have appeared in several scholarly journals. His current research activities include two book projects: *Globalization, Postcoloniality and Critical Management Studies,* and *Against the Grain: Advances in Postcolonial Organization Studies* (as editor).

Pushkala Prasad is the Zankel Chair Professor of Management & Liberal Arts at Skidmore College, and Visiting Professor of Corporate Social Responsibility at Lund University in Sweden. She is the author of *Crafting Qualitative Research* (M.E. Sharpe, 2005), and has published widely in *Organization Science,* the *Academy of Management Journal* and the *Journal of Management Studies*. She is currently researching the management of legitimacy by the tobacco, beef and gun industries.

Alison Pullen is Associate Professor of Organization Studies at the School of Management and The Centre of Management and Organization Studies (CMOS), University of Technology, Sydney, Australia. Alison has previously worked at the Universities of Leicester, Essex, Durham and York, UK. She is author of *Managing Identity* (Palgrave, 2006), and co-editor of *Thinking*

Organization (Routledge, 2005), *Organization and Identity* (Routledge, 2005), *Exploring Identity* (Palgrave, 2007) and *Bits of Organization* (Liber, 2009). She writes on corporeality, gender, ethics, and identity, and her work is informed by post-feminist methodologies and philosophies.

Alannah E. Rafferty is a Lecturer in the School of Psychology at The University of Queensland, Australia. Her research interests include organizational change and development, readiness for change, transformational leadership, and job attitudes. Alannah has extensive experience in the development, administration, and use of surveys to inform leadership development and strategic change, and within a range of private and public sector organizations. Alannah has published in a number of international high quality peer-reviewed journals, including the *Journal of Applied Psychology*, *The Leadership Quarterly*, and the *Journal of Occupational and Organizational Psychology*.

Monder Ram is Professor of Small Business and Director of the Centre for Research in Ethnic Minority Entrepreneurship (CREME), De Montfort University, UK. He is author of *Managing to Survive: Working Lives in Small Firms* (Blackwell, 1994), and *Ethnic Minorities in Business* (with T. Jones, Small Business Enterprise Trust, 2008). He has published widely on employment relations, ethnic minority entrepreneurship, informal economic activity, and small firm policy. Recent articles have been published in a range of journals, including *Journal of Management Studies*, *Organization*, *Work and Occupation*, and *Work, Employment and Society*. Monder's current research projects include new migrant business activity, supplier diversity, enterprise policy, and work relations in small firms.

Michael I. Reed is Professor of Organizational Analysis (Human Resource Management Section) and Associate Dean (Research), Cardiff Business School, Cardiff University, Wales, UK. He has published widely in major international journals, and book length monographs in the areas of organization theory and analysis, expert work and knowledge organizations, public services organization and management, and organizational futures. He is a member of several leading international academic associations, such as the Academy of Management, the European Group for Organization Studies, the British Sociological Association, and the British Academy of Management (Council Member from 2004). He is one of the founding editors of the international journal, *Organization*, published by Sage.

Carl Rhodes is Professor of Organization Studies, School of Management, University of Technology Sydney, Australia. His current research focuses on critically interrogating the narration and representation of organizational experience in practice and culture, with a particular concern with the possibilities for organizational ethics and responsibility. His most recent books are *Critical Representations of Work and Organization in Popular Culture* (Routledge, 2008, with Robert Westwood), *Humour, Work and Organization* (Routledge, 2007, with Robert Westwood) and *Management Ethics-Contemporary Contexts* (Routledge, 2006, with Stewart Clegg). His work can also be found in journals such as *Organization*, *Organization Studies*, *The Leadership Quarterly*, and *Qualitative Inquiry*. Carl is currently editing a volume entitled *Bits of Organization* (Liber, 2009) with Alison Pullen.

Charles A. Scherbaum is an associate professor of psychology at Baruch College in the City University of New York, USA. He has been an author/co-author on numerous published articles and chapters, including those appearing in *Personnel Psychology*, *Organizational Research Methods*, *Educational & Psychological Measurement*, and *Leadership Quarterly*. His current research focuses on personnel selection, cognitive ability testing, quantitative methods, and applied psychometrics.

Linda Smircich (PhD Syracuse University) is Professor of Organization Studies at the Isenberg School of Management at the University of Massachusetts, Amherst, USA. She teaches Organizational Behavior and Theory to undergraduates and to MBAs, and doctoral courses in Qualitative Research, and Alternative Paradigms in Organizational Analysis. Her earlier scholarly writing centred on organizational culture; she now would describe herself as pursuing a cultural and critical perspective on organization and management. Her research, in collaboration with Marta B. Calás, applies insights from cultural studies and feminist theorizing to organizational topics such as business ethics, globalization, and issues of work and family. In 2006, Linda and Marta received the Sage Award for scholarly contributions from the Gender, Diversity and Organization division of the Academy of Management. Linda is part of the founding editorial team of *Organization: The critical journal of organization, theory and society.*

Paul E. Spector is a distinguished university professor of industrial/organizational (I/O) psychology and I/O doctoral program director at the University of South Florida, USA. He is also director of the NIOSH funded Sunshine Education and Research Center's Occupational Health Psychology program. He is the Associate Editor for Point/Counterpoint for *Journal of Organizational Behavior*, and is on the editorial boards of *Journal of Applied Psychology*, *Journal of Occupational and Organizational Psychology*, *Organizational Research Methods*, *Personnel Psychology*, and *Work & Stress*. His research interests include methodology, counterproductive work behavior, occupational stress, personality, and violence. In 1991, the Institute For Scientific Information listed him as one of the 50 highest impact contemporary researchers (out of over 102,000) in psychology worldwide.

Eugene F. Stone-Romero is Professor of Management at the University of Texas at San Antonio, USA. He has a PhD from the University of California-Irvine, and he is a Fellow of the Society for Industrial and Organizational Psychology, the Association for Psychological Science, and the American Psychological Association. The results of his research have appeared in such outlets as the *Journal of Applied Psychology*, *Organizational Behavior and Human Performance*, *Personnel Psychology*, *Journal of Vocational Behavior*, *Academy of Management Journal*, *Journal of Management*, *Educational and Psychological Measurement*, *Journal of Educational Psychology*, *International Review of Industrial and Organizational Psychology*, *Research in Personnel and Human Resources Management*, *Applied Psychology: An International Review*, and the *Journal of Applied Social Psychology*. He is also the author of numerous book chapters dealing with issues germane to the related fields of research methods, human resources management, industrial and organizational psychology, organizational behavior, and applied social psychology. Finally, he is the author of a book titled *Research Methods in Organizational Behavior*, and the co-author of books titled *Job Satisfaction: How People Feel about Their Jobs and How It Affects Their Performance*, and *The Influence of Culture on Human Resource Management Processes and Practices.*

Antonio Strati is Professor of Sociology of Organization and lectures at the Universities of Trento and Siena, Italy. His work has been published in several international journals. His book *Organization and Aesthetics* (Sage, 1999) has appeared also in French (PUL, 2004), in Portuguese (FGV, 2007), and in Italian (Mondadori, 2008). He is author of the textbook *Theory and Method in Organization Studies* (Sage, 2000). His main research interests focus on qualitative methods and practice-based theorizing to understand aesthetics, tacit knowledge, and symbolism in organizational life.

Roy Suddaby is a Professor of Management and Organization and Rice Faculty Fellow at the Alberta School of Business and an Adjunct Professor in the Department of Sociology, University of Alberta, Edmonton, Canada. He is the author/co-author of numerous articles and book chapters. Professor Suddaby is an Associate Editor of the *Academy of Management Review*, and is the co-editor of the *Sage Handbook of Organizational Institutionalism* (2007) and *Institutional Work* (Cambridge University Press, 2009). His research focuses on managing change in the professions and creative industries; current projects include a study of corporate art collections and changes in professional regulation.

Sharmi Surianarain is a PhD student at the Department of Management and Organizations, Kellogg School of Management, Northwestern University, USA. Her areas of research focus include public-private partnerships in the development of HIV/AIDS drugs; organizational culture in multi-party alliance organizations such as healthcare consortia; partnership strategies between government, private sector, and non-governmental sector organizations; and study of the shareholder and ownership trends in the African telecoms industry. Sharmi also holds two degrees from Harvard University, where her key areas of focus were education and social policy.

David Tranfield was Professor of Management and Director of Research and Faculty Development at Cranfield School of Management, UK, from 1998 to 2008, and is now Professor Emeritus. He was elected a Fellow of the British Academy of Management in 2001 and is one of four inaugural Sunningdale Fellows (2005) of the UK National School for Government having served on the Commissioning Group of the Fellowship. He has served on the Council and Research Policy Committees of the British Academy of Management (1993 to 2003) and on the UK Engineering and Physical Sciences Research Council College (1993 to 2009). He specializes in the management of strategic change, particularly its design, implementation and evaluation. He is a champion of practice-based and practitioner-focused research and his 1998 paper with Ken Starkey ('The nature, social organization and promotion of management research') in the *British Journal of Management* has endured as the definitive statement of British Academy of Management research policy for the last ten years. His pioneering work on evidence-based management continues to extend his 'theory/practice' agenda.

Haridimos Tsoukas is the George D. Mavros Research Professor of Organization and Management at the Athens Laboratory of Business Administration (ALBA Graduate Business School), Greece, and a Professor of Organization Studies at Warwick Business School, University of Warwick, UK. He has published widely in several leading academic journals, and is the author of *Complex Knowledge: Studies in Organizational Epistemology* (OUP, 2005), and *If Aristotle Was a CEO: Essays on Leadership and Management* (in Greek, Kastaniotis, 2005). He has edited/co-edited several books, including *The Oxford Handbook of Organization Theory: Meta-theoretical Perspectives* (OUP, 2003), *Organizations as Knowledge Systems* (Palgrave Macmillan, 2004), and *Managing the Future: Foresight in the Knowledge Economy* (Blackwell, 2004). He is a former editor-in-chief of *Organization Studies*. Research interests include: knowledge-based perspectives on organizations; the management of organizational change and social reforms; the epistemology of practice; and epistemological issues in organization theory.

Samantha Warren is Senior Lecturer in Organizational Behaviour and Human Resource Management at the University of Surrey, UK. She is a founding member of the International Network for Visual Studies in Organizations (inVisio), and is a member of the executive board of the Standing Conference on Organizational Symbolism (SCOS). Her research interests centre on the aesthetic realm of organizational life, with particular emphasis on the use of visual methods as a route to organizational knowledge. She is also interested in the visuality-materiality-identity nexus – exploring the role of objects in 'identity-work' at work. Her work can be found in academic journals, including *Human Relations*, *Organization Studies*, and the *Accounting, Auditing & Accountability Journal (AAAJ)*. She is currently co-editing a special issue of *AAAJ* on 'Accounting and the Visual' with Dr Jane Davison, due for publication in 2009.

Colin C. Williams is Professor of Public Policy, School of Management, University of Sheffield, UK. He is author/co-author of numerous articles and books, including *The Hidden Enterprise Culture* (Edward Elgar, 2008), *Re-thinking the Future of Work* (Palgrave-Macmillan, 2007), *A Commodified World?* (Zed, 2005), and *Cash-in-Hand Work* (2004, Palgrave-Macmillan). Research interests include the informal economy, entrepreneurship, and economic development. His current projects are on evaluating policy initiatives for tackling undeclared work, and promoting entrepreneurship.

Edward Wray-Bliss is Senior Lecturer in Management at the School of Management, University of Technology, Sydney, Australia. His writing on the ethics and politics of research is published in *Organization Studies (2008) Human Relations* (2005), *Organizational Research Methods* (2002), *Tamara* (2003), *Ephemera* (2004), and elsewhere. Other research interests include all things (un)ethical, and have ranged across the issues of discrimination, business ethics, call centres, ethical theory, and latterly, drugs, drug testing and alcohol at work.

Dvora Yanow holds the Strategic Chair in Meaning and Method at the Vrije Universiteit, Amsterdam, the Netherlands. Her research has been shaped by an overall interest in the communication of meaning in organizational and policy settings, focusing on the role of built space in communicating meaning, organizational learning from an interpretive-cultural perspective, and the links between improvisation and research methods and management practices. Her publications include *How does a policy mean? Interpreting policy and organizational actions* (Georgetown University Press, 1996); *Conducting interpretive policy analysis* (Sage, 2000); *Constructing American 'race' and 'ethnicity': Category-making in public policy and administration* (M.E. Sharpe, 2003, winner of the 2004 ASPA and 2007 Herbert A. Simon-APSA book prizes); the co-edited *Knowing in organizations* (M.E. Sharpe, 2003), *Interpretation and method: Empirical research methods and the 'interpretive turn'* (M.E. Sharpe, 2006), and Organizational ethnography: Studying the complexities of everyday organizational life (Sage, 2009).

Sierk Ybema is Assistant Professor of Organizational Science at Vrije Universiteit, Amsterdam, the Netherlands. He is author/co-author of various articles and co-editor of books and special issues, including *Contradictions in Context: Puzzling over Paradoxes in Contemporary Organizations* (with Willem Koot and Ida Sabelis, 1996), *Organizational Ethnography: Studying the Complexities of Everyday Organizational Life* (with Dvora Yanow, Harry Wels and Frans Kamsteeg, 2009), and *Constructing Identity in Organizations* (with Tom Keenoy et al., a special issue for *Human Relations*, 2009). His research focuses on cultural dynamics, discourse, and identity in organizational life. His current interests include ethnographic methodology, (inter)organizational conflict and collaboration, and collective identity change crisis.

Preface

The overriding purpose of this *Handbook* is to give organizational researchers an indispensable reference work, a litmus for issues of current and future methodological significance, a grounding in the terrain's history which conditions contemporary thinking and practice, a well-spring of ideas and inspiration. Our specific aims are to:

- provide a comprehensive critical review of contemporary issues, debates, field practice, and trends in organizational research methods;

- locate current thinking, debates, and methods in the history of organizational research, demonstrating how current thinking and practice are influenced by earlier perspectives;

- identify trends, theories, and issues which have the potential to shape the underpinning epistemologies, theories, methodologies, and where appropriate the subject matter, of organizational research into the medium-term future;

- explore strategies for bridging the gap between researchers, and those who are in a position to act on research findings to influence organizational practice.

Our main readership includes professional academic researchers in faculty, doctoral, and postdoctoral positions. The contents and authorship are designed to appeal to a wide disciplinary and international readership, by including a range of contributors balancing Australasian, European and North American perspectives. The content also addresses the international dimensions of the subject, such as cross-cultural and comparative research, transferability issues with culture-specific findings, and the management of international research teams.

Organization studies is a broad subject area, extending far beyond the narrow confines of the traditional subject of organizational behaviour. It is important also to recognize that interest in organizational research methods extends to settings beyond conventional commercial concerns, to a range of organized settings, issues, themes, and topics that are not commonly found on introductory business and management studies programmes. This broadening of the field is reflected, for example, in *The Sage Handbook of Organization Studies* (Clegg et al., 2006). The current project thus addresses the interests, concerns, and needs of a widening range of researchers, whose objectives encompass a variety of questions and problems, covering a diversity of settings, unconstrained by conventional discipline boundaries.

We hope that this *Handbook* will also be of interest to two other groups of readers.

First, the postgraduate Masters degree student community. There are now numerous specialist Masters degree programmes in research methods, and almost all postgraduate Masters degree programmes in business, management, and related subject areas require candidates to complete a field-based research project. While these readers are already well-served with a range of generic and more specialized texts, this *Handbook* aims to provide more depth and wider contextualization in specific areas.

Second, the management consultancy community. This includes the larger management consultancies, which have specialist organization development and change units, and the internal change and organization development departments of larger concerns. The aims and methods of management consultancy overlap with those of academic research, and many faculty researchers, particularly in business schools, are involved in consultancy work.

THE RESEARCH METHODS CONTEXT

One of the aims of this *Handbook* is to locate the more technical aspects of research methods in the wider context of the many other influences on research design and methods, which are often bypassed by conventional accounts, but which also influence the conduct of research in organizational settings. In addition, the distinctive properties of organized human activity as a site of interest to researchers are often overlooked, despite the observation that those properties trigger research interest in the first place, and affect approaches to data collection.

One of the central themes running through this project concerns the diverse and eclectic nature of contemporary organizational research. The field is no longer dominated or constrained by positivist epistemology and its traditional extended family of primarily quantitative hypothetico-deductive methods. Organizational research today also embraces, and reflects the influence of, critical, phenomenological, constructivist, interpretative, institutionalist, feminist, realist, and postmodern perspectives. In this regard, organizational research has come to resemble other branches of the social sciences. It is not surprising that diversity and eclecticism have involved the generation of new research topics and agendas, the creation of novel terminology, the use of innovative research methods, the development of combined or mixed methods research, the collection of non-traditional forms of evidence, the development of fresh approaches to measurement, analysis, conceptualization and theory building, and the acceptance of modes of generalizability of findings other than statistical.

One consequence of this flurry of creativity is that the language and the evidence base of published output are increasingly bewildering to non-academic consumers of research findings. This is probably one factor (among others) fuelling the popularity of evidence-based management (see Learmonth, Chapter 6, and Denyer and Tranfield, Chapter 39, this volume) as commentators representing both the academy and practice rush to accuse researchers of pursuing irrelevant inquiries and being unable to develop useful conclusions. Why should this be a cause for concern, when academic output in many other fields attracts such criticisms? The answer begins with the observation that the organizational research voice by definition often attempts to reach both academic and practitioner ears. Researchers are often motivated by a desire to challenge organizational practice, to trigger intervention, to effect change. Why investigate power if not to identify ways to deploy it more effectively, address its consequences, or recommend strategies to reduce power inequalities? Why study job satisfaction and quality of working life if not to prescribe methods for their enhancement? Why research harassment, bullying, and discrimination at work if not to expose these practices and help bring them to an end?

Some researchers will complain, with justification, that the preceding paragraph makes unwarranted assumptions about their research aims, which lie elsewhere. An increasingly common answer to the question, 'why study?', concerns simply the accurate description of social and organizational phenomena. To capture the richness and complexity of social and organizational experience can be a valuable goal in its own right. Some researchers take their aspirations beyond description to address explanations relating to the phenomena under investigation. However, this does not necessarily extend to the identification of hypotheses, or to the establishment of causal links. The topic of causality is complex and controversial, and discussion of the processes of causal inference is beyond the scope of this preface.

However, for many organizational members unfamiliar with contemporary debates in social science philosophy, epistemology, and methodology, the concept of 'explanation' relates to more familiar notions of 'what causes what', and 'what works', sometimes reflecting a misguided but perennially popular concern with 'best practice'. An inability, or perhaps worse, a confessed unwillingness, to identify causality in either a technical or a popular sense, can be a further source of confusion and frustration in the view of non-academic users of organizational research findings.

Novel research aims, concepts, methods, evidence, and theories are not merely unfamiliar. They may be seen as untrustworthy. Ears accustomed to the notion that 'proof' relies on the analysis of data from controlled experiments, or from large, representative samples, may listen with suspicion to reports of findings based on opportunistically chosen qualitative studies of single cases, where participants were involved as co-researchers, and the researcher sought to change organizational practices during the study. The aspirations of organizational research with respect to change, improvement, and development are unlikely to be fulfilled if the segment of the audience in a position to act on the findings cannot understand the methods or the message. Those aspirations will suffer more significant damage if that audience does not trust the message, believing it to be based on 'unscientific' or otherwise flawed methods.

This line of reasoning is complicated by the observation that the linkages between problem definition, data collection, research conclusions, prescription, and consequent changes to practice, are not as linear as this sentence construction implies. Even findings that are regarded as trustworthy do not always find immediate application. The relationships between evidence and practice in most fields (including medicine, where the concept of 'evidence-based medicine' is a popular theme), are considerably more complex, for reasons beyond the scope of this introductory discussion. Relations between researchers, and the consumers of findings, therefore, are problematic. Recent innovations in epistemology, methodology, and terminology appear to have increased the distance between these communities, and this is a fundamental challenge for organizational researchers.

Finally, the distinction is often made between method and theory as discrete if related stages of research practice. First, define problem or question. Second, gather data. Third, analyse and interpret data. Finally, develop theory, or explanation, based on what the data reveal. It has long been recognized that this linear path from problem definition to explanation does not reflect the conduct of research, particularly qualitative research, and that the distinction between theory and method is oversimplified and misleading, for a number of reasons.

First, it is difficult to gather 'raw' data unless one has a tacit theory concerning which kinds of information are likely to be relevant in the first place. For example, it is difficult to frame questions concerning the concept of 'professional identity' without an approximate understanding of the dimensions of this construct, and the factors that might be significant in shaping it, or even to decide whether this topic is best approached through the use of, say, qualitative interviews, same- or mixed-profession focus groups, a diary study, or by observation. Second, a research method can itself be viewed as an implicit theory. At its simplest, this implicit theory states that, if I gather my data in this manner, I will find out what I want to know. Researchers studying organizational change from a processual-contextual perspective thus begin with a theory of method which states that, if we gather longitudinal data from case study sites using multiple methods (interviews, documents, observation), at different levels of analysis (individual, team, organization, external context), we will expose the complex, iterative, politicized nature of the change process and the multiple interacting forces determining its outcomes. Third, there are numerous examples of research method influencing the dimensions of the theory derived from the data analysis. One infamous example is Fredrick Herzberg's two-factory theory of work motivation, derived from the critical incident interview method, which generated narratives which, when content analysed, suggested that the factors leading to low job satisfaction, poor motivation, and low performance were different from, and not merely opposite to, the factors leading to high satisfaction, motivation, and performance. Researchers studying the same question with different methods generated results inconsistent with Herzberg's findings, which have been attributed to the phenomenon of projection; when we perform well, we congratulate ourselves, but when we perform badly, we project the blame onto factors beyond our control.

A clear distinction between substantive theory (e.g., leadership theory, institutional theory) and theories that are employed in relation to research practice, is therefore difficult to sustain. Choice of method is conditioned by (sometimes tacit) theory, method itself is (often implicit) theory, and the development of theory can be conditioned by the choice of method, which in turn influences the nature and scope of the data gathered. As already indicated, one of the overriding purposes of this *Handbook*, therefore, is to *recontextualize* the organizational research methods field, demonstrating both the range of issues that influence the choice and use of methods, and also the substantive consequences of methods choices. Our aim is to establish that this field is more complex, more challenging, and indeed more interesting than conventional treatments allow, and that the development of this field depends to a large extent on whether and how those complexities and challenges are addressed.

WHAT'S IN A METHOD?

One of our first challenges was to define the *scope* of this handbook, an issue that generated debate with members of our editorial board, some of whom argued for a more inclusive approach than we proposed. For example, one member of the board noted that, 'I was surprised by your definition of research methods as procedures for data collection. My understanding is that methods includes analysis and interpretation also, not simply data collection. I suggest developing a more inclusive definition'. That inclusive definition of research methods is widely presumed. For example, the majority of papers published in *Organizational Research Methods*, a journal sponsored by the Research Methods Division of the Academy of Management, deal with developments in (primarily quantitative) data *analysis* techniques, and only a small number of papers consider data collection *methods*.

As this debate will also concern many readers, we should explain how we have addressed the matter, and the thinking behind our resolution. We have adopted, *in the first instance*, a narrow definition of research method simply as a tool or technique or approach for collecting and collating data. Social science has only three methods; observation, asking questions, and inspecting documents, although these can be used and combined creatively in a number of different ways. This approach appears to draw a boundary around a set of research practices distinct from epistemological concerns, and deliberately excludes data analysis techniques. Data analysis can be regarded as a closely related but separate field, with its own specialist literature, such as the *Handbook of Data Analysis* (Hardy and Bryman, 2004), and widening the scope and length of this project to incorporate data analysis would have been unrealistic. Does this imply a focus on qualitative methods at the expense of quantitative techniques? It can be argued that perhaps all organizational (and social) research methods are qualitative, based as they are on observation, asking questions, and analysing documents. Even the conventional Likert-scaled tick-box self-report survey relies on ordinal measurements with language labels (although statistical tools are often applied to the resultant numbers).

Nevertheless, this is a definition of convenience. Research methods as data collection tools cannot be divorced from the wider set of considerations involving research objectives, epistemological choices, and the opportunities and constraints presented by the organizational setting in which research will be conducted. This wider contextualization of method is the argument of chapter 1, and is one of the central arguments of this project; data collection methods are part of a systematic web of influences – personal, interpersonal, epistemological, theoretical, historical, contextual, ethical, temporal, political – and cannot be regarded as isolated technical choices determined exclusively or even primarily by research aims.

A distinction between research methods and data analysis techniques is also an artificial one, in at least two other respects. First, the techniques of data analysis that a researcher employs are often (but not always) implicated in the methods that have been used to collect the data in the first place. This is illustrated, for example, by the collection and collation of qualitative and quantitative longitudinal case study data to develop process theoretical explanations of phenomena such as organizational change (Pettigrew, 1990; Dawson, 1997 and 2003; Suddaby and Greenwood, Chapter 11, this volume; Langley, Chapter 24, this volume) and innovation (Van de Ven et al., 1999; Van de Ven and Poole, 2002). Second, some data collection methods have embedded analytical procedures, such as grounded theory (see Goulding, Chapter 22, this volume), and action research and other collaborative approaches (see Denis and Lehoux, Chapter 21, this volume). Consequently, a narrow definition of research method does not lead us to *exclude* issues of epistemology, data analysis, interpretation, and theory development, but instead allows us to *locate* those factors, or rather those mutual interdependencies, more clearly in the context of a distinct primary focus on data collection tools and techniques.

This debate arises from the somewhat casual manner in which the associated terminology is often used. Many commentators use the terms methodology, design, strategy, and method synonymously, inclusively as already noted, and often without precise definition. Gill and Johnson (2000) use the phrase 'research methods' to encompass the research process from inception to communication. In their introductory text, Saunders et al. (2003) similarly use *research methodology* to describe the unfolding steps across the research process as a whole, defining *research strategy* as a 'general plan of how the researcher will go about answering the research question' (p. 488), and *research methods* as 'tools and techniques used to obtain and analyse research data, including for example questionnaires, observation, interviews, and statistical and non-statistical techniques' (p. 481). While casual, broad, and inclusive usage can lead to confusion, precise distinctions can create artificial categories which in turn blur interdependencies. In the context of organization studies, a multidisciplinary and interdisciplinary field which encompasses the full spectrum of ontological, epistemological, and methodological perspectives, it has perhaps become more important to be explicit in the use of these terms, given the potential for misinterpretation. Exploring what his title describes as *research design* in organization studies, Grunow (1995) uses the terms *research methodology*, *research design*, and *research strategy* as synonyms, discusses multimethods designs (and strategies), and asks, 'how are research strategies designed?', (p. 97). However, he identifies case studies, comparative case studies, surveys, combined surveys and case studies, and experiments, as *forms of study*, contrasted with interviews, observation, content analysis, document analysis, and group discussion, which are *techniques of data collection*.

In their analysis of current trends in organization and management research, Scandura and Williams (2000) use the term *research methodology* in their title, observe that, 'it is important for researchers to assess the *methods* they employ' (p. 1248), then advise that, 'researchers should be mindful of what *methodological procedures* are being rewarded by top journals' (p. 1248), then note that their study focused on *research strategies*, including formal theory/literature reviews, sample surveys, laboratory experiments, experimental simulations, field studies, field experiments, judgement tasks, and computer simulations (emphasis added). Incidentally, Scandura and Williams (2000, p. 1263) note an increase in the use of case studies, arguing that 'Management researchers need to rethink their apparent predisposition towards field studies, the most common research strategy now employed. They need to question whether studies with ambiguous conclusions can say much about the settings in which they occur. It may be that, without rigour, relevance in management research cannot be claimed' (see Tsoukas,

Chapter 17, and Fitzgerald and Dopson, Chapter 27, this volume). For Scandura and Williams, evidently, the popularity of a research strategy, or form of study, or research method, is not to be confused with its acceptability.

Adopting a more structured approach, Bryman and Bell (2007) distinguish between research strategy, design, and method. *Research strategy* concerns 'a general orientation to the conduct of research' (p. 28), distinguishing quantitative and qualitative strategies, while recognizing the limitations of such a basic classification. *Research design* is 'a framework for the collection and analysis of data' (p. 40). Designs include experiments, surveys, case studies, and longitudinal and comparative studies. *Research method*, then, is defined as 'simply a technique for collecting data' (p. 40). These are the usages reflected in the title and editorial contributions to this *Handbook*, although we leave it to individual contributors, where appropriate, to adopt and explain their own terminology.

WHAT'S IN THIS HANDBOOK?

Our editorial introduction first identifies some of the main contemporary characteristics of organization studies research, with regard to its widening boundaries, multi-paradigmatic profile, and methodological inventiveness. Choice of research methods is then set in the context, not only of research aims, epistemological concerns, and norms of practice, but also with regard to a range of organizational, historical, political, ethical, evidential, and personal factors, which are often treated as problems to be overcome, rather than as issues to be addressed systematically, and perhaps exploited to the benefit of the research process.

Our editorial board members questioned the presence of chapters exploring the ontological and epistemological aspects of research; conventionally, one might confine 'thinking about research' to another volume, and focus on 'doing research'. But this is unrealistic. One of the implications of the pluralistic approach to epistemology and methods that has emerged is the increasing need for researchers to make their own positions explicit, particularly in cross- or inter-disciplinary work of the kind that arises in organization studies. Epistemology and methods must now be addressed simultaneously, in both the conduct and writing of research, and we feel that it is appropriate to combine these issues within the same covers.

We have then divided the main contents of the *Handbook* into five sections.

Part 1, *Dilemmas: the shifting context of organizational research*. These six chapters focus on the issues, debates, tensions, and dilemmas which define the historical, epistemological, and practical contexts in which organizational research occurs.

ch	authors, short title	contents, arguments
1	David A. Buchanan and Alan Bryman **contextualizing methods**	Organizational research is now characterized by widening boundaries, a multiparadigmatic profile, and methodological inventiveness. Choice of research method relies not only on research aims and epistemological stance, but also on organizational, historical, political, evidential, and personal factors, which are not 'problems to be solved', but factors to be woven effectively into practical research designs.
2	Stanley Deetz **research discourses**	Researchers adopt differing approaches to the construction of knowledge. The concept of incommensurable paradigms is replaced with four discourses of research, normative, interpretive, critical, and dialogic, based on the type of subject interaction researchers prefer (local/emergent, or elite/a priori), and on whether the focus is with closure or indeterminacy (seeking consensus, or seeking dissensus). This creates a 'rotation of contestabilities', as these orientations are useful for different types of research question. Ideally, researchers would move across orientations with ease. However, a multiperspectival approach leads to shallow interpretations, and good work within one orientation is valuable.

Part 2, *Agendas: the broadening focus of organizational research*. These ten chapters explore influential traditions in organizational research, that is areas that have helped to define and characterize the field, exemplifying methodological approaches, developments, and trends, taking methodology into new territory.

	Stewart Clegg (*Cont'd*)	power', and the way in which power is constituted over time, is exemplified with incidents from the author's work and research experiences.
10	Robert David and Alexandre Bitektine **institutional theory**	The growth in popularity (i.e., institutionalization) of institutional theory has been accompanied by a shift in the agenda from a traditional focus on stability, similarity, and constraint, towards attempts also to explain change, diversity, and action. The field has also welcomed the use of qualitative research methods. But institutional theory has limited relevance to management practice, beyond institutionalizing change. The fragmentation of an approach that seeks to explain everything with little practical output may contribute to the deinstitutionalization of the perspective.
11	Roy Suddaby and Royston Grenwood **researching institutional change**	Institutional explanations of change offer an alternative to economic accounts which overlook the normative systems through which social arrangements arise and evolve. Institutional researchers have traditionally relied on *multivariate* methods to develop variance-based explanations. However, *interpretive*, *historical*, and *dialectical* approaches using a range of qualitative methods are increasingly used to understand processes of institutional change, such as movements in world views, complex path dependency, and political struggle. These approaches each offer a partial account. Exemplary research typically deploys two or more perspectives, one dominant (foreground) and one subordinate (background). This multi-theoretic stance, recognizing the tensions and benefits of competing paradigms, is likely to characterize developments in this field in future.
12	Alannah Rafferty and Mark Griffin **job satisfaction and motivation research**	Job satisfaction is one of the most studied concepts in those domains of enquiry that emphasize organizational behaviour, employing a variety of research methods and designs. The field has been dominated by a quantitative research approach and great strides have been made to improve the quality of measurement of job satisfaction. Although a 'traditional' topic, current trends and developments affecting the nature and experience of work mean that the significance of this field remains high.
13	Glenn Carroll, Mi Feng, Gael Le Mens and David McKendrick **studying organizational populations**	Outlines the rationale for a focus on populations of organizations rather than on organizations as such, as well as the analytic choices available to researchers. Discusses the kinds of archival data that are typically employed in population ecology research and the different approaches to evaluating the quality of such data. Delineates the issues involved in targeting and sampling particular populations, in particular from the perspective of the biases generated through one approach rather than another. Presents the case for examining 'vital events' in organizational populations, such as founding and mortality.
14	Antonio Strati **organizational aesthetics**	Research in organizational aesthetics (architecture, dress, product design, furnishings, equipment, 'atmosphere') is well established in Europe, but not in North America. This perspective offers a new methodological awareness giving theoretical value to notions of ugliness and the sublime, beauty and pathos. An 'aesthetic style' of research challenges the dominance of cognitive understanding with four approaches which transgress traditional methods: archaeological, empathic-logical, aesthetic, and artistic. Opposing alienating and manipulative processes, an aesthetic approach is critical of positivist perspectives, challenging the distinction between the value of research and the pleasure of doing it. Critical also of managerial standpoints, aesthetic research is concerned with emancipation and the exercise of aesthetic judgement.
15	Marta B. Calás and Linda Smircich **feminist perspectives**	The role of feminism concerns the social transformation of unequal gender and power relations. Feminist theory is thus philosophical, political, and plural, and research method derives from a theoretical understanding of what we want to know. Organization studies has incorporated feminist meta-theory in three main ways: researching *conditions of women* (feminist empiricism), *gendering relations* (feminist standpoint), and the *discursive processes of gendering* (feminist postmodernism). It is the researcher's orientation and purpose, not research method, that make research feminist; several examples are explored. The aims of feminist research, as with critical management studies, do not always coincide with other organization and management scholarship, where business case takes priority over social justice. However, feminist organization

Part 3, *Strategies: approaches to organizational research.* These nine chapters deal with approaches to achieving research aims, illustrating links between topic, aims, strategy, analytical framework, and theoretical development, also demonstrating the range of choice and degree of creativity as well as technical knowledge underpinning research strategies.

	Jean-Louis Denis and Pascale Lehoux (*Cont'd*)	these designs depends on the participants' commitment to each others' agendas as well as to their own.
22	Christina Goulding **grounded theory**	Grounded theory is an approach to data collection and analysis that is primarily associated with qualitative research. Notes that the origins of this approach lie in the quest in sociology for an approach to theory generation from qualitative data, but that the originators of grounded theory – Barney Glaser and Anselm Strauss – later parted company over how it should be practised. As a result, there are subtle differences among practitioners in how grounded theory should be conducted. The author uses a detailed illustration from her own work, which is closer to Glaser's than to Strauss's rendition, to examine the main elements of grounded theory.
23	Michael Moss **archival research**	The internet has revolutionized information-seeking behaviour and distribution channels, as internet engines widen access to research resources. But do we mistake noise for music? Digital content is not mediated by editorial controls, or appraised by custodians as in the analogue world, raising questions of integrity and provenance. This implies freedom, creativity, and sharing of ideas. But an audit and compliance culture encourages organizations to destroy potentially incriminating evidence, on which strict conditions may apply in terms of access and publication. The US Patriot Act requires archives and libraries to report readers and the materials they consult. The careful drafting and filing of written records is replaced with the haphazard storage of electronic communications. Rather than opening the view, the information landscape may in future be narrowed by technological, social, and geopolitical trends.
24	Ann Langley **process theory**	Process theories explore the temporal dynamics of evolving sequences of events rather than synchronic relationships among independent and dependent variables. Where variance theories reveal covariation, process theory is often required to explain how and why. Process perspectives are particularly relevant to organization studies where time is critical, where the diachronic patterns of events, behaviours, and choices shape outcomes. Using predominantly qualitative methods, process theorists often study the untidy and iterative nature of organizational changes, and links to practice are clearer than with variance theory. Process perspectives raise three challenges affecting the production of knowledge; temporal orientation (past, present, future), conceptual products (patterns, mechanisms, meanings), and researcher perspective (site relationships, academic careers). Strategies for establishing the trustworthiness of process research are explored.
25	Mike Reed **critical realism**	Presents critical realism as an alternative to both positivism and constructivism. This is apparent in its social ontology which, while acknowledging an external and extant social reality, argues that reality 'cannot be reduced to a discrete set of observable events or a discursively manufactured inter-subjective construct'. Depicts the main contribution of the approach as its commitment to the identification of generative mechanisms and their operation in specific socio-historical situations. Examines challenges to critical realism, such as the questionable role of agency within its purview.

Part 4, *Methods: data collection in organizational research*. These fifteen chapters focus on specific methods of data collection, demonstrating the inventiveness and innovation that now characterizes this field, and the widening range of possibilities concerning the development of data collection tools.

| 26 | Timothy Hinkin and Brooks Holtom **survey design** | Focuses on two aspects of survey administration that are seen as crucial to the reliability and validity of measurement: the factors that affect willingness to participate, and how respondents can be encouraged to participate. Applies an organizational perspective to the factors that inhibit willingness to participate, arguing that the ideal is for the organization to become a partner in data collection. This approach has significant implications for collaboration between academic researchers and practitioners. |

34	Carl Rhodes and Alison Pullen **narrative-based methods**	Narrative is a way of representing the connections between a series of events. One of the roles of narrative analysis in organizational research is to develop an understanding of sensemaking. Stories are the building blocks for a narrative analysis, providing insight into organizations as social constructions. Shows how narrative analysis can turn its attention to the research process itself, demonstrating that research is a realm in which stories are told and which can themselves be subjected to narrative analysis. Examines the conventions that are employed in telling research stories.
35	Gary Alan Fine, Calvin Morrill and Sharmi Surianarain **organizational ethnography**	Qualitative research has always been with us, and is frequently seen as making major contributions to the field of organizational research. Unlike many other research methods, ethnography allows for a detailed understanding of context and multiple perspectives and gives a stronger sense of process. Examines some of the main contributions of ethnographic research in the field. Shows how ethnographers manage accusations of bias through techniques like member checks and triangulation. Also examines the dilemmas an ethnographer faces, such as knowing when to finish collecting data.
36	John Hassard and David A. Buchanan **feature films as data**	Feature films can be viewed not only as illustrating aspects of work, management, and organization, but as documentaries coding cultural myths, values, preoccupations, anxieties, and patterns of social change, and as process explanations linking antecedents to consequences in context through narrative. Viewing 'movie as thesis', film is a source of creative theoretical insight, as well as a platform for theory testing, and has significant untapped potential as one component of visual organization studies.
37	Charles Scherbaum and Adam Meade **measurement**	The importance of measurement lies with objectivity, quantification, communication, efficiency of observation, consistency, and link to theory. However, measurement is often treated casually by organizational researchers, who tend to rely on classical techniques, overlooking contemporary developments, such as generalizability theory, item response theory, logistic models, graded response models, and measures of social cognitions such as implicit association and conditional reasoning tests.
38	Colin C. Williams and Monder Ram **researching 'off the books' work**	While one might assume difficulties in researching the informal, shadow, underground, 'black', economy, involving 'cash-in-hand' deals, working family members, and ethnic minorities, this is not the case. Off-the-books work is readily accessible to research through a range of indirect (proxy) and direct (more conventional) methods, and such studies are empirically and theoretically rewarding, and also inform policy and practice in significant ways.
39	David Denyer and David Tranfield **systematic review**	Systematic review is a research methodology that entails searching and synthesizing the literature relating to a specific area in order to arrive at definitive conclusions about what is known. Outlines the distinctive approach of systematic review, and links this to evidence-based management, noting that the impetus for systematic review in organization studies is often associated with the growing use of it in medicine. Points to some of the criticisms that are levelled at systematic review for organization studies and suggests how the method can be modified to take into consideration the distinguishing features of organizational research.
40	Ken Parry and Maree Boyle **organizational autoethnography**	Organizational autoethnography is a new approach located in the traditions of both case study and ethnography, and which seeks to link the personal and the organization in organizational research. Organizational autoethnography is a highly reflexive approach that locates the researcher firmly within the overall research process. Organizational autoethnographies must be written in an evocative manner in order to maximize the impact on readers.

Part 5, *Conclusion: the future of organizational research.* The final chapter offers our editorial assessment of the main themes, developments, trends, and challenges facing the field of organizational research methods.

41	Alan Bryman and David A. Buchanan **present and futures of organizational research**	The methodological inventiveness that has become a hallmark of organizational research is now threatened by multiple institutional pressures. The multiparadigmatic nature of the field once stimulated debate, but we are now witnessing a 'Balkanization' of organization studies, in which the previously 'warring' factions no longer even

Alan Bryman and David A. Buchanan (*Cont'd*)	exchange views. The field is also characterized by different approaches to the use of case studies, and by contrasting perspectives on the nature of causality, the latter being potentially bewildering for potential users of research findings. The writing of organizational research and the role of reflexivity are also explored. In the light of this discussion, is the future of organizational research methods bright, or bleak?

1

The Organizational Research Context: Properties and Implications

David A. Buchanan and Alan Bryman

INTRODUCTION

The field of organizational research displays three trends: widening boundaries, a multiparadigmatic profile, and methodological inventiveness. Choice of research methods, shaped by aims, epistemological concerns, and norms of practice, is thus also influenced by organizational, historical, political, ethical, evidential, and personal factors, which are typically treated as problems to be overcome. This chapter argues that those factors constitute a system of inevitable influences, and that this contextualization of methods choice has three implications. First, it is difficult to argue that methods choice depends exclusively on links to research aims; choice of methods involves a wider, more complex, interdependent set of considerations. Second, it is difficult to view method as merely a technique for snapping reality into focus; choice of methods frames the data windows through which phenomena are observed, influencing interpretative schemas

and theoretical development. Third, research competence thus involves addressing coherently the organizational, historical, political, ethical, evidential, and personal factors relevant to an investigation.

Methods out of context

Choice of methods tends to be presented as a step in the research process between setting objectives and commencing fieldwork. Consequently, methods are characterized in terms of finding the 'appropriate tool' in relation to research topic and questions. Partially accurate, this depiction decontextualizes method, providing an incomplete basis for explaining the approach deployed in a particular study. This chapter aims to demonstrate how choice of methods is shaped not only by research aims, norms of practice, and epistemological concerns, but also by a combination of organizational, historical, political, ethical, evidential, and personally significant characteristics of this field of research. While often acknowledged as difficulties facing the field researcher, we argue instead that these factors are naturally occurring and unavoidable influences, which must be accommodated in decisions concerning choice of methods, as they cannot simply be overcome through diligent planning. This perspective locates method as an integral component of a wider, iterative, and coherent research system, influencing the social possibilities of data collection, as well as the substantive nature of data collected, and the nature and direction of theory development. Those organizational, historical, political, ethical, evidential, and personal factors are not just unwelcome distractions. They are core components of the data stream, reflecting generic and specific properties of the research setting, central to the analysis and interpretation of results and to the development of theoretical and practical outcomes. We thus portray the research process in a less linear manner than is typically depicted in textbooks, arguing that our alternative characterization more effectively captures the realities of research methods decisions, and that this perspective will be instructive for students and novice researchers.

Our argument has three steps. First, to establish the platform for the argument that follows, we outline three significant trends in organizational research: the widening boundaries of this field, its multiparadigmatic profile, and its methodological inventiveness. Second, we consider the range of factors influencing methods decisions. Finally, we consider the implications of this perspective for the theory and practice of organizational research.

Boundaries, paradigms, and inventiveness

This section argues that organizational research has since its inception widened its boundaries dramatically, has developed (as other social sciences) a multiparadigmatic profile, and has been extraordinarily inventive with regard to the development of data

collection methods. A more restricted domain, with a broad epistemological consensus, would perhaps display less methodological creativity and present a narrower range of methods problems and choices. But the growth in popularity of mixed methods research has problematized, if not ruptured, the relationship between epistemology and method, weakening confidence in, and preoccupation with, those links (Teddlie and Tashakkori, 2003; and see Bryman, Chapter 30, this volume). Consequently, method is increasingly located in the context of wider and more fluid intellectual currents, discouraging rigid adherence to epistemological positions and encouraging a more pragmatic 'do whatever necessary', or 'pick and choose' approach to methods choice.

Widening boundaries

The term organizational behaviour was coined by Fritz Roethlisberger to suggest the widening scope of 'human relations'. So, in 1957, the Human Relations Group (previously the Mayo Group) at Harvard Business School was renamed the Organizational Behavior Group, and organizational behaviour was recognized as a subject at Harvard in 1962, with Roethlisberger (1977) as the first area head. Research at that time focused on work design, motivation, job satisfaction, rewards, groups, technology, leadership, and performance. Four decades later, in the introduction to the first edition of their *Handbook of Organization Studies*, Clegg, Hardy, and Nord (1996) argued that the 'traditional' label no longer reflected the scope of the subject or captured the work of those outside business and management with an interest in organizational issues. We now see research in topics such as aesthetics, bullying, change processes, creativity, cross-cultural communication, discourse, e-commerce, emotion, empowerment, ethics, fear (and loathing), feminism, femininity, gender, harassment, innovation, institutions, language, learning organizations, masculinity, narrative, organizational memory, political behaviour, power, psychological contract, reflexivity, sexuality, storytelling, sustainability, symbolism, and work-life balance. While this caricature of a once narrowly-defined field is inevitably unfair in some respects (the employee counselling programme at the Hawthorne plant, for example, addressed domestic and emotional concerns; Roethlisberger and Dickson, 1939), the argument concerning the broadening of boundaries is valid. It could be argued that our illustrative topic list is incomplete, and that the field of organizational research is now unbounded.

Researchers across this field also embrace diverse aims. Some are concerned to establish covariation, identify causal links, build models, and test hypotheses. Others are more preoccupied with rich description, capturing the complex texture of the organizational world as a valuable goal in its own right. For example, Goes and Park (1997) offer a compelling demonstration of the relationships between interorganizational networks and healthcare innovation, using methods (survey and published performance data), which reveal little or nothing of how those networks function or how they trigger and develop innovation processes. In contrast, O'Leary (2003) presents four competing narrative constructions, based on employee accounts from a newspaper company, depicting widely divergent perspectives on organizational life, using methods (participant observation and interviews) which reveal little or nothing of how those constructs and stories may be related to individual satisfaction, motivation, employee behaviours, management-employee relations, or organizational effectiveness. In one case, we see the links, but not the underlying mechanisms, while in the other, the mechanisms are displayed, but what these are connected to is unclear. These remarks are not intended as criticism of either of those contributions, but simply to illustrate the implications of contrasting research objectives and their coexistence in this field.

Multiple paradigms

The field of organizational research is no longer dominated or constrained by positivist (or neo-positivist) epistemology and its extended family of primarily quantitative hypothetico-deductive methods (Campbell and Stanley, 1966; Cook and Campbell, 1979; Shadish, Cook, and Campbell, 2001). Relatively few researchers today support the notion of a fixed hierarchy of evidence, with the double-blind randomized controlled trial as the ultimate model of proof (Tranfield, Denyer, and Smart, 2003). Nor is it possible to capture the range of epistemological positions with the distinction between variance and process theories (Mohr, 1982; Langley, 1999; see Langley, Chapter 24, this volume). Organizational research displays a variety of positivist, critical, phenomenological, constructivist, interpretative, feminist, and postmodern perspectives. Developing the work of Burrell and Morgan (1979) on paradigms, Deetz (1996; 2000) identifies four research orientations based on 'dimensions of contrast'. One dimension is 'local/emergent' versus 'elite/*a priori*', based on the sources of ideas and concepts, either in dialogue with respondents or established by the researcher on theoretical grounds. The second is 'consensus' versus 'dissensus', based on relationships between research aims and the dominant social discourse, with the aim either to confirm unity of understanding or to expose conflicts and tensions.

These dimensions produce four 'analytic ideal types' (Deetz, 1996: 195; see Deetz, Chapter 2, this volume) or different ways of engaging in research. Deetz also observes interplay, as researchers are adept at 'dodging criticism by co-optation' of other orientations (but adherents to more or less extreme versions of these positions can disagree fiercely). A normative (positivist) discourse assumes progressive enlightenment, rationalization and control, with concerns for codification, with establishing covariation and causal relations through hypothesis testing, with cumulative evidence, and with nomothetic laws (e.g., Hamel, 2000). An interpretative (constructivist, phenomenological) discourse regards sense-making individuals as engaged participants, as cocreators of social structures, using ethnographic and hermeneutic methods to establish local meanings, grounded in social and organizational practices (e.g., Fincham, 2002; Huxham and Vangen, 2003). A critical (neo-Marxist) discourse views organizations as sites of political struggle. The research aim is to unmask modes of domination and distorted communication by showing how these are reproduced, to highlight how social practices and institutional structures create and sustain power differences, obscuring alternative perspectives (e.g., Knights and McCabe, 1998). A dialogic (postmodern, Foucauldian) discourse focuses on the role of language in the constructed and polyvocal nature of social reality. Organizations are viewed as disjointed narratives that fail to establish a coherent reality. Dialogic discourse seeks to expose the pervasive and fluid nature of power relations in contemporary society, to unpack taken-for-granted realities, to uncover their complexities, lack of shared meaning, and hidden resistances (e.g., Collins and Rainwater, 2003). When publishing, researchers are usually encouraged, implicitly or explicitly, to locate their work on such a map, potentially straddling more than one quadrant.

It is important to recognize that such a typology is a helpful organizing framework, but that other perspectives remain possible. For example, as Deetz notes, it is possible to combine or to co-opt orientations for different purposes. In addition, it can be argued that realist perspectives are not captured in this space at all (see Reed, Chapter 25, this volume).

Methodological inventiveness

The 'paradigm wars' of the 1980s have thus turned to 'paradigm soup', and organizational research today reflects the paradigm diversity of the social sciences in general. It is not surprising that this epistemological eclecticism has involved the development of novel terminology, innovative research methods, nontraditional forms of evidence, and fresh approaches to conceptualization, analysis, and theory building. Examples of inventiveness in method include the use of organizational stories (Boje, 1991, 2001; Barry and Elmes,

1997; Taylor, 1999; Kolb, 2003), narratives (Czarniawska, 1999; Pentland, 1999; Doolin, 2003), visual, pictorial, and photographic images (Meyer, 1991; Harper, 1994, 2000; Suchman, 1995; Emmison and Smith, 2000; Buchanan, 2001; Stiles, 2004), feature film (Foreman and Thatchenkery, 1996; Hassard and Holliday, 1998; Champoux, 2001; Buchanan and Huczynski, 2004), creative dialogue, drawings and art, poetry, and theatre (Broussine, 2008), discourse analysis (Dick, 2004), Internet-based or 'online' research methods (Fielding et al., 2008), and collaborative strategies involving respondents as coresearchers and cointerpreters of findings (Denis and Lomas, 2003; Heller, 2004). These innovations are particularly evident in the domain of qualitative and interpretative methods (Prasad and Prasad, 2000). Meyer (1991: 218) observed that a 'burst of innovation' and a 'new pluralism in methodology' in organization science had not affected data collection methods; that criticism now appears to have been addressed. Traditional preoccupations with representative sampling and statistical generalization have long been complemented by arguments for the value of small-n studies, and for the epistemology of the singular, based on naturalistic (Stake, 1994) and analytical generalization (Mintzberg, 1979a; Mitchell, 1983; Eisenhardt, 1989; Tsoukas, 1989; Dyer and Wilkins, 1991; Buchanan, 1999; Yin, 2003; Butler, 1997; Stake, 2000).

One reason for this paradigmatic diversity and methodological innovation is that this field is a meeting point for numerous disciplines – mainstream and political psychology, social psychology, sociology, ethnography, economics, public policy, history, anthropology, and the business areas of strategy, finance, marketing, human resources, and operations management. Each of these disciplines and related subdisciplines brings its own distinct perspectives and traditions. Further, there is a growing acceptance, if not endorsement, of studies that combine quantitative and qualitative research. Such a mixed methods approach potentially provides opportunities for greater insight than can be achieved by one approach alone (e.g., Currall and Towler, 2003; see Bryman, Chapter 30, this volume). This development further contributes to the sense of paradigm soup, as researchers using such approaches tend to set aside the epistemological and ontological divisions, and because this questions the appropriateness of traditional research quality criteria (such as validity and reliability), as well as qualitative alternatives (Lincoln and Guba, 1985). Consequently, the field is fragmented, with no central core of traditions, frameworks, and concepts, and no unified theoretical or practical proposal.

Trends in the field of organizational research thus include a widening of boundaries, adoption of a range of orientations (epistemologies), and methodological innovation. The following section locates method in the context of a number of other properties of the organizational research field, which can systematically, and unavoidably, influence choice of method.

Field properties

While personal experience sits at the bottom of the hierarchy of evidence, to be treated with caution, if not discarded, it is personal research experience that informs this discussion. We consider features, challenges, and tensions that have coloured, indeed determined, our own methodological decisions, but which tend to be regarded as 'problems' in most accounts, not considered as legitimate influences on those decisions. In particular, we consider the organizational, historical, political, ethical, and evidential properties of the research field and the resources or personal properties of the researcher. Figure 1.1 summarizes this argument, illustrating the broad system of influences on choice of organizational research methods, beyond traditional concerns with the link to research topic, question, and objectives. In practice, this system of influences has multiple interrelationships, and the arrows

for presentational purposes indicate only the primary influences on methods choice.

Organizational properties

The logistics of fieldwork will always be more or less significantly influenced by properties of the focal organization such as size, location (single or multisite), and whether it is a commercial organization or a professional bureaucracy (Mintzberg, 1979b). Choice of method can also be heavily contingent on the stability of the research site or sites. Predetermined and inflexible methods are less appropriate (perhaps inappropriate) where the organizational context is changing. However, one significant contemporary feature of most medium and large-size organizations concerns the scale and frequency of role and structure change. For example, a tracking study of large British firms found that they experienced major changes on average every three years and that a third engaged in large-scale reorganizations annually (Whittington and Mayer, 2002). While such studies focus on the organizational repercussions (e.g., on the need to develop management skills in 'adaptive reorganization'), they have implications for research method. For example, the simple question, 'what is your job title?', is often met with a bemused smile, as many managers have portfolios of responsibilities, which change frequently (Buchanan, 2003). Establishing a sampling frame, or a list of key informants, or constructing an organization chart, can be problematic. On several occasions, in different settings, we have returned within a matter of weeks to reinterview a respondent, to find that they have assumed another role, or set of roles, and that our line of questioning is no longer relevant. Growth in 'outsourcing' of key services and the development of network forms of interorganizational collaboration mean that members of 'partner' organizations may be unsure which organization or project they are being questioned about. Taking static measurements to establish covariation is of limited relevance, rendering process theoretical perspectives, based on contextualized event sequence analysis, more appropriate (Poole et al., 2000; Pettigrew et al., 2001).

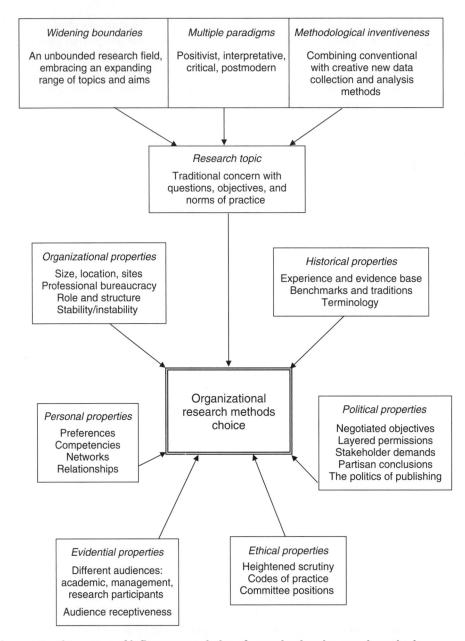

Figure 1.1 The system of influences on choice of organizational research methods

Depending on the research topic, the flux and patterns of change become substantive data observations, and the role of the researcher may be to 'catch reality in flight' (Pettigrew, 1990). In these kinds of rapidly changing organizational settings (Eisenhardt and Bourgeois, 1988; Buchanan, 2000), research methods must be regularly reviewed and adjusted in a flexible manner, as initial plans become inappropriate and as fresh lines of inquiry become apparent. As discussed next, such flexibility is problematic where ethical guidelines require researchers to detail methods in advance and to adhere rigidly to those plans.

Historical properties

The history of a research field conditions contemporary methods decisions by providing an experience and evidence base, benchmarks, departure points, and traditions. Consequently, the ghosts of the Hawthorne studies continue to haunt researchers in the twenty-first century, having made durable contributions to research agendas, methodology, and terminology. In natural and biomedical science, new research builds on previous work, rendering it obsolete. Organizational research is rarely cumulative in this respect, and researchers ignore at their peril the historical record, the concepts and evidence from long-running research streams, and past contributions in their field. For example, although research into leadership traits was abandoned in the 1950s, following contradictory and inconclusive findings, similar studies still surface in popular, academic, and professional literature (Leigh and Walters, 1998; Charm and Colvin, 1999; Kamp, 1999; Department of Health, 2002). Organizational researchers may thus be advised to allow past experience, frameworks, conceptualizations, and findings, to influence contemporary choices of research focus and appropriate methods.

Political properties

As organizations are political systems (Mintzberg, 1983; Pfeffer, 1992), it is difficult for researchers to respect conventional norms of observer neutrality by avoiding entanglement in power and political issues (see Clegg, Chapter 9, this volume). Researchers are routinely engaged in political actions in at least four ways – when negotiating research objectives, obtaining permissions to access respondents, aligning with stakeholder groups, and when attempting to publish findings.

Negotiated objectives

Researchers often find themselves negotiating their objectives with the 'gatekeepers' who can sanction or block their work (Korczynski, 2004). A gatekeeper is anyone in a position to decide whether or not a research project can proceed at a given site. From a methods perspective, this can be problematic, in at least two respects. First, in many organizational settings, the field researcher may be faced not with a single gatekeeper, but with many individuals who can either allow or deny research access. Second, the researcher may often (not always) have choice with regard to which gatekeepers to approach, choosing (say) the most senior or the one with whom they have the closest relationship; it may be politically unwise to approach more than one gatekeeper simultaneously. However, gatekeepers can make their consent contingent and the spirit of free inquiry is jeopardized when certain themes and topics are discouraged and others welcomed. One solution involves the overt description of a study in innocuous terms (a study of interpersonal relations and team dynamics) while wording data collection instruments to incorporate related themes (age, race, and sex discrimination in promotions), tailoring observations and document collection accordingly. This approach raises ethical concerns relating to appropriate degrees of openness and honesty on the part of the researcher, and the degree to which gatekeepers and respondents may be misled with regard to the researcher's intentions, implying that fully informed consent may not have been given. For example, in their study of management perceptions of organization politics, Madison et al. (1980: 83) argue that the topic is, 'too sensitive for use in direct investigations', and that researchers should cloak the term 'politics' with an appropriate euphemism (managers in this instance were asked to talk about their 'total experience' of work with several employers). In our experience, funding can be linked to the researcher's willingness to address specific themes, questions, and problems in a particular manner. Failure to comply with such expectations has predictable implications for the success of research grant submissions, which may be magnified when funding bodies insist that organizational research access is secured before financial support can be released.

Layered permissions

Organizational researchers can rarely approach respondents directly with requests to participate in their studies. Permission typically has to be obtained first from a senior management gatekeeper, who may often refer such requests to other senior colleagues and in some instances to a management committee or board. In turn, once a general warrant to proceed has been granted, unit or department managers may then have to be approached with further requests to access 'their' staff in a particular manner. Individual respondents can, of course, then refuse to collaborate, despite that cascade of management concessions. This layering of permissions has at least two consequences for method. First, this can delay the start of data collection, and second, this can again compromise research objectives and methods. Permission may be constrained in terms of the topics that can be investigated, the questions that can be asked, the materials that can be collated, and the timing and manner in which data collection is allowed to unfold.

Partisan conclusions

One of the dilemmas of organizational research concerns the extent to which researchers align (or are encouraged by circumstances to align) their agendas with the interests of specific stakeholder groups. Support for managerial agendas, implicit or explicit, direct or indirect, attracts accusations of partisanship, captured by the phrase, 'servants of power'. As management permission is typically a prerequisite for organizational access, it is often difficult to avoid linking research aims explicitly to managerial interests in a way that could potentially damage the interests of other stakeholder groups; for example, assessing process redesign options that would reduce staffing, skill, and payment levels.

Researchers are often asked to report their findings to those who granted access, as a form of *quid pro quo*, for providing documentation and allowing staff to be interviewed, to complete questionnaires, or to attend focus groups, for example. Such reporting implies a tacit acceptance of managerially defined themes and problems. The consequences of failing to meet gatekeeper expectations in this respect can be damaging to the researcher's local reputation, may restrict publication of findings, occasionally leads to the censorship of reports, and can close that research site to other investigators. For example, O'Connor (1995) studied written accounts of change authored by internal organization development (OD) groups in a high technology manufacturing company. The texts praised the efforts of the OD function, whose members had authored the accounts in 25–30 page case studies, presenting the OD function and key individuals as 'pivotal' in change initiation and implementation. In her conclusions, however, O'Connor observes how 'involvement' in key decisions was limited to a small group of 'key' managers; how 'disagreement' was treated as resistance and lack of understanding rather than as 'involvement'; how change narratives revolved around a 'heroic' figure with 'adversaries'. The host organization did not welcome O'Connor's interpretations. Her gatekeeper denied her account, describing it as shocking, outrageous, and unacceptable, and never met with her again. Such a candid account is unusual, but almost certainly reflects a relatively common organizational field research experience.

The politics of publishing

There is a further dimension to the presumed link between research questions and methods, concerning the wider politics of getting one's findings into print. In book publishing, most editors adopt an eclectic approach to their authors' epistemological standpoints, seeking variety in this respect for sound commercial reasons. However, such openness is less common in refereed journals whose editors often privilege particular epistemologies and forms of knowledge. Thus, Huy (2001) establishes his credentials as a normative managerialist commentator in a *Harvard Business Review* article, but identifies himself as an interpretative sociologist in *Administrative Science Quarterly* (Huy, 2002). Knights and

McCabe (1998) adopt a critical labour process perspective in *Human Relations*, but Knights (2002) establishes a postmodern identity in *Organization*. Such 'credentialling' is typically accomplished subtly through a combination of language use and appropriate referencing. To expose more clearly the artifice behind such stylistic manipulations, some authors have deliberately resorted to publishing their findings using several different 'voices' (e.g., Rhodes, 2001; Collins and Rainwater, 2003). Sutton (1997) argues that he has had to play down the significance of his qualitative data in order to get his papers published in journals that prioritize quantitative research, and that he has become a closet qualitative researcher, 'because some editors, reviewers, and journals remain unfairly biased against qualitative research' (Sutton, 1997: 99). The quality of authors' arguments about the appropriateness of their research methods should resolve such disputes, were those decisions based just on links to aims. However, Sutton's experience suggests that bias against one orientation or another is sometimes so strong, and that researchers are disadvantaged, as editors and reviewers discount claims for the appropriateness of particular methods regardless of the cogency of the supporting case.

Further light on this issue is shed by Herman and Egri (2002) describing the background to their research on environmental leadership (Egri and Herman, 2000). In a revealing discussion about their research planning, they note that one of the main reasons they chose to combine their qualitative approach with a survey was that they 'understood that qualitative research alone would not satisfy many mainstream academics' (Herman and Egri, 2002: 132). One of the traditional advantages of mixed methods research concerns the potential for triangulation combining quantitative and qualitative data streams in relation to the same issue. If methods flowed primarily from questions, researchers would not feel compelled to employ techniques they would otherwise prefer not to use. It is apparent that the politics of publishing pull investigators in directions which may be 'politically correct', but with which they may not always feel comfortable, observations that further undermine the textbook connection between research questions and methods.

The political dimensions of organizational field research mean that claims to observer neutrality, as across the social sciences, are hollow. Researchers are occasionally motivated not only to develop understanding, but also to challenge management practices, to trigger intervention, and to effect organizational change. Why investigate power if not to identify ways of addressing its consequences or to reduce power inequalities? Why study quality of working life or sexual harassment unless one wishes to improve the one and overcome the latter? Stakeholder alignment has fundamental, if rarely reported, implications for method concerning, for example, respondent selection, modes of observation, and lines of questioning, with respect to issues that are included and topics which are considered beyond the boundaries of the study.

Ethical properties

Organizational research has attracted an increasing level of ethical scrutiny (see Bell and Wray-Bliss, Chapter 5, this volume). Several bodies (Academy of Management, British Sociological Association, British Psychological Society, European Market Research Association, Social Research Association, etc.) have long-standing research ethics codes, although there is little or no evidence to suggest that those codes are even occasionally contravened. However, in Britain, the Department of Health (2001a, 2001b, 2001c, 2005) Research Governance Framework applies the standards for biomedical research (drug trials, new treatments) to organizational research in health and social care, even where patients or clients are not implicated. This involves a protracted application process policed by local and multisite research ethics committees, concerned primarily with issues of informed consent, right of withdrawal, and respondent anonymity. However, policy guidelines clearly invite ethics review committees to challenge (and reject) methods choices, stating that, 'research which is not of sufficient quality to contribute something useful to existing knowledge is unethical' (Department of Health, 2005: 13). In addition to traditional concerns, therefore, committees also consider aspects of method where, in their judgement, inappropriate choices may have been made. In our experience, an ethics review panel rejected a proposal for a study of management processes where the main data collection methods were scrutiny of documentation and observation of management committee meetings. Some members of those committees, the panel argued, could come under undue social pressure to consent to observation, which thus rendered the method unethical. In two other separate instances involving qualitative inductive multimethod case studies of healthcare service improvement initiatives, ethics committees challenged proposals for lacking precision with regard to sampling and questioning strategies, unimpressed by arguments concerning the need to adjust methods in a flexible manner during fieldwork, in the light of emerging themes, findings, and unanticipated organizational changes.

The open-ended nature of qualitative inquiry thus surfaces ethical concerns. Some research modes, such as grounded theory, discourage the specification of research questions in advance of data collection, privileging issues emerging during the investigation (Locke, 2001; see Goulding, Chapter 22, this volume). In America, institutional review boards (IRBs) make life difficult for qualitative researchers who advocate flexible methods in order that new questions can emerge and be pursued effectively. This has led to clashes between researchers and IRBs, which often employ biomedical research standards, prohibiting flexible methods on ethical grounds, because the investigator does not know exactly how the research will be done (Lincoln and Tierney, 2004). Lynn (2004) reports the case of an IRB which successfully argued that a hospital quality improvement project, led by managers, but

leading to publication of the lessons derived, constituted research activity, and should thus have been subject to prior ethical review (a judgement, which, if applied consistently, would in Lynn's view present insurmountable barriers to most quality improvement projects). Moreover, the growing tendency, following the Belmont Report, for matters of research design, quality, and ethics effectively to become fused, magnifies the problem when biomedical criteria for research quality and ethics are applied (Sieber, 2004). These trends parallel the consequences of the British Department of Health Research Governance Framework (Truman, 2003), whereas the implications of the Belmont rules are much broader. Indeed, there are calls in Britain for the 'light touch' approach to ethical vetting in nonhealth fields to become more rigorous (Kent et al., 2002). The notion that research methods depend only on research questions is untenable when considering the open-ended nature of qualitative research, and the ethical context in which many researchers ply their trade, requiring them to mould methods to sometimes inappropriate criteria.

The increased intensity of ethical scrutiny is perhaps not surprising. There has been growth in public concern with the process and outcomes of all scientific enquiry, and researchers must be able clearly to justify their approach. Researchers must also comply with legislation concerning, for example, discrimination, privacy, and data protection, to protect themselves as well as informants. Some social and organizational research involves vulnerable respondents who deserve protection from researchers who may cause unwitting harm. Some social and organizational research focuses on controversial and sensitive issues, about which some respondents may be reluctant to speak openly, and where researchers must avoid exerting pressure on individuals to submit to a project's requirements.

Ethical scrutiny generates other challenges for method. It may not always be practicable to gain prior consent from every respondent likely to be involved in a study where some form of observation will be used, thus breaching the principle of right to withdraw. Some researchers may be concerned about contamination by presensitizing respondents with knowledge of the research aims; this can be avoided by misleading respondents, breaching the principle of informed consent. In publishing, a researcher may be required to omit information, which, although relevant to the development of an explanation of the phenomenon under investigation, would disclose individual or organizational identity, breaching the principle of anonymity. We were once asked to omit discussion of a conference that had contributed to an organizational change process; participants had reacted unfavourably to the style and content of some presentations. However, several delegates were prompted by that experience to develop their own approach to the issues in hand, thus securing their commitment to the change agenda. Discussion of this incident was proscribed, because it would 'unnecessarily embarrass the conference organizers, who had already learned from that mistake'.

The spotlight of ethical scrutiny is currently focused on the proposal stage. Should the research process as a whole become subject to ethical monitoring, as has been informally suggested, field researchers may face even more constraints with regard to choice of appropriate, and acceptable, data collection methods.

Evidential properties

Organizational researchers often have to consider how their findings will be used, and by whom, before making methods choices, so that their approach will be perceived by relevant audiences as having been appropriate. Researchers thus have to take into account the potentially conflicting interests and expectations of their academic, managerial, and research participant audiences. Academic colleagues expect new knowledge and theoretical insight. Organization managers anticipate practical recommendations. Research participants typically wish to know that their contributions have been interpreted

and used in an appropriate manner, and are presented anonymously. The process, which leads from problem definition, to data collection and evidence, conclusions, prescription, and subsequent changes in organization practice, may appear to be linear, but is problematic. The relationships between evidence and practice in most fields (including medicine, where 'evidence-based medicine' is now mandatory) are complex (Fitzgerald et al., 2002), and the external validity of organizational research remains contentious. Qualitative researchers often have a limited interest in statistical generalization, emphasizing instead analytical (link to theory) and naturalistic (link to experience) generalization. Findings generated in one setting (acute medical care) may not generalize to others (bespoke furniture manufacture). Researchers must judge the scope conditions for their findings, or derive *moderatum* generalizations, indicating that aspects of a situation or context can be viewed as 'instances of a broader recognizable set of features' (Williams, 2000: 215). Feeding back 'acceptable' findings in the context of a professional organization (Mintzberg, 1979b; Brock, Powell, and Hinings, 1999), such as healthcare, presents challenges not commonly faced by researchers in commercial settings. Doctors and engineers, for example, schooled in the norms of biomedical and natural science research practice, are understandably suspicious about research findings based on methods that do not appear to follow those familiar protocols. Evidence thus has to meet a receptive audience, whose members have adequate organizational authority, for findings to transfer into practice. That combination of factors is rare. It may even be the case that the researcher has to offer to conduct an enquiry specifically in a manner that gatekeepers regard as credible; for example, to secure access to a General Motors factory, Milkman (1997) agreed to conduct a survey that would provide 'hard quantitative data', even though her research required a qualitative approach.

Research evidence rarely reveals clear causal links. For all but the most closely bounded topics, the field is multivariate and multilayered. For example, does total quality management improve organizational effectiveness? The main terms in this question are difficult to define with precision, they mean different things in different contexts, and to different stakeholders, and the number of interacting factors involved, over time, at various levels of analysis (individual, team, business unit, organization, and external context) defies simplistic attempts at theorizing (Iles and Sutherland, 2001; Øvretveit and Gustafson, 2002). Establishing cause and effect across complex, iterative, and multidimensional processes over time is challenging. Several commentators have turned to process theories to handle such phenomena (Pettigrew, 1985; Langley, 1999; Van de Ven and Poole, 2002; Dawson, 2003). Process theories tend to adopt a narrative form, and focus on local causality, rather than seek to identify universal laws linking dependent and independent variables. A further complication is that different stakeholders hold contrasting views of the nature, definition, and significance of organizational problems. However, audiences for research findings are often interested mainly in, 'what works?'. Researchers who can answer this question may find that their enterprise shares some of the attributes of the work of management consultants, but without the financial rewards. The respective roles of researchers and consultants are more closely intertwined than is often acknowledged. Researchers interested in, for example, total quality management, or business process re-engineering, can argue that they are studying novel organizational forms, but they are also studying the nature and implications of the commercial products of management consulting firms. The findings from such studies may be used both by host organizations and consulting firms, to influence organizational change processes.

Decisions about method may thus have to consider the nature of the evidence ultimately required to inform practice, and also assess the acceptability of different forms and sources of evidence to specific audiences responsible for implementing recommendations (see Learmonth, Chapter 6, this volume for a critical discussion of evidence-based management).

Personal properties

Researchers commonly study topics in which they have a personal interest, using methods in which they are trained and competent, and with which they feel comfortable. Some researchers enjoy in-depth face-to-face encounters and the challenge of identifying pattern and order in qualitative data; others find satisfaction discovering at a computer screen associations in quantitative data sets. A researcher's training and skills can thus influence both choice of research topic and how it is investigated. Novice researchers are typically instructed not to allow personal preference and bias to intrude on 'technical' decisions concerning research methods. Should researchers be encouraged to experience guilt with respect to personal beliefs and passions, with respect to the skills that they have acquired, practised and honed? As many commentators have advocated, reflexivity should be encouraged in making and in reporting decisions concerning research methods.

Departing from the convention that relationships with research participants contaminate data, Dutton and Dukerich (2006) argue that the researcher's social networks and interpersonal skills ('relational practices') are critical to designing and sustaining interesting organizational research. While the contribution of friends and acquaintances with regard to accessing organizations as research sites and gathering relevant 'inside' information may be widely appreciated, these issues are rarely recognized in published accounts as factors influencing research design (Buchanan, Boddy and McCalman, 1988; Dutton and Dukerich, 2006: 21).

Package deals and the unseen: implications for method

This chapter began with the argument that the field of organizational research displays at least three significant trends. The first concerns a widening of the scope of the agenda, embracing a growing range of themes, issues, problems, and settings. A second theme, common across the social sciences, concerns an eclectic, multiparadigmatic approach, which has contributed to a weakening of the traditional dominance (but not necessarily the influence) of positivist orientations. While blurred at the margins, those competing orientations have generated intense debate. Consequently, the field is fragmented, with little or no consensus around concepts, frameworks, theories, or practical propositions. A third trend concerns the creative approach to method, which now deploys a diverse array of data collection methods, with more novel techniques standing alongside, and often complementing established approaches. We then sought to demonstrate that choice of research methods is shaped not only by technical and theoretical considerations related to the research topic, objectives, and norms of practice, but also by a number of other characteristics of organizational field research:

Attributes of the organizational research setting or context

The research tradition or history relevant to a particular study

The inevitable politicization of the organizational researcher's role

Constraints imposed by a growing concern with research ethics

Theoretical and audience-related issues in translating evidence into practice

Personal preferences and biases with regard to choice of method

While these attributes of organizational research have been widely acknowledged, they are typically represented as problems or difficulties, interfering with choice of methods, to be avoided through careful planning. However, as Figure 1.1 seeks to illustrate, those factors, taken together, instead constitute an interrelated system of inevitable influences on research methods choices. Contextualizing methods choice in this web of influence has at least three implications. First, it is difficult to sustain a model of the researcher as neutral observer. Even the selection of an underpinning paradigm is a politically inspired act, not merely an intellectually informed choice, as this can involve an implicit alignment with particular stakeholder interests, overlooking or marginalizing issues that may be more important to others. Neutrality is often further compromised in feeding back to gatekeepers reports of research findings, conclusions, and practical recommendations, as 'politically incorrect' conclusions may be omitted. Researchers claiming neutral status are often pursuing agendas that are implicitly aligned with partisan interests. The concept of researcher as detached and disinterested has already been widely discredited (e.g., Van de Ven and Poole, 2002).

Second, it is difficult to sustain a model of the research process in which method relies solely on links to objectives, the advantages and limitations of one approach weighed objectively against others. We have sought to show that methods choice is a multicriteria decision, involving a more complex, interrelated, and iterative series of considerations. Method in this perspective is part of a 'package deal', an integral component of a comprehensive research system where, in the pursuit of particular aims in a given setting, theoretical, epistemological, organizational, historical, political, ethical, evidential, and personal factors are combined in a coherent manner. Choice of method is not a 'stand alone' decision reached at an early stage in the research process, but evolves as a project unfolds, as the researcher's understanding of the issues, and also of the organizational research setting, develops. The widely-espoused view, reinforced in methods texts and elsewhere, that the research process (sampling, data collection methods, analysis, etc.) flows logically and inexorably from research questions, is an oversimplification when this range of influences on an investigation is considered (Bryman and

Bell, 2007). It is not surprising that, when Grunow (1995) conducted a content analysis of organization studies articles, he found that only 21 percent discussed the relationship between the research topic or problem and the methods employed in the investigation.

Third, it is difficult to sustain a concept of method as neutral technique for bringing reality into focus. Shaped by a comprehensive web of influences, decisions concerning method frame the data windows through which organizational phenomena are observed. Methods choices determine the unseen as well as the documented, thus linking organizational, historical, political, ethical, evidential, and personal factors with the development of both theoretical and practical conclusions. Consequently, those factors can be considered as data, rather than as features of the research setting of problematic concern. Advocates of reflexivity (Woolgar, 1988; Alvesson and Sköldberg, 2000) advise openness and honesty with regard to the position and identity of the researcher, accompanied by critical self-appraisal. The argument here suggests that reflexive appraisal should be extended to incorporate discussion of the sweep of factors influencing methods choices for a given project, as these in turn both influence and contribute to the evidence base on which conclusions are constructed.

It is thus important to understand more fully, and to articulate more openly, the basis of research methods choices. The factors affecting those choices could perhaps be more widely reported to support methods training by providing a widely informed overview of the nature of the craft and to promote productive dialogue across a research community that seems to be increasingly fragmented by differences in orientation. Despite the web of constraints and influences, the design of organizational research work and the choice of data collection methods remain in part a creative process. This complex package of issues can be combined and configured in a variety of different ways. It is important, therefore, to recognize not only the technical skills and knowledge of

the researcher, but also the role of personal interests, preferences, biases, prejudices, and creativity.

Competence in research method has traditionally, and narrowly, been expressed in terms of selecting methods consistent with research topic and objectives, while avoiding or resolving those annoying practical field-work problems. We conclude that competence in method must now also encompass the ability to address, systematically and coherently, the organizational, historical, political, ethical, evidential, and personal influences identified in this chapter.

NOTES

*An earlier version of this chapter was first published in *Organizational Research Methods*; see Buchanan and Bryman (2007).

REFERENCES

Alvesson, M. and Skoldberg, K. (2000) *Reflexive Methodology: New Vistas for Qualitative Research*, London: Sage Publications.

Barry, D. and Elmes, M. (1997) 'Strategy retold: toward a narrative view of strategy discourse', *Academy of Management Review*, 22(2): 429–52.

Boje, D.M. (1991) 'The storytelling organization: a study of story performance in an office-supply firm', *Administrative Science Quarterly*, 36(1): 106–26.

Boje, D.M. (2001) *Narrative Methods for Organizational and Communication Research*, London: Sage Publications.

Brock, D.M., Powell, M.J. and Hinings, C.R. (eds) (1999) *Restructuring the Professional Organization: Accounting, Health Care and Law*, London and New York: Routledge.

Broussine, M. (2008) *Creative Methods in Organizational Research*, London: Sage Publications.

Bryman, A. and Bell, E. (2007) *Business Research Methods*, (second edn), Oxford: Oxford University Press.

Buchanan, D.A. (1999) 'The logic of political action: an experiment with the epistemology of the particular', *British Journal of Management*, 10 (special conference issue): 73–88.

Buchanan, D.A. (2000) 'The lived experience of high velocity change: a hospital case study', American Academy of Management Conference, Symposium on Strategy as Dynamic and Pluralistic, Toronto, August.

Buchanan, D.A. (2001) 'The role of photography in organizational research: a re-engineering case illustration', *Journal of Management Inquiry*, 10(2): 151–64.

Buchanan, D.A. (2003) 'Demands, instabilities, manipulations, careers: the lived experience of driving change', *Human Relations*, 56(6): 663–84.

Buchanan, D.A. and Bryman, A. (2007) 'Contextualizing methods choice in organizational research', *Organizational Research Methods*, 10(3): 483–501.

Buchanan, D.A. and Huczynski, A. (2004) 'Images of influence: twelve angry men and thirteen days', *Journal of Management Inquiry*, 13(4): 312–23.

Buchanan, D.A., Boddy, D. and McCalman, J. (1988) 'Getting in, getting on, getting out and getting back', in Alan Bryman (ed.), *Doing Research in Organizations*, London: Routledge, pp.53–67.

Burrell, G. and Morgan, G. (1979) *Sociological Paradigms and Organizational Analysis*, London: Heinemann.

Butler, R. (1997) 'Stories and experiments in social inquiry', *Organization Studies*, 12(6): 927–48.

Campbell, D.T. and Stanley, J.C. (1966) *Experimental and Quasi-Experimental Designs for Research*, Chicago: Rand McNally & Company.

Champoux, J.E. (2001) *Organizational Behaviour: Using Film to Visualize Principles and Practices*, Cincinnati, OH: South-Western College Publishing/Thomson Learning.

Charm, R. and Colvin, G. (1999) 'Why CEOs fail', *Fortune*, 139(12): 69–78.

Clegg, S.R., Hardy, C. and Nord, W.R. (eds) (1996) *Handbook of Organization Studies*, London: Sage Publications.

Collins, D. and Rainwater, K. (2003) 'Riders on the storm: a sideways look at a celebrated tale of corporate transformation', British Academy of Management annual conference, Harrogate, September.

Cook, T.D. and Campbell, D.T. (1979) *Quasi-Experimentation: Design and Analysis Issues for Field Settings*, Chicago: Rand McNally College Publishing Company.

Currall, S.C. and Towler, A.J. (2003) 'Research methods in management and organizational research: toward integration of qualitative and quantitative techniques', in A. Tashakkori and C. Teddlie (eds), *Handbook of Mixed Methods in Social and Behavioral Research*, Thousand Oaks: Sage Publications, pp.513–26.

Czarniawska, B. (1999) *Writing Management: Organization Theory as a Literary Genre*, Oxford: Oxford University Press.

Dawson, P. (2003) *Reshaping Change: A Processual Approach*, London: Routledge.

Deetz, S. (1996) 'Describing differences in approaches to organization science: rethinking Burrell and Morgan and their legacy', *Organization Science*, 7(2): 191–207.

Deetz, S. (2000) 'Describing differences in approaches to organization science: rethinking Burrell and Morgan and their legacy', in Peter J. Frost, Arie Y. Lewin and Richard L. Daft (eds), *Talking About Organization Science: Debates and Dialogue from Crossroads*, Thousand Oaks, CA: Sage Publications, pp.123–52.

Denis, J.L. and Lomas, J. (2003) 'Convergent evolution: the academic and policy roots of collaborative research', *Journal of Health Services Research and Policy*, 8(2): 1–5.

Department of Health (2001a) *Good Practice in Consent Implementation Guide*, London: Department of Health.

Department of Health (2001b) *Governance Arrangements for NHS Research Ethics Committees*, London: Central Office for Research Ethics Committees (COREC).

Department of Health (2001c) *Research Governance Framework for Health and Social Care*, London: Department of Health.

Department of Health (2002) *NHS Leadership Qualities Framework*, London: NHS Modernization Agency Leadership Centre.

Department of Health (2005) *Research Governance Framework for Health and Social Care*, (second edn), London: Department of Health.

Dick, P. (2004) 'Discourse analysis', in Catherine Cassell and Gillian Symon (eds), *Essential Guide to Qualitative Methods in Organizational Research*, London: Sage Publications, pp.203–13.

Doolin, B. (2003) 'Narratives of change: discourse, technology and organization', *Organization*, 10(4): 751–70.

Dutton, J.E. and Dukerich, J.M. (2006) 'The relational foundation of research: an underappreciated dimension of interesting research', *Academy of Management Journal*, 49(1): 21–6.

Dyer, W.G. and Wilkins, A.L. (1991) 'Better stories, not better constructs, to generate a better theory: a rejoinder to Eisenhardt', *Academy of Management Review*, 16: 613–19.

Egri, C.P. and Herman, S. (2000) 'Leadership in the North American environmental sector: values, leadership styles, and contexts of environmental leaders and their organizations', *Academy of Management Journal*, 43(4): 571–604.

Eisenhardt, K.M. (1989) 'Building theories from case study research', *Academy of Management Review*, 14(4): 532–50.

Eisenhardt, K.M. and Bourgeois, L.J. (1988) 'Politics of strategic decision making in high-velocity environments: towards a mid-range theory', *Academy of Management Journal*, 31(4): 737–70.

Emmison, M. and Smith, P. (2000) *Researching the Visual: Images, Objects, Contexts and Interactions in Social and Cultural Inquiry*, London: Sage Publications.

Fielding, N., Lee, R.M. and Blank, G. (eds) (2008) *The Sage Handbook of Online Research Methods*, London: Sage Publications.

Fincham, R. (2002) 'Narratives of success and failure in systems development', *British Journal of Management*, 13(1): 1–14.

Fitzgerald, L., Ferlie, E., Wood, M. and Hawkins, C. (2002) 'Interlocking interactions, the diffusion of innovations in healthcare', *Human Relations*, 55(12): 1429–49.

Foreman, J. and Thatchenkery, T.J. (1996) 'Filmic representations for organizational analysis: the characterization of a transplant organization in the film Rising Sun', *Journal of Organizational Change Management*, 9(3): 44–61.

Goes, J.B. and Park, S.H. (1997) 'Interorganizational links and innovation: the case of hospital services', *Academy of Management Journal*, 40(3): 673–87.

Grunow, D. (1995) 'The research design in organization studies: problems and prospects', *Organization Science*, 6(1): 93–103.

Hamel, G. (2000) 'Waking up IBM: how a gang of unlikely rebels transformed Big Blue', *Harvard Business Review*, 78(4): 137–46.

Harper, D. (1994) 'On the authority of the image: visual methods at the crossroads', in Norman K. Denzin and Yvonna S. Lincoln (eds), *Handbook of Qualitative Research*, Thousand Oaks, CA: Sage Publications, pp.403–12.

Harper, D. (2000) 'Reimagining visual methods: Galileo to *Neoromancer*', in Norman K. Denzin and Yvonna S. Lincoln (eds), *Handbook of Qualitative Research* (second edn.), Thousand Oaks, CA: Sage Publications, pp.717–32.

Hassard, J. and Holliday, R. (eds) (1998) *Organization Representation: Work and Organization in Popular Culture*, London: Sage Publications.

Heller, F. (2004) 'Action research and research action: a family of methods', in Catherine Cassell and Gillian Symon (eds), *Essential Guide to Qualitative Methods in Organizational Research*, London: Sage Publications, pp.349–60.

Herman, S. and Egri, C.P. (2002) 'Triangulation in action: integration of qualitative and quantitative methods to research environmental leadership', in K.W. Parry and J.R. Meindl (eds), *Grounding Leadership Theory and Research: Issues, Perspectives, and Methods*, Greenwich, CT: Information Age Publishing, pp.129–48.

Huxham, C. and Vangen, S. (2003) 'Researching organizational practice through action research: case studies and design choices', *Organizational Research Methods*, 6(3): 383–404.

Huy, Q.N. (2001) 'In praise of middle managers', *Harvard Business Review*, 79(8): 72–9.

Huy, Q.N. (2002) 'Emotional balancing of organizational continuity and radical change: the contribution of middle managers', *Administrative Science Quarterly*, 47(1): 31–69.

Iles, V. and Sutherland, K. (2001) *Organizational Change: A Review for Health Care Managers, Professionals and Researchers*, London: National Co-ordinating Centre for NHS Service Delivery and Organization Research and Development.

Kamp, D. (1999) *The 21st Century Manager: Future-Focused Skills for the Next Millennium*, London: Kogan Page.

Kent, J., Williamson, E., Goodenough, T. and Ashcroft, R. (2002) 'Social science gets the ethics treatment: research governance and ethical review', *Sociological Research Online*, 7(4): www.socresonline.org.uk/7/4/williamson.html.

Knights, D. (2002) 'Writing organizational analysis into Foucault', *Organization*, 9(4): 575–93.

Knights, D. and McCabe, D. (1998) 'When "life is but a dream": obliterating politics through business process re-engineering?', *Human Relations*, 51(6): 761–98.

Kolb, D.G. (2003) 'Seeking continuity amidst organizational change: a storytelling approach', *Journal of Management Inquiry*, 12(2): 180–83.

Korczynski, M. (2004) 'Access', in M.S. Lewis-Beck, A. Bryman and T.F. Liao (eds), *The Sage Encyclopedia of Social Science Research Methods (Vol.1–3)*, Thousand Oaks, CA: Sage Publications, pp.2–3.

Langley, A. (1999) 'Strategies for theorizing from process data', *Academy of Management Review*, 24(4): 691–710.

Leigh, A. and Walters, M. (1998) *Effective Change: Twenty Ways to Make it Happen*, London: Institute of Personnel and Development.

Lincoln, Y.S. and Guba, E. (1985) *Naturalistic Inquiry*, Beverly Hills, CA: Sage Publications.

Lincoln, Y.S. and Tierney, W.G. (2004) 'Qualitative research and institutional review boards', *Qualitative Inquiry*, 10(2): 219–34.

Locke, K. (2001) *Grounded Theory in Management Research*, London: Sage Publications.

Lynn, J. (2004) 'When does quality improvement count as research ?: human subject protection and theories of knowledge', *Quality and Safety in Health Care*, 13: 67–70.

Madison, D.L., Allen, R.W., Porter, L.W., Renwick, P.A. and Mayes, B.T. (1980) 'Organizational politics: an exploration of managers' perceptions', *Human Relations*, 33(2): 79–100.

Meyer, A.D. (1991) 'Visual data in organizational research', *Organization Science*, 2(2): 218–36.

Milkman, R. (1997) *Farewell to the Factory: Auto Workers in the Late Twentieth Century*, Berkeley & Los Angeles: University of California Press.

Mintzberg, H. (1979a) 'An emerging strategy of "direct" research', *Administrative Science Quarterly*, 24(4): 582–89.

Mintzberg, H. (1979b) *The Structuring of Organizations: A Synthesis of the Research*, Englewood Cliffs, NJ: Prentice Hall.

Mintzberg, H. (1983) *Power in and Around Organizations*, New Jersey: Prentice Hall.

Mitchell, J.C. (1983) 'Case and situational analysis', *Sociological Review*, 31(2): 187–211.

Mohr, L.B. (1982) *Explaining Organizational Behaviour: The Limits and Possibilities of Theory and Research*, San Francisco: Jossey-Bass Publishers.

O'Connor, E.S. (1995) 'Paradoxes of participation: textual analysis and organizational change', *Organization Studies*, 16(5): 769–803.

O'Leary, M. (2003) 'From paternalism to cynicism: narratives of a newspaper company', *Human Relations*, 56(6): 685–704.

Øvretveit, J. and Gustafson, D. (2002) 'Evaluation of quality improvement programmes', *Quality and Safety in Health Care*, 11: 270–75.

Pentland, B.T. (1999) 'Building process theory with narrative: from description to explanation', *Academy of Management Review*, 24(4): 711–24.

Pettigrew, A.M. (1985) *The Awakening Giant: Continuity and Change in ICI*, Oxford: Basil Blackwell.

Pettigrew, A.M. (1990) 'Longitudinal field research on change: theory and practice', *Organization Science*, 1(3): 267–92.

Pettigrew, A.M., Woodman, R.W. and Cameron, K.S. (2001) 'Studying organizational change and development: challenges for future research', *Academy of Management Journal*, 44(4): 697–713.

Pfeffer, J. (1992) *Managing With Power: Politics and Influence in Organization*, Boston, MA: Harvard Business School Press.

Poole, M.S., Van de Ven, A.H., Dooley, K. and Holmes, M.E. (2000) *Organizational Change and Innovation Processes: Theory and Methods for Research*, Oxford and New York: Oxford University Press.

Prasad, A. and Prasad, P. (2002) 'The coming of age of interpretive organizational research', *Organizational Research Methods*, 5(1): 4–11.

Rhodes, C. (2001) *Writing Organization: (Re)presentation and Control in Narratives at Work*, Amsterdam/Philadephia: John Benjamins Publishing Company.

Roethlisberger, F.J. (1977) *The Elusive Phenomenon: An Autobiographical Account of My Work in the Field of Organizational Behaviour at the Harvard Business School*, Boston, MA: Harvard University Press.

Roethlisberger, F.J. and Dickson, W.J. (1939) *Management and the Worker*, Cambridge, MA: Harvard University Press.

Shadish, W.R., Cook, T.D. and Campbell, D.T. (2001) *Experimental and Quasi-Experimental Designs for Generalized Causal Inference*, Boston, MA: Houghton Mifflin.

Sieber, J.E. (2004) 'Ethical principles', in M.S. Lewis-Beck, Alan Bryman and T.F. Liao (eds), *The Sage Encyclopedia of Social Science Research Methods*, Thousand Oaks: Sage Publications, pp.323–25.

Stake, R.E. (1994) 'Case Studies', in Norman K. Denzin and Yvonna S. Lincoln (eds), *Handbook of Qualitative Research*, Thousand Oaks: Sage Publications, pp.236–47.

Stake, R.E. (2000) 'Case studies', in Norman K. Denzin and Yvonna S. Lincoln (eds), *Handbook of Qualitative Research* (second edn), Thousand Oaks: Sage Publications, pp.435–54.

Stiles, D.R. (2004) 'Pictorial representation', in Catherine Cassell and Gillian Symon (eds), *Essential Guide to Qualitative Methods in Organizational Research*, London: Sage Publications, pp.127–39.

Suchman, L. (1995) 'Representations of work: making work visible', *Communications of the ACM*, 38(9): 56–61.

Sutton, R.I. (1997) 'The virtues of closet qualitative research', *Organization Science*, 8(1): 97–106.

Taylor, S.S. (1999) 'Making sense of revolutionary change: differences in members' stories', *Journal of Organizational Change Management*, 12(6): 524–39.

Teddlie, C. and Tashakkori, A. (2003) 'Major issues and controversies in the use of mixed methods in the social and behavioral sciences', in A. Tashakkori and C. Teddlie (eds), *Handbook of Mixed Methods in Social and Behavioral Research*, Thousand Oaks, CA: Sage Publications, pp.3–50.

Tranfield, D., Denyer, D. and Smart, P. (2003) 'Towards a methodology for developing evidence-informed management knowledge by means of systematic review', *British Journal of Management*, 14(3): 207–22.

Truman, C. (2003) 'Ethics and the ruling relations of research production', *Sociological Research Online*, 8(1): www.socresonline.org.uk/8/1/truman.html.

Tsoukas, H. (1989) 'The validity of idiographic research explanations', *Academy of Management Review*, 14: 551–61.

Van de Ven, A.H. and Poole, M.S. (2002) 'Field research methods', in Joel A.C. Baum (ed.), *The Blackwell Companion to Organizations*, Malden, MA and Oxford: Blackwell Publishing, pp. 867–88.

Whittington, R. and Mayer, M. (2002) *Organizing for Success in the Twenty-First Century: A Starting Point for Change*, London: Chartered Institute of Personnel and Development.

Williams, M. (2000) 'Interpretivism and generalization', *Sociology*, 34: 209–24.

Woolgar, S. (ed.) (1988) *Knowledge and Reflexivity: New Frontiers in the Sociology of Knowledge*, London: Sage Publications.

Yauch, C.A. and Steudel, H.J. (2003) 'Complementary use of qualitative and quantitative cultural assessment methods', *Organizational Research Methods*, 6(4): 465–81.

Yin, R.K. (2003) *Case Study Research: Design and Methods* (second edn.), Thousand Oaks: Sage Publications.

PART I

Dilemmas: The Shifting Context of Organizational Research

Focusing on the issues, debates, tensions, and dilemmas, which define the historical, epistemological, and practical contexts in which organizational research occurs

2

Organizational Research as Alternative Ways of Attending To and Talking About Structures and Activities

Stanley Deetz

INTRODUCTION

Over the past thirty years, the number of approaches to studying organizations has grown rapidly. We have moved from a time characterized by competing theories to one filled with metatheoretical debates, which pose more radical questions regarding the nature of the world and the best ways to do research. The presence of such fundamental differences has encouraged reflection on research practice, creating difficulty in assessing the quality of different works. Judging which work does the job better is hard when the job each is intended to do is different. Understanding the differences in ways of doing research is essential for understanding as well as critical judgements.

In the 1990s, I developed a characterization of research programme differences that was designed to be more helpful than the popular representation of paradigms by Burrell and Morgan (1979). While certainly more, and in many ways better, research has been conducted since then, I have found little reason to revise that characterization. In many ways, recent conflicts have tended to confirm that the identified dimensions of contrast are useful ones. Following that previous work (Deetz, 1996), this chapter reflects on research practices and debates, sorting out the differences that make some programmes different from others. As an analogy, the chapter tries to determine what games are being played, and what makes them different, so that we can attribute different approaches to different teams competing in the same basic game. This essay hopes to trigger discussion regarding how different scholars construct knowledge and justify research practices and also about the values, hopes, and groups interests that they support.

To discuss different programmes of work, I must myself accept a metatheoretical position. A version of social constructionism allows a way to talk about alternative programmes and how they are constructed without prejudicing one over the others (see Parker, 1998; Mir and Watson, 2000). This chapter begins with a discussion of this version of constructionism. I will argue that knowledge is constructed from alternative ways of attending to and talking about organizational life. This will be contrasted with relativist and objectivist claims.

This chapter will reproduce my two-dimensional scheme for directing attention to similarities and differences among research programmes. I will argue that the most interesting differences can be displayed through looking at, first, the type of inter-action researchers favour with individuals and events in the research site – characterized as local/emergent versus elite/a priori conceptions. And second, the moves the research activity and report make toward closure or indeterminacy in that interaction – characterized as consensus-seeking versus dissensus-seeking. These dimensions generate a two-by-two matrix; I will discuss each of four 'ideal type' research programmes as discourses, or as community-based ways of engaging and talking about the world, and conclude by considering the researcher's choices.

I do not believe that different research programmes are usefully referred to as 'paradigms'. Such a spatial bounded metaphor favours building boxes and placing individuals and their work in them. Rather, most of us ask and answer very different questions at different points in time. There are enough human and organizational problems, of radically different sorts, impacting on enough different stakeholders, to require radically different ways of conception and research. We each need different approaches to address them.

For example, when I was a department head, I carefully counted the number of students 'majoring' with us. The count was important to getting staff and other resources. I also wanted to be able to assess the impact of different educational initiatives and

predict the success of 'majors'. This requires particular modes of research. However, I also knew that the idea of a major was a social construction, and that how and when one was counted, as well as concepts of success, were relatively arbitrary. Moreover, particular departments and ways of learning were respectively advantaged and disadvantaged by the constitution of majors and the practices surrounding them. To understand these issues required a different notion of research. My research processes were not so much competitive as simply addressing different levels and types of concerns at different moments. They are not practiced at once but rotated through my life. And they each impact on each other. If counting majors did not have consequences, we would not be concerned with the nature of their social construction, and in looking at their social construction, we often come to constitute and count them differently.

Consequently, in the practice of organizational research, comparing different theories and their knowledge claims requires a *rotation of contestabilities*. Different discourses are not well conceived as incommensurable paradigms – as boxes, fixed justifications, or safe places not needing conversation. Rather, they can be usefully thought of as languages and practices each attending to different concerns and problems, each partial and directional open to translations, which, when done well, enrich and complicate alternative languages (Chia and King, 2001). The question is not which is right or better, but which languages and processes address whose and which problems, and the consequences of addressing them in this way. This is similar to the argument advanced by Tsoukas (2000, 2004).

Social construction as a prior interactive production

Scientific observation has long been considered a compound, an irreducible outcome of a relation between a way of attending to and talking about the world, and a world that can be attended to and talked about in this way. This fundamental understanding arises across our various discussions of research and science as well as in everyday life. In philosophy, Husserl demonstrated the irreducibility of the productive moment where a particular way of attending, to the world and the world attended, to interact to form experience. Understanding the irreducibility of this formed unity requires a longer philosophical argument than is possible here. Basically, this means that the world can only be experienced in approaching it in some way, using some senses or sense extending instrument. All claims are grounded in this contact where a not-yet-determined world becomes determined in a specific way. Neither the way of encountering the world, nor the external world, can be given priority since they exist in relation to each other. Neither objectivist nor relativist claims can avoid an appeal back to the moment of interaction. Heidegger also demonstrated the linguisticality of this, showing that all 'seeing' is 'seeing as' (Rorty, 1979; Deetz, 1992, 2000). Following the earlier example, a 'department major' is not relative or easily wished away, but a real person with needs and goals; seeing the person as a major requires encountering them in a particular way. Both the person and the constitutive processes are necessary for there to be a 'department major'.

In the radically different tradition of the philosophy of the natural sciences, the Heisenberg principle suggests the inseparability of the means of observation and the observed. Hanson (1965) shows that all seeing is theory laden; observation is like a fabric with a 'warp' and 'woof'. By the end of the twentieth century such an understanding had moved from the realm of philosophy to define the epistemological struggles of science and everyday life in 'culture wars', 'paradigm debate', 'articulatory practices', and 'standpoint epistemology'. Whether they like to or not, independent of their preferred philosophy of science, all organizational researchers must begin from here (Astley, 1985). The myth of immaculate perception is dead, but questions of the preferencing of research community or managerial conceptions and struggles over objectivity and subjectivity are not.

Many researchers, however, especially in America, and following neopositivist traditions, do not spend much time thinking about this. They accept the world as it appears to them in their science, procedures, and language, as simply real and there. The rest is often treated as philosophical and prescientific. While naive empiricism may be gone, methodological determinism is not. Research in these traditions is rarely reflexive, and the consequences of particular positionings and the constructionist qualities of conceptions, instruments, and procedures are rarely made explicit. This chapter intends to aid the process of making background constructionist activities explicit and discussible, also connecting evaluation to issues of stakeholder preference and consequences.

Fundamental assumptions about the nature of the world, methods of producing knowledge, and values, are developed through the discourse of researchers. Such assumptions are necessary to produce any kind of understanding and knowledge and are usually most contested during periods of rapid change. While fundamental assumptions themselves are not open to refutation, they are open to exploration. Scholars rightfully ask of any research program, 'to solve what problems?'; 'to what ends?'; 'whose meanings?'; 'whose knowledge?'.

Various contemporary social constructionist positions seem obvious to many, but heretical to some. Much of the concern is justified by appeals to fears of relativism. Most often, this arises from the retention of subject-object dualism, and the definition of truth specific to unreflected common sense or their own epistemological preferences. Certainly, much of the current debate between social constructionist and critical realists is continued as each side advances basically over-characterized views of the other position based in subject-object dualism (Willmott, 2005; Contu and Willmott, 2005; Gergen 1998). While some social constructionists are relativists, the stronger version social constructionisms are not. To say that a community-based construction relative to particular perspectives and values (which are not reducible to personal preference or opportunistic claims) must be known before truth and falsity can be adjudicated, is not tantamount to making truth irrelevant or relativist (Deetz, 2000). Conceptions of truth and falsehood linked to a particular epistemology and group-based preconceptions do not provide a useful vocabulary for discussing competing truth claims in an increasing global and heterogeneous society. We need to begin rather than end the discussion of knowledge.

Understanding our alternative research approaches from a constructionist stance leads us to be less concerned with the relation of the constituted subject and constituted world, and more with the *constituting activity*, the original codeterminative interaction from which subjects and objects are later abstracted and treated as natural. As already indicated, all seeing, including that of science, is a seeing as; the important questions are seeing as what, and how is that seeing possible. This space of indeterminacy before either subjects or objects are made determinate is a space of openness and mutuality – coconstruction – which gets lost in the 'present object' treated as naturally occurring in both science and everyday life.

That every science has a 'seeing as' – concepts and methods based on its time and place – does not make scientific activity or results subjective or relative in any ordinary use of those terms. Rather, the social location of science makes science socially relevant in specific ways, and for better and worse, relevant often in ways preferable for dominant groups. Science loses and gains in this understanding. On the one hand, science loses broad claims to universality and timelessness, and the implied privilege of claiming to understanding nature as nature prefers to be understood. On the other hand, science gains in that the only way it can hope to break its cultural limitations is to re-enter the space of indeterminacy. Without this re-entry, scientific practice becomes engineering (application of concepts to a presumed world) rather than full science (creation of concepts

in relation to the world). Constructionism is a two-way street. It hopes to reclaim the world against subjective domination carried in culture-based scientific conceptions and methods and enable alternative subjectivities. Rather than joining the relativism-subjectivism versus objectivism battle, the position here presents an opposition to both (see Natter, et al., 1995; Bernstein, 1984). Against the preference of either side, the hope is to reclaim the interactional, codeterminative formation that each inhibits. Considering alternative theories aids the process of interaction and codetermination by revealing the cultural taken-for-grantedness that lead presumed natural objects to be formed and understood in specific ways, and the way that social privilege is built into scientific observation through concepts, methods and technologies of data collection and production.

Perhaps these discussions would seem unimportant (or would at least remain invisible) if we had wide consensus on what is important in organizations, but in admitting our heterogeneity we open questions as to preference, not just truth. We must ask whose, and not just what. To say that a research programme is based in specific conceptions of nature, humanity, sociality, and preference for certain forms and functions, does not render organization science untrue or simply relativistic. However, it is relative and relevant to particular social desires and conceptions. I find a programme of work useful, precisely because I share in many of those conceptions. Moreover, I believe that investigating those conceptions, and considering alternatives, advances both our cultural understanding and often our science.

Science is best seen as a three-part relation, between a researcher with methods and concepts, a changing indeterminate world, and communities from which problems and conceptions are drawn and challenged. The most 'rigorous' science can cover up (in fact the more rigorous, the more likely the cover up), but not deny that the world can be 'seen as' in many interesting and useful ways, all of which have a truth. Only the excess of the world over its description can object to the culturally enabled and limited researcher and community. Only the discussion of the community can define problems and examine cultural preferences in its science. And only a conception of rigor, which is informed by knowledge of perceptual attending, cultural presuppositions, and power relations can overcome the native presumptions, biases, and opinions of the community about the world. Science must be seen as in the world, not simply about it. Science's truth loses its value otherwise.

Alternative ways of attending to the world

The aim in this chapter is to elucidate the process of research and knowledge production rather than to classify different people's work, to produce a lens for seeing different ways of doing research than to offer a mirror for representation. Admittedly, no matter how hard one works to think of words as ways of attending to the world, or focusing on a way of understanding it, others will quickly turn words into names and means of classification. Some of these problems and paradigm debates arise from the tendency to reify concepts, especially in educational programmes and materials. Here, I will suggest that dimensions of contrast can be used as ideal types, as ways of focusing attention on differences that make a difference rather than as a means of classification.

The question is not, 'are these the right categories or who fits in each?' It is, 'are these differences that make a difference?' Do these dimensions provide insight into genuine differences in research programmes? I hope to aid rethinking the differences and similarities among different research approaches, making our conflicts and discussions more productive rather than simply replacing some boxes with different boxes. The two dimensions together produce four idealized ways of talking about and doing research. However, people or research programmes do not fit into them well. As suggested earlier, many researchers rotate through them. Where there

is consensus regarding conceptions of organizational goals, problems, and events (the community produces them in the same way rather than having contesting conceptions), research often operates like normal science or what will be called normative research. And still, researchers can turn to investigate the social historical power dynamics by which such consensus arises and is sustained. In so doing, they would understand more fully the social constructions that make possible normal science.

From the constructionist metaperspective taken here, the core process in understanding alternative research programmes is to understand their discourse – how they perceive, think and talk about organizational life. Understanding a discourse includes identification of the object distinctions they make, whose language is used in making those object distinctions, what and whose values and interests are carried with those distinctions, and how the conflicting descriptions of the world are handled, as well as exploring their processes of self-justification and distinction from alternative research programmes. Further, research programmes differ in the extent to which they recognize and make explicit their own constitutive activities. Many researchers assume that they are merely discovering and naming real world objects. To the extent that this is done, much of the micropractice of research is missed. I follow Bourdieu's (1991: 106) advice that, 'The social sciences deal with prenamed, preclassified realities, which bear proper nouns and common nouns, titles, signs, and acronyms. At the risk of unwittingly assuming responsibility for the acts of constitution of whose logic and necessity they are unaware, the social sciences must take as their object of study the social operations of naming and the rites of institution through which they are accomplished'.

Dimensions for contrasting research programmes

Research programmes can be described by locating differences in 'discourses', that is, the linguistic systems of distinction, the values enacted in those distinctions, the orientations to conflict, and relations to other groups. Two dimensions of contrast will be developed here. Later, four prototypical discourses or research approaches: normative, interpretive, critical, and dialogic, will be developed from these conceptions (Figure 2.1).

First, differences among research orientations can be shown by contrasting 'local/emergent' research conceptions with 'elite/a priori' ones. This dimension focuses on the origin of concepts and problem statements as part of the constitutive process in research. Second, research orientations can be contrasted in the extent to which they work within a dominant set of structurings of knowledge, social relations, and identities (a reproductive practice), called here a 'consensus' discourse, and the extent to which they work to disrupt these structurings (a productive practice), called here a 'dissensus' discourse. This dimension focuses on the relation of research practices to the dominant social discourses within the organizations studied, the research community, and/or wider community. I see these dimensions as analytic ideal types in Weber's sense, mapping two distinct continua. While categories of research are derivatively produced by the dimensions, the intent is to bring attention to meaningful differences and similarities among different research activities, rather than classification.

The local/emergent–elite/a priori dimension
The key questions addressed by this dimension concern where and how research concepts arise, and thus implicitly whose conceptions are used. Either concepts are developed in relation with organizational members and transformed in the research process, or they are brought to the research 'interaction' by the researcher and held static through the research process. This dimension can be characterized by a set of paired conceptions, which flesh out contrasts embedded in the two poles. Table 2.1 presents an array of these contrasts. The choice of and stability of the language system is of central importance since the linguistic/conceptual system directs the statement of problems, the observational process itself in producing objects, and highlighting and hiding potential experiences, the type of claims made, the report to external groups, and the likely generalizations (appropriate or not) readers will make.

The local/emergent pole draws attention to researchers who work with an open language system and produce a form of knowledge characterized more by insight into empirical events than large scale generalizations. Central to their work is the situated nature of the research enterprise. Problem statements, the researcher's attention, and descriptions are worked out as a play between communities. The theoretical vocabulary carried into the research activity is often considered as sensitizing, or as a guide to getting

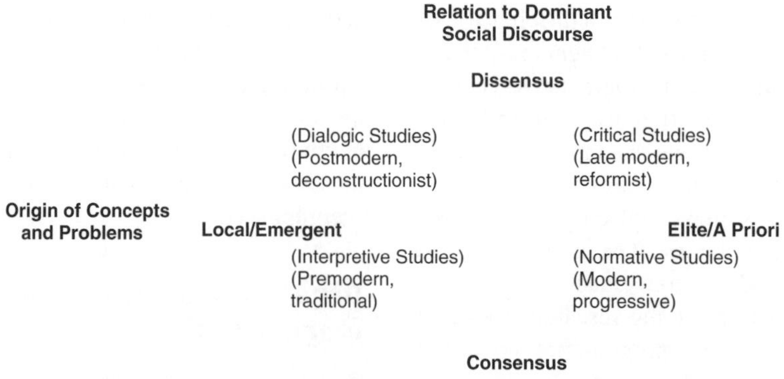

Relation to Dominant
Social Discourse

Dissensus

(Dialogic Studies)   (Critical Studies)
(Postmodern,   (Late modern,
deconstructionist)   reformist)

Origin of Concepts
and Problems   Local/Emergent   Elite/A Priori
                    (Interpretive Studies)   (Normative Studies)
                    (Premodern,   (Modern,
                    traditional)   progressive)

Consensus

Figure 2.1   Contrasting dimensions from the metatheory of representational practices

Table 2.1 Characterizations of the local/emergent–elite/a priori dimension

Local/emergent	Elite/a priori
Comparative communities	Privileged community
Multiple language games	Fixed language game
Particularistic	Universalistic
Systematic philosophy as ethnocentric	Grounded in hoped for systematic philosophy
Atheoretical	Theory driven
Situational or structural determinism	Methodological determinism
Nonfoundational	Foundational
Local narratives	Grand narrative of progress and emancipation
Sensuality and meaning as central concerns	Rationality and truth as central concerns
Situated, practical knowledge	Generalizable, theoretical knowledge
Tends to be feminine in attitude	Tends to be masculine in attitude
Sees the strange	Sees the familiar
Proceeds from the other	Proceeds from the self
Ontology of 'otherness' over method	Epistemological and procedural issues rule over substantive assumptions

started, constantly open to new meanings, translations, and redifferentiation based on interactions in the research process. Produced insights into organization processes may be particularistic, regarding both time and place, even though the emerging analytic frame is designed to aid in the deeper understanding of other settings. Cumulative understanding happens in providing stories or accounts, which may provide insight into other sites, rather than cumulative universal claims. The research attends to the feelings, intuitions, and multiple forms of rationality of both the researched and researcher rather than using a single logic of objectification or purified rationality. The study is guided more by concept formation than concept application. Distantiation and the 'otherness' of the other (the way people and events exceed categories and classifications of them) is sought by the researcher to force reconception and linguistic change. This is considered more valuable than the identification and naming of preconceived traits, attributes, or groupings. Objectivity, to the extent that it is considered at all, arises out of the interplay and the constant ability of the researched to object and correct. The researcher is more a skilled collaborator in knowledge production than an expert observer.

The elite/a priori pole draws attention to the tendency in some research programmes to privilege the language system of the researcher and the expertise of the research community, as well as hold that language system constant throughout the research process. Such research tends to be heavily theory-driven with careful attention to definitions prior to the research process. The experiences of the researched become coded into the researcher's language system. Demands of consistency and/or reliability require changes in the conceptual system to occur outside of rather than in the research process.

Whether intentional or not, the conceptual system of the researcher is considered as better or as more clearly representing what 'really' is the case, than that of everyday people and seeks generality beyond the various local systems of meaning. In privileging a language system, there is a tendency to universalize and justify such moves by appeals to foundations or to essentialist assumptions. Research claims, thus, are seen as freed from their local and temporal conditions of production. In most cases, these approaches follow an enlightenment hope for producing rational knowledge not constrained by tradition or particular belief systems of the researcher or researched. The knowledge produced is treated as progressive or reformist in conception, leading to increased capacities or well-being. The more 'normative' versions openly proclaim 'objectivity' and value neutrality based on a shared language game and research methods and tend to overlook the positions of their own community or alliances with other groups. The more 'critical' versions note the presence of values and distortions in normative work and hold out the hope for a better, purer form of knowledge based on processes that include more interests and means of analysis in the work.

Focusing on the origin of concepts and problems using a dimension of 'local/emergent–elite/a priori' allows three important gains. First, it acknowledges linguistic/social constructionism in all research positions and directs attention to whose concepts are used in object production and determination of what is problematic. Second, the focus on the origin of concepts helps distinguish fundamentally different kinds of knowledge. Elite/a priori conceptions lead to the development of 'theoretical codified' knowledge, to 'book' knowledge or 'knowing about.' Local/emergent conceptions lead to the development of 'practical' knowledge, to 'street wisdom' or 'knowing how.' Third, this dimension emphasizes that both the application and discovery of concepts can demonstrate implicit or explicit political alliances with different organizational or social groups. For example, to the extent that researchers' concepts align with managerial interests and problem statements and are applied a priori, knowledge claims are intrinsically biased toward these interests. The knowledge claims become part of the processes that are being studied, reproducing worldviews, personal identities, and fostering particular organizational interests (Knights, 1992).

The consensus–dissensus dimension

The 'consensus–dissensus' dimension draws attention to the relation of research to existing social orders and presumption of an orderly or conflict-filled universe. Consensus or dissensus should not be understood as agreement and disagreement but rather as presentation of unity or of difference, the continuation or disruption of prevailing discourse (Table 2.2). This dimension is similar to the traditional sociological distinction made by Burrell and Morgan (1979) between 'change' and 'regulation,' but has some advantages.

Rather than being class-based, contemporary concerns with conflict and power focus on the ways dominant discourses (though often disorganized and tension-filled) place limitations on people, including managers, and limit the successful functioning of organizations in meeting human needs. The focus is more on the suppression of diverse values and the presence of destructive control processes than on group conflict. The processes of domination today are less often seen as macrosociological and more often seen as arising in normative or unobtrusive controls (Barley and Kunda, 1992; Barker, 1993) and instantiated as routine micropractices in the work site (Deetz,1998; Fleming and Spicer, 2008). The focus on discursive rather than group relations aids the understanding of domination and the various ways organizational stakeholders are left out of discussions as well

Table 2.2   Characterizations of the consensus–dissensus dimension

Consensus	Dissensus
Trust	Suspicion
Hegemonic order as natural state	Conflicts over order as natural state
Naturalization of present	Present order is historicized and politicized
Integration and harmony are possible	Order indicates domination and suppressed conflicts
Research focuses on representation	Research focuses on challenge and reconsideration (re-presentation)
Mirror (reflecting) dominant metaphor	Lens (seeing, reading as) dominant metaphor
Validity central concern	Insight and praxis central concern
Theory as abstraction	Theory as opening
Unified science and triangulation	Positional complementarity
Science is neutral	Science is political
Life is discovery	Life is struggle and creation
Researcher anonymous, out of time and space	Researcher named and positioned
Autonomous, free agent	Historically/socially situated agent

as the ways such forms of decisional skewing are reproduced.

The consensus pole draws attention to the way some research programmes both seek order and treat order production as the dominant feature of natural and social systems. With such a conception, the primary goal of the research is to display a discovered order with a high degree of fidelity or verisimilitude. The descriptions hope to 'mirror' entities and relations that exist 'out there' in a relative fixed state, reflecting their 'real' character. In the 'normative' version, this reality is treated like the natural world, while in 'interpretive' work it is a social world. Language is treated as a system of representations, to be neutralized and made transparent, used only to display the presumed shared world. Existing orders are largely treated as natural and unproblematic. To a large extent, through the highlighting of ordering principles, such orders are perpetuated. Random events and deviance are down-played in significance in looking at norms and the normal, and attention is usually to processes reducing deviance, uncertainty, and dissonance. In most cases, where deviance is itself of attention, it tends to be normalized through looking at the production of deviant groups (i.e., other orders). Conflict and fragmentation are usually treated as system problems and attention is given to how orders deal with them in attempts at maintenance.

The dissensus pole draws attention to research programmes that consider struggle, conflict, and tensions to be the natural state. Research itself is seen as inevitably a move in a conflictual site. The existing order indicates the suppression of basic conflicts and along with that the domination of people and their full variety of interests. Research aims at challenging mechanisms of order maintenance to reclaim conflicts and tension. The non-normative aspects of human conduct and extraordinary responses are emphasized along with the importance of largely random and chance events. Rather than language naming and describing, researcher conceptions are seen as striking a difference, de- and redifferentiating, 'rearticulating' experience

(Laclau and Mouffe, 1985). The 'mirror' gives way to the 'lens' as the dominant metaphor for language and theory, noting the shifting analytic attempt to see what could not be seen before and showing the researcher as positioned and active (Rorty, 1979; Deetz, 1992). For dissensus-style research, the generative capacity (the ability to challenge guiding assumptions, values, social practices, and routines) of an observation is more important than representational validity (Gergen, 1978). The research is, in Knights' (1992) sense, 'anti-positive'. Dissensus work does not deny the significance of an ordered observed world; rather it takes it as a powerful (power filled) product, and works to break reifications and objectifications to show fuller potential and variety than is immediately apparent. For example, consensus orientations in cultural studies may seek to discover the organizational culture or cultures. Dissensus orientations show the fragmentation inherent in any claim of culture and the work required for site subjects to maintain coherence in the face of this as well as subjects' own forms of resistance (Prasad and Prasad, 2000; McCabe, 2007). Consensus orientations apply role and identity classifications and relate them to other variables; dissensus orientations see identity as multiple, conflictual, and in process.

While these differences can be characterized clearly in abstraction, in continuous time every consensus arises out of and falls to dissensus, and every dissensus gives way to emerging (if temporary) consensus. The issue is not the ultimate outcome desired or likely but rather which part of this flow through time is claimed in the research process. For example, while critical theorists clearly seek a social consensus, which is more rational, their research tries to produce this through the creation of dissensus in place of dominant orders. Ideological critiques in the critical theory conception of the negative dialectic aim to reclaim conflict and destroy a false order rather than produce a new one. Thus, I place them on the dissensus end. Critical theories differ from many dialogic or 'postmodern' positions in the production of dissensus. In critical theories, dissensus is produced by the use of a priori conceptions and procedures that are intentionally designed to discover asymmetries and domination of particular forms (Alvesson and Willmott, 2003; Alvesson and Ashcraft, Chapter 4 this volume). In dialogic research, a priori conceptions are themselves considered as potential disguises. Deconstructive processes are used to unmask these conceptions thereby allowing organizational activities to be given new, multiple and conflicting descriptions (Kilduff, 1993). The dialogic outcome requires a constant dedifferentiation and redifferentiation for the sake of demythologizing and enriching natural language, and consequently opening to reconsideration the most basic and certain experiences of everyday work life.

Ideal types of ways of attending to the world

The grid produced from these two dimensions provides a spatially and visually convenient discursive four-space solution (hence we should easily be reminded of its arbitrary and fictive character). I will describe these as different discourses to note a way of articulating arguments and engaging in research practices rather than a means of reconstructive self-naming. Each discourse provides an orientation to organizations, a way of constituting people and events, and a way of reporting on them. I hope that this also leads us to think about which discourse is being used or how it is joined with others rather than pigeonholing specific authors. Table 2.3 offers prototypical descriptions of each orientation related to a dozen dimensions of interest shaping organizational communication research programs.

These orientations are idealizations not structures. First, each of these four discourses, which are provisionally held apart for viewing, are filled with internal conflict and strife – including theory debates, moments of incommensurability, dilettantes, and tyrants. Second, the edges are not demarcated. Most researchers and teachers do not cluster around a prototype, but gather at the crossroads,

Table 2.3 Prototypical discursive features

Issue	Normative	Interpretive	Critical	Dialogic
		Discourse		
Basic goal	Law-like relations among objects	Display unified culture	Unmask domination	Reclaim conflict
Method	Nomothetic science	Hermeneutics, ethnography	Cultural criticism, ideology critique	Deconstruction, genealogy
Hope	Progressive emancipation	Recovery of integrative values	Reformation of social order	Claim a space for lost voices
Metaphor of social relations	Economic	Social	Political	Mass
Organizational metaphor	Marketplace	Community	Polity	Carnival
Problems addressed	Inefficiency, disorder	Meaninglessness, illegitimacy	Domination, consent	Marginalization, conflict suppression
Concern with communication	Fidelity, influence, information needs	Social acculturation, group affirmation	Misrecognition, systematic distortion	Discursive closure
Narrative style	Scientific/technical, strategic	Romantic, embracing	Therapeutic, directive	Ironic, ambivalent
Time identity	Modern	Premodern	Late modern	Postmodern
Organizational benefits	Control, expertise	Commitment, quality of work life	Participation, expanded knowledge	Diversity, creativity
Mood	Optimistic	Friendly	Suspicious	Playful
Social fear	Disorder	Depersonalization	Authority	Totalization, normalization

mixing metaphors, borrowing lines from other discourses, and dodging criticism by co-optation. Practicing researchers often move happily from one discourse to another without accounting for their location. They operate like other organizational members, borrowing discourses that suit their immediate purposes and the fashions of the moment (Deetz, 1994). More and less serious plays across the lines exist, but the issue is not crossing but the seriousness of the play. And third, the discourses are not themselves sealed off from each other. They pose problems for each other and steal insights across the lines. For example, the philosophical fights between Habermas and Gadamer, Habermas and Lyotard, Habermas and Luhmann, Foucault and everybody, left their traces in the work of each. From these struggles, the various organizational research programmes based in these works have gained enriched conceptions of power, knowledge, agency, and political action (Martin, 1990; Ashcraft and Mumby, 2004).

Provisional ordering of discourses is not to police the lines, but to provide a view of the social resources from which researchers draw and an understanding of the stock of arguments used in developing and justifying research activities and claims. The ideal types aid the understanding of differences that matter and that are hard to see in the flow of research activity. Clarifying the tendencies in specific types of research positions helps clarify debates and the relation of different groups to them. For example, the interpretive, critical, and dialogic critiques of normative research are quite different. Normative researchers accustomed to making arguments against subjectivity and traditionalism simply miss the point of each of these critiques; they often reduce them to abstract and confused presentations of what they think 'opponents' should be saying rather than concrete but different arguments from what they expected.

Further, while most researchers are not purists, their work carries assumptions and responsibilities, which are central to understanding and evaluating their work, but are rarely explicit in reports. For example, many feminists' writings carry a general sympathy with the conceptual and analytic power of dialogic research programmes, while they still wish to have a political agenda that requires critical preconceptions which assume social divisions and gender-based domination to be general (Thomas and Davies, 2005; Ashcraft and Mumby, 2004). Such works can be classified as dialogic, but the ethical and political character of many of these studies cannot be justified easily with dialogic conceptions alone. The distinctions developed in this chapter can expose the tensions and resources from which researchers draw to conduct and justify their work.

I often draw in my own work on conceptions from critical and dialogic writings. For me, critical theory notions of ideology and distorted communication provide useful sensitizing concepts and an analytic framework for looking for micropractices of unwarranted control, discursive closure, ideology, and skewed representation in organizational sites (Deetz, 1998 and 2003). But rarely are these conceptions closely tied to the full critical theory agenda. They require considerable reworking in specific sites and the results of my studies aim more at finding and giving suppressed positions a means of expression than realizing an ideal speech situation or reaching a purer consensus. What is important is not whether I am a late-modern critical theorist or a dialogic postmodernist, but rather the meaning and implications of concepts that I draw from these two competitive research orientations. My degree of consistency is of less interest than how I handle the tension, and whether the two conceptual resources provide an interesting analysis or intervention. Some clarity and understanding in alternative research orientations provides guidance and accountability, or at least a common stock of material for building and evaluating new arguments. Further, exploring general orientations can reveal assumptions hidden in one's own way of working since they remain unproblematic in one's research community.

In an ideal research programme, we might identify a complementary relation among orientations, with each asking different questions at different moments and each, at the appropriate moment, answering to the specific criteria of a particular orientation. This might operate in a rotation among orientations without any one being privileged or reduced to a preliminary or supplementary role. For example, my work relies on a conception of discursive closure, which draws attention to places where cooperative decision-making is hampered by arbitrary limits enacted in the discussion. As a critical researcher, I must show how these closures are intrusions of power relations usually based in or supporting social divisions, which lead to distorted communication and a false consensus. My study appeals to reason, logical analyses, and a coherent demonstration. As a dialogic researcher, I see these closures as the suppression of conflicts and see my own concerns with consensus and appeals to reason as simply different acts of privilege and potential closure. My analysis is now judged by the way indeterminacy is allowed to re-emerge and the compelling quality of recovered claims and voices. But at another moment, I may well pose normative questions – Which means of closure are used most often? Who uses them? When are they used? Can people be taught to avoid them? A study designed to answer such questions appeals to standards of definition, measurement, sampling, and quantitative data analysis. And further yet, there are interpretive concerns – What sense do these discursive moves have in a community? To what ends are they used? How are they self-understood and justified? What are their consequences in specific circumstances? Interpretive research standards are now relevant.

One can easily see how such a rotation through orientations might be constant and productive without losing the separation and tensions among them. Such tensions could enrich work from each orientation. Yet, few research programmes are treated this way and most researchers, like myself, follow their own lines of interest, commitments, and training, which either leads to an eclipse of questions and concerns from other orientations, or leaves them for someone else

who is interested in those problems. Taking seriously other works does not mean that we find other groups' issues and procedures as necessarily interesting or helpful, nor should we naively believe that all of them are. But our claims and the relation between our claims and study procedures should be clear, so that objections and conflicts can be on those grounds rather than on imposed traditional problem statements and methods. The point is for the researcher to be clear about what type of questions or claims drive the work at any particular time, and how the work addresses the standards and criteria appropriate to it.

A basic understanding of alternative research orientations enables shorthand accounts and helps distinguish intentional and/or productive ambiguities from careless and/or unproductive ones. As a reviewer, I am often frustrated by nonreflective mixing of metaphors and conceptions in submitted papers. Often the claims made would require a different kind of study based on different assumptions and research activities. I think this arises, partly, from authors trying to anticipate reviewer needs for normative-type generalizations, while being committed to a non-normative research orientation, but it also comes from inattention to what makes different kinds of research different. Clearly, a balance must be struck between (1) reifying research orientations through simplistic grids and subsequent over-characterizations and rigid standards, or (2) having each study try to be totally self-justifying and cut loose from any community. While I do not think that there is any easy way out of this tension, having good dimensions of contrast and good characterizations helps. A brief sketch of the four orientations aids highlights the differences and similarities in these community discourses along the suggested dimensions of difference.

The discourse of normative studies

The researchers producing this discourse have been described as methodological determinists, functionalists, covering law theorists, or as simply practicing the variable analytic tradition. This discourse is still dominant in North American research and in applied organizational research throughout the world. It is reconstructed and justified in Donaldson, (1985, 2003). I describe this discourse as 'normative' to emphasize the centrality of codification, the search for regularity, normalization of experience, and a strategic/directive control orientation. Conceptions of operationalization, 'objectivity,' and law-like relations are merely the most obvious forms of practice. The research practices mirror nineteenth century conceptions of the natural sciences, often involving recent advances in operationalization, hypothesization, statistical reduction, and 'pattern recognition' processes. Conventional practices and methodological determinism have in most cases replaced strong allegiance to the positivist philosophy of science that grounds many of the methods and assumptions. The 'objects' constructed by these practices are given qualities of constancy and permanence as if given specific attributes by nature. The combination of a priori conceptions and focus on consensus leads the artefacts of these practices to be described as facts (Natter et al., 1995).

The discourse is decisively modern in Gergen's (1992) sense, and knowledge is considered positive, cumulative, and progressive. A grand narrative of emancipation is shaped by a commitment to make a better world through discovery of fundamental processes and the increase of production. The organization is an existing object created for instrumental ends, usually making money, though some concept of the invisible hand integrates that with the social goals of development and widespread availability of goods and services.

This discourse is present in classical management theories, theories of leadership, contingency theory, most systems theories, and other places described by Burrell and Morgan (1979) in their discussion of 'functionalism'. However, it is also present in those advocating the management of culture (Schein, 1992) conceived as a variable or an object to be strategically deployed (Barley et al., 1988). Many of those working with conceptions of

organizations as 'post-modern' (rather than postmodern) have a discourse primarily structured in a normative fashion (Bergquist, 1993). Many Marxist studies utilize normative themes. Most academic Marxist works depend on privileging particular social communities and employ economic and structural explanations based on normative conceptions. Lenin's embrace of scientific management was not inconsistent. In managed economies, the managerial elite giving rise to these concepts is quite different, of course, from the managerial elite accepted by most Western European and North American studies. Elite planning and strategic management are generally dependent on this discourse (Knights and Morgan, 1991).

The discourse of interpretive studies

For interpretive researchers, the organization is a social site, a type of community, which shares important characteristics with other types of communities. The emphasis is on a social rather than economic view of organizational activities. Traditional methods of studying communities are seen as especially useful. The discourse often draws on traditional and premodern themes (Gergen, 1992). This is not to suggest a focus on the past as much as a concern with those aspects of life which have not yet been systematized, instrumentalized, and brought under the control of modernist logics and sciences. Interpretive studies accept much of the representational and consensual view of science seen in normative writings, but shift the relation between theoretical conceptions and the talk of the subjects under study. People are not considered to be objects like other objects, but are active sensemakers like the researcher. Theory is given a different conception and role. While theory may provide important sensitizing conceptions, it is neither a device of classification, nor is it tested in any simple and direct manner. The key conceptions and understandings must be worked out with the subjects under study. Theory can be inductive and grounded. Research subjects can collaborate in displaying key features of their world. However, like normative research, the pressure is to get it right, to display unified, consensual culture in the way that it 'actually' exists, a present 'integrated' culture in Martin's (1992) terms. The aim is to display convincingly a unified way of life with all its complexities and contradictions.

Most researchers use forms of ethnography, phenomenology, or hermeneutics in a rigorous way as the principal means of study. Research is usually done in the field, based on a prolonged period of observation and depth interviewing. The interest is in the full person in the organization, thus social functions beyond the work process are considered. The workplace is seen as a site of human activity, one of those being 'work' proper. The goal of interpretive studies is to show how particular realities are socially produced and maintained through norms, rites, rituals, and daily activities. In much of the writings, a preservationist, communitarian, or naturalist tone exists. It moves to save or record a life form with its complexity and creativity that may be lost to or overlooked in modern, instrumental life. Gergen (1992) describes the romantic sense of this discourse with its depth and connection to the inner life. Cultural studies in organizations are interpretive to the extent that they have not been captured by normative, modernist co-optations. Most interpretivists have taken culture to be an evocative metaphor rather than a variable or thing that an organization has.

Gradually, researchers doing interpretive work began to question the logic of displaying a consensual unified culture and have attended more to its fragmentation, tensions, and processes of conflict suppression (Martin, 1992). And similarly, much more attention has been paid to the politics of representation and the role of the report author (Lindlof and Taylor, 2002). Interpretivists have thus become more critical and dialogic in conception, reporting, and practice.

The discourse of critical studies

Critical researchers see organizations as social historical creations accomplished in conditions of struggle and domination that hides and suppresses meaningful conflict.

Organizations are described as political sites, thus general social theories, and especially theories of decision making in the public sphere, are seen as appropriate. While commercial organizations could be positive social institutions providing forums for the articulation and resolution of important group conflicts over the use of natural resources, distribution of income, production of desirable goods and services, the development of personal qualities, and the direction of society, various forms of power and domination have led to skewed decision making and fostered social harms and significant waste and inefficiency. Either explicit or implicit in critical work is a goal to demonstrate and critique forms of domination, asymmetry, and distorted communication through showing how social constructions of reality can favour certain interests, and alternative constructions can be obscured and misrecognized. If these can be overcome, conflicts among different interests can be reclaimed, openly discussed, and resolved with fairness and justice. The research aims at producing dissensus and providing forums for and models of discussion to aid in the building of more open consensus. Of special concern are forms of false consciousness, consent, systematically distorted communication, routines, and normalizations, which produce partial interests and keep people from genuinely understanding, expressing, or acting on their own interests (Alvesson and Willmott, 2003). Of the four orientations, critical studies have the most explicit set of value commitments and most direct attention to moral and ethical issues. Much of the discourse has a suspicious and therapeutic tone, but also a theory of agency, which adds an activist tone. People can and should act on these conditions through improved understanding as well as access to communication forums.

Studies have focused on the external relations of organizations to the wider society, especially the effects of corporate colonization, rationalization of society, and the domination of the public sphere, and on internal relations in terms of the domination by instrumental reasoning, discursive closures, and consent processes (Thackaberry, 2004). Critical research includes a large group who differ in theory and conception, but who share discursive features in their writing. They include Frankfurt school critical theorists (Alvesson and Willmott, 2003; Veak, 2006), conflict theorists (Dahrendorf, 1959), versions of feminist work (Ferguson, 1984), and versions of labour process theory (Braverman, 1974; Knights and Willmott, 1990). Most researchers work either with a kind of critical ethnography (Alvesson and Deetz, 2000) or critical discourse analysis (Fairclough, 2005). While not necessarily so, in practice researchers working from the later, more explicitly political and moral writings of Foucault engage in a critical discourse (Knights, 1992; Wray-Bliss, 2003).

The discourse of dialogic studies

I have chosen the term 'dialogic' rather than the more obvious 'postmodernist' to organize this discourse, because it attends to key features of this work and because of the growing commercial use of the term 'postmodern,' making it increasingly difficult to distinguish between realist assumptions about a changing world (a postmodern world, which could also be postindustrial, postFordist, or ad hoc) and a postmodern or dialogic discourse, which denies realist assumptions. The term also makes it easier to include older theories like Bahktin's. Their themes include focusing on the constructed nature of people and reality, emphasizing language as a system of distinctions, which are central to the construction process, arguing against grand narratives and large-scale theoretical systems such as Marxism or functionalism, emphasizing the power/knowledge connection and the role of claims of expertise in systems of domination, emphasizing the fluid and hyper-real nature of the contemporary world and role of mass media and information technologies, and stressing narrative/fiction/rhetoric as central to the research process. Examples include Chia (2003); Covaleski et al. (1998); Willmott (2005); Ashcraft and Mumby (2004); Cooper and Burrell 1998; Burrell (1988); and Cunliffe, 2002.

Dialogic studies focus on the fragmentation and potential disunity in any discourse. Like critical studies, the concern is with asymmetry and domination, but unlike the critical studies' predefinition of groups and types of domination, domination is considered mobile, situational, not done by anyone. Group and personal identity cannot be seen as fixed or unitary. The intention is to reclaim conflicts suppressed in everyday realities, meaning systems, and self-conceptions, and the enhancement of local forms of resistance (Barge and Little, 2002; Fleming and Spicer, 2008). Fixed conceptions give way to the appeal of that beyond conception, the 'otherness' of the world and other. Rather than critical theory's reformation of the world, they hope to show the partiality (the incompletion and one-sidedness) of reality and the hidden points of resistance and complexity (Collinson, 2003; Taylor and Bain, 2003; Thomas and Davies, 2005). In place of an active political agenda and often-utopian ideals, attention is given to the space for a continually transforming world by recovery of marginalized and suppressed groups.

A look to the future

Clearly, different organizational research programmes have different goals and assumptions and provide different forms of evaluation. I hope to have displayed differences that give insights into the diverse discourses in organizational studies, displaying some of the ways that they are alike and different. The relations among these options are not well developed in exclusionary, supplementary, or integrative terms. Often, these differences are seen as different perspectives, as if one elephant existed with each seeing a part. Difference then could be overcome with triangulation, integration, and addition. Rather we have many animals, each seen in giving up another. Each orientation creates a vision of social problems and tries to address them. Different orientations have specific ways of answering the types of questions they pose and do not work terribly well in answering the questions of others.

I am not alone in wishing that we were all multilingual, that we could move across orientations with grace and ease, but this type of Teflon-coated multiperspectival cosmopolitan envisioned by Morgan (1986) or Hassard (1991) is both illusionary and weak. Good scholars have deep commitments. Multiperspectivalism often leads to shallow readings and leaves basic assumptions unexamined. Some scholars are more multilingual than others are, but doing good work within an orientation still must be prized first. Ideally, alternative research programmes complement each other. Consensus without dissensus is stifling and finally maladaptive. Elite/a priori concepts are necessary and probably inevitable, but we can make them temporary and open to reconfiguration.

Most organizational scholars are doubtless becoming both more knowledgeable about alternatives and more appreciative of the differences. This development allows us to get beyond unproductive theoretical and methodological arguments to more basic and serious questions. The choice of orientation, to the extent that it can be freed from training and department/discipline politics, can probably be reduced to alternative conceptions of social good and preferred ways of living. This acceptance grounds theory and method debate in a moral debate that has been neither common nor explicit in organizational studies. I agree with Gergen (1992), that organizational research and theory needs to be evaluated as much by a question of 'how shall we live?' as by verisimilitude and methodological rigor. Studies need to be understood and evaluated on their own terms, but should also appeal to the larger social concerns in which both the needs and means of accomplishment are contested.

REFERENCES

Alvesson, M. and Deetz, S. (2000) *Doing Critical Management Research*, London: Sage.

Alvesson, M. and Willmott, H. (eds) (2003) *Studying Management Critically*, London: Sage.

Ashcraft, K.L. and Mumby, D.K. (2004) *Reworking Gender: A Feminist Communicology of Organization*, Thousand Oaks, CA: Sage.

Astley, G. (1985) 'Administrative science as socially constructed truth', *Administrative Science Quarterly*, 30(3): 497–513.

Barge, J.K. and Little, M. (2002) 'Dialogical wisdom, communicative practice, and organizational life', *Communication Theory*, 12(4): 375–97.

Barker, J. (1993) 'Tightening the iron cage - concertive control in self-managing teams', *Administrative Science Quarterly*, 38(3): 408–37.

Barley, S., Meyer, G. and Gash, D. (1988) 'Cultures of culture: academics, practitioners and the pragmatics of normative control', *Administrative Science Quarterly*, 33(2): 24–60.

Barley, S. and Kunda, G. (1992) 'Design and devotion: surges of rational and normative ideologies of control in managerial discourse', *Administrative Science Quarterly*, 37(3): 363–99.

Bernstein, R. (1984) *Beyond Objectivism and Relativism*, Philadelphia: University of Pennsylvania Press.

Bergquist, W. (1993) *The Postmodern Organization: Mastering the Art of Irreversible Change*, San Francisco: Jossey-Bass.

Bourdieu, P. (1991) *Language and Symbolic Power*, Cambridge, MA: Harvard University Press.

Braverman, H. (1974) *Labor and Monopoly Capitalism*, New York: Monthly Review Press.

Burrell, G. (1988) 'Modernism, postmodernism and organizational analysis: the contribution of Michel Foucault', *Organization Studies*, 9(2): 221–35.

Burrell, G. and Morgan, G. (1979) *Sociological Paradigms in Organizational Analysis*, London: Heinneman.

Chia, R. (2003) 'Organization theory as postmodern science', in H. Tsoukas and C. Knudsen (eds), *The Oxford Handbook of Organization Theory: Meta-Theoretical Perspectives*, Oxford: Oxford University Press, pp.113–40.

Chia, R. and King, I.A. (2001) 'The language of organization theory', in R. Westwood and S. Linstead (eds), *The Language of Organization*, London: Sage, pp.310–28.

Collinson, D. (2003) 'Identities and insecurities: selves at work', *Organization*, 10(3): 527–47.

Contu, A. and Willmott, H. (2005) 'You spin me round: the realist turn in organization and management studies', *Journal of Management Studies*, 42(8): 1645–62.

Cooper, R. and Burrell, G. (1988) 'Modernism, postmodernism and organizational analysis', *Organization Studies*, 9(1): 91–112.

Covaleski, M.A., Dirsmith, M.W. and Samuel, S. (1998) 'The calculated and the avowed: techniques of discipline and struggles over identity in big six public accounting firms', *Administrative Science Quarterly*, 43(2): 293–27.

Cunliffe, A.L. (2002) 'Social poetics: a dialogical approach to management inquiry', *Journal of Management Inquiry*, 11(2): 128–46.

Dahrendorf, R. (1959) *Class and Class Conflict in Industrial Society*, Stanford, CA: Stanford University Press.

Deetz, S. (1992) *Democracy in the Age of Corporate Colonization: Developments in Communication and the Politics of Everyday Life*, Albany, NY: State University of New York Press.

Deetz, S. (1994) 'Representative practices and the political analysis of corporations', in B. Kovacic (ed.) *Organizational Communication: New Perspectives*, Albany, NY: State University of New York Press, pp.209–42.

Deetz, S. (1996) 'Describing differences in approaches to organizational science: rethinking Burrell and Morgan and their legacy', *Organization Science*, 7(2): 191–207

Deetz, S. (1998) 'Discursive formations, strategized subordination, and self-surveillance: an empirical case', in A. McKinlay and K. Starkey (eds), *Managing Foucault: A Reader*, London: Sage, pp.151–72.

Deetz, S. (2000) 'Putting the community into organizational science: exploring the construction of knowledge claims', *Organization Science*, 11(6): 732–8.

Deetz, S. (2003) 'Disciplinary power, conflict suppression and human resource management', in M. Alvesson and H. Willmott (eds), *Studying Management Critically*, London: Sage, pp.23–45.

Donaldson, L. (1985) *In Defense of Organizational Theory: A Reply to Critics*, Cambridge: Cambridge University Press.

Donaldson, L. (2003) 'Organization theory as positive science', in H. Tsoukas and C. Knudsen (eds), *The Oxford Handbook of Organizational Theory: Meta-Theoretical Perspectives*, Oxford: Oxford University Press, pp.39–62.

Fairclough, N. (2005) 'Discourse analysis in organization studies: the case for critical realism', *Organization Studies*, 26(6): 915–39.

Ferguson, K. (1984) *The Feminist Case Against Bureaucracy*, Philadelphia: Temple University Press.

Fleming, P. and Spicer, A. (2008) *Contesting the Organization: Struggle, Power and Resistance in Organizations*, Cambridge: Cambridge University Press.

Gergen, K. (1978) 'Toward generative theory', *Journal of Personality and Social Psychology*, 36(11): 1344–60.

Gergen, K. (1992) 'Organizational theory in the postmodern era', in M. Reed and M. Hughes (eds), *Rethinking Organization*, London: Sage, pp.207–26.

Gergen, K. (1998) 'Constructionism and realism: how are we to go on?', in I. Parker (ed), *Social Constructionism, Discourse, and Realism*, Thousand Oaks, CA: Sage Publications.

Hanson, N. (1965) *Patterns of Discovery*, Cambridge: Cambridge University Press.

Harding, S. (1991) *Whose Science? Whose Knowledge?*, Ithaca, NY: Cornell University Press.

Hassard, J. (1991) 'Multiple paradigms and organizational analysis: a case study', *Organization Studies*, 12(2): 275–99.

Kilduff, M. (1993) 'Deconstructing organizations', *Academy of Management Review*, 18(1): 13–31.

Knights, D. (1992) 'Changing spaces: the disruptive impact of a new epistemological location for the study of management', *Academy of Management Review*, 17(3): 514–36.

Knights, D. and Morgan, G. (1991) 'Corporate strategy, organizations, and subjectivity: a critique', *Organization Studies*, 12(2): 251–73.

Knights, D. and Willmott, H. (eds) (1990) *Labour Process Theory*, London: Macmillan.

Laclau, E., and Mouffe, C. (1985) *Hegemony and Socialist Strategy: Towards a Radical Democratic Politics*, London: Verso.

Lindlof, T.R. and Taylor, B.C. (2002) *Qualitative Communication Research Methods* (2nd ed.), Thousand Oaks, CA: Sage.

Martin, J. (1990) 'Deconstructing organizational taboos: the suppression of gender conflict in organizations', *Organization Science*, 1(4): 339–59.

Martin, J. (1992) *Cultures in Organizations: Three Perspectives*, Oxford: Oxford University Press.

McCabe, D. (2007) *Power at Work: How Employees Reproduce the Corporate Machine*, London: Routledge.

Mir, R. and Watson, A. (2000) 'Strategic management and the philosophy of science: the case for a constructivist methodology', *Strategic Management Journal*, 21(9): 941.

Morgan, G. (1986) *Images of Organizations*, Thousand Oaks, CA: Sage.

Mumby, D. (2005) 'Discourse, power, and ideology: unpacking the critical approach', in D. Grant, C. Hardy, C. Oswick, N. Phillips, and L. Putnam (eds),

The Handbook of Organizational Discourse, London: Sage Publications, pp.237–58.

Murphy, A.G. (1998) 'Hidden transcripts of flight attendant resistance', *Management Communication Quarterly*, 11(4): 499–535.

Natter, W., Schatzki, T. and Jones III, J.P. (1995) *Objectivity and its Other*, New York: Guilford Publications, Inc.

Prasad, P. and Prasad, A. (2000) 'Stretching the iron cage: the constitution and implications of routine workplace resistance', *Organization Science*, 11(4): 387–403.

Parker, I. (ed.), (1998) *Social Constructionism, Discourse and Realism*, London: Sage.

Rorty, R. (1979) *Philosophy and the Mirror of Nature*, Princeton, NJ: Princeton University Press.

Schein, E. (1992) *Organizational Culture and Leadership* (2nd edition), San Francisco: Jossey-Bass.

Taylor, P. and Bain, P. (2003) ' "Subterranean worksick blues": humour as subversion in two call centres', *Organization Studies*, 24(9): 1487–509.

Thackaberry, J.A. (2004) 'Discursive opening and closing in organizational self study: culture as the culprit for safety problems in wildland fire-fighting', *Management Communication Quarterly*, 17(3): 319–59.

Thomas, R. and Davies, A. (2005) 'What have feminists done for us?: feminist theory and organizational resistance', *Organization*, 12(5): 711–40.

Tsoukas, H. (2000) 'False dilemmas in organization theory: realism or social constructivism?', *Organization* 7(3): 531–5.

Tsoukas, H. (2004) *Complex Knowledge: Studies in Organizational Epistemology*, Oxford: Oxford University Press.

Veak, T. (2006) *Democratizing Technology: Andrew Feenberg's Critical Theory of Technology*, Albany, NY: State University of New York Press.

Willmott, H. (2005) 'Theorizing contemporary control: some post-structuralist responses to some critical realist questions', *Organization*, 12(5): 747–80.

Wray-Bliss, E. (2003) 'Research subjects/research subjections: exploring the ethics and politics of critical research', *Organization*, 10(2): 307–25.

3

Interpretivism in Organizational Research: On Elephants and Blind Researchers

Dvora Yanow and Sierk Ybema

INTRODUCTION

The old Sufi tale about the blind men discovering the elephant has been drawn on by many (Waldo, 1961; Westerlund and Sjostrand, 1979; Morgan, 1986; Adams, 1994) to illustrate an argument about perception and social realities. The details change from one version to another, as befits an orally transmitted story, but in outline, for those unfamiliar with it, the plot proceeds along these lines. Townspeople hear that an elephant has arrived, but as they have never encountered one before, they send five (or six) men (never women, in the versions we have read or heard) to scout the thing out. The creature is in a barn that is completely dark, and so the men cannot see it (or it is not dark, but they are blind, although we do not quite understand how they got there, then, or why). One, feeling its flank, says the elephant must be a brick wall. A

second, touching the tail, says it must be a rope. Another, encountering an ear, is sure the elephant is a very large leaf. Happening on a leg, the fourth declares the elephant the trunk of a tree. And the fifth, climbing onto the beast's trunk, is sure the elephant is a sturdy vine meant for swinging from tree to tree. (The versions with a sixth man depict him stroking the tusk and envisioning a spear.) The men return to the town and tell about their discovery, but the townspeople are no more enlightened for the conflicting details about 'what an elephant really is'. The moral of the story is that what you see depends on where you stand: perspective is all when it comes to knowing and knowledge.

Whereas we find the story engaging and have used it ourselves in our teaching to illustrate this same point, the tale masks certain features of what it seeks to illuminate. We find both morals and maskings characteristic of the methodological state of organizational studies debates. However, the methodological arguments have been, and still are, intertwined with substantive theoretical debates within disciplinary subfields; and both are linked, intricately, with the construction of the field of study as a scientific discipline, including its curricula, professional associations and conferences, and journals. In reflecting on the state of interpretivism within organizational studies, then, we find ourselves taking a 'science studies' approach (e.g., Latour, 1987; Latour and Woolgar, 1979) that shifts attention not to one organization or another, but to the discipline as a whole as a research site (Yanow, 2005a). This builds on an understanding of a scientific paradigm, and the not unrelated concept of the hermeneutic circle, as entailing not merely a particular way of looking at the world, but also the community of scientists sharing in that way of seeing, together with the research methods that comprise the way of knowing accepted within that epistemic-interpretive community. To this are added the enactments of theoretical and paradigm debates in the professional practices that constitute and structure the discipline (such as graduate curricula, conferences, journals, and the like).

Hermeneutics is one of the two major philosophical-conceptual underpinnings of interpretive approaches to the study of organizations. As with other aspects of interpretivism, it is at once a theoretical approach and a set of methods for carrying out that approach. With its focus on, initially, the Bible; later, other written texts; later still, spoken words, film, and the like; and then built spaces and other non-word-based artefacts (though possibly containing words) and acts treated as 'text analogues' (Taylor, 1971; see also Ricoeur, 1971), hermeneutics posits a relationship between such artefacts and their 'underlying' meanings. It also encompasses the set of typically unspoken, yet tacitly known 'rules' shared by members of an interpretive-practice community for making sense of those literal or other texts. Each time an artefact is created, its creators embed within it what is meaningful to them. Each time an artefact is used, its

underlying meanings are reinstantiated and sustained – or changed. The relationship is a symbolic one, with artefacts representing their associated meanings. This, then, is why participant-observer, ethnographic, semiotic, ethnomethodological, and other such methods start with acts, physical objects, and/or texts, treating them as the embodiments and vehicles for the expression of human meaning and seeking to draw out, through systematic observation sustained over time, the unspoken, tacitly known, everyday, commonsensical values, beliefs, and/or feelings/sentiments that comprise those meanings.

Phenomenology, the second central source, focuses on accounting for processes of sense-making and the role therein of intersubjectivity, lived experience, and prior knowledge. Phenomenologists argued that humans make sense drawing on 'more' or other than merely sense data; a whole interpretive scheme (whether called a lens, a frame, a paradigm, a *weltanschaaung*, a worldview, or some other term) is called into play in the process of making sense of the world we encounter. Here, too, interpretive research methods seek to track the processes through which meaning/s is/are created.

In both cases, interpretive analysis asks after multiple, and potentially conflicting, meanings made or held by different interpretive-discourse-practice communities using and interpreting the same artefact(s). Critical theorists have criticized phenomenologists, in particular, for ignoring power dimensions; but whereas this point may hold at the level of philosophy, in application to organizations, public policies, and many other areas of social scientific study, interpretive approaches engage various aspects of the political, including silences in discourse, whether silent by choice or silenced by force of some sort. In sum, this interpretive turn in theorizing has provided the grounding for methodologies within the social sciences more broadly and organizational studies in particular that are ontologically constructivist (rather than realist) and epistemologically interpretive (rather than objectivist).

Looking at developments over the last two decades of the twentieth century, we sketch out four different takes on the position of interpretivism in organizational studies, each with its own blindspots. We describe (i) how the field opened up for interpretive research, embracing a polyphony of different voices; (ii) how it might be seen as having taken an 'interpretive turn'; (iii) how these two aspects were in part marked by some paradigm struggle or 'war'; as well as (iv) how efforts at 'peacemaking' were advanced across those divides. To make the distinctions vivid, we designate these, tongue in cheek, as *pluralists*, *revolutionaries*, *warriors*, and *peacemakers* in Table 3.1, which summarizes the argument we develop here.

The elephant tale helps us explicate this argument. Ours is not, then, primarily a chronological tale, but one of framing and reframing; in our view, these four aspects unfolded in an intertwined, perhaps even at times Hegelian fashion (of thesis, antithesis, and synthesis). What is clearest is that these two decades were a marked departure from the prior state of affairs; there, it is easier to see a rupture in time. So before sketching out these four 'blind man's' takes on the position of interpretivism in organizational studies, we first narrate a history of the entrance of interpretivism into the field, as that tale is frequently told.

One caution: we have struggled to present a picture that, if not quite 'global', at least captures developments on both sides of the Atlantic, rather than the more usual US-dominated view. We are hampered in this, however, by our own lived experiences: each of us was schooled in a different academic era and location and in different approaches to the field (neither of them a now-standard business or management approach). One of us was 'disciplined' at the hands of the pre-interpretive hegemony; the other, by some interpretivists themselves. An additional factor shaping our narrative comes from the development of the discipline itself: despite its Germanic origins (in Weberian bureaucracy theory), at a certain point in time the field of study became largely

nation- and/or language-based; and so it is inaccurate, really, to speak of a single field of study. When conferences and journals began to bring those borders down, US journals and publishers exerted tremendous influence on the shape and perceptions of the field. Our narrative reflects these limitations. Someone else might tell this history, or its parts, differently. Then again, that is part of our story.

The elephant in the organizational studies barn: pre-interpretivist history

A common narrative about the history of scientific ideas suggests that in the 1960s and 1970s, a behaviouralist-functionalist approach came to dominate the social sciences, organizational studies included. It took the groundbreaking studies of 'paradigms' and perspectives in the history, philosophy, and sociology of science and knowledge – starting with Kuhn's (1970/1962) unintended popularizing of the first term – to challenge that hegemony. Drawing the idea of paradigms into organizational studies, Burrell and Morgan (1979) suggested that, rather than manifesting a single, overarching paradigm, organizational studies' theoretical arguments reflected a set of underlying methodological presuppositions, each with its own ontological and epistemological perspectives. Along with functionalism, they included 'interpretive', 'radical humanist', and 'radical structuralist' paradigms. The parable of the blind men and the elephant was taken up by many, as it nicely expressed this image of competing paradigmatic views of social realities, along with the possibility of paradigm-plurality.

From the vantage point of the late 1970s–1980s, various authors (e.g., Astley and Van de Ven, 1979; Burrell and Morgan, 1979; Bolman and Deal, 1984; Morgan 1986), looking back at the field during the first two-thirds of the twentieth century, argued that it consisted of several 'blind' epistemic communities, each looking at a different part

Table 3.1 The position of interpretivism in the organizational studies paradigm debates: four perspectives

	Position of interpretivism	Identity position	Methods	Contributions	Limitations
I. 'Pluralists': Breaking with the paradigm hegemony of 'normal science'	One of several separate 'blind' perspectives living in peaceful coexistence with alternative perspectives	The 'new kid on the block' (re)claiming territory/sovereignty	(Re)turn to field research (participant observation; ethnography)	Proliferation, democratization, emancipation of 'minority paradigms'	Plurality without dialogue or cross-fertilization
II. 'Revolutionaries': Claiming the 'interpretive turn' as a decisive, paradigmatic shift	The new, arguably-dominant (in its own eyes) mode of thinking about theories, methods, and methodologies	'Winner' crowing over (future) victory	Assertive exploration of various 'interpretive' methods, including critical-theoretical modes (e.g., semiotics, abduction)	New epistemological awareness, reflexivity	Relativism as the new truth claim ('everything is a subjective construction – except this statement'); simplified dichotomy (positivism/interpretivism)
III. 'Warriors': Fighting paradigm hostilities	Resistance struggle against the dominance of pre-existing 'normal science'	'Warrior' fighting the uphill battle of a 'minority science' against 'normal' science	[as above]	Energizing vitality, clear demarcation of differences	Claims of superiority vis-à-vis alternative paradigms, theories, methodologies
IV. 'Peacemakers': Advocating multi-perspectivism and paradigm interplay	Hegemonic attempt to bring different interpretations together in a unified, multi-perspectival view	'Peacemaker', enlightened leader, m/paternalistic; a metastance, an external, omniscient narrator offering omniscient view from a distance	Assertion of 'mixed methods' (meaning 'mixed methodologies'), triangulation as solution to 'problem'	Acknowledgement of alternative views; creative interplay	Neglect or denial of paradigm incommensurability; espoused constructivism hides underlying realism (seeing an elephant; unaware of own blindnesses)

of the organizational beast, each arguing that it had the right view – the universal Truth – of what made an organization an organization.

Drawing attention to differences between theories, several of these reflective authors theorized disciplinary history in terms of four or five different lenses (e.g., Bolman and Deal, 1984; Shafritz and Ott, 1996; Yanow, 1987). From the start – according to this historical narrative – the key dimension of organizations was their structure, building on Weberian bureaucratic and public administration ideas concerning hierarchical levels, spans of control, position definitions and tasks, and so forth (e.g., the work of Fayol, Gulick and Urwick, and others). The translation into English and spread of Freud's ideas in the 1930s, the Hawthorne experiments' 'discovery' of the informal organization, and Homans' ideas about the group as a basic unit of analysis introduced a new contender in the form of human relations theories, concerned with roles, interpersonal relationships, and other social psychological concepts. Still other features of the 'organizational elephant' came into view when systems theories developed by the military during World War II added complexity to structural theories, situating departments and organizations in their respective 'environments'. Similarly, the enhanced level of general political activity in the 1970s generated its organizational studies counterpart in a more complex human relations theory, putting contesting interests, power, and negotiation at the centre of analytic focus in a way that accommodates neither human relations theories' emphasis on the dysfunctionality of conflict nor structural and systems theories' ideas about authority and control.

In this retrospective view, each of the four sets of theories or 'lenses' competed for standing as the best explanation of what constituted the organizational elephant – e.g., much as 'norms' could not explain inputs, outputs, and feedback loops, 'bargaining' did not describe very well technology or task. What emerges from this reflective narrative of the history of the field is an understanding that the logic underlying early battles

among contending theoretical approaches was essentially ontological, concerned with the 'reality status' of their focus. The four lenses or frames could be seen, at heart, as competing frames of analysis, each intended to provide the correct answer to the question, 'what is an organization?' That logic assumes that organizations are empirical entities with factual characteristics existing in the 'real' world; and it looks for the 'nature' – the essential character – of these organizational realities *as if they were* facts existing in nature. Organizational facts are objective, in this view, and they are discoverable; the essence of 'organization' was to be grasped by analysing its attributes through some form of objective – quantitative – analysis, shaped by the (structural-) functionalism that held sway at the time, itself marked – although not in any recognized way – by the ontological and epistemological legacy of early twentieth century logical positivism (and its heritage from earlier, nineteenth century forms of positivist thought; for further discussion see Bernstein, 1983; Polkinghorne, 1983, 1988; in organizational studies, Burrell and Morgan, 1979; Hatch and Yanow, 2003).

In other words, organizational studies through the late 1970s was diverse and divided, carved up by theoretical differences. Many scholars hoped for a single orientation – what later would be called a paradigm – that would unite various contending parties. Drawing on what today we identify as a Kuhnian view of science, they argued that a one-paradigm approach would enhance the field's theoretical development and help it to 'mature'. Commenting on the battles between sociologically informed 'organizational theory' (drawing also on bureaucracy theory, which was tied to public administration and political science) and (social-) psychologically informed 'organizational behaviour' in the 1970s, a former president of the Academy of Management illuminates what seems to have been, at that time, the dominant perspective:

> One source of the multiple identities that affect organizational behaviour is the fact that

members [of the Academy] are psychologists and/or sociologists as well. *If these disciplines could be collapsed into organizational behavior,* ... many identity conflicts would be removed, *a major source of fragmentation in the study of organizations would be eliminated*, and the combined discipline would not only be more powerful but larger and more effective as well (Miner, 2007: 314; emphases added)

The sentiment underlying this desire for unity stems from an understanding of science as intimately tied to the notion of progress, which could only be achieved through adopting one, unifying set of principles. Kuhn's influential treatment of 'paradigm' associated the 'possession' of a paradigm with disciplinary maturity. In his view, the social sciences were without a paradigm. By logical inference, that must mean that they are immature. The power of the rhetoric challenged social scientists; who wants to be allied with such a status? As the erstwhile Academy of Management president put it, looking at the fragmented 'picture of the organization field' suggested by analysis of his 1977 data, '[I]n my mind the field was still quite immature and had done little at that time to progress' over the previous twenty years (Miner, 2007: 314). Whether under the influence of a Kuhnian view of paradigmatic science or of the more general search for scientific unity within the discipline, the various theoretical approaches to the study of organizations battled over what the key tool was that would join them all together and enable scientific 'progress'.

What was not recognized at the time, at least not in the US, was that there was, in fact, a paradigm in play that united these competing theoretical approaches and their attendant methods – one informed by ontological and epistemological assumptions emanating from positivist philosophies (especially logical positivism) as these had taken root in social science research methods. The theoretical debate, in other words, had its methodological counterpart, a then-dominant objectivist-realist paradigm that came to hold hegemonic sway within organizational studies. This was amply manifested within

US disciplinary structures, ranging from graduate school curricula to the kinds of research that could be funded and accepted for presentation at Academy of Management panels or for publication in its and other leading journals. The empirical data remain to be gathered, but analysis of one of the premier journals provides evidence that is, we warrant, suggestive of the field as a whole. Publication of qualitative studies of work and organizations available in the 1950s and early 1960s fell off precipitously in the then-leading journals between 1965 and 1975, at least as reflected in the first 40 volumes of *Administrative Science Quarterly* (Van Maanen, 1998: xviii), recovering only slightly over the next two decades, but never reaching their previous height.

To this point, our history has been narrated largely from a North American perspective (one likely to be familiar to organizational studies scholars in other parts of the world which have enjoyed the 'globalization' of US academic textbooks and theories). However, this is only a partial history – or a perspectival one. The view from Europe and from those North American fields not dominated by the business orientation toward organizations that developed in the 1980s and 1990s is rather different. Within bureaucracy studies, developed through the middle of the twentieth century, organizational analyses both included treatments of the political within organizational life, and held on to a participant-observer, ethnographic, meaning-focused 'case study' approach (e.g., Blau, 1953/1963; Becker et al., 1961; Crozier, 1964; Dalton, 1959; Gouldner, 1954; Kaufman, 1960; Selznick, 1949, 1957; in subsequent generations, Allison, 1971; Lipsky, 1980; Ingersoll and Adams, 1992, to name a few). But while such studies also remained part of the European organizational studies curriculum (e.g., Burrell and Morgan, 1979; Lammers, 1991 [1983]), they mostly disappeared on the other side of the ocean.

With the development of the disciplines in US higher education, the late 1970s 'take-off' of business and management schools and departments, and the growing marginalization of public administration schools and departments, along with the increasing hegemony of behaviouralism, survey research, and quantitative methods, qualitative studies of bureaucracies were largely severed from the organizational studies curriculum and consigned to the public administration dust-heap (itself a topic of study quarantined from business management curricula). Because of the structures of their university programmes, European and British faculties did not hive off public sector organizations from corporate ones; studies of governmental, nonprofit, and other such agencies were (and are) still considered part of the field. European organizational studies scholars were still versed in the philosophical and methodological issues undergirding claims to knowledge; 'ontology', 'epistemology', 'phenomenology', 'hermeneutics', and their theoretical proponents were not foreign names and concepts. It is no accident that Burrell and Morgan's 1979 book came from the pens of two scholars schooled in Britain – few US organizational studies scholars could have written such a book at that time – or that studies of the symbolic dimensions of organizational life took off in Europe more rapidly (e.g., through the first few years of the Standing Committee on Organizational Symbolism – SCOS – established in the 1980s) and achieved a centrality that they still lack in the US.

The new appreciation in the US for epistemological polyphony, joined with European visions of organizational symbolism, enabled a shift in the vision of organizational studies as a science in search of an overarching theoretical paradigm to seeing it as having grown up with a dominant methodological paradigm that was ontologically realist, epistemologically objectivist, and procedurally following 'the scientific method'. The awareness of divergent and contradictory philosophical presuppositions underlying organizational analyses not only provided useful ways of reconceptualizing the history of the field's ideas as a contending set of theories each vying for dominance. It also marked a crucial step in a fundamentally different way of thinking about theories and theorizing – and about methodologies and methods. This 'crucial step' can be narrated from at least four different angles. Each narrative casts the role of interpretivism in the field of organizational studies somewhat differently.

Paradigm proliferation: from an elephant to brick walls, ropes, leaves, tree-trunks, spears, and vines

The first take on interpretivism follows from the seminal statement by Burrell and Morgan (1979) about multiple paradigms being present in organizational studies. This led to a rise in reflexivity concerning claims to knowledge and their sources, including a growing awareness and understanding of the variety of ontological-epistemological perspectives used in analysing organizations. In addition to their analysis, several other books and articles advanced perspectival approaches, adding frames, metaphors, perspectives, and lenses to the paradigm terminology (e.g., Astley and Van de Ven, 1979; Scott, 1981; Bolman and Deal, 1984; Morgan, 1986). Together with functionalism and critical perspectives, interpretivism figures in the Burrell and Morgan framework as one of the 'characters' that helped to break through the hegemonic normalcy of single paradigm science.

A sense of 'peaceful co-existence' among paradigms, a 'live and let live' mentality that some read into the quadrant dividers in the portrayal by Burrell and Morgan of 'paradigm incommensurability', is central to this shift from paradigm unity to paradigm plurality. In this quadrant-based view, no single paradigm can win the revolution, displace the others, and lay claim to 'the' truth. In this sense, adopting a multiperspectival view means considering different theories – or metaphors, frames or 'images' – of organizations *in a non-hierarchical order*; the elephant's leg, for instance, claims no privilege over its trunk or its ear or any other component. From the perspective of understanding what comprises the elephant, all appendages have equal standing.

This view opened theorizing itself to alternative, contrasting interpretations coexisting within a larger framework; each and every theory, by implication, had to share its hitherto-hegemonic claim to 'the' truth with other theories. Rather than fuelling each theory's ambition to discover and describe the 'true' elephant, this approach fostered a growing awareness of the inherent partiality of any and every truth claim. It instructed scholars of organizations – us – that our own sight is limited and that that limited sight can blind us to alternative interpretations. This view also suggested, to many, an equivalence between 'paradigms' and 'eyeglasses', as if switching paradigms were no more complicated than replacing one pair of glasses with another.

However, a multiparadigm view itself rests on a philosophical foundation that is interpretivist in nature. It holds that paradigms are more firmly rooted within individuals than eyeglasses, and it also denies the absolute authority of each and every truth claim, including that of 'normal science'. The dawning of epistemological perspectivalism within organizational studies brought with it a critical awareness of the field's hitherto ontological realism. This is the apparent moral of the elephant story: that what one understood an organization to 'be' depended on what part of the organization one studied, and that there could be different ways of looking at an elephant. It helped to grow a perception of inherent blind spots in the field's various ways of seeing and knowing – indeed, an awareness that theorizing itself is a way of worldmaking, to borrow Nelson Goodman's (1978) phrase. In this sense, the turn away from a single-paradigm organization science was a radical departure from the positivist paradigm that was now seen as having dominated the field of organizational studies almost since its inception. It was the beginning of a new era.

The interpretive turn as 'paradigm revolution': we are all blind wo/men

Paradigm plurality 'matured the minds' for a fundamentally different way of thinking about theories and theorizing – and about methodologies and methods. Without much exaggeration, this second take on interpretivism depicts its role in organizational studies as a paradigmatic revolution. The recognition that our thinking about organizational and other social realities is itself shaped by our theoretical presuppositions radically undermined the realist-objectivist foundations of functionalism and occasioned what has been referred to as an 'interpretive turn' within the social sciences (Rabinow and Sullivan, 1979, 1985; Hiley et al., 1991). The interpretive turn occasioned other turns – among them the linguistic turn (e.g., Van Maanen, 1995a); the rhetorical turn (e.g., McCloskey, 1985); and more recently the practice turn (Schatzki et al., 2001), among others. Together, these various turns brought the questions of knowledge claims and knowledge production to the fore – the quintessential concerns of methodologies and their practical translation into everyday methods. They shifted the terrain of analytic inquiry from an ontological focus on what an organization really is to providing reflective epistemological accounts of its 'knowability' – how that knowledge was developed and known (including the roles of positionality and reflexivity in knowledge-creation). Such questioning itself engendered a shift from the search for universal, generalizable principles or laws of human behaviour to more situated, contextual knowledge, in which both 'knowers' and 'knowns' (Jacobson and Jacques, 1990) are understood to embody situation-specific characteristics. What these ideas and arguments showed us was that, ultimately, we are all blind women and men.

In this view, organizations, like other 'social realities,' have no *ab origine* objective status. They are to be understood, instead, as objectifications of an intersubjective, social process of constructing realities (Berger and Luckmann, 1966).

And that understanding would come about not through external, objective, sense-based observation following the 'rigorous' steps of 'the scientific method', but through subjective, hermeneutic and phenomenological, systematically interpretive sense-making – that conducted through participant-observer, ethnographic, and other interpretive methods (on interpretive methodology and methods and the differences between qualitative and interpretive methods, see Yanow and Schwartz-Shea, 2006). In organizational studies, Weick's (1979) shift from organization to organizing (organizational processes), Van Maanen's (1979) reclaiming of qualitative methods, and new attention to organizational culture and symbolism (Pettigrew 1979) marked this interpretive turn.

Such a position has profound implications not only for 'truth claims' but also for the research methods that generate them: it provides the philosophical rationale for constructivist-interpretive methods. The number of qualitative studies in *Administrative Science Quarterly*, after falling off dramatically through the mid-1970s, rallied slightly between 1976 and 1995 (Van Maanen, 1998: viii). According to some organizational scholars (e.g., Clegg and Hardy, 2006; Prasad, 2005), the interpretive turn occasioned a 'methodological turn' within organizational studies from positivist-inflected quantitative methods to more constructivist-interpretive methods. Looking at several special issues in leading journals and the contents of various handbooks, Clegg and Hardy (2006: 432) recently concluded that 'new ways of doing and thinking about research are clearly emerging and, increasingly, receiving some degree of blessing from bastions of orthodoxy, such as the Academy of Management'. Organizational sciences, like the social sciences at large (Lincoln and Guba, 2000: 163), have taken a distinct turn toward more interpretive, postmodern, and criticalist research practices along with their attendant theorizing.

These developments gave organizational studies a new taxonomy – an interpretivist approach alongside a positivist approach that insisted on universal principles derived through objective analysis, among other things. In methodological terms, this binary was more commonly labelled 'qualitative' and 'quantitative', without engaging the philosophical presuppositions undergirding the duality (see Bryman, Chapter 30, this volume). Interpretive science often positioned itself as an alternative to mainstream science. In doing so, it offered itself, implicitly, as a perspective that had at least equal value and insight – as just another appendage on the elephant. But in some writings, interpretively-oriented scholars adopted a more defensive (or, from another perspective, offensive) mode, implicitly laying claim to having a 'better truth', in the form of more adequate methodologies or theories than those offered by the methods or canons of 'positivist' organizational science. And the latter, finding their hegemony threatened and feeling themselves under attack, fought back. These attacks, taking place also in the social sciences more broadly, launched very explicit 'paradigm wars' between positivists and interpretivists, making evident hitherto unarticulated underlying tensions.

Paradigm wars and warriors: duelling blind scholars

Paradigm plurality – the notion that we are all partially-sighted – not only held out the promise of a peaceful proliferation and democratization of different approaches and perspectives within the organizational (and other social) sciences. It also set in motion the emancipation of 'minority paradigms', growing the awareness of paradigmatic divides. Such paradigm differences surfaced and collided in the 1980s across a number of organizational studies' subfields, first and foremost around the topic of culture in organizational life. The appearance of 'organizational culture' as a field of study constituted a revolution in the organizational sciences as it itself embodied the ontological and epistemological polyphony promised by the interpretive turn, awareness of which came to many organizational culture scholars later, through the vehicle of the 'cultural revolution' (see Prasad and Prasad, Chapter 8, this volume). The latter enabled a perception of the paradigmatic unity of the field's preceding schools of thought; their shared positivist presuppositions now came clearly into view (and, in fact, organizational culture as a concept and field of study itself split between realists and interpretivists, as we discuss below). The colliding of paradigm differences may have been occasioned by the development of organizational culture as a field of study, but it precipitated them for the discipline as a whole; many of the paradigm battles that were played out initially on organizational culture's pages came to mark the broader field of study.

As the scope of the discipline is too large to trace these methodological developments in all its areas, we use organizational culture and its related domain, organizational symbolism, as a lens through which to portray these developments, and then note in brief their appearance in a couple of other subfields. This narrative illustrates that the 'interpretive turn' in organizational studies did not simply add another appendage of equal weight but also, at times, occasioned rather heated debate. The examples show that the interpretive turn was not about organizational scholars quietly embracing a new, more interpretivist view, but rather involved 'blind scholars' openly arguing over the 'true' organizational reality, continuing the battle for ideational supremacy that had marked the field's early history, although now on new grounds.

'Organizational culture' was heralded as a new paradigm in organizational studies, a theoretical and methodological revolution that built on the new awareness of possible alternatives to dominant modes of theorizing. Viewing culture as a new 'root metaphor' (Smircich, 1983), a new way of seeing and understanding organizational life, many scholars positioned it against 'mainstream thinking', proclaiming it a more vital, more grounded alternative to the lifeless, people-less systems and other theories that largely ignored human agency and the 'subjective' dimensions of everyday organizing. But the functionalist and generalizable side of the coin was also still present; others saw 'corporate culture' as a tool that managers could use to control employees and improve organizational efficiency and/or effectiveness by creating 'stronger' cultures, assuming that organizations had a unitary culture and that it was subject to control by executives and upper level managers (e.g., Deal and Kennedy, 1982; Peters and Waterman, 1982; Ouchi, 1981; see Kunda, 1992 for a critique of this view). This contrasted with the more interpretive view of culture as potentially less unitary, also reflecting 'subcultural' groupings existing within a single, bounded organization along professional, managerial, race-ethnic, gender, and other work-related occupational and demographic lines. And this orientation drew different methods into play.

For those more inclined to take an interpretive approach to the topic than a positivist-functionalist one, doing organizational culture studies was often an act of academic resistance played out methodologically as well as theoretically, even to the point (at that time) of signalling membership on the radical fringe of the discipline. Both the subject of study and the researcher were understood to be situated in specific contexts; generalizable typologies were judged not possible in this view. 'Culture' came to stand in for a different ontological, epistemological, and methodological position, one that broke with the functionalist, positivistically-influenced paradigm that dominated organizational studies. Whereas the latter could be prosecuted through objective fact-gathering means, generating 'laws' or principles that are (posited to be) generalizable across organizations, an interpretive position approaches culture as *a way of seeing* organizations: theorizing and methods are joined.

In this view, 'organizational culture' meant not only theories of culture(s) operating within organizations, but also 'cultural' analyses of organizations: the use of those methods that generated situation-specific knowledge reflecting both organizational actors' understandings of their situations and researchers' interpretations of those understandings as well as of their own experiences. To see and perhaps even experience 'other' cultural groupings within an organization – subcultures, countercultures, etc. – and the values, beliefs, and feelings (or sentiments) that were meaningful to them required a researcher to become familiar with the internal workings of the organization under study, from the shop floor level in lieu of or in addition to the executive suite. In opposition to the large-scale survey research of contingency theorists and those who wished to promulgate generalizable laws of organizational life, organizational culture scholars oriented toward situation-specific, meaning-focused studies began to reclaim the ethnographic and other qualitative and interpretive methods that had characterized earlier (but largely forgotten) bureaucracy, work, and workplace studies. Exposure to the various angles of sight afforded by studying managerial, sub-, and countercultures reinforced an appreciation for the range of multiple possible meanings that could be encompassed within and interpreted from the same organizational slogan, award trophy, ceremony, or other symbol.

Treating culture as an approach, rather than as a variable to be studied, situated methodological concerns within their related questions of knowledge and reality. This linked 'cultural' studies of organizations to other contemporaneous theoretical developments, among them feminist, critical, literary, postcolonial, and postmodern theoretical approaches. (These often linked to a new field called 'cultural studies'; including that here makes clear that we are using the phrase with a different meaning.) Feminist, critical, and postcolonial theorists called attention to the fact that much of what is presented as neutral and universal knowledge is actually based on an assumed norm; for feminist theorists, males; for critical theorists, a power-based status resting typically on class and/or race and/or gender; for postcolonial theorists, a viewpoint from North-Western Europe. These critiques call attention to the situatedness – the 'positionality' – of the researcher producing knowledge, as well as to the subject of knowledge. Analyses of

theoretical writings underscored this point, arguing that the text is as much, if not more, an interpretive representation created by the author, as it is a realist reflection of the subject of the study. In sociology and anthropology, initially this extended to the recognition that scholarly theorizing is itself shaped by societal metaphors (e.g., Brown, 1976; Gusfield, 1976) and that writing, too, is a way of worldmaking that constitutes the very subject being (re)presented (Clifford and Marcus, 1986; Geertz, 1988; Richardson, 1994; Van Maanen, 1988; similar arguments engaged museum exhibiting practices, e.g., Karp and Lavine, 1991). This perspective was soon adopted in organizational studies as well (e.g., Brower et al., 2000; Golden-Biddle and Locke, 1993, 1997; Hatch, 1996; Van Maanen, 1995a; Yanow, 1995).

Similar battles are still being fought in other subfields. In organizational identity scholarship, for example, the fundamental position established by Albert and Whetten (1985) stakes a claim to an a priori definition: organizational identity is central, enduring, and distinctive. Those who challenge that definition, whether on theoretical or empirical grounds, point out that nowhere does this treatment, whether by its authors or those who have sought to build upon it, take into account the situatedness of organizations and their actors, let alone of the researcher (see, e.g., Hatch and Schultz, 2002; Hatch and Yanow, 2008; Ybema et al. 2009). In a similar vein, organizational learning scholars have been battling over whether that term designates learning undertaken by individuals within the organization on its behalf or whether it can also designate collective action on the part of the organization as a whole (for explication and overviews, see Antonacopoulou, 1999; Cook and Yanow, 2006/1993; Easterby-Smith and Araujo, 1999; Gherardi, 2000; Popper and Lipshitz, 2000; Weick and Westley, 1996). Advocates of the first position tend to take an ontologically realist approach with respect to the concept of learning (seeing it as something that can *only* be done by individuals who can, in the view of these scholars, be observed learning), and to search for generalizable knowledge. Those advancing the latter position tend to focus on the situatedness of analysis and the more subjectivist epistemology of workplace practices (Nicolini, Gherardi, and Yanow, 2003) – a more interpretive approach.

The battles between the two approaches in each of these subfields seemingly are disagreements about theoretical argumentations. However, underlying this surface engagement is in some sense a 'deeper' paradigm war between conceptualizations that retain a (logical) positivist influence in their methods and goals or intentions for their truth claims, and those influenced by hermeneutic-phenomenological presuppositions. The theoretical debates can usefully be seen as a surrogate for these methodological differences. The seriousness of the debate, which has been echoed more broadly across the social sciences as a whole, was captured in a series of plenary addresses and subsequent panels at the Academy of Management and then in print (for the basic lines of argument, see Pfeffer, 1993; Van Maanen, 1995b; see also Perrow, 1994). Organizational studies seemed caught, trapped between two, if not more, incommensurable methodological – philosophical – positions. For those who believed that the lack of a single paradigm stood in the way of scientific progress, this was an untenable situation.

Multi-perspectival peace-makers' offensives: seeing an elephant?

While the discovery and description of different paradigms or perspectives sparked wars among some scholars, it inspired others to try (once again) to achieve a single-perspective, unified paradigmatic approach, launching what might in retrospect be called a 'peace offensive'. Burrell and Morgan (1992, 1979: 25) had argued that synthesis across paradigms was impossible – that they needed to remain separate because they are based on incommensurable ontological and epistemological assumptions. Others, however, argued that the position set out by Burrell and Morgan led, paradoxically, to an

approach 'that acknowledges a wider field of vision but is no less myopic' (Willmott, 1990: 49), constraining analysis within a single paradigm and excluding the possibility of forms of analysis that transcend that paradigm's limitations. For such scholars, acknowledging the existence of different paradigms and perspectives created the need to remove the blinders embedded in 'one-sided', monocular perspectives and bridge the boundaries of paradigmatic differences, thereby arguing against 'hermeticism' (Hassard, 1988) and paradigm closure (Willmott, 1990) and engaging in 'paradigm crossing' or 'cross fertilization' (e.g., Gioia and Pitre, 1990; Hassard, 1991; Lewis and Kelemen, 2002; Willmott, 1990, 1993). From such a point of view, organizational theory was in need of boundary-transcending contributions: 'There are many ringing denunciations of opposing viewpoints, but too few attempts at bridging or synthesis' (Van de Ven and Poole, 1988: 25).

In order to build a case for boundary-crossing, these 'multi-perspectivists' typically followed a rhetorical strategy in which they first established a view of the field as being 'at war', its factions struggling for intellectual dominance (Martin and Frost, 1996), after which they argued in favour of 'peace-making', offering a multiperspectival hand holding out a treaty that would bring the warring factions together in an overarching framework or metatheory House of Peace of their devising. Among those advocating for cross-paradigmatic bridge-building were Scott (1981) and Morgan (1986) in organizational theory at large, and Martin (1992) in the subfield of organizational culture, while in the literature on organizational research methods, some sounded a similar call for combining, 'triangulating' or 'mixing' methods (Jick, 1979; Lee, 1991; Martin, 1990; Rousseau, 1990; see Bryman, 2008; Buchanan and Bryman, 2007).

In his three-part treatment of organizational systems theories, Scott (1981) distinguished among rational, natural, and open systems theories of organizations, suggesting that analysis drawing on all three frames provided a fuller view of the organization being studied. Morgan (1986), in an argument parallel to that of Brown (1976), who saw sociological theories as influenced by various metaphors of the social world, advanced the idea that different organizational theorists developed the analyses they did because of some underlying perception – he saw these images in metaphoric terms – of the organizational world. But, unlike Brown, Morgan made the largely implicit assumption that scholars and practitioners could and would achieve a better understanding of organizations if they – we – could step out of our single-metaphor perspectives and see the organizational world as a combination of all of the metaphoric images he outlined, as if they could be synthesized into a superior vision (Burrell, 1996: 652). It is a view similar to Schön's (1979), who argued that making explicit the metaphors shaping our perceptions (of actions, policies, and the like) would yield a more accurate rendering of social reality, a move that Miller (1985) critiques as impossible.

Martin (1992) also challenged the one-sidedness of a single perspective view, arguing that this enabled seeing certain aspects sharply but at the same time blinded visions of others. She advocated for a multiperspective approach to overcome those shortcomings and avoid drawing a one-sided picture of cultural reality. Although at times she seems to be claiming that integration, differentiation, and fragmentation perspectives are part of organizational realities and at other times treats them as if they were theorists' views, the overarching theme of her argument is that in order to make for more effective theories and understandings of organizational life, theorists need to articulate all three approaches, integrating them into a single analysis in order to capture the social reality that is the organization (Ybema, 1996, 1997).

Joining different perspectives within an overarching framework, as advocated by these and other theorists, offers a wider metastance with respect to methodological and theoretical differences. It suggests the possibility of being outside of theories and theorizing, allowing an external, omniscient view from a distance that sees more clearly the differences among various theoretical positions in terms of their assumptions, opinions, emphases, characteristics, methods, and so on and is, therefore, able to bridge those differences and unite them under an overarching umbrella. This is in keeping with another moral embedded in the tale of the elephant that contrasts quite strongly with the 'partial views of each individual blind man' moral. By suggesting that there *is*, in actual fact, something recognizable as an elephant, this telling of the tale holds out the promise that we – or, at least, the narrator – may deduce the true nature of the thing by adding up or combining the different reports from various blind men. The structure of the narrative posits a perspective outside of and above the events it narrates. It has, after all, an omniscient narrator who is external to the unfolding events; otherwise, how would we know that the creature that came to town and that was perceived by the blind men, however hands-on in fashion their observation, was, in fact, an elephant?

From *this* perspective, the story tells an objectivist tale, rather than the constructivist one it is usually used to illustrate it! The moral of the story in this telling is that perfect, complete, objective knowledge is, after all, possible – if we could but remove those (silly) blinders and turn on the lights. Then we could learn how to look in the correct way, as we would see how to combine the various partial views into the greater whole. In terms of Scott's, Morgan's or Martin's theorizing, *this* moral of the elephant story is that the researcher needs to use all three frames, all nine metaphors, all three perspectives. For those holding their work out as exemplary of interpretivist presuppositions, such a claim poses a paradox: it renders those presenting a unifiable multiperspectival view as not much different, in a sense, from those who advanced paradigm wars, both groups advocating for the unity of science, each holding out their own 'worldview' as the more realistic, and therefore better, understanding.

A similar realism underlies Plato's story of the men in the cave seeing their shadows.

It is a position that appears to want things both ways – an ontological realism coupled with an epistemological constructivism. This is the stance of critical realists (e.g., Collier, 1994), and it has its counterpart in research methods. Murphy's (1980) qualitative methods analogy (or at least, some interpretations of it) to the mid-nineteenth century Wild West wagons in the US circling the campfire at the end of the day, read as implying that capturing views from the perspective of each wagon will enable a complete portrayal of the finite and very real (and therefore knowable) fire (see also Reed, Chapter 25, and Ackroyd, Chapter 31, this volume). As with the elephant and the cave, such an approach suggests that there is an organizational reality, which can, at the end of the day (so to speak), be rendered as the ethnographer or other interpretive researcher captures all possible perspectives and voices on the research question.

Picasso-ian portraiture expresses a similar multiplicity of viewpoints; but instead of an unnatural realism showing various angles of his subjects' faces as if the observer could take multiple perspectives at once, Picasso sought to capture time's motion on the two-dimensional canvas, thereby conveying a more natural view closer to real life than that presented by earlier renderings that froze time and motion, as contemporary artist David Hockney noted (cited in Hatch and Yanow, 2008). This is the kind of dynamism that interpretive methodologies seek to capture. Yet, even in such methodological positions, the complexities of organizational life and the partiality of scientific knowledge of them are, in the end, often resolved by omniscient researchers who, through the tools of reflexivity (that considers and explores their positionality) and negative case analysis and member-checking (that safeguard against premature analytic closure), explain away its chaos by imposing pattern and order (Law, 2004).

This is, we think, where things stand in organizational studies with respect both to its theorizing and to its methods and methodological positions: ranged opposite

those who would still argue for universal principles and scientific laws, but not comfortable with the seeming nihilism of much postmodernist theorizing and research, are those who are contending with shadows on the cave wall, trying through ethnographic, ethnomethodological, practice-grounded, and other sorts of studies to achieve, as Hockney put it about Picasso's methods and their results, a view that is not 'always from a distance and [not] always in a kind of stopped, frozen time' (quoted in Hatch and Yanow, 2008: 27).

Blind-sided by the elephant?: or, elephants and turtles all the way down

There is an Indian story ... about an Englishman who,
having been told that the world rested on a platform
which rested on the back of an elephant
which rested in turn on the back of a turtle,
asked ..., what did the turtle rest on?
Another turtle.
And that turtle?
'Ah, Sahib, after that it is turtles all the way down.'

Clifford Geertz (1973: 28–9; line breaks not in original)

No man stands on truth.
They are merely banded together as usual,
one leaning on another and all together on nothing;
as the Hindoos made the world rest on an elephant,
and the elephant on a tortoise,
and had nothing to put under the tortoise.

Henry David Thoreau (1852, 4 May; line breaks not in original)

What do we learn from these debates over paradigms and perspectives? What good have 'paradigm pluralists' (emphasizing the incommensurable of partiality knowledge generated through different paradigms, à la Burrell and Morgan), 'paradigm revolutionaries' (those who see in the 'interpretive turn' a revolutionary transformation, with interpretivism the new, dominant way of thinking), 'paradigm warriors', and 'multi-perspectival peacemakers' brought us? Our treatment of the topic so far, despite our use of terms such as war and battle, presents the topic in a rather antiseptic way. We ourselves have practised the blind men and elephant story in the way we presented the four different views on interpretivism in organizational studies by outlining the characteristics and contributions of each 'argumentational move' in the paradigm debates, whether aimed at 'pluralistic co-existence', 'revolution', 'war' or 'peace'. If, however, we are to take Kuhn's observations seriously, claiming the status of 'paradigm' is a political statement. To see its implications, we need to return to the reflective stance on our discipline's professional practices that constitutes the science studies perspective.

From one point of view, the paradigm debates have certainly served a purpose; for interpretive scholars, at least, paradigm 'plurality' and the 'interpretive turn' created space and legitimacy for alternative approaches, and 'paradigm wars' were invigorating, productive, and thought-provoking. Within organizational culture, for example, the debates opened analysis up to the symbolic, meaning-making dimensions of organizational life and, more generally, to interpretive methodological approaches. Culture was set apart from 'mainstream' thinking, and the debates (Is culture manageable? Is it a unifying force?) helped to articulate arguments and gain new insights. Those who sought to include multiple paradigms or perspectives in their thinking – the 'peacemakers' – provided useful overviews and opened up different perspectives, persuading some to get out of the trenches and think 'outside the box'. Paradigm 'wars' in this context were, at times, positive in their outcomes and inspiring of further work.

On the other hand, within the context of academic departments and their hiring and promotion practices, professional associations and 'air-time' for presenting papers at meetings, and journals' editorial positionings, which view of the elephant scholars took had implications for their professional lives. Nowhere is this clearer than in the contrasts between another binary, imperfect as it might be: those schools and departments, associations, and journals on either side of

the Atlantic, where deep divides between interpretivism and positivism have hardly been bridged at all and the US positivist-informed and/or inflected methodological hegemony still prevails (as it does there in political and other social sciences, as well).

US scholars trying to do interpretive research on the whole still feel beleaguered, facing opposition from the hiring front to getting published. A glance at almost any issue of *Organizational Research Methods*, the journal of the Academy of Management's Research Methods Division, confirms their invisibility: interpretive (or qualitative) methods articles have been rare, the exceptions being two special issues (Volume 5:1, in 2002, and Volume 11:3, in 2008), along with a handful of qualitative-interpretive articles that appeared in a recent volume, including a themed issue on ethnostatistics. Although the Academy of Management's Critical Management Studies Interest Group has become a platform for interpretive research, those methods are still difficult to find in the pages of the Academy's journals, and such research is likely to be held to standards more appropriate to positivist science (see, e.g., Eden, 2003). The first US conference devoted to qualitative methods in organizational studies (organized by Ann Cunliffe, at the University of New Mexico, in March 2008) had as its purpose, at least in part, to give these methods a visibility (and hence legitimacy) that they have not been accorded since the 1960s.

Indeed, US scholars conducting interpretive research are more likely to find readership, and colleagues, on the other side of the ocean, where researchers are at least more or less versed in the terminology ('ontology' and 'epistemology'), concepts, and arguments, even when they oppose interpretivist positions. Ocean-crossing largely began with the development of the SCOS conference and its celebration of organizational culture and symbolism. Others have been drawn by the more theoretically inclined European Group on Organizational Studies (EGOS) conferences, which have made space for feminist and critical theories as well; a more recent creation, the British-based Critical

Management Studies (CMS) conference; and the ongoing [Metaphor and] Organizational Discourse conference in London/Amsterdam. EGOS' journal, *Organization Studies*, and the independent (and intentionally ocean-crossing) *Organization* have, since their respective inceptions, been outlets for inter-pretive theoretical and/or methodological scholarship, the likes of which would be hard to find in an Academy of Management journal. On the US side, only the frame-breaking *Journal of Management Inquiry* (JMI) and, occasionally, *Organization Science*, publish articles of similar theoretical or methodologi-cal orientation and scope.

At the same time, European and British scholars typically find it difficult to have work accepted for publication in US journals. JMI created the position of European editor some years ago in an effort to counteract this invisible boundary – but no leading US journal has followed suit. The issue is one of style, best expressed in terms of epistemic communities and their 'paradigms': scholars largely write in separate worlds, speaking past each other even when trying to engage one another's arguments (see Bryman and Buchanan, Chapter 41, this volume).

We have, unfortunately, minimal sense of the state of affairs in other parts of the world. Australia, New Zealand, India, Latin America – all have active and growing organi-zational studies scholarly communities. Asian and Pacific Researchers in Organizational Studies (APROS) has sought to bring many of these together, and interpretive research has been well represented there. At the same time, there is considerable pressure on scholars in these areas, as elsewhere, to adopt US models of scholarship, driven by textbook and journal publishing as well as by conferences (e.g., the British Academy of Management and EURAM; see Prichard et al., 2007). What this bodes for interpretive methodologies is unclear.

Writing from their institutional location in New Zealand, Prichard et al. (2007: 27) note the dominance and centrality of North Atlantic journals, conferences, and societies in management and organizational studies,

observing the extent to which 'North Atlantic Theories of Organisation' (NATO) are equated with 'international studies of organizations'. (For a related argument noting the 'over-whelmingly western' roots of management and organizational studies scholarship, see Frenkel and Shenhav, 2006; see also Yanow, 2005b; Weir, 2009; and the emerging literature on 'Afrocentric management'.) Another arti-cle reflects on the effect of such hegemony on scholarship, linking theoretical orientations to research methods in noting the role of 'nationality' among the elements shaping a researcher's positionality with respect to the study of organizational discourses:

> [In] North American business schools … [which] are dominated by positivist approaches to science … ODA [organizational discourse analysis] will be an interesting but marginal, even odd, approach to the study of organization. Training, senior faculty support and co-authors may be hard to come by. In the absence of exposure to qualitative research training, one may feel too insecure to proceed, or one can suffer the hubris of assuming that anyone who can talk and read can do discourse analysis. In the UK and Europe, ODA fits well with the more mainstream interpretive and critical traditions. In Australasia, 'refugees' from North American and UK systems mix with Kiwis and Aussies in more intellectually diverse departments. All of the non-US researcher positions must relate to the American domination of the intellectual field, hierarchical ranking of journals, etc. (Prichard et al., 2004: 216).

We can only hazard some guesses as to how to explain these differences. Unlike the US, Britain and Europe have not (yet) experienced the wholesale colonization of organizational studies by business and management faculties, and scholarship is still often found within social science faculties (although Britain's Research Assessment Exercise and EU-driven reward structures instantiate increas-ingly constricting productivity measures that threaten to change this). In Britain and Europe, faculty and students seem still to be close to their countries' blue collar backgrounds, social democratic governments, and/or still more level socio-economic-class playing fields (although all of this is also changing), leading perhaps to a greater inclination to conduct the shop floor studies that have drawn, historically, on interpretive methods and which enjoy a rich tradition there (e.g., in early Tavistock Institute studies).

That said, the paradigm divisions are not without cost, too, to the culture of scholarship. What interpretivism initially brought to the table was a certain playfulness. That playfulness introduced alternative paradigms, opened our eyes to our own blindnesses, started 'wars', wrote 'peace treaties', and debated new boundaries, without ever taking itself too seriously, at first. When debates on organizational culture, for example, were alive and kicking, academic life was enjoyable – for some; it was intellectually challenging, and one could feel part of a movement. For others, seeking to explore 'interpretive' positions that run counter to normative business school traditions, led to an often-punitive disciplining, manifested in various areas of disciplinary practices, among them hiring, tenure, and publication processes. This led to a sense of not belonging (see, e.g., Cunliffe, 2008: 9–10; she also cites an article by David Boje referring to his feelings of being an 'outcast'). At times, some 'paradigm pluralists', 'paradigm revolutionaries', 'paradigm warriors', and 'paradigm peacemakers', in their more hegemonic efforts to establish paradigmatic dominance in the field, or simply to defend a theory or claim space for a different perspective, seemed to want to colonize the entire discipline. Despite the proclaimed openness of interpretivism to multiple rather than universal-generalizable versions of social realities, some of the advocates of a multiperspectival position tended to advance claims to the whole research enterprise, not just arguing for 'equal' space and time – and to do so with charged rhetoric (a more adequate explanation is, *ipso facto*, a more 'advanced' one), which lent the arguments a feeling of superiority.

In not acknowledging their own blindnesses, those interpretive scholars alienated themselves from the underlying assumptions of interpretivism by forgetting to put their own 'truths' in quotation marks, and in the plural. Remembering the self-contradiction of this position could render ironic the sense of superiority inherent in all points of view that see themselves as having a corner on the market of Truth. In the meantime, however, the presence of this variety of perspectives – including pre-interpretivist positivism-informed studies – within contemporary organizational studies, explains why it is necessary today to be so explicit in detailing methodological groundings for research. As long as one does research within a single epistemic community, one need not spell things out quite as much or in the same way; but with increasingly cross- (not to say inter-) disciplinary work, such as in organizational studies, being more explicit and more transparent seems called for. 'Testability', one of the two hallmarks of science (the other being sytematicity), cannot be carried out at the level of theory and methods alone; and engaging it methodologically requires a reflective transparency with respect to the presuppositions on which those theories or methods stand.

Are debates in the field of organizational studies today open and playful, showing an awareness of potential blindnesses as well as the potential of alternative interpretations? As we have argued, interpretivism has certainly gained prominence in the field. In Europe, interpretive analysis is no longer (if it ever was) a counterculture or a discriminated-against 'minority' voice; in the US-based and -influenced academy, where positivist-inflected methods and arguments (still) hold sway (even, as Ann Cunliffe reminds us [personal communication, 5 June 2008], within qualitative research), oppositional theoretical voices seem no longer quite as isolated as they were 20 years ago, thanks in no small part to the space created for them by the Critical Management Studies group within the Academy of Management. Their methodological presence, however, continues in many departmental curricula and in the halls of science to have to battle for airtime and legitimacy. And some of our British colleagues note that, while from the western side of the Atlantic, academic practices might appear more accepting of interpretive and/or pluralistic approaches as valuable research, the Research Assessment measurement system that privileges publication in tier-1 journals, with its own implications for controlling tenure, promotion, and scholarly respect, is heavily slanted away from such work. Even funding for attending workshops on interpretive and other theoretical and methodological topics is discouraged in many British business schools as being 'not the kind of thing that we should be doing'. Interpretive scholarship is, in a word, 'dissed' – disrespected, dismissed – as being not true scholarship, and those British scholars manning the barriers often turn to US journals and scholars to back up their claims privileging positivist-informed research over other forms (Christine Coupland, personal communication, May 2008).

Although the hostilities may have lessened, then, the paradigm wars continue (Bryman 2008); but this is now largely a cold war, having lost its initial playful vitality. Rivals have retreated to safety in the trenches (on different sides of the Atlantic, for instance), writing in separate worlds, in many ways successfully ignoring each other. Interpretive approaches have proliferated into different strands of research (such as practice theory, discourse analysis, or organizational identity), abandoning a term like organizational culture in favour of seemingly more vivid terms like 'discourse', 'hegemony', 'institutions', 'identities', 'aesthetics' or 'practices'. The retreat into one's own 'community of interest' established what looks like a dominant 'cold war' style 'paradigm peace' – no overt fights and a somewhat phony peace – that hides paradigmatic contentions from view, deadening the lively and thought-provoking debates of the 1980s and 1990s.

Although it is still hard to tell, today's 'cold war' seems to add a new chapter to the story of interpretivism in organizational studies. We wonder what a newly enrolled doctoral student, coming of age in a post-interpretive-turn world, would make of this narrative. If interpretivists do not derive their identity as much from offering an alternative or an addition to mainstream functionalism any more, the challenge for interpretive approaches to studying organizational life today remains giving voice to alterity, because these approaches still retain the potential to enable a continuous running commentary on our theory constructions, smiling ironically at our neatly crafted frameworks and clear-cut distinctions.

ACKNOWLEDGEMENTS

We are grateful to Christine Coupland, Ann Cunliffe, Mary Jo Hatch, and Peregrine Schwartz-Shea, as well as the two editors, for comments on earlier drafts of this chapter. A section of the chapter draws on previously published material (Yanow, 1987; Yanow and Adams, 2000/1997).

REFERENCES

Adams, G.B. (1994) 'Blindsided by the elephant', *Public Administration Review*, 54(1): 77–83.

Albert, S. and Whetten, D.A. (1985) 'Organizational identity', in L.L. Cummings and B.M. Staw, (eds), *Research in Organizational Behavior*, Greenwich, CT: JAI Press, pp.485–503.

Allison, G. (1971) *Essence of Decision*, Boston, MA: Little-Brown.

Antonacopoulou, E. (1999) 'Developing learning managers within learning organizations', in Mark Easterby-Smith, John Burgoyne, and Luis Araujo, (eds), *Organizational Learning and the Learning Organization*, London: Sage, pp.217–42.

Astley, W.G. and Van de Ven, A.H. (1979) 'Central perspectives and debates in organization theory', *Administrative Science Quarterly*, 31: 78–108.

Becker, H.S., Geer, B., Hughes, E. and Strauss, A. (1961) *Boys in White*, Chicago: University of Chicago Press.

Berger, P.L. and Luckmann, T. (1966) *The Social Construction of Reality*, New York: Anchor Books.

Bernstein, R.J. (1983) *Beyond Objectivism and Relativism*, Philadelphia: University of Pennsylvania Press.

Blau, P. (1963) [1953] *The Dynamics of Bureaucracy*, Chicago: University of Chicago Press.

Bolman, L. and Deal, T. (1984) *Reframing Organizations*, San Francisco: Jossey-Bass.

Brower, R., Abolafia, M.Y. and Carr, J.B. (2000) 'On improving qualitative methods in public administration research', *Administration and Society*, 32: 363–97.

Brown, R.H. (1976) 'Social theory as metaphor', *Theory and Society*, 3: 169–97.

Bryman, A. (2008) 'The end of paradigm wars?', in Pertti Alasuutari, Leonard Bickman, and Julia Brannen, (eds), *The Sage Handbook of Social Research Methods*, London: Sage, pp.13–25.

Buchanan, D.A. and Bryman, A. (2007) 'Contextualizing method choice in organizational research', *Organizational Research Methods*, 10(3): 483–501.

Burrell, G. (1996) 'Normal science, paradigms, metaphors, discourses and genealogies of analysis', in Stewart R. Clegg, Cynthia Hardy, and Walter R. Nord, (eds), *Handbook of Organization Studies,* London: Sage, pp.642–58.

Burrell, G. and Morgan, G. (1992)[1979] *Sociological Paradigms and Organisational Analysis*. Aldershot: Ashgate.

Clegg, S. and Hardy, C. (2006) 'Representation and reflexivity', in Stewart R. Clegg, Cynthia Hardy, Thomas B. Lawrence, and Walter R. Nord, (eds), *The Sage Handbook of Organization Studies*, (second edn.), London: Sage, pp.425–43.

Clifford, J. and Marcus, G.E. (eds) (1986) *Writing Culture: The Poetics and Politics of Ethnography*, Berkeley: University of California Press.

Collier, A. (1994) *Critical Realism: An Introduction to Roy Bhaskar's Philosophy*, London: Verso.

Cook, S.D. and Yanow, D. (2006) [1993] 'Culture and organizational learning', in Barbara Czarniawska, (ed.), *Organization Theory*, vol. 1, Cheltenham: Edward Elgar, pp.259–76.

Crozier, M. (1964) *The Bureaucratic Phenomenon*, Chicago: University of Chicago Press.

Cunliffe, A.L. (2008) 'Alterity, Ricoeur, and the poetics and politics of self and scholarship', Inaugural Lecture, University of Hull Business School (12 May).

Dalton, M. (1959) *Men Who Manage*, New York: Wiley.

Deal, T.E. and Kennedy, A.A. (1982) *Corporate Cultures: The Rites and Rituals of Corporate Life*, Reading, MA: Addison-Wesley.

Donaldson, L. (2003) 'Organization theory as a positive science', in Christian Knudsen and Haridimos Tsoukas, (eds), *The Oxford Handbook of Organization Theory: Meta-theoretical Perspectives*, New York: Oxford University Press, pp.39–62.

Easterby-Smith, M. and Araujo, L. (1999) 'Organizational learning: current debates and opportunities', in Mark Easterby-Smith, John Burgoyne, and Luis Araujo, (eds), *Organizational Learning and the Learning Organization*, London: Sage, pp.1–22.

Eden, D. (2003) 'Critical management studies and the Academy of Management Journal', *Academy of Management Journal*, 46: 390–4.

Frenkel, M. and Shenhav, Y. (2006) 'From binarism back to hybridity: a postcolonial reading of management and organization studies', *Organization Studies*, 27: 855–76.

Geertz, C. (1973) *The Interpretation of Cultures*, NY: Basic Books.

Geertz, C. (1988) *Works and Lives: The Anthropologist as Author*, Stanford, CA: Stanford University Press.

Gherardi, S. (2000) 'Practice-based theorizing on learning and knowing in organizations', *Organization*, 7: 211–23.

Gioia, D.A. and Pitre, E. (1990) 'Multiparadigm perspectives on theory building', *Academy of Management Review*, 15(4): 584–602.

Golden-Biddle, K. and Locke, K. (1993) 'Appealing work: an investigation of how ethnographic texts convince', *Organization Science*, 4: 595–616.

Golden-Biddle, K. and Locke, K. (1997) *Composing Qualitative Research*, Thousand Oaks, CA: Sage.

Gouldner, A.W. (1954) *Patterns of Industrial Bureaucracy*, Glencoe, IL: Free Press.

Goodman, N. (1978) *Ways of World-making*, Indianapolis, IN: Hackett.

Gusfield, J.R. (1976) 'The literary rhetoric of science', *American Sociological Review*, 41: 16–34.

Hassard, J. (1988) 'Overcoming hermeticism in organization theory: an alternative to paradigm incommensurability', *Human Relations*, 41: 247–59.

Hassard, J. (1991) 'Multiple paradigms and organizational analysis: a case study', *Organization Studies*, 12: 275–99.

Hatch, M.J. (1996) 'The role of the researcher: an analysis of narrative position in organization theory', *Journal of Management Inquiry*, 5: 359–74.

Hatch, M.J. (2004) 'Dynamics in organizational culture', in Marshall Scott Poole and Andrew Van de Ven, (eds), *Handbook of Organizational Change and Innovation*, Oxford: Oxford University Press, pp.190–211.

Hatch, M.J. and Schultz, M. (2002) 'The dynamics of organizational identity', *Human Relations*, 55: 989–1019.

Hatch, M.J. and Yanow, D. (2003) 'Organizational studies as an interpretive science', in Christian Knudsen and Haridimos Tsoukas, (eds), *The Oxford Handbook of Organization Theory: Meta-theoretical Perspectives*, New York: Oxford University Press, pp.63–87.

Hatch, M.J. and Yanow, D. (2008) 'Methodology by metaphor: ways of seeing in painting and research', *Organization Studies*, 29: 23–44.

Hiley, D.R., Bohman, J.F. and Shusterman, R. (eds) (1991) *The Interpretive Turn*, Ithaca, NY: Cornell University Press.

Ingersoll, V.H. and Adams, G.B. (1992) *The Tacit Organization*, Greenwich, CT: JAI Press.

Jacobson, S. and Jacques, R. (1990) 'Of knowers, knowing and the known', Presented to the Academy of Management Annual Meeting, August.

Jick, T.D. (1979) 'Triangulating on mixing qualitative and quantitative methods: triangulation in action', *Administrative Science Quarterly*, 24: 602–11.

Karp, I. and Lavine, S.D. (eds) (1991) *Exhibiting cultures: the poetics and politics of museum display*, Washington, DC: Smithsonian Institution Press.

Kaufman, H. (1960) *The Forest Ranger*, Baltimore, MD: Published for Resources for the Future by Johns Hopkins Press.

Kuhn, T. (1970) *The Structure of Scientific Revolutions* (second edn.), Chicago: University of Chicago Press.

Kunda, G. (1992) *Engineering Culture*, Philadelphia: Temple University Press.

Lammers, C.J. (1991) [1983] *Organisaties vergelijkenderwijs: Ontwikkeling en relevantie van het sociologisch denken over organisaties* [Organizations in comparison: Development and relevance of sociological thinking about organizations], Utrecht: Het Spectrum.

Latour, B. (1987) *Science in Action: How to Follow Scientists and Engineers Through Society*. Cambridge, MA: Harvard University Press.

Latour, B. and Woolgar, S. (1979) *Laboratory Life: The Construction of Scientific Facts*. Beverly Hills, CA: Sage.

Law, J. (2004) *After Method: Mess in Social Science Research*, London: Routledge.

Lee, A.S. (1991) 'Integrating positivist and interpretive approaches to organizational research', *Organization Science*, 2: 342–65.

Lewis, M.W. and Kelemen, M.L. (2002) 'Multiparadigm inquiry: exploring organizational pluralism and paradox', *Human Relations*, 55(2): 251–75.

Lincoln, Y.S. and Guba, E.G. (2000) 'Paradigmatic controversies, contradictions, and emerging confluences', in Norman K. Denzin and Yvonne S. Lincoln, (eds), *Handbook of Qualitative Research*, (second edn.), London: Sage, pp.163–88.

Lipsky, M. (1980) *Street-level Bureaucracy*, New York: Russell Sage.

Martin, J. (1990) 'Breaking up the mono-method monopolies in organizational analysis', in John Hassard and Denis Pym (eds), *The Theory and Philosophy of Organizations: Critical Issues and New Perspectives*, London: Routledge, pp.30–43.

Martin, J. (1992) *Cultures in Organizations: Three Perspectives*, Oxford: Oxford University Press.

Martin, J. and Frost, P.J. (1996) 'The organizational culture war games: a struggle for intellectual dominance', in Stewart R. Clegg, Cynthia Hardy, and Walter R. Nord (eds), *Handbook of Organization Studies* London: Sage, pp.599–621.

McCloskey, D.N. (1985) *The Rhetoric of Economics*, Madison: University of Wisconsin Press.

McGregor, D. (1957) 'The human side of enterprise', *The Management Review*, 46(11): 22–8.

Miller, D.F. (1985) 'Social policy: an exercise in metaphor', *Knowledge*, 7(2): 191–215.

Miner, J.B. (2007) 'Where is organizational science headed?' in Gavin M. Schwarz, Stewart Clegg, Thomas G. Cummings, Lex Donaldson, and John B. Miner, 'We see dead people? The state of organization science', *Journal of Management Inquiry*, 16(4): 300–17.

Morgan, G. (1986) *Images of Organization*, Beverly Hills, CA: Sage.

Murphy, J.T. (1980) *Getting the Facts*, Santa Monica: Goodyear.

Nicolini, D., Gherardi, S. and Yanow, D. (2003) 'Toward a practice-based view of knowing and learning in organizations', in Davide Nicolini, Silvia Gherardi, and Dvora Yanow (eds), *Knowing in Organizations: A Practice-based Approach*, Armonk, NY: M. E. Sharpe, pp.3–31.

Ouchi, W.G. (1981) *Theory Z: How American Business Can Meet the Japanese Challenge*, Reading, MA: Addison-Wesley.

Perrow, C. (1994) 'Dialogue: Pfeffer slips!', *Academy of Management Review*, 19: 191–4.

Peters, T.J. and Waterman, R.H. (1982) *In Search of Excellence*, New York: Harper and Row.

Pettigrew, A.M. (1979) 'On studying organizational cultures', *Administrative Science Quarterly*, 24(4): 570–81.

Pfeffer, J. (1993) 'Barriers to the advance of organizational science: paradigm development as a dependent variable', *Academy of Management Review*, 18(4): 599–620.

Polkinghorne, D.E. (1983) *Methodology for the Human Sciences*, Albany, NY: SUNY Press.

Polkinghorne, D.E. (1988) *Narrative Knowing and the Human Sciences*, Albany, NY: SUNY Press.

Popper, M. and Lipshitz, R. (2000) 'Organizational learning: mechanisms, culture, and feasibility', *Management Learning*, 31(2): 181–96.

Prasad, P. (2005) *Crafting Qualitative Research: Working in the Postpositivist Traditions*, Armonk, NY: M. E. Sharpe.

Prichard, C., Jones, D. and Stablein, R. (2004) 'Doing research in organizational discourse: the importance of researcher context', in David Grant, Cynthia Hardy, Cliff Oswick, and Linda Putnam (eds), *Sage Handbook of Organizational Discourse*, London: Sage, pp.213–36.

Prichard, C., Sayers, J. and Bathurst, R. (2007) 'Franchise, margin and locale: constructing a critical management studies locale in Aotearoa New Zealand', *New Zealand Sociology*, 22(1): 22–44.

Rabinow, P. and Sullivan, W.M. (eds) (1979) *Interpretive Social Science*, Berkeley: University of California Press.

Rabinow, P. and Sullivan, W.M. (eds) (1985) *Interpretive social science*, (second edn.), Berkeley: University of California Press.

Rein, M. and Schön, D.A. (1977) 'Problem setting in policy research', in Carol Weiss (ed.) *Using Social Research in Policy Making*, Lexington, MA: Lexington Books, pp.235–51.

Richardson, L. (1994) 'Writing: a method of inquiry', in Norman K. Denzin and Yvonna S. Lincoln (eds), *Handbook of Qualitative Research*, Thousand Oaks, CA: Sage, pp.516–29.

Ricoeur, P. (1971) 'The model of the text', *Social Research*, 38: 529–62.

Rousseau, D.M. (1990) 'Assessing organizational culture: the case for multiple methods', in Benjamin Schneider (ed), *Organizational Climate and Culture*, San Francisco: Jossey Bass.

Schatzki, T.R., Knorr-Cetina, K. and von Savigny, E., (eds) (2001) *The Practice Turn in Contemporary Theory*, New York: Routledge.

Schein, E.H. (1985) *Organizational Culture and Leadership*, San Francisco: Jossey-Bass.

Schein, E.H. (1992) *Organizational Culture and Leadership* (second edn.), San Francisco: Jossey-Bass.

Schön, D.A. (1979) 'Generative metaphor', in Andrew Ortony, (ed.), *Metaphor and Thought*, Cambridge: Cambridge University Press, pp.254–83.

Scott, W.R. (1981) *Organizations: Rational, Natural, and Open Systems*, Upper Saddle River, NJ: Prentice-Hall.

Selznick, P. (1949) *TVA and the Grass Roots*, Berkeley: University of California Press.

Selznick, P. (1957) *Leadership in Administration: A Sociological Interpretation*, New York: Harper and Row.

Schultz, M. and Hatch, M.J. (1996) 'Living with multiple paradigms: the case of paradigm interplay in organizational culture studies', *Academy of Management Review*, 21(2): 529–57.

Shafritz, J.M. and Ott, J.S. (eds) (1996) *Classics of Organization Theory*, (4th edn), Belmont, CA: Wadsworth.

Smircich, L. (1983) 'Concepts of culture and organizational analysis', *Administrative Science Quarterly*, 28: 339–58.

Taylor, C. (1977) [1971] 'Interpretation and the sciences of man', in Fred R. Dallmayr and Thomas A. McCarthy (eds), *Understanding and Social Inquiry*, Notre Dame, IN: University of Notre Dame Press, pp.101–31.

Thoreau, H.D. (1852) *Journals*, part IV (excerpts). Available at http://www.sniggle.net/Experiment/index.php?entry=excerpts04#04May52 (last accessed 20 May 2008).

Tuana, N. (1989) 'The weaker seed: the sexist bias of reproductive theory', in Nancy Tuana (ed.), *Feminism and Science*. Bloomington, IN: Indiana University Press.

Van de Ven, A.H. and Poole, M.S. (1988) 'Paradoxical requirements for a theory of organizational change', in Robert E. Quinn and Kim S. Cameron (eds), *Paradox and Transformation: Toward a Theory of Change in Organization and Management*, Cambridge MA: Ballinger, pp.19–63.

Van Maanen, J. (1979) 'The fact of fiction in organizational ethnography', *Administrative Science Quarterly*, 24: 539–50.

Van Maanen, J. (1988) *Tales of the Field: On Writing Ethnography*, Chicago: University of Chicago Press.

Van Maanen, J. (1995a) 'Style as theory', *Organization Science*, 6: 133–43.

Van Maanen, J. (1995b) 'Fear and loathing in organization science', *Organization Science*, 6: 687–92.

Van Maanen, J. (ed.) (1998) *Qualitative Studies of Organizations*, Thousand Oaks, CA: Sage.

Waldo, D. (1961) 'Organization theory: an elephantine problem', *Public Administration Review*, 21(4): 210–25.

Weick, K. (1979) *The Social Psychology of Organizing*, (second edn), New York: Random House.

Weick, K.E. and Westley, F. (1996) 'Organizational learning: Affirming an oxymoron', in Stewart R. Clegg, Cynthia Hardy, and Walter R. Nord, (eds), *Handbook of Organization Studies*, London: Sage, pp.440–58.

Weir, D. (2009) *Management in the Arab World*. Cheltenham: Edward Elgar (forthcoming).

Westerlund, G. and Sjostrand, S.-E. (1979) *Organizational Myths*. NewYork: Harper and Row.

White, J.D. (1992) 'Taking language seriously: toward a narrative theory of knowledge for administrative research', *American Review of Public Administration*, 22: 75–88.

Willmott, H. (1990) 'Beyond paradigmatic closure in organizational enquiry', in John Hassard and Denis Pym (eds), *The Theory and Philosophy of Organizations: Critical Issues and New Perspectives*, London: Routledge, pp.44–60.

Willmott, H. (1993) 'Breaking the paradigm mentality', *Organization Studies*, 14: 681–721.

Yanow, D. (1987) 'Ontological and interpretive logics in organizational studies', *Methods*, 1(2): 73–89.

Yanow, D. (1995) 'Writing organizational tales', *Organization Science*, 6: 225–6.

Yanow, D. (2005a) 'In the house of "science", there are many rooms: Perestroika and the "science studies" turn', in Kristen Renwick Monroe (ed.), *Perestroika! The Raucous Rebellion in Political Science*, New Haven: Yale University Press, pp.200–17.

Yanow, D. (2005b) 'Public administration in "translation": Non-Western and other administrative practices. introduction to the symposium on "Non-Western administrative practices"', *Administrative Theory & Praxis*, 27: 81–5.

Yanow, D. and Adams, G.B. (2000/1997) 'Organizational culture', in Jay Shafritz (ed.), *Defining Public Administration*, New York: Westview Press, pp.137–46.

Yanow, D. and Schwartz-Shea, P. (eds) (2006) *Interpretation and Method: Empirical Research Methods and the Interpretive Turn*, Armonk, NY: ME Sharpe.

Ybema, S. (1996) 'A duckbilled platypus in the theory and analysis of organisations: combinations of consensus and dissensus', in Willem Koot, Ida Sabelis, and Sierk Ybema (eds), *Contradictions in Context: Puzzling over Paradoxes in Contemporary Organizations*, Amsterdam: VU University Press, pp.39–61.

Ybema, S. (1997) 'Telling tales. contrasts and commonalities within the organization of an amusement park: confronting and combining different perspectives', in Sonja A. Sackmann (ed.), *Cultural Complexity in Organizations: Inherent Contrasts and Contradictions*, Newbury Park, CA: Sage, pp.160–85.

Ybema, S., Keenoy, T., Oswick, C., Beverungen, A., Ellis, N. and Sabelis, I. (2009) 'Articulating identities', *Human Relations*, 62(3) (in press).

4

Critical Methodology in Management and Organization Research

Mats Alvesson and Karen Lee Ashcraft

INTRODUCTION

Of course, the term 'critical' carries many meanings. In one sense, all research is critical in that scholars strive to avoid speculative arguments and erroneous conclusions. In a more specific sense, this chapter invokes 'critical' to capture the sort of extensive reflection upon established ideas, ideologies, and institutions that can stimulate liberation from or at least reduce repression, self-constraint, and suffering. Critical scholarship tends to stand on the side of 'weaker' parties when studying or commenting upon relations of dominance, although many objects of critique – such as environmental catastrophe, consumerism, and the seduction of other mainstreaming notions – go far beyond a neat dichotomy of dominating and dominated. Critical theory is referred to as a tradition of social science, including the Frankfurt School and later mingled with related authors and lines of thought, such as Foucault, critical poststructuralism, neo-Marxism, and many versions of feminism.

A label that has become increasingly popular and a source of affiliation for many researchers is critical management studies (CMS). Although used in different ways, this broad moniker generally unites a diverse constellation of critical approaches to the study of organization. Threaded through such variety is an interest in the 'underbelly' of organizing, typically viewed as negative aspects of management and organization. CMS tends to call into question established social orders – dominating practices, discourses, ideologies, and institutions. The idea is to contribute to the disruption of ongoing social reality for the sake of rousing resistance to relations of constraint and domination. Typically, critical studies place a local object of study in a wider cultural, political, and economic context, relating a focused phenomenon to broader discursive and material formations like class, late capitalism, affluent/postscarcity society, and male domination. While there are also more micro-oriented critical studies, these too tend to consider societal context, even if it does not take centre stage (e.g. Rosen, 1985, who places a company-sponsored breakfast in a luxury restaurant within the context of capitalism and class relations).

Traditionally, methodology has not been the strongest side of CMS. At least in part, this is because 'mainstream' empirical projects in management and organization studies are held in some suspicion for not always delivering the most interesting and trustworthy results. CMS scholars contend that the 'science' of organization reflects managerial leanings, such that conventional empirical studies designed for academic and practitioner audiences are in themselves worthy objects of critical investigation. Not surprisingly, then, theoretical analyses and metacritique have been more common in CMS than original empirical research, and the literature has historically offered little assistance in facilitating a move from the comfortable 'armchair' of critical theory to the unsettling ambiguities of empirical work in 'the field' of nonacademic organizational settings. Writings on critical method have tended to express broad methodological principles with general relevance for (but little specific bearing on) fieldwork (e.g. Kincheloe and McLaren, 2005; Morrow, 1994), or to follow fairly conventional qualitative models and adjust with critical elements (e.g. Thomas, 1993).

As empirical projects in CMS have grown in recent years, they have mostly embraced qualitative methods aligned with interpretivist stances, particularly in the arena of 'data collection' (Given the misleading impression of empirical representations as solid facts and the problematic nature of the idea that we can just collect/pick up these, we signal some distance and irony to this dominant view of doing empirical work). Critical influences tend to enter the scene more prominently in 'data analysis', supplying theoretical frameworks and vocabularies for sifting through empirical materials in ways that challenge participants' taken-for-granted realities. It remains difficult, however, to ambitiously rethink and revise methodology through the lens of critical-philosophical insights, particularly at the level of 'data'

and technique. To be sure, the paucity of work in this area has recently changed somewhat, as authors in feminism (Olesen, 2000; Skeggs, 1997), critical organization research (Alvesson and Deetz, 2000), and methodology more broadly (Alvesson and Sköldberg, 2009) have begun to elaborate critical qualitative methodologies. CMS scholars increasingly call for critical reflexivity on relations of power in the research process, and many discussions of method in critically oriented empirical work have begun to reflect such accountability (e.g. Bell, 1999). Nonetheless, CMS critiques of science have historically reserved their strongest fire for quantitative methods of management research, whereas qualitative methods continue to be generally regarded as amen(d)able to critical aims.

Our aim in this chapter is to synthesize and characterize common methodological themes in CMS. Because of the predominance of qualitative approaches in the empirical work emerging from CMS thus far, we emphasize issues in the design, conduct, analysis, and representation of fieldwork and interviews, particularly from a critical ethnographic stance. Along the way, we call for a stronger and more systematic integration of critical theoretical principles and CMS research practices, urging reflexive fieldwork and interviewing, as well as a sharp eye for the ways in which critical analysis and writing can function ironically to speak for and sometimes silence participant voices. We also observe the recent growth of historical and visual methods in CMS, which are serving to expand the current scope of qualitative approaches.

Even as we stress the pervasiveness of qualitative approaches, we also wish to question the common notion that certain methodologies are inherently more and less compatible with CMS. We cannot here address *how* most methods might be creatively deployed for critical purposes, but we do argue that such innovative uses are possible and productive. Accordingly, we encourage CMS researchers to consider and develop counterintuitive applications and combinations of methodologies – for example, questionnaires or surveys conducive to quantitative analyses in support of Foucauldian-inspired 'genealogies' of discourse and meaning – while remaining mindful of their respective political tendencies and consequences. Overall, then, we seek to advance the methodological contributions of CMS by intensifying critical reflection in and about qualitative approaches, as well as by provoking curiosity and imagination regarding methodological alternatives, including those long held in suspicion as antithetical to critical aims.

What is critical management studies (CMS)?

We begin by identifying with greater precision some core characteristics that distinguish the literature known as CMS, or critical management (or organization) studies. Of course, there are many ways to depict this literature, and scholars hailing from poststructuralist, feminist, or critical realist positions, for example, would likely portray key features quite differently. For the broad synthesizing purpose of this chapter, we extend a previous account (Alvesson, 2008) of defining characteristics with relevance, albeit variable, to most substreams of critical organization scholarship. Generally speaking, CMS entails:

(1) The critical questioning of ideologies, institutions, interests, and identities (what might be called 'the 4 I's') deemed dominant, in some way harmful, and/or under-challenged.
(2) Through some form of denaturalization and/or rearticulation.
(3) With the aim of inspiring social reform in the presumed interest of the less-privileged and/or majority – particularly resistance to 'the 4 I's' that tend to fix people into unreflectively receiving and reproducing limited ideas, selves, motives, and practices.
(4) While also maintaining at least some degree of recognition that 'real' (i.e., lived and living) conditions constrain choice and action in the contemporary organizational world.

We explore each of these elements in the following section.

Focus of study

Critical questioning means that one carefully picks a theme or phenomenon that is assessed to deserve the whip – and curiosity – of CMS. Of course, societies are full of negative things: Individuals and institutions are imperfect; and social relations inevitably engender conflict, pain, misunderstanding, and failure. Of most interest from a CMS perspective are dominant (as opposed to idiosyncratic or sporadic) phenomena surrounding organization and work that appear to reign un(der)-challenged – that is, when a quality of 'taken-for-grantedness' guides the usual stance toward or representation of something. It is thus systematic but not easily recognizable forms of repression or constraint that tend to capture CMS attention.

Method of study

Although empirical inquiry within CMS could conceivably be conducted through any number of techniques, most prevalent are qualitative forms of fieldwork entailing interviews and/or participant observation. In part, CMS' affiliation with qualitative, interpretivist methodologies can be understood to follow critical theories of social science, which serve to debunk images of objective researchers safely insulated in experimental environments, manipulating human dynamics and reducing their context-specific complexity into fixed and measurable variables, statistics, and aggregates. For perhaps obvious reasons, critical theory cultivates deep suspicion of research motives like prediction and control, of research tools that mechanize human action and erase the inherent contingency of meaning. It is thus not surprising that critical scholars felt more affinity with research motives like understanding and research methods attuned toward hermeneutics, the preservation of participant voices and meanings, and the inherent vulnerability of both knower and known. Still in need of careful reconsideration, however, are the negative, even re-/oppressive tendencies of qualitative methods presumed compatible with CMS aims, as well as the potential for creative critical adaptations of quantitative approaches assumed hostile to CMS agendas. In short, we suggest the time has come to rethink prevalent scripts regarding 'appropriate' critical methods.

Whatever the method of seeking and analyzing empirical material, some kind of denaturalization methodology tends to distinguish the overall interpretive approach of critical scholars. This could range from radical deconstruction and reconstruction to more subtle portrayals that reveal the partial and contingent character of phenomena. The key is to articulate an alternative position that challenges conventional representations and critically probes (rather than taking at face value) the reported views and experiences of research participants. This entails confronting the ways in which researchers as well as participants habitually naturalize, reify, or in other ways freeze culturally dominant understandings. More specifically, this critical endeavour may be accomplished through such analytical practices as negation, deconstruction, revoicing, or defamiliarization (Alvesson and Deetz, 2000).

Purpose of study

While critique, challenge, and provocation may seem valuable in themselves, and while means-ends reasoning may be suspect through a critical lens, it is also worthwhile to consider the larger objective(s) of CMS. Even as social engineering and managerialism – involving a legitimation of expertise and the turning of subjects into objects of managerial intervention and control – are justified favourite themes for critique, this need not exclude the idea of CMS attempting to influence social and managerial practices. Indeed, participation, reduction of hierarchy, and communicative action (the latter referring to effort to clarify meanings through critical scrutiny in dialogue form) are key features in CMS oriented projects aimed at reforming institutions (e.g. Forester, 2003; Meyerson and Kolb, 2000). This suggests a positive, affirming pole of CMS, different from critique based on fault-finding and the raising of red flags. Emancipation in this sense entails efforts to break away from structures and ideologies that tend to constrain forms of consciousness into prespecified routes that stifle imagination. For CMS scholars of postmodernist convictions, goals like autonomy and self-clarification can appear as the antiquated, arrogant projections of researchers, but a parallel quest for meaningful space alive with possibility rather than predefinition through the critical investigation of various discursive traps can still be a possible route. For example, the notion of microemancipation has been proposed to balance the Foucauldian notion of persistent and ever-present localized politics against grandiose Marxist and other radical, large-scale emancipatory projects (Alvesson and Willmott, 1996). Another possible route toward transforming relations of power is *resistance*, in the sense of multiple, always indeterminate and ongoing defensive, reactive, or alternative projects, fuelled by the ambiguities and multi-discursivity of power, at least in postmodern-inspired writings (e.g. Thomas and Linstead, 2002). (There are, of course, also more traditional and broader views on resistance, e.g. Ackroyd and Thompson, 1999; Prasad and Prasad, 1998.) Such variations on the very purpose of CMS – knowledge input to reform, emancipation and resistance – all target some sort of repressive or otherwise disadvantageous organizational practices and encourage movement of a different kind.

Accountability to context

CMS scholarship usually entails at least some appreciation of the conditions and constraints that mark organizational and management contexts. Conventional ideas and expectations from taxpayers and university management, colleagues, and students, as well as other organizational practitioners, generate pressures to consider practical relevance. By acknowledging this feature of CMS, we do not mean to imply the necessity of a pro-managerial position, but we do mean to signal the legitimacy of requests for knowledge relevant to organizational life and effective production of goods and services. Of course, there are debates within CMS about the virtues and problems of 'anti-managerial' positions, and some see a trend to demonize those viewed, however erroneously, as possessing or exercising institutional power (e.g. managers) (Clegg et al., 2006).

To us, it seems sensible to take management seriously; to recognize some legitimacy to values like productivity, quality, and customer service; and to grant that some degree of coordination, control, division of labour, hierarchy, and exercise of authority can be reasonable and even helpful. In the absence of such features, for example, social and organizational relations can also face a 'tyranny of structurelessness' (Freeman, 1972–3) that can feel as impractical and unpleasant as the hyperstructured conditions they seek to redress, as evidenced in some experiments with feminist organization that eschew all forms of hierarchy and bureaucracy (Ashcraft, 2001; Morgen, 1994). Innovative hybrid forms of organizing, less ideologically pure but more responsive to practical dilemmas, might better aid institutional reform, emancipatory changes, or resistant actions (Adler, 1999; Ashcraft, 2006). Some consideration of specific organizational missions is also pertinent to empirical work in CMS. As Alvehus (2006) notes, organizations in this literature often appear primarily to produce (unhappy, imprisoned, or at least normalized) subjects rather than also socially valued products or services.

We suggest that CMS analyses of the possibilities for social reform, emancipation, and resistance should demonstrate mindfulness of surrounding organizational, societal, and economic contexts and related dilemmas and restrictions. In this sense, highly utopian, revolutionary, and other radical models may be less helpful for CMS than for critical enterprises more broadly. In other words, the demand to relate ideas for social transformation to the needs of living managers, workers, and organizations is a potentially distinctive feature of CMS, as a specific branch of critical social science oriented toward those acting amid the circumstances of contemporary organizational life (Spicer et al., 2009). This does not imply that all critical research should be 'realistic' or simply adapt to organizational settings and regimes, but rather that CMS seeks to acknowledge how realizing ideals such as class, gender, race, and ecological justice may have drastic consequences for the material functioning of organizations alongside effects on member subjectivities.

Three major moves in CMS research

Like many critical scholarly enterprises, CMS research can be divided into three central and often overlapping activities that follow from the above description of overall focus, method, purpose, and accountability, generating (1) insight (hermeneutic understanding in the critical tradition, archaeology to Foucault), (2) critique (genealogy to Foucault, deconstruction to the poststructuralists) and (3) transformative redefinition (Alvesson and Deetz, 2000). The first endeavour points at hidden or less obvious dimensions of some chunk of social reality; the second shows the problematic nature of these dimensions and the symbolic and material orders they indicate; and the third undermines their apparent robustness by encouraging alternative ways of constructing reality. Typically, CMS research emphasizes the first two activities; while the third may be addressed implicitly or explicitly, much of the extant literature does not step far beyond critique.

Insight
This term denotes the process of investigating and exposing the ways in which social knowledge and the seemingly 'objective' or 'natural' character of objects, events, and people are formed and sustained. Insight summons a hermeneutic view of language as constitutive and disclosive, opening a field of consideration, rather than a representational view, which tends to support 'knowledge as truth' claims. In other words, language use and social texts are seen as consequential acts of social construction that yield clues to underlying meanings and tensions, not as accurate mirrors of or transparent windows on reality. Insight generally entails constructing empirical material about a phenomenon of

interest, then reading that material in light of, and to shed light on, the social and political conditions (e.g. traditions, assumptions, and historical and economic contexts) that produced it. Specifically, CMS scholars tend to take interest in localized meanings and relations to the extent that these inform the larger organizational and societal systems that enable them; that is, particular sites and situations offer a useful means of accessing the broader meaning systems that activate situated quandaries and link them to the cultural milieu. For example, how are particular identities, practices, and truths created and sustained, and what social forces (e.g. available discourses and ideologies, enduring institutions, and economic and technological shifts) facilitate such constructions? In this sense, insight entails interpretation, in that it aims to generate meaning out of apparent ambiguity, or to transform seeming certainty into indefinite complexity – in short, to draw attention to the plural yet readable nature of phenomena. For many CMS scholars, then, an insightful interpretation is one that enriches understanding of the obscure or concealed. As we elaborate in our later discussion of methodological dilemmas, this expectation of critical insight also engenders some risk – for instance, of hastily concluding that local realities merely exhibit favoured 'scripts' of critical theories (e.g. 'the usual' class and/or patriarchal relations, managerialist, or consumerist ideologies) instead of curiously exploring local nuances for what else might be at stake.

Critique: Deconstruction and the genealogy of knowledge

CMS scholars generally maintain that organizational arrangements, relationships, and member perceptions cannot be assumed to naturally occur. Rather, they arise historically in response to social, political, and economic exigencies; and they reflect systematic relations of power that tend to privilege and disadvantage certain bodies. It is thus not enough to produce insightful descriptions of social realities; it is also the researcher's job to criticize the political relations embedded

in such realities. As this suggests, critique cannot be separated from insight, for insight as defined above entails a challenge to some prior understanding. Critique builds upon insight, explicitly connecting interpretations of reality to conditions and relations of power that freeze certain ways of organizing the world without fuller consideration of alternatives. As this suggests, CMS critique is distinct from other forms of evaluation in that it seeks to unravel the ideological and institutional roots of sedimented meaning systems while exposing marginalized possibilities for review (Alvesson and Deetz, 2000).

Many CMS scholars acknowledge that knowledge can guide domination and participation, and that the line between the latter two is often blurred, as in the case of participatory decision-making processes that engender discursive and ideological closure, or when people feel liberated by ideas that arguably further constrain them (e.g. Barker, 1993). In other words, so-called emancipation can amount to the exchange of one prison for another, and this can hold true for knowledge produced and held by critical researchers as much as that espoused by research participants. From this view, the point is not to try and locate power-free truth (as Habermas might), but to critically examine the simultaneity of as well as thin, roving line between liberation and subordination, autonomy and dependence. Critique is thus directed at the conventions of social orders and the privileged forms of knowledge, which are complicit with such orders. Hence, critiques of organizational domination and participation must always include a critique of the social science (for CMS, management, and organization science) that accompanies it. Critique in this sense is a participative, communicative act aimed at reopening dialogue while remaining mindful that all forms of knowing (dialogue included) are inevitably political.

Transformative redefinition: Concept formation and moves beyond resistance

Reconstruction toward social transformation is a logical extension and counterpart to insight and critique. It can easily be claimed that critical writings, in both enlightenment and postenlightenment veins, have placed too much faith in awareness and not enough stock in alternative responses. The hope that seeing systems of constraint will activate knowledge of how to act differently seems optimistic at best, for interests and identities lack the sort of straightforward and robust character presupposed by such hope. Contemporary forms of control formulate subjectivity in multiple, shifting and dynamic ways, and although critical research can retain its usual suspects – such as managerialism, technocracy, capitalism, patriarchy, bureaucracy, and US imperialism – stable objects of critique fail to account for (post)modern forms of power that work on many levels concurrently and in diverse, even contradictory ways. Consider, for example, the rise of cynical consciousness, wherein people take comfort in their articulate understanding of problematic social and organizational features while continuing to act in ways that support those features (Fleming and Spicer, 2003; Sloterdijk, 1984).

In this light, emphasizing critique, raised consciousness, and attitudes of resistance becomes clearly insufficient for effecting social change. Instead, meaningful change must also reside in the micropractices that constitute the innumerable sites of power relations (Alvesson and Willmott, 1996; Foucault, 1980). While much CMS research stresses resistance, as noted in the preceding section, it is currently conceived as a mainly defensive project reacting to extant political relations. The idea of transformation points to a more positive or reconstructive development; for example, microemancipation means locating pockets of activity, decision, self-definition, and initiative that are grounded in conscious consideration and response. Such pockets seldom arise in isolation but are part of loosely affiliated, parallel, or sympathetic (although sometimes in tension as well) participatory processes and communication (Deetz, 1992; Forester, 2003). They do not result from some new social and organizational 'solution' (read: regime) but entail ongoing tasks of struggle and decision as new forms of control

continually evolve. Through this lens, higher education, including management, must be involved in the production and distribution of what might be called political competence – i.e. encouraging critical reflection on and analysis of how institutions and forms of power constrain us, broadening the range of choices to include not only means for accomplishing of received goals, but also social and ethical sensitivity about drawbacks of any goals and instrumental actions (French and Grey, 1996).

Methods behind the moves: Generating insight, critique, and transformative redefinition

While we certainly think that quantitative research has its place within CMS, there is not much to be said about critical quantitative methodology. Given the options currently available for integrating ideas and insights from critical theory into the research process, we will concentrate on the prominence of qualitative critical research.

Critical listening across the research process

Having broadly characterized CMS research and its core activities, we move increasingly closer to the conduct of empirical work. As argued from the outset, at the more 'technical' level of methods, particularly in terms of interactions with research participants and gathering artefacts, CMS has been less distinctive. Although critical researchers have tended to conduct fieldwork in ways similar to other qualitative researchers, a bit later we will consider how such research practices can become more tailored to critical philosophies. We begin, however, with the point that critical methods have thus far most come into play in the analytic process, as suggested by our above discussion of generating insight, critique, and transformative self-definition. It is worth underscoring that these analytic activities occur throughout the research process. That is, they are not undertaken merely after empirical materials have been gathered; for example, they shape the selection of empirical materials as well as the questioning and recording of research participants. Across the many moments of research, critical analytic practice requires a particular sort of listening that can be distinguished from more descriptive interpretations bent primarily on understanding participant understandings. Specifically, critical listening seeks:

(1) To hear not only the social realities of participants, but also the pivotal modes of order(ing) embedded therein, including dominant discourses and the accounts, assumptions, values, vocabularies, and so forth that constitute local formations of power.

(2) To identify local themes of significance to participants that also link up to the political, moral, or ethical phenomenon of topical and theoretical interest.

(3) To explore those themes for variation and subtlety, both in terms of preserving multiple and even competing participant voices as well as pursuing alternative and nuanced theoretical explanations.

Preferably, CMS insight and critique stems from such careful and sustained acts of listening, introducing politically sensitized accounts without dismissing or silencing participant realities. Transformative rearticulation can then bring a positive, constructive turn to the negative, desconstructive moves of critique by indicating new possibilities for creating and engaging social realities. Insight, critique, and redefinition that flow from vigilant critical listening also tend to be more responsive to participants' lived experiences and, thus, to provide more feasible, actionable alternatives. In this sense, the desired effects of CMS analytical activities are closer to surprise and stimulation prompted by novel political readings rather than shame and defensiveness wrought by heavy-handed lessons in the researcher's political reality. Cautious and thorough critical listening is perhaps the most crucial path to these effects.

In terms of utilizing and configuring empirical material, the desired effects may be accomplished in a number of ways that vary by source, force, and directness of intervention. For example, one possibility is to produce a variety of empirically grounded discourses, such as local actors' varied voices on the subject matter, with particular attention to surfacing voices deemed absent, weak, obscured, or peripheral. Another option entails the use of empirical examples that illustrate the diversity of available or possible social forms, thereby opening a particular setting to previously concealed alternatives. Such examples may emerge from within or beyond the bounds of particular societies. Progressive change projects, in which transformation is not just imagined at a distance but pursued by researchers and participants in the field, can also offer useful material. Typically, such projects are more localized and directly accountable to the particular setting in question – for instance, more subject to managerial goals like increased efficiency (Meyerson and Kolb, 2000).

Thus far, we have advocated critical listening as a vital and ongoing research practice that enables the production of 'good' critique, insight, and transformative redefinition throughout the conduct of an empirical project. A more conventional way of organizing the research process is to examine the key ingredients of various stages, such as formulating research questions, doing fieldwork, conducting analysis, and writing and representing. As we indulge this accessible and seemingly discrete and linear format below, we must hasten to add that, of course, the so-called phases of research interweave and rarely if ever unfold in a neatly linear fashion. Particularly in much qualitative research, research questions shift; analysis and writing occur while the researcher is in the field as well as afterward; and such overlap is a matter of design rather than error.

Formulating research questions

As already established, CMS research is generally motivated by questions of power, organization, and society. Hence, research problems with clear potential to disrupt received patterns of thinking and acting are regarded as most promising. Specific problems typically emerge from reading critical theoretical literatures alongside observations of contemporary organizational formations in, for example, public discourse and everyday work life.

Research questions can also emerge from placing critical theories of certain phenomena in conversation with more conventional theories and empirical studies. In this case, a critical reading of available scholarship is a crucial starting point, so that the focus, assumptions, categories, vocabularies, and logics of 'mainstream' research are not uncritically adopted and reproduced – and, thus, their ideological leanings and political functions unchallenged – in the formulation of research questions. The norm in science is one of knowledge accumulation, where researchers advance extant constructs to further test and build knowledge, for example, by identifying surface gaps or controversies (Sandberg and Alvesson , 2008; Locke and Golden-Biddle, 1997). From a CMS perspective, however, scholarly constructions of phenomena are not so much a reliable map for present knowledge and future research as an interesting object for problematization. Asking research questions that identify and challenge conventional scholarly assumptions thus becomes a common critical practice.

That said, it is not as if CMS scholarship is somehow off the hook of scrutiny in favour of indicting 'mainstream' research. Critical research questions can also stem from sceptical readings of critical theories. In other words, researchers should take care not to unreflectively reproduce 'sacred critical wisdom' in generating guiding questions. For example, rather than asking how employees of a particular organization are oppressed by dominant entrepreneurial discourses demanding disciplined bodies, a careful critical researcher might ask if and how entrepreneurial discourse is in local circulation; if so, what varied forms it tends to take; and how employees experience and respond to these variations in light of contextual pressures. Note how, in contrast to the former framing of the inquiry, curiosity about the relationship between participant experience and critical theory – as well as openness to mystery, surprise and 'critically counterintuitive' findings – are built into the research question itself (Alvesson and Kärreman, 2007), thereby illustrating how critical listening is a crucial analytic activity in even the earliest 'phases' of the research process.

As a general template, it is fair to say that CMS research tends to share at least some key questions with fairly traditional interpretive, qualitative research: What goes on here? What do 'the natives' think they are up to? But CMS research also tends to sharpen the inquiry with a critical edge, pushing researchers to challenge participant sensemaking and commonsense understandings: What in *the hell* do the natives think they are up to? In other words, how can we understand the problematic aspects of the natives' understandings, the assumptions, and constructions that they may be seen as being caught in? To be sure, formulating a sufficiently novel and challenging research question usually entails a combination of effort, innovation, and luck. Although most critical research begins with a guiding question, the more precise question typically shifts and unfolds during fieldwork and analysis. Sometimes, an excellent research question can in itself pose a major contribution. Burawoy's (1979) reframing of the question 'why don't the workers work more?' to 'why do the workers work as much as they do?' can be seen as an example.

Conducting fieldwork: Spotlight on interviews and ethnographic observation

Because interviews and participant observation have been the most common qualitative research methods among CMS researchers, we focus our discussion here accordingly, concluding with a brief consideration of emerging trends.

Conventionally, interviews are seen as tapping people for information about something, such as their attitudes toward certain phenomena, or their perceptions of how a decision was made or the consequences of a merger. Broadly speaking, a neopositivist or realist take on interviews holds that, when conducted well, they offer transparent gateways to realities inside and beyond individuals. From a more interpretive view, interviews are seen as expressing not so much actual events as the experiences and meanings of participants. Some sceptics express doubt about the capacity of interviews to reveal anything other than how people perform in interview situations. Radical critics advocate taking interviews as cultural sites for empirical study rather than as mirrors of something else (Silverman, 2001), while more moderate critics propose great care in drawing inferences that exceed interview settings based on interview conversations (Alvesson and Kärreman, 2000). Alvesson (2003) suggests that researchers consider a set of key ingredients and interpretive options before determining a reasonable reading of interview talk. Interviews may, for example, be seen as political action, in which participants express group (e.g. organizational, racial, gender, and occupational) identities and favourable 'truths', or as revealing shared social scripts about gender, leadership, corporate strategy, or whatever the particular topic may be. Although it may be tempting to take as fact accounts of bad management, racism, sexism, or other oppressions, critical listening is again of utmost importance, for, in many cases, interview conversations are most appropriately cast as story-telling and sense-making, loosely connected to other sorts of realities.

For some CMS researchers, a related temptation arises to embrace the stories of 'weaker' or subordinated participants (e.g. lower-level female service workers) while holding in suspicion the voices of elite or dominant members (e.g. white male executives). Feminist standpoint theories, among others, provide useful guides for CMS researchers in this regard, for they articulate the need to critique and minimize dominant voices and to expose and privilege marginalized perspectives without romanticizing the latter in ways that abdicate a critical, political consciousness (Aptheker, 1989; Harding, 1991; Smith, 1987). Nonetheless, issues related to trusting and romanticizing voices are far from

unproblematic in many such feminist studies (Alvesson and Billing, 2009). Another option that can assist in resisting this temptation is to frame interviews with all participants as opportunities to investigate the extent to which and ways in which people integrate dominant discourses with their sense of self. Through this lens, the issue is not so much what marked or predetermined bodies are speaking (e.g. the white male manager or the female domestic worker), but the extent to which the speaker hails their own body and those of others in particular ways with effects for subjectivity and power. This is a distinctive interpretive move for critical research, which draws attention to the openness and fluidity, tensions, and contradictions of identity work in interviews. For example, P. Y. Martin (2006) explores dynamics surrounding male interviewees who exhibit little or limited gender reflection, while Alvesson and Sveningsson (2003) show how managers relate to leadership in a confusing way, using leadership more for legitimation and ego-boosting (identity work) than as a guide for practice.

Contrasted with interviews, ethnographic or participant observation is typically viewed as an ambitious research practice offering rich and in-depth access to organizational life. Less dependent than interviews on individual report and recollection, and less removed from organizational practice, ethnographic observation seems to draw a higher credibility rating from CMS scholars than primarily interview-based studies. In part, this is because participant observation allows researchers to see organizing in action and, thus, to assess how interview accounts 'hold up to' practice and to witness firsthand phenomena discussed in or omitted by interviewees. And yet, considerable critique has been levied at the often arbitrary authority associated with 'having been there' (Van Maanen, 1995). Often cited by CMS scholars, Thomas' (1993) account of critical ethnography illustrates our earlier claim that critical research often follows the basic outline of a traditional interpretive, inductive approach to participant observation but adds an element of critical character. For example, Thomas suggests that critical ethnography emphasizes subject matter concerned with control and injustice, accentuates the repressive and circumscribing aspects of cultural phenomena, is more inclined to scepticism of data and information, and adopts a defamiliarizing mode of interpreting common language and sense-making. Thomas adds that critical researchers should reflect on relations of power in the research process itself in order to disrupt the faith in professional technique and authority that permeates the social sciences, although he mostly limits the call for critical reflexivity to accounting for how the researcher's participation shaped the data and for the broader relevance of the research.

It is likely, in part because of the extra burdens which follow scepticism of 'normal' social science, that empirical projects in CMS have been slower to develop. Adequately studying and integrating the historical and cultural context of localized interactions, developing accounts that probe beneath the immediately evident and rupture entrenched constructions, extending insight and critique to the politics of the research process itself – such worthy critical endeavours add considerable time and energy demands to an already taxing qualitative research process. Nonetheless, some of the most influential qualitative empirical work in organization studies has stemmed from critically informed ethnographies (e.g. Jackall, 1988; Kunda, 1992). 'Critical' here comes less from the explicit use of a strong theoretical vocabulary, but more in how these studies unpack how organizational cultures and norms tend to constrain individuals and make ethical action difficult. In particular, Jackall shows how firms create dependencies and traps – e.g. the strong pressure on managers not to deviate and the risk of appearing unreliable if one is not seen as loyal to the boss – and how people in organizations consequently have great problems in acting based on ethical convictions. Interesting here is the exploration of how ethics really work in specific settings, where the reader can follow the considerations

and faith of people encountering ethical dilemmas – seldom to be solved in a morally and politically unproblematic way.

Stretching beyond the usual interviews and ethnographic observations, CMS scholars work with textual artefacts as well, such as organizational documents. Increasingly, CMS research investigates fragments of popular and trade discourse about work and organization, and these analyses may include historical and/or contemporary texts, written word and visual image (e.g. Ashcraft and Flores, 2003; Carlone and Taylor, 1998; Czarniawska-Joerges and Monthoux, 1994; Jacques, 1996). Some researchers combine these methods with the more conventional qualitative empirical approaches described in the preceding section (e.g. Holmer Nadesan and Trethewey, 2000). As we elaborate later, such methodological trends follow the rise of postmodernist conceptions of discourse and indicate productive expansions in available CMS approaches to empirical research; these trends also engender new methodological dilemmas that, we suspect, will require increasingly sophisticated theorizing and training.

Writing and representing

For many audiences, a key feature of CMS writing is abstruse jargon. Employing the constructs of critical theories and enhancing accessibility while calling attention to the norms, boundaries and associated politics of social scientific representation are thorny challenges for CMS researchers. The vocabularies of many critical theories could be said to serve a mystifying function that ironically reserves access to insight, critique, and transformative redefinition primarily to intellectuals trained in critical traditions. Arguably, we have all read critical works that seem primarily dedicated to demonstrating the theoretical dexterity of the author, thereby maximizing this effect. Moreover, academic journal publication conventions, even some tailored to CMS, tend to domesticate scholarly writing such that research texts sometimes contradict the espoused orientation. For example, some studies drawing on Foucauldian and other poststructuralist ideas ironically rest on 'depersonalized, third-person and apparently objective and authoritative representations' (Wray-Bliss, 2002: 20). Not only critical analyses but also overt accounts of research methods, typically required for scholarly publications that report empirical studies, are particularly interesting sites for the manifestation of related tensions – a point to which we return in our discussion of dilemmas below.

Generally, there is a booming literature on the possibilities, merits, and difficulties of alternative forms of ways of writing (e.g. Van Maanen, 1988; Watson, 2000; Wolf, 1992). Some of the most successful – in the sense of influential – work in critical studies on organizational and business practices and their consequences manages to make the reader identify and feel engaged by characters and situations in the text. In particular, we have Klein (2000) and Sennett (1998) in mind, but within the more academically traditional texts, work such as Rosen (1985), Jackall (1988) and Kunda (1992) score very well in terms of the ability to present texts that are in harmony with the ideals of critical research and elicit the reader's engagement. For example, Kunda's (1992) in-depth ethnography uses one (fictional?) episode to provide an intensive, concentrated miniportrait on the relationship between self and organization in a firm that employs corporate culture as a strong regulatory force. This episode involves the researcher meeting an informant, a middle level manager, on the company parking place and walking with him to the office. Corporate life is vividly presented during this brief tour: the reader meets the differentiation of employee classes and encounters the massive communication of corporate messages, as well as ambivalence about being sucked into corporate culture while trying to maintain an independent position. The seemingly mundane takes on analytical significance, as Kunda and the manager observe decals on the cars in the parking lot, such as a heart accompanied by the text: 'I love Tech' (= the firm). The manager comments, 'that shit is everywhere.

I have it on my car as well'. Generally speaking, critical work tends to use tragedy as a narrative form, but one could imagine the use of ironic narratives with much more frequency and greater (political) effect (Alvesson, 2008).

Dilemmas and controversies of critical reflexivity: Politics, ethics, and humility in the research process

As implied by our earlier discussion of critical listening, cutting across the critical research process are vexing issues of reflexivity, ethics and politics. Although these concerns are hardly unique to CMS, they assume particular shape and are increasingly pressing matters in that context.

As a methodological construct, reflexivity references many things, such as examining the broader social and political context of knowledge production, interrogating the role of the researcher and the relation of researcher and 'researched', challenging one's preferred perspective and language through deployment of alternative viewpoints and vocabularies, and so on (Altheide and Johnson, 1994; Alvesson, Hardy and Harley, 2008). Despite its sensitivity to relations of power, CMS has no monopoly on reflexivity. Indeed, the avowed political stance of critical research and attendant critique of supposed scientific neutrality may actually render CMS scholars especially strained to see how 'insightful' and 'emancipatory' readings can be ironically imposed with iron fists or velvet gloves on participants and readers. In our view, any claim that critical scholars 'enter into an investigation with their assumptions on the table, so no one is confused concerning the epistemological and political baggage they bring with them to the research site' (Kincheloe and McLaren, 2005: 306–7) should be read as a sign of some worry, as it is impossible to exercise full knowledge and control over the content of such baggage, beyond confessing its general existence. In other words, as vulnerable humans and cultural actors working within the very meaning systems they critique, critical researchers may not fare better than others with respect to reflexivity. However, because CMS scholars are committed to challenging dominant systems of power, reflexivity regarding the researcher's participation in institutionalized relations of knowledge production and the politics of the research process is an essential component of critical empirical research. In fact, innovative work in critical reflexivity is increasingly regarded as a valuable contribution of its own, parallel to conventional empirical studies yielding results based on the methodical 'collection' and detached analysis of 'data'. Here, we discuss four major dilemmas of critical reflexivity implicated at various points in the foregoing discussion; we intend this as a provocative rather than exhaustive list.

Illuminating the relation between the research process and reported findings

Critical scholars are often quick to acknowledge that research relations shape the knowledge produced. Generally speaking, they are less adept at accounting for that relationship, particularly in published descriptions of the research process – for example, in the ubiquitous 'research methods' section required by most academic journals that feature empirical work. As hinted earlier, many CMS scholars continue to write in voices of decided analytic distance, as if the researcher and research process are somehow exempt from the politics that plague other social relations. Another approach entails various forms of methodological 'confession' or so-called 'positionality' work, wherein researchers relate emotional dimensions of knowing; situate their research role and performances in terms of gender, race, class, and sexuality relations; and weigh their participation in the politics of research. Typically, however, such admissions remain textually separated from the presentation of findings, such that the emotional, political aspects of knowing and truth claims remain unmarked. Arguably, feminist scholars have taken the lead in modelling workable alternatives to these common habits, specifically by exploring the relation between epistemologies

of intimacy and distance and by explicating the politicized relation between knowledge claims and the bodies and activities that produced them (e.g. Behar, 1996; Kauffman, 1992; Luttrell, 2003).

The right/duty to be critical or refrain from telling people what to think (or, 'wielding a moral hammer')

Difficult questions concerning the researcher's moral position and responsibility abound. In the related activities of insight, critique, and transformative redefinition, critical researchers attempt at once to honour, challenge and change participant perspectives – certainly no simple balancing act. As Czarniawska (2005) argues, 'as researchers it is our moral right to reveal everything that harms people or makes them suffer. At the same time I believe that researchers have no moral right to decide that something is wrong or absurd if the involved actors do not think so' (p. 159). Not limited to the arena of critical research, the dilemma is not easily resolved. At one end lurk the risks of arrogance and elitism; at the other, the dangers of affirming damaging social orders. Moreover, the ethical requirements of most forms of social science, such as informed consent and transparent research goals, sometimes work at odds with the aims of CMS. For example, gate keepers and interviewees may be less likely to grant access to researchers overtly espousing a critical lens and investigating the underside of organizational life. And yet, however enabling of CMS objectives, 'critical deceptions' can understandably cast the CMS enterprise as an arrogant if not ironically unethical and oppressive project.

Rather than engage such dilemmas in the abstract, we advocate grounded, practical, localized negotiation. This process might involve, for instance, challenging participants by encouraging them to consider 'hidden' consequences and alternatives to their current realities. Of equal importance, it entails the researcher's openness to receiving and absorbing as well as delivering challenge

(Spicer et al., 2009). Additionally, researchers can be encouraged to extrapolate gradually and cautiously from local to global contexts and discouraged from facile analytical moves that brandish a critical 'hammer'. Put another way, we advise against empirical projects that primarily utilize local realities to illustrate already determined critical claims – for example, by hastily imposing the usual suspects and ready-made scripts of CMS on complex tensions without first seeking to comprehend the situated struggles of those who live them.

Finding a feasible stance for intervention

As should be evident by now, few, if any, CMS researchers could claim neutrality with a straight face. But appropriate postures from which to claim involvement continue to fuel heated debate. Among the more common positions, for example, are claims to obligatory situational relevance, summarized earlier as 'accountability to context'; 'purist' claims, wherein critique should not be compromised by pragmatic constraints; what might be called 'mediating' claims, which acknowledge the researcher's active and invested role in weaving a critical tale but shy away from directive intervention; 'change agent' standpoints, from which researchers 'roll up their sleeves' and collaborate with participants in attempting to coordinate social transformation; as well as managerially relevant (Clegg et al., 2006) and anti-managerial claims (Fournier and Grey, 2000), which diverge over the appropriate place of organizational and managerial imperatives like productivity and efficiency in critical research. Not surprisingly, choices regarding authorial voice are in some ways related to one's stance on intervention. As a general rule, for instance, the more one is bent on practical, contextual applicability, the more one is likely to stress accessibility and minimize critical jargon. However, there appears to be no easy match between philosophies of intervention and those of critical reflexivity; scholars across intervention perspectives don voices that range in degrees and kinds of reflexivity.

Navigating methods suited to contemporary theories of discourse

A final methodological challenge appears to be growing in response to postmodernist accounts of discourse as fragmented over time and space. These theories challenge traditional notions of research site (e.g. a particular physical organization), suggesting the relevance of multiple and loosely affiliated sites of organizing (e.g. discourses of occupational identity that emerge not only in workplaces, but also in families, general education, industry and trade circles, popular culture, legal arenas, and professional associations, to name a few), as well as the importance of tracking the historical evolution of discursive formations surrounding organization and work. As briefly noted earlier, CMS scholars are increasingly rising to these challenges with varied forms of text- and image-based research. These developments bring with them dilemmas of adequate methodological preparation and experience, as conventional training in qualitative empirical methods does not necessarily include critical rhetorical, textual, archival approaches. More germane to this discussion, such methodological innovations in CMS are already introducing new twists on dilemmas of critical reflexivity, such as practicing site immersion in multiple locations of organizing, developing vocabularies to assess the politics of text inclusion, and demonstrating accountability to nonliving participant voices in historical research.

Moving between the text and the reality 'out there', or how constructionistic should one be?

Another problematic issue entails positioning critical claims in relation to 'reality' – for instance, emphasizing an extreme discursive lens that rejects any form of 'positivism', endeavouring to capture or mirror something 'real', or asserting bold claims about social phenomena 'as such'. One approach is to concentrate on representations (i.e. texts and discourses); another is to focus on constructions and meanings (addressing the level 'beneath' the 'surface' level of representations); and a third involves considering mechanisms, structures and practices that extend 'beyond' the first two more 'idealistic' foci. CMS researchers, to a higher degree than many other camps, are caught between different ideals and critics. For example, a recent controversy between the poststructuralist and critical realism wings of CMS is unfolding, particularly occupying some critical scholars in the UK (e.g. Fleetwood, 2005; Thompson, 2004; Willmott, 2005).

SUMMARY

Drawing on Alvesson and Deetz (2000) as a starting point, we emphasized three pivotal activities in critical management and organization research – generating insight, critique, and transformative redefinition – all of which necessitate careful critical listening and reflexivity in order to perform well. Expressed a bit differently, insight homes in on a particular chunk of social reality and reveals previously obscured understandings of it; critique explores the problematic nature of these understandings and the larger symbolic and material arrangements in which they are embedded; and transformative redefinition undermines their vitality by facilitating visions of other possible realities.

Thus far, empirical projects in CMS have stressed the suitability of qualitative paths to and through these activities. In the spirit of critical reflexivity, we have sought here to subtly model these activities by directing them at critical methodologies as a useful subject/object of critical consideration. On the one hand, for example, we respected enduring assumptions of critical-qualitative fit by devoting the bulk of our energies to reviewing common elements and manifestations of qualitative approaches in CMS research. Simultaneously, we attempted to reveal key limitations and tensions endemic to such approaches and to gently challenge the critical-qualitative match as an adequate guide for the future. By noting trends already on the horizon, and by claiming the

potential viability of creative methodological combinations that have long been tacitly proscribed, we sought to stimulate at least some imaginative unrest in the terrain of critical methodologies.

REFERENCES

Ackroyd, S. and Thompson, P. (1999) *Organizational Misbehaviour,* London: Sage.

Adler, P. (1999) 'Building better bureaucracies', *Academy of Management Executive,* 13(4): 36–47.

Altheide, D. and Johnson, J. (1994) 'Criteria for assessing interpretive validity in qualitative research', in N. Denzin and Y. Lincoln (eds), *Handbook of Qualitative Research,* Thousand Oaks, CA: Sage.

Alvehus, J. (2006) *Paragrafer och Profit,* Lund: Lund Business Press.

Alvesson, M. (2003) 'Beyond neo-positivism, romanticism and localism. a reflexive approach to interviews', *Academy of Management Review,* 28(1): 13–33

Alvesson, M. (2008) 'The future of critical management studies', in D. Barry and H. Hansen (eds), *The Sage Handbook of New Perspectives on Organization Studies,* London: Sage

Alvesson, M. and Billing, Y. (2009) *Understanding Gender and Organization* (second edn.), London: Sage.

Alvesson, M. and Deetz, S. (2000) *Doing Critical Management Research,* London: Sage.

Alvesson, M., Hardy, C. and Harley, B. (2008) 'Reflecting on reflexivity: reappraising reflexive practice in organisation and management theory', *Journal of Management Studies,* 43: 480–501.

Alvesson, M. and Kärreman, D. (2000) 'Taking the linguistic turn in organizational research: challenges, responses, consequences', *Journal of Applied Behavioural Science,* 36(2): 134–56

Alvesson, M. and Kärreman, D. (2007) 'Creating mystery: empirical matters in theory development', *Academy of Management Review,* 32(4): 1265–81.

Alvesson, M. and Sköldberg, K. (2009) *Reflexive Methodology* (second edn.), London: Sage.

Alvesson, M. and Sveningsson S. (2003) 'The good visions, the bad micro-management and the ugly ambiguity: contradictions of (non-)leadership in a knowledge-intensive company', *Organization Studies,* 24(6): 961–88.

Alvesson, M. and Willmott, H. (1996) *Making Sense of Management: A Critical Analysis,* London: Sage.

Alvesson, M. and Willmott, H. (eds) (2003) *Studying Management Critically*, London: Sage.

Aptheker, B. (1989) *Tapestries of Life: Women's Work, Women's Consciousness, and the Meaning of Daily Experience*, Amherst: University of Massachusetts Press.

Ashcraft, K.L. (2001) 'Organized dissonance. feminist bureaucracy as hybrid form', *Academy of Management Journal*, 44(6): 1301–22.

Ashcraft, K.L. (2006) 'Feminist-bureaucratic control and other adversarial allies: how hybrid organization subverts anti-bureaucratic discourse', *Communication Monographs*, 73: 55–86.

Ashcraft, K.L. and Flores, L.A. (2003) 'Slaves with white collars: decoding a contemporary crisis of masculinity', *Text and Performance Quarterly*, 23: 1–29.

Barker, J. (1993) 'Tightening the iron cage: concertive control in self-managing teams', *Administrative Science Quarterly*, 38: 408–37.

Behar, R. (1996) *The Vulnerable Observer: Anthropology That Breaks Your Heart*, Boston, MA: Beacon Press.

Bell, E. (1999) 'The negotiation of a working role in organizational ethnography', *International Journal of Social Research Methodology*, 2: 17–37.

Burawoy, M. (1979) *Manufacturing Consent*, Chicago: University of Chicago Press.

Carlone, D. and Taylor, B. (1998) 'Organizational communication and cultural studies', *Communication Theory*, 8: 337–67.

Clegg, S., Kornberger, M., Carter, C. and Rhodes, C. (2006) 'For management?', *Management Learning*, 37: 7–27.

Czarniawska, B. (2005) *En Teori om Organisering*, Lund: Studentlitteratur.

Czarniawska-Joerges, B. and Monthoux, P.G. (1994) *Good Novels, Better Management: Reading Organizational Realities in Fiction*, New York: Gordon & Breach.

Deetz, S. (1992) *Democracy in the Age of Corporate Colonization: Developments in Communication and the Politics of Everyday Life*, Albany, NY: State University of New York Press.

Fleetwood, S. (2005) 'Ontology in organization and management studies: a critical realist perspective', *Organization*, 12, 197–222.

Fleming, P. and Spicer, A. (2003) 'Working at a cynical distance', *Organization*, 10(1): 157–9.

Forester, J. (2003) 'On fieldwork in a Habermasian way: critical ethnography and the extra-ordinary character of ordinary professional work', in M. Alvesson and H. Willmott (eds), *Studying Management Critically*, London: Sage.

Foucault, M. (1980) *Power/Knowledge*, New York: Pantheon.

Foucault, M. (1983) 'Structuralism and post-structuralism: an interview with Michel Foucault', by G. Raulet. *Telos*, 55: 195–211.

Foucault, M. (1995) 'The art of telling the truth', in Kelly, M. (ed.), *Critique and Power*, Cambridge, MA: MIT Press.

Fournier, V. and Grey, C. (2000) 'At the critical moment: conditions and prospects for critical management studies', *Human Relations*, 53(1): 5–32.

Freeman, J. (1972–3) 'The tyranny of structurelessness', *Berkeley Journal of Sociology*, 17: 151–64.

French, R. and Grey, C. (1996) *Rethinking Management Education*, London: Sage.

Grey, C. and Willmott, H. (eds) (2005) *Critical Management Studies*, Oxford: Oxford University Press.

Harding, S. (1991) *Whose science? Whose Knowledge? Thinking from Women's Lives*, Ithaca, NY: Cornell University Press.

Holmer Nadesan, M. and Trethewey, A. (2000) 'Performing the enterprising subject: gendered strategies for success (?)', *Text and Performance Quarterly*, 20: 223–50.

Jackall, R. (1988) *Moral Mazes. The World of Corporate Managers*, Oxford: Oxford University Press.

Jacques, R. (1996) *Manufacturing the Employee: Management Knowledge From the 19th to 21st Centuries*, London: Sage.

Kauffman, B. (1992) 'Feminist facts: interview strategies and political subjects in ethnography', *Communication Theory*, 2: 187–206.

Kincheloe, J. and McLaren, P. (2005) 'Rethinking critical theory and qualitative research', in N. Denzin, and Y. Lincoln. (eds), *Handbook of Qualitative Research* (third edn.), Thousand Oaks, CA: Sage.

Klein, N. (2000) *No Logo*, London: Flamingo.

Kunda, G. (1992) *Engineering Culture. Control and Commitment in a High-Tech Corporation*, Philadelphia: Temple University Press.

Locke, K. and Golden-Biddle, K. (1997) 'Constructing opportunities for contribution: structuring intertextual coherence and "problematizing" in organizational studies', *Academy of Management Journal*, 40(5): 1023–62.

Luttrell, W. (2003) *Pregnant Bodies, Fertile Minds: Gender, Race, and the Schooling of Pregnant Teens*, New York: Routledge.

Martin, P.Y. (2006) 'Practicing gender at work: Further thoughts on reflexivity', *Gender, Work and Organization*, 13(3): 254–76.

Meyerson, D. and Kolb, D. (2000) 'Moving out of the armchair: developing a framework to bridge the gap between feminist theory and practice', *Organization*, 7(4): 553–71.

Morgen, S. (1994) 'Personalizing personnel decisions in feminist organizational theory and practice', *Human Relations*, 47(6): 665–84.

Morrow, R. (1994) '*Critical Theory and Methodology*', Thousand Oaks, CA: Sage.

Olesen, V. (2000) 'Feminisms and qualitative research at and into the millennium', in Denzin and Y. Lincoln (eds), *Handbook of Qualitative Research* (second edn.), Thousand Oak, CA: Sage.

Prasad, P. and Prasad, A. (1998) 'Everyday struggles at the workplace', in *Research in the Sociology of Organizations*, 15: 225–57. JAI Press.

Rosen, M. (1985) 'Breakfirst at Spiro's: dramaturgy and dominance', *Journal of Management*, 11(2): 31–48.

Sandberg, J. and Alvesson, M. (2008) 'Routes to research. beyond gap-spotting', Working paper. Univ. of Queensland Business School.

Scarbrough, H. and Burrell, G. (1996) 'The axeman cometh: the changing roles and knowledges of middle managers', in S. Clegg, and G. Palmer (eds), *The Politics of Management Knowledge*, London: Sage.

Sennett, R. (1998) *The Corrosion of Character*, New York: Norton.

Silverman, D. (2001) *Interpreting Qualitative Data* (second edn.), London: Sage.

Skeggs, B. (1997) *Formations of Class and Gender*, London: Sage.

Sloterdijk, P. (1984) 'Cynicism – The Twilight of False Consciousness', *New German Critique*, Fall 1984, 33, 190–206.

Smith, D. (1987) *The Everyday World as Problematic: A Feminist Sociology*, Boston, MA: Northeastern University Press.

Spicer, A., Alvesson, M. and Kärreman, D. (2009) 'Critical performativity: the unfinished business of critical management studies', Human Relations (forthcoming).

Thomas, J. (1993) *Doing Critical Ethnography*, Newbury Park: Sage.

Thomas, R. and Linstead, S. (2002) 'Losing the plot? Middle managers and identity', *Organization*, 9(1): 71–93.

Thompson, P. (1993) 'Post-modernism: fatal distraction', in J. Hassard and M. Parker (eds), *Postmodernism and Organizations*, London: Sage, pp.183–203.

Thompson, P. (2004) 'Brands, boundaries and bandwagons. a critical reflection on critical management studies', in S. Fleetwood and S. Ackroyd (eds), *Critical Realism in Action in Organisation and Management Studies*, London: Routledge.

Van Maanen, J. (1988) *Tales of the Field. On Writing Ethnography*, Chicago: University of Chicago Press.

Watson, T. (2000) 'Ethnographic fiction science', *Organization*, 7: 489–510.

Willmott, H. (2005) 'Theorizing contemporary forms of control. some poststructural responses to some critical realist questions', *Organization*, 12: 747–80.

Wolf, M. (1992) *A Thrice-Told Tale. Feminism, Postmodernism and Ethnographic Representation*, Stanford: Stanford University Press.

Wray-Bliss, E. (2002) 'Abstract ethics, embodied ethics: the strange marriage of Foucault and positivism in labour process theory', *Organization*, 9(1): 5–39.

5

Research Ethics: Regulations and Responsibilities

Emma Bell and Edward Wray-Bliss

INTRODUCTION: SCIENCE NOT ETHICS?

We wish to begin this chapter with a characterization of academic research, which seems to leave little space, or have little need, for ethical reflexivity.

> Proper academic research is a process defined by scholarly detachment from the subject studied. It is a rational, dispassionate, and largely technical endeavour, not emotional, ideological, or personal. It is characterized by value freedom and the eradication of biases. It is properly distanced from political debates about the purposes to which such research might be put. If asked how ethics comes into the frame then, apart from avoiding the obvious issues of falsification of data or blatant abuse of subjects, questions of ethics, like other emotive or subjective issues such as biases, values, and political or religious views, should be largely expunged from the research process lest they taint the dispassionate pursuit of knowledge.

For some readers this characterization might appear to be a 'straw man', a bald caricature of the disengaged academic. For others, given the disparate nature of academic research on organizations, it may approximate an ideal to aspire to. We present it here to begin what we intend to be a questioning, at times sceptical, examination of research ethics across the paradigmatically diverse field of organizational research: starting with this view which, perhaps more than any other, seems to pit academic research – presented as 'science' – against or, perhaps more tellingly, *above* ethics.

Such a view of science can trace its history to European eighteenth-century Enlightenment thinkers, their popularization of a fifteenth- to seventeenth-century scientific world view and extension of such views from the areas of natural science to the study of humanity (Christians, 2005). Located within a political struggle with the landed aristocracy and church hierarchy over the distributions of privileges, inequalities, and social status and an ideological struggle with the Aristotelian-Christian ideas, which legitimized these, the Enlighteners promoted reason, observation, facts, and the autonomy of the individual as a direct counter to the church's imposition of an incontestable moral and religious authority. In such a context, that which was apprehended by revelation or superstition, or imposed by tradition or domination, was representative of the old order, of the church's and the landed aristocracies' claims to divine rights. To free people from such constraints, reason was to be divided from and elevated above faith, facts from values, the material from the spiritual, truth from belief, 'is' from 'ought'. We have here the emergence of a view of science, the legacy of which we operate with today, where the scientific pursuit of hard facts appears largely separate to and divorced from the realm of morals or ethics.

However, this apparently clear cut picture of Enlightenment science as separate from, or in antithesis to, morality or ethics, is more ambivalent than may at first appear. Woven within this view of the liberating force of reason and science is a strong normative, ethical, commitment to the values of progress, truth, and freedom. The freedom of the sovereign individual, acting through reason, freed from domination by religious or other traditional moral authority was upheld as the highest ethical end. Thus, though the *process* of science was understood to be necessarily freed from issues of beliefs, values or such, science itself was strongly wedded to a liberal humanist ethics. Science and reason were cast as key forces through which humankind would move to a progressively less preju-diced, less hierarchical, more rational social order. Seidman (1998: 21–2), summarizing the views of the eighteenth-century European thinker *Condorcet*, for example, presents this era as asserting that 'the very nature of science – its reliance upon facts and observation, its openness to criticism and revision – inevitably promotes individualism, tolerance, equality, and democracy. Hence the progress of science automatically translates into social progress'.

Though still perhaps an inspiring ideal for many – and, we suggest, the enduring implicit justification for science and academic research more generally – faith in the inherently liberal, humanist, or progressive ethics of science has been seriously tested in more recent times through historical revelations, which have implicated scientists in atrocities against humanity (Punch, 1994).

Neither is *social* science free from charges of complicity in deeply ethically problematic practices. Prasad (2005: 76–78), for instance, charts how ethnography, considered by many to be the pre-eminent qualitative method-ology, has its roots deep in the politics of colonial and American frontier expansion. Urgently needing more information about the 'native' populations so as to subjugate, pacify and/or better exploit them, colonial powers and frontier administrators commissioned and supported ethnographic field work to provide invaluable 'authentic' accounts of the 'natives'. Prasad perceptively highlights how the problematic legacy of colonialism still runs like a seam through contemporary ethnographic research and writing. Such a legacy surfaces, for instance, in quasi-colonial assumptions about the ability of the expert academic researcher to apprehend the native's point of view – to, one might argue, treat the researched as a colonized people or subject race such that the expert researcher can assume to 'know them and what is good for them better than they could possibly know themselves' (Said, 1978: 35; also Wray-Bliss, 2002b: 94).

For some critics, particularly those drawing on feminist and postmodernist traditions, such examples where science has functioned in the service of oppression are not merely dismissible as 'bad' science. They also raise deeper ethical questions with the understand-ings of academic research methods and the authority of academic knowledge, which we have inherited from the Enlightenment. The researcher's detachment and distance – from research subjects, from values or biases, from consideration of the ends that knowledge may be put to – are not, according to these critics, markers of an impartial scientific process that enhances human knowledge and progress. Rather, such detachment repre-sents a discredited, even dangerous, way of apprehending the world that distances the researcher or scientist from an appreciation of their and others' humanity. Glover (2001) provides a compelling, far-reaching account of the consequences of detachment or divorce from humanity during the twentieth century.

He argues that this century's atrocities, wars, and genocides compel us to re-examine our ethical assumptions and ethical philosophies. Included amongst the historical experience he considers is the following correspondence between scientists at the I.G. Farben Chemical Trust and officials at the concentration camp, Auschwitz, regarding the procurement of research subjects:

> In contemplation of experiments with a new soporific drug, we would appreciate your procuring for us a number of women ... We received your answer but consider the price of 200 marks a woman excessive. We propose to pay not more than 170 marks a head. If agreeable, we will take possession of the women. We need approximately 150 ... Received the order of 150 women. Despite their emaciated condition, they were found satisfactory ... The tests were made. All subjects died. We shall contact you shortly on the subject of a new load. (Glover, 2001: 338–9)

While such horrific examples of the divorce of humanity from the pursuit of knowledge are most thankfully rare, a number of other critics have also raised strong ethical objections to more subtle forms of researchers' detachment from the subject and objects of their research. Included amongst such criticisms are arguments linking the treatment of subjects in research as passive objects of study, to the broader objectification and oppression of women and marginalized members of society (Hooks, 1989; Said, 1978; Stanley and Wise, 1993). Critics have also highlighted how conventional practices in academic writing – including writing in the third person, excluding from the text data that is ambivalent or contradictory to the main argument, perfunctory technical sounding summaries of research methods used, and the citing of an author's qualifications and institutional allegiances in biographical notes – push for the elevation of the authority of the 'dispassionate' and 'objective' academic voice (Smith, 1990). Such authority, while useful in making the academic voice heard, may also have the effect of rendering research subject's voices subordinate and subject to that of experts and thereby less able to contest or contradict academics' and other experts' representation or appropriation of their lives (Opie, 1992). For some, the critiques of the Enlightenment view of science and scientific method are of a magnitude that obliges us to overturn the historical separation of science and ethics and make the explicit articulation and debate about our ethical positions and intentions central to our research practices (Bauman, 2005; Seidman, 1998).

From the preceding broad brush discussion we can perhaps begin to appreciate how matters of ethics intertwine with research both through the *process* of carrying out research and its *legitimacy* or whether it should be conducted at all. In organizational research, these areas of ethical consideration are no less pertinent. First, in relation to the process of research, the dominance of quantitative research practices which draw on a positivist epistemology, may serve to reduce the status of research populations from that of active, knowledgeable, and diverse subjects to passive, easily categorized objects of knowledge. The reproduction of the distanced, detached voice of the author in published texts, in both quantitative and qualitative research, 'mainstream' and 'critical' studies, can obscure the normative and inherently contestable basis of research and push for the presumption of academic authority over the lives of those studied (Wray-Bliss, 2002a). This may render less-powerful members of organizations, who already have few opportunities to have their voices and views publicly aired, more silent still.

Second, in relation to the legitimacy of organizational research as a worthwhile project, this can be argued to rest, as did the Enlightenment view of science before it, upon largely unexamined assumptions about the goodness of its ends – in this case the 'goodness' of organization. For though each research topic and subdiscipline or field will have its own local rationale – extending our knowledge of organizational strategy, for instance, or optimizing distribution and supplier networks – organizational research in general is validated by an implicit appeal to the furtherance of organizational effectiveness.

This constitutes an assumed ethical end that serves to legitimize the organizational research arena. However, some critics have argued that such assumptions cannot continue to underpin the ethical legitimacy of organizational research. For example, the view that the rightful purpose of organizational research is to aid us in a movement toward progressively more rational and efficient organization, expressed through notions of evidence based practice (Learmonth, *this book*), may itself be questioned. Critical organizational researchers (Alvesson and Deetz, 2000), working in such fields as labour process theory and critical management studies (Grey and Willmott, 2005) have highlighted and critiqued the normative, pro-managerial, pro-western (Griseri, 2002) and masculine (Gherardi, 1995) interests and assumptions underpinning and directing mainstream management and organizational research. Such concerns around the unacknowledged normative assumptions of organizational research, the systemic privileging of managerial concerns and voices and the silencing of the interests of a range of other organizational participants and stakeholders are longstanding. Writing in 1974, Braverman, for instance, was highly critical of the failure of industrial sociologists to examine the degradation of the working conditions and processes faced by nonmanagerial labour. He attributed this failure to sociologists' own unacknowledged managerial assumptions. By sharing with management 'the conviction that this organization of the labour process is "necessary" and "inevitable"', Braverman argued:

This leaves to sociology the function, which it shares with personnel administration, of assaying not the nature of the work but the degree of adjustment of the worker. Clearly for industrial sociology the problem does not appear with the degradation of work, but only with overt signs of dissatisfaction on the part of the worker. (Braverman, 1974: 29)

Difficulties concerning the ethical legitimacy of organizational research driven by partial, managerial interests may be rendered particularly acute in the contemporary climate, when the majority of organizational research takes place within the context of business schools which, as Parker (2002: 130) observes, are 'pressed up hard against the utilitarian reality of corporate managerialism'. Researchers working in this context may feel, in innumerable material and symbolic ways, the need to be 'relevant to' and 'in the service of' business impressed upon them – rendering re-examination of the 'goodness' of commercial organizational ends that much more difficult. Yet some critics have called for a re-examination of largely taken-for-granted assumptions about the goodness of modernist organization per se. Echoing and extending concerns regarding the rationalizing and homogenizing pressures in western society and large scale bureaucratic organization, the postmodern social critic Zygmunt Bauman has powerfully questioned the beneficence of the modern organizational form. His work has linked treasured modernist features of organization – its complex hierarchy, focus upon procedures, instrumental orientation, delineation of responsibilities, and removal of personal sentiment from the efficient performance of organizational roles – with the potentially catastrophic, systematic erosion of moral responsibility in organization (Bauman, 1989/1991). Following Bauman, even the goal of more rational or efficient organization, an end upon which the legitimacy of organizational research at least implicitly relies, cannot be assumed to be an unquestionable good. Furthermore, the nature of goodness itself – or more specifically questions of how we are to decide on matters of ethics – is also contested. The long history of moral philosophy, while aspiring to some universal and eternal understanding of goodness, has achieved the production of multiple well-reasoned but contested and at times conflicting formulations of ethics (MacIntyre, 1998). The modern citizen, including of course the academic, is the inheritor of this legacy, which has become structured into our institutions, laws, customs, and individual moral subjectivities. Such that now, notions including duty, virtue, responsibility, fairness, consequence, and even happiness carry echoes of different philosophical ethical traditions that each encourage us to place different weight on different outcomes, intentions, customs, or contexts in our deliberations of what is ethical.

From the preceding discussion, several points emerge, which we wish to carry forward in this chapter. First, research ethics is informed by wider philosophical debate and discourse, but it is not an abstract, peripheral, or principally philosophical concern. Instead, it encompasses a set of empirically and theoretically driven issues that permeate the entire research process. Second, organizational research has a cumulative, and sometimes immediate, effect upon participants, which cannot be assumed to be necessarily beneficial. Third, ethical considerations run through all types of organizational research, both quantitative and qualitative, affecting choices of method, degree of detachment from or relationship with the researched, the way that the organization, data, or other's experience is represented in the text and the way that the academic voice is authorized. Finally, the credibility and authority of organizational research rests on either an implicit or explicit ethical warrant, which ensures its ongoing support. One of the principal ethical warrants on which organizational research is founded is the assumed goodness of a managerial agenda and/or the beneficence of modernist organization. These assumptions in turn draw on the historical legacy of the Enlightenment. This legacy is wedded to liberal humanist notions of progress, reason, and the furtherance of humanity and which understands science to be at the heart of this process. It has passed down a view that the researcher's detachment from central aspects of their own and others' humanity is at the core of the scientific method. However, we have suggested that we can no longer, in the current context, make assumptions about the progressive nature of this detached scientific process, of science and research itself, or indeed of the goals of modernist organization. This is not to say that researching organization or organizational research processes are inherently

unethical or harmful – far from it. At a time when the reach, power, and complexity of organizations risks outpacing our traditional processes of democratic accountability, intellectual comprehension, and moral imagination, understanding organization is, we would argue, fundamental to wellbeing and survival. Rather, the implication of the above would seem to be that we, as a community of organizational researchers, need to subject our research practices, agendas and assumptions to continual and sustained ethical scrutiny. In the following section, we explore how the organizational research community currently engages with such matters.

The status of ethics in organizational research

Within organizational research, we can identify what we might call implicit and explicit engagements with ethics. Implicit engagements include a myriad of choices and assumptions, which may not be explicitly articulated as ethical issues but which nevertheless imply ethical choices. These include a researcher's choice of topic, the nonfalsification of research data, avoidance of plagiarism, judgements around whose 'voice' will be represented in the research and how (Wray-Bliss, 2004), even decisions regarding where or if to publish the research and how it will be written up imply choices that may impede or enable other's access to the research, to knowledge about their world or access to how they have been represented and understood in the wider society (Parker, 2002; Grey and Sinclair, 2006). However, the above issues are seldom explicitly articulated or engaged with as ethical issues. More often than not, they will be seen as merely matters of academic convention in the particular organizational research field. Instead, 'research ethics' are normally understood more narrowly and discretely as concerned with the need to follow a set of clearly defined precepts concerning appropriate and acceptable research conduct. These explicit engagements with ethics involve consideration of how researchers should treat the people who form the subjects of their investigation and whether there are certain actions that should or should not be taken in relation to them. This approach tends to result in the generation of a set of ethical principles, which organizational researchers are expected to show that they have considered, usually at the design stage of the research. Failure to adequately address these issues may result in censoring by the organizational research community.

The main mechanisms for ensuring compliance to such ethical precepts have traditionally been self-disciplinary. These have taken the form of adherence to codes of ethical practice developed by professional associations to which organizational researchers belong. The origins of these codes and the ethical precepts within them can be traced to the military tribunal known as the 'Nuremburg Trial' involving twenty-three German physicians and administrators who were accused of war crimes and crimes against humanity for their participation in inhuman experimentation on those deemed unworthy of life during the Second World War. The appalling nature of these atrocities, and the shock of the international community at the role of science in their perpetration, led the trial judges to formulate a universal standard for human experimentation in an attempt to pave the way for a reconstituted moral vision (Katz, 1992). Argument submitted to the United States Counsel for War Crimes by doctors for the prosecution sought to define legitimate research on human subjects and to protect them from potential harm through the principle of voluntary informed consent. In a section entitled '*Permissible Medical Experiments*', the verdict established ten points, which covered the areas of: (i) ensuring the voluntary consent of the subject; (ii) experiments must be for the good of society; (iii) sufficient prior research must have been conducted; (iv) unnecessary suffering or harm must be avoided; (v) experiments with the chance of injury or death are prohibited; (vi) the risk should never outweigh the humanitarian importance of the problem studied; (vii) preparation and facilities must be in place

to avoid harm or injury; (viii) only properly qualified persons may conduct the research; (ix) the subject can withdraw consent; and (x) the scientist must terminate the experiment if the risk of harm warrants it. These ten points have subsequently become known as the 'Nuremburg Code' and have informed both biomedical and social science ethics codes since.

For nonmedical organizational researchers, professional bodies such as the *Academy of Management*, or related social science disciplines like the *Social Research Association*, *American Psychological Association*, or *British Sociological Association* set out the main ethical issues that researchers tend to face and provide guidance on how they should respond to them. That there has been relatively little variation in the content of these codes since the 1960s (Bryman and Bell, 2003; Bell and Bryman, 2007) suggests that a broad consensus has emerged surrounding the definition of ethical issues in social science research founded on the principles established by the Nuremburg Code. Such codes universally specify the avoidance or minimization of harm or risk of harm, whether physical or psychological, and the need to ensure that research subjects are fully informed about the nature of the research and give their consent to being involved with it. In addition, they stress the necessity to maintain the privacy of research subjects, ensuring the confidentiality and anonymity of data where appropriate, minimizing the possibility for deception at all stages of the research process, from data collection to dissemination. There may also be an obligation to declare sources of funding and support that have the potential to affect the affiliations of the researcher or cause a potential conflict of interest. In each case, it is the researcher's responsibility to ensure that these ethical issues have been considered and that steps have been taken to address them where necessary.

Despite, or perhaps because of, the convergence of ethics codes there has, in recent years, been an increase in attention and debate concerning ethics in social scientific research (Sin, 2005; Truman, 2003; Kent et al., 2002; Nelson, 2004; Wiles et al., 2007). Such sensibilities have informed a terminological shift away from a focus 'on hapless research participants, conventionally termed, *subjects,* a word reflecting the concept that research participants have things done to them' (Lincoln and Guba, 1989: 222, emphasis in original) towards the use of the term 'participants' (Birch and Miller, 2002). These debates have been most vocal amongst qualitative and reflexive researchers who draw on feminist, postmodern, and postcolonial critiques to critically re-examine the ethics of their own research practices. This may have had the unintentional effect of encouraging more positivist and/or quantitatively minded researchers to assume, mistakenly, that consideration of ethical issues is more relevant to, or only becomes problematic in relation to, qualitative research.

In comparison to the broader social sciences, organizational researchers have been more reticent in reflecting on the implications of these debates for research practice (see Brewis and Wray Bliss, 2008; Bell and Bryman, 2007). Yet, there is little doubt that their impact is likely to be significant, not least because they have been paralleled by a rise in ethical governance, as the agencies and institutions that fund or disseminate organizational research or employ organizational researchers have become more active in seeking to regulate ethical conduct. For example, recent revisions to the code of ethics produced by the Academy of Management allow researchers to be penalized for ethical breaches through a process of formal adjudication, which can result in their exclusion from the Academy (although it should be borne in mind that there is no requirement on organizational researchers to belong to this or any other professional association). In addition, academic institutions that employ researchers, driven in part by a concern to avoid potentially costly litigation, are taking a more active role in overseeing the ethical conduct of their members. Within universities, research ethics committees (RECs) or, in North America, institutional review boards

(IRBs) have been established with responsibility for judging adherence to ethical precepts in research proposals submitted by research students and academics. These developments signal the establishment of ethical governance structures, which are more formalized and less 'light touch' in comparison to former voluntarist systems (Kent et al., 2002). Such developments may be interpreted on one level as a welcome indication that the academic research community is engaged in a serious and sustained way with ethics. However, a number of concerns have been expressed regarding the current trend toward greater formalization of ethical accountability in the social sciences, which we outline in the section that follows.

Critiques of ethical formalism: Committees and codes

Characterizing the historical treatment of issues of morality and ethics in civil society, Bauman (1993) argues that we have tended to reduce matters of ethics – understood as that unending innermost compulsion to seek to do what is *right*, to know one's own heart, to be responsible toward the Other – to matters of following predefined rules, laws or codes. In so doing, a small proportion of the population have been granted the moral status to reflect, philosophize, and codify what is ethical while the rest have been allotted the roles of merely following these rules and norms, socialized into doing so through the mechanisms of organizational and state bureaucracy. For Bauman, such rule-following, bureaucratized behaviour does not represent ethics but rather its antithesis – the abdication of individual ethical agency and its replacement with conformity. Whether we take Bauman's broad-brush depiction of society at face value or not, we can begin to appreciate that the formalization or bureaucratization of ethics may be questioned. Such a critique focuses on whether ethical formalism enhances accountability and responsibility or limits and constricts our engagement with matters of ethics.

If we apply these considerations to research ethics we can perhaps begin to appreciate some of the concerns that have been voiced regarding ethical governance as promoting a rigid and inflexible understanding of ethics, one that encourages the ticking of boxes rather than ongoing ethical reflexivity. Critiques of ethical formalism in social scientific research are driven by concerns about the disciplinary effects associated with these mechanisms and by the possibility that this will lead to the imposition of a hegemonic view of what constitutes 'good' research. Critics seek to argue that social science research operates differently from other research involving human subjects (Coomber, 2002) and that the principles that are used to regulate the community need to reflect this. One of the criticisms that can be made of the standardization of research governance is that it does not necessarily encourage or support researchers in the process of becoming morally-active individuals, since it is only through conducting and writing up research that we develop a full awareness of ethical issues. A further critique is that they may be functioning so as to prohibit, or make significantly more difficult, valuable forms of research that do not readily conform to a narrowly defined set of bureaucratic norms,

'if the ways of ensuring ethical research are heavily reliant on RECs, this may not serve research practice well. This seems to be especially the case where processes are rigid and concerned only with assessing the ethical issues prior to the project start, when the information needed to make the assessment is not available' (Richardson and McMullan, 2007: 1127).

These points can be illustrated in relation to the principle of informed consent, where the role of the REC typically is to:

...a) make sure that the research proposals passed by the committee are appropriate and safe, and b) that the prospective participants are fully appraised of the research and of their rights (e.g. to anonymity or to stop the research at any time without prejudice). The method increasingly used to achieve the second of these concerns is that of the signed consent form. (Coomber, 2002, section 1.1)

The adequacy of form-filling as a method of ensuring that participants understand the implications of consenting to participate in a research investigation has been questioned by several commentators (c.f. Edwards and Mauthner, 2002; Bhattacharya, 2007). Sin (2005) and Wiles et al. (2007) suggest that consent is contingent and situated, varying according to whom one is dealing with and how definitions are operationalized, a process that relies on an ongoing process of negotiation, which cannot be adequately addressed by getting participants to sign a form. This is a particular issue for qualitative researchers and those working with theoretical perspectives that seek to overcome traditional knowledge hierarchies and power relations in the research process through, for example, the adoption of feminist, participatory or decolonizing methodologies (Bhattacharya, 2007; Boser, 2007). RECs tend to be predicated upon a medical model of the research process that is insensitive to more flexible, emergent research strategies (Truman, 2003; Wiles et al., 2007; Lincoln and Tierney, 2004; van den Hoonard, 2001). Methods such as participatory action research (*Chapter 2, this volume*) make it virtually impossible to anticipate all conventional ethical issues in advance of a study being undertaken (Bell and Bryman, 2007). The problematic nature of informed consent is also apparent in relation to ethnographic research, where the researcher's daily participation and routine appearance in the lives of those she or he researches can encourage participants to forget that their interactions and conversations are the subject of study.

Bhattacharya (2007: 1110) argues that there needs to be space within regulative structures for addressing 'the implications of fluidity and the contingent nature of qualitative research'. In such research, relationships with participants are continually deferred and not necessarily defined purely in terms of a short-term, instrumental academic need to collect data. Although it is also important to note that all types of research can deal with complex ethical issues, which may not become apparent until after the study has begun. The requirement to obtain signed consent also has the potential to adversely affect the participation of particular groups in research, such as those who wish or need to remain anonymous because for example they are involved in committing illegal acts, by increasing rather than reducing their anxiety about participating in a research investigation (Coomber, 2002; Nelson, 2004). Ethical regulation based on principles intended to protect vulnerable research subjects from harm has the potential to make it more difficult to study organizations and individuals who do not want their activities to be studied, using covert methods for example (Galliher, 1982; Herrera, 2003). Finally, while informed consent protects research participants from harm, it does not allow for the possibility of participants causing harm to others (Koro-Ljungberg et al., 2007).

Ethical formalism has also resulted in the widespread convention that research should be anonymized in publication to protect participants from the risk of potential harm (Cassell, 1978). While this might initially seem to be a clear-cut ethical good, Grinyer (2002) has questioned this assumption, noting that in some cases it can be extremely important to participants that their accounts are not anonymized so as to maintain their authenticity. While in organizational research there are many instances where organizations that authorize research access are not anonymized in publication, increased ethical formalism poses a challenge to this convention. Furthermore, an argument may be made not to anonymize research subjects on the grounds of a felt ethical responsibility to expose and document forms of organizational exploitation, abuse or malpractice. Within organizational research, there has been only limited acknowledgement of the implications of unequal power relations in the research process. Relating to participants in organizational research as vulnerable subjects can unwittingly serve to reproduce existing power relations and hierarchies (Wray-Bliss, 2003a). Uncritically adopting, or being compelled to adopt, research protocols that have been specifically designed to protect

vulnerable subjects may institutionalize forms of practice that take-for-granted and merely seek to mitigate the effects of assumed power inequalities between 'researcher' and 'the researched'. In organizational research, the majority of participants are adult, employed, and often highly educated. This potentially enables them to exert considerable influence in shaping the nature, direction, and outcomes of the research to a far greater extent than ethics codes generally allow for.

Such discussions fuel concerns about the rise of an audit culture (Power, 1997) within research ethics where having been seen to have 'done ethics' becomes more important than meaningful engagement with the issues raised. This encourages a view of ethics as a separate component in the research process that is dealt with at a certain point, potentially having the effect of discouraging researchers from continuing to reflexively engage with ethical issues throughout the research process (Mason, 1996). As Sin (2005: 289) argues, 'the tick-box approach to ensuring compliance in ethical standards … is an oversimplistic representation of the "messy" realities surrounding the research process'. Moreover, the formalization of ethical governance is by no means consistent, as Richardson and McMullan (2007: 1126) note, 'RECs vary greatly from institution to institution and there is no consistency even about whether the research ethics committee operates at the level of the discipline, the level of department/school, at faculty level or the level of institution'. The apparent inability of ethical governance structures to deal with certain types of qualitative research is suggested to have led some RECs to reject qualitative research projects for being unscientific and ungeneralizable. The disciplinary effects associated with such a discourse are, therefore, potentially significant:

> Narrow definitions of scientific inquiry – and evidence – serve ultimately to circumscribe painfully and dangerously the range of what is considered useful knowledge and, consequently, to limit the kinds of studies supported by a range of

administrative and managerial structures, including IRBs, funding agencies, foundations, and state governments and agencies. The long-term results are systematic constriction of academic freedom (for individual researchers) (Akker, 2002), a seeping loss of institutional autonomy (for institutions of higher education), and a loss of needed epistemological perspectives on persistent social justice issues. (Lincoln, 2005: 173)

Within UK health research, there is evidence that the rigidity of ethical governance structures is causing researchers to modify their research strategies or even to stop doing research in this type of organization altogether (Richardson and McMullan, 2007). Since ethical governance structures in health are increasingly being used as a model for other disciplines, it is entirely possible that over time this pattern will also affect researchers studying other types of organizations.

As the preceding discussion illustrates, by defining what is acceptable or 'good' organizational research, ethical governance structures have significant disciplinary effects (Lincoln and Cannella, 2004a, 2004b), their power being derived from having the ability to change the way that research is conducted. Funding bodies may make grant awards conditional on the researcher having demonstrated that ethical issues have been considered while RECs may grant researchers conditional approval, requiring modifications to be made in advance of the study. Such structures have the ability to restrict researchers' ability to follow research questions they wish to pursue. There are fears that in so doing academic researchers' independence and ability to speak 'truth to power' may be diminished. For some, this has evoked a concern about academic research being manipulated to support government, executive, or other institutional or organizational interests – what in the US has come to be known as 'Bush Science' (Lather, 2004). As Koro-Ljungberg et al. (2007) argue, the notion of 'value-free science' disguises a subtle form of oppression, which is based on the notion that those in power act neutrally to defend the 'common good'. Adopting a Foucauldian perspective, they argue that IRBs constitute

a type of 'examining apparatus' through which the 'normalization' of researchers and research projects is achieved as a form of control.

Lincoln (2005) suggests that researchers need either to communicate with RECs or to serve on them as a means of representing their interests and getting their voices heard, or even to try to work in partnership to try to understand their worldview (Boser, 2007). Similarly, Bell and Bryman (2007) argue that the organizational research community needs to become more actively engaged in these debates if they are going to be able to influence ethical governance structures in a way that ensures that the particular issues it faces are taken into account. These concerns find additional purchase for organizational researchers when we consider the way that ethical codes are being shaped by bodies such as funding councils. For example, the Research Ethics Framework launched in 2005 by the Economic and Social Research Council, the main funding body for UK social science research, is concerned to minimize the risk of harm to not only individual research participants but also their organizations or businesses. This constitutes organizations as well as individuals as the subject of ethical considerations (Bell and Bryman, 2007) and in so doing potentially recasts ethics in a way that restricts the ability of researchers to examine critically certain issues such as forms of oppression within organizational structures, which are subordinated to the organization's right to be protected from critique.

Given that ethics codes originated with the Nuremburg Trial's concern to give justice to human subjects who suffered at the hands of those who were integrated into the organized atrocity of the Nazi holocaust (Bauman, 1989/1991), the extension of definitions of harm to include protection of organizations might seem a perverse departure. However, it must be acknowledged that the definitions of goodness upon which ethical oversight regimes are based are not neutral – they are founded upon a modernist, Enlightenment view of science outlined at the start of this chapter. Ethical formalism can encourage a view of ethics as a series of abstract, neutral, objectively measurable principles, which can be universally applied, rather than a series of politicized judgements about the legitimacy of research as a worthwhile project based on assumptions concerning the goodness of academic knowledge about organization. We end this chapter by considering the implications of this final point and suggesting some possible responses to the issues we have raised in this chapter so far. As part of the organizational research community ourselves, these proposals are of course informed by our own theoretical and epistemological affiliations. We, therefore, offer them for debate and consideration, rather than in any attempt to set an agenda for others to follow.

Relating to and representing the other

Throughout this chapter we have sought to emphasize the importance of ethics, not only in relation to the *process* of doing organizational research, but also in terms of what is perceived to be the legitimacy of its *purpose*. How we as an academic community respond to the rise of ethical governance structures is in large part determined by the answers to these broader questions. Addressing them involves evaluating the ethical intentions that underpin organizational research; in other words, why we do it and the purposes it serves. This not only entails sustained examination of the relationships between the researcher and individuals and organizations who become participants in organizational research – the traditional focus of discussions about research ethics. It also involves exploration of the relationships that organizational researchers have with other groups, including audiences of managers and students who read and apply organizational research, universities and funding bodies that provide financial support and other researchers whose work informs it or who continue to develop it.

Some initial insights into these issues can be gained from considering how organizational researchers have responded to ethical oversight regimes and critiques of research ethics. One potential response has been simply to push for the reduction or even the rejection, of ethical formalism. This is justified on the grounds that either there is a commonality of interests between organizational researchers and those individuals and organizations that constitute the focus of their research, or that the professional integrity of researchers is such that no such external disciplinary mechanisms are required. This latter point would seem to evoke a deontological ethical position, where the researcher searches their own heart and reason to determine their ethical obligations. If this assumption is correct, it may seem to follow that formal guidelines on research ethics, developed in large part to protect the interests of the researched, may be dispensed with. Alternatively, we might argue, drawing implicitly upon a utilitarian ethical formulation and weighing up the moral worth of consequences for the majority, that the goals of scientific research have an importance that overrides issues of research ethics. However, in the context of the postpositivist questioning of the modernist faith in science, truth and ideology in recent decades discussed earlier in this chapter, we suggest the political naivety of the first position and arrogance of the second are dangerous bases upon which to assume a commonality of interests or to override ethical concerns.

If we accept that the formalization of research ethics is a trend that cannot be reverted then another response would be to engage directly with ethical oversight regimes to ensure that the concerns of organizational researchers are effectively represented. This response introduces other dynamics since it potentially lends ethical oversight regimes greater authority through which to require researchers' conformity to predefined ethical codes. Furthermore, while the representation of different ethical issues or academic disciplines may mitigate the narrowness of definitions and applications of ethics, the constitution and function of such bodies tends to suggest pressures toward universalising and normalizing research ethics. This generates the same problems of exclusion, the application of potentially inappropriate ethical criteria and questions of how to apply such criteria across disciplinarily, methodologically, and politically diverse fields and subfields of organizational research. In short, we remain unconvinced that such processes are the only or indeed the best way of encouraging organizational researchers to actively and routinely engage with the complex range of ethical issues that doing research generates.

A further strategy would be for the organizational research community to move away from the ethical universality implied by compliance-oriented ethics codes and instead to embrace ethical pluralism. This approach would involve different communities of organizational researchers attempting to articulate ethical practices for their specific communities; positivist organizational researchers could have one set of ethical practices, interpretive researchers another, critical researchers yet another (a situation which some may suspect already pertains though is rarely explicitly articulated). However, the adoption of a strategy of ethical pluralism introduces other challenges, for if we follow the logic that ethical responsibilities vary according to the research community studied, we can envisage arguments for responsibilities not only to be enhanced when, for instance, vulnerable or historically silenced organizational subjects are studied but also diminished when the research subjects constitute a community that, in some way, has forfeited our normal ethical regard. For organizational researchers drawing upon postmodernism and Critical Theory, acutely conscious of the political inequalities of organization and the dangers of universal truth claims, for example, a localized or selective research ethics, one that could vary according to the political status of the community studied, might not be inconceivable. Such selective ethics, however, raises difficult issues about the nature of ethics and politics of academic research, which have yet to be systematically explored (Collins and Wray-Bliss, 2005).

Any movement toward ethical pluralism will have to engage with the historical context of the attempt to universalize research ethics. The Nuremburg Code was devised as a universal code precisely so that groups of individuals – be they Jews, the disabled, or indeed those whose politics one vehemently disagrees with – could not be removed from the status of moral beings. Movements toward dismantling the aspiration to universality – the desire to write a code that says to all humanity for all time that the potential atrocities and abuses of science are not to be tolerated in sciences' name – will need to think carefully about what protections or prohibitions have the gravity to take its place.

While we find ourselves having some sympathy with each of these arguments we believe that there is still a need for greater transparency and reflexivity than these approaches invite and that this necessitates a process of cultivating greater ongoing critical self awareness in relation to ethics. Our final suggestion, therefore, entails shifting the emphasis away from approaches that are informed by teleological and deontological theories and concerned with 'what to do', toward an approach which instead seeks to develop dispositions such as honesty, sensitivity, respectfulness, reciprocity, and reflexivity, driven by a concern with how the researcher should 'be' (Wax, 1982; Lather, 1986; Lincoln, 1995; Wray-Bliss, 2003b; Bell and Bryman, 2007; Richardson and McMullan, 2007; Brewis and Wray-Bliss, 2008). This invites conceptualization of the ethical relationship between the researcher, their topic, and those whom they research as an ongoing, active, personal, and relational responsibility. In addition, it encourages a shift away from a controlling orientation to ethics as primarily involving formalized compliance to bureaucratic rules, toward one that is a more enabling and aspirational. It entails a focus on how organizational researchers choose to conduct themselves, casting ethics as a matter of beliefs, thoughts, and values as well as actions. For critical management researchers who are concerned with exposing and redressing the political inequalities of organization an approach to research ethics, which takes into account the relative power and influence of the groups represented in the research might seem particularly appropriate (Bell and Bryman, 2007; Brewis and Wray-Bliss, 2008; Wray-Bliss 2003b). Such a position also evokes feminist and postmodern approaches to ethics that emphasize responsibility to the Other (Bauman, 1993; Benhabib, 1987) through valuing connectedness with the actual researched populations who may be particularly vulnerable or have historical reasons for being particularly suspicious of the intentions of academic researchers (McLaughlin and Tierney, 1993; Bishop, 2005). This approach might further necessitate organizational researchers devoting more attention to ethics. For example, by particular journals becoming more proactive in specifying ethical standards to which their prospective contributors must attend and encouraging greater discussion of ethical issues in published articles, or through the education of organizational researchers in a way which casts ethics as an ongoing aspect of their professional development. Most fundamentally, however, rather than only being relevant to certain methodological approaches, ethics would be treated as a central aspect of the conduct of all research involving organizations.

We have, in this final section, outlined a number of possible responses to ethical formalization in relation to organizational research. We do not regard any of these responses as ideal. Nor do we envisage the possibility of an ideal response, either for the communities of organizational researchers or for individual researchers. This is because matters of ethics centre on the fundamental question of how we should live. Moreover, while much moral philosophy has aspired to universal ethical pronouncement on the good life, we are wary of the potentially subordinating power effects of such claims. For us then, research ethics involves explicit consideration of how we should relate to research participants, other researchers, institutions that support research, and research

audiences, including those who read and apply our research. Such questions, as we have sought to emphasize throughout this chapter, do not lend themselves to easy solutions. Our position here has been, therefore, to suggest that ethical issues permeate the entire research process for all researchers whether positivist, interpretivist, postmodernist, and whether dealing with quantitative and/or qualitative data. Furthermore, while ethical formalization is a trend which in our view cannot be easily avoided, the way that each of us, as individual organizational researchers, engages with such challenges has the potential to vary enormously. We can all, of course, fall back on the path of least resistance and minimally comply with whatever research ethics principles are prescribed to us by our funding bodies, journals, supervisors, or university ethics committees. Alternatively, we can seek to embrace the possibilities that ethics introduces for reinvigorating and redefining the way that we think of and do organizational research.

REFERENCES

Akker, J. (2002) 'Protecting academic freedom worldwide', *Academe*, 88(3): 44–5.

Alvesson, M. and Deetz, S. (2000) *Doing Critical Management Research*, London: Sage.

Bauman, Z. (1989/1991) *Modernity and the Holocaust*, Cambridge: Polity Press.

Bauman, Z. (1993) *Postmodern Ethics*, Oxford: Blackwell.

Bauman, Z. (2005) 'Afterthought: on writing, on writing sociology', in N. Denzin and Y. Lincoln (eds) *Sage Handbook of Qualitative Research* (third edn.), London: Sage, pp.1089–98.

Bell, E. and Bryman, A. (2007) 'Ethical codes and management research: a comparative content analysis', *British Journal of Management*, 18(1).

Benhabib, S. (1987) 'The generalised and the concrete other', in E. Frazer, J. Hornsby and S. Lovibond (eds), *Ethics: A Feminist Reader*, Oxford: Blackwell.

Bhattacharya, K. (2007) 'Consenting to the consent form: what are the fixed and fluid understandings between the researcher and the researched', *Qualitative Inquiry*, 13(8): 1095–15.

Birch, M. and Miller, T. (2002) 'Encouraging participation: ethics and responsibilities', in M. Mauthner,

M. Birch, J. Jessop and T. Miller (eds), *Ethics in Qualitative Research*, London: Sage, pp.91–106.

Bishop, R. (2005) 'Freeing Ourselves from neocolonial domination in research: a kaupapa Māori approach to creating knowledge', in N.K. Denzin and Y.S. Lincoln (eds), *Sage Handbook of Qualitative Research*, (third edn.), Thousand Oaks, CA: Sage, pp.109–38.

Boser, S. (2007) 'Power, ethics and the IRB: dissonance over human participant review of participatory research', *Qualitative Inquiry*, 13(8): 1060–4.

Braverman, H. (1974) *Labour and Monopoly Capitalism: The Degradation of Work in the Twentieth Century*, London: Monthly Review Press.

Brewis, J. and Wray-Bliss, E. (2009) 'Re-searching ethics: towards a more reflexive critical management studies', *Organization Studies*, 29(11): 1–20.

Bryman, A. and Bell, E. (2003) *Business Research Methods*, Oxford: Oxford University Press.

Cassell, J. (1978) 'Risk and Benefit to Subjects of Fieldwork', *American Sociologist,* 13: 134–43.

Christians, C.G. (2005) 'Ethics and Politics in Qualitative Research', in N. Denzin and Y. Lincoln (eds), *Sage Handbook of Qualitative Research* (third edn.), London: Sage.

Collins, H. and Wray-Bliss, E. (2005) 'Discriminating Ethics', *Human Relations*, 58(6): 799–824.

Coomber, R. (2002) 'Signing Your Life Away', *Sociological Research Online*, 7(1). <http://www.socresonline.org.uk/7/1/coomber.html>.

Edwards E. and Mauthner, M. (2002) 'Ethics and feminist research: theory and practice', in M. Mauthner, M. Birch, J. Jessop and T. Miller (eds), *Ethics in Qualitative Research*, London: Sage, pp.14–31.

Galliher, J.F. (1982) 'The protection of human subjects: a re-examination of the professional code of ethics', in M. Bulmer (ed.), *Social Research Ethics: An Examination of the Merits of Covert Participant Observation*, London: Macmillan.

Gherardi, S. (1995) *Gender, Symbolism and Organizational Cultures*, London: Sage.

Gillies, V. and Alldred, P. (2002) 'The ethics of intention: research as a political tool', in M. Mauthner, M. Birch, J. Jessop and T. Miller (eds), *Ethics in Qualitative Research*, London: Sage, pp.32–52.

Glover, J. (2001) *Humanity: A Moral History of the Twentieth Century*, London: Pimlico.

Grey, C. and Sinclair, A. (2006) 'Writing differently', *Organization,* 13(3): 443–53.

Grey, C. and Willmott, H. (eds) (2005) *Critical Management Studies: A Reader*, Oxford: Oxford University Press.

Grinyer, A. (2002) 'The anonymity of research participants: assumptions, ethics and practicalities', *Social Research Update*, issue 36.

Griseri, P. (2002) *Management Knowledge: A Critical View*, Basingstoke: Palgrave.

Hearn, J. (2004) 'Personal resistance through persistence to organizational resistance through distance' in R. Thomas, A. Mills and J.H. Mills (eds), *Identity Politics at Work: Resisting Gender, Gendering Resistance*, Abingdon: Routledge, pp.40–63.

Herrera, C.D. (2003) 'A clash of methodology and ethics in "undercover" social science', *Philosophy of the Social Sciences*, 33(3): 351–62.

Hooks, B. (1989) *Talking Back: Thinking Feminist, Thinking Black*, London: Sheba Feminist Publishers.

Katz, J. (1992) 'The consent principle of the nuremberg code: its significance then and now' in G.J. Annas and M.A. Grodin (eds), *The Nazi Doctors and the Nuremberg Code: Human Rights in Human Experimentation*, New York: Oxford University Press.

Kent, J., Williamson, E., Goodenough, T. and Ashcroft, R. (2002) 'Social Science Gets the Ethics Treatment: Research Governance and Ethical Review', *Sociological Research Online*, 7(4). <http://www.socresonline.org.uk/7/4/williamson.html>.

Koro-Ljungberg, M., Gemignani, M., Winton Brodeur, C. and Kmiec, C. (2007) 'The technologies of normalization and self: thinking about IRBs and extrinsic research ethics with foucault', *Qualitative Inquiry*, 13(8): 1075–94.

Lather, P. (1986) 'Research as praxis', *Harvard Educational Review*, 56(3): 257–77.

Lather, P. (2004) 'This is your father's paradigm: government intrusion and the case of qualitative research in education', *Qualitative Inquiry*, 10(1): 15–34.

Lincoln, Y.S. (1995) 'Emerging qualitative criteria', *Qualitative Inquiry*, 1: 275–89.

Lincoln, Y.S. (2005) 'Institutional review boards and methodological conservatism', in N.K. Denzin and Y.S. Lincoln (eds), *Sage Handbook of Qualitative Research*, (third edn.), London: Sage.

Lincoln, Y.S. and Cannella, G.S. (2004a) 'Dangerous discourses: methodological conservatism and governmental regimes of truth', *Qualitative Inquiry*, 10(1): 5–14.

Lincoln, Y.S. and Cannella, G.S. (2004b) 'Qualitative research, power and the radical right', *Qualitative Inquiry*, 10(2): 175–201.

Lincoln, Y.S. and Guba, E.G. (1989) 'Ethics: the failure of positivist science', *The Review of Higher Education*, 12(3): 221–40.

Lincoln, Y.S. and Tierney, W.G. (2004) 'Qualitative research and institutional review boards', *Qualitative Inquiry*, 10(2): 219–34.

MacIntyre, A. (1998) *A Short History of Ethics*, London: Routledge.

Mason, J. (1996) *Qualitative Researching*, London: Sage.

McLaughlin, D. and Tierney, W. (eds) (1993) *Naming Silenced Lives: Personal Narratives and Processes of Educational Change*, London: Routledge.

Nelson, C. (2004) 'The brave new world of research surveillance', *Qualitative Inquiry*, 10(2): 207–18.

Opie, A. (1992) 'Qualitative research, appropriation of the "other" and empowerment', *Feminist Review*, 40(Spring): 52–69.

Parker, M. (2002) *Against Management*, Cambridge: Polity Press.

Power, M. (1997) *The Audit Society: Rituals of Verification*, Oxford: Oxford University Press.

Prasad, P. (2005) *Crafting Qualitative Research: Working in the Postpositivist Traditions*, London: M.E. Sharp.

Punch, M. (1994) 'Politics and ethics in qualitative research', in N. Denzin and Y. Lincoln (eds), *Sage Handbook of Qualitative Research* (first edn.), London: Sage, 83–97.

Richardson, S. and McMullan, M. (2007) 'Research Ethics in the UK: what can sociology learn from health?', *Sociology*, 41(6): 1115–32.

Said, E. (1978) *Orientalism: Western Conceptions of the Orient*, London: Penguin.

Seidman, S. (1998) *Contested Knowledge: Social Theory in the Postmodern Era*, (second edn.), Oxford: Blackwell.

Sin, C.H. (2005) 'Seeking informed consent: reflections on research practice', *Sociology*, 39(2): 277–94.

Smith, D (1990) *Texts, Facts and Femininity: Exploring the Relations of Ruling*, London: Routledge.

Stanley, L. and Wise, S. (1993) *Breaking Out Again: Feminist Ontology and Epistemology*, London: Routledge.

Truman, C. (2003) 'Ethics and the Ruling Relations of Research Production', *Sociological Research Online*, 8(1) <http://www.socresonline.org.uk/8/1/truman.html>.

van den Hoonard, W.C. (2001) 'Is research-ethics review a moral panic?', *Canadian Review of Sociology and Anthropology*, 38(1): 19–36.

Wax, M.L. (1982) 'Research reciprocity rather than informed consent in fieldwork', in J.E. Sieber (ed.), *The Ethics of Social Research: Fieldwork, Regulation and Publication*, New York: Springer-Verlag.

Weems, L. (2006) 'Unsettling politics, locating ethics: representations of reciprocity in postpositivist inquiry', *Qualitative Inquiry*, 12(5): 994–1011.

Wiles, R., Crow, G., Charles, V. and Heath, S. (2007) 'Informed Consent and the Research Process: Following Rules or Striking Balances?', *Sociological Research Online*, 12 (2). <http://www.socresonline.org.uk/12/2/wiles.html>.

Wray-Bliss, E. (2002a) 'Abstract ethics, embodied ethics: the strange marriage of Foucault and positivism in LPT', *Organization*, 9(1): 5–39.

Wray-Bliss, E. (2002b) 'Interpretation – appropriation: (making) an example of labour process theory', *Organizational Research Methods*, 5(1): 80–103.

Wray-Bliss, E. (2003a) 'Research subjects/research subjections: the politics and ethics of critical research', *Organization*, 10(2): 307–25.

Wray-Bliss, E. (2003b) 'Ethical discriminations? representing the reprehensible', *Tamara*, 2(3): 7–22.

Wray-Bliss, E. (2004) 'The right to respond? the monopolisation of voice in CMS', *Ephemera*, 4(2): 101–20.

6

Rhetoric and Evidence: The Case of Evidence-Based Management

Mark Learmonth

INTRODUCTION

Evidence-based management has become a particularly hot topic, now, in the early years of the twenty-first century. And this chapter is in line with some of its ambitions; for example, it is intended, in part, to be a call for academics (and practitioners) to use more forms of evidence to inform practice. However, the chapter is also concerned to provide a critical exploration of some of the ideas about 'evidence' and 'management' that have become associated with evidence-based management. Or at least, evidence-based management in its most prominent form – which is to say the version that promises applications of science to management through which we can: 'hear and act on the facts [in order] to make more informed and intelligent decisions' (Pfeffer and Sutton, 2006: 14).

Curiously, however, for a movement that is so 'now', this promise is based on a version of science and evidence that is somewhat dated. For in today's intellectual environment, it is only rather traditional versions of science that fail to question the idea that scientific facts are the products of impersonal, disinterested, and rigorous observations concerning the evidence. This traditional view of science and evidence was most influentially propounded by Robert Merton (1973/1942) for whom science's 'truth-claims, whatever their source, are to be subjected to *preestablished impersonal criteria*; [t]he acceptance or rejection of claims entering the list of science is not to depend on the personal or social attributes of their protagonist; [o]bjectivity precludes particularism' (1973/1942: 270; italics in original). Evidence, in this traditional view, can be misunderstood, it can even be falsified or invented; nevertheless, the only judge we need of the facts of science is reality itself – because evidence produced and understood according to established scientific criteria of objectivity will, *ipso facto*, reflect that reality.

In contrast, a rather more radical view of scientific knowledge seeks to give us 'methods for studying the fabrication of scientific facts' (Latour, 1987: 21). In this view, the rhetorical devices scientific accounts use – their deployments of terms like 'facts' and 'evidence' for example – are analysed as part of a project concerned with showing how scientific facts come to be accepted as facts. For example, Potter (1996) points to the way in which formulations like 'the results show', or the 'evidence suggests', attributes agency to the evidence itself, while simultaneously removing agency from the investigator who makes the claim. For Potter, this is 'a cardinal feature of the empiricist repertoire' (1996: 157) – a repertoire central to science in its production of forms of knowledge widely accepted as true. It is not that scientific truth and facts are being denied in this view; rather, such work seeks to bracket off questions about whether scientists are 'really' being objective, whether their findings are 'actually' true, and so on, in order to focus on how (what counts as) knowledge is produced and, importantly, the effects of its use in society.

The radical view of scientific knowledge has become commonplace in social studies of scientific knowledge since the 1980s (Mulkay, 1981). Indeed, for proponents like Potter, work in the tradition of Merton's sociology of science 'now seems striking in its conservatism and its resistance to a thoroughgoing exploration of the social basis and context of facts' (Potter, 1996: 17). Unsurprisingly then, the importance of the social basis and context of the knowledge produced by the social scientific community has become a central concern for many social scientists – as seen, for example, in the emphasis on reflexivity in much contemporary work – an emphasis which has meant, 'studies have paid particular attention

to the researcher and the research subject and, particularly, the limitations of researchers in representing the subjects under study and their effect on the creation of "knowledge"' (Hardy et al., 2001: 532–3). That said, the traditional view still represents a widely held 'commonsense' set of epistemological and ontological positions, even among some social scientists. Indeed, it remains possible for prominent social scientists to write about the nature of social science and evidence without any reference to the more radical views of scientific knowledge briefly sketched above, and to do so, what is more, in the pages of what are generally taken to be high-quality social scientific journals.

I think this is a sad state of affairs – and, what is more, a state of affairs that matters – not least because of the conservative political implications that the commonsense model of science and knowledge typically has when it is taken for granted in social research. Thus, my aim in this chapter is to provide a study of the nefarious effects that ignoring the radical view of scientific knowledge can have. I do so using the case of evidence-based management within organization studies, an issue about which there is a growing body of literature seeking to promote it: see, for example, Axelsson (1998); Briner (2000); Davies et al. (2000); Stewart (2002); Dopson (2006); Hewison (1997); Kovner et al. (2000); Ozcan and Smith (1998); Tranfield et al. (2003); Walshe and Rundall (2001) (and see Denyer and Tranfield, Chapter 39, this volume). Indeed, in recent times, evidence-based management has been advocated in particularly high-profile ways. For example, at the 2005 Academy of Management Conference, Rousseau, the outgoing President of the Academy, chose to entitle her presidential address: 'Is There Such a Thing As 'Evidence-Based Management'?' (Rousseau 2006a). A few months later, Pfeffer and Sutton (2006) published *Hard Facts, Dangerous Half-Truths and Total Nonsense: Profiting from Evidence-based Management*. Perhaps not coincidentally, evidence-based management has now got its own entry on Wikipedia (2006); an entry, which contains a prominent link to a website run by Pfeffer and Sutton, described on the Wikipedia site as 'dedicated to the [evidence-based management] movement'.

The rhetoric of evidence-based management

Rousseau's address was aimed principally at the academic community, Pfeffer and Sutton's book (and web pages) at practicing executives. What they share, however, is the aim of convincing their respective audiences of the benefits of evidence-based management, and they both do so by providing more or less unconditional praise – virtual panegyrics upon evidence-based management for managerial practice. However, as panegyrics, neither discussed the contestation surrounding the nature of 'facts', 'evidence' and so on within the social sciences. Both also appear to share an unremittingly pro-top management tone – to the exclusion of any 'evidence' that might cause us to reflect in a serious and sustained manner on the legitimacy of conventional management goals (profitability, control and so on). Thus, for Rousseau (2006a: 258), evidence-based practice is a (theoretically unproblematic) 'paradigm for making decisions that integrate the best available research evidence with decision-maker expertise and client/customer preferences to guide practice toward more desirable results'.

To be clear, I believe that 'evidence' can (and should) inform practice. And in fact, I can welcome some of the broadly liberal sentiments expressed by the proponents of evidence-based management; Rousseau's (2006b: 1092) championing of evidence-based management as 'a counterforce to the arbitrariness and self-serving bias observed in how firms are organized and managed today', for instance, or Pfeffer and Sutton's (2006: 222) ambition for a better use of evidence to be an 'antidote to the smart talk, self-aggrandizement, and bullshit that pollute so much of business life'. However, I am much less sympathetic to their wider, more axiomatic assumptions (which they

leave implicit and unexplored) because they apparently adopt an unexamined Mertonian view of science and its applications in organization and management. For in a social science like organization studies, 'evidence' is never just there, waiting for the researcher to find. Rather it is always necessary to construct it in some way – a process that is inherently ideological and always contestable – not merely a technical, 'scientific' task (Alvesson and Deetz, 2000). This means that questions such as what counts as evidence; what organizational practices (which is to say not merely *management* practices) the evidence might, ethically and politically, inform; what interests different constructions of the evidence support and deny (and so on) – are questions that, for most major issues in our field, are the subject of radical dispute. That is to say, the grounds on which the disputes can be conducted are themselves contested (Burrell and Morgan 1979; Grey 2004; Learmonth 2006). Under such circumstances, therefore, as Jack and Westwood (2006: 481) argue, 'research must become reflexive and aware of its ontological and epistemological assumptions, political positioning and ethical obligations'. But where, one might ask, is any reflexivity concerning the political positioning of research and evidence in, for example, this statement from Rousseau's (2006a: 256) speech to the Academy:

> Through evidence-based management, practicing managers develop into experts who make organizational decisions informed by social science and organizational research – part of the zeitgeist moving professional decisions away from personal preference and unsystematic experience toward those based on the best available scientific evidence.

This rhetoric of 'the best available evidence' can only plausibly be created by an elision of the more radical critiques of scientific knowledge – an elision Rousseau achieves, in part, by failing to ask the question: 'the best scientific evidence – according to whom'? Indeed, one can also ask further questions, for example: 'the best scientific evidence – according to which (of many, often contested) criteria'? Thus, the absence of any revealed awareness of the political positioning of this statement allows Rousseau's assertion to lionize managers as 'experts', while suggesting that, when associated with science and evidence, managerial decisions are above dispute (Willmott, 1997). Her assertion can be understood, therefore, as an example of how, following Grey (1996: 601), 'the ideological nature of management is obscured by the way in which it appears to be based upon objective knowledge independent of political or social interests and moral considerations'. In Rousseau's account then, the ideological nature of management is obscured by the rhetoric of 'evidence' – an evidence constructed in line with the interests of the people in charge of organizations, while giving itself out to be neutral and universal (Learmonth and Harding, 2006).

Nevertheless, while it is important to make these theoretical objections, my primary concern in this chapter is *not* to contest evidence-based management on intellectual grounds. Of course, contesting evidence-based management on intellectual grounds is worthwhile – I have attempted it myself (Learmonth and Harding, 2006), as have others, most recently Morrell (2008). However, I am de-emphasizing such critique here, largely because I suspect that the advocates of evidence-based management are not particularly concerned to be thought intellectually credible by social scientists. Indeed, it seems to me that Van Maanen's (1995) (gentle) comments on an earlier article by Pfeffer (1993) might equally apply to Pfeffer's own (and much other similar) more recent work on evidence-based management – at least, that is, if we were to read it as an intellectual project:

> ...insufferably smug; pious and orthodox; philo-sophically indefensible; extraordinarily naive as to how science actually works; theoretically foolish, vain and autocratic; and – still being gentle – reflective of a most out-of-date and discredited father-knows-best version of knowledge, rhetoric and the role theory plays in the life of any intellectual community (Van Maanen, 1995: 133).

Instead, my concern is to contest evidence-based management as a *political project*. As I have argued elsewhere (Learmonth, 2006: 1090), proponents like Rousseau appear to be set on using their own versions of 'evidence' and 'management', 'as a means to further a particular set of interests and values in organizational life while doing so under cover – the cover provided both by the prestige of science and by the enthusiasm, in certain quarters, for (a narrow rhetoric of) evidence'. Indeed, once we read the pronouncements of proponents of evidence-based management as political manoeuvrings (and, what is more, under cover) they no longer seem so 'extraordinarily naive'; in fact, I suggest, they become rather sophisticated. Thus, while winning the argument against evidence-based management may be necessary, it will hardly be sufficient, given that the rhetoric of evidence-based practices is being recognized by its proponents to provide them with a new political resource, which they can deploy (more or less surreptitiously) to resist the philosophical and ideological pluralism to which they object. Indeed, Rousseau (2006b) has made this resource explicit; for her, the promotion of evidence-based management 'would *counter* the current organizational research bias toward novelty and fragmentation' (2006b: 1091; italics added). All in all then, the rhetoric of evidence-based management seems capable of nurturing and reinvigorating an optimistic faith in (a managerially-orientated version of) 'science' – a version of science, we should not forget, that still remains influential (and often dominant) in many business schools throughout the world, despite the more radical theories of scientific knowledge advanced during the last generation.

Evidence-based medicine: A model for evidence-based management?

Pfeffer and Sutton (2006: 13) claim that their 'interest in evidence-based *management* was inspired and, to some extent, guided by the evidence-based *medicine* movement' (italics in original). So what is evidence-based medicine?

According to Harrison (1998: 15), it is, 'the doctrine that professional clinical practice ought to be based upon sound biomedical research evidence about the effectiveness of each diagnostic or therapeutic procedure'. This doctrine has an intuitive, seemingly incontestable appeal, and during the 1990s its worldwide popular success among health care professionals was rapid and dramatic (Trinder, 2000). Evidence-based medicine has now enjoyed well over ten years of popularity in most fields of health care across the globe, such that today, it seems virtually axiomatic that all clinical practice can, and should, be evidence-based. That is to say, that practice should integrate individual clinical expertise 'with the best available external clinical evidence from systematicresearch' (Sackett et al., 1996: 71). Furthermore, evidence-based medicine *can* work – at least when work means (quite specifically) that aggregate clinical outcomes get improved. Indeed, in this specific sense (and taking account of the problematizations that are beginning to emerge from social scientists (Lambert et al., 2006) certain clinical evidence-based practices are widely acknowledged to work impressively. However, its overall successes are often overdrawn (evidence-based medicine rarely, if ever, provides categorical, recipe-style answers for individual clinical situations) such that much optimistic hype is accumulating about it, with unintended consequences.

For example, whether or not clinical practice can be said to be evidence-based is taking on a significance that is wider than its mere effectiveness. As Morse (2006: 80) suggests, today, '*[e]vidence* and *evidence-based practice* have become the new mantras for health care' (italics in original). So, to be able to claim that practice is 'evidence-based' typically provides a significant source of prestige and legitimacy that contributes to the construction of professional identity (Traynor, 2004; Green, 2000). This also seems to be the case, incidentally, for health care managers. The Department of

Health in England, for instance, produced a guide for management development called the *National Health Service* (NHS) *Leadership Qualities Framework* that contains a prominent claim that the framework is 'evidence based, grounded in research with 150 NHS chief executives and directors' (Department of Health, 2004). So the same sorts of ideas that underpin evidence-based medicine have come to be central, not only merely in guiding individual clinicians' practice, but also in shaping research agendas, formulating health policy (Gordon, 2006), and allocating resources (Lambert et al., 2006). In sum, evidence-based practices have taken on a legitimatory and symbolic role that has created a cultural environment in health care in which *any* problematization of using 'evidence' – virtually regardless of context – can be constructed (and dismissed) as reminiscent of early arguments against evidence-based medicine.

But leaving aside the debates about evidence-based medicine, I now want to turn to the question of whether this enthusiasm for evidence makes sense in the context of the rather different discipline of management and organization. And I do so using the work of a thinker who has proved influential within the social studies of science – Thomas Kuhn.

Normal science?: Medicine and management

The desire to make any kind of practice evidence-based relies on a particular intellectual framework being widely accepted by those involved. Significant disagreements about fundamental issues, and especially disagreements about what counts as 'evidence', would self-evidently make appeals to evidence ineffective as a persuasive device, and probably incoherent. However, Kuhn (1970) argued that a state of consensus about such fundamentals characterizes what he called *normal science*. For him, at any given point in history, the question of what counts as evidence and other matters basic to the conduct of science are usually more or less uncontroversial within a particular discipline of natural science. Kuhn's claim was empirically based:

[I]n the early stages of the development of any science different men confronting the same range of phenomena ... describe and interpret them in different ways. What is surprising, and also unique in its degree to the fields we call science, is that such initial divergences should ever largely disappear. For they do disappear to a very considerable extent and then apparently once for all (Kuhn, 1970: 17).

And to explain the disappearance of divergence, he argued that shared intellectual frameworks develop among natural scientists. For Kuhn, scientists typically come to share what he called a paradigm – a set of axiomatic conventions, which 'some particular scientific community acknowledges for a time as supplying the foundation for its further practice' (Kuhn, 1970: 10). The accepted conventions of the scientific community (such as what counts as evidence) are the more or less unexamined rules that enable scientists to come to a consensus about both what counts as a problem and the conditions to be met for a problem to be seen as solved. Ordinarily then, scientists do not question the very rules or foundations of the game, only certain moves within it – disagreement and competition are within certain parameters and limits that are unquestioned, at least for the time being (Fuchs and Ward, 1994). So normal science is able to produce what is widely accepted to be knowledge, Kuhn argues, by virtue of the fact that at any given point in history, members of the relevant scientific community can normally (more or less) agree on the foundational rules concerning how knowledge should be constituted.

Following Kuhn, it is apparent that a claim that clinical practice should be evidence-based only makes sense given the existence of a more or less unified paradigm that clinicians and researchers in a given health care discipline acknowledge as forming the foundation for their own knowledge. Indeed, proponents of evidence-based health care typically aim to ensure that only those studies produced within their paradigm can influence clinical decision-making. The principal method for assuring this – critical appraisal (for a description see Newman and Roberts, 2002) – can be interpreted after Kuhn, as a means of policing paradigmatic boundaries to ensure that only studies operating within the paradigm count as 'evidence'. That critical appraisal is generally represented as testing the quality of a study in what appear to be absolute terms, reflects the status and taken-for-grantedness of the paradigm in scientific and clinical thinking.

Outside normal science, on the other hand, the lack of an agreed paradigm means that disputes and divergences over foundations (for example about what counts as evidence and quite possibly about what count as problems) are likely to arise with such regularity that appeals to evidence as a means to resolve these disputes would become worthless. Outside normal science, criticism is not restricted to routine disagreement – it turns principled and radical (Fuchs and Ward, 1994). And Kuhn explicitly limited his empirical observations of the operation of normal science to the natural sciences. Indeed, he mentioned that as a natural scientist himself, he:

[W]as struck by the number and extent of the overt disagreements between social scientists about the nature of legitimate scientific problems and methods ... [T]he practice of astronomy, physics, chemistry or biology [might we add medicine?] normally fails to evoke the controversies over fundamentals that today often seem endemic among, say, psychologists or sociologists' (Kuhn, 1970: viii).

As Burrell and Morgan (1979) developed at length after Kuhn, organizational research is framed within a range of conflicting understandings of foundational knowledge – the nature of the social world, what is worth knowing, judgements about appropriate moral conduct and so on. (For a recent reformulation of that work see Deetz, Chapter 2, this volume.) In management theory, therefore, as in psychology and sociology, 'controversies about fundamentals' are endemic. The human sciences, including management, can never rely merely on instrumental reason, because they always and necessarily connect with the contested politics, values, and beliefs that arise from particular ideas about the good society and different ways of being in the world that precede empirical inquiry and shape what is seen 'out there'.

So while some orientations to the study of management and organization are more popular and influential than others, as in sociology and psychology, there is no single, unified approach to any matter that is widely accepted by scholars within the discipline. There are voices in management studies articulating theoretical stances that include, for example, varieties of critical theory (Alvesson and Willmott, 1996), neo-Marxism (Thompson and Smith, 2001), postmodernism (Linstead, 2004), social constructionism (Harding, 2003), and feminism (Walby, 1986), that have a prominence that is far greater than in medicine or most natural sciences. As Burrell (1996: 394) has put it:

> [T]he normal state of organizational science is pluralistic. This does not mean that organizational analysis is 'immature' or is awaiting its normal science phase with bated breath. It is simply that a plurality of legitimate and competing perspectives is to be expected.

Of course, my own representations of the controversies in the disciplines of medicine and management are likely to reproduce my perspectives and interests, positioned as I am in particular ways within the debates. As a management academic on the 'critical' wing of British business schools (Fournier and Grey, 2000), I no doubt have a self-serving predisposition to emphasize the extent to which management studies is fractured by political controversies. And I am aware that a small number of medical academics have expressed concerns about the dominant assumptions on which medicine as science is built (for example, Greenhalgh and Hurwitz, 1998; Tonelli, 1998). Nevertheless, I believe this picture of the level of contestation within the two disciplines is broadly fair, such that a range of contrasts between the academic study of the clinical health care disciplines (especially medicine) and

the study of management arise from the differences between the two fields in the levels of contestation surrounding their knowledge claims.

For example, it is widely believed that students in health care professions can be taught many techniques that allow for a high degree of confidence about the probability of their effects; for managers, techniques of agreed effectiveness are few in number, largely because there is no settled idea of what constitutes management effectiveness (Grey, 2004). Relatedly, and in a further contrast to the health care professions, managers are not obliged to undergo any kind of university-based training; indeed, countries that make extensive use of university business schools for management education like America and Britain do not seem to gain any particular advantage when compared to those that do not – say Germany or Japan (Grey and Willmott, 2002).

I submit, therefore, that within organization theory, it is hazardous, if not perverse, to expect a plurality of legitimate but competing theoretical perspectives and political orientations to converge in ways that enable (à la evidence-based medicine) the conscientious, explicit and judicious use of current best evidence in making decisions. Not because organizational questions are too complex to be susceptible to the sort of evidence-based measures now seen as axiomatic in clinical fields, but because, in organizational theory, what counts as evidence and how it should be understood are never merely technical questions. These sort of questions are posed outside a normal science framework so they inevitably have controversial epistemological, moral and political dimensions that make radical dispute – including dispute about what counts as evidence – nearly ubiquitous.

Evidence as catchphrase

Nevertheless, in spite of these arguments, the new *slogan* of 'evidence-based practice' is proving attractive to all sorts of people – including, perhaps particularly important, bodies responsible for the governance and funding of social research. For example, Britain's leading social science research funding body, the Economic and Social Research Council has a Centre for Evidence-based Policy and Practice (http://www.evidencenetwork.org/). And though (presumably) most of the social scientists who deploy terms like 'evidence-based practice' appreciate the complexities of the debates surrounding what evidence might be, the impact of this slogan-like rhetoric on others should not be underestimated. In particular, the idealized and overly optimistic representations of evidence-based medicine that the 'evidence-based' catchphrase seems to encourage are beginning to heighten expectations among politicians, policymakers, and others about the extent to which social research evidence can deliver useful technical fixes for them. Policymakers are starting to ask: 'if medical research can do it, why can't social research provide us with similarly categorical answers?'.

So, it is not entirely surprising that the Coalition for Evidence-based Policy (2006), for example, a body which advises American federal and state policymakers, claims at the head of its web-site:

> In the field of medicine, public policies based on scientifically-rigorous evidence have produced extraordinary advances in health over the past 50 years. By contrast, in most areas of social policy – such as education, poverty reduction, labor and employment, crime and justice, and health care financing and delivery – government programs often are implemented with little regard to evidence, costing billions of dollars yet failing to address critical needs of our society. [So the Coalition has organized] one of the leading web-sites on evidence-based programs – *Social Programs that Work* (www.evidencebasedprograms.org) – which provides policymakers and practitioners with clear, actionable information on 'what works' in social policy, based on evaluations that meet the highest level of scientific rigor.

Of course, these sorts of claims, concerned as they are with social settings, are vulnerable to a range of criticisms. One such criticism might follow Fox (2003: 81) in his critique of similar evidence-based

practices – the proponents of which he sees as typically seeking to claim an 'unmediated knowledge of reality'. Furthermore, and more directly political, an emphasis on 'what works' typically assumes that the current circumstances are a given. Thus, subjecting the circumstances *themselves* to sustained and detailed critical examination is beyond the ambitions of the model of science taken for granted in the Coalition's statement. Indeed, we might go as far as to argue that this inability to scrutinize the political interests served by the rhetoric of 'what works' can give politicians cover to pursue their partisan objectives, while appearing to be gathering objective, reliable, generalizable evidence (Majone, 1989) – a critique made particularly prominent in response to conservative regime during the Bush era (Denzin and Giardina, 2006; Mooney, 2005). And in a British context, evidence-based practices are, at the least, as Pawson (2006: 2) points out 'strongly associated with the so-called pragmatic, anti-ideological turn in modern [British] politics', that is, since New Labour came to power.

These sorts of objections to a natural science model being transferred to social settings have, of course, been well rehearsed in the social sciences over the years. But I want to emphasize again that the cultural context created by the evidence-based movement has rendered these arguments more or less redundant – at least in terms of the practical business of contesting a misplaced confidence in 'science' amongst those attracted by evidence-based practice. As Torrance (2006: 127) suggests, government agencies that commission social research now share 'an almost global "new orthodoxy" [which] seems perversely and wilfully ignorant of many decades of debate over whether, and if so in what ways, we can conduct enquiry and build knowledge in the social sciences, pausing only to castigate social researchers for not being more like (supposedly unproblematic) medical research'. Furthermore, the evidence-based rhetoric reinforces other longer-term trends – in particular the trend for the governance of social scientific research to be conducted as if the social sciences were just another natural science. For, as Donovan (2005: 611) argues:

> [T]he point here is not what social scientists do or do not believe to be genuine social science, but the fact that at the policy level this decision has been taken out of their hands and is being externally regulated by non-social scientists. The policy preference is to model social science upon idealized natural science practice, favouring user-orientated, fact-finding, 'positivistic' approaches and their associated (and preferably quantitative) empirical methods.

Consequently, as far as people like those who control research funding, policymakers and practitioners are concerned, it would hardly be surprising if attempts to find evidence-based solutions became increasingly popular. A new twist, perhaps, on the debates about relevance – Mode 1 and Mode 2 knowledge, and all that (Gibbons et al., 1994; Grey, 2001; Starkey and Maddan, 2001; Starkey, 2001).

Practicing managers are unlikely (to say the least) to be much influenced by the critiques of science in critical theory, and from their perspective one can easily understand the attractions of a promise like that of the Coalition for Evidence-based Policy, to provide 'clear, actionable information on "what works"'. One can also understand why 'evaluations that meet the highest level of scientific rigor' would be attractive, in that the commonsense understanding of 'scientific rigor' might reasonably be assumed (however paradoxical this assumption might sometimes turn out to be) to result in advice untainted by ideology or sectional interests (Donovan, 2005). While one would not want to overstate the appetite managers and policy makers will ever likely have for academic evidence, nevertheless, as Trinder (2000: 5) argues, the central concerns of the evidence-based movement resonate with and mirror 'significant contemporary issues and concerns, namely those of risk, audit and effectiveness, rationalism, transparency, professional accountability, consumerism, empowerment, and the needs of the information society'.

So, to return to the proponents of evidence-based management, their optimistic claims for the efficacy of evidence start to make more sense when understood within a cultural context that has been influenced by the over-hyped successes of the evidence-based movement in medicine and elsewhere; an influence reinforced by trends in research governance, and by ideas about relevance, that continue to influence the research environment for organizational studies. Thus, on the back cover of the book by Pfeffer and Sutton (2006), David Kessler, the Dean of the School of Medicine at the University of California, San Fransisco writes:

> This book convinced me that the time is ripe for an evidence-based management movement. Just as medical decisions are better for patients when they are based on sound evidence, this same idea ought to be applied to management. Understanding the effects of your actions is critical, and both physicians and leaders who take this scientific approach will do a superior job of practicing their craft.

Evidence-based management's effect(s)

In the light of these developments, I suggest that the growing confidence in science and evidence for management – as if management were more or less analogous to medicine – may well start to have tangible effects on organization studies. Of particular importance, the sort of environment that encourages practitioners to believe certain types of academic research can directly improve decisions would, presumably, increase the monies that research councils and other bodies (such as commercial companies) were prepared to invest in management research. This is an observation unlikely to be lost on the advocates of evidence-based management. Indeed, one of Pfeffer's (1993: 599) key justifications for his original proposal to enforce paradigmatic unity was to improve the ability of organization studies, 'to compete successfully with adjacent social sciences such as economics in the contest for resources'. So it is, perhaps, not entirely cynical to read Pfeffer and Sutton's (2006) book on evidence-based management as a sales pitch for what academic management research can offer business executives.

Of course, any increases in research funds made available via evidence-based management would represent an important development for *all* organizational researchers – whatever their stance on evidence-based management – especially in the current climate in universities, where an individual scholar's ability to attract external research funding brings considerable institutional and personal advantages (Cheek, 2005). However, funding increases from evidence-based management would, no doubt, continue to be administered through the now well-established model for commissioned research; competitive tenders for projects that are specified in some detail, with evaluation procedures following the mantra that only 'useful' research should be funded (Donovan, 2005; Cheek, 2005). As Pawson (2006: 3) comments:

> In the UK, much if not most, policy inquiry is conducted by units and centres that perch on the edge of mainstream university departments and whose existence depends on winning the *next* contract. Oftentimes, this means that the policy-research relationship is financially circular, with one arm of government providing the funds for another to supply the evidence base … [T]he increasing role of the private sector should [also] be noted, as both recipients and providers of information. Unhappily, one also observes that this new function for auditors coincided with the outbreak of corporate scandals about their traditional role as independent regulators.

It is hard, therefore, to be optimistic about the effects of such increased funding on management researchers who might want to resist the impact of managerialism. Indeed, it seems likely that we would either become increasingly torn between the demands of funders and our preferred methodological and political orientations – or face a greater marginalization because of a relative failure to generate research income. The key point about either scenario is that they would both represent a surreptitious move toward the paradigmatic unity that Pfeffer (1993) proposed; surreptitious because there would be no need for individual scholars to be seen

directly imposing their views – rather the imposition would occur *de facto* – largely through the demands of research funders and the incentives they have in their gift to encourage (and discourage) various forms of research.

Such processes are already particularly advanced in much of the research carried out, for example, in American education policy research and in organizational research in British health care. If we want to see the potential effects of evidence-based management on a pluralistic, critically-orientated organizational research we might start by looking in these areas. In American education, in spite of a strong tradition of qualitative research in this sector in the past (House, 2006; Lather, 2006), federally funded policy research is now being dominated by randomized control trials and the other quantitive, experimental designs that are widely used in medical research. Today, such methods effectively more or less exclude funding from any form of qualitative research – a phenomenon that Lincoln and Cannella (2004: 7) call 'methodological fundamentalism'. This is a fundamentalism imposed by politicians with the encouragement of those educational scholars whose interests are served by the domination of quantitive methodologies. Indeed, House (2006: 103) points to the moral fervour with which some American education researchers object to certain qualitative methods:

> Experimental advocates regard such studies as blasphemous and lament the disrespect to scientific truth. In their view, they are re-establishing the authority of social science, particularly the authority of the methodology they learned as graduate students and nurtured as professors.

Another, somewhat different, example is health care in Britain, where the government research-funding agency, the NHS Service Delivery and Organization (SDO) Programme, has since 2000 been commissioning, 'research evidence directed at improving the organization and delivery of health services and to promote the uptake and application of that evidence in policy and practice'

(SDO, 2006: 1). SDO work has become important to organizational research in British health care because of the relatively large amounts of additional funding it has made available to researchers. While the agency often does commission qualitative work, its explicit policy is to develop research that *managers* find useful (Edwards, 2003). Thus, a senior health care executive chairs the programme board, and other health managers are well represented on it (SDO, 2006: 3). Furthermore, its research funding is administered through closely specified tenders that give researchers little freedom in the sorts of reports that they produce (Learmonth and Harding, 2006). Perhaps, then, in place of the *methodological* fundamentalism of American education policy research, what can be seen in health care organizational research in Britain is a managerialist orientation that effectively produces an *ideological* fundamentalism. As Learmonth (2003: 110–11) has argued, the SDO:

> ...appear[s] to be orientated towards an uncritical acceptance of managerialist literature, including 'popular' management titles [such that] it is not implausible to believe that the [largely pro-management] orientations [of organizational research in the UK health sector] are caused by the demands of funders rather than scholars' preferred intellectual commitments.

Indeed, in a recent personal conversation about some of the arguments in this chapter, the head of a university research centre, heavily reliant on funding from bodies like the SDO, told me that he felt a certain sympathy toward much of my analysis. However, he believed that his current institutional position effectively precluded him from publicly criticizing the funding bodies on which the centre relied. And anyway, people in bodies like the SDO seem to me to have become more or less impervious to any criticism of their stance on evidence-based management. My guess is that their very *raison d'être* has become so closely aligned with evidence-based management that it is now difficult for them to do anything other than stonewall or dismiss all invitations to rethink their position.

DISCUSSION AND CONCLUSION

So what would I like to see instead? Perhaps the most important thing, in contrast to developments in America and Britain, would be the encouragement of a radical heterogeneity, both in the nature of research questions, and in the research traditions employed. So it is not that I am denying the importance of running organizations efficiently and effectively. Indeed, I think that evidence will always have an important role in helping us to change organizations in beneficial ways. However, against the current trend to homogenize evidence within conservative frameworks – conservative because they do not examine received ideas about organizational realities – I am advocating that forms of evidence should be as broad as possible, including those forms that explicitly challenge managerialist beliefs and assumptions. Such challenges, it seems to me, are likely to provide opportunities for bringing new sources of creativity to organizing as well as encouraging more open debates that represent wider constituencies and interests.

However, the practical difficulties faced in adopting this position are considerable, not least because of the resistance that powerful groups with an interest in evidence-based management might offer. Governments, managers, and others usually look to academics to give them straightforward answers to their difficulties and dilemmas; they may well be reluctant to fund research that does not provide these answers, or that explicitly opposes their interests. On the other hand, however, should academics acquiesce to pressures to produce work that simply serves management purposes, then in the longer term, I think we risk failing society at large. Such acquiescence could even remove incentives to comment outside institutionally approved discourses. And if it were to do so, academic work would ultimately not be in the interests of *anyone* in organizations, including its top managers. So my concern – that the popularization of evidence-based management has the potential to bring strong incentives into play for critically orientated researchers to compromise their work – is a concern that has significance well outside universities themselves.

For example, I already come under (gentle) pressure to seek grants from bodies like the SDO. Indeed, it seems to be standard advice to someone in my position, that for the purposes of career progression, one should apply for grants from these bodies – provide them with the managerially orientated reports they require – then write separate, critical academic papers from the data. But one of the problems with this advice is that reports to such bodies are in the public domain; indeed, they are considerably more likely to be read by practitioners than articles in scholarly journals (Learmonth and Harding, 2006). It seems, therefore, that the political risks of this action suggest that critical researchers should think long and hard before compromising, though our promotion prospects would undoubtedly be enhanced by compromise.

So, I have been pondering ways of resisting the worst of the negative possibilities that any further popularization of evidence-based management might have in store for people like me. I suggest that 'attack' may be the best form of defence. For as Fox (2003: 97) points out, the logic of evidence-based practice 'does not demand that all research stops if it is not immediately "relevant"'. In fact, rather the opposite is the case – the rhetoric of 'evidence' can, in principle at least, provide new opportunities for all types of empirically-orientated researchers to get more of a hearing – research and evidence are open equally to be constructed as subversive as to be constructed managerially. Even Pfeffer and Sutton (2006: 230) (though they 'hesitate to recommend' it) briefly discuss the value of what they say 'might be called *evidence-based misbehavior*' (italics in original). They realize that the logic of their position on evidence-based management means that it would be legitimate for subordinates, more aware of the evidence than their managers, to subvert orders in the (evidence-based) interests of the company.

Thus, one response to evidence-based management, in line with more radical sensibilities, would be to develop Pfeffer and Sutton's own suggestions about evidence-based misbehaviour, only with less hesitancy. Indeed, Fox (2003: 89) commends what he calls 'transgressive research' to researchers confronted with evidence-based rhetoric, arguing that it represents 'practice-orientated research that is constitutive of difference, challenges power and constraint, and encourages resistance and new possibilities'. Transgressive research seems to be potentially of great value for activists and others involved in organizations (including, perhaps many people with manager in their job title), unhappy with the status quo and seeking ways to resist the norm and bring about radical change. However, the results of rigorous social scientific work will seldom provide evidence that gives activists evidence-based advice about how to 'misbehave'. As Weick (2001: 73) argues: 'when people experience uncertainty and gather information to reduce it, this often backfires and uncertainty increases. As a result … the more information is gathered, the more doubts accumulate about any option'. Therefore, if research is 'relevant' it will probably be in its ability to change thinking about so-called 'transgressive' activities, or about the acceptability of standard managerial practices. I suggest that practicing managers and others in organizations need to be rather wary of academics presenting what they do as if it were consultancy.

Nevertheless, I wonder whether conducting forms of transgressive research might be one way for academics to survive within evidence-based discourses while having the chance to subvert its political intentions, and still carry on doing the kind of work that I think is important. It might even be a way, furthermore, following Grey (2001: 32), in which to:

…reimagine relevance so [that business school academics] see themselves at the centre stage of working with all the complexities of knowledge, free from the demands of relevance – or, more accurately, free from the current restricted, persecuted and persecutory imaginations of what relevance might be.

Nevertheless, I am not naive enough to imagine that transgressive research will be the quickest route to career and other conventional forms of institutional 'success'. I guess we would have to work very hard indeed for it to become acceptable to bodies like the SDO, even though it produces 'evidence' that many (nonmanagerial and marginalized) groups would find 'relevant'. But I think, politically, it is imperative to keep trying.

REFERENCES

Alvesson, M. and Willmott, H. (1996) *Making Sense of Management: A critical introduction*, London: Sage Publications.

Alvesson, M. and Deetz, S. (2000) *Doing Critical Management Research*, London: Sage Publications.

Axelsson, R. (1998) 'Towards an evidence-based health care management', *International Journal of Health Planning and Management*, 13: 307–17.

Briner, R. (2000) 'Evidence-based human resource management', in L. Trinder (ed.), *Evidence-Based Practice: A Critical Appraisal*, Oxford: Blackwell, pp.184–211.

Burrell, G. (1996) 'Normal science, paradigms, metaphors, discourses and genealogies of analysis', in Stewart Clegg and Cynthia Hardy (eds), *Handbook of Organization Studies: Theory & Method*, London: Sage Publications, pp.388–404.

Burrell, G. and Morgan, G. (1979) *Sociological Paradigms and Organisational Analysis: Elements of the sociology of corporate life*, London: Heinemann.

Cheek, J. (2005) 'The practice and politics of funded qualitative research', in Norman K. Denzin and Yvonna S. Lincoln (eds), *The Sage Handbook of Qualitative Research (Third Edition)*, Thousand Oaks, CA: Sage Publications, pp.387–409.

Coalition for Evidence-based Policy (2006) http://coexgov.securesites.net/index.php?keyword=a432fbc34d71c7 (accessed 21 December 2006).

Davies, H.T.O., Nutley, S.M and Smith, P.C (2000) 'Introducing evidence-based policy and practice in public services', in Huw T. O. Davies; Sandra M. Nutley and Smith, Peter C. (eds), *What Works? Evidence-based policy and practice in public services*, Bristol: The Policy Press, pp.1–12.

Deetz, S. (1996) 'Describing differences in approaches to organization science: rethinking Burrell and Morgan and their legacy', *Organization Science*, 7(2): 191–207.

Denzin, N.K. and Giardina, M.D (eds) (2006), *Qualitative Inquiry and the Conservative Challenge*, Walnut Creek, CA: Left Coast Press.

Department Of Health (2004) *National Management Development Initiative*, [Accessed 01.12.04]: www.modern.nhs.uk/1115/20946/posters.pdf.

Donovan, C. (2005) 'The governance of social science and everyday epistemology', *Public Administration*, 83(3): 597–615.

Dopson, S. (2006) 'Debate: why does knowledge stick?: what we can learn from the case of evidence-based health care', *Public Money and Management*, (April): 85–6.

Edwards, N. (2003) 'What type of research do NHS managers find useful?', Keynote Speech at the Second National SDO Conference: Delivering Research for Better Health Services, 19 March 2003.

Fournier, V. and Grey, C. (2000) 'At the critical moment: conditions and prospects for critical management studies', *Human Relations*, 53: 7–32.

Fox, N.J. (2003) 'Practice-based evidence: towards collaborative and transgressive research,' *Sociology*, 37(1): 81–102.

Fuchs, S. and Ward, S. (1994) 'What is deconstruction and when does it take place?: making facts in science, building cases in law', *American Sociological Review*, 59: 481–500.

Gibbons, M. Limoges, C., Nowotny, H., Schwartzman, S., Scott, P., and Trow, M. (1994) *The New Production of Knowledge: The Dynamics of Science and Research in Contemporary Societies*, London: Sage Publications.

Gordon, E. (2006) 'The political context of evidence-based medicine: policymaking for daily haemodialysis', *Social Science & Medicine*, 62: 2707–19.

Green, J. (2000) 'Epistemology, evidence and experience: evidence-based health care in the work of accident alliances', *Sociology of Health & Illness*, 22(4): 453–76.

Greenhalgh, T. and Hurwitz, B. (1998) *Narrative-Based Medicine: Dialogue and Discourse in Clinical Practice*, London: BMJ Publishing Group.

Grey, C. (1996) 'Towards a critique of managerialism: the contribution of Simone Weil', *Journal of Management Studies*, 33(5): 591–611.

Grey, C. (2001) 'Re-imagining relevance: a response to Starkey and Maddan', *British Journal of Management*, 12: s27–s32.

Grey, C. (2004) 'Reinventing business schools: the contribution of critical management education', *Academy of Management Learning and Education*, 3(2): 178–86.

Grey, C. and Willmott, H. (2002) 'Contexts of CMS', *Organization*, 9: 411–18.

Grey, C. and Willmott, H. (2005) *Critical Management Studies: A Reader*, Oxford, England: Oxford University Press.

Harding, N. (2003) *The Social Construction of Management*, London: Routledge.

Hardy, C., Phillips, N. and Clegg, S. (2001) 'Reflexivity in organization and management theory: a study of the production of the research 'subject'', *Human Relations*, 54: 531–60.

Harrison, S. (1998) 'The politics of evidence-based medicine', *Policy and Politics*, 26(1): 15–31.

Hewison, A. (1997) 'Evidence-based evidence-based management?', *Journal of Nursing Management*, 5: 195–8.

House, E.R. (2006) 'Methodological fundamentalism and the quest for control', in Norman K. Denzin and Michael Giardina (eds), *Qualitative Inquiry and the Conservative Challenge*, Walnut Creek, CA: Left Coast Press, pp.93–108.

Jack, G. and Westwood, R. (2006) 'Postcolonialism and the politics of qualitative research in international business', *Management International Review*, 46(4): 481–501.

Kovner, A.R., Elton, J.J. and Billings, J. (2000) 'Evidence-based management', *Frontiers of Health Services Management*, 16(4): 3–24.

Kuhn, T.S. (1970) *The Structure of Scientific Revolutions*, (second edn.), Chicago: Chicago University Press.

Lambert, H., Gordon, E. and Bogdan-Lovis, E. (2006) 'Introduction: gift horse or Trojan horse?: social science perspectives on evidence-based health care', *Social Science & Medicine*, 62(11): 2613–20.

Lather, P. (2006) 'This is your father's paradigm', in *Qualitative Inquiry and the Conservative Challenge*, Norman K. Denzin and Michael Giardina (eds), Walnut Creek, CA: Left Coast Press, pp.31–55.

Latour, Bruno (1987) *Science in Action*, Cambridge MA: Harvard University Press.

Learmonth, M. (2003) 'Making health services management research critical: a review and a suggestion', *Sociology of Health & Illness*, 25(1): 93–119.

Learmonth, M: (2006) 'Is there such a thing as 'evidence-based management?: a commentary on Rousseau's 2005 presidential address', *Academy of Management Review*, 31(4): 1089–91.

Learmonth, M. and Harding, N. (2006) 'Evidence-based management: the very idea', *Public Administration*, 84(2): 245–66.

Lincoln, Y.S. and Cannella, G.S (2004) 'Dangerous discourses: methodological conservatism and governmental regimes of truth', *Qualitative Inquiry*, 10(1): 5–14.

Linstead, S. (ed.) (2004) *Organization Theory and Postmodern Thought*, London: Sage Publications.

Majone, G. (1989) *Evidence, Argument and Persuasion in the Policy Process*, New Haven, CT: Yale University Press.

Merton, R.K. (1973/1942) 'The normative structure of science', in Norman W. Storer (ed.), *The Sociology of Science: Theoretical and Empirical Investigations*, Chicago: University of Chicago Press, pp.267–78.

Mooney, C. (2005) *The Republican War on Science*, New York: Basic Books.

Morrell, K. (2008) 'The narrative of evidence-based management: a polemic', *Journal of Management Studies*, 45(3): 613–35.

Morse, J.M. (2006) 'The politics of evidence', in Norman K. Denzin and Michael Giardina (eds), *Qualitative Inquiry and the Conservative Challenge*, Walnut Creek, CA: Left Coast Press, pp.79–92.

Mulkay, M. (1981) 'Action and belief or scientific discourse?: a possible way of ending intellectual vassalage in social studies of science', *Philosophy of Social Science*, 11: 163–71.

Newman, M. and Roberts, T. (2002) 'Critical appraisal I: is the quality of the study good enough for you to use the findings?', in J.V. Craig and R. Smyth L (eds), *The Evidence-based Practice Manual for Nurses*, Edinburgh: Churchill Livingstone, pp. 86–112.

Ozcan, Y.A. and Smith, P. (1998) 'Towards a science of the management of health care', *Health Care Management Science*, 1: 1–4.

Pawson, R. (2006) *Evidence-based Policy: A Realist Perspective*, London: Sage Publications.

Pfeffer, J. (1993) 'Barriers to the advance of organizational science: paradigm development as a dependent variable', *Academy of Management Review*, 18(4): 599–620.

Pfeffer, J. and Sutton, R. (2006) *Hard Facts, Dangerous Half-Truths and Total Nonsense: Profiting from Evidence-based Management*, Boston, MA: Harvard Business School Press.

Potter, J. (1996) *Representing Reality: Discourse, Rhetoric and Social Construction*, London: Sage Publications.

Rousseau, D. (2006a) 'Is there such a thing as 'evidence-based management?', *Academy of Management Review*, 31(2): 256–69.

Rousseau, D. (2006b) 'Keeping an open mind about evidence-based management: a reply to Learmonth's commentary', *Academy of Management Review*, 31(4): 1091–3.

Sackett, D.L., Rosenberg, W.M.C., Gray, J.A.M., Haynes, B. and Richardson, S. (1996) 'Evidence-based medicine: what it is and what it isn't', *British Medical Journal*, 312: 71–2.

SDO (2006) *Annual Report 2006: NHS Service Delivery and Organisation R&D Programme*, London: NCCSDO.

Smith, V. (2001) 'Ethnographies of work and the work of ethnographers', in P. Atkinson, A. Coffey, S. Delamont, J. Lofl and L. Lofl (eds), *Handbook of Ethnography*, London: Sage Publications, pp. 220–33.

Starkey, K. (2001) 'In defence of modes one, two and three: a response', *British Journal of Management*, 12: s77–s80.

Starkey, K. and Maddan, P. (2001) 'Bridging the relevance gap: aligning stakeholders in the future of management research', *British Journal of Management*, 12: s3–26.

Stewart, R. (2002) *Evidence-Based Management: A Practical Guide for Health Professionals*, Abingdon, Oxon: Radcliffe Medical Press.

Thompson, P. and Smith, C. (2001) 'Follow the redbrick road: reflections on pathways in and out of the labor process debate', *International Studies of Management & Organization*, 30: 40–67.

Tonelli, M.R. (1998) 'The philosophical limits of evidence-based medicine', *Academic Medicine*, 73: 1234–40.

Torrance, H. (2006) 'Research quality and research governance in the United Kingdom: from methodology to management', in Norman K. Denzin and Michael Giardina (eds), *Qualitative Inquiry and the Conservative Challenge*, Walnut Creek, Ca: Left Coast Press, pp.127–48.

Tranfield, D., Denyer, D. and Smart, P. (2003) 'Towards a methodology for developing evidence-informed management knowledge by means of systematic review', *British Journal of Management*, 14(3): 207–22.

Traynor, M. (2004) 'Nursing, managerialism and evidence-based practice: the constant struggle for influence', in M. Learmonth and N. Harding (eds), *Unmasking Health Management: A Critical Text*, New York: Nova Science, pp.117–28.

Trinder, L. (2000) 'Introduction: the context of evidence-based practice', in Liz Trinder and Shirley Reynolds (eds), *Evidence-Based Practice: A Critical Appraisal*, Oxford: Blackwell, pp.1–16.

Van Maanen, J. (1995) 'Style as theory', *Organization Science*, 6(1): 133–43.

Walby, S. (1986) *Patriarchy at Work*, Cambridge: Polity Press.

Walshe, K. and Rundall, T.G. (2001) 'Evidence-based management: from theory to practice in health care', *The Milbank Quarterly*, 79(3): 429–57.

Weick, K.E. (2001) 'Gapping the relevance bridge: fashion meets fundamentals in management research', *British Journal of Management*, 12: s71–s75.

Wikipedia (2006) http://en.wikipedia.org/w/index.php?title=Evidence-based_management&direction=next&oldid=79420854 (accessed 30 October, 2006).

Willmott, H. (1997) 'Management and organization studies as science?', *Organization*, 4(3): 309–44.

Willmott, H. (1998) 'Re-cognizing the other: reflections on a 'new sensibility' in Robert Cooper, Robert Chia (ed.), social and organizational studies', in *In the Realm of Organization: Essays for* London: Routledge, pp.213–41.

PART II

Agendas: The Broadening Focus of Organizational Research

Focusing on influential traditions in organizational research, on areas that have helped to define and characterize the field, exemplifying methodological approaches, developments, and trends, taking methodology into new territory

7

Leadership Research: Traditions, Developments, and Current Directions

Michael D. Mumford, Tamara L. Friedrich, Jay J. Caughron, and Alison L. Antes

Few topics in the area of organizational research are as important as leadership (Bass, in press; Yukl, 2002). Consider just a few of the tasks we expect leaders to accomplish. Leaders must help create cohesive and motivated teams (DeCremer, 2006). They must sell, or champion, new initiatives (Howell and Boies, 2004). They must help people make sense of crises (Drazin et al., 1999). And leaders must establish, and direct, the strategy being pursued by the organization (Finkelstein, 2003). Clearly, leadership makes a difference, a big difference, with respect to the nature of organizational behavior and the performance of organizations (Yukl, 2002). Accordingly, leadership may be one of the most intensively studied phenomena in the field of organizational behavior.

Traditionally, studies of leadership have employed a reasonably straightforward paradigm. This paradigm was derived form the Ohio State Leadership Studies (e.g., Fleishman, 1951, 1953b; Fleishman and

Harris, 1962). Essentially, in this method a construct held to account for certain aspects of leader behavior, for example consideration and initiating structure, is defined. Subsequently, a set of behaviors to be applied in describing the leader with regard to this construct is generated and scaled, with these scales being used to predict various outcomes of leadership. In fact, this same basic method underlies the development of multiple measures of leadership, including measures of leader-member exchange (Graen and Uhl-Bien, 1998) and transformational leadership (Bass, 1997; Bass and Avolio, 1989).

Although few scholars would dispute the value of the paradigm as a basis for certain studies of leadership, it is a paradigm that has often been questioned. Some of these questions involved the ability of these kinds of behavior surveys to adequately assess certain aspects of leadership. For example, it is difficult to see how behavioral surveys can be used to assess leaders' mental models (Mumford et al., in press). Moreover, questions have been raised about the construct validity of the information provided by the surveys (Brown and Keeping, 2005). These questions have, in turn, given rise to both new methods for survey based studies of leadership and the application of new methods in studies of leadership.

In the present chapter, we will review some of the major methods currently being employed in studies of leadership. We will begin by considering recent revisions to standard survey methods. Subsequently, we will consider the alternative methods currently being applied in studies of leadership. More specifically, we will consider attribute, experimental, qualitative, and historiometric studies. In this review, we will consider both the strengths and weaknesses of each approach from a substantive perspective, as well as critical issues that need to be addressed to improve the methods being applied.

Survey studies

As already noted , the method most commonly applied to studies of leadership may be found in behavioral surveys. The key assumption underlying this approach, a nontrivial assumption, is that what is of interest in the study of leadership are behaviors exhibited by people who hold leadership roles. What should be recognized here, however, is that a variety of models, or theories, might be applied to specify the particular behaviors of interest.

One illustration of this approach is provided by studies of leader-member exchange. The theoretical model underlying this research holds that relationships are dyadic and that leaders form relationships of differential quality with different individuals (Dansereau et al., 1973). Differential quality of the relationship formed between leaders and followers is measured through questions such as 'Do you know where you stand with the leader?', 'Does the leader understand your problems and needs?', and 'Does the leader recognize your potential?'. Responses to these questions

typically load on one factor producing internal consistency coefficients in the 70s to 80s. Another illustration of this approach may be found in studies of transformational leadership (Bass, 1997). Within this theory, leadership is held to be a result of four transformational behaviors – charisma, inspirational motivation, individualized consideration, and intellectual stimulation, along with three transactional dimensions – contingent reward, active management by exception, and passive management by exception. Followers are asked to rate leaders on questions such as 'expresses confidence that goals will be achieved,' 'treats each member as an individual,' and 'avoids making decisions' (Bass and Avolio, 1998). Typically, these scales yield adequate internal consistency.

The first point to be borne in mind with regard to behavioral survey studies concerns an assumption implicit in this approach. More specifically, survey studies assume that relevant leadership behaviors can, in fact, be observed. For many leadership behaviors, for example, leader-member exchange or transformational leadership, this assumption does appear to hold. For other phenomena known to be important to leadership, such as planning (Marta et al., 2005) or leaders' mental models (Calori et al., 1992), it is not clear that relevant manifestations will necessarily be observed by followers. Thus, in applying survey methods, it is important to bear in mind that only certain aspects of leadership can be studied.

The next question that arises with regard to behavioral survey measures concerns the level at which the behaviors of interest are likely to be observed (Dansereau and Yammarino, 1998). For some theories, for example leader-member exchange, the level of analysis is a particular, individual, follower's perceptions. For other theories, for example, charismatic and transformational leadership (Klein and House, 1998) the level at which hypotheses are framed pertains to the group. This group level framing implies that agreement should be observed among multiple followers in their perceptions of leaders. Moreover, when hypotheses are framed in terms of these group-level, or organizational-level, effects, analyses should be based on within and between (WABA) methods or hierarchical linear modeling.

A more central concern with regard to behavioral survey methods arises from another question. Just what is it that is really being measured? Brown and Keeping (2005), in one study along these lines, examined the transformational leadership measures of Bass and Avolio (1989). They also examined liking for the leader. It was found that liking accounted for relationships between transformational leadership and outcomes such as organizational citizenship and affective organizational commitment. Moreover, evidence was provided that liking for the leader might operate as a method bias factor. These findings are noteworthy for three reasons. First, they point to the need to measure and control for potential biasing factors such as liking, observational opportunity, and socially desirable responding in survey studies. Second, they broach the question as to whether new methods are needed for collecting follower reports of leader behavior. For example, behavioral comparison with regard to behaviors of similar favorableness may be required. Third, and finally, the Brown and Keeping (2005) study reminds us that there is risk in imputing causal relationships based on survey data until alternative explanations can be ruled out.

Along related lines, in many, although not necessarily all, survey studies, only survey data is collected. This reliance on survey reports for both predictors and criteria opens up the possibility that method bias may have resulted in inflated correlational relationships (Podsakoff et al., 2003). One obvious response to this problem is to apply alternative measures of outcomes as well as survey-based measures. When the use of alternative measures does not prove possible, however, requisite control analyses should be conducted before seeking to establish predictor criterion relationships.

These observations about the biasing factors that need to be taken into account in survey studies point to another concern of some importance. More specifically, inferences about causality must be made with respect to relevant controls. For example, in studies of leader influences on organizational growth, prior size and market expansion both represent controls that need to be taken into account before drawing strong conclusions about the influence of leader behavior. Similarly, in a study of leader emergence on team tasks, team member familiarity, and team cohesiveness, again, represent controls that may need to be taken into account. Unfortunately, in many survey studies controls are not widely, and appropriately, applied.

These observations about the need to take controls into account underscore the importance of the strength of inferences allowed by study design. As the depth and complexity of verified relationships increase, it becomes possible to place greater confidence in the conclusions emerging from the study (Sosik, 2005). In fact, in recent years, we have seen the emergence of studies examining more complex mediational and moderator relationships. For example, Carmeli and Schaubroeck (2006) examined the mediational impact of the quality of decisions arising from behavioral integration of top management teams on organizational decline. Similarly, Kacmar and her colleagues (Kacmar et al., in press) have examined the influence of work context on the satisfaction and performance of individuals receiving high and low scores on a measure of leader-member exchange.

The importance of models, and well developed model tests, in survey studies brings us to a final observation. Often, although not always, behavioral survey studies are based on an idealized model of leader behavior. Illustrations of this approach can be found in recent research on spiritual leadership (Fry, 2005) and authentic leadership (Avolio and Gardner, 2005). What should be remembered with regard to the idealized models is that inferential standards will necessarily differ from normative studies. More specifically, in the case of idealized models, relevant comparison conditions must be specified. Moreover, gains in relevant outcomes, for example, follower commitment or follower performance, must be demonstrated vis-à-vis select normative comparison models (Schriesheim et al., 2006).

Attribute studies

Although much of the leadership literature continues to apply survey methods focusing on leader behavior, the questions remain as to what attributes of people, and their lives, give rise to leadership. Essentially, the questions being asked in these studies concern what individual characteristics, or situational experiences, influence leader emergence and performance, and how these individual and situational characteristics shape leader behavior. For example, Paunonen et al. (2006) examined the influence of narcissism on peer nominations of leaders. In contrast, Sosik (2005) examined the influence of leader values on transformational leadership behavior.

These two illustrative trait studies underscore a key decision that must be made in all attribute studies. More specifically, what measure, or measures, of leadership will be used as the criterion variable? As noted earlier, one choice that might be made in this regard is to examine behavior, performance, or both behavior and performance. What should be recognized here, however, is that the distinction made between behavior and performance is, in a sense, overly simplistic. For example, one might examine growth in leadership skills (Mumford et al., 2000). Alternatively, one might examine a select outcome of leader performance, such as increased innovation rates (Amabile et al., 2004). Still another option involves the examination of network structures (Mehra et al., 2006). What should be recognized here, however, is an important, and often overlooked, point. The criteria being examined in attribute studies determine both the nature and potential importance of the conclusions that can be drawn.

As important as the criteria being applied are to attribute studies, the focus of these studies is on identifying a set of attributes (individual, group, or contextual attributes) that influence the criteria of concern. Strong attribute studies explicitly tie attributes under consideration to a particular set of criteria of interest. One classic illustration of this approach may be found in studies by Vroom and his colleagues (Vroom and Jago, 1988). Here the focus was on the speed and acceptance of leader decisions with leader interaction strategies (e.g., consultation versus autocratic) being appraised with respect to situational influences (e.g., time pressure and information availability). In fact, the evidence accrued in these studies suggests that this model does provide a plausible basis for accounting for leader decisions and leader performance in decision-making.

The importance of defining criteria and relevant predictors in attribute studies brings to the fore a new question. What attributes should we be studying as potential predictors? Traditionally, debate in this regard has swirled around individual predictors in contrast to situational predictors (Bass, 1990). In fact, this person versus situation dichotomy has broken down in recent years as the complex nature of leadership and leader behavior has received more attention. Although many studies focus solely on traits, other studies examine the interaction of traits with situational influences. Some studies, moreover, focus on developed skills and expertise seeking to link more acquisition of skills and expertise to relevant environmental influences on growth (McCauley et al., 1994).

Nonetheless, with attribute studies certain key considerations will influence the likely success of the effort. First, and foremost, attributes influencing leadership behavior, leader performance, or other criteria have long been studied (Bass, 1990). Thus, the key question at hand in attribute studies is often not general effects. We know that leaders are typically intelligent (Bass, 1990), an individual attribute, and that leaders emerge under conditions of crisis (Hunt et al., 1999), a situational attribute. As a result, studies examining leader idea evaluation, a component of intelligence, will typically prove of greater value than a study of intelligence per se (Lord and Hall, 2005; Mumford et al., 2003).

Similarly, studies examining how leaders shape group perceptions of and team cohesion under crisis conditions will typically have greater value than a study of crisis conditions per se (Drazin et al., 1999).

In addition to specificity, a second consideration often evident in viable studies of individual and situational attributes involves examination of the mechanisms giving rise to observer effects. Many, perhaps most, attributes do not exert their effects directly on leader behavior and performance. Thus, the identification and assessment of mediators is often integral to the success of these studies. An illustration of this point may be found in a recent study of genetic influences on leadership by Arvey et al. (2006). Here leadership was measured by movement into leadership roles among identical and fraternal twins.

This study of genetic influences points to another issue that affects the success of attribute studies. The influence of attributes is often not immediate. Unfortunately, most leadership studies are based on cross-sectional data. The assumption underlying the use of cross-sectional data is, of course, straightforward. It is assumed that, due to prior operation of either individual or situational attributes, effects will be observed in a cross-sectional investigation. Although this assumption does hold in the case of many studies, it is also true that interpretations of causation become clouded. More centrally, some phenomena of interest are simply not amenable to those kinds of inferences. For example, studies of the career development process for leaders often do not meet this assumption (Howard and Bray, 1988). This same caveat also applies to other investigations. For example, Rowe et al. (2005) were interested in the effect of leader turnover on baseball team performance, with different effects being postulated for leaders operating at different levels. To investigate these effects a time series study of coaches and general managers was conducted.

At least three other methodological considerations also influence the success of attribute studies. Perhaps the most important of these concerns pertains to the amount of variation extant among the attributes being studied. In studies of individual attributes this phenomenon is referred to as range restriction. Although situational and developmental studies evidence less concern with the amount of variation being examined, from a design perspective, a similar concern applies. Unless variation exists among the situational variables of concern, it is difficult to demonstrate effects. Moreover, organizations often take actions that are through either direct, or indirect, mechanisms intended to restrict the range of relevant situational variables operating. This rather straightforward observation has a direct and an indirect implication. The direct implication is that studies of leadership attributes should be conducted under conditions where adequate variability exists, or can be corrected for, given the attributes of interest. The indirect implication is that the operation of phenomena that rise to limited variation in select variables may actually be marking phenomena of interest for students of leadership – albeit phenomena that may need to be studied using different research methods. Additionally, these observations underscore the need for certain studies to examine, and test, shifts in variance – asking the question: what factors are giving rise to these changes in variance?

Related to the issue of variance is the need for attribute studies to take another consideration into account. Attribute studies of leadership are typically conducted in organizations where leadership is not a neutral phenomenon, given the manifold effects of leadership on real-world outcomes. For example, most organizations seek to train central aspects of leadership, and most organizations have explicit and implicit policies in place intended to improve employee and thus, presumably, follower satisfaction. These contextual influences, accordingly, represent potential confounds that must be measured and controlled for in attribute studies examining leader development and follower motivation. Clearly, these confounds need to be specified and measured before strong conclusions can be drawn with respect to the effects of either individual or situational attributes on leader emergence and performance.

The third concern likely to arise in most attribute studies pertains to the boundary conditions under which individual or situational variables exert their effects on leader emergence and performance. Although leadership research is typically framed in terms of general effects, a variety of contextual variables operate that make it possible to observe certain effects, both with regard to those attributes influencing leadership and the effects of leadership on the criterion of interest. For example, the level of leadership under consideration is known to influence the skills that leaders must posses (Mumford et al., 2000), the amount of discretion leaders have in selecting their behavior (Finkelstein, 2003), and the appropriateness of applying organizational performance criteria (Jaques, 1976). Similarly, the setting in which leadership occurs, either business or nonprofit, may have significant effects on the relevance of both predictors and criteria.

The first, and most obvious, implication of these observations is that in conducting studies of leader attributes, and to some extent survey based studies of leader behavior, the conditions of the study must be clearly described and the limitations these conditions place on the generality of conclusions to be drawn noted. More centrally, however, development and testing of theories with regard to leadership often requires specifying the boundary conditions under which attributes influencing leader behavior will operate.

Experimental studies

Survey and attribute studies are typically 'real-world' studies. Research along these lines has, in fact, been the single most common approach applied by those of us interested in leadership. Nonetheless, growing recognition of the aforementioned problems has led many investigations to begin to question the field's reliance on these methods. Moreover, some aspects of leadership, for example, leader thought processes or leader decision-making, are quite often not amenable to 'real-world' investigation. These two concerns have given rise to a renewed interest in experimentally based studies of leadership. Two recent studies illustrate the potential value of experimental studies to the field of leadership.

Strange and Mumford (2005) were interested in the cognitive variables giving rise to the development of a leader's vision. Specifically, they argued that leaders' reflection on case events in relation to descriptive mental models, coupled with self-reflection on personal experience, gives rise to the formation of a prescriptive mental model which is the basis for vision formation. Notably, however, Strange and Mumford (2005) argued that reflection and analysis giving rise to visions might consider either key causes embedded in case events or key goals embedded in these events.

To test this model, Strange and Mumford (2005) asked undergraduates to assume the role of principal of a new experimental school. They were to prepare a speech to be delivered to students, parents, and teachers describing their vision for the school. Prior to preparing the vision statement, statements that were evaluated by actual students, parents, and teachers, these undergraduates were (1) exposed to strong and weak models through a consultant's report, (2) were then asked to think about their own past experiences, and (3) analyze either causes or goals. The vision statements that they produced were then rated by expert judges.

Another recent experimental study by Bono and Ilies (2006) was concerned with affect rather than cognition. More specifically, they argued that leader charisma would contribute to the expression of positive emotions by the leader. Leaders' expression of positive emotions would, in turn, influence follower mood, attraction to the leader and behavior outcomes. A series of experimental studies involving graduate students were conducted. In the first experiment, it was shown that a behavioral measure of charisma was related to expression of positive emotions in vision statements. In the second study, raters watched speeches given by leaders and evaluated positive emotions, effectiveness, and attractiveness, along with charisma. In the third study, again based on video tapes, follower moods before and after emotional or nonemotional statements by leaders were assessed.

Not only do these studies tell us something about charismatic leaders, but they also tell us something about the characteristics of well designed experimental studies. First, and foremost, viable experimental studies in the area of leadership typically employ low fidelity stimulation tasks (Hunt et al., 1999). In the case of the Strange and Mumford (2005) study, this was the formation of a school vision, while in the case of Bono and Ilies (2006) it involved videotapes of leader speeches. What should be recognized here, however, is that the low fidelity simulations do not seek to replicate leader performance. Instead, they seek to create conditions that simulate a *select* aspect of leader performance of theoretical concern.

Second, these studies illustrate the importance of theory in the design and conduct of viable experiments. Theory is, as noted in the preceding section, used to isolate those aspects of leadership of particular interest. However, in well designed experimental studies, theory serves another critical role. More specifically, it identifies the specific variables to be manipulated. What is of note in this regard, however, is that a well designed experiment's manipulations occur in a 'naturalistic' flow. As a result, order effects with regard to manipulations are typically not of overwhelming concern.

Third, viable experiments must be appropriate to the population at hand. Thus, in the Strange and Mumford (2005) study, a high school curriculum design task was used, in part, because undergraduates had experience to reflect on, and, in part, because undergraduates had the requisite background knowledge. Other tasks that might be used include group project tasks (Marta et al., 2005), consulting scenarios (DeCremer, 2006), and assessment center exercises (Kellet al., 2006). Although

a variety of tasks can be used in experimental studies, the relevance and realism of the task to the target population must be a critical concern if viable information is to be obtained with respect to leadership.

Even bearing these key characteristics of viable experimental studies in mind, a number of issues are likely to arise in application of this technique. Of course, the traditional criticism of experimental methods has been the fact that experiments, at least as classically conceived, examined only variables subject to manipulation. This criticism, however, has become less significant with the more widespread application of mixed design – designs examining the interactions between select individual differences variables and situational manipulations (DeCremer, 2006). A more telling criticism, however, arises from the limitations placed on 'real-world' complexity in experiments. Experiments necessarily examine only a few manipulations, or individual variables, in a limited context. As a result, generalizability to real-world effects is necessarily limited.

Accordingly, in experiments generalization is, more often than not, driven by the theoretical model under consideration. An important, albeit often overlooked, aspect of experimental studies is the strength of the argument that can be made for the theory being proposed. Of course, the strength of these arguments depends in part on the controls applied and the clarity of the variables being manipulated. However, in the interpretation of experiments, the strength of the conclusions that may be drawn often depends on the *pattern* of the interactions observed vis-à-vis extant theory. Unfortunately, in many experimental studies, the manipulations being examined are not those that will produce theoretically meaningful interactions, thus limiting confidence in the model and, hence, potential generalizability.

Another set of concerns with regard to experiments pertains to characteristics of the experimental method. In this regard, two key characteristics of any experimental study must be borne in mind. First, the level of leadership phenomena that can be studied using experimental methods is inherently limited to individual, dyadic, or group phenomena. Organizational and environmental phenomena are simply not amenable to experimentation. Second, experiments are necessarily short term events. Thus, long-term emergent phenomena, or developmental phenomena, are typically not readily amenable to experimental investigation in the study of leadership.

Qualitative studies

Survey, attribute, and experimental studies are all inherently quantitative in nature. In recent years, however, one of the more important trends to emerge in studies of leadership has been the more widespread application of qualitative methods (Bryman, 2004). There are, in fact, a number of aspects of qualitative methods that make this approach attractive in studies of leadership. First, qualitative methods, at least in principle, allow for studies of leadership *in situ*. These context based studies, of course, allow for the assessment of multiple influences, which operate at different levels (e.g., individual, dyadic, group, and organizational), on leader behavior and performance. Second, qualitative studies permit examination of how leaders weigh and respond to different variables in a real-world context where effects emerge over time. Third, qualitative studies allow for the examination of exceptional cases of leader behavior and performance – exceptional cases that may prove of unique value for theory development.

One example of the application of qualitative methods may be found in a recent study by Cha and Edmondson (2006). In this study, the concern at hand was the negative consequences of charismatic leadership. More specifically, they argued that strong organizational values may, through follower sensemaking, result in a hypocrisy attribution, which acts to undermine the influence exerted by charismatic leaders. To test this hypothesis, in-depth interviews and extensive observations were conducted in a small advertising firm directed by a charismatic chief executive officer (CEO). Multiple visits to the organization were conducted where interviews and observational data were collected in two phases. In phase one, general observations concerning the organization were collected. In phase two, interviews and observations focused on the maintenance of employee commitment and creativity. These data were then content coded with respect to sent values, expanded values, and hypocrisy attributions.

Another example of the application of qualitative methods may be found in a study by Boje and Rhodes (2006) that was concerned with the use of corporate advertising as a 'substitute' for leadership. In this study the concern at hand was McDonald's development of the concept of Ronald McDonald. Corporate records were used to trace the development of the concept of Ronald McDonald as a corporate symbol. Notably, the conclusions reached in this study indicated that Ronald McDonald emerged as a symbol of post-transformational leadership after the company's founder, Ray Kroc, had left the organization.

These studies, of course, are partly of interest because they illustrate the diversity of qualitative studies of leadership. They are also of interest, because they point to the characteristics of successful qualitative studies from both a substantive and a methodological perspective. Both Cha and Edmondson (2006) and the Boje and Rhodes (2006) studies point to one of the great strengths of qualitative studies. Qualitative research, when well conducted, serves an important role in the study of leadership by providing a grounded basis for the development of new theoretical concepts – in the case of Cha and Edmondson (2006) the role of hypocrisy, and, in the case of Boje and Rhodes (2006) the use of corporate symbols as a substitute for leaders in defining and communicating integrative beliefs and values. Not only do qualitative studies provide a basis for theory development, but these efforts also illustrate another unique strength of qualitative studies. More specifically, as noted earlier, they allow for the integration of phenomena operating at multiple levels. Thus, in the Cha and Edmondson (2006) study, organizational level variables in combination with dyadic, or group, level leadership behavior are seen as giving rise to individual-level follower behaviors.

Finally, as illustrated in the Boje and Rhodes (2006) study, the examination of unusual, salient, events – in the case of this study Ronald McDonald – may reveal important, albeit overlooked, aspects of leadership. This use of unusual, salient events as a basis for theory development, however, raises a question. How generalizable are these events to more routine forms of leadership? This observation, of course, brings to the fore a key aspect of well designed qualitative studies focusing on extreme events. Such studies are most likely to prove useful if they illustrate a particular phenomenon that might occur in less extreme forms or if they are intended to illustrate exceptions to general rules and the conditions giving rise to these exceptions (Maslin-Wicks, in press).

These observations about extreme cases, however, point to a key characteristic of well done qualitative studies. More specifically, successful qualitative studies do not represent blind, open-ended, observations. Instead, they are theoretically driven, with theory providing both a basis for generalization and selection of the particular set of observations being examined (Mumford and Van Doorn, 2001). This structuring of observations is of concern in qualitative studies because of the wide array of information that is available and the number of different lenses that might be applied in attempts to understand these observations. Accordingly, clarity with regard to theory and the particular observations (e.g., interview questions and historic documents) used to test this theory is of particular concern in qualitative studies.

Along related lines, observations obtained in qualitative studies must be interpreted. Interpretation of observations in terms of an underlying set of constructs can occur through either explicit or implicit content coding schemes. What is of note in this regard is that the strength of the inferences that may be derived from qualitative studies increases when explicit procedures for coding observations are applied. This evidence becomes substantially more compelling when multiple judges are used in this content analysis and evidence bearing on agreement of these judges is provided. Alternatively, studies might employ qualitative analysis programs. Although application of qualitative analysis software is potentially useful, application of these procedures requires evidence bearing on both the validity of 'search terms' applied and the reliability of conclusions flowing from application of these 'search terms.'

Often, but not always (Mumford and Van Doorn, 2001), qualitative studies occur with respect to a single case event with multiple informants being asked to provide information with regard to this event. As a result, when describing qualitative studies, the context of the case is important as it can result in limitations on the generalizability of the conclusions that may be drawn. Unfortunately, in many qualitative studies, those aspects of the case context that set noteworthy limitations on the generalizability of the conclusions that may be drawn are not expressly articulated. Failure to recognize unique limiting conditions, of course, undermines the strength of the conclusions that may be drawn from qualitative studies.

Along related lines, many qualitative studies are based on a single case event. Clearly, examination of a single case event limits the potential generalizability of conclusions. In well designed qualitative studies, this issue is addressed through theory, with theory providing the basis for generalization, or through the examination of multiple cases, with cross-case replication providing a basis for generalization. In fact, use of multiple informants serves to provide this generalizability data in many qualitative studies. However, qualitative studies often fail, because they do not explicitly consider the generalizability of the conclusions flowing from the study design.

A final limitation evident in qualitative studies concerns the nature of the criteria, or outcomes, of interest. One of the great strengths of qualitative studies is that they permit the examination of multiple criteria, or outcomes, of leadership, and they permit examination of interactions among outcomes over time and across levels of analysis. Although the examination of multiple outcomes unfolding over time is of great potential value in studies of leadership, qualitative studies often do not explicitly define the criteria of interest and fail to examine these outcomes over time. Without explicit definitions of criteria, or outcomes of interest, the value of qualitative studies to leadership research, in fact, is limited.

There are several additional qualitative approaches that have been taken towards the study of leadership that present their own potential contributions. As previously mentioned, one limitation of qualitative research is the focus on single events, which results in a lack of evaluation of outcomes across time. A narrative approach to the study of leadership is one methodology that may avoid this limitation. Detailed leader narratives are a means by which the sequential relationship of causes, critical events, and ultimate consequences can be evaluated, in addition to providing the richness of information with regard to the social context (Court, 2004).

A second qualitative approach emerging in leadership research is the use of discourse analysis – the assumption that aspects of reality are embedded within the specific language of the account (Alvesson and Kärreman, 2000; Alvesson, 1996). This assumption has multilevel implications, because the analysis of the discourse can be conducted with regard to the individual (the leader), the institution, and the environmental context. More specifically, the words used to describe a particular event are indicative of both the leader, him or herself, and, in addition, can be used to understand the social context of the institution. As interest in a more integrative approach to leadership research grows, a qualitative approach such as this, which contains multilevel information, may prove quite valuable (Yukl, 2002).

Historiometric studies

Leadership differs from many other phenomena of interest to students of organizational behavior with regard to available historic information. In other words, leaders leave a track record. This record may be reflected in archival data (Rowe et al., 2005), speeches given by the leader (Fiol et al., 1999), historical biographical material (Strange and Mumford, 2002), or leader autobiographies (Welch, 2001). These sources, of course, open up the possibility of historiometric studies.

Historiometric studies represent an attempt to quantify historic observations on historic data bearing on leadership behavior and performance (Simonton, 1991). Traditionally, historiometric studies have not played a large role in leadership research primarily as a result of three key considerations. First, historic records are selective and do not consider all aspects of leader behavior and performance. Second, the selective nature of historic records implies that filtering has occurred. This filtering, in turn, brings into question whether the material included in these documents accurately reflects the behavior and performance of the leader or the archivist's *beliefs* about the leader behavior and performance. Third, archival records are typically available only from select types of leaders – typically historically, or organizationally, notable leaders.

Although these limitations in historic data are widely recognized, in recent years, with the growth of interest in outstanding leadership, historiometric studies have begun to receive more attention. For example, in one study along these lines, Mumford (2006) was interested in contrasting the behaviors and performance of outstanding charismatic, ideological, and pragmatic leaders. He obtained academic biographies of 120 leaders falling into one of these types where biographies were screened for historic accuracy. Subsequently, select sections of these biographies examining developmental influences as well as performance, problem-solving behavior, leader-follower interactions, political behavior, and communication strategies were identified.

Judges were then asked to rate the extent to which these passages reflected a given construct of interest. The effects found in these studies held even when multiple controls, such as the time when the biography was written or the theoretical perspective of the author, were taken into account.

While some historiometric studies contrast different leaders, other historiometric studies examine the behavior or performance of a single leader. For example, Bligh and Hess (in press) examined the content of addresses given by Alan Greenspan during his tenure as chairman of the Federal Reserve. These speeches were analyzed using content analysis software with respect to noteworthy economic events. Other studies, for example Fiol et al. (1999), have also examined leader speeches. In this study, the use of specific words (e.g., 'we') was applied to examine leader sensemaking and sensebreaking.

These studies illustrate the potential value of historiometric research. They also serve to illustrate certain key characteristics of successful historiometric studies. Viable historiometric studies are ultimately contingent on the quality of the historiometric data being examined. In some cases, this is accomplished through the use of first hand leader products – as illustrated in studies based on speeches (e.g., Bligh and Hess, in press). In other cases, for example the Mumford (2006) study, historiometric studies may be based on secondary sources – albeit secondary sources of known validity. In fact, frequently, these secondary sources prove especially attractive due to the richness of the information provided.

Historic studies, like qualitative studies, moreover, typically provide an unusually rich body of evidence about leader behavior and the context in which this behavior emerged. The richness of historical data, however, leads to a key requirement imposed on historiometric studies. More specifically, these studies are based on the development of viable measures for assessing behaviors of interest *within* the context of the documents being worked with. Thus, one might analyze speeches for the presence and timing of certain words, or, alternatively, one might analyze the early chapters of biographies for evidence of the frequency of exposure to certain types of life events, such as anchoring or contaminating events, as illustrated in Ligon et al. (in press). What is critical in this regard is not content per se but rather the reliability and validity of the coding scheme being used to provide measures of this content.

With regard to measurement, however, it is important to bear in mind a unique characteristic of historiometric studies. More specifically, measures applied in these studies are typically source specific. Thus, the measures of sensemaking applied in studies of biographies will differ from the measures of sensemaking applied in studies of leader speeches. This nonequivalence of measures, while necessary in content analysis of material drawn from qualitatively different sources, opens up questions with regard to measure equivalence and places a premium on demonstration of reliability and validity of the particular measures being applied.

The importance of development of viable measures applying to a particular type of source document, however necessary, does not directly address the critical question arising in virtually all historiometric investigations. Here, we refer to the issue as to what comparisons are to be made to draw inferences about leadership. In virtually all historiometric studies, the people of interest are leaders. Thus, historiometric studies have little to say about what makes someone a leader. Instead, historiometric studies seek to answer questions about changes in leader behavior or performance with respect to: (1) differences among different types of leaders (Mumford, 2006), (2) differences among leaders operating in different contexts or settings (Mumford et al., 2003), or (3) changes in leader behavior as a function of time or changes in context (Bligh and Hess, in press). What is of note is that the value of historiometric studies depends on the systematic sampling of both comparison groups as well as the target group of interest (Simonton, 1991).

These observations about comparison groups point to one of the more significant limitations of historiometric studies. His-toriometric studies are most useful for examining conditions giving rise to vari-ation in leader behavior or performance. Historiometric studies, however, have less to say about leadership per se—statements that require a comparison of leaders to nonleaders. Another limitation of historiometric studies concerns the nature of the material available for study. Although it does not hold in the case of close followers (Strange, 2004), historiometric data typically focuses on the leader, his or her behavior, or performance. Thus, historiometric data may tell us about the influence tactics used by a leader and the outcomes of these tactics. It will not, however, typically, have much to say about followers' reactions to these tactics. Thus, historiometric data will not have much value for studies concerned with relationships.

Although this limitation is endemic to his-toriometric data, it often evidences two advan-tageous characteristics. First, multiple criteria or outcomes are available for most historically notable leaders. Second, historiometric data is available over time. The temporal, multiple outcome aspect of historiometric data allows these studies to examine the origins and development of leader behavior and leader performance. Although these studies allow examination of developmental effects with respect to multiple criteria, it is open to question whether historiometric studies have commonly been designed to allow effective capitalization on this unique characteristic of historic data.

CONCLUSIONS

We have not, in the present effort, sought to examine every method that might be employed in studies of leadership. For example, we have provided no description of in-depth psychoanalytic procedures (Bartone et al., in press). Little has been said about designs for evaluating leadership develop-ment interventions (McCauley and Hughes-James, 1994). And we have not here sought to examine cross-cultural research on leadership

(e.g., Resick et al., 2006). Instead, in this chapter, we have examined the methods being applied in the major types of studies, behav-ioral, attribute, experimental, qualitative, and historiometric, currently being applied in attempts to understand leadership.

Moreover, it should be noted that we have not attempted to provide a detailed methodological review of each of these techniques. For example, we did not address observer training (Kazdin, 1982) or measure-ment and modeling issues (Scherbaum et al., 2006). However, we have not provided an in-depth examination of this topic. Rather, in this effort we have focused on those methodological issues of greatest relevance to drawing inferences about leadership.

Along related lines, we have not delved deeply into general leadership research issues or debates that have great methodological implications. Briefly, there are several points of contention with regard to the study of leadership that may impact methodological directions. These debates include, but are not limited to, whether there is a difference between management and leadership, whether leadership can be distributed, what the appropriate level of study is for leadership research, and finally, whether it is important to consider the 'dark side' of leadership.

With regard to the debate whether lead-ership and management are distinct, the discussion has revolved around both dif-ferences in processes and behaviors of leadership versus management (Fairholm, 2004; Kotter, 1990) and differences in the individual characteristics of leaders versus managers (Ackerman, 1985; Zaleznik, 1993). For instance, Kotter (1990) outlined the differences in the processes of managers and leaders and the ultimate outcomes they seek to accomplish. If this is the case, the differing goals of these two groups must be taken into account when determining what sample would be appropriate for a given research question, and in experimental studies, what variables should be manipulated. It is clear that more research needs to be conducted to determine if managers and leaders are, in fact, different (Bedeian and Hunt, 2006).

At this point it may be advisable to approach leadership broadly as to be able to provide information for both groups (Yukl, 1989).

A second area in which debate has methodological implications is whether leadership can be distributed amongst two or more individuals and, if so, if that still constitutes leadership. The essence of this debate is who is, in fact, the focus of leadership studies. The traditional approach to leadership research focuses on a central leader who influences subordinates. Recent efforts have argued that leadership is more than just this top-down influence, but is rather an influence process among individuals that can be bottom-up or lateral as well as top-down (Pearce and Conger, 2003). The presence of leadership influences other than a central leader may warrant more controls in studies of centralized leadership. The greater methodological impact, however, would be a necessary shift in the level of study. Studies of distributed leadership would require group level interactions whereas studies of centralized leadership can be conducted at the individual level (Avolio et al., 2003). Along related lines, there is also debate as to what level of leadership researchers should be studying.

Most researchers would agree that leadership does not exist in a vacuum (Yukl, 2002), however, there is no clear consensus as to what levels of influences and processes are most critical to understanding leadership. Matching the level of analysis to the level of conclusions being drawn is critical. For instance, group level conclusions could not be directly drawn based on surveys of individuals, it would be necessary to employ multilevel analyses (Dansereau and Yammarino, 2006).

Finally, a more recent trend in the leadership research is in the direction of the 'dark side' of leadership. Many leadership scholars recognize a long standing 'heroic' bias towards which leaders are studied, what characteristics lead to successful leadership and the development of successful leaders (Alimo-Metcalfe and Alban-Metcalfe, 2005; Conger, 1997; Luthans et al., 1998; Manz and Sims, 1991). In light of recent instances of CEO corruption (e.g., Enron and WorldCom), there is greater debate over the value in understanding the environments in which harmful leaders emerge, what leader characteristics these leaders share and the conditions under which leader errors may occur, not to mention the resulting impact on subordinates. Although potentially all of the methodologies discussed in the current work could be applied to the study of 'bad' leaders, the criterion of interest would greatly influence the viability of approaches. For instance, it is more likely that a leader's failure would be manifested at the group or organizational levels and therefore need to be measured as such. Historiometric studies may prove particularly useful in studying leader failure, because judgments of failure rely on historical information. With regard to conducting research on leader errors, it would first be necessary to determine what the 'correct' processes are, or the processes and behaviors that result in desired outcomes. Therefore, studies of errors would either need to be strongly tied to prior research on desirable outcomes with regard to leadership, or involve multistudy designs. These debates, and their resulting methodological implications, demonstrate the necessity for an adaptive field of leadership research built on multiple methodologies.

Bearing these caveats in mind, we believe that the present effort leads to some noteworthy conclusions about the nature of leadership research. Perhaps the first and most important conclusion that may be drawn in this regard is that leadership research has changed from a field dominated by survey studies of leader behavior (Yukl, 2002) to a multimethod field. In fact, the widespread application of multimethod approaches in the study of leadership has represented one of the most important advances in recent years, resulting in a more compelling description of the complex phenomenon of leadership.

The widespread acceptance of this multimethod framework has, itself, begun to influence the design of leadership studies. For example, Tsui, Zhang, Wang, Xin, and Wu (2006) applied a multimethod framework in examining the relationship between leadership and organizational culture. In this study, both behavioral surveys and qualitative methods were applied, resulting in a stronger understanding of how leaders work within and change cultures. In another study, applying this multimethod approach, Sosik et al. (1999) conducted experimental studies of transformational leadership behavior – demonstrating that transformational behaviors influence team performance in an 'online' work environment. This multimethod approach has, in fact, resulted in a stronger body of evidence with regard to the generality of findings and the strength of resulting theoretical conclusions.

Not only does the present review tell us something about the importance of a multimethod approach in studies of leadership, but it also tells us something about when and how these approaches should be applied. For example, experimental methods are simply not likely to provide value in areas that lack adequate theory development. Clearly, without strong underlying theory, it is too difficult to construct the kind of low-fidelity simulations that provide the basis for much of this research. When theory is available, however, experimental studies have proven of great value. Survey studies may be useful for examining normative leadership behaviors. However, historiometric studies are likely to prove more useful in examining phenomena of interest for truly outstanding leaders. Attribute studies, both trait and situational studies, play a key role in identifying the variables giving rise to leader behavior and performance.

Although the present effort tells us something about the unique strengths of each of the major methodological techniques applied in studies of leadership, it also reminds us that certain issues, key issues, must be addressed to permit effective application of these techniques. For example, qualitative studies require strong theory to guide observation and coding. Attribute studies typically require control measures to rule out competing explanations. Survey studies must take into account considerations about both level of analysis and relevant boundary conditions.

Experimental studies must be applicable within the population being examined. Historiometric studies require careful specification of relevant comparison conditions or comparison groups. Clearly, the quality of leadership research will improve if investigators carefully attend to the unique requirements imposed by the method being applied.

Not only does the present effort point to some unique characteristics of each method in studies of leadership, but also, we believe, the present effort reminds us of certain key characteristics of any viable leadership study. First, viable leadership studies formulate a theory with regard to some distinct aspects of leader behavior or performance. They do not seek to describe a universal leader. Second, viable studies carefully specify the level at which this theory operates and conduct studies at the appropriate level. Third, the observations to be taken, or the measures to be applied, are carefully specified in relation to theory and level. Fourth, the right variables are measured and appropriate controls are applied.

These four 'rules' may come as no surprise to most scholars. However, in implementing these rules one must remember that the devil is in the details – details that must be evaluated with respect to the theory of concern and the method being applied. Hopefully, the present effort will provide the background needed by researchers as they begin to address these issues.

ACKNOWLEDGMENTS

We would like to thank Sam Hunter and Katrina Bedell-Avers for their contributions to the present effort. Correspondence should be addressed to Dr. Michael D. Mumford, Department of Psychology, The University of Oklahoma, 73019 or mmumford@ou.edu.

REFERENCES

Ackerman, L. (1985) 'Leadership vs. Managership', *Leadership and Organization Development Journal*, 6: 17–19.

Alimo-Metcalfe, B. and Alban-Metcalfe, J. (2005) 'Leadership: time for a new direction?', *Leadership*, 1: 51–71.

Alvesson, M. (1996) 'Leadership studies: from procedure and abstraction to reflexivity and situation', *The Leadership Quarterly*, 7: 455–85.

Alvesson, M. and Kärreman, D. (2000) 'Varieties of discourse: on the study of organizations through discourse analysis', *Human Relations*, 53: 1125–49.

Amabile, T.M., Schatzel, E.A., Moneta, G.B., Kramer, S.J. (2004) 'Leader behaviors and the work environment for creativity: perceived leader support', *The Leadership Quarterly*, 14: 5–32.

Arvey, R.D., Rotundo, M., Johnson, W., Zhang, Z., and McGue, M. (2006) 'The determinants of leadership: genetics and personality factors', *The Leadership Quarterly*, 17: 1–20.

Avolio, B.J. and Gardner, W.L. (2005) 'Authentic leadership development: Getting to the root of positive forms of leadership', *The Leadership Quarterly*, 16: 315–38.

Avolio, B.J., Sivasubramanian, N., Murry, W.D., Jung, D., and Garger, J.W. (2003) 'Assessing shared leadership: development and preliminary validation of a team multifactor leadership questionnaire', in Pearce, C.L., and Conger, J.A. (eds), *Shared Leadership: Reframing the How and Whys of Leadership*, Thousand Oaks, CA: Sage Publications.

Bartone, P.T., Snook, S.A., Forsythe, G.B., Lewis, P., and Bullis, R.C. (in press) 'Psychosocial development and leader performance of military officer cadets', *The Leadership Quarterly*.

Bass, B.M. (1990) *Bass and Stogdill's handbook of leadership: Theory, research, and managerial applications*, New York: Free Press.

Bass, B.M. (1997) 'Personal selling and transactional/transformational leadership', *Journal of Personal Selling & Sales Management*, 17: 19–28.

Bass, B.M. (In Press) *Handbook of Leadership*, New York: Free Press.

Bass, B.M. and Avolio, B.J. (1989) 'Potential biases in leadership measures: How prototypes, leniency, and general satisfaction related to ratings and rankings of transformational and transactional leadership constructs', *Educational and Psychological Measurement*, 49: 509–27.

Bass, B.M. and Avolio, B.J. (1998) *Manual for the Multifactor Leadership Questionnaire*, Redwood, CA: Mindgarden, Inc.

Bedeian, A.G. and Hunt, J.G. (2006) 'Academic amnesia and vestigial assumptions of our forefathers', *The Leadership Quarterly*, 17: 190–205.

Bligh, M. and Hess, G. (in press) 'The power of leading subtly: Alan Greenspan, rhetorical leadership, and monetary policy', *The Leadership Quarterly*.

Boje, D.M. and Rhodes, C. (2006) 'The leadership style of Ronald McDonald: double narrations and stylistic lines of transformation', *The Leadership Quarterly*, 17: 94–103.

Bono, J.E. and Ilies, R. (2006) 'Charisma, positive emotions and mood contagion', *The Leadership Quarterly*, 17: 317–34.

Brown, D.J. and Keeping, L.M. (2005) 'Elaborating the construct of transformational leadership: the role of affect', *The Leadership Quarterly*, 16: 245–72.

Bryman, A. (2004) 'Qualitative research on leadership: a critical by appreciative review', *The Leadership Quarterly*, 15: 729–69.

Calori, R., Johnson, G. and Sarnin, P. (1992) 'French and British top managers' understanding of the structure and the dynamics of their industries: A cognitive analysis and comparison', *British Journal of Management*, 3: 61–78.

Carmeli, A. and Schaubroeck, J. (2006) 'Top management team behavioral integration, decision quality, and organizational decline', *The Leadership Quarterly*, 17: 441–53.

Cha, S.E. and Edmondson, A.C. (2006) 'When values backfire: Leadership, attribution, and disenchantment in a values-driven organization', *The Leadership Quarterly*, 17: 57–78.

Conger, J.A. (1997) 'The dark side of leadership', in Vecchio, R.P. (ed.), *Leadership: Understanding the dynamics of power and influence in organizations*, Notre Dame, IN: University of Notre Dame Press.

Court, M. (2004) 'Using narratives and discourse analysis in researching co-principalships', *International Journal of Qualitative Studies in Education*, 17: 579–603.

Dansereau, F., Cashman, J. and Graen, G. (1973) 'Instrumentality theory and equity theory as complementary approaches in predicting the relationship of leadership and turnover among managers', *Organizational Behavior & Human Performance*, 12: 184–200.

Dansereau, F. and Yammarino, F. J. (1998) *The Multiple-level Approaches: Classical and New Wave*, Stamford, CT: Elsevier Science/JAI Press.

Dansereau, F. and Yammarino, F.J. (2006) 'Is more discussion about levels of analysis really necessary? When is such discussion sufficient?', *The Leadership Quarterly*, 17: 537–52.

De Cremer, D. (2006) 'When authorities influence follower's affect: the interaction effect of procedural justice and transformational leadership', *Journal of Work and Organizational Psychology*, 15: 322–51.

Drazin, R., Glynn, M.A. and Kazanjian, R.K. (1999) 'Multilevel theorizing about creativity in organizations: a sensemaking perspective', *Academy of Management Review*, 24: 286–307.

Fairholm, M.R. (2004) 'Different perspectives on the practice of leadership', *Public Administration Review*, 64: 577–90.

Finkelstein, S. (2003) *Why Smart Executives Fail and What You Can Learn From Their Mistakes*. New York: Portfolio.

Fiol, C.M., Harris, D. and House, R.J. (1999) 'Charismatic leadership: strategies for effecting social change', *The Leadership Quarterly*, 10: 449–82.

Fleishman, E.A. (1951) *Leadership Climate and Supervisory Behavior*, Columbus, OH: Personnel Research Board, Ohio State University.

Fleishman, E.A. (1953b) 'The description of supervisory behavior', *Journal of Applied Psychology*, 37: 1–6.

Fleishman, E.A. and Harris, E.F. (1962) 'Patterns of leadership behavior related to employee grievances and turnover', *Personnel Psychology*, 15: 43–56.

Fry, L.W. (2005) 'Editorial: introduction to *The Leadership Quarterly* special issue: toward a paradigm of spiritual leadership', *The Leadership Quarterly*, 16: 619–22.

Graen, G.B. and Uhl-Bien, M. (1998) 'Relationship-based approach to leadership: development of leader-member exchange (LMX) theory of leadership over 25 years: applying a multi-level multi-domain perspective', in Dansereau, F. and Yammarino, F. J. (eds), *Leadership: The Multiple-level Approaches: Contemporary and Alternative*, Stamford, CT: Elsevier Science/JAI Press, pp.103–55.

Howard, A. and Bray, D.W. (1988) *Managerial Lives in Transition: Advancing Age and Changing Times*, New York: Guilford Press.

Howell, J.M. and Boies, K. (2004) 'Champions of technological innovation: the influences of contextual knowledge, role orientation, idea generation, and idea promotion on champion emergence', *The Leadership Quarterly*, 15: 130–49.

Hunt, J.G., Boal, K.B. and Dodge, G.E. (1999) 'The effects of visionary and crisis- responsive charisma on followers: an experimental examination of two kinds of charismatic leadership', *The Leadership Quarterly*, 10: 423–48.

Jacques, E. (1976) *A General Theory of Bureaucracy*. London: Heinemann.

Kacmar, M., Zivnuska, S. and White, C.D. (in press) 'Control and exchange: The impact of work environment on the work effort of low relationship quality employees', *The Leadership Quarterly*.

Kazdin, A.E. (1982) *Single-case Research Designs: Methods for Clinical and Applied Settings*, New York: Oxford University Press.

Kellet, J.B., Humphrey, R.H. and Sleeth, R.G. (2006) 'Empathy and the emergence of task and relations leaders', *The Leadership Quarterly*, 17: 146–62.

Kernberg, O.F. (1984) 'The couch at sea: psychoanalytic studies of group and organizational leadership', *International Journal of Group Psychotherapy*, 34: 5–23.

Klein, K.J. and House, R.J. (1998) 'On fire: charismatic leadership and levels of analysis', In Lord, R.G. & Hall, R.J. (2005), Identity, deep structure and the development of leadership skill, *The Leadership Quarterly*, 16: 591–615.

Kotter, J.P. (1990) *A Force for Change: How Leadership Differs from Management*, USA: Free Press.

Ligon, G.S., Hunter, S.T. and Mumford, M.D. (in press) 'Development of outstanding leadership: A life narrative approach', *The Leadership Quarterly*.

Lord, R.G. and Hall, R.J. (2005) 'Identity, deep structure and the development of leadership skill', *The Leadership Quarterly*, 16: 591–615.

Luthans, F., Peterson, S.J., Ibrayeva, E. (1998) 'The potential for the "dark side" of leadership in post-communist countries', *Journal of World Business*, 33: 185–201.

Manz, C.C., and Sims, H.P. (1991) 'SuperLeadership: beyond the myth of heroic leadership', *Organizational Dynamics*, 19: 18–35.

Marta, S., Leritz, L.E. and Mumford, M.D. (2005) 'Leadership skills and the group performance: situational demands, behavioral requirements, and planning', *The Leadership Quarterly*, 16: 591–615.

Maslin-Wicks, K. (in press) 'Forsaking transformational leadership: Roscoe Conkling, the Great Senator from New York', *The Leadership Quarterly*.

McCauley, C.D. and Hughes-James, M.W. (1994) *An Evaluation of the Outcomes of a Leadership Development Program*, Greensboro, NC: Center for Creative Leadership.

McCauley, C.D., Ruderman, M.N., Ohlott, P.J. and Morrow, J.E. (1994) 'Assessing the developmental components of managerial jobs', *Journal of Applied Psychology*, 79: 544–60.

Mehra, A., Smith, B.R., Dixon, A.L. and Robertson, B. (2006) 'Distributed leadership in teams: the network of leadership perceptions and team performance', *The Leadership Quarterly*, 17: 232–45.

Mumford, M.D. (2006) *Pathways to Outstanding Leadership; A Comparative Analysis of Charismatic, Ideological, and Pragmatic Leadership*, Mahwah, NJ: Erlbaum.

Mumford, M.D., Connelly, S. and Gaddis, B. (2003) 'How creative leaders think: experimental findings and cases', *The Leadership Quarterly*, 14: 411–32.

Mumford, M.D., Friedrich, T.L., Caughron, J.J. and Antes, A. (in press) 'Leadership training and assessment: rethinking the state of the art', in K.A. Ericsson (ed.), *The Development of Professional Performance*.

Mumford, M.D., Marks, M.A., Connelly, M.S., Zaccaro, S.J. and Reiter-Palmon, R. (2000) 'Development of leadership skills: Experience and timing', *The Leadership Quarterly*, 11: 87–114.

Mumford, M.D. and Van Doorn, J.R. (2001) 'The leadership of pragmatism: Reconsidering Franklin in the age of charisma', *The Leadership Quarterly*, 12: 274–309.

Paunonen, S.V., Lönnqvist, J., Verkasalo, M., Leikas, S. and Nissinen, V. (2006) 'Narcissism and emergent leadership in military cadets', *The Leadership Quarterly*, 17: 475–86.

Pearce, C.L. and Conger, J.A. (2003) *Shared Leadership: Reframing the How and Whys of Leadership*, Thousand Oaks, CA: Sage Publications.

Podsakoff, P.M., MacKenzie, S.B., Lee, J. and Podsakoff, N.P. (2003) 'Common method biases in behavioral research: a critical review of the literature and recommended remedies', *Journal of Applied Psychology*, 88: 879–903.

Resick, C.J., Hanges, P.J., Dickson, M.W. and Mitchelson, J.K. (2006) 'A cross-cultural examination of the endorsement of ethical leadership', *Journal of Business Ethics*, 63: 345–59.

Rowe, W.G., Cannella, A.A., Rankin, D., and Gorman, D. (2005) 'Leader succession and organizational performance: integrating the common-sense, ritual scapegoating, and vicious-circle succession theories', *The Leadership Quarterly*, 16: 197–219.

Schriesheim, C.A., Castro, S.L., Zhou, X., and DeChurch, L.A. (2006) 'An investigation of path-goal and transformational leadership theory predictions at the individual level of analysis', *The Leadership Quarterly*, 17: 21–38.

Scherbaum, C.A., Finlinson, S., Barden, K. and Tamanini, K. (2006) 'Applications of item response theory to measurement issues in leadership research', *The Leadership Quarterly*, 17: 366–86.

Simonton, D.K. (1991) 'Personality correlates of exceptional personal influence: a note on Thorndike's (1950) creators and leaders', *Creativity Research Journal*, 4: 67–78.

Sosik, J.J. (2005) 'The role of personal values in the charismatic leadership of corporate managers: a model and preliminary field study', *The Leadership Quarterly*, 16: 221–44.

Sosik, J.J., Kahai, S.S. and Avolio, B.J. (1999) 'Leadership style, anonymity, and creativity in group decision support systems: the mediating role of optimal flow', *Journal of Creative Behavior*, 33: 227–56.

Strange, J.M. (2004) 'Exceptional leaders and their followers: an in-depth look at leader-follower interactions', *Dissertation Abstracts International*, 65 (1-B): 470. (UMI No.AAT 3120032).

Strange, J.M. and Mumford, M.D. (2002) 'The origins of vision: Charismatic versus ideological leadership', *The Leadership Quarterly*, 13: 343–77.

Strange, J.M. and Mumford, M.D. (2005) 'The origins of vision: Effects of reflection, models and analysis', *The Leadership Quarterly*, 16: 121–48.

Tsui, A.S., Zhang, Z., Wang, H., Xin, K.R. and Wu, J.B. (2006) 'Unpacking the relationship between CEO leadership behavior and organizational culture', *The Leadership Quarterly*, 17: 113–37.

Vroom, V.H. and Jago, A.G. (1988) 'Managing participation: a critical dimension of leadership', *Management Learning*, 36: 299–316.

Wayne, S.J., Liden, R.C. and Sparrowe, R.T. (1994) 'Developing leader-member exchanges: the influence of gender on ingratiation', *American Behavioral Scientist*, 37: 697–714.

Welch, J. (2001) *Jack: Straight From the Gut*, New York: Warner Business Books.

Yukl, G. (1989) 'Managerial leadership: a review of theory and research', *Journal of Management*, 15: 251–89.

Yukl, G. (2002) *Leadership in organizations*, Upper Saddle River, NJ: Prentice- Hall.

Zaleznik, A. (1993) 'Managers and leaders: are they different?', in Rosenbach, W.E. and Taylor, R.L. (eds) *Contemporary Issues in Leadership*, Boulder, Colorado: Westview Press.

8

Endless Crossroads: Debates, Deliberations and Disagreements on Studying Organizational Culture

Pushkala Prasad and Anshuman Prasad

INTRODUCTION

Organizational culture's popularity within the field of management has been closely marked by intense controversy over how to study it. Culture's swift ascendancy as a central concept in organization theory has been accompanied by serious questions relating to methodological choices and conceptual clarifications over its nature and role in economic institutions (Martin and Frost, 1996). One can easily argue that students of organizational culture have faced an endless series of crossroads offering diverse possibilities for theorizing organizational culture and empirically examining it.

Almost two decades after the emergence of organizational culture as a key concept in management studies, this chapter revisits these conceptual and methodological crossroads and offers further deliberations on studying it. We find this to be a fitting moment for this exercise for several reasons. First, *organizational* culture has demonstrated a remarkable staying power and now occupies a taken-for-granted place within the landscape of organization studies. Discussions of workplaces, corporations, and institutions routinely refer to their cultural attributes and practices and their significance for organizational capabilities and functioning. Organizational culture is thus so ingrained in our everyday consciousness that we may be in danger of treating it as self-evident and unproblematic. This chapter renews our awareness of the complexities inherent in conceptualizing and examining organizational culture.

Second, the intense heat generated by the early organizational culture debates has largely died down. Hence, revisiting contested epistemological and methodological considerations in a cooler intellectual climate may well yield fruitful insights that can usefully be applied to current understandings of organizational culture. And finally, earlier formulations of organizational culture took place in an epoch that could arguably be characterized as less globalized – when national boundaries were relatively impermeable and when local organizational boundaries had far more immediate meaning (Gelinas, 2003). Globalization has undoubtedly changed the nature of economic institutions by infusing them with more transnational populations and influences. Our approaches to understanding organizational culture, therefore, need to change in order to mirror these wider structural transformations. This chapter accordingly revisits many of the epistemological, ontological, and methodological crossroads that have faced researchers of organizational culture and reflects on them in terms of today's globalized world.

Organizational culture at the crossroads: a brief overview

The organizational culture phenomenon in management studies is commonly viewed as being a by-product of the Japanese economic miracle that took the Western world by surprise in the 1970s. A major emerging assumption of the times centred around the idea that Japanese national culture was a source of successful alternative approaches to interacting with people and resources in economic enterprises, and therefore, *management* itself was subject to cultural influences (Adler and Jelinek, 1986). While the initial interest of management researchers was in *national* cultures, this very quickly transformed into an interest in *organizational* culture (Morgan, 1986), particularly through the work of Peters and Waterman (1982). If nations were cultural entities, it followed that organizations would have to be so too. This assumption triggered a wave of studies that tested and examined organizational cultures, and theorized relationships between organizational culture and a multitude of organizational dimensions, including effectiveness, performance, leadership and so on (Denison, 1990; Schein, 1985).

While the first wave of studies approached organizational culture somewhat simplistically, it swiftly became apparent that culture was a far more complex and elusive phenomenon than had been initially surmised. From the early eighties, questions and debates about organizational culture turned into relatively heated intellectual contestations that Martin and Frost (1994) describe as academic 'war games'. These war games were played around a number of crossroads that offered researchers diverse options around formulations and examinations of organizational culture. This section provides a brief overview of some of these crossroad positions.

The crossroads of methods

One of the most visible crossroads centres around the choice of data collection methods for studying organization culture. The principal choice being made here is between quantitative and qualitative methods, with some combination of mixed methods being a third option. Quantitative methods mostly involve the use of large-scale surveys of employee attitudes and assessments of organizational life as well as inventories of employees' value orientations to work (Cooke and Rousseau, 1988; Hofstede et al., 1993; O'Reilly et al., 1991; Schneider, 1990). It is possible to argue that these efforts are remnants of the earlier workplace 'climate' studies of the 1930s and 1940s, which were concerned with the measurement of employee attitudes and satisfaction. Currently, when quantitative methods are used, the main goal appears to be an assessment of organizational cultures as being either strong or weak (Schneider, 1990), or falling into a particular category type, such as production cultures, bureaucratic cultures, or professional cultures (Jones, 1983). Surveys are also used to establish relationships between organizational cultures and a host of other elements such as performance and leadership (Denison, 1990; Schein, 1985).

Among quantitative researchers, disagreements also surface about the variable status of organizational culture. Should organizational culture be operationalized as an independent or dependent variable? In other words, is it more useful to estimate the predictive potential of organizational culture, or to understand how culture itself can be transformed by a range of factors (Adler, 1983)? Some researchers advocate treating organizational culture as an intervening variable that mediates the effects of other variables on specific organizational outcomes, while others assert that organizational culture may be most relevant if treated as a residual variable – i.e., the source of all variance that is unaccounted for by other variables in the researcher's model (Adler, 1983).

In formulating organizational culture as a variable, researchers collapse a number of complex phenomena and intricately interlinked dynamics into a single unit that is then statistically manipulated to serve as a predictor of certain organizational outcomes, or to establish specific relationships between multiple social dimensions in organizations. Central to the quantitative research agenda is some kind of generalization and a claim of universal applicability (Denison et al., 2003). A major assumption (though frequently unstated) of the research is that the survey instruments can be transported and used in different locations, both nationally and internationally.

Qualitative methods of data collection typically include in-depth interviews with key subjects, extended periods of observation by researchers, and various forms of document analysis. A favoured research tradition in studying organization culture is ethnography (Agar, 1986; Van Maanen, 1998) – an import from the discipline of anthropology that is noticeably wedded to an *emic* or endogenous style of inquiry privileging the standpoints of organization members or 'natives' over those of the researchers or any outside 'expert'.

Qualitative data tends to be focused on organizational activities and processes that are believed to be particularly rich in symbolism. Organizational rites and ceremonies (Trice and Beyer, 1984), organizational stories and legends (Clark, 1972; Martin et al., 1983),

organizational rituals (Weeks, 2004), and organizational occasions (Rosen, 1985), are all seen as relevant data points for qualitative researchers of organizational culture. The goal of qualitative research is primarily to gain insights into organizational functioning and interactions through an examination of cultural processes at the workplace. Their focus is on the local organizational context, and they have little faith or interest in replicating their studies or generalizing their findings.

Qualitative studies of organizational culture tend to be influenced and inspired by anthropology and sociology (Turner, 1986; Van Maanen, 1988), while quantitative studies tend to be influenced by intellectual developments in psychology (Hofstede, 1998). These disciplinary influences have interesting effects on the study of organizational culture. Somewhat paradoxically, quantitative researchers who are committed to 'objective' measures of organizational culture focus on individual mindsets and cognitive structures, in keeping with Hofstede's (1998) assertion that culture is, 'a collective programming of the mind'. Qualitative researchers who typically adopt a more 'interpretative' approach, on the other hand, look for cultural expression in empirically observable actions and behaviours, such as organizational stories, rituals, and public displays (ceremonies and formal announcements). Clearly, divisions about method and data sources actually reflect more fundamental differences about the nature and characteristics of organizational culture that have provenance in different academic disciplines. These diverse disciplinary orientations inevitably place researchers of organizational culture before other conceptual crossroads as well.

The crossroads of unity and diversity

One of the more prominent and unavoidable sets of crossroads presents researchers with choices about the singularity and diversity of organizational culture. The early and somewhat more popular view tends to be 'integrationist' (Martin and Frost, 1994) – seeing culture as essentially a *shared* set of values, work habits, and symbolic orientations to organizational realities (Deal and Kennedy, 1982; Ott, 1989; Pettigrew, 1979). Martin and Frost (1994: 602) argue that integrationist studies, 'define culture as an internally consistent package of cultural manifestations that generates organization-wide consensus, usually around some set of shared values'. From this perspective, organizational culture is almost by definition a common, shared, and hence uniform phenomenon (Hofstede, 1998; Ott, 1989) that is implicitly responsible for bringing organizational members together and building a sense of organizational kinship and community.

Integrationist visions of culture are largely responsible for generating ideas of 'strong' organizational cultures (Deal and Kennedy, 1982; Sørensen, 2002) as a desirable condition. Strong cultures are believed to enhance organizational performance (Sørensen, 2002; Wilkins and Ouchi, 1983), while, conversely, 'weak' cultures are assumed to be detrimental to organizational functioning. Often, the notion of 'strong' culture appears to be inseparable from organizational culture itself. Whether using quantitative or qualitative methods, integrationist researchers look for common work values and shared organizational realities and consensus when studying organizational culture, with differences and dissonances being regarded as evidence of weak organizational cultures.

This homogeneous model of organizational culture is sharply questioned by a number of scholars, who Martin (1992) refers to as the *differentiationists*. Fundamentally, differentiationist views of culture reject the unitary approach (Gregory, 1983). Organizational cultures, they assert, are much more likely to be made up of a number of sub-cultures, which are themselves shaped in part by diverse environmental pressures and influences (Gregory, 1983; Sackman, 1992). From this view, an organization's culture, 'is a *nexus* where environmental influences intersect, creating a nested, overlapping set of sub-cultures with a permeable organizational boundary' (Martin, 1992: 114).

Within the differentiation approach itself, this nexus position is at one end of a spectrum that argues for acknowledging heterogeneity as an intrinsic element of organizational culture. At the other end of the spectrum, some researchers posit that organizational cultures are constantly *contested* by diverse social identity groups who are engaged in redefining shared expectations and routine organizational practices in keeping with their own interests (Ray, 1986; Van Maanen and Kunda, 1989). The position is succinctly articulated by Rose (1988: 142) who points out that, 'though it is possible for an organization to have a unitary culture, several factors often militate against such a possibility, especially as organizations become large and complex'. In sum, organizational cultures emerge out of conflicts between different groups (be they occupational, divisional, ethnic, or gender based), and are reproduced and redefined through negotiations between them. In this view, organizational cultures tend to be dynamic rather than static with even seemingly stable cultures concealing a host of tensions and struggles behind their production.

Between the compartmentalized culture position and the contested culture position are a number of more nuanced approaches to differentiated organizational cultures. Martin and Siehl (1983) offer one such vision – conceptualizing any organization as comprised of a range of relatively distinct subcultures that operate in relation to a 'core' or 'umbrella' culture. Some of these subcultures may be closer to the core culture (enhancing subcultures) while others may be more distant (orthogonal subcultures) or even oppositional (countercultures). In essence, Martin and Siehl (1983) recognize that organizations are complex cultural amalgamations rather than singular cultural entities with variations in terms of how intra-organizational groups/subcultures interact with a core or dominant culture. Yet another nuanced view is proposed by Young (1989), who argues that even dominant and presumably shared cultural values and practices can be interpreted and experienced differently by members of different organizational subcultures. This position calls into question the notion that culture equals homogeneity because of the prevalence of differential experience.

Methodologically, differentiationist views of culture tend to favour emic qualitative techniques, though quantitative measures are used when organizational subcultures are conceptualized as informal groups clustering around core value sets and work orientations (Hofstede, 1998; Liu, 2003). The more complex differentiationist positions, however, are almost always drawn to ethnography, because of their emphasis on sense-making and subjective experience (Prasad, 1997, 2005). Further, any study that focuses on paradox (e.g., Martin et al., 1983) or ambiguity (Meyerson, 1991; Young, 1989) requires the use of interpretive methods, because they facilitate a grasp of complicated cultural constructions. In other words, when researchers investigate organizational culture as a complex and somewhat 'messy' phenomenon, ethnography is the method of choice. However, when organizational cultures are studied as being comprised of relatively neat and discrete units or subcultures, both quantitative and qualitative methods can be used.

The crossroads of cultural sensitivity and blindness

Studies of culture are themselves conducted against a backdrop of assumptions, perspectives, and prescriptions. For decades, anthropologists – the specialists in culture research – have been mindful of the cultural baggage that researchers bring to any study. Organizational culture research is not exempt from this either. One path often taken by researchers is more *provincial* – concerned only with immediate and local interactions, and largely indifferent to the impacts of the larger geographical context on the culture. Adler (1983) makes a useful distinction between parochial and ethnocentric studies within the provincial paradigm. Parochial studies examine organizational cultures within single firms (typically in the US or Western Europe), and then assume

that these findings are applicable to firms across the industrialized world. Ethnocentric research (which is the more prevalent) uses instruments, surveys, interview protocols, etc., developed to examine organizational culture is one country to study firms in other countries. Adler (1983) characterizes such studies as being ethnocentric, because (a) they fail to recognize the culturally biased nature of their own assumptions in designing and conducting their research, and (b) they assume that such research is easily transferable across a range of national and cultural boundaries.

In a related critique, Adler and Jelinek (1986) argue that several studies of organizational culture are parochial in their ability to ignore wider cultural influences on the formation of organizational culture itself. As they point out, organizational cultures are frequently treated as if they exist in 'splendid isolation' from outside influences. Ethnocentrism, on the other hand, can also take place on account of researchers' inability to see or to notice elements of their own culture, because their extreme familiarity makes them virtually invisible. This kind of 'cultural blindness' (Alvesson, 1993: 47) pervades studies of organizational culture, because researchers (who are often at home in contemporary organizations) take central features of organization so completely for granted that they fail to notice them as significant cultural artifacts and practices.

Organizational researchers, however, can choose to introduce greater cultural sensitivity into their work by paying conscious attention to cultural differences embedded in the contexts of organizations being studied. One way of doing this is to adopt a *comparative* approach that explicitly compares organizations in one cultural context with organizations in another (Adler, 1983). Comparative studies are designed to distinguish between aspects of organizations that appear to be universal from dimensions that are culturally specific. Even more cognizant of cultural specificity are approaches that Adler (1983) clarifies as *polycentric*. The starting point for these studies is the notion that organizations can only be understood in terms of their own cultures and cultural contexts (Gregory, 1983).

In essence, polycentric studies incline towards ethnographies and methodologically require researchers to cultivate a native point of view (Gregory, 1983). Polycentric approaches to organizational culture are *emic* rather than etic (Prasad, 1997), implying an endogenic orientation that posits that the only meaningful way of understanding culture would be through the experiences and interpretations of its natives. At heart, polycentric approaches are in pursuit of authenticity and are methodologically committed to the cultural immersion of researchers in native worlds (Tedlock, 1991). One accusation periodically levelled at polycentric approaches is that they exemplify a high degree of cultural relativism that is at odds with the scientific paradigm. A second is that 'going native' brings with it its own dangers of cultural blindness, because researchers become so much a part of the culture they are studying that they are unable to 'see' it with any kind of objectivity or detachment (Prasad and Prasad, 2002; Tedlock, 1991).

Here again, an interesting paradox is in play. On the one hand, provincial approaches put a great deal of *cultural distance* between researchers and their subject worlds thereby fostering one form of cultural blindness. On the other hand, polycentric approaches call for high degrees of familiarity with their subject worlds, turning researchers into sympathetic natives who develop a different kind of cultural blindness. No matter which pathway is taken, researchers, it appears, run the risk of developing some form of cultural blindness.

The crossroads of cohesion and control

Researchers invariably face choices about deciphering organizational cultures in terms of their functionality. At one end of the spectrum, organizational cultures are viewed as holding high cultural value for organizations since they provide coherence and lend collective meaning to organizational actions and events (Pettigrew, 1979; Schein, 1985). From this perspective, organizational culture becomes the metaphoric glue that holds an organization together and instils a sense of collective belonging among its employees. Culture is able to accomplish this mainly because of its symbolic capabilities to infuse meanings across organizations through innumerable shared rituals and ceremonies (Dandridge, 1986; Trice and Beyer, 1993) such as organizational meetings and the annual Christmas party (Rosen, 1988), and through the stories and legends that are told and retold in different organizational situations (Alvesson, 2002; Clark, 1972). In other words, these ceremonies, stories, and rituals engender a sense of collective purpose and carve out a distinct organizational image with which employees can closely identify. In the long run, a 'strong' organizational culture is also believed to foster a sense of solidarity and result in superior organizational performance.

It is worth observing that, within the paradigm of functionality, even those researchers who are cognizant of the more dysfunctional possibilities of organizational culture, either treat such dysfunctionalities as primarily aberrant (Trice and Beyer, 1993), or show how seemingly dysfunctional cultures can still serve as mechanisms for employee solidarity and identification. Weeks' (2006) study of the ritualistic nature of complaint in a British bank is an example of the latter, where he argues that the culture of complaint that pervaded the organization ultimately served to foster a sense of group membership at the workplace, and organizational loyalty toward the local branch office.

At the other end of the spectrum, some researchers see organizational culture as an ideological sphere that is manipulated by managerial elites in order to elicit employee compliance. Designated by Carol Axtell Ray (1986) as 'the last frontier of control', organizational culture in this paradigm is seen in a more critical light (Burawoy, 1979; Kunda, 1992). This entails viewing organizational culture as a nexus of material and symbolic relations that creates a spurious sense of collective identity among employees that in turn discourages them from voicing dissent or subverting the prevailing organizational order. From a critical perspective, organizational cultures can also play a role in constituting employee identities, and therefore have an emotional claim on individuals (Du Gay, 1996). In many ways, organizational cultures are seen as ideologically powerful, because they are so hard to resist considering how deeply ingrained they are in everyday rules and routines (Mills, 1988).

The central methodological implications of this divergence regarding the role of culture in organizations are to be found at the level of analysis and representation. Whether one favours a functionalist or critical view of culture inevitably influences the *interpretation* of data. The study of organizational ceremonies starkly illustrates this tendency. Functionalists such as Trice and Beyer (1993), for instance, see organizational ceremonies and rituals as integrative phenomena, providing coherence to organizational experiences and fostering a sense of organizational community. Critical scholars such as Rosen (1985) and Rosen and Astley (1988), on the other hand, see organizational ceremonies such as awards banquets and office Christmas parties as liminal events orchestrated by management in order to provide a *ludic space*, in which employees can fleetingly experience a social freedom that is denied to them in their everyday work lives. Paradoxically, however, as Rosen and Astley (1988) assert, these ceremonies simultaneously validate and legitimize the very hierarchies they purport to disrupt. The salient point here is that a reading of organizational culture is substantially coloured by one's theoretical inclinations and less driven by so-called empirical 'facts'.

Making choices at the cultural crossroads

The question raised by all these culture debates cannot be meaningfully addressed without serious consideration of the nature of organizational culture itself. What is organizational culture and how can we usefully understand it are central questions

that can influence one's choice of pathways at each set of crossroads. The definitive statement on the nature of organizational culture was made by Smircich (1983), who suggested that the fundamental choice a researcher makes is between conceptualizing culture as a set of properties that an organization *has*, and conceptualizing culture as something that an organization *is*. The first approach sees culture as a set of attributes and characteristics that can be listed and eventually summarized as being either 'strong' or 'weak', or falling into some kind of typification such as professional or bureaucratic (Jones, 1983). Smircich's (1983) second approach is far more comprehensive, seeing culture as the relatively enduring, complex organization of symbolic and material relationships through which an organization is constituted or *is*.

We concur with Smircich that the second approach is likely to yield more useful insights into organizational functioning. It is sometimes argued that one's approach to culture should really be determined by the kind of research question that is being asked. Our position, however, is that one's fundamental conceptualization of organizational culture will inevitably shape the questions being asked, and that Smircich's (1983) approach is likely to yield more relevant questions. Why is this the case? We would argue that the notion of culture as a set of properties is an incomplete one that takes a relatively simplistic and static view of organizations. In practice, this approach has tended to treat employee attitudes and work values as the cornerstones of organizational culture (Cooke and Rousseau, 1988; Hofstede, 1980; Hofstede, 1991), and is psychologistic in orientation. In essence, this approach equates *collective mindsets* (at national or organizational levels) with culture, and is methodologically committed to providing collective and cognitive inventories that are believed to be adequate proxies for culture (e.g. Hofstede, 1991).

While acknowledging collective cognition as an element of culture, the second approach (seeing culture as something an organization or nation is) is more focused on the process of *cultural enactment* through which mindsets are routinely expressed and sanctioned in the public domain (Geertz, 1973). Drawing substantially on anthropology, this approach is methodologically focused on the production and reproduction of social/organizational arrangements, and the collective actions and evens that hold symbolic potency for organizational members – the ceremonies, stories, icons, myths, and heroes that give meaning to everyday work lives, and make each organization/nation a distinctive space in which to work or reside (Kunda, 1992; Martin, 1992; Smircich, 1983). In our view, this approach is superior, because (a) it is more comprehensive with its focus on collective enactments rather than solely on cognitions, and (b) it is more dynamic with its focus on the processes whereby culture is produced and reproduced – through traditions, rituals, and collective sense-making.

Understanding culture as something an organization is carries some serious methodological implications. First, the absolute scope of the concept suggests that culture is very much a *totality* (Geertz, 1973; Williams, 1977) encompassing a number of dimensions of organizational life. This makes it extremely difficult – virtually impossible – to document and represent an organization's culture in its entirety. At most, what we can explore in our research is a *cultural slice* of an organization. Researchers should, therefore, be careful about claiming to have understood an organization's entire culture, or about classifying organizations into somewhat simplistic cultural types. What we can offer is an understanding of *cultural tendencies* that may vary from organization to organization.

Second, the notion that organizations are cultural entities problematizes the idea that cultural aspects or cultural dimensions of organizations are somewhat distinct or separate from other organizational dimensions, notably political, economic, or communicative ones. This point has been theoretically endorsed by prominent anthropologists such as Marcus (1999), Roseberry (1989) and Sahlins (1978), who emphasize the inextricable relationship of culture to economy (i.e., material culture) and politics (i.e., kinship governance networks). Organization researchers, however, have by and large tended to isolate culture and treat it either as a variable or a discrete sphere of activity.

Understanding culture as something organizations are, however, implies seeing organizational activities as cultural practices, be they corporate strategizing, the exercise of executive leadership, mergers and acquisitions or problems of organizational communication. What is more relevant than studies of organizational culture are *cultural analyses* of organizations – using culture as a prism for examining organizational activities and interactions. An example of such work is Aboulafia's (1996) study of Wall Street, in which he analyses bond traders as tribes participating in a number of ritual exchanges and kinship relationships that have deep cultural significance for them. This kind of cultural analysis is helpful in appreciating the ways in which the noninstrumental and symbolic dimensions of life permeate and even shape those dimensions we consider purely rational – e.g., engaging in corporate strategy, communicating within bureaucracies and so on.

Let us now look at how adopting cultural analysis might influence our choice of pathways at each of the crossroads discussed in the preceding section. When it comes to choosing between quantitative and qualitative methods, cultural analysis clearly favours the latter. This is because at its core, cultural analysis emerges out of the hermeneutic tradition – i.e., it sees culture as taking place through both the shared and contested interpretations of its participants. The focus on interpretation implies that researchers of culture not only examine collective actions but also the meanings that such actions hold for multiple members – what Geertz (1973) refers to as the 'webs of significance' that underpin even routine interactions and events. Given this emphasis on meaning, *language* as a medium for understanding and representing organizational culture is more appropriate than measurement. We use the term language here rather broadly, seeing it as being expressed and woven into a multitude of social texts such as conversation, argument, symbolic artifacts, ceremonial rituals, conventional practices, and spatial arrangements. The reasons for this are somewhat self-evident but still bear repeating. Primarily, language allows for nuance, ambiguity, and complexity in a way that measurement does not. At its core, measurement is all about simplifying connections between social variables while cultural analysis is fundamentally concerned with understanding and exploring complexity. Quantitative methods in the social sciences are also aimed at detaching social relationships from their contexts while cultural analysis tries to weave contexts into the fabric of narrative analysis. Thus, at both the level of data collection and data analysis, narration is likely to be more effective than numerical analysis. We would like to be quite clear that we are not opposed to the use of quantitative methods in organization and management studies. We merely consider them to be ineffective in the study of organizational culture, because culture is not meaningful as a measurable concept. In fact, we would go as far as to suggest that quantitative measures do not 'capture' organizational culture, but merely represent fragmented and disparate elements of culture. Further, as long as culture is equated solely with values or specific work attitudes, one can see how quantitative surveys might hold some attraction. However, once we recognize the substantial behavioural component of culture, ethnography, with its traditional emphasis on observation and interpretation, becomes a far more suitable methodology than quantitative survey instruments.

When it comes to the second set of crossroads options, the uniformity versus differentiation perspectives of organizational culture are not easily resolved through the adoption of cultural analysis. Cultural analysis is more likely to suggest that any organizational culture is likely to be constituted of a variety of subcultures, be they occupational, departmental, regional, ethnic, or generational, which might share certain key tendencies, while differing profoundly on a number of others at the same time. Singularity and differentiation are more likely to be matters of degree that are contingent on a multiplicity of factors including historical trends, policy imperatives, material conditions, and structural arrangements. In general, however, cultural analysis would tend to be more skeptical of claims of cultural homogeneity except under unique conditions (e.g., the Amish), and be more predisposed to accept the presence of a multiplicity of subcultures existing in various states of conflicts and coexistence in organizations and societies (Gregory, 1983; Young, 1989).

When confronted with the questions of ethnocentrism and polycentrism found at the third crossroads, cultural analysis favours a more endogenic or emic view that places native accounts and interpretations at the centre of data collection and analysis. At the same time, more recent developments in cultural analysis, especially within anthropology, have problematized unquestioned notions about 'insiders' and 'outsiders', suggesting that especially under conditions of globalization, transnationality, and isomorphic institutionalization, easy distinctions between even 'natives' and 'foreigners' are harder to sustain (Marcus, 1999; Inda and Rosaldo, 2002). A major segment of contemporary cultural analysis also suggests that questions about the validity of polycentric versus ethnocentric analyses are best understood when foregrounded against the matrices of power that engulf them (Kondo, 1990; Prasad and Prasad, 2002; Tedlock, 1991). Inevitably, such questions force researchers toward the contemplation of matters of *representation* – asking themselves why certain subject groups are being studied, whose interests such studies might serve, and what responsibilities might accrue to the researcher in representing these groups in emic or etic ways.

In arriving at the fourth crossroads, cultural analysis is not necessarily predisposed to choose between cohesion and control, but to see culture as always holding both possibilities. Since culture is viewed as a source of deep collective meaning and group identification, it is clearly also a source of internal cohesion and integration. For the same reasons, however, it also lends itself to manipulation by corporate leaders, managerial elites, and occupational and professional groups (Rosen and Astley, 1988; Willmott, 1993) who attempt to garner culture's symbolic effects to influence organizational compliance with specific agendas, policies, or structural changes. The two positions are thus not mutually exclusive, but exist instead in an uneasy relationship with each other.

Culture on the move: re-tooling cultural analysis for the twenty-first century

Our discussion so far indicates that engaging in cultural analysis has implications for the directions we take at the different culture crossroads. These crossroads, however, are very much part of the 1980s landscape of organization studies, and have been insufficiently revisited since then. Regrettably, a once lively debate conducted by articulate and compelling voices (Martin, 1992; Ray, 1986; Smircich, 1983; Van Maanen, 1998) is at something of a standstill within organization studies, seemingly impervious to vigorous discussions on studying culture in disciplines such as communication and anthropology, and reluctant to acknowledge that exponential transformations at a global level might hold implications for how we conceptualize and examine organizational culture. Debates on organizational culture are almost entirely confined to a small group of European researchers (Grafton Small, 2005; Linstead and Mullarkey, 2003) who advocate the use of literary and aesthetic approaches to studying culture.

We would argue that such intellectual isolation and inertia serve organizational cultural analysis poorly, and once again is in danger of rendering organization culture research 'dominant but dead' (Calás and Smircich, 1987).

The first step in reviving organizational cultural analysis is to examine how organizations and their cultural dynamics may have altered with the onset of globalization. In general, we can understand globalization as referring to the intensification of contact between different regions of the world, mainly brought about by specific technological developments such as fibre-optics, and unique structural changes such as the liberalization of national economies and an unprecedented mobility of capital (Friedman, 2003; Inda and Rosaldo, 2002). Globalization invariably refers to the enormous scale of *flows* – of people, capital, ideas, images, and technology that are occurring on an ongoing basis (Appadurai, 1996). These flows, moreover, are neither predictable nor unidirectional, and frequently move out of unexpected sources in unforeseen directions. We can witness, for instance, how Chinese capital buys up shopping malls in Scandinavia, American business school graduates intern in Bangalore in India, Indian companies farm out surplus call centre work to Uruguay, and Nigeria becomes a major market for Bollywood movies as well as American country and western music. Described by Appadurai (1996) as 'flows in disjuncture', this phenomenon is a predominant feature of globalization.

What does all this mean for organizations, culture, and cultural analysis of organizations? More than anything else, it suggests that organizational cultures are no longer as stable or containable as we are used to thinking of them as being. The idea of culture has traditionally been predicated on certain key assumptions of semipermanence and endurability. Cultures are commonly seen as tied to habit, convention, and routine and are, therefore, also seen as relatively stable and enduring. This view of culture has implicitly guided most organizational ethnographies, be they concerned with engineering firms (Kunda, 1992), wall street brokers (Aboulafia, 1996), or flight attendants (Hochschild, 1983). Contemporary organizations, however, are increasingly unstable places, filled as they are with itinerant and nomadic populations (Ong, 1987), and operating around electronic technologies that require less face-to-face contact among employees and with clients, suppliers, and customers.

At the same time, organizations have become much more permeable than ever before, being exposed to influences from the media, the internet, a host of vital institutions (e.g., universities and government bodies), and their own shifting transnational populations (Barber, 1995; Pieterse, 2004). The contained distinctiveness of organizations that was captured by organizational ethnographies of the early culture research era (Gregory, 1983; Kunda, 1992) may be less relevant now given the more transient and hybridized nature of organizations and the nations in which they are located (Inda and Rosaldo, 2002; Pieterse, 2004).

If there is a single constant in our times, it is that culture itself is on the move. It is our position that cultural analyses of organizations should be able to engage with these dynamic and extended movements of culture. Conventional ethnographies of single organizations or individual departments (while often rich in local detail) are likely to miss out on a huge segment of cultural influences on organizations, and to overlook the fact that the cultural life of organizations is frequently found outside its formal boundaries.

A growing movement in a number of disciplines such as anthropology, communication, education, sociology, and history is to recognize that organizations are very much embedded in a 'world system' (Wallerstein, 2000), and to, therefore, conduct cultural analyses of organizations in different but relevant social spheres. The term given by Marcus (1999) to this kind of research is *multi-sited ethnography*, and it has been gaining considerable adherence in different disciplinary and interdisciplinary fields.

In essence, multisited ethnography expands the contours of traditional ethnography (along dimensions of time and space) so that cultural narratives of organizations are no longer rigidly circumscribed by imagined organizational or workplace boundaries. At the same time, these cultural narratives are consciously connected to significant events and trends in the world system. As Marcus (1999: 79) succinctly observes, cultural analysis needs to 'move out from the single sites and local situations of conventional ethnographic research designs to examine the *circulation* of cultural objects, meanings, and identities in diffuse timespace' (emphasis added). This emphasis on circulation is critical to multisited ethnography which recognizes that today's global reality is overwhelmingly characterized by the endless movement and flows of ideas, objects, and people across homes, organizations, nations, neighbourhoods, universities, and world bodies. We should note that this heightened focus on circulation and movement is not intended to displace the *local* (which occupies an almost sacred place within the ethnographic tradition), but to reconnect it (in analysis and representation) to the wider global system from which it draws both structure and meaning. In this reframed cultural analysis, therefore, a study of maquiladora cultures, for instance, would also have to incorporate an understanding of global treaties (e.g., North American Free Trade Agreement – NAFTA) and power relationships, and connect the maquiladora workforce with community life in Mexico (though remittances and so on).

Multisited ethnographies require researchers to break out of the confinements of organizational and workplace boundaries in following specific cultural narratives. Marcus' (1999) own guidelines for doing this are quite useful. In essence, he recommends that researchers pursue or *follow* specific people, objects, conflicts, life histories, discourses, or myths with salient connections to diverse organizations. In following these phenomena over relevant time/space contexts, one can produce useful and meaningful cultural analyses of organizations and their effects. The central argument for adopting this approach is a growing sense (in anthropology, communication studies, and other disciplines) that conventional notions of culture as being rooted in singular locations is no longer apposite. Until recently, culture was viewed as a relatively stable phenomenon, preserved through traditions and enduring over notable periods of time. Innovations in technology have rendered cultural phenomena much more transitory and malleable, calling for methodologies that capture their dynamic nature.

Following people would involve ethnographically tracking the lives and movements of a specific group of people, be they migrant workers, expatriate managers, or transnational professionals, as they traverse across diverse geographic regions and organizations. Ong's (1987) brilliant ethnography of women workers in Malaysian electronic chip factories is a case in point. Ong tries to understand the phenomenon of spirit possessions that were prevalent in these factories through an ethnography of multiple cultural sites, including the factories, the rural areas from which the woman workers were displaced, the patriarchal managerial system across the industry, and the wider world system of offshoring of which they were a part. Similarly, Mirchandani's (2004) study of call centres in India examines processes of identity formation and contestation across work, training, and community sites.

Following material objects as they are gathered, produced, and distributed can also serve as valuable source of cultural insight into organizations which are conduits for the production and circulation of most objects. Mintz' (1985) classic study of the emergence of sugar as a major commodity in the global market travels through many historical spaces, including slavery and colonialism, to weave a complex picture of power and cultural practice in different parts of the world. A more recent multisited ethnography of an object is Issenberg's (2007) study of the global sushi industry, following it from Japan to Newfoundland and then to California and Peru, and tracing the complex networks of production and distribution that simultaneously make sushi a fast food and gourmet item. Issenberg's study also explores the symbolic significance of sushi for different communities across the globe, showing how the immense flexibility of the product to adapt to local conditions gives sushi its enormous

staying power in a volatile and competitive food market.

Marcus (1999) also recommends following life histories through diverse cultural sites and institutions. This is not to be confused with traditional biographies, but is more of an in-depth cultural analysis of organizations and institutions through the lens of one or more life histories. Sennett's (1998) ethnography of a blue-collar worker and his professional son twenty years later is a study not only of their lives but also of the changing nature of capitalism and its effects on personality developments in the US.

Multisited ethnographies can also revolve around discourses that originate in and/or shape organizations. Focusing on discourses is one way of following ideas and images as they circulate through various organizational sites. Du Gay's (1996) work on changes in British organizational cultures traces the emergence and diffusion of the discourse of privatization – what he labels 'enterprise culture' – from policy circles to a major British retailing firm, showing how this discourse was responsible for reconstituting employee identities as consumers rather than workers. In a study of diversity management in the Canadian Petroleum industry, Prasad et al. (2007) examine the effects of the discourse of fashion on managerial responses to diversity by studying human resource divisions in five different petroleum companies, salient consulting firms, and key professional conferences. The authors are able to trace the emergence of fashionable managerial practices to vested interests and networked interactions, which in turn led to a widespread organizational cynicism about them.

In all these studies, efforts are made to ground local stories, lives, and circumstances in wider trends and events such as policy initiatives, trade flows, changing demographics, and global ideologies. The central goal here is to rupture our own socially constructed demarcations between the micro and the macro, the local and the global, and organizations and their environments. In taking up such a course of action, organizational ethnographers would be well advised to become theoretically more venturesome, and to draw on intellectual traditions such as discourse analysis, poststructuralism, feminism, postcolonialism, and praxeology – which have all approached culture as a series of struggles and predicaments situated in a wider world of material and symbolic relationships. Undoubtedly, these new ethnographic ventures will also generate different methodological crossroads as well, but they will hopefully also revive and enliven older debates while keeping cultural analyses of organizations relevant in a changing world.

REFERENCES

Aboulafia, M.Y. (1996) *Making Markets: Opportunism and Restraint on Wall Street*, Cambridge, MA: Harvard University Press.

Adler, N. (1983) 'A typology of management studies involving culture', *Journal of International Business Studies*, 14: 29–47.

Adler, N. and Jelinek, M. (1986) 'Is 'Organizational Culture' culture bound?', *Human Resource Management*, 25: 73–90.

Agar, M. (1986) *The Professional Stranger*, New York: Academic Press.

Alvesson, M. (1993) *Cultural Perspectives on Organizations*, Cambridge: Cambridge University Press.

Alvesson, M. (2002) *Understanding Organizational Culture*, London: Sage Publications.

Appadurai, A. (1996) *Modernity at Large: Cultural Dimensions of Globalization*, Minneapolis, MN: University of Minnesota Press.

Barber, N. (1995) *Jihad vs. MacWorld*, New York: Times Books.

Burawoy, M. (1979) *Manufacturing Consent: Changes in the Labor Process under Monopoly Capitalism*, Chicago: University of Chicago Press.

Calás, M., and Smiricich, L. (1987) 'Post culture: is the organizational culture literature dominant but dead?', Paper presented at the International Conference on Organizational Symbolism and Corporate Culture. Milan.

Clark, B. (1972) 'The organizational saga in higher education', *Administrative science Quarterly*, 17: 178–84.

Cooke, R.A. and Rousseau, D.M. (1988) 'Behavioral norms and expectations: a quantitative approach to the assessment of culture', *Group and Organizational Studies*, 13: 245–73.

Dandridge, T. (1986) 'Ceremony as an integration of work and play', *Organization Studies*, 7: 159–70.

Deal, T. and Kennedy, A. (1982) *Corporate Culture: The Rites and Rituals of Corporate Life*, Reading, MA: Addison-Wesley.

Denison, D. (1990) *Corporate Culture and Organizational effectiveness*, New York: Wiley.

Denison, D., Haaland, S. and Goelzer, P. (2003) *Corporate Culture and Organizational Effectiveness: Is There a Similar Pattern Around the World?*, Greenwich, CT: JAI Press.

Du Gay, P. (1996) *Consumption and Identity at Work*, London: Sage Publications.

Geertz, C. (1973) *The Interpretation of Cultures*, New York: Basic Books.

Gelinas, J.B. (2003) *Juggernaut Politics: Understanding Predatory Globalization*, London: Zed Books.

Grafton Small, R. (2005) 'Asymmetry and the assault on order', in A. Linstead and S. Linstead (eds), *Organization and Identity*, London: Routledge, pp.63–77.

Gregory, K. (1983) 'Native-view paradigms: multiple cultures and culture conflicts in organizations', *Administrative Science Quarterly*, 28: 359–76.

Hofstede, G. (1980) *Culture's Consequences: International Differences in Work-Related Values*, London: Sage Publications.

Hofstede, G. (1991) *Cultures and Organizations: Softwares of the Mind*, London: McGraw-Hill.

Hofstede, G. (1998) 'Identifying organizational subcultures: an empirical approach', *Journal of Management Studies*, 35: 1–12.

Inda, J.K. and Rosaldo, R. (2002) 'A world in motion', in. J,K. Inda and R. Rosaldo (eds), *The Anthropology of Globalization: A reader*, Chicago: University of Chicago Press, pp.1–34.

Issenberg, S. (2007) *The Sushi Economy: Globalization and the Making of a Modern Delicacy*, New York: Gotham Books.

Jones, G.R. (1983) 'Transaction costs, property rights and organizational culture: an exchange perspective', *Administrative Science Quarterly*, 28: 254–67.

Kunda, G. (1992) *Engineering Culture: Control and Commitment in a High-Tech Corporation*, Philadelphia: Temple University Press.

Linstead, S. and Mullarkey, J. (2003) 'Time, creativity and culture: introducing Bergson', *Culture and Organization*, 9: 3–13.

Liu, S. (2003) 'Cultures within culture: unity and diversity of two generations of employees in state-owned enterprises', *Human Relations*, 56: 387–417.

Marcus, G. (1999) *Ethnography Through Thick and Thin*, Princeton: Princeton University Press.

Martin, J. (1992) *Cultures in Organizations: Three Perspectives*, Oxford: Oxford University Press.

Martin, J. Feldman, M. Hatch, M. and Sitkin, S. (1983) 'The uniqueness paradox in organizational stories', *Administrative Science Quarterly*, 28: 438–53.

Martin, J. and Frost, P. (1996) 'The organizational culture war games: a struggle for intellectual dominance', in S. Clegg, C. Hardy and W. Nord (eds), *Handbook of Organizational Studies*, London: Sage, pp.599–620.

Martin, J. and Siehl, C. (1983) Organizational Culture and Counter-Culture: An Uneasy Symbiosis. *Organizational Dynamics*, 12: 52–64.

Meyerson, D. (1991) 'Normal' ambiguity? a glimpse of an occupational culture', in P. Frost, L. Moore, M. Louis, C. Lundberg and J. Martin (eds), *Reframing Organizational Culture*, Newbury Park, CA: Sage Publications, pp.131–44.

Mills, A.J. (1988) 'Organization, gender and culture', *Organization Studies*, 9: 351–69.

Mirchandani, K. (2004) 'Practices of global capital: gaps, cracks and ironies in transnational call centers in India', *Global Networks*, 4: 355–73.

Morgan, G. (1986) *Images of Organization*, London: Sage Publications.

O'Reilly, C., Chatman, J. and Caldwell, D. (1991) 'People and organizational culture. a q-sort approach to assessing person-organization fit', *Academy of Management Journal*, 34: 48–516.

Ong, A. (1987) *Spirits of Resistance and Capitalist Discipline: Factory Women in Malaysia*, Albany, NY: State University of New York Press.

Ott, J. (1989) *The Organizational Culture Perspective*, Pacific Grove, CA: Brooks and Cole.

Peters, T.J. and Waterman, R.H. (1982) *In Search Of Excellence: Lessons from America's Best-Run Companies*, New York: Harper and Row.

Pettigrew, A. (1979) 'On studying organizational cultures', *Administrative Science Quarterly*, 24: 570–81.

Pieterse, J.N. (2004) *Globalization and Culture: Global Melange*, New York: Rowman and Littlefield Publishers.

Prasad, P. (1997) 'Systems of meaning: ethnography as a methodology for the study of information technologies', in A. Lee, J. Liebenau and J. DeGross (eds), *Information Systems and Qualitative Research*, London: Chapman and Hall, pp.101–18.

Prasad, P. (2005) *Crafting Qualitative Research: Working in the Postpositivist Traditions*, Armonk, NY: M. E. Sharpe.

Prasad, P. and Prasad, A. (2002) 'Casting the native subject: ethnographic practice and the (re)production of difference', in B. Czarniawska and H. Hopfl (eds), *Casting the Other: The Production and Maintenance of Inequalities in Work Organizations*, London: Routledge, pp.185–204.

Prasad, P., Prasad, A. and Mir, R. (2007) 'One mirror in another: managing diversity and the discourse of fashion', Working Paper.

Ray, C.A. (1986) 'Corporate culture: the last frontier of control', *Journal of Management Studies*, 23: 287–96.

Rose, R. (1988) 'Organizations as multiple cultures: a rules theory analysis', *Human Relations*, 41: 139–70.

Rosen, M. (1985) 'Breakfast at Spiros: dramaturgy and dominance', *Journal of Management*, 11: 31–48.

Rosen, M. (1988) 'You asked for it: christmas at the bosses' expense', *Journal of Management Studies*, 25: 463–480.

Rosen, M. and Astley, W.G. (1988) 'Christmas time and control: an exploration in the social structure of formal organizations', *Research in the Sociology of Organizations*, 6: 159–82.

Rosenberg, W. (1989) *Anthropologies and Histories: Essays in Culture, History and Political Economy*, New Brunswick, NJ: Rutgers University Press.

Sackman, S.A. (1992) 'Culture and subcultures: an analysis of organizational knowledge', *Administrative Science Quarterly*, 37: 140–61.

Schein, E. (1985) *Organizational Culture and Leadership*, San Francisco: Jossey Bass.

Schneider, B. (ed.) (1990) *Organizational Climate and Culture*, San Francisco: Jossey Bass.

Sennett, R. (1998) *The Corrosion of Character: The Personal Consequences of Work in the New Capitalism*, New York: W.W. Norton and Co.

Smircich, L. (1983) 'Concepts of culture and organizational analysis', *Administrative Science Quarterly*, 28: 339–58.

SØrensen, J. (2002) 'The strength of corporate culture and the reliability of firm performance', *Administrative Science Quarterly*.

Tedlock, B. (1991) 'From participant observation to the observation of participation: the emergence of narrative ethnography', *Journal of Anthropological Research*, 47: 69–74.

Trice, H. and Beyer, J. (1984) 'Studying organizational cultures through rites and ceremonials', *Academy of Management Review*, 9: 653–9.

Trice, H. and Beyer, J. (1993) *The Cultures of Work Organizations*, Englewood Cliffs, NJ: Prectice-Hall

Turner, B. (1986) 'Sociological aspects of organizational symbolism', *Organization Studies*, 7: 101–15.

Van Maanen, J. (1988) *Tales of the Field*, Chicago: University of Chicago Press.

Van Maanen, J. and Kunda, G. (1989) 'Real feelings: emotional expression and organizational culture', *Research in the Sociology of Organizations*, 11: 43–103.

Weeks, J. (2004) *Unpopular Culture: The Ritual of Complaint in a British Bank*, Chicago: University of Chicago Press.

Wilkins, A.L. and Ouchi, W.G. (1983) 'Efficient cultures: exploring the relationship between culture and organizational performance', *Administrative Science Quarterly*, 28: 468–81.

Williams, R. (1977) *Marxism and Literature*, Oxford: Oxford University Press.

Willmott, H. (1993) 'Strength is ignorance, slavery is freedom: managing culture', *Journal of Management Studies*, 30: 515–52.

Young, E. (1989) 'On the naming of the Rose: interest and multiple meanings as elements of organizational culture', *Organizational Studies*, 10: 87–206.

9

Doing Power Work

Stewart Clegg

INTRODUCTION

In this chapter, I will introduce the notion of the researcher, especially as a doctoral student, as someone who is expected to think for a living. Thinking for a living, it will be suggested, means following ideas – even if they take us out of what we define as our intellectual paddock and lead us to stray into neighbouring or even distant terrain.

For organizational scholars, however, thinking for a living is not sufficient. We have to relate how our thinking for a living relates to the way that others are working for a living in relation to those organizations that employ them, that they relate to and work with. Thus, the second movement is to consider the relation between thinking for a living and working for a living.

Researchers work. They do researching for a living. Hence, the third movement of the chapter is to address how we can connect that thinking that we do with the worlds of organizations and work on which we work – doing researching for a living. In essence, this kind of work entails making sense of others working for a living, and the organizations within which they do this working, and which they relate to in the process. There are many ways that one might make these connections.

If one is studying power relations, then one of the best ways is to focus on the discursive moves that actors make in context. Practically, this means gaining access to key decision-making and issue-addressing meetings in which people's managing largely consists of talking through, round and about issues. Theoretically, there are a number of ways of addressing such talk; the one that I shall focus on derives from the notion that people are engaged in complex language games in everyday organizational life.

Of course, for researchers, the ideas they develop in one project should feed and nurture subsequent ones, subsequent significations one might say, and so for the fourth movement of the chapter I consider how the earlier conjunction of empirical experience and theoretical insight led to subsequent theoretical signification.

All research takes place in space and time as the abstract coordinates of its construction. Typically, researchers focus more on one axis than on the other; most survey researchers take a small, often static slice of time, and bring reports from a large number of discrete spaces at more or less one moment. If they do this more than once, then they may be said to bring back snapshots that form an elapsed sequence, often referred to as a panel study.

Case study researchers vary enormously in the amount of time that they spend in the field. Because I understand that this book is meant to be a useful tool for practising researchers, I have decided to discuss an exemplary case study, one that records a detailed length of time in the field, measured in terms of quite a number of years. I am well aware that such a level of detail may be out of reach of many hard-pressed research students and apprentice researchers, but Flyvbjerg's (1998) work sets a benchmark of which all case study researchers should be aware.

Finally, in the last movement, there are a few words summing up the themes that have been scored into this account, and the lessons that it might teach.

Thinking for a living

Becoming a researcher means getting a PhD. I chose to do my research on 'power in organizations'. The first thing that one does as a researcher is to try and define the parameters for a literature search. At the time that I started the research, there did not appear to be a great deal of literature to search. Max Weber (1968) had written about power; David Hickson and his colleagues (1971) had done a masterful job of pulling together much of the more recent thinking into a 'strategic contingencies theory of intraorganizational power', which accommodated major contributions such as those of Crozier (1963; also see the later development by Crozier and Friedberg 1980). In passing, they had referenced a definition of power by the American political scientist, Robert A. Dahl (1957). Following this up entailed reading some of the political science literature, in which I found debates about power and nondecision-making that were entirely pertinent to organization theory, and almost entirely absent.

Two main debates had preoccupied the American political science literature concerned with power. One was a debate that Dahl (1958, 1971) had had with C. Wright Mills (1957), the author of the famous study of *The Power Elite*. Mills provided an institutional history of the construction of the military

industrial complex that many commentators, including President Eisenhower, saw as dominating the Cold War United States in the 1950s. Dahl countered that Mills had not clearly determined that this elite existed; for him to do so, he said, one had to establish that its preferences routinely prevailed in decision-making in specific arenas of power. Having a reputation for being powerful was insufficient, he said. We have to be able to say that we have observed someone doing power, which would consist of making someone do something with respect to a decision that was different from what they would have done had the other not interceded. 'My intuitive idea of power', Dahl (1957: 203) said, occurs when someone whom he nominates as an A, can do something to someone else, whom he nominates as a B: 'A has power over B to the extent that he can get B to so something B would not otherwise do'.

Such a definition has immediate organizational application; as Dahl (1957: 203) says, an 'A' could be any kind of agency – a person, group, roles, office, government, nation-state or other human aggregate. The agency expressed in power will depend on mobilizing some resources; these will be expressed through means or instruments of power and, empirically, be rendered as a probability that A's power will prevail over a specific scope of B's behaviour. For instance, an organization such as the Greater London Council may be able to mobilize resources, such as cameras, parking patrol officers, and legislation, to dissuade drivers from entering central London unless they are prepared to pay a congestion charge. The power of the council would be rendered in terms of the probability that a certain percentage of drivers will obey the new rules and a certain percentage will break them.

However, the astute reader will have already picked up the reference to rules. As the rules change, behaviour changes in response to their enforcement. Somehow, it seems to be the rules that represent the changed power. Looked at this way, the opportunities for analysis become more promising. We might, for instance, compare different cities and ask why and when congestion charging was, or was not, introduced. In the city of Sydney, where I am writing at this moment, there is no congestion charge, even though the roads are highly congested and traffic circulation and movement is widely acknowledged as a problem. Why is it the case that the city of London was able to introduce this change of rules while many other cities that are equally afflicted with the same problems have not? Once we start to enquire into these questions, we probably have to relax the focus on decision making. For one thing, the key issue may be that there has been no decision making; that, for whatever reasons, the issue of congestion charging has not arisen. In exploring these reasons, we would need to expand our reading somewhat, and catch up with a second major set of debates that were occurring in political science.

Dahl's (1961) empirical work rapidly attracted criticism of the assumptions on which it was based. The chief protagonists were Bachrach and Baratz (1962: 948) who question whether a 'sound concept of power' can be 'totally embodied and fully reflected in "concrete decisions" or in activity bearing directly upon their making?' Is there not such a phenomenon as 'non-decision-making', they suggest? One can capture this concept by investigating how an 'A devotes his energies to creating or reinforcing social and political values and institutional practices that limit the scope of the political process to public consideration of only those issues which are comparatively innocuous to A' (Bachrach and Baratz 1962: 948). In the case in point, this could take us into quite diverse territory. We might want to compare the organizational structure and scope of operations of city councils: are they weak and fragmented because they are small and premised on historical neighbourhoods, or are they large and unified as a result of amalgamation? What role do developers and road lobbies play in constructing a climate of opinion? What is the state of public transport? What are the boundaries of the city, and how do these map onto the patterns of wealth and social demography of the citizens[1]? Answers to these questions might indicate forms of bias

that may be mobilized in the existing structure of things (Schattschneider, 1960: 71) and shape action about the issue – or non-issue – at hand.

What constitutes an issue cannot simply be read off, observationally, from what happens. What does not happen also needs to be considered. The 'dominant values and the political myths, rituals, and institutions which tend to favour the vested interests of one or more groups, relative to others' (Bachrach and Baratz, 1962: 950) need to be considered. These constitute the rules of the game, and it is through these rules that power possibilities will be shaped and framed.

Three major ways of nondecision-making present themselves. First, the powerful may choose not to hear issues articulated by the less powerful, and in this way, they never make it on to the formal agenda of decision-making. Second, there may be a 'rule of anticipated reaction' (Friedrich, 1937) in play. The relatively weak might anticipate the likely reaction to an issue and choose not to raise it, anticipating the likely outcome, so the issue remains unacknowledged publicly. Third, nondecision-making may occur through the mobilization of bias, evident in 'those situations where dominant interests may exert such a degree of control over the way in which a political system operates, and over the values, beliefs, and opinions of less powerful groups within it, that they can effectively determine not only whether certain demands come to be expressed and needed, but also whether such demands will even cross people's minds' (Saunders, 1979: 30).

Debates in a field are often quite hermetically sealed; researchers read specific journals in the field that they define themselves as working in and do not, on the whole, read journals from other fields, even if they are cognate to their field of interest. It was certainly the case that when I began to read widely in the power literature, I discovered debates there that had not, at the time, made any impact in organization theory. What was important next was to work out how these could be translated into data collection and interpretation. About the answer to this question, I was less confident than in my ability to have tracked down interesting ideas in the literature.

One thing was for sure: I did not feel that, after moving into these more subtle accounts of power and the rules of the game, that the standard questionnaire approach which generated data on a number of predetermined response sets would furnish the quality of data that was required to address these issues. For one thing, any such approach would have to have incorporated quite a large sample across a wide number of organizations to be statistically valid; meeting this requirement would have meant a considerable degree of abstractness and lack of context in any questions that could be asked, if only because, as a researcher, I could not possibly know in advance what the contextual issues and nonissues would be across a wide range of organizations. Of necessity, it seemed that a case study approach would be necessary.

That case studies should be preferred was not the conclusion that early organization theory studies of power, such as Hickson et al. (1971) and Hinings et al. (1974) came to. The power of numbers overwhelmed the power of context, even when the numbers were fairly meaningless, because they referred to hypothetical rather than real situations. The preference for numbers runs deep in organization theory, in a somewhat intellectually stunted way. No better instance of this can be found than in the continuing fascination of organization theorists for measuring things that do not happen other than as an artefact of the questions that are asked in a survey by way of responses to hypothetical questions. The numbers are generated by individual responses to Likert-scale type questions. The answers of all the individuals are then aggregated and a mean score for 'organizational politics' derived from these, which is taken, somewhat bizarrely, to represent the organization that the individuals are situated in. Of course, the data represent no such thing: any score is merely an artefact of the questions, the scales and the individuals coming into collusion to generate data which, when averaged, are meaningless as a measure

of anything other than of the 'average sense' that a number of discrete individuals make of a set of hypothetical questions such as 'rewards come only to those who work hard in this organization'. Using such data, a Perception of Organization Politics score (POPs) can be generated. Quite what the value of such data is escapes me entirely. For one, it breaches Durkheim's (1964) *Rules of Sociological Method*. The average of aggregate individual data about noncontextually specific and hypothetical questions that generate replies from any number of individuals, which tap into their delusions, disconnects, or their ability to parrot corporate lines means nothing real. If this work has any merit, it as a kind of ritual incantation that will keep simple-minded positivist supervisors happy and ensure that you never have to speak to managers about how they use, view, and are abused by organizational politics in their own terms. Instead, all that the respondents might think has already been curtailed by the thinking that goes into the questions that collect the data. It is lazy research; the researcher does hardly any translational work and just leaves it to trust that the respondents are capable of doing it without any reality checks on their ability to do so. If this kind of research interests you and is what you wish to do, I suggest you give up reading this chapter now and go and read something such as Vigoda (2003) or Ferris et al. (2007; 2005). It will be far more to your taste, even though I believe it to be a complete waste of time other than as an object lesson in how *not* to research power and politics in organizations.

Working for a living

Perhaps typically of most research students, my experience of the world of work was fairly limited. While many of my contemporaries were gaining business and organizational experience, I was reading obscure debates about power in libraries of journals and books. That was the nature of my work at that time. As a research apprentice, it was what one is expected to do. However, I had worked at other things in the past. One of these was as a seasonal worker on a construction site, working as a labourer for a group of joiners or carpenters as they are sometimes called. As I worked away in the library or at my desk at home my thoughts often turned back to this work experience, wondering how I could translate the terms of debate that I was grappling with into an understanding of something concrete.

Looking back on that experience of my early induction at the bottom of the organizational hierarchy, I did what the joiners told me to do, whether it was applying fish oil to shuttering – a particularly unpleasant job – brewing up the tea, fetching the fish and chips at lunch time, going to the bookie's office to put bets on, hammering nails – and screws – into formwork, or downing tools. Downing tools – when I would carry nail boxes and other equipment back to the joiners hut – normally occurred at the end of the day, or at a lunch break – 'snap time' – but on one occasion it occurred more irregularly.

The 'lads' with whom I worked were skilled labourers and good sorts. Jokes and observations on the young women passing by the site were one currency of work time relations. Doubtless, we were a bastion of working class masculinity and sexism, but at a time when hardly any of us thought much about the latter and rarely connected it to the former. The other main currency of conversation concerned pay rates. These were very complex and consisted of several allowances such as a journey to work allowance and a shower and clean up allowance, as well as conditions that had been won for the joiners as a part of a collective industrial relations award. There was an hourly rate, and a piece-rate system that delivered a productivity bonus if the joiners exceeded the norms that were established for the metres of shuttering that were constructed as form work in a given time period. Additionally, there were contractual agreements about when joiners could work. One of these was that 'joiners shall not work in inclement weather'.

A recurrent theme of conversation among the joiners was the inadequacies of the project and project manager. One day we were on the site and it started to flake with snow, the temperature dropped, and our hands became blue with cold. The ganger, the leader of the work team, called us all off the job saying, 'Eh up, 'appen weather's turned inclement', and we trooped back to our hut, where I brewed the tea, and the lads studied the racing form, the page three girls, and the rest of the paper. After we had been there for about thirty minutes, the foreman came down and said, 'What's up wi' you lot then? Get thee sen back on site'. The ganger replied, 'No, no, joiners don't work in inclement weather'. The foreman looked hostile and left. Ten minutes later, the project manager came down to the hut and said, 'Why aren't you out there working? What do you think we're paying you for?'

Now, with mention of pay, it appeared as if we were getting somewhere. The issue turned out not to be about the weather at all; it was really about pay, which the project manager had raised as an issue. Sure enough, the joiners did have a collective agreement that they should not work in inclement weather, but there was no operational definition of what constituted inclemency. The weather was not that bad – unpleasant but not so severe that you could not work. 'Well, point is', came the reply, 'it's not worth it, for what thee's paying us in shutterage, there's nought in it for us'. And that was the nub; the site was badly managed; the project manager was not doing his job well.

It was widely known that his wife had left him because of his 'fancy woman', his 'bit on the side', and that he was having trouble looking after his children, getting them to school and picking them up, and himself to work. The job was ill-managed; this manifested itself mainly from the joiners' point of view in a lack of coordination in the flow of materials aligned with the flow of work on the site. Hence, they were making very little or no bonus – not because of their laziness but because, as they saw it, of the project manager's incompetence – or at least distraction. They had little to do because of the lack of effective coordination. Raising the inclemency rule was merely a way of putting pressure on the project manager;

instantiating a legitimate rule to establish a legitimate grievance without establishing a formal dispute.

Some time later, I realized that I had learnt a lot from this incident. Things did not get done and buildings were not accomplished without a great deal of coordination, communication, consent, and control – the 'four Cs' of management. Looking back on this experience some time after it had happened, I thought that if understanding power in organizations required detailed contextual understanding, the conclusion I had come to, then why not go back to construction sites to study it? At least I knew something about them as an insider.

Researching for a living

Making sense of working for a living

I re-entered the world of construction sites, this time as a nonparticipant observer. I was not working on the site, other than to connect what I knew from the library with what I could grasp on site. I spent all my time on the site, wandering around, sitting in on meetings, and tape-recording conversations. As well as reading Max Weber (1968), Georg Simmel (1971), Michel Crozier (1963), and David Hickson (1971) on power, in addition to the contributions to the Community Power Debate by Dahl (1961) and Bachrach and Baratz (1970), I had also been reading in the areas of methodology and philosophy of enquiry. I read Garfinkel (1967) on ethnomethodology, and I read Wittgenstein, (1972a) on language games. Wittgenstein fascinated me. I had first met him in an undergraduate philosophy subject. I knew about the *Tractatus Logico-Philosophicus* (Wittgenstein 1994), and I knew of his renunciation of its problematic and the adoption of the language game approach of the *Philosophical Investigations*. And I had read about the builders who made an appearance early on in the *Blue and Brown Books* (1972b). They were quite impoverished, linguistically, seeming to respond best to gestures and short, sharp imperative commands. I knew that Wittgenstein – an engineer by training – had

built a family home in his native Vienna for his sister and could only conclude that his wealthy background meant that he took only a very patrician interest in how it was built. Certainly, the language games that we had played on site were much richer, much more multifaceted, and much more tangential to the task of construction.

Still, together with my interest in ethnomethodology, this interest in Wittgensteinian language games shaped a research method in my mind. I would go back on site, I would lurk in the corners and shadows, I would blend in, and I would capture the naturally occurring conversations I chanced upon. I would do so using some new technology – that of a portable cassette player. But there were some problems. Construction sites are very noisy; conversation is shouted and snatched by the wind, covered by the sound of machinery, and fragmented by motion around the site. Thus, I retreated to the project office, where at least it was warm, where I had a table in the corner, strewn with technical drawings that I could hide behind, read philosophy, and where conversation could be captured.

Each day I might capture anything up to six hours of taped material. So much talk, heated arguments, conspiratorial planning and plotting, multiple issues and agendas, different points of view, irreconcilable interests, sexual flirtation, everyday dramas; all human life was there. And I had much of it on my cassette tapes. I sat up till late at night transcribing it, slept a few hours, and then was back on the site to collect more. I did this for three months – not every day, but about three or four days a week on average. From the point of view of the builders, I was studying how managers actually managed – hence the tape recordings. And, in a way, I was, because my ways of making sense of these materials were increasingly being steered by my ways of making sense of Wittgenstein. My earlier thoughts of using conversational analysis methods that had developed out of Garfinkel's (1967) ethnomethodology (see Greatbatch, Chapter 28, this volume) increasingly seemed inadequate to my research question of how power, nondecision-making and the rules of the game were constituted and accomplished in organizations. Turn-taking did not seem to be the trick (Sacks et al., 1974). To answer my needs, I turned to ideas that I had encountered in Wittgenstein.

Language games and power in construction

Wittgenstein's analysis of language games in his scattered texts, notably the *Philosophical Investigations* (1972a), was thin. Central concepts for thinking about language were introduced, including the notions of 'form of life' and 'language game', but were analytically underdeveloped. That this should be the case was hardly surprising given that the texts come from notes that his students took in his lectures, and were only constituted as books subsequent to his death in 1951. It was part of what made them so useful – that they were underdeveloped provided ample room for subsequent theorists to be creative (see for instance Pitkin, 1972).

Taking a cue from ethnomethodology, but not using its conversation analysis approach, I was probably one of the earliest researchers to realize that the world of organizations is a world that is essentially rich in discourse; whatever else managers may do a large part of their work consists of the interpretation of key texts and the articulation and rationalization of different accounts of these (Clegg, 1975). Power came into the analysis in a way that blended Wittgenstein (1972a) with Garfinkel (1967). One of the key concepts of the latter was the notion of 'indexicality', a term that originated from linguistics, where an indexical term would be defined as one that could only be understood in context. Classically, indexical terms would be 'it' and 'this'. For instance, in the following sentence one cannot know what either mean without an appropriate context being supplied: '*It is this, then*'. *It* could be an interrogative or a factual statement referring to the relation of two terms – but without a context being provided, then the meaning of the terms is utterly inscrutable. One could as easily imagine the sentence to be one spoken by an explorer, a lover, or a politician, or, indeed, almost any identity.

What relates indexicality to power is context. In the context of construction sites, the contract and its associated documents are the central framework shaping managerial discourse. The contract in question was of the kind that is referred to in the construction industry as a hard money contract – where the construction being undertaken was bid for on the basis of the specifications in the contract, for a definite price, and where the most competitive tender wins the contract. What this does is to set up a constitutive framework in which the *meaning* of the contract plays an essential role. Despite recommendations in the procedural handbooks of the industry, the contracts are never unindexical; that is, they cannot be read simply as a precise and unequivocal set of instructions for building a building. There are at least two reasons for this (Clegg, 1975). Both are questions of context – one immanently material to the conditions in which the specific contract is enacted, and the other transcendentally constitutive of all contracts.

The immanent reasons are simple. Contractual specifications, typically, are large and complex bodies of documentation. Not only are there the documents on which the work is bid, but there is also an associated 'bill of works', comprising detailed consultants reports and associated documents. In an ideal world these would exist in an absolute and seamless correspondence of all detail from one document to another such that no document ever contradicted another or was in conflict with it. Given the vast amount of paper – comprising detailed specifications, reports, and projections – associated with relatively complex construction projects, that there actually is such correspondence is a large assumption to make. Many hands, at many times, using many distinct skills, produce the papers. More often than not, there will be points of ambiguity or even disagreement between them. The precise meaning of them is not stipulated in the documents themselves; in Wittgenstein's (1972a) terms there is no metarule that provides the rules for how the meaning embedded in the documents should be interpreted. It is this that provides the immanent grounds for indexicality, and substantial opportunity for extensive language games to be conducted between project managers and other significant actors on construction sites, in which the precise meaning of what is often imprecise documentation is translated into contested action.

One distinction is central to Wittgenstein's thought – that between the 'surface' and the 'deep' structure. The classic case of the difference between surface and deep structure is one that Wittgenstein uses on several occasions, and it involves the relation between any given instances of speech and the idea of grammar. Speech is on the surface; it is what one hears or reads in a written form. Underlying it, however, are the rules of grammar.

Wittgenstein thought of the deep structure in terms of grammar. I argued that the texts that I recovered through audio-taping from the construction site had a social grammar underlying them – one that was embedded in their 'form of life', another Wittgensteinian concept. Quite what Wittgenstein meant by 'form of life' is not entirely clear. On some occasions it seems to mean no more than a mode of life; on other occasions, the meaning is more inscrutable, possibly even genetically constitutive. The form of life, I argued, was transcendentally constitutive, and with this move brought together the surface structure and the deep structure. On the surface was what people said; underlying this was a deep structure of rules in the use of which players were more or less skilled game-players, using a social grammar as a generative device for making sense of what it was that was being said and what it was that could – and should – be said. Skill is the crucial issue in this regard – and the skills were basically a mastery of rhetoric, of being able to make something out of the opportunities presented by the contractual documents. Deeper still was a transcendental frame, the form of life, which made what was constituted by the grammar, the deep structure, sensible and rational, by stipulating the need for the organization to be as profitable an enterprise as it could be.

The action was played out in specific arenas. Project meetings were the main arenas. These meetings were held to discuss issues. Sometimes they had fairly formal agendas, other times they were impromptu. Many of these were taped over a three-month period of intensive fieldwork. The issues invariably related some actions, or absence of actions, to the contractual documents contained in the bill of works. Thus, much of what was said in these meetings was said in relation to some putative but contested state of affairs in terms of the alignment of that state of affairs with the state that should have pertained in terms of the contractual specifications. The gap between these states was the matter at issue. Hence, the discourses involved attributions of responsibility for variance. What got to be said was spoken from different positions of material interest in the contract; for the head contractor, the main issue was to find indexical particulars in the contract that could be exploited in order to win some contribution to the profitability of the site through processing variation orders for which additional payments could be demanded. The architect and client team sought to see that what they thought they had designed and were paying for was actually constructed for the price contracted. That is the point of hard money contacts – they are supposed to provide for a 'what you contracted for is what you get at the price agreed' outcome – at least in theory. In practice, industry people know that skilled and shrewd project managers will find ways of creating significant – and costly – variance.

It can be seen that the rules underlying the surface production of text were quite clear; the project manager and his team sought systematically to exploit any indexicality in the contract in order to maximize profitability while the architect and the client team sought to resist this at every turn. In turn, that these were the rules of the game only made sense in terms of a form of life of capitalism – one in which the creation of profit was the fundamental aim.

To make it more concrete, the matter under discussion in a project meeting might be something apparently simple such as the

Table 9.1   Power, rule and domination: Three dimensions of power

Concept	Level of analysis	Structural level	Ethnographic questions	Primacy of analytic focus	Focus
Power	Situated actions as empirical texts	Surface structure	Who wins?	Episodic action	Immanent relations
Rules	Constitutive rules	Deep structure	What are the rules?	Enacted mediation	Rhetorical skills
Domination	The aim of the game	Form of life	Why these rules?	Structurational framing	Transcendent taken-for-grantedness

meaning of clay. But while the meaning of clay may appear simple, it soon becomes apparent that, from a perspective that sees the talk as exhibiting a surface structure, deep structure, and form of life, that in fact the meaning is, precisely, a matter of power. The actually recorded material – what people said in situated action – provides the surface structure of the text. The contested matter was the depth of clay that should have been excavated to prepare the site for foundation pillars that were to be constructed out of poured concrete. The issue was simple. The consultant engineers' drawings instructed excavation to a minimum of 600 mm into 'sandy, stony clay'. They did not specify the depth at which such clay could be found. Accompanying the drawings was a series of reports from drilled test bore holes done as a site survey of the ground that had to be built on. These recommended excavation to a depth of two meters into clay. The project manager argued that there were different qualities of clay across the site, running at variable depths. There was 'puddle clay' and 'sandy, stony clay'. He defined 'normal clay' as 'sandy, stony clay'. The resulting depth of the excavations done became the subject of an acrimonious letter from the clients' architect to the construction company. The points at issue resulted from investigation of the claimed excavation levels, which, as the letter put it, revealed little or no consistency. The counter claim from the project manager was that the normal clay substrata varied in level across the site – hence the need for additional – and unauthorized – excavation. It was a complicated dispute (Clegg 1975, appendix 2 and 4).

The analytical importance of the case is that it demonstrates that, in everyday organizational life, language games can be inherently political. First, the contestation that occurs – the discourse of the site meetings – is not random. Second, contestation is patterned by the skilful use of the underlying rules for constituting issues – searching for indexicality in the meaning of the documents – by the participants in the arena. These comprise a mode of rationality – a way of acting that is, within the situated action context, rational. Third, this patterning only makes sense where the ultimate aim is the maximization of profit. The analysis can be represented in the terms displayed in Table 9.1.

Subsequent significations

The stress on situated and plural rationalities that developed out of my interest and appreciation of Garfinkel's (1967) ethnomethodology and Schutz's (1967) phenomenology was subsequently to be fed by the work of the French historian of ideas, Michel Foucault. Foucault (1977: 27–28) says 'power produces knowledge … power and knowledge directly imply one another … there is no power relation without the creative constitution of a field of knowledge, nor any knowledge that does not presuppose and constitute at the same time power relations'. In such a view, rationalities and powers are fused. Rationalities are always situational. And because they are always contextually situational, they are always implicated with power. No context stands outside power. If that were the case, then power would exist nowhere, outside of understanding, outside of possibility, outside of sense. Different power actors operate in and through different rationalities, which have different rules for producing sense and, at the more formal outer limits, for producing truth. In fact, sense and truth cannot be separated from the ensemble of rules that constitute them – and their obverse – as such.

To adopt a discursive analysis of rationality is to see what people say as the means whereby rationality and power become interwoven. People may be in a position to say anything, given the infinity of discourse, but they rarely surprise the well-grounded analyst with their discursive moves. Language games are not predictable but they are explicable. We can understand and constitute the senses that are being made as well as the conditions of existence and underlying tacit assumptions that make such sense possible. And in this way we can begin to understand the different forms of agency that find expression in organizational contexts, where the players make sense of rules that they actively construct and deconstruct in the context of their action.

I have used the idea of 'circuits of power' to represent the ways in which power may flow through different modalities (Clegg, 1989). Relatively simple is transitive power, where one agency seeks to get another to do what they would not otherwise do. Power in this sense usually involves fairly straightforward episodic power, oriented towards securing outcomes. The two defining elements of episodic power circuits are agencies and events of interest to these agencies. Agencies are constituted within social relations; in these social relations they are analogous to practical experimentalists who seek to configure these relations in such a way that they present stable standing conditions for them to assert their agency in securing preferred outcomes. Hence, relations constitute agents that agents seek to configure and reconfigure; agencies seek to assert agency and do so through configuring relations in such a way that their agency can be transmitted through various generalized media of communication, in order to secure preferential outcomes. All this is quite straightforward and familiar from what

Lukes (1974; 2005) termed one-dimensional accounts of power.

Episodes are always interrelated in complex and evolving ways. No 'win' or 'loss' is ever complete in itself, nor is the meaning of victory or defeat definitely fixed as such at the time of its registration, recognition, or reception; such matters of judgment are always contingent on the temporalities of the here-and-now, the reconstitutions of the there-and-then, on the reflective and prospective glances of everyday life (Schutz, 1967). If power relations are the stabilization of warfare in peaceful times, then any battle is only ever a part of an overall campaign. What is important from the point of view of the infinity of power episodes stretching into a future that has no limits, are the feedback loops from distinct episodic outcomes and the impact that they have on overall social and system integration. The important question is whether episodic outcomes tend rather more to reproduce or to transform the existing architectonic – the architecture, geometry, and design – of power relations. How they might do so is accommodated in the model through the circuit of social integration in episodic outcomes, which serve either more or less to transform or to reproduce the rules fixing extant relations of meaning and membership in organizational fields; as these are reproduced or transformed they fix or refix those obligatory passage points, the channels, conduits, in the circuitry of extant power relations. In this way, dispositional matters of identity will be more or less transformed or reproduced, affecting the stability of the extant social relations that had sought to stabilize their powers in the previous episodes of power. As identities are transformed then so will be the social relations in which they are manifested and engaged (see Figure 9.1).

System integration also needs to be considered. Changes in the rules fixing relations of meaning and membership can facilitate or restrict innovations in the techniques of disciplinary and productive power which, in turn, will more or less empower or disempower extant social relations that seek to stabilize the episodic field, recreating existing

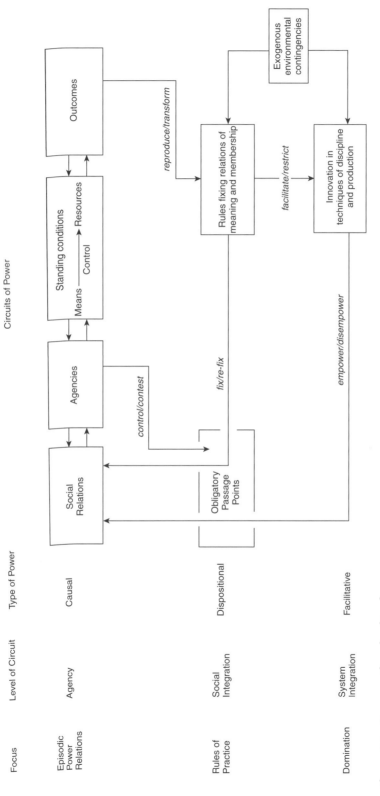

Figure 9.1 Representing circuits of power

obligatory passage points or creating new ones, as the case might be. (Clegg, 1989, Chapters 8 and 9, discusses the model in detail, applying it also to matters of state formation.)

Bringing time in to play

The study discussed earlier (Clegg, 1975), was not concerned with a large slice of temporality, and this was a real weakness in terms of providing an account of how power was constituted across time. The later formal model of circuits of power was intended to be a way of making sense not just of events that were 'here-and-now' but of how the present was constituted. Fortunately, there is an exemplary and detailed case study of planning in Aalborg conducted by Bent Flyvbjerg (1998), which is easily interpretable in terms of the later 'circuits' model, even though it does not use it explicitly. Clegg (1989) and Flyvbjerg (1998) were both influenced by Foucault, albeit that both use the resources that he provides creatively. Clegg, especially, recognized that there is no fundamental power that should be seen as constitutive of nearly anything and everything. Power should not be seen as ubiquitous. It flows through different circuits of social relations, with different effects.

High-level city officials initiated the Aalborg Project in October 1977, as a plan intended to limit the use of cars in the city centre. Soon after its initiation, several agencies – trade unions, police, local and national consultants, the business community, private corporations, the media, and interested citizens – became involved in order to decide on issues such as redirecting traffic by creating a rational local and national bus traffic system. A task force was established to formulate a three-year plan. The first conflict arose between architects and the bus company over the location and size of a bus terminal. Originally just a minor disagreement, the discussion turned into embittered conflict and division among the main players. There was a public hearing and the production of a counter-plan by the Aalborg Chamber of Industry and Commerce, which produced a revised plan that was approved in 1980.

Small business people with retail outlets in the planning precinct grew increasingly dissatisfied with the original urban renewal plan. Without a constant stream of cars coming in to the city centre they feared they would lose business. They succeeded in halving the original plan to construct the bus terminal. The Environmental Protection Agency then began to question the environmental hazards and impact of the proposed bus terminal, while another source of local conflict concerned a subplan designed to try and maintain the authentic charms of the old shopping streets. The Town Council forbade all nonretail businesses (banks, insurance companies, and offices) from occupying ground floor premises, to try and preserve the street's character. However, nonretail business leaders were also present in the local Chamber of Industry and Commerce, and they agitated against this plan. In its first four years, the Aalborg Plan underwent six rounds of reconstruction and modification. Although the overall plan was never actually rejected, specific projects became more and more minute, as well as more problematic in content and scope, generating further subordinate and specific episodes of power between local factions, such as cyclists and planners; planners and small business people; motorists and public transport, and so on.

Unexpected and unanticipated environmental contingencies had an impact on the project, such as the mayor and several high-level local officials being jailed on bribery charges, thus challenging the overall legitimacy of the urban renewal plan. By this time the original plan had undergone its eleventh revision. The Chamber of Industry and Commerce reversed its original stand and began arguing that redirecting traffic would hurt businesses by causing falling revenues. However, the city council survey rejected this fear by revealing that retail profits were increasing. Meanwhile, new social democratic politicians came on the scene, deciding to bolster the urban renewal project by emphasizing positive aspects of the original plan adopted a decade earlier, which led the Aalborg Project into a total impasse.

The outcomes were not what any factions wanted. Instead of reducing car traffic, it increased by 8 percent; instead of creating an integrated system of bicycle paths, unconnected stretches were built; instead of reducing traffic accidents, the number of fatalities and injuries among cyclists increased 40 percent; instead of reducing noise, the levels substantially exceeded Danish and international norms, with increasing air pollution the result.

Flyvbjerg's (1998) main theme is that power shapes rationality. At various stages in the project, as the various political actors sought to steer the project through their preferences, they sought to structure what the circuits of power model terms obligatory passage points. Different claims were made for participation in different committees; differential participation produced different outcomes at different times, favouring different preferences. Small battles were fought over who, and what, could be introduced in which arenas and meetings. In this way, the relations of meaning and membership in the various locales were contested, reproduced, or transformed. As these changed, then the obligatory passage points shifted; as these shifted, the relations of power that had prevailed shifted also, most dramatically when the mayor and officials were indicted and imprisoned. Thus, small wins in specific episodes of power had the capacity to shift the configuration of the overall circuitry through which power relations flowed. The actors engaged in the plans were constantly seeking to fix and refix specific schemes, and although the play of power was very fluid, the underlying social integration of the small business people with each other, the Chamber of Industry and Commerce, and the editorial views of the local newspaper, seemed to mean that the small business people were the prevailing winners in the many struggles. The attempts to respecify the system integration of the traffic plan in Aalborg consistently foundered on the reef of social integration. How Aalborg was planned, designed, and looked, as well as how it was not planned, not designed, and did not look, was an effect of power relations.

Flyvbjerg (1998) alerts us to one very important fact of power relations and rationalities. When power and knowledge are entwined, then the greater the power the less the need for rationality, in the sense of rational means-end justifications. The relation between rationality and power was an uneven relation. Power clearly dominated rationality. That is, those who presently configured power sought to continue doing so, and were quite ready to define the reality of the project in any way that seemed to them to further their preferences, using whatever strategies and tactics were available to them. In this sense, what was defined as rationality and reality was an effect of power, as it defined and created 'concrete physical, economic, ecological, and social realities' (Flyvbjerg 1998: 227). What was advanced and argued as rationality depended wholly on power relations; the more disadvantaged in these the agents were, the more they were liable to have recourse to conceptions of rationality that downplayed power and sought to position themselves through factual, objective, and reasoned knowledge. The most powerful rationalities took the form of rationalizations rather than authoritatively grounded accounts. Often, these were public performance of rationality which other agents who were witness to the rationalizations felt compelled not to reveal, because they lacked the powers to do so; they anticipated and feared the reaction that their actions would in all probability produce; should they move, dangers lurked in open conflict and identification of differences.

The greater the facility with which agencies could have recourse to power relations, the less concerned they were with reason, and the less they were held accountable to it. Access to more power produced less reason. In other words, the more that they were able to seduce, manipulate, dominate, induce, and rationalize, the less likely that they would be amenable to the authority of reasoned argument. The Enlightenment project of a rational public sphere is a strategy of the weak and opposed by the strong, according to Flyvbjerg's analysis. Power relations were, on the whole more marked by the gentle arts of power – persuasion, inducements, and seduction – than by antagonistic strategies. The antagonisms were the most visible and publicly reported aspects of power, but they were hardly the most typical. They rarely are. The necessity to throw one's weight around usually signals a position of relative weakness rather than strength, such that if one needs to use force, one is demonstrating that one is weak. Establishing agreements between agents creates the power of ongoing action, a much stronger relation of power than specific episodes enacted in response to conditions of crisis.

In Aalborg, what was most typical was the constant attention to the small things of power relations that continually reproduced the status quo; rather than attempts at transformation, it was largely reproduction that prevailed, and the most skilled strategists of power were those for whom reproduction was their preferred strategy. In the case of Aalborg, this was the small business community, whose institutionalized voice was much more actively represented to governmental rationality than that of the various citizen groups, including the cyclists, greens, and so on. In turn, these relations were embedded in deeply held local loyalties and relations defined by the forms of symbolic and cultural capital that Bourdieu analyses. When, in openly antagonistic settings, these relations came up against contrapoints of view that were well researched and represented in rational terms, power-to-power relations dominated over those defined in terms of knowledge or rationality against power. Mostly, power relations were both stable and inequitable, characterized by consensus and negotiations, such that rationality could gain a greater toehold. The more power relations became antagonistic the easier it was to deploy arguments and strategies that elided rationality but relied on other strategies, such as personal connections. Thus, if rationality is to influence existing circuits of power, it must try to keep the power circuitry intact. To challenge the rationality of the circuit within which one's actions are being coconstructed is often to play a losing hand, if one does not have recourse to some external circuit-breakers, such as kith, kin, or community connections that provide relations for extra-circuitry mobilization.

Circuits of power in practice

The theorization of circuits of power has been used in a number of other studies; Cerny (1994); Hallsworth and Taylor (1996); Hallsworth et al. (1997); Coopey et al. (1997); Orssatto and Clegg (1999); Orssatto et al. (2002); Lycett and Paul (1999); Lagendijk and Cornford (2000); Taylor and Hallsworth (2000); Lucio (2000); Tantoush et al. (2001); Prasad and Eylon (2001); May (2001); Bathelt and Taylor (2002); Bathelt (2002); Clegg et al. (2002); Clegg and Ray (2003); Leiser and Backhouse (2003); Rodrigues and Child (2003); Johnston (2004); Muir (2004); Latimer (2004); Marshall and Rollinson (2004); Vaara et al. (2005). However, the one that we shall discuss here is a recent study of 'Circuits of power in practice: strategic ambiguity as delegation of authority', by Sally Davenport and Shirley Leitch (2005). It is a study of positive power enacted through the facilitative circuit, which is the reason that we have chosen to discuss this particular application. It pulls together an analysis of power with an analysis of strategic ambiguity to empower stakeholders. Strategic ambiguity (Eisenberg, 1984) involves deliberate use of ambiguity to create a 'space' in which multiple interpretations and responses by stakeholders are enabled and made possible (Davenport and Leitch, 2005). The case study analyses the attempt by the Foundation for Research, Science and Technology, a public sector research funding body in New Zealand, to transform the national science system. Given that unclear goals, restive and sometimes resistant stakeholders, and a process of creative engagement between the organization and its stakeholders marked the attempt, the use of strategic ambiguity was highly appropriate.

In 1999, New Zealand research funding changed from being a very explicit rules-based model in which power relations were highly episodic, with strong noncollaborative competition between grant getters. What changed the situation was the fashion for a 'knowledge economy' that had blown across the Pacific and into New Zealand. In the new knowledge economy, the idea was to create facilitative knowledge sharing and building capacities rather than encourage zero-sum games between researchers in a very small country (less than four million people). Policy statements were issued; things were going to change and things *had* to change. What was changing was that the foundation was moving from funding research to investing in innovation. Where previously there had been disciplinarily-defined fiefdoms, there was now to be one investment operation in an innovation strategy, accompanied by 'disinvestment' in existing areas of research that failed to show promise for future wealth creation.

The focus of this research is on the third circuit of power, the positive facilitative circuit, which comes into play when the existing rules of practice characterizing a power arena are changed or destabilized in some way, either by authorities or others internal to the circuits of power, or by some exogenous contingency that has an impact on these circuits. When the existing rules of practice fixing relations of meaning and membership change, then relations of power in the circuit may be either empowering or disempowering of members, stakeholders, and others. Here the focus is on stakeholders who are particularly susceptible to the central paradox of power: 'the power of an agency is increased in principle by that agency delegating authority; the delegation of authority can only proceed by rules; rules necessarily entail discretion and discretion potentially empowers delegates' (Clegg, 1989: 201). The use of strategic ambiguity is one way of achieving 'high discretionary strategic agency' through enabling creativity in sensemaking about what changing meanings mean. Strategic ambiguity introduces purposeful discretion into the space between organization and delegates. Contested sensemaking shifts the circuits of power in unanticipated but partially creative ways. For anyone familiar with university research circles, the immediate results were predictable – confusion, resentment, and resistance. However, researchers who were involved in research institutes that already had a private sector funding orientation saw

it quite differently and much more positively. The Foundation sought to engage research providers and end users of research in a creative dialogue into which those institutes jumped with alacrity, while the universities were far more hesitant about what the changed conditions meant. Previously they never had to negotiate; they just submitted research applications and were either funded or not, according to the recommendations of expert panels in a very small national system. Now the priorities were being set by the Foundation in terms of investment criteria which were opaque to the community of researchers until they entered negotiation with the Foundation. The researchers speculated that perhaps, as the rules became more fixed, as meanings settled down and settled in with the new system of funding, the system of relations might shift back into a more episodic mode of circuitry. In which case, one might expect periodic bouts of reformed purpose and renewed use of new sources of strategic ambiguity.

CONCLUSION

Researching power and politics in organizations is best done through case study. Only case study can provide the fine-grained contextual detail necessary to begin to appreciate the finer points of theoretical arguments that have developed since the early days of organization and political science accounts of power. Moreover, it is only through the contribution of liberal doses of theory that one can overcome the spatial limitations of any case study research; that it tells us about a very limited piece of space, even when it is studied in depth and over time. What can connect the specificities of a case to the generalities of a field is the work of theory. The case must be theorized; it must be read through theory, it must help build theory, otherwise it becomes just another, hopefully interesting, story. Local stories are important; they are how we learn who we are and what we relate to in terms of stocks of knowledge, but in modernity stories in themselves are regarded as insufficient if they do not connect to those larger stories that are illuminated in theory.

My introduction to stories about power began with simple mechanics, where an A got B to do something that B would not otherwise have done. Through this contribution, I hope to have been able to persuade the reader of the value of both more complex stories and of more complex theories for rendering the complexity of these stories more manageable and comprehensible (and see Clegg, 1975, 1989; and Clegg et al., 2006).

NOTES

*Shortly before the time that I read the proof copies of this chapter the State government did introduce a 'congestion charge' - but only for motorists using the Harbour Bridge and Harbour Tunnel. These motorists travel from the northern suburbs. The state government is Labor; almost every seat in the northern suburbs is held by the political opposition. Drivers from the western suburbs where all seats are held by Labor do not have to pay this congestion charge; in fact, their tollway charges are subsidized. The politics of congestion charging are very clear in this case.

REFERENCES

Bachrach, P. and Baratz, M.S. (1962) 'Two faces of power', *American Political Science Review*, 56: 947–52.

Bachrach, P. and Baratz, M.S. (1963) 'Decisions and non-decisions: an analytical framework', *American Political Science Review*, 57: 641–51.

Bachrach, P. and Baratz, M.S. (1970) *Power and Poverty: Theory and Practice*, Oxford: Oxford University Press.

Bathelt, H. (2002) 'The re-emergence of a media industry cluster in Leipzig', *European Planning Studies*, 10(5): 583–611.

Bathelt, H. and Taylor, M. (2002) 'Clusters, power and place: inequality and local growth in time space', *Geografiska Annaler: Series B, Human Geography*, 84(2): 93–109.

Cerny, P.G. (1994) 'The dynamics of financial globalization: technology, market structure, and policy responses', *Policy Sciences*, 27(4): 319–42.

Clegg, S.R. (1975) *Power, Rule and Domination: A Critical and Empirical Understanding of Power in Sociological Theory and Organizational Life*, London: Routledge and Kegan Paul.

Clegg, S.R. (1989) *Frameworks of Power*, London: Sage Publications.

Clegg, S.R., Courpasson, D. and Phillips, N. (1989) *Power and Organizations*, London: Sage Publications.

Clegg, S. R., Courpasson, D. and Phillips, N. (2006) *Power and Organizations*, Thousand Oaks, CA: Sage Foundations of Organization Science.

Clegg, S.R. and Ray, T. (2003) 'Power, rules of the game and the limits to knowledge management: lessons from Japan and Anglo-Saxon alarms', *Prometheus*, 21(1): 23–40.

Clegg, S.R., Pitsis, T.S. Rura-Polley, T. and Marosszeky, M. (2002) 'Governmentality matters: designing an alliance culture of inter-organizational collaboration for managing projects', *Organization Studies*, 23(3): 317–37.

Coopey, J., Keegan, O. and Emler, N. (1997) 'Managers' innovations as "sense-making"', *British Journal of Management*, 8(4): 301–15.

Crozier, M. (1964) *The Bureaucratic Phenomenon*, Chicago: University of Chicago Press.

Crozier, M. and Friedberg, E. (1980) *Actors and Systems*, Chicago: University of Chicago Press.

Dahl, R.A. (1957) 'The concept of power', *Behavioral Science*, 20: 201–15.

Dahl, R.A. (1958) 'A critique of the ruling elite model', *American Political Science Review*, 52(June), 563–9.

Dahl, R.A. (1961) *Who Governs?*, New Haven, CT: Yale University Press.

Dahl, R. A. (1971) *Modern Political Analysis*, Englewood Cliffs, NJ: Prentice-Hall,

Davenport, S. and Leitch, S. (2005) 'Circuits of power in practice: strategic ambiguity as delegation of authority', *Organization Studies*, 26(11): 1603–23.

Durkheim, E. (1964) *The Rules of Sociological Method*, London: Routledge and Kegan Paul.

Eisenberg, E. (1984) 'Ambiguity as a strategy in organizational communication', *Communication Monographs*, 51: 227–42.

Ferris, G.R., Treadway, D.C., Kolodinsky, R.W., Hochwarter, W.A., Kacmar, C.J., Douglas, C. and Frink, D.D. (2005) 'Development and validation of of the Political Skills Inventory', *Journal of Management*, 31(1): 126–52.

Ferris, G.R., Treadway, D.C., Perrewe, P.L., Brouer, R.L., Douglas, C. and Lux, S. (2007) 'Political skill in organizations', *Journal of Management*, 33(3): 290–320.

Flyvbjerg, B. (1998) *Rationality and Power: Democracy in Practice*, Chicago: University of Chicago Press.

Foucault, M. (1977) *Discipline and Punish: The Birth of the Prison* (ed. A. Sheridan), London: Allen & Lane.

Friedrich, C.J. (1937) *Constitutional Government and Democracy*, New York: Gipp.

Garfinkel, H. (1967) *Studies in Ethnomethodology*, Englewood Cliffs: Prentice-Hall.

Hallsworth, A. and Taylor,M. (1996) 'Buying power: interpreting retail change in a circuits of power framework', *Environment and Planning A*, 28: 2125–37.

Hallsworth, A., Taylor, M., Jones, K. and Muncaster, R. (1997) 'The US food discounter's invasion of Canada and Britain: a power perspective', *Agribusiness*, 13(2): 227–35.

Hickson, D.J., Hinings, C.R., Lee, C.A., Schneck, R.E. and Pennings, J.M. (1971) 'A strategic contingencies theory of intraorganizational power', *Administrative Science Quarterly*, 16(2): 216–29.

Hinings, C.R., Hickson, D.J., Pennings, D.J. and Schneck, R.E. (1974) 'Structural conditions of intraorganisational power', *Administrative Science Quarterly*, 12: 22–44.

Johnston, P. (2004) 'Outflanking power, reframing unionism: the basic strike of 1999–2001', *Labor Studies Journal*, 28(4): 1–24.

Lagendijk, A. and Cornford, J.R. (2000) 'Regional institutions and knowledge: tracking new forms of regional development policy', *Geoforum*, 31: 209–18.

Latimer, J. (2004) 'Commanding materials: (re)legitimating authority in the context of multidisciplinary work', *Sociology*, 38(4): 757–75.

Leiser, S. and Backhouse, J. (2003) 'The circuits-of-power framework for studying power in institutionalization of information systems', *Journal of the Association for Information Systems*, 4, online.

Lucio, M.M. (2000) 'European works councils and flexible regulation: the politics of intervention', *European Journal of Industrial Relations*, 6(2): 203–16.

Lukes, S. (1974) *Power: A Radical View*, London: Macmillan.

Lukes, S. (2005) *Power: A Radical View*, (second edn.), London: Palgrave-Macmillan.

Lycett, M.P. and Paul, R.J. (1999) 'Information systems development: a perspective on the challenge of evolutionary complexity', *European Journal of Information Systems*, 8(2): 127–35.

Marshall, N. and Rollinson, J. (2004) 'Maybe Bacon had a point: the politics of interpretation in collective sensemaking', *British Journal of Management*, 15(1): 71–86.

May, T. (2001) 'Power, knowledge and organizational transformation: administration as depoliticization', *Social Epistemology*, 15(3): 171–85.

Mills, C.W. (1957) *The Power Elite*, New York: Oxford University Press.

Muir, J. (2004) 'Public participation in area-based urban regeneration programmes', *Housing Studies*, 19(6): 947–66.

Orssatto, R.J. and Clegg, S.R. (1999) 'The political ecology of organizations: toward a framework for analyzing business–environment relations', *Organization and Environment*, 12: 263–79.

Orssatto, R., den Hond, F. and Clegg, S.R. (2002) 'The political ecology of automobile recycling in Europe', *Organization Studies*, 23(4): 639–66.

Pitkin, H.F. (1972) *Wittgenstein and Justice*, Berkeley: University of California Press.

Prasad, P. and Eylon, D. (2001) 'Narrating past traditions of participation and inclusion: historical perspectives on workplace empowerment', *The Journal of Applied Behavioral Science*, 37: 5–14.

Rodrigues, S. and Child, J. (2003) 'Co-evolution in an institutionalized environment', *Journal of Management Studies*, 40(8): 21–37.

Sacks, H, Schegloff, E.A. and Jefferson, G. (1974) 'A simplest systematics for the organization of turn-taking for conversation', *Language*, 50: 696–735.

Saunders, P. (1979) *Urban Politic: A Sociological Interpretation*, London: Hutchinson.

Schattschneider, E.E. (1960) *The Semi-Sovereign People: A Realist's View of Democracy in America*, New York: Holt, Rinehart & Winston.

Schütz, A. (1967) *The Phenomenology of the Social World*, Evanston Ill. Northwestern Press.

Simmel, G. (1971) *Georg Simmel on Individuality and Social Forms*, edited by Donald N. Levine, Chicago: University of Chicago Press.

Tantoush, T., Clegg, S.R. and Wilson, F. (2001) 'CADCAM integration and the practical politics of technological change', *Journal of Organizational Change Management*, 14(1): 9–27.

Taylor, M. and Hallsworth, A. (2000) 'Power relations and market transformation in the transport sector: the example of the courier services industry', *Journal of Transport Geography*, 8: 237–47.

Vaara, E., Tienari, J., Piekkari, R. and Santti, R. (2005) 'Language and the circuits of power in a merging multinational corporation', *Journal of Management Studies*, 42(3): 595–623.

Vigoda, E. (2003) *Developments in Organizational Politics: How Political Dynamics affect Employee Performance in Modern Work Sites*, Cheltenham: Edward Elgar.

Weber, M. (1968) *Economy and Society: An Outline of Interpretive Sociology*, New York: Bedminster Press.

Wittgenstein (1994) *Tracatus Logico-Philosophicus*, London: Routledge.

Wittgenstein, L. (1972a) *Philosophical Investigations*, translated from the German by G.E.M. Anscombe, Oxford: Blackwell.

Wittgenstein, L. (1972b) *The Blue and Brown Books*, Oxford: Blackwell.

10

The Deinstitutionalization of Institutional Theory? Exploring Divergent Agendas in Institutional Research

Robert J. David and Alex B. Bitektine

INTRODUCTION

The growth of institutionalist research within organizational studies has been nothing short of remarkable. The institutional perspective has come to dominate submissions to the Organization and Management Theory Division of the Academy of Management Annual Meetings (Thompson, 2004; Davis, 2005), and occupies an increasingly large space in leading academic journals. As Tolbert and Zucker (1996) suggested in their review over a decade ago, institutional theory seems on its way to becoming institutionalized itself within organizational studies. The core argument of this chapter is that the increase in institutional theory's prominence has been due to its theoretical and methodological malleability. Whereas early theoretical statements in neoinstitutionalism emphasized stability, homogeneity, and constraint, more recent work celebrates the polar opposite: change,

diversity, and strategic action. This has allowed for a far greater range of empirical phenomena to be addressed under the 'institutional' rubric. We find, moreover, that the expansion of institutional research is associated with a corresponding rise in the use of qualitative empirical methods. We suggest that, together, these theoretical and methodological trends may in fact signal a coming *de*institutionalization of institutional theory.

There is little doubt that institutional theory has increased in popularity since the core theoretical statements of the 1970s and 1980s. As Figure 10.1 shows, the percentage of articles dealing with some element of institutions has risen steadily in leading organizational-studies journals, from about 4% in the period 1980–1984 to almost 14% by 2007 (see Appendix for search details). While this search of only article titles and abstracts does not capture the full volume

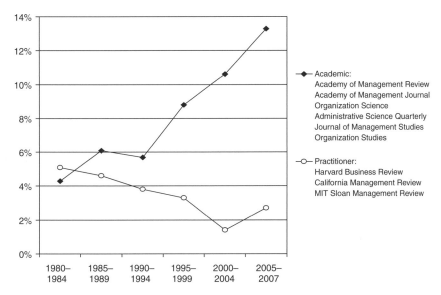

Figure 10.1   Percent of academic and practitioner papers discussing institutions and/or institutional theory

of institutional scholarship, it reflects a clear trend in the growth of institutional theory within the organizational-studies community. In additional analysis not shown, we also found an expansion of institutional articles in specialized journals within management information systems (MIS) and international business (IB), which suggests that the institutional perspective has spilled into adjacent areas from its core organizational-theory base.

A secondary goal of this chapter is to explore the influence of institutional theory on management practice. To our surprise, we found no evidence that institutional theory's increased prominence within the academic community has had any corresponding effect on its prevalence within the practitioner literature. In fact, Figure 10.1 shows a declining interest in the perspective within practitioner-oriented publications and suggests that institutional theory currently has little relevance for practitioners. Moreover, our review of those few practitioner papers that make use of institutional theory and its concepts shows that an overwhelming majority of them explore intraorganizational processes, which contrasts with the interorganizational focus of most institutional articles within the academic

literature. More troubling is that many of the articles within practitioner journals identified by our search made only loose and superficial use of institutional theory. This suggests a major 'disconnect' between academic and practical use of the perspective.

Before examining the practitioner literature in more detail, we first turn our attention to the increasing prominence of the institutional perspective within academic journals. What explains the growth shown in Figure 10.1, and what are its implications? In their review, Tolbert and Zucker (1996) noted this upswing in popularity and worried about the lack of consensus regarding variables, measures, and types of analysis within institutional research. In this chapter, we argue that the continued growth of the institutional perspective within organization theory has resulted not from empirical success but rather from an expansion in the range of phenomena that institutional researchers have sought to address and from a broader spectrum of methods that are now being used in institutional research. Indeed, one of the characteristics of institutionalist research is its sweeping breadth. This expansion comes with a risk of fragmentation, however, to an extent that endangers the very essence of the perspective. As we discuss in the following section, the perspective now displays even more clearly the fragmentation that concerned Tolbert and Zucker a decade ago.

To appreciate the expansion of institutional theory, it is first necessary to provide some ordering of the vast body of institutional work. There are multiple ways of doing this. Scott's (1995) well-known approach segments institutional research according to the bases, or 'pillars,' of institutionalization (see also Suchman, 1995). Tolbert and Zucker (1996), meanwhile, distinguish between works that treat institutionalization as an outcome versus as a process. Others take a temporal approach and discuss the similarities and differences between older and newer institutional work (DiMaggio and Powell, 1991; Hirsch and Lounsbury, 1997). In their recent review, Schneiberg and Clemens (2006) focus on the array of methodological approaches within the institutional perspective and classify these according to the level of analysis studied. Suddaby and Greenwood (Chapter 11, this volume) also focus on differences in methodological approach and classify extant work according to one of four ontologies.

While all of these lenses provide a fruitful way of ordering the institutional literature, they do not fully expose the breadth of the perspective and its theoretical evolution over the past decade. In the next section, we outline core differences in what studies labeled 'institutional' seek to explain, with reference to exemplars. In doing so, we show how works under the 'institutional tent' may in fact have very little in common. Our objective is not to critique any one approach, but rather to highlight the high level of fragmentation within institutional research and some of the risks inherent in this. We then discuss how this theoretical evolution relates to methodological trends, and seek to connect the scope of the questions posed by institutionalist research with the scope of methodological approaches used to address them. Following this, we discuss further the status of institutional theory within

the practitioner literature. We conclude by suggesting that the trends we outline in theoretical emphasis, methodology usage, and practical application signal the potential for the deinstitutionalization of institutional theory and provide some suggestions on how this risk can be mitigated.

The evolution of divergent agendas within institutional research

The stream of research known as 'neoinstitutionalism' was spurred by two landmark works: Meyer and Rowan's (1977) theory of formal organizational structure, and DiMaggio and Powell's (1983) theory of organizational homogeneity. These papers were very explicit in their theoretical agenda: they challenged the then-dominant view that organizational structure is driven by technical imperatives, and instead argued that organizational structures and practices are explained by the need for legitimacy rather than efficiency. These papers sought to explain organizational stability and similarity, and gave a very limited role to strategic action. Both sets of authors were little concerned with organizational performance, beyond survival. And, as sociologists, they had little interest in the actual practice of management; instead, their interest was with field-level, rather than organizational, processes and outcomes.

Spawned by these two works, the institutional approach blossomed into a fertile, although still small, stream of literature through the 1980s and early 1990s. Neoinstitutional theory at that time had become largely associated with the idea of explaining similarity among organizations as driven by social and cognitive forces. Facilitated by the availability of historical records and registries of different types of organizations, research on formal organizational structure proliferated. The focus on observable elements of organizational structure (as opposed to more difficult-to-observe organizational actions and behavioral patterns) permitted neoinstitutional researchers to document patterns of adoption and the diffusion of various organizational forms.

With the explosion of research through the 1990s self-classifying itself under the term 'institutional', however, came a series of departures from the theoretical agenda of Meyer and Rowan (1977) and DiMaggio and Powell (1983). We discuss here three major shifts in emphasis: from stability to change, from isomorphism to diversity, and from constraint to action.

Stability versus change

As noted above, a core objective of institutional research has been to explain the emergence of stability, either within or between organizations. Indeed, this is the core meaning of the term 'institutionalization.' Highly stable, or institutionalized, structural arrangements are those that are perceived as objective, exterior facets of social life and have become taken for granted (Berger and Luckmann, 1966; Tolbert and Zucker, 1996). Stability stems from the legitimacy imperative, or the fact that organizations often choose to perpetuate institutional activities in anticipation of acquiring or sustaining social approval (DiMaggio and Powell, 1983; Oliver, 1992). In Scott's (1995) typology, stability can rest on any of three foundations: *regulative*, which includes the laws and administrative guidelines that constitute the basic rules governing relationships within and between organizations; *normative*, or 'expert' beliefs and value judgments; and *cognitive*, meaning shared perceptions of social life. In their seminal paper, Meyer and Rowan (1977) argued that change in highly institutionalized structures can occur only through coercion, such as that mandated by the state or prominent organizations.

Considerable institutional research has studied how stability comes about, or how organizational fields take shape and stabilize. For example, DiMaggio (1991) studied how art museums became widespread and accepted, and identified the importance of the creation of a common body of knowledge, the formation of professional associations, and the consolidation of a professional elite.

Rao (1994) studied the emergence of the automobile industry and highlighted the role of certification contests in legitimating the new field. Rao (1998) also showed how nonprofit consumer watchdog organizations emerged as a stable, recognized organizational form once a 'truce' developed between competing forms. In their study of the emergence of electric power organizations, Granovetter and McGuire (1998) highlighted the importance of industry associations in defining and stabilizing the boundaries of new sectors of activity. These studies are consistent with early work by Zucker (1977), who used a lab experiment to show that stability is rooted in shared cognitive understandings (see also Tolbert and Zucker [1996], who build on this view of institutionalization). In sum, the research agenda of many institutionalist studies through the 1980s and 1990s was to explain how structures and patterns of behavior became stable, persistent features of the social environment.

Recently, however, an increasing number of institutional studies have sought to explain the exact opposite phenomenon: how stable structures and patterns of behavior change or are discarded. In a paper that precipitated this shift in institutionalists' attention, Oliver (1992) argued that such 'deinstitutionalization' can be triggered by political, functional, or social forces. Hoffman (1999: 351) criticized extant institutional work for having 'only stability and inertia as its central defining characteristics,' and showed how organizational fields (in this case the US chemical industry) changed as a result of disruptive events. Several recent studies have examined change in long stable structures and practices. For instance, Scott, Ruef, Mendel, and Caronna (2000) described how the American healthcare system underwent a transformation from professional dominance to legislative dominance (in the mid 1960s), and then to managerial control and market dominance (in the mid 1980s). Ahmadjian and Robinson (2001) showed how poor performance triggered the abandonment of permanent-employment guarantees by Japanese firms. Greenwood, Suddaby, and

Hinings (2002) chronicled how changes in client expectations led to change in the organizational form of accounting firms in Alberta, Canada. Sine and David (2003) described how functional pressures stemming from the oil crisis led to the erosion of the long-dominant regional monopoly form of electric utility in the United States.

This shift—from studying stability to studying change—is not simply a movement along a continuum. It reflects a fundamental difference in what researchers consider important and interesting, and ultimately what research agenda they wish to pursue and what empirical settings they choose to study. Whereas an emphasis on homogeneity and stability was an attempt to show that the quest for technical efficiency does not drive formal structure and behavior (organizations facing different technical imperatives might well adopt the same structures and behaviors), an emphasis on change, that organizations can and do change (e.g., abandon institutionalized structures) when faced with pressures to do so.

Similarity versus diversity

In their seminal article, DiMaggio and Powell (1983) wondered why organizations in the same field are so similar. These authors posited that, as organizational fields evolve, three forces promote similarity among constituent organizations. First are coercive forces, or informal and formal pressures imposed on organizations by institutions (such as the state) on which they rely for resources and legitimacy. Organizations often adopt a new practice as a legitimate feature of a field if prominent players endorse or require that practice. Second are mimetic forces, or pressures that drive organizations to mimic the actions of peers that are perceived as legitimate and successful. Under conditions of uncertainty, 'organizations tend to model themselves after similar organizations in their field that they perceive to be more legitimate or successful' (DiMaggio and Powell, 1983: 152). Third are normative forces, which arise from rules and norms (such as those found in professions) that define goals and

designate appropriate means to pursue them. Principally, professionalism, in the form of formal education and the growth and elaboration of professional networks, can promote the diffusion of organizational structures and practices through organizational fields.

This theorizing sparked a great deal of empirical research on how organizations become more similar. In their pioneering study, Tolbert and Zucker (1983) found that structures mandated by the state diffused more rapidly through municipalities than structures not so mandated. Meyer, Scott, Strang, and Creighton (1988) showed how public schools in the United States became increasingly similar from 1940 to 1980 as a result of professional standardization and legislative developments. Galaskiewicz and Wasserman (1989) examined the charitable contributions of 75 firms and found that these firms mimic firms in their peer networks when selecting the recipients of their donations. D'Aunno, Sutton, and Price (1991) revealed that isomorphism of drug abuse treatment centers with the broader mental health sector (e.g., use of standardized mental health practices) increased their likelihood of resource acquisition. Han (1994: 637) found that 'a dynamic of imitation' led firms to select similar auditing firms. Corporations were more likely to adopt the multidivisional form when others in their industry had done so (Fligstein, 1985); savings and loans were more likely to expand into new service areas when large and profitable firms were active there (Haveman, 1993); and hospitals were more likely to adopt standardized (as opposed to customized) total quality management (TQM) programs as TQM adoption increased (Westphal, Gulati, and Shortell, 1997). In short, there is considerable evidence that organizations within fields become more similar over time.

More recently, however, researchers have shifted their attention from similarity to diversity within fields. Lounsbury (2001) showed how variation in college and university recycling programs was driven by a national social movement organization that promoted these recycling programs.

Sine, Haveman, and Tolbert (2005) found that regulative and cognitive institutions increased rather than decreased the diversity of organizational foundings in the US electric power sector. In their study of the American pharmaceutical industry from 1800 to 2004, Goodrick and Reay (2005) found that the field moved from a situation where a single, market logic (consumer choice) overwhelmed professional (specialized knowledge) and organizational (efficiency) logics, to one where a constellation of market, professional, and organizational logics coexist. Similarly, Ierfino (2006) described how multiple logics (and associated practices) coexist within the Canadian wine industry. And most recently, Marquis and Lounsbury (2007) showed how efforts to introduce a widespread, unified logic in the field of banking triggered foundings of new organizational forms that preserved diversity within the field.

This change in emphasis is striking. Institutions, according to DiMaggio and Powell (1983) and Meyer and Rowan (1977), are drivers of *similarity*, and considerable support for this core tenet has been found. However, recent research suggests something quite different: the institutional environment can be a source of *diversity* rather than isomorphism. In other words, recent research focuses on how institutional environments are capable of sustaining diversity among organizations. What, then, is institutional theory's answer to DiMaggio and Powell's question of 'why are organizations so similar?'

Constraint versus action

A core premise of neoinstitutionalism is that institutions constrain action. Institutions are said to confront the individual as social facts: 'by the very fact of their existence, [institutions] control human conduct by setting up predefined patterns of conduct, which channel it in one direction as against the many other directions that would be theoretically possible' (Berger and Luckmann, 1966: 55). In their paper, Meyer and Rowan (1977: 340) described the institutional environment as comprising 'powerful institutional rules which function as highly rationalized myths

that are binding on particular organizations.' Zucker's (1977) lab experiment provided a striking example of conformity in the face of institutional pressures. She showed that actors tended to provide conformist evaluations of 'light transmission' when placed in a highly institutionalized context (i.e., one characterized by organizational or authoritative conditions). In a field study, Ritti and Silver (1986: 34) described the development of an institutionalized pattern of exchange between a state utility commission and consumer advocate bureau whereby the parties followed established 'rituals' in order to obtain outcomes they saw as 'safe and predictable.' Tolbert (1985) showed how the structural differentiation of colleges and universities was constrained by institutionalized patterns of dependence. Baron, Dobbin, and Jennings (1986) showed how government agencies, unions, and personnel professionals constrained organizational-level variation in personnel practices. The implication of these studies for the scope of action—individual or organizational—is clear: actors are highly constrained, and must conform to institutional demands or face deleterious outcomes.

The notion of institutions as constraints on action has slowly eroded within the institutional literature, however. Whereas DiMaggio noted the neglect of action within neoinstitutionalism in 1988, Oliver (1991) provided a theoretical framework with which to view strategic responses to institutional pressures. She argued that organizations could do more than simply acquiesce to institutional demands, but could also defy, avoid, and manipulate them. More recently, Lawrence (1999) outlined a theory of 'institutional strategy,' or pattern of action for managing the institutional environment. Principally, these include defining standards and rules of membership within a field. And Bitektine (2008) showed how incumbent organizational populations could strategically manipulate social norms to create entry barriers against new entrants with a different organizational form.

Considerable empirical work has investigated these ideas, especially the importance of rhetorical skill in countering institutional pressures and altering institutional environments. A study of attempts to repair legitimacy after a public relations crisis in the cattle-ranching industry demonstrated the efficacy of verbal accounts (Elsbach, 1994). Similarly, skillful framing by actors in the Canadian accounting field facilitated the broadening of accounting firms' professional scope (Greenwood, Suddaby, and Hinings, 2002). Social and political skills allowed Sun Microsystems to institute standards associated with its Java technology (Garud, Jain, and Kumaraswamy, 2002). Actors in the HIV/AIDS-treatment field framed new practices of consultation and information exchange among community organizations and pharmaceutical companies in ways that integrated the interests of many different stakeholders and that were consistent with existing routines (Maguire, Hardy, and Lawrence, 2004). And entrepreneurs in the nascent independent power sector convinced regulatory authorities to establish a certification system that raised the confidence constituents had in their organizations (Sine, David, and Mitsuhashi, 2007).

In other words, institutional research now attends to (a) the availability of conflicting institutional norms that offer actors a choice of different legitimating accounts, and (b) the possibility of intentional, self-interested behavior on the part of actors that choose to deviate from institutional norms. Actors are no longer simply bound by institutional rules, but can modify and even create them. This fundamental shift represents a marked departure from earlier conceptions, which left little scope for purposive action (DiMaggio and Powell, 1991). It also entails an expansion in levels of analysis: whereas organizational and interorganizational levels were the focus of early work, individuals are now also the subject of inquiry.

Coevolution of theoretical and methodological shifts

In this section, we argue that the changes in theoretical agendas discussed in the preceding section have been accompanied by important trends in empirical methodology. As has been observed in the natural sciences (Kuhn, 1970), the evolution of research in the social sciences can be regarded as a path-dependent process. This process often follows a path of least resistance, rather than unfolding along a straight line of a clearly defined research agenda that was established early on in seminal papers that brought a particular theory or research stream into existence. In such 'opportunistic' evolution, the research questions within a given theory that can be explored using readily available, legitimate analytic methods get addressed first, generating relatively high returns to researchers in terms of publication acceptance. At the same time, other, equally important, questions, that require greater resource investments, deployment of less legitimate research methods, or development of novel (and, therefore, 'risky') methodological approaches often get addressed much later or sometimes remain unaddressed in empirical research for decades, until a major change in research paradigm (Kuhn, 1970) legitimates new methodologies or draws the attention of researchers to other questions and theories. In other words, theory and methods constantly interact with each other, affecting researchers' choices of research questions and methods in a way that cannot be explained by theoretical or methodological considerations alone.

Whereas the 'old' institutionalism of Selznick (1949) and Gouldner (1954) attended to agency and relied on qualitative methods, as did the 'Scandinavian School' of institutionalism (e.g., see Scott and Christensen, 1995), leading organization-theory journals had a decidedly quantitative focus in the 1980s. This facilitated the study of structural stability and similarity, which could be accomplished through data collection on the total number of organizations that share a particular structural feature over time. However, a study of the often-chaotic processes of change, especially with a focus on agency, could not rely to the same extent on quantification of organizational features. For instance, since entrepreneurial action aimed at changing prevailing social norms is much more difficult to observe and quantify than structural homogeneity in an organizational field, most recent research on institutional entrepreneurship has relied on richer, qualitative research methodologies requiring extensive fieldwork. Thus, while the recognition of the ability of individual actors to effect changes in their institutional environment had been addressed at the theoretical level in the 1960s (Berger and Luckmann, 1966; Stinchcombe, 1965), consideration of agency within institutional theory accelerated only in the mid-1990s which coincided with the time when qualitative empirical research methods gained greater legitimacy and became more popular within organizational theory.

In this respect, the evolution of institutional theory over the last two decades can be seen as an instance of coevolution of theoretical agendas and empirical methods: developments at the theoretical level were facilitated by the dissemination and growing legitimacy of qualitative research methods in organizational studies, and *vice versa*. While the theoretical shifts have been discussed above, the methodological side of this coevolution can be seen in Figure 10.2, which tracks the prevalence of qualitative research methods in organizational studies based on content analysis of citations and abstracts of six leading academic journals in organizational theory. As with the search presented in Figure 10.1, the data were retrieved in five-year periods starting from 1980. The counts obtained using this methodology were then divided by the universe of papers published in the six journals in a given five-year period, which produced a percent share of papers mentioning qualitative methods in the citation or abstract.

The figure shows that the presence of organizational-theory papers that use or discuss qualitative research methods has almost doubled since the 1980s: it has grown from about 5% in the early 1990s to almost 10% in 2005–2007. At the same time, the adoption of qualitative research methods in institutional theory was lagging behind the broader trend in the 1980s, caught up with the rest of the field through the 1990s, and surpassed the average to reach 14% in 2005–2007.

Thus, the decade following the publication of the influential paper on institutional entrepreneurship by DiMaggio (1988), which called for institutional research on agency and change, was characterized by the increasing use of qualitative methods in institutional research and in organizational studies as a whole. The greater popularity of qualitative approaches, we argue, stimulated research on difficult-to-quantify aspects of the institutional environment and permitted researchers to address questions that could not be explored using statistical methods and operationalizations. For example, qualitative field studies by Greenwood et al. (2002) and Maguire et al. (2004) could not (in our opinion) have provided the rich insights they did on the complex and multifaceted role of agency in institutional change through quantitative methods. The outcome of this positive feedback loop between theoretical agendas and qualitative research methods produced a strong increase in the number of qualitative studies within institutional theory (see Figure 10.2). At the same time, the increasing use of qualitative methods within institutional research itself contributed to the increasing legitimacy of these methods more generally.

In sum, the kinds of research questions that are explored empirically reflect to a large extent the research methods that are most readily available. If researchers believe quantitative methods to be more legitimate (and thus more likely to lead to publication), they will in the aggregate favor research questions that can best be addressed quantitatively. This could lead to some questions (e.g., about organizational structure) receiving more attention than others (e.g., about power and conflict). In the case of institutional theory, greater methodological pluralism has coevolved with a greater diversity in research questions. This 'methodologically diverse' institutional theory has proven very pliable,

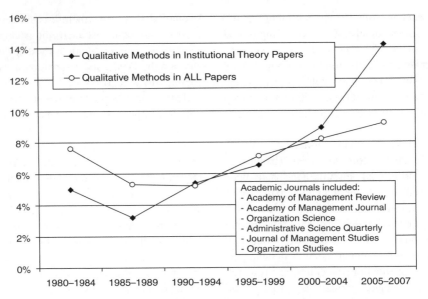

Figure 10.2   Percent of academic papers discussing or using qualitative methods.

especially when seen in comparison to related perspectives such as organizational ecology (see Haveman and David, 2008), which remain loyal to quantitative methods and to operationalizations of organizational processes through 'coarse' measures such as foundings and failures. The result is that institutional theory represents a very large tent that houses a great variety of theoretical agendas and methodological approaches.

Practical applications of institutional theory

We now turn our attention to how these theoretical and methodological shifts have affected institutional theory's influence on management practice. In its original statement, neoinstitutional theory did not lend itself well to practical application. With an emphasis on stability, homogeneity, and constraint, there was little scope for managerial action and thus little relevance for managers. In their 1991 review, DiMaggio and Powell acknowledge that the emphasis of neoinstitutional work at that time was disciplinary rather than prescriptive. The shifts outlined above, however, to the study of change, diversity,

and agency could be expected to render the institutional perspective more amenable to practical application. Indeed, the notion of 'change agents' seems to be of widespread managerial interest. It is surprising, therefore, that Figure 10.1 fails to confirm an increase in the use of institutional theory within the practitioner literature: if anything, the proportion of articles taking an institutional perspective in leading practitioner journals has declined at the same time as the proportion in leading academic journals has risen. In searching further for the use of institutional theory within practitioner journals, we were struck by how few papers adopt the perspective and by how thinly institutional theory is used by those that do. Before suggesting some reasons for this, we briefly review how institutional theory has been used by those writing for practitioners.

Institutional concepts tend to be used in two main ways within practitioner journals: to understand processes of new practice adoption, and to describe organizational environments. The practitioner-oriented papers in the 1980s and 1990s tended to regard the process of institutionalization as 'formalization' or 'ensuring persistence' of certain practices. For example, Gilad and Gilad (1986) discussed how the practice of business intelligence (i.e., systematically collecting information on competitors) spread through the business community. Epstein (1987) discussed how to institutionalize corporate social policies such as business ethics, value-based moral reflection, corporate social responsibility, and corporate social responsiveness within an organization. Beer, Eisenstadt, and Spector (1990) used institutional reasoning to discuss how their concept of 'revitalization' can be embedded in formal policies, systems, and structures.

The most prominent theme in practitioner-oriented publications that draw on institutional theory is that of institutionalization of change within organizations. Blumenthal and Haspeslagh (1994) argued that a successful organizational transformation is one in which management has succeeded in institutionalizing behavioral change. Tichy and Ulrich (1984) suggested that such institutionalization of change requires not only that new realities, action, and practices be shared throughout the organization, but also that, at a deeper level, a new culture that fits with the transformed organization be shaped and reinforced. Human resource management tools, such as selection, development, appraisal, and reward systems, play an important role in institutionalizing change according to these authors. The role of formal processes in institutionalization of new practices and operating procedures within companies is of particular importance to practitioner-oriented researchers. Prokesch (1997) described how the top management in British Petroleum used formal processes to 'institutionalize breakthrough thinking' in the organization. Relatedly, Nadler and Tushman (1990) suggested that the responsibility for managing in turbulent environments must initially be institutionalized throughout the management system to ensure success. Using a case study of a large clothing retailer, Roberto and Levesque (2005) uncovered four critical processes that facilitate institutionalization of a strategic change initiative: chartering, learning, mobilizing, and realigning.

In work that both recalls the older, Selznick (1949) tradition as well as anticipates further development of institutional entrepreneurship research, Hamermesh developed a concept of institutional strategy which deals with organizational intangibles and determines 'how a company defines and shapes its basic character and vision, what builds a sense of purpose among employees and creates commitment to the goals and mission of the enterprise' (1986: 116). Hamermesh regards institutional strategy as one of the three levels of strategy, along with business strategy, or 'competitive strategy of a particular business unit', and corporate strategy, or 'decisions affecting what businesses the company will compete in and how it will allocate resources among those businesses' (1986: 116).

Institutional processes at the interorganizational or population/industry level of analysis have received relatively little attention in practitioner-oriented research drawing explicitly on institutional theory. Among notable examples is the work by Guillen (1994) and Carroll and Hannan (2000). Guillen (1994) explored the techno-economic and institutional factors that led to the adoption of three basic models of organizational management in the twentieth century: scientific management, human relations, and structural analysis. The author concludes that 'as paradigms of ideas, management models are adopted in practice only when institutional circumstances conspire with them' (Guillen, 1994: 84) and calls for a balance between techno-economic variables and institutional factors in organizational analysis. Carroll and Hannan (2000) highlighted the practical importance of corporate demography as an academic field and as an important component of corporate policy making. The applications of a corporate-demographic approach, as described in their article, demonstrate the potential value of corporate demography and institutionally informed research for understanding the changing roles of corporations and populations of corporations.

Why has institutional theory had little impact on management practice, and why has this not increased with the theoretical developments discussed in the preceding section? We point here, speculatively, to three closely related reasons, which continue to apply to institutional theory despite the theoretical and methodological shifts outlined earlier. First, current institutional work seems no more concerned with organizational performance than was previous work. Recent institutional studies of change and agency using a qualitative approach focus no more— and often less—on profit, return on investment, or other standard measures of performance than did earlier studies of structure and homogeneity employing statistical analysis. Second, the motivations of institutional scholars remain predominantly theoretical. In other words, influencing practice is not central to the research agenda of institutional scholars of *any* theoretical or methodological stripe. As a result, the research and writing style of institutional theorists remains largely geared to other academics rather than to practicing managers. Finally, these factors are reflected in the choice of publication outlets that institutionalists choose. Institutional theory retains a strong sociological orientation, and as such studies often appear in sociology journals with little managerial readership. Even the management journals favored by institutional scholars, such as *Administrative Science Quarterly* and *Organization Science*, have little managerial readership compared to other management journals such as *Strategic Management Journal*. Moreover, little effort is made by institutional scholars (as compared, for example, with those in the field of organizational behavior) to translate and publish their work in journals with a practitioner readership such as *Harvard Business Review* or *California Management Review*. As a result, the disjuncture between institutional theory's academic prominence and its practical application is likely to remain wide for at least the near future.

Discussion

The early emphasis of neoinstitutional theory was on stability, similarity, and constraint.

A very different theoretical focus exists within the institutional literature today, however. Organizational fields are conceived of being diverse and in constant flux, and actors are seen as being able to create and modify institutions according to their interests. These changes in theoretical emphasis have been accompanied by an increase in the diversity of empirical methods. In addition to an increase in the use of qualitative methods (Figure 10.2), there has also been a shift in the means of data collection. Whereas most institutional studies of stability and conformity relied on archival records of organizational structure (e.g., Tolbert and Zucker, 1983; Fligstein, 1985; Han, 1994), recent studies of agency and change typically rely (at least in part) on data collected from field interviews (e.g., Greenwood et al., 2002; Maguire et al., 2004). Both theoretically and methodologically then, institutional theory has proven very flexible, especially when seen in comparison to related perspectives such as organizational ecology (see Haveman and David, 2008). This flexibility, we argue, has contributed to the marked increase in prominence of the institutional perspective (Figure 10.1) within organizational theory. In many ways, this is a triumph and serves as a welcome counterweight to the rationalist perspective that still dominates other areas of management theory.

This increased prominence comes with a potential danger, however. While the flexibility of institutionalism has led to increased breadth of application, it also entails a blurring of the institutionalist agenda. It is less clear today what makes institutional research distinctive, and what its core theoretical message is. If institutional theory is to explain everything—stability, change, structure, action, homogeneity, and diversity—then it risks explaining nothing. What is the core message of the institutionalist approach today? How are we to recognize institutional research, beyond the presence of the label? Because there are no clear answers to these questions, institutional theory risks engendering disillusionment among scholars. We know from research on management fashion that a sharp upswing in popularity, coupled with increased ambiguity in meaning, is often followed by a sharp decline in usage (Abrahamson, 1996; David and Strang, 2006; Giroux, 2006). Seen in this light, it is quite possible that institutional theory has peaked, and may soon experience a downturn as leading organizational theorists seek to 'stand out from the crowd' and develop more focused approaches (Abrahamson and Fairchild, 1999). At the same time, despite its current prominence among academics, it appears that institutional theory has little impact on management practice. This precludes the fruitful interplay between theory and practice that can prevent perceptions of irrelevance from surrounding a research stream.

As institutionalists ourselves, however, we prefer to maintain a more optimistic outlook for the perspective, and offer the following related prescriptions to avoid the dangers we outlined above. First, we urge greater precision in meaning within institutional research. Core constructs and ideas such as 'organizational field', 'ceremonial conformity', and 'institutional entrepreneurship' are often used loosely and with little precision. As the diversity of theoretical and methodological approaches increases, this laxity risks getting worse. By returning to core theoretical statements and attending more carefully to their use of terms and proposed relationships, empirical researchers—both qualitative and quantitative—can make more focused contributions and build cumulatively on one another's work. Doing so can also prevent the perspective from losing academic coherence.

Second, and related to the need for greater precision, we argue for increased use of experimental research designs within institutional theory. Although this may seem an odd prescription, given the increased diversity of methods observed earlier, we note that only two prominent institutional studies have been lab experiments Zucker (1977) and Elsbach (1994). We call for greater use of experiments, because these can effectively confirm (or disconfirm) cause and effect relationships that are often suggested but

difficult to isolate in contextually-rich field studies. At present, much of the theoretical insight of institutional theory goes untested— we believe laboratory work along the lines of Zucker (1977) and Elsbach (1994) would allow researchers to 'get to the bottom' of many posited relationships. Given that most institutionalists have little training in experimental designs, however, this may necessitate collaboration with colleagues from other disciplines (e.g., psychology).

Third, we call for a loosening of the tight coupling that exists within the institutional literature of quantitative methods with deductive theory testing and qualitative methods with inductive theory building. Most qualitative field studies in institutional theory, we observe, set out to develop new theory. This is valuable, of course, but much of it goes untested in subsequent work, perhaps because of the difficulty in finding or collecting sufficient appropriate data to perform statistical analyses. We argue that, given this situation, qualitative tests of theory can be informative. This approach is not unheard of in management studies: for example, Keil (1995) used a single case study of an IT project in a large computer company to provide a comparative test of three theories of escalating commitment, and Shane (2000) used a series of case studies to test the explanations of entrepreneurial opportunity discovery provided by Austrian economics. While we recognize that such approaches do not provide *statistical* tests of theories, we believe there is considerable value in uncovering even single cases of a theory being confirmed or disconfirmed—especially in a domain such as institutional theory that tends to favor developing new theory to testing its existing theoretical repertoire.

And finally, institutional theorists should attempt to reduce the gap between the perspective's theoretical prominence and its practical relevance. From our discussions with managers of all types, it is clear that institutional theory applies well to many managerial situations; yet, few managers are familiar with institutional research (in contrast, most *are* familiar with research in organizational behavior). Institutional theorists could certainly become more attentive to the interest of practitioners in intraorganizational processes, such as organizational leadership and decision making. In this respect, research informed by institutional theory and based on research methods used for intraorganizational studies in organizational behavior, may constitute a promising direction for increasing the practical relevance of institutional research. In addition, we believe that institutionalists can do a better job of highlighting to practitioners the relevance of interorganizational institutional processes and organizations' interactions with the superordinate social system. This could involve publishing 'research briefs' or translations in outlets such as the *Academy of Management Perspectives* that are targeted to practicing managers. Doing so would provide a necessary 'reality check' and would reveal the potential of institutional theory to inform practice.

APPENDIX: SEARCH METHODOLOGY

Methodology—figure 10.1

The searches were conducted in December, 2007 at McGill University using Proquest ABI/Inform Global using the keyword *institution** in the title or abstract to identify journal papers that discuss institutions and/or institutional theory ("*" refers to any subsequent word ending). Searching on titles and abstracts allowed us to retrieve those papers where institutional theory is central to the paper. Of course, many institutional *themes* (such as regulatory and political change) may be present without use of the word institution, but our interest here is in trends, not absolute numbers of articles.

The data were retrieved in five-year periods starting from 1980. By constructing five-year windows, we smooth year-to-year variation to reveal general trends. The search was performed on a set of six leading academic journals in the field of management and on three leading practitioner journals. The

Table 10.1   Journals used in the analysis

Academic journals 1980–2007	Practitioner journals 1980–2007
• Academy of Management Review	• Harvard Business Review
• Academy of Management Journal	• California Management Review
• Organization Science	• MIT Sloan Management Review
• Administrative Science Quarterly	
• Journal of Management Studies	
• Organization Studies	

'Publication title' text box was used, with the 'OR' operator between the journal titles. The journals are listed in Table 10.1.

The counts obtained using this methodology were then divided by the universe of papers published in these academic and practitioner journals in a given five-year period, which produced a percent share of papers that discuss institutions and/or institutional theory in citation or abstract. The universe of papers published in these journals was estimated for each of the five-year periods by performing a search with the string 'a OR the' in citation or abstract. The use of these two most frequent English words in the search string was necessary to exclude nonarticle journal content: the blank 'Citation and Abstract' textbox in Proquest fetched also tables of contents, acknowledgements, editorial board lists, etc., which were unduly inflating the total counts of papers in journals.

Methodology—figure 10.2

The searches were conducted in December, 2007 at McGill University on Proquest ABI/Inform Global using the following string to identify the mentions of qualitative methods in journal citations and abstracts: *'qualitative*' OR 'case study' OR 'field work' OR 'field study'*. The same six leading management journals were included:

• Academy of Management Review
• Academy of Management Journal
• Organization Science

- Administrative Science Quarterly
- Journal of Management Studies
- Organization Studies

While Academy of Management Review (AMR) is focused on theoretical papers, rather than empirical research, the journal has published a number of papers on research methods in organizational studies. The mentions of a particular method in AMR signify a certain level of researchers' familiarity with this method and its acceptance in the management research community. For this reason, we believe that the mentions of qualitative methodologies in AMR can also be used as a proxy for the interest in and popularity of these methods.

As with the search presented in Figure 10.1, the data were retrieved in five-year periods starting in 1980. The counts obtained using this methodology were then divided by the universe of papers published in these six journals in a given five-year period, which produced a percent share of papers mentioning qualitative methods in citation or abstract. As before, the universe of papers published in these six journals was estimated by performing a search with the string 'a OR the' in citation or abstract.

REFERENCES

Abrahamson, E. (1996) 'Management fashion', *Academy of Management Review*, 21(1): 254–85.

Abrahamson, E. and Fairchild, G. (1999) 'Management fashion: lifecycles, triggers, and collective learning processes', *Administrative Science Quarterly*, 44(4): 708–40.

Ahmadjian, C.L. and Robinson, P. (2001) 'Safety in numbers: downsizing and the deinstitutionalization of permanent employment in Japan', *Administrative Science Quarterly*, 46: 622–54.

Baron, J.N., Dobbin, F.R. and Jennings, P.D. (1986) 'War and peace: the evolution of modern personnel administration in U.S. industry', *American Journal of Sociology*, 92(2): 350–83.

Beer, M., Eisenstat, R.A. and Spector, B. (1990) 'Why change programs don't produce change', *Harvard Business Review*, 68(6): 158–66.

Berger, P.L. and Luckmann, T. (1966) *The Social Construction of Reality*, Garden City, NY: Anchor Books.

Bitektine, A. (2008) 'Legitimacy-based entry deterrence in inter-population competition', *Corporate Reputation Review*, 11(1): 73–93.

Blumenthal, B. and Haspeslagh, P. (1994) 'Toward a definition of corporate transformation', *Sloan Management Review*, 35(3): 101–6.

Carroll, G.R. and Hannan, M.T. (2000) 'Why corporate demography matters: policy implications of organizational diversity', *California Management Review*, 42(3): 148–63.

D'Aunno, T., Sutton, R.I. and Price, R.H. (1991) 'Isomorphism and external support in conflicting institutional environments: a study of drug abuse treatment units', *Academy of Management Journal*, 34(3): 636–61.

David, R.J. and Strang, D. (2006) 'When fashion is fleeting: transitory collective beliefs and the dynamics of TQM consulting', *Academy of Management Journal*, 49: 215–33.

Davis, G.F. (2005) 'The prevalence of "theory" among OMT submissions', Presentation made at Academy of Management Annual Meetings, Honolulu, HI.

DiMaggio, P.J. (1988) 'Interest and agency in institutional theory', in L.G. Zucker (ed.), *Institutional Patterns and Organizations: Culture and Environment*, Cambridge, MA: Ballinger, pp. 3–22.

DiMaggio, P.J. (1991) 'Constructing an organizational field as a professional project: U.S. art museums, 1920–1940', in W.W. Powell and P.J. DiMaggio (eds), *The New Institutionalism in Organizational Analysis*. Chicago: University of Chicago Press, pp. 267–92.

DiMaggio, P.J. and Powell, W.W. (1983) 'The iron cage revisited: institutional isomorphism and collective rationality in organizational fields', *American Sociological Review*, 48(2): 147–60.

DiMaggio, P.J. and Powell, W.W. (1991) 'Introduction', In W. W. Powell, and P.J. DiMaggio (eds), *The New Institutionalism in Organizational Analysis*, Chicago: University of Chicago Press, pp. 1–40.

Elsbach, K.D. (1994) 'Managing organizational legitimacy in the California cattle industry', *Administrative Science Quarterly*, 39(1): 57–88.

Epstein, E.M. (1987) 'The corporate social policy process: beyond business ethics, corporate social responsibility, and corporate social responsiveness', *California Management Review*, 29(3): 99–114.

Fligstein, N. (1985) 'The spread of the multi-divisional form among large firms', *American Sociological Review*, 50: 377–91.

Galaskiewicz, J. and Wasserman, S. (1989) 'Mimetic processes within an interorganizational field: an empirical test', *Administrative Science Quarterly*, 34(3): 454–79.

Garud, R., Jain, S. and Kumaraswamy, A. (2002) 'Institutional entrepreneurship in the sponsorship of common technological standards: the case of Sun Microsystems and Java', *Academy of Management Journal*, 45(1): 196–214.

Gilad, T. and Gilad, B. (1986) 'Business intelligence— the quiet revolution', *Sloan Management Review*, 27(4): 53–61.

Giroux, H. (2006) 'It was such a handy term: management fashions and pragmatic ambiguity', *Journal of Management Studies*, 43(6): 1227–60.

Goodrick, B. and Reay, T. (2005) 'Constellation of institutional logics: U.S. pharmacy 1800-2004', Paper presented at Administrative Sciences Association of Canada Annual Meetings, Toronto.

Gouldner, A. (1954) *Patterns of Industrial Bureaucracy*, Glencoe, IL: Free Press.

Granovetter, M. and McGuire, P. (1998) 'The making of an industry: electricity in the United States', in M. Callon (ed.), *The Law of Markets*, Oxford: Blackwell Publishers, pp. 147–73.

Greenwood, R., Suddaby, R. and Hinings, C.R. (2002) 'Theorizing change: the role of professional associations in the transformation of institutional fields', *Academy of Management Journal*, 45(1): 58–80.

Guillen, M.F. (1994) 'The age of eclecticsm: current organizational trends and the evolution of managerial models', *Sloan Management Review*, 36(1): 75–86.

Hamermesh, R.G. (1986) 'Making planning strategic', *Harvard Business Review*, 64(4): 115–20.

Han, S.-K. (1994) 'Mimetic isomorphism and its effect on the audit services market', *Social Forces*, 73(2): 637–63.

Haveman, H.A. (1993) 'Organizational size and change: diversification in the savings and loan industry after deregulation', *Administrative Science Quarterly*, 38(1): 20–50.

Haveman, H.A. and David, R.J. (2008) 'Ecologists and institutionalists: friends or foes?', in R. Greenwood, C. Oliver, K. Sahlin-Andersson and R. Suddaby (eds), *Handbook of Organizational Institutionalism*, London: Sage, pp. 573–90.

Hirsch, P.M. and Lounsbury, M. (1997) 'Ending the family quarrel: toward a reconciliation of "old" and "new" institutionalisms', *American Behavioral Scientist*, 40(4): 406–18.

Hoffman, A.J. (1999) 'Institutional evolution and change: environmentalism and the U.S. chemical industry', *Academy of Management Journal*, 42(4): 351–71.

Ierfino, L. (2006) 'Understanding de-stabilization and re-stabilization within mature organizational fields: the case of niche logic spillover to mainstream markets', Paper presented at the Academy of Management Annual Meetings, Atlanta.

Keil, M. (1995) 'Escalation of commitment in information systems development: a comparison of three theories', *Academy of Management Journal*, 38(2): 348–52.

Kuhn, T.S. (1970) *The Structure of Scientific Revolutions*, Chicago: University of Chicago Press.

Lawrence, T.B. (1999) 'Institutional strategy', *Journal of Management*, 25(2): 161–87.

Lounsbury, M. (2001) 'Institutional sources of practice variation: staffing college and university recycling programs', *Administrative Science Quarterly*, 46: 29–56.

Maguire, S., Hardy, C. and Lawrence, T.B. (2004) 'Institutional entrepreneurship in emerging fields: HIV/AIDS treatment advocacy in Canada', *Academy of Management Journal*, 47(5): 657–79.

Marquis, C. and Lounsbury, M. (2007) 'Vive la resistance: competing logics and the consolidation of U.S. community banking', *Academy of Management Journal*, 50(4): 799–820.

Meyer, J.W. and Rowan, B. (1977) 'Institutionalized organizations: formal structure as myth and ceremony', *American Journal of Sociology*, 83(2): 340–63.

Meyer, J.W., Scott, W.R., Strang, D. and Creighton, A.L. (1988) 'Bureaucratization without centralization: changes in the organizational system of U.S. public education, 1940–1980', in L. Zucker (ed.), *Institutional Patterns and Organizations*. Cambridge, MA: Ballinger, pp. 139–68.

Nadler, D.A. and Tushman, M.L. (1990) 'Beyond the charismatic leader: leadership and organizational change', *California Management Review*, 32(2): 77–97.

Oliver, C. (1991) 'Strategic responses to institutional processes', *Academy of Management Review*, 16(1): 145–79.

Oliver, C. (1992) 'The antecedents of deinstitutionalization', *Organization Studies*, 13: 563–88.

Prokesch, S.E. (1997) 'Unleashing the power of learning: an interview with British Petroleum's John Browne', *Harvard Business Review*, 75(5): 146–68.

Rao, H. (1994) 'The social construction of reputation: certification contests, legitimation, and the survival of organizations in the American automobile industry: 1895–1912', *Strategic Management Journal*, 15: 29–44.

Rao, H. (1998) 'Caveat emptor: the construction of nonprofit consumer watchdog organizations', *American Journal of Sociology*, 103(4): 912–61.

Ritti, R.R. and Silver, J.H. (1986) 'Early processes of institutionalization: the dramaturgy of exchange in interorganizational relations', *Administrative Science Quarterly*, 31(1): 25–42.

Roberto, M.A. and Levesque, L.C. (2005) 'The art of making change initiatives stick', *Sloan Management Review*, 46(4): 53–60.

Schneiberg, M. and Clemens, E.S. (2006) 'The typical tools for the job: research strategies in institutional analysis', *Sociological Theory*, 24(3): 195–227.

Scott, W.R. (1995) *Institutions and Organizations*, Thousand Oaks, CA: Sage.

Scott, W.R. and Christensen, S. (eds) (1995) *The Institutional Construction of Organizations*, Thousand Oaks, CA: Sage.

Scott, W.R., Ruef, M., Mendel, P. and Caronna, C.A. (2000) *Institutional Change and Organizations: Transformation of a Healthcare Field*, Chicago: University of Chicago Press.

Selznick, P. (1949) *TVA and the Grassroots*, Berkeley: University of California Press.

Shane, S. (2000) 'Prior knowledge and the discovery of entrepreneurial opportunities', *Organization Science*, 11(4): 448–472

Sine, W.D. and David, R.J. (2003) 'Environmental jolts, institutional change, and the creation of entrepreneurial opportunity in the US electric power industry', *Research Policy*, 32(2): 185–207.

Sine, W.D., Haveman, H.A. and Tolbert, P.S. (2005) 'Risky business: entrepreneurship in the new independent-power sector', *Administrative Science Quarterly*, 50(2): 200–32.

Sine, W.D., David, R.J. and Mitsuhashi, H. (2007) 'From plan to plant: effects of certification on operational start-up in the emergent independent power sector', *Organization Science*, 18(4): 578–94.

Stinchcombe. (1965) 'Social structure and organizations', in J.G. March (ed.), *Handbook of Organizations*, Chicago: Rand McNally, pp. 142–93.

Suchman, M.C. (1995) 'Managing legitimacy: strategic and institutional approaches', *Academy of Management Review*, 20: 571–610.

Thompson, T. (ed.) (2004) *OMT Newsletter, Fall 2004*, Briarcliff Manor, NY: Academy of Management.

Tichy, N.M. and Ulrich, D.O. (1984) 'SMR forum: the leadership challenge—a call for the transformational leader', *Sloan Management Review*, 26(1): 59–68.

Tolbert, P.S. (1985) 'Institutional environments and resource dependence: sources of administrative structure in institutions of higher education', *Administrative Science Quarterly*, 30(1): 1–13.

Tolbert, P.S. and Zucker, L.G. (1983) 'Institutional sources of change in the formal structure of organizations: the diffusion of civil service reform, 1880–1935', *Administrative Science Quarterly*, 28(1): 22–39.

Tolbert, P.S. and Zucker, L G. (1996) 'Institutionalization of institutional theory, In Clegg, S., Hardy C. and Nord, W. (eds), *The Handbook of Organizational Studies*, Thousand Oaks, CA: Sage, pp. 175–90.

Westphal, J.D., Gulati, R. and Shortell, S.M. (1997) 'Customization or conformity? an institutional and network perspective on the content and consequences of TQM adoption', *Administrative Science Quarterly*, 42(2): 366–95.

Zucker, L.G. (1977) 'The role of institutionalization in cultural persistence', *American Sociological Review*, 42: 726–43.

11

Methodological Issues in Researching Institutional Change

Roy Suddaby and Royston Greenwood

INTRODUCTION

Institutions now occupy a central position in most accounts of macro-organizational change (Greenwood et al., 2008). Institutional theory posits that organizations are subject not only to economic pressures, but also to social and cultural pressures that arise from interactions between organizations in their institutional environment (Meyer and Rowan, 1977). As a result, organizations often act in ways that are not necessarily 'rational', but are consistent with the 'rules, norms and ideologies of the wider society' (Meyer and Rowan, 1977: 84). That is, organizations adopt forms and practices that are isomorphic with norms of appropriate conduct or 'rationalized myths.' Part of the attraction of institutional explanations in organization theory is that they offer an alternative explanatory framework to economic accounts, which, based on assumptions of rational efficiency and motives of self-interest, fail to fully explain organizational action. As a result, institutional theory has

attracted an eclectic array of researchers who work from many different methodological perspectives but are engaged in the common enterprise of understanding how institutions produce both homogeneity and heterogeneity in organizational practices.

An institution, in this theoretical context, is understood to be 'more-or-less taken-for-granted repetitive social behavior that is underpinned by normative systems and cognitive understandings that give meaning to social exchange and thus enable self-reproducing social order' (Greenwood et al., 2008, pp. 4–5). Institutions may take the form of rules or codified social arrangements, norms of conduct, or cognitive structures that provide understanding and give meaning to social arrangements. A social arrangement is said to be institutionalized when it is widely practiced, largely uncontested, and resistant to change. Institutional change, which is the focus of this chapter, is the displacement of one set of institutionalized arrangements by another, or, the significant modification of prevailing arrangements, either substantively (in that the arrangements themselves change) *or* symbolically (in that the meanings associated with the arrangements change).

Organizations are analytically distinct, but are derived from institutions. Organizations, in this sense, are manifestations of explicit rule systems and implicit value clusters. As North (1990) observed, researchers should distinguish between their analysis of the underlying rules, or institutions, and the players of the game, i.e., organizations. In Selznick's (1957) terms, organizations absorb the influence of institutions as their purely technical activities become infused with the significance and meaning of distinctive values. Organizations and institutions thus exist in a state of mutual reinforcement where, on the one hand, organizations inculcate and reflectively manifest norms, values, and meanings drawn from the institutions that surround and support them; and, on the other hand, institutions are reproduced through the actions of organizations. Institutional processes may exist at multiple levels of analysis (i.e., the individual, the group, the organization, the community, the organizational field, the State, and even world society), but in this chapter we are interested in pressures for change that occur at the level of the organization within an organizational field. Our focus, in other words, is that of 'organizational institutionalism.'

DiMaggio and Powell (1983: 148) define an organizational field as consisting of domains of organizations that, 'in the aggregate, constitute a recognized area of institutional life: key suppliers, resource and product consumers, regulatory agencies and other organizations that produce similar services or products.' Scott (1994: 208), more succinctly, refers to the field as a community of organizations that 'interact frequently and fatefully with each other.' Organizational fields are typically associated with institutional 'logics' (Friedland and Alford, 1991) or broad belief systems that specify the boundaries of a field, its rules of membership, and the role identities and appropriate organizational arrangements of its constituent communities. All fields are, to a greater or lesser extent, subject to multiple logics arising from core institutions of society (Friedland and Alford, 1991; Thornton, 2002).

Institutional theory has evolved from an early preoccupation with showing the effects of institutional forces to an analysis of how those processes and their underlying institutions evolve and change. Agency has become recognized in some institutional accounts (Oliver, 1991; Lawrence and Suddaby, 2006). Despite this progress, critics express serious concerns about the theory's future direction. One concern is that research has become problem- rather than theory-driven, with an obsessive focus on drawing statistical relationships between variables, but without a substantive theoretical story that might allow understanding and generalizations (Davis and Marquis, 2005; Sorenson, 1998). Another concern is that institutional theory has become diffracted, without any attempt to draw coherent relationships between core puzzles, constructs, or ideas (Lawrence and Suddaby, 2006). Some argue that core constructs, such as institutions, logics, and even legitimacy, remain weakly defined and, as a result, are often inappropriately operationalized (Donaldson, 1995).

Others point out that prevailing approaches tend to minimize the phenomenological underpinnings of institutions (Barley, 2008; Zilber, 2008), because they are not easily amenable to quantitative analysis. The unfortunate consequence is that, while we may have impressive evidence of the effects or outcomes of institutional pressures, we lack understanding of the processes whereby those effects occur (e.g. Barley and Tolbert, 1997). Still others have pointed to an inability to separate institutional from other theoretical explanations such as organizational learning theory or resource dependence theory (Haunschild and Miner, 1997), making institutional theory too often a weak and unconvincing 'default option' for understanding change (Greenwood et al., 2008: 16).

Many of the problems identified in the preceding paragraphs are the result of a reliance on a relatively narrow range of methodological tools. Most researchers adopt multivariate methods which give attention to discrete and observable elements of organizations that change in response to changes in institutional pressures. Multivariate methods, necessarily, address the observable and countable elements of change, attending to the frequency of appearance or absence of discrete structural practices. These methods are powerful but are limited in the theoretical questions they can address.

A growing number of institutional researchers view institutional change as predicated on shifts in values, meanings and norms, and have begun to move beyond observable outcomes in order to attend to the ways in which institutional pressures are subjectively perceived and acted upon. Institutional change, in this view, is less about shifts in structures of institutional control and more about change in the shared meanings and understandings attributed to structures of control. That is, researchers are adopting tools that can address the phenomenological and ideational dimensions of institutional processes.

These tools we classify as *interpretive*, *historical*, and *dialectical* methods. We argue that the processes of institutional change are more fully understood when they are examined from these methodological perspectives, thus complementing the more common multivariate procedures that demonstrate the outcomes of change. We also argue that particular themes or aspects of change are best revealed by a particular perspective. Thus, institutional change conceived as a shift in taken-for-granted views of the world is best studied with *interpretive* methods; change as a complex phenomenon in which multiple political and economic pressures coincide is best studied with *historical* methods; change as a conflicted struggle over ideology and meaning is best analyzed with *dialectical* methods. Each of these mechanisms or dynamics of change (i.e., movements in world views, complex path dependence, or political struggle) generates changes in the discrete and observable facets of organization and reveals different aspects of the relationship between institutions and organizations. We argue, thus,

for the adoption of more varied or pluralistic techniques in order to capture a more holistic and balanced understanding of institutional change.

We present our argument in four parts. Following Alford (1998), we first review the four major epistemological categories of institutional research—the multivariate, the interpretive, the historical, and the dialectical. We illustrate how each has been used to study institutional change, and how each provides a useful but partial account. Second, we argue that most exemplary research incorporates elements of at least two of the four epistemologies. Third, we demonstrate how institutional research might benefit from combining methodological approaches in foreground and background elements of a single study. We conclude with a discussion of implications and future directions.

Four epistemologies

This section reviews the advantages and disadvantages of four methodological approaches and some of their associated techniques to the study of institutional change. The first—the use of multivariate analysis—differs from the other three in important ways, but notably in that it focuses upon variance rather than process. *Variance* methods seek to understand institutional change through 'causal analysis of independent variables' (Van de Ven and Poole, 2005: 1387; and see Langley, Chapter 24, this volume). Researchers using the variance approach assume that institutions and organizations are relatively fixed and stable arrangements best analyzed by observing how arrangements change when contextual conditions are varied. Causal relations between context and institutional outcomes are assumed to be relatively unitary and linear, but the time ordering of events is not considered to be particularly important (Van de Ven and Poole, 2005). The remaining three approaches, interpretive, historical, and dialectical, are largely qualitative in nature, and seek to understand institutions as relatively emergent clusters of interactions among and between social actors. Each of the four approaches has particular strengths.

Multivariate

Multivariate methods dominate research in institutional theory. They are most often used in studies that trace the diffusion of a particular practice or structural feature across a population or field of organizations. This diffusion model builds upon the core of an early observation of institutional thought that, over time, organizations become more similar to each other as they respond to their common institutional context (DiMaggio and Powell, 1983). Multivariate methods have been used to describe the conditions under which organizations adopt antitakeover provisions (Davis, 1991), engage in unrelated diversification (Haveman, 1993), adopt new managerial practices (Tolbert and Zucker, 1983; Westphal et al., 1997), enter new markets (Greve, 1995, 1996), construct alliances (Garcia-Pont and Nohria, 2002), engage particular advisors (Haunschild and Miner, 1997), or engage in decoupling of core and peripheral activities (Westphal and Zajac, 1994).

Multivariate methods draw from a functional epistemology, in which institutions and organizations are viewed as discrete and relatively autonomous elements of a broader social system. Typically, multivariate studies characterize, as a dependent variable, the extent to which some organizational practice or structural feature is adopted throughout a defined population of organizations. Institutional change is thus implicitly defined as diffusion of a new practice or procedure. So, for example, in Haveman's (1993) study of mimetic isomorphism, the dependent variable was the rate of entry into new markets by savings and loan organizations. Similarly, the study by Westphal et al. (1997) measured the adoption of total quality management practices by general medical surgical hospitals in the US from 1985 to 1993.

The independent variable in most of these studies typically involves factors thought to promote or inhibit diffusion of a practice. One line of research, consistent with ecological theory, treats the number and rate of previous adoptions as the independent variable. In this sense, extensive diffusion indicates that the practice has attained cognitive legitimacy. Other studies emphasize the links between organizations (such as interlocking boards—e.g., Davis and Greve, 1997), the role of professional networks (e.g., Baron et al., 1986), the influence of particular organizations that act as models or exemplars (e.g., Haunschild, 1993) *and* attributes, such as status and age, that inhibit diffusion (e.g., Ahmadjian and Robinson, 2001).

Multivariate methods are especially useful for capturing the blunt outcomes of institutional change, and have been important in validating some of the central premises of institutional theory. But these methods contain some implicit and limiting assumptions. Foremost, they treat institutions and organizations as discrete structural objects. These methods attend to overt and easily measurable elements of organizations that change as a result of shifting institutional pressures. What these methods cannot do, however, as we elaborate below, is capture the processes and the motivation of adoption. Nevertheless, there have been sophisticated attempts to do so (e.g., Westphal et al., 1997). By contrast, qualitative methods are necessary to trace the norms, values, and ideologies that underpin the overt elements of organizational structure and thus offer a more compelling test of whether and why patterns of diffusion *are* the consequences of institutional dynamics (rather than, for example, organizational learning). Further, institutional processes may be at work *without* overt changes in structure. For example, Zilber's (2002) ethnographic account of institutional change in a rape crisis center demonstrated that large-scale shifts can occur in the meanings and interpretations attributed to a practice, but without change in the practices themselves. Such forms of institutional change are difficult to detect by multivariate analysis.

Multivariate research often masks the 'messy' elements of institutional change. Adoption of a practice is typically coded as a binary fact; 'adoption' or 'non-adoption,' offering no room for nuanced analyses of the microelements of diffusion that fall between the 'adoption' and 'non-adoption' such as partial adoption (Zbaracki, 1998), adoption and subsequent rejection (although see Davis and Greve, 1997) or adoption with translation (Brunsson, 1989; Sahlin-Andersson, 1996).

In fact, the process of adoption or non-adoption is, itself, socially constructed. Munir (2005) offers this insight in his historical study of digital photography, where he observes that the 'precipitating event' of the introduction of digital technology in 1981 was an artificial construction of the rivalry between Kodak and Sony. The new practice had been introduced several years earlier and was still in the process of incremental refinement. Kodak's competitors, however, required a defining 'event' to promote the innovation and thus constructed, rather artificially, a discrete 'change' in technology. Munir's (2005) analysis demonstrates well the difficulty in imposing a discrete moment of change on what was a gradual and relatively incremental process.

Similarly, multivariate analyses of institutional change *infer* the causality between dependent and independent variables. In most multivariate studies, the question of causality is addressed through the presentation of proxies or 'intervening variables' that 'theorize about the mechanisms that explain *why* the independent and dependent variables are related' (Alford, 1998: 39). Many multivariate diffusion studies fail to posit intervening variables, relying on the correlation between changes in environmental conditions and the act of adoption to explain processes of isomorphic diffusion. This approach, quite rightly, has been criticized as treating institutional processes as a 'black box' in which researchers leave out the agents or individual activity that promote or inhibit diffusion, that create or reinterpret rational myths, and that legitimate or delegitimate possibilities of change (DiMaggio, 1988).

Multivariate diffusion studies, similarly, have been criticized for using weakly operationalized variables (Baum and Powell, 1995; Boxenbaum and Johnsson, 2008;

Zucker, 1989). Donaldson (1995), for example, objects to the use, by Tolbert and Zucker (1983), of relatively distant proxies to measure technical accomplishment in their exposition of the two-stage model of diffusion. Tolbert and Zucker (1983) found that economic and organizational factors such as size, age, city expenditures, and characteristics of the city population (proportions of the population that are illiterate, immigrant, and employed in manufacturing) were useful in predicting the adoption of civil service reforms for early adopters, but not for late adopters. They concluded that the loss of predictive power for later adopters means that they adopt for fear of losing legitimacy rather than from the hope of gaining efficiency. Donaldson (1995: 30), however, points out that, 'the fact that these variables predict adoption less among later than among earlier adopting cities is not evidence that the civil service regulations are less effective for later adopting cities, as no assessment is made of effectiveness for adopters, either late or early.' Others have noted that the diffusion of a practice across a population of organizations *may* be an outcome of institutional processes, but it might also be the outcome of organizational learning (Haunschild and Chandler, 2008). Mizruchi and Fein (1999) were especially critical of the tendency to use weak indicators of institutional effects. In short, the inferences drawn from use of multivariate procedures have been questioned.

Poor proxies create similar problems in multivariate studies of nonisomorphic change. There is reasonably strong evidence that profound institutional change, such as the adoption of a new organizational form, is usually preceded by changes in institutional logics (Leblebici et al., 1991; Scott et al., 2000; Thornton, 2002; Thornton and Ocasio, 1999). Therefore, many empirical studies count the number of prevalent new organizational forms as a proxy for measuring the degree to which logics have changed. A difficulty with this approach, however, is that actors may adopt similar structures, but for different reasons. Some may adopt for reasons of technical efficiency, while others may do so to seek legitimacy. In fact, if we take seriously the totalizing cognitive influence of institutions, the adoptive actors may not fully comprehend their own motivations for adoption. Still, the researcher cannot tease apart the technical/mimetic distinction that forms the nub of institutional theory accounts without capturing the motivations of adopters.

Part of the reason researchers struggle with proxy measures is that the boundary between 'institutional' and 'technical' environments is, itself, a product of socially constructed categories and institutionalized assumptions about the world. There is an historical/cultural component that may shift the boundary between these categories, depending upon where and when the research occurs. So, for example, Dobbin (1994) demonstrates that in nineteenth century France, sociopolitical conditions concentrated resources in the state and made the model of state owned railroads to be more efficient. In England, by contrast, sociopolitical conditions favored the individual and promoted a model of railroads owned by private corporations. That two different templates of railroad ownership could each produce efficient modes of transportation suggests that our definition of technical efficiency is really a product of culture.

In summary, because they rely on correlational evidence, multivariate procedures are better equipped to describe the outcomes of institutional change than to identify the motivations for change or the processes by which change is precipitated and unfolded. That is, these procedures address questions of 'whether' and 'when' but not questions of 'whom' or 'why' and 'how.' To address these latter questions, researchers have expanded their research toolkit. That is, with apologies to those who advocate hard epistemological boundaries between paradigms, institutional researchers must begin to draw upon more pragmatic and pluralistic methods that take seriously the processual and phenomenological elements of institutional change by incorporating interpretive, historical, and dialectical explanations.

Interpretive

Interpretive methods are the second most common approach to studying organizations (Gioia and Pitre, 1990) and were, arguably, the first to be applied to the study of institutionalization in organizations (Scott, 2001; Tolbert and Zucker, 1996). In contrast to multivariate methods, interpretive methods are distinctly subjective in focus, attending to the ways in which institutions are experienced by actors (Gephart, 2004). Drawing from phenomenologists such as Schutz (1962), and Berger and Luckmann (1967), interpretivists focus on how subjective experiences such as social roles, routines, and patterns of interaction, become typified so as to appear as an objective reality. Interpretive methods thus pay close attention to the ways in which actors make sense of, or apply meaning to, institutionalized practices and structures.

Interpretivist assumptions form the core of early institutional theory, often referred to as the 'old' institutionalism (Selznick, 1996; Stinchcombe, 1997). In old institutional theory, organizational change is predicated on how actors interpret organizational values in the context of broader social commitments. Selznick's (1949) analysis of the ways in which the Tennessee Valley Authority (TVA) adapted to external threats is, perhaps, the best illustration of the 'old' institutionalism. For Selznick (1996), a key contribution of the TVA study was recognition that individuals interpret bureaucratic objectives by drawing upon their social context. Organizational goals, as a result, often become subverted to cultural pressures by acquiring surplus social meaning, a process Selznick (1957: 17) described as 'the infusion with value beyond the technical requirements of the task at hand.' Organizations are thus as likely to adapt in ways dictated by societal concerns—such as conformity with culturally prescribed norms—as they are to change in ways that might improve productive efficiency.

Early proponents of 'new' institutionalism were also interpretivist. Meyer and Rowan (1977: 341) describe institutionalization as the process by which classifications become 'built into society as reciprocated typifications or interpretations.' Their central construct of 'rational myths,' or the shared meanings and understandings associated with institutional constructs, is inherently interpretive. DiMaggio and Powell (1983) also draw attention to the powerful cognitive or ideational forces that derive from common understandings and which form the engine for institutional isomorphism. The central idea spawned by interpretive assumptions is that institutional change is *invariably* accompanied by shifts in meaning, understandings, and values.

Researchers have adopted a number of different techniques to analyze shifts in meaning. Some use traditional ethnographic techniques (Barley, 1986; Zilber, 2002); others use participant observation (Bartunek, 1984), longitudinal case studies (Fligstein, 1990; Hinings and Greenwood, 1988), discourse analysis (Lawrence and Phillips, 2004; Phillips and Malhotra, 2008), content analysis (Suddaby and Greenwood, 2005; Zilber, 2006), symbolic interactionism (Barley, 2008), and cultural framing analysis (Hirsch, 1986). Zucker (1977) offers one of the most creative interpretive approaches by adapting the traditional experimental methodology from social psychology to assess how different organizational contexts contribute to the persistence of institutional effects.

An exemplary contemporary example of an interpretivist approach is Zilber (2002). Her account of the reinstitutionalization of an Israeli rape crisis center is unique on three counts. First, she employs an ethnographic technique which allows the researcher to concentrate analytic attention on how people within organizations subjectively experience organizational reality, and how they collectively negotiate their interpretation of that reality as conditions change (e.g., a shift in funding arrangements or the employment of individuals with different backgrounds). This technique offers a 'real-time' assessment of institutional change at an individual level of analysis.

Second, Zilber carefully distinguishes between changes in meaning and the outcomes that become manifest as a result of those changes. While we have understood for some time that institutional change requires a shift in both the structural and ideational elements of organizations (Greenwood and Hinings, 1996; Ranson et al., 1980), most research prior to Zilber's study focused on the structural elements of change as evidence of, and a proxy for, changes in the underpinning values and meanings. But Zilber's study demonstrates that organizations can experience a change in underpinning meaning systems without an accompanying, overt change in structure. It is only by using ethnographic procedures that this combination of a shift in meaning, without structural manifestations, could be observed.

Finally, Zilber's method led to the identification of *internal* dynamics that produced and shaped the direction of change. Zilber's focus on endogenous sources of change is in contrast with most multivariate studies, which tend to focus attention on external forces 'smacking into stable institutional arrangements and causing indeterminancy' (Clemens and Cook, 1999: 447). These 'jolts' arise from diverse sources such as regulatory change, technological disruptions, competitive exigencies, changes in social preferences, and war (Baron et al., 1986; Fox-Wolfgramm et al., 1998; Garud et al., 2002; Haveman, 1993; Lounsbury, 2002; Russo, 2001). Zilber's approach, by contrast, not only looks internally to identify dynamics of change, it also recognizes that the classification of a source of change as being 'external' or 'internal' is highly dependent upon the interpretation of individuals who become subject to the change.

Zilber's study (2002) illustrates not only the advantages of interpretive methods but also demonstrates the shortcomings. The standards of validity and reliability for interpretive studies (authenticity, resonance, and trustworthiness; Gephart, 2004) are clearly different from more positivist research (see Fitzgerald and Dopson, Chapter 27, this volume). From the perspective of multivariate research, such studies lack generalizability. Those trained in historical methods might also question the degree to which Zilber's causal sources of change are, indeed, endogenous. Meaning systems, although expressed in the interactions of small groups, may actually be derived from the moral and intellectual trends of an era, a generational or sociocultural period (i.e., a *zeitgeist*). Meyer and Rowan (1977), for example, might explain the shift from feminist to therapeutic logics observed by Zilber as an extension of the historical zeitgeist of overarching rationalization or a 'rationalized myth' derived not from internal interactions of individuals but from the broader sociocultural context. And from the point of view of researchers employing a dialectical perspective, interpretive research may be critiqued for privileging the insights of individuals who, because of their subject positions, may lack the reflective capacity to recognize the totalizing hegemony of institutional power.

Historical

Researchers who adopt historical methods view institutions (and organizations) as the outcome of complex phenomena in which multiple causes interact (Eisenstadt, 1964; Selznick, 1949). The goal of using an historical methodology is to identify stages of continuity, diversity, and change by analyzing how varying historical conditions produce different institutional and organizational arrangements. Historical methods focus systematically on past events, using archival documents and retrospective interpretations of actors in an effort to understand the processes by which institutions emerge, self-maintain, and erode.

Historical methods offer three distinct advantages over multivariate and interpretive approaches. First, historians adopt a distinctly *processual* view of institutional change. That is, they avoid overly simplistic notions of linear causality, and see organizational change as the outcome of multiple and often messy causes. Second, historical approaches offer the construct of *path dependency*, or the notion that the range of strategic choices of present-day actors is shaped and limited by past events. Third, historical methods take seriously the notion that institutional

arrangements are *socially* constructed, and allow researchers to avoid *their own* capture by a prevailing institutional logic. It is only by looking back in time that the researcher becomes aware that the present taken-for-granted social and organizational arrangements are actually historically contingent arrangements.

Attentive to process

Historians are uniquely sensitive to time and context and, as a result, view institutions, and the organizational arrangements that flow from them not as concrete things of stable durability, but as historically contingent, temporal processes (Tsoukas and Chia, 2002). This viewpoint is in distinct contrast to multivariate approaches which tend to view institutions, and the organizational arrangements that arise from them, as fixed entities with distinct attributes that are of relatively universal applicability. Researchers using multivariate methods look for stochastic explanations of change. They assume that instances of institutional change are driven by external contingencies that are relatively random and independent of each other.

Institutional theorists who adopt a historical perspective understand institutional outcomes as the result of causes that vary in number and influence across different contexts of time and place. Institutions are complicated, causal sources are often messy (Bennett and Elman, 2006; Schneiberg, 2005), and are best understood in terms of the interaction of multiple processes in which the time ordering of events is critical (Van de Ven and Poole, 2005). And, in order to uncover those processes, the historical dynamics and events that generate one set of institutional and organizational arrangements are compared and contrasted to those of a different time or place. So, for example, Dobbin (1994) compared the different structural organization of railroads that occurred in Britain, France, and the United States and concluded that cultural meaning, particularly the core understanding of how to secure social order, played a critical role in shaping the markedly different public policy arrangements (notably, the preference given to private versus public ownership) in these nation states.

Historical methods also tend analytically to arrange processes into distinct periods or phases (Van de Ven and Poole, 2007). Phases are identified as relatively distinct and coherent clusters of activity, temporally bracketed, and organized around common themes (Abbott, 1984, 2001). Identifying suitable start and end points and identification of historical turning points, however, is challenging (Rowlinson, 2005). But periods are useful analytic devices for imposing a degree of separation on the multiple influences affecting the relative stability of institutional arrangements at particular moments of time. Fligstein (1987) was an early exponent of the comparison of historical periods, showing how changing cultural conceptions of control affected the backgrounds of CEOs of large corporations over the course of 60 years. Leblebici et al. (1991) identified distinct stages in the evolution of the radio broadcasting industry in the US. These stages varied according to which focal actor (or 'institutional entrepreneur') had adopted a leading role in the organizational field.

Path dependence

A related and equally important concept introduced to studies of institutional change by historical researchers is the notion of 'path dependence'. Krasner (1984: 225) first described the construct of path dependence in historical institutionalism as the ways in which the institutional arrangements of today are limited and shaped by choices made in the past:

> Current institutional structures may be a product of some peculiar historical conjuncture rather than contemporaneous factors. Moreover, once an historical choice is made, it both precludes and facilitates alternative future choices. Political change follows a branching model. Once a particular fork is chosen, it is very difficult to get back on a rejected path. Thus the kinds of causal arguments appropriate for periods of crises when institutions are first created may not be appropriate for other periods.

Path dependence introduces into organizational institutionalism a different source of constraint on rational choice with the notion that existing institutional arrangements result from both conscious agency and historical accretion (Raadschelders, 2007), and that 'the weight of existing institutions' (Schneiberg, 2005) generates incremental change.

A useful example of how path dependence has been used in institutional analysis comes from Biggart and Guillen (1999) who show how historical methods can be used to reveal the path dependent influence of national institutions. They studied the auto assembly industry in four countries (South Korea, Taiwan, Argentina, and Spain) and explained their varying success by differences in public policy institutions that allowed domestic manufacturers to establish alliances with resource importers in some countries but not others. Another example of path dependent arguments is Schneiberg's (2007) analysis of cooperatives in the US economy between 1900 and 1950. Schneiberg shows how a distinct variant of capitalism, based on cooperative ownership and publicly shared models of governance, developed concurrently but quite separately from the dominant model of US neoliberal capitalism of dispersed ownership of publicly traded corporations. He argues that the coexistence of two quite dissimilar models of capitalism demonstrates the dynamics of path dependence in which the less dominant approach emerged from the detritus or cast-off models abandoned by the pursuit of what ultimately became the dominant model of corporate capitalism.

The notion of path dependence also usefully focuses attention on the founding conditions of institutions and organizations. There is a long standing assumption, particularly amongst the 'old' institutional scholars, that the historical institutional conditions under which a particular organizational arrangement is founded, serves to 'imprint' that organization with distinct characteristics that are relatively resistant to change. As Stinchcombe (1965: 169) simply stated, 'organizations formed at one time typically have a different social structure from those formed at another time.'

'Imprinting' for some organizational theorists has become a catchphrase for the inherent rigidity of organizations, but a more accurate usage within institutional theory is that it captures the notion that the institutional context within which an organization is founded radically proscribes the range of options available to that organization (and others occupying the organizational field) for change. That is, attempts to change the organization must be sensitive to the 'cultural repertoires' or 'genres' available to that organization (Clemens, 1996). Imprinting is typically considered at the level of the organization, but there are interesting extensions of Stinchcombe's basic idea to other levels of analysis. Burton and Beckman (2007), for example, examine the influence of imprinting and institutional factors upon the turnover of incumbents of particular functional positions. Another interesting extension of the 'imprinting' thesis is Phillips' (2005) study of Silicon Valley law firms. Phillips shows that founders from parent firms in which women in senior positions is an institutionalized norm are more likely to found firms with similar promotion practices. In effect, founders are 'imprinted' by their early organizational experiences and act as carriers of those norms.

Social construction

Historical research is particularly sensitive to the process of social construction. There is an inherent understanding that narratives, documents, and residual artefacts used to construct histories are often products of dominant social groups and the primary concern is with exposing these interests by careful examination of these materials (Carr, 1964). Historical studies usefully demonstrate how motives for the adoption of new templates of organizing can be retrospectively reconstructed. An excellent illustration of this is the historical analysis by Rowlinson and Hassard (1993) of the 'enlightened' labor management practices and traditions at the British confectioner, Cadbury. They show how Cadbury reconstructed its corporate history, inaccurately, to claim that its use of 'Garden Cities' to house workers was motivated by a religiously inspired regard for employee interests, when in fact a detailed historical analysis of Cadbury reveals that the company's actual motivation was to create a captive labor source. Over time, however, the 'invented' version of Cadbury's history as an enlightened religious employer became taken for granted by both internal and external constituencies.

As a result, historically motivated institutional research helps the researcher escape the cognitive influence of extant institutions. One of the core challenges in researching institutions is the degree of reflexivity, not only of actors, but also of researchers. Actors and researchers are embedded in institutional contexts and, in so far as those contexts are taken-for-granted, it is difficult for us as researchers to recognize, measure, and interpret institutional effects. From a historical perspective, this problem is substantially reduced, though not entirely removed. Viewed retrospectively, as illustrated by the example of Cadbury, the totalizing influence of institutions and processes of institutionalization are more easily traced and observed.

Historical research techniques are many and varied but inevitably focus on archival documentation (Ventresca and Mohr, 2002) of both primary and secondary sources, and retrospective interviews. Historiography is, 'an empirical research paradigm using an interpretive or qualitative approach which focuses on a chronology over a substantial period of time in order to obtain a fuller and richer understanding of a situation or set of circumstances' (O'Brien et al., 2004). Historiography is, therefore, not to be confused with merely longitudinal studies, time series analyses, or 'evolutionary' studies, in that each of these lacks an interpretive element by the researcher who must critically evaluate the data sources and offer an analysis that goes beyond simply 'confirm[ing] or refut[ing] the efficiency of some contemporary causal relationship' (Jacques, 2006).

Despite the advantages of the historical approach, its use for understanding institutional change is surprisingly infrequent. When used, however, it can provide powerful insights across multiple empirical contexts. Fligstein (1985) employs historical methods to describe the causal sources of the diffusion of the multidivisional form. Holm's (1995) historical account of changes in the Norwegian fishing industry reveals institutionalization and field formation as a dynamically complex and inherently political process and reveals the powerful insight that actors are simultaneously subject to multiple institutional pressures. The historical account by Hargadon and Douglas (2001) of Edison's work identifies key tactics required to legitimate new technologies. Leblebici et al. (1991) provide an intriguing account of the emergence of radio broadcasting and highlight the complex causality underlying it. And Schneiberg (2007) uses historical methods to demonstrate how abandoned institutional projects can be cobbled together to create new and innovative institutions in his sweeping analysis of institutional change in the US economy from 1900 to 1905.

A particularly influential exemplar of how historical methods can be used to study institutional change is the account by Leblibici et al. (1991) of the emergence of the field of radio broadcasting. The paper's main contribution is to demonstrate the role of peripheral actors in shaping the path dependent evolution of an organizational field. Their analysis illustrates many of the advantages of detailed historical work, particularly the notion that institutional change is the result of complex (i.e., multiple) causality. The paper also effectively demonstrates how retrospective analysis of institutional change overcomes cognitive barriers to interpreting institutions. By viewing the field over time, Leblebici et al. avoided the common trap of seeing the institutional structure of the field as reified or given and, instead, identified the institutional structures that ultimately shaped the field as contingent and relatively unstable structures that emerged as a result of negotiation and competition between actors.

Historical research methods are not without their pitfalls. A common analytic challenge for historical researchers is periodization, i.e., the identification of suitable start and end points for the span of study, and the identification of significant historical turning points (Rowlinson, 2005). Historical research has also been criticized for overemphasizing detail at the expense of theoretical coherence. Critics have also pointed to flaws inherent in some techniques of historical research, such as the use of retrospective interviews which are dependent upon the sometimes imperfect or self-serving memories of participants (Golden, 1992). There are, however, common remedies for these problems. Golden (1992) offers a useful summary. First, researchers should try to focus on verifiable actions and facts rather than beliefs and intentions. Second, as with all research, one should try to triangulate data sources (Jick, 1979). Third, one should be careful with relatively recent events where interview subjects and data may still be constrained by emotions and interests.

There is a growing awareness among institutional theorists that institutions are the outcome, not of discrete choices between alternative arrangements, but rather of long stretches of sedimentation, in which the overt features of an organizational form are the product of complex layers of historical conflicts, crises and erosions (Cooper et al., 1996). Historical research methods are appealing for their richness and ability to embrace the sedimentary nature of institutions. Historiography offers a unique but underutilized method for the archaeological investigation of the complex and varied influences of institutions on organizational outcomes.

Dialectical

Drawing from Marxist (Benson, 1977) and critical theory (Hasselbladh and Kallinikos, 2000), researchers, using dialectical methods, work on the assumption that institutions are manifestations of power relations in society. In the process of institutionalization, structures of power and conflicts between powerful actors become incorporated into taken-for-granted routines, practices, and norms of social relations. As a result, previously overt expressions of power become normalized and absorbed into everyday practices and thus hidden (Gephart, 2004). The primary goal of dialectical research methods is thus to uncover these hidden interests, and to expose hegemonic forms of domination and inequalities that have become taken-for-granted. Subsidiary goals include the exposure of contradictions that arise during the process of institutionalization when overt conflicts and struggles become embedded in pragmatic interests and the consolidation of power.

Dialectic researchers employ many different methodological techniques (Morrow, 1994). Some researchers, acting on the assumption that hegemonic power is revealed in language, focus on discourse (Hardy et al., 2003; Oakes et al., 1998). Others attend to the contradictions inherent in overt symbols and artifacts, such as dress (Creed et al., 2002). A particularly useful dialectical technique is the 'extended case method' which originated in the Manchester School of Social Anthropology in the 1950s and has been reintroduced to social theory by Burawoy (1998). This method is based on reflective or hermeneutic techniques that tap into macrocultural phenomena by using microlevel data, particularly the everyday interpretations, experiences, and practices of individuals. Data are extracted through narrative interviews in which informants are encouraged to reflect on macrosocial forces that shape or influence their behavior.

Although the extended case method has similarities to interpretive techniques, such as ethnography or participant observation, it differs from these approaches in several important respects. First, while most interpretive approaches try to capture the subjective perceptions of the subject *in situ* and seek to minimize the impact of the researcher, the extended case method openly acknowledges, and embraces, the intervention of the researcher. The researcher is viewed as a 'stimulus' whose task is to provoke the subject and to create a reaction. As such, the act of interviewing a respondent is designed to disrupt the 'lived experience' of the subject. It is through this disruption that we learn about

the nature of institutions because, as Burawoy (1998: 14; see also Gephart, 1993) observes, 'institutions reveal much about themselves when in stress or in crisis, when they face the unexpected as well as the routine'. We learn much about institutionalized social orders, according to Burawoy, by seeing how they respond to challenge and pressure. A key task of the researcher, therefore, is to challenge the subject's assumptions about the ways in which expressions of power become objectified or are made to appear natural.

The extended case method is distinguishable from traditional grounded theory methods in that its goal is not to discover new theories by aggregating from multiple observations, but rather to extend existing theories by abstracting a single data point (or local knowledge) into aggregate social processes (or situational knowledge) that become institutionalized as structures of power. So, for example, Burawoy (1998) identifies Kanter's (1977) study of situational power in organizations as an illustrative form of extended case research, in that Kanter abstracts from local case studies the observation that individual work attitudes and behaviors are not inherent personality characteristics of individuals but, rather, are situational responses to structural determinants of power.

Perhaps the most significant advantage offered by dialectic techniques in researching institutional change is that they suggest ways of overcoming the cognitive dilemma of how we, as researchers, can objectively study institutional processes. The cognitive dilemma is this; if institutions are cognitively totalizing structures that determine the world views of both actors and researchers, 'it is not at all easy to adjudicate between "institutions as constraints on action" and "institutions as culturally constitutive of actors" ' (Schneiberg and Clemens, 2006: 196).

Dialectical methods offer several solutions to the cognitive dilemma. First, there are clearly periods of unrest and disruption when the institutional fabric is torn and the totalizing influences, inherent contradictions, and hegemonic power of institutional structures reveal themselves. Second, the sedimentary effects of institutionalization (and the hidden structures of power) can be discerned in language. Because the evolution of language does not occur at the same pace as practice, archival records often preserve the process by which institutions 'sediment over' conflict and struggle. As a result, the 'contested ascent' (Blackler and Regan, 2006) of abstract ideas into codified routines and practices can be observed in texts, archives and discourse.

Despite the advantages of dialectical methods, they have been rarely used to study institutional change. However, recent work indicates growing recognition of their possibilities. Seo and Creed (2002) provide a compelling account of how organizational fields have inherent contradictions that amplify as fields mature and become the locus of potential disruption and change. Greenwood and Suddaby (2006) elaborate the framework of Seo and Creed through an empirical analysis of how large accounting firms legitimated new practices that served their interests, and how those practices arose from field-level contradictions. A third illustration is the recent analysis by Blackler and Regan (2006) of institutional change in family services in the UK. These researchers developed a detailed case study through a process of 'participatory action' in which the researchers were actively engaged in the project that formed the basis of their study. This involvement is a form of the action research advocated by Silverman (2001) and Bartunek (1984) in which the researchers act not as detached observers but become involved as agents of change. Researchers actively provoke change by engaging in a process of 'dialectical review' in which they openly question extant institutional arrangements.

Blackler and Regan's (2006) case study depicts a clear connection between rhetoric (or discourse) and action (see also Heracleous and Barrett, 2001; Phillips et al., 2004; Sillince, 2005; Suddaby and Greenwood, 2005). It also highlights the critical conditions under which some forms of 'talk'

become objectified or institutionalized. The study serves as an exemplary illustration of how dialectic methods can be used to distil the linkages between macroinstitutional constructs (i.e., the ideational elements of institutions) and microinstitutional behaviors (i.e., the practical actions of individuals).

Combining methods: background and foreground uses

Although research on institutional change can be categorized into the above four methodological approaches, studies that make a central contribution often use a pluralistic synthesis of methods, with one dominant methodology in the foreground and another, more subordinate method, in the background. So, for example, Haveman's (1993) study of mimetic behavior amongst savings and loans organizations, while clearly a multivariate study, contains within it an important, albeit brief, element of the historical methodology. A similar combination of historical overview, followed by multivariate analysis, is characteristic of Edelman's work (e.g., Edelman et al., 1999). Rao et al. (2003) combine an historical overview with multivariate methods to show complex society-wide processes that contextualize and give insight into changes (which they analyze using multivariate analysis) occurring at the level of the field or industry (in their case, French cuisine). Zilber's (2002) interpretive account of changes experienced in an Israeli rape crisis center, similarly presents the interpretive data against a backdrop historical study. And the Blacker and Regan (2006) analysis of change in family support services, while clearly dialectical in the foreground, includes many 'behind the scenes' elements of interpretive methodology.

Our sense is that serious contributions to understanding institutional change arise from the theorization of institutions as complex phenomena. To do so, we need to see institutions as both nouns and verbs (Van de Ven and Poole, 2005; Weick, 1979). Barley and Tolbert (1997), for example, adopt a strong processual view of institutions and suggest they may be best studied by using methods that focus analytic attention on processes of structuration. They suggest a series of methods based on viewing institutions as 'scripts' or 'grammars of action' in which institutions are understood as an algorithm or social software that enables and constrains social action.

Interestingly, the specific methods that Barley and Tolbert (1997) identify as appropriate for studying the various elements of institutional scripts fit comfortably within the four part schema identified in this chapter. They suggest, first, that institutional researchers should attend to charting the flows of action within scripts or attending to 'who interacts with whom at what times.' This component of institutionalization can be effectively captured through multivariate techniques that view actors and institutions as relatively concrete structures whose features can be observed and counted. Second, Barley and Tolbert suggest that it is equally important to assess how these interactions are understood, not only by the researcher, but also by the participants engaged in them. To capture these understandings requires use of interpretive techniques that attempt to capture process narratives. Barley and Tolbert (1997) also point out that historical techniques are important, because they capture the unfolding of scripts over long time periods and that archival documents are frequently the only practical means through which a researcher can capture the collective narrative that explains why certain scripts of action were selected over others. Finally, Barley and Tolbert (1997) note that institutional scripts are typically most apparent in times of conflict and struggle, or where an event has disrupted a pre-existing interaction order and caused actors to shed taken-for-granted roles, status positions, and patterns of authority. Such attention to change in socially embedded power structures would, ideally, draw upon the procedures of dialectic research.

Treating institutions as complex entities that interact across multiple levels of analysis implies that researchers should expand their range of methodological tools. The notion that

institutions are comprised, simultaneously, of content and process elements directs us, necessarily, to the notion that the use of multivariate methods must be complemented by an equal use of qualitative methods, particularly those that focus on the interpretations and categorization of events by the participants, when studying processes of institutional change.

In order to accomplish the goal of encouraging more pluralistic methods in researching institutional change, the traditional model of writing and presenting management research must be adapted. Management journal articles follow an established genre. Journal articles are terse and precisely focused on a single issue or aspect of organizations. Similarly, they tend to draw from a relatively focused range of literatures. As a result, it is highly unusual for a management journal to publish an article that employs multiple or mixed methods. Mixing qualitative and quantitative elements in a single manuscript would violate highly institutionalized norms of presentation.

Yet in literature, music and science, genre mixing has been identified as a critical element of creative discovery (Brown, 1990; Bazerman, 1987). As we note in the preceding section, much exemplary research on institutional change has, similarly, engaged in genre mixing. The high impact multivariate research articles are often the product of considerable 'behind-the-scenes' qualitative research and strong instances of content analysis skilfully embrace both manifest (i.e., word frequency) and latent (i.e., word meaning) elements. The skill is both in employing mixed methods and in adopting Alford's (1998) notion of foreground and background modes of presentation. We believe that this modest variation in the institutionalized template of presenting management research should be expanded and, perhaps, formalized.

We see several specific possibilities for adopting pluralistic methods in studying institutional change. *Attitude survey analysis*, for example, is a technique that employs both multivariate and interpretive elements that seems ideally suited for the study of institutional logics. Survey analysis is widely used in political science and was, once, a popular technique in sociology. Its use has declined among social scientists, partly because of technical issues, but largely because its application has been under-theorized (Splichal, 1999). One of the more common criticisms of survey analysis is that the methodology depends upon an interpretive component (the interpretation of the questions) and a multivariate com-ponent (the statistical interpretation of the results).

From our perspective, however, it is precisely this mix of interpretive and mul-tivariate elements that make the technique attractive for studying aspects of change in institutional logics. Although institutional theory has developed strong theoretical arguments about the relationship between underlying beliefs or attitudes and changes in institutional structure, there has been very little attempt to use opinion survey techniques to map or locate the sources of changes in attitudes about dominant institutional structures (but see Suddaby et al., 2009, for an attempt to do this).

Another technique that usefully combines qualitative and quantitative elements is *semantic field analysis* (Kittay and Lehrer, 1992). This technique combines quantitative elements of structural network analysis with the interpretive elements of discourse analysis by analyzing and mapping the use of words across an institutionalized field. The method is based on the assumption that institutional logics become embedded in language, and that words applicable to a common conceptual or ideological domain can be identified and mapped through space. Semantic field analy-sis thus creatively combines the structural and ideational elements of organizational fields and institutional logics. They can also be usefully combined with historical research methods to analyze how field logics evolve through time.

We note that pluralistic research extends beyond the four categories of method we describe here. It might, for example, be instructive to mix levels of analysis in

studying institutional change. As Weick and Quinn (1999: 362) observe, the difference between those who see institutions as rela-tively stable, isomorphic structures, and those who see institutions as subject to bouts of revolutionary, divergent change, might be simply explained by the point of view of the researcher:

> The contrast between episodic and continuous change reflects differences in the perspective of the observer. From a distance (the macro level of analysis), when observers examine the flow of events that constitute organizing, they see what looks like repetitive action, routine and inertia dotted with occasional episodes of revolutionary change. But a view from closer in (the micro level of analysis) suggests ongoing adaptation and adjustment. Although these adaptations may be small, they tend to be frequent and continuous across units, which means they are capable of altering structure and strategy.

It is this mix of approaches, methods, or genres that frees the researcher from recreat-ing dominant views and which produces true insight. This argument is not to be taken as an overt call for paradigm commensurability. There are well-articulated epistemological issues in doing so (Burrell and Morgan, 1979) as well as pragmatic problems of presenting complex methodologies in the restrictive format of a journal article. In fact, we believe that research benefits from the intellectual tension generated from the use of competing paradigms. What we do suggest, however, is that papers that succeed in making a signifi-cant contribution to understanding processes of institutional change often have an inherent sensitivity to the idea that institutional change should be theorized broadly and involves use of multiple methodological paradigms. As Alford (1998: 122) suggests:

> Pay attention to multiple kinds of arguments. Don't confuse statistical summaries and reductions of the data with causal inference. Do pay serious attention to the historical context of the data and the actual social processes and interactions that constitute the meaning of the data to human actors.

By problematizing institutional change in a multitheoretic way, we may be able better to identify and then answer the central questions of institutional change. Are organizations becoming more or less similar? Where do institutional templates and logics come from? How do logics shift? How are shifts in logics manifest and understood at the organizational level?

REFERENCES

Abbott, A. (1984) 'Event sequence and event duration: colligation and measurement', *Historical Methods*, 17: 192–204.

Abbott, A. (2001) *Time Matters: On Theory and Method*, Chicago: University of Chicago Press.

Ahmadjian, C.L. and P. Robinson, (2001) 'Safety in numbers: downsizing and deinstitutionalization of permanent employment in Japan', *Administrative Science Quarterly*, 46: 622–54.

Alford, R.R. (1998) *The Craft of Inquiry: Theories, Methods, Evidence*, Oxford: Oxford University Press.

Barley, S.R. (1986) 'Technology as an occasion for structuring: evidence from observations of CT scanners and the social order of radiology departments', *Administrative Science Quarterly*, 31 (1): 78–108.

Barley, S.R. (2008) 'Coalface institutionalism', in R. Greenwood, C. Oliver, K. Sahlin and R. Suddaby (eds), *Handbook of Organizational Institutionalism*, London: Sage.

Barley, S.R. and Tolbert, P. (1997) 'Institutionalization and structuration: studying the links between action and institution', *Organization Studies*, 18 (1): 93–117.

Baron, J.N., Dobbin, F.R. and Jennings, P.D. (1986) 'War and peace: the evolution of modern personnel administration in U.S. industry', *American Journal of Sociology*, 92 (2): 350–83.

Bartunek, J. (1984) 'Changing interpretive schemes and organizational restructuring: the example of a religious order', *Administrative Science Quarterly*, 29 (3): 355–72.

Baum, J.A.C. and Powell, W.W. (1995) 'Cultivating an institutional ecology or organizations: comment on Hannan, Carroll, Dundon and Torres', *American Sociological Review*, 60: 529–38.

Bazerman, C. (1987) 'Codifying the social scientific style. the APA Publication Manual as a behavioralist rhetoric', in John S. Nelson, Allan Megill and Donald N. McCloskey (eds), *The Rhetoric of the Human Sciences. Language and Argument in Scholarship and Public Affairs*, Madison: University of Wisconsin Press, pp. 125–44.

Bennett and Elman (2006) 'Complex causal relations and case study methods: the example of path dependence', *Political Analysis*, 14: 250–67.

Benson, K. (1977) 'Organizations: a dialectical view', *Administrative Science Quarterly*, 22(1): 1–21.

Berger, P.L. and Luckmann, T. (1967) *The Social Construction of Reality: A Treatise on the Sociology of Knowledge*, New York: Anchor.

Biggart, N. and Guillen, M. (1999) 'Developing difference: social organization and the rise of the auto industries of South Korea, Taiwan, Spain and Argentina', *American Sociological Review*, 64(5): 722–47.

Blackler, F. and Regan, S. (2006) 'Institutional reform and the reorganization of family support services', *Organization Studies*, 27(12): 1843–61.

Boxenbaum, E. and Johnsson, S. (2008) 'Isomorphism, diffusion and decoupling', in R. Greenwood, C. Oliver, K. Sahlin and R. Suddaby (eds), *Handbook of Organizational Institutionalism*, London: Sage.

Brown, R.H. (1990) 'Social science and the poetics of truth', *Sociological Forum*, 5(1): 55–74.

Brunsson, N. (1989) *The Organization of Hypocrisy*, Chichester: Wiley.

Burawoy, M. (1998) 'The extended case method', *Sociological Theory*, 16(1): 4–33.

Burrell, G. and Morgan, G. (1979) *Sociological Paradigms and Organizational Analysis*, London: Heinemann.

Burton, M.D. and Beckman, C.M. (2007) 'Leaving a legacy: position imprints and successor turnover in young firms', *American Sociological Review*, 72(2): 239–67.

Carr, E.H. (1964) *What is History?*, London: Pelican.

Clemens, E. (1996) 'Organizational form as frame: collective identity and political strategy in the American labor movement, 1880–1920', in, D. McAdam, J.D. McCarthy and M.N. Zald (eds), *Comparative Perspectives on Social Movements*, Cambridge: Cambridge University Press, pp. 205–26.

Clemens, E.S. and Cook, J.M. (1999) 'Politics and institutionalism: explaining durability and change', *Annual Review of Sociology*, 25: 441–66.

Cooper, D.J., Hinings C.R., Greenwood R. and Brown. J. (1996) 'Sedimentation and Transformation in Organizational change: the case of Canadian law firms', *Organization Studies*, 17(4): 623–47.

Creed, W.E.D., Scully, M. and Austin, J. (2002) 'Clothes make the person: the tailoring of legitimating accounts and the social construction of identity', *Organization Science*, 13(5): 475–96.

Davis, G.F. (1991) 'Agents without principles? the spread of the poison pill through the intercorpora network', *Administrative Science Quarterly*, 36(4): 583–613.

Davis, G.F. and Greve, H.R. (1997) 'Corporate elite networks and governance changes in the 1980s', *The American Journal of Sociology*, 103(1): 1–37.

Davis, G.F. and Marquis, C. (2005) 'Prospects for organization theory in the early twenty-first century: institutional fields and mechanisms', *Organization Science*, 16(4): 332–43.

DiMaggio, P. (1988) 'Interest and agency in institutional theory', in L. Zucker (ed.), *Institutional Patterns and Organizations: Culture and Environment*, Cambridge, MA: Ballinger, pp. 3–22.

DiMaggio, P. and Powell, W.W. (1983) 'The iron cage revisited: institutional isomorphism and collective rationality in organizational fields', *American Sociological Review*, 48(2): 147–16.

Dobbin, F. (1994) *Forging Industrial Policy: The United States, Britain and France in the Railway Age*, Cambridge: Cambridge University Press.

Donaldson, L. (1995) *American Anti-Management Theories of Organization: A Critique of Paradigm Proliferation*, Cambridge: Cambridge University Press.

Edelman, L.B., Uggen, C. and Erlanger, H.S. (1999) 'The endogeneity of legal regulation: grievance procedures as rational myth', *The American Journal of Sociology*, 105(2): 406–54.

Eisenstadt, S. (1964) 'Social change, differentiation and evolution', *American Sociological Review*, 29(2): 235–47.

Fligstein (1985) 'The spread of the multidivisional form, 1919–1979', *American Sociological Review*, 50: 377–91.

Fligstein (1987) 'The intraorganizational power struggle: the rise of finance presidents in large corporations, 1919–1979', *American Sociological Review*, 52: 44–58.

Fligstein, N. (1990) *The Transformation of Corporate Control*, Cambridge, MA: Harvard University Press.

Fox-Wolfgramm, S.J., Boal, K.B. and Hunt, J.G. (1998) 'Organizational adaptation to institutional change: a comparative study of first-order change in prospector and defender banks', *Administrative Science Quarterly*, 43(1): 87–126.

Friedland, R. and Alford, R.R. (1991) 'Bringing society back in: symbols, practices and institutional contradictions', in W.W. Powell and P.J. DiMaggio (eds), *The New Institutionalism in Organizational Analysis*, Chicago: University of Chicago Press, pp. 232–66.

Garcia-Pont, C. and Nohria, N. (2002) 'Local versus global mimetism: the dynamics of alliance formation in the automobile industry', *Strategic Management Journal*, 23: 307–21.

Garud, R., Jain, S. and Kamaraswamy, A. (2002) 'Institutional entrepreneurship in the sponsorship of common technological standards: the case of Sun Microsystems and Java', *Academy of Management Journal*, 45: 196–214.

Gephart, R.P. (1993) 'The textual approach: risk and blame in disaster sensemaking', *Academy of Management Journal*, 36(6): 1465–514.

Gephart, R.P. (2004) 'From the editors: qualitative research and the Academy of Management Journal', *Academy of Management Journal*, 47(4): 454–62.

Gioia, D. and Pitre, E. (1990) 'Multiparadigm perspectives on theory building', *Academy of Management Review*, 15(4): 584–602.

Golden, B. (1992) 'The past is the past—or is it? The use of retrospective accounts as indicators of past strategy', *Academy of Management Journal*, 35(4): 848–60.

Greenwood, R. and Hinings, C.R. (1996) 'Understanding radical organizational change: bringing together the old and the new institutionalism', *Academy of Management Review*, 21(4): 1022–54.

Greenwood, R., Oliver, C., Sahlin, K. and Suddaby, R. (2008) 'Introduction', in R. Greenwood, C. Oliver, K. Sahlin and R. Suddaby (eds), *Handbook of Organizational Institutionalism*, London: Sage.

Greenwood, R. and Suddaby, R. (2006) 'Institutional entrepreneurship in mature fields: The Big Five accounting firms', *Academy of Management Journal*, 49(1): 27–48.

Greve, H.R. (1995) 'Jumping ship: the diffusion of strategy abandonment', *Administrative Science Quarterly*, 40(3): 444–73.

Greve, H.R. (1996) 'Patterns of competition: the diffusion of a market position in radio broadcasting', *Administrative Science Quarterly*, 41(1): 29–60.

Hardy, C., Phillips, N. and Lawrence, T. (2003) 'Resources, knowledge and influence: the organizational effects of inter-organizational collaboration', *Journal of Management Studies*, 40(2): 321–47.

Hargadon, A.B. and Douglas, J.Y. (2001) 'When innovations meet institutions: Edison and the design of the electric light', *Administrative Science Quarterly*, 46(3): 476–501.

Hasselbladh, H. and Kallinikos, J. (2000) 'The project of rationalization: a critique and reappraisal of neo-institutionalism in organization studies', *Organization Studies*, 21(4): 697–720.

Haunschild, P.R. (1993) 'Interorganizational imitation: the impact of interlocks on corporate acquisition activity', *Administrative Science Quarterly*, 38(4): 564–92.

Haunschild, P. and Chandler, D. (2008) 'Institutional-level learning: learning as a source of institutional change', in R. Greenwood, C. Oliver, K. Sahlin and R. Suddaby (eds), *Handbook of Organizational Institutionalism*, London: Sage.

Haunschild, P. and Miner, A. (1997) 'Modes of interorganizational imitation: the effects of outcome saliency and uncertainty', *Administrative Science Quarterly*, 42(3): 472–500.

Haveman, H. (1993) 'Follow the leader: Mimetic isomorphism and entry into new markets', *Administrative Science Quarterly*, 38(4): 593–627.

Haveman, H.A. and David, R.J. (2008) 'Ecologists and institutionalists: friends or foes?', in R. Greenwood, C. Oliver, K. Sahlin and R. Suddaby (eds), *Handbook of Organizational Institutionalism*, London: Sage.

Heracleous, L. and Barrett, M. (2001) 'Organizational change as discourse: communicative actions and deep structures in the context of information technology implementation', *Academy of Management Journal*, 44(4): 755–78.

Hinings, C.R. and Greenwood, R. (1988) *The Dynamics of Organizational Change*, London: Basil Blackwell.

Hirsch, P.M. (1986) 'From ambushes to golden parachutes: corporate takeovers as an instance of cultural framing and institutional integration', *American Journal of Sociology*, 91(4): 800–37.

Holm, P. (1995) 'The dynamics of institutionalization: transformation processes in Norwegian fisheries', *Administrative Science Quarterly*, 40(3): 398–422.

Jacques, R.S. (2006) 'History, historiography and organization studies: the challenge and the potential', *Management and Organizational History*, 1(1): 31–49.

Jick, T.D. (1979) 'Mixing qualitative and quantitative methods: triangulation in action', *Administrative Science Quarterly*, 24(4): 602–16.

Kanter (1977) *Men and Women of the Corporation*, New York: Basic Books.

Kittay, E.F. and Lehrer, A. (1992) 'Introduction', in A. Lehrer and E.F. Kittay (eds), *Frames, Fields and Contrasts*, Hillsdale, NJ: Lawrence Erlbaum and Associates, pp.1–18.

Krasner, S.D. (1984) 'Approaches to the state: alternative conceptions and historical dynamics', *Comparative Politics*, 16(2): 223–46.

Lawrence, T.B., Hardy, C. and Phillips, N. (2002) 'Institutional effects of interorganizational collaboration: the emergence of proto-institutions', *Academy of Management Journal*, 45(1): 281–90.

Lawrence, T.B. and Phillips, N. (2004) 'From *Moby Dick* to *Free Willy*: macro-cultural discourse and institutional entrepreneurship in emerging institutional fields', *Organization*, 11(5): 689–711.

Lawrence, T.B. and Suddaby, R. (2006) 'Institutions and institutional work', in S.R. Clegg, C. Hardy, T.B. Lawrence and W.R. Nord (eds), *The Sage Handbook of Organizations Studies* (second edn.), London: Sage, pp. 215–54.

Leblebici, H., Salancik, G.R., Copay, A. and King, T. (1991) 'Institutional change and the transformation of interorganizational fields: an organizational history of the U.S. radio broadcasting industry', *Administrative Science Quarterly*, 36(1): 333–63.

Lieberman, M.B. and Asaba, S. (2006) 'Why do firms imitate each other?', *Academy of Management Review*, 31(2): 366–85.

Lounsbury, M. (2001) 'Institutional sources of practice variation: staffing college and university recycling programs', *Administrative Science Quarterly*, 46: 29–56.

Lounsbury, M. (2002) 'Institutional transformation and status mobility: the professionalization of the field of finance', *Academy of Management Journal*, 45(1): 255–66.

Meyer, J. and Rowan, B. (1977) 'Institutionalized organizations: formal structure as myth and ceremony', *American Journal of Sociology*, 83(2): 333–63.

Mizruchi, M.S. and Fein, L.C. (1999) 'The social construction of organizational knowledge: a study of the uses of coercive, mimetic, and normative isomorphism', *Administrative Science Quarterly*, 44(4): 653–83.

Morrow, R. (1994) *Critical Theory and Methodology*, Newbury Park, CA: Sage.

Munir, K.A. (2005) 'The social construction of events: a study of institutional change in the photographic field', *Organization Studies*, 26(1): 93–112.

North, D.C. (1990) *Institutions, Institutional Change and Economic Performance*, Cambridge: Cambridge University Press.

Oakes, L., Townley, B. and Cooper, D. (1998) 'Business planning as pedagogy: language and control in a changing institutional field', *Administrative Science Quarterly*, 43(2): 257–92.

O'Brien, J., Remenyi, D. and Keaney, A. (2004) 'Historiography—a neglected research method in business and management studies', *Electronic Journal of Business Research Methods,* 2(2): 135–44.

Oliver, C. (1991) 'Strategic responses to institutional processes', *Academy of Management Review*, 16: 145–79.

Phillips, D.J. (2005) 'Organizational genealogies and the persistence of gender inequality: the case of Silicon Valley law firms', *Administrative Science Quarterly*, 50(3): 440–72.

Phillips, N., T.B Lawrence and C. Hardy, (2004) 'Discourse and institutions', *Academy of Management Review*, 29: 635–52.

Phillips, N. and Malhotra, N. (2008) 'Taking social construction seriously: extending the discursive approach in institutional theory', in R. Greenwood, C. Oliver, K. Sahlin and R. Suddaby (eds), *Handbook of Organizational Institutionalism*, London: Sage.

Raadschelders, J.C.N. (2007) 'Abraham Lincoln's presidency as the foundation of the modern administrative state?', *Public Administration Review*, 67(5): 943–46.

Ranson, S., Hinings, C.R. and Greenwood, R. (1980) 'The structuring of organizational structures', *Administrative Science Quarterly*, 2(2): 1–12.

Rao, H., Monin, P. and Durand, R. (2003) 'Institutional change in Toque Ville: Nouvelle cuisine as an identity movement in French gastronomy', *American Journal of Sociology*, 180(4): 795–843.

Rowlinson, M. (2005) 'Historical research methods', in R. Swanson and E.F. Holton III (eds), *Research in Organizations*, San Francisco, CA: Barrett-Kohler, pp. 295–314.

Rowlinson, M. and Hassard, J. (1993) 'The invention of corporate culture: a history of the histories of Cadbury', *Human Relations*, 46(3): 299–326.

Russo, M.V. (2001) 'Institutions, exchange relationships, and the emergence of new fields: regulatory policies and independent power production in America, 1978–1992', *Administrative Science Quarterly*, 46(1): 57–86.

Sahlin-Andersson, K. (1996) 'Imitating by editing success: the construction of organizational fields', in B. Czarniawska and G. Sevon (eds), *Translating Organizational Change*, Berlin: Walter de Gruyer, pp. 69–92.

Schneiberg, M. (2005) 'Combining new institutionalisms: explaining institutional change in American property insurance', *Sociological Forum*, 1: 93–137.

Schneiberg, M. (2007) 'What's on the path? path dependence, organizational diversity and the problem of institutional change in the US economy, 1900–1950', *Socio-Economic Review*, 5(1): 47–80.

Schneiberg, M. and Clemens, L. (2006) 'The typical tools for the job: research strategies in institutional analysis', *Sociological Theory*, 3: 195–227.

Schutz, A. (1962) *Collected Papers*, Vol. I. The Hague, Netherlands: M. Nijhoff.

Scott, W.R. (1994) 'Conceptualizing organizational fields: Linking organizations and societal systems', in H.U. Derlien, U. Gerhardt and F.W. Scharpf (eds), *Systemrationalitat und partialinteresse [Systems rationality and partial interests]*, Nomos Verlagsgellschaft: Baden-Baden, pp. 203–11.

Scott, W.R. (2001) *Institutions and Organizations* (second edn.), Thousand Oaks, CA: Sage.

Scott, W.R., Reuf, M., Mendel, P.J. and Caronna, C.A. (2000) *Institutional Change and Healthcare Organizations: From Professional Dominance to Managed Care*, Chicago: University of Chicago Press.

Selznick, P. (1949) *TVA and the Grassroots*, Berkeley: University of California Press.

Selznick, P. (1957) *Leadership in Administration*, New York: Harper and Row.

Selznick, P. (1996) 'Institutionalism "old" and "new"', *Administrative Science Quarterly*, 41(2): 270–7.

Seo, M.G. and Creed, W.E.D. (2002) 'Institutional contradictions, praxis and institutional change: a dialectical perspective', *Academy of Management Review*, 27(2): 222–47.

Sillince, J.A.A. (2005) 'A contingency theory of rhetorical congruence', *Academy of Management Review*, 30(3): 608–21.

Silverman, D. (2001) *Interpreting Qualitative Data: Methods for Analyzing Talk, Text and Interaction*, London: Sage.

Sorenson, A.B. (1998) 'Theoretical mechanisms and the empirical study of social processes', in, P. Hedstrom and R. Swedberg (eds), *Social Mechanisms: An Analytical Approach to Social Theory*, New York: Cambridge University Press, pp. 238–66.

Splichal, S. (1999) *Public Opinion: Developments and Controversies in the Twentieth Century*, Lanham, MD: Rowman & Littlefield.

Stinchcombe, A.L. (1965) 'Social structure and organization', in March, J.G. (ed.), *Handbook of Organizations*, Chicago: Rand McNally, pp. 142–93.

Stinchcombe, A.L. (1997) 'On the virtues of the old institutionalism', *Annual Review of Sociology*, 23: 1–18.

Suddaby, R. and Greenwood, R. (2005) 'Rhetorical strategies of legitimacy', *Administrative Science Quarterly*, 50(1): 35–57.

Suddaby, R., Gendron, Y. and Lam, H. (2008) 'The organizational context of professional work', *Accounting Organizations and Society*, (In press).

Thornton, P. (2002) 'The rise of the corporation in a craft industry: conflict and conformity in institutional logics', *Academy of Management Journal*, 45 (1): 81–101.

Thornton, P. and Ocasio, W. (1999) 'Institutional logics and the historical contingency of power in organizations: executive succession in the higher-education publishing industry, 1958–1990', *American Journal of Sociology*, 105(3): 801–43.

Tolbert, P.S. and Zucker, L.G. (1983) 'Institutional sources of change in the formal structure of organizations: the diffusion of civil service reform, 1880–1935', *Administrative Science Quarterly*, 28(1): 22–39.

Tolbert, P.S. and Zucker, L.G. (1996) 'The institutional-ization of institutional theory', in S. Clegg, C. Hardy and W. Nord (eds), *Handbook of Organization Studies*, London: Sage, pp. 175–90.

Tsoukas, H. and Chia, R. (2002) 'On organizational becoming: rethinking organizational change', *Organization Science*, 13(5): 567–82.

Van de Ven, A.H. and Poole, M.S. (2005) 'Alternative approaches for studying organizational change', *Organization Studies*, 26(9): 1377–404.

Ventresca, M.J. and Mohr, J.W. (2002) 'Archival research methods', in J.A.C. Baum (ed.), *The Blackwell Companion to Organizations*, Oxford: Blackwell Publishers, pp. 805–28.

Weick, K. (1979) *The Social Psychology of Organizing*, Reading, MA: Addison-Wesley.

Weick, K.E. and Quinn, R.E. (1999) 'Organizational change and development', *Annual Review of Psychology*, 50: 361–86.

Westphal, J.D., Gulati, R. and Shortell, S.M. (1997) 'Customization or conformity? an institutional and network perspective on the content and conse-quences of TQM adoption', *Administrative Science Quarterly*, 42(2): 366–94.

Westphal, J.D. and Zajac, E.J. (1994) 'Substance and symbolism in CEO's long term incentive plans', *Administrative Science Quarterly*, 39(3): 367–90.

Zbaracki, M. (1998) 'The rhetoric and reality of total quality management', *Administrative Science Quarterly*, 43(3): 602–38.

Zilber, T.B. (2002) 'Institutionalization as an interplay between actions, meanings and actors: the case of a rape crisis center in Israel', *Academy of Management Journal*, 45(1): 234–54.

Zilber, T.B. (2006) 'The work of the symbolic in institutional processes: translations of rational myths in Israeli hi-tech', *Academy of Management Journal*, 49(2): 279–301.

Zilber, T.B. (2008) 'The work of meanings in institutional processes and thinking', in, R. Greenwood, C. Oliver, K. Sahlin and R. Suddaby (eds), *Handbook of Organizational Institutionalism*, London: Sage.

Zucker, L.G. (1977) 'The role of institutionalization in cultural persistence', *American Sociological Review*, 42(5): 726–43.

Zucker, L.G. (1989) 'Combining institutional theory and population ecology: no legitimacy, no history', *American Sociological Review*, 54: 542–5.

12

Job Satisfaction in Organizational Research

Alannah E. Rafferty and Mark A. Griffin

INTRODUCTION

Job satisfaction is one of the most frequently studied aspects of organizational life in the psychological sciences (Cranny et al., 1992; Fisher, 2000; Landy, 1989; Locke, 1969, 1983). Psychologists have argued that the way that an individual feels about work and the meaning that work holds in his or her life is a critical element of the employment experience (e.g., Judge et al., 2001a; Tait et al., 1989). The degree of interest in job satisfaction is reflected in the number of studies that have been published in the area. Entry of the search term 'job satisfaction' in the psycLIT database reveals well over 5,500 published studies in refereed journals. Importantly, however, as reflected in our analysis of articles published in the *Journal of Applied Psychology* and the *Journal of Organizational Behavior* since 2000, relatively few studies have focused on the job satisfaction construct itself.

As noted by Locke (1983), it is impossible to conduct a comprehensive review of the job satisfaction literature in a single chapter. We adopt a psychological perspective on job satisfaction and focus on methodological issues that have emerged in the literature in the last few decades. We begin our review by exploring why job satisfaction has been the subject of such interest. Next, we examine classic studies, including the Hawthorne Studies (Roethlisberger and Dickson, 1939), Hoppock's (1935) and Schaffer's (1953) study, and Herzberg and colleagues' (1957, 1959) work. We then define the construct of job satisfaction, noting some of the methodological debates in the area. Next, we discuss the distinction between global and facet job satisfaction. We then examine the major methodological approaches and measurement instruments that have been used when studying satisfaction. Our analysis then turns to recent empirical research. We conduct a review of articles published since 2000 in two major organizational psychology journals, the *Journal of Applied Psychology* and the *Journal of Organizational Behavior*. Finally, we identify some emerging issues in the job satisfaction literature, including dispositional approaches to job satisfaction and multilevel research.

Why study job satisfaction?

There are a number of perspectives that motivate the study of job satisfaction. While our review of recent empirical studies reveals that job satisfaction is often treated as a dependent variable, some authors argue that job satisfaction is a crucial construct, because it mediates relationships between working conditions and organizational and individual outcomes (e.g., Dormann and Zapf, 2001). Researchers have been particularly interested in exploring relationships between job satisfaction and individual performance. The satisfaction-performance relationship has been the subject of hundreds of studies, and a number of meta-analyses have summarized results of these studies (Bowling, 2007; Iaffaldano and Muchinsky, 1985; Judge et al., 2001b; Petty et al., 1984). Landy (1989) described the ongoing search for confirmation of the link between job satisfaction and job performance as the 'Holy Grail' of Industrial and Organizational Psychology. Indeed, researchers have persevered despite evidence that there is only a weak relationship between these constructs. In the most recent meta-analytic review, Bowling (2007) concluded that the satisfaction-performance relationship is largely spurious and is influenced by individuals' dispositional characteristics. Researchers have also studied other outcomes, including voluntary turnover (e.g., Hom et al., 1992; Wright and Bonett, 2002), absenteeism (e.g., Tharenou, 1993), and counterproductive behaviors (e.g., Gottfredson and Holland, 1990), to name just a few.

A second perspective that has motivated research on job satisfaction is interest in the link between job and life satisfaction. Some researchers have argued that since work is a central life activity it is likely to influence individuals' satisfaction with life (e.g., Rain et al., 1991; Rode, 2004; Tait et al., 1989). Empirical research indicates that there is moderate positive relationship between job and life satisfaction (r=.44; Tait et al., 1989). However, as with research looking at satisfaction-performance relationships, authors have suggested that the job-life satisfaction relationship is influenced by dispositional factors, which are related to both constructs (e.g., Heller et al., 2002; Judge and Hulin, 1993). We examine research exploring the relationship between dispositional characteristics and job satisfaction in greater detail later in this chapter. In the following section, we examine some classic studies that have had an important impact on the methodologies and approaches used when studying job satisfaction.

Historical perspectives

Research exploring job satisfaction began in the 1920s and 1930s with the Hawthorne Studies (Roethlisberger and Dickson, 1939) and work by Hoppock (1935). Although these two sets of studies were conducted at roughly the same time, the Hawthorne Studies have had the most enduring influence on job satisfaction research (Locke, 1983). We also describe studies conducted by Schaffer (1953) and Herzberg and his colleagues (1957, 1959).

The Hawthorne Studies

The Hawthorne Studies were a series of studies conducted from 1924 to 1932, which provided the impetus for research focused on psychological and social factors in the workplace and are generally acknowledged as one of the starting points of the Human Relations school of thought (Judge and Larsen, 2001; Locke, 1969, 1983). This series of studies was initially designed to study the effects of work conditions, such as the timing of rest breaks, the length of the working day and pay rates, and on worker fatigue. However, the emphasis soon shifted to the study of 'attitudes,' as workers did not respond in expected ways to systematic changes in working conditions. Roethlisberger and Dickson's (1939) use of the term 'attitudes' encompasses operators' attitudes to management, their moods in the workplace, and the reactions to their supervisor and the experimental team.

We draw on one of the early studies, the Relay Assembly Room study, to provide an example of how 'attitudes' were assessed in the Hawthorne Studies. The Relay

Assembly Room study involved a small group of female workers who were isolated in a room from the rest of employees. In one of the 13 experimental periods, a survey consisting of eight questions was administered to operators. This initial questionnaire assessed whether operators had experienced any changes in their 'mental health habits and mental attitudes.' An additional questionnaire was then administered that focused on specific issues in the test room that could be responsible for these positive responses to the test room. Twenty-one questions were asked of operators, who suggested that they liked the smaller group in the test room, liked having 'no bosses,' enjoyed the 'freedom' available in the test room, and 'the way they were treated.' In summary, in the Relay Assembly Test Room study researchers were beginning to focus on individuals' cognitive and affective responses to their job and were interested in determining the particular aspects or facets of work that were responsible for these responses.

The Hoppock Study

Hoppock (1935) published the first intensive study of job satisfaction, based on interviews with adults in a small town and 500 schoolteachers. Hoppock's research was driven by two underlying questions (Landy, 1989). First, are workers happy? Second, are some workers happier than others are? Hoppock used verbal self-reports collected via interviews to assess job satisfaction. When summarizing his findings, he identified many factors that could influence job satisfaction, including worker fatigue, job conditions such as monotony, supervision, and autonomy. Results indicated that only 12% of workers could be classified as dissatisfied and that occupational groupings influenced satisfaction with higher status occupational groups reporting higher satisfaction. In summary, Hoppock began to systematically analyze job satisfaction and identified a range of factors contributing to job satisfaction that are still studied today (e.g., Rose, 2003).

Schaffer (1953)

Schaffer (1953) argued that whatever psychological mechanisms make people satisfied or dissatisfied in life also make them satisfied or dissatisfied in their work. He suggested that the amount of dissatisfaction experienced by an individual is determined by; a) the strength of an individual's needs or drives; and b) the extent to which an individual can perceive and use opportunities in the situation for the satisfaction of those needs. Schaeffer identified 12 needs that need to be met and overall satisfaction was said to be predicted by the two most important needs held by a person. If the individual's two most important needs are met by the job then they are satisfied.

Based on his analysis, Schaffer (1953) developed a questionnaire measure to assess the strength of each of the 12 needs, the degree to which each of the needs were satisfied by the individual's job, and the individual's overall satisfaction. The overall satisfaction scale consisted of three items, two of which were based on the work of Hoppock (1935), while the third item was an open-ended question. In summary, Schaffer's work acknowledged that individual differences are an important antecedent of job satisfaction, a topic that has recently received considerable attention.

Herzberg: The two-factor theory

By the late 1950s, Herzberg and colleagues (1957) were able to review the available job satisfaction literature in a systematic way. They concluded that there was sufficient evidence to confirm a relationship between satisfaction and outcomes such as performance, turnover, absence, and psychosomatic illnesses. In addition, Herzberg et al. (1957) concluded that satisfaction and dissatisfaction were two distinctly different phenomena. Herzberg et al. (1959) conducted a follow-up study to explore this idea, and they interviewed 203 accountants and engineers. Herzberg et al. (1959) concluded that specific factors were related to feeling positive about the job, including: achievement and recognition, the work itself, responsibility, advancement or promotion opportunities, and salary.

In contrast, dissatisfaction with a job was related to another set of factors, including: company policies and administration, technical supervision, salary, relationships with supervisors, and working conditions.

On the basis of this study, Herzberg and his colleagues (1959) proposed the two-factor theory or the motivator-hygiene theory and a number of empirical tests of the two-factor model were conducted (e.g., Ewen et al., 1966; Graen, 1966). Ewen et al. tested the theory using a sample of 793 male employees from a range of different jobs and failed to support the theory. Subsequent research also failed to support the two-factor theory and research on this topic declined dramatically. Landy (1989) suggests that while this theory is probably reasonable at the descriptive level, it is not an explanation of how job satisfaction develops and of its relationships with other constructs. Despite the limitations of the theory, it stimulated research into job satisfaction and prompted new directions of investigation.

Defining job satisfaction

The definition of job satisfaction has been debated throughout its history. Many researchers have defined job satisfaction as an emotional reaction to the job (e.g., Cranny et al., 1992; Locke, 1969; Spector, 1997). Cranny and colleagues (p. 1) state that 'there is general agreement that job satisfaction is an affective (that is, emotional) reaction to a job that results from the incumbent's comparison of actual outcomes with those that are desired (expected, deserved, and so on).' Locke (1969: 316) defined job satisfaction as 'the pleasurable emotional state resulting from the appraisal of one's job as achieving or facilitating the achievement of one's job values.' Although job satisfaction is usually described as an affective response, it is usually measured as an evaluative assessment of job attitudes compared to an individual's internal or external standards (Fisher, 2000; Niklas and Dormann, 2005; Pekrun and Frese, 1992).

The distinction between affect and evaluation has been addressed by research in the social psychology of attitudes, and recently, scholars have begun to draw explicitly on the attitudes literature when defining job satisfaction (e.g., Fisher, 2000). Fisher identified two components of job attitudes, an affective or emotional component and a cognitive component. Weiss (2002) identified three distinct, but related aspects, of job satisfaction. He argued that job satisfaction incorporates an individual's evaluation of their job, their beliefs about their job, and their affective experiences on the job. Importantly, however, Weiss identifies evaluation as the central component of job satisfaction and in line with this statement, he defined job satisfaction as 'a positive (or negative) evaluative judgment one makes about one's job or situation' (p. 175). An important consequence of this perspective is that affect and beliefs are understood to be different causes of job satisfaction.

The definitional debates in the job satisfaction literature have important implications for how we measure job satisfaction and the most appropriate research designs to use. Weiss (2002) argues that current job satisfaction measures are limited, because they do not enable researchers to assess the three component model of job satisfaction that he identified. He argues that since affective states and beliefs structures have important behavioral and cognitive consequences, then they are likely to have added value over the cognitive evaluations, which have been the focus of measurement efforts to date.

Some empirical research has explored the extent to which existing job satisfaction measures capture cognitive versus affective information. Brief and Roberson (1989) conducted a study with 144 students, and explored the extent to which the Job Descriptive Index (JDI; Smith et al., 1969), the Minnesota Satisfaction Questionnaire (MSQ; Weiss et al., 1967, and the female Faces Scale (Dunham and Herman, 1975) captured cognitions and positive and negative affect. The different measures of job satisfaction varied in the extent to which they captured the affective and cognitive aspects of job satisfaction. Brief and Roberson suggest their results as suggesting that the Faces measure is the 'most balanced' of the scales as it displayed relationships with cognitions *and* positive and negative affect.

Similarly, Fisher (2000) argued that it is useful to think of existing job satisfaction measures as lying on a continuum assessing the cognitive component of job attitudes to assessing a combination of cognitive and affective components. Based on an empirical study that used an experience sampling methodology to collect data from 121 employees over a two-week period, Fisher concluded that most job satisfaction measures only assess affect to a limited degree. In contrast to other researchers, Judge and Larsen (2001) argued that it is not productive to classify job satisfaction measures as either cognitive or affective. They argued that there is no need to measure new, affectively laden job satisfaction measures or to supplement or replace job satisfaction measures with measures of affect. Judge and Larsen argue that while cognition and affect can help us better understand the nature of job satisfaction, separate measures of these aspects of job satisfaction are not likely to prove useful.

Niklas and Dormann (2005) argue that findings suggesting that existing job satisfaction measures primarily tap the cognitive components of satisfaction have important implications. While cognitions are relatively stable over time, affective reactions are unstable, so different methodologies are required to assess cognitions and affect. In addition, while the issue of time frame is relatively unimportant when measuring cognitions, this issue is critical when assessing affect, as retrospective reports of affect tend to be biased. As such, there is a need to assess affect on a time-contingent basis. To date, however, researchers studying relationships between trait and state affect and job satisfaction have retrospectively measured affect over the last weeks, months, or years (Niklas and Dormann, 2005). This is a critical limitation of existing approaches, because people tend to overestimate the intensity and frequency of positive and negative affect in retrospective measures, and retrospectively reported affect

is likely to be affected by current affect (Fisher, 2002). In addition, negative affect is more easily recalled than positive affect (e.g., Baumeister et al., 2001).

In summary, there is still considerable debate concerning how to define job satisfaction. This debate has important methodological implications. Our review suggests that the different definitions of job satisfaction require authors to develop different measures of satisfaction. For example, if we define job satisfaction as an attitude that consists of cognitive evaluations, affect, and beliefs then theorists argue that there is a need to develop measures of affect and beliefs independent of evaluations. Niklas and Dormann's (2005) work highlight the fact that affective reactions are unstable, which means that different methodologies are required to assess cognitions and affect. Researchers have recently begun to address the methodological issues associated with assessing affect when studying relationships between dispositional factors and job satisfaction.

Facet satisfaction versus overall job satisfaction

Most scholars recognize that job satisfaction is a global concept that also comprises various facets (Ironson et al., 1989; Judge and Larsen, 2001; Smith, 1992). Researchers have examined relationships between global job satisfaction and facet satisfaction (Smith, 1992; Weiss, 2002), the impetus for which lies with Locke (1969). He suggested that overall job satisfaction is the sum of the evaluations of the elements of which satisfaction is composed. Global or overall job satisfaction scales ask an individual to combine his or her reactions to a job in an overall or integrated response (e.g., all things considered, how satisfied are you with your job?). In contrast, facet satisfaction scales are designed to examine specific aspects of job within the more general domain (Ironson et al., 1989). The most typical categorization of facets was proposed by Smith et al. (1969), who identified five facets, including: pay, promotion, co-workers, supervision, and the work itself. Another common distinction is between extrinsic and intrinsic satisfaction. Satisfaction with pay and promotions has been considered forms of extrinsic satisfaction. In contrast, satisfaction with co-workers, supervisors, and the work itself are considered to reflect intrinsic satisfaction (Judge and Larsen, 2001).

Empirical studies have indicated that global measures of job satisfaction and facet satisfaction measures are only weakly to moderately related (e.g., Aldag and Brief, 1978). These findings have resulted in a debate as to why global measures of job satisfaction are not equivalent to the sum of facet satisfactions (e.g., Highhouse and Becker, 1993; Scarpello and Campbell, 1983). Scarpello and Campbell examined relationships between single item global measures of job satisfaction and facet measures of satisfaction taken from the short-form of the MSQ (Weiss et al., 1967). These authors concluded that it is not appropriate to use the sum of the facet measures as a measure of overall job satisfaction as global measures of job satisfaction appear to capture information relating to satisfaction with occupational choice, life off the job, in addition to capturing information about job satisfaction. As such, global evaluations of job satisfaction are more complex than the sum of the job satisfaction facets that are typically measured. In summary, empirical research findings suggest that global satisfaction and facet satisfaction measures assess distinctly different issues and are not equivalent measures of job satisfaction.

The facet satisfaction and global job satisfaction distinction also becomes problematic if we consider Weiss's (2002) discussion of job satisfaction. In particular, if job satisfaction is a cognitive evaluation then Weiss argues that the facets of job satisfaction are not distinguishable from the overall job satisfaction evaluation. Rather, Weiss suggests that there 'are only discriminable objects in the work environment that we evaluate' (p. 186). The basic argument being proposed by Weiss is that while we may evaluate issues such as how satisfied we are with our supervisor or our pay, these

evaluations combine to create an overall evaluation of how satisfied we are in the workplace. This argument suggests that what have been called facets of job satisfaction are simply evaluations that individuals make about their work environment. In summary, an analysis of existing research suggests that global measures of job satisfaction appear to tap a broad domain of satisfaction that incorporates life satisfaction. In contrast, while facet job satisfaction measures are designed to assess a broad domain they appear to assess a more limited and focused aspect of job satisfaction involving specific evaluations. In addition, the recent emphasis on job satisfaction as an evaluation that is caused by affect and beliefs also calls into question the facet versus global satisfaction distinction.

Research design issues in the study of job satisfaction

The predominant methodological approach that has been used when studying job satisfaction is the field study, with authors using both cross-sectional and longitudinal approaches. While early research on job satisfaction used qualitative data collection approaches such as interviews, very little recent research has adopted this approach. In addition, a number of quasi-experimental field studies have also been conducted that assess job satisfaction. However, job satisfaction has not been the key variable of interest in these studies. More recently, with increasing interest in the role of affect in job satisfaction, a number of studies have focused on intraindividual processes. These studies have used experience sampling methodologies. In the following section, we focus on exploring early research that used interviews, quasi-experimental studies and studies using experience methodologies to study intraindividual processes.

Qualitative studies
Qualitative studies are typically conducted in applied settings are and are generally broadly focused studies that are exploratory in that they are not driven by explicit hypotheses.

These studies are designed to gather data on individual experience and meaning, and many different methods such as interviews, conversations, observations, personal experiences, and textual analysis can be used to collect data. Qualitative studies emphasize depth of information and analysis as opposed to breadth of information and analysis (Kidd, 2002). Next, we explore studies that have adopted qualitative approaches when exploring job satisfaction.

A number of early researchers used techniques such as interviews in order to develop an understanding of the nature and antecedents of job satisfaction (e.g., Hoppock, 1935; Herzberg et al., 1959). For example, Hoppock interviewed adults in a small town and 500 schoolteachers in order to explore whether workers were happy in their jobs and whether some individuals were happier than others. However, a search of recent studies using PsycLIT revealed that very few authors have used qualitative approaches to study job satisfaction. In those studies that we did identify that used some type of qualitative approach, interviews were generally used as a supplement to quantitative analyses rather than the primary data collection approach (e.g., Lyons and O'Brien, 2006). For example, Lyons and O'Brien conducted a study in order to explore the determinants of job satisfaction for a sample of African-American employees. These authors collected data using surveys and also collected data using an interview to administer an open-ended question ('what makes you or would make you a satisfied employee?'). Lyons and O'Brien concluded that the interview data was consistent with the quantitative results.

We identified one study that did use an interview as the primary data collection tool. Bussing and Bissels (1998) conducted an exploratory study to test a model of work satisfaction and conducted semistructured interviews with 46 German nurses. Participants were asked to give a detailed description of issues such as their working situation and their overall satisfaction or dissatisfaction in the workplace. Bussing and Bissels argue that the use of qualitative

analysis allowed them to identify substantially different qualities of work satisfaction. In addition, the authors argue that they were able to identify apparently inconsistent statements that reflected the contradictory experiences and pressures placed on nurses in the workplace. In summary, we identified very few recent studies that have used qualitative methods when studying job satisfaction. One potential explanation for the lack of such studies is that the amount of qualitative work published in APA journals in the last 50 years is quite small (Marchel and Owens, 2007). Despite this, however, Bussing and Bissels' (1998) work suggests that there are important benefits to be gained from using qualitative methods when studying job satisfaction.

Quasi-experimental field studies

A number of researchers have conducted quasi-experimental studies where job satisfaction has been included as a measure of interest (e.g., Lam and Schaubroeck, 2000a, 2000b; Logan and Ganster, 2005; Seibert, 1999; Workman and Bommer, 2004). A quasi-experiment is an 'experiment[s] that ha[ve]s treatments, outcome measures, and experimental units, but do[es] not use random assignment to create the comparisons from which treatment-caused change is inferred' (Cook and Campbell, 1979: 6). Rather, comparisons occur between a nonequivalent control group and an experimental group or groups who differ in many ways apart from the treatment of interest. One of the challenges of using a quasi-experimental approach involves determining what effects are attributable to the treatment of interest versus those effects due to the initial noncomparability of the experimental and control group. However, quasi-experimental studies are important, because they allow researchers to study causal relationships in a complex field setting. In addition, these studies also allow us to determine whether results obtained in the laboratory generalize to real world environments. In the case of job satisfaction and many other organizational constructs, it is essential that we study these variables *in situ* using rigorous methods that allow us to consider issues of causality. In the next section, we examine one quasi-experimental study that incorporated job satisfaction.

Seibert (1999) conducted a pretest-posttest nonequivalent control group quasi-experimental design, which was designed to test the effectiveness of a formal mentoring program in a Fortune 100 company over a one year period. Job satisfaction was a key outcome variable in this study. Results suggested that the facilitated mentoring program had a significant effect on job satisfaction. One year after the initiation of the program, employees who had been mentored reported significantly higher job satisfaction than their nonmentored counterparts. In summary, we could only identify a small number of quasi-experimental studies that assessed job satisfaction as one of many outcomes of interest. While quasi-experimentation has been discussed as a powerful tool for drawing casual inferences in applied settings (Cook and Campbell, 1979; Cook et al., 1992), researchers do not seem to have fully utilized this approach when studying job satisfaction. We argue that one issue that researchers can focus on when studying job satisfaction is the use of quasi-experimental research.

Intraindividual processes

The majority of job satisfaction research has focused on differences between individuals. In recent years, however, increasing attention has been paid to the way individuals' job satisfaction changes over time. Although earlier research had investigated the stability of satisfaction (e.g., the genetic basis of job satisfaction; see Arvey et al., 1989), little attention had been paid to the fluctuations in satisfaction from month to month, day to day, or within even shorter time periods. The development of diary studies and other experience sampling methodologies has encouraged a better understanding of these fluctuations within individuals. The traditional cross-sectional, between-subjects approach used in job satisfaction research assumes that constructs are stable over time

and that variations around the average level of a variable are random (Ilies and Judge, 2002). Experience sampling methods allowed the possibility that this within-person variance is systematic and meaningful. From this perspective, job satisfaction might develop over time, change in response to transient events, be moderated by more stable factors, and might itself influence diverse within-person factors such as insomnia for example. We discuss one study that has explored intraindividual processes in the following section.

As described by Ilies and Judge (2004) experience sampling methodologies ask individuals to report on their momentary feelings or their subjective feeling states, and/or to report on their current physiological state. This approach has been said to be beneficial, because it eliminates error associated with selective recall processes. An example of what experience methodology involves can be seen in a study conducted by Ilies and Judge. These researchers conducted a study involving 33 participants from two state universities in the United States. In the first phase of data collection, participants completed a measure of trait affectivity and asked a significant other to complete the same measure. In Phase 2, one week later, participants reported their momentary mood and job satisfaction three times a day, for two weeks, using a diary method. That is, participants were asked to record their responses to survey questions assessing mood and job satisfaction at regular intervals throughout the day. The measure of job satisfaction collected through this approach was called 'experience-sampled' job satisfaction. In the final phase of the study, Phase 3, which occurred two months after Phase 2, participants responded to an overall job satisfaction survey and reported on their beliefs about their job. The results of this study revealed that experience-sampled job satisfaction was associated with the overall job satisfaction measure collected in Phase 3. In summary, a number of research studies have studied intraindividual processes and job satisfaction. This methodology offers an important means by which to understand the impact of affect on job satisfaction.

Measurement of job satisfaction

A number of different techniques have been adopted when studying job satisfaction. By far the most common approach involves the use of questionnaires. A variety of questionnaire measures have been developed over the last 70 years. Some of the most commonly used and well-validated measures are the JDI (Smith et al., 1969) and the MSQ (Weiss et al., 1967). Two other measures that are commonly used when assessing job satisfaction include the Michigan Organizational Assessment Questionnaire (MOA; Cammann, Fichman, Jenkins, and Klesh, 1983), and Brayfield and Rothe's (1951) Overall Job Satisfaction Measure. In the next section, we discuss these measures in some detail.

Questionnaire measures
Job Descriptive Index   The JDI was developed by Smith et al. (1969) and the original scale consisted of 72 items that assessed five facets of job satisfaction, including: satisfaction with work itself, pay, promotion opportunities, supervision, and co-workers. Roznowski (1989) assessed the JDI and made a number of changes to the measure. In particular, modifications were made to reflect issues such as changes in technology that have occurred since the original scale was developed. Roznowski demonstrated that the items loaded on five factors and that the scales have good reliability, which has been supported by other researchers (e.g., Judge and Hulin, 1993).

Minnesota Satisfaction Questionnaire   The 'long-form' of the MSQ consists of 100 items that assess 20 subscales, such as individuals' satisfaction with the extent to which they get to use their abilities on the job, achievement, advancement, moral values, and so on. Twenty of the items in the MSQ have been used to assess general job satisfaction and form the 'short-form' of the MSQ. The short-form consists of 12 questions assessing

intrinsic satisfaction. Intrinsic satisfaction items measure issues such as accomplishment obtained from one's job and opportunities to use abilities on one's job. Eight items assess extrinsic satisfaction. Examples of issues assessed in the extrinsic scale include satisfaction with promotion opportunities, and satisfaction with pay. The short-form of the MSQ has been shown to have good reliability (Mathieu, 1991; Wong et al., 1998).

Michigan Organizational Assessment Questionnaire   Cammann et al. (1983) developed a measure of overall job satisfaction when they developed the Michigan Organizational Assessment Questionnaire. The satisfaction scale consists of three items such as 'all in all, I am satisfied with my job.' This scale had demonstrated adequate reliability (e.g., McFarlin and Sweeney, 1992).

Brayfield and Rothe's (1951) Overall Job Satisfaction Measure   Brayfield and Rothe (1951) developed an 18-item measure of job satisfaction. However, a number of researchers have adopted a 6-item version of this measure and this measure has displayed adequate reliability (e.g., Aryee, Fields and Luk, 1999). The 18-item measure has also demonstrated adequate reliability (Pillai, Schriesheim and Williams, 1999).

Graphic measures
Faces Scales   Kunin (1955) developed the General Faces Scale because he stated that attitude surveys, which translate 'one man's feelings into another man's words' (p. 65), result in distortion of meaning. To address this issue, Kunin conducted research to establish scale values for two series of faces that varied on a continuum from happy to unhappy. Respondents are asked to circle the face that reflects the way that they are feeling about their job. Dunham and Herman (1975) developed a female version of the faces scale, and demonstrated that the male and female versions can be used interchangeably to measure job satisfaction. The Faces Scales have been used by a number of researchers (e.g., Dunham, Smith, and Blackburn, 1977;

Niklas and Dormann, 2005; Rousseau, 1978). Authors such as Fisher (2000) and Niklas and Dormann argue that the faces scales are affectively laden measures, as they found that job satisfaction as assessed by the General Faces Scale is strongly determined by state affect.

Recent empirical research

To assess the range and focus of recent job satisfaction research, we conducted a review of studies published since 2000 in the *Journal of Applied Psychology* (*JAP*) and the *Journal of Organizational Behavior* (*JOB*). We identified 84 studies assessing job satisfaction with fifty of these empirical studies published in *JAP*, while 34 studies were published in *JOB*. In the following section, we outline some of the methodological characteristics of these studies. Job satisfaction was treated as a dependent variable in the majority of these studies. Specifically, in 41 of the 50 studies published in *JAP* and 29 of the 34 studies published in *JOB*, job satisfaction was treated as a dependent variable. Only nine *JAP* studies and four *JOB* studies treated job satisfaction as an independent variable. Studies where satisfaction acted as a mediator or moderator were included in the independent variable study count. Researchers in two of the major organizational psychology journals appear to use job satisfaction primarily as a broad outcome measure and have paid less attention to the meaning of the construct and its impact on other outcomes.

Next, we summarized the measures that were used to assess job satisfaction in *JAP* and *JOB* since 2000. Analysis revealed that 15 studies used either the Michigan Organizational Assessment Questionnaire (Cammann et al., 1983) or Brayfield and Rothe's (1951) measure. The next most commonly used measure was the JDI (Smith et al., 1969), which was used six times. The MSQ (Weiss et al., 1967) was used in four of the studies. Importantly, however, 13 studies used measures specifically designed for the research or did not clearly identify where the job satisfaction measure was obtained

from. Another notable feature of the measures used was that over 40 separate measures of satisfaction were used in the 84 studies. This result indicates that there is little consistency in the use of job satisfaction measures.

Finally, we reviewed the research methodology used when conducting job satisfaction studies in *JAP* and *JOB*. Our analysis suggests that both cross-sectional and longitudinal field studies were used. Of the studies published in *JOB*, 26 adopted a cross-sectional survey approach while seven studies used a longitudinal survey methodology. One study (Workman and Bommer, 2004) used a quasi-experimental methodology when collecting data in the field. There was a very even split between cross-sectional survey studies and longitudinal survey studies in *JAP*.

Emerging issues

Our review of the job satisfaction literature reveals that interest in this construct has not waned in the 80 years since its inception. Indeed, researchers have continued to study questions concerning the relationship between job satisfaction and performance relationship despite discouraging results (e.g., Bowling, 2007). Recent theoretical developments regarding the dispositional influences on job satisfaction and methodological advancements concerning the measurement of the affective aspects of job satisfaction, suggest that interest in satisfaction will continue to grow. Our review of recent job satisfaction literature reveals a number of emerging trends. In particular, increasing attention has been devoted to exploring the role of dispositional factors as antecedents of job satisfaction and as third variables responsible for job satisfaction-outcome relationships. A second theoretical issue that has emerged in recent research are multilevel studies of job satisfaction. Next, we explore these issues in some detail.

The role of dispositional factors

In the past, cognitive judgement approaches (e.g., Locke's (1976) needs-values conflicts approach) and social influence approaches (e.g., Salancik and Pfeffer, 1978) have dominated the field as explanations for the causes of job satisfaction. In the past two decades, however, increasing attention has focused on the dispositional bases of job satisfaction (e.g., Staw et al., 1986; Staw and Ross, 1985; Weiss, 2002). Staw and Ross stimulated interest in this perspective when they argued that previous research had overestimated the influence of the situation on job satisfaction and underestimated the impact of an individual's dispositional characteristics. The dispositional approach suggests that a person's job satisfaction reflects their tendency to feel good or bad about life in general. This tendency to feel good or bad is independent of the job itself and its positive or negative features (Weiss and Cropanzano, 1996).

Researchers interested in the satisfaction-performance relationship have begun to explore the role of dispositional characteristics as an explanation for the relationship between these two constructs. Bowling (2007) concluded that the relationship between satisfaction and performance is largely spurious. Results of this meta-analysis revealed path coefficients of 0.09 to 0.23 between satisfaction and performance after personality was controlled. Judge et al. (2002) conducted a meta-analytic review of relationships between job satisfaction and the 'Big 5' personality traits (Goldberg, 1990). This review indicated that neuroticism, extraversion, and conscientiousness, displayed moderate relationships with job satisfaction. Neuroticism was most strongly associated (negatively) with job satisfaction, followed by conscientiousness, which displayed a positive association with job satisfaction. However, the 80% credibility interval for conscientiousness included zero, suggesting that this result may not be replicable. Other dispositional characteristics that have been the subject of considerable attention in recent times include trait affectivity (Thorensen et al., 2003), and core self-evaluations (Judge et al., 2005; Judge and Bono, 2001). Below, we examine research on positive and negative affectivity and then we

examine the research addressing the role of core self-evaluations.

Positive affectivity and negative affectivity

A great deal of attention has been directed towards examining relationships between positive affectivity (PA) and negative affectivity (NA) and job satisfaction (e.g., Thorensen et al., 2003). People high on positive affectivity tend to be sociable, lively, and are often in a positive mood. In contrast, people who are high on negative affectivity tend to be more distressed, unhappy, and irritable (Watson et al., 1988). A number of theoretical models have been developed to explain the relationship between job satisfaction and trait affectivity. Weiss and Cropanzano (1996) developed Affective Events Theory (AET), which focuses on affective experiences at work as proximal drivers of affective reactions, which influence attitudes and behaviors. This model implies that job events mediate relationships between dispositional affectivity and job satisfaction. Judge and Larsen (2001) proposed the stimulus-organism-response (SOR) model. The basis of this model is that PA and NA influence individuals' responses and judgements by moderating relationships between a stimulus and the organism. In addition, this model argues that affect mediates relationships between an organism and their responses. Finally, Forgas and George (2001) proposed the affect infusion model (AIM). This approach suggests that individual's attitudes to their job are partially a function of the affect that 'infuses' their cognitive processing when they are forming evaluations of objects. As such, the AIM is a direct effects model.

A number of empirical studies have explored relationships between trait and state affect and job satisfaction. These studies involve intraindividual processes described previously in this chapter. For example, Ilies and Judge (2002) examined the within-person relationship between mood (state affect) and job satisfaction, and also examined the role of personality in moderating these relationships. Twenty-seven employees completed mood and job satisfaction surveys at four different times a day for four weeks. The results of this study indicate that 36% of the total variance in job satisfaction was due to within-person factors and mood explained 29% of this within-person variance. In addition, mood and job satisfaction were related both within and across individuals. Results also indicated that within-person variability in mood was related to within-person variability in job satisfaction and variability in mood and job satisfaction was predicted by neuroticism. Finally, individuals who scored higher on neuroticism were more likely to have their mood affect their job satisfaction.

A number of meta-analyses have summarized relationships between trait affectivity and state affect and job satisfaction (e.g., Thorensen et al., 2003). In the most recent review, Thorensen et al. reported an estimated corrected mean population correlation of 0.27 between trait PA and satisfaction, while state PA had an estimated mean population correlation of 0.38 with satisfaction. Trait NA had an estimated mean population correlation of −0.27 with job satisfaction while state NA had an estimated mean population correlation of −0.31. However, Niklas and Dormann (2005) argue that the conclusion that there is a relationship between trait affectivity and state affect and job satisfaction is problematic for a number of reasons. While results have been interpreted as suggesting that state affect is a result of job events, which then causes job satisfaction, these relationships are open to interpretation, because trait affectivity was not controlled when estimating relationships between state affect and job satisfaction. As such, the correlation between state affect and job satisfaction may in fact be spurious. In addition, Niklas and Dormann argue that there is a need to determine whether state affect only influences job satisfaction at the time when it is measured or whether state affect has a lasting influence on satisfaction.

Niklas and Dormann (2005) conducted a two week diary study with 91 employees to address these concerns. Participants completed questionnaires four times a day. Facet job satisfaction was assessed as was general satisfaction using the Faces Scales. Trait job satisfaction and trait affect were measured and participants were asked to indicate how satisfied they usually are with work and how they usually feel. When state job satisfaction and state affect were assessed, participants were asked to indicate their current attitude toward their job and their current affect. The results of this study revealed that within-person aggregated state job satisfaction was strongly correlated with generalized job satisfaction. In addition, state affect and state job satisfaction were related even when trait affect and generalized satisfaction are controlled. Niklas and Dormann suggest that this study provides evidence that the relationship between state affect and job satisfaction is not due to the influence of a third factor, trait affectivity. Rather, they conclude that positive or negative work events lead to state affect, which has an impact on job satisfaction above and beyond that of affective disposition. Importantly, Niklas and Dormann state that job satisfaction depended more on affect elicited by current affairs than on personality dispositions. Because trait affectivity was controlled, Niklas and Dormann argue that state affect does not merely represent a mediator between trait affect and satisfaction. Rather, there must be situational factors that elicit state affect, which lead to changes in job satisfaction.

Core self-evaluations (Judge et al., 2005) defined core self-evaluations as fundamental, subconscious conclusions that individuals reach about themselves, other people, and the world. Four core self-evaluations – self-esteem, generalized self-efficacy, neuroticism, and locus of control – have been identified. Core self-evaluations can help elucidate the psychological processes underlying the dispositional source of job satisfaction. A growing number of empirical studies have explored the influence of core self-evaluations on job satisfaction. For example, Judge et al. (1998) conducted an empirical study and reported that core self-evaluations have consistent effects on job satisfaction, independent of the attributes of the job itself. Judge and his colleagues state that results indicated that core self-evaluations had an indirect influence on job satisfaction, via their impact on individuals' perceptions of their job's attributes. These perceptions then influence job satisfaction.

Despite the progress that has been made in accounting for dispositional influences on job satisfaction, Johnson, Rosen, and Levy (in press) identified a number of theoretical and measurement issues with the core-self evaluation construct that are of particular concern. We focus on just two of the issues identified. First, Johnson et al. argue that, to date, core self-evaluation has been discussed as a superordinate construct with effects indicators, such that this construct is responsible for levels of self-esteem, generalized self-efficacy, locus of control, and neuroticism. In such models, causality flows from the construct to the traits, which are manifestations of the construct. However, Johnson et al. argue that core self-evaluation is more accurately modeled as an aggregate construct. In an aggregate model, core self-evaluation would not cause the traits but be caused by them. This is a critical distinction, because if core self-evaluation is modeled as a superordinate construct, then the likelihood of uncovering true effects is reduced. Second, the measurement of core self-evaluation does not align with how it is conceptualized. The use of summed scores is inappropriate, as an aggregate construct cannot be adequately represented by a summed score.

Multi-level studies of job satisfaction

Job satisfaction has also been incorporated in multilevel processes involving teams and organizations. Many permutations of relationship are possible when complex mediational processes are considered at multiple levels of analysis. We consider two broad and important types of multilevel problems that involve job satisfaction. The first multilevel problem involves top down processes whereby team and organizational processes shape the experience of job satisfaction of individuals. In these studies, predictors at the team and organization level of analysis influence individual experiences of job satisfaction. For example, Jex and Bliese (1999) found that the collective self-efficacy of 36 US army companies positively influenced individual experiences of job satisfaction. In addition, collective self-efficacy moderated the relationship between work overload and job satisfaction such that work overload was less negatively related to job satisfaction in units with higher levels of collective self-efficacy. Other multilevel studies have investigated the way individual satisfaction has been shaped by aggregate processes such as leadership (Griffin et al., 2001), organizational justice (Mossholder et al., 1998) group racial composition (Mueller et al., 1999), and demographic diversity (Wharton et al., 2000).

Second, researchers have incorporated job satisfaction as an aggregate construct within systems of other variables that are assessed beyond the individual level. This approach seeks to extend theoretical relationships obtained at the individual level to higher levels of analysis (Chen et al., 2005). Ostroff (1992) invigorated research of this kind when she proposed that aggregate job satisfaction would be related to organizational performance. Her study extended the satisfaction-performance debate to the organizational level of analysis and provided a theoretical framework for understanding how individual attitudes might influence organizational outcomes. Patterson, Warr and West (2004) further extended this thinking to show that aggregate job satisfaction mediated the link between a company's organizational climate and objective measures of company performance. They argued that aggregate job satisfaction captured affective experiences that arose from the practices and procedures enacted in the company. In summary, researchers are increasingly concerned with studying multilevel relationships between job satisfaction and team and organizational variables. This research has opened up a whole new realm of possibilities concerning the role and the importance of job satisfaction.

CONCLUSION

Job satisfaction has been an active and productive area of research since the 1930s. Our review has revealed that there is still considerable interest in job satisfaction and that a growing number of methods are being used to study satisfaction. In particular, we reviewed studies using methodologies such as interviews, questionnaires, and diary studies. Recent developments in the methods used to study the affective aspects of job satisfaction reflect the continuing growth and sophistication of research methods and designs in the area. Overall, our review suggests that while working roles change for individuals and theoretical perspectives fade or rise for scholars, the experience of job satisfaction continues to play a central role in understanding life at work. We expect that this interest will continue across the spectrum of issues raised in this chapter. Debate regarding the definition and nature of job satisfaction will continue as insights grow from new methodologies, cross-cultural perspectives, and changing theoretical paradigms. This debate is important and will generate new methodologies as researchers seek to explore the implications of new definitions for theory, measurement, and practice. Recent advances in intraindividual and multilevel designs suggest that enormous scope remains for embedding the notion of job satisfaction within broader theories and practices. We conclude that the study of job satisfaction is a healthy topic of research that will continue to enhance understanding of how people interact with organizations.

REFERENCES

Aldag, R.J. and Brief, A.P. (1978) 'Examination of alternative models of job satisfaction', *Human Relations*, 31(1): 91–8.

Arvey, R.D., Bouchard, T.J., Segal, N.L. and Abraham, L.M. (1989) 'Job satisfaction: environmental and genetic components', *Journal of Applied Psychology*, 74(2): 187–92.

Aryee, S., Fields, D. and Luk, V. (1999) 'A cross-cultural test of a model of the work-family interface', *Journal of Management*, 25(4): 491–511.

Baumeister, R.F., Bratslavsky, E., Finkenauer, C. and Vohs, K.D. (2001) 'Bad is stronger than good', *Review of General Psychology*, 5(4): 323–70.

Bowling, N.A. (2007) 'Is the job satisfaction-job performance relationship spurious? a meta-analytic examination', *Journal of Vocational Behavior*, 71(2): 167–85.

Brayfield, A.H. and Rothe, H.F. (1951) 'An index of job satisfaction', *Journal of Applied Psychology*, 35(5): 307–11.

Brief, A.P. and Roberson, L. (1989) 'Job attitude organization: an exploratory study', *Journal of Applied Social Psychology*, 19(9): 717–27.

Bussing, A. and Bissels, T. (1998) 'Different forms of work satisfaction: concept and qualitative research', *European Psychologist*, 3(3): 209–18.

Cammann, C., Fichman, M., Jenkins, D. and Klesh, J. (1983) 'Assessing the attitudes and perceptions of organizational members', in S. Seashore, E. Lawler, P. Mirvis and C. Cammann (eds), *Assessing Organizational Change: A Guide to Methods, Measures, and Practices*, New York: John Wiley.

Chen, G., Bliese, P.D. and Mathieu, J.E. (2005) 'Conceptual framework and statistical procedures for delineating and testing multilevel theories of homology', *Organizational Research Methods*, 8(4): 375–409.

Cook, T.D. and Campbell, D.T. (1979) *Quasi-experimentation: design and analysis issues for field settings*, Chicago: Rand McNally College Publishing Company.

Cook, T.D., Campbell, D.T. and Perracchio, L. (1992) 'Quasi-experimentation', in M.D. Dunnette and L.M. Hough (eds), *Handbook of Industrial and Organizational Psychology* (Second edn., Vol. 1), CA: Consulting Psychologists Press.

Cranny, C.J., Smith, P.C. and Stone, E.F. (1992) 'The construct of job satisfaction', in C.J. Cranny, P.C. Smith and E.F. Stone (eds), *Job Satisfaction: How People Feel About Their Jobs and How It Affects Their Performance*, New York: Lexington Books.

Dormann, C. and Zapf, D. (2001) 'Job satisfaction: a meta-analysis of stabilities', *Journal of Organizational Behavior*, 22(6): 483–504.

Dunham, R.B. and Herman, J.B. (1975) 'Development of a female faces scale for measuring job satisfaction', *Journal of Applied Psychology*, 60(5): 629–51.

Dunham, R.B., Smith, F.J. and Blackburn, R.S. (1977) 'Validation of the index of organizational reactions with the JDI, the MSQ, and Faces Scales', *Academy of Management Journal*, 20(3): 420–32.

Ewen, R.B., Smith, P.C., Hulin, C.L. and Locke, E.A. (1966) 'An empirical test of the Herzberg two-factor theory', *Journal of Applied Psychology*, 50(6): 544–50.

Fisher, C.D. (2000) 'Mood and emotions while working: missing pieces of job satisfaction', *Journal of Organizational Behavior*, 21(Spec Issue): 185–202.

Fisher, C.D. (2002) 'Antecedents and consequences of real-time affective reactions at work', *Motivation and Emotion*, 26(1): 3–30.

Forgas, J.P. and George, J.M. (2001) 'Affective influences on judgements and behavior in organizations: an information processing perspective', *Organizational Behavior and Human Decision Processes*, 86(1): 3–34.

Goldberg, L.R. (1990) 'An alternative "description of personality": the big-five factor structure', *Journal of Personality and Social Psychology*, 59(6): 1216–29.

Gottfredson, G.D. and Holland, J.L. (1990) 'A longitudinal test of the influence of congruence: Job satisfaction, competency utilization, and counterproductive behavior', *Journal of Counseling Psychology*, 37(4): 389–98.

Graen, G.B. (1966) 'Addendum to "an empirical test of the Herzberg two-factor theory"', *Journal of Applied Psychology*, 50(6): 551–55.

Griffin, M.A., Patterson, M.G. and West, M.A. (2001) 'Job satisfaction and teamwork: the role of supervisor support', *Journal of Organizational Behavior*, 22(5): 537–50.

Heller, D., Judge, T.A. and Watson, D. (2002) 'The confounding role of personality and trait affectivity in the relationship between job and life satisfaction', *Journal of Organizational Behavior*, 23(7): 815–35.

Herzberg, F., Mausner, B., Peterson, R.O. and Capwell, D.F. (1957) *Job Attitudes: Review of Research and Opinion*, Pittsburgh, Psychological Service of Pittsburgh.

Herzberg, F., Mausner, B. and Snyderman, B.B. (1959) *The Motivation to Work*, New York: John Wiley and Sons.

Highhouse, S. and Becker, A.S. (1993) 'Facet measures and global job satisfaction', *Journal of Business and Psychology*, 8(1): 117–27.

Hom, P.W., Caranikas-Walker, F., Prussia, G.E. and Griffeth, R.W. (1992) 'A meta-analytical structural equations analysis of a model of employee turnover', *Journal of Applied Psychology*, 77(6): 890–909.

Hoppock, R. (1935) *Job Satisfaction*, New York: Harper.

Iaffaldano, M.T. and Muchinsky, P.M. (1985) 'Job satisfaction and job performance: a meta-analysis', *Psychological Bulletin*, 97(2): 251–73.

Ilies, R. and Judge, T.A. (2002) 'Understanding dynamic relationships among personality, mood, and job satisfaction: a field experience sampling study', *Organizational Behavior and Human Decision Processes*, 89(2): 1119–39.

Ilies, R. and Judge, T.A. (2004) 'An experience-sampling measure of job satisfaction and its relationship with affectivity, mood at work job beliefs, and general job satisfaction', *European Journal of Work and Organizational Psychology*, 13(3): 367–89.

Ironson, G.H., Smith, P.C., Brannick, M.T., Gibson, W.M. and Paul, K.B. (1989) 'Construction of a job in general scale: a comparison of global, composite, and specific measures', *Journal of Applied Psychology*, 74(2): 193–200.

Jex, S.M. and Bliese, P.D. (1999) 'Efficacy beliefs as a moderator of the impact of work-related stressors: a multilevel study', *Journal of Applied Psychology*, 84(3): 349–361.

Johnson, R.E., Rosen, C.C. and Levy, P.E. (In Press), 'Getting to the core of core self-evaluation: a review and recommendations', *Journal of Organizational Behavior*.

Judge, T.A. and Bono, J.E. (2001) 'Relationship of core self evaluations traits–self-esteem, generalized self-efficacy, locus of control, and emotional stability–with job satisfaction and job performance: a meta-analysis', *Journal of Applied Psychology*, 86(1): 80–92.

Judge, T.A., Bono, J.E., Erez, M. and Locke, E.A. (2005) 'Core self-evaluations and job and life satisfaction: the role of self-concordance and goal attainment', *Journal of Applied Psychology*, 90(2): 257–68.

Judge, T.A., Bono, J.E., Ilies, R. and Gerhardt, M.W. (2002) 'Personality and leadership: a qualitative and quantitative review', *Journal of Applied Psychology*, 87(4): 765–80.

Judge, T.A. and Hulin, C.L. (1993) 'Job satisfaction as a reflection of disposition: a multiple causal analysis', *Organizational Behavior and Human Decision Processes*, 56(3): 388–421.

Judge, T.A. and Ilies, R. (2004) 'Affect and job satisfaction: a study of their relationship at work and home', *Journal of Applied Psychology*, 89(4): 661–73.

Judge, T.A. and Larsen, R.J. (2001) 'Dispositional affect and job satisfaction: a review and theoretical extension', *Organizational Behavior and Human Decision Processes*, 86(1): 67–98.

Judge, T.A., Locke, E.A., Durham, C.C. and Kluger, A.N. (1998) 'Dispositional effects on job and life satisfaction: the role of core evaluations', *Journal of Applied Psychology*, 83(1): 17–34.

Judge, T.A., Parker, S., Colbert, A.E., Heller, D. and Ilies, R. (2001a) 'Job satisfaction: a cross-cultural review', in N. Anderson, D.S. Ones, H.K. Singangil and C. Viswesvaran, (eds) *Handbook of Industrial* and Organizational Psychology, London: Sage Publications.

Judge, T.A., Thorensen, C.J., Bono, J.E. and Patton, G.K. (2001b) 'The job satisfaction-job performance relationship: a qualitative and quantitative review', Psychological Bulletin, 127(3): 376–407.

Kidd, S.A. (2002) 'The role of qualitative research in psychological journals', Psychological Methods, 7(1): 126–38.

Kunin, T. (1955) 'The construction of a new type of attitude measure', Personnel Psychology, 8: 65–77.

Lam, S.S.K. and Schaubroeck, J. (2000a) 'A field experiment testing frontline opinion leaders as change agents', Journal of Applied Psychology, 85(6): 987–95.

Lam, S.S.K. and Schaubroeck, J. (2000b) 'The role of locus of control in reactions to being promoted and to being passed over: a quasi experiment', Academy of Management Journal, 43(1): 66–78.

Landy, F.J. (1989) 'Job satisfaction: the meaning of work', Psychology of Work Behavior (fourth ed.), Pacific Grove, CA: Brooks/Cole Publishing Company.

Locke, E.A. (1969) 'What is job satisfaction?', Organizational Behavior and Human Performance, 4(4): 309–36.

Locke, E.A. (1976) 'The nature and causes of job satisfaction', in M. Dunnette (ed.), The Handbook of Organizational Psychology, Chicago, Rand McNally.

Locke, E.A. (1983) 'The nature and causes of job satisfaction', in M. Dunnette (ed.), Handbook of Industrial and Organizational Psychology, New York: John Wiley and Sons.

Logan, M.S. and Ganster, D.C. (2005) 'An experimental evaluation of a control intervention to alleviate job-related stress', Journal of Management, 31(1): 90–107.

Lyons, H.Z. and O'Brien, K.M. (2006) 'The role of person-environment fit in the job satisfaction and tenure intentions of African American employees', Journal of Counseling Psychology, 53(4): 387–96.

Marchel, C. and Owens, S. (2007) 'Qualitative research in psychology', History of Psychology, 10(4): 301–24.

Mathieu, J.E. (1991) 'A cross-level nonrecursive model of the antecedents of organizational commitment and satisfaction', Journal of Applied Psychology, 76(5): 607–18.

McFarlin, D.B. and Sweeney, P.D. (1992) 'Distributive and procedural justice as predictors of satisfaction with personal and organizational outcomes', Academy of Management Journal, 35(3): 626–37.

Mossholder, K.W., Bennett, N. and Martin, C.L. (1998) 'A multilevel analysis of procedural justice context', Journal of Organizational Behavior, 19(2): 131–41.

Mueller, C.W., Finley, A, Iverson, R.D. and Price, J.L. (1999) 'The effects of group racial composition on job satisfaction, organizational commitment, and career commitment: the case of teachers', Work and Occupations, 26(2): 187–219.

Niklas, C.D. and Dormann, C. (2005) 'The impact of state affect on job satisfaction', European Journal of Work and Organizational Psychology, 14(4): 367–88.

Ostroff, C. (1992) 'The relationship between satisfaction, attitudes, and performance: an organizational level analysis', Journal of Applied Psychology, 77(6): 963–74.

Patterson, M. Warr, P. and West, M. (2004) 'Organizational climate and company productivity: the role of employee affect and employee level', Journal of Occupational and Organizational Psychology, 77(2): 193–216.

Pekrun, R. and Frese, M. (1992) 'Emotions in work and achievement', in C.L. Cooper and I.T. Robertson, (eds), International Review of Industrial and Organizational Psychology, Chichester: John Wiley and Sons.

Petty, M.M., McGee, G.W. and Cavender, J.W. (1984) 'A meta-analysis of the relationships between individual job satisfaction and individual performance', Academy of Management Review, 9(4): 712–21.

Pillai, R., Schriesheim, C.A. and Williams, E.S. (1999) 'Fairness perceptions and trust as mediators for transformational and transactional leadership: a two-sample study', Journal of Management, 25(6): 897–933.

Quinn, R.P. and Staines, G.L. (1979) The 1979 Quality of Employment Survey, Institute for Social Research, University of Michigan, Ann Arbour, Michigan.

Rain, J.S., Lane, I.M. and Steiner, D.D. (1991) 'A current look at the job satisfaction/life satisfaction relationship: review and future considerations', Human Relations, 44(3): 287–306.

Rode, J.C. (2004) 'Job satisfaction and life satisfaction revisited: a longitudinal test of an integrated model', Human Relations, 57(9): 1205–30.

Roethlisberger, F.J. and Dickson, W.J. (1939) Management and the worker: an account of a research program conducted by the Western Company, Hawthorne Works, Chicago, Cambridge, MA: Harvard University Press.

Rose, M. (2003) 'Good deal, bad deal? job satisfaction in occupations', Work, Employment, and Society, 17(3): 503–30.

Rousseau, D. (1978) 'Relationship of work to nonwork', Journal of Applied Psychology, 63(4): 513–17.

Roznowski, M. (1989) 'Examination of the measurement properties of the Job Descriptive Index with experimental items', *Journal of Applied Psychology*, 74(5): 805–14.

Salancik, G.R. and Pfeffer, J. (1978) 'A social information processing approach to job attitudes and task design', *Administrative Science Quarterly*, 23(2): 224–53.

Scarpello, V. and Campbell, J.P. (1983) 'Job satisfaction: are all the parts there?', *Personnel Psychology*, 36(3): 577–600.

Schaffer, R.H. (1953) 'Job satisfaction as related to need satisfaction in work', *Psychological Monographs: General and Applied*, 67(14): 1–29.

Seibert, S.E. (1999) 'The effectiveness of facilitated mentoring: a longitudinal quasi-experiment', *Journal of Vocational Behavior*, 54(3): 483–502.

Smith, P.C. (1992) 'In pursuit of happiness', in C.J. Cranny, P.C. Smith and E.F. Stone (eds), *Job Satisfaction*, New York: Lexington Books.

Smith, P.C., Kendall, L.M. and Hulin, C.L. (1969) *The Measurement of Satisfaction in Work and Retirement*, Chicago: Rand McNally.

Spector, P.E. (1997) *Job Satisfaction: Application, Assessment, Causes, and Consequences*, Thousand Oaks: Sage Publications.

Staw, B.M., Bell, N.E. and Clausen, J.A. (1986) 'The dispositional approach to job attitudes: a lifetime longitudinal test', *Administrative Science Quarterly*, 31(1): 56–77.

Staw, B.M. and Ross, J. (1985) 'Stability in the midst of change: a dispositional approach to job attitudes', *Journal of Applied Psychology*, 70(3): 469–80.

Tait, M., Padgett, M.Y. and Baldwin, T.T. (1989) 'Job and life satisfaction: a reevaluation of the strength of the relationship and gender effects as a function of the date of the study', *Journal of Applied Psychology*, 74(3): 502–7.

Tharenou, P. (1993) 'A test of reciprocal causality for absenteeism', *Journal of Organizational Behavior*, 14(3): 269–87.

Thorensen, C.J., Kaplan S.A., Barsky, A.P. and de Chermont, K. (2003) 'The affective underpinnings of job perceptions and attitudes: a meta-analytic review and integration', *Psychological Bulletin*, 129(6): 914–45.

Watson, D., Clark, L.A. and Tellegen, A. (1988) 'Development and validation of brief measures of positive and negative affect: the PANAS scales', *Journal of Personality and Social Psychology*, 54(6): 1063–70.

Weiss, D.J., Dawis, R.V., England, G.W. and Lofquist, L.H. (1967) *Manual for the Minnesota Satisfaction Questionnaire: Minnesota Studies in Vocational Rehabilitation*, University of Minnesota, Vocational Psychology Research.

Weiss, H.M. (2002) 'Deconstructing job satisfaction: separating evaluations, beliefs and affective experiences', *Human Resource Management Review*, 12(2): 173–94.

Weiss, H.M. and Cropanzano, R. (1996) 'Affective events theory: a theoretical discussion of the structure, causes and consequences of affective experiences at work', *Research in Organizational Behavior*, 18: 1–74.

Weiss, H.M., Nicholas, J.P. and Daus, C.S. (1999) 'An examination of the joint effects of affective experiences and job beliefs on job satisfaction and variations in effective experiences over time', *Organizational Behavior and Human Decision Processes*, 78(1): 1–24.

Wharton, A.S., Rotolo, T. and Bird, S.R. (2000) 'Social context at work: a multilevel analysis of job satisfaction', *Sociological Forum*, 15(1): 65–90.

Wong, C.S., Hui, C. and Law, K.S. (1998) 'A longitudinal study of the job perception-job satisfaction relationship: a test of three alternate specifications', *Journal of Occupational and Organizational Psychology*, 71(2): 127–46.

Workman, M. and Bommer, W.H. (2004) 'Redesigning computer call center work: a longitudinal field experiment', *Journal of Organizational Behavior*, 25(3): 317–37.

Wright, T.A. and Bonett, D.G. (2002) 'The moderating effects of employee tenure on the relation between organizational commitment and job performance: a meta-analysis', *Journal of Applied Psychology*, 87(6): 1183–90.

13

Studying Organizational Populations Over Time*

Glenn R. Carroll, Mi Feng, Gaël Le Mens,
and David G. McKendrick

INTRODUCTION

Most social scientists agree that formal organizations occupy a central role in modern society in that most collective action occurs within them. There is also an emerging consensus, evidenced by the research designs organizational scientists typically use, that a powerful way of studying organizations involves the collection and analysis of data over time. Yet, issues about how to study organizations over time sometimes engender confused debate. In this chapter, we aim to clarify some of the main issues involved, with a special focus on studying organizational populations over time. Throughout the chapter, we illustrate our general points with specific examples drawn from our ongoing study of the historical worldwide population of tape drive producers.

What is an organizational population?

Early studies of organizational populations were often simply called an 'industry study.'

In a typical study of this kind, analysts study a single industry over time by collecting information on all the firms or other organizations operating in a market. For instance, Epstein (1927) conducted a study of failure among American automobile producers. Such studies continue today (see Klepper, 2002; Mitchell, 1994; Tripsas, 1997). The definition of industry or market used in industry studies may be explicit and clear. However, it is usually not theoretically reasoned in any depth and often simply follows common sense or convention, as incorporated in directories, reports, or archives (used as sources for data). As a result, what is regarded as the relevant organizational population varies significantly from one study to the next – e.g., in some cases, it implies legal incorporation, in others, the production of goods or services, in yet others, the sale of goods or services possibly produced by other parties.

Attention to the conceptual foundations of the population-based design can be traced to the population ecology perspective on organization. Specifically, Hannan and Freeman (1977: 935–6) reasoned that,

'Systems relevant to the study of organization-environment relations are usually defined by geography, by political boundaries, by market, or product considerations, etc. Given a systems definition, a population of organizations consists of all the organizations within a particular boundary that have a common form. That is, the population is the form as it exists or is realized within a specified system.' This construction presupposes two conceptual feats. First, it presumes that system boundaries are clearly identifiable and relatively unambiguous. Second, the Hannan and Freeman (1977) construction also presupposes a definition of organizational form.

In fact, although system boundaries may not be unambiguously identifiable in a particular context, delineation of system boundaries is usually something that is left up to the investigator and has not been the subject of much debate or analysis among researchers. (The exceptions are occasional studies of geographically shifting boundaries (see, for example, Carroll and Wade, 1991; Bigelow et al., 1997; Sorenson and Audia, 2000).

By contrast, with respect to organizational forms, quite a bit has changed as ecology developed. Initially, Hannan and Freeman (1977) suggested that 'an organizational form is a blueprint for organizational action, for transforming inputs into outputs.' They mentioned three general ways that blueprints might be inferred: (1) from formal organizational structures; (2) from patterns of activity; and (3) from the normative order. Hannan and Freeman (1984) reconsidered further the form concept and noted that analogies to genes, niches, and exchange patterns have all been used in defining forms; they also suggested a focus on the boundary-defining processes creating and merging forms.

This somewhat loose approach to defining systems and forms fostered much organizational ecology research. Fueled by the clever use of archival and other source material, ecologists conducted scores of studies involving the collection and analysis of purported organizational populations in particular places over long periods of time (see Carroll and Hannan, 2000).

Although ecological research generated impressively cumulative theory and findings on certain issues, in retrospect this accomplishment seems at least mildly surprising. Like prior industry studies, ecological studies of organizations varied substantially in delineation of market boundaries and especially in the operational definitions of forms. In particular, studies often elided over differences in products, establishments, organizations, and firms. They also differed in how they defined the date of entry into and exit from the population.

Some current research in ecology embraces an alternative view of organizational forms as collective identities. Pioneered by Rao et al. (2003), Ruef (2000) and Zuckerman (1999), this approach implies that for researchers to identify forms, they need to understand the ways that contemporaneous participants and relevant audience members see forms and distinguish among them. This approach contrasts markedly with the (implicit) prior view that forms are a purely analytical or theoretical construct of the researchers. Hannan et al. (2007) go further and argue that form membership is often partial; that some organizations are seen as full members of a collective identity, while others are seen as 'kind of' or 'sort of' members. Accordingly, they regard populations as fuzzy sets rather than crisp classical sets and they associate a grade-of-membership (GoM) that varies from 0 (nonmembers) to 1 (full members) with each potential member organization.

Using collective identity to define forms matters a lot in terms of which organizations get chosen for study in a given context and how they are treated numerically. For example, among national labor unions in the U.S., the organizational distinction between craft (wherein workers are organized by their skills) and industrial union (wherein workers are organized across all skills within an industry) has usually been considered important. Yet, as Hannan et al. (2007) point out, certain cases such as the Brotherhood of Carpenters and Joiners prove difficult to classify, because they are best considered as 'hybrids,' albeit with shifting tilt in one direction or the other. In the collective identity framework, such a union can have a time-dependent GoM associated with both craft and industrial union forms, whereas in previous approaches the union would have been classified into one form or the other, or left to a nonmeaningful residual category.

The difference in approaches carries implications for population counts and other commonly used measures. By the traditional view, an organizational population is 'crisp' in the sense that every organization is either in it or not, and counting members or density is straightforward once the inclusion rules are set. By the collective identity view, familiar counts such as density are weighted by the GoM, implying very different measures for the population. The earlier approach suffers from forcing a black-white coding rule on situations that even contemporary participants regard as genuinely ambiguous. The newer approach makes stronger demands on data collection and renders some previously diamond quality source material as incomplete. For instance, with each organization with a nonzero GoM, analysts must now devise a measure of the GoM for each organization. Moreover, Hannan et al. (2007) propose new measures for population density, contrast, and others based on the collective identity definition to forms.

For tape drive producers, we have not yet succeeded in fully implementing a fuzzy approach to population membership. As described in the following section, our sources allow us to identify firms involved in the sale of tape drive products in the market. These facts allow a crisp definition of membership, but we hope that we might be able to use other available information to weight it by the degree to which a firm might have been considered a 'full-fledged' tape drive producer for data storage. For instance, we know whether a firm was involved in only the design or manufacture of tape drives or both. We also know whether the firm produced a predigital analog tape drive. In addition, we know the early technological background of each firm in terms of whether it produced drives for computer applications, for digital instruments, for audiovisual applications, for military applications, or combinations thereof. Finally, we know whether a firm is a new start-up in tape drives (a de novo firm) or whether it previously operated in another market (a de alio firm). Each of these factors is plausibly related to population membership, as viewed by contemporaneous market participants. To generate a fuzzy measure for the GoM for tape drive producers would require theorizing about how the participants used this information to determine which firms are 'really' tape drive producers and which firms are 'kind of' tape drive producers. Similar challenges confront analysts studying other historical populations who wish to use a fuzzy conception of forms.

Why study organizational populations?

Within contemporary organizational theory, researchers interested in testing theories increasingly choose between a population research design, and a design that uses representative data from the largest organizations in the economy or a sector (e.g., Fortune 500). In the population design, data are collected on all the organizations of a particular type for (almost) the entire period of the organizational form's existence, while the other popular design takes data from many different kinds of organizational populations, usually for a relatively short period. What are the issues involved in choosing between these designs? What are the trade-offs?

Contemporary theory on organizations assigns central roles to various environmental agents, including strategic competitors, resource providers, governmental regulators, and social institutions. Typically, these agents are governed by complex processes, at times envisioned as nonlinear and network-based. In addition, research suggests that organizations are often path dependent, meaning that prior (possibly random) behaviors influence subsequent actions.

Three aspects of this theoretical posture usually make the population design better suited than its alternative for researching organizations, in our view (Carroll and Hannan 2000). First, samples of very diverse types of organizations likely display the effects of many different processes, probably mixed in ways that follow at least in part from the context. With a sample of diverse organizations, the only hope of detecting these widely varying processes would entail an intractable large sample. Second, complexity in organization-environmental processes requires researchers to observe many dimensions of an organization's specific context. Such demands can often be satisfied efficiently by constructing variables from the population elements themselves: relative size, density (number of organizations), competitive history, niche overlap, ordering of competitive moves, etc. This option typically is not viable with highly diverse samples, because there will be only one or several units from any given population. Third, sampling schemes incorporating great organizational diversity rarely obtain adequate information on vital events such as founding and mortality, because updating the sampling frame is very costly.

The population design does carry certain drawbacks, however. The most obvious, of course, is its inability to provide data for estimation of the means and proportions of characteristics of the multipopulation universe. Analytically, the greatest potential defect involves the possibility that the particular population examined behaves peculiarly with respect to the issues of interest. Another potential defect occurs when the researcher misinterprets – or incorrectly attributes – developments to a single population that would easily be seen as otherwise in a study with greater diversity in sampling. Accordingly, it is important to recognize that cumulative theoretical progress depends on the study of many and varied populations, not just a few, regardless of how important they may be. Ideally, comparison of findings across many different population studies makes aberrant findings obvious and at the same time greases the wheels of the theory mill. Meta-analyses, therefore, feature

centrally in the development of cumulative knowledge.

In attempting to assess these tradeoffs, Carroll and Hannan (2000) designed a series of computer simulations where the true parameters of processes are known and then estimated from different data with different design characteristics, including observation windows. Their findings show that observation plans based on diversity at the costs of temporal and organizational coverage often produce inferior result. By contrast, the population study covering a long period performs much better, despite lacking overall representativeness. In their view, the population design does much better than many analysts would expect, even on processes related to internal organizational structure.

Identifying and collecting population data

Organizational populations typically differ in the kinds of data and sources available about them. This variation makes it hard to know in advance what kinds of unique sources might be found. A librarian or an automated search usually uncovers only the most obvious sources; finding unusual ones often requires a good 'nose,' hard work, and luck. Nothing substitutes well for exploring library stacks and examining old documents. Nevertheless, it is worth it: a single good source can allow a researcher to reconstruct the past for an entire organizational population.

Criteria for evaluating sources

How should population source data be evaluated? Demographers of human populations evaluate censuses in terms of coverage (those related to persons missed or counted incorrectly) and content (inaccurate classification of a person based on characteristics). For organizational-population data, Carroll and Hannan (2000) propose consideration of four issues: (1) organizational coverage (the degree to which a source includes information about all organizations that fit the definition of the population); (2) temporal coverage (whether the observation window of the sources includes crucial periods of population history); (3) precision in the timing information (the dating of events); and (4) availability of accurate organization-specific information. The first two might be considered coverage issues and the last two content issues.

Obviously, real sources rarely match the ideal of providing a complete accurate representation of the population history. Although the ideal will be unknown in most research settings, external information can often be used to uncover clues about the quality of a source. Historical references sometimes tell when the first organization began operating in a population. With the tape drive producers, for instance, we know that in 1951 Remington Rand's Uniservo magnetic tape drive was the first tape drive for digital data recording shipped to a commercial customer (along with the first electronic stored-program computer, their Univac (Rosen, 1969; Daniels et al., 1999). (Both the computer and the tape drive were developed by Eckert-Mauchly Computer Corporation, which Remington Rand acquired the previous year (*New York Times*, 1950).) Even if previous attempts were made to record data on tape, these did not lead to commercial products until the Uniservo. So, this information can be used to evaluate a source's coverage: if it begins at a later date, then it is incomplete.

Sometimes external information about a set of well-known cases can be used for validation. This kind of test is a weaker one, because information on well-known cases is much easier to come by than information on short-lived and unimportant ones. Perhaps a more helpful use of external information would involve taking a random sample of information from an incomplete but authoritative source to validate a more complete source whose quality is unknown. This procedure entails comparing a sample from the source against a set of independent facts known or believed to be accurate. In both cases, external information provides an efficient way to evaluate a source prior to actual coding and cleaning of the data in a source, which can be expensive and time-consuming.

Another efficient method for evaluating a source involves comparing aggregate numbers or marginal distributions tabulated from it with those reported elsewhere. Sometimes aggregate counts on, say, the number of firms in an industry in a particular year (and perhaps by size class) appear in the summary data provided by governments, industry associations, or trade publications. For instance, in 1975, *Modern Data*, a trade journal, reviewed the fastest growing segment of the tape drive industry, the digital cassette tape drive market, and identified all of the manufacturers and their products (*Modern Data*, 1975).

A third way to evaluate a source prior to data collection involves polling industry experts. Generally speaking, an expert is someone who knows the industry and its firms; this might include industry historians, industry analysts in the investment banking and stock brokerage industries, employees of firms, and customers or suppliers of the industry. Experts usually can provide valuable information about the design of a source and also assess its accuracy. For instance, with tape drives we emailed knowledgeable persons who formerly worked for some of the companies involved in the early industry.

A fourth method of assessing the quality of data sources applies only after the data have been collected. It involves estimating known baseline models of organizational and population processes with the data (e.g., the model of density dependence) and comparing these estimates to the range of previously reported findings. Data generating estimates on baselines within the range expected should often be regarded as acceptable (certainly, the exercise supports this assessment). Although estimates that fall outside the range might signal flawed data, they might also be the result of a unique population of organizations. Only additional study could lead to a firm conclusion.

Commonly used data sources

Carroll and Hannan (2000) describe the following commonly used types of sources for population data on organizations: Industry

Directories; Encyclopedic Compilations; Governmental Registries; Censuses: Governmental and Other; Restricted-Inclusion Databases; and Lists of Prominent Firms.

Single authoritative sources such as annual directories and encyclopedic compilations cannot always be found for particular industries or populations. On close inspection, sources that appear to be authoritative are often found to be lacking in completeness of coverage or accuracy of reports on dates of events or on organizational characteristics. Thus, organizational analysts often find themselves using multiple sources, including disparate sources discovered by a more open-ended archival search. The dataset we compiled on tape drives is partly the result of this kind of process, as we describe in the following section.

Illustration: collecting data on tape drive producers

Over the past seven years, we used a range of sources to identify and compile information on tape drive producers. Our first step involved contacting a market research company, Freeman Associates, in Santa Barbara, California, which had tracked the tape drive industry since the 1980s. In July 2000, we sent a letter to Freeman describing our research goals and requesting copies of the company's annual reports. The president of the company invited us to meet with him to discuss our project and the terms for using the data. Shortly thereafter, Freeman sent us a full complement of the reports. We began to review the reports in early 2001, and in the summer, a doctoral student began to code data, which covered industry and firm revenue and unit shipments by product category as well as product technical specifications, including dates of first shipment. Coding and cleaning these data extended into 2006.

Parallel to this effort, we pored over trade and business journals and newspapers in the libraries of the University of California, San Diego, and Stanford University in an effort to identify all companies that ever manufactured a magnetic digital tape drive.

As explained in the preceding section, we marked the start of the tape drive industry as 1951. We then went through every publication (and issue) we thought relevant to computers and data storage between 1951 and 1980, when Freeman issued its first report and electronic sources became more widely available. These publications included *Electronic News, Datamation, Computers & Automation, Data Management, Modern Data, Computers & Data Processing, Mini-Micro Systems, and Business Automation.* They reported on individual firms, product announcements, industry trends, and the like. Information from these sources constituted the initial firm-level event file.

We also searched electronic databases through our respective university libraries, both for digital content and for additional hard-copy material. Searching WorldCat and OCLC enabled us to find and borrow a handful of useful marketing and consultant reports from libraries around the United States. These included reports from the Venture Development Corporation, Auerbach, Quantum Science Corporation, Frost & Sullivan, and Computer Industry Annual and covered the tape drive market from the late 1960s through the early 1980s. Additionally, electronic versions of the *Wall Street Journal, New York Times, Business Week*, and other newspapers and magazines provided important facts about changing ownership, firm size, production locations, business segments, key managers, and related information back to 1951. For information about firms, their products, and the tape drive industry in the 1980s and 1990s, we relied on Factiva and Lexis-Nexis, both of which had digital text articles from computer-related newspapers (*Electronic News*), magazines (*Computer Reseller News, Macworld, Computerworld,* etc) and press releases (*Business Wire, PR Newswire*), as well as regional newspapers (e.g., *San Diego Business Journal, Tulsa World*) that provided better coverage of local business.

After exhausting these sources, we came to have a good understanding of what we thought was the population of tape drive manufacturers. Then, in 2004 and 2005, we visited two archives for several days each to search for additional firm- and product-level information – the Charles Babbage Institute at the University of Minnesota, and the Hagley Museum and Library in Wilmington, Delaware. From these, we were able to collect various presale product information (such as brochures and specification sheets, occasional newspaper clippings, and annual reports) as well as postsale information (such as operating manuals, programming manuals, and the like). Additionally, we found some extensive records on a few prominent corporations (from antitrust complaints against IBM), some market research reports, and some reports and newsletters from consultants and financial and securities companies tracking tape drive producers.

A few academic journals proved helpful in rounding out the picture of key technological milestones, events and personalities in the industry. These include *IEEE Annals of the History of Computing, Computer Surveys, Business History, and IBM Journal of Research and Development*. Some books and theses on the computer industry were similarly useful for filling some gaps in our knowledge, although no book documented the history of the tape drive industry. Fisher et al. (1983) provided an excellent overview of the firms involved in the computer and peripherals market during the 1960s and 1970s. Other informative sources include Phister (1979), Forman (1980), Bashe et al. (1986), Flamm (1987), Lundstrom (1987), Hendry (1989), Pugh et al. (1991), and Daniels et al. (1999).

Finally, it was sometimes the case that the sources we used offered incomplete or even contradictory information about the firms' involvement in the industry. A prevalent concern was whether we accurately identified a tape drive producer. It could be difficult to discern whether a firm, in fact, produced a tape drive or had instead purchased a tape drive from another company and added electronics. Through web-based searches, we were almost always able to clarify this issue by finding and contacting former employees

and then emailing them questions. We were able to find people who worked for companies in our population as far back as the early 1960s. Nonetheless, for about 35 companies that advertised a tape drive or subsystem, or received some otherwise oblique mention, we were unable to confirm that they sold the drive mechanism. So, we did not include them in our database.

Designing a population study

Which organizational population(s) should one choose to study and why? Often this choice is made for idiosyncratic or personal reasons based on a person's passion or interests. In our view, that course of action is fine and likely proves useful in motivating the analyst to delve deeply into the institutional background of the population, something which we think is important. However, even if personal taste drives the initial choice, sooner or later the researcher needs to advance some substantive or theoretical ideas elaborating the implications of the choice.

A common substantive motivation for choosing a population involves its purported social or economic significance. For example, in response to the complaint that ecological theory applies mainly to small and powerless organizations, Hannan and Freeman (1987) chose to study national labor unions, because 'Some labor unions … have managed to amass millions of members and have accumulated enormous political power' (1987: 912). Likewise, Mitchell (1989) chose to study medical imaging machine producers, because 'imaging techniques … are important diagnostic medical tools' (1989: 208).

Even though choosing to study important populations seems sensible and even wise to many, Denrell and Kovacs (2008) show that this decision can often generate serious analytical problems. Why? Important populations tend to be long-lived and grow to substantial sizes; choosing a sample on this basis likely introduces sample selection bias into studies intended to explain factors related to population growth and size. In essence, the more important the population, the less typical it probably is. Denrell and Kovacs (2008) show in simulations that commonly estimated models such as that of density-dependent legitimation and competition are indeed biased when estimated from single realizations of long-lived populations.

A number of research strategies might be taken to mitigate against the sample selection bias identified and analyzed by Denrell and Kovacs (2008). These include: (1) choosing to study multiple realizations of the same kind of population, i.e., examine multiple environments where the same process is believed to have operated; (2) choosing to study some populations that have reached extinction e.g., the Norwegian automobile industry; (3) identifying potential populations at an early stage and studying them prospectively.

The strongest rationales for choosing to study any particular organizational population involve claims that characteristics of the population appear especially helpful in testing some theoretical claim or in isolating the effects of some particular process of interest. For example, Dobrev (2001) chose to study Bulgarian newspapers after the collapse of state socialism, because he wanted to see how legitimacy was restored.

For the tape drive population, our main motivation was to study an ecological community of separate interdependent populations. We chose data storage because of the functional similarity of its underlying populations (tape drives, floppy drives, hard disk drives, disk drive arrays, and optical drives), their different technological and scientific bases, and the availability of data. Tape drives are especially interesting, because they are the initial population in this community. We hope that this population might illuminate some of the identity and form emergence issues as well. In particular, we hope to be able to study how the technology and its associated organizational population emerged from audio and instrument tape applications.

Table 13.1 shows the distributions of entries and exits by type of event for the tape drive population. For entry mode, classification as a de novo entrant means that the firm was founded as a tape drive producer;

Table 13.1   Entries and exits into tape drive market by type

Entries		Exits	
De novo	72	Number of absorptions	21
De alio	122	Number of liquidations	165
Joint venture start-up	8		
Subsidiary start-up	12		
Other kinds of entry	1		
Total	215	Total	186

classification as a de alio entrant means that the firm had a presence in some other market before starting to produce tape drives (many were computer producers). For exit types, most exits result from liquidations.

Figure 13.1 plots the evolution of the number of tape producers (population 'density'). While the market began with a handful of de alio producers, a number of de novo entrants entered as early as 1957. The smaller number of de novo producers suggests, however, that they hardly thrived in the market conditions at that time. Not until the end of the 1960s did de novo producers consistently account for more than a quarter of the producers.

Figure 13.2 displays the annual number of entries and exits. It suggests that uncertainty characterized the decade around 1970: many firms entered (among these, many de novo), but many also failed. The surge in failures around 1975 suggests that the many entries in the years 1968–1974 resulted in heightened competition (or enhanced acquisition activities) in the following years. After 1982, the number of exits is almost consistently higher than the number of entries, suggesting a maturing market.

Figure 13.3 shows the evolution, from 1983 onward, of the number of producers of seven types of tape drives. The plots suggest that changes in the 'high-end' market (varieties of 1/2 inch format, depicted on the right quadrant) were smoother than that in the other segments (left quadrant). Variations of the number of producers of QIC (Quarter Inch Cartridge) drives were particularly large.

Table 13.2 provides a more detailed look at the dynamics within a technological type.

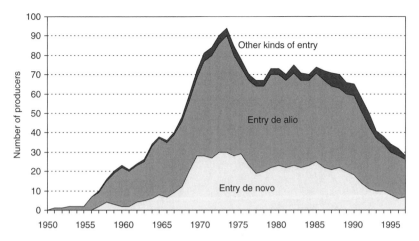

Figure 13.1   Density of tape drive producers by entry mode. Copyright © 2007 by G.R. Carroll and D.G. McKendrick. Used by permission. All rights reserved.

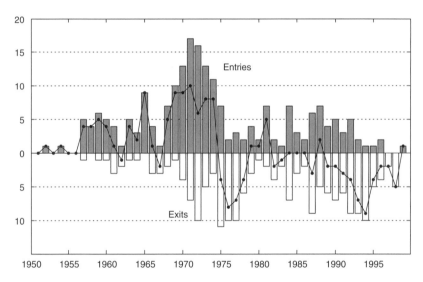

Figure 13.2   Yearly entries and exits into tape drive production. Copyright © 2007 by G.R. Carroll and D.G. McKendrick. Used by permission. All rights reserved.

Note: The number of entries in each year is given by the length of the bar above the x-axis. The number of exits in each year is given by the length of the bar below the x-axis. The solid line shows the annual difference between the number of entries and exits

It lists the producers of QIC drives operating in 1983 and compares it to a listing of those operating in 1995. Of the 33 producers of QIC drives in 1983, 24 (73%) had exited this segment by 1995. This fact might be explained by a shrinking appeal of QIC drives and a corresponding decrease of the market size of this segment between 1983 and 1995. However, it is also interesting to notice that

7 of the 15 QIC drive producers operating in 1995 were not operating in 1983. Therefore, while this technological segment experienced high turnover among firms, the aging of the technology might not uniquely account for the failure of so many of the producers that operated in 1983.

Figure 13.4 shows that most producers specialized in only one type of tape drive.

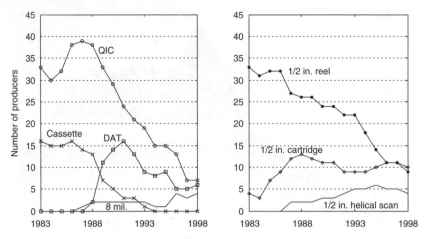

Figure 13.3   Density of producers by type of tape drive. Copyright © 2007 by G.R. Carroll and D.G. McKendrick. Used by permission. All rights reserved.

Table 13.2   Tape drive producers operating in 1983 and 1995

Producers of QIC drives		
Operates in 1983		Operates in 1995
3M	*Kennedy / Allegheny*	Anritsu
Amilon	*International*	Archive / Conner
Anritsu'	*Mohawk Data*	Peripherals
Archive	*Moya*	**ComByte**
Basic Four	Penny and Giles	Datamec / Hewlett Packard
Bright Industries / Datapoint	Perex (Sintrom Group)	**DDF Pertec**
Burroughs	Philips	**Exabyte**
Cipher Data Products	*Quantex (North Atlantic Industries)*	**Georgens Industries**
Control Data	*Raymond Engineering*	**Iomega**
Data Electronics	*Sankyo Seiki*	Penny and Giles
Datamec / Hewlett Packard	Siemens	Perex (Microvitec)
Digi-Data	*Sycor / Northern Telecom*	Siemens
Digital Equipment	TEAC	**Sony**
Electronic Processors Inc.	*Tektronix*	**Tandberg Data**
Exatron	*Transaction Management*	TEAC
Feedback Data	Wangtek	Wangtek
Genisco Technology		
Irwin Magnetics		

Note: 1983 producers who had exited by 1995 are in italics. 1995 producers who did not make QIC drives in 1983 are in bold.

In the latter years, however, a larger proportion of producers are offering several types of drives. This might be explained by the emergence of new drive types (e.g. DAT and 8 millimeters) in the 1980s and the uncertainty about which one would become dominant. In the face of such uncertainty, it was surely safe to develop a presence in several market segments. Another explanation might lie in the tendency to continue production of decaying drive types to allow clients to read tapes recorded years earlier.

Analyzing vital rates in populations

Population data allow for the study of organizational vital events such as founding and mortality. In analyses of these events, organizational vital rates are typically specified as continuous-time rate or hazard

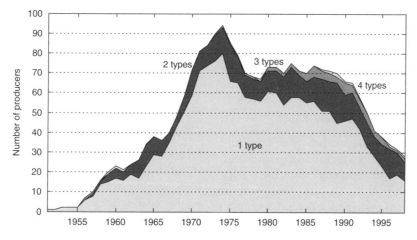

Figure 13.4 Evolution of the distribution of the number of product types offered by producers. Copyright © 2007 by G.R. Carroll and D.G. McKendrick. Used by permission. All rights reserved.

function models. For mortality, the organization is treated as the unit at risk, and the 'dependent variable' is the instantaneous rate of an organization's disappearance from the population, defined as:

$$r(t) = \lim_{\Delta t \to 0} \frac{P[t < T < t + \Delta t | T > t]}{\Delta t},$$

where T is a random variable for the time of the mortality event, t is the tenure of the organization in the population, and $P(.)$ is the conditional probability of the organization's departure from the populations over the interval $[t, t+\Delta t]$ given that the organization was still in the population at time t. Analysts commonly use the continuous-time framework, because they believe it more accurately reflects the actual process (rather than the structure of the data), whereby firms might leave the population at any moment in time. For founding, a similar setup is typically used – except that here the unit at risk is the population itself, conditional on the first founding; the rate is then defined as the rate of founding experienced by the population. If certain assumptions are invoked, rate models can be estimated with a variety of data structures, including event-count and event-history data.

For founding events, data often come aggregated to the year, meaning that observations often contain more than one event. One could, of course, artificially disaggregate the data and estimate the durations between events by say, distributing events equally throughout the year (so if there are two events, the durations would be a half year, three events, a third year, etc.). However, a preferred course of action is to use only the information contained in the data and estimate rate models from the event-count data using appropriate estimators such as Poisson regression and negative binomial regression.

For mortality, the data typically constitute event-history data on individual organizations. Contemporary analysts often use the *piecewise exponential* function to represent variation in the timing of organizational disappearance from the population to allow a flexible specification of dependence on tenure u or time since market entry:

$$r(u) = exp[\overset{q}{\underset{p=0}{\Sigma}} m_p A_p(u)],$$

where $A_p(u) = 1$ when u belongs to interval $(u_p, u_{p+1}]$ and 0 if otherwise. A *piecewise exponential* model represents a widely used strategy that splits the time-axis into time-pieces determined by an analyst (Carroll and

Hannan 2000: 136–8). It specifies the organizational mortality rate $r(u)$ as a function of organizational tenure (u) in the population, and other measured covariates (X). The general class of models we will estimate has the form:

$$\ln r(u) = m_p + \gamma X_{iu},$$

where m_p denotes tenure-specific effects, and X_{it} summarizes time-varying covariates. Parameters are frequently estimated using the method of maximum likelihood as implemented with a user-defined routine in STATA (Sørensen, 1999). To estimate rate models with time-varying covariates, 'split-spell' data are constructed, breaking observed durations in year-long periods with the values of covariates updated every year.

Examining duration dependence in mortality now typically involves an iterative fitting process to find the best piecewise exponential model. The goal of the process is to determine the length of the time-pieces. Table 13.3 illustrates the approach with mortality estimates for the tape drive data. It examines duration dependence in mortality where duration is defined as tenure in the industry. We first cut organization tenure into the smallest possible pieces permitted by the data structure, which here is one year. There is no need to examine the time-pieces for old organizations in as great detail as those for young organizations, because the variation in the constant hazard rate is much smaller in later stages of the lifetime of an organization. (A graph of smoothed cumulative hazard rate verifies this statement.) Therefore, we start with a specification using ten one-year time-pieces for the first ten years of industry tenure, and another piece for tenure greater than ten years. The estimates of this model are shown in Table 13.3 as Step 1. These estimates show

Table 13.3   Iterative fitting of piecewise constant rate exponential models

Step 1		Step 2		Step 3		Step 4		Step 5	
Tenure	m_p	Tenure	m_p	Tenure	m_p	Tenure	m_p	Tenure	m_p
Year 0–1	−1.55* (0.151)	Year 0–1	−1.55* (0.151)	Year 0–1	−1.55* (0.151)	Year 0–1	−1.55* (0.151)	Year 0–1	−1.89* (0.349)
Year 1–2	−2.13* (0.224)	Year 1–3	−2.18* (0.167)	Year 1–3	−2.18* (0.167)	Year 1–3	−2.18* (0.167)	Year 1+	−2.55* (0.360)
Year 2–3	−2.23* (0.250)	Year 3–4	−2.69* (0.333)	Year 3–6	−2.58* (0.189)	Year 3–7	−2.50* (0.160)		
Year 3–4	−2.69* (0.333)	Year 4–6	−2.53* (0.229)	Year 6–7	−2.25* (0.302)	Year 7+	−2.82* (0.122)		
Year 4–5	−2.52* (0.316)	Year 6–7	−2.25* (0.302)	Year 7–9	−2.87* (0.316)				
Year 5–6	−2.54* (0.333)	Year 7–8	−2.91* (0.447)	Year 9–10	−2.98* (0.500)				
Year 6–7	−2.25* (0.302)	Year 8–9	−2.83* (0.447)	Year 10+	−2.80* (0.137)				
Year 7–8	−2.91* (0.447)	Year 9–10	−2.98* (0.500)						
Year 8–9	−2.83* (0.447)	Year 10+	−2.80* (0.137)						
Year 9–10	−2.98* (0.500)								
Year 10+	−2.80* (0.137)								
d.f.	11		9		7		4		2
No. of Obs	2329		2329		2329		2329		2329
Log Likelihood	−346.4		−346.5		−346.6		−347.1		−351.8
Likelihood Ratio			0.086		0.184		1.030		9.426*
p–value			0.958		0.911		0.794		0.009

* p<0.05.

that the mortality rate decreases over industry tenure, all significant at the 0.01 level. It is also shown that the difference in the estimate of hazard rate for tenure 1–2 (−2.13) and 2–3 (−2.23), and tenure 4–5 (−2.52) and 5–6 (−2.54) are very small. So, we likely may collapse these tenure cells without losing any statistical power. Step 2 presents the results after the collapse. The value of the likelihood ratio test statistics of Step 2 against Step 1 is 0.086, with two degrees of freedom. Thus, the null hypothesis that the hazard rate is constant in tenure groups 1–3 and 4–6 respectively cannot be rejected.

The collapsing procedure can be applied repeatedly until any further collapse substantially undermines the overall model fit. The comparison between Step 4 and Step 5 illustrates the stopping point. In Step 4, we break the duration scale in tenure years at 1.0, 3.0, and 7.0, which is not significantly different from a more detailed cut shown in Step 3. In Step 5, however, dividing tenure pieces into the 0–1 and 1 plus groups drops the log likelihood a lot. The likelihood ratio test confirms that Step 5 decreases the model fit significantly as compared to Step 4, which means that we have oversimplified the specifications of tenure dependence.

From the above steps, we conclude that the appropriate breaking points for the worldwide tape drive organizations are 1.0, 3.0, and 7.0. The four tenure pieces thus provide the baseline model for subsequent analyses of this population.

In most studies, organizational analysts also want to know how environmental variation affects the exit rate. The best way to do this is to measure environmental variables directly and estimate their effects as covariates in a rate model. However, an indirect way is to construct periodizations of environmental change, based on historical information. Table 13.4 illustrates this method, using two periodizations of environmental change in tape drives, one developed from studying the technological developments and the other from examining the influence and postures of IBM (especially with respect to governmental antitrust

actions), a phenomenal player in computer and related industries.

The variable labeled Timeline 1 delineates how key technological and market advancements in the history of the tape drive industry affected the life chances of producers. As previously mentioned, the tape drive industry started in 1951 with the shipment by Remington Rand Inc. of the first tape drive to commercial customers, the Uniservo I. Twelve years later, in 1963, Philips launched the first audio cassette, which initiated development activities directed at data storage, although commercially successful devices did not appear for several years. We chose it as the first period cut, because it led to a fundamental segmenting in the market, extending the application of digital tape storage to smaller computer systems and making storage portable. The second cut is 1965, when tape drives began to handle the sort and merge applications that became commonplace in modern computing. Our third cut comes immediately following this technological advancement, in 1966, when Telex jump-started the so-called IBM 'plug-compatible' market. Previously, independent tape drive producers sold their products primarily to mainframe manufacturers rather than directly to end users of computers; use of peripherals from sources other than the mainframe makers normally involved special 'black box' interfaces and costly adaptations of the standard software (Datapro, 1971). Telex was then marketing the standard M4000 digital tape transport, and it decided to modify it so that it could be an IBM-compatible machine. It became the first IBM plug-compatible tape drive (Fisher et al., 1983). While competition raged in the IBM plug-compatible market, a number of competing formats and standards proliferated in other market segments, especially for smaller devices that endeavored to improve upon the Philips-type cassette tape drive. In 1973, 3M introduced a milestone product, the quarter-inch cartridge tape drive, becoming the fourth cut in our timeline. Although cartridge tape drives were in use before the cassette recorder, with several companies making these more sophisticated cartridge systems, none gained the widespread acceptance of 3M's DC-300A Data Cartridge and associated drive. The product conferred on cartridge tapes a legitimacy and standardization they never before had. The final period in our technological timeline started with the introduction of the digital audio tape (DAT) tape drive by Sony and HP and the 8 mm videocassette format by Exabyte, both in 1987. These innovations took tape drive capacity, performance, and reliability to a new frontier.

The variable named Timeline 2 analyzes such a situation with IBM. IBM's actions shaped the competitive environment for all other tape drive producers for almost 30 years. Founded in 1911 with the name of Computing-Tabulating- Recording Company, IBM quickly secured the position as the largest player in electronic computing industry due to its innovation, customer service, and steady product expansion. Beginning in 1964, the great success of IBM in the mainframe computer market (referred to as the System/360 era) stimulated tremendous interest among other firms to design peripheral devices to work with IBM's machines, ushering in the plug-compatible market described in the preceding section. As plug-compatible peripherals manufacturers began to capture market share, IBM reacted with a series of strategic actions that its competitors thought violated antitrust laws, and they filed a number of private antitrust suits against IBM beginning in 1968 (Fisher et al. 1983). For its part, the U.S. Department of Justice filed its own antitrust complaint in 1969, alleging that IBM violated Section 2 of the Sherman Act by attempting to monopolize the general-purpose electronic digital computer system market, specifically computers designed primarily for business. The trial in the government case, US v. IBM, began in 1975. After six years of trial, the case was withdrawn in 1982 by William F. Baxter, assistant attorney general in charge of the Antitrust Division, Department of Justice. So, we decided to use 1969, 1975, and 1982 to divide the industry history into four periods. While we do not know *a priori* how individual tape drive producers

responded to the government's suit against IBM, we expect the scrutiny it brought to IBM to create a somewhat favorable environment for non-IBM producers.

The estimates of the piecewise constant rate are shown in Model 1 in Table 13.4; in Model 2 we add population age as a control. The significant positive coefficient of population age indicates that the tape drive industry becomes increasingly formidable to new entrants as it evolves. Population age significantly improves the model fit on the basis of Model 1, as the likelihood ratio test tells.

Model 3 in Table 13.4 estimates the effect of these key technological advancements in the tape drive industry on the mortality rate of the market players. The comparison between Model 3 and Model 4 tells us that the population age effect disappears after we controlled for the timeline, shown by the likelihood ratio test statistics of 0.384. This result implies that the effect of population age is almost fully captured by the period effects along the technical dimension.

Model 5 in Table 13.4 estimates the effect of the IBM antitrust timeline. There is no clear evidence that the antitrust investigation made it any easier for tape drive manufacturers to survive; indeed, the mortality rate among tape drive firms becomes higher between 1969 and 1975, and after 1982. When we look at the antitrust timeline together with the population age in Model 6, the age effect, though not significant by itself, significantly improves the overall model fit. The comparison between Model 5 and Model 6 informs us that the evolutionary dynamics of the tape industry do not apparently hinge on the legal reaction of government towards IBM. This finding also implies that the technology advancements provide more useful and relevant framework to examine the development of the tape drive industry over time.

CONCLUSION

In this chapter, we have provided a short overview of why and how organizational

Table 13.4 Effects of timelines (periodizations) on exit rates

	Baseline Model			Timeline 1			Timeline 2	
	Model 1	Model 2		Model 3	Model 4		Model 5	Model 6
Year 0–1	−155* (0.151)	−2.30* (0.253)	Year 0–1	−1.89* (0.349)	−2.00* (0.394)	Year 0–1	−2.04* (0.255)	−2.43* (0.362)
Year 1–3	−2.18* (0.167)	−2.97* (0.270)	Year 1–3	−2.55* (0.360)	−2.66* (0.400)	Year 1–3	−2.70* (0.270)	−3.10* (0.373)
Year 3–7	−2.50* (0.160)	−3.35* (0.279)	Year 3–7	−2.89* (0.370)	−3.00* (0.415)	Year 3–7	−3.05* (0.272)	−3.47* (0.381)
Year 7+	−2.82* (0.122)	−3.85* (0.297)	Year 7+	−3.38* (0.370)	−3.51* (0.429)	Year 7+	−3.54* (0.273)	−3.97* (0.390)
Population Age		0.03* (0.008)	Post 1963	−1.32 (1.055)	−1.37 (1.059)	Post 1969	0.47† (0.279)	0.19 (0.329)
			Post 1965	1.57 (1.155)	1.55 (1.156)	Post 1975	0.04 (0.237)	−0.15 (0.266)
			Post 1966	−0.01 (0.604)	−0.07 (0.613)	Post 1982	0.36† (0.199)	−0.01 (0.309)
			Post 1973	0.09 (0.217)	−0.03 (0.294)	Population Age		0.03 (0.021)
			Post 1987	0.55* (0.170)	0.38 (0.317)			
			Population Age		0.01 (0.022)			
d.f.	4	5		9	10		7	8
No. of Obs	2329	2329		2329	2329		2329	2329
Log Likelihood	−347.1	−339.3		−337.0	−336.8		−340.2	−338.9
Likelihood Ratio		15.62*			0.384			2.48
p–value		0.0001			0.535			0.016

* $p < 0.05$.

analysts use longitudinal data on organizational populations to investigate basic theoretical questions. We have addressed philosophical, theoretical, substantive and methodological issues involved in the study of organizational populations over time. Throughout the discussion, we have attempted to illustrate abstract matters with specific illustrations from our ongoing study of tape drive producers. Although the population design is popular and has remarkable power, it also faces a number of challenges in keeping up with contemporary theory, especially those presented by the fuzzy or partial conception to organizational forms and populations.

NOTES

*We appreciate financial support for this project from the Stanford Graduate School of Business and the Durham Business School. We thank Raymond Freeman, Jr. for copies of the Freeman Reports, and Robert Abraham, who continued the business upon Freeman's retirement, for his help in understanding the industry. We also thank the Charles Babbage Institute, especially Carrie Seib, and the Hagley Museum and Library, especially Carol Lockman and Marjorie McNinch, for access to their respective collections.

REFERENCES

Amburgey, T.L., Kelly, D. and Barnett, W.P. (1993) 'Resetting the clock: the dynamics of organizational transformation and failure', *Administrative Science Quarterly*, 38: 51–73.

Bashe, C., Johnson, L., Palmer, J. and Pugh, E. (1986) *IBM's Early Computers*, Cambridge, MA: MIT Press.

Bigelow, L., Carroll, G.R., Tsai, L. and Seidel, M.D. (1997) 'Geography and Organizational Density: Regional Patterns of Foundings of American Automobile Producers, 1885–1981', *Social Science Research*, 26: 377–98.

Carroll, G.R., Bigelow, L.S., Seidel, M-D.L. and Tsai, L.B. (1996) 'The fates of De Novo and De Alio producers in the American automobile industry, 1885–1981', *Strategic Management Journal*, 17: 117–37.

Carroll, G.R. and Delacroix, J. (1982) 'Organizational mortality in the newspaper industries of Argentina and Ireland: an ecological approach', *Administrative Science Quarterly*, 27(1982): 169–98.

Carroll, G.R. and Hannan, M.T. (2000) *The Demography of Corporations and Industries*, Princeton: Princeton University Press.

Carroll, G.R. and Wade, J.B. (1991) 'Density dependence in the organizational evolution of the American brewing industry across different levels of analysis', *Social Science Research*, 20: 271–302.

Daniels, E., Mee, C.D. and Clark, M.H. (eds) (1999) *Magnetic Recording: The First 100 Years*, New York: IEEE Press.

Datapro (Datapro Research Corporation) (1971) *All About Independent Tape and Disk Drives*, datapro70, March.

Denrell, J. and Kovacs, B. (2008) 'Selective sampling of empirical settings in organizational studies', *Administrative Science Quarterly*, 53: 109–44.

Dobrev, S.D. (2001) 'Revisiting organizational legitimation: cognitive diffusion and sociopolitical factors in the evolution of Bulgarian newspaper enterprises, 1846–1992', *Organization Studies*, 22: 419–44.

Epstein, R.C. (1927) 'The rise and fall of firms in the automobile industry', *Harvard Business Review*, 2: 157–174.

Fisher, F.M., McKie, J.W. and Mancke, R.B. (1983) *IBM and the U.S. Data Processing Industry*, NY: Praeger.

Flamm, K. (1987) *Targeting the Computer: Government Support and International Competition*, Washington, DC: The Brookings Institution.

Forman, R.L. (1980) *Tales in Peripheral Enterprise: The Rise of Dataproducts Corporation in the Computer Industry 1962–1972*, M.A. Thesis, UC Santa Barbara.

Freeman Reports (1983–1999) *Tape Drive Directories*.

Freeman, J. and Hannan, M.T. (1983) 'Niche width and the dynamics of organizational populations', *American Journal of Sociology*, 88: 1116–45.

Hannan, M. T. and Freeman, J. (1977) 'The population ecology of organizations', *American Journal of Sociology*, 82: 929–64.

Hannan, M.T., and Freeman, J. (1984) 'Structural inertia and organizational change', *American Sociological Review*, 49: 149–64.

Hannan, M.T. and Freeman, J. (1987) 'The ecology of organizational mortality: American labor unions', *American Journal of Sociology*, 92: 910–43.

Hannan, M.T., Pólos, L. and Carroll, G.R. (2007) *The Logics of Organizational Theory: Audiences, Codes and Ecologies*, Princeton: Princeton University Press.

Haveman, H. (1993) 'Organizational size and change: diversification in the savings and loan industry after deregulation', *Administrative Science Quarterly*, 38: 20–50.

Hendry, J. (1989) *Innovating for Failure*, Cambridge, MA: MIT Press.

Klepper, S. (2002) 'The capabilities of new firms and the evolution of the US automobile industry', *Industrial and Corporate Change*, 11: 645–66.

Lundstrom, D.E. (1987) *A Few Good Men From Univac*, Cambridge, MA: The MIT Press.

McKendrick, D.G., Jaffee, J., Carroll, G.R. and Khessina, O.M. (2003) 'In the bud? analysis of disk array producers as a (possibly) emergent organizational form', *Administrative Science Quarterly*, 48: 60–93.

Mitchell, W. (1989) 'Whether and when: probability and timing of incumbents' entry into emerging industrial subfields', *Administrative Science Quarterly* 34: 208–30.

Mitchell, W. (1994) 'The dynamics of evolving markets: the effects of business sales and age on dissolutions and divestitures', *Administrative Science Quarterly*, 39: 575–602.

Modern Data (1975) 'Cassette drives and systems', October: 58–63.

New York Times (1950) 'Computer unit sold to Remington Rand', March 2: 46.

Petersen, T. (1991) 'Time-aggregation bias in continuous-time hazard-rate models', in Masden, P. (ed.), *Sociological Methodology*, 21: 263–90. Oxford: Basil Blackwell.

Phister, M. Jr. (1979) *Data Processing Technology and Economics* (Second edn.), Santa Monica Publishing Company and Digital Press.

Pugh, E., Johnson, L. and Palmer, J. (1991) *IBM's 360 and Early 370 Systems*, Cambridge, MA: MIT Press.

Rao, H., Monin, P. and Durand, R. (2003) 'Institutional change in Toque Ville: nouvelle cuisine as an identity movement in French gastronomy', *American Journal of Sociology*, 108: 795–843.

Rosen, S. (1969) 'Electronic computers: a historical survey', *Computing Surveys*, 1(1): 7–36.

Ruef, M., (2000) 'The emergence of organizational forms: a community ecology approach', *American Journal of Sociology*, 106: 658–714.

Sørensen, J. (1999) 'Stpiece: a program for the estimation of piecewise-constant rate hazard models in STATA 6.0', Unpublished ado-file. University of Chicago: Graduate School of Business.

Sorenson, O. and Audia, P. (2000) 'The social structure of entrepreneurial activity: geographic concentration of footwear production in the United States, 1940–1989', *American Journal of Sociology*, 106: 424–62.

Tripsas, M. (1997) 'Unraveling the process of creative destruction: complementary assets and incumbents survival in the typesetter industry', *Strategic Management Journal*, 18: S119–42.

Zuckerman, E. (1999) 'The categorical imperative: securities analysts and the illegitimacy discount', *American Journal of Sociology*, 104: 1398–438.

14

'Do You Do Beautiful Things?': Aesthetics and Art in Qualitative Methods of Organization Studies

Antonio Strati

INTRODUCTION

Studies and research on the aesthetic dimension of organizational life first appeared with the 'cultural turn' in organizational studies that occurred during the 1980s. These analyses concern themselves with a range of subjects, from the internal and external architectures of organizations to the discipline imposed on the bodies of the people working in them or on their behalf. They exhibit a distinctive feature: whilst they study the aesthetic dimension of the organization concerned, they develop aesthetic awareness of organizational phenomena. Put otherwise, research on organizational aesthetics is grounded at the same time on an 'aesthetic style' in the research methods used to study organizations. This chapter describes the aesthetic quality of such study in terms of a new methodological awareness comprised in the critical analysis of work and management practices in organizations. Such analysis is conducted using four approaches – archaeological, empathic-logical, aesthetic, and artistic – and it is traversed by two main themes: that of aesthetics (understood as sensible knowledge and aesthetic judgment) and organizational life; and that of art and management.

Aesthetic understanding as new methodological awareness in the study of organizational life

Awareness has only recently come about that use can be made of aesthetic as well as cognitive understanding in the empirical analysis and theoretical study of organizations. This concerns the methodologies of organizational analysis; and therefore also, in many respects, both their privileged object of study, and the research epistemology and theoretical paradigms in which this new methodological awareness finds the taste for study mixed variously with base assumptions and value premises.

A recent Europe-centred methodological awareness

For around ten years – the most recent in the century-long history of organizational theories and management studies – field studies and theoretical reflections on the aesthetic dimension of organizations, the methods used to study it, and the 'aesthetic' nature of approaches to organizational study, have been discussed at international conventions and seminars, and they appear with increasing frequency in prestigious international journals and publications. This has been observed by several scholars (Minahan and Cox, 2007) and, amongst them, by Pasquale Gagliardi in his chapter on organization aesthetics in the *Handbook of Organization Studies*, revised for its second edition. During the ten years since that handbook's first edition, studies on the topic had proliferated, and organizational aesthetics were no longer a neglected area of organization studies. There is, on the contrary:

> a growing body of literature on aesthetic themes, one in which systematic reflection is conducted on the relationships between these and organization (Dean et al.,1997; Strati,1999) and between art and management (Guillet de Monthoux, 2004); there are research anthologies as well as special journal issues (*Organization* 3/2, 1996; Linstead and Höpfl, 2000; *Human Relations* 55/7, 2002), which have resulted from seminars and conferences expressly devoted to analysis of the methodological implications of taking an aesthetic approach to the study of organizations. The aesthetics of organization is therefore taking shape as a distinct field of inquiry within organizational studies [...]. (2006: 702)

I consider organizational aesthetics research to be not merely a series of theories and methodological treatments, but rather a postsocial collective phenomenon in which organizational scholars investigate the capacities for action of people and artefacts in organization at the level of the *pathos*

of sensible knowledge and aesthetic judgement. It is a strand of organizational analysis with its 'barycentre' in Europe – as Ramirez (2005: 31) notes – because the 'main writings on this matter have been done by European scholars; in particular from Italy, Scandinavia, and France'. Thus, the main characteristics of this 'new methodological awareness', may be summarized as follows:

- It has not been subject to the strong influence of North American organizational scholars on organization theory and management studies.
- It is critical of the normative and prescriptivist stance apparent in organizational theories and management studies, and thus reprises the methodologies of organizational analysis that arose with the 'cultural turn' of the 1980s (Gherardi and Turner, 1987).
- It wages a polemic against the positivist and neopositivist methodologies of organization analysis and disputes the sharp separation among science, art and mythical thinking, thus displaying continuity with symbolist studies of organizations, as well as its own theoretical-methodological specificity.
- It also strongly controverts the interpretationist methodologies that privilege causal explanations of organizational life – such as the causal cognitive maps used by the cognitivist approach to the study of organizations (Strati, 1998) – although it shares their underlying interpretative paradigm.
- It endeavours to bring out the new humanism in organizations that opposes alienating and manipulative processes.

Methodological choices and paradigmatic controversy

If proper account is to be given of aesthetic methodological awareness in organizational theories and management studies, one must relate methodological choices – from empirical research methods to theory-building, to communication of research results – to epistemological issues and paradigmatic controversies. Striking in this regard is what I have called elsewhere (Strati, 2007) 'the maturity of the beginnings' of the aesthetic discourse on organizations: namely the collective phenomenon which, at the end of the 1980s:

- Laid the bases for definition of what is meant by 'organizational study'. Art and aesthetics, and the notions of beauty and *pathos*, gave theoretical value and scientific meaning to the evocative knowledge-creation process – obscured by the dominance of the logical-analytical process – and art acquired theoretical-methodological legitimacy, rather than circumscribing one type of social world.
- Redefined the organization by emphasising 'materiality' as its distinctive feature. The corporeality of people at work, the physicality and/or aesthetic impalpability of organizational artefacts, feelings, and emotions give materiality to organizations.
- Raised the methodological issue of how empirical research can grasp the aesthetic dimension of an organization as a whole, as well as the aesthetics of the work and organizational practices performed within it.
- Brought to light the aesthetic phenomenon constituted by organizational management, given that the members of organizations are people, not concepts or instruments, and consequently know and act through their senses, formulating aesthetic judgments.
- Stressed personal knowledge and differences among organizational actors in opposition to the organizational manipulation intended to standardize them aesthetically by means of art and taste.
- Highlighted the collective dynamics of aggregation with others and/or distinction from others via the aesthetics of both the content and form of work.
- Recast the status of objects, showing their capacity for subtle and intense action in socializing people into work cultures and organizational cultures, and also in regard to the sensible, aesthetic, and emotional control exercised by dominant organizational cultures. In those same years, at the end of the 1980s, but in very different theoretical frameworks, this capacity for action was attributed to objects by other studies which re-examined the status itself of the organizational actor, notably Workplace Studies (Hindmarsh and Heath, 2007; Nicolini et al., 2003) and those inspired by Actor Network Theory (Latour, 2005).

However, this is not to imply that the new methodological awareness is grounded on a univocal definition of aesthetics, that is, a 'single lens' through which organizations can be examined. Although the concept of aesthetics dates back only to the mid-1700s – when the term was first used to denote a relatively unitary discipline comprising the aesthetics of the sensible, the aesthetics of the sentiment of the beautiful, and the space of the apparition of art works of and reflection on art (Escoubas, 2004: 5–6) – poetry and art, the beautiful and the sublime, have been debated for millennia, and in diverse cultures and civilizations. But even if one goes no further back than the aesthetic philosophy developed approximately three centuries ago, one already finds debates and controversies on what constitutes aesthetics. What, therefore, is the aesthetic philosophy that underpins aesthetic studies on organizational life? It is the body of thought produced from Aristotle to Immanuel Kant, from Plotinus to Susanne Langer, or from Dewey to Luigi Pareyson. It is, therefore, a doctrine to which numerous philosophers have contributed; but pre-eminent among them are Giambattista Vico (1725) and Alexander Gottlieb Baumgarten (1750–8):

- The former because of his antagonism against the Cartesian rationalist tradition, and his proposal of 'a new science' founded on a 'poetic logic', where reasoning by metaphors, the imagination, evocative knowledge, and mythical thinking are legitimate ways to understand the world and social life,
- The latter because of his emphasis on sensible knowledge and the sensible-aesthetic judgement yielded by the perceptive faculties of sight, hearing, smell, taste, and touch which produce an art of the analogy of reason (*ars analogi rationis*) ancillary to the latter but independent from it.

These two aesthetic philosophies focus on forms of knowing and acting which are not rooted in methods of analysis embedded in cognition or analytic rationality, although they are always in dialogue – and often in dispute – with them.

Methodological awareness in the plural

The aesthetic philosophies of Vico and Baumgarten stress that aesthetics has not been confused with art in the debate on the theoretical and epistemological foundations of organizational aesthetics research in any of the methodological frameworks developed. These exhibit a variety of methodological and substantive nuances and details, which give sense to the aesthetic understanding of organizations as qualitative inquiry. They are now briefly described – and shaped – in terms of the four main aesthetic approaches to study of organizational life: archaeological, empathic-logical, aesthetic, and artistic.

The archaeological approach

The *archaeological approach* (Berg, 1987) is the first of them, both in time and in its capacity for action and persuasion. The reference to archaeology denotes the metaphorical operation by which, on adopting this approach, the scholar assumes the guise of an archaeologist and/or historian of art and observes organizational aesthetics in regard to the organizational cultures and symbologies that they bring to light.

For example, the aesthetics of the architectures of organizational buildings – argue Per Olof Berg and Kristian Kreiner (1990) – constitute the 'traces' used by researchers to show the predominant values of the managerial philosophy, owing to their ability to evoke individual and collective memories. By observing the aesthetics of the buildings and constructions that house organizations, as well as their internal architectures, researchers are able to demonstrate the symbolic conditioning exerted by those aesthetics on organizational action, insofar as they set value on creativeness, transparency, connectedness and openness, or conversely, on standardization, hierarchy, formal power, and prestige due to status. Moreover, the aesthetics of architectural features are able to signal, via the building, its facade, a meeting room or a workplace, the organization's institutional value as a 'totem'; that is, as a unifying symbol which stands as a central organizational referent for organizational symbols and cultures.

The approach has developed within the mainstream of symbolist studies on organizational cultures (Turner, 1990) and still

forms a bridge between aesthetic study and organizational symbolism. It has been widely adopted and adapted to the requirements of field research, in many cases implicitly rather than explicitly. It does not address the issue of methodology except in the conventional terms of research design (Bryman, 1989: 28–30) in qualitative research.

The empathic-logical approach

The *empathic-logical* approach (Gagliardi, 1990; 2006) has had wide impact, because it highlights the organizational control exercised at the level of aesthetics, beginning with the *pathos* of the organizational artefacts constituting the symbolic landscape of the tangible organization. This approach has studied 'the objects that are used in managing – premises […], their furnishing […], office equipment […], public relations materials […], and products of all type' – writes Ramirez (2005: 31) – observing 'that considerable effort was spent on rendering them attractive […] that the physical manifestations work were systematically utilized as means to render the aesthetic appeal of cooperation'.

The attention paid by the researcher to the aesthetics of organizational architectures, however, does not focus directly and almost exclusively on organizational symbols, and in this it differs from the archaeological approach. Witkin's (1990) study of the aesthetics of a large multinational's conference rooms illustrates how the physical arrangement induced a two-dimensional understanding of reality and instead blunted the three-dimensional understanding of it. Put otherwise, the *pathos* of that organizational artifact exerted an influence at the level of the aesthetic understanding of the organization's members: on the level, that is, of what is sensorially perceivable before symbolic-valorial systems. By their nature – writes Gagliardi (2006: 714) – perceptive premises evade control by the mind, while at the same time they constitute a further level of organizational control which adds to and combines with those of (i) the directly imparted order, (ii) programmes and procedures and

(iii) the ideological premises of organizational action identified by Charles Perrow (1972).

Unlike the archaeological approach, this one divides the research into three main phases:

(a) In the first, the researcher immerses him/herself empathetically in organizational life and inter-rogates the feelings aroused in him or her by organizational artefacts and gives them names. Thus, immersion in organizational interaction and examination of the aesthetic sense of the experience concludes this research phase of observing organizational phenomena.

(b) The second phase involves interpretation of what has been observed, giving names to the experiences acquired, and balancing the passive 'intuition' deriving from immersion in the texture of organizational interactions with the 'active' analysis prompted by detachment from them. However, this phase should not be seen as clearly distinct from the other two, given the qualitative nature of this approach that – contrary to what happens in quantitative study – does not separate one phase from the others, but rather is in search of continuous dialogues between them.

(c) In the third phase, empathy gives way to the logical-analytical rigour with which the research is 'eloquently' reported, writes Gagliardi (2006: 720), 'without any pretence to the production of literary artifacts aimed at communicating only or mainly on the aesthetic plane'.

The aesthetic approach

Also the *aesthetic approach* (Strati, 1992, 1999) has been influential in shaping the aesthetic discourse on organizations. The aesthetic approach shows how the aesthetics from which the organization acquires its form are negotiated. It emphasizes the quotidian construction, reconstruction and destruction of the aesthetics specific to the organizational context studied. It focuses on the organizing of aesthetics, and it studies how the aesthetic categories – from the ugly to the sublime, from the comic to the sacred, from the picturesque to the *prestissimo* or *adagio* of the agogic categories – mark out the organizational specificities of the social practices examined.

For example, the aesthetic judgements on beauty expressed by the employees and collaborators of a prestigious Italian photography firm (Strati, 1999) brought into focus numerous aspects and organizational dimensions through which the beauty of their organization acquired its form: (i) the firm's nature as a flowing and interweaving microcosm of beautiful relations in every-day work, (ii) its 'opening of doors' to external interlocutors and other organizations, making the people with which it interacted 'smile', (iii) improving, with its production and promotion of a photographic style, the life-quality of people in external society, (iv) being one of the beautiful Italian things, (v) showing a renewed vitality in comparison to the past, (vi) becoming a myth if it closed. Here it was the category of beautiful that gave this specific form to the organization. Nevertheless, it is not always thus. Indeed, the aesthetic category of ugly, grotesque, or disgusting often emerges from empirical research. Its organizational meaning has been shown, for instance, by Patricia Martin (2002), who illustrates how aesthetic feelings, even those aroused by the unpleasant odours of persons and rooms in residential homes for the elderly, organized – though not unequivocally – organizational life, and that this depended on the style of organizing aesthetics in use in the old people's home.

Unlike the archaeological approach, the aesthetic approach does not consider aesthet-ics as ancillary to the symbolic understanding of organizational cultures, but rather as a distinctive characteristic of a specific and free-standing form of organizational under-standing. And unlike the empathic-logical approach, it does not proceed through three main phases – observation/immersion, inter-pretation, and the 'eloquent' report – nor does it shift from empathic understanding of the observation to the analytical understanding that arises from interpretation and then charac-terizes the description of results. It grasps the dynamics of organizational power in the nego-tiation of organizational aesthetics and high-lights how the researcher 'does' aesthetics.

The research process critically directs the attention of organization scholars to the fact that often, though not always, the researcher:

(a) Chooses a topic, style, and subject of analysis according to his/her taste and personal preferences for method and theory.

(b) Activates his/her sensory faculties and aesthetic judgment upon immersing him/herself in the texture of organizational interactions and empathizing with the organizational actors as they act and interact.

(c) Observes the interactions among the organizational actors and, when appropriate, also assumes the role of an imaginary participant observer, that is, using the empathic knowledge-creation process (Weber, 1922) which involves 'putting oneself in the place of' and experiencing sensorially, but always imaginarily, fragments of the organizational life under consideration.

(d) Listens for emphases and overtones in the sense constructions of the organizational actors and critically reflects on the power which accompanies their attractiveness.

(e) When the materials collected and processed – which is not a specific and freestanding phase of research but is instead confused with other aspects of the aesthetic study – lets the experiences gathered in the course of the research re-emerge so that they can be relived sensorially and rejudged aesthetically.

(f) When communicating the research results uses the evocative knowledge process, drawing on art and aesthetic philosophy, employing metaphors, leaving contradictions and ambiguities unresolved, resorting to vivid accounts of the organizational dynamics, and processes studied. So that those who read and/or listen to the results must activate their own perceptive-sensory faculties and sensible-aesthetic judgement in order to interpret and make sense of those results.

The artistic approach

The *artistic approach* (Guillet de Monthoux, 2004) has been influential in proposing views of the organization through the eyes – disenchanted – of the artist and/or the art promoter, gallery owner, museum director, or orchestra conductor. More than the other three, this approach critically focuses on the experience of art in organizing. It comprises the sensible-aesthetic experience of the empathic-logical and aesthetic approaches, and the symbolic-cultural experience that characterizes all the three other approaches – the archaeological one especially. Artistic performance is its central concern, as highlighted by its close attention to styles of leadership in organizations, their merging beyond the dualisms that separate art and science, their transmuting into styles of 'liedership' – from lieder in classical music – evocative of the crucial importance of having 'voice' in organizational communication (Putnam et al., 1996). It is, however, an approach critical of the 'popular American notion of "the experience economy" (Pine and Gilmore, 1999) (where companies attempt to produce emotionally intensive offerings to increase profits), arguing that all too often this notion ignores, and even denies, the deeper creative potential which the tension between the rational and the artistic offers' (Ramirez, 2005: 32).

If the aesthetic approach asks the interviewee 'Do you do beautiful things?', or 'What is beautiful in your organization?' – and therefore investigates how social practices within the organization and the organization itself are interpreted and enacted on the basis of the aesthetic judgment – the artistic approach instead asks: 'What is art to you?', 'Who is the artist, then?', 'How did you conceive the "art firm" you founded?' Pierre Guillet de Monthoux (2004: 352–3) asks these questions in awareness of their exploratory-colloquial character in his section on the 'Cittadellarte' (Artcity), an art foundation created by Michelangelo Pistoletto – an artist of international renown and proponent of *Arte Povera* – and his partner Maria Pioppi. ' "But what is art to you, Michelangelo?" I asked stupidly, and I heard John Dewey laugh at me in the back of my head', writes Guillet de Monthoux (p. 352), and by means of these questions gathered information on the entrepreneurial style of Cittadellarte; a style that constitutes this art firm as 'concrete action for a new kind of socially responsive-responsible art' and sees it as 'a modern version of the studios of Renaissance artists where science, production and economy were inextricably bound up with imagination, philosophy, and spirituality' (Guillet de Monthoux, p. 353). On the other hand, a study may examine research on the role of the straight line in perspectival art to deduce its influence on early writings in the theory of organization and management. 'It may seem unusual to some to discuss paintings as a means of understanding studies of management and organizations but frequently they offer us a view that is somehow more vivid', Ian King maintains (2007: 226). It is the exploration of new forms of scholarly inquiry and framing able to configure themselves by drawing upon – Daved Barry argues (2008, p. 40) – both the underlying assumptions and the 'lively qualities' of contemporary art, so as to make the working and organizational practice of research 'work done in delightful, imaginative ways'. When aesthetic issues are examined, the aesthetic form is a means both to use 'artistic methods to explore sensory experiences' – write Steven Taylor and Hans Hansen (2005: 1223–4) – and to communicate the research results by representing them in forms which draw on the wide range of genres and styles of artistic expression, i.e. the artistic performance (Scalfi, 2007; Steyaert and Hjorth, 2002). The aesthetic object of study for artistic methods consists in the artistic forms 'used to present the direct sensory day-to-day experience in organizations', continue Taylor and Hansen. These are highly promising in that they capture the feeling of the event or the organizational process being examined and, at the same time, 'work with traditional intellectual analysis to give to richer, fuller, more-embodied understanding', specify Taylor and Hansen (2005: 1224), as in the case of Laura Brearley's work (2001) 'on the experience of transition in organizational life. She tracked the experiences of managers as they went through a difficult merger. Part of her research process is creating poems, songs, and multimedia tracks from interview data and images that the managers created'.

This approach, like the archaeological approach and unlike the empathic-logical one, does not proceed through research phases; nor does it articulate the research process into several interweaving activities, as does the aesthetic approach. On the contrary, this approach envisages the hybridization of artistic creative energy and ratiocinative capacity in the performative conduct of both research and organization. It draws indiscriminately on methods of artistic understanding and those used by the social sciences. It is not, in fact, particularly concerned with the issue of the qualitative methodology of organizational analysis, unlike the empathic-logical and aesthetic approaches. Instead, it 'pragmatically overcomes' the issue of the methodology most appropriate to the aesthetic study of organizations by mixing artistic sensibility and cognitive rationality. It projects the scholar into the playfulness, improvisation, and sensuality of the research experience, and the performance distinctive of the research process until dissemination of the results.

Issues of method traversing organizational aesthetics research

All four approaches take a critical stance towards the traditional distinction between the usefulness of research and the pleasure of doing it, as well as the taste for transgressing the traditions of study accredited in organizational theories and management studies. Also shared by all four approaches is criticism of assuming a managerial standpoint. Rejection of the corporate standpoint, indeed, constitutes the specificity of European research on the aesthetic dimension of organizational life. This concern with emancipation is particularly marked in the European debate because of the aestheticizing effects (Hancock and Tyler, 2000; Pelzer, 2002; Marquard, 1989) that art and aesthetics exert on the sensibility, and on the ability to activate the perceptive-sensory faculties and aesthetic judgment that distinguish the personal knowledge of organizational actors. Moreover, all four approaches conduct an epistemological polemic against absolute belief in rationality and against the predominance of cognitivism and positivism in organizational theories and management studies. 'Much of the early work in organizational aesthetics' – write Steven Taylor and Hans Hansen (2005: 1219) – 'primarily draws on the epistemological conceptualization of aesthetics to make an argument for the importance and reasonableness of an aesthetic approach to organizations'. The methodological question is internal to the epistemological one, and it has been expressly addressed in various works. But it has been treated in diverse ways, so that studies which reflect on the qualitative methods employed – notes Samantha Warren (2008: 564) – alternate with others which 'remain strangely silent on the complexities of the methodologies employed to do this – subsuming them under the banner of "case study" or "ethnography"'.

Table 14.1 shows the distinctive features of each approach, its differences in research style, and what constitutes its emphasis, strengths, and limitations. Brief discussion is required of these latter, whilst the other points have already been treated. Each of the four approaches has limitations, which concern different areas of the methodological discourse.

The limitation of the archaeological approach resides in the symbolic and culturalist studies of organizations (Turner, 1990). Within this theoretical and methodological domain that constituted its original humus, it continues to produce studies and research. The archaeological approach is not the only one to extend its roots into the organizational symbolism approach to the study of organizations. So too do both the empathiclogical and aesthetic approaches – but less so to the artistic one, because, unlike the other three approaches, it gives equal importance to debates on how to do, promote, manage, and teach art. However, both these two approaches envisage aesthetic understanding as an autonomous branch of the qualitative study of organizational life. The methodological choice of pursuing logical-analytical rigour already in the second phase of analysis, and then especially in the third, is the limitation set on the empathic-logical approach. In this way, the aesthetic understanding of organizational life is not freed from the supremacy of the rational reasoning, but is instead constrained

Table 14.1 The four approaches of aesthetic organizational research

Research approach	Researcher's style	Emphasis on	Strengths	Limitations
Archaeological	Guise of an archaeologist and/or an historian of art using qualitative research design and methods	The symbolism of art and aesthetics in organizational life	The aesthetic side of organizational cultures and of the symbolic management of organizations	Aesthetics are ancillary to symbolism
Empathic-logical	Empathic immersion followed by emphatic and logical interpretation, and by a logical-analytical illustration of the outcomes	The *pathos* of organizational artefacts	Precognitive knowledge of organizations and the organizational control based on the *pathos* of artefacts	Aesthetics are translated into logical-analytical descriptions
Aesthetic	Empathic understanding, imaginary participant observation, aesthetic judgement, evocative process of knowing, 'open text' for communicating the outcomes	The collective everyday negotiation of organizational aesthetics	The materiality of quotidian organizational life and also of the researcher's interactions with both organizational actors and organizational scholars	Aesthetics are grounded on connoisseurship
Artistic	Hybridization of artistic creative energy and ratiocinative capacity	The creativity and playfulness of organizational interactions	The artistic performance in managing organization processes	Aesthetics are 'art-bounded'

by the latter. Connoisseurship is the limitation of the aesthetic approach, because aesthetic expertise is its object of study and so too, at the same time, are the skills required to study it. This gives elusiveness both to aesthetic experience in organizations and to research practices in use. Finally, the shortcoming of the artistic approach is its use of art as a stimulus and inspiration for the understanding of organizational life and for communicating such understanding.

These four approaches raise issues of method which to some extent traverse organizational aesthetics research in its entirety:

- The issue of method has 'a modernist musty taste' more in the artistic approach to organizations than in the others. This issue is discussed with transgressive intent and theoretical provocation in the aesthetic approach; with exploratory intent and to understand organizational life in the empathic-logical one; and taking the form of a question that traverses the entire body of analysis of organizations as cultures and symbolic constructs in the archaeological approach.
- The distinction between the construction of aesthetic knowledge about organizations and the study of organizational aesthetics with a view to intervening in organizational contexts and in organizational management is simply a 'nonsense' in the artistic approach, while it gives pre-eminence to understanding in the aesthetic approach, and has the sense of 'intervene only if it has been understood' in the empathic-logical one, and of 'symbolic management' in the archaeological one.

These are the main features of organizational aesthetics research. There now follows more detailed discussion of certain of its aspects, beginning with one shared by all four approaches to the aesthetic study of organizations: the epistemological controversy centred on the object that these approaches study.

Object of study, point of view, and sensible-aesthetic judgement

This part of the chapter illustrates and discusses the relations that connect the 'aesthetic' connotation of the four approaches outlined above with the object of study privileged by empirical and theoretical research, and with the researcher's point of view in the aesthetic study of organizations.

The polemic inherent in the object of study of aesthetic approaches

Enquiring as to what constitutes the object studied by a theoretical-methodological system is almost routine practice in the social sciences and organization theory. However, it has the merit of highlighting the specific characteristics of the theorizations generated by study of that object. Of course, this does not mean that the study object 'determines' both the research methodology and the organizational theory. It only implies that, by reflecting on the object of study, it is possible to characterize and, in part, describe important aspects of the methodological contribution made by aesthetic approaches to organizational analysis.

The object studied by organizational aesthetics research is the aesthetic dimension of organizational life. Nevertheless, what is this 'aesthetic dimension' exactly? Moreover, why does it provoke epistemological controversy among organization scholars?

If we address these two questions together, we are forced *to exclude* that 'aesthetic dimension' means *solely* what is beautiful in an organization. Beauty is certainly essential to the aesthetic dimension; but why should it give rise to epistemological controversy? Studying the beauty of the design of an organization's product – for example, the design for an Alfa Romeo automobile produced by the Pininfarina agency, or the architecture of the building at Cleveland University designed by Frank Gehry – does not in itself involve epistemological controversy, but instead a choice between competing methodologies.

But, if beauty is linked to aesthetics, and if one grasps its reflections in philosophy, art history, and semiotics, as well as in sociology, anthropology, psychology, and economics, then the epistemological controversy does emerge. This is evidenced by the etymology of the word 'aesthetic', which stems from the Ancient Greek root *aisth* and the verb *aisthánomai*. Thus emphasized is sensible knowledge as 'action' performed through the senses of sight, hearing, smell, taste, and touch, and which – stresses Baldine Saint Girons (2008: 22) – is synonymous with neither 'artistic' nor beautiful. These are perceptive-sensory faculties, not the mere terminal sensors of some sovereign conscience; they are 'places of the flesh where the flesh of the world becomes visible', writes Rosella Prezzo (2004: 8), when commenting on the work of the French phenomenologist philosopher Maurice Merleau-Ponty. That is to say, they are ways for individuals to be sensitive to the world amid their social and postsocial interactions in organizational settings. Knowing is thus sensible action, as argued – from the point of view of Deweyan pragmatic philosophy by Shusterman (2008) with his proposal of a philosophy of somaesthetics. Note, though, that it too is subject to the evocative knowledge-creation process activated by the imagination. Conceptual art forcefully reminds us of this, both with its artistic production, and with its theoretical contention that if it is legitimate to display an ordinary object – one thinks of Duchamp's ready-mades – as a work of art, it is equally legitimate to present an abstract idea, preferably drawn from daily life, as the source and content of an artistic experience (Lenain, 2006–7). This is what makes us feel an emotion, or presense it, as when we imagine the scrape of chalk on a blackboard. It immerses us, through the imagination, in the already-felt experience, not merely on the cognitive level but also on the experiential one, so that we rehear the screech of the chalk on the blackboard and our body sensorially relives the jarring sensation. It is the way in which – as Rancière (2003) puts it – certain configurations of the perceivable and the imaginable, or particular forms of experiencing and inhabiting the sensible world, come to define themselves. To conclude, the object of study constituted by the corporeality of feeling through the senses,

and by the ensuing judgement, calls into question, on the one hand, the predominance of mental processes, rational-legal norms and analytic logic, and on the other, the instrumental view of corporeality whereby people and artefacts are means to attain organizational ends.

Impalpable corporeality of aesthetics

Now examined will be the salient characteristics of the object of study in organizational aesthetics research, while bearing in mind the epistemological controversy that it provokes. Organizations have their own specific materiality made of the corporeality of persons and artefacts, but which also comprises something impalpable and invisible that can be emblematically denoted here as 'the atmosphere of the organization' – as suggested by such commonplace expressions in organizations as 'there's something in the air', 'a heavy atmosphere', 'there's an ill wind blowing', 'see which way the wind blows' or 'let in some fresh air'. The atmosphere of an organization is a study object, which:

- Is mundane, is 'everyone's' – except in person-less organizations – and pervades organizational life. It constitutes the latter and belongs, in principle, to those who participate in organizational life. It does not characterize particular organizational processes, tasks, levels, or roles, but is distinctive of everyday work and organizational practices in organizations.
- Is felt and judged by being experienced. Not, that is, through the cognitive or rational knowledge process, but through the feeling of being immersed in the air being breathed, with all the senses and the capacity for sensible-aesthetic judgment that enable identification of beauty, ugliness, and grotesqueness through the aesthetic categories of the language in-use in the organization.
- Has corporeality, even when it is evoked by the organization's language with images, metaphors, or judgements like 'there was a heavy atmosphere at the meeting'.
- Is never identical, because the air breathed in organizations is never the same, not even when it is 'stale'. It is constantly changed by being breathed, or when a window is opened, a computer is switched on, or a machine or a car is started up. In fact, if we consider the moment

when the two corporealities – that of a person's sensory abilities and that of the air – meet, there emerges a connection-in-action between them that takes the form of an interactive change process. For, as we change the air by breathing and rebreathing it, we are changed by what the air brings with it: pleasure at its freshness, distaste at its smells, and the bad humours of its tension.

- Is a hybrid object of study, rather than a pure one. We emit organizational artifacts into the organizational air that we breathe. Our breath mixes our scents, the odours of the fabrics that we are wearing, the leather of our shoes and handbags, the paint on the walls, the materials and the work instruments we are using – in a meeting room, for instance, the wood of the tables, the metal of the chairs, warm OHP projectors, the ink of board markers, printed paper, and photocopies.

The air breathed in organizations is an object of study that acquires and changes sense, meaning and value in the course of organizational interaction: it is not objectively beautiful or ugly, and it is not always subjectively so for those who breathe it. Nor is there a mechanical, deterministic unidirectional relation whereby the beauty or ugliness of the air breathed in organizations affects all their members in the same way and in the same terms. It all depends on the sensibility – and therefore again on the corporeality of the sensory faculties – of those who breathe the air, who may feel its aesthetic qualities more or less intensely. The corporeality of personal knowledge also gives rise to the paradoxical situation where the freshness of springtime air gives hay fever sufferers the sensation of suffocating rather than breathing: they open a window, take a lungful of air, and begin to weep and cough. An attractive organizational setting may be equally suffocating for those who are particularly sensitive: it bores them to death with its tedium; it is so beautiful that 'it takes your breath away'. Just as 'we can't catch our breath' when we are overwhelmed with work and cannot 'take a breather'.

Hence, if the object studied by organizational aesthetics research is the atmosphere of organizations, it is a 'common' object of study that highlights the subjective conditions of the organizational knowledge process. The air breathed in organizations is judged sensorially and aesthetically. It is judged in terms of the taste of those who breathe it and their sensibility; or in other words, by the sensible action of the knowing subject in the postsocial interactions that characterize the organization. Moreover, this knowing subject is both the organizational actor and the researcher, which shifts our attention to the point of view assumed in aesthetic research in organizations, and the communication of its results.

Point of view and aesthetic understanding

As we have seen, the object studied by organizational aesthetics research is the connection-in-action between the personal knowledge of individuals – acquired, forged, and performed in the organizational interactions that immerse them in the sociality of collective action and in a multitude of relations with artefacts – and the action of artefacts at the level of *pathos*. This connection gives salience to the taste of the researcher, doing so in the material determination of aesthetic feeling. Taste, taste judgement, or aesthetic judgement on aesthetic experiences in organizations direct the organization scholar's attention to the subjective conditions of organizational theory-building, in that they involve 'personal knowledge' (Polanyi, 1958) activated by the researcher as s/he engages in aesthetic study of the organization at hand.

Sensorial and aesthetic forming

The issue of the point of view – that is, of position in the complex of postsocial relations among organizational actors, and between them and the organizational scholar – therefore does not concern one's place in an ongoing process as if it were a road; but rather the construction of that road, not alone but collectively in postsocial organizational interaction. It is a sensorial and aesthetic 'forming' amid the postsocial interactions of organizational life. The Italian existentialist philosopher Luigi Pareyson (1954: 23) wrote that every 'human operation is always formative, and even a thought process and a practical undertaking demand the exercise of formativity'. Every interaction comprises invention of how to proceed: 'one cannot think or act without forming' and every action 'cannot be itself without forming'. Those who conduct empirical research in organizations are acquainted with the *formativity* described by Pareyson in his essay on aesthetics: they observe what can be observed, they jump from one organizational phenomenon to another, and they switch from examining an organizational event from beginning to end to watching snatches of another event. There are also research situations in which communication with the actors of the process under investigation abruptly ceases. If one considers field research, it more frequently proceeds in fits and starts than in a linear progression yielding the sensation of completeness. However, the researcher constantly 'gives form' through doing what as it is being done invents the method to do it:

> Productive force and inventive capacity are therefore required by thought and action, because speculative and practical operations consist of a formative activity which, in a specific field, does things at the same time as it invents how they should be done. (Pareyson, 1954: 23)

Form and 'giving form' have been treated by the sociologist Georg Simmel in his reflections on art (1916; Eng. trans. 2005: 155): he writes that 'there is no human work, beyond pure imitation, that is not simultaneously fashioning and creating'. This has also been stressed by Rafael Ramirez, drawing on the aesthetic philosophy of Susanne Langer:

> It is in fact very hard to think of organizations without thinking of form – people in organizations per*form*; managers re*form* and trans*form* organizations; are concerned about subordinates in*form*ally de*form*ing their views; so they *form* their personnel and ensure they wear uni*form*s that manifest their *form*al selves to others, who become in*form*ed. (2005: 32)

Imaginary shadowing

Let us now imagine that we have an opportunity to conduct 'shadowing' in an organization; that is, observe organizational life as the shadow of some organizational actor. In order to show further how the point of view can be sensorially grounded, let us imagine – also for the sake of controversy and transgression – that we have decided to observe the aesthetic understanding and action of the organization's cleaning staff. This point of view shows a general stance, since cleaning is work probably common to all organizations; but it is also very specifically situated and ambiguous, given that it concerns the experiential and not solely cognitive activity performed by most of us – organizational scholars and otherwise – of cleaning the house and tidying the workplace. This ambiguity may be heightened by aesthetic feelings due to previous experiences in other organizational contexts. There will in fact be researchers who have worked as cleaners when they were students. Even the mere idea of shadowing a cleaner in the organization considered will evoke these previous experiences, so that the researcher relives and re-experiences the work and organizational practice done previously with all his/her sensible-aesthetic senses and judgements. On the other hand, there will be those who, like me, did not work as cleaners when they were students, but experienced something similar when they did military service. Thus re-emergent in their memories is the experience of being on fatigue – cleaning kitchens, barracks, latrines, parade grounds, and guard posts – which is only in certain respects similar to that of the cleaning staff in the organization where the shadowing is to take place but whose mere imagining is able to evoke the latter. Latent feelings return to the surface on contact with the smells, shapes and materiality of soaps, waters, brushes, rags, dirt, and dust. As they re-emerge, they are 'affectively' marked because – as the French phenomenologist Henry (1963) reminds us – there is no feeling which is impassive, nor any aesthetic feeling that is not affective. Moreover, feelings are relived experientially, yet not exactly, as they were but marked by the mythical thinking evoked by the memory of gestures, fatigue and disgust felt on cleaning, and on submitting to the command of military organizational life.

This command distinguishes and separates two social practices: doing the cleaning in the organization/being on fatigue and cleaning the barracks. It gives them different flavours in the experiential episode that 'forms' the researcher's point of view as s/he does the shadowing, although, in many other respects, they are similar in terms of sensible knowledge and sensible action in organizations. They cannot be made equal by the materiality of sensory contact in both situations with the smells and colours of the soiled, dilapidated organizational spaces more exposed to the ravages of people or the weather, ugliness and filth, alternated with aestheticizing embellishments, repulsive or gracious styles of organizational life. Choice, though constrained within the limits of work opportunities, gives a different flavour to cleaning, as opposed to the absence of choice when on army fatigue – a flavour, not the product of analytical thought, but which derives from reliving prior organizational experience with all the senses.

The choice vividly illustrates the aesthetic dimension of social practice in organizations, for we can ask, while 'forming' our point of view, if we would like to do cleaning work and if it would appeal to us to the extent that we could envisage it as our life's work; or if, conversely, it is work that does not appeal to us and that we would never contemplate doing, even less devoting the rest of our life to it. These are mundane issues, but they sometimes elicit responses felt 'with all one's being', 'with all one's body'.

Giving form to the point of view

We now 'know' a great deal about this work practice in the organization. We know the practice insofar as it is 'felt' experientially and in the interaction between cleaning work in the organization and the point of view being formed for the empirical research. Formativity takes place in the imagination and in sensible experience: we

have assumed a point of view and formed it sensorially before the shadowing begins. This is the 'imaginary participant observation' performed by projecting oneself into the situation through empathic understanding, and studying it by means of the evocative knowledge-creation process (Strati, 1999). As a method of organizational analysis to prefigure the future development of research, 'imaginary participant observation' activates all the senses, with their capacities for aesthetic judgment, rather than operating at the level of cognition and analytical-rational logic, and it constitutes the 'felt' personal knowledge which Michael Polanyi (1958) called the tacit dimension of knowledge.

What we now know about the work and organizational practice of cleaning predicates our point of view on the issue of whether its purpose is to improve quality and conditions through aesthetics and by operating on the aesthetic dimension. The issue arises at the level of sensible knowledge and aesthetic understanding, less on that of ethical or logical-analytical reflection, owing to the aesthetic feelings aroused by the questions concerning whether the cleaning work would appeal to us, perhaps for a lifetime. The issue is not a new one, and it has been framed in terms of concern about the deterioration in the quality of the organizational life due to both managements' failure to develop organizational aesthetics (Ackoff, 1981) and business consultants' failure to do so. Some decades ago, Fred Steele (1973) suggested in fact that consultants, by seeking the collaboration of designers, broke down the resistance of business managements and introduced organizational learning and training schemes to develop employees' abilities to make appropriate changes to the organization's aesthetic dimension. In Human Resources Development the aesthetic is precious, asserts Stephen Gibb (2006: 164), since it is 'a source of making sense of conduct' in organizations, even though science and technology render it precarious by claiming that it has little economic and political value.

Again, what we know about evoked and relived prior sensible-aesthetic knowledge of cleaning work in organizations raises the issue of choosing a paradigm. 'Forming' the researcher's point of view in this respect recalls Thomas Kuhn's (1962: 154) observation concerning aesthetic considerations which, although 'rarely made entirely explicit', have a sometimes decisive importance for the choice of theoretical paradigm for the research.

If we reprise the sociological paradigms of organization studies identified by Burrell and Morgan (1979) – 'radical humanist', 'radical structuralist', 'interpretative' and 'functionalist' – we can only base the aesthetic understanding of organizational life on those for which the organization is an artefact, inexplicable apart from the symbolic interactions among the subjects involved: the interpretative and radical humanist paradigms. This latter paradigm, in particular, enables one to reaffirm that examining the materiality of organizational life and rooting the methodologies of organizational aesthetics research in sensible experience is also to lay the epistemological bases for critical analysis of what prevents people from fulfilling themselves in organizational routine, beginning with their aesthetic-sensory sensibility, the subjective differences that they enact in interactions, and their creativity. Moreover, the aesthetic understanding of organizations shares with the radical humanism paradigm its privileging of intuition rather than analytical logic, and the evocative knowledge-creation process rather than the one based on causal explanation.

The foregoing discussion has shown that 'giving form' to the aesthetic point of view in the study of the organizational life is rooted in the corporeality and materiality of postsocial interactions, and not only in the ratiocination of cognitive processes. Moreover, it leaves nothing as it was before, as illustrated by the words to this Neapolitan song written by Pino Daniele (2007):

Il ricordo di un amore	*The memory of a love*
viaggia nella testa	*journeys in the mind*
e non c'e' una ragione	*and there is no reason*
quando cerchiamo quel	*when we look for what*
che resta	*remains*

e' come un vento di	*it is like a wind of*
passione o una	*passion or a*
rosa rossa	*red rose*
il ricordo di un amore	*the memory of a love*
ci cambia e non ci lascia	*changes us and does*
	not leave us

Love, the feminist philosopher Carla Locatelli (2007) maintains, is also an important component of organizational life: love for what one is doing; doing things 'with love'. Love is also apparent in the social practices of conducting organizational search, as revealed by the different and multifaceted passions of knowledge, learning, and invention (Gherardi et al., 2007). This may give the impression that aesthetic analysis romanticizes the understanding of organizational life (Hancock, 2005). However, it is not so much this, I believe, that is done with the aesthetic discourse on organization; rather, it is understanding of organizational life in terms of a new humanism that is achieved.

CONCLUSIONS

This chapter has illustrated organizational aesthetics research in terms of a new methodological awareness in the qualitative study of organization. The four aesthetic approaches to the study of organizations described – 'archaeological', 'empathic-logical', 'aesthetic', and 'artistic' – have illustrated the diverse features that methods of analysis – from those more consolidated in the social sciences in general (the 'intellectual' ones) to the more innovative methods rooted in the arts (the 'artistic' ones) – have assumed and may assume in the methodological debate. Their principal feature in common is that researchers immerse themselves in the life of the organization studied, activating their perceptive-sensory faculties and then detaching themselves from the context in order to judge it aesthetically and sensorially. The understanding of organizational life thus obtained is rooted in sensible knowledge constantly in dialogue and/or controversy with cognitive knowledge, and which is primarily characterized as the researcher's personal knowledge. This is a distinctive theoretical node in the aesthetic understanding of organizational life. I believe it to be of considerable importance for the study of organizations for the following reasons:

- It gives due prominence to the fact that researchers learn much more from organizational research than they are able to express and communicate in logical-analytical terms.
- It shows that aesthetics furnishes the language – metaphorical and nuanced; based on intuition and imagination; that develops between poetic logic, art, semiotics and aesthetic philosophy; and constituted by the evocative process of knowledge creation – able to 'give form' to the tacit dimension of the understanding of organizational life by both the organizational actor and the researcher.
- Rebalances relations between researcher and organizational actor, thereby giving full citizenship to researchers in the organizational interactions through which the research process is configured. The researcher is thus not obscured by the light shone on the organizational actors, and the collective and postsocial construction of organizational knowledge and organizational discourse is not subordinated to that of organizational life. This rebalance is unstable, however, because it is achieved through a sequence of everyday imbalances in research, primarily the power asymmetries which the aesthetic approach brings to the fore.
- It drives the epistemological polemic against the dominance of cognitivism, of causal explanation, the myth of rationality, and the belief in the corporate management of the aesthetic dimension of organizational life.

REFERENCES

Ackoff, R. (1981) *Creating the Corporate Future: Plan or be Planned For*, New York: Wiley.

Barry, D. (2008) 'The art of …', in D. Barry and H. Hansen (eds), *The Sage Handbook of New Approaches in Management and Organization*, London: Sage, pp. 31–41.

Baumgarten, A.G. (1750–8) *Aesthetica I-II*. Frankfurt am Oder: Kleyb (Photostat: Olms: Hildesheim, 1986).

Berg, P.O. (1987) 'Some notes on corporate artifacts', *Scos Note-Work*, 6(1): 24–8.

Berg, P.O. and Kreiner, K. (1990) 'Corporate architecture: turning physical settings into symbolic resources', in P. Gagliardi (ed.), *Symbols and Artifacts: Views of the Corporate Landscape.* Berlin: de Gruyter, pp. 41–67.

Brearley, L. (2001) 'Foot in the air: an exploration of the experience of transition in organizational life', in C. Boucher and R. Holian (eds), *Emerging Forms of Representing Qualitative Data*, Melbourne: RMIT University Press, pp. 151–84.

Bryman, A. (1989) *Research Methods and Organization Studies*, Boston: Unwin Hyman.

Burrell, G. and Morgan, G. (1979) *Sociological Paradigms and Organizational Analysis*, Aldershot: Gower.

Daniele, P. (2007) 'Vento di passione', in *Il mio nome è Pino Daniele e vivo qui.* CD Music Aim, Sony BMG Music Entertainment.

Dean, J.W., Ramirez, R. and Edward O. (1997), 'An aesthetic perspective on organizations', in C. Cooper and S. Jackson (eds), *Creating Tomorrow's Organizations: A Handbook for Future Research in Organizational Behavior*, Chichester: Wiley, pp. 419–37.

Escoubas, É. (2004) *L'Esthétique*, Paris: Ellipses.

Gagliardi, P. (ed.) (1990) *Symbols and Artifacts: Views of the Corporate Landscape*, Berlin: de Gruyter.

Gagliardi, P. (2006) 'Exploring the aesthetic side of organizational life', in Clegg, S.R., Hardy, C., Lawrence, T.B. and W.R. Nord (eds), *The Sage Handbook of Organization Studies* (second edn.), Sage: London, pp. 701–24.

Gherardi, S. and Turner, B.A. (1987, partial reprint 1999) *Real Men Don't Collect Soft Data*, Trent: Dipartimento di Politica Sociale, Quaderno 13. Reprint 1999 in A. Bryman and R. Burgess (eds), *Qualitative Research I-IV*, London: Sage, pp. 103–8.

Gherardi, S., Nicolini, D. and Strati, A. (eds) (2007) Special issue on 'the passion for knowing and learning', *Organization*, 14 (3).

Gibb, S. (2006) *Aesthetics and Human Resource Development*, London: Routledge.

Guillet de Monthoux, P. (2004) *The Art Firm: Aesthetic Management and Metaphysical Marketing from Wagner to Wilson*, Stanford: Stanford Business Books.

Hancock, P. (2005) 'Uncovering the semiotic in organizational aesthetics', *Organization*, 12(1): 29–50.

Hancock, P. and Tyler, M. (2000) ' "The look of love": gender and the organization of aesthetics', in J. Hassard, R. Holliday and H. Willmott (eds), *Body and organization*, London: Sage, pp. 108–29.

Henry, M. (1963) *L'Essence de la Manifestation*, Paris: PUF.

Human Relations (2002) 55/7. Special Issue on 'Organizing aesthetics', A. Strati and P. Guillet de Monthoux (eds).

Hindmarsh, J. and Heath, C. (2007) 'Video-based studies of work practice', *Sociology Compass*, 1: 1–17.

King, I.W. (2007) 'Straightening our perspective: the logos of the line', *Organization*, 14(2): 225–41.

Kuhn, T. (1962) *The Structure of Scientific Revolutions*, Chicago: University of Chicago Press.

Latour, B. (2005) *Reassembling the Social. An Introduction to Actor-Network-Theory*, Oxford: Oxford University Press.

Lenain, T. (2006–2007) 'Du mode d'existence de l'oeuvre dans l'art conceptuel', *La Part de l'Oeil*, Special Issue on Esthétique et phénoménologie en mutation, 21–22: 53–69.

Linstead, S. and Höpfl, H. (eds) (2000) *The Aesthetics of Organization*, London: Sage.

Locatelli, C. (2007) 'Women's Way of Knowing: It Is All About Love!', *Organization*, 14(3): 339–50.

Marquard, O. (1989) *Aesthetica und Anaesthetica. Philosophische Uberlegungen*, Paderborn: Schoningh.

Martin, P.Y. (2002) 'Sensations, bodies, and the "Spirit of the Place": aesthetics in residential organizations for the elderly', *Human Relations*, 55(7): 861–85.

Minahan, S. and Wolfram Cox, J. (eds) (2007) *The Aesthetic Turn in Management*, Ashgate: Gower.

Nicolini, D., Gherardi, S. and Dvora Y. (eds) (2003) *Knowing in Organizations: A Practice-Based Approach*, New York: M.E. Sharpe Armonk.

Organization (1996) 3/2. Special Issue on 'Aesthetics and Organization', E. Ottensmeyer (ed.).

Pareyson, L. (1954) *Estetica. Teoria della formatività*, Turin: Giappichelli. Reprinted 1988, Milan: Bompiani.

Pelzer, P. (2002) 'Disgust and organization', *Human Relations*, 55(7): 841–60.

Perrow, C. (1972) *Complex Organizations: A Critical Essay*, Glenview, IL: Scott, Foresman.

Pine, J.B. and Gilmore, J.H. (1999) *The Experience Economy*, Cambridge, MA : Harvard Business School Press.

Polanyi, M. (1958) *Personal Knowledge. Towards a Post-Critical Philosophy*, London: Routledge & Kegan Paul.

Prezzo, R. (2004) 'Il primato di un paradosso', in M. Merleau-Ponty, *Il primato della percezione e le sue conseguenze filosofiche*, Milan: Medusa, pp. 5–14.

Putnam, L., Phillips, N. and Pamela C. (1996) 'Metaphors of communication and organization', in S. R. Clegg, C. Hardy and W. R. Nord (eds), *Handbook of Organization Studies*, London: Sage, pp. 375–408.

Ramírez, R. (2005) 'The aesthetics of cooperation', *European Management Review*, 2: 28–35.

Rancière, J. (2003) *Le destin des images*. Paris: La fabrique éditions (Eng. transl. *The Future of the Image*, London: Verso, 2007).

Saint Girons, B. (2008) *L'acte Esthétique*, Paris: Klincksieck.

Scalfi, A. (2007) 'Untitled 2004 # Paris', *Aesthesis. International Journal of Art and Aesthetics in Management and Organizational Life*, 1(1): DVD, 20' 38".

Shusterman, R. (2008) *Body Consciousness. A Philosophy of Mindfulness and Somaesthetics*, Cambridge: Cambridge University Press.

Simmel, G. (1916) *Rembrandt, Ein kunstphilosophischer Versuch*, Leipzig: Kurt Wolff Verlag (Eng. trans.: *Rembrandt. An Essay in the Philosophy of Art*. Translated and edited by A. Scott and H. Staubmann. New York: Routledge).

Steele, F.I. (1973) *Physical Settings and Organization Development*, Reading, MA: Addison-Wesley.

Steyaert, C. and Hjorth, D. (2002) "'Thou art a scholar, speak to it …'" – on spaces of speech: A script', *Human Relations*, 55(7): 767–97.

Strati, A. (1992) 'Aesthetic understanding of organizational life', *Academy of Management Review*, 17(3): 568–81.

Strati, A. (1998) '(Mis)understanding cognition in organization studies', *Scandinavian Journal of Management*, 14(4): 309–29.

Strati, A. (1999) *Organization and Aesthetics*, London: Sage.

Strati, A. (2007) 'Sensations, impressions and reflections on the configuring of the aesthetic discourse in organizations', *Aesthesis. International Journal of Art and Aesthetics in Management and Organizational Life*, 1(1): 14–22.

Taylor, S. and Hansen, H. (2005) 'Finding form: looking at the field of organizational aesthetics', *Journal of Management Studies*, 42(6): 1210–31.

Turner, B.A. (ed.) (1990) *Organizational Symbolism*, Berlin: de Gruyter.

Vico, G. (1725) *Principi di una scienza nuova*, Naples: Mosca (third edn.), (1744), (Eng. trans.: *The New Science of Giambattista Vico*, ed. T.G. Bergin and M.H. Fisch. Ithaca, NY: Cornell University Press, 1968).

Warren, S. (2008) 'Empirical challenges in organizational aesthetics research: towards a sensual methodology', *Organization Studies*, 29(4): 559–80.

Weber, M. (1922) *Wirtschaft und Gesellschaft. Grundriß der verstehenden Soziologie*. Tübingen: Mohr. (Eng. trans.: *Economy and Society: An Outline of Interpretive Sociology. I-II*. Berkeley: University of California Press, 1978).

Witkin, R.W. (1990) 'The aesthetic imperative of a rational-technical machinery: a study in organizational control through the design of artifacts', in P. Gagliardi (ed.), *Symbols and Artifacts: Views of the Corporate Landscape*. Berlin: de Gruyter, pp. 325–38.

15

Feminist Perspectives on Gender in Organizational Research: What is and is Yet to be

Marta B. Calás and Linda Smircich

INTRODUCTION

> Feminism is about the social transformation of gender relations … feminism has always, to some extent and in some way, been philosophical. That it asks how we organize life, how we accord it value, how we safeguard it against violence, how we compel the world, and its institutions, to inhabit new values, means that its philosophical pursuits are in some sense at one with the aim of social transformation (Judith Butler, 2004: 204–205).

Feminist theorizing is philosophical, it is political, and it is plural. As a global social movement, feminism turns critical eyes on the institutions of society, asking profound questions about the conditions of inequality under which people live. As an intellectual movement, its main epistemological contribution is theorizing gender. This means confronting the nature and consequences of gendered embodiment, exploring what it means to be a woman or man in terms of the material conditions of existence, and questioning the ways in which a gendered world affects the nature of knowledge production. Feminism calls attention to approaches to knowledge production that separate knower and known, the mind from the body, cognition from affect, as well as the language through which knowledge is constituted and the purposes towards which it works. Altogether, feminist theorizing involves redressing gender and other social injustices, and is transformative in intent. Even in its tamest forms, feminist analyses are concerned with social change.

The singular term 'feminist theorizing' is, in actuality, rather plural. It refers to a complex body of theoretical perspectives ranging from the better-known liberal feminism, emphasizing equal rights, to the most caricatured, radical feminism, often seen as separatist and extreme. It includes, as well, both materialist theorizing and the contemporary 'post' trends, and more recently, transnational theorizing that engages directly with conditions of globalization.

Rather than discounting older theories to favour recent trends, feminist theorizing acknowledges the different historical, social, and political contexts from which theories emanate, while always considering different epistemological locations in terms of their adequacy towards social change. For instance, it would be a mistake to discard the equality aims of early liberal feminism, as gender inequality is *still* a concern around the world. However, the philosophical inspiration under which liberal feminist theorizing emerged, the social context it spoke to, and the analyses thus developed, may no longer be adequate for understanding contemporary conditions contributing to inequality. Thus, the continuing need for addressing conditions of inequality generates other feminist theorizing and analyses, as well as ways to articulate new issues and questions.

Feminist theorizing is also plural in that it recognizes the difficulty of placing the singular term 'woman' at the centre of its representations. Actual women, and their experiences, are multiple, according to their social and cultural locations, and this multiplicity needs to be acknowledged and unravelled. In general, most contemporary feminist theorizing focuses on the social construction and reproduction of gender relations and intersections with race, class, ethnicity, sexualities, and other relevant social processes underlying the production of differences and inequalities in various contexts.

Altogether, feminist analyses are intended to make us see the problematic nature of much that we, collectively, may take for granted in conventional social relations. Given their sensitivity to contingent conditions and emphasis on social transformation, feminist analyses are intended to question from the outset the apparent naturalness and inevitability in the status quo. Further, contemporary feminist theorizing no longer treats *gender* as a demographic variable distinguishing human beings based on apparently essential characteristics

due to sex or to gender roles. Rather, feminist theorizing understands gender as a central axis around which social life revolves; it is an axis of inequality/domination-subordination, where gender relations are hierarchical power relations. While there are fundamental differences in the conceptualization of gender among the various strands of feminist theorizing and thus in how power is conceptualized, a focus on power is part and parcel of feminist analyses, and underlies calls to action towards social transformation. How would these ideas play out in organizational and management research addressing gender issues? What difference may they make in contemporary organizational research more generally? We aim to answer these questions in the rest of the chapter.

Gender arrived as an explicit focus in organization studies in the person of 'woman' during the 1970s, when attention was drawn (again) to her subordinate status in modern society by the second wave women's movement. Since then, the woman-in-management research, mostly in the US, has explored the exclusion or under-representation of women at higher levels of organizations, while other research, primarily in Europe, has explored the gendering of organizations more broadly. Yet, despite what could be called 'progress' on numerous fronts, persistent patterns of gendered exclusion and segregation in organizations continue to draw the attention of researchers and policy makers. Worldwide inequality in representation and in pay persists (e.g., Hausmann et al., 2007), including a motherhood wage penalty (e.g., Budig and England, 2001). As well, women worldwide continue to be overrepresented among the poor, including in industrialized 'rich' nations (UNIFEM, 2007).

Thus, bringing feminist perspectives to the study of organizations today implies more than a focus on women; it implies recognizing that organizations, as core institutions of society, are centrally involved in the production and maintenance of social relations of inequality and subordination, including gender, race, ethnic, class, and sexuality relations. Organizational research, supported by feminist theorizing and analyses, would start by regarding gender as a central axis around which organizing/organization occurs. Observation and study of organizations informed by feminist theorizing would be guided by critical awareness of possible relations of domination/subordination and would bring a focus on emancipatory change.

It is to these issues – social transformation implicating organizations – that feminist research on gender in organization studies is directed. But, what is feminist research? In the following section, *Feminist thinking about gender and research*, we move away from questions of method to emphasize instead questions of meta-theory. We thus highlight assumptions about the ontological status of *gender* within feminist theorizing. Understanding differing ontologies facilitates discussion of the various epistemological and methodological arguments usually developed in feminist analyses. From this brief general discussion, we proceed to explore *Feminist research on gender in organizational studies*. Here we discuss how some organization and management studies scholars have incorporated feminist epistemological strategies in their research. We consider several examples and, in a few instances, contrast them with nonfeminist work on similar topics. Three subsections then describe the particulars of organization and management research that may be conducted under each of these feminist epistemological strategies:

- Feminist empiricism: researching conditions of women in organizations
- Feminist standpoint theory: researching the gendering of organizations
- Feminist postmodernism: researching the gendering of organizational knowledge

In the final section, *The yet to be?: Feminist analyses and the potential for social transformation in organization studies*, we conclude with what we regard as some unrealized possibilities for organization studies made available by feminist analyses.

Feminist thinking about gender and research

A rich and expanding interdisciplinary literature reflects on questions of ontology, epistemology, and methodology for performing feminist research (e.g., Harding, 1991; Fonow and Cook, 1991; 2005; Reinharz, 1992; Letherby, 2003; Hesse-Biber and Yaiser, 2004; *Signs*, 2005; Hesse-Biber, 2007). Collectively these discussions underscore that the ontological status granted to gender and the epistemological strategies that follow from it have methodological consequences. That is, theoretical understandings deriving from ontological and epistemological locations orient researchers to frame their research questions in specific ways. Once this is decided (and only then), a discussion about method would follow. Thus, method is a technical derivative – the 'how to' – of a theoretical understanding about what is to be known.

Is there a feminist methodology? Is there a feminist method?

Some think that feminist research equates with qualitative research, but feminist research in actuality can be quantitative or qualitative. For instance, if concerned with influencing public policy, feminist research would tend to favour quantitative and statistical forms of presentation and argument (see Fonow and Cook, 2005). Examples abound in economic geography where quantitative research documents spatial and temporal inequalities in women's lives, including in association with race, ethnicity, and class (e.g., McLafferty, 1995). Examples can also be found in economics (e.g., Strassman, 2008) and sociology (Misra et al., 2007). Yet, there are other methodological considerations not traditionally connected with 'method', such as for what purposes are the methods used? In this light, one can see how problematic it is to focus primarily on the quantitative-qualitative distinction, for it sidesteps the philosophical discussions of epistemology and methodology in favour of a focus on technique. Instead, feminist researchers understand epistemology, methodology, and method as interconnected within the course of research projects.

Shulamit Reinharz (1992), for example, emphasizes that feminism is a perspective not a method; therefore, feminists use a multiplicity of research methods. Yet for research to be feminist, it must be guided by feminist theory, involve an ongoing criticism of nonfeminist scholarship, and aim to create social change. Also, what many feminist scholars would identify as central features of feminist research is expressed by philosopher Sandra Harding (1987): first, it should be for women and towards their interests, and second, it should place the gender, race, class, culture, etc. of the researcher explicitly – i.e., establish her/his presence – within the frame of the research. That is, the researcher should be part of the research activity, visible as a real, concrete, historical individual with interest and desires. Finally, feminist research should be reflexive in that the presence, cultural beliefs and behaviours of the researcher must become part of the empirical evidence for the claims advanced in the results. The latter point includes acknowledging and addressing the power relations between researcher and researched, and how these impact the interpretative process.

Importantly, there is a difference between feminist research and research on gender done by women. The latter may be as androcentric as any other nonfeminist research, regardless of who is the researcher or what the subject matter may be. For instance, research comparing men and women in organizations is unlikely to be considered feminist unless its theoretical framing and design shows a concern for the possible disadvantages facing women and it seeks to address how research findings may help change those disadvantages. Thus, a central question for our purpose in this chapter is, how would traditional disciplinary frameworks and research practices change if they reflected the interests of those excluded from them? Adding women to the tradition is not enough; much more needs to change.

Is there a feminist ontology?

What is *gender*? The ontological status granted to the concept of gender differs according to feminist theoretical perspective. If we focus on the commonalities regarding gender among the varieties of feminist theorizing, rather than the particularities of their arguments, we can organize them into three distinctive groups. Readers interested in learning more about the specifics of each theory should consult, for instance, Jagger (1983), Tong (1998), and in organization studies, Calás and Smircich (1996 and 2006).

The first group approaches gender as a condition of social differentiation between men and women and comprises liberal, radical, and psychoanalytic feminist theory, including women of colour's critiques of these theories. Each presumes the equal social status of men and women as human beings and, therefore, assumes at a minimum that women's subordination in society must be redressed through demands to gender equity.

In this regard, earliest theories of liberal feminism were concerned with inequality between 'the sexes', i.e., between two categories of persons ('males' and 'females') denoted by biological characteristics. Later, distinctions were made between biologically-based 'sex' and 'gender' as a product of socialization and experience. Yet, feminist theorizing differs over what aspects of experience are viewed as most important in constituting gender. For instance, liberal feminism focuses on socialization into sex/gender roles; radical feminism addresses cultural practices that value men's experiences over women's; psychoanalytic feminism is concerned with experiences acquired in early developmental relations. Meanwhile, black 'womanists', and other 'women of colour' theorists, question these theories by asking which 'women's experiences' are constitutive of 'gender'. They note that an appeal to 'women' often conceals a white, privileged, heterosexual woman image, rather than the diversity of women's experiences arising from their different positions in culture and society.

By contrast, in the second group gender is understood differently, becoming more distanced from 'women's experience'. Theories in this group, including socialist feminist and some transnational feminist theorizing, approach gender as historical relational processes among members of patriarchal capitalist societies. They also focus on contemporary conditions, such as neoliberal globalized capitalism, which transform but also reproduce such historical processes. Here, *gender(ing)* as a dynamic relational process is part of a contested terrain in the material production of social inequalities, including, for instance, processes and practices embedded in institutions through which asymmetric gender relations are reproduced. It is from the naturalization of these relationships that gender oppression and subordination are produced and reproduced, such as the gendered division of labour, which also includes processes of class relations and practices of racialization, sexualization, and so on.

Finally, a third group of theoretical approaches, including poststructuralist and (post)colonial approaches and other approaches to analysis emerging in the wake of various 'posts', such as 'queer theory', understand gender as discursive processes and practices. Each of these problematize the notion of 'experience' insofar as it invests 'sex' and 'gender' with a certain stability as analytical categories. These perspectives note that subjectivity and identity are constructed linguistically, historically, and politically, and are therefore flexible and multiple. From these perspectives, gender differentiations are produced through language and representation, and thus through the process of producing knowledge itself. Here the notion of *gender* – i.e., its ontological status – is in question as a product of modern philosophies, which rely on stable categorizations to justify knowledge claims.

Our chapter does not favour any of these ontological considerations as most desirable for feminist gender research in organization studies. To the contrary, we highlight these differences to clarify their implications in conducting research; that is,

to clarify those epistemological strategies and methodological approaches necessary for understanding what kind of questions can be asked, the reasons for asking those questions, and the kind of research that can better answer them.

Is there a feminist epistemology?

Given these ontological considerations, what difference do they make when thinking about producing knowledge? Epistemology, a philosophical metatheoretical perspective defining what can be regarded as knowledge, derives from the ontological status accorded to phenomena and serves to justify knowledge claims about them. Traditional epistemological claims privileged 'man as knower', as if he were a disinterested and objective observer of a world whose laws and regularities would eventually be rendered evident and universally applicable to all (Lloyd, 1984). For the purposes of this knowledge enterprise, women were disqualified as inherently unable to occupy the position of knower because of their emotional proclivities and intellectual limitations.

Therefore, feminist epistemology is, at the outset, a critique of these traditional epistemological arguments (for a more in-depth discussion, see Anderson, 2007/2008 forthcoming). It asks particular questions. Do traditional epistemologies authorize as knowledge only certain views of the world and not others? Whose world is represented under particular epistemological justifications? Can knowledge ever be 'objective' in the sense that it makes no difference who the agent of knowledge production is? Doesn't it matter who produced the questions defining what problems should be investigated? Doesn't it matter whose point of view is taken into account when interpretations about causes and solutions to those problems are proposed? (e.g., Anderson, 1995; Code, 1991; Longino, 1990; Nelson, 1990). Feminist epistemological arguments, in general, note that all this *does* matter.

Specifically, feminist epistemology emphasizes that there is no disinterested knowledge. Rather, traditional epistemology can be thought of as representing men's social experiences, deriving from privileges accorded to certain men in relationship to women, and other men, in societies where producing knowledge has been a high status enterprise. Feminist epistemology starts, thus, from observing that all knowledge is situated; that is, arising from the particular position of the knowing subject (Haraway, 1991; Harding, 1987). Concurrently, feminist epistemology observes that gender is part of the social situation of the knowing subject, not as individual knower but as member of specific social groups with particular views of the world. These caveats do not exclude men from doing feminist research, but not all feminist epistemological claims, such as knowledge based on women's experiences, are open to men.

Harding (1987, 1991, 1998) identifies three different feminist epistemological strategies attending to these issues: feminist empiricism, feminist standpoint epistemology, and feminist postmodernism, which roughly correspond to the ontological differences regarding gender in feminist theorizing previously discussed. Each epistemological strategy highlights concerns raised by the questions just posed. In particular, feminist empiricism emphasizes the possibility of different notions of objectivity that may be derived from relations among differently situated knowers; standpoint theory privileges the value of knowledge attained by knowers in specific nondominant social situations, i.e., knowledge 'from below'; and feminist postmodernism focuses on the instability of the subjects of knowledge and therefore problematizes, altogether, conventional legitimation of knowledge claims. In the following section, we showcase the value of each of these epistemological strategies for research on gender in organizational studies with examples from organization and management literature.

Feminist research on gender in organizational studies

Through brief discussions of several published studies, we exemplify the ways feminist theories and epistemological strategies can frame research on gender in organization studies. Also, we show how each feminist analytical approach is directed to 'social change', yet the nature and scope of the envisioned changes differs according to theoretical frame. We aim to make apparent that it is the research questions, the orientation of the researcher, and the purpose of the work that makes it feminist.

Feminist empiricism: Researching the conditions of women in organizations

Feminist empiricism begins from the philosophical position that knowledge producers are embodied beings whose particular location matters in the world they observe; therefore, the notion of 'objectivity' as a view from 'nowhere' is suspect (Haraway, 1991). Men's historical privilege as knowledge producers and their experiences in this regard, have limited recognition of women's experiences as equally worthy of consideration. Thus, feminist empiricists highlight those taken-for-granted social practices, maintaining gender, race, class, and other inequalities also impact how enquiry has been and is still performed and how its results become normalized. Once women and others traditionally left out of the knowledge production enterprise become agents of knowledge production, it should be expected that justificatory claims for what counts as knowledge will also change. More generally, feminist empiricists would claim that knowledge so produced is less biased, more complete, and more truthful to the original ideals of a 'scientific enterprise'. Specifically, claims to objectivity under traditional epistemologies are seen as partial views, excluding many other human experiences by not noticing, for instance, that apparently neutral theoretical frameworks have original and unrecognized androcentric biases.

Feminist empiricism follows Quine's (1963) revision of traditional epistemology in considering that observation is theory-laden. Thus, all observations are underdetermined by theoretical frames and subject to revision by new theories and different interpretations, while all research renders partial views of a more complex, plural, and messy world, rather than complete understanding of phenomena. Feminist empiricism also rejects a sharp division between fact and values, for such a division masks the historical and social conditions that made it a normative ideal during the Newtonian science era, benefiting those who could deny the value-ladenness of 'facts'. Therefore, rather than hiding the values that guide research, these values should be exposed and subject to scrutiny, for research is not the product of any individual inquirer but the product of norms and practices embedded in communities of inquiry, and epistemology is a socialized endeavour whose guiding values should be made explicit for all to see.

In organization studies empiricism is the dominant form of research, including research on gender and management; however, most of this research is not feminist. The apparent interest in women's situation in 'women in management' research may lead some to assume this research is also feminist, yet this is not necessarily the case, and its focus on 'management' is sometimes even contrary to feminist interests.

To illustrate and contrast feminist approaches with nonfeminist ones, we begin with research examples on the general topic of women and careers, where attention has been paid recently to two related issues: whether professional women are 'opting-out' of their careers because of child-related responsibilities (Belkin, 2003), and what happens if, after a period of career interruption, they want to return to the workplace. Interestingly, the topic of women's 'opting-out' has been taken up by both organizational and feminist literatures, yet the questions and assumptions from which they start are not identical nor are their analyses of the conclusions that they reach.

The organization and management articles, by Lisa Mainiero and Sherry Sullivan (2005) and Sylvia Hewlett and Carolyn Luce (2005), start by accepting the 'opt-out' premise that professional women are leaving their careers

in noticeable numbers. Both see the 'opting out' situation as detrimental for women and for organizations – i.e., a 'brain drain' for Hewlett and Luce; and a 'talent drain' for Mainiero and Sullivan – at a time when a labour shortage is forecast. Mainiero and Sullivan support this claim with a report from the US Department of Labor, indicating the shortage will occur by 2012. Hewlett and Luce are less specific about timing but maintain that market and economic factors are aligning for a labour shortage. In these articles, professional women 'opting-out' is seen as an organizational problem to be solved, which requires understanding its causes better and making the appropriate organizational adjustments for amelioration.

To understand why professional women are leaving their careers beyond the simple explanation of having children, both sets of authors collected data via surveys from professional women but also from professional men as a means for comparison. The articles reach similar conclusions. Women leave their careers to have children, but also because of other family obligations, such as taking care of elderly parents, and because of traditional gender division of labour where husbands do less household work. At the same time, women who leave also report lack of opportunities and lack of meaningful work as factors contributing to their decisions. Both articles note that women and men report different career paths, with men having a more linear 'up the hierarchy' approach with deviations, primarily to look for better career opportunities.

The two articles differ, however, in explaining the underlying factors affecting women's 'opt-out' decisions. Hewlett and Luce acknowledge that only privileged women can actually choose to leave without thinking too much about the financial repercussions. They also focus on the cost of this decision for women's careers over time. In fact, they found that most women return to their careers after one or two years of time-out, but also that they pay a high price in terms of lost earnings potential and further career opportunities. Thus, the emphasis of their analysis is on structural conditions that disadvantage women.

In contrast, Mainiero and Sullivan describe women's careers as different from men's, but they paint an almost benign picture for women, highlighting behavioural explanations. Because women are relational, they claim, what is missed by employing organizations and by some academic research is observing how their careers are patterned differently, for over time they have different priorities in their search for authenticity, balance, and challenge in their lives. In the words of Mainiero and Sullivan (2005: 114), women's careers are like kaleidoscopes, where "'opting-out', becomes a natural decision based on the fit of the colours of her kaleidoscope at that point in time. Her career does not dictate her life. Instead, she shapes her career to fit her life as marked by her distinct and changing personal kaleidoscope patterns over her life span'. The authors further argue that men also value family and flexibility, but their timing is different; they value relationships more once they have made progress in their careers. In this argument, women are choosing what they see as best for them, including caring for others; organizations, however, are missing out by not understanding them, and therefore not providing accordingly for this very different career path.

Both articles have very similar advice for organizations: at a minimum employers must fix their retention problems and talent losses, as women will need to take time out one way or another. Both articles advise more flexible jobs and career paths; for instance, options to work reduced hours, less face time, and telecommuting. They emphasize that organizations must proactively create cultures that encourage employees to make use of flexible jobs, including personal leave, without stigmatizing those who do. For those who leave, organizations must maintain contact and encourage them to return without marginalization, even offering rewards, mentoring, networking, and advancement opportunities so that their career ambitions are nurtured. Mainiero and Sullivan also

recognize that women pay a 'motherhood tax' if they take time out or choose flexible and/or part-time jobs, and therefore advise a more fair compensation system which pays for project outcomes rather than hours, and that includes nonwork outcomes in the evaluation method. These authors also advise organizations to lobby for governmental support of policies for working parents and a shorter workweek.

From our descriptions, some might conclude that this is feminist research. We agree that several aspects could be judged as feminist, in particular the recognition by Hewlett and Luce of the structural conditions making 'the choice' of opting-out such a high cost decision for women, as well as both articles' suggestions for organizational changes to improve the situation for parents. Yet, the possible feminist impetus to benefit women is weakened by other aspects of this research. A feminist reading of these articles would note, first, that the topic of careers refers primarily to white-collar employees from mid- to top-levels of organizations, usually managerial or professional employees, which comprise the organizational elite. Neither article spoke about other women in organizations, usually lower paid and with many fewer choices and probably facing more burdens if they quit their jobs, other things being equal. Further, if all the advice about retaining, encouraging, rewarding, and benefiting a certain group of women were implemented, the disparity between elite 'career women' and all other women in organizations (and in society) would become even more glaring. Second, not much is made either of the fact that men's achieving 'linear careers' might also be connected to the possibility of mothers' 'opting-out' – i.e., sustained by a traditional patriarchal culture which discriminates against women occupying high level positions while making things much easier for men in the workplace, who also benefit from the wife-at-home support.

Third, the logic behind the advice, and behind both articles, includes a certain commodification of 'valuable women' whose talents are needed, making all women potentially disposable items when no longer needed. A feminist reading would also note an additional problem with this supporting logic: if the main reason to retain 'valuable women' is that organizations would lose talent given an assumed labour shortage, this also assumes that organizations actually are interested in maintaining at least the same size of labour force. That is, it assumes organizations would want to maintain an equal or higher proportion of high-paid employees over time – women in particular – and that they have a willingness to invest even more in them. But, why assume such is the case?

Our first feminist example by economist Heather Boushey (2008) has something to say on these matters. Titled 'Opting out?', her article addresses whether a woman 'with a child in the home in the US is any less likely to be working today than she was at earlier points in the last two decades simply because she has a child in her family' (Boushey, 2008). Analyses of historical data from the US Bureau of Labor Statistics, 1980 to 2006, and additional data for highly-educated professional women (i.e., the typical subjects of the 'opting-out' articles), demonstrate that whether married or single, highly educated or not, professional or working class, motherhood does not reduce women's labour force participation. In fact, a higher proportion of women with children were working in full time jobs in 2005 than in 1980, and increasingly most women with children are working full rather than part time.

Importantly, Boushey notes that the 2001 recession in the US was very hard on women workers, who lost more jobs than in prior recessions, even though fewer than men. Further, by 2007, employment rates for both men and women had not returned to the levels before 2001, a remarkable slow job recovery that economists are still trying to understand. Thus, in Boushey's (2008: 31) words, 'the opting-out story may be an illusion due to the lower employment rates for workers overall since 2000'. And, we add, due to the unwarranted assumption on which the advice in the prior articles hinged: that organizations would be adding rather than

replacing labour over time, in particular, high priced labour.

Beliefs about labour force expansion or contraction aside, Boushey highlights that *if* women *were* opting-out of the labour force to have children – all women and particular groups of women, as the article tested for – this *would be* a feminist concern, for it would indicate society's failure to accommodate to the realities of its workforce rather than be a signal of mothers' 'true' preferences. And, in fact, a reduction in mothers' labour force participation over time would have been expected given the increasing cost of childcare, and the lack of benefits and inflexible schedules they face, adding to the difficulties of parenthood for workers. But, given these difficulties, what is remarkable is that mothers *continue* to enter the labour force, which reiterates that economic inequality, declining economic mobility and falling real wages for men since the 1970s fuel the need for dual-earning families. And thus, the article's closing observations are almost a direct feminist response to the two careers articles above: 'Focusing on the needs of the millions of US parents who are working, rather than questioning whether professional mothers are at work, would be a fruitful course forward for academic research and policy-makers alike' (Boushey, 2008: 31–32).

Our second feminist article, a report from the Center for WorkLife Law of the University of California by Joan Williams, Jessica Manvell, and Stephanie Bornstein (2006), looks at the 'opt-out' argument from yet another angle by focusing on media representations. Content analysing US print news stories published between 1980 and 2006 about women leaving the workplace, their research shows that news stories focus overwhelmingly 'on psychological or biological "pulls" that lure women back into traditional roles, rather than workplace "pushes" that drive them out' (Williams et al., 2006: 6). Equally overwhelming is the focus on white, affluent women with white-collar jobs – about only eight percent of all American women workers. As well, these often appear as soft, human interest stories, rather than stories highlighting how female unemployment carries serious economic consequences for society, women, and families.

The report acknowledges the feminist literature documenting the lack of an 'opt-out' trend, also citing earlier work by Boushey (2005) in this regard. Yet, it further notes that such analyses do not go far enough in telling stories of mothers who do leave or stay home because of workplace inflexibility, lack of family support, and workplace bias against mothers. Thus, the report aims to expose what is behind media stories and provide the media with accurate information. To this effect, the report draws on recent research data to document realities the news media could and should represent to introduce new story lines, explaining and documenting why and how US women are being pushed out of the paid workforce. These include an unrealistic workplace structure dating from the 1950s, which fosters a particular concept of the Ideal Worker; workplace bias, and discrimination against mothers and a failure of US public policy to help workers balance work and family responsibilities.

The work of Boushey and of Williams et al. exemplify many aspects of feminist empiricist research, including demonstrating the underdetermination of data and the possibilities of reinterpreting 'the facts' based on other theories and analyses, as well as reminding us to acknowledge that there is no simple explanation for a complex, plural, and messy world. Importantly, and in particular in the report by Williams et al., these works show that there is no sharp distinction between 'facts' and 'values', but rather that the values underpinning any 'fact' should also be the object of research, because they define the directions social change may take.

For instance, all our examples conclude that US workplaces are inflexible and that more support is needed for workers trying to balance work and family life. Yet, the nonfeminist articles appear almost naive in expecting that simply invoking 'loss of women's talents' and 'labour shortage' are sufficient for organizations to change in the recommended directions. By contrast, the feminist articles highlight that a focus on professional women 'opting-out' is almost a distraction from the real problems of most parents in US workplaces today – e.g., extraordinary expectations about working hours with a concurrent reduction of as many high paying jobs, jobs benefits, and benefited jobs as possible. Organizations are not blind to these issues; rather they have created benefit from them. Public policy follows along, aided by media stories, and possibly the help of the managerial bias in organization and management research.

Feminist empiricists would thus note that the values of the community of inquirers guiding research should also be made explicit rather than hidden behind the veil of 'objectivity'. For instance, the work of Williams et al. could be read as a challenge to media organizations to be explicit about the values and experiences lurking behind their 'facts'. One passage is quite telling when speculating why the opt-out media story resurfaces over the years: 'Perhaps it rings true to the editors who assign it over and over again … Opt Out stories depict the dramatic failure of high-hours, high pressure workplaces (such as newspapers) to retain and promote proportionate numbers of women as nobody's fault; in fact, it's inevitable given that the 'brains of men and women light up differently'. The Opt Out story line sends the reassuring message that nothing needs to change (Williams et al., 2006: 9).

We have used these comparative illustrations to make clear differences between feminist and nonfeminist research focused on women in organizations. While each is supported with quantitative data, note that because the assumptions being made and the interests the research is intended to serve are different, the data vary as they are used to support different types of analysis. Also, the feminist articles used so far follow along the lines of liberal feminist assumptions about women's equality in society, but feminist empiricism may be guided by other than liberal feminist premises, as our next two examples demonstrate.

Jan Thomas and Mary Zimmerman (2007) examine the evolution, dilution, and co-optation of one aspect of the feminist movement: grassroots feminist women's health centres. Originally developed in the 1960s and early 1970s as alternatives to the mainstream health care system, feminist health centres sought to empower women with greater control over their wellbeing. With roots in radical feminism, and an emphasis on participatory practice, their goals included demystifying medical processes, educating and supporting women in their health choices, providing widely accessible women-centred services, and advocating for women and their health issues. The authors' historical analysis for the period 1982–2002 revealed how the aims of a feminist women's health centre model, originally conceived to challenge 'the patriarchal and hierarchal medical model of care', were blunted as hospitals appropriated features of this model and used them as marketing tools for revenue production (Thomas and Zimmerman, 2007: 374).

A database from in-depth interviews, participant observation, and multiple forms of documentary material was assembled into case studies of four types of service delivery: programmes, pavilions, centres, and medi-spas, developed by hospitals in the context of changing social, economic, and political conditions. Beginning in the 1980s, hospital-based women's health centres increasingly brought inside the corporate system formerly alternative practices, such as birthing centres with water tubs and home-like decor, with more recent developments including gourmet meals and luxury linens, as a way of marketing hospital services especially to insured women. By the 1990s, managed care, declining reimbursement from insurance companies, and continued competition, spurred development of the medi-spa model, featuring spa and aesthetic services, tapping into the 'self-pay market' as sources of revenue generation. Through various co-optation processes, the feminist transformative potential was lost as certain feminist practices were appropriated into profit-centered systems. The authors observe that these processes apply to other situations, where the 'driving force of change is revenue production rather than gender equity' (Thomas and Zimmerman, 2007: 380).

Marking this research as distinctively feminist is the kind of organization it studied and the argument it makes about them. It aligns with radical feminism ontologically and with feminist empiricism epistemologically, seeking to present a 'more truthful', less celebratory account about developments in women's health programmes of particular interest to radical feminists. Their historical approach allows them to document contradictory processes by which a movement to put health care into women's hands was transformed, with women again becoming the objects of capitalist enterprise. Their findings are consistent with many other case studies detailing the struggles faced by feminist businesses, and other alternative organizations, as they try to forge alternative modes of practice that challenge extant power relations within capitalism (e.g., Ferree and Martin, 1995). The researchers convey their orientation and commitments in concluding that, 'The profit motive would have to be substantially reduced, and operational goals shifted from financial outcomes to health outcomes, before real feminist changes could be expected' (Thomas and Zimmerman, 2007: 380).

Consistent with a substantial body of feminist empiricism premised on Joan Acker's (1990) theory of gendered organizations, the next example, by Marjukka Ollilainen and Toni Calasanti (2007), examines ways in which gendering is achieved and sustained via structural, interactional, and symbolic processes (e.g., Benschop and Doorewaard, 1998). It also draws upon insights and argumentation stemming from psychoanalytic/gender cultural feminist analyses, showing the connections among gender socialization patterns, traditional division of labour in the western family, and organizing in the workplace.

Specifically, the authors examine gendering processes in the context of self-managing teams, an organizational form assumed to weaken old hierarchies in favour of bringing about more egalitarian practices. In their study of four mixed-sex teams engaged in service work, the authors show how the gender division of labour is reflected in, and reproduced, by the women's and men's experiences in their teams, especially through the processes of emotion work. Through interviews and observations, the researchers found the metaphor of family repeatedly invoked to describe what was going on. While 'harmonious, family-like relations … appear to facilitate efficiency and productivity' (Ollilainen and Calasanti, 2007: 19), their analysis shows how the family metaphor also positioned people in gender stereotypical ways, preserving gender connotations and reinscribing gender as a status with traditional role expectations.

Metaphors of family and marriage, 'played into gender inequalities within these teams' (p. 24), reintroducing 'a patriarchal hierarchy' (p. 6). Older women were seen as 'mothering' the younger men, promoting their career mobility, and sacrificing their own. Women were praised for their compassion and superior ability to soothe angry customers, while men distanced themselves from those tasks associated with the feminine, in favour of focusing on more highly valued activities. Thus, the task sharing expected in teams gave way to stereotypical patterns of work distribution, mirroring patterns of domestic labour. The researchers use their evidence to counter arguments that gender salience would diminish through mixed sex work groups. The authors note (p. 24) that 'the cultural aspects of the metaphors team members use introduce a conservative element that can inhibit equality'.

The authors' feminist analyses evaluate organizational forms showing that what may ostensibly be considered equalizing tendencies at work, such as team based work design, cannot be isolated from the wider societal context of unequal gender relations. Psychodynamic and cultural features of the family are invoked and to some extent replayed inside the workplace, threatening moves to democratize

organizations. Organizations are shown as sites of ongoing production/reproduction of gender relations, with gender as an axis around which organizing occurs. Thus, the research effort offers a sceptical view of corporate practices proclaimed to be equalizing, while reproducing in practice patterns of gender inequality. Implicitly their argument is that changes in the workplace towards greater gender equality will not occur separate from changes in society's gender relations.

Feminist standpoint epistemology: Researching the gendering of organizations

Based on the theoretical premises of socialist and/or forms of transnational feminist theorizing, research based on feminist standpoint epistemologies considers gendering processes as part of the historical relational processes constituting a society – where inequality, conflict, and power struggles are the norm. This research is explicit in seeing knowledge production as a contested practice, noting that those in different social locations 'tend to generate distinctive accounts of nature and social relations' (Harding, 1997: 384). With origins in Marxist analysis, standpoint epistemologies emphasize knowledge as reflecting embodied experience under specific historical and material conditions. Consistent with its epistemological assumptions, research from an explicitly feminist standpoint seeks to be 'corrective' by producing knowledge from the vantage point of those subjugated by dominant knowledge claims, including women, people of colour, and poor people.

Traditional justificatory strategies for knowledge claims are seen as power moves, sustaining privilege for some. Following from this, feminist standpoint epistemologies address not only the issue of partial view stemming from the vantage point of the privileged, but also further the notion that the ways of seeing of the disadvantaged may offer a better and more complete understanding. This feminist argument, thus, includes as part of the epistemological strategy a struggle to achieve ways of seeing 'the world' from the position of those disadvantaged by traditional epistemologies.

'Standpoint' is not the same as the 'perspective' of an individual speaker, as might be obtained through a phenomeno- logical interview. Rather, an epistemological standpoint is an achievement derived from intellectual and political struggles by groups who have been subjugated by dominant knowledge claims. Here, standpoint episte- mologies have an affinity with consciousness raising groups originating in radical feminism, in that connections between 'the personal' and 'the structural' become evident. Insofar as the experiences and knowledge of women – in all their differences of race, class, sexual orientation, etc. – are often disregarded or subjugated, a feminist standpoint would use these differences towards unmasking what have been so far privileged understandings.

Importantly in this regard, Patricia Hill Collins (1990) develops black feminist stand- point epistemology based on black women's personal experiences of racism and sexism. Drawing from the notion of 'bifurcated consciousness' from W.E.B. DuBois, her approach addresses the ability of certain marginalized groups to experience their social conditions both from their standpoint and that of the privileged among which they reside, enabling a side by side comparison of conditions of advantage and disadvantage. In this sense, black women are 'outsiders within' a social order they know from the inside but with sufficient distance to enable critique.

Harding's (1993) notion of 'strong objec- tivity' further defends standpoint episte- mologies as capable of improving research objectivity on two counts. First, it improves reflexivity in that researchers must make explicit their social positions, interests, back- ground assumptions, and biases in relation- ship to those they research, and therefore acknowledge the partiality of their views. Further, inclusion of marginalized groups into inquiry will improve reflexivity insofar as these would be most likely to question dominant representations as partial truths. Thus, strong objectivity does not privilege the epistemological standpoint of the oppressed but that of communities of inquiry which include them.

One prominent advocate of standpoint epistemological positions is Dorothy Smith, whose research approach, institutional ethnography, stems from Marxist, feminist, and ethnomethodological roots (e.g., Smith, 1987 and 2005; Griffith and Smith, 2005; Rankin and Campbell, 2006; DeVault, 2007). Marjorie DeVault (2007: 5) describes it as follows: 'Combining theory and method, institutional ethnography emphasizes connections among the sites and situations of everyday life, management/professional practice, and policy making, considered from people's location in everyday life ... but the research is not confined to the everyday life of the anchor group at this point of entry. Rather, the institutional ethnographer traces how those lives are organized through the social relations of their context'.

Texts occupy an important position in these analyses. People activate all kinds of texts in ways that create linkages across sites, and thus texts are often the sources of translocal coordination, by creating relationships among people, institutions, and their demands, in ways usually invisible in other types of analyses. Dorothy Smith coined the term 'ruling relations' to describe a complex web of discourses and practices in a formation of textually-based power which emerged and became dominant with the development of corporate capitalism. Ruling relations coordi- nate and objectify lived experiences of people, which thus become amenable to management. Methodologically, institutional ethnography is probably the most clearly defined research approach arising from standpoint epistemolo- gies, but feminist standpoint researchers use other methodological approaches.

The first example, by Patricia Y. Martin (2001), researches professional women's experiences with, and interpretations of, men at work, and from their accounts develops theory on the ways in which men 'mobilize' masculinities. As part of her research on diver- sity in for-profit companies, Martin conducted interviews with professional women working in male dominated workplaces. From these exchanges, Martin selected stories containing gender dynamics that were somewhat puzzling to the six women who told them. As she observes, 'The women's uncertainty, and "theorizing" about what they were observing, provided a space for me, as sociologist, to also theorize their experiences with men and masculinities in organizations'(Martin, 2001: 594). The women told stories in which men were seen to be 'peacocking', 'self-promoting', 'expropriating others' labour', 'protecting', 'sucking up', 'deciding based on liking or disliking', and so on (pp. 601–603).

Martin worked inductively with these accounts to identify features of men's masculinities mobilizing practices. She identified 'contesting masculinities' and 'affiliating masculinities' (Martin, 2001: 604). Further, she noted that when men mobilize masculinity/ies in meetings or interactions at work, they 'conflated masculinity/ies processes with working processes', i.e., masculinities and working were fused so that work fosters masculinities (Martin, 2001: 605). For their part the women described themselves as drained by having to spend energy and time coping with 'men acting like men', and at other times feeling excluded, as the targets of men's actions were other men. Martin (2001: 605) theorizes that, 'It is perhaps noteworthy that men are able to conflate working and masculinities, because they predominate in the powerful positions, and because men and masculinity have more legitimacy (than do women and femininity) in work contexts'.

Martin's work demonstrates the value of feminist standpoint theory for producing new knowledge from the position of less privileged groups. She is careful not to suggest that this reflects the experience of all women, or that the men intended to harm women, or that they even actually behaved as the women described. Rather, the research brings to visibility dynamics of gendering of which people may be only liminally aware. She asks, 'if men were more aware of women's accounts, especially the costs that their mobilizing

exacts, would it matter? Would men become more reflexive about their behaviour and/or change?' (Martin, 2001: 610).

The second example, by Brenda Allen (1996), is also concerned with producing new knowledge from the standpoint of a marginalized group subject to multiple oppressions: women of colour. Her focus is on organizational socialization, the process by which new employees learn workplace expectations and become integrated, or not, within their organizations. As part of a larger project on socialization of faculty women of colour, Allen performed a self-interview recording her own responses to the questions she planned to pose to participants (Allen, 1996: 261–262). Her article interweaves autobiographical data and personal narrative into a critical feminist rereading of one model of organizational socialization prominent in her field, showing how organizational socialization is not only about learning the ropes, it is a process 'fraught with issues of oppression and resistance' (Allen, 1996: 267).

As a communication studies scholar, Allen also speaks as an African American, heterosexual woman raised in a lower class community. She frames herself as an 'outsider within' the predominantly white university and discipline. She builds upon the feminist critiques of the literature regarding the universalizing tendencies of organizational scholarship that does not capture women's experiences. Instead, she offers scenes from her everyday life, in particular as these shed a different light on processes featuring in the organizational socialization literature. As she observes, work on 'anticipatory socialization' fails to stress how sources of communication through which individuals learn about work settings depict and reinforce societal stereotypes about occupations that contain racist, sexist, and classist aspects. Upon entering the workplace, organizational practices oriented toward assimilating newcomers are offered as 'for your own good', and are perhaps well meaning: for instance, warning academics who are 'tokens' against serving on many committees as damaging to their careers. Yet these warnings can be seen at the same time as exclusionary and limiting, and working against social change.

In Allen's experience, not considered in socialization theory is the racism and sexism with which some newcomers must cope, taking energy and time away from what the organization regards as valuable and productive. The details of her experience point to the situatedness of knowledge, showing as well the gendering /racing/classing of knowledge professed as general or universal in organization studies.

As these examples show, feminist standpoint work is explicit in using women's lives as a foundation for constructing knowledge with transformative capacities, particularly when women speak about their struggles. Allen intends her scholarship not only to instigate change in organizational practices, especially in universities but also to inspire change on the part of researchers, noting how the act of doing feminist standpoint work can serve emancipatory ends – as she reports her own feelings of empowerment achieved through this form of eliciting knowledge. Martin is concerned with subverting gender practices that harm people, to which Allen adds a concern for practices of race-ing and class-ing. In each of these studies, the researcher-author reflexively counts herself as among the studied. Each sees their work as making aspects of the gender order visible in ways they were not before. Each envisions their research as raising consciousness.

Finally, we briefly describe a research project opening another angle into issues of motherhood and work missed by the 'opt-out' discussions in the feminist empiricism section. Jill Weigt (2006) uses institutional ethnography to explore the social organization of mothers' carework after welfare reform. Welfare reform refers to a 1996 law restructuring the US welfare system, which from 1935 had guaranteed cash assistance to poor families. This restructuring ('welfare-to-work') required a high number of welfare recipients to move quickly into the labour market, and was in fact noted by Boushey (2008) in her historical tracking of women with children entering the US labour force.

Poor mothers comprised a large portion of those affected by welfare-to-work, and most ended up employed in low pay jobs near or below the poverty level. Under these circumstances, the question of how children would be cared for when their mothers went to work in low paid jobs took centre stage.

The research was based on data from interviews of a large sample of individuals affected by the restructuring, followed by in-depth interviews with a smaller sample, and an intensive study of a few women with children who were followed for a period of three to four years after leaving the welfare programme. Weigt (2006: 333–334) asked questions such as, 'What do her assertions and her decisions under these conditions tell us about the social relations that shape her carework? To what social relations is she accountable? How do they shape the ways she cares for her children? How does she participate in these social relations? And whose interests do they serve?' She then explored how her respondents navigated the tensions between low-wage work and the unpaid carework of their children, and documented ways 'carework' is organized by forces originating outside these women's lives. Following the aim of institutional ethnography, as well as standpoint theory in general, this research was intended to help participants understand their circumstances as influenced but not determined by power relations (i.e., ruling relations) operating beyond their individual experience of everyday life. Recognizing these relations enables knowing and experiencing the world in other ways, a form of consciousness raising that can help to disrupt limitations and foster possibilities for the pursuit of other options.

Weigt's analyses drew connections between local moments – the narratives of participants' experiences – and the translocal origins of these discourses. She found that the mothers' narratives revealed ruling relations linked to the discourse of neoliberalism, including dismantled welfare policies and a low-wage labour market, complemented by the ideology of the traditional middle class nuclear family, representations of 'good' and 'bad' mothers in the media, and the discourse of work enforcement. As such, these women interpreted their difficulties as their personal failings rather than as failures of policies and the limited jobs available to them. Further, all this legitimated the hierarchy of access to resources (i.e., who deserves which resources), producing social inequalities while upholding the social relations of privilege and subordination required to sustain a neoliberal economy.

In the spirit of institutional ethnography, this research signals the intertwined nature of ideologies of motherhood with ideologies of the market supporting contemporary business organizations. The 'opt-out' arguments are only one set in lines of discourses legitimating the institutional outcomes of these ideologies, and so are the 'welfare-to-work' narratives. As expressed by Weigt (2006: 348), 'failing to address private obligations, neoliberal welfare policies and employment arrangements' depend on individual women 'to take up carework with little institutional support, regardless of their material circumstances'. A neoliberal economy is simply a contemporary incarnation of patriarchal capitalism, where mothers continue to be the ultimate cheap labour. Institutional ethnographies highlight the details of these interconnections, which must be made visible before anything can change.

Feminist postmodernism: Researching the gendering of organizational knowledge

Feminist postmodernism would be sceptical of the justificatory strategies offered by feminist empiricism and feminist standpoint epistemologies. From a postmodernist perspective, these epistemological strategies are to be critiqued in that they derive from modern political philosophy, generally from liberal political thought in the first case and from Marxian theories in the second. Postmodernist feminist work argues that both assume a certain universal knowledge that can be arrived at through reason, observation, and

progressive politics, and therefore end up in a place not very different from the traditional epistemologies they criticize.

What if the world is more ambiguous and unstructured, more fluid, and the knowledge production enterprise directly implicated in the illusion of mastery over this? From such a perspective, the only epistemological strategy available is to be continuously involved in deconstructing this illusion and, paradoxically, in opening spaces for those in the margins of the epistemological enterprise to stay in the margins as deconstructors of mastery. Women in their multiplicity, and others left outside this enterprise, may thus claim their marginal positions for such purposes. At the same time, however, they cannot claim authority for their deconstructive strategies from those same marginal positions, for in these arguments nobody, dominant or marginal, has a solid position on which to legitimate their claims.

That is, following poststructuralist philosophical approaches, the subjects of these analyses are discursive effects of language and other practices of signification, attempting to fix the elusive nature of a fluid world which includes the fluid subjectivities of those involved in any kind of knowledge production. Research from this perspective understands that differentiation along gender configurations is produced and reproduced through the process of producing knowledge itself. Researchers pay careful attention to how knowledge is constructed in order to deconstruct, not to destroy, but rather to reveal or make undecidable, naturalized aspects of gender. Knowledge justified on the basis of 'experience' (e.g., women's experience) is particularly amenable to deconstruction, as there is no fixed subject behind such experience. Either linguistically or historically, the subject is always changing as the boundaries of self-understanding are being redrawn in relation to others (e.g., woman as the other of man, women of colour as the other of white women, and so on).

Not surprisingly, feminist theorizing shows some ambiguity about these arguments. There are concerns with lost political power for knowledge based on 'women's claims' and therefore for social change to improve women's social situation based on these claims. Yet, there have been also important theoretical developments regarding other subjectivities where fluidity rather than fixity is the norm, while maintaining agency for fluid subjectivities. Notable among these is Haraway's (1985) conceptualization of the 'cyborg', calling into question the notion of humans independent from technologies; Alcoff's (1988) notion of 'positionality' locating subjectivity in historical and social contexts; Butler's (1990) 'performativity', addressing and problematizing gender as a cultural performance; and Barad's (2003) 'agential realism' which questions several of these alternatives as still privileging the human subject. In each of these, new notions of agency for social change are thought possible without taking resort to identity politics.

Generally, research drawing upon post-structuralist feminism pays attention to discourse and language as constitutive of social reality, and to how gender has been stabilized as male/female dualisms in that 'reality'. Language and other practices of signification privilege the male and masculine through devaluing the female and feminine, and therefore they are a prime focus of analysis. How is that done? What else is possible? There is a fairly identifiable organizational literature drawing from feminist postmodern analyses. Much of it has examined how scholarly knowledge is constituted in organizational theories through language that privileges the stereotypically masculine over the stereotypically feminine (e.g., Ahl, 2004; Brewis, 2001; Calás and Smircich, 1991; Kark and Waismel-Manor, 2005; Mumby and Putnam, 1992). Others have considered practices of everyday life and their interplay with organizational discourses (e.g., Martin, 1990; Runté and Mills, 2006). Still others have delved into popular texts, such as media representations, together with bodies of academic knowledge, to investigate the former's gendered organizational aspects (e.g., Bowring, 2004).

One example of these works is an early attempt of ours at feminist postmodern analyses (Calás and Smircich, 1991). We choose it not to privilege what we do, but because we took an approach to analysis seldom repeated in our field. Basically, we argued that the topic of leadership in organization studies is actually seduction dressed up as rational masculinity, and it is a condition that reproduces itself overtime. Thus, despite calls for 'advancing' knowledge on the topic, there is little else to be said about the meaning of leadership. To make this point, we began by following in parallel the dictionary history of the words 'leadership' and 'seduction', which many would consider to be opposites. We traced how 'the leader' acquired a masculine persona precisely by feminizing its other, 'the seductor', a term now obsolete, but remaining in the dictionary in its feminine version – seductress. In this dictionary history, the meaning of seduction has become 'to lead astray'; we, therefore, wonder if that means that leading is to seduce properly. And what would that mean?

In other words, we were arguing that on the surface of leadership theory there was an attempt to hide its sexualized nature, but that the constitution of this knowledge has become so taken for granted as proper, rational discourse, and as 'real' knowledge about 'real' leadership by institutionalized scholarly expectations that any other interpretation has become out of bounds. In all this, we suspected, there were various subtexts where the rational becomes a hypermasculinity concealing desire for a homosocial order. Of course, we don't make this argument outright, but rather through deconstructive demonstration (readings) where we explore seminal (and we mean it) writings about leadership in the course of the modern history of the field, exemplified with classic texts between 1938 and 1982.

In some analyses, we pair textual descriptions of leadership with contemporary writings on sexuality, and examine their intertextual relationships as anxieties of the times. In others, we return to the dictionary for alternative, not so innocent, meanings in the words used, and rewrite paragraphs with these alternative wordings. We also add parallel commentaries from feminist theorists on questions of sexuality. In each case we reconstitute these texts on the basis of other possible meanings, recognizing as we go that they all result in a very similar sense of what could be seen as leadership. There is homosocial pleasure in what they do, and so it is in the community of scholars that do it. No wonder the field keeps asking for 'advances' in knowledge about leadership, but cannot get beyond repeating itself. Can anything be done about this? What about bringing the excluded female into this picture?

We end by writing two utopias drawn from feminist fiction to explore the possibility of a seductive feminine leadership, but conclude by recognizing that 'the alternative' is untenable. None of it looks like 'leadership', which further makes the point about the homosocial masculinity that leadership has become. Yet, we had one more 'trick' to perform and thus wrote Utopia Three, where we announced that on writing 'this whole paper *as if* we were going to be able to articulate an alternative for the dilemma of leadership/seduction – we can tell you that finding an alternative was never our purpose. Our purpose, rather, was *the very action of writing this improbable paper*' (Calás and Smircich, 1991: 597). Deconstructing 'leadership' in a feminist key was an occasion for denoting the closure around what organizational scholars could think and say as organizational theory and research. Thus, we were dislodging 'the *masculinist monologic* in which we have encased our organizational signifiers' by allowing its *absurdity* to appear. We thus reiterated that trying to fix 'knowledge' (e.g., about the meaning of leadership) was at least part of the problem, while part of the solution might be allowing for the pleasure of writing differently when writing organizational texts.

In our next example, Michèle Bowring (2004) analyses a television series, part of the *Star Trek* franchise, where the leader of the starship Voyager was a woman, Captain Janeway. Bowring opens her discussion observing that framing a strong female leader was a pressing problem for the producers of the series, who wanted to portray a future where gender equality had been attained. They finally settled for a character whose body/appearance was sufficiently feminine but far from overtly sexualized. Bowring sees the dilemma the producers faced as closely tied to debates in the social sciences over power and political implications of gendered roles where the body has taken a central place. And thus, the author's underlying purpose for the article is 'to uncover the way in which research about leadership has been constrained by a reliance on the categories male-female, and/or masculine-feminine … and instead refigure it as one of an infinite number of positions' (Bowring, 2004: 383).

Bowring highlights the work of Butler, using her ideas on the body and sexuality as well as other works examining the body as a fluid construct, and focuses on two versions of the Voyager series. The television series is analysed by addressing the difficulties through the years of maintaining the female leader character without falling into stereotypical representations. This effort ultimately fails; the series ends having portrayed throughout a lonely and sad figure, whose life is compartmentalized into public/private domains with little private life, and a public life that keeps her separated from the rest of her crew as a way of maintaining her authority. In Bowring's view, the series reflects the common understanding of gender and leadership.

She then focuses on a second version of the series from a popular slash fiction website, and analyses the 50 stories written and posted over the final three years of the series. These are subversive stories, which pose Janeway as a queer character, with a private romantic life entangled with a cyborg female character, also from the series. The focus of the analysis is again on Janeway's leadership, which is portrayed as happy and flexible, capable of stepping outside rigidly defined gender roles, and also a more complete person as a fluid character. The article concludes by remarking that it is not calling for 'queer leadership' as another stereotype for gender-based ideas about leadership. Rather, its aim was to dislodge 'presuppositions and expectations at the heart of binary distinctions … so prevalent in positivist research … replacing these presuppositions with the acknowledgment that gender, identity, and leadership are constituted of many parts: body, culture, desire, experience, and relationships are some of them' (Bowring, 2004: 402–403). Further, there is no natural relationship among the parts as all are always in the process of becoming.

Our final example, from Mary Runté and Albert Mills (2004) puts another twist on motherhood and work dilemmas. Through a feminist poststructuralist critique, based on Weedon's focus on discourse via Foucault's arguments, they show how the organizational literature around work-family conflict 'serves as a powerful discourse in which work is privileged over home-life' (p. 237). They examine extant literature and arguments about the 'conflict' and notice that, while in contemporary terms we continue to act as if there is a public-private life separation, we have forgotten that such is merely a spatial separation resulting from the industrial revolution. While people's lives are not easily compartmentalized, the work-family discourse makes us believe it to be so, allowing for work-life to encroach upon family-life and concealing that family-life has become an accessory to work. That is, the 'balance' emphasized in the 'work-family conflict' literature is skewed toward benefiting work. Their analyses employ the metaphor of 'paying the toll' to examine how the discursive transit between work and family exacts this toll, who pays it and for what purposes.

Various aspects of this are highlighted, including how the discourse builds a bridge between work and family, and how speeding over the bridge in the direction of market work–as if *work* consisted of only financially remunerated activities–usually disadvantages 'working women' more than 'working men'. Yet, Runté and Mills turn the traffic in the other direction. They note that the work-family conflict discourse has focused almost exclusively on the consequences for employer, spouse, and children of mothers' engagement in the market work domain. Meanwhile, the consequences of fathers' involvement in the market work domain for employers and the family are seldom addressed and, if addressed, they usually tag on to issues in mother's market work. Thus, the dominant literature makes all problems regarding the family side of things the mother's fault.

Further, the increased emphasis on a balancing act in favour of employer's profitability, implicitly fosters creating new businesses to substitute for family work–such as the work of raising children–which almost seems to ask for parents to disconnect from their families. Thus, the family has become commodified, and such commodification extends to the lives of children, now highly formalized, structured and speeded-up, with preschoolers competing for high academic standards as a 'competitive-edge' for their future work life, a point similarly made by Williams et al. (2006).

To this effect, Runté and Mills (2004: 246) also comment that day care and schooling have become vocational domains and are 'another example of how the work sphere has colonized and dominates the family domain to such a point that the pretence that these are separate spheres is not only analytically unsound, but actively propagandistic'. They conclude by emphasizing that their analyses are not arguing for a stronger stress on the family in the work-family literature, or for a nostalgic return to the traditional family. Rather, their deconstructions provoke a rethinking of what people care about, and therefore reconsideration of how the taken for granted work-family discourse is in effect part of the creation of subjectivities that we may also want to rethink.

Examples of feminist analyses in the postmodern mode help reveal how organizational studies constructs its subject, be it leadership or work-family issues, on very shaky grounds. Notice, as well, that the deconstructive work in each case results not in alternative answers but in displacement of the argument to an undefined possibility, which nonetheless calls into question dominant understandings. As such, we are also demonstrating that no organization work is beyond feminist deconstruction as well as no feminist work is beyond the dominant organizational world we all inhabit. What else to do?

The yet to be?: Feminist analyses and the potential for social transformation in organization studies

We have discussed possibilities for research on gender in organization studies by incorporating feminist meta-theory, analyses, and research approaches. We intended to highlight how organization studies could contribute to social transformation by first calling attention to how noncritical organizational studies generally reiterates a social order that privileges a few and disadvantages many. To show how it could be otherwise, we followed three approaches to feminist epistemology and then presented examples from literature that already engages critically with organization studies through feminist lenses. In this section, we raise some additional considerations. First, we address areas where we believe the organizational literature could benefit further from incorporating feminist epistemologies, including more research in certain areas and new research in others. Second, we revisit briefly the three feminist epistemologies to discuss how they have become closer, their boundaries not as clearly drawn now, which offers additional analytical possibilities. Finally, we reflect on what it would mean for organization studies more generally to rethink the field along feminist lines and consequences of doing so.

In considering areas where organizational research on gender could benefit from feminist epistemologies, we observe that feminist standpoint analyses are almost nonexistent. That is, despite some gestures in this direction, the full standpoint argument, from recognition of the particular standpoint to the advocacy of empowerment for change, is seldom developed, which also creates additional

confusion with the commonplace use of the word 'standpoint' to imply any perspective. We also believe that, theoretically and methodologically, institutional ethnography has much to offer to standpoint analyses in organization studies and that its use should be more widely discussed.

Similarly, and perhaps surprisingly, we would encourage more feminist empiricism. Given the emphasis on empirical research in organization studies, feminist empiricism contributes, in particular, to correcting old positivist notions about evidence as separate from theoretical framing by reiterating the underdetermination of data, and by questioning the separation of facts and values and traditional assumptions about the nature of objectivity. Much of this has also been stated in post-Kuhnian science, to which feminist empiricism has contributed. In advocating feminist empiricism, we are also underscoring that the vast majority of conventional organization and management research on gender, in the US in particular, is not feminist. The mere act of addressing women's situation and/or citing a feminist theorist (Carol Gilligan is a usual choice) is not sufficient to frame research as feminist. Unfortunately, such actions often pay lip service to feminist analyses while leaving in place what feminism is trying to redress, such as when the organizational literature instrumentally deploys women's values to make 'the business case'.

Finally, and perhaps not too seriously, we are calling for a moratorium on feminist postmodern organizational research of which there is no shortage. One reason is fairly pragmatic in light of feminist concerns about the loss of strength of political intervention if there was 'no-body' on which to base a knowledge claim. In our view, the Po-Mo turn in organization studies, not only feminist, at a time when careerism in the field accelerated, contributed to depoliticizing much of the critical force of critical management studies, including feminist work. The Po-Mo focus on the 'pyrotechnics' of discursive analyses, joined with an almost competitive interest in the latest in philosophical trends, has tended to turn possibilities for social and cultural critique into a 'macho' game of duelling citations, with attention to emancipatory implications all but lost. Navigating the political implications of such a game is a difficult enterprise, as survival in the game depends on publishability. Therefore, what gets published may define much of what is written, turning into an alibi for doing 'critical but not too critical' work in the field.

The other reason is not merely a pragmatic one. Today, the subject of postmodernism – i.e., 'the western subject' – has been thoroughly deconstructed. But postmodernism via postcolonial critique brought recognition of other subjectivities – e.g., subaltern – beyond the purview of western philosophies. Postcolonial feminism has been a strong contributor to these latter interests, first in literary studies and now even stronger in its more recent social science modality of transnational feminist studies. This work partakes of critiques of western humanism from postcolonial theories, but goes beyond its discursive and historical/cultural emphasis to include materialist analyses and critiques of relationships between the west and the rest (e.g., Kim-Puri, 2005). Attention is paid, in particular, to questions of parity and justice when women and others relate worldwide, i.e., transnationally, within and beyond the nation-state, under differentiated material conditions. A focus is on new subject configurations worldwide, appearing in the intersections (plural) of gender, race, class, ethnicity, sexuality, religion, and so on. There is a dearth of research of this type in organization studies despite the fact that new subjects are constantly being produced in the interstices of contemporary activities of globalized capitalisms (e.g., new economic activities engaged in by immigrant communities and relational conditions of labour between first and third world populations, as in domestic labour).

This brings us to our second concluding point. There is rapprochement among feminist empiricism, standpoint theory, and postmodernism reflecting wider concerns in feminist studies. While differences remain, in particular regarding methodological tools, Anderson (2007/2008, forthcoming) notes that at present all three feminist epistemological projects have embraced pluralism in theoretical representations and reject a transcendent subject of knowledge viewpoint – all knowledge is situated, there is no 'view from nowhere'. At the same time, the postmodernist critique of standpoint theory and critiques from women of colour and postcolonial analyses, have instigated moves away from claiming the superiority of 'women's standpoint' toward acknowledging multiple epistemic positions, including those of subjugated men. Pluralism in standpoint epistemology is also joined at present with a pragmatic interest in solving particular problems from the perspective of contingent standpoints; for instance, discovering morally or politically significant truths for subjugated groups, which joins feminist empiricism concerns. Similarly, some feminist postmodernist theorizing has moved toward a more stable middle ground for knowledge claims, sharing the interests of standpoint and feminist empiricism, and envisioning critical theory as a constructive, not merely a deconstructive project.

What to make of all this? *Are feminist perspectives and organization studies antagonistic? Should they be?* We acknowledge that feminist research on gender is no longer unusual in organization and management studies; there are scholars who, like us, identify themselves as feminist and produce feminist work. Yet, the aims of feminism do not sit comfortably with much of organization and management scholarship. On the one hand, insofar as organization studies are framed for management rather than for people, and 'the business case' is emphasized over the case for social justice or social transformation, the more committed the field is likely to be to 'normal science' with a view of researchers as detached observers, and the more likely it will continue to serve, unreflectively, extant privileged interests rather than the interests of all. As such, our answer to the questions posed would be a definite 'yes', and for that reason we would advocate continuing and increasing feminist organization research as acts of resistance for an ongoing deconstruction of the dominant.

On the other hand, insofar as critical management studies do have a space at the organization studies and management academic 'table', and insofar as there is a possibility for a feminist organization studies to be part of it, the more likely it is that practices of capitalist and patriarchal modes of organizing will be critically examined as a matter of course, maintaining the impetus for a transformative organization studies.

Thus, our preferred but very qualified answer to the questions above is that while there are contradictory features in doing feminist organization research, there is a continued need to navigate spaces between co-optation and emancipatory possibilities when doing such work. More generally, therefore, we encourage advancing the presence of feminist epistemologies in organization and management inquiry to gain in intellectual richness and social engagement, no matter how difficult this may be. Examples in this regard from the other social sciences, as well as some natural sciences, could further guide our way. As such, our field would be enriched in its capacity for contributing to a positive transformation of our world today, and so would be its relevance for the future of our planet.

REFERENCES

Acker, J. (1990) 'Hierarchies, jobs, bodies: a theory of gendered organizations', *Gender & Society*, 4(2): 139–58.

Ahl, H. (2004) *The Scientific Reproduction of Gender Inequality: A Discourse Analysis of Research Texts on Women's Entrepreneurship*, Copenhagen: Copenhagen Business School.

Ahmed, S. (2000) 'Whose counting?', *Feminist Theory*, 1(1):97–103.

Alcoff, L. (1988) 'Cultural feminism versus post structuralism: the identity crisis in feminist theory', *Signs*, 13 (3): 405–36.

Allen, B.J. (1996) 'Feminist standpoint theory: a Black Woman's (re) view of organizational socialization', *Communication Studies*, 47(4): 257.

Anderson, E. (1995) 'Knowledge, human interests, and objectivity in feminist epistemology', *Philosophical Topics*, 23: 27–58.

Anderson, E. (2007/forthcoming 2008) 'Feminist Epistemology and Philosophy of Science', *The Stanford Encyclopedia of Philosophy* (Fall 2008 Edition), Edward N. Zalta (ed.), forthcoming URL = <http://plato.stanford.edu/archives/fall2008/entries/feminism-epistemology/>.

Barad, K. (2003) 'Posthumanist performativity: toward an understanding of how matter comes to matter', *Signs*, 28(3): 801–31.

Belkin, L. (2003) 'The opt-out revolution', *New York Times Magazine*, Available online at http://www.nytimes.com/2003/10/26/magazine/26WOMEN.html.

Benschop, Y. and Doorewaard, H. (1998) 'Six of one and half a dozen of the other: the gender subtext of Taylorism and team-based work', *Gender, Work & Organization*, 5(1): 5–18.

Boushey, H. (2005) *Are Women Opting Out? Debunking the Myth*, Washington, DC: Center for Economic and Policy Research.

Boushey, H. (2008) 'Opting out?': the effect of children on women's employment in the United States', *Feminist Economics*, 14(1): 1–36.

Bowring, Michele A. (2004) 'Resistance is not futile: liberating Captain Janeway from the masculine-feminism dualism of leadership', *Gender, Work & Organization*, 11(4): 381–405.

Brewis, J. (2001) 'Foucault, politics and organizations: (re)-constructing sexual harassment', *Gender, Work & Organization*, 8(1): 37–60.

Budig, M.J. and England, P. (2001) 'The wage penalty for motherhood', *American Sociological Review*, 66(2): 204–25.

Butler, J. (1990) *Gender Trouble: Feminism and the Subversion of Identity*, New York: Routledge.

Butler, J. (2004) *Undoing Gender*, New York: Routledge.

Calás, M.B. and Smircich, L. (1991) 'Voicing seduction to silence leadership', *Organization Studies*, 12(4): 567–602.

Calás, M.B. and Smircich, L. (1996) 'From the "Woman's point of view": feminist approaches to organization studies', in S.R. Clegg, C. Hardy and W. Nord (eds), *Handbook of Organization Studies*, London: Sage, pp. 218–57.

Calás, M.B. and Smircich, L. (2006) 'From the "Woman's point of view" ten years later: Towards a feminist Organization Studies', in S.R. Clegg, C. Hardy, T.B. Lawrence and W.R. Nord (eds) *The Sage Handbook of Organization Studies*, London: Sage, pp. 284–346.

Code, L. (1991) *What Can She Know?* Ithaca, NY: Cornell University Press.

Collins, P.H. (1990) *Black Feminist Thought*, Boston, MA: Unwin Hyman.

DeVault, M. (1991) *Feeding the Family: The Social Organization of Caring as Gendered Work*, Chicago: University of Chicago Press.

DeVault, M.L. (ed.) (2007) *People at Work: Life, Power, and Social Inclusion in the New Economy*, New York: NYU Press.

Ferree, M.M. and Martin, P.Y. (eds) (1995) *Feminist Organizations: Harvest of the New Women's Movement*, Philadelphia: Temple University Press.

Fonow, M.M. and Judith, A.C. (1991) *Beyond Methodology: Feminist Scholarship as Lived Research*, Bloomington, Indiana: Indiana University Press.

Fonow, M.M. and Judith, A.C. (2005) 'Feminist methodology: new applications in the academy and public policy', *Signs*, 30(4):2211–36.

Gherardi, S. (1995) *Gender, Symbolism and Organizational Culture*, London: Sage.

Gilligan, C. (1982) *In a Different Voice*, Cambridge, MA: Harvard University Press.

Griffith, A.I. and Smith, D.E. (2005) *Mothering for Schooling*, New York: Routledge Falmer.

Haraway, D. (1985) 'A manifesto for cyborgs: science, technology, and socialist feminism in the 1980s', *Socialist Review*, 80: 65–107.

Haraway, D. (1991) 'Situated knowledges: the science question in feminism and the privilege of partial perspective', in D. Haraway (ed.) *Simians, Cyborgs, and Women*, New York: Routledge, pp. 183–202.

Harding, S. (1987) 'Introduction: is there a feminist method?', in S. Harding (ed.), *Feminism & Methodology*, Bloomington, IN: Indiana University Press, pp. 1–14.

Harding, S. (1991) *Whose Science? Whose Knowledge?*, Ithaca: NY: Cornell University Press.

Harding, S. (1993) 'Rethinking standpoint epistemology: "What is Strong Objectivity?"', in L. Alcoff and E. Potter (eds), *Feminist Epistemologies*, New York: Routledge, pp. 49–82.

Harding, S. (1997) 'Comment on Hekman's "Truth and method: feminist standpoint theory revisited": whose standpoint needs the regimes of truth and reality,' *Signs*, 22(2): 382–91.

Harding, S. (1998) *Is Science Multicultural? Postcolonialisms, Feminisms, and Epistemologies*, Bloomington, IN: Indiana University Press.

Hausmann, R., Tyson, L.D. and Zahidi, S. (2007) *The Global Gender Gap Report*, Geneva, Switzerland: The World Economic Forum.

Hesse-Biber, S.N. (2007) *Handbook of Feminist Research: Theory and Praxis*, Thousand Oaks, CA: Sage.

Hesse-Biber S.N. and Yaiser, M.L. (2004) *Feminist Perspectives on Social Research*, New York: Oxford University Press.

Hewlett, S.A. and Luce, C.B. (2005) 'Off-ramps and on-ramps: keeping talented women on the road to success', *Harvard Business Review*, March.

Jagger, A.M. (1983) *Feminist Politics and Human Nature*, Totowa, NJ: Rowman & Allanheld.

Kark, R. and Waismel-Manor, R. (2005) 'Organizational citizenship behavior: what's gender got to do with it?', *Organization*, 12(6): 889–917.

Kim-Puri, H-J. (2005) 'Conceptualizing gender-sexuality-state-nation', *Gender & Society*, 19(2): 137–59.

Letherby, G. (2003) *Feminist Research in Theory and Practice*, Buckingham: Open University Press.

Lloyd, G. (1984) *Man of Reason: 'Male' and 'Female' in Western Philosophy*, Minneapolis, MN: University of Minnesota Press.

Longino, H. (1990) *Science as Social Knowledge*, Princeton, NJ: Princeton University Press.

Mainiero, L.A. and Sullivan, S.A. (2005) 'Kaleidoscope careers: an alternative explanation for the "opt-out" revolution', *Academy of Management Executive*, 19(1): 106–23.

Martin, J. (1990) 'Deconstructing organizational taboos: the suppression of gender conflict in organizations', *Organization Science*, 1(4): 339–59.

Martin, P.Y. (2001) 'Mobilizing masculinities: women's experiences of men at work', *Organization*, 8(4): 587–618.

McLafferty, S.L. (1995) 'Counting for women', *Professional Geographer*, 47(4): 436–42.

Misra, J., Budig, M.J. and Moller, S. (2007) 'Reconciliation policies and the effects of motherhood on employment, earnings and poverty', *Journal of Comparative Policy Analysis*, 9(2):135–55.

Mumby, D.K. and Putnam, L.L. (1992) 'The politics of emotion: a feminist reading of bounded rationality', *Academy of Management Review*, 17(3): 465–86.

Nelson, L.H. (1990) *Who Knows: From Quine to a Feminist Empiricism*, Philadelphia: Temple University Press.

Ollilainen, M. and Calasanti, T. (2007) 'Metaphors at work: maintaining the salience of gender in self-managing teams', *Gender & Society*, 21(1): 5–27.

Quine, W.V.O. (1963) 'Two Dogmas of empiricism', In *From a Logical Point of View*, New York: Harper & Row.

Rankin, J.M. and Campbell, M.L. (2006) *Managing to Nurse: Inside Canada's Health Care Reform*, Toronto: University of Toronto Press.

Reinharz, S. (1992) *Feminist Methods in Social Research*, New York: Oxford University Press.

Runté, M. and Mills, A.J. (2004) 'Paying the toll: A feminist post-structural critique of the discourse bridging work and family', *Culture and Organization*, 10(3): 237–49.

Signs (2005 Special Issue) 'New Feminist Approaches to Social Science Methodologies', Sandra Harding and Kathryn Norberg (eds), *Signs*, 30 (4).

Smith, D.E. (1987) *The Everyday World as Problematic*, Toronto: University of Toronto Press.

Smith, D.E. (2005) *Institutional Ethnography: A Sociology for People*, Lanham, MD: AltaMira.

Strassmann, D. (2008) 'Editorial: feminist economic methodologies', *Feminist Economics*, 14(2): 1–2.

Thomas, J.E. and Zimmerman, M.K. (2007) 'Feminism and profit in American hospitals: the corporate construction of women's health centers', *Gender & Society*, 21(3): 359–83.

Tong, R.P. (1998) *Feminist Thought: A More Comprehensive Introduction*, Boulder, CO: Westview.

UNIFEM (2007) *Annual Report 2006–2007*, New York: United Nations.

Weigt, J. (2006) 'Compromises to carework: the social organization of mothers' experiences in the low-wage labor market after welfare reform', *Social Problems*, 53(3): 332–51.

Williams, J., Manvell, J. and Bornstein, S. (2006) ' "Opt-out" or pushed out?: how the press covers work/family conflict. the untold story of why women leave the workplace', The Center for WorkLife Law, University of California, Hastings College of the Law.

16

Researching Work and Institutions through Ethnographic Documentaries

John S. Hassard

INTRODUCTION

The aim of this chapter – which complements the discussion of feature films in Chapter 35 – is to describe and analyse the methods and methodology of ethnographic documentary for organizational research. This is achieved predominantly through an historical appreciation of the development of styles and schools. In so doing, we note how, in the British tradition, the ethnographic documentary has been deployed to provide grounded sociological insights into the 'real world' of institutions and occupations. The dynamic of this method is one of the attempts to gain evermore direct and unmediated images of organizations and work.

The chapter adopts the following structure. Initially, we introduce the methods and methodology of ethnographic documentary in order to prepare the way for an historical review of anthropological studies of work, occupations, and organizations. Subsequently, we document how such ethnographic evidence has been realized under four main

filmic styles – the *world-of-labour film*, the *free cinema film*, the *modern television documentary*, and the *video diary/blog* – and analyse each as a case example of *cinéma vérité*, or film-truth. Finally, we discuss the representational nature of ethnographic documentary and examine the extent to which the film-truth method achieves its objective of offering privileged access to the everyday reality of work and organizations.

History and method of ethnographic documentary

In *The Cinema and Social Science*, de Heusch (1962: 13) writes, 'When Lumiere definitely established a technique and sent his cameramen all over the world, the ethnographic and sociological cinema was born'. Elsewhere Morin (1956: 14) notes how the precursors of the cinema intended to develop the cinematograph as a 'research' instrument in order to study the 'phenomena of nature'. While the ingenuity of Lumiere's techniques made it likely that the cinematograph could, potentially, become a methodologically 'objective' instrument with which to research social and organizational behaviour, Morin (1956: 15–16) notes, however, that it was not long before the 'illusionists' had taken this new type of 'microscope' away from the 'scientists' and transformed it into a 'toy', thereby reviving the 'tradition of the magic lantern and the shadow play'.

It is against this backdrop of methodological and technical development in which, as Morin suggests, the cinematograph becomes 'snatched away' from science, that we find 'cinema truth' – for Morin, one of the basic aims of early film-making – being reintroduced into the film-maker's art. Over the decades the century, documentary film-makers, in particular, have addressed the problem of how to make anthropological films more 'real' and 'truthful'. The history of ethnographic documentary filmmaking has seen a range of styles emerge in this quest. For the most part these have been subsumed under one generic title – *cinéma vérité* (film-truth).

Philosophy and method

According to its proponents, the aim of *cinéma vérité* is simply to present the 'truth'. In his *French Cinema since 1946*, Roy Armes (1966: 125), for example, argues that *cinéma vérité* offers a 'rejection of the whole aesthetic in which the art of the cinema is based. An interesting visual style and striking beautiful effects are rejected as a hindrance to the portrayal of the vital truth'.

Over the years, however, critics have pointed to confusion about the basic aims of *cinéma vérité*, and suggested that under its banner all kinds of films have been made, many of which are unrelated to the original philosophy. Debate over the value and purpose of *cinéma vérité* was particularly heated in the early 1960s, and notably around the time of the 1963 Lyon 'summit' conference on *cinéma vérité*, organized by *Radio Television Francaise* and attended by such notables of the ethnographic film as Jean Rouch, Edgar Morin, Robert Drew, Richard Leacock, Michel Brault, and Albert and David Maysles. While proponents such as Armes

heralded *cinéma vérité* as the 'true art of cinema', critics branded it as 'anti-art'. Among the critics, James Lipscombe (1964: 62), for example, argued that the term *cinéma vérité* had become used so loosely that most of the films produced in its name 'have absolutely nothing in common except celluloid'. In a similar vein, Charles Ford claimed that *cinéma vérité* was the 'biggest hoax of the century', and that 'nothing is more fabricated, more prepared, more licked into shape, than the so-called improvisation of *cinéma vérité*' (Natta, 1963, quoted in Issari and Paul, 1979). Such diversity of views has made *cinéma vérité* one of the most controversial methods in film studies, with this controversy enduring to the present day.

While we explain later how, as a philosophy and method, *cinéma vérité* ostensibly starts with Dziga Vertov's work on the concept of kino-eye in 1919, it was during the 1960s that the style became widely adopted and discussed in film-making circles. When it was adopted, it was in fact as a tribute to Vertov's work that the term *cinéma vérité* was first used in a stylistic sense, in fact to describe *Chronique d'un Été* (1962), a film collaboration between the anthropologist Jean Rouch and the sociologist Edgar Morin. According to Issari and Paul (1979: 6), such was the impact of *Chronique d'un Été* that the term 'spread like wildfire', one result being a proliferation of definitions in which *cinéma vérité*:

…acquired different names from its founders, practitioners and critics in accordance with their understanding of the style. To Jean Rouch and Edgar Morin it was *cinéma vérité*; Richard Leacock called it 'living camera'; Mario Ruspoli, the Maysles brothers, and Louis Marcorelles were amongst those who favoured 'direct cinema'. William Bleum designated the style as 'mobile camera', but William Jersey selected the term 'realistic cinema'. Italians named it 'film inquiry'. To Armondo Plebe it became 'synchronous cinema'; to Colin Young, 'cinema of common sense'; to Jean Claude Bringuier, 'cinema of behaviour'; to Norman Swallow, 'personal documentary' or 'telé-vérité'. Others dubbed it 'film journalism', 'truth film', 'direct shooting' and 'free cinema' (Issari and Paul, 1979: 7).

Of all the terms coined, however, two have proved the most enduring – *cinéma vérité* and 'direct-cinema'. Although methodologically they stem from largely similar historical roots, and while their associated films have many similarities, their proponents often testify to separate philosophies, the main difference residing in the function of the film-maker (and by extension 'film-researcher'). While the practitioner of *cinéma vérité* (in the Rouch and Morin style) deliberately intervenes, hoping that greater spontaneity and 'truth' will be stimulated by the 'subjective' participation of the film-maker in the event filmed, the 'direct' film-maker claims to take an 'objective' stance, merely standing by in the hope that a situation of anthropological or sociological interest will resolve itself in a dramatic way (see Barnouw, 1975; Nelmes, 2003).

In terms of stylistic influence, it is 'direct-cinema' that has become the exemplar for the film-truth method generally. In this style, the film-maker tries above all to avoid sociological judgement and subjectivity. The aim is to convey the phenomenology of a social situation; to film people as they live their everyday lives. The philosophy suggests that the filmmaker's role is to reveal the most essential parts of this reality, not to create a new one. The 'direct' filmmaker should dispense with those elements of method which serve to distort 'truth'; that is, with the professional 'camouflage' of conventional film-making, such as scripts, scenes, studios, actors and so forth. Films are to be made of ordinary people in real situations, the only acceptable aids being portable cameras and sound equipment. As the filmmaker is only interested in events as they naturally unfold, no direction is permitted. In the more 'pure' forms, there is no plot, no preconceived dialogue, and no questions are either posed or answered. The philosophy states that, in shooting a film, the crew's task should be confined to following subjects and filming their moments of personal drama. Decisions concerning action should rest with the subject – the filmmaker merely decides whether or not to film a particular piece of action (Issari and Paul, 1979; Nelmes, 2003).

Pioneers and schools

We have noted how a range of ethnographic documentary approaches have been subsumed under the general heading of *cinéma vérité*. We will now attempt to place structure on the development of these approaches, first, by discussing the ideas and works of two of its founders, Dziga Vertov and Robert Flaherty, and second, by describing how *cinéma vérité* has been shaped in what we will call the French, American, and British schools of ethnographic documentary. We will show how each of these schools offers a distinctive approach to ethnographic filmmaking and, especially in the British tradition, with regard to work, institutions, and occupations.

Dziga Vertov and kino-pravda

As noted, it was in the hands of the Russian film-maker Dziga Vertov (1896–1954: real name Denis Arkadievitch Kaufman) that an ethnographic documentary style based on 'film-truth' or *kino-pravda* is first developed in theory and practice (Petric, 1978). Vertov is associated with what has been termed the 'extremist theory' of the ethnographic film, the view that the cinema should rid itself, as Sadoul (1940: 172) says, 'of everything which has not been taken from life'.

In line with the prevailing philosophy of socialist realism in early Soviet film making, Vertov argued that *kino-pravda* required the nonparticipation of the filmmaker as a fundamental condition of attaining ethnographic authenticity. If the movie camera was to be an effective tool in influencing the masses, it was necessary to present realistic images of their everyday lives. Instead of staged sets, real locations would be used, in which peasants played peasants and workers played workers. If filmmaking was to become a truly proletarian art, Vertov believed its function was to portray the life of the people in all its intense and intimate detail (Lawson, 1964: 73). Given the technology available, however, Vertov was perhaps somewhat overambitious in his claims to be providing a *kino-pravda* approach for anything more than short sequences of film. In order to achieve 'truthful' images with cumbersome technology, his early films saw the use of hide-aways and telephoto lenses, as in his famous filming of a family weeping at a grave. Written in the early 1920s, at a time when filmmaking technology was in its infancy, his original ideas on the ethnographic film reflect prophecy more than practice. Vertov, however, remains the father figure of *cinéma vérité* in that his philosophies reflect the core ideas of the movement.

Robert Flaherty's Nanook of the North

The other founding father of the *cinéma vérité* documentary was the American trapper-prospector Robert Flaherty, who in 1920 and 1921 spent fifteen months making a publicity film in Hudson's Bay for the French fur company *Revillon*, a film screened in 1922 as *Nanook of the North*. In its original version, Nanook is a silent 38-minute portrait of the world of the eskimo. The story develops through scenes, which alternate between descriptions of the everyday struggle for existence and the tenderness of family life. The first American film in the *cinéma vérité* style, Nanook remains highly acclaimed and widely screened (Nelmes, 2003).

The high quality of *Nanook*, however, is often attributed to the large amount of preparatory work undertaken by Flaherty (as also with his *Man of Aran*, 1934: see Calder-Marshall, 1963). Unlike in 'purist' forms of direct observation, where subjects receive a minimal briefing, Flaherty studied Nanook and his family in detail before filming. As de Heusch (1962: 35) notes, 'Flaherty does not follow Nanook about in order to take pictures: he enters into conversation with him, he asks him to cooperate closely in the sociological portrait'. Because of the elaborate manner in which the scenes are reconstructed, the extent to which Nanook represents film-truth is obviously questionable. The well-known scene where Nanook and his family wake up in an igloo, for example, is achieved by Flaherty

removing the roof in order to have enough space and light to shoot (Winston, 1979). In Flaherty's hands, the documentary becomes 'a work of art imbued with rationality and truth' (de Heusch, 1962: 35–6). Nanook is constructed like a fictional film in which the main character acts the part of himself within the framework of a prepared story. The story is conveyed in accordance with the demands of the director.

The French School: Rouch and Morin's Chronique d'un Été

Historians of *cinéma vérité* commonly claim that the development of increasingly unobtrusive film-making technologies will bring the notion of the 'cinema eye' closer to reality (see Barnouw, 1975; Issari and Paul, 1979; Nelmes, 2003). It is claimed, for example, that a classic example of such technological progress was witnessed in the development of the 16 mm camera with portable sound equipment, notably in the work of the French anthropologist turned filmmaker Jean Rouch. Rouch is often considered the founder of ethnographic cinema, because he overcame a number of traditional filmmaking handicaps simply by using lighter technology. Synonymous with the so-called 'French School' of the ethnographic documentary film, Rouch is the figure most readily associated with the term *cinéma vérité* (Issari and Paul, 1979; Aitken, 2005).

As noted earlier, Rouch is best known for a film made in collaboration with Edgar Morin (and the French-Canadian film-maker Michel Brault) on the lives of Parisians, *Chronique d'un Été* (Chronicle of a Summer, 1961). According to Rouch, *Chronique d'un Été* was an attempt to combine 'Vertov's theory' and 'Flaherty's method' (Armes, 1966). Initially twenty-one hours long, but later cut to one hour and forty five minutes, the film begins by showing the reactions of passersby to the question, 'Are you happy?', and continues by interviewing them in detail about, for example, their likes, dislikes, hopes, and anxieties. In the final scenes, we witness the participants themselves viewing the film in a screening room, the footage describing their reactions to the interview process.

Although technically *Chronique d'un Été* benefits from the development of real-time (rather than post-synchronization) sound recording, it appears to suffer methodologically from the fact that most of its subjects appear uneasy in front of the camera. More than any other landmark documentary, *Chronique d'un Été* highlights the issue of whether the camera should be used to 'record' action or to 'stimulate' it. In hands of Rouch and Morin, the *cinéma vérité* film becomes not so much a recording of what would happen if the camera was not there, as what happens because the camera *is* there.

The American School: Drew Associates' Primary

In contrast, the American tradition of *cinéma vérité*, based on the 'direct-cinema' approach, adopts a more Cartesian orientation. The exemplar of this is found in the collaborative work of Robert Drew, Richard Leacock and colleagues (including filmmakers Albert Maysles, Donn Pennebaker, and Gregory Shuker) – or Drew Associates – and their classic documentary in the 'living-camera' style, *Primary* (1960).

Providing funds to develop sufficiently mobile 16 mm equipment, the living-camera project was commissioned by *Time-Life*, for whom Drew Associates were to make a news-film equivalent of the magazine's well known news-spreads. To this end, Drew and Leacock negotiated an agreement with Senators John F. Kennedy and Hubert Humphrey to record their political campaigns in the 1960 Winsconsin primary election. The plan was to follow the candidates and film their activities 'without intruding'. No lighting was to be used; the crew would film only what was in front of them; they would go into situations 'cold'.

By employing this method, Drew felt that not only would the facts of a situation be revealed, but also the essence or feeling. The 'living' camera would report the emotional as well as the intellectual truth. 'Internal forces' would be revealed by studying 'external forces' (Leacock, 1992). Like Vertov, Drew Associates presumed that the essence of a situation would be captured when subjects were too tired, relaxed, or involved to protect themselves from the scrutiny of observers. The film is commonly considered a break-through in that, with relatively small, quiet, and portable technology, the camera operator could now 'walk in and out of buildings, up and down stairs, film in a taxi or limousine', and all the time 'get sound and pictures as events occurred' (Leacock, 1992). Frequently screened, *Primary* is a film with a strong Vertovian flavour, in which the subject matter is treated in a largely disinterested fashion, the action following no plot other than the train of events which leads to Kennedy winning the election.

Work and institutions in the ethnographic documentary

Having described the basic philosophy and method of the ethnographic documentary, and offered a review of landmark contributions, we now offer a case account linked to researching work and organizations, that of the ethnographic description of occupations and institutions. From the 1930s to the present, and especially since the advent of television, large audiences have been found in Britain for documentary films, which centre upon the relationship between individuals and their workplaces. We document how such work has been developed under four main styles – the *world-of-labour film*, the *free cinema film*, the *modern television documentary*, and the *video diary/blog* – and discuss each as a case example.

World-of-labour films (1930s/1940s)

The origins of work-related ethnographic documentary in Britain lie in the early world-of-labour films of producer-theorist John Grierson (see Manvell, 1946; Barnouw, 1975; Beveridge, 1979; Forsyth, 1979; Aitken, 1990 and 1998; Nelmes, 2003). In his 1929 silent film on the herring industry, *Drifters*, Grierson effectively screened the first European occupational documentary. *Drifters* was revolutionary in European film-making in that for the first time the focus for large screen entertainment was nothing more exotic than the work of fishermen. In important respects, Grierson's work reflects the influence of both Vertov and Flaherty. While the Soviet style is evident in Grierson's concern for social problems, Flaherty's romantic style underpins the quest to record the heroic nature of ordinary existence (Aitken, 1990 and 1998). Holder of a doctorate in social sciences from Glasgow University, Grierson's work is driven by a concern for the ethical and sociological purpose of the documentary film. As Agel (1953: 45) notes, Grierson's aim is 'to exalt human toil and civic virtues' and above all 'to magnify the unconscious beauty of the physical effort involved in labour'.

Grierson's work subsequently influenced the social and industrial documentaries of Paul Rotha, whose work represents an early attempt to demystify the structure of British industrial society, especially the role of the state. Among Rotha's best known films are *Shipyard* (1935), concerning the construction of a ship and the reactions of the community in which the shipyard is based, and *Rising Tide* (1935, later retitled *Great Cargoes*), which deals with extensions to the Southampton docks and the interdependence of various commercial activities (see Rotha, 1967; Aitken, 1990, 1998 and 2005). In his theoretical treatise, *Documentary Film Art* (1936), Rotha explains his approach to the ethnographic film through praising Flaherty's technique and commitment, but criticizing his over-romantic and idyllic conception of a primitive struggle with nature, an image far removed from, and with little to say about, the alienating realities of the modern industrial world. Rotha's view was that serious ethnographic documentaries should focus on the social realism of industrial civilization; they should concentrate on issues that confront large masses of the world's population (Rotha, 1967). For Rotha, the idyllic documentary largely avoids any conscious, critical social analysis.

Other quality documentaries set in industrial or other work-related settings find Grierson in collaboration with Alberto Cavalcanti or Harry Watt. For example, it was Grierson who produced Cavalcanti's *Coal Face* (1936), a study of the lives of miners, while Cavalcanti in turn produced Watt's *North Sea* (1938), a study of seafarers. The latter film departs, however, from the early requirements laid down by Grierson, in that it employs actors and tells a scripted story. This was also the case with Watt's classic of the period, *Night Mail* (1936), which tells the story of the night run by the postal train between London and Glasgow, and centrally the work of postal workers receiving, sorting, and dispatching mail during the run. A collaboration with Grierson and Basil Wright, like *North Sea*, the film was produced by the esteemed Film Unit of the General Post Office (see Aitken 1998 and 2005).

Free cinema movement (1950s/1960s)

In the post-World War Two era, the British ethnographic documentary escaped from its role in creating a largely propagandist view of British society through what came to be known as the 'free cinema' movement, whose aim was to return to a more direct approach to the, notably working-class, documentary. The origins of free cinema lie in the pages of the short-lived Oxford University magazine, *Sequence* (1949–52: 14 issues). The editors of *Sequence*, Lindsay Anderson and Gavin Lambert (and later Karel Reisz), severely criticized British filmmaking for presenting a view of the nation from the perspective of the pre-1914 bourgeoisie. It was Anderson's view, in particular, that British filmmaking was devoid of critical analysis, especially regarding the class system. According to Robinson (1973: 292), the *Sequence* view was that British film-makers had characterized 'the function of the working class [as] to provide "comic relief" to the sufferings of their social superiors'.

The term 'free cinema' was first coined in February 1956 as the headline for a National Film Theatre programme of short films. The notes for the programme explain how the movement's films are 'free in the sense that their statements are entirely personal. Though their moods and subjects differ, the concern of each of them is with some aspect of life as it is lived in this country today'. The attitude is one of 'a belief in freedom, in the importance of people and in the significance of the everyday' (quoted in Robinson, 1973: 294). The *Sequence* philosophy was to show the way 'ordinary people' enact their 'everyday lives'. The objective was for these films to possess a 'feeling of freshness' in documenting the 'real environment in which people work and play' (Robinson, 1973: 294).

The classic of the Free Cinema movement is undoubtedly Anderson and Reisz's *Every Day Except Christmas* (1957), a film mainly about night workers at London's Covent Garden Market. The film begins with the image of a shed somewhere far out of London, in which a lorry is being loaded with food and flowers at the very moment when the BBC announcer is saying 'goodnight' to listeners. From every corner of the country, similar vehicles speed towards the capital and Covent Garden Market. While the lorries are unloaded, dealers prepare their stands: boxes are opened; apples are polished; workers pause for tea and a chat. A large well-dressed man gives orders; the major retailers arrive and bargain; and a small trader loads a handcart. Housewives and itinerant merchants buy after the retailers have gone; an old woman sells flowers; tramps pick up any damaged fruit. Finally, the lorries are loaded with empty packing cases and depart for the four corners of Britain.

In recording these scenes, the camera carefully studies the faces of traders, customers and the like and catches their subtle yet commonplace gestures. In so doing, *Every Day Except Christmas* achieves an ethnographic montage in which each face contributes to the sociological effect. As in much of Anderson and Reisz's work, it is the class structure of Britain that is reflected primarily in scenes which document the ebb and flow of work and rest. The philosophy leans firmly upon Vertov's theories in that the goal is to bring to the audience critical reflections on the world in which it lives.

Modern television documentary (1960s–present)

From the 1960s onwards, television replaced the short or feature length film as the main medium for disseminating ethnographic documentaries in Britain. Indeed, since *The Family* (1974) made nationally famous the Wilkins' of Reading, British television has played host to a wealth of film-truth series. The advent of mass television, however, did not alter the trend for ethnographic filmmakers to be preoccupied with understanding the nature of work, occupations, and institutions.

The 1990s, in particular, saw British audiences bombarded with *cinéma vérité* studies of work and organizations, with large audiences being found for series such as *Flying Squad* (police officers, BBC, 1990), *The Duty Men* (customs officers, BBC, 1991), *Fire* (firefighters, Thames, 1991), *D.E.A.* (drug enforcement officers, BBC, 1992), *Town Hall* (town councillors, BBC, 1992), *The Ark* (zoo keepers, BBC, 1993), *The Adventurers* (venture capitalists, BBC, 1993), *Turning the Screws* (prison officers, Channel 4, 1993), *Skipper* (trawlermen, BBC, 1993), *Coal* (coalminers, BBC, 1994), *The Factory* (factory workers and managers, Channel 4, 1995), and *When Rover Met BMW* (car workers and managers, BBC, 1996), for example.

Stylistically, British television-based ethnographic documentaries have been influenced considerably by the work of the American film-maker Frederick Wiseman, who in the mid-1960s made a series of investigations for US television into the relationships between individuals and institutions. As much as John Grierson, it has been Wiseman's technique of using documentary film for observing social relationships that has influenced a generation of high profile British *cinéma vérité* filmmakers, including Roger Graef, Nick Broomfield, Diane Tammes, Chris Oxley, and Molly Dineen.

An early expression of Wiseman's influence was found in Graef's series, *The Space Between Words* (BBC, 1972), which looked at 'communication' in five institutional settings; the family, school, work, diplomacy, and politics. The series was innovatory for British television in that it focused on 'ordinary situations' and presented the images with the minimum of introduction. Graef's idea was to 'let viewers develop their own theories of communication'. In filming the series, Graef's policy was 'never to use lights, or staged scenes, to keep the equipment out of sight, and to have the minimum of people in the room'. To remain as anonymous as possible, Graef even had a rule of 'never looking any of the subjects being filmed in the eye'. A radical venture at the time, Graef has noted, with irony, how the response of the media was to interview academics and critics in order to obtain 'professional' explanations of the issues raised by the films, a practice completely anathema to the project (Graef, 1992).

Graef is better known, however, for documentaries which examine the relationship between organizational practices and institutional politics. Examples here are his films on investment in new technology at British Steel, and the allocation of spare beds in the National Health Service. His most notorious work in this style, however, was a series documenting the lives and work of members of the Thames Valley Police Force (*Police*, 1982, with Charles Stewart). In this series, Graef wished to combine the apparent objectivity of direct-cinema methods with the analysis of contemporary social issues, which, in the case of one episode, 'A Complaint of Rape', led to widespread public debate. The *Police* series laid new ground for British ethnographic documentary in that it opened up issues which the subjects themselves were not aware of, thus instigating a self-discovery process.

During the 1990s, the institutional documentaries of Diane Tammes also reflected a direct-cinema style. In her series, *Casualty* (Channel 4, 1991), for example, an institution is described with relatively few edits or guiding commentaries. The film reflects that variant of the direct-cinema philosophy associated with the British National Film School, which suggests that the longer a sequence is allowed to run the more 'truthful' the images are likely to be. Tammes, however, has admitted to becoming 'less strict' with herself as her career as a documentary filmmaker has progressed. While she suggests her early work was 'purist', in that, 'the camera was there simply to see how people interacted', subsequent work has often involved dialogue with subjects from behind the camera. 'Truth', she argues 'is about what people actually come away with at the end of the film'. The problem is that 'everyone who makes a film is just putting their own truth on the screen' (Tammes, 1992).

An interventionist style was also evident during the 1990s in the work of Molly Dineen, and in particular her highly popular series on zookeepers, *The Ark* (BBC, 1993). Originally aiming to make 'a film about a zoo', Dineen ultimately told 'a story about a British institution undergoing radical change'. Dineen explains how, as financial problems loomed at London Zoo, it became a case of 'suits versus beards' – in other words, 'the management men and the financiers against the scientists and academics' (*The Guardian*, 1993: 53). As the crisis came to a head, she documents how problems of 'human resource' management began to take priority over 'animal' management. Consequently, her style of filmmaking became increasingly investigative, critical, and interactive, with Dineen, from behind the camera, probing to uncover the layers of political intrigue underlying, for example, decisions on redundancy and restructuring.

From the mid-1980s, a further step away from the philosophy and practice of 'objective' or 'purist' ethnographic documentary was signalled in works which actually made overt the construction of the *cinéma vérité* film. This is nowhere better represented than in works by the celebrated film-maker Nick Broomfield. When in 1990, for example, Broomfield (with Joan Churchill) made a follow up for Channel 4 of his earlier institutional film *Juvenile Liaison* (1975), he brought to the fore his own problems as a filmmaker, especially that of tracing the original participants and gaining their renewed consent. This style of focusing on what goes on behind the scenes was subsequently used by Broomfield to great effect in his film, *The Leader, The Driver and the Driver's Wife* (Channel 4, 1991) where, exploiting the off-screen drama, Broomfield documented his difficulties in trying to secure an interview with the South African right-wing politician Eugene Terreblanche, the result being a black comedy of trial and tribulation – one somewhat reminiscent of Michael Moore's attempt to hold an interview with General Motors CEO Roger Smith in *Roger and Me* (1989). This style of filmmaking could not be further removed from Broomfield's earlier work, for here the camera is anything but anonymous. Broomfield has remarked that, as his filmmaking style has 'matured', he has felt increasingly hide-bound by having to keep to a 'pure' *cinéma vérité* approach, for in the filmmaking process, 'things don't happen when they are supposed to happen'. Broomfield argues that the associations you make throughout a film are often much richer than simply documenting what happened. For Broomfield, therefore, 'the notion of objectivity is no longer tenable' in ethnographic filmmaking. By keeping the 'pretence of objectivity' and thus 'failing to share personal experiences', he argues that the audience is 'less able to evaluate your final product' (Broomfield, 1992).

Video diaries and video blogs (1990s – present)

The important film makers of the future will be amateurs (attributed to Robert Flaherty, c.1925, by Jean Rouch, 1992)

Since the mid-1990s, one of the most popular forms of television *cinéma vérité* has seen both professional film-makers and also members of the public use 8 mm video camera technology to record personal 'diaries'. It can be argued that the personal documentaries which accrue from these diaries reflect many of the ethnographic qualities the *cinéma vérité* pioneers sought in terms directness and authenticity.

In work and organizational settings, the use of the video diary form has been regularly employed in the Channel 4 series *Cutting Edge*. Films in this series frequently take the form of covert ethnographies broadcast under the title *Undercover*. An early example of a programme employing this method, one that aroused considerable media attention, was *Low Paid Work* (1993), in which former BBC film-maker Sima Ray spent three months undertaking covert observation in shops, factories, restaurants, and nursing homes throughout Lancashire. Concealing a camcorder in a shoulder bag, Ray filmed the situations she encountered as a young Asian woman in search of employment and accommodation. During the period of observation, all the jobs she managed to secure were remunerated at less than the legal minimum rate, employers showing scant regard for the law. One of the lowest paid jobs Ray obtained was, in fact, obtained through the local Job Centre, a State-run agency. Through covert observation of the relationship between employers and employees – a method that would, perhaps, today fail to gain permission from a university research ethics committee – Ray's film portrays vividly the feelings of hopelessness and depression experienced by low paid workers, in this case during a period of high unemployment. The film drew a sharp contrast between the low paid worker's struggle for existence and the luxurious lifestyles enjoyed by many employers, these contrasting images being silhouetted against a background in which the State frequently failed to prosecute employers who broke the law, and where the Government was concerned to veto European Community legislation on minimum wages.

The most ambitious British video diaries project, however, has undoubtedly been the BBC's *Video Nation* series, a television project in social anthropology and audience interactivity. Starting in 1993, the BBC has encouraged people to record their lives on video, with a subset of these video diaries being shown on television. Originally created in the Community Programme Unit for BBC 2, and founded and coproduced between 1993 and 2001 by Chris Mohr and Mandy Rose, the series initially involved a diverse group of fifty people, selected from across the UK, being trained in the use of camcorders and invited to record aspects of their everyday lives during the course of a year. The BBC team selected extracts from these recordings and presented them as short films immediately before *Newsnight*. More than 10,000 tapes were ultimately submitted to the BBC, from which approximately 1,300 films were edited and shown on television. Viewing figures were high (1 to 9 million) and led to themed series of *Video Nation* films, such as *African Shorts, Hong Kong Shorts, Coming Clean, Bitesize Britain*, and others. In 2000, BBC 2 decommissioned the series and built a website from the archive at http://www.bbc.co.uk/videonation/. As the website shows, a significant proportion of the *Video Nation* contributions concern either the relationship between people and their employment or personal commentaries on the organizations they work for. Such films often reflect extremely intimate and emotional impressions of the relationships between people, work, and organizations.

From around 2003, a Web-based continuation and expansion of video diaries has emerged in the form of video blogging or 'vlogging'. During the mid-1990s, when the *Video Nation* project was being developed, the bandwidth and processing power required to operate video online made it an extremely difficult operation for most amateurs. With the advent of greater computer and connection speeds, however, vlogging has witnessed a significant increase in popularity. For example, the Yahoo! Videoblogging Group saw its membership increase dramatically in 2005, while the most expansive video-sharing site to date, YouTube, founded in February 2005, was launched publicly between August and November 2005. In turn, the BBC launched its first official video blog in October 2006. Currently, many open source content management systems, like WordPress or Drupal, enable posting of video content, thus allowing bloggers to host and administer their own video blogging sites. Furthermore, the convergence of mobile phones with digital cameras now allows publishing of video content on the Web almost as it is recorded. While the potential of vlogging for academic research into work and organizations appears exciting and significant, in comparison to earlier forms of ethnographic filming, a formal methodological philosophy is yet to be established. However, in terms of practical impact, *The Economist* on 15 March 2008 – in a side-bar titled 'On strike, virtually' – cited examples of management being under pressure from 'virtual workforce protests' in a piece that highlighted the use of video blogging for orchestrating protest and dissent.

Ethnographic documentary, realism, and representation

It has become more difficult to think of ethnographic films as definitive representations of events, independent of the process that produced them, and ethnographic film-makers have begun to look upon their work as more tentative forays into cultural complexity [and as] parts of a continuing enquiry (MacDougal, 1978: 415).

Having described the philosophies and aims of ethnographic documentary, and also the forms it has taken in producing studies of work, institutions, and organizations, we finally examine the integrity of the approach in relation to methodological constructs of 'representation' and 'reality'.

In contrast to the philosophies of Vertov and Grierson, a key argument of recent theoretical writing on film-truth is to regard the 'truth' claims of the genre as in some way 'fictional'. In contrast to the early 'purist' assumptions of direct-cinema, which rest upon the Cartesian belief that reality enjoys an independent existence 'out there', current methodological assessments of the professional ethnographic documentary suggest that its products are in many ways as artificial as those of popular cinema. It is argued, for example, that through editing and associated processes, both genres come to contain similar elements of plot, character, situation, and event (Renov, 1986; Hall, 1991; Nicholls, 1991; Nelmes, 2003). As such, both offer cultural images, which present the viewer with challenges or dilemmas, build heightened tensions and dramatic conflicts, and ultimately terminate with resolution and closure. In sum, it is claimed that ethnographic documentaries operate with reference to a 'reality' that is constructed, one that is, above all, the product of signifying systems.

In being so constructed, we find the signification process of ethnographic documentary, like that for other fictional accounts, being subject to scrutiny over its role in (re)producing hegemony. The claim of film-truth to be accessing some privileged reality 'out there' becomes treated itself as an ideological effect (Nicholls, 1991). Acknowledging this constructed basis serves to undermine, for example, the claims to moral superiority of, for example, Vertov, Flaherty, the British world-of-labour filmmakers, and the proponents of direct-cinema. It serves also to suggest that *cinéma vérité* offers access to *a* world rather than to *the* world. While *cinéma vérité* films appear to direct us toward the world, it can be argued that they remain constructed texts, offering representations rather than replications. Such representations reflect truth claims not only of what we discover in the social world, but also of what interpretations, meanings and explanations can be assigned. The social world is made manifest through agencies of external authority, through representatives. What we experience is an historical world made available through picture windows in which social practices are telescoped, dramatized, and reconstructed.

One of the main hegemonic products of this process is our impression of encountering the *cinéma vérité* world as if it were being presented for the first time. The world made available to us is one we perceive as Newtonian and Cartesian; a world comprised of reason, realism, and common sense; a world waiting to be discovered through advances in technology. We discover that which we take to be the only thing we can discover. We are presented with a universe which fits within the framework of its representations. In this representational process, elements of style, structure, and perspective freely mix. When the filmic argument takes shape, we move beyond the factual world to that of the construction of meaning through a system of significations. In so doing, we never experience a pure correspondence between evidence and perspective, for facts become fashioned by arguments, which in turn rely on strategies and conventions for their accomplishment (Shotter, 1993).

The so-called methodological 'objectivity' of the ethnographic documentary can, therefore, be read as an ideological representation which operates in the guise of 'common-sense'. Barthes (1974) calls this institutionally enforced nature of representation the 'zero-degree style', for it adopts a posture of innocence and neutrality in the face of systems which provide the foundations upon which institutional perspectives represent themselves. The direct-cinema documentaries of, for example, Wiseman and Graef are never as neutral as they appear, for they embody a distinctive view of institutions like hospitals and prisons in a way which reflects strategies of resistance over a mechanistic and bureaucratic logic. The 'third dimension' (Lukes, 1974) of this hegemonic process is that which is accomplished without overt commentary. In ethnographic documentary, we tend to perceive only the particular arrangements of sound and image. Objectivity is constrained by decisions of what should, and should not, merit being commented upon.

In sum, these representational and ideological arguments suggest that ethnographic documentaries always present *a* truth rather than *the* truth. *Cinéma vérité* films contain authorial voice and, as such, what we experience is less the world 'reproduced' as 'represented'. This is so, 'even if the evidence they recruit bears the authenticating trace of the historical world itself' (Nicholls, 1991: 118).

CONCLUSION

I think this objective-subjective stuff is a lot of bullshit. I don't see how a film can be anything but subjective (Frederick Wiseman, quoted in Levin, 1971: 321).

As the basis for considering its potential use in organizational research, this chapter has offered description and analysis of a range of ethnographic documentary filmmaking styles. In the main, these styles have followed the early philosophies of Dziga Vertov and John Grierson in advocating a progressively 'direct' and 'natural' approach to filmmaking in which everyday events are recorded without the traditional, cinema-based props of scripts, staging, lighting, and so on. Proponents traditionally explain their development by recourse to a determinist theory in which technological innovations (e.g., mobile 16 mm technology with synchronized sound in the early 1960s and 8 mm video technology in the 1980s) provide for the capture of increasingly unobtrusive images through the eyes of a metaphoric fly-on-the-wall.

The chapter has addressed this technical and stylistic history at two main levels, research methodology and sociological analysis. For the former, film-truth may appear initially appealing to organizational research in that it appears to promise progressive reduction in levels of obtrusiveness and reactivity in the observation process. Also methodologically, *cinéma vérité* seems to offer a textual layer additional to, yet different from, those employed in traditional organizational research investigations. The suggestion is that a film record can add to the diversity and richness of data collected on, for example, work, occupations and institutions. As such, there appears potential for ethnographic documentary to contribute to a spirit of triangulation through providing more 'immediate' images than can be obtained by other research methods.

This methodological review, however, was in turn complemented by a critical sociological analysis of the relationship between 'realism and representation' in ethnographic documentary. This led to an awareness of significant shortcomings in the technological determinist argument, which underpins much of the methodological argument for *cinéma vérité*. Initially from the standpoint of method, but increasingly from that of deconstruction, it became apparent that an equally appropriate metaphor for fly-on-the-wall documentaries could be 'fly-in-the-soup'! Critical reviews of the ethnographic documentary, together with work on authority and knowledge, proved influential in directing the argument toward an appreciation of the ideologically enforced nature of representation. In the process, earlier methodological concerns with overcoming obtrusiveness became defused by discussions of the relativity of authorial presence and the ideology of 'common-sense'. Awareness of the ideological effects of *cinéma vérité* helped deconstruct many of the methodological assumptions upon which 'purist' approaches were founded. It was argued, accordingly, that *cinéma vérité* documentaries operate with reference to a reality that is essentially the product of signifying systems.

REFERENCES

Agel, H. (1953) 'Esthetique du cinema', *Positif*, 7, 45–52.

Aitken, I. (1990) *Film and Reform; John Grierson and the Documentary Film Movement*, London: Routledge.

Aitken, I. (1998) 'The Documentary Film Movement', in J Hassard and R Holliday (eds) *Organization/Representation: Work and Organizations in Popular Culture*, London: Sage.

Aitken, I. (ed.) (2005) *Encyclopedia of the Documentary Film*, London: Routledge.

Armes, R. (1966) *French Cinema Since 1946: Vol II: The Personal Style*, Amsterdam: Ellerman Harms.

Barnouw, F. (1975) *Documentary: A History of the Non-Fiction Film*, New York: Oxford University Press.

Barthes, R. (1974) *S/Z*, New York: Hill and Wang.

BBC (British Broadcasting Corporation) (1983) Arena – 'The GPO'.

Beveridge, J. (1979) *John Grierson: Film Maker*, London: Macmillan.

Broomfield, N. (1992) (interview with) 'The Late Show', BBC Television, March.

Calder-Marshall, A. (1963) *The Innocent Eye: The Life of Robert J Flaherty*, London: W H Allen.

Cameron, I. and Shivas, M. (1963) 'Interviews', *Movie*, 8: 15–22.

Flaherty, F. (1972) *The Odyssey of a Film Maker*, New York: Arno Press.

Forsyth, H. (1979) *John Grierson: A Documentary Biography*, London: Faber and Faber.

Graef, R. (1992) (interview with), 'The Late Show', *BBC Television.*

Guardian, The (1993) 'The Ark in the Storm', 17 January.

Hall, J. (1991) 'Realism as a style in cinema verite: critical analysis of primary', *Cinema Journal*, 30, 424–46.

Heusch, L. de (1962) *The Cinema and Social Science*, Paris: UNESCO.

Issari, M. and Paul, D. (1979) *What is Cinema Verite?*, Methuen, NJ: The Scarecrow Press.

Lawson, J. (1964) *Film: The Creative Process*, New York: Hill and Wang.

Leacock, R. (1992) (interview with), 'The Late Show', *BBC Television,* March.

Levin, R. (1971) *Documentary Explorations*, New York: Doubleday.

Lipscombe, J. (1964) 'Correspondence and controversy', *Film Quarterly*, 18(2): 60–8.

Lukes, S. (1974) *Power: A Radical View*, London: Macmillan.

MacDougal, D. (1978) 'Ethnographic film: failure and promise', *Annual Review of Anthropology*, 7: 402–25.

Manvell, R. (1946) *Film*, London: Macmillan.

Morin, E. (1956) *Le Cinema ou L'Homme Imaginaire*, Paris.

Natta, E. (1963) 'Pro e Contro il Cinema-verite', *Rivista del Cinematografo*, November, 415–20.

Nelmes, J. (ed.) (2003) *An Introduction to Film Studies*, London: Routedge.

Nicholls, B. (1991) *Representing Reality: Issues and Concepts in Documentary*, Bloomington, IN: Indiana University Press.

Petric, V. (1978) 'Dziga Vertov as Theorist', *Cinema Journal*, 1: 41–2.

Renov, M. (1986) 'Rethinking documentary: towards a taxonomy of mediation', *Wide Angle*, 8(3/4): 71–7.

Robinson, D. (1973) *The History of World Cinema*, New York: Doubleday.

Rollins, J. (1985) *Between Women: Domestics and Their Employers*, Philadelphia: Temple University Press.

Rotha, P. (1936) *Documentary Film Art*, London: Faber and Faber.

Rotha, P. (1967) *The Film Till Now: A Survey of World Cinema*, London: Spring Books.

Rouch, J. (1992) (interview with), 'The Late Show', *BBC Television,* March.

Sadoul, G. (1940) *Histoire d'un Art: Le Cinema*, Paris: Flammarion.

Shotter, J. (1993) *Cultural Politics of Everyday Life*, Buckingham: Open University Press.

Tammes, D. (1992) (interview with), 'The Late Show', *BBC Television,* March.

Winston, B. (1979) 'Documentary: I think we are in trouble', sight and sound', *International Film Quarterly*, 48(1): 2–7.

PART III

Strategies: Approaches to Organizational Research

Focusing on approaches to achieving research aims, illustrating links between topic, aims, strategy, analytical framework, and theoretical development, and also demonstrating the range of choice and degree of creativity as well as technical knowledge underpinning research strategies

Craving for Generality and Small-N Studies: A Wittgensteinian Approach towards the Epistemology of the Particular in Organization and Management Studies

Haridimos Tsoukas

INTRODUCTION

Small-N studies in the social sciences usually attract the question of external validity; how confident are we that findings can be applied beyond the boundary of a particular investigation? How far can one generalize from a particular ethnography or case study or even set of case studies? How unique is the phenomenon studied? To what extent can it be seen as an instance of a broader pattern of phenomena caused by general causal forces? Admittedly, the suspicion one detects towards small-N studies in post-War organization and management studies (OMS) (see Thompson, 1956–57) has been weakened over the years. Indeed, one of the most pleasing aspects of academic journal publishing today is to see hitherto bastions of positivist OMS, such as the *Academy of Management Journal*, gradually opening up to small-N studies and increasingly accepting papers with a case study or ethnographic research design (Anand et al., 2007; Maitlis, 2005; Plowman et al., 2007).

The near-fatal question 'can these particular findings be generalized?' is increasingly less being asked of small-N studies in the way it used to, mainly because we have, today, a more refined view of what generalization means. Developments in post-Kuhnian philosophy of science made us see the historical contingency of scientific claims. The Newtonian style of thinking, namely the style of thinking aiming at the 'decontextualized ideal' (Toulmin, 1990: 30–6), according to which science is the search for the universal, the general, and the timeless, has gradually given way, or at least has made room for, the 'ecological style' (Toulmin, 1990, Chapter 5), namely the style of thinking that embraces complexity by reinstating the importance of the particular, the local, and the timely. From the statistical notion of generalization, implied by the question 'can these particular findings be generalized?', we have gradually moved to notions such as 'analytical generalization' (Yin, 1994) and 'naturalistic generalization' (Stake, 2000), both novel 'conceptual combinations' (Wisniewski, 1997) invented to articulate different notions of generalization. More pragmatically, the common acknowledgement that some of the best social science has been conducted in the form of small-N studies has clearly helped to legitimate this research design.

The craving for generality has not gone away (and arguably it should not), but it has taken a different form. The core issue is how the particular and the general are related, a largely philosophical question. The dominant conception has been that the particular is subsumed by—is a manifestation of—the general. However, the opposite view that aims to reinstate the epistemic significance of the particular still suffers from a creeping Newtonianism. Our research practice may have shifted and become more accepting of small-N research designs, but our epistemology has not necessarily done so. For some scholars, small-N studies should aim at imitating the logic of large-N or experimental research designs (Yin, 1994; Eisenhardt, 1989; Eisenhardt and Graebner, 2007). For others, small-N studies, undoubtedly useful as they may be, they are rhetorically, though not necessarily epistemologically, indispensable—properly done, they provide more persuasive arguments about causal forces than cross-sectional empirical research (Siggelkow, 2007). However, if small-N studies research is to be accorded the status that, it is increasingly realized it deserves, a bolder defense for it is required. The

underlying question that needs to be tackled is that of epistemology; what is the status of the particular vis-à-vis the general? How are we to preserve the epistemic significance of the particular without losing sight of the general?

The purpose of this chapter is to advance such an epistemological defense of small-N studies, in the context of OMS, by drawing on Wittgenstein. In a nutshell, my argument is as follows.

Organizational and management research adopting small-N research designs is conducted within a space demarcated by two questions: 'What is going on here?,' and 'What is this a case of?' The first question calls for situational specificity, the second for theoretical reasoning. These questions, by being simultaneously posed, create dialogical tension and call for trade-offs. The more researchers are concerned with capturing situational uniqueness, the more descriptive they become and the more theoretically open-ended their accounts will be. By contrast, the more researchers try to situate their study within what is already known about the phenomenon of interest, in order to decide what a particular case is a case of, the more they will describe the phenomenon in terms that have already been defined in the literature. The distinctive *theoretical* contribution of small-N studies stems from seeing particular cases as opportunities for further refining our hitherto conceptualization of general processes. Particular cases share family resemblances rather than an overarching feature. Concepts are empirically underdetermined. Theorizing is an *analogical* process: small-N studies researchers notice analogies with processes described in other studies and, in an effort to account for the specificity of the *particular* case under study, they draw new distinctions and, thus, further refine what is currently known. Without the specificity of the particular case, new distinctions will not be possible. And without the aid of hitherto available conceptualizations, conceptual refinement will be limited. It is not so much analytical generalization that small-N studies aid, as *analytical refinement* (or *heuristic generalization*). By doing so, the craving for generality is not the craving for subsuming particular instances under general laws or mechanisms, but the craving for a clearer view—higher elucidation. The analytical refinement achieved does provide general concepts, which, however, are inherently open-ended—generalizations are heuristic. They aid generic understanding without annihilating the epistemic significance of the particular.

The chapter is organized as follows. In the next section, Wittgenstein's view of generic concepts and particular cases is described. Wittgenstein, it is argued, shows us a way to preserve the epistemic significance of the particular without losing sight of the general. This is followed by an application of relevant Wittgensteinian ideas to small-N studies, drawing in particular on the work of Lakoff (1987), which highlights the radial structure of concepts. Next, a description, along with an assessment, of the different ways for achieving generalizability in small-N studies is offered. Four overlapping approaches are briefly described: the experimental method logic, causal mechanisms, critical realism, and analytical generalization. None of these is found adequate, mainly because they underestimate the epistemic significance of the particular. In the penultimate section, an epistemology of the particular is sketched and the case for analytical refinement (or heuristic generalization) is made, followed finally by the conclusions. Throughout the paper several examples from organizational and management studies research are used to illustrate aspects of the argument.

Generic concepts and particular cases: A Wittgensteinian view

In *The Blue and Brown Books*, Wittgenstein (1969: 17) condemns what he calls the 'craving for generality' and 'the contemptuous attitude towards the particular case,' whereby an analytical definition of a concept aims at articulating what is common in all its empirical instances. His view is different. Elaborating his notion of

'language games,' for example, Wittgenstein persistently refrains from saying what a language game *is*. His imaginary interlocutor is unhappy. 'You take the easy way out!,' he complains. 'You talk about all sorts of language-games, but have nowhere said what the essence of a language-game, and hence of language, is: what is common to all these activities, and what makes them into language or parts of language' (Wittgenstein, 1958: 64). Wittgenstein readily concedes: 'And this is true,' he says. 'Instead of producing something common to all that we call language, I am saying that these phenomena have no one thing in common which makes us see the same word for all, but that they are *related* to one another in many different ways. And it is because of this relationship, or these relationships, that we call them all 'language' (Wittgenstein, 1958: 65).

Take the concept of 'game'. All sorts of different games may be described by it: card games, athletic games, board games, etc. Do they all have something in common? If we *look* at games, as opposed to thinking about them, we will see that they are not united by a single defining feature, but rather they have lots of overlapping similarities in common, just like members of a family share similarities in terms of facial features, bodily build, eye color, and so on. Games are like a family; the similarities they have are 'family resemblances' (Wittgenstein, 1958: 67). What holds the concept of 'games' together is not an overarching feature, a single thread running through them all, but an overlapping set of different fibres, as in a rope (Wittgenstein, 1958: 67). To put it more formally, no analytic definition of 'games' may be given in terms of necessary and sufficient conditions (Glock, 1996: 121).

The craving for generality makes us treat the concepts we use first, as if they were tightly bounded, and second, as general pictures of the specific phenomena at hand containing all that is common in them. The particular is thought to be merely a manifestation of the general, just like particular leaves are thought to make up the general term 'leaf'

(Wittgenstein, 1969: 19). By extension, theory is seen as a conceptual map—a specification of concepts and their relationships—that abstracts the workings of an empirical phenomenon in such a way that it is revealed what is really going on. Theory digs out what we did not know was going on; it reveals a reality behind the scenes, as it were. Theory is like a calculus; concepts are precisely defined and related and, ideally, any empirical phenomenon is explained by the operation of the theoretical calculus.

A late Wittgensteinian view of theory does not deny the value of concepts but sees their functioning differently. When we are initiated into particular forms of life and language games, we are initiated into the use of concepts such as 'promise,' 'diagnosis,' 'professionalism,' 'service,' and so on. But such a use has not been taught us by strict rules; it has rather been taught in the context of social practices in which we have been *practically* shown to make certain distinctions, use certain tools, and utter certain words in certain circumstances. Thus, when we are asked to specify the concepts and the rules we use them with, we are unable to do so.

While we are free to draw boundaries around concepts, boundaries 'will never entirely coincide with the actual usage, as this usage has no sharp boundary' (Wittgenstein, 1969: 19). 'We are unable clearly to circumscribe the concepts we use; not because we don't know their real definition, but because there is no real "definition" to them. To suppose that there *must* be would be like supposing that whenever children play with a ball they play a game according to strict rules' (Wittgenstein, 1969: 25). In other words, the usage of concepts is partly bounded and partly open-ended. Through usage, we necessarily revise concepts—'extend' their reach (Wittgenstein, 1958: 67–8) and redraw their blurred boundaries. Concrete cases help us better understand the use of general concepts. Particular cases are opportunities for potentially extending our hitherto understandings of a phenomenon at hand. The particular is not subsumed into the general; it rather further specifies the general.

As mentioned above, we understand general concepts because we have been taught to *use* them in particular cases, although we find it difficult to define them. Definition, however, is not a precondition for concept use. On the contrary, we first *use* concepts and then reflect on them. 'But if the concept "game" is uncircumscribed like that, you don't really know what you mean by a "game",' asks Wittgenstein's incredulous interlocutor. Wittgenstein does not reply by resorting to a formal argument, but through appealing to common sense, that is to say, to the way we *use* ordinary language; 'When I give the description: "The ground was quite covered with plants"—do you want to say I don't know what I am talking about until I can give a definition of a plant?' (Wittgenstein, 1958: 70). I may not be able to define a 'plant' but I know perfectly well, what I mean by the statement, 'The ground was quite covered with plants'. We use language in an intelligible manner even when we are unable to define some of the concepts we employ. Our definitional difficulty with the concept 'game' makes it open-ended and susceptible to further specification.

And if I am asked by someone to explain what a 'game' is, how can I do it? 'I imagine that we should describe *games* to him,' notes Wittgenstein, 'and we might add: This *and similar things* are called "games." Do we know more about 'games,' although we may not be able to explain precisely the concept to our questioner?' No, it is not a question of ignorance, remarks Wittgenstein (1958: 69): 'We do not know the boundaries because none have been drawn' or, to be more precise, because there are no clear boundaries and, whatever boundaries there are, they have been drawn for a special purpose, and may thus be re-drawn for another purpose. It is our 'primitive' capacity to see similarities rather than grasping a transcendent pattern and applying it in particular circumstances that enables us to both grasp and teach the concept of a 'game.' 'Being able to see that one activity is similar to another and is, therefore, a game is not something that stands in need of further analysis. It is primitive. There is no reason behind our use of words for classifying something as a game. The reason lies in our seeing similarities. We cite examples and, as we become competent with the concept, we learn to see activities as similar. We see one activity as another and call it a game. But the seeing of the similarity cannot be underpinned by an explicit rule, there is none. Seeing the similarity is primitive' (Luntley, 2003: 81).

Particular cases and general concepts in small-N studies

What has the preceding Wittgensteinian view of concepts and their instantiations to do with small-N studies? Put it this way; one of the traditional criticisms against small-N studies is that they fail to *generalize*, namely that the claims they make are drawn from a limited sample and are not, therefore, representative. By implication, such claims are not generalizable to a broader population. Such a view rests on a statistical view of generalization; we can make inferences from case material, provided the cases at hand are representative instances of a general population. That is the reason why, from such a perspective, every effort is made to break an empirical phenomenon into its analytical components and their relationships, and rigorously define and operationalize them in order to be able to verify the frequency of their occurrence in a representative sample drawn from a population. Since small-N studies are, usually, case studies and ethnographies, a statistical view of generalization is clearly not applicable. Case studies are selected primarily because they are genuinely interesting, novel, poorly understood, rare, deviant, unique, and/or easily accessible (Siggelkow, 2007). Often, their richness preserves the contextual background, the temporality of events, and actors' perspectives (Weick, 2007).

If what constitutes a 'case of something' is seen through the lens of the classical theory of categories, we would expect a case to have all the properties of the category it belongs

to. To call, say, the organizational form of McDonald's a case of the process of 'rationalization,' would presuppose that the concept 'rationalization' is exhaustively defined and we look for instances of it so that when a particular organization such as McDonald's has all the relevant features, it is seen as an instance of the concept. However, if we take Wittgenstein seriously, this is impossible. Like 'games,' 'rationalization' has no fixed boundaries—it is not bounded in any natural way. It rather consists of multiple instances, all of which form relationships of family resemblance, namely instances are similar to one another in a wide variety of ways and not through a well-defined collection of common properties. Moreover, some of those instances are more central than others—they are more representative (more typical—prototypical) of the concept than others (Lakoff, 1987). The organization of an industrial plant or an administrative bureaucracy is more typical of 'rationalization' than is the organization of a consulting firm or a university.

The history of the concept is a useful guide in the research on 'rationalization.' The study of rationalized institutions shows the precursors to McDonald's and McDonaldization to be Weber's bureaucracy, Taylor's scientific management, and Ford's assembly line (Ritzer, 1993 and 1998), all of which constitute the prototypical cases of rationalization. McDonaldization, through its emphasis on efficiency, predictability, calculability, and control, extends and further develops the process of rationalization. The nonprototypical case at hand (e.g., McDonald's) is *similar* to the prototypical cases of rationalization, and it is our ability to spot similarities between the nonprototypical and prototypical cases that enables us to include McDonald's under the concept of rationalization. By doing so, through the study of fast-food restaurants, shopping malls, and credit card organizations, all of which are associated with the consumer orientation of late modern capitalism, we *revise* the concept of rationalization—introduce new distinctions (emotional labor, panoptic forms of control, and ironic forms of resistance) and thus extend its boundaries.

Particular cases, such as fast-food restaurants, developed at certain moments of historical time, help us to extend our hitherto understanding of rationalization. The particular case—McDonald's—is not merely subsumed into the generic notion of rationalization; it further specifies it.

Let me put it in a different way. Commenting on family resemblances among kinds of number, Wittgenstein asks: 'Why do we call something a 'number'?' And he replies: 'Well, perhaps because it has a—direct—relationship with several things that have hitherto been called a number; and this can be said to give it an indirect relationship to other things we call the same. And we extend our concept of number as in spinning a thread we twist fibre on fibre. Moreover, the strength of the thread does not reside in the fact that some one fibre runs through its whole thread, but in the overlapping of many fibres' (Wittgenstein, 1958: 67). It is because we see a *similarity* between the organization of fast-food restaurants (a phenomenon of relatively recent origins, around the mid-1950s) and industrial factories and state administration (phenomena much older, originating the nineteenth century, which provided the prototypical core of 'rationalization') that we are able to regard the former as having a family-resemblances relation to the latter, namely as being a nonprototypical member of 'rationalization.' By so doing, we further extend our understanding of 'rationalization,' and thus redraw its boundaries. Particular cases help further to specify generic concepts. To the extent this happens, accumulation of knowledge becomes possible.

How are generic concepts further specified? As researchers of formal organization, we have been *practically* shown in our scholarly communities, namely we have been shown through the study of concrete examples in our academic social practices (Tsoukas, 2005: 324–5), to recognize prototypical 'bureaucratic' forms of organization and prototypical processes of 'rationalization.' Through the further empirical investigation of nonprototypical instances of those concepts we potentially extend their reach. The radial

structure of concepts, namely that concepts consist of a historically established core that includes prototypical members and 'belt-on' nonprototypical members that bear family resemblances to the core (Lakoff, 1987), gives epistemological significance to particular cases, since the latter are seen as occasions for *further* specifying concepts. As an early student of sociological method and strong proponent of the use of qualitative methods, Florian Znaniecki (1934: 250), put it:

> [O]f course the inductive scientist continuously goes on investigating objects or processes already defined and classified even though he does not doubt the validity of his former definition, for there is always something to learn about individual data: concrete reality [...] is an inexhaustible source of new knowledge.

Concrete reality is an inexhaustible source of new knowledge, because the boundaries we draw around concepts are necessarily limited, malleable, and derive from concrete examples in historical time. The more we look for concrete data, especially idiosyncratic data which provide nonprototypical members of the conceptual categories implicated in our investigation, the more likely it is that we will be compelled to revise (to a smaller or larger extent) the boundaries we have hitherto drawn around concepts, in order to accommodate the new data. The more interesting the new data are, namely the more nonprototypical cases we investigate, the more likely it is that they will make us *re*-think what we know (Benbya and McKelvey, 2007). In that sense, the strategic selection of cases, namely choosing data that have the potential to surprise us, is conducive to extending what we already know (Flyvbjerg, 2004: 395–8). Idiographic data are epistemologically significant to the extent that we regard our concepts as radially structured and, therefore, malleable and underdetermined.

Achieving generalizability in small-N studies: An assessment

Efforts to achieve generalizability in small-N studies can be classified in four overlapping approaches: the experimental method logic, causal mechanisms, critical realism, and analytical generalizations.

Experimental method logic

An attempt to overcome the problems of generalizability associated with small-N studies has been to apply Mill's (2002) 'method of agreement' and 'method of difference.' We may call both of them the 'method of covariance' (see Nichols, 1986; Lieberson, 1991 and 1994; Savolainen, 1994). The method of agreement starts with a common outcome in two or more cases, which is explained in terms of an independent variable that is constant across cases, whereas all the other variables vary. The method of difference deals with situations in which the outcome is not the same across cases; the outcome is explained in terms of an independent variable that is perfectly correlated with the dependent variable (namely, it varies in a way that is causally efficacious on the outcomes), whereas all other independent variables remain constant. This is possibly the most widely used method in qualitative comparative organizational research. For example, Burns and Stalker (1961) explored the causal antecedents of mechanistic and organic organizational structures. Woodward (1981) studied how different types of production technology impact upon organizational structure. Lawrence and Lorsch (1986) studied the overall orientation and structure of three different departments in ten corporations operating in different environments.

Mill's methods utilize the logic of the experimental method in emphasizing the controlled comparison of cases, and are grounded on a Humean understanding of causality as regularity of association. However, as Mill himself was clearly aware and pointed out accordingly, the covariance method faces serious obstacles in the investigation of social phenomena.

First, social phenomena, being open-ended and language-dependent, are hardly ever sufficiently similar to be included in a controlled comparison of cases. As Winch (1958: 108) notes, several religions use water in their rites of faith, but an act of Christian baptism is essentially different from a similar pagan act, despite their surface similarities— practices derive their meaning from the contexts and ways of life in which they are embedded.

Second, experimental control is a large-N method, because it is assumed that most causal relations are probabilistic, and therefore require repeated tests, which are not possible in small-N studies (Steinberg, 2007: 192).

Third, the covariance method does not take into account *interaction effects*, namely that the influence of each independent variable on the dependent variable is affected by the level of other independent variables (Lieberson, 1991: 312–3). In other words, most social phenomena have complex multiple determinants rather than single independent variables. If independent variables interact, it means that the influence of a particular independent variable upon an outcome may be ascertained only through experimental or statistical controls (George and McKeown, 1985: 27; Lieberson, 1991: 309 and pp.312–3).

Causal mechanisms

The second major attempt to overcome the problems of generalizability associated with small-N studies is the delineation of causal mechanisms that bring about the outcomes under investigation. Hedström (2005), one of the major proponents of this view, describes the mechanistic approach as follows:

> The core idea behind the mechanism approach is that we explain not by evoking universal laws, or by identifying statistically relevant factors, but by specifying mechanisms that show how phenomena are brought about. [...] A social mechanism, as here defined, describes a constellation of entities and activities that are organized such that they *regularly* bring about a particular type of outcome. We explain an observed phenomenon by referring to the social mechanism by which such phenomena are *regularly* brought about' (Hedström, 2005: 24–5, emphasis added).

Mechanists argue that covering-law explanations do not explain, since they merely register correlations and constant conjunctions of events, rather than showing the processes (to be precise, the events and activities) that bring about those correlations and conjunctions in the first place. Mechanists argue that such events and activities must be sought in social interaction, namely in individuals interacting over time. Mechanists are, usually, methodological individualists; they postulate that the core entities involved in the explanation of social-level phenomena are individuals along with their actions, which constitute the core activities. Further down the explanatory ladder, the core entities postulated in individual-level explanations are actors' beliefs, desires, and opportunities. For mechanists, statistical explanations do not really explain, since 'a statistical analysis is a *test* of an explanation, not the explanation itself' (Hedström, 2005: 23). The question still remains, what is the mechanism that brings about a statistical regularity?

Promising though a mechanism-based explanation may be, it has limitations insofar as it aspires to offer generalized explanations. The problem is that macrolevel regularities may be realized through a variety of underlying mechanisms (Sawyer, 2004). A mechanism to explain the rise of youth unemployment in Stockholm, for example, to take an example used by Hedström (2005: 119–42), would not necessarily explain the rise of youth unemployment in other cities; the realizing mechanisms may be different. Even a mechanistic explanation cannot avoid the problem of accounting for regularity since the extent to which a particular mechanism *regularly* brings about the phenomenon to be explained is still an unresolved issue. As Sawyer (2007: 260) notes, 'in the future, the debate will turn on how generalizable a given mechanistic explanation is: exactly what is the nature of the relationship between a mechanistic explanation of one observed case, and more general macrolevel regularities.'

Critical realism

A third attempt to overcome the problem of generalizability associated with small-N

studies is the causal powers approach suggested by critical realists (Ackroyd and Fleetwood, 2000; Tsoukas, 1989 and 1994; see Reed and Ackroyd, Chapters 25 and 31, respectively, this volume). Here, generality is seen not as a feature of the empirical domain (namely, how often something happens) but as a property of the necessary relations in structures operating in the real domain. Critical realists argue that, ontologically, the world consists of real, complex structures that exist independently of our knowledge of them. Causal powers reside in structures and constitute their necessary ways of acting. Causal powers endure even when they are not acting and they act even when the consequences of their acting are not realized, due to countervailing causal powers or contingencies. Causal powers operate as tendencies whose activation, as well the effects of their activation, are contingent. Case studies and idiographic research in general, have external validity, namely they are generalizable insofar as they are concerned with the explication of the causal powers which are at work and which, only contingently, are capable of producing the observed phenomena (Tsoukas, 1989).

Although realists and mechanists posit the operation of mechanisms at work to account for empirical phenomena, they differ in terms of their ontological commitments. Insisting on the ontological primacy of structures over and above individuals, realists are methodological collectivists, whereas, as already noted, mechanists tend to be methodological individualists.

Analytical generalization

A fourth approach towards achieving generalization in small-N studies has been offered by those researchers who argue for the value of 'analytical generalization' (Yin, 1994: 36–7) or 'analytical induction' or 'causal inference' (Mitchell, 1983: 200–1) or 'theoretical inference' (Williams, 2000: 216). For Yin (1994: 36), 'in analytical generalization, the investigator is striving to generalize a particular set of results to some broader theory.' In analytical generalization, the researcher aims at clarifying the theoretically necessary links between two or more characteristics of the phenomenon at hand in terms of a broader theoretical scheme. Insofar as the analysis is sound, it is inferred that the logical links established in one case will be present in other cases too. For example, from Goffman (1961) we have learned about the importance of personal territory control by inmates in asylums as a form of total institution. Insofar as this is a behavior that has been postulated to be a theoretically necessary feature of total asylums, we would expect it to hold widely, although its precise form may vary.

Similarly, Weick and Roberts (1993) developed the notion of collective mind in order to explain the organizational performance of high reliability organizations (HRO). Drawing on their own as well as on earlier case-based empirical research on a US aircraft carrier, Weick and Roberts argue that in an HRO, individuals contribute their actions while envisaging a system of joint actions (representation) and interrelate their actions with the system that is envisaged (subordination). In other words, the authors postulate theoretically necessary links between contribution, representation, and subordination to explain effective group performance. Their argument draws on Ryle's (2000) conceptualization of mind as a disposition to act in a certain manner, and Asch's (1952) properties of group performance.

Following Yin's argument, the small-N study of Weick and Roberts is an instance of analytical generalization; the links between group performance and high reliability have been made in terms of how heedfully the activities of each group member, namely the activities of contributing, representing, and subordinating, are interrelated. The more heedful the pattern of interrelations, the more developed the collective mind and the higher the organizational ability to cope with unexpected events. These conceptual links, forged in the empirical study of a particular aircraft carrier, are inferred to hold true in other cases in which group behavior is a strong determinant of high organizational reliability.

Notice that, in analytical generalization, what matters is the 'cogency of theoretical reasoning' (Mitchell, 1983: 207). Whereas statistical (or enumerative) generalization works by extrapolating surface relationships to a broader population, analytical generalization specifies theoretically necessary relations (such as those specified by Weick and Roberts) which, insofar as they are shown to be necessary, are presumed to hold in other similar cases (Gobo, 2004: 422). As Znaniecki (1934: 250–1) eloquently remarks:

> While both forms of induction tend to reach general and abstract truths concerning particular and concrete data, enumerative induction abstracts by generalization, whereas analytical induction generalizes by abstracting. The former looks in many cases for characters that are similar and abstracts them conceptually because of their generality, presuming that they must be essential to each particular case; the latter abstracts from the given concrete case characters that are essential to it and generalizes them, presuming that insofar as essential, they must be similar in many cases.

Towards the epistemology of the particular: The case for analytical refinement

Despite the redefinition of generalization as abstraction (rather than enumeration, which has been the hitherto dominant view) by proponents of critical realism and analytical generalization, the inductive inference question remains; how confident can we be that the theoretically salient features of a particular case hold in other cases too? Or, to put it differently; how can one be sure that another case, similar though it may appear to be to the one that has already been studied is, indeed, a case of the same phenomenon? After all, it can plausibly be argued that organization theorists (and social scientists at large) do not simply offer mere descriptions of particular phenomena; they rather presume that the cases they study are indicative of some *general* features of the world (Williams, 2000: 219). Or, to put it differently, they assume that some general forces operating in the world take a particular form in a particular case (Walton, 1992: 121).

For example, Mintzberg's (1973) classic study of managerial work is not just a study of the daily routines of five individuals who simply occupy managerial posts; it claims to be a study of what managers do—it elucidates some *general* features of managerial roles and tasks (in Mintzberg's terms 'the *nature* of managerial work'). The same applies to Orr's (1996) ethnographic study of photocopier technicians, Feldman's (2000) case study of organizational routines in a US university, the study of flute makers by Cook and Yanow (1996), and Buchanan's (1999) study of a single manager's political behavior in the process of organizational change. All such case studies inevitably make broader claims concerning, respectively, the way technical specialists carry out their work within a formal organizational context; the way organizational routines are enacted; the development, maintenance, and perpetuation of organizational culture in a craft company; and the logic of managerial political action. All of these studies, by offering thick descriptions of the respective phenomena at hand, reveal generic processes operating in a microcosm. Although they are not representative samples of broader populations, they nonetheless are reflections of larger phenomena (Gerring, 2006: 709).

Insofar as this is the case, case study researchers will inevitably be asked: 'To what extent does this hold in other cases?' Note, however, that this is an enumerative question, which cannot be answered with a small-N research design. It cannot be known, through a small-N research design, to what extent, say, 'the logic of political action' also holds in other change management situations, similar to the one Buchanan studied. Moreover, and this is crucial, the very formulation of the question is problematic. The 'logic of political action' is not cast in stone; it is not something given—defined once and for all—so that all we have to do is merely look for the frequency of its appearance in different settings. We recognize managerial

'political' activity when we see it, but cannot exhaustively define it. What holds 'the logic of political action' together is not an overarching feature but overlapping similarities—family resemblances.

Particular instances that we, prima facie, regard to be prototypical members of 'managerial political action,' such as the use of covert and power-based means to realize certain self-serving ends, furnish the intersubjectively recognizable core of this concept. Nonprototypical instances identified by Buchanan (1999) such as, for example, the covert use of power to advance organizational (as well as individual) ends and protect one's professional reputation, provide occasions for further extending the concept. Indeed, what Buchanan has done is to have used his study of a single manager to offer a *re*conceptualization of organizational political behavior in the context of change implementation to include new distinctions, such as the often necessary, rational and defensible-in-context, covert use of power to advance *collective* ends. This is a new distinction.

Alternative notions of generalizability in organization and social studies (that is, notions other than statistical generalization) do not hold up particularly well. Problems with the generalizing capability of 'mechanisms' have already been mentioned. The argument advanced by critical realists and supporters of analytical generalization alike, namely that, from the perspective of small-N research design, generalization is synonymous with abstraction, while partly true, does not go far enough insofar as it collapses empirical research with theoretical reasoning. This argument is couched from within the epistemology of the general; because empirical research is implicitly seen in primarily quasi-enumerative terms, and given that critical realists and analytical generalizers justifiably want to get away from it, they opt to formulate their support for generalization in terms of abstraction—the theoretical (the general) is given priority over the empirical (the particular). It is as if they say, 'we do not know whether the theoretical links we postulate in this particular case hold true in other cases; please judge our argument in terms of its theoretical persuasiveness.' What such an argument misses is the *epistemic* role of the empirical as a precondition for the development of the theoretical. A more rounded view would highlight both poles of the loop; the empirical as a precondition for the development of the theoretical, and the theoretical as an indispensable tool for the exploration of the empirical. It is the *dialogicality* between the theoretical and the empirical that is crucial which, however, tends to be underestimated by those elevating abstraction as the yardstick for the assessment of small-N research findings. To appreciate the contribution of the concretely empirical for the development of the abstractly general, one needs to grasp the epistemic significance of the concretely empirical, which cannot be done within the epistemology of the general that is motivated by the Newtonian ideal.

The defense of 'analytical generalization' in particular, the most widespread epistemological justification of small-N research designs in OMS, by its supporters, has been particularly problematic. What does it means 'to generalize a particular set of results to some broader theory' (Yin, 1994: 36)? Yin, the main proponent of this view, adopts the 'replication logic,' namely that a theory should be tested through replication of the findings in more than one setting. But then, the replication logic is not really different from a quasi-enumerative view of generalization; the more empirical studies we have, the more we can have faith in the findings. To liken the replication logic with the experimental logic as Yin does is of doubtful effectiveness; social theories are not simply refuted or confirmed through experiments. The logic of experiments presupposes that we can create a closed system in which all other variables, except for those of critical interest, are held constant. In social life, given the language-dependent character of social systems, this is hardly ever possible. Meanings both vary across contexts and change due to actors' reflexivity (Tsoukas and Knudsen, 2002). Moreover, the replication logic applied in the social sciences suffers from all the weaknesses that the covariance method does, namely the inability to take into account interaction effects and stochastic processes. The experimental logic is a large-N method, because 'experimental scientists recognize that most causal relations of interest are probabilistic and therefore require repeated tests' (Steinberg, 2007: 192).

Small-N research is better justified if the second half in the distinction 'statistical' vs. 'analytical/theoretical generalization' is dropped, and replaced by 'analytical refinement.' Simply put, small-N studies are not so much designed to offer analytical generalization as analytical refinement. Or, if the language of generalization must be maintained, small-N studies offer *heuristic generalization*: opportunities for refining our analytical understanding of certain phenomena, namely opportunities for making more incisive distinctions than hitherto available. Conceptual frameworks generated from small-N research are *generalizations* insofar as they abstract from concrete data and are related to them in a type-token relationship. However, they are *heuristic* generalizations insofar as concepts are empirically underdetermined, with nonprototypical tokens offering occasions for extending the radius of application of concepts. Heuristic generalizations are guides towards a better understanding of organizational and social life, while remaining open to change through their encounter with nonprototypical cases— they are self-designing maps, so to speak. Heuristic generalizations are more than just limited (due to the logical problem of inductive inference and the ontological problem of categorical inequivalence as Williams, 2000: 219 points out); crucially, they are *open-ended*. Even within the same horizon of meaning in a social system—within the same symbolic order—there are nonprototypical cases, which call for the revision of concepts.

Small-N studies, being usually rich in thick descriptions, make it possible not only to think concretely *about* what Geertz (1973: 23) called 'mega-concepts,' such as 'modernization,' legitimacy,' 'conflict,' and 'structure,' but more importantly to think 'creatively and imaginatively *with* them' (Geertz, 1973: 23). To think *about* a concept is to seek to capture all its empirical manifestations, to treat particular instances as being uniform instantiations of an underlying reality, which all share the same features. By contrast, to think creatively *with* a concept is to look for the family resemblances suggested by it and heuristically search for the manifold similarities as well as differences among the empirical phenomena indicated by the concept. On this account, concepts point at things, and are thus malleable. Every new empirical exploration is seen as potentially further specifying what is already known. On the traditional account, by contrast, concepts exhaustively define the way things are and are thus stable.

For example, Orr's study made us see, among other things, the importance of story-telling among front-line employees for organizational learning and collective identity. Feldman's study drew our attention to the malleability of organizational routines. Buchanan's study showed that political behavior on the part of managers is neither necessarily irrational nor self-serving, but an essential feature of managers concerned with being both effective change agents and maintaining their professional reputation. Such small-N studies refine what we already know about the respective phenomena of interest by further specifying the generic concepts they employ. Each empirical study is not aimed at confirming or refuting a particular theory but at further refining it. By doing so, such studies refine the terms of the debate and sensitize us to seeing new aspects of, namely, making ever finer distinctions in, the phenomenon at hand. Just like Geertz argued for anthropology more than three decades ago, the epistemology of the particular to which small-N studies are committed, 'is marked less by a perfection of consensus than by a refinement of debate. What gets better is the precision with which we vex each other' (Geertz, 1973: 29).

Several workplace studies since the 1930s have focused on informal groups in organizations, but they tended to see them as organizationally dysfunctional. Orr's detailed ethnography, however, made us see the organizational importance of knowledge held by technicians, the narrative mode through which it circulated in technicians' lifeworld, and the necessary improvisation, which technicians must undertake for their knowledge to become organizationally useful. Through the refined vocabulary of 'improvisation,' 'narrative knowledge,' and 'communities of practice,' Orr gave us a more refined understanding of what is going on in the workplace. The challenge for similar studies in future is not simply to confirm or to refute those insights as to elaborate further distinctions, which make us see things we could not see before. It is not analytical generalization that is at work here but conceptual and perceptual elucidation.

In small-N studies, researchers begin with a sense of bewilderment as to what is going on but they do not enter the field 'intellectually empty-handed' (Geertz, 1973: 27). On the contrary, the researcher is sensitized by prior studies and relevant concepts are adopted from earlier research (Weick, 2007: 16). Buchanan (1999), for example, was not the first to study managerial politics at work and his empirical exploration of a single manager was self-consciously guided by earlier notions of political behavior as being oriented towards self-serving outcomes, covert, devious and power-based means, and unsanctioned. But a theoretically-minded small-N studies researcher will sooner or later confront the questions, 'what is really going on here?,' 'what more general process may be responsible for the phenomenon at hand?,' and 'what is it a case of?' (Weick, 2007: 16).

Prior concepts may be too limited or unproductive or insufficiently revealing to account for what is going on in a particular case. The task of the researcher is precisely to make the argument for the case in hand, namely to demonstrate that the phenomenon investigated is a case of some larger forces that take a particular shape and give results in a particular setting. Theorizing, on this view, is an *analogical* process; researchers develop theories by, initially, seeing analogies with processes described in other similar cases and, later, since all analogies are partly inexact, reformulating the case in hand so that it either *re*specifies what is currently known or fashions a new perspective to make sense of the puzzling phenomenon (Walton, 1992: 126–35). For example, whereas Roethlisberger and Dickson (1939) saw informal work-group norms as an attempt by workers to control the production process, Burawoy (1979) saw them as helping to manufacture workers' consent in the interest of the bosses. Similarly, whereas Orr (1996) saw technicians' improvizational activity as an essential component of their professional identity, Contu and Willmott (2006: 1776), through a Marxian-Lacanian lens, see it as an 'ideological fantasy' that sustains the capitalist labor process.

Thus, in reflecting on what a phenomenon is a case of, a researcher notes analogies with earlier studies and, insofar as those analogies fail to explain adequately the phenomenon of interest, the researcher reformulates their case in order to make sense of it. In other words, by pursuing the question, 'a case of what?,' a researcher contrasts the case in hand with other case models and, by so doing, reconceives the case as an instance of some new or previously misapprehended general process (Stinchcombe, 1978: 21–2; Walton, 1992: 135). As Abbott (2001: 129) remarks, 'it is precisely in the reflection about what x is a case of that real theory begins.'

On this account, therefore, theorizing is an inherently *incomplete* process. To be precise, it is a profoundly dialogical enterprise in the sense that the process is completed any time another researcher sees analogies with, and borrows concepts from, earlier studies in an attempt to make sense of a particular phenomenon by which they are puzzled. The process then starts afresh and becomes, again, incomplete, waiting for another researcher to join in and continue the borrowing. As Bakhtin (1981: 293) aptly remarks, 'The world in language is half someone else's. It becomes

one's own only when the speaker populates it with his own intention, his own accent, when he appropriates the word, adapting it to his own semantic and expressive intention'.

Moreover, the process is not only incomplete but, as Geertz (1973: 29) notes with regard to cultural ethnographic analysis, 'the more deeply it goes the less complete it is.' When a researcher seeks to offer a thick description of a particular phenomenon, keeping the overall theoretical framing to a minimum, their account lends itself to multiple theoretical framings—the account becomes less complete, more open-ended, and is susceptible to several interpretations (Flyvbjerg, 2004: 400). As Bechky (2006: 1759) notes, commenting on the reception of Orr's (1996) ethnographic work, the theoretical restraint of his ethnography helped diffuse his ideas, leaving ample room for other researchers to take Orr's work in new directions. The same applies to the now famous case of Honda's expansion into the US motorcycle market (Pascale, 1984 and 1996). The more one stays at the level of narrative description of what took place, the more incomplete the case is, namely the more difficult it is to ascertain what Honda's expansion is a case of (Runde and de Rond, 2007).

Thus, small-N researchers need to make a choice. The more they are concerned with singularity, namely with making phenomenological sense of particular events, the more descriptive they become and the more they tie their account to the uniqueness, idiosyncrasies, and contingencies of the settings they study. On the other hand, the more they seek to make their case comparable to other cases in order to draw analogies from other case models that will enable them to address the question, 'what is this a case of?,' the more they will seek to conduct their thick descriptions in terms that have already been defined in the literature (Gerring, 2006: 715). A comparative orientation brings a theoretical bent to a small-N study at the expense of situational uniqueness. A phenomenological orientation brings a situational bent at the expense of theoretical synopsis.

An epistemology that takes the particular seriously is forced to strike a balance between the two extremes. Too much concern with situational uniqueness does not allow one to assess the *significance* of the phenomenon at hand, which may be obtained by contrasting it with what is already known (Mitchell, 1983: 203). Too much concern with fitting situational idiosyncrasy into already defined categories does not enable one to make creative use of the case, namely use it to extend what is already known and further specify generic concepts.

Again, Orr's (1996) ethnography is a good case in point. His ethnographic account is not a mere description of technicians' work practices, and one can safely assume that it is rather different from how technicians themselves would have described their work should they have chosen to do so in, say, a book. Orr's account, rather, is a theoretically-informed narrative that is organized around certain theoretical notions, such as 'bricolage,' 'narratives,' 'communities of practice,' and 'situated action,' which have enabled Orr to let technicians speak for themselves in a way that suited his purposes. Orr, however, does not merely give voice to his technicians; through his narrative, he rather *organizes* their voices so that a theorized storyline emerges (Golden-Biddle and Locke, 2006), which further extends what organizational and management theorists have known about story-telling, improvisation, and communities of practice at the work place. Practitioners are *in* the phenomenon—they are the case. Theorists move between two questions; 'what is going on here?,' and 'what is this a case of?.' The first calls for descriptive mastery, the second for theoretical craftsmanship.

CONCLUSIONS

The craving for generalization has been a characteristic of mainstream social science and has, historically, constituted part of the canon for assessing relevant research. This has been reflected in the sometimes understandably apologetic tone small-N organization and management theorists have adopted in defending their work. Generalization has been considered a good thing in itself and the distinction between 'statistical' and 'analytical generalization' has been widely adopted, with small-N researchers usually aligning themselves with the latter. But the craving for analytical generalization creates more problems than it solves. The main problem is that it treats particular cases as mere manifestations of generic concepts—the particular is subsumed into the general—thus missing the *epistemic* significance of the *particular* potentially to shape the general.

It has been argued here that the distinctive contribution of small-N studies is better appreciated if it is seen through the epistemology of the particular, rather than through the epistemology of the general. From the epistemology of the particular, specific cases under research (the very stuff of small-N studies) share family resemblances rather than an overarching feature. Concepts are necessarily empirically underdetermined; concrete cases aid the understanding the use of general concepts. Particular cases are opportunities for potentially extending our hitherto understandings of a phenomenon at hand. The particular is not subsumed into the general; it rather further specifies the general.

Small-N studies help us to refine the distinctions through which we understand general processes and by so doing provide heuristic generalizations. The latter are generalizations in so far as they include conceptual abstractions from concrete data. But they are heuristic in so far as those conceptual abstractions have a radial structure, whose nonprototypical members offer opportunities for extending the radius of application of the concepts at hand, thus helping to make new distinctions. New distinctions are made when the researcher, helped by noting inescapably inexact analogies with other similar cases, cannot fit the case material to those analogies and is, therefore, compelled to reformulate the case at hand. Small-N studies are uniquely capable for helping researchers to achieve this because, through the intense familiarity with the reality at hand, researchers create advanced forms of learning which are conducive to generating new insights, namely making more incisive distinctions. If the real mark of expertise is the move from rule-based knowledge to intuitive understanding that comes with extensive experience with context-dependent knowledge (Dreyfus and Dreyfus, 2005; Dreyfus, 1991), small-N researchers have a better chance to be creative since proximity to reality and feedback from the object of study force researchers to test out analogically derived conceptions of what is going on (Flyvbjerg, 2004: 392).

From such a point of view, the question, 'how far do those distinctions apply?' does not arise since particular cases share family resemblances, which means that, despite similarities, each case preserves its own particularity. From within the epistemology of the particular, the critical question, rather, is 'how far can you go with those distinctions?.' Notice that this question applies to both researchers and practitioners alike. Researchers are invited to think analogically and see whether currently used distinctions help them make sense of a particular case and, thus, reformulate accordingly their understanding. Similarly, practitioners are invited to reformulate distinctions relevant to reported cases to take account of their own experiences and thus make even more refined distinctions (Stake, 2000; Lincoln and Guba, 1985).

Insofar as life is experienced by concrete individuals in concrete cases, even the most general concepts (Geertz's 'mega-concepts') take their particular shape in particular settings. Small-N studies do not present a map but a portrait of the world that acts as an aid to perception (Shotter and Tsoukas, 2007: 21). We notice aspects previously unnoticed and see connections previously unseen. But such aspects and such connections are not 'out there' (and it is in that sense that such knowledge does not produce a map); rather we—researchers and practitioners alike— bring them forth by asking, 'what is this a case of?.' Moving up and down between experienced reality and conceptual grasp, we potentially refine our understanding of

the phenomenon in hand. If small-N studies achieve anything, it is to help create a more refined debate—to keep the conversation going.

ACKNOWLEDGEMENTS

I would like to thank Ann Langley, Alan Bryman, and David Buchanan for their extremely helpful comments and suggestions on an earlier draft of this chapter.

REFERENCES

Abbott, A. (2001) *Time Matters: On Theory and Method*, Chicago: Chicago University Press.

Ackroyd, S. and Fleetwood, S. (eds) (2000) *Realist Perspectives on Management and Organisations*, London: Routledge.

Anand, N., Gardner, H.K., and Morris, T. (2007) 'Knowledge-based innovation: emergence and embedding of new practice areas in management consulting firms', *Academy of Management Journal*, 50: 406–28.

Asch, S.E. (1952) *Social Psychology*, Englewood Cliffs, NJ: Prentice-Hall.

Bakhtin, M.M. (1981) *The Dialogic Imagination*, M. Holquist (Ed.); C. Emerson and M. Holquist (trans.), Austin, TX: University of Texas Press.

Bechky, B.A. (2006) 'Talking about machines, thick description, and knowledge work', *Organization Studies*, 27: 1757–68.

Benbya, H. and McKelvey, B. (2007) 'Using Pareto-based science to enhance knowledge for practical relevance', Paper presented at the Third *Organization Studies* Summer Workshop, Crete, 7–9 June 2007.

Buchanan, D. (1999) 'The logic of political action: an experiment with the epistemology of the particular', *British Journal of Management*, 10: S73–S88.

Burawoy, M. (1979) *Manufacturing Consent*, Chicago: Chicago University Press.

Burns, T. and Stalker, G.M. (1961) *The Management of Innovation*, London: Tavistock.

Contu, A. and Willmott, H. (2006) 'Studying practice: situating talking about machines', *Organization Studies*, 27: 1769–82.

Cook, S.D. and Yanow, D. (1996) 'Culture and organizational learning', in M.D. Cohen and L.S. Sproull (eds), *Organizational Learning*, Thousand Oaks, CA: Sage, pp. 430–59.

Dreyfus, H. (1991) *Being-in-the-world*, Cambridge, MA: MIT Press.

Dreyfus, H. and Dreyfus, S. (2005) 'Expertise in real world contexts', *Organization Studies*, 26: 779–92.

Eisenhardt, K. (1989) 'Building theories from case study research', *Academy of Management Review*, 14: 532–50.

Eisenhardt, K. and Graebner, M.E. (2007) 'Theory building from cases: opportunities and challenges', *Academy of Management Journal*, 50: 25–32.

Feldman, M. (2000) 'Organizational routines as a source of continuous change', *Organization Science*, 11: 611–29.

Flybjerg, B. (2004) 'Five misunderstandings about case study research', in C. Seale, G. Gobo, J.F. Gubrium, and D.D. Silverman (eds), *Qualitative Research Practice*, London: Sage, pp. 390–404.

Geertz, C. (1973) *The Interpretation of Cultures*, New York: Basic Books.

George, A.L. and McKeown, T.J. (1985) 'Case studies and theories of organizational decision making', *Advances in Information Processing in Organizations*, 2: 21–58.

Gerring, J. (2006) 'Single-outcome studies: a methodological primer', *International Sociology*, 21: 707–34.

Glock, H-J. (1996) *A Wittgenstein Dictionary*, Oxford: Blackwell.

Gobo, G. (2004) 'Sampling, representativeness and generalizability', in C. Seale, G. Gobo, J.F. Gubrium, and D.D. Silverman (eds), *Qualitative Research Practice*, London: Sage, pp. 405–26.

Goffman, E. (1961) *Asylums*, New York: Anchor.

Golden-Biddle, K. and Locke. K. (2006) *Composing Qualitative Research* (second edn.), London: Sage.

Hedström, P. (2005) *Dissecting the Social*, Cambridge: Cambridge University Press.

Lakoff, G. (1987) *Women, Fire, and Dangerous Things*, Chicago: The University of Chicago Press.

Lawrence, P.R. and J.L.Lorsch (1986) *Organization and Environment*, (Revised edn.), Cambridge, MA: Harvard Business School Press.

Lieberson, S. (1991) 'Small N's and big conclusions: an examination of the reasoning in comparative studies based on a small number of cases', *Social Forces*, 70: 307–20.

Lieberson, S. (1994) 'More on the uneasy case for using Mill-type methods in small-N comparative studies', *Social Forces*, 72: 1225–37.

Lincoln, Y.S. and Guba, E.G. (1985) 'Naturalistic Inquiry', Newbury Park, CA: Sage.

Luntley, M. (2003) *Wittgenstein: Meaning and Judgment*, Oxford: Blackwell.

Maitlis, S. (2005) 'The social processes of organizational sensemaking',*Academy of Management Journal*, 48: 1–49.

Mill, J.S. (2002) *A System of Logic*, University Press of the Pacific.

Mintzberg, H. (1973) *The Nature of Managerial Work*, New York: Harper and Row.

Mitchell, J.C. (1983) 'Case and situation analysis', *Sociological Review*, 31: 187–211.

Nichols, E. (1986) 'Stocpol on revolution: Comparative analysis vs. historical conjuncture', *Comparative Social Research*, 9: 163–86.

Orr, J.E. (1996) *Talking About Machines*, Ithaca, NY: ILR Press/Cornell University Press.

Pascale, R.T. (1984) 'Perspectives on strategy: the real story behind Honda's success', *California Management Review*, 26: 47–72.

Pascale, R.T. (1996) 'The Honda effect', *California Management Review*, 38: 80–91.

Plowman, D., Baker, L.T., Beck, T.E., Kurlkarni, M., Solansky, S. and Travis, D. (2007) 'Radical change accidentally: the emergence and amplification of small change', *Academy of Management Journal*, 50(3): 515–43.

Ritzer, G. (1993) *The McDonaldization of Society*, Thousand Oaks, CA: Pine Forge Press.

Ritzer, G. (1998) *The McDonaldization Thesis*, London: Sage.

Roethlisberger, F.J. and W.K. Dickson (1939) *Management and the Worker*, Cambridge, MA: Harvard University Press.

Runde, J. and M. de Rond (2007) 'Evaluating causal explanations of samples of one', Paper presented at the Third *Organization Studies* Summer Workshop, Crete, 7–9 June 2007.

Ryle, G. (2000) *The Concept of Mind*, Chicago: Chicago University Press.

Savolainen, J. (1994) 'The rationality of drawing big conclusions based on small samples: in defense of Mill's methods', *Social Forces*, 72: 1217–24.

Sawyer, K.R. (2007) 'Book review of *Dissecting the Social: On the principles of Analytic Sociology*' by Peter Hedström, *Philosophy of the Social Sciences*, 37: 255–60.

Shotter, J. and Tsoukas, H. (2007) 'Theory as therapy: towards reflective theorizing in organization studies', Paper presented at the Third *Organization Studies* Summer Workshop, Crete, 7–9 June 2007.

Siggelkow, N. (2007) 'Persuasion with case studies', *Academy of Management Journal*, 50: pp. 20–24.

Stake, R.E. (2000) 'Case studies', in Denzin, N.K. and Lincoln, Y.S. (eds), *Handbook of Qualitative Research*, (second edn.), Thousand Oaks, CA: Sage, pp. 435–54.

Steinberg, P.F. (2007) 'Causal assessment in small-N policy studies', *The Policy Studies Journal*, 35: 181–204.

Stinchcombe, A.L. (1978) *Theoretical Models in Social History*, New York: Academic Press..

Thompson, J.D. (1956–7) 'On building an administrative science', *Administrative Science Quarterly*, 1:102–11.

Toulmin, S. (1990) *Cosmopolis: The Hidden Agenda of Modernity*, Chicago: The University of Chicago Press.

Tsoukas, H. (1989) 'The validity of idiographic research explanations', *Academy of Management Review*, 14: 551–61.

Tsoukas, H. (1994) 'What is management? an outline of a metatheory', *British Journal of Management*, 5: 289–301.

Tsoukas, H. (2005) 'The practice of theory: a knowledge-based view of theory development in organization studies', in H. Tsoukas, *Complex Knowledge*, Oxford: Oxford University Press, pp. 321–39.

Tsoukas, H. and Knudsen, C. (2002) 'The conduct of strategy research', in A. Pettigrew, H. Thomas and R. Whittington (eds), *Handbook of Strategy and Management*, London: Sage, 411–35.

Walton, J. (1992) 'Making a theoretical case', in C.C. Ragin and H.S. Becker (eds) *What is a Case?*, Cambridge: Cambridge University Press, pp. 121–38.

Weick, K. (2007) 'The generative properties of richness', *Academy of Management Journal*, 50: 14–19.

Weick, K. and Roberts, K. (1993) 'Collective mind in organizations: heedful interrelating on flight decks', *Administrative Science Quarterly*, 38: 357–81.

Williams, M. (2000) 'Interpretivism and generalization', *Sociology*, 34: 209–24.

Winch, P. (1958) *The Idea of a Social Science and its Relation to Philosophy*, London: Routledge and Kegan Paul.

Wisniewski, E.J. (1997) 'Conceptual combination: possibilities and esthetics', in Ward, T.N., S.M. Smith, J. Vaid. (eds), *Creative Thought*, Washington, DC: American Psychological Association, pp. 51–82.

Wittgenstein, L. (1958) *Philosophical Investigations*, (second edn.), Oxford: Blackwell, translated by G.E.M. Anscombe.

Wittgenstein, L. (1969) *The Blue and Brown Books*, (second edn.), Oxford: Blackwell.

Woodward, J. (1981) *Industrial Organization*, (second edn.), New York: Oxford University Press.

Yin, R.K. (1994) *Case Study Research: Design and Methods*, (second edn.),Thousand Oaks, CA: Sage.

Znaniecki, F. (1934) *The Method of Sociology*, New York: Rinehart.

18

Implications of Research Design Options for the Validity of Inferences Derived from Organizational Research

Eugene F. Stone-Romero

With little exception, advances in both science and practice in the organizational sciences (e.g., human resource management, industrial and organizational psychology, organizational behavior, organizational communication, organization theory) hinge on the existence of findings from sound empirical research (referred to hereinafter as research). Research is used in (a) testing predictions about organizational phenomena (e.g., individual behavior and group processes), (b) developing theory concerned with such phenomena (e.g., expectancy theory and resource-dependency theory), and (c) designing and implementing interventions for changing variables (e.g., job enrichment and survey feedback) that are assumed to influence outcomes associated with individuals, groups, and organizations (e.g., worker well-being

and performance, group effectiveness, and organizational efficiency). Overall, sound research is critical to both the development and application of knowledge about organizational phenomena, and good research design is vital to both the soundness of research and the validity of inferences derived from it. In view of this, the overall purpose of this chapter is to consider the factors that influence the validity of inferences derived from research, especially those concerned with causal connections between variables. Consistent with this purpose, the chapter has sections that deal with (a) research design, (b) the purposes of research, (c) the facets of validity in research, (d) the types of settings in which research is conducted, (e) the types of experimental designs that can be used in research, (f) examples of the intersection of experimental designs and research settings, (g) the important distinction between experimental design and statistical methods, and (h) some conclusions about the design and conduct of research on phenomena of interest to organizational researchers.

Research design

Research or study design is an overall plan for conducting a study that considers several components (Cook and Campbell, 1979; Fromkin and Streufert, 1976; Kerlinger and Lee, 2000; Rosenthal and Rosnow, 2008; Runkel and McGrath, 1972; Shadish et al., 2002; Stone, 1978). First, the researcher must specify the units (e.g., individuals, groups, and organizations) that will be studied. Second, he or she must decide on the type of *experimental design* that will be used in the study. Here, the options include nonexperimental, quasi-experimental and randomized experimental. In randomized experimental or quasi-experimental research, the researcher must devise strategies for manipulating independent variables, and in nonexperimental research, he or she must determine how *assumed* independent variable will be measured. Third, depending on the experimental design associated with a study, the researcher must specify the strategies that will be used in manipulating or measuring actual or assumed independent, mediating, moderating, and dependent variables. Fourth, the researcher must determine how the studied units will be sampled (e.g., randomly and nonrandomly). Fifth, he or she must decide if the study is to be conducted in a special purpose or a nonspecial purpose setting. Sixth, and finally, he or she must specify the methods (statistical versus nonstatistical) that will be used in analyzing the data produced by the study. As is explained in the following section, there is a very important distinction between experimental design and statistical methods, and contrary to what many researchers appear to believe, statistical methods are virtually always an *unacceptable* substitute for good experimental design in

terms of a researcher's ability to make valid inferences about causal connections between variables.

General purposes of research

Research on phenomena of relevance to organizations is conducted for a number of major purposes, most of which involve assessing the relation between and among unobservable constructs using manipulations or measures of variables that serve to operationally define the constructs (Guion, 2002; Nunnally, 1978; Shadish et al., 2002; Stone, 1978). Some examples of relations that might be tested are those between: (a) worker ability and job performance, (b) the demographic composition of work teams and team performance, and (c) the monthly sales of department stores by geographical regions in the U.S. In many such studies, the researcher has no immediate interest in determining if the observed relations are causal in nature. However, having found a relation in one such study, the researcher may be interested in testing causal hypotheses in subsequent investigations.

A second major purpose of research is to determine the effects of various types of manipulations (interventions, treatments) of unobservable constructs on criteria of interest to a researcher. Some examples include the effects of (a) job enrichment on job satisfaction, (b) realistic job previews on employee turnover, (c) structured (as opposed to unstructured) pre-employment interviews on biases of various types (sex, race, age, etc.). In such studies, causality is an important concern.

A third major purpose of research is to determine if causal or noncausal relations between variables that were found in one set of circumstances (e.g., with a given set of units and measures in a specific setting) generalize to other sets of circumstances (e.g., with other types of units and measures in other settings). For example, will a stress-reduction program be as effective for police officers in SWAT units as it is for nurses working in trauma centers?

Facets of validity in research

A major objective in research is to generate valid inferences (conclusions) about issues addressed by it. Thus, researchers must be concerned with inferences associated with four facets of validity, i.e., internal, statistical conclusion, construct, and external (Cook and Campbell, 1979; Shadish et al., 2002). The better the overall design of a study, the greater the degree of confidence a researcher can have about the validity (correctness, truth value, etc.) of his or her research-based inferences.

A model of research-based inferences

A comprehensive model of factors that influence the validity of research-based conclusions is shown in Figure 18.1. Arrow 1 links the operational definitions of cause and effect constructs, and relates to *internal validity* inferences. Arrows 2 and 3 deal with factors that affect *construct validity*, i.e., the relation between constructs and their operational definitions. Arrow 4 is concerned with the correctness of statistical inferences about the relation between the operational definitions, and deals with *statistical conclusion validity*. Finally, arrow 5 has do with factors that moderate the causal relation

between X and Y, thus having a bearing on *external validity*. These facets of validity are considered next.

Construct validity

Construct validity has to do with the degree of correspondence between a given construct (e.g., incentive) and the measures and/or manipulations that are used to operationally define it (Cronbach and Meehl, 1955; Guion, 2002; Nunnally, 1978; Shadish et al., 2002; Stone-Romero, 1994). This facet of validity is critical in both types of operational definitions. Research tests for relations between variables using operational definitions that are of two basic types, i.e., manipulations and measures. *Manipulations* are actions taken by a researcher to vary the value of an independent variable (Aronson et al., 1990; Fromkin and Streufert, 1976; Shadish et al., 2002). Some organizational examples include: redesigning jobs, introducing quality control procedures, installing a computerized human resource information system, and implementing absence control procedures. *Measures* are observations of the values of variables. There are numerous strategies for measuring variables, including questionnaires, personality inventories, and aptitude and/or ability measures.

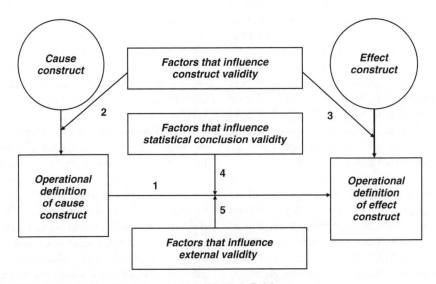

Figure 18.1 The construct validity of operational definitions.

Figure 18.2 illustrates construct validity and the factors that detract from it in terms of variance in an unobservable, focal construct (σ_C^2) and its operational definition (σ_O^2). As shown in the figure, the variance shared by these is construct validity (σ_v^2). Several factors detract from it. One of these is *bias*, i.e., systematic variance in an operational definition that is unrelated to the focal construct (σ_b^2). For example, a questionnaire measure of organizational citizenship behavior may be biased by the motives of respondents to respond to items in a socially desirable manner. Construct validity would also be reduced by *unreliability*, i.e., nonsystematic (random) variance in an operational definition (σ_e^2). For example, the just-mentioned measure may not be internally consistent (Nunnally, 1978). However, even if an operational definition were free from bias and unreliability, it may still have a low level of construct validity, because it may be deficient; that is, it may not fully capture the essence of the focal construct. For example, a measure of job enrichment would be deficient if it had items that dealt with feedback, but lacked items that had to do with autonomy, task significance, task identity, and feedback. In Figure 18.2, deficiency is represented by the portion of variance in the focal construct that is unshared with the operational definition (σ_d^2).

The construct validity of any given operational definition can be adversely affected by such problems as (a) an inadequate preoperational definition of the construct, (b) a single operational definition of the construct (e.g., a specific measure), (c) a manipulation that motivates research participants to respond in a biased manner (e.g., demand characteristics-based responding and evaluation apprehension-based responding), and (d) an operational definition that fails to capture the actual degree of variability in the focal construct (Nunnally, 1978; Rosenthal and Rosnow, 2008; Shadish et al., 2002; Stone-Romero, 1994).

Internal validity

Internal validity has to do with the correctness of inferences about causal connections between focal constructs (Cook and Campbell, 1979; Shadish et al., 2002), for example, the inference that X causes Y (symbolically: $X \rightarrow Y$). It is important to note that there is a nontrivial distinction between *actual* versus *assumed* causal relations between constructs. Research that uses randomized experimental designs provides the firmest basis for demonstrating that an independent variable (X) causes (i.e., produces changes in) a dependent variable (Y). The validity of causal inferences is somewhat weaker in research that uses quasi-experimental designs, and weakest in research that uses nonexperimental designs. In virtually all nonexperimental research, a cause is assumed (X_A) as opposed to actual (X), and an effect is assumed (Y_A) as opposed to actual (Y).

Inferences about cause are most justified when a researcher can show that: (a) the cause preceded the effect in time (temporal precedence), (b) the cause and effect are related to one another (covariation), and (c) there are no rival explanations of the covariation between the cause and effect (absence of confounds). These conditions are most likely to be satisfied in research that uses randomized experimental designs and least likely to be satisfied in research that uses nonexperimental designs.

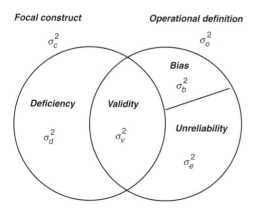

Figure 18.2   Validity facets in empirical studies.

Statistical conclusion validity

Researchers typically use statistical methods (e.g., correlation, regression, and analysis of variance) to test for relations between variables (Hays, 1994). For example, using data from a nonexperimental study, they infer that there is a nonzero relation between X_A and Y_A. Or using data from a randomized experimental study, they infer that the average score for units in a treatment condition (M_T) is greater than the average for units in a control condition (M_C). In both cases, statistical inferences are critical to inferring that the studied variables are related to one another (Cook and Campbell, 1979; Hays, 1994; Shadish et al., 2002). As such, the validity of the same inferences will be adversely affected by a number of factors, including low statistical power, failing to meet the assumptions of statistical tests, and conducting large numbers of statistical tests using a nominal Type I error rate that is far lower than the actual (effective) Type I error rate (Cook and Campbell, 1979; Hays, 1994; Shadish et al., 2002).

External validity

External validity has to do with the correctness of inferences about the existence of a causal relation between two variables *across* different sampling particulars of units, settings, treatments, and outcome measures.

For example, will a goal setting program that has been shown to improve the performance of salespeople in retail stores in the U.S. improve the performance of comparable workers in Mexico?

External validity is threatened by any factors that serve to moderate (Stone, 1988; Stone-Romero and Liakhovitski, 2002) the causal relation between a cause and an effect (Shadish et al., 2002). Stated somewhat differently, external validity is an issue when there are interactions between a treatment (X) and one or more of the other sampling particulars of a study (e.g., units, treatments, settings, and outcomes).

Types of variables in assumed causal models

Research aimed at testing assumed causal models typically considers more than a simple, two-variable sequence. For example, it may involve assumed exogenous (i.e., independent), and endogenous (i.e., mediator dependent) variables. Figure 18.3, which is based on the Theory of Reasoned Action (Ajzen, 1988), is an illustration of such a model. It considers six exogenous variables (i.e., behavioral beliefs, evaluation of outcomes, normative beliefs, moral beliefs, perceived behavioural control, and motivation to comply), four mediator variables (attitude

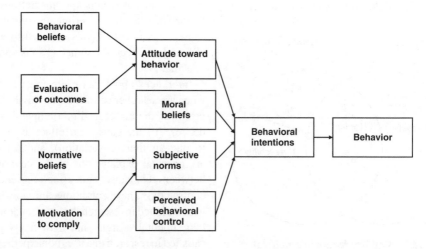

Figure 18.3   The theory of reasoned action.

toward behavior, subjective norms, perceived behavioral control, and behavioral intentions), and one dependent variable (i.e., behavior).

Timing of measurement in research

In studies of assumed causal models (e.g., the model shown in Figure 18.3), it is critical that assumed mediators and effects be measured at appropriate times (Mathieu and Taylor, 2006; Shadish et al., 2002). The reason for this is that typically, the influence of causes on mediators and effects is not instantaneous. For example, in a study aimed at testing the effects of feedback from a supervisor on worker behavior, it may take several weeks for feedback (the cause) to influence the worker's behavioral intentions, and for these to affect the worker's behavior (i.e., his or her task performance). Thus, it is critical that there be appropriate lags between the times at which (a) causes are varied (either naturally or experimentally) and (b) mediators and effects are measured.

Experimental design versus research setting

Prior to describing the three afore noted types of experimental designs, it is important to distinguish between experimental designs and research settings (Stone-Romero, 2002, 2007c; Stone-Romero and Rosopa, 2008). Thus, this section focuses on three setting-related issues, i.e., the 'laboratory' versus 'field' distinction, the influence of setting type on internal validity, and the types of realism that are important in research. Taken together these issues are very important in research aimed at testing for the existence of causal relations between variables. As such, they have very important implications for internal validity.

The often inappropriate laboratory versus field distinction

Frequently, a distinction is made between laboratory and field research settings (e.g., Kerlinger and Lee, 2000; Locke, 1986).

Regrettably, the same distinction is *not* very informative (Campbell, 1986; Stone-Romero, 2007c; Stone-Romero and Rosopa, 2008). As Stone-Romero (2007c) noted, a more appropriate distinction is between *special purpose* (SP) and *non-special purpose* (NSP) research settings. Settings of the former variety are created for the specific purpose of doing research (e.g., a laboratory room at a university or a simulated work setting in an industrial park). In contrast, settings of the latter type are created for purposes other than research (e.g., organizations such as Microsoft, Mercedes Benz, Matsushita, and Sony).

SP settings have two major attributes. First, they are created for the purpose of conducting research and cease to exist when it has been completed. Second, they are designed so as to allow for the *effective* (unconfounded) manipulation of one or more independent variables. In general, SP settings have only a subset of the features or elements that are found in NSP settings (Aronson et al., 1990; Berkowitz and Donnerstein, 1982; Fromkin and Streufert, 1976; Runkel and McGrath, 1972).

Setting type and the validity of causal inferences

Inferences about cause (e.g., $X \rightarrow Y$) vary as a function of the setting in which research is conducted. Because SP settings are created specifically for the purpose of conducting a study, research in such settings typically provides for a much greater degree of control over confounding (nuisance) variables than research in NSP settings. The important implication of this is that to the degree that the influence of confounding variables can be controlled, a researcher can be more confident about the internal validity of a study (Cook and Campbell, 1979; Shadish et al., 2002; Stone, 1978; Stone-Romero, 2007c). As such, it is generally the case that inferences about cause are more justified when research is conducted in SP than NSP settings (Stone-Romero and Rosopa, 2008).

Realism in research

It is important that SP settings be designed with two properties in mind. More specifically, it is essential that such settings have *experimental realism*. In addition, it is often desirable for them to have *mundane realism* (Aronson et al., 1990; Fromkin and Streufert, 1976). For example, a researcher interested in studying the effects of variations in job design on critical psychological states and job satisfaction could create a SP setting in a university-based laboratory. Note that the assumed causal model in this study is job design → critical psychological states → job satisfaction. For this study, it would be important to have job design manipulations (e.g., autonomy and feedback) that had desired degrees of *impact* on research participants, thus insuring *experimental realism* (Aronson et al., 1990). However, it would *not* be very important to have other elements that would be found in an actual organization (e.g., performance-based compensation, health care benefits, and retirement plans). Nevertheless, the greater the degree to which these and other elements that are common to work organizations were part of the SP setting, the greater would be the study's *mundane realism* (Aronson et al., 1990). As a consequence, the greater would be the study's potential to test the assumed causal model in terms of its capacity to operate in NSP organizational settings.

It merits adding that the just-described job design study also could be conducted in a NSP setting (e.g., an actual work organization). However, for several reasons, it would typically be much more difficult to conduct it in this type of setting (Cook and Campbell, 1979; Shadish et al., 2002). One reason for this is that in most NSP settings it is very difficult to bring about changes in existing organizational arrangements (e.g., physical layout of facilities, assignment of workers to jobs, and pay and fringe benefits provided to workers) that are needed to provide for the effective manipulation of independent variables. As a consequence, research in NSP settings that uses randomized experimental or quasi-experimental designs typically results in lower levels of control over extraneous or confounding variables than studies using the same types of designs in SP settings. Therefore, inferences about cause are typically more problematic for research in NSP settings than for research in SP settings.

In general, studies conducted in NSP settings have higher levels of mundane realism than those conducted in SP settings. This often serves as a basis for the claim that external validity inferences (Shadish et al., 2002) are more appropriate for studies in NSP settings than in SP settings. However, the legitimacy of this argument appears questionable (Dipboye and Flanagan, 1979; Fromkin and Streufert, 1976; Locke, 1986; Stone-Romero, 2002). There are several reasons for this. One is that even when studies are conducted in NSP settings, they typically involve non-representative samples of subjects, settings, and operational definitions of manipulations and/or measures. Thus, the external validity of such studies is suspect. The fact that they were conducted in NSP settings often does nothing to strengthen external validity inferences. Another reason is that a major purpose of research is to show that there is a relation between two or more variables. In this regard, numerous chapters in a book on generalizing from 'laboratory to field settings' (Locke, 1986) provide clear evidence that relations that are found in SP settings are also found in NSP settings. The findings apply to relations involving numerous variables of interest to organizational researchers, including attributions, goal setting, participation in decision making, financial incentives, reinforcement schedules, job satisfaction, job characteristics, and job performance.

It deserves adding that the degree to which a study has experimental realism is very important for studies that test assumed causal models. There is a very important reason for this, which is that tests of such models may fail to show support for causal connections between variables if independent variables are operationally defined in such a way as to have insufficient impact on study participants (Aronson et al., 1990; Fromkin and Streufert, 1976; Shadish et al., 2002).

Thus, even though there actually may be a causal relation between X and Y, a study that used an operational definition of X that lacked experimental realism may fail to provide evidence of it. In addition, to the extent that a study lacks mundane realism, an effect found in a SP setting may not be found in a NSP setting. For example, the effect of X may be present when a SP setting isolates it from all of the other variables that are likely to be found in NSP settings. However, in a NSP setting the influence of X may be too weak to allow for an adequate test of the causal model.

Types of experimental designs

Experimental designs used in research are of three basic types, i.e., randomized experimental, quasi-experimental, and nonexperimental. These are described next.

Randomized experimental designs

Studies that use randomized experimental designs have four major attributes (Shadish et al., 2002; Stone-Romero, 2007c). Taken together, the results of studies using such designs tend to have high levels of internal validity (Cook and Campbell, 1979; Shadish et al., 2002; Stone-Romero, 2002, 2007c).

1. Manipulation of independent variables

In research that uses randomized experimental designs, the levels of one or more independent variables are manipulated by the researcher. For example, in a study concerned with the effects of temperature and humidity on the performance of workers, a researcher would experimentally vary each of them. He or she would have to use least two levels of each independent variable that differed enough from one another to produce changes in performance. With such a design, the researcher could test for the main effects of each variable and their interaction. Note, in addition, that if there were enough research subjects to allow for adequate statistical power, the researcher could have far more than two levels of each variable. This would increase his or her ability to accurately

model the relations between the independent variables and the dependent variable.

The capacity to manipulate levels of one or more independent variables serves to strengthen inferences about cause; that is, it leads to relatively high levels of internal validity. One reason for this is that in a study that used a randomized experimental design, the researcher can be confident about the cause(s) preceding the effect(s) in time (i.e., temporal precedence). In addition, assuming a properly conducted randomized experiment, he or she can be confident that changes in one or more dependent variables were the result of the manipulations.

2. Random assignment of units to study conditions

A second attribute of a randomized experimental study is that units (e.g., individuals) are randomly assigned to study conditions. Assuming a sufficient number of units and effective randomization procedures, the researcher can be highly confident of the equivalence of individuals in each of the conditions (in terms of mean levels of any and all measured and unmeasured potentially confounding variables) prior to the time that subjects were exposed to the study's manipulations. As a result, he or she can be confident that posttreatment levels of the dependent variables for each of the conditions resulted from the study's manipulations, as opposed to confounds (Cook and Campbell, 1979; Shadish et al., 2002; Stone-Romero, 2002, 2007c).

3. Measurement of dependent variables

A third characteristic of studies using randomized experimental designs is that levels of dependent variables are measured. For example, in the just-described study, the researcher would measure the performance levels of workers in each of the conditions. The researcher also could measure subjects' beliefs about the levels of manipulations they experienced. Such *manipulation checks* are especially important in terms of inferences about the construct validity of the manipulations (Aronson et al., 1990; Shadish et al., 2002).

When tests of assumed causal models are based on data from well-designed and properly conducted randomized experimental research: (a) causal paths are well-known, (b) confounds are not an issue, and (c) model misspecification is typically not a concern. Thus, inferences about cause rest on a very firm foundation.

The latter argument is predicated on the assumption that the randomized experiments are properly designed and executed. However, there may be instances when randomized experiments 'break down.' This is more likely to be a problem in NSP than SP settings (Cook and Campbell, 1979; Shadish et al., 2002). Among the many causes of this are such threats to internal validity as differential attrition across treatment conditions, diffusion of treatments, compensatory equalization, resentful demoralization, testing, instrumentation, and the interaction of these threats. To the extent that these threats are present in a randomized experiment, the validity of inferences about causal connections between variables in mediation models will suffer. For example, consider a study to test the mediating effect of motivation to perform (M) on the relation between task-related incentives (X) and job performance (Y). An experiment designed to test the $X \rightarrow M$ path would yield flawed inferences if the observed relation between X and M were a function of resentful demoralization (a confound) as opposed to X.

4. Some limitations on the use of research using randomized experimental designs

In spite of the value of randomized experiments for internal validity inferences, it may be difficult or impossible to use this type of design in many circumstances (see, for example, Cook and Campbell, 1979; Rosenthal and Rosnow, 2008; Shadish et al., 2002). First, some variables are not subject to manipulation (e.g., the actual age and sex of study participants). Second, although it may be possible to manipulate other variables (e.g., the personality, physical health, and mental health of study participants), such manipulations would be unacceptable on ethical grounds if they resulted in physical or psychological harm to participants. Third, in research that takes place in NSP settings (e.g., work organizations), a researcher may not have the ability to randomly assign units (e.g., workers, teams, and plants) to treatment conditions. Fourth, in research in NSP settings, it may not be possible to isolate units from one another (spatially), leading to the breakdown of randomized experiments aimed at testing assumed causal models. Fifth, research participants may refuse to be assigned to experimental conditions on a random basis. Sixth, it may be unethical to withhold beneficial treatments from units (e.g., those in a no-treatment control group). As a result of these and other factors, researchers who are interested in examining relations among variables that are assumed to be causes, mediators (Stone-Romero and Rosopa, 2004, 2007, 2008), and effects, may have to use either quasi-experimental or non-experimental designs (Cook and Campbell, 1979; Rosenthal and Rosnow, 2008; Shadish et al., 2002).

Quasi-experimental designs

There are five major types of quasi-experimental designs, i.e., single group designs without a control condition, multiple group designs that lack one or more pretest measures, multiple group designs that have a control condition and use pretest measures, time series designs, and regression discontinuity designs. Details on these designs are available in several works (e.g., Cook and Campbell, 1979; Rosenthal and Rosnow, 2008; Shadish et al., 2002). Whatever their specific nature, quasi-experimental designs have several attributes. Taken together, they lead to internal validity inferences that are typically weaker than those stemming from research using randomized experimental designs, but stronger than those derived from studies using nonexperimental designs.

Manipulation of independent variables In research using quasi-experimental designs, the researcher manipulates the levels of independent variables. Typically, however, quasi-experimental designs tend to have a very small number of manipulated variables. In addition, in quasi-experimental designs of the time series variety, an independent variable may be introduced and then removed several times, with the expectation that measured levels of the dependent variables will covary with these changes. However, whatever the specific type of quasi-experimental design, the fact that independent variables are manipulated strengthens internal validity inferences (Cook and Campbell, 1979; Shadish et al., 2002; Stone-Romero, 2002, 2007b; Stone-Romero and Rosopa, 2004, 2008).

Nonrandom assignment of units to conditions
Unlike what is true of randomized experiments, in quasi-experiments units are *not* randomly assigned to study conditions. For example, in a quasi-experiment using a nonequivalent control group design in a NSP setting, subjects in one operating unit of a firm may be exposed to a goal setting manipulation, while individuals in another, geographically remote unit may serve as no-treatment controls. Because intact units are used in the study, they may differ from one another on a host of variables prior to the time the treatment is introduced in the first unit. This serves to reduce the researcher's confidence about internal validity inferences (Cook and Campbell, 1979; Shadish et al., 2002; Stone-Romero, 2002, 2007b).

Measurement of assumed dependent variables
In quasi-experimental research, the researcher measures the values of one or more *assumed* dependent variables. The assumed qualifier is used because units are not randomly assigned to study conditions. As a result, in research using several specific types of quasi-experimental designs, there is no assurance that across-condition differences in such variables resulted from the treatments. For example, they may have been a product of one or more unmeasured confounding variables.

Some limitations on the use of quasi-experimental designs
A number of conditions limit the use of quasi-experimental designs in tests of causal models. They include most of the factors noted above that pertain to randomized experimental designs. In the interest of brevity, the same factors are not considered in this subsection.

Nonexperimental designs
Nonexperimental studies are the most frequently used in organizational research (Austin, Scherbaum and Mahlman, 2002; Scandura and Williams, 2000; Stone-Romero, Weaver, and Glenar, 1995). Research using such designs studies has several defining attributes. Taken together, they serve to greatly reduce the validity of causal inferences (Cook and Campbell, 1979; Shadish et al., 2002; Stone-Romero, 2002, 2007a).

Measurement of assumed independent variables
In nonexperimental research, variables that are assumed to be causes are measured, as opposed to manipulated. For example, a researcher interested in studying the relation between job enrichment and job satisfaction would measure the former variable, operating on the assumption that differences in observed levels of job enrichment reflected actual differences of this variable. However, because job enrichment was measured, as opposed to manipulated, inferences about a causal connection between it and job satisfaction would rest on a very shaky empirical foundation. Stated somewhat differently, the same study would *not* have a high level of internal validity. In addition, as is detailed in a section that follows, inferences about cause would *not* be strengthened *whatsoever* by the application of so called 'causal modeling procedures' to data derived from the study. This point is echoed by methodologists in numerous academic disciplines (Brannick, 1995; Cliff, 1987; Freedman, 1987; Holland, 1986; Ling, 1982; Millsap, 2002; Rogosa, 1987; Rosopa and Stone-Romero, 2008; Stone-Romero and Rosopa, 2004, 2007, 2008).

Nonrandom assignment of units to assumed conditions A second attribute of nonexperimental studies is that study participants are *not* randomly assigned to study conditions. Rather, the researcher collects data from individuals who have levels of assumed independent variables that may have resulted from various unknown causes. For example, in the just-described job enrichment study, the researcher would have to assume that the self-reported levels of measured job enrichment corresponded to the actual levels of enrichment of subjects' jobs. This assumption would, for example, be erroneous if the reports varied systematically as a function of factors other than objective levels of enrichment (e.g., the cognitive ability levels of subjects; see Stone et al., 1990).

Measurement of assumed dependent variables As is true of research using quasi-experimental designs, studies using nonexperimental designs deal with measured levels of what are assumed to be dependent variables. As a result, relative to studies that use either randomized experimental or quasi-experimental designs, studies that use nonexperimental designs typically have very low levels of internal validity.

Some limitations on the use of nonexperimental designs It is generally the case that research using nonexperimental designs is easier to conduct than is research that uses either randomized experimental or quasi-experimental designs. This is especially true of studies conducted in NSP settings (e.g., work organizations). One important reason for this is that organizations (and other types of social systems) are far more willing to allow for studies in which assumed causes are measured as opposed to manipulated. However, because nonexperimental designs afford a very poor basis for inferences about causal connections between variables, researchers who are interested in testing such connections shy away from the use of nonexperimental designs.

The value of longitudinal, nonexperimental designs In longitudinal, nonexperimental research, assumed causes, mediators, and effects are measured. Because of this, it is virtually always the case that two of the three requirements for making causal inferences can not be satisfied (i.e., temporal precedence and ruling out rival explanations). For example, McDonald (1999) noted that longitudinal studies are 'open to the objection that an apparently causal relation between an earlier and a later measure may just represent a relation of temporally stable traits of the person, or perhaps aspects of an unfolding developmental sequence that does not allow conceptual manipulation of the earlier measured attribute' (p. 370). As a result, the internal validity of longitudinal studies of the nonexperimental variety is typically quite low.

Intersection of research settings and experimental designs

As noted above, in any given study, a researcher has to make decisions about a number of important issues, two of which are types of experimental design and type of research setting. This section considers the combinations of these two design features. For each combination we consider an example of a study that used the design. In addition, we consider the relative strengths and weaknesses in terms of factors that influence various facets of validity.

Randomized experiments in NSP settings

It is possible to conduct randomized experiments in NSP settings. However, studies of this type are relatively rare, because organizations are typically reluctant to allow research of this type because of its potential to disrupt ongoing activities. However, Cook and Campbell (1979) and Shadish et al. (2002) noted that several factors may serve to enhance the likelihood of doing experimental research in NSP settings. The conditions are when: (a) the demand for a given treatment (e.g., a labor-saving device) is greater than its supply, (b) an innovation (e.g., new computers) is to be introduced, but it cannot be delivered to all units at once, (c) units are isolated from one another in time (e.g., in basic training units in the military), (d) units are separated geographically and the level of inter-unit communication is low (e.g., fast food restaurants in various regions of the country), (e) there is a need for change and multiple treatments of unknown efficacy can be introduced, (f) units can be assigned to conditions randomly as opposed to on the basis of need or merit, (g) units have no preferences for the type of treatment they are to receive, (h) it is possible to create an organization for the sole purpose of conducting an experimental study, (i) the organization gives the researcher control over units for the purpose of a study, and (j) units expect to be assigned treatments on a random basis. Note that in some of the just-noted cases, what was originally a NSP setting is temporarily converted to a SP setting for the duration of a study.

Example of the use of the design

Research by Stone Gueutal, Gardner, and McClure (1983) conducted a randomized experiment in a NSP setting. They were interested in the degree to which the type of organizations with which data subjects had dealings (the independent variable) influenced their privacy-related values, beliefs, attitudes, and several other outcome variables (the dependent variables). Thus, they conducted a randomized experiment in which study participants were randomly selected from several geographical regions within the State of Indiana. Participants were randomly assigned to conditions in which they were asked to consider their dealings with one of six types of organizations (e.g., their employer, the Internal Revenue Service, and law enforcement agencies). They then responded to structured interview items dealing with the dependent variables in terms of a specific type of organization. Results of univariate and multivariate analyses revealed that organization type affected their privacy-related values, beliefs, and attitudes.

Relative strengths of study in terms of validity facets

Because the just-described study used a randomized experimental design, it allowed for strong inferences about the effects of organization type on the dependent variables. In addition, because the respondents were randomly sampled from the population (i.e., adults in the State of Indiana) who responded to interview items in terms of their actual values, beliefs, and attitudes, the study's results appeared to be reasonably strong in terms of construct validity. In addition, the study's sample size was large enough to detect effects, and the univariate statistical analyses used Scheffe-based Type I error rates. Thus, the study was strong in terms of statistical conclusion validity. However, the study had at least two potential weaknesses that relate to external validity. First, because respondents were sampled from a single state, the extent to which the findings might generalize to residents of other states is an open question. Second, the data were collected using structured interviews. As a result, it was not possible to infer how the results might have been affected by alternative measurement strategies (e.g., questionnaires).

Randomized experiments in SP settings

Randomized experiments are frequently conducted in SP settings. One important reason for this is that such settings allow the researcher to manipulate independent variables, while controlling for possible confounds through strict control over the study's setting. Although the label is not a good one (Campbell, 1986; Stone-Romero, 2007c; Stone-Romero and Rosopa, 2008), the term laboratory experiment is commonly used to describe research using this type of design (Locke, 1986).

Example of use of the design

Stone and Stone (1985) were interested in factors that affected individuals' beliefs about the accuracy of performance feedback and their self-perceived task competence (i.e., task-based esteem). Based on relevant theory and research, they hypothesized that self-esteem would be influenced by both the favorability of feedback and its consistency. In order to test these hypotheses, they conducted a randomized experimental study in a special purpose setting (i.e., a university laboratory facility). The study involved manipulations of (a) feedback favorability (acceptable vs. superior) and (b) the consistency of feedback (consistent vs inconsistent) from two feedback agents. After working on an in-basket task, subjects were randomly assigned to one of the four study conditions. After receiving performance feedback, they completed measures of the dependent variables. Results of analyses of variance showed support for virtually all of the hypothesized relations, including those concerned with interaction effects.

Relative strengths of study in terms of validity facets

The just-described study was strong in terms of internal validity; that is, because of the use of a randomized experimental design, the researchers were able to make confident inferences about causal relations between the independent and dependent variables. It also was strong with respect to construct validity in that operational definitions of the independent variables were clearly related to the underlying constructs. Statistical conclusion validity was not an issue in the study, because the size of the sample was large enough to detect almost all hypothesized effects. In addition, as a result of the strength of the manipulations, effect sizes were relatively large for both of the dependent variables. However, because the study was performed in a SP setting using student subjects who worked on a task for a one-hour period, external validity was a concern. Thus, the researchers recommended that the study's hypotheses be tested in NSP settings (e.g., actual work organizations).

Quasi-experiments in SP settings

Although it is possible to conduct quasi-experimental organizational research in SP settings, studies of this type are very rare. A search of the social science literature using the PsycInfo database from 1872 to June 2007 failed to reveal a single published study of this

nature. However, quasi-experimental research in SP settings is not at all uncommon in a number of other disciplines. For example, research using quasi-experimental designs is common in clinical psychology. Thus, this subsection considers a study in this psychological specialty area.

Example of use of the design

Blanchard et al. (1997) were interested in determining the effects of thermal biofeedback interventions for the treatment of vascular headaches. The research took place in a SP setting, i.e., a laboratory created for the study of stress and anxiety disorders and associated treatments. There were four experimental conditions: (a) thermal biofeedback for hand warming (TBFHW), (b) thermal biofeedback for hand cooling (TBFHC), thermal biofeedback for temperature stability (TBFTS), and (c) suppression of alpha brain waves (SABW). In order to assess the effects of the treatments, the researchers conducted a randomized experiment in which 70 patients were randomly assigned to one of four treatment conditions. Results of repeated measures t-tests showed reductions in headache intensity for all but the subjects in the TBFTS condition.

Although the overall experimental design was randomized experimental, within each of the treatment conditions the design could be regarded as quasi-experimental in that subjects completed premeasures of headache intensity, were exposed to the treatment, and then completed postmeasures of headache intensity. In addition, Blanchard et al., conducted within-condition internal analyses (Aronson et al., 1990) with subsets of the subjects in the thermal biofeedback conditions who they referred to as 'learners' (i.e., those who demonstrated a criterion level of proficiency at controlling their hand temperature). The use of the internal analyses converted what was initially a randomized experiment to a quasi-experiment. Results of the same analyses showed that subjects in the TBFHC and TBFTS conditions showed reductions in headache intensity, whereas those in the TBFHW condition did not.

Relative strengths of the study in terms of validity facets   First, the internal validity of the randomized experimental component of the study was high. However, it was reduced considerably by the fact that the internal analyses were conducted only for the learners. Second, the construct validity of both the manipulations and measures used in the study appeared to be quite high. Third, there were problems with the statistical conclusion validity of the study. Within-condition sample sizes were relatively small for the randomized experimental portion of the study. As a result, some of the *t*-tests failed to yield statistically significant results. In addition, the sample size problem was exacerbated by the internal analyses, which used only a subset of the initial study participants. Moreover, there were Type I error rate problems, because the researchers performed numerous post-hoc tests without making downward adjustments to the per-comparison Type I error rate. Fourth, and finally, the external validity of the study's results is questionable, because the study's participants were restricted to individuals who volunteered for treatment. Thus, there's no assurance that similar results would obtain with other sample of subjects (e.g., nonvolunteers).

Quasi-experiments in NSP settings

There are numerous instances of studies using quasi-experimental designs in NSP settings. Quasi-experiments are far more common than randomized experiments in such settings. This is especially true of research in the organizational sciences. One important reason for this is that quasi-experiments are far less disruptive of ongoing organizational structures and process than are randomized experiments.

Example of use of the design   Hackman et al. (1978) were interested in the effects of changes in job design (the independent variable) on measures of several job characteristics, job performance, and absenteeism (the assumed dependent variables). In order to determine the effects of such changes, they conducted a quasi-experimental study

using 94 employees of a bank. Data on the assumed dependent variables were collected before and after changes in the jobs. Results showed that the job design manipulations resulted in expected changes in measures of several job characteristics and absenteeism. However, changes in performance between the pre- and postintervention periods were found only for employees who were relatively high in terms of growth need strength. The researchers noted that the results of their study needed to be replicated using studies with randomized experimental designs.

Relative strengths of study in terms of validity facets   Because the study used a quasi-experimental design, inferences about causal relations between the changes in job characteristics and the assumed dependent variables were much more plausible than they would have been in a study using a nonexperimental design. Nevertheless, the researchers lacked control over a host of factors that might have affected the study's results. For example, scores on the postchange measures may have been affected by sensitization stemming from completion of the pretest measures. As a consequence, the internal validity of the study was not as great as it would have been with a randomized experimental design.

Most of the measures used in the study appeared to have a high degree of construct validity; that is, that they had been used in numerous other studies on job design. Unfortunately, however, there were serious statistical conclusion validity problems with the study. More specifically, the researchers performed a large number of statistical tests, using a nominal Type I error rate of 0.05 for each. Thus, the effective Type I error rate for each test was considerably higher than the nominal level of 0.05. The researchers should have used a more stringent per-test Type I error rate than 0.05 for each statistical test. Note, in addition, because the study was conducted with employees of a single organization, its results have a low level of external validity. Fortunately, however, relations between actual job characteristics and various assumed outcomes have been shown in numerous studies.

Non-experiments in NSP settings

Nonexperimental studies in NSP settings are very common in organizational research (Austin et al., 2002; Scandura and Williams, 2000; Stone-Romero, Weaver, and Glenar, 1995). In fact, a study by Stone Romero et al. (1995) showed that for 1,929 articles published in the *Journal of Applied Psychology* for the period of 1975 to 1993, the percentage of studies that used nonexperimental designs was much greater than that of studies using either randomized experimental or quasi-experimental designs.

Example of use of design Stone-Romero Stone, and Hyatt (2003) were interested in determining the degree to which individuals viewed 12 personnel selection procedures (e.g., application blank, interview, mental ability test, and work sample) to be invasive of their privacy. In order to obtain data on this issue, they conducted two nonexperimental studies in NSP settings. In Study 1, Thurstone-type scaling procedures were used to obtain invasiveness scale scores for each of the 12 procedures, and in Study 2, participants provided direct ranks of the invasiveness of each of the same procedures. In addition, in Study 2, participants ranked the 12 procedures in terms of a number of factors that were viewed as possible antecedents of invasiveness (e.g., procedure reveals negative information, procedure invades the body, and procedure erroneously discredits applicants). Results of Study 1 revealed considerable differences in the relative invasiveness of the procedures. In addition, the results of Study were highly consistent with those of Study 1. Moreover, Study 2 showed a number of very strong correlations between invasiveness and its assumed antecedents.

Relative strengths of the study in terms of validity facets In view of the fact that the Stone et al. (2003) studies used nonexperimental designs, they had relatively low levels of internal validity; that is, no strong inferences were possible about the factors responsible for the invasiveness scale scores (Study 1) or the average ranks of the procedures (Study 2). In addition, it was not possible to infer that the assumed antecedents of invasiveness (Study 2) were actually causes of invasiveness. Although internal validity inferences were problematic, the same was not true for the construct validity of the measures used in the studies. More specifically, in both studies, the measures were straightforward and subjects were provided with brief descriptions of each of the selection procedures as well as with a definition of invasiveness.

Statistical conclusion validity was not an issue in Study 1, because it used scaling procedures, and no statistical tests were performed. In addition, in order to avert Type I error rate problems in Study 2, all statistical tests were performed using a 0.01 (as opposed to a 0.05) Type error rate. The external validity of the findings of the two studies also deserves consideration. In Study 1, the participants were employed adults living in two mid-western states, and in Study 2, they were graduate students at universities in Wisconsin and New York. Neither of the samples was randomly selected from any larger population. As a result, confident inferences to other samples of subjects were not possible. However, given that Studies 1 and 2 used different scaling methods for assessing the invasiveness of the procedures and the studies produced highly similar findings, the external validity of the results with respect to measures appears high. Finally, the results of the studies do not appear to be context (setting) specific in that the data of Study 1 were collected at the residences of subjects, whereas the data of Study 2 were collected in classrooms. Although both of these are NSP settings, they differ considerably from one another on a number of dimensions.

Nonexperiments in SP settings

Nonexperimental research is often conducted in SP settings. A common example of this is questionnaire-based research collected in university facilities that are dedicated to research (e.g., a behavioral laboratory).

Example of use of design A considerable body of research shows that perceptions of various types of stimuli are related to field independence, i.e., an individual difference dimension that deals with the ability of individuals to perceive stimuli independent of the context in which they are embedded. On the basis of a review of this literature, Stone (1979) hypothesized that field independence (i.e., an assumed cause) would be related to individuals' perceptions of task characteristics (i.e., assumed effects). Thus, he performed two nonexperimental studies in which subjects (a) completed a measure of field independence, (b) performed a task in a SP setting (i.e., a university-based laboratory room), and perceptions of the characteristics of the task. Note that all subjects performed the same task. Thus, Stone hypothesized that variations in perceptions of task characteristics would have to be a function of individual differences (e.g., in field independence). Among the various findings were that field independence correlated positively with perceptions of task variety, task identity, and feedback in both studies. In addition, several other correlation coefficients were of modest magnitude (e.g., −0.24), but were not statistically significant.

Relative strengths of the study in terms of validity facets In view of the fact that both studies were nonexperimental, they had very low levels of internal validity. As opposed to being the cause of task characteristics perceptions, field independence may simply have been correlated with one or more actual but unknown causes. In contrast to its standing on internal validity, the studies were high on construct validity. One reason for this is that both field independence and perceptions of task characteristics were measured with instruments for which there was considerable construct validity evidence. However, for two reasons, there are problems with the statistical conclusion validity of both studies. First, the sample size of Study 1 was too small to detect several relations. Second, the researcher tested several correlation coefficients for significance using a nominal Type

I error rate of 0.05, and failed to use a per-significance test Type I error rate that would have held the study-wise rate at 0.05 or below. Finally, the external validity of the results of the studies is questionable. One reason for this is that the subjects worked on a specific task in a SP setting. Thus, there's no assurance that the findings of the study would generalize to other tasks in other settings (e.g., NSP).

Independent of the experimental design used in a study and the type of setting (SP versus NSP) in which it takes place, a researcher must determine the degree to which its data provide support for one or more hypotheses. In quantitative (as opposed to qualitative) research, this determination is typically based on the results of statistical tests. Thus, the chapter next considers the distinction between statistical methods and experimental design. Of particular interest and importance is the use of the findings of statistical tests as a basis for supporting inferences about causal relations between (among) variables.

Statistical methods versus experimental design

Although three basic types of experimental designs (i.e., randomized experimental, quasi-experimental, and nonexperimental) were considered above, the statistical methods that might be used to analyze data from studies using such designs were not mentioned. However, the joint consideration of experimental design and statistical methods gives rise to an extremely important issue. The type of experimental design used in a study is *independent* of the statistical methods that can be used to analyze data from it. Thus, for example, data from a simple randomized experiment involving a control group and a treatment group can be analyzed with a number of statistical methods, including (a) an independent groups t-test, (b) analysis of variance, (c) bivariate correlation, using dummy codes for the independent variable, (d) path analysis (PA), and (e) structural equation modeling (SEM). Note, in addition, that the F stemming from the

ANOVA (analysis of variance) will equal the squared t from the t-test. In addition, the estimate of the proportion of variance explained by the ANOVA and the t-test will equal the r^2 derived from the bivariate correlation analysis. Moreover, in PA using a correlation matrix as the input, the path coefficient from the independent variable to the dependent variable will equal the bivariate correlation coefficient and will result in the same t-value as that obtained from the t-test.

One very important implication of the foregoing is the test of an assumed causal model using data from a nonexperimental study and statistical methods that purport to yield information about causality does *nothing whatsoever* to change the nature of the study's experimental design. Stated somewhat differently, 'causal modeling' methods are incapable of converting data from a nonexperiment into data that provide a firm basis for inferences about mediation.

Causal modeling

Although data from virtually all nonexperimental studies provide a very weak basis for making causal inferences, a number of so called causal modeling techniques are currently being used with such data to test assumed causal models, including PA, hierarchical multiple regression (HMR), and SEM (Baron and Kenny, 1986, 1979; Blalock, 1964, 1971; Bollen, 1989; Cohen et al., 2003; Kenny, 1979; Maruyama, 1998; Millsap, 2002). A large number of examples of such analyses can be found in articles published in the major journals in the organizational sciences (e.g., *Academy of Management Journal, Personnel Psychology, Journal of Applied Psychology, and Administrative Sciences Quarterly*) in the last four decades. In view of this, it is important to consider the conditions that are vital to valid inferences about causal relations between variables.

Conditions vital to inferences about cause

As indicated in the preceding section, inferences about cause are most justified in the case of studies that use randomized experimental designs, considerably less justified in studies that use quasi-experimental designs, and almost never justified in studies that use nonexperimental designs. The reason for this is that the conditions vital to causal inferences (i.e., temporal precedence, correlation, and absence of confounds) are most likely to be satisfied in research that uses randomized experimental designs, less likely to be satisfied in studies that use quasi-experimental designs, and virtually never satisfied in studies that use nonexperimental designs.

Even if one relaxed the temporal precedence requirement, the validity of causal inferences using data from nonexperimental studies would hinge on the assumed causal model being properly specified. Among the relevant specification considerations are the proper ordering of variables in the model, the inclusion of all important causes (exogenous variables) and mediator variables, the correct specification of the form (e.g., linear, nonlinear) of the relations considered by the model, the correct specification of the causal paths in the model (including those associated with reciprocal causation), and the use of measures of variables that have high levels of construct validity. It is impossible to satisfy these model specification requirements in virtually all nonexperimental studies. As a consequence, inferences about the validity of assumed causal models that are based upon such research rest on a very weak empirical foundation. As such, they are virtually never justified. In this regard, Cliff (1987) noted, that when a researcher is analyzing data from nonexperimental research 'it is not possible to isolate the empirical system sufficiently so that the nature of the relations among variables can be unambiguously ascertained' (p. 119). Consistent with this view, Rogosa (1987) wrote that 'Attempts to answer experimental … research questions with nonexperimental data seem fundamentally askew' (pp. 193–194). And, in accordance with these arguments, Ling (1982) argued that 'causal inference[s] from correlational [i.e., nonexperimental] data (in the absence of controlled experiments) … are at best a form of statistical fantasy' (p. 490).

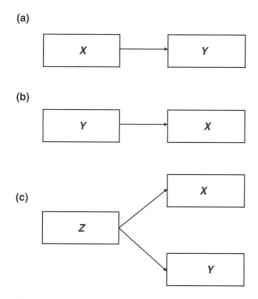

Figure 18.4 Alternative causal models that are consistent with an observed _X − Y_ correlation.

Model-data consistency versus model-reality consistency

It is quite common for researchers who use causal modeling procedures to argue that they have shown support for an assumed causal model as a result of model-data consistency, i.e., showing consistency between it and the covariances among variables considered by a nonexperimental study. The model-data consistency issue is considered in relation to Figures 18.4a–18.4c, which show several possible causal model possibilities for an observed relation between variables X and Y.

The general argument used by researchers who test assumed causal models using data from nonexperimental research has three parts:

(1) _The premise_: If my assumed causal model (e.g., that shown in Figure 18.4a) is correct, then the findings of my nonexperimental study will be consistent with it.

(2) _The research findings_: The findings of my study are consistent with my assumed causal model; that is, there is a nonzero correlation between X and Y.

(3) _The conclusion_: Therefore, my assumed causal model is correct.

Unfortunately, this conclusion is not based on sound reasoning. More specifically, it is an instance of the logical fallacy of _affirming the consequent_ (Kalish and Montague, 1964; Stone-Romero and Rosopa, 2008).

It is easy to see why the just-noted conclusion is unwarranted. The reason is that the data also may be consistent with a number of other possible causal models. For example, it is also consistent with (a) the model shown in Figure 18.4b which posits that $Y \rightarrow X$, and (b) the model shown in Figure 18.4c which specifies that $Z \rightarrow X$ and $Z \rightarrow Y$, thus the correlation between X and Y is noncausal. Assuming that the other models (Figures 18.4b and 18.4c) fit the data as well as the researcher's assumed causal model (Figure 18.4a), the researcher will _not_ be able to show that his or her preferred model is superior to the others.

However, in order to buttress the argument that his or her assumed causal model is correct, the researcher may argue that it is _theory consistent_. Unfortunately, this is of little or no help in terms of supporting claims about cause. The reason for this is that a number of different theories may be used to explain any observed covariance. Stone-Romero and Rosopa (2008) provide several illustrations of this. One has to do with the relation between job satisfaction and job performance. Researchers associated with the human relations movement argued that job satisfaction is the cause of job performance (see Pinder, 1989). However, expectancy theorists viewed job satisfaction as a consequence of job performance (e.g., Porter and Lawler, 1968). Still others posited that job satisfaction and job performance are reciprocally related to one another. Given these competing views, the researcher is in no position to argue that one theory is more supported by the data than another.

A second example of competing theoretical explanations concerns the relation between job satisfaction and organizational commitment. One group of theorists argued that organizational commitment causes job satisfaction (e.g., Bateman and Strasser, 1984; Koslowsky, 1991; Lance, 1991; Vandenberg and Lance, 1992; Wiener and Vardi, 1980). Another set of researchers asserted that job satisfaction causes organizational commitment (e.g., Williams and Hazer, 1986). Yet another group of researchers concluded that job satisfaction and organizational commitment are reciprocally related to one another. Finally, some opined that the relation between these two variables is spurious (e.g., Currivan, 1999). Again, a researcher who found a positive relation between these two variables would be hard-pressed to claim that one theoretical stance was superior to the alternatives.

Overall, it should be clear that the invocation of a theory is of little or no help in supporting the conclusion that the findings of a nonexperimental study have internal validity. Thus, theories are of little or no value in terms of buttressing claims about the correctness of an assumed causal model for such a study. Clearly, the best strategy for showing support for such a model is to perform one or more randomized experiments that test model-based predictions. Stone-Romero and Rosopa (2008) explain how such experiments can be used to support causal inferences for a simple causal model in which the relation between X and Y is mediated by M; that is, $X \rightarrow M \rightarrow Y$.

Prediction versus causation

Tests of assumed causal models often lead to results that can be used for prediction purposes. In this context, the term *prediction* is used in a statistical sense (Hays, 1994; Pedhazur, 1982). That is, information on a set of predictor variables can be used to predict the value of a criterion of interest. The fact that such prediction is possible does *not* imply that the predictor is a cause of the predicted variable (Bollen, 1989; Brannick, 1995; Cliff, 1987; Freedman, 1987; Holland, 1986; Kelloway, 1998; Ling, 1982; Millsap, 2002; Rogosa, 1987; Stone-Romero and Rosopa, 2004, 2008). For example, (a) the Zip Codes of individuals can be used to predict their annual income levels, (b) the weights of individuals can be used to predict

their heights, and (c) the heights of individuals at age 10 can be used to predict their heights at age 30. In each of these instances, the fact that the first variable can be used to predict the second does *not* serve as a basis for inferences about cause. Indeed, one can use statistical methods for post-dictive purposes; that is, a researcher can use data from a currently measured variable to post-dict events that took place *in the past* (Blum and Naylor, 1968; Stone-Romero, 2007a) For example, current assessments of neurological damage in Viet Nam veterans can be used to post-dict their previous level of exposure to neurotoxins (e.g., Agent Orange).

The very important implication of the above is that the ability to predict, in a statistical sense, has no necessary implications for the understanding of causal processes. Regrettably, there is considerable evidence of the fact that many researchers do not understand this fact. This issue is considered in the subsection titled '*Unwarranted causal inference in organizational research.*'

Causal inferences associated with nonmanipulable variables

In randomized experimental studies, researchers can manipulate such characteristics of stimulus of people as their age, race, biological sex, and ethnicity. As such, they can test for the effects of such variables on measured outcomes. As a result, they can support inferences about the impact of such variables on the outcomes. However, in nonexperimental studies the same variables are measured, as opposed to manipulated, and they are often *assumed* to have a number of roles. One of these is that of a moderator (Stone, 1988; Stone-Romero and Liakhovitski, 2002). For instance, in criterion-related validation studies, race has been studied as a moderator of the validity of predictors of job performance (e.g., Boehm, 1972; Schmidt and Hunter, 1974). A second role is that of an assumed independent variable. For example, numerous studies have examined the relation between sex and altruistic motives and/or behaviors (e.g., Fletcher and Major, 2004). Third, and finally, such variables are often used as controls in statistical analyses. Interestingly, however, it is typically the case that researchers fail to provide a sound rationale for this use of nonmanipulable variables.

An important issue in the nonexperimental studies is the degree to which researchers can make valid inferences about the effects of nonmanipulable variables. Clearly, in nonexperimental research, causal inferences are almost never justified. Thus, in research of this type it is inappropriate to argue about the *effects* of various nonmanipulable variables. It deserves adding that the vast majority of nonmanipulable variables that are studied in nonexperimental studies represent little more than surrogates for other nonmanipulable variables. For example, biological sex is a 'stand-in' for a number of variables (values, motives, attitudes, aptitudes, and abilities) that differ between men and women. Thus, in such research, it would be far better to measure such variables directly, as opposed to measuring the surrogate of sex.

Causal inferences from research using longitudinal, nonexperimental designs

In longitudinal studies, data on one or more variables are collected from the same set of subjects at two or more time periods (Rosenthal and Rosnow, 2008; Stone, 1978). In such studies that are of the nonexperimental variety, assumed causes, mediators, and effects are all measured. Because of this, it is virtually always the case that two of the three requirements for making causal inferences can not be satisfied (i.e., temporal precedence and ruling out rival explanations). In this regard, McDonald (1999) noted that longitudinal studies are 'open to the objection that an apparently causal relation between an earlier and a later measure may just represent a relation of temporally stable traits of the person, or perhaps aspects of an unfolding developmental sequence that does not allow conceptual manipulation of the earlier measured attribute' (p. 370). As a result, the internal validity of longitudinal studies of the nonexperimental variety is typically very low. Unfortunately, many researchers don't seem to be cognizant of this fact. More specifically, they assume that causal inferences are justified when a variable measured at one point in time covaries with a variable measured at a later point in time. Indeed, the Discussion sections of many nonexperimental studies of the cross-sectional variety (i.e., all variables measured at a single point in time) often offer ill-advised calls for longitudinal research to better understand causal mechanisms. Assuming that the same research is nonexperimental in nature, it will do nothing whatsoever to elucidate an understanding of causal connections between variables. The most effective way of developing such an understanding is to study such connections using randomized experimental research (Cook and Campbell, 1979; Shadish et al., 2002; Stone-Romero, 2002, 2007c; Stone-Romero and Rosopa, 2004, 2007, 2008). A generally less effective strategy is quasi-experimentation.

Unwarranted causal inference in organizational research

As noted above, causal inferences are most justified for studies that use randomized experimental designs, considerably less warranted for studies that use quasi-experimental designs, and virtually never justified for studies that use nonexperimental designs. Unfortunately, however, inappropriate inferences about causal connections between variables (i.e., inferences that are not justified by the type of experimental design of a study) are quite common in reports of the findings of nonexperimental research.

Unwarranted causal language (i.e., such terms as causes, effects, and influences) can be found in very large percentages of the articles published in the major journals in the organizational sciences. Evidence of this comes from a study by Stone-Romero and Gallaher (2006) that content analyzed 161 randomly sampled articles that were published in 1988, 1993, 1998, and 2003 volumes of *Personnel Psychology*, *Organizational Behavior and*

Human Decision Processes, the *Academy of Management Journal*, and the *Journal of Applied Psychology*. The articles reported the findings of studies that used randomized experimental, quasi-experimental, and nonexperimental designs. They were searched for instances of the inappropriate use of causal language in their Title, Abstract, and Results and/or Discussion sections. The analysis revealed that unwarranted causal language was used one or more times in 58 of the 73 articles that reported the results of research that used nonexperimental designs (79% of such articles), and 14 of the 18 articles that reported the findings of research that used quasi-experimental designs (78% of such articles). A few examples of the articles that contained inappropriate causal inferences are offered next.

Salanova, Agut, and Piero (2005)

The authors used SEM procedures and data from a nonexperimental study to test an assumed causal model involving two hypothesized mediating effects: (a) work engagement as a mediator of the relation between organizational resources and service climate and (b) customer loyalty as a mediator of the relation between employee performance and service climate. In the Results section of their article they stated that 'These results show that engagement fully mediated the relationship between organizational resources and service climate. In addition, employee performance mediated the relationship between service climate and customer loyalty' (p. 1222). They went on to report that 'Thus, the influence of organizational resources and engagement on employee performance was fully mediated by service climate' (p. 1222). The Discussion section of the article had several questionable causal claims: One is 'To sum up, a partial mediation effect of performance between service climate and customer loyalty has been identified' (p. 1224). To their credit, the authors noted that 'The research design was cross-sectional, and hence, the 'potential' reciprocal relationships between employees and customers cannot be fully interpreted causally' (p. 1225). Regrettably, this caution

does not serve to negate the unwarranted causal claims made in the article. It would have been far better for the authors to describe the findings of their study in a more circumspect manner than to make unwarranted claims about cause and then suggest that not all of them may be justified.

Hui, Lee, and Rousseau (2004)

The authors used data from a nonexperimental study and SEM to test an assumed causal model in which instrumentality was posited to be a mediator of relations between several types of psychological contracts (i.e., relational, balanced, and transactional) and a number of putative consequences (i.e., altruism, conscientiousness, civic virtue, courtesy, and sportsmanship). In the article's Abstract they wrote that 'The authors found evidence that instrumentality mediates the relationship of relational and balanced forms with OCB; however, the transactional contract form is directly related to OCB' (p. 311). Their Results section had two clear statements about causal connections between variables: First, 'This indicated that the transactional contract had a direct effect on OCB, a finding contrary to Hypothesis 1' (p. 317). Second, 'The transactional contract form had direct effects on OCB, but balanced and relational contracts did not, contrary to Hypothesis 1' (p. 317). Interestingly, the findings of their study led them to conclusions about effects that differed from their assumed causal model. In view of the fact that causal modeling is intended to confirm (as opposed to generate) causal models, the validity of these conclusions seems especially problematic. Finally, the Discussion section of their article had several conclusions about causal effects: First, 'Our results showed that the transactional contracts measured in China had a direct effect on OCB, whereas the relational and balanced contract forms were related to OCB only through instrumentality beliefs' (p. 318). Second, 'Instrumentality mediates the effects of relational and balanced contracts on OCB' (p. 318). Having offered these inferences, they went on to offer one design-related caution. More specifically, because their study used a nonexperimental design, 'Longitudinal research designs are needed to test the causal effects of psychological effects of psychological contracts on outcomes' (p. 319). As indicated above, unless longitudinal designs involve experimentation, they are generally of little or no value in showing causal connections between variables. It's not the time at which variables are measured that allows for causal inferences. Rather, as is noted above, it is a design that involves random assignment of units to conditions, the manipulation of causal variables, and design-based control of confounds.

Brown, Jones, and Leigh (2005) Using data from a nonexperimental study of representatives of an office supply manufacturer, the authors tested an assumed causal model in which self-efficacy was viewed as a mediator of relations between (a) the assumed antecedents of previous performance and organizational resources and (b) the hypothesized consequence of current performance. The data were analyzed using the Baron and Kenny (1986) regression-based strategy. In the Abstract of the article, the authors wrote 'the results reveal a pattern of *moderated mediation,* in which goal level mediates the indirect effect of self-efficacy on performance when role overload is low, but not when it is high' (p. 972; italics in original). Consistent with the same inference, in the Results section of the article, the authors stated that their findings indicated support for 'the moderated mediation effect in Hypothesis 4. In other words, goal level mediates the effect of self-efficacy on performance, but only when role overload is low' (p. 977). And, in the Discussion section of the article, the authors specified that 'The results indicate a pattern of moderated mediation, in which goal level mediates the indirect effect of self-efficacy on performance when role overload is low, but not when role overload is high. When role overload is low, self-efficacy has both direct and indirect effects on performance …, but high role overload negates both types of effects' (p. 977). The Discussion section did not contain a single caution

about using the findings of a nonexperimental study as a basis for making causal inferences.

CONCLUSIONS

Research design and validity inferences

A researcher has many options when designing a study, including those that pertain to its experimental design, which is the most important determinant of its *internal validity*. As noted in the preceding section, the experimental design of a study should be governed by its major purpose(s). If the sole interest of a researcher is to determine if two or more variables are related to one another, he or she can conduct a study that uses a nonexperimental design. However, if the researcher is concerned with determining causal relations between or among variables, he or she should opt for one or more randomized experimental studies (Stone-Romero and Rosopa, 2008). And, in instances where experimentation is possible, but units can not be randomly assigned to treatment conditions, one or more quasi-experimental studies should be conducted (Stone-Romero and Rosopa, 2008). In short, if causal inferences are an important issue, research that uses randomized experimental designs is the most appropriate means of developing evidence on which to base them.

Irrespective of the experimental design used in a study, a researcher must devote attention to the other facets of validity. First, to bolster inferences about *construct validity*, he or she must take care to insure that the sampling particulars of a study (e.g., setting, units, measures, and manipulations) are faithful representations of the relevant constructs. For example, it is of virtually no value to show that a manipulation of X leads to changes in Y if a researcher has little or no knowledge about the constructs associated with these variables. In addition, the construct validity of a study would be questionable if it dealt with the decision-making processes of neurosurgeons, but used undergraduate business students as subjects.

Second, a researcher has to be concerned about the validity of inferences derived from statistical analyses, i.e., *statistical conclusion validity*. It is of virtually no value for a researcher to claim that a study showed support for a hypothesized relation between two variables if this finding was based on a study that used inflated study-wise Type I error rates. In addition, the study would be of no value if there truly was a relation between the variables, but the study lacked the statistical power to detect it.

Third, and finally, a study might be very strong in terms of internal validity, construct validity, and statistical conclusion validity, but weak with regard to *external validity*. Thus, if it is important to make inferences about a casual relation to sampling particulars other than those considered by a study (e.g., to other sets of units, manipulations, measures, and settings), the researcher must conduct additional studies to support claims about external validity. However, external validity is not always an important concern in research (Mook, 1983).

Experimental design and data analytic strategies

From the foregoing it should be clear that there is a very important distinction between experimental design and the methods used to analyze data from a study. Regrettably, large numbers of publications in the organizational sciences and many other disciplines provide clear evidence of a very prevalent problem: Researchers who are interested in showing causal relations between (among) variables seem to think that statistical methods are an appropriate substitute for sound experimental design. That is, they base conclusions about causal connections between (among) variables on the results of applying causal modeling procedures (e.g., HMR, PA, and SEM) to data from nonexperimental research (see Stone-Romero and Gallaher, 2006; Stone-Romero and Rosopa, 2004, 2005, 2008). However, valid inferences about cause

stem from sound experimental design, *not the use of causal modeling procedures*. Consequently, when nonexperimental research is reported, researchers must be careful to avoid causal interpretations of their findings. Recall, for example, that an observed relation between two variables (e.g., X and Y) can be consistent with multiple assumed causal models (see Figure 18.4), and a researcher typically has no basis for legitimately arguing that one such model (e.g., Figure 18.4a) is superior to the alternatives (e.g., Figures 18.4b, 18.4c, and 18.4d).

Methodological pluralism

In studies of virtually all phenomena in the organizational sciences, methodological pluralism is highly desirable. In early stages of research on a phenomenon, nonexperimental studies may offer valuable clues about the correlates of a variable that is of interest to an investigator. In addition, the results of nonexperimental research may provide a basis for the formulation of hypotheses about causal connections between the same variable and its assumed antecedents. However, such hypotheses are best tested using randomized experimental designs.

Another highly important dimension of methodological pluralism relates to the empirical realization of the constructs considered by a study. In any given study, it is vital to demonstrate that there is a clear connection between any given construct and its sampling particulars (e.g., manipulations and/or measures of variables). However, in subsequent studies it is critical to demonstrate that the relation that was observed between the variables was not an artifact of specific sampling particulars. Thus, for example, if a researcher used a specific measure of an assumed effect construct in one study, he or she should conduct follow-up research that uses alternative measures. In addition, if the researcher manipulated an independent variable in a particular way in one study, he or she should use alternate manipulations in subsequent studies.

A final word

Randomized experimental research is vital to developing an understanding of causal relations between a specific variable and its assumed antecedents and consequences. The findings of such research can contribute significantly to the development of both models and theories. In addition, they afford the firmest basis for the formulation and application of appropriate interventions aimed at changing organizational processes and practices. In terms of multiple criteria that are highly important to both scientists and practitioners, it is critical that research on relations between variables have high levels of internal, construct, external, and statistical conclusion validity. However, of these types of validity, internal is the *sine qua non* (Campbell Stanley, 1963).

REFERENCES

Ajzen, I. (1988) *Attitudes, Personality, and Behavior*, Chicago, IL: Dorsey Press.

Aronson, E., Ellsworth, P., Carlsmith, J.M. and Gonzales, M.H. (1990) *Methods of Research in Social Psychology* (second edn.), New York: McGraw-Hill.

Austin, J.T., Scherbaum, C.A. and Mahlman, R.A. (2002) History of research methods in industrial and organizational psychology: measurement, design, analysis. In S. G. Rogelberg (Ed.), *Handbook of Research Methods in Industrial and Organizational Psychology* Malden, MA: Blackwell, pp. 1–33.

Baron, R.M. and Kenny, D.A. (1986) 'The moderator-mediator variable distinction in social psychological research: conceptual, strategic, and statistical considerations', *Journal of Personality and Social Psychology*, 51: 1173–82.

Bateman, T.S. and Strasser, S. (1984) a longitudinal analysis of the antecedents of organizational commitment, *Academy of Management Journal*, 27: 95–112.

Berkowitz, L. and Donnerstein, E. (1982) 'External validity is more than skin deep: some answers to criticisms of laboratory experiments', *American Psychologist*, 37: 245–57.

Blalock, H.M. (1964) *Causal Inferences in Nonexperimental Research*, New York: W.W. Norton.

Blalock, H.M. (1971) *Causal Models in the Social Sciences*, Chicago: Aldine.

Blanchard, E.B., Peters, M.L., Hermann, C., Turner, S.M., Buckley, T.C., Barton, K. and Dentinger, M.P. (1997) 'Direction of temperature control in the thermal biofeedback treatment of vascular headache', *Applied Psychophysiology and Biofeedback*, 22: 227–45.

Blum, M. and Naylor, J.C. (1968) *Industrial Psychology: Its Theoretical and Social Foundations*, New York: Harper and Row.

Boehm, V.R. (1972) 'Negro-white differences in validity of employment and training selection procedures: summary of research evidence', *Journal of Applied Psychology*, 56: 33–39.

Bollen, K.A. (1989) *Structural Equations with Latent Variables*, New York: Wiley.

Brannick, M.T. (1995) 'Critical comments on applying covariance structure modeling', *Journal of Organizational Behavior*, 16: 201–13.

Brown, S.P., Jones, E. and Leigh, T.W. (2005) 'The attenuating effect of role overload on relationships linking self-efficacy and goal level to work performance', *Journal of Applied Psychology*, 90: 972–9.

Campbell, J.P. (1986) 'Labs, fields, and straw issues', in E.A. Locke (ed.), *Generalizing From Laboratory to Field Settings: Research Findings From Industrial-Organizational Psychology, Organizational Behavior, and Human Resource Management*, Lexington, MA; Lexington Books, pp.269–79.

Campbell, D.T. and Stanley, J.C. (1963) *Experimental and Quasi-Experimental Designs for Research*, Chicago: Rand McNally.

Cliff, N. (1987) 'Comments on Professor Freedman's paper', *Journal of Educational Statistics*, 12: 158–60.

Cohen, J., Cohen, P., West, S.G. and Aiken, L.S. (2003) *Applied Multiple Regression/Correlation Analysis for the Behavioral Sciences* (third edn.), Mahwah, NJ: Erlbaum.

Cook, T.D. and Campbell, D.T. (1979) *Quasi-experimentation: Design and Analysis Issues for Field Settings*, Boston, MA: Houghton Mifflin.

Cronbach, L.J. and Meehl, P.E. (1955) 'Construct validity in psychological tests', *Psychological Bulletin*, 52: 281–302.

Currivan, D.B. (1999) 'The causal order of job satisfaction and organizational commitment in models of employee turnover', *Human Resource Management Review*, 9: 495–524.

Dipboye, R.L. and Flanagan, M.F. (1979) 'Research settings in industrial and organizational psychology: are findings in the field more generalizable than in the laboratory?', *American Psychologist*, 34: 141–50.

Fletcher, T.D. and Major, D.A. (2004) 'Medical students' motivations to volunteer: an examination of the nature of gender differences', *Sex Roles*, 51(1–2): 109–14.

Freedman, D.A. (1987) 'As others see us: a case study in path analysis', *Journal of Educational Statistics*, 12: 101–28.

Fromkin, H.L. and Streufert, S. (1976) 'Laboratory experimentation', in M.D. Dunnette (ed.). *Handbook of industrial and organizational psychology*, Chicago, IL: Rand McNally, pp. 415–65.

Guion, R.M. (2002) 'Validity and reliability', in S.G. Rogelberg (ed.), *Handbook of Research Methods in Industrial and Organizational Psychology*, Malden, MA: Blackwell, pp. 57–76.

Hackman, J.R., Pearce, J.L. and Wolfe, J.C. (1978) 'Effects of changes in job characteristics on work attitudes and behaviors: a naturally occurring quasi-experiment', *Organizational Behavior and Human Performance*, 21: 289–304.

Hays, W.L. (1994) *Statistics* (fifth edn.), Ft. Worth, TX: Harcourt Brace.

Holland, P.W. (1986) 'Statistics and causal inference', *Journal of the American Statistical Association*, 81: 945–60.

Hui, C., Lee, C. and Rousseau, D.M. (2004) 'Psychological contract and organizational citizenship behavior in China: Investigating generalizability and instrumentality', *Journal of Applied Psychology*, 89: 311–21.

Kalish, D. and Montague, R. (1964) *Logic: Techniques of formal reasoning*, New York: Harcourt, Brace, & World.

Kenny, D.A. (1979) *Correlation and Causality*, New York: Wiley.

Kerlinger, F.N. and Lee, H.B. (2000) *Foundations of Behavioral Research* (fourth edn.), Belmont, CA: Wadsworth.

Kelloway, E.K. (1998) *Using LISREL for Structural Equation Modeling: A Researcher's Guide*, Thousand Oaks, CA: Sage.

Koslowsky, M. (1991) 'A longitudinal analysis of job satisfaction, commitment, and intention to leave', *Applied Psychology: An International Review*, 40: 405–15.

Lance, C.E. (1991) 'Evaluation of a structural model relating job satisfaction, organizational commitment, and precursors to voluntary turnover', *Multivariate Behavioral Research*, 26: 137–62.

Ling, R.F. (1982) 'Review of *correlation and causality* by David A. Kenny', *Journal of the American Statistical Association*, 77: 489–91.

Locke, E.A. (1986) *Generalizing From Laboratory To Field Settings: Research Findings From Industrial-Organizational Psychology, Organizational Behavior, and Human Resource Management*, Lexington, MA: Lexington Books.

Maruyama, G.M. (1998) *Basics of Structural Equation Modeling*, Thousand Oaks, CA: Sage.

Mathieu, J.E. and Taylor, S.R. (2006) 'Clarifying conditions and choice points for mediational type inferences in organizational behavior', *Journal of Organizational Behavior*, 27: 1031–56.

McDonald, R.P. (1999) *Test Theory: A Unified Treatment*, Mahwah, NJ: Erlbaum.

Millsap, R.E. (2002) 'Structural equation modeling: a user's guide', in F. Drasgow and N. Schmitt (eds), *Measuring and Analyzing Behavior in Organizations*, San Francisco: Jossey-Bass, pp. 257–301 .

Mook, D.G. (1983) 'In defense of external invalidity', *American Psychologist*, 38: 379–387.

Nunnally, J.C. (1978) *Psychometric theory* (second edn.), New York: McGraw-Hill.

Pedhazur, E.J. (1982) *Multiple regression in behavioral research: Explanation and prediction* (second edn.), New York: Holt, Rinehart and Winston.

Pinder, C.C. (1998) *Work Motivation in Organizational Behavior*, Upper Saddle River, NJ: Prentice-Hall.

Porter, L.W. and Lawler, E.E. (1968) *Managerial Attitudes and Performance*, Homewood, IL: Irwin-Dorsey.

Rogosa, D. (1987) 'Causal models do not support scientific conclusions: a comment in support of Freedman', *Journal of Educational Statistics*, 12: 185–95.

Rosenthal, R. and Rosnow, R.L. (2008) *Essentials of Behavioral Research* (third edn.), New York: McGraw-Hill.

Rosopa, P.J. and Stone-Romero, E.F. (2008) Problems with detecting assumed mediation using the hierarchical multiple regression strategy, *Human Resource Management Review*, 18: 294–310.

Runkel, P.J. and McGrath, J.E. (1972) *Research On Human Behavior: A Systematic Guide to Method*, New York: Holt, Rinehart, & Winston.

Salanova, M., Agut, S. and Piero, J.M. (2005) 'Linking organizational resources and work engagement to employee performance and customer loyalty: the mediation of service climate', *Journal of Applied Psychology*, 90: 1217–27.

Scandura, T.A. and Williams, E.A. (2000) Research methodology in management: current practices, trends, and implications for future research, *Academy of Management Journal*, 43: 1248–64.

Schmidt, F.L. and Hunter, J.E. (1974) 'Racial and ethnic bias in psychological tests: divergent implications of two definitions of test bias', *American Psychologist*, 29: 1–8.

Shadish, W.R., Cook, T.D. and Campbell, D.T. (2002) *Experimental and quasi-experimental designs for generalized causal inference*, Boston, MA: Houghton Mifflin.

Stone, E.F. (1978) *Research Methods in Organizational Behavior*, Santa Monica, CA: Goodyear.

Stone, E.F. (1979) 'Field independence and perceptions of task characteristics: a laboratory investigation', *Journal of Applied Psychology*, 64: 305–10.

Stone, E.F. (1988) 'Moderator variables in research: a review and analysis of conceptual and methodological issues', in G.R. Ferris and K.M. Rowland (eds), *Research in Personnel and Human Resources Management*, Vol. 6, Greenwich, CT; JAI Press, pp.191–229.

Stone, D.L. and Stone, E.F. (1985) 'The effects of feedback favorability and feedback consistency on self-perceived task competence and perceived feedback accuracy', *Organizational Behavior and Human Decision Processes*, 36: 167–85.

Stone, E.F., Gueutal, H.G., Gardner, D.G. and McClure, S. (1983) 'A field experiment comparing information-privacy values, beliefs, and attitudes across several types of organizations', *Journal of Applied Psychology*, 68: 459–68.

Stone, E.F., Stone, D.L. and Gueutal, H.G. (1990) 'The influence of cognitive ability on responses to questionnaire measures', *Journal of Applied Psychology*, 75: 418–27.

Stone-Romero, E.F. (1994) 'Construct validity issues in organizational behavior research', in J. Greenberg (ed.), *Organizational Behavior: The State of the Science*, Hillsdale, NJ: Lawrence Erlbaum Associates, pp.155–79.

Stone-Romero, E.F. (2002) 'The relative validity and usefulness of various empirical research designs', in S.G. Rogelberg (ed.), *Handbook of Research Methods in Industrial and Organizational Psychology*, Malden, MA: Blackwell, pp.77–98.

Stone-Romero, E.F., Stone, D.L. and Hyatt, D. (2003) 'Personnel selection procedures and invasion of privacy', *Journal of Social Issues*, 59: 343–68.

Stone-Romero, E.F. (2007a) 'Non-experimental designs', in S. Rogelberg (ed.), *The Encyclopedia of Industrial and Organizational Psychology*, Beverly Hills, CA: Sage Publishing, pp. 519–21.

Stone-Romero, E.F. (2007b) 'Quasi-experimental designs', in S. Rogelberg (ed.), *The Encyclopedia of Industrial and Organizational Psychology*, Beverly Hills, CA: Sage Publishing, pp. 655–57.

Stone-Romero, E.F. (2007c) 'Experimental designs', in S. Rogelberg (ed.) *The encyclopedia of Industrial and Organizational Psychology*, Beverly Hills, CA: Sage Publishing, pp. 239–41.

Stone-Romero, E.F. and Gallaher, L. (2006) *Inappropriate Use of Causal Language in Reports of Non-Experimental Research*, Paper presented at the meeting of the Society for Industrial and Organizational Psychology, Dallas, TX.

Stone-Romero, E.F. and Liakhovitski, D. (2002) 'Strategies for detecting moderator variables: a review of theory and research', *Research in Personnel and Human Resources Management*, 21: 333–72.

Stone-Romero, E.F. and Rosopa, P.J. (2004) 'Inference problems with hierarchical multiple regression-based tests of mediating effects', in J. Martocchio (Series ed.), *Research in Personnel and Human Resources Management*, Greenwich, CT: Elsevier, pp. 249–90.

Stone-Romero, E.F. and Rosopa, P. (2007) 'Tests of mediating effects', in N.J. Salkind (ed.) *The Encyclopedia of Measurement and Statistics*, Beverly Hills, CA: Sage Publishing, pp. 995–9.

Stone-Romero, E.F. and Rosopa, P. (2008) 'The relative validity of inferences about mediation as a function of research design characteristics', *Organizational Research Methods*, 11: 326–52.

Stone-Romero, E.F., Weaver, A.E. and Glenar, J.L. (1995) 'Trends in research design and data analytic strategies in organizational research', *Journal of Management*, 21: 141–57.

Vandenberg, R.J. and Lance, C.E. (1992) 'Examining the causal order of job satisfaction and organizational commitment', *Journal of Management*, 18: 153–67.

Wiener, Y. and Vardi, Y. (1980) 'Relationships between job, organization, and career commitments and work outcomes: an integrative approach', *Organizational Behavior and Human Performance*, 26: 81–96.

Williams, L.J. and Hazer, J.T. (1986) 'Antecedents and consequences of satisfaction and commitment in turnover models: a reanalysis using latent variable structural equation methods', *Journal of Applied Psychology*, 71: 219–31.

19

Cross-Cultural Comparative Studies and Issues in International Research Collaboration

Mark F. Peterson

INTRODUCTION

The methods issues in cross-cultural organizational research are linked with the distinctive characteristics of the phenomena studied, the theoretical and metatheoretical perspectives taken by researchers, and the social process of collaborating across culture and distance. Whereas most organizational research can be simplified by assuming that the phenomena encountered in one's own part of the world are all that matter, cross-cultural research draws attention to phenomena that are sometimes different in nuance and at other times profoundly different. The methods for studying culture, the choice of theories and constructs, and the intellectual traditions in which researchers understand them vary not only with personal idiosyncrasies, but also with the societies in which researchers are geographically located. The need to access diverse populations to do global research

means that researchers increasingly find advantage in forming collaborative groups, which are challenging to participate in and to manage due to communication constraints, variability in preferred methods, theories, and traditions, and global differences in work situations and personal lives.

The aim of this chapter is to identify major controversies in cross-cultural organizational research methods, particularly those that rely on questionnaires, as well as in the social process of doing such research. I will first consider basic technical issues that produce ongoing controversies and common misunderstandings. Since even researchers who share a basic methodological perspective rarely agree about all of these issues, international teams struggle with technical controversies. Attention then turns to methodological implications of perspectives on culture and controversies in cross-cultural research. Third, the interplay of ideals about how to conduct cross-cultural research, with the researcher's cultural and personal situation will be considered, and ways to work successfully with a multinational research team will be suggested. Given space constraints, readers are referred to further studies of cultural differences involving, for example, hierarchical moderated regression, multigroup structural models, and hierarchical linear modelling, and also for research using qualitative methods (Easterby-Smith and Malina, 1999; Raudenbush and Bryk, 2002; Van de Vijver and Leung, 1997).

Technical issues

Construct equivalence and level of analysis present the greatest technical challenges in cross-cultural research. Equivalence issues plague researchers who wish to compare one phenomenon, say an attitude like commitment, across several nations based on some theoretically meaningful aspect of national culture, such as individualism (Gelade et al., 2006). Here, we find that we are also comparing languages, thought patterns, social norms, regulatory environments, social structures, and probably other issues of which we are unaware. Consequently, the ability to control for factors that confound the substantive comparison of interest with the degree of precision that is typical in domestic research is only possible when comparing a few select phenomena in small numbers of nations (Leung, 2008).

Translation equivalence

The technical literature concerning equivalence starts from careful translation checking (Brislin et al., 1973). For example, *back translation* requires having one party translate a survey, another translate it back to the source language, and then both to engage in a process of comparison and correction. *Parallel translation* is achieved by having two people separately translate a survey into a target language, and then either the translators or others compare the translations and make corrections. Back translation is more consistent with current norms in most parts of the world, but the decision concerning which to use is an issue of power as much as research norms. In practice, back translation puts power for making final judgments about translation adequacy in the hands of the party who designed the survey, usually in English. Parallel translation puts this power in the hands of the parties who are fluent in the target language.

The translation procedure used is important, but is now seen as secondary to quantitative indicators of translation quality. In the early years of comparative research, documenting the careful conduct of translation was considered state of the art for achieving equivalence. However, greater confidence is now placed in indicators of equivalence in measurement structures. Equivalence is assessed by comparing reliability coefficients or by using the measurement portions of structural equation modelling programs (Van de Vijver and Leung, 1997). The availability of quantitative indicators means that the results of a pilot study to evaluate measure equivalence is likely to be more meaningful than are debates about the virtues of back translation or parallel translation.

Most discussions of translation equivalence in comparative survey research assume that the structures of different languages are similar, leaving translation adequacy as the main explanation for nonequivalence. However, languages have long been known to differ, often in surprising ways (Nisbett et al., 2001; Sapir, 1921). Many controversies about the implications of phrasing questionnaire items in the generic (English) organizational literature concern the distinctive characteristics of English, such as whether pronouns are singular or plural. For example, how my superior treats *me* may be different from how my superior treats *us*. In comparative studies of leadership with colleagues in Japan, we faced the problem of communicating such differences in Japanese, where the subject of a sentence is often implicit, especially when the subject is personal like I, me, we, or you (Peterson, Maiya and Herreid, 1993). The awkwardness of explicitly representing the 'me' versus 'us' distinction in Japanese is likely to evoke responses different from those one would expect from survey research in English. Researchers who collaborate in a multiple-language project also need to discuss whether their goal is to extend work that is established in one language into another. In that case, the success of a translation might be evaluated relative to the language of origin. Where a measure is being more substantially redesigned, as in a study that redesigned role stress measures (Peterson et al., 1995), or a new measure is created for global use (Leung et al., 2002), overall similarity among the translations being studied may be more important.

A full treatment of language structures is outside the scope of the present chapter. However, it would be surprising if any survey measure that has been carefully tailored to promote both reliability and validity in one language will have precisely the same meaning in languages from radically different language groups. Still, languages tend to be sufficiently analogous that effective communication is typically possible (Pike, 1982, pp. 132–133). A host of comparative survey-based projects show that measures which were designed to have optimal psychometric properties in one language can be effectively translated into many others with only a modest loss of precision. The reduction in a reliability coefficient from 0.80 for a measure in one language to 0.70 in another adds imprecision, but such differences are often treated as sufficiently manageable to allow comparison (Leung, 2008).

Conceptual equivalence

Issues of translation equivalence merge with issues of conceptual equivalence since both are rooted in language. Concepts correspond between societies to different degrees. For example, Farh et al., (2004) report an inductive study of organization citizenship behaviour (OCB) in China. Their analysis indicates that some constructs, such as 'taking initiative', appear to be almost identical to US concepts, such as 'conscientiousness'. Other Chinese concepts, such as 'helping coworkers', shows nuances of a US concept, in this case 'altruism'. However, others, such as 'interpersonal harmony', are more uniquely linked to China's heritage. Smith (2008) reviews indigenous management concepts from understudied parts of the world that only roughly correspond to ideas familiar in the English literature.

As with measure equivalence, discussions of conceptual equivalence are increasingly framed in statistical terms. That is, conceptual equivalence is evident when a measure fits into a set of relationships with other measures in theoretically meaningful ways, such as a nomological net, in the same way in different parts of the world. When viewed in this way, discussions of conceptual equivalence are typically reflected in hypothesis development and testing rather than in validity assessment. Data analysis techniques used to establish such relationships range from showing that regression slopes are equivalent in different nations to applying even more complex multigroup structural models (Van de Vijver and Leung, 1997). Controversies about the technical merits of different methods for assessing cultural differences in relationships among measures concern the strengths and limitations of regression, structural equation modelling, and hierarchical linear modelling (Raudenbush and Bryk, 2002).

Response bias

Language differences suggest that item phrasing is likely to affect inter-item covariance, reliability coefficients, or measurement model equivalence. However, language equivalence issues and culturally linked communication style preferences can also affect the tendency to use high, low, or intermediate values in responses (Smith, 2004). Significant anecdotal evidence has been collected concerning cultural differences in response patterns (Van de Vijver and Leung, 1997). National differences have recently been explained in part by a link to Hofstede's (2001) concept of power distance (Smith, 2004). Average responses to surveys in large power distance nations are generally found to be more positive than those in small power distance nations.

In addition to cultural patterns in response tendencies, nuances reflecting *degree* in specific words can create language differences for particular items. The sensitivity of responses to the phrasing of alternatives is well recognized for English-language surveys (Bass et al, 1974). However, adverbs of degree may not match precisely between languages. For example, in a set of response alternatives ranging from 'strongly agree' to 'strongly disagree', the English 'slightly' agree can convey slightly more agreement than the Chinese *you dian* agree. Similarly, the phrasing of the question stem may have a different degree of positive, neutral, or negative connotation in two languages. In a simple question like 'How hungry are you?', a Dutch translation that represents hunger as *honger* relates to the upper ranges of this phenomenon (overlapping with starving), whereas the alternative Dutch *trek* relates more closely to the more ordinary degrees of hunger experienced in developed nations.

One solution has been to design measures using forced-choice alternatives or rankings that make response patterns difficult or impossible. For example, the *Meaning of Working* project (1987) asked respondents to rank a set of fourteen goals to avoid possible cultural differences in the propensity to say that all work goals are very desirable. Even if respondents would like to say that each goal is the most important, the answering system only allowed a respondent to rank one as the most important. Another approach has been to adjust responses to Likert-scale measures using within-subject standardization or mean-centring. Within-subject standardization requires subtracting the average for each respondent across all items from the score of each item, and dividing the result by the standard deviation of the respondent's answer across all items (Hofstede, 2001). Some researchers have, then, helpfully rescored the result so that it corresponds to the original response alternatives (Hanges and Dickson, 2004). Mean-centring takes the first step of subtracting each respondent's overall mean, but leaves out the second step of dividing by each respondent's standard deviation.

Unfortunately, these solutions to the response pattern problem have significant limitations. They all produce dependencies among items that limit the reliability of indices that combine items (except when adjustments are made to Likert-scaled items after indices are formed), and create covariances among the adjusted items that may not be meaningful. Consider, for example, two questions from the Organizational Commitment Questionnaire (Mowday et al., 1979) about which most people are likely to have similar attitudes; 'My values and the values of this organization are quite similar', and 'I am proud to work for this organization'. If respondents were asked to rank these obviously similar items as '1' and '2', their answers would necessarily have a correlation of -1.0. A similar negative correlation appears if respondents answer these questions using Likert scales, and the researcher then standardizes the responses within subjects as described in the preceding section.

The extent to which such within-subject adjustments are troublesome is affected by two considerations. One is the number of items, such that the dependencies produced are smaller as the number of items increases. The other is the original covariances among the items, such that the tendency to reduce meaningful variance is increased as the original covariances increase (Saville and Willson, 1991; Smith, 2004).

Sample equivalence

Cross-cultural researchers also face the problem of sample equivalence. Referring to the example of commitment, one would not want comparisons to be confounded by other demographic characteristics besides nation. Demographic confounds are readily resolved in domestic research by statistically controlling for factors such as age or gender before comparing commitment levels across organizations. Such controls, though, typically assume that any implications of age and gender are reasonably consistent across organizations. Such an assumption is generally reasonable within a single nation, but is less reasonable across nations. Cultural variability in the meaning of demographics is reflected in showing respect for age and gender (Peng and Peterson, 2008). For example, in Japan, only those women who are extraordinarily committed to remaining employed tend to continue working for a major employer beyond their mid-20s. It is also unusual for a man to remain with a major employer beyond age 55 unless he holds a senior management position. Glazer and Beehr's (2005) study of nurses in four nations indicates that simple statistical controls for other sample characteristics such as occupation or employer type are similarly problematic where the social status or employment conditions affecting a group vary by nation. The consequence is that implications of demographic characteristics may well need to be considered, but the limitations of the simple statistical controls used in domestic research must be recognized.

Data collection process equivalence

National or cultural differences can also affect the meaning of data collection procedures. In some nations, postal systems work efficiently, but in others mail surveys can be lost or delayed. In some places, personal interviewers who come to a private home are viewed as normal visitors, but elsewhere they are viewed as potential threats and may be at risk themselves. In some nations, research that includes separate-source performance evaluations or access to personnel records requires respondents to sign a consent form, but in other nations, it does not. In a study of local governments, I found that if a Japanese organization agrees to participate, then nearly all employees will voluntarily participate as well; in the United States, however, organization consent and employee consent tend to be separate issues. Superficially equivalent data collection procedures are not the same as substantive equivalence, and a degree of nonequivalence in the data collection process

is likely in comparative projects (Lincoln and Kalleberg, 1990).

Adapting to equivalence constraints

How do we solve issues of limited equivalence? The magic of randomization (Campbell and Stanley, 1963) is typically out of reach in cross-cultural research. We are left with the partially satisfactory recourse of making statistical adjustments to our measures, matching respondents as best we can, and interpreting the likely implications of uncontrolled contextual differences. Precise equivalence gives way to sufficient comparability to allow reasonably meaningful comparisons with caveats and needs for replication (Leung, 2008). Subjectively evaluating context to give meaning to comparisons can require even a quantitatively oriented researcher to be something of a linguist, anthropologist, economist, sociologist and psychologist, or to invite collaborators from other disciplines (House et al., 2004).

Level of analysis

Is culture a characteristic of a society or of its members? As a theoretical question, I will deal with this again in the following section, but it also has a technical side.

Many cross-cultural projects collect survey data from individuals then aggregate those data to create measures that are typically used to represent a national collective. The mechanics of creating nation scores is simple; take an average across a set of items and across a set of people. The basis for making decisions about what items to combine to create nation scores, however, is frequently misunderstood even by experienced scholars. Researchers typically create measures based on individual-level measurement structures, then perform a second set of analyses to see whether there is sufficient variance among units at a higher level (groups, organizations, nations, etc.) to aggregate the individual-level measures to that level (Peterson and Castro, 2006). Hofstede (2001), however, notes that the correlations and covariances between items on which measure decisions are based differ depending on the level of analysis at which they are calculated.

Consider, for example, a hypothetical study that seeks to create measures to represent the aspects of individualism and collectivism that Oyserman et al. (2002) identify in their meta-analytical review of individualism-collectivism. In principle, one might be able to construct ten items that provide face-valid indicators of individualism and another ten relevant to collectivism. It is frequently reported that, when such items are analysed at the individual level, two or more constructs emerge that are internally homogenous and only modestly correlated with one another (Kirkman et al., 2006; Oyserman, et al., 2002). That is, it is not unusual for one person to express both individualistic and collectivistic values, or indeed to express neither individualistic nor collectivistic values. However, when such items are aggregated to the nation level, and correlations among these items are calculated, the items tend to combine into one rather than two dimensions (Hofstede, 2001; Kirkman et al., 2006). That is, societies in which many people express individualistic values also tend to be societies in which few people express collectivistic values.

More generally, measurement structures are often affected by level of analysis (Peterson and Castro, 2006) and need to be assessed at each level at which they are to be used (Inglehart and Baker, 2000). Whether or not individual-and nation-level measurement structures differ depends on the topic of concern. Personality measures seem to have similar structures at both levels (Gelade et al., 2006), while measures of values often seem to differ by level (Hofstede, 2001). The measures of managers' use of social structures as sources of meaning show some tendency to collapse into a smaller number of dimensions at the national level compared with the individual level (Smith et al., 2002). Decisions about what items should be combined to create measures of personal perceptions, attitudes, or values related to culture will differ from decisions about what items should be combined based

on nation-level measurement structures to create nation-level measures of culture.

Perspectives and controversies

The technical issues of equivalence and level of analysis tend to be the focus of most commentary on cross-cultural research methods, but these are expressions of more basic issues concerning the nature of culture and its representation. Cross-cultural studies have progressed from the 1980s when culture was treated as an amorphous concept evoked to describe differences between nations without providing an explanation (Child, 1981; Roberts, 1970). Subsequently, controversies have centred on which ways of understanding and representing culture are most useful. These debates often concern the adequacy of Hofstede's (2001) conceptualization of culture as 'the collective programming of the mind' (based on the dimensions of individualism-collectivism, power distance, uncertainty avoidance, masculinity-femininity, and short-long term orientation), and the utility of cultural distance and country cluster research that is closely tied to these constructs.

Although these controversies continue, others have recently arisen. One set of controversies concerns the relative utility of alternative systems for categorizing cultural values compared to the one that Hofstede proposed. A second concerns whether organization studies will benefit more by comparing societies based on value dimensions, or whether it is better to compare belief systems, social structures, or concepts suggested by neoinstitutional theory or theories of institutional systems (see David and Bitektine, Chapter 10, this volume). Another is whether national culture analysis should be abandoned in favour of research about the values and the cognition of individuals, or whether collective culture characteristics can instead provide a better basis than surveys of individuals for drawing inferences about cognition. A further controversy concerns whether there is so much variability within nations, or such strong patterns of multiple-nation similarity, that other boundaries around culture should be considered. I will deal briefly with each of these after discussing Hofstede's view of culture and cultural dimensions.

Culture and the 'collective programming' metaphor

Many of the controversies surrounding Hofstede's project relate to theoretical perspectives on the nature of culture. Researchers often cite Kroeber and Kluckhohn's (1952) review of competing definitions. The metaphor of 'collective programming' does not derive from any particular line of theory, although it suggests several. Currently, the many definitions of culture in use reflect major theoretical perspectives. For psychologists who study attitudes, values, or personality, Hofstede's metaphor draws attention to constructs that will have adequate psychometric properties in a given society, indicating that individuals use them frequently and understand them intuitively (Kirkman et al., 2006). The metaphor also evokes ways of thinking that are shaped by the social norms reflected in what children are rewarded and punished for by their parents, teachers, and childhood friends (Rokeach, 1968, 1973). For psychologists who are closer to theories of scripts, schemas, and cognitive structures, it implies that the way in which such ideas are structured are shaped by socialization (Markus and Kitayama, 1991; Nisbett et al., 2001). For linguists and anthropologists, the idea of mental programming invokes the Sapir-Whorf view that language is an aspect of culture that shapes what people intuitively understand (Sapir, 1921; Whorf, 1956). For sociologists and political scientists using survey methods, the metaphor suggests the sort of nation-level measures of societal norms noted in the preceding discussion of level of analysis. For sociologists and political scientists interested in social institutions, collective programming might call to mind the sort of influence that institutions like governments and churches generate (Whitley, 1999), as well as the influence of less tangible institutions such as normative systems (Kostova and Roth, 2002).

"Hofstede proposed *the idea of collective programming at a time when dimension-based theories were prominent in psychology and sociology, and this idea has* frequently ..." frequently been interpreted in terms of value dimensions. Many of the alternative theoretical perspectives developed later could not have been anticipated when Hofstede presented his perspective in 1980. These alternatives, however, permit useful reformulations of the 'collective programming' metaphor, each of which is likely to produce different responses to the issues discussed in this chapter.

Dimensions and nation scores

Challenges to uses of Hofstede's nation scores are many and well known. The use of these scores is criticized for relying on old data about phenomena that are susceptible to change, for being collected in a single company (IBM), for being based on items that have little face validity, and for being too quantitative and missing too much about the most important aspects of culture. The responses are also well known. Researchers who seek to explain culture tend to consider aspects of a nation's heritage reaching much longer into the past than the date of the IBM survey, studying a single company controls for many extraneous variables, the measures have construct validity in relation to a host of external criteria, and the measures are useful but are incomplete compared to the insight gained from learning a language and living and working in a society. Hofstede reviews and responds to these controversies in depth in the second edition of *Culture's Consequences* (Hofstede, 2001).

Alternative national culture dimensions schemes

The first edition of *Culture's Consequences* in 1980 established a paradigm for national culture research. One key characteristic of the paradigm is that questionnaire surveys can be used to collect individual data, which are then combined based on nation-level measurement structures. The dimensions measured are indicators of values that characterize the national norms and institutions that societies use to fulfil generic social functions. A number of projects fall within this paradigm, but do so creatively by proposing alternative systems of dimensions.

The four most influential are projects based on the *Schwartz Value Survey* (Schwartz, 1994; Schwartz and Ros, 1995), the *Riding the Waves of Culture* model (Trompenaars and Hampden-Turner, 1998), the *World Value Survey* (Inglehart and Baker, 2000), and the *Global Leadership and Organizational Behaviour Effectiveness* project (GLOBE; House et al., 2004). The Schwartz Value Survey project introduces seven nation-level culture dimensions, which contrast with one another—conservatism-intellectual autonomy and affective autonomy, hierarchy-egalitarianism, and mastery-harmony. Nation-level scores based on data from secondary school teachers and university students are available for a number of these (Schwartz, 1994; Schwartz and Ros, 1995). Trompenaars and Hampden-Turner (1998) collected an extensive consulting-based data set that identified seven variables, the first five of which are based on the 'theory of action' developed by Parsons and Shils (1951); universalism-particularism, individualism-communitarianism, specific-diffuse, affective-neutral, achievement-ascription, sequential-synchronic, and internal-external. Smith et al. (1996) applied multidimensional scaling to this data set to identify two dimensions; egalitarian commitment and utilitarian involvement, contrasted with loyal involvement—an interesting nuance on the individualism-collectivism theme. The GLOBE project (House et al., 2004) augments Hofstede's project by creating nine culture dimensions; power distance, uncertainty avoidance, future orientation, institutional collectivism, in-group collectivism, performance orientation, gender egalitarianism, assertiveness, and humane orientation. Inglehart and Baker (2000) identify two national cultural dimensions; traditional/secular versus rational, and survival versus self expression.

The illustrations of culture dimensions drawn from these projects should not discount

their significance as alternatives to Hofstede's original dimensions. Each project is at least as extensive in the number of individuals surveyed and nations represented, as was the Hofstede project. Each is also linked to a significant theoretical tradition, and they each provide alternatives within the paradigm of nation-level research about culture dimensions.

Alternatives to cultural value dimensions

The paradigm of national dimensions based on values competes with a reasonably compatible set of alternatives. The social axioms model, for example, represents cultural differences in attribution propensities or systems of beliefs (Leung et al., 2002). Another approach renews a neglected theme in comparative sociology, organization studies, and social psychology concerning the analysis of societal differences in emphasis on a set of social structures including roles, rules, and norms that influence the behaviour and thinking of the society's members (Peterson and Smith, 2000 and 2008; Smith et al. 2002). This research identifies five organizational role categories—superiors, subordinates, colleagues, staff specialists, and one's self, as well as organizational rules and organizational and societal norms.

Individual level research on cultural themes

Several cross-cultural researchers have suggested that the field should move away from studying national culture dimensions. Instead of treating national culture as an indicator of a range of experiences that shape cognitive structures, characteristics of individuals should be measured using personal values surveys, and these measures should be used to test individual-level hypotheses. A recent review (Kirkman et al., 2006) suggests that many if not most studies that evoke Hofstede's (2001) conceptual basis and culture dimensions proceed in this way by linking the values of individuals, rather than national culture values, to various criteria.

The challenge of research into individual expressed values is that such constructs represent the more rationalized but less behaviourally influential aspects of cognition (Peterson and Wood, 2008). It is tempting to extend the value label too far by interpreting expressed values as implicit, taken-for-granted aspects of cognition. People do think deliberately and act based on conscious values or beliefs under circumstances that are unfamiliar, threatening, or emotional. The argument for representing national culture by aggregating responses to attitude and value surveys rests on the effects of socialization on such conscious thought. Unfortunately, using expressed personal values as *indicators* of culture has made it tempting for researchers to mistakenly *equate* culture with patterns of conscious thought. Cognition research since the 1970s suggests that most aspects of behaviour are driven by less accessible cognitive mechanisms (Kahneman, 2003; Nisbett and Willson, 1977). Indicators of the culture in which a person has been socialized may be better indicators of aspects of these cognitive processes than are the values that individuals overtly express.

Extending the national culture paradigm to individuals

The distinctions in meaning reflected in differences between the structures for measures of values at individual and national levels make it challenging to connect levels of analysis. Since the structure of values at the nation level differs from that at the individual level, it is inappropriate to conclude without testing that research findings at one level apply to the other. For example, if societal values of individualism and gross national product are associated at the *nation* level, then preferences for individualism may or may not be associated with wealth at the *individual* level. Nevertheless, individuals are certainly exposed to, experienced in, and socialized into the cultures of their nations, so it is reasonable to expect that societal culture does affect individuals. How, then, does one do research that connects levels?

Studies that connect societal culture characteristics to nonconscious cognitive characteristics other than attitudes or values

typically follow cognitive psychology research paradigms (Peterson and Wood, 2008). Individuals are randomly assigned at birth to a cultural group. In experimental studies, a researcher then assigns them to more immediate experimental conditions to study the joint effects of culture and other experimental manipulations. Although just like any other experimental manipulation, individuals respond differently to the culture to which birth assigns them, culture can be treated as a quasi-experimental condition to which they have been exposed (Campbell and Stanley, 1963). As in any quasi-experimental context, the analogy with experimental manipulation is approximate; cultural groups are more complex than any ordinary experimental manipulation, and those who participate in research are often atypical of their cultural group. Nevertheless, experimental studies of culture and cognition often treat the implications of national culture for structuring the cognitive processes of a society's members as more relevant than the values that individuals express in surveys.

Studies that include a method to check the applicability of national values dimensions provide one option that can be useful for individual level research that evokes culture explanations. Brett and colleagues (1997), for example, report several negotiation studies using Japanese and US managers attending executive training as participants. These researchers recognize that the participants in their studies are not a random sample of the participants' national cultures, but a sample of people who have found their way into managerial roles. Nevertheless, the researchers recognize that their participants live and work in a national cultural environment. The researchers, therefore, expect group differences with respect to participants' cultural values, but do not expect individual participants' expressed cultural values to act as mediators. Brett and her colleagues use their participants' cultural values as a form of quasi-experimental sampling check to evaluate whether the relative positioning of the national samples of managers is consistent with cultural theory (Jeanne M. Brett, personal communication, October 2007). This approach is most evident among psychologists who emphasize cognitive structures, such as Markus and Kitayama (1991) and Nisbett et al. (2001). However, a similar logic of looking for ways to evaluate the validity of society-level culture implications for individuals can also be found in research emphasizing values in the Rokeach (1968) tradition.

Nation, subculture, or region

Studying individuals rather than cultural groups is not the only alternative to studying national cultures (Peterson and Smith, 2008). Although some subcultures are typically recognized as exceptions in the major comparative studies of nations, the significance of within-nation subcultures is sometimes advocated even more strongly (Lenartowicz and Roth, 2001). Projects advocating the analysis of within-nation subcultures have emphasized the use of regions for explaining variance in the values of individuals and have studied relatively small segments of the world. Further work of this kind must progress beyond these limitations to develop and validate measures based on subculture-level measurement structures that are analogous to those that have been used for developing nation-level measures. This work also needs to compare within-nation variability to between-nation variability on a global scale.

Studies of multiple-nation regions, sometimes referred to as 'civilizations' (Huntington, 1993), are another alternative for analyzing cultural groups (e.g., Ronen, 2006). Ordinarily, however, multiple-nation regions are proposed as a way of identifying global cultural forces that supplement and explain rather than replace analyses of national cultures.

International research collaboration

Handling the technical and metatheoretical issues in international research is a social process as well as an intellectual one. Two issues that remain in the background of most domestic research surface in debates in international collaborative teams. One is the way researchers need to interact in order to move between theory and experience. Polanyi (1958/1962, pp. 69–131) discusses this in his chapter about 'articulation' as a social process of explicating tacit knowledge. A second issue concerns bringing ideas, theories, and methods developed in one part of the world into contact with the system of meanings used in another (Peterson and Pike, 2002). These issues appear in international collaboration in part due to issues of conceptual equivalence; ideas that researchers from one locale find important are seen as less important or omit the concerns of researchers in other locales. Hofstede (1996) and Erez (1990) identify topical preferences in different parts of the world, and these also occur due to the cultural basis of intellectual traditions that influence preferred theories and methods (Weber, 1951).

Two other contingencies that affect international research team dynamics are the researchers' institutional context and their project aims (Peterson, 2001). Unpleasant politics can develop when viewpoints become tied to the images and identities of particular parties (Dutton and Dukerich, 1991). From the GLOBE project, Hanges et al. (2005) provide examples of how viewpoints and identities can become linked in international collaborative projects.

Normative and descriptive international collaboration

The literatures about international research collaboration include both normative material about how such research should be conducted, and descriptive reports about the experiences of international teams. Normative commentary includes recommendations about how to avoid over-reliance on concepts and theory from one nation, particularly United States (Boyacigiller and Adler, 1991; Peng et al., 1991; Peterson, 2001), and how input from the locales in which data are to be collected should be obtained. Some recommended procedures focus on how to draw the most from *researchers* from different nations (Brett et al., 1997), while others focus on how best to learn from *respondents* in different locales (Morris et al., 1999). These approaches to de-centring international research are complementary.

The effectiveness of procedures for de-centring research is also now debated as part of a descriptive literature on international team dynamics (Hofstede, 2006; Javidan et al., 2006). A few international teams have been reflective about their dynamics. Easterby-Smith and Malina (1999) describe the conduct of an ethnographic project. Graen et al. (1997), Hanges et al. (2005), IDE (1981), MOW (1987), and Teagarden et al. (1995) describe the dynamics of very large-scale projects. Mezias et al. (1999) illustrate what can happen when US researchers study the global programmes of a US multinational organization. Tannenbaum et al. (1974) provide an example of how to incorporate different researchers' interpretations of the same data. Peterson (2001) provides a useful review of these projects. An analogous descriptive literature about handling process issues in international management teams is also relevant (Baba et al. 2004; Maznevski and Chudoba, 2000). Current commentary on international research collaboration suggests that normative models should be seen as alternatives. No model is universally optimal. The recommendations that follow draw both from the normative and descriptive literatures of international collaboration.

Research purposes affect collaboration

At least four purposes affect why researchers become involved in leading or participating in an international collaborative research project (Peterson, 2001). A collaborative group is composed of people who are likely to have a variety of purposes, and groups as a whole are likely to vary in the level of agreement about purposes. Choices about the methods, concepts, and viewpoints discussed in the foregoing section are influenced by the purposes of individual collaborators. The distinction among the first three of the following purposes has been frequently discussed (Boyacigiller and Adler, 1991).

First, research that focuses on *replication* is constrained to repeat procedures followed in the original research. To the extent that this purpose is accepted, debates about methods and concepts derail the project. Previously fixed procedures are so central that even the personal involvement of the researcher or group that did the original work can be limited to providing advice rather than directing the new team. An example would be continuing use of the Schwartz Value Survey (Schwartz and Sagiv, 1995) once the measures had become established.

Second, some research uses a dispersed set of collaborators to develop insight into *a research problem that is viewed as universal*. This purpose characterizes particular members of many research teams, although it is less often characteristic of a team as a whole. In this case, it is the theoretical and technical views of the collaborators that are treated as central, rather than the unique qualities of their cultural backgrounds, or the context in which they will collect data. For example, at the time of writing, I am collaborating with a group of negotiation researchers to contribute ideas about culture research methods where this knowledge is viewed as not being based on my cultural background (Metcalf et al., 2007).

Third, international collaborative research frequently draws upon the *cultural knowledge and setting of collaborators*. That is, a collaborator is part of a group, either because of a personal intuition for how a research problem is likely to be best formulated in their setting, or because of the ability to collect data in a particularly setting. This is consistent with integrating multiple methods and perspectives. For example, the negotiation study that I am assisting includes researchers from several nations who have an intuition about how negotiation works in their country, and whose contribution reflects the purpose of promoting the project's applicability in many nations.

Fourth, *intended outlets and audience* influence project design and conduct. Universities in United States and Europe are increasingly driven by criteria from accrediting and funding agencies that base faculty resources and rewards on research that is published in a list of frequently cited journals. The functioning of international teams is then shaped by personal values and reward systems that influence the importance that their members place on conforming to the norms associated with producing such publications.

Those who manage or collaborate in international teams must recognize that these purposes create very different ways of operating. Purposes for being involved in a project, though, are not personality traits. One can be involved simultaneously in multiple projects that have quite different mixes of these purposes.

Resource implications

The normative literature on international collaborative research tends to be abstract and idealistic, while the descriptive literature tends to be selective in focus. Figure 19.1 attempts to remedy both problems by drawing attention to the elements in setting up a research project. Most of these elements are present in any project, but are easily overlooked when researchers are so intent on a normative model of how to conduct good cross cultural research that they lose track of the resources that are needed to do any kind of research. Resources designated in Figure 19.1 as 'social' are those typically not contracted in exchange for money, but are based on networks, understandings, and relationships. Contracted resources are those that typically require funds. Theory resources and data analysis resources represent the body of knowledge and practice that the group will need to access. Organizing skills are those needed to coordinate a project group and link it to outside parties in its academic discipline(s). Collaborators from different nations typically contribute to different subsets of these elements.

The process of setting up a group oscillates between finding collaborators, negotiating purposes, and assembling resources. If these elements seem to be in sequence, such that one is needed before the other, this is not intended. They are set out randomly to indicate that in crystallizing a research project, these tend to

Social influence processes

- Collaborators
- Commentators
- 'Close' audience
- 'General' audiences
- Research participants ('subjects')

Research design ideals: pragmatics

- Participant access
- Funding
- Computing resources
- Assistants
- Travel support
- Email knowledge
- Data collection

Research design ideals: theory

- Literature knowledge
- Theory orientation
- Development/critiquing skills
- Writing ability

Organizing skills

- Promoting collaboration
- Gatekeeper roles
- Conference organizing

Data analysis

- Personal understanding
- Assistants
- Support resources

Plus

- Administrative support
- Personal and distant communication skills
- Personal and collective persistence

Figure 19.1 Elements in a research project.

occur chaotically. At some point, through the deliberate, proactive efforts of an individual, a few collaborators, or occasionally a larger group, the elements of a research project come to be formulated with sufficient clarity that the project can be announced. Other collaborators are then recruited and focused work can begin. Whichever elements remain indeterminate are either worked out or remain to haunt the project and threaten its completion.

Regardless of research process ideals or the explicit plan for a project, power considerations suggest that collaborators are likely to have credibility and influence to the extent that they can contribute the resources for handling one or more of the elements in Figure 19.1 that others in the group find important. The ability to provide those resources makes it predictable that large multiple nation projects will become centralized. If most project organizing experience, resources, and research skill comes from one or two people, any project is likely to reflect the preferences of a few individuals. Anyone joining an international research team would do well to consider what resources they bring, and any group taking an ideological stance about how the research process should unfold might consider whether its ideals are consistent with the distribution of resource contributions from its various members.

Project coordination

What are the options for coordinating an international collaborative project if one is in a high-power position, or for influencing the group where one's power is more limited or spread more evenly? Theories of social structures help identify these options (Peterson, 2001; Peterson and Smith, 2000; Smith and Peterson, 1988). Rules or norms about science, rules and norms negotiated by the group, guidance from an experienced leader, or ongoing collegial adjustments among experienced colleagues, all provide alternatives.

Two normative theories about how to manage international collaboration from Brett et al. (1997) and Morris et al. (1999) rely on universal arguments about the nature of doing good social science to develop a set of procedures. As normative theories, they rely on *norms* of science to guide social behaviour, specifically variants on Berry's (1969) adaptation of Pike's (1960) ideas about emics and etics, concerning the use of cross-cultural surveys. As attempts to promote particular scientific norms, these views do not directly discuss the issue of whether the members of a collaborative research team will accept them. The variant proposed by Morris et al. (1999) applies best when a project includes a substantial replication element as well as including the potential for adaptation. The Brett et al. (1997) variant applies best where new theory and new measures are being designed. If a team genuinely accepts one of these or some other normative model, the model can well provide a procedure to follow that will combine prior research, the unique cultural intuition of collaborators, and the input of research participants in a fruitful way.

Considering other aspects of social structure besides norms provides other alternatives for guiding a collaborating group's work. Drenth and Wilpert (1980) explain the process for crystallizing and transforming local group *norms* into a system of *rules* by creating an explicit social contract. Such working rules have the potential to make explicit many of the issues in Figure 19.1. Easterby-Smith and Malina (1999) describe the process of relying heavily on norms based on the trust that individual collaborators develop through experience.

Relying on a strong group leader can also prove useful. Many cross-cultural projects are known by the name of the person who coordinated them. The GLOBE project (House et al. 2004) provides an example of how to coordinate a project based on a clear *leader* and carefully thought out *explicit hierarchy* of roles and responsibilities. Hanges et al. (2005) describe a number of challenges faced by the GLOBE project, and how the senior leader and leadership group addressed them, in part by relying on norms about how to do good social science, rules in the form of social contracts, and other social structures such as collaborators chosen to fit the purposes of the project.

International research without questionnaires

This discussion has centred on survey research, principally because that is the dominant approach to cross-cultural organizational research. There are other extensive international literatures that deal with explicit systems of rules, laws, and economic indicators that do not evoke the concept of culture. These draw from literatures of neoinstitutional theory (Kostova and Roth, 2002), national business systems (Whitley, 1999), and sovereignty (Krasner, 1988). One challenge in such work is to contrast laws in nations where they tend to be followed and enforced, with laws in nations where they are public expressions of ideals. Another challenge is to know how to interpret economic data where those providing information about, say, wages paid or received, operate in a system that rewards distorting the information reported. Collaboration with local researchers with a through knowledge of the local business context is likely to be particularly useful in these cases.

A certain amount of qualitative ethnographic analysis is built into survey-based projects when the modes of decentring methods described in the preceding section are followed (Morris et al., 1999). Occasionally, distinct ethnographic projects also appear in the cross-cultural management literature. To date, these have tended to be conducted by relatively small groups and represent only a few nations (Baba et al., 2004; Farh et al., 2004; Maznevski and Chudoba, 2000). Easterby-Smith and Malina (1999) describe the social aspects of their research process in some depth. One larger and more loosely coordinated international comparative analysis of psychological contracts relied on a combination of historical analysis, ethnography, and survey research (Rousseau and Schalk, 2000). The collaborators in that case worked from a core of basic constructs and a loose analytical framework, but the researchers from each nation conducted their analyses in individualized ways. This project merges with a larger literature in which a researcher edits a book that includes chapters on a particular theme, including contributions from multiple nations.

A challenge for research relying heavily on local concepts is to find a basis for comparison. To the extent that much survey research is introduced or informed by historical and ethnographic analysis, survey studies implicitly provide this sort of comparative framing. If a large number of ethnographic projects conducted separately in multiple nations were to produce the sort of fragmentation that characterized anthropology in the mid-twentieth century, the *post hoc* coordination provided by the Human Relations Area File (Murdock, 1940) would be useful for establishing an accessible index and facilitating comparisons.

CONCLUSIONS

International collaborative research has a technical side, a methodological and theoretical orientation side, and a social process side. The purpose of this chapter has been to identify issues and literatures that can help to think through each of these. International collaborative studies bring together researchers whose cultural backgrounds and intercultural experiences lead them to make different assumptions about how the group will operate. It also brings together people who have different degrees of skill and different views about technical issues, who are likely to have different perspectives about methodological and theoretical issues, and who bring unique personal research interests, career plans, and resources. A review of international collaborative projects suggests that those which produce influential research seldom met all of the ideals of any normative model about how they should operate (Peterson, 2001). A clear sequence of moving back and forth between prior theory and new experience is rarely followed, but both inputs are typically included in some way. All collaborators rarely contribute equally to the research design or execution, most typically because many have other interests and other demands on their time apart from the interests of a core group.

Human nature can be helpful in international research collaboration. People are able to use different theoretical and methodological tools at different times for different purposes. We are able to use a map containing representations of roads even when such maps do not recognize trees and houses. We can also refer to a photograph without worrying whether or not map making is incommensurate with photography, and vice versa. Similarly, social scientists are frequently able to see analogies between quite different ways of analysing cultural characteristics and understanding societies. Whereas theories can be incommensurate such that one does not recognize the existence of central elements of another, people collaborating in international teams are likely to be more successful if they seek elements of complementarity. Ideologies and attitudes about how research *should be* conducted tend to give way to pragmatic considerations of personal necessity and resource limitations about how research *can be* conducted.

In order to become involved in an international project in a way that is likely to be satisfactory to all concerned, the considerations identified here suggest that one should look for a project having several characteristics. It should have:

- Members with adequate technical skills
- A constructive way to develop technical agreements
- Basic methodological and theoretical orientations where differences are viewed as complementary rather than incommensurable
- Compatible purposes
- A working consensus about the norms, rules, and roles that will guide the research process

To the extent that these qualities are lacking, as they always will be to some degree, efforts to improve the project group need to attend to all of these, and not just to a preferred subset.

REFERENCES

Adler, N.J. and Boyacigiller, N. (1995) 'Global organizational behaviour: going beyond tradition', *Journal of International Management*, 1: 73–86.

Baba, M., Gluesing, J., Ratner, H. and Wagner, K.H. (2004) 'The contexts of knowing: natural history of a globally distributed team', *Journal of Organizational Behaviour*, 25: 547–87.

Bass, B.M., Cascio, W.F. and O'Connor, E.J. (1974) 'Magnitude estimations of expressions of frequency and amount', *Journal of Applied Psychology*, 59: 313–20.

Berry J.W. (1969) 'On cross-cultural comparability', *International Journal of Psychology*, 4: 119–28.

Boyacigiller N. and Adler N.J. (1991) 'The parochial dinosaur: organizational science in a global context', *Academy of Management Review*, 16: 262–90.

Brett, J.M., Tinsley, C.H., Janssens, M., Barsness, Z.I. and Lytle, A.L. (1997) 'New approaches to the study of culture in industrial/organizational psychology', in P.C. Earley and M. Erez (eds), *New Perspectives on International/Organizational Psychology*, San Francisco: Jossey-Bass, pp. 75–129.

Brislin, R.W., Lonner, W. and Thorndike, R.M. (1973) *Cross-Cultural Research Methods*, New York: John Wiley and Sons.

Campbell, D.T. and Stanley, J.C. (1963) *Experimental and Quasi-Experimental Designs for Research*, Skokie, IL: Rand-McNally.

Child, J. (1981) 'Culture, contingency and capitalism in the cross-national study of organizations', *Research in Organizational Behaviour*, Vol. 3. Greenwich, CT: JAI Press, pp. 303–56.

Drenth, P.J.D. and Wilpert, B. (1980) 'The role of "social contracts" in cross-cultural research', *International Review of Applied Psychology*, 29: 293–305.

Dutton, J.E. and Dukerich, J.M. (1991) 'Keeping an eye on the mirror: image and identity in organizational adaptation', *Academy of Management Journal*, 34: 517–54.

Earley, P.C. (2006) 'Leading cultural research in the future: a matter of paradigms and taste', *Journal of International Business Studies*, 37: 922–31.

Easterby-Smith, M. and Malina, D. (1999) 'Cross-cultural collaborative research: toward reflexivity', *Academy of Management Journal*, 42: 76–86.

Erez, M. (1990) 'Toward a model of cross-cultural industrial and organizational psychology', in H.C. Triandis, M.D. Dunnette and L.M. Hough (eds), *Handbook of Industrial and Organizational Psychology*, (second edn.), Vol. 4. Palo Alto, CA: Consulting Psychologists Press, pp. 559–608.

Farh, J.L., Zhong, C.B. and Organ, D.W. (2004) 'Organizational citizenship behaviour in the People's Republic of China', *Organization Science*, 15: 241–53.

Gelade, G.A., Dobson, P. and Gilbert, P. (2006) 'National differences in organizational commitment: effect of economy, product of personality, or consequence of culture?', *Journal of Cross Cultural Psychology*, 37: 542–56.

Glazer, S. Beehr, T.A. (2005) 'Consistency of implications of three role stressors across four countries', *Journal of Organizational Behaviour*, 26: 467–87.

Graen, G.B., Hui, C., Wakabayashi, M. and Wang, Z.M. (1997) 'Cross-cultural research alliances in organizational research: cross-cultural partnership making in action', in P.C. Earley and M. Erez (eds), *New Perspectives on International Industrial/Organizational Psychology*, San Francisco: Jossey-Bass, pp. 160–89.

Hanges, P.J. and Dickson, M.W. (2004) 'The development and validation of the GLOBE culture and leadership scales', in R.J. House, P.J. Hanges, M. Javidan, P.W. Dorfman and V. Gupta (eds) *Culture, Leadership, and Organizations: The GLOBE Study of 62 Societies*, Thousand Oaks, CA: Sage, pp. 122–51.

Hanges, P., Lyon, J. and Dorfman, P. (2005) 'Managing a multinational team: Lessons from project GLOBE', in D. Shapiro, M.V. Glinow and J. Cheng (eds), *Managing Multinational Teams: Global Perspectives*, Vol. 18. Oxford: Elsevier, pp. 337–60.

Hofstede, G. (1996) 'An American in Paris: the influence of nationality on organization theories', *Organization Studies*, 17: 525–37.

Hofstede, G. (2001) *Culture's consequences: international differences in work related values*, (second edn.) Thousand Oaks, CA: Sage.

Hofstede G. (2006) 'What did GLOBE really measure? researchers' minds versus respondents' minds', *Journal of International Business* Studies, 37: 882–96.

House, R.J., Hanges, P.J., Javidan, M., Dorfman, P.W. and Gupta, V., (eds) (2004) *Culture, Leadership, and Organizations: The GLOBE Study of 62 Societies*, Thousand Oaks, CA: Sage.

Huntington, S.P. (1993) 'The clash of civilizations', *Foreign Affairs*, 72(3): 22–49.

IDE International Research Group (1981) *Industrial democracy in Europe*, Oxford: Clarendon Press.

Inglehart, R. and Baker, W.E. (2000) 'Modernization, cultural change, and the persistence of traditional values', *American Sociological Review*, 65: 19–51.

Inkeles, A. and Levinson, D.J. (1969) 'National character: the study of modal personality and sociocultural systems', in G. Lindzey and E. Aronson (eds), *The Handbook of Social Psychology*, Reading, MA: Addison-Wesley, pp. 418–506.

Javidan M., House, R.J., Dorfman, P.W., Hanges, P.J. and de Luque, M.S. (2006) 'Conceptualizing and measuring cultures and their consequences: a comparative

review of GlOBE's and Hofstede's approaches', *Journal of International Business Studies*, 37: 897–914.

Kahneman, D. (2003) 'A perspective on judgment and choice', *American Psychologist*, 58: 697–720.

Kirkman, B.L., Lowe, K.B. and Gibson, C.B. (2006) 'A quarter century of *Culture's Consequences*: a review of empirical research incorporating Hofstede's cultural values framework', *Journal of International Business Studies*, 37: 285–320.

Kostova, T. and Roth, K. (2002) 'Adoption of an organizational practice by subsidiaries of multinational corporations: institutional and relational effects', *Academy of Management Journal*, 45: 215–33.

Krasner, S.D. (1988) 'Sovereignty: an institutional perspective', *Comparative Political Studies*, 21: 66–94.

Kroeber, A.L. and Kluckhohn, C. (1952) 'Culture: a critical review of concepts and definitions', *Papers of the Peabody Museum of American Archaeology and Ethnology*, 47 (1), Cambridge, MA: Harvard University.

Lenartowicz, T. and Roth, K. (2001) 'Does subculture within a country matter? A cross-cultural study of motivational domains and business performance in Brazil', *Journal of International Business Studies*, 32: 305–25.

Leung, K. (2008) 'Methods and measurements in cross-cultural management', in P.B. Smith, M.F. Peterson and D.C. Thomas (eds), *Handbook of Cross-Cultural Management Research*, Thousand Oaks, CA: Sage, pp. 59–73.

Leung, K., Bond, M.H., Reimel de Carrasquel, S., Muñoz, C., Hernádez, M., Murakami, F., Yamaguchi, S., Bierbrauer, G. and Singelis, T.M. (2002) 'Social axioms: the search for universal dimensions of general beliefs about how the world functions', *Journal of Cross-Cultural Psychology*, 33: 286–302.

Lincoln, J.R. and Kalleberg, A.L (1990) *Culture, control and commitment: a study of work organization and work attitudes in the United States and Japan*, Cambridge: Cambridge University.

Markus. H., and Kitayama, S. (1991) 'Culture and self: Implications for cognition, emotion and motivation', *Psychological Review*, 98: 224–53.

Maznevski, M. and Chudoba, K. (2000) 'Bridging space over time: Global virtual team dynamics and effectiveness', *Organization Science*, 11: 473–92.

Metcalf, L.E., Bird, A., Peterson, M.F., Shankarmahesh, M. and Lituchy, T. (2007) 'Cultural influences in negotiation: a four-country comparative analysis', *International Journal of Cross Cultural Management*, in press.

Mezias, S.J., Chen, Y.R. and Murphy, P. (1999) 'Toto, I don't think we're in Kansas anymore: some footnotes to cross-cultural research', *Journal of Management Inquiry*, 8: 323–33.

Morris, M.W., Leung, K., Ames, D. and Lickel, B. (1999) 'Views from inside and outside: integrating emic and etic insights about culture and justice judgment', *Academy of Management Review*, 24: 781–96.

MOW (Meaning of Working International Research Team) (1987) *The Meaning of Working*, London: Academic Press.

Mowday, R.T., Steers, R.M. and Porter, L.W. (1979) 'The measurement of organizational commitment', *Journal of Vocational Behaviour*, 14: 224–47.

Murdock, George P. (1940) 'The cross-cultural survey', *American Sociological Review*, 5: 361–70.

Nisbett, R.E., Peng, K., Choi, I. and Norenzayan, A. (2001) 'Culture and systems of thought: holistic vs. analytic cognition', *Psychological Review*, 108: 291–310.

Nisbett, R.E. and Willson, T.D. (1977) 'Telling more than we can know: verbal reports on mental processes', *Psychological Review*, 84: 231–59.

Oyserman, D., Coon, H.M and Kemmelmeier, M. (2002) 'Rethinking individualism and collectivism: evaluation of theoretical assumptions and meta-analyses', *Psychological Bulletin*, 128: 3–72.

Parsons, T. and Shils, E.A. (1951) *Toward a General Theory of Action*, Cambridge, MA: Harvard University Press.

Peng, T.K., Peterson, M.F. and Shyi, Y.P. (1991) 'Quantitative issues in cross-cultural management research: trends and equivalence issues', *Journal of Organizational Behaviour*, 12: 87–108.

Peng, T.K. and Peterson, M.F. (2008) 'Nation, demographic, and attitudinal boundary conditions on leader social rewards and punishments in local governments', *Journal of Organizational Behaviour*, 29: 95–117.

Peterson, M.F. (2001) 'International collaboration in organizational behaviour research', *Journal of Organizational Behaviour*, 22: 59–81.

Peterson, M.F. and Castro, S.L. (2006) 'Measurement metrics at aggregate levels of analysis: implications for organizational culture research and the GLOBE project', *Leadership Quarterly*, 17: 506–21.

Peterson, M.F., Maiya, K. and Herreid, C. (1993) 'Adapting Japanese PM leadership field research for use in Western organizations', *Applied Psychology: An International Review*, 43: 49–74.

Peterson, M.F. and Pike, K.L. (2002) 'Emics and etics for organizational studies: a lesson in contrast from linguistics', *International Journal of Cross Cultural Management*, 2: 5–19.

Peterson, M.F. and Smith, P.B. (2000) 'Sources of meaning, organizations, and culture: making sense of organizational events', in Ashkanasy, N.M., Wilderom, C.P.M. and Peterson, M.F. (2000) *Handbook of Organizational Culture and Climate*, Thousand Oaks, CA: Sage, pp.101–16.

Peterson, M.F., Smith, P.B. and 44 coauthors. (2005) 'Role conflict, ambiguity, and overload: a 21-nation study', *Academy of Management Journal*, 38: 429–52.

Peterson, M.F. and Smith, P.B. (2008) 'Social structures and processes in cross-cultural management', in P.B. Smith, M.F. Peterson and D.C. Thomas (eds), *Handbook of Cross Cultural Management Research*. Thousand Oaks, CA: Sage, in press.

Peterson, M.F. and Wood, R. (2008) 'Cognitive structures and processes in cross-cultural management', in P.B. Smith, M.F. Peterson and D.C. Thomas (eds), *Handbook of Cross Cultural Management Research*, Thousand Oaks, CA: Sage, in press.

Pike, K.L (1960) *Language in Relation to a Unified Theory of the Structure of Human Behaviour* (third edn.), Glendale, CA: Summer Institute of Linguistics.

Pike, K.L. (1982) *Linguistic Concepts: An Introduction to Tagmemics*, Lincoln, Nebraska: University of Nebraska.

Polanyi, M. (1958/1962) *Personal Knowledge: Towards a Post-Critical Philosophy*, Chicago: University of Chicago.

Raudenbush, S.W. and Bryk, A.S. (2002) *Hierarchical Linear Models: Applications and Data Analysis Methods* (second edn.), Thousand Oaks, CA: Sage.

Roberts, K.H. (1970) 'On looking at an elephant: an evaluation of cross-cultural research related to organizations', *Psychological Bulletin*, 74: 327–50.

Rokeach M. (1968) 'A theory of organization and change within value-attitude systems', *Journal of Social Issues*, 24: 13–33.

Rokeach, M. (1973) *The Nature of Human Values*, New York: Free Press.

Ronen, S. (2006) *The New Cultural Geography: A Meta-Analysis of Country Clusters*, Invited address, 26th congress of the International Association for Applied Psychology, Athens, July.

Rousseau, D.M. and Schalk, R. (2000) *Psychological Contracts in Employment: Cross-National Perspectives*, Thousand Oaks, CA: Sage.

Sapir, E. (1921) *Language*, New York: Harcourt, Brace and Co.

Saville, P. and Willson, E. (1991) 'The reliability and validity of normative and ipsative approaches in the measurement of personality', *Journal of Occupational Psychology*, 64: 219–38.

Schwartz, S.H. (1994) 'Beyond individualism-collectivism: new cultural dimensions of values', in U. Kim, H.C. Triandis, C. Kagitçibasi, S.C. Choi and G. Yoon (eds), *Individualism and collectivism: Theory, Method and Applications*, Newbury Park, CA: Sage, pp. 85–119.

Schwartz, S.H. and Ros, M. (1995) 'Values in the West: a theoretical and empirical challenge to the individualism-collectivism cultural dimension', *World Psychology*, 1: 91–122.

Schwartz, S.H. and Sagiv, L. (1995) 'Identifying culture-specifics in the content and structure of values', *Journal of Cross-Cultural Psychology*, 26: 92–115.

Scott, W.R. (1995) *Institutions and Organizations*, Thousand Oaks, CA: Sage.

Smith, P.B. (2004) 'Acquiescent response bias as an aspect of cultural communication style', *Journal of Cross Cultural Psychology*, 35: 50–61.

Smith, P.B. (2008) 'Indigenous aspects of management issues', in P.B. Smith, M.F. Peterson and D.C. Thomas (eds), *Handbook of Cross-Cultural Management Research*, Thousand Oaks, CA: Sage, pp. 319–32.

Smith, P.B., Dugan, S. and Trompenaars, F. (1996) 'National culture and the values of organizational employees: a dimensional analysis across 43 nations', *Journal of Cross-Cultural Psychology*, 27: 231–64.

Smith, P.B. and Peterson, M.F. (1988) *Leadership, Organizations and Culture*, London: Sage.

Smith P.B., Peterson M.F. and Schwartz S.H. with 44 coauthors (2002) 'Cultural values, sources of guidance and their relevance to managerial behaviour: a 47 nation study', *Journal of Cross Cultural Psychology*, 33: 188–208.

Tannenbaum, A.S., Kavcic, B., Rosner, M., Vianello, M. and Wieser, G. (1974) *Hierarchy in Organizations*, San Francisco: Jossey-Bass.

Teagarden, M.B., Von Glinow, M.A., Bowen, D.E., Frayne, C.A., Nason, S., Huo, Y.P., Milliman, J., Arias, M.E., Butler, M.C., Geringer, J.M., Kim, N.M., Scullion, H., Lowe, K.B. and Drost, E.A. (1995) 'Toward a theory of comparative management research: an idiographic case study of the best international human resources management project', *Academy of Management Journal*, 38: 1261–87.

Trompenaars, F. and Hampden-Turner, C. (1998) *Riding the Waves of Culture: Understanding Diversity in Global Business* (second edn.), New York: McGraw Hill.

Usunier, J.C. (1998) *International and Cross-Cultural Management Research*, London: Sage.

Van de Vijver, F. and Leung, K. (1997) *Methods and Data Analysis for Cross-Cultural Research*, Thousand Oaks, CA: Sage.

Weber, M. (1951) *The Religion of China*, New York: Free Press.

Whitley, R. (1999) *Divergent Capitalisms: The Social Structuring and Change of Business Systems*, Oxford: Oxford University Press.

Whorf, B. (1956) *Language, Thought and Reality*, Cambridge, MA: MIT Press.

20

Common Method Variance or Measurement Bias? The Problem and Possible Solutions

Paul E. Spector and Michael T. Brannick

The ubiquitous self-report questionnaire is perhaps the most popular method for conducting research in organizations. Researchers using questionnaires have long been aware of problems with the approach, but none is perhaps more dreaded than the idea that resulting correlations are due to common method variance (CMV), which is known by other names such as monomethod bias or same-source bias. The charge that observed relationships among variables are spuriously due to the single method employed is routinely leveled by reviewers and editors of submitted work. Authors themselves feel compelled, or are compelled, to devote at least a paragraph of virtually every article to a disclaimer that of course, the results in the research report are likely biased by the methods used, and that 'caution' must be exercised in interpreting results, whatever it means to be cautious in such cases. One occasionally wonders why journals fail to put the disclaimer on the bottom of the contents page of each issue, rather than wasting space by repeating it in each paper.

Given the widespread belief in the insidious action of CMV, one might expect that there is a great deal of evidence documenting its existence and effects on observed results. In point of fact, there is little credible evidence that CMV accounts for observed correlations with self-reports (see Spector, 2006 for a review), and a great deal of evidence to the contrary. Why then do sophisticated researchers persist in assuming the existence of something in the absence of confirming scientific evidence? The answer is twofold. First, CMV is common knowledge among researchers. It is an urban legend that people have heard so often and so long that they simply accept it as true. Akin to groupthink, people find confirmation, not in empirical findings, but in the expert opinions of accomplished researchers who affirm its existence in their written work. Such confirmation occurs both in papers that describe yet another method to test for and control CMV, and in individual papers that note CMV as a limitation. Second, there is a confusion between CMV and invalidity due to biases and other factors that might influence the observed measure. It is the action of these additional influences on a measured variable that represents a significant limitation to the use of any method in conducting organizational research, and not just questionnaires. Thus the question we should be asking is not whether the observed correlations among variables were inflated by CMV, but rather what feasible alternative explanations there are for observed correlations among variables due to the action of factors other than those presumed.

In this chapter we address three issues. First, we will discuss what CMV is and briefly cover the empirical findings that suggest it does not exist, at least in a meaningful way. Second, we will contrast CMV with bias that affects the assessment of particular constructs using specific methods. Bias, as we will show, is a more significant problem than CMV in that it does not lend itself to any general approaches to achieve its control. Finally, we will talk about specific methodological approaches to identifying and controlling bias. As we will discuss, the idea of CMV is a vast oversimplification that obscures the complex interplay between constructs and assessment, especially when one wishes to explore relationships among theoretical constructs.

Common method variance

Method variance is systematic variance in measurement attributable to the specific method used to assess a construct. Campbell and Fiske (1959) are credited with having focused attention on this issue, giving as examples of things causing method variance the format of a psychological test as well as characteristics of Skinner boxes. Of particular concern is the situation in which the same method is used to assess two or more constructs. It is presumed that the method variance component will affect all variables using that method, and therefore, the method variance components will be common across constructs assessed with the same method. Thus, common method variance is variance shared by different variables that is attributed to sharing a common method. Many people appear to consider the self-report questionnaire to be a method (indeed, it is usually such questionnaires that come under attack for problems with CMV). Following the standard argument, if we survey people with such a questionnaire, then the responses to all items would be affected by the common self-report questionnaire method, resulting in an inflation of correlations among items and scales. The interpretive difficulty is that when we find that our scales of interest (e.g., autonomy and job satisfaction) are correlated, we cannot tell whether the correlation is due to relations among the constructs of interest, common method variance, or both.

What is a method?

One reason that CMV is still being debated and researched may be that the term *method* has not been well defined, particularly when it comes to deciding what to worry about when invoking common method variance as an explanation of an observed correlation. *Method* may be defined quite narrowly or quite broadly, and the choice of definition influences the definition of CMV and thus its examination and control. On the narrow side, method means apparatus, items, or specific stimulus situation as designed by the researcher for data collection. One might use a paper-and-pencil survey, the same questions and general format for the survey administered over the web, the identical questions and general format in an interview, alternate wordings of questions, alternate arrangements of sequences of scales, and so forth. Quite a bit of research has been completed on this conception of method, and the effects of method have generally been small and rarely pose a threat to the interpretation of observed correlations.

For example, it is not likely that we find the correlation between autonomy and job satisfaction is positive on the paper version, but not on the web version or the interview version. It is not likely we will find that autonomy and job satisfaction only correlate positively if one uses all positively worded items or only if the autonomy questionnaire precedes the satisfaction questionnaire or only if both scales are administered with Likert scales rather than faces scales.

On the broad side of the continuum, method may be conceived as the process by which numbers are generated, that is, method is the process of measurement. This conception of method includes not only the stimulus material, such as the items in the questionnaire, but also the respondent (a job incumbent, the incumbent's supervisor, a coworker, and a job analyst), the larger, general context of measurement, including location and time of day, and especially the purpose of measurement as it is understood by the respondent. The result of the measurement process is a distribution of numbers that can be described in part by its variance. Part of the variance will be due to the trait of interest to the researcher, and part of the variance will be due to factors other than the trait of interest. That variance which was not intended by the researcher is method variance. We find it useful to consider method variance from this perspective; such a conception avoids the stipulation that method variance be produced in equal amounts or even by the same things across variables.

In the middle ground is the respondent, or source of information. One objection to the questionnaire administered as a survey may be that the same person (typically the job incumbent) essentially provides both the independent and dependent variables for a study. Unlike the effects of item formats, the effects of respondent have sometimes been substantial. Incumbent and supervisor often disagree about the job performance of each. Unfortunately, when there is disagreement between sources of information, there is typically no gold standard to serve as referent and thus is not always clear who (if anyone)

is correct. Therefore, although it is usually desirable, using different respondents for the independent and dependent variables is not always the best choice.

Evidence against common method variance

If CMV is a ubiquitous inflator of observed relationships, one would expect that finding evidence for it would be straightforward and easy. There is amazingly little evidence available to support the possibility of CMV as a universal inflator of correlations, and considerable disconfirming evidence (Spector, 1987; 2006; Spector and Brannick, 1995). Perhaps the only evidence in support of CMV comes from confirmatory factor analysis studies in which multiple traits are assessed with multiple methods. Each observed measure is allowed to load on one trait and one method factor, while it is assumed that traits are related with one another and methods are related with one another. Such analyses have led to estimates of the proportion of variance attributable to traits and methods (e.g., Bagozzi and Yi, 1990; Williams, Cote, and Buckley, 1989).

There are two important limitations with this line of research. First, they estimate the proportion of method variance, and do not speak to the issue of CMV and how it might inflate correlations. Second, this technique has computational difficulties when both traits and methods are intercorrelated. Such models often will fail to converge, and when they do in almost all cases impossible parameter estimates are produced, such as negative variances, and correlations far greater than 1.0 in magnitude. This has led several critics to question the results it yields (e.g., Brannick and Spector, 1990; Marsh, 1989). Spector (2006) summarized the case against CMV, providing several forms of evidence to refute the idea that there is shared variance due to method that permeates all measured variables.

Perhaps most importantly, if CMV exists, we should find that all variables assessed within a single self-report questionnaire are correlated. Spector (2006) provided as an example Boswell, Boudreau, and Dunford

(2004) from *Journal of Applied Psychology*, a top-tier journal that certainly favors significant over nonsignificant findings. With a sample of 1601, certainly large enough to detect significance for even trivial sized relationships, 40% were nonsignificant and half the significant ones accounted for no more than 1% of the variance. To show this was not a fluke, one of us (Spector) grabbed the latest issue of *Journal of Organizational Behavior* and scanned articles for a correlation matrix from a survey study. Lester, Kickul and Bergmann (2007) reported correlations among six variables in their study of social contract. With a sample size of 195, 5 of 15 (one-third) of correlations were nonsignificant. It should be kept in mind that studies such as these two examples include variables that are expected, based on prior research and theory, to be correlated. So, under conditions expected to maximize significant findings, and with a review process that disfavors null results, articles in major journals often report nonsignificant correlations.

Furthermore, if CMV is the insidious inflator of correlations, as many believe it to be, the use of multiple methods should result in smaller correlations between variables than the use of a single method, especially the self-report questionnaire. Evidence to address this issue has been provided by Crampton and Wagner (1994) who conducted an extensive meta-analysis comparing single-source with multisource studies of the same phenomena. They collected more than 40,000 correlations from 581 articles that allowed for a comparison of 143 variable pairs. In only 26.6% of cases were correlations from single-source studies significantly larger than from multisource, with a median correlation difference of 0.14. In 11.2% of cases they were smaller, with a similar 0.15 median correlation difference, and in 62.2% of cases there were no significant differences. Again, the facts fail to support the idea of CMV.

Biases in organizational research

According to classical test theory (Lord and Novick, 1968), a measured variable consists of two components: True score and error.

$$O = T + E$$

It is assumed that the systematic true score part reflects the variable of interest, assuming construct validity evidence, and the nonsystematic part is random errors of measurement. For the most part, it is reliability that defines the true score portion, with the remaining unreliable part representing error. Of course, it has long been recognized that a measured variable can be affected by biases. In our view, it is best to conceptualize an observed measure as reflecting a set of true scores plus error, in other words,

$$O = \Sigma T + E$$

with ΣT representing a variety of potential influences on an observed measure that combined determine each individual's score. Thus an observed score might reflect not only the construct of interest, but response styles, personality (including social desirability), mood, environmental factors, and a host of other potential influences. In theory, psychological measures are unidimensional scales tapping a single construct except for random errors of measurement (trait score is synonymous with true score). In practice, psychological measures are composites of many things, only some of which are intended by the researcher (trait score is not synonymous with true score; true score is all systematic sources of variance). Bias is that part of the trait score that represents things unintended.

Considered from another perspective, bias represents invalidity of a measure. It is the systematic portion of a measure that represents something unintended. Given a constant level of reliability, measures can vary in their levels of validity in that the amount of variance due to unintended influences (i.e., biases) can vary. Two measures might both reflect a theoretical construct, but one has more bias than the other, and one might contain biases not contained by the other. Interpretation of a measure's meaning must consider sources of invalidity and how they affect relationships with other measures.

As with method variance, bias can affect the observed relationships between two measures. If a bias is unshared, it will act like error and serve to attenuate the correlation of an observed measure with another variable (Podsakoff, MacKenzie, Lee and Podsakoff, 2003; Williams and Brown, 1994). If a bias is shared on the other hand, it will tend to inflate correlations between two observed measures. The extent to which observed correlations are attenuated or inflated is determined by the relative strength of true relationship between the constructs of interest, how well the measures reflect those constructs, and the magnitude and nature of biases that are shared and unshared. There are a number of factors in both the measurement situation and nature of underlying construct that cause bias. These factors can reside in the design of the measure, individual differences in respondents, or the nature of the assessment situation. Furthermore, the construct itself can affect the extent to which it is subject to particular biases. A particular measure of a particular construct can be affected by a host of influences that contribute to the observed measure.

With measures that rely on people's reports, either self-reports or other-reports, there are factors that determine how accurately the participant is able to respond. Again, the nature of the construct and design of the instrument are key determinants. The ease with which an individual is able to form a judgment about the construct level for a given target is relevant to bias, where the more difficult the judgment, the more room there is for additional influences on the report. Constructs that are ambiguous or reflect things that are unobservable leave room for outside influences on reports. Thus, the proper design of a scale in which the judgment task and responses are unambiguous will minimize bias. Furthermore, the ability of the individual to observe and make judgments also affects whether or not bias will occur.

Response styles

There are patterns of response to paper-and-pencil measures for both self-report and other-report that are interpreted as response styles. Such patterns vary across people, with some responding in systematic ways that might well be forms of measurement bias. Thus, response styles represent individual difference variables that can be tied in some cases to personality. However, it is not always clear-cut whether a given pattern represents a response style or not.

Some response styles are found primarily in self-reports, whereas others can be found in other-reports. Two styles that have been studied extensively concerning the former is acquiescence and social desirability. The latter includes halo and leniency patterns that are common when people make evaluative ratings of others, such as in performance appraisal.

Acquiescence

Acquiescence is the tendency to agree with all items regardless of content. It occurs with scales that ask for agreement, such as in measures of attitudes or personality. It is perhaps most prominently seen with scales in which people agree strongly with items that are phrased in opposite directions, such as a job satisfaction scale in which one item asks 'I like my job' and another asks 'I hate my job.' Clearly individuals should not agree with both, but sometimes they do. Although such patterns are clearly of concern, Rorer (1965) provided convincing evidence that acquiescence tends to be limited to particular scales. That is, the acquiescence bias tends not to be universally shared, and thus is not a general inflator of relationships across scales. In many cases it would tend to attenuate rather than inflate observed correlations.

Social desirability

Social desirability is an individual difference in the tendency to endorse items that are socially acceptable and to fail to endorse items that are socially unacceptable. Scales have been devised to assess social desirability, the most popular being Crowne and Marlowe's

(1964). These authors have discussed social desirability, not as a bias, but rather as the personality trait of need for approval. The possibility of social desirability as a bias has led to concerns about the validity of measures of personality and other variables that have been shown to relate to it.

The importance of social desirability as a general biasing factor in organizational research is open to question. Moorman and Podsakoff (1992) conducted a meta-analysis of organizational studies that included a measure of social desirability. They found across 36 samples from 33 studies that the mean correlation between social desirability and organizational variables was 0.05, with the largest being only 0.17. Likewise, Ones, Viswesvaran and Reiss (1996) investigated the potential biasing effect of social desirability on the relationship between personality and job performance using meta-analysis. They also found quite small correlations between social desirability and other variables. In both cases, the authors found little evidence that observed correlations were affected by social desirability by comparing results with and without social desirability controlled.

Halo

A halo pattern exists when a rater tends to rate each individual the same across different dimensions. This is seen in performance appraisals when one individual is given all outstanding ratings whereas another is given all below satisfactory ratings. Such patterns might reflect either an intended or unintended bias that could be due to a number of mechanisms. On the intended side, supervisors might give ratings to support decisions they have made about each individual employee, for example, those favored would be given all high ratings and those unfavored would be given all low. On the unintended side, raters might have limited information about individual dimensions and use a global schema to make all judgments (Dalal, 2005). In either case, halo would represent a source of bias.

It should not be assumed, however, that similarity of ratings across dimensions

reflects bias. It has been pointed out that observed relationships among dimensions of performance are sometimes accurate and that there can be 'true halo' (e.g., Murphy, Jako, and Anhalt, 1993). Some individuals might be outstanding across all dimensions, whereas others are unsatisfactory across all dimensions. Thus more evidence than the halo pattern is needed to determine whether or not bias is likely.

Leniency

A leniency pattern is most commonly seen when individuals are rating the quality of individuals in some domain or activity, such as job performance. Distributions of such ratings are typically skewed toward the top, with relatively few individuals receiving ratings below the middle of a scale. Such distributions are often thought to be biased toward the top due to the hesitancy of raters to give individuals poor ratings. This is particularly the case in organizational settings with performance appraisals that have ramifications beyond the accurate assessment of performance. Although such patterns of relationships are often considered to reflect biased ratings, this is not always the case. As with halo, in some instances it is likely that most individuals are above the middle of the scale, as selection and training systems of organizations are designed to produce a distribution of performance that is skewed toward the outstanding end. Individuals who fail to perform adequately are dismissed or encouraged to leave, thus cutting off the real bottom of the distribution.

Negative affectivity

Negative affectivity (NA) is a personality variable that has been suggested to be a source of bias in the assessment of many organizational variables, particularly concerning job stress (Watson, Pennebaker, and Folger, 1987). The argument is that individuals who are high on NA are predisposed to experience distress and negative emotions across situations, even in the absence of objective stressors. Their reports about their experiences and perceptions are biased by their tendency to report things in a negative way. The finding that NA relates to other variables in and of itself is not evidence that it is a bias. Spector, Zapf, Chen, and Frese (2000) discussed several nonbias mechanisms through which NA would relate to various organizational variables. For example, they summarized evidence that the job conditions of those high in NA might be objectively different from those who are low. Thus one cannot assume that relationships between organizational variables that relate to NA are inflated by a biasing factor.

Survey design biases

With questionnaire studies and other methods that rely on people's reports, measurement bias can be introduced by the methods used. Priming occurs when a question presented at one point in time affects subsequent responses. Such biases can be introduced by the use of leading or loaded questions, by the use of inflammatory language, or by including messages in the instructions that might influence people's responses. For example, one might conduct a study of experience with workplace bullying and include items that ask if the individual has been subject to one of a list of abusive acts, and how one feels about coworkers and supervisors. It is likely that including in the instructions statements intended to draw attention to the issue can have a biasing effect, for example, 'Each year millions of people are the innocent victims of workplace bullying, perpetrated by coworkers and supervisors who enjoy abusing their power over others. Such individuals have no place in the modern workplace.' Responses are likely to be influenced by such messages when questions concern experiences with bullying and attitudes or perceptions about coworkers and supervisors.

Priming can also occur in more subtle ways when responses to one question might influence responses to another (Harrison, McLaughlin, and Coalter, 1996). For example, if one set of questions asks about a number of negative behaviors by supervisors, answers to subsequent questions about satisfaction with supervision could be affected. Priming influences are least likely to occur with multi-item measures such as those often used in organizational research (Harrison and McLaughlin, 1993). Despite using multi-item measures, care should be taken in separating items that have the potential to influence one another.

Item overlap occurs when the same or similar items are used in scales designed to assess different constructs. This can occur at times because the constructs themselves are overlapping, but they also can occur because of inadequate precision in operationalizing constructs. For example, Dalal (2005) has documented how measures of counterproductive work behavior (CWB) and organizational citizenship behavior (OCB) can share items although the constructs are not intended to be bipolar opposites. Thus, having good attendance is OCB and having poor attendance is CWB; speaking well of the employer is OCB and speaking ill is CWB. As Dalal (2005) demonstrated, item overlap likely inflated relationships between CWB and OCB measures.

Conclusions about measurement bias sources

A theme running through our discussion of these five sources or types of measurement bias is that it is not always clear when and if they are operating in a given situation. The relation between a measure and a measurement bias source, such as NA, or the existence of a response pattern, is insufficient evidence from which to conclude there is measurement bias. Even more difficult is drawing the conclusion that measurement biases were shared across measures, thus producing an inflated relationship. What is needed are strategies that can control and eliminate potential measurement biases so that one can reach more confident conclusions that observed correlations reflect relationships among constructs of interest. This is a tall order, and requires a systematic strategy of ruling in or out potential measurement biases and alternative explanations for results. For the remainder of this chapter we will discuss various attempts to solve the problems posed by measurement bias.

Controlling measurement biases in organizational research

Design approaches

The essence of the design approach to controlling measurement bias is to vary features of methods. So, for example, if single source (respondent) is a criticism of the study, then one can use different sources for the independent and dependent variables in the study. One could use supervisors or job analysts to assess work autonomy, and the incumbent to measure satisfaction with the work, for example. In any case, the question one must ask is not principally what features or elements are common to the independent and dependent variables. Rather, the questions deal with what causes variance in the response distribution and how extraneous variables that produce measurement bias might contaminate both the independent and dependent variables. It is not enough to just choose two different methods (e.g., incumbent versus supervisor reports). Those methods must be chosen to enable a comparison of measurement with and without some feature expected to produce measurement bias. It is only when one method contains the feature and the other does not that the action of the measurement bias can be investigated. We suggest asking the following questions:

1. What are the social consequences of the responses? Research indicates that social pressure can influence responses (e.g., conformity, Bond and Smith, 1996), and respondents may wish to either help or thwart investigators (e.g., Orne, 1962).

2. To what degree do the stimulus conditions provoke defensiveness or threaten esteem? Asking people about sensitive topics such as their weight and sexual behavior is likely to result in nuisance variance that can contaminate observed relations among variables. Such measurement biases need not be conscious; the large majority of people appear to believe that their job performance is above average (e.g., Meyer, 1980: Thornton, 1980) and (apparently) to present an overly optimistic assessment of their marriage (e.g., Edmonds, 1967; Fowers, Applegate, Olson, and Pomerantz, 1994).

3. Are there other payoffs or costs to the respondent for responding in particular ways? Job applicants tend to respond to personality tests differently than do job incumbents (e.g., Birkeland, Manson, Kisamore, Brannick, and Smith, 2006), and individuals who are instructed to complete such surveys under multiple conditions (tell the truth, fake good, and pretend you are applying for a job) respond differently (Vishwesvaran and Ones, 1999). Note that this is neither a source effect nor a stimulus effect, as the same individuals complete the same survey items under different measurement contexts. Grocery checkers show very different performance under test conditions and typical performance conditions (Sackett, Zedeck, and Fogli, 1988).

The result of asking such questions is a potential list of hypotheses regarding nuisance variables that might produce distorted correlations. Some of these variables can be controlled through the design of the study. For example, it is common in social psychology for participants to be blind to the experimenter's hypotheses, and thus the impact from nuisance variables related to our first question can be minimized. Of course, in the absence of information about the purpose of the study, the participant is likely to generate his or her own, which can produce a different kind of measurement bias.

It is also important to remember that in order to be the sort of problem addressed in this chapter, the nuisance variable must be shared by the independent variable and dependent variable. Suppose we approach a person and ask them to taste a new soft drink. If we ask them to rate their satisfaction with the drink, this is unlikely to be affected by defensiveness. Liking or disliking a soft drink is hardly something people will find personally threatening. It may instead be affected by the social context (e.g., they may try to please the marketers by saying they like the drink), conformity (if others are also tasting the soft drink, the person might conform to their ratings), and if they are being filmed for a commercial while they taste the beverage (they might be concerned with how their response might affect airing of their film on television). Measures of other satisfactions might share some, but not all, of these influences. For example, a measure of marital satisfaction would be unlikely to be affected by attempts to please the marketer, but would be affected if they think they are being filmed and their spouse might see their response.

It should be kept in mind that the main strength in the design approach is in being able to rule out a potential measurement bias as the explanation for relationships among variables. If we find, for example, that correlations between autonomy and job satisfaction are more or less the same whether both are assessed via incumbent reports, or one is assessed from incumbents and the other from supervisors, we can be fairly certain that measurement biases residing within the individual incumbent were not the reason for the observed relationships. This of course assumes that supervisors did not share measurement biases with the incumbents. On the other hand, a failure to rule out measurement biases is likely to be inconclusive. If the relationship between autonomy and job satisfaction observed with incumbent reports fails to be maintained with supervisor reports of autonomy, one cannot know if the reason is measurement bias within the incumbent reports, or lack of validity of the supervisor reports. We would need far more data than just lack of confirmation to draw a definitive conclusion.

Nevertheless, the design approach can be relatively strong, particularly when the design involves manipulation of features of method chosen in a systematic way based on sound theory. The design approach is not always practical, however. For example, if one is really interested in facets of incumbent job satisfaction, surveying respondents other than the incumbent is possible, but problematic. If the incumbent is the sole source of data, it will be difficult to control measurement biases related to individual differences such as personality or defensiveness using the design approach. In the choice of design versus statistical approaches to controlling method variance, we agree with Podsakoff et al. (2003), who stated:

> In general, we recommend that researchers first try to prevent method biases from influencing their results by implementing any of the procedural remedies that make sense within the context of their research (p. 899)

Statistical approaches

A number of techniques to identify and control method variance can be found in the literature (see the thorough review by Podsakoff et al., 2003). There are two main approaches to the statistical control of method variance, both of which use partialling. The *nuisance variable* approach is to measure specific nuisance variables such as social desirability and negative affectivity (NA). Method variance is controlled in this approach by partialling the nuisance variable(s) from the relationship between the focal variables (the independent and dependent variables of interest) using either multiple regression or partial correlation. The *method factor* approach is to create a nonspecific factor corresponding to 'method' upon which one loads all the relevant observed variables. In this approach, method variance is controlled by partialling the method factor from the correlation between the focal variables. There are advantages and disadvantages to each approach.

Observed vs. latent variables

In practice, the nuisance variable approach is most often applied to observed variables and the method factor approach is most often applied to unobserved variables (i.e., factors). That is, to apply the nuisance variable approach, one must know what those variables are and assess them so as to remove their possible effects. With the method factor approach, the nuisance variables are inferred from the observed correlations using factor analysis. The important distinction is not whether the corrections are applied to factors or observed variables, but rather whether the shared measurement bias is hypothesized (nuisance variables) or inferred (method factors).

Nuisance variable approach

The nuisance variable technique is a straightforward application of multiple regression or partial correlation as described in many textbooks (e.g., Pedhazur, 1997). Such an approach has been used, for example, by Williams, Gavin, and Williams (1996) to explore the potential biasing effect of negative affectivity. It is closely related to the general use of control variables in nonexperimental research, where factors such as socioeconomic status are often applied as statistical controls (see Meehl, 1971).

Lindell and Whitney (2001) recommended a variation of this approach that involves adding an extra scale to a survey that is theoretically expected to be unrelated to the variables of real interest. The smallest correlation of this measure with one of the others is taken as an upper bound estimate of the amount of method variance. The effect of that extra measure can be partialled from the relationships of interest using partial correlation or regression, thus removing CMV.

Evaluation of the nuisance variable approach

The nuisance variable approach has the advantage of specifying and testing for the effects of specific unwanted hypothetical causes of an observed relationship. The chief virtue of the approach is that should the correlation between the focal variables remain large after applying the partial, then the nuisance variable can be ruled out (or at least reduced in force) as the explanation of the observed relations. The disadvantage of the nuisance variable approach is that it is not

certain that the correct measurement biases or all measurement biases have been considered. If the researcher omits the nuisance variable that is the real culprit in a spurious correlation, the measurement bias effect will remain unchecked. Also, some nuisance variables are difficult to measure directly, for example, item order and item format effects, or cognitive structures such as implicit theories of performance that might be used by raters. The nuisance variable approach appears most useful with individual differences such as defensiveness, personality, or social motives.

The Lindell and Whitney (2001) approach is based on the presumption that there is a constant method inflation effect that can be estimated and controlled. However, what if this conception of method variance is not correct and there is no constant correlation inflation effect? As we have shown, it is often the case that variables within questionnaires are uncorrelated, so finding a variable that will have a small relationship with other variables is relatively easy. In such cases, the Lindell and Whitney adjustment will have little effect, leading to the conclusion that CMV did not significantly inflate observed correlations, and producing a false sense of security that one can assume observed correlations reflect relationships among intended traits.

An important point to keep in mind when employing the nuisance variable approach is that what gets partialled from what, or even whether something ought to be partialled at all depends upon the researcher's theory about the causal relations among constructs of interest (Pedhazur, 1997). As Pedhazur (1997) noted, 'controlling variables without regard to the theoretical considerations about the pattern of relations among them may yield misleading or meaningless results' (p. 170; see also Meehl, 1971; Spector et al., 2000). Gordon (1968) cautioned that by using two similar independent variables, researchers may partial a relation out of itself, and thus falsely conclude through partial correlation that no relations exist between the focal variables. If we consider social desirability (the need for approval) as a nuisance variable, for example, we might conclude, for a hypothetical example, that satisfaction with coworkers and satisfaction with supervision are unrelated. However, a person's inter-actions with others at work are doubtless influenced by the need for approval, and so part of the correlation between satisfaction with coworkers and supervision may actually be due to incumbent behavior driven by the approval motive. Therefore, the observed relation may be causal and legitimate rather than spurious. Such considerations are not unique to the nuisance variable approach. When dealing with latent variable (factor) models, the analogous problem is discussed by many authors under specification errors.

Method factor approach

Although there have been several different conceptions of method factors (see Kumar and Dillon, 1992, for descriptions), we confine our discussion to additive models in which method factors act to inflate observed corre-lations, because this conception corresponds best to the CMV criticism. The method factor approach comes in two main varieties, the sin-gle method factor approach and the multiple method factor approach. In the single method factor approach, one essentially removes the first factor or first principal component from all the correlations among all the measures of interest in a survey. The inspection of focal variables under such an approach is essentially one of deciding whether the focal variables are related beyond what one would expect from the general level of correlation among scales. The reasoning behind such an approach is that CMV produces variance that is shared among all the variables that are measured by it; such shared variance produces the first common factor.

The multiple factor approach is usually applied to mutitrait-multimethod (MTMM) data, in which each of several traits is measured by two or more methods. A method factor is hypothesized for each method (as we noted earlier, method is seldom defined theoretically and is defined operationally simply as the researcher's choice of data collection procedures). As with the single method factor approach, the multiple method

factors are essentially partialled from the observed correlations to determine whether there is correlation remaining between the focal variables after the method factor has been removed.

Illustration of the method factor approach

An illustration of the multiple method factor approach is shown in Figure 20.1. The numbers in the figure are based on the results of Cote and Buckley (1987), who modeled 70 different MTMM matrices. Their overall average showed 41.7 percent trait variance, 26.3 percent method variance, 32.0 percent error variance, an average trait correlation of 0.674, and an average method correlation of 0.484. If one takes the estimates seriously (we do not for reasons we describe shortly), one would expect to see the relations between factors and observed variables shown in Figure 20.1 (all factor loadings for methods are equal to one another at 0.512, and all trait loadings are equal to one another at 0.646).

Several interesting results follow from this illustration. First, the correlation between the latent trait factors is substantial (0.674) even after removing the effects of method. Second, we can derive the expected correlation between observed measures of the two traits both within and between methods. (We used the tracing rule from path analysis to find the expected correlations.) Within methods, the expected observed correlation is:

$$(0.646)(0.674)(0.646)+$$
$$(0.512)(1)(0.512) = 0.54.$$

Note that this correlation, even though it is affected by method variance, is actually smaller than the correlation between trait factors (0.674).

Between methods, the expected observed correlation is:

$$(0.646)(0.674)(0.646)+$$
$$(0.512)(0.484)(0.512) = 0.41,$$

which is 0.13 lower. This observed correlation is also lower than the correlation between

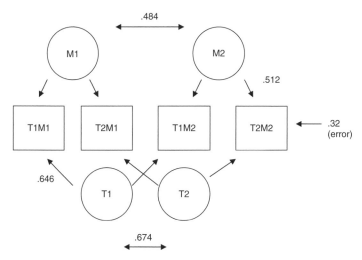

Figure 20.1 Structural model for average of all studies by Cote and Buckley, 1987
Note: All method loadings equal 0.512, all trait loadings equal 0.646, and all uniqueness values (error variances) = 0.32.

trait factors. Further, if one were to collect data both between and within sources, both observed correlations (0.54 and 0.41) would result in the same conclusion that the traits are positively related. Finally, consider that the between-method observed correlation should be free of CMV (at least as the authors considered method), but it shows only a modest reduction compared to the correlation within methods.

Both observed correlations underestimate the factor correlation (correlation between true scores) because of measurement error, so the relationships among the underlying traits will be larger than those observed. However, the important point is that the observed correlations do not support the notion of a spurious correlation between traits that should be properly attributed to method variance. Furthermore, the observed correlations understate the relations between the true scores, so that the potential inflating effects of method variance were counteracted by unreliability. It should be kept in mind that the reason for smaller between methods correlations might also be attributable, at least in part, to invalidity in the alternative sources which might further attenuate observed correlations.

Evaluation of the method factor approach

The method factor approach has the benefit that whatever methods effects are present, they are thought to be captured by the method factor. Unlike the nuisance variable approach, in which one must specify in advance the source of method variance, the method factor approach allows one to extract the method variance post hoc. There are both practical and logical problems with the method factor approach, however. In practice, the single method factor approach tends to attribute too much of the variance to method, thus, over-adjusting for CMV (e.g., Kemery and Dunlap, 1986; Podsakoff and Organ, 1986; Podsakoff and Todor, 1985). As noted earlier, the most general problem of the multiple method factor models, which is typically fit to MTMM data, is severe estimation problems (e.g., Brannick and Spector, 1990; Kenny and Kashy, 1992; Marsh, 1989; Widaman, 1985; Wothke, 1987) such that most of the models of such data contain estimates that are either constrained to the boundary of admissibility (for example, variances constrained to zero, because otherwise they would be negative) or are inadmissible (for example, an estimated correlation is greater than 1.0). In models that produce constrained or inadmissible estimates, the estimates that are admissible are suspect (Bentler, 1976; Fornell and Bookstein, 1982). The estimation problem is one reason we do not take seriously the estimates provided by Cote and Buckley (1987).

There are also theoretical problems in the application of the method factor approach. There is a fundamental ambiguity in assigning a general level of correlation among observed measures to either trait or method factors. Either or both could produce a general level of observed correlations. The central difficulty can be seen in Figure 20.1, in which the correlation between any two observed variables could be explained by either trait or method factors. It may be possible to solve the estimation problems given sufficient traits, methods, and sample size (e.g., Marsh and Bailey, 1991). However, because of the fundamental ambiguity involved in assigning a general level of correlation to either traits or methods, the application of the method factor approach is likely to be problematic unless the researcher can design a study in which at least some traits or methods can be known *a priori* to be independent. If one thinks of method as a bundle of features describing the data collection, then it should be clear that most data collection procedures share some features. So if we test different item formats, we typically use the same individuals in both 'methods.' But the effects of method cannot be examined when the method is constant. This is one reason that the MTMM method factors are estimated to be correlated—at least part of the variance due to method will be shared. Consider using a pencil as a method. We could give the same people the same survey twice and just change the pencil they were using (e.g., from a wooden pencil to a mechanical pencil). We could generate an MTMM matrix estimate method variance using factor analysis for such a design. What would the result be and what would it tell us? Presumably, the estimated method variance would be quite small; respondent effects could not be estimated, though, so if they are present they would be treated as trait effects. In this case, we would likely conclude that method variance is not a problem since it is unlikely

that correlations would vary much within versus between pencil methods.

One might find it difficult to publish the MTMM study in which the pencil was the method, but it illustrates our point that in the method variance literature *method* is rarely defined and the mechanisms for its effects are rarely explained. A quick look at the literature on the MTMM matrix reveals that 'method' varies widely across studies. Method appears to be whatever the researcher has in mind; statements about what data collection procedures must be sufficiently different to constitute different methods are hard to find. Method has included distinctions among raters, scale formats, behavioral exercises, and occasions. Consider using a set of raters as methods, either as job analysts, where the job is the focal entity, or as assessors in an assessment center, where the behavior of an individual in a performance exercise is the object of interest. We could construct a MTMM matrix with rater as a method. If by chance all the raters have the same erroneous mental representation of jobs or of performance, then the resulting matrix will not be able to distinguish method from trait variance.

Surprisingly, in the literature distinctions about method are treated interchangeably; any MTMM matrix is described as informative regarding construct validity. A second reason that we do not take the estimates of Cote and Buckley (1987) seriously is that no attention is paid to the definition of method; the various differences such as item format and source are averaged so that *method variance* has neither theoretical nor practical bases for interpretation.

Method variance and the research question

As we have shown, there are strong and weak points associated with both design and statistical approaches to controlling method variance. In this section, we consider the problem of measurement bias and construct validity of measures in relation to our goals as researchers. Some problems are more tractable than others. Questions about the relations of constructs of interest range from relatively simple to complex. We may simply wish to know whether the focal variables are related at all. We may wish, in addition, to know the degree or magnitude of the relations and the functional form of the relations. At the complex end of the spectrum, we may wish to understand the focal variables in the context of a nomological net in which the focal variables are embedded in a set of causes and effects.

Any correlation

Perhaps the most basic question for a research is whether or not observed correlations reflect relationships among constructs of interest. If the study can be properly designed, then potential measurement biases are controlled directly, and the test of the zero order (raw) correlation among observed variables produces a direct test of the association of the focal constructs. If the design cannot be used to preclude measurement biases, both the nuisance variable approach and the method factor approach produce estimates of the partial correlation between focal variables holding the effects of the extraneous variables constant. The partials then represent the unbiased relationships among variables of interest. Because of specification problems described earlier, both the nuisance variable and method factor approaches yield con-servative tests of the association of focal traits. In other words, showing that the focal traits are related after controlling for method variance is a strong argument that the measurement biases fail to account for the observed relations. Thus, methods of controlling for CMV tend to produce strong (conservative) results regarding the question of whether focal traits are related.

If the measurement bias tests wipe out the focal associations, it is still possible that the focal traits are related, but additional work is needed to understand why the association appears under some measurement conditions but not others (and, of course, what conditions do and do not produce the association). If it turns out that the focal relations are entirely explained by the conditions of measurement, this is still worth knowing.

If the observed variables show an association after controlling for measurement bias, then the factors must also be related, because random errors of measurement only attenuate observed correlations on average. Of course, it is possible that the factors might be associated, but the observed variables still show relations that are essentially zero, because of the magnitude of measurement error. However, the test of whether the focal variables are related at all appears to be the question for which current methods of controlling method variance are best suited.

A caveat to the strong test notion is that the important sources of method variance are contained in the control variables (nuisance variables or method factors). If pencil is our method variable, it will not control for incumbent defensiveness, for example. We are counting upon the researcher to be thoughtful about the possible reasons for the spurious relations, that is, we encourage the researcher to develop and test plausible alternative hypotheses for the association between focal variables.

Practical significance

Are the relations between independent and dependent variable large enough to warrant continued interest (of practical significance)? When the researcher has an applied interest, the question of measurement bias and CMV becomes entangled with the use of the measures. If our test scores, performance ratings, questionnaire scale scores, or other organizational measures are being used for some purpose such as hiring, promotion, training, job evaluation, or organizational change, it becomes an issue whether to remove measurement bias from scores used in deci-sion making. Corrections for measurement bias are likely to meet with resistance in such cases.

Functional relations among constructs

Researchers using covariance structure mod-els are often interested in questions about the causal relations among constructs. Another, similar research agenda item is to deter-mine the relations between independent and dependent variables measured with perfectly valid and reliable scales. Such questions are often of interest in psychological research, but usually cannot be answered to any reasonable degree of certainty, because issues of construct validity, statistical control, and theory are inseparable. Theory depends upon valid measurement, and statistical corrections to improve the validity of measurement depend upon theory. In our view, the statistical approaches to CMV are not particularly helpful when functional relations (theory development) is the main goal. In such cases, it is better to use the design approach to deal with measurement bias.

Finally, when dealing with issues of theory development (the nomological net), measurement and theory evolve jointly through a dialog with data. Only through a process of sophisticated investigations that minimize sources of invalidity can we become confident that our findings are due to genuine relations among constructs and not to features or aspects of the measurement process. No single study can simultaneously demonstrate that both measures and theory are valid.

SUMMARY AND CONCLUSIONS

Rather than objecting to questionnaire results on the basis of common method variance, we ask that critics be more specific in their objections. Is the problem likely due to specifics of the measurement, respondent effects, or the context of measurement? Why (by what mechanism or proximal cause) is the problem likely to occur? Similarly, we ask researchers who are attempting to control or eliminate measurement bias and 'CMV' to describe more specifically what effects they think are likely in their particular research context, and what they have done to examine or control such effects.

Simple conceptions of CMV and its effects are unlikely to be accurate or helpful in the control of measurement biases. A more complex approach is needed to attack reasonable doubt regarding spurious correlations. Format (apparatus) effects are not likely to produce sufficiently strong measurement biases that

explain spurious correlations among focal variables with conventional questionnaires, and so controlling such effects is not going to be particularly helpful. We encourage researchers to consider both respondent consequences for providing data, and their ability to report on the constructs of interest as sources of hypotheses regarding measurement biases.

Research design is preferable to statistical methods for controlling the effects of measurement biases. The two main statistical approaches to controlling measurement biases (the nuisance variable and method factor approaches) have both strengths and weaknesses. Both types of approach provide tests of whether observed correlations are spurious. They do not provide good evidence of the practical value of traits measured without measurement biases due to method, nor do they allow the researcher a crystal ball with which to observe relations that would have been possible with bias-free measurement.

To summarize, we conclude, based on a weighing of the evidence, that common method variance is a myth or urban legend. There is not a constant inflation of correlations among all variables attributable to the use of a single method. However, the lack of CMV does not mean that measurement biases are not at play, and do not themselves affect the magnitude of observed correlations. The idea of simple CMV adjustment procedures is seductive, but simple adjustments are unlikely to be helpful, because they adjust for a constant inflation, something that is not there. We encourage researchers to consider the possibility that measurement bias is specific and not universally shared across all traits assessed with a particular method. Only by the application of multiple methods to control and identify measurement biases will we gain confidence in our conclusions that underlying constructs of interest are related.

REFERENCES

Bagozzi, R.P. and Yi, Y. (1990) 'Assessing method variance in multitrait-multimethod matrices: The case of self-reported affect and perceptions at work', *Journal of Applied Psychology*, 75: 547–60.

Bentler, P.M. (1976) 'Multistructure statistical model applied to factor analysis', *Multivariate Behavioral Research*, 11: 3–25.

Birkeland, S.A., Manson, T.M., Kisamore, J.L., Brannick, M.T. and Smith, M.A. (2006) 'A meta-analytic investigation of applicant faking on personality measures', *International Journal of Selection and Assessment*, 14: 317–35.

Bond, R. and Smith, P.B. (1996) 'Culture and conformity: a meta-analysis of studies using Asch's (1952b, 1956) line judgment task', *Psychological Bulletin*, 119: 111–37.

Boswell, W. R., Boudreau, J.W. and Dunford, B. B. (2004) 'The outcomes and correlates of job search objectives: searching to leave or searching for leverage?', *Journal of Applied Psychology*, 89: 1083–91.

Brannick, M.T. and Spector, P.E. (1990) 'Estimation problems in the block diagonal model of the multitrait-multimethod matrix', *Applied Psychological Measurement*, 14: 325–39.

Campbell, D.T. and Fiske, D.W. (1959) 'Convergent and discriminant validation by the multitrait-multimethod matrix', *Psychological Bulletin*, 56: 81–105.

Cote, J.A. and Buckley, M.R. (1987) 'Estimating trait, method, and error variance: generalizing across 70 construct validation studies', *Journal of Marketing Research*, 24: 315–18.

Crampton, S.M. and Wagner, J.A. III. (1994) 'Percept-percept inflation in microorganizational research: an investigation of prevalence and effect', *Journal of Applied Psychology*, 79: 67–76.

Crowne, D.P. and Marlowe, D. (1964) *The Approval Motive*, New York: John Wiley.

Dalal, R.S. (2005) 'A meta-analysis of the relationship between organizational citizenship behavior and counterproductive work behavior', *Journal of Applied Psychology*, 90: 1241–55.

Edmonds, V.H. (1967) 'Marital conventionaliation: Definition and measurement', *Journal of Marriage and the Family*, 29: 681–8.

Fornell, C. and Bookstein, F.L. (1982) 'Two structural equation models: LISREL and PLS applied to consumer exit-voice theory', *Journal of Marketing Research*, 19: 440–452.

Fowers, B.J., Applegate, B., Olson, D.H. and Pomerantz, B. (1994) 'Marital conventionalization as a measure of martial satisfaction: a confirmatory factor analysis', *Journal of Family Psychology*, 8: 98–103.

Gordon, R.A. (1968) 'Issues in multiple regression', *American Journal of Sociology*, 73: 592–616.

Harrison, D.A. and McLaughlin, M.E. (1993) 'Cognitive processes in self-report responses: tests of item context effects in work attitude measures', *Journal of Applied Psychology*, 78: 129–40.

Harrison, D.A., McLaughlin, M.E. and Coalter, T. M. (1996) 'Context, cognition, and common method variance: psychometric and verbal protocol evidence', *Organizational Behavior and Human Decision Processes*, 68: 246–61.

Kemery,. E.R. and Dunlap, W.P. (1986) 'Partialling factor scores does not control method variance: a reply to Podsakoff and Todor', *Journal of Management*, 12: 525–30.

Kenny, D.A. and Kashy, D.A. (1992) 'Analysis of the multitrait-multimethod matrix by confirmatory factor analysis', *Psychological Bulletin*, 112: 165–72.

Kumar, A. and Dillon, W.R. (1992) 'An integrative look at the use of additive and multiplicative covariance structure models in the analysis of MTMM data', *Journal of Marketing Research*, 29: 51–64.

Lester, S.W., Kickul, J.R. and Bergmann, T.J. (2007) 'Managing employee perceptions of the psychological contract over time: the role of employer social accounts and contract fulfillment', *Journal of Organizational Behavior*, 28: 191–208.

Lindell, M.K. and Whitney, D.J. (2001) 'Accounting for common method variance in cross-sectional research designs', *Journal of Applied Psychology*, 86: 114–21.

Lord, F.M. and Novick, M.R. (1968) *Statistical Theories of Mental Test Scores*, Reading, MA: Addison-Wesley.

Marsh, H.W. (1989) 'Confirmatory factor analyses of multitrait-multimethod data: many problems and a few solutions', *Applied Psychological Measurement*, 13: 335–61.

Marsh, H.W. and Bailey, M. (1991) 'Confirmatory factor analyses of multitrait-multimethod data: a comparison of alternative models', *Applied Psychological Measurement*, 15: 47–70.

Meehl, P.E. (1971) 'High school yearbooks: a reply to Schwartz', *Journal of Abnormal Psychology*, 77: 143–8.

Meyer, H.H. (1980) 'Self-appraisal of job performance', *Personnel Psychology*, 33: 291–5.

Moorman, R. H. and Podsakoff, P.M. (1992) 'A meta-analytic review and empirical test of the potential confounding effects of social desirability response sets in organizational behavior research', *Journal of Occupational and Organizational Psychology*, 65: 131–49.

Murphy, K.R., Jako, R.A. and Anhalt, R.L. (1993) 'Nature and consequences of halo error: a critical analysis', *Journal of Applied Psychology*, 78: 218–25.

Ones, D.S., Viswesvaran, C. and Reiss, A.D. (1996) 'Role of social desirability in personality testing for personnel selection: the red herring', *Journal of Applied Psychology*, 81: 660–79.

Orne, M.T. (1962) 'On the social psychology of the psychological experiment: with particular reference to demand characteristics and their implications', *American Psychologist*, 17: 776–83.

Pedhazur, E.J. (1997) *Multiple Regression in Behavioral Research*, (third edn.), Orlando, FL: Harcourt Brace.

Podsakoff, P.M., MacKenzie, S.B., Lee, J.Y. and Podsakoff, N.P. (2003) 'Common method biases in behavioral research: a critical review of the literature and recommended remedies', *Journal of Applied Psychology*, 88: 879–903.

Podsakoff, P.M. and Organ, D.W. (1986) 'Self-reports in organizational research: problems and prospects', *Journal of Management*, 12: 531–44.

Podsakoff, P.M. and Todor, W.D. (1985) 'Relationships between leader reward and punishment behavior and group processes and productivity', *Journal of Management*, 11: 55–73.

Rorer, L.G. (1965) 'The great response-style myth', *Psychological Bulletin*, 63: 129–56.

Sackett, P.R., Zedeck, S. and Fogli, L. (1988) 'Relations between measures of typical and maximum job performance', *Journal of Applied Psychology*, 73: 482–6.

Spector, P.E. (1987) 'Method variance as an artifact in self-reported affect and perceptions at work: myth or significant problem?', Journal of Applied Psychology, 72: 438–43.

Spector, P.E. (2006) 'Method variance in organizational research: truth or urban legend?', *Organizational Research Methods*, 9: 221–32.

Spector, P.E. and Brannick, M.T. (1995) 'The nature and effects of method variance in organizational research', in C.L. Cooper and I.T. Robertson (eds), *International Review of Industrial and Organizational Psychology: 1995*, West Sussex, England: John Wiley, pp.249–74.

Spector, P.E., Zapf, D., Chen, P.Y. and Frese, M. (2000) 'Why negative affectivity should not be controlled in job stress research: don't throw out the baby with the bath water', *Journal of Organizational Behavior*, 21: 79–95.

Thornton, G.C. III (1980) 'Psychometric properties of self-appraisal of job performance', *Personnel Psychology*, 33: 263–71.

Vishwesvaran, C. and Ones, D.S. (1999) 'Meta-analysis of fake ability estimates: implications for personality measurement', *Educational and Psychological Measurement*, 59: 197–210.

Watson, D., Pennebaker, J.W. and Folger, R. (1987) 'Beyond negative affectivity: measuring stress and satisfaction in the workplace', in J.M. Ivancevich, and D.C. Ganster (eds), *Job stress: From Theory to Suggestion* New York: Haworth Press, pp.141–57.

Widaman, K.F. (1985) 'Hierarchically nested covariance structure models for multitrait-multimethod data', *Applied Psychological Measurement*, 9: 1–26.

Williams, L.J. and Brown, B.K. (1994) 'Method variance in organizational behavior and human resources research: effects on correlations, path coefficients, and hypothesis testing', *Organizational Behavior and Human Decision Processes*, 57: 185–209.

Williams, L.J., Cote, J.A. and Buckley, M.R. (1989) 'Lack of method variance in self-reported affect and perceptions at work: reality or artifact?', *Journal of Applied Psychology*, 74: 462–68.

Williams, L.J., Gavin, M.B. and Williams, M.L. (1996) 'Measurement and non-measurement processes with negative affectivity and employee attitudes', *Journal of Applied Psychology*, 81: 88–101.

Wothke, W. (1987) 'Multivariate linear models of the multitrait-multimethod matrix', Paper presented at the American Educational Research Association Conference, Washington, DC.

21

Collaborative Research: Renewing Action and Governing Science

Jean-Louis Denis and Pascale Lehoux

INTRODUCTION

Collaborative research refers to a broad range of research activities in the service of various practical and developmental goals. It has been defined as 'a deliberate set of interactions and processes designed specifically to bring together those who study social problems and issues (researchers) with those who act on or within those societal problems and issues (decision-makers, practitioners, citizens, and so on)' (Denis and Lomas, 2003, p. S2:1). Collaborative research implies the involvement of nonresearchers in the conduct of research, and its expected benefits include:

- Broadening the range of choices in defining problems and assembling methodologies
- Enriching the interpretation of research findings
- Fostering the use and application of research findings in action or decision-making contexts
- Changing the thinking and behaviors of researchers and practitioners regarding the purpose and practice of their work

The picture is not, however, entirely rosy. That is because collaborative research may also have some shortcomings and undesirable effects. These hold the potential to threaten the autonomy of the research process and, ultimately, of researchers themselves. Indeed, there is a risk in collaboration of reducing the originality and specificity of research as well as jeopardizing the entire knowledge production process.

We begin this chapter by exploring some of the varieties of collaborative research in terms of research goals, links to experiential knowledge, and attributes of the research process. We then discuss some of the challenges involved in practicing collaborative research, including the tension between rigor and relevance, and the transformative potential of collaborative research in contemporary organizations. We then introduce briefly the institutionalization of collaborative research through networks of scientists and practitioners. We argue that these networks hold the potential to increase the supply of collaborative research and present opportunities to transform the relationship between science and practice in organizations and institutional settings. We also suggest that network science ought to become an important instrument in the governance of science and research practices and the exposure of scientific knowledge to new normative imperatives.

Throughout our discussion of collaborative research, we focus more on the social arrangements and institutional underpinnings of this approach than on its technical aspects. Along the way, we emphasize the challenges that face collaborative research as well as the practices and processes that hold the most potential for increasing its benefits. In order to illuminate our argument, we occasionally draw on salient examples from the healthcare field.

Understanding collaborative research

In this section, we examine the *action research* tradition and its derivatives in order to define scholarly archetypes of collaborative research in terms of goals, links to experiential knowledge, and conceptions of the research process. The generic properties of action research are as follows (Cullen, 1998):

- A need for close interactions with practitioners through the research process
- Experiential knowledge as a critical asset for understanding and transforming organizations
- A close connection between objectivity and subjectivity in human action
- The potential of research to contribute to the construction and reconstruction of social or organizational realities
- The fundamental role of reflexivity in developing new organizational forms and social arrangements
- A close link between the practice of research and the development of new ideas

Different approaches to action research each have their own weightings and conceptions of these properties. In our discussion of contemporary methodologies, we draw on work by Whyte, Reason, Argyris,

Checkland, and Patton – all landmarks in the development of systematic and collaborative forms of inquiry. According to Whyte (1991), the action research model finds its roots in the work of Kurt Lewin and North American social scientists at the end of World War II. At that time, the conduct of field experiments – as opposed to laboratory experiments – was seen as a major asset for social theories and social science knowledge. When compared with the classical approach to scientific inquiry, the added value of action research is based on the need to create and diffuse 'social inventions'; that is to say, new organizational and social structures, new patterns of relationships and exchanges, and new roles and procedures that shape human interactions (Whyte, 1989, 1991; Whyte et al., 1989). Through action research, innovative knowledge and practices are simultaneously developed as a result of an explicit articulation among three theoretical systems that are always at play in efforts to understand processes of organizational or social changes:

- Local theory within a concrete system of action
- Formal theory (i.e., espoused principles in the conduct of human affairs)
- Scientifically grounded theory (i.e., generalizations of processes that produce or impede learning and change)

More precisely, action research aims at understanding how local and formal theories are connected in real-life contexts, and how participatory processes involved in research form a basis on which to create social innovations that affect the content of and balance between the two theories. Consequently, action research combines and confronts various sources of knowledge, such as experiential and so-called scientific knowledge (Whyte, 1991). The coexistence of experiential and scientific knowledge materializes through cooperation and deliberation between researchers and practitioners.

The primary assumption behind action research is that in order to develop and learn innovative practices, people should be in a position to contemplate alternatives, access resources necessary for their own development, and be stimulated by competition or comparisons with others' performance (Whyte, 1991). Work and organizational arrangements (Pasmore and Khalsa, 1993) are not the result of strict determinism, but can be regenerated through self-governing processes and industrial democracy (Gustavsen, 1998) that value positive exchanges among organizational actors and also value joint pay-off relationships over strict control (Whyte, 1991). The success of action research is measured by its capacity to bring about long-term change in organizations beyond the timeframe of a given research initiative (Greenwood, 1996; Whyte et al., 1989: 535).

A form of inquiry called *participatory action research* (PAR) has recently been popularized by Reason (1994, 2006) and others (Heron and Reason, 2001; Reason and McArdle, in press). PAR is closely related to the emancipatory agenda of the liberationist movement, as exemplified by Paulo Freire (1972). The distinction between Whyte's take on action research and Reason's work on PAR seems more a matter of nuance than fundamental difference. Reason's approach emphasizes the need for a joint commitment of researchers and practitioners to a developmental and transformative agenda:

> Co-operative inquiry is a way of working with other people who have similar concerns and interests to yourself, in order to: understand your world, make sense of your life and develop new and creative ways of looking at things; learn how to act to change things you may want to change and find out how to do things better (Heron and Reason, 2001: 182).

On this account, the ultimate aim of collaborative research is to contribute to the emergence and maintenance of a more cooperative world. According to Reason, traditional researchers are overly theoretical and insufficiently practical. Under PAR, cooperative inquiry leads to the dissolution of boundaries between the roles of researchers and practitioners, and research should lead to the creative action of people rather than to propositional knowledge.

Two other variants of action research have been developed with the aim of contributing to organizational learning and development: Checkland's (1994, 1999) *Soft Systems Methodology* (SSM) and Argyris's *action science* (Argyris et al., 1985). SSM is based on the conception of an organization as a 'continually changing product of human processes' (Checkland, 1994: 77). The inquiry process at the root of SSM is based on a continuous dialectic between judgements and actions organized as a system. For SSM, the target of change is the standards that guide a system's operations. Any organizational setting, according to Checkland (1994: 85), is the product of conflicting appreciative statements and norms. Within this conflictual universe, organizational members strive for purposeful action. The object of SSM inquiry is to deal with problem situations by identifying and debating the standards that guide actions (Checkland, 1994: 86). Checkland (1994, 1999) proposes to use metaphors of a given action setting to identify issues and map out competing representations in order to find more consensual and effective modes of action.

Checkland's focus on changing standards resembles Argyris's action science perspective. Action science uses participants' speech acts to identify the assumptions behind theories-in-use and to assess the incongruence between espoused theories and practice. In doing so, action science aims at increasing a sense of individual causal responsibility in organizations and social systems (Edmondson, 1996). For Argyris and Schön (1989), participants' defensive routines (i.e., their theories-in-use) risk blocking desirable courses of action discovered by collaborative inquiry. The action science perspective is collaborative in the sense that its goals cannot be achieved without close collaboration by and openness of concerned organizations and participants. Findings generated by the action science approach are also subject to disconfirmation by concerned practitioners. However, a highly structured process driven by researchers guides the generation of those models. Action science and SSM are probably more intrusive and under researchers' control than the forms of inquiry developed by Whyte and Reason.

While not focusing strictly on the interface between research and organizations, the field of evaluation research has been largely concerned with the development of more collaborative forms of inquiry. In his book on *utilization-focused evaluation*, Patton (1997) suggests that evaluation as applied research should be geared to the needs of clients or principal stakeholders in order to increase the use and application of knowledge. In their study of naturalistic evaluation, Lincoln and Guba (1985) apply this preoccupation to a broader diversity of stakeholder groups, including ones threatened by evaluation results and disadvantaged groups that have generally had less input into the research process and interpretation of findings (Themessl-Huber and Grutsch, 2003). Recently, the term *empowerment evaluation* has been coined to refer to this broader objective of social improvement and democracy (Gregory, 2000; Mark et al., 2000; Patton, 1997) and to issues of ownership, relevance, understandability, access, involvement, improvement, and capacity building associated with evaluative processes (Patton, 1997: 147). The ultimate aim of participatory/empowerment evaluation is to help people to learn how to think critically and to evaluate information (Patton, 2002). In accord with this perspective, process use (e.g., learning, capabilities development) is as important as evaluation's substantive impact.

By comparing these various forms of collaborative inquiry, we can derive five research archetypes (Table 21.1) differentiated according to the goals they pursue, their conceptions of experiential knowledge, and the ways in which they organize the research process. The ultimate aim of Whyte's version of action research is to bring about sustainable social inventions within organizational settings. For Reason, the goal of PAR is to increase the level of cooperation among a broad diversity of actors within organizations and societies.

Both Checkland's SSM and Argyris's action science aim, through systematic inquiry, at changing standards and norms that guide behaviors in organizational contexts in order to improve practices. Finally, Patton and his colleagues aspire to increase concerned actors' abilities to benefit from the evaluative experience and to develop critical-thinking skills.

The main goals pursued by these various theories shape their proponents' views of the role of experiential knowledge in formal inquiry. Whyte's approach highly values experiential knowledge as a critical resource for learning and practice changes. Reason emphasizes the role of the experiential knowledge of both researchers and practitioners jointly involved in cooperative forms of inquiry. Checkland and Argyris, meanwhile, use concerned actors' experiential knowledge to identify key normative elements that need to change in order to make practice change possible. And Patton sees in evaluation a pedagogical device whereby the confrontation of systematic evaluation and experiential knowledge brings mutual enrichment.

Collaborative research is shaped according to the goals and relations to experiential knowledge that characterize these five archetypes. For Whyte, researchers play the role of facilitators by structuring the different research steps and by providing data and insights on a diversity of participatory processes and experiences. For Reason, PAR is based on an iterative, cooperative form of inquiry, whereby researchers and practitioners engage equally in each phase of the research process in order to expose publicly their own thoughts and experiences regarding contexts, problems, and solutions. Checkland's SSM, meanwhile, is based on a highly structured, research-driven process geared to identifying plausible metaphors of organizational situations that can be used to reveal practice standards. And for his part, Argyris developed a process for elucidating assumptions behind practitioners' behaviors and to stimulate new patterns of interaction. Finally, the utilization approach and its derivatives emphasize the

Table 21.1 Five collaborative research archetypes

	Action research (Whyte)	Participatory action research (Reason)	Soft system methodology (Checkland)	Action science (Argyris)	Utilization-focused evaluation (Patton)
Goals	Create sustainable social inventions within organizations.	Increase cooperation among diverse organizational and social actors.	Modify organizational and professional norms and improve established practices.	Modify organizational and professional norms and improve established practices.	Increase organizational permeability to evaluation-based learning and critical thinking.
Conception of experiential knowledge	A critical resource for learning and change.	Something possessed by both researchers and practitioners that forms the basis of cooperative inquiry.	Examining experiential knowledge helps reveal normative assumptions (tacitly and explicitly) deployed in practices.	Examining interactions and experiential knowledge should lead to challenges to the norms that impede practice change.	When evaluation and experiential knowledge are mutually enriched they serve as learning devices.
Research process	The researcher is a facilitator who organizes and provides data and insights to the participatory process.	Researchers and practitioners are equal, cooperative participants who contribute to each step in the process.	A research-driven, highly structured process is required to elucidate and challenge established organizational practices.	New patterns of interaction are stimulated through a formal analysis of established normative assumptions.	The evaluator maintains a pedagogical role while each step in the process is negotiated with the evaluation's users.

joint negotiation of each research step while maintaining a strong pedagogical role for evaluators.

Challenges to implementing a collaborative action research agenda

Our brief review of the five archetypes of collaborative action research shed light on some of the fundamental challenges at the heart of conducting research in partnerships. In order to illuminate those challenges, we have formulated three questions:

1. How can reflexivity be introduced into practice?
2. Who should lead and frame the research process?
3. How can one strike a balance between scientific and practical relevance?

Action research is based on the assumption that the experience of conducting research is, in itself, a source of learning. It suggests that reflexivity will be a key component of any collaborative inquiry (question 1). As we saw, collaborative research is also based on the principle of shared responsibility among researchers and practitioners. Consequently, the roles of researchers and practitioners should be negotiated and addressed explicitly (question 2). Finally, agreeing on what the outcome of a research process should be is critical to assessing its potential (question 3).

Question 1: How can reflexivity be introduced into practice?

Reflexivity implies deliberate thinking about how the research process (or other forms of practice) shapes its outcomes (Cutcliffe, 2003; Easterby-Smith and Malina, 1999; Hardy et al, 2001; Schön, 1983). In the context of collaborative research, one may expect that learning from practice will be a main result of the reciprocal influence between researchers and nonresearchers (Whyte, 1991). As we noted previously, despite their differences, all five collaborative research archetypes use deliberate processes to mix and confront researchers' and practitioners' norms

and knowledge. In this subsection, we explore various pathways through which the collaborative research experience can stimulate learning through practice for researchers and nonresearchers.

The potential for collaborative research to generate conditions suitable for reflexivity is a complex and controversial issue. For some authors (e.g., Reason, 1994, Whyte, 1991), reflexivity emerges almost naturally from interactions and open dialogue among a diversity of participants, including researchers and nonresearchers; it is a shared responsibility and a collective endeavor. For others (e.g., Argyris, 1993; Argyris et al., 1985), reflexivity is produced under the strong guidance of researchers who set up systematic processes to unveil the implicit logic of actions and interactions within organizations. The action science perspective also represents a vigorous critique of the usual mode of scientific inquiry by inviting researchers to reflect on their practices.

Reflexivity, defined as learning from practice, can be generated through various pathways: immersion, confrontation, and diffusion. The first pathway – *immersion* – develops through close, long-term connections between researchers and practitioners in organizations. Its purpose is to achieve a thicker knowledge of context and practices. Immersion implies that researchers become the main data instruments (Wadsworth, 2005) and that through conversations and group involvement (e.g., participating in committees and training sessions) they become actors whose actions have immediate effects on their research settings. This pathway to reflexivity resembles the traditional approach to ethnography adapted for and transplanted to contemporary organizations. By being immersed in a practice setting, a researcher accepts being intrusive. The benefits of such a process are tangible for researchers and nonresearchers; for example, researchers may become a resource for stimulating learning in organizations by providing divergent insights into current practices and contingencies. In addition, such research experience may push researchers to become more aware of the limits and potential of current methodologies to inform practices (Hardy et al., 2001).

Somewhat paradoxically, immersion has the potential to increase the capacity to detach oneself from observed practices and to adopt a critical stance. Work by Finlay and Gough (2003), Lascoumes (1996), and Giddens (1986), for example, suggests that close connections among actors may motivate them to improve the social monitoring of practices and, consequently, improve their capacity to make significant changes. Bate et al. (2000a, 2000b) provide a convincing account of a research methodology called 'culturally sensitive restructuring,' whereby researchers work closely with practitioners to develop strategies to make changes to hospitals' social fabric. Similarly, the integration of researchers in primary care organizations during periods of strategic change helps management teams identify and understand the links between knowledge production and the development of innovative practices such as need assessments and community involvement. Immersion can stimulate reflexivity as long as people are open to rethinking how they deal with others' positions and contingencies.

A second pathway to reflexivity – *confrontation* – conceives of collaborative research as the meeting point between potentially conflicting expectations regarding the respective roles of researchers and nonresearchers, the shaping of the research process, and desirable research outcomes. Reflexivity depends on the capacity to benefit from and regulate tensions among participants; for example, because of the threats it may represent for key stakeholders, evaluative research (a type of research popular in organizational settings) is often framed initially in collaborative terms, but risks becoming confrontational. In such situations, the use of research to stimulate learning from practice partly depends on researchers' and nonresearchers' abilities to clarify their mutual roles and expectations and to engage in deliberation (Denis et al., 2003). In a study we conducted of an emerging network in the field of genetics, tensions among

academic public-agency researchers provided an opportunity to formalize follow-up rules (i.e., format, frequency, and framing of issues): to maintain links among a large, multidisciplinary team and to learn from research results in order to support network management. Cooperation among research participants was repositioned in a context in which different epistemic standpoints could coexist (Lehoux et al., 2008). The deliberate creation of an intermediary zone between groups of researchers from different institutions and disciplines is an example of adaptation based on learning from practice (Knorr-Cetina, 1999).

A third pathway – *diffusion* – exists somewhere between the previous two. This pathway is well trod in situations involving organizational change. Denis et al. (2001), for instance, found that each project they studied was supported by a cooperative agreement, whereby researchers were open and considered it necessary to confront their research findings with the views of concerned actors and practitioners in the field. In diffusion situations, researchers debate findings not only with involved practitioners but also with practitioners in other similar contexts. This approach to linkages and exchanges aims at increasing the learning potential of the research experience while at the same time being much less intrusive. Some organizational settings (in particular, participating research sites) may perceive diffusion as not entirely satisfying because of the distance investigators deliberately maintain with the field. This third pathway to reflexivity has, however, caused ideas generated through the research experience to circulate in broad policy and managerial contexts and has contributed to closer links between researchers and practitioners. Diffusion seems to make researchers and nonresearchers more sensitive to the learning that both communities may derive from each other. Key ingredients of diffusion-based reflexivity are long-term but less intense interactions among researchers and practitioners as well as maintenance of researchers' credibility in practice settings.

In our description of these three pathways to reflexivity, we left aside the question of potential gridlock or blockage of the inquiry and exchange processes that occasionally result from conflicting interests and some participants' determination to dominate the research process. This potential brings to the fore the conditions necessary for achieving reflexivity in practice. At the basis of any reflexive process is the requirement that cooperation among individuals and groups can be maintained despite any controversies that might arise. Reflexivity also implies that deliberative mechanisms can be developed and used to counteract phenomena associated with asymmetrical power relations. In our own study of organizational change and innovation in health care, we have found that the source of financial support for research is one of the key elements affecting the equilibrium of relationships between researchers and practitioners, as well as between research programs' theoretical and practical aims. Most of our research is funded by independent peer-review agencies. While these agencies advocate collaborative research and partnerships, the fact that we do not depend on the collaboration of partners to obtain funding fosters – at least in our view – a healthy balance between curiosity-driven research and practical and instrumental considerations.

Nevertheless, researchers' financial autonomy does not exclude the need for close partnerships with practice settings. On the contrary, all of our research endeavors involve and rely on such alliances. These kinds of partnerships make possible both access to fine-grained data on organizational processes and joint interpretations of findings.

In a majority of our research, such collaboration has been relatively smooth and constructive. In most cases, this has been due not to independent financial support but, instead, has arisen because of clear definitions of respective roles and expectations. Our research has taught us, for instance, to avoid formulating any kind of prescriptions regarding either best or recommended practices.

This is at odds with a widespread expectation among practice settings that we will offer consultant-style advice. Instead, we typically use our research results to identify key issues affecting practitioners and to propose new perspectives for thinking about promising or innovative methods. We have found that these steps result in a clear delineation between researchers' and consultants' roles and we have learned to accept that there will likely be some dissatisfaction among practice settings' elite members. However, we believe this is a necessary evil, because getting too close to organizations' systems and imperatives would eventually compromise our scholarly independence.

There is, of course, no magic recipe for counteracting the propensity of some elites to discredit or attempt to control research processes and interpretations. In exceptional cases, we have faced highly conflictual situations, and our research team has been obliged to proceed without the support of key partners. In these instances, while we began with agreements between researchers and practitioners around research processes, those processes eventually ceased to be at all cooperative. These sorts of relationship implosions bring to the fore the issue of the independence of researchers and their findings. Such situations frequently culminate in a split between investigators and practitioners and a termination of collaborative inquiry.

On a more optimistic note, the three pathways to reflexivity we have identified suggest factors that can help to prevent termination of the research experience. In the immersion mode, anticipation by researchers and key participants of sources of misunderstanding and their implementation of mechanisms to counteract imbalances in interactions (e.g., the PAR approach) may help to attenuate counterproductive dynamics. In the confrontational mode, researchers' ability to formulate and propose formal rules of the game – including expectations regarding deliverables and rules for cross-validation of findings and interpretations – can contribute to the maintenance of collaboration.

Finally, in the diffusion mode, the validation of findings and interpretations by concerned participants is essential because of the broad circulation of research results in diverse practice settings. Concerned organizations and participants should, after all, be comfortable with the research product that will be used to stimulate reflexivity through a diffuse network.

Question 2: Who should lead and frame the research process?

Different approaches to collaborative research hold different views of the roles of researchers and nonresearchers in shaping the research process. Recent research policies formulated, for example, by the Canadian Health Services Research Foundation and various service delivery organizations, have fostered the blending of roles to stimulate innovation in both research and practice. At a more micro level, collaborative research is based on the assumption that negotiation among research participants at each research step will, at the very least, increase knowledge use and application (Patton, 2002). Action research's valuation of relationality (i.e., recognizing intrinsic values in interactions between researchers and those being researched; Bradbury and Bergmann Lichtenstein, 2000) increases the odds that practitioners will concern themselves with the impact of the research process itself and will seek a direct voice in the process. In addition, through such involvement, non-researchers can increase their competency in the framing of research problems and, consequently, be better equipped to make demands of the research community (Denis et al., 2003).

The negotiation of research roles is probably more fundamental and has a greater impact on research outcomes than does the negotiation of research operations. Negotiating the research process with concerned stakeholders can have certain pitfalls; for example, it might put the research at risk of capture by local interests (Argyris and Schön, 1989). Research conducted in organizations is often negotiated with organizational elites who may frame problems and the search for solutions or alternatives according to highly particular views, thereby restricting the plurality of perspectives that will be considered. By focusing on the dilemmas of top managers involved in major change processes (Denis et al., 2001), for instance, researchers might neglect the viewpoints of a broader organizational base (e.g., workers, and service providers). This oversight may not be an issue for the generation of sound propositional knowledge such as leadership theories in highly professionalized organizations. It may, however, be a limitation from the point of view of the transformational ideal that informs many approaches to collaborative research.

While collaborative research is fundamentally based on the creation of partnerships between researchers and nonresearchers, there may be possibilities to reduce the consequences of negotiation on the research experience by developing effective mediating structures. The use of advisory committees is a widespread technique for ensuring input from concerned nonresearchers. Our reliance on such committees in some of our research has been largely positive. In those instances, people whom we invited engaged voluntarily in this process. Along the way, they increased their sensitivity to the potential of emerging research results, and by representing various types of expertise and locations, they helped us to expand our research agenda and to fine-tune its methodologies. They also helped us to extract practical implications from our empirical findings and to suggest further avenues of inquiry.

Such benefits appear to arise in contexts in which there are fewer direct negotiations involving research processes and roles. Advisory committees often take a stance that differs from that of their immediate clients, and they can be thought of as a technique to generate an intermediary space between the research and the nonresearch communities. In this sense, they can also be seen as a resource for collective reflexivity that can help to orient direct negotiations between researchers and nonresearchers.

Question 3: How can one strike a balance between scientific and practical relevance?

It can often be difficult to reconcile the pursuit of scientific and practical relevance. *Scientific relevance* refers broadly to the contribution of research to the knowledge stock of a given field. Scientific relevance levels thus depend on the originality of research questions and findings and on the attributes of the production processes that generate findings. It should also be kept in mind that the definition of scientific rigor varies across positivist, postpositivist, and constructivist paradigms (among others, see Lincoln and Guba, 1985).

Practical relevance refers to the benefits that concerned practitioners perceive in research processes and findings. It may, for instance, include the emancipatory or transformational goals promoted by PAR. Well-known work by Patton (1997) on utilization-focused evaluation, and Campbell (1971/1989) on the experimenting society, suggest that researchers have a pedagogical role to play in explaining the attributes of systematic inquiry processes to concerned stakeholders, while also taking into account their insights when adjusting research processes and interpretations. In such cases, both scientific and practical relevance can be simultaneously achieved.

This view coheres with the work of Cheo and Trent (2006) on the concept of 'transactional validity,' which is 'an interactive process between the researcher, the researched, and the collected data that is aimed at achieving a relatively higher level of accuracy and consensus by means of revisiting facts, feelings, experiences, and values and beliefs collected and interpreted' (p. 321). In other words, interactions are a resource for seeking agreement about what will be considered an accurate account. Interactions between researchers and practitioners involve a constant logic of 'member checking,' whereby researchers invite participants to express their opinions regarding the accuracy of findings and the adequacy of the research process. Incorporating participants' viewpoints is seen as a fundamental ingredient for enriching the research process and its

validity while simultaneously increasing the practical relevance of its findings. Validated research reports and related publications that draw on key informants can also be considered a form of member checking.

Again, however, we want to emphasize the need to install effective deliberative processes in order to avoid the discrediting of research by powerful interest groups. Such processes are particularly useful when the framing of a problem, research findings, or even researchers' views conflict with interest groups' expectations and the strategic goals they are pursuing through their participation in formal inquiries. Our previous discussion of reflexivity suggests that elements such as independent financial support and clear definition of researchers' roles can alleviate the threat of external control and distortion of the research process. The discussion by Argyris and Schön (1989) of the production of nonmanipulative knowledge in the context of collaborative research lends further credence to our assertions.

The capacity to resist distortion of the research process or results varies across the five archetypes. When collaborative research is closely associated with an emancipatory and transformational agenda, the pursuit of scientific relevance, at least in terms of the generation of propositional knowledge, is probably more in tension with practical relevance. As Reason (2006: 191) suggests, conflicting views of validity in research are at stake:

> Thus, the movement in qualitative research has been away from validity criteria that mimic or parallel those of empiricist research toward a greater variety of validity considerations that include the practical, the political and the moral; and away from validity as policing and legitimation toward a concern for validity as asking questions, stimulating dialogue, making us think about just what our research practices are grounded in, and thus what are the significant claims concerning quality we wish to make.

According to this view, criteria used to assess the quality of a collaborative research process will be based on the valuation of choice, transparency, social relevance, participation, and practical outcome (Kvale, 1995; Maginn, 2007; Reason, 2006). In fact, many experts consider the quality of the interaction process to be the fundamental ingredient in achieving transformational validity, which has been defined 'as a progressive, emancipatory process leading toward social change that is to be achieved by the research endeavour itself' (Cheo and Trent, 2006: 321; see also LeCompte, 2002). According to this logic, the validity of a collaborative research project is assessed by the ameliorative or social improvement process (Mark et al., 2000) that emerges from its implementation. Further, pragmatic and communicative concerns take precedence over the validity of a representation as defined within the empiricist tradition (Kvale, 1995), and local validity takes precedence over other forms of validity in scientific inquiry.

From this perspective, the main outcome of collaborative research is to stimulate long-term, sustainable development processes from the points of view of concerned actors. The search for benefits through research in terms of learning and capability-building (Patton, 2002) and substantive change (Whyte, 1991) dominates. Scientific and practical relevance can be achieved by such research if those efforts generate sound theoretical contributions to and rich empirical findings about potential links among systematic forms of inquiry, cooperative interactions, and learning in organizational settings (Whyte, 1991). Organizational researchers must, therefore, seek to generate rich and focused process data on mechanisms that are conducive to change, including the role of research processes in inducing transformation.

As we underscored in the first section of this chapter, the action science perspective places scientific relevance at the service of practical relevance. Argyris et al. (1985) hold that researchers should help practice settings develop and test refutable propositions regarding local contexts and the logic of certain actions. The validity of proposition formulation and testing depends on researchers' capacity to use 'talk data'

and theories of organizational learning in order to generate valid empirical maps of organizational systems. The validity of inferences is, meanwhile, based on the strength of observational data, participants' (including researchers) willingness to publicize their reasoning, dedication to seeking alternative explanations and sources of refutation, and the degree of value ascribed to the use of errors and poor performance as learning opportunities. The action science perspective advocates researchers' maintenance of independent standards in order to assess the validity of knowledge claims and inferences. However, its proponents use these standards in real-life settings to act upon dominant action logics and to achieve practical relevance.

In collaborative research, there is no unanimous view of the ideal balance or mix of scientific and practical relevance. The epistemological foundations of different types of collaborative research produce varying weightings and definitions. When the objectives of representational accuracy and the ability to test the plausibility of inferences dominate, collaborative research strives for a balance between these two types of relevance. When the cooperative agenda takes precedence over more conventional empiricist criteria to assess the quality of research, collaborative research aims mainly at practical relevance. Some approaches to collaborative action research (e.g., to varying degrees, Argyris, 1993; Checkland, 1994 and 1999; Whyte, 1991) seem to strive for a dual role for researchers, one that involves simultaneous engagement with scientific and practical relevance. Considering the reality of organizational settings, it seems reasonable to maintain in collaborative research a preoccupation with researchers' independence or, at least, with pluralism in the assessment of research quality.

Collaborative research engages researchers in journeys that can transform the very practice of research itself. Such endeavors require framing research processes in concert with multiple stakeholders and may, in some cases, achieve a high level of scientific and practical relevance. These aspects of collaborative research underscore the challenges of 'engaged scholarship' (Van de Ven and Johnson, 2006), whereby strong connections with practice settings need to be coupled with strategies aimed at achieving sound and nonmanipulative knowledge of organizational transformation processes.

The institutional basis of collaborative research

In this final part of our chapter we move on to a discussion of the institutional basis for the increased interest in collaborative research. In organizational and other social sciences, collaborative research regained popularity as a result of the call for large-scale adoption of research partnerships as an ideal model for contemporary scientific inquiries. More precisely, three contextual factors appear to play roles in promoting the partnership model:

- Debate within the scholarly community about the need for and value of usable knowledge.
- Current research policies that push toward formalized partnerships between researchers and nonresearchers.
- Popular notions of evidence-informed management and decision-making in organizations.

These factors do not, of course, function independently of one another; each one influences the others and their joint impact suggests that any analysis of the promises of collaborative research should account for the context in which a given research strategy takes shape. We will now briefly explore each of these factors in order to gain a clearer picture of the partnership model's institutionalization.

Debates taking place in the scientific community over the legitimacy of organizational scholarship and researchers' social responsibility have stimulated interest in collaborative research (Mohrman et al., 2001; Bartunek et al., 1993; Rynes et al., 2001). Some scholars have raised the issue of the growing distance between organizational research's current foci and the needs and preoccupations

of organizations and their workers. Organizational scholarship has, therefore, been reframed, by some, as an applied research endeavor that needs to connect more closely with organizational problems and processes. Adherents of this point of view see in research partnerships a vehicle for achieving a new equilibrium between the quest for independent and scholarly knowledge and the goal of increased practitioner relevance.

This view is somewhat countered by other scholars (Clegg, 2002; Hinings and Greenwood, 2002) who believe that the dominant trend in organizational research has entailed a move away from its sociological foundations and a colonization by organizational or corporate interests (see Learmonth, Chapter 6, this volume). This account emphasizes the importance of investigator-driven research, and suggests that careful attention should be paid to the types of partnerships that are developed in the context of 'network science.' If research partnerships are desirable, they should not be instituted at the cost of subservience to organizational or economic elites. Institutionalizing research partnerships can be a legitimate trend, but such alliances should be based on a new social contract between organizational scholars, practicing managers, and organizations.

This concern over the capture of the research process by organizational elites brings us back to the issue of the role that critical thinking plays in contemporary organizational research (see Alvesson and Ashcraft, Chapter 4, this volume). While it is not our goal here to define the attributes of critical thinking in organizational research and its implications for research practices, we maintain that a sustained focus on theorization as a priority helps to alleviate the danger of such capture. On this view, generating and sharing ideas favors the maintenance of the specificity of the research endeavor. In addition, sharing research results with audiences beyond one's immediate research partners may also help to preserve a more critical and independent stance toward findings and their relation to practice. In general, we believe that closer linkages between researchers and practitioners can, under the proper conditions, be achieved while safeguarding genuine research. Accomplishing these goals implies – even requires – a determination by research policy-makers and funding agencies not to transform researchers into clients of the organizations in which they pursue their work. While this chapter focuses on the strengths and weaknesses of collaborative research, it is nevertheless essential to maintain and develop curiosity-driven organizational research that excludes nonacademic partners. We do not believe that collaborative research should be framed as a 'paradigm shift' to which everyone should adhere. The quality of organizational research as a whole can only be increased by further developing these two different knowledge production modes.

A second contextual factor that pushes for the institutionalization of research partnerships is found in contemporary research and scientific policies. Gibbons et al. (1994) have written about the possible shift of knowledge production in contemporary science from Mode I to Mode II, a transformation based on a delocalization of scientific production, the setting up of interdisciplinary teams (O'Connor et al., 2003), the predominance of problem-driven research, and the systematic incorporation of nonresearchers as research partners and as assessors of research priorities and outcomes. Their analysis certainly coheres with many well-documented innovations in research policies and practices (Denis, Lehoux and Champagne, 2004; Gibbons et al., 1994; Nowotny et al., 2001; Pettigrew, 2003).

A fundamental assumption behind Mode II knowledge production is that strong incentives for orienting research toward strategic decision-making priorities or practice settings tend to increase the relevance of knowledge production and the dividends of resources invested in research. Pressures arising from an increased heterogeneity of the social organization of research/knowledge production do not derive exclusively from a utilitarian view of the value of knowledge. These pressures also spring out of the search for a collective control of science in contexts characterized by an emerging complexity and interdependence

of problems, the spreading of risks, potential adverse consequences of applied science, and uncertainties about the proper course of action in organizations or society at large (Callon et al., 2001; Lascoumes, 1996; Nowotny et al., 2001). From this perspective, institutionalizing research partnerships can also mean institutionalizing shared responsibility and control in the development of research and the use of scientific knowledge.

Looking at contemporary science policies, Maasen and Lieven (2006) suggest that the call for Mode II knowledge production might represent a decrease in the autonomy of research and science. Some have worried, in this light, that increased demands for scientific accountability (Maasen and Lieven, 2006) may give preeminence to a problem-solving approach to knowledge production and use (Denis et al., 2004), and could put science under the control of extra-academic interests that might not respond positively to the ideal of research democratization. In such contexts, science and research regain their autonomy by being more *entrepreneurial* – identifying the needs of client organizations, framing research to respond to those needs, competing on the market for applied research – while at the same time accepting more heteronomy in the form of additional layers of control.

Entrepreneurial research that is focused on client needs is necessarily collaborative in the sense that it is based on a joint strategic alliance between researchers and organizational settings. If the confinement of research appears to be no longer desirable for the reasons we presented earlier, the current role of research in the institutionalization of partnerships puts the collaborative research agenda into a novel context that requires closer scrutiny. The ambitions of those who would renew the governance of research do not necessarily coincide with the ideals of those who advocate collaborative designs. Early work on collaborative research sought more lateral and voluntary collaboration between researchers and nonresearchers and had a genuine interest in theorizing collaborative processes as the basis for social learning and innovation.

Entrepreneurial research may not value those principles. Hinings and Greenwood (2002) distinguish between a sociology of organizations that focuses on the control and the consequences of organizational forms, and a business school approach that focuses on the design of efficient organizations from the perspective of senior management. Their criticism of the latter perspective applies also to collaborative entrepreneurial research. The proximity of scholarship to organized interests may compromise the contribution of research and knowledge to social and organizational innovation.

Implementation of Mode II knowledge production has an impact on the craft and practices of research. Managing partnerships involving multiple individuals and organizations, for instance, requires setting up clear transactional rules between researchers and nonresearchers (Pettigrew, 2003). Further, pressures to institutionalize research partnerships favor a more bureaucratic framing of relationships and large-scale research partnerships imply establishing complex coordinating mechanisms (Cummings and Kiesler, 2005; Denis et al., 2004; Maasen and Lieven, 2006). Researchers need to develop mechanisms to manage these partnerships, even at the risk of less personal immersion in the craft of research. In this light, it should be noted that collaborative research is, in the end, based on close and somewhat personal links between researchers and nonresearchers and that trust plays a critical role in the functioning of such an approach (Denis and Lomas, 2003). Managing research and being accountable for the use of resources may become the core concerns of the current reshaping of research production. If this is a reasonable hypothesis, the next challenge for collaborative research will be to develop strategies and policies to regulate larger and more formal exchanges among researchers and nonresearchers.

Another factor that favors the dissemination of collaborative research is the growing interest within the field of management for the use of research-based evidence to improve practice (Champagne et al., 2004; Kovner and Rundall, 2006; Pfeffer and Sutton, 1999;

Rousseau and McCarthy, 2007; Walshe and Rundall, 2001). In brief, the trend for more evidence-informed practice pushes toward a systematization of the process of involving nonresearchers in defining research priorities and framing research steps. It also promotes development of links between researchers and nonresearchers aimed at increasing practitioners' perceptions of benefits as well as strengthening organizations' receptivity to research results and their eventual incorporation or development of their own research capabilities. For the purposes of this chapter, we need only note that the evidence-based trend in management militates for increased relationships between researchers and nonresearchers, a move that will likely contribute to the expansion and systematization of research partnerships.

In previous sections, we analyzed microlevel collaborative research practices. In this section, we explored various contextual factors that promote a formal embedding of collaborative research in broader institutional contexts. Evidence indicates that research may move from small-scale, local, and cooperative commitments to more formal and transactional forms. Such a transformation will not necessarily be opposed to an increased mobilization of research-based evidence in the conduct of organizational affairs. However, it will likely influence the craft of collaborative research and the implementation of partnerships.

CONCLUSION

In one of the final chapters of a book about a large collaborative research program on changing organizational forms, Pettigrew (2003) discusses the characteristics of the program's principal nonresearch participants: 'All three of these individuals had strong conceptual abilities, were interested in ideas, and took a positive view of the potential of management research to have an impact on scholarships and on practice' (p. 370). In the context of network science, it seems useful to note that one of the key elements of successful collaborative research rests, at least in part, on the commitment of nonresearchers to the value of science, their understanding of the specificities and constraints of research production, and their interest in conceptual material. Similar conclusions can be reached for the desirable attributes of researchers involved in collaborative research. The propensity of researchers to take organizational problems and contingencies seriously and to have a genuine commitment to the development of managerial practices seems critical. Such openness also implies the capacity to avoid any premature and normative statements about desirable modes of organizing and practice.

The adoption of any approach to collaborative research should be guided by the following pragmatic considerations related to organizational context:

- Levels of cooperation
- Availability of levers for change and learning
- The experience of researchers and nonresearchers with partnerships
- An organization's expectations regarding the outcomes of the research process

When an organization is seeking tangible utility and resource-use accountability, it may be preferable to frame collaborative research in more transactional terms that predefine key components of the research process and outcomes. In a more expanded and somewhat less formalized type of collaborative research, agreement between researchers and nonresearchers will correspond more closely to a relational contract based on a more negotiated and emerging research process coupled with an encompassing view of the relevance of research results. In such cases, and quite paradoxically, there will probably be more opportunities for experiential knowledge to shape research processes and outcomes than would be possible with a more transactional model. However, as we observed earlier, current pressures to institutionalize research partnerships can constrain the capacity of researchers and nonresearchers to implement relational models. To go

beyond those constraints, both researchers and nonresearchers should experiment with and reflect on models that can simultaneously expand the collaborative research agenda and foster its organic properties.

Another question raised by our analysis of collaborative research is how best, through the research process, to achieve cooperation and nonmanipulative knowledge (see Argyris and Schön, 1989). There is, unfortunately, no definitive answer to this dilemma. At the very least, researchers should pay careful attention to the organizational contexts in which research is developed, the types of concerns that are at the basis of a given research effort, and the concrete rules of participation within those contexts. We believe it is reasonable to suggest that researchers involved in collaborative research should balance trust, distance, and immersion within their organizational settings.

Finally, it is important to keep in mind that collaborative research should, ultimately, produce results that are valuable, innovative, and somewhat exciting. In a discussion of research richness, Weick (2007) recently suggested that researchers should obtain intimate knowledge of their investigative contexts and that they ought to examine them using a variety of theories in order to avoid producing simplistic accounts. Such advice fits well with our discussion of collaborative research, according to which researchers' involvement need not come at the expense of specificity. By engaging in close interactions with practice settings, researchers and nonresearchers alike should be able to generate significant findings. Moreover, in order to extract the benefits of their research experience, the commitment of researchers and, ideally, nonresearchers to theorization is necessary. This final point returns us, quite naturally, to our earlier observations on the value of reflexivity in practice.

REFERENCES

Argyris, C. (1993) *Knowledge for Action: A Guide to Overcoming Barriers to Organizational Change*, San Francisco: Jossey-Bass.

Argyris, C., Putnam, R. and McLain Smith, D. (1985) *Action Science: Concepts, Methods, and Skills for Research and Intervention*, San Francisco: Jossey-Bass.

Argyris, C. and Schön, D.A. (1989) 'Participatory action research and action science compared: a commentary', *American Behavioral Scientist*, 32(5): 612–23.

Bartunek, J.M., Bobko, P. and Venkatraman, N. (1993) 'Toward innovation and diversity in management research methods', *Academy of Management Journal*, 36(6): 1362–73.

Bate, P., Khan, R. and Pyle, A.J. (2000a) 'Culturally sensitive structuring: an action research-based approach to organization development and design', *Public Administration Quarterly*, 23(4): 445–70.

Bate, P., Khan, R. and Pyle, A.J. (2000b) 'Towards a culturally sensitive approach to organization structuring: where organization design meets organization development', *Organization Science*, 11(2): 197–211.

Bradbury, H., and Bergmann Lichtenstein, B.M. (2000) 'Relationality in organizational research: Exploring the space between', *Organization Science*, 11(5): 551–64.

Callon, M., Lascoumes, P. and Barthe, Y. (2001) *Agir dans un Monde Incertain – Essai sur la Démocratie Technique*, Paris: Seuil.

Campbell, D.T. (1989) 'The experimenting society', in E.S. Overman (ed.), *Methodology and Epistemology for Social Science*, Chicago: University of Chicago Press (Original work published 1971), pp. 290–314.

Champagne, F., Lemieux-Charles, L. and McGuire, W. (2004) 'Introduction: towards a broader understanding of the use of knowledge and evidence in health care', in L. Lemieux-

Charles and F. Champagne (eds) (2004) *Using Knowledge and Evidence in Health Care: Multidisciplinary Perspectives*, Toronto: University of Toronto Press, pp. 3–17.

Checkland, P. (1994) 'Systems theory and management thinking', *American Behavioral Scientist*, 38(1): 75–91.

Checkland, P. (1999) *Systems Thinking, Systems Practice: Includes a 30-Year Retrospective*, Chichester: John Wiley and Sons.

Cheo, J. and Trent, A. (2006) 'Validity in qualitative research revisited', *Qualitative Research*, 6(3): 319–40.

Clegg, S.R. (2002) '"Lives in the balance": a comment on Hinings and Greenwood's "Disconnects and consequences in organization theory?"', *Administrative Science Quarterly*, 47: 428–41.

Cullen, J. (1998) 'The needle and the damage done: research, action research, and the organizational and social construction of health in the "Information Society"', *Human Relations*, 51(12): 1543–64.

Cummings, J.N. and Kiesler, S. (2005) 'Collaborative research across disciplinary and organizational boundaries', *Social Studies of Science*, 35(5): 703–22.

Cutcliffe, J.R. (2003) 'Reconsidering reflexivity: introducing the case for intellectual entrepreneurship', *Qualitative Health Research*, 13(1): 136–48.

Denis, J-L., Lamothe, L. and Langley, A. (2001) 'The dynamics of collective leadership and strategic change in pluralistic organizations', *Academy of Management Journal*, 44(4): 809–37.

Denis, J-L., Lehoux, P. and Champagne, F. (2004) 'Knowledge utilization on fine-tuning dissemination and contextualizing knowledge', in L. Lemieux-Charles and F. Champagne (eds), *Using Knowledge and Evidence in Health Care: Multidisciplinary perspectives*, Toronto: University of Toronto Press, pp. 18–40.

Denis, J-L., Lehoux, P., Hivon, M. and Champagne, F. (2003) 'Creating a new articulation between research and practice through policy? the views and experiences of researchers and practitioners', *Journal of Health Services Research and Policy*, 8(4, Suppl. 2): S2:44–S2:50.

Denis, J-L. and Lomas, J. (2003) 'Convergent evolution: the academic and policy roots of collaborative research', *Journal of Health Services Research and Policy*, 8(4, Suppl. 2): S2:1–S2:6.

Easterby-Smith, M. and Malina, D. (1999) 'Cross-cultural collaborative research: toward reflexivity', *Academy of Management Journal*, 42(1): 76–86.

Edmondson, A.C. (1996) 'Three faces of Eden: the persistence of competing theories and multiple diagnoses in organizational intervention research', *Human Relations*, 49(5): 571–95.

Finlay, L. and Gough, B. (eds) (2003) *Reflexivity: A Practical Guide for Researchers in Health and Social Sciences*, Oxford: Blackwell.

Freire, P. (1972) *The pedagogy of the Oppressed*, Harmondsworth: Penguin.

Gibbons, M., Limoges, C., Nowotny, H., Schwartzman, S., Scott, P. and Trow, M. (1994) *The New Production of Knowledge: The Dynamics of Science and Research in Contemporary Societies*, London: Sage.

Giddens, A. (1986) *The Constitution of Society*, Berkeley, CA: University of California Press.

Greenwood, D.J. (1996) 'Participation in human inquiry', *Human Relations*, 49(9): 1253–9.

Gregory, A. (2000) 'Problematizing participation: a critical review of approaches to participation in evaluation theory', *Evaluation*, 6(2): 179–99.

Gustavsen, B. (1998) 'From experiments to network building: trends in the use of research for reconstructing working life', *Human Relations*, 51(3): 431–48.

Hardy, C., Phillips, N. and Clegg, S. (2001) 'Reflexivity in organization and management theory: a study of the production of the research "Subject"', *Human Relations*, 54(5): 531–60.

Heron, J. and Reason, P. (2001) 'The practice of co-operative inquiry: Research with rather than on people', in P. Reason and H. Bradbury (eds), *Handbook of Action Research: Participative Inquiry and Practice*, London: Sage. pp. 179–88.

Hinings, C.R. and Greenwood, R. (2002) 'Disconnects and consequences in organization theory?', *Administrative Science Quarterly*, 47: 411–21.

Knorr-Cetina, K. (1999) *Epistemic cultures: How the Sciences Make Knowledge*, Cambridge, MA: Harvard University Press.

Kovner, A.R. and Rundall, T.G. (2006) 'The promise of evidence-based management', *Frontiers of Health Services Management*, 22(3): 3–22.

Kvale, S. (1995) 'The social construction of validity', *Qualitative Inquiry*, 1: 19–40.

Lascoumes, P. (1996) 'Rendre gouvernable: De la "traduction" au "transcodage" L'analyse des processus de changement dans les réseaux d'action publique', in CURAPP (ed.), La gouvernabilité, Paris: Presses Universitaires de France, pp. 325–38.

LeCompte, M. (2002) 'The transformation of ethnographic practice: past and current challenges', *Qualitative Research*, 2(3): 283–99.

Lehoux, P., Daudelin, G., Denis, J-L. and Miller, F. (2008) 'Scientists and policymakers at work: listening to epistemic conversations in a genetics science network', *Science and Public Policy*, 35(3): 207–20.

Lincoln, Y.S. and Guba, E.G. (1985) *Naturalistic Inquiry*, Beverly Hills, CA: Sage.

Maasen, S. and Lieven, O. (2006) 'Transdisciplinarity: a new mode of governing science?', *Science and Public Policy*, 33(6): 399–410.

Maginn, P.J. (2007) 'Towards more effective community participation in urban regeneration: the potential of collaborative planning and applied ethnography', *Qualitative Research*, 7(1): 25–43.

Mark, M.M., Henry, G.T., and Julnes, G. (2000) *Evaluation: An Integrated Framework for Understanding, Guiding, and Improving Policies and Programmes*, San Francisco: Jossey-Bass.

Mohrman, S.A., Gibson, C.B. and Mohrman, A.M., Jr. (2001) 'Doing research that is useful to practice: a model and empirical exploration', *Academy of Management Journal*, 44(2): 357–75.

Nowotny, H., Scott, P. and Gibbons, M. (2001) *Re-Thinking Science: Knowledge and the Public In an Age of Uncertainty*, Cambridge: Polity Press.

O'Connor, G.C., Rice, M.P., Peters, L. and Veryzer, R.W. (2003) 'Managing interdisciplinary, longitudinal research teams: extending grounded theory-building methodologies', *Organization Science*, 14(4): 353–73.

Pasmore, W. and Khalsa, G.S. (1993) 'The contributions of Eric Trist to the social engagement of social sciences', *Academy of Management* Review, 18(3): 546–69.

Patton, M.Q. (1997) 'Toward distinguishing empowerment evaluation and placing it in a larger context', *Evaluation Practice*, 18(2): 147–63.

Patton, M.Q. (2002) 'A vision of evaluation that strengthens democracy', *Evaluation*, 8(1): 125–39.

Pettigrew, A.M. (2003) 'Co-producing knowledge and the challenges of international collaborative research', in A.M. Pettigrew, R. Whittington, L. Melin, C. Sanchez-Runde, F. van den Bosch, W. Ruigrok, et al. (eds), *Innovative Forms of Organizing: International Perspectives*, London: Sage, pp. 352–74.

Pfeffer, J. and Sutton, R.I. (1999) *The Knowing-Doing Gap: How Smart Companies Turn Knowledge into Action*, Cambridge, MA: Harvard Business School Press.

Reason, P. (1994) 'Three approaches to participative inquiry', in N. K. Denzin and Y. S. Lincoln (eds.), *Handbook of Qualitative Research*, Thousand Oaks, CA: Sage, pp. 324–39.

Reason, P. (2006) 'Choice and quality in action research practice', *Journal of Management Inquiry*, 15(2): 187–203.

Reason, P. and McArdle, K.L. (in press) 'Action research and organization development', in T.G. Cummings (ed.), *Handbook of Organization Development*, Thousand Oaks, CA: Sage.

Rousseau, D.M. and McCarthy, S. (2007) 'Educating managers from an evidence-based perspective', *Academy of Management Learning and Education*, 61(1): 84–101.

Rynes, S.L., Bartunek, J.M. and Daft, R.L. (2001) 'Across the great divide: knowledge creation and transfer between practitioners and academics', *Academy of Management Journal*, 44(2): 340–55.

Schön, D.A. (1983) *The Reflective Practitioner: How Professionals Think in Action*, New York: Basic Books.

Themessl-Huber, M.T. and Grutsch, M.A. (2003) 'The shifting locus of control in participatory evaluations', *Evaluation*, 9(1): 92–111.

Van de Ven, A.H., Johnson, P.E. (2006) 'Knowledge for theory and practice', *Academy of Management Review*, 31(4): 802–21.

Wadsworth, Y. (2005) '"Gouldner's child?" some reflections on sociology and participatory action research', *Journal of Sociology*, 41(3): 267–84.

Walshe, K. and Rundall, T.G. (2001) 'Evidence-based management: from theory to practice in health care', *The Milbank Quarterly*, 79(3): 429–57.

Weick, K. (2007) 'The generative properties of richness', *Academy of Management Journal*, 50(1): 14–19.

Whyte, W.F. (1989) 'Introduction', *American Behavioral Scientist*, 32(5): 502–12.

Whyte, W.F. (1991) *Social Theory For Action: How Individuals and Organizations Learn to Change*, Newbury Park, CA: Sage.

Whyte, W.F., Greenwood, D.J. and Lazes, P. (1989) 'Participatory action research: through practice to science in social research', *American Behavioral Scientist*, 32(5): 513–51.

22

Grounded Theory Perspectives in Organizational Research

Christina Goulding

INTRODUCTION

Grounded theory is a methodology largely associated with the qualitative school of enquiry. It was developed in the 1960s by two American sociologists, Barney Glaser and Alselm Strauss and their book *The Discovery of Grounded Theory* (1967) remains a touchstone for researchers interested in exploring the social processes that impact on behavior. Essentially, the role of grounded theory was, and is, the generation of new theory that accounts for the relationship of the individual or collective experience to society, to history, the group or the organization. With its origins in symbolic interactionism the researcher attempts to determine what symbolic meanings, artifacts, words, and gestures have for people as they interact with one another and how individuals construct their notions of social reality through these symbolic meanings (Cutcliffe, 2000). Indeed the seductive appeal of grounded theory lay largely in the fact that it offered a structured approach to exploring the social, the symbolic, and context specific behaviors.

Although primarily used by sociologists it has since spread to other related disciplines. Today, 'grounded theory has gone global, seriously global among the disciplines of nursing, business, and education' (Glaser 1999: 837). Recent years have also seen a rapid adoption in the field of management and organizational studies and more recently within disciplines that have a long history of quantitative research such as marketing. Not surprising, given that most organizational research is concerned with behavior at one level or another and grounded theory is a methodology that stresses the significance of social processes or a concern with human beings in their relations to each other (Parry, 1999a). As such grounded theory is well suited to the analysis of data collected within organizations by means of participant observation, direct observation, semi structured or unstructured interviews, or case studies, as most users of it will be concerned with situations in which they are able to observe organizational behavior in naturalistic settings (Turner,1983; Martin and Turner, 1986). Today the range of organizational studies applying grounded theory is vast. A recent Google Scholar search using the words 'grounded theory and organizational research' revealed 17,600 hits ranging in scope from studies of knowledge based views of the organization (Sousa and Hendriks, 2006), inter-organizational systems based on electronic data interchange (Crook and Kumar, 1998), organizational processes (Orton, 1997), managers' interpretation of processes and organizational change (Isabella, 1990), analysis of management action (Partington, 2000), leadership (Parry 1998, 1999, 1999a; Parry and Meindl, 2002), corporate turnaround (Pandit, 1996), and management knowledge (Trim and Lee, 2004).

In this chapter, I attempt to lay out some of the issues surrounding the use of grounded theory in studies of behavior. I start by looking at theory development in qualitative research. This is followed by a brief overview of some of the fundamental processes inherent in any grounded theory study, before moving on to discuss the evolving nature of the methodology. Here I place particular emphasis on the split between the two originators of grounded theory which has resulted in two versions; one associated with Glaser, the other with Strauss and Corbin. In order to offer an example of grounded theory in practice, I next present a 'snapshot' of a grounded theory study, which is followed by a discussion of writing and presenting grounded theory research. I conclude by looking at some of the key debates and critiques of grounded theory as a methodology.

Theory generation in qualitative research

The emphasis behind grounded theory is one of 'new' theory generation. It was intended as a methodology for developing theory that is grounded in data which is systematically gathered and analyzed. In keeping with its principles, the theory evolves during the research process itself and is a product of

continuous interplay between analysis and data collection (Glaser and Strauss, 1967; Glaser, 1978, 1992). A further proposition was that the theory should be readily understandable to sociologists of any viewpoint and that it should 'fit' the situation being researched. By 'fit' it is meant that the categories developed must be applicable to, and indicated by the data. These categories should also 'work'; defined as, 'they must be relevant to, and be able to explain the behavior under study' (Glaser and Strauss, 1967: 3).

According to Strauss and Corbin (1994) the sources of data gathered in the majority of qualitative studies, including grounded theory, are usually the same. These are most commonly interviews and observations, although grounded theory may utilize many types of data; it 'transcends' specific forms of data type (Glaser and Strauss, 1967). However, grounded theorists have refined the usual scientific canons for the purpose of studying behavior such as coding, verification, and testing procedures. Essentially, grounded theory has a built in mandate to strive toward verification through the process of category 'saturation' which basically involves staying in the field until no further evidence emerges.

Fundamental processes

It is important to note that the original intent of grounded theory was a methodology specifically for sociologists. In recent years, the diffusion across a number of disciplines has meant the adaptation of the methodology in ways that may not be completely congruent with all of the original principles. Nevertheless, regardless of discipline or persuasion, there remain a set of fundamental processes that need to be followed if the study is to be recognized as a product of the methodology.

(1) *Theoretical sampling*: Unlike other methodologies where the samples are specified in terms of location, characteristics of the participants, and numbers, with grounded theory, sampling is an emergent and ongoing process that evolves as the theory develops

from the data. It is in fact the findings and emergent questions that direct the researcher to different contexts, people, and places in order to saturate the data.

> Theoretical sampling is the process of data collection for generating theory whereby the analyst jointly collects, codes and analyses the data and decides what data to collect next and where to find it, in order to develop the theory as it emerges. This process of data collection is 'controlled' by the emerging theory (Glaser, 1978: 36).

(2) *Constant comparison*: This is a fundamental feature of grounded theory and requires the researcher to engage in data interpretation at the same time as the data are collected. Like its name implies, constant comparison is a process by which the researcher transcribes interviews or analyses memos comparing like with like and looking for emerging patterns and themes. Throughout the process, it is not unusual to apply a form of triangulation in terms of data collection in order to cross check and verify emergent findings (see, for example, Herman and Egri, 2002; Kan and Parry, 2004). The search for similarities is important as is the search for differences, as differences in behavior need to be accounted for and explained theoretically through the application of theoretical sensitivity. This means that the presentation of grounded theory research must go beyond thick description to offer an explanation of the phenomenon under study.

(3) *Open coding*: Open coding involves the breaking down, conceptualization, and categorization of data. This may start with taking a transcript of an interview and scrutinizing it 'line by line' in order to identify key words and phrases that give some insight into what is happening in the data. At this stage coding is unstructured and hundreds of codes may be identified. Inevitably these need to be reduced as coding moves on to a more abstract level in the search for patterns and themes that suggest a relationship.

(4) *Memos*: Memo writing is vital as they provide a bank of ideas which can be revisited. They help map out the emerging theory. Essentially memos are ideas which have been noted during the data collection process which help to reorient the researcher at a later date. However, ideas can also occur away from the data and should be written down. Memos may be a few lines or several pages long.

(5) *Axial coding:* This involves the appreciation of open coded categories or concepts in terms of their dynamic interrelationships. These should form the basis for the construction of a coherent matrix of associations. These concepts are initially clustered into descriptive categories. They are then re-evaluated for their interrelationships and through a series of analytical steps are gradually subsumed into higher order categories (or one underlying core category) which suggests an emergent theory. They should, however, remain open to reappraisal.

(6) *Selective coding*: Selective coding subsumes the data further into a core category which the researcher has to justify as the basis for the emergent theory. This is normally when the theory is written up and integrated with existing theories to show relevance and new perspective. Nevertheless there are dangers to beware of when using this methodology. There is general acknowledgement of the danger of placing too much emphasis on identifying codes as the exclusive feature, without theoretically coding which involves explaining how codes relate to each other (Glaser, 1978; Strauss, 1991; Glaser, 1992). The researcher must also ensure that constant comparison is an ongoing feature of the process. Theoretical sampling should direct the researcher to further individuals, situations, contexts, and locations and the theory should only be presented as developed when all core categories are saturated.

The evolving nature of grounded theory

There are many textbooks dealing with the process and practice of grounded theory. Glaser and Strauss's (1967) *The Discovery of Grounded Theory*, lays out the principles of grounded theory and details the difference between inductive and deductive research procedures. In 1978,

Glaser published *Theoretical Sensitivity*, which elaborated on the original methodology, stressing the role of theory development and, as the title suggests, the importance of applying sensitivity to theory development. In 1990, Anselm Strauss and Juliet Corbin published *Basics of Qualitative Research: Grounded Theory Procedures and Techniques* which is the most commonly used text by business and organizational researchers, largely because of its highly descriptive and prescriptive detailing of the key procedures. However, it is also the book that precipitated a major rift between the two originators of the methodology and saw the split of grounded theory into two camps. As a reaction to the text, Glaser published a book in 1992 entitled *Basics of Grounded Theory: Emergence versus Forcing*, in which he implored Strauss to withdraw his publication on the grounds that it grossly misrepresented the original principles of the methodology; namely, replacing the stress on theoretical emergence from the data with strategies that involve forcing data into preconceived categories. From here the scene was set, and it is now normal for researchers to specify which version of grounded theory they have applied.

Glaser versus Strauss: choosing the methodology

According to Skodol-Wilson and Ambler-Hutchinson (1996), researchers in the area of nursing where the method is widely used, are now obliged to specify whether the grounded theory approach they employed was the original 1967 Glaser and Strauss version, the 1990 Strauss and Corbin rendition, or the 1978 or 1992 Glaser interpretation. A comparison of the original *Discovery of Grounded Theory* (Glaser and Strauss 1967), with Glaser's 1978, *Theoretical Sensitivity*, and Strauss's 1990 *The Basics of Qualitative Research*, demonstrates the subtle but distinct differences in perceptions of the method between the two authors since its inception. Not only are there differences in style and terminology, but also Strauss's version of the method has been reworked to incorporate a strict and complex process of systematic coding.

Glaser's reaction to these developments was vociferously documented in the publication of *The Basics of Qualitative Research* (Glaser 1992) which is a rather damning critique of Strauss and Corbin's 1990 work. Pages 1–2 detail letters from Glaser to Strauss imploring him to withdraw his text for revision on the basis that what it contained was a methodology, but it was not grounded theory. He stated in fact that it ignored up to 90 percent of the original ideas and proceeded with the accusation that:

> Strauss's book is without conscience, bordering on immorality ... producing simply what qualitative researchers have been doing for sixty years or more: forced, full conceptual description (Glaser, 1992: 3).

Other grounded theory researchers have reiterated this, arguing that Strauss has modified his description of grounded theory from its original concept of emergence to a densely codified operation. Essentially Strauss and Corbin introduced a new coding process with a strong emphasis on conditions, context, action/interaction strategies, and consequences. Glaser's response was to deny that this constituted true grounded theory due to its stress on preconceived and forced discovery, centering primarily on these preordained categories at the expense of allowing the theory to emerge. In effect, Glaser's model favors creativity and openness to unanticipated interpretations of data while Strauss and Corbin have gone down a much more prescriptive and mechanical road (Hall and Callery, 2001; Suddaby, 2006). The differences can also be attributed to divergence in the epistemological implications of the methodology, with Strauss and Corbin endorsing Dewey's instrumentalism by introducing a form of hypo-deductivism, while Glaser insists that grounded theory involves only the inductive phase of inquiry (Rennie, 1998).

Nevertheless, there have been further discrepancies in the development of the method from those other than the two key figures. These include the number of academics with no first hand contact of either Glaser or Strauss who have independently invented rigid rules for judging the credibility of grounded theory products. These 'cooked up' translations are often guilty of breaching the essence of the method and the inherent creativity of the original. Such later additions include the requirement of a visual diagram with all grounded theories, and a statement that a sample size of twelve be the minimum for any grounded theory study (Skodal-Wilson and Ambler- Hutchinson, 1996), although it is unclear how this rather arbitrary figure was reached. This in itself appears to go against the whole philosophy of theoretical sampling as it dictates and directs the research design from the start. This inflexibility has given rise to accusations of distortion of the method.

In organizational studies and business and management in general, the dominant text of reference is Strauss and Corbin. This may be because its tightly prescribed procedures enticingly suggest that, if followed, a theory is guaranteed. Glaser on the other hand emphasizes the need to 'wallow' in the data with the promise that if you stick with it, a theory will emerge. However, in practice both have their limitations. As Partington observes; 'doctoral students working in the field of organization and management who have attempted to follow the Strauss and Corbin approach have abandoned it due to its bewildering complexity' (2000: 95)' On the other hand, Glaser's stress on 'emergence' can appear daunting and risky. The notion of extended 'wallowing' can go against the principles of much research training and smack of a lack of empirical rigor when compared with the more prescribed method. Moreover the fear of the unknown can, and does, deter many from tying their masts to a Glaserian approach. In practice, most will usually adopt a middle ground approach to the application of the methodology, although, regardless of this grounded theory, research requires certain qualities of the researcher; confidence, creativity, and experience, and as such does not necessarily favor the novice researcher (Pandit, 1996).

Grounded theory: an illustrative case

The following is based on my own experiences of using grounded theory. The context of the research was the heritage industry, with a focus on consumer experiences of visiting particular types of museums. The roots of the original research stem back to the 1990s, a time when there was much debate about the growth in the number of museums, especially 'living' recreations of our industrial past. The rapid expansion of museums in the UK from the late 1980s resulted in a position adopted by a small group of cultural commentators wedded to the idea that Britain was in danger of becoming one large heritage theme park, that the only industry left in operation was that found in our industrial museums. Moreover, much of the published work focused on the nature of how the past was interpreted and was aimed at museum professionals—or the production side. The limited work on the nature of the experience—the consumption perspective, tended to consist of the obligatory visitor survey or painted a picture of contemporary heritage consumers as passive dupes who accepted the 'themed' as authentic in their ever growing quest for the novel, ready made experience (see, for example, Hewison, 1987). Whilst much of this work was stimulating and provocative there was very little that examined, in-depth, the motivational influences and the actual on-site experiences of the growing number of heritage consumers. These two factors of motivation and experience became the general questions driving the research.

In choosing the methodology, given the lack of existing theory and literature, a grounded theory approach was selected in order to develop theory that emerged directly from the data. More specifically, a Glaserian approach was considered the most appropriate given the stress on 'emergence.'

Theoretical sampling

In accordance with grounded theory principles, the researcher should, in the first instance, go to those people and places that are most likely to provide early insights. In this case, given the debate about themed heritage and consumer experiences, the first port of call was an open air museum that was a reconstructed nineteenth century industrial town, situated in the Midland region of the UK. The museum employed a number of permanent demonstrators as well as a body of volunteers. All of these dressed in period Victorian costume and worked in the many shops, businesses and houses. These consisted of a bank, a printers, a chemist complete with dentist chair, a wood yard, an iron smelting furnace, a school, a candle-makers, doctor's surgery, a fairground, a bandstand, squatters cottage and various dwellings. Very little information was provided textually and historical stories emerged largely through an interactive process between demonstrator and visitor. Initially the director of the museum was contacted and he proved to be very cooperative, granting permission to conduct the research and providing free passes and unlimited access to the site. He also participated in an interview in order to provide background. Other demonstrators were also interviewed in order to give the provider perspective. However, the bulk of the data were collected through a process of participatory observation and a series of interviews with visitors of all ages, social class, varying party composition and both genders.

Data collection

Observations were recorded in memo form and these provided a valuable insight into the nature of the on-site experience. This tended to vary depending on party composition, the nature of interactions between individuals, the group, and demonstrators. They also allowed for noting how individuals dealt with such issues as crowding, weather conditions, routing, as well as nonverbal signals such as expressions of boredom, interest, excitement, reflection, and so on. In short, they provided a rich bank of information that could be revisited. However, useful as these observations were in relation to the actual experience, they offered little insight into the motivations behind the visit. These became more transparent through the interviews with visitors which explored participants' backgrounds, their expectations, their perceptions of authenticity, and their personal identification with the resource.

Constant comparison

These interviews were transcribed as soon as possible after they had taken place and were compared like with like in order to identify recurring themes, patterns, similarities and importantly, differences. During the early stage, a line-by-line analysis was conducted which revealed hundreds of codes and key words. The main task was to search for meaning and look for the relationship between them in order to reduce these codes into a series of themes that made sense, had fit, could be traced directly back through the data, and had explanatory power. After some time, the interpretation started to focus on seven key concepts. These included:

Concept development:

1. The experience of alienation in the present
2. The degree of personal and cultural identification with the heritage setting
3. The stimulation of nostalgia
4. The desire for authenticity
5. The desire for education
6. The desire for social interaction
7. Environmental comfort

Concepts, properties, and dimensions

Each of these concepts had properties. For example, alienation depended on such properties as the individual's role repertoire, their sense of control in the present, their feelings of independence, and the nature of their social affiliations. Personal and cultural identification depended on the level of personal significance, cultural significance, and personal meaning. The intensity of nostalgia was based on such factors as withdrawal from the present, rose tinted remembrance, and the transposition of life experiences. The question of authenticity was again related to individual expectations and the judgment criteria against which the resource was evaluated. For some, any transgression from historical accuracy was deemed unacceptable, whilst others accepted the limitations and suspended disbelief accordingly. At the other end of the scale some visitors came to be entertained and simply enjoyed the spectacle of the performance. This in turn was linked to the educational aspects of the experience and how the visitor engaged in problem solving, either through social interaction with the group, interaction with demonstrators or in isolation. The issue and importance of social interaction again varied, depending on motivation. For some the entire experience was a social event, for others the presence of crowds was an unwanted intrusion that impinged on the power of imagination and individual contemplation. With regard to the setting itself, the environment and environmental comfort was highly important, but reaction to such factors as crowding, queuing, and environmental noise again varied, from cheerful tolerance to complete frustration. The properties that supported each of the seven concepts had, in turn, their own dimensions, ranging from high to low. These allowed for the categorization of consumer types depending on their intensity.

Striving for saturation

At this stage in the research, however, it was too premature to claim saturation. The research had been conducted at only one site, and it was only one of a number of forms of heritage interpretation. In keeping with the principles of theoretical sampling, as the data are analyzed and the concepts emerge, the researcher should be willing to take the research into different contexts and talk to a wider variety of people who can shed further light on the problem and offer a rounded explanation. To this end two further sites were selected. The first was an orthodox city museum with a mixture of traditional static displays and interactive computer assisted games and virtual experiences. The second was an English heritage site with no means of

interpretation or information apart from one small leaflet. The three sites used in the study allowed for a comparison of behavior across heritage that was:

1. Fully interpreted (living museum)
2. Semi-interpreted (city museum)
3. Noninterpreted (English heritage site)

Once again interviews were conducted on site and observations noted in memo forms. The fresh data were then compared with existing transcripts and were scrutinized for any new information. Whilst no new concepts emerged, the significance of those identified were reinforced and strengthened with further examples in different contexts. These concepts paved the way for categorization or a higher level of abstraction. 'Routinely grounded theory is a third perceptual level theory. Data go to concepts, and concepts get transcended to a core variable or category, which is the underlying pattern' (Glaser, 1999). Analysis on this level forces the generation of core categories and guides further theoretical sampling.

Categorization

The final process of categorization involved the identification of three consumer behavioral types, comprising:

1) The Existential visitor
2) The Purist visitor
3) The Social visitor

The following is an example of the development of one of the three core categories that was developed through the analysis. It focused primarily on the behaviour of elderly visitors of which there were a significant number. This category does not, however, offer a generic explanation of this age group. It is important when using grounded theory to look for cases that do not fit. Whilst this category did stand up when compared to others with similar social and psychological characteristics, opposite cases were also identified which were diverse enough to warrant their own categories.

EXAMPLE OF CONCEPT DEVELOPMENT

Code/concept properties category	Dimensions	Concept
Multiple role loss	high	
Social contact	low	
Dissatisfaction with the present	high	alienation
Disempowerment	high	
Role stripping	high	
Infirmity	medium	
Loss of significant others	high	
Selective recall	high	
'rose' tinted remembrance	high	
Rejection of the present	high	nostalgia
Ability to distort the past	high	
E		
X		
		I
		S
Past interpreted in the light of personal experiences	high	identification
T		
		E
		N
		T
criteria for authenticity = objects	high	perceived
I		
acceptance of artificial	high	authenticity
A		
		L
education	low	
strong escapist tendencies	high	personal/cultural
imagination creates experience involvement	medium	
need for interaction others & tangible objects	high	social interaction
environmental tolerance mechanisms	high	filtering

These codes provided guidance for future analysis using the constant comparison method.

Labeling behavior

Whilst most texts on grounded theory advise the avoidance of literature directly related to the area of study until the theory is developed, it is important to incorporate existing theories in order to extend them in the final analysis. Furthermore, labels devised by other theorists may be used if they provide a comparable conceptual base. At this stage the literature should be used to enhance theoretical sensitivity. The following is an example, drawn from the analysis of behavior labelled 'existential'.

Extract from analysis of core category 'Existential' visitor

This category retains a number of similar common characteristics as those proposed by Cohen (1988) to describe the existential tourist. According to Cohen, the existential tourist is highly alienated. He/she will spiritually abandon modernity and embrace the 'other,' thus turning it into his/her elective centre. Such a tourist will seek existential experiences and will be deeply concerned with authenticity. However, in this case, the category focuses more specifically on a particular age group, namely the aged and usually infirm. Here, the basic social process centers around a high degree of alienation and dissatisfaction with the present as a consequence of changes over time (loss of others, role stripping, and physical deterioration) resulting in self perceptions of vulnerability, disempowerment, and isolation.

They are existential by virtue of their ability to construct their own values and ideologies regarding particular systems (providing a degree of escapist self determination) and then to transpose these values to another time belonging to their own experiences, whether real or partially reconstructed. They further exhibit tendencies associated with 'first order simple nostalgia' (Davis, 1979). The unquestioned belief that things were better in the past. It is a form of 'simple' nostalgia that manifests itself in a longing to return to this preferred state, but also the recognition that this is impossible.

This group finds themselves locked into a pseudocultural dichotomy, alienated from their immediate center (the present) in which they retain very little power, but alienated also from their 'ideal' center (the past) through distance in time and space. The motivation behind the consumption of contemporary heritage, therefore, becomes one of searching for an 'elective' centre. Ideally, this 'alternative' is one which alleviates dissonance and transcends the perceived amoralism of modernity. It is one through which the themization, museumization, and conflation of a particular era into a sanitized simulacrum of a remembered earlier life serves as a platform for vicarious rediscovery and nostalgic escapism. As such the quest for 'personal' authenticity is high. The invisibility of the negatives and frequent aggregation and fusing of various periods into a near 'Disney' fantasy reconstruction is often overlooked. The discovery of familiar objects and settings becomes the prime satisfier and serves to verify the authenticity of the interpretation.

A final note

With regard to interpretation of data it is important to give consideration to the labeling of identified 'types.' Glaser (1978) suggests that categories should indicate behavioral type, not people 'type.' This allows the actors to walk in and out of many behavioral patterns. The emphasis is therefore on behavioral, not personal patterns. So for example, the 'existential' may be nostalgic when faced with themed stimuli, but may not be, once removed from the situation. It is important to recognize that most actors engage in a type of behavior without being typed by it; they engage in other behaviors as well. It is this complexity that often leads to increased output from the research. With regard to publishing, most grounded theory studies will have identified in depth a number of influential concepts. It is very rare to see an entire study published in a single paper due to the complex issues that usually arise from the analysis. These may be viewed as 'theory bits' (Glaser, 1999), and may be a concept or hypotheses arising from the theory. In the case of the heritage study, a number of concepts formed the bases of individual papers that were published in their own right. These included nostalgia and museum visiting (Goulding, 2001), nostalgia and age related cultural consumption (Goulding, 1999), the museum environment and the visitor experience (Goulding, 1999, 2000) and perceptions of and experiences of authenticity in museums (Goulding, 2000a). The concepts and categories also acted as building blocks

and paved the way for subsequent research in completely different cultural contexts in an ongoing process of theory development.

Writing the theory

One of the questions that comes up time and time again is the issue of writing and presenting grounded theory research. One general belief is that it should be written as it were conducted. That is as a process of presenting the research questions, a discussion of data collection and codes followed by findings, theory, and recontextulization in the literature. However, this seldom works. The end result of such endeavors tends to be a confusing array of method mixed with early theory, mixed with literature. In reality, grounded theory is usually written up in a conventional manner. That is, contextual literature, methodology, interpretation, and theoretical findings. Some get so obsessed with writing the study 'as it happened' that they lose sight of the fact that grounded theory is not a theory in itself, it is a methodology, and a means to an end. Suddaby (2006) makes some very interesting observations from the reviewer perspective.

> Even though grounded theory research is conducted iteratively, by analyzing and collecting data simultaneously, it is usually presented sequentially. This gap occurs because the norms of presentation in management (and other academic) journals have positivist origins and impose discrete and sequential categories of data collection and analysis on authors trying to present grounded theory research. In pure form grounded theory research would be presented as a jumble of literature consultation, data collection and analysis conducted in ongoing iterations that produce many relatively fuzzy categories that, over time, reduce to fewer, clearer conceptual structures. Theory would be presented last. Presenting grounded theory in this pure form, however, would neither be efficient, nor comprehensible to the majority of researchers who work in the positivist paradigm (p. 637).

The norm that has evolved is to present grounded theory in the same sequence as quantitative research. This, however, can lead to accusations of methodological mixing or imitation of positivist research. Suddaby goes on to suggest means of overcoming this; namely by making clear the means of data collection and analysis. These should be made apparent to the reader in the methodology section, along with examples of coding and illustrative representations of conceptual developments through diagrams or tables. Importantly, it is incumbent upon the researcher to state that although they are presenting their study in a traditional manner, the concepts did, in fact, emerge from the data.

Debates surrounding grounded theory

According to Charmaz (1983) both the assumptions and analytical methods of grounded theory have been criticized by some qualitative researchers on a number of accounts. For example, the suggestion that grounded theorists fail to give proper attention to both data collection techniques and to the quality of the gathered material. Such criticisms misinterpret the aims and methods of grounded theory and arise as a result of certain features of the methodology such as the language, which to a large extent relies heavily on terms commonly associated with quantitative research (coding, comparison groups, theoretical sampling, etc.) and can elicit images of logico-deductive quantitative procedures. However, while language has been an issue that has shaped perceptions of grounded theory, it is not the worse slur on its character. One of the main criticisms is the overly generic use of the label grounded theory, often applied to studies that have ignored most, or in some cases all of the basic principles. In response to this problem occurring in submissions to *Academy of Management Journal*, Roy Suddaby (2006) published an insightful paper detailing what grounded theory 'is not.' Essentially he sums up six common misconceptions which lead to papers being rejected. These include:

1) Grounded theory is not an excuse to ignore the literature
2) Grounded theory is not presentation of raw data

3) Grounded theory is not theory testing, content analysis, or word counts
4) Grounded theory is not simply routine application of formulaic technique to data
5) Grounded theory is not perfect
6) Grounded theory is not easy

These six headings neatly summarize the main misconceptions about grounded theory and in the following section I have taken the liberty of adding my own thoughts and readings to Suddaby's analysis.

Grounded theory is not an excuse to ignore the literature

This is an issue that has caused debate and division across disciplines and is one that has led to criticism of the methodology in general. However, it is now widely accepted that although grounded theory is inductive, developing theory largely from the data, it is impossible to wipe the slate clean of all prior knowledge, theories, and conceptual positions. Charmaz (1983) points to the fact that unlike deductive research, grounded theorists do not rely directly on the literature to shape their ideas, since it is expected that the theory will emerge independently from the analysis. This, however, should not be misinterpreted as commencing from a position of total ignorance. Rather the researcher should read in related areas from the start and allow the data to direct the literature to inform the emerging theory and vice versa. At the very least, a general reading of the literature should be carried out in order to get a feel for the issues in question and identify the gaps to be filled (Cutcliffe, 2000), but it is also important that the researcher does not become too immersed in the literature and thus become theoretically contaminated. Glaser (1978) discusses the role of theory and its importance in sensitizing the researcher to the conceptual significance of emerging concepts and categories, observing that knowledge and theory are used as if they were another informant. This is vital, for without this grounding in extant knowledge, pattern recognition would be limited to the obvious and the superficial, depriving the analyst of the conceptual leverage from which to develop theory (Glaser 1978). As Suddaby (2006) suggests: 'totally unstructured research procedures produces totally unstructured manuscripts that are unlikely to make it past the desk editor at any credible journal of social science' (p. 634). The challenge is how to make the familiar new and to be aware of the possibilities of existing theory and its influence upon the work being undertaken.

Grounded theory is not presentation of raw data

Here the problem lies with the lack of conceptualization or theoretical abstraction which leads to trite findings such as 'entrepreneurs are risk takers, change is difficult and leaders are charismatic' (Suddaby, p. 635). This may be down to an inability to lift the analysis above the descriptive level, or possibly the fact that the researcher either stopped collecting data too early, or stopped interrogating the data too early. This issue of premature closure is a well debated area although it is often simply taken to mean leaving the field too early. It is not, as it may also include the under analysis of textual or narrative data. The method requires that the researcher move through a succession of stages starting with in vivo codes, or open codes which are codes derived directly form the data, through to more abstract or second level categorical codes, and finally to the last stage of conceptual and theoretical codes which are the building blocks of theory (Skodol-Wilson and Ambler-Hutchinson, 1996). At each of these levels the theory should become more refined, integrating abstract concepts that cover behavioral variation. Therefore, premature closure can also occur in situations where the researcher has collected a wealth of data if the analyst does not move beyond describing what is in that data.

Grounded theory is not theory testing, content analysis, or word counts

This is often the result of methodological muddling, using interpretivist methods to analyze 'realist' assumptions. Such manuscripts may start off with hypotheses and then proceed to report how these were tested through interviews or word counts. Whilst there is nothing wrong with combining multiple methods, or quantitative and qualitative techniques, and indeed there are cases where this should be encouraged (Suddaby, 2006), there has to be some congruence between the research question, the underpinning ontology, and the methods used. A good example of this is Parry's (1999) hierarchy of abstraction modeling in which he offers an illustration of using quantitative techniques to validate qualitatively derived grounded theories of social processes of leadership. In this he traces the process of theory development and matches questions with method in a manner that transcends quantitative or qualitative debates of supremacy. This is the important factor, not the nature of the data itself as 'any kind of data can be constantly compared' (Glaser, 1999: 842) and is often based on triangulation (see, for example, Herman and Egri, 2002; Kan and Parry, 2004). The main problem lies in methodological transgression. Such transgressions refer to 'the frank violation of the grounded theory philosophy and methodology' (Skodal Wilson and Ambler Hutchinson, 1996: 224). These methodological transgressions also pertain to cases where the canons of quantitative method are modified and applied to interview or textual data, and where the outcome is a study described in positivist terms such as random sampling, reliability, validity statistics, independent and dependent variables, and so on. Indeed, as Suddaby points out, grounded theorists do engage in a system of theory testing only, not in the Popperian sense of falsification. Rather, theory testing is conducted through the rigorous application of the constant comparison method.

Grounded theory is not simply routine application of formulaic technique to data

Again, this is a misconception that has arisen as a result of newly imposed rules regarding such things as the number of interviews needed before one can claim theoretical saturation (Goulding, 2002; Suddaby, 2006).

Essentially saturation is reached when there are no new insights arising from fresh data. A further problem arises out of an obsession with coding and the presentation of codes and concepts that lack creative and theoretical insight (Suddaby, 2006). 'The grounded theorist does not wish to parade in a very obvious way the very low-level kinds of conceptual descriptions which make up the bulk of the analysis ... The concepts which have been taken out, made explicit, and defined rigorously, need then to be "hidden" again in the theoretical/descriptive account' (Turner, 1983: 347).

Grounded theory is not perfect

In addition to the foregoing, Suddaby discusses the growing rift between academic purists who seek to develop and improve the methodology and pragmatists who are more actively engaged in applying it. He warns of the need to bear in mind that grounded theory was developed as a practical methodology for providing understanding of complex social phenomenon, and as a way of occupying a middle ground between 'slippery epistemological boundaries' (p. 638) and as such its techniques are inherently messy and require a tacit understanding, of, for example, when saturation is reached, which only comes with experience. Another feature of grounded theory that has been challenged, is the over emphasis on induction (method, data, findings, and theory), as a position that stands in direct opposition to deduction (theory, method, data, and findings). Strauss and Corbin (1994) acknowledge the over emphasis on induction in the original *Discovery* (1967) which played down the role of theoretical sensitivity. Indeed the very nature of induction as a pure process has itself been challenged:

What field researchers actually do when they use analytical induction would be described more properly by philosophers of science as 'retroduction' than as induction. A double fitting or alternative shaping of both observation and explanation, rather than an ex post facto discovery of explanatory ideas ... (Katz, 1983: 133–4)

Informally most researchers readily admit that research is a function of both inductive and deductive analysis and that most adopt a middle path. Accordingly there is scope for the development and explication of a more 'iterative' as averse to purely 'inductive' approach to theory development (Orton, 1997).

Grounded theory is not easy

As largely discussed earlier in this chapter, possibly one of the reasons that so many are drawn to grounded theory lies in the fact that its procedures have been so well documented and described in the numerous texts that now abound on the subject. These can sometimes offer the false belief that if the steps outlined in their pages are followed to the letter, a theory will emerge. This is not necessarily the case. It is possible to develop hundreds of codes, but fail to grasp the connection between them. Glaser (1978) likens this to a 'drugless trip' whereby the researcher lives in a dream-like state, submerging him/herself in the data with no revelatory insights, until, if one is lucky, a 'light bulb' comes on and the connections become clearer. This may take months, but until it happens, the end result may seem a lifetime away. Again, this is linked to the theoretical sensitivity of the researcher and the depth of experience in using the methodology. Glaser (1999) sums up the essence of the grounded theory researcher:

The grounded theory researcher has three important characteristics: an ability to conceptualize data, an ability to tolerate some confusion, and an ability to tolerate confusion's attendant regression. These attributes are necessary because they enable the researcher to wait for the conceptual sense making to emerge from the data. This is just a fact ... Students who attempt grounded theory but cannot tolerate confusion and regression, and who need to continually feel cognitively in control, fall by the wayside. They get fed up (p. 838).

CONCLUDING REMARKS

In this chapter, I have attempted to address some of the key issues surrounding the use of grounded theory. My intention was not to present a detailed account of all the nuances and intricacies involved in applying the methodology. There are numerous texts that offer this and it is down to the individual to draw their own conclusions and decide on which version they are most comfortable with. Neither was the intention to discourage researchers from adopting grounded theory. Rather, my aim was to highlight some of the potential pitfalls so that they can be considered and hopefully avoided. Ultimately the goal of most researchers working within organizational studies is publication in a top flight journal, and as this chapter demonstrates, reviewers are becoming increasingly fastidious in how they judge the credibility of grounded theory manuscripts. Consequently, whether it is a PhD under examination or a paper submitted for publication, the main concern is that a clear logic is shown and the principles and processes involved in the generation of the findings are applied and made explicit.

REFERENCES

Charmaz, K. (1983) 'The grounded theory method: an explication and interpretation', in Emerson, R. (ed.), *Contemporary Field Research: A Collection of Readings*, Boston, MA: Little Brown Company.

Cohen. E (1988) 'Authenticity and commoditization', *Annals of Tourism Research*, 15(3): 371–86.

Crook, C.W and Kumar, R.L (1998) 'Electronic Interchange: a multi-industry investigation using Grounded Theory', *Information and Management*, 34(2): 75–89.

Cutlciffe, J.R. (2000) 'Methodological issues in Grounded Theory', *Journal of Advanced Nursing*, 31(6): 1476–84.

Davis. F. (1979) *A Yearning for Yesterday: A Sociology of Nostalgia*, London: Collyer MacMillan.

Gersick, C.J. (1988) 'Time and transition in work teams: toward a new model in group development', *Academy of Management Journal*, 31: 9–41.

Glaser, B. (1978) *Theoretical Sensitivity: Advances in the Methodology of Grounded Theory*, Mill Valley, CA: Sociology Press.

Glaser, B. (1992) *Basics of Grounded Theory: Emergence versus Forcing*, Mill Valley, CA: Sociology Press.

Glaser, B. (1999) 'The future of grounded theory', *Qualitative Health Research*, 9(6): 836–45.

Glaser, B. and Strauss, A. (1967) *The Discovery of Grounded Theory: Strategies for Qualitative Research*, Chicago: Aldine.

Goulding, C. (1999) 'Heritage, nostalgia, and the 'Grey' consumer', *The Journal of Marketing Practice: Applied Marking Science*, 5 (6/7/8): 177–99.

Goulding, C. (1999) 'Museum culture and consumer behaviour', *Journal of Marketing Management*, 15 (November): 647–72.

Goulding, C. (2000) 'The museum environment and the visitor experience', *European Journal of Marketing*, 34(3/4): 433–52.

Goulding, C. (2000a) 'The commodification of the past, postmodern Pastiche, and the search for authentic experiences at contemporary heritage attractions', *European Journal of Marketing*, 34(7): 835–53.

Goulding, C. (2001) 'Romancing the past: heritage visiting and the nostalgic consumer', *Psychology and Marketing*, 18(June): 565–92.

Goulding, C. (2002) *Grounded Theory: A Practical Guide for Management, Business and Market Researchers*, London: Sage.

Goulding, C. (2005) 'Grounded theory, ethnography and phenomenology: a comparative analysis of three qualitative strategies for market research', *European Journal of Marketing*, 39(3/4): 294–308.

Hall, W. and Callery, P. (2001) 'Pearls, pith and provocation: enhancing the rigor of grounded theory: incorporating reflexivity and relationality', *Qualitative Health Research*, 11(2): 257–72.

Herman, S. and Egri, C.P. (2002) 'Triangulation in action: integration of qualitative and quantitative methods to research environmental leadership', in Parry, K and Meindl, J. (eds), *Grounding Leadership Theory and Research: Issues, Perspectives and Methods*, Greenwich, CI: Information Age Publishing, pp.129–48.

Hewison, R. (1987) *The Heritage Industry: Britain in a Climate of Decline*, London: Mathuen.

Isabella, L.A. (1990) 'Evolving interpretations as change unfolds: how managers construe key organizational events', *Academy of Management Journal*, 33(1): 7–41.

Kan, M. and Parry, K. (2004) 'Identifying paradox: a grounded theory of leadership in overcoming resistance to change', *The Leadership Quarterly*, 15(4): 467–91.

Katz, J. (1983) 'A theory of qualitative methodology: the social system of analytical fieldwork', in Emerson, R. (ed.), *Contemporary Field Research: A Collection of Readings*, Boston, MA: Little Brown Company.

Martin, P.Y. and Turner, B. (1986) 'Grounded theory and organizational research', *Journal of Applied Behavioral Science*, 22(2): 141–57.

Orton , J.D. (1997) 'From inductive to iterative grounded theory: zipping the gap between process theory and process data', *Scandinavian Journal of Management*, 13(4): 419–38.

Pandit, N. (1996) The creation of theory: a recent application of the grounded theory method', *The Qualitative report*, 2(4) http://www.nova.edu/Ssss/QR/QR2-4/pandit.html (last accessed 16/01/07).

Parry, K.W. (1998) 'Grounded theory and social process: a new direction for leadership research', *Leadership Quarterly*, 9(1): 85–106.

Parry, K.W. (1999) 'Hierarchy of Abstraction Modelling (H.A.M) and the psychometric validation of grounded theory research', *International Journal of Organizational Behavior*, 5(5): 180–94.

Parry, K.W. (1999a) 'Enhancing adaptability: leadership strategies to accommodate change in local government settings', *Journal of Organizational Change*, 12(2): 134–56.

Parry, Ken. W. (1998) 'Grounded theory and social process: a new direction for leadership research', *Leadership Quarterly*, 9(1): 85–106.

Parry, K.W. and Meindl, J. (Eds) (2002) *Grounding Leadership Theory and Research: Issues and Perspectives*, Greenwich: Information Age Publishing.

Partington, D. (2000) 'Building grounded theories of management action', *British Journal of Management*, 11(2): 91–102.

Rennie, D. (1998) 'Grounded theory methodology: the pressing need for a coherent logic of justification', *Theory and Psychology*, 8(1): 101–19.

Skodol-Wilson, H. and Ambler-Hutchinson, S. (1996) 'Methodological mistakes in grounded theory', *Nursing Research*, 45(2): 122–4.

Sousa, C.A and Hendriks, P.H. (2006) 'The diving bell and the butterfly: the need for grounded theory in developing a knowledge-based view of organizations', *Organizational Research Methods*, 9(3) 315–38.

Stern, P.N. (1994) 'Eroding Grounded Theory, in Morse', J.M (ed.) *Critical Issues in Qualitative Research Methods*, Thousand Oaks, CA: Sage.

Strauss, A. (1991) *Qualitative Analysis for Social Scientists*, Cambridge: Cambridge University Press.

Strauss, A. and Corbin, J. (1990) *Basics of Qualitative Research: Grounded Theory Procedures and Techniques*, Newbury Park: Sage.

Strauss, A. and Corbin, J. (1994) 'Grounded theory methodology: an overview', in Denzin, N. and Lincoln, Y. (eds) *Handbook of Qualitative Research*, California: Sage.

Strauss, A. and Corbin, J. (1997) *Grounded Theory in Practice*, Thousand Oaks, CA: Sage.

Suddaby, R. (2006) 'From the Editors: what grounded theory is not', *Academy of Management Journal*, 49(4): 633–42.

Sutton, R.I. (1987) 'The process of organizational death: disbanding and reconnecting', *Administrative Science Quarterly*, 32: 542–69.

Trim, P. and Lee, Y.L. (2004) 'A reflection on theory building and the development of management knowledge', *Management Decision*, 42(3/4): 473–80.

Turner, B. (1983) 'The use of grounded theory for the qualitative analysis of organizational behaviour', *Journal of Management Studies*, 20(3): 333–48.

23

Archival Research in Organizations in a Digital Age

Michael Moss

THE CHANGING NATURE OF THE SEARCH FOR RESOURCES

For many scholars, search engines (predominantly Google) are now their gateways to research resources, 'making what was familiar appear strange and what was natural seem arbitrary' (Burke, 2000: 2). A decade ago, it would have been unthinkable that entering a search term in a search engine with global reach would produce satisfying results; now it is surprising if it does not. No longer do we consult encyclopedias and guides on our shelves; instead we 'Google it' (Hargittai, 2007a). As a result, it is now accepted best practice to distribute on the web information that was previously published in analogue form, such as reports of government inquiries, corporate reports and accounts, and a good deal of supporting material. In a research university, much journal content is now accessible in this way, often without even having to enter sites through the library. Consequently, content legitimized by the editorial process and peer review becomes submerged in the tide of global information that lacks such familiar mediation.

This dramatic change in the distribution channel and in information seeking – behaviour has destabilized much accepted practice, leading the professions that engage with such resources to seek to redefine their role and function (Buckland, 1998). Bruce Winston (2006: 280) considers the library will continue to exist but, 'may look more like museums where one-of-a-kind archives are held, such as the Library of Congress. Patrons of the university library would spend time studying archives as one might do in a museum, but the traditional book would be available by electronic access', through subscription services. David Levy (2003: 36) believes that libraries and library practices need to be refashioned where 'a single medium as representational format [ones and zeroes] is now capable of representing all the forms of talk we have so far managed to create: textual graphics, voice, and moving images.

And a single device is capable of making all these formats manifest'.

Be that as it may, in the analogue the very terms archive, library, and museum imply a sense of place, with collections of material that had been selected, appraised, or privileged by custodians – mediated in some fashion. Although the algorithms in search engines privilege some information over others, the process is not comparable, and has led some commentators to question whether the term 'digital library' can in any meaningful sense be applied to content captured from the web (Miksa and Doty, 1994). In this environment, coloured as it is by postmodern and poststructuralist thinking, the term archive (more commonly employed than library) is coming to mean much more than simply the physical holdings of paper records. It extends to the whole sweep of evidence marshalled in any argument, and can include physical objects, landscape, and digital material that might have previously been considered to be within the print culture of a library, or objects stored in museums. This uncertainty has serious repercussions for research, particularly in the social sciences and humanities that lack the technical infrastructures of science and medicine that accompany well-resourced initiatives, such as the e-science agenda.

Mike Featherstone (2006: 594) postulates that the archive that is the internet is an antithesis of its analogue equivalent; 'the repository of material which has only been loosely classified; material whose status is as yet indeterminate and stands between rubbish, junk, and significance; material which has not been read and researched', and which thus becomes for him 'the activity of individuals in everyday life who seek to preserve documents, photographs, diaries, and recordings to develop their own archives as memory devices'. Therefore, 'In this dream, new technologies play a central role as the means by which all documents might be put online, linked by a vast hypertextual network' (Sawchuk and Johnson, 2001). This utopian techno-conception is reinforced and extended by the Internet Archive founded by Brewster

Khale in 1996 to build 'a digital library of Internet sites and other cultural artefacts in digital form' (Internet Archive, 2007). Khale's premise is that: 'Advances in computing and communications mean that we can cost-effectively store every book, sound recording, movie, software package, and public web page ever created, and provide access to these collections via the Internet to students and adults all over the world' (ITConversations, 2004). Such a claim begs many questions, particularly of redundancy, which is reduced in the analogue world where content is selected for permanent preservation and made accessible by librarians and archivists. And what is implied by 'ever created'? Does this mean literally for ever, or at least as long as information has survived in the analogue, which is well over 2,000 years? If that is the case, then the phrase is meaningless and requires qualification through selection. Arguments for appraisal by archivists and privileging by librarians expressed in terms of physical space rather than intellectual access have been negated by the possibility of mass digital storage, and have been replaced by more robust concepts of 'intermediation' of information by professionals for future user communities (Lee, 2000). Clifford Lynch (2003: 196), the director of the US Coalition of Networked Information, dismisses such as an approach as special pleading or, the 'haphazard historical gerrymandering of knowledge into institutional collections belonging to communities'. Nevertheless, there remains an issue about the authenticity and integrity of digital objects that was first raised in respect of film by Walter Benjamin (1935/6) in the 1930s. At one level, practice in the print culture has simply been translated to the digital with a raft of books and articles made available online from publishing houses. Technical solutions have been developed to sustain the authenticity and integrity of the original using such utilities as LOCKSS (2007; Lots of Copies Keep Stuff Safe) that began life in 1999 and seeks 'to insure important scholarly assets remain available in a distributed, self-repairing, robust, digital preservation system'. It is not quite as simple as that, as many digital resources have embedded 'behaviours'; for example, the uniform resource locators (urls) cited here, which cannot be expected to function over time, are an excellent example of the problem.

Mediation or creative commons?

Much web content, however, lacks such mediation, which appeals to many commentators, because it chimes with the postmodern perspective of the 'other'. Charles Leadbetter in his experimental book, *We Think: Why Mass Creativity is the Next Best Thing*, which he posted to the internet before publication for comment, goes further in contending that this will lead to a paradigm shift in the social construction of knowledge, and as a result in the behaviour of organizations and in the way in which we perceive them. He is excited by the concept of a creative commons that he compares with Henry Ford's introduction of factory technology using low skilled labour:

> Thanks to the relatively low cost of technology many consumers can become producers at least some of the time. Good ideas will come from amateurs as well as professionals. Innovation will not just flow down a pipeline, from experts working in their labs and studios, to passive consumers waiting in the line. Innovation is a social, cumulative and collaborative activity; ideas will flow back up the pipeline from consumers and they will share them amongst themselves. That is why the next big thing will be us: our power to share and develop ideas, without having to rely on formal organisations to do it for us. (Leadbetter, 2006).

If this is the case, and there is evidence to suggest that it is, then such content becomes important not simply as cultural artefact, but as an essential research resource. In its Christmas 2006 issue (page 30), *Time Magazine* voted 'us' as its person of the year – 'Yes, you. You control the Information Age. Welcome to your world.' Somewhat romantically, it counterpoised Carlyle's 'great men' view of history with 'a story about community and collaboration on a scale never seen before. It's about the cosmic compendium

of knowledge, *Wikipedia*, and the million-channel people's network. *YouTube* and the online metropolis *MySpace*. It's about the many wrestling power from the few and helping one another for nothing and how they will change the world, but also change the way the world changes'. Having made these wild claims, there was no exploration of the consequences of such atomization, except a comment made by the editor on the *BBC Today* programme that there would be still a need for the press to 'fire hose' the junk. For *YouTube*, such mediation is unnecessary, 'As more people capture special moments on video, *YouTube* is empowering them to become the broadcasters of tomorrow' (*YouTube*, 2007), while *MySpace* is more modestly demotic – 'a place for friends' – but it does have resonances with Leadbetter's organizational vision by including in its target community, 'business people and co-workers interested in networking' (*MySpace*, 2007). There is evidence that it is used for such purposes, and by organizations seeking to gain new customers or to promote products and services (McLaughlin, 2006). *Flickr* (2007), the online photograph site, has homely aspirations that are similar to *MySpace*: 'We want to help people make their photos available to the people who matter to them'. The interesting feature of all these sites is that they resemble libraries in their organization with content allocated to subject areas or categories. In 2007, Mike Wesch (2007) of Kansas State University poked fun at this apparent paradox in a posting to *YouTube* with the witty title 'YouTube R/evolution' that raises some challenging questions.

The audit society and the constructed archive?

The concept of a dialogic construction of knowledge has a long pedigree that was most recently articulated by Gibbons et al. (1994) in *The New Production of Knowledge: The Dynamics of Science and Research in Contemporary Societies*. The sociologist Helga Nowotny (2004: 179) revisited the topic in a special issue of the journal *Minerva* that explores the relationship between science and scholarship, in which she explained that:

> The old paradigm of scientific discovery ('Mode 1') – characterized by the hegemony of theoretical or, at any rate, experimental science; by an internally-driven taxonomy of disciplines; and by the autonomy of scientists and their host institutions, the universities – was being superseded by a new paradigm of knowledge production ('Mode 2'), which was socially distributed, application-oriented, trans-disciplinary and subject to multiple accountabilities.

The anthropologist Marilyn Strathern (2004) tested these assumptions in her study of the Cambridge Genetics Knowledge Park that also embraces her interest in the impact of the audit culture on organizational behaviour. This concept, developed by Michael Power (1997), has, as Daniel Miller (1998, pp. 204–5) pointed out, profound implications for the resulting record:

> The paradox is that, while consumption is the pivot upon which these developments in history spin, the concern is not the cost and benefits of actual consumers, but of what we might call virtual consumers, which are generated by management theories and models … [And] the rise of auditing in Britain [is thus] symptomatic not of capitalism, but of a new form of abstraction that is emerging, a form more abstract than the capitalism of firms dealing in commodities.

We might also add government and substitute the world for Britain. Strathern (1997) explored this critical audit culture from the perspective of her own Cambridge College and the Research Assessment Exercise in British Higher Education introduced by the Conservative government in 1986 where, as she puts it, the 'ought' becomes 'is' and things do indeed work backwards, where 'the form in which the outcome is to be described is known in advance' (Strathern, 2000). Jacques Derrida (1996: 16) warned of such entanglement when he wrote that, 'the technical structure of the *archiving* archive also determines the structure of the *archivable* content even its very coming into existence and in its relationship to the future'. This circularity

is on the one hand reinforced by the digital, as the processes become faster, and because of the way the systems work, the 'loose ends' (inconsistencies, aberrant behaviour and so on) disappear, and on the other is subverted by it, as we have seen. An extreme example is the 9/11 site that includes no references to those from the far right who blamed the attacks on abortionists and homosexuals, or those caught up in the events who were illegal immigrants into America (Frendo, 2007, pp. 23–31).

Such a binary opposition within the archive has far-reaching consequences for organizational research, particularly as the 'audit process' 'encourages a form of reflexivity', but 'the reflexive subject is caught within tightly fixed parameters that appear to render opposition futile' (Shore and Wright, 2000: 78). In its most extreme form, it ironically negates good governance by insisting that all information, the archive if you will, belongs to the organization. The Ford Motor Company's standard of corporate governance in 2007 was unambiguous: 'Please be aware that all Company information belongs to the Company, not to you'. This covers 'any information that you acquire or record in performing your job duties. It includes such documents as written memoranda, hand-written notes, computer files, voice mail, and e-mail notes'. Any violation is subject 'to disciplinary action which may include termination of contract'. (Ford Standards of Corporate Conduct, 2007). As Foucault put it, 'visibility is a trap', and the resulting record will indeed convert the 'ought' into 'is' (Foucault, 1977: 200). Frendo cites Spivak's chilling observation that, 'as we produce the official explanations we reproduce the official ideology, the structure of possibility of a knowledge whose effect is that very structure' (Frendo, 2007, citing Spivak, 1987: 108). The occlusion of the individual voice makes it increasingly difficult to rely on organizational records to investigate the dynamics of leadership, corporate strategy, and modes of operation, except by inference and, even then, there is a risk of running foul of the regulatory environment.

The voice of the individual in the audit culture

In both the public and private sector, however, it is difficult to control, at least in open societies, disclosures by individuals that might spring the trap, even if they are employed under conditions that prohibit the retention and release of information. The explosion of the internet has made disclosure much simpler, much harder to prevent, and potentially much more anonymous than before. The United States Military has had to accept blogging by its servicemen as a feature of the war in Iraq, and the concomitant release of information that previously would have been redacted by the censor, or, if it escaped, only confined to private space. Such resources themselves raise further difficult issues about authenticity and veracity that were encountered in the analogue world, but where it is much simpler to detect falsification and identify culprits. If the corporate sector can manipulate social networks to its advantage so can everyone else from, in the case of Iraq, the Pentagon to Osama Bin Laden. There are those who reject all such web content as unreliable, condemning much of it as mere plagiarism, and look back fondly to the time when knowledge was held bound in libraries. This is to deny the pervasive ubiquitousness of the aptly named worldwide web that enables globalization and through its chaordic structure has encouraged a revival in interest in networked organizations. Verne Harris (2001: 1), writing from the perspective of postapartheid South Africa, addressed the asymmetry between the archival outputs of audit and creative commons that in his case are voices of the oppressed and tortured: 'Under apartheid the terrain of social memory, as with all social space, was a site of struggle. In the crudest sense this was a struggle of remembering against forgetting, of oppositional memory fighting a life-and-death struggle against a systematic forgetting engineered by the state'. This resulted in the selective destruction not only of the records of government, but also the erasure by 'confiscation or destruction' of individuals and organizations involved in resisting it.

Although an extreme example of how the record can be subverted, it resonates with the concerns of Strathern and Foucault, and is the inevitable consequence of the policy of the Ford Motor Company. Even in open societies, disclosure is not always straightforward, and poses difficult moral and ethical questions, both for the researcher and the individual. This can be illustrated from an organizational perspective by the experience of Dr. Jeffrey Wigand (2005), former vice president for research and development for Brown & Williamson, and the tobacco-industry whistle-blower who admitted in 1993 that the link between nicotine and addiction was well known. He summed up his dilemma in an interview:

> You feel a very deep, inner conflict between your loyalties, your loyalty to your family, and supporting and protecting your family, the supposed loyalty that you're supposed to have through the corporation that's actually paying you to support your family.

In the public sector, this ethical dilemma has been greatly exacerbated by the war on terror, which has allowed governments to introduce measures that erode personal freedoms and which are open to abuse, particularly by neoconservatives who believe that 'truth is not salutary, but dangerous, and even destructive to society – any society', and we could substitute the archive for truth (Drury, 2005: 1). The Patriot Act introduced by George W. Bush in 2001, just forty-three days after the 9/11 attack, deeply troubles the library and archival communities in America because of the threat it poses to intellectual freedom by requiring disclosure to law enforcement agents of the names of readers and the material consulted (USA Patriot Act, 2007). The American Library Association is unequivocal in condemnation:

> The USA Patriot Act threatens your privacy in bookstores and libraries. It gives the FBI the power to apply to a secret court for an order compelling the surrender of records of the books you purchase

or borrow. The government does not have to produce any evidence that you are a terrorist – or even that you are suspected of any crime. The order also gags booksellers and librarians, making it illegal to reveal that your records have been searched.

In the United Kingdom, such contingency led to the suicide of the weapons inspector Dr. David Kelly in July 2003. The government record that was uniquely revealed to the public in the subsequent inquiry served to confirm Harris's (2002) perception of an inadequate and contested record, not in a coercive totalitarian regime, but in a supposedly free democratic society (Moss, 2005). Jonathan Powell, the Prime Minister's chief of staff at the time, was forced to admit under cross-examination that minutes of meetings were only taken if actions were to follow (Hutton, 2004; transcripts for 18 August, 2003). The moral philosopher Onora O'Neill (2004: 92) suggests that this betrays a lack of 'epistemological fussiness' in keeping the record that is expected, particularly in public life, and will only serve to confuse, whether intentionally or not, future users.

Record keeping in the digital environment

Because the processes designed to guarantee authenticity and trust in record keeping and publication in the analogue have been abandoned in the digital environment, such fiduciary concerns have attracted much scholarly attention (Bishop et al., 2003). They are not new. Newspapers have always been biased, as we all know and accept. The record is always partial, even when it is apparently complete; as Jenkinson, the doyen of British archival thinkers, noted over fifty years ago, they serve as 'substitution not merely for the spoken word but for the fallible and destructible memory of the people who took part in whatever the transactions may have been that gave rise to them' (Jenkinson, 1980, pp. 321–2). Minute books have been kept in Britain since at least the sixteenth century by the state and organizations, which operated either to provide common services

or for mutual advantage. Although they were mandated during the nineteenth century in Britain by legislation, in both the public and private sector, more often than not they disguise more than they reveal. By their very nature they are an expression of collective decision making, and only exceptionally do individuals appear in the record and then usually to express dissent. Reference to individuals has become even more problematic with the introduction in many jurisdictions of legislation to protect personal data. When minutes are open to either public scrutiny or inspection by external regulators, such as the Security and Exchange Commission in America, or the Competition Committee in Britain, or under freedom of information legislation, they can become opaque to a fault and, paradoxically, fiduciary behaviour gives way to obsessive secretiveness. This is only part of the explanation for the decline in the quality of minute taking, evidenced in the Hutton report. In many organizations, the minute in the analogue was the pinnacle of integrated record keeping systems that included correspondence, often arranged systematically in files, financial records, papers relating to the production and delivery of products and services, and records of employment. In large organizations, such as government departments, health services, and big companies, these could be of considerable complexity, with practices and procedures that evolved over time to meet particular needs and circumstances, leading to the creation of the sources employed in research (Yates, 1989; Menne-Haritz, 2004a; Moss, 2005). The introduction of networked computing from the mid-1980s had a fundamental and deleterious impact on such practices.

In the analogue culture, reports and letters were usually drafted or dictated and a fair copy made by a clerk for signature or filing. In government departments in many jurisdictions, and in other large organizations, registries drew up filing plans, referenced filed documents, and were responsible for their subsequent control and disposal (Moss, 2005; Tough and Moss, 2003). Such practices separated back and front office and gave fiduciary protection to executives and government officials, but were expensive to operate. For the external user, the resulting archive was remarkably reliable and complete, allowing for the reconstruction of events, and the way that organizations were managed and functioned, with precision and certainty. With Edwin Green, the present author was able to unravel from the files in The National Archives at Kew, at the Bank of England, and in the hands of the successors of the voting trustees, the complex organizational structure of the Royal Mail Group that collapsed in 1931 (Green and Moss, 1982). The authenticity of, and trust in, the record was not in question. Pressures to cut costs combined with the invention of the personal computer to shatter such integrated systems. Executives began to both draft and complete their own correspondence, and reports and email began to replace letters as the preferred mode of communication with little consideration of the consequences for the business process. Any consideration of fiduciary responsibility was forgotten in the pell-mell race for efficiency. Although the telephone had prefigured some of these developments, the practice of minuting on file conversations was not carried over into the new digital environment. Clerks and secretaries disappeared, registries were abandoned, and the back office was collapsed into the front office with no thought of the risks involved. Filing became haphazard, evident from the Hutton Inquiry and the 40 million emails from the Clinton White House (1993–2001) that are in effect stand-alone objects (Electronic Records, 2001). Technical solutions to address the problem through electronic records and document management systems (ERDMS) have not proved effective, largely because electronic records are 'fluent and not fixable recordings' and have the 'capacity of being timeless without any traces of changes or external influences' raising doubts about authenticity and trust (Menne-Haritz, 2004b: 10). It is not surprising that there are concerns that the resulting 'archive' will be deficient, even as a current management tool, let alone as a resource for researchers.

Although financial records have always had to be trustworthy because they are subject to scrutiny, practice has been equally transformed in the digital environment. They have been used to manage the state, organizations, and enterprises for centuries, and detailed procedures have been developed to prevent fraud and misallocations, both internal and external. In the paper world, transactions were registered and summarized in account books that were elaborately cross-referred to mark the audit trail, and as time went on to allow them to be used as a management tool. They were surrounded by security, both to prevent tampering, and to prevent unauthorized access to sensitive information. The ledgers containing details of entries in the balance sheet and profit and loss account were often locked and described as private. The evidence of how these series were used to control an organization can often only be inferred from the way in which they were constructed, the records entered, and from marginal jottings and calculations. Since most transactions have a financial expression, it is much more difficult to dissemble than in the narrative contained in minutes and correspondence, even in cases where disguise or fraud was deliberately intended. Although there were variations of practice between and across organizations, once the principles have been understood they are easy to interpret by an external user. In digital financial systems, books of account have been replaced for almost forty years by large databases that record individual transactions that can be aggregated and disaggregated at will to produce summary outputs such as the balance sheet, profit and loss accounts and other views of activities. Although procedures must be as robust as in the analogue to satisfy external scrutiny, they present the researcher with just as formidable a challenge as Clinton's email, particularly as aggregation is dependent on codes embedded in the record of the transaction. Without the codebook they become meaningless accumulations. In many organizations, these individual records are linked to other data to gain competitive advantage. It is not difficult to guess that

Tesco and WalMart owe their success in the retail market to their effectiveness in leveraging information that they collect about customer preferences and their suppliers, but how it is done is closely guarded. Google collects click streams, which, by providing invaluable evidence for their clients and advertisers, is an essential source of revenue (Battelle, 2005). Such data are not normally accessible to outside researchers and then often under terms that compromise its validity. There are exceptions, such as Digg.com, that provides a real time view of its user community (http://labs.digg.com).

Access and preservation

If use of such digital assets is problematic, access may prove difficult for two reasons. Organizations are increasingly aware of the dangers of hidden contingent liabilities within record series, and there is as yet no agreement about long-term preservation. The American tobacco manufacturer Brown & Williamson was a subsidiary of British American Tobacco (BAT) when the Food & Drugs Administration (FDA) took the company to court in 1999. The FDA was able legally to discover 6 to 7 million documents held in Britain by its parent company, many of which should possibly have been destroyed as they were outside the period of statutory limitation (FDA, 2000; BAT, 2004). In 2003, the Securities and Exchange Commission prosecuted Henry Blodget of Merrill Lynch for publicly recommending a stock that he had described in a private email as a 'pos – a piece of shit' (Securities and Exchange Commission, 2003). This was discovered by Eliot Spizer, then the attorney general for the State of New York, when he investigated a private action brought against Merrill Lynch by a private investor, Debases Kanjilal, who had lost $500,000 on a stock recommended by Blodget (Callahan, 2004). This led to a $100 million fine for Merrill Lynch and instruction to put its house in order. These and other high profile cases, many involving Eliot Spizer, together with a tightening compliance environment consequent on the war on terror

and the collapse of Enron in 2001, have made organizations much more aware of the possibility of 'smoking guns' in their records (Langley, 2003; McKemmish, 1998). As a result, audit and risk management committees are more likely to insist on the destruction of records as soon as they are time-expired or no longer of commercial use, in order to extinguish any contingent liability. They will also impose conditions on access that may compromise research and prevent publication. It is possible that the only record left by a private sector organization will be those mandated by international regulation and local jurisdictions. Such an approach to risk management is no longer confined to the private sector and raises serious questions about the accountability of governments whose liabilities cannot be limited to the same degree (HM Treasury, 2004; Moss, 2006).

These pressures on the archive are compounded by the problems of the long-term preservation of digital content. As Seamus Ross (2006: 143) concludes, 'Digital preservation should ensure that we pass usable, authentic and reliable evidence to the future. Current approaches are inadequate'. Embedded behaviours present major obstacles. At a simple level, links are permanently fractured, evident from the Internet Archive; but, more seriously, underlying applications, for example macros, cease to function, as software is no longer available. There are many well-resourced projects worldwide to investigate the issue, such as the Digital Curation Centre (DCC) in Britain and the Coalition for Networked Information (CNI) in America, but no immediate solutions are in prospect. Every national library and archive has initiatives to address the problem, and in some instances to harvest content from the web. What is clear is that, despite the potential for cheap mass storage, preservation of digital objects will be much more expensive than analogue equivalents. No organization will adopt preservation strategies unless there is a convincing business case, often compliance with external regulation, or in the case of government the need to be seen to be accountable. Only rarely can a long-term purely business case be made. Although there will be greater constraints, both legal and financial, on the ability to retain information for research, it will still be incumbent on the established networks of libraries and archives (however redefined) to collect digital assets. Approaches to appraisal and privileging are challenging the authority of archivists and librarians to make these decisions on behalf of the academy, within the mediated analogue environment, in favour of participation by domains in reaching decisions, particularly about the mass of disintermediated material on the web (Yakel and Torres, 2003). This will become increasingly necessary as all disciplines mimic the behaviour of the scientific community in conducting their discourse in virtual communities that have been made more tractable and visible by the web without the need to resort to publishers' distribution channels. An element of archiving is in some senses implicit in the declaration of content in such communities that we might characterize as epistemic, whose mode of working Eric Raymond (1999), a major player in the open-source community, well describes as being akin to a bazaar.

The archive and the accumulation of knowledge

Inspired by Derrida's ideas and perhaps influenced by the secret negotiations between the apartheid regime and the African National Congress (ANC) in the early 1990s, Harris (2001: 6) explored the intentions that weld such bazaars, deepening the analysis, and making it less asymmetrical:

> The structure of archiving, then, involves a trace being consigned to a substrate, a place (and it can be a virtual place) of consignation. And consignation, structurally, involves the exercise of power, what Derrida calls archontic power: the power to consign; the power over the place of consignation; so that in all archiving, the diarist making an entry, the rock painter at work, the person sending an e-mail to a friend, archontic power is in play. And archivists, from the beginning and always, are political players. Of course, they can strain against the forces of archontic power.

Not everyone is willing to concede to this equation that translates all archival information into political action. Latour struggled to find a word to characterize his centres of calculation (the archive), dismissing political power as having little to do with the tedious task of 'reckoning'. He rejected categorization as it divided 'a cloth that we want seamless in order to study it as we choose', but his concept of how knowledge (the archive) is accumulated is predicated on actions that are never neutral and from some perspectives could be considered 'political' (Latour 1987, pp. 220 and 223). Such problematizing of the record by drawing attention to its inevitable social construction raises fresh difficulties, particularly the danger of a collapse into relativism that Nowotny (2004) and others recognized. Rather than retreating into a positivist past, they chose to explore the characteristics of the paradigm they had described. The features that have most implications for the archive, particularly in its digital expression, are its trans-disciplinarity, by which is meant 'the mobilization of a range of theoretical perspectives and practical methodologies to solve problems'; 'the much greater diversity of the sites of production at which knowledge is produced and in the types of knowledge produced'; 'it is highly reflexive'; 'research has become a dialogic process'; and lastly, 'novel forms of quality control' (Nowotny, 2004: 180). These features are writ large in Wikipedia, the disintermediated online encyclopedia, which has been the subject of intense debate and a well-publicized disagreement between its cofounders Jimmy Wales and Larry Sanger. Sanger left in March 2002 after Wales refused to allow him to exercise 'expert' editorial control. Four years later he set up the expert-edited Citizendium, a 'citizens' compendium of everything', which with its global group of collaborators will 'create the most reliable and largest encyclopedia that they can' and, unlike Wikipedia, all entries will be attributed (Citizendium, 2007). As researchers at the IBM Visual Communications Lab have shown, Wikipedia is itself moving spontaneously in this direction (Viégas, 2006), confirming the finding of Susan Bryant et al. (2005) that 'For experts or Wikipedians, the Wikipedia as whole becomes more important than any single article or set of articles ... In the move from novice to Wikipedian, goals broaden to include growing the community itself and improving the overall quality and character of the site' (Bryant, 2005). Such developments do nothing to lesson the criticism of much internet content by Jaron Larnier (2006) as 'online fetish site[s] for foolish collectivism' in the 'race to erase personality' that hearken back to a positivist past with embedded principles of peer group review.

Questions of trust and value in digital content

This question of trust is at the heart of perceptions about web content. Some commentators, by analyzing users' clickstreams, have drawn a distinction between information seeking behaviour in the analogue and digital environments, suggesting that there is a much greater degree of triangulation in establishing trust in the digital than in the analogue (Nicholas, 2007). There are good reasons for doubting such conclusions for all but the most inexperienced users of information resources. To scholars in the humanities and social sciences trained in the careful comparison of sources, triangulation and contextualization are second nature. What appears to differentiate some web content is the much greater lack of context than ever before, but that in itself poses the question of how useful much of this disintermediated content will be in testing hypotheses and constructing arguments as the web becomes more and more flooded with information. Hargittai (2007b: 3) concluded that, 'Evaluating the credibility of online content itself poses a challenge to the utility one might be able to derive from time spent online'. Are the contents of *YouTube* and *MySpace* and a mosaic of blogs worth referencing, let alone preserving? Are we in danger of mistaking noise for music with a score, however atonal in character? What the argument may really be about is shifting

the parameters of information management away from a hierarchical linear approach that arbitrarily classified knowledge into subject domains, towards 'the rediscovery of ordinary transactions between self and world', that enable rather than stifle trans-disciplinarity (McLuhan, 1962: 187). In other words, there is a danger of mistaking cause for effect, and by so doing following the example of *Time Magazine* in exaggerating the importance of the mass of personal content that floods the web. In the past, there was probably not any less information in circulation; it was just much less visible, confined to conversations, notes, letters, and private personal reflection in diaries. Much of this content never got as far as even being considered as archival, worthy of short-term, let alone long term, preservation, but some did to add depth to understanding. As Keene puts it:

> [A]rchives are often structured by discourses of power and come to be used in the cause of public or scientific truth. But at the same time the archive, as an institution, has a way of accommodating quirky details, narratives and even entire collections that seem to have little to do with its formal or original purpose. Exaptive elements, such as these, are a vital element in the archive's long-term value as a site for understanding and for establishing sympathy with our fellow human beings (Orlow and Maclennan, 2005: A8).

What survives of such exaptive elements or loose ends is a narrow haphazard fraction or in Harris's (2002) words 'a sliver of a sliver'. The web has made what was private reflection public and presents the information professions and their users with an enormous challenge.

In the context of an encroaching audit and compliance culture, the loose ends will be essential in contextualizing resources, but there is little agreement or guidance on what to keep (Strathern, 2000). There is no evidence that, despite their claims to social empowerment, sites such as *MySpace*, *YouTube*, *Facebook* or *Flikr*, have any concept as to what commitments might be involved in long-term digital curation. Although it is probable that many loose ends will continue to survive haphazardly in an analogue form, it would be imprudent to make such an assumption, particularly if it is believed that public web content can have a significant impact in much the same way as newspapers did. There is potential here for the traditional skills of archivists and librarians in selecting (appraising and privileging) material for permanent preservation, but in partnership with user communities, rather than in seeking to enhance access where much professional effort has been directed and then negated by Google (Breivik and Gee, 2006; Yakel and Torres, 2003). There is much debate and little agreement in the information professions about the role of collecting and collections in the digital environment (Currall et al., 2006; Geisler et al., 2002). Some commentators believe that collecting can be automated by using metadata (catalogue information), but that presupposes it to be present, which is unlikely for much disintermediated data apart from that resident on sites such as *YouTube* and *MySpace* where it has been loosely categorized (Lagoze and Fielding, 1998). Others consider that selection could be made heuristically by consumer preferences in much the same way as Amazon privileges books or Tescos and Wall Mart the goods in their stores. Some form of heuristic must be part of the solution in much the same way as viewing panels have for some time been used by television and radio archives to decide what content should be captured (Currall et al., 2006: 110). This approach was adopted in 2004, using institutional recommendations, by the National Library of Australia's Pandora project on the grounds that other approaches, such as random web harvesting, are prohibitively expensive. Although the library's criteria for collecting may give cause for some concern, for example a decision not to collect datasets or online newspapers, they are explicit and address the research community, as arguably a national library should (Phillips, 2003). By making the criteria public, they leave room for other communities to collect material to fill the gaps, as happened in the analogue world.

The threat to research resources and the need for dialogue

For those who make use of such resources to research organizational behaviour, like the other social sciences, they are threatened by the interaction of the digital with the audit culture and disintermediated content that it enables, which is compounded by the consequences of the war on terror leading to greater secrecy, a tightening compliance environment as a result of business scandals in America, leading to an enhanced awareness of contingent liability, and data protection that can be used to hinder access to any information that names individuals. Worryingly, this combination of factors that restricts access and might be thought to be a feature of the private sector is extending to the public sector as private sector practice encroaches on the public sphere and more public sector functions are transferred to the private. In these circumstances, it may no longer be possible to gather data from either the private or public sphere except of the crudest aggregations, hampering research into many aspects of organizational behaviour. Paradoxically, as Foucault so accurately predicted, freedom of information and transparency have the reverse effect in the public sector, if politicians wish only to be seen to be accountable rather than having acted responsibly.

Access that is predicated on permission raises ethical concerns, as it likely to be conditional, and could lead to a prohibition on disclosure or publication. It is not unrealistic to suppose that, in future, access to the private and public archive will only be permitted for consultants if it can be proved to be in the public interest. While the limitation of liability and therefore control of disclosure is essential for the functioning of the private sector, this should not extend to the same degree to the public sphere where there are far fewer checks and balances. It is the duty of the courts to ensure that rights of access to the public record are maintained and that the executive in democratic societies take seriously this responsibility. In America and Britain, the behaviour of the Bush and Blair administrations give cause for concern, as does the tendency for the activity of archiving to become confused with that of the management of information or knowledge for organizational purposes. The academy is weakened in addressing these issues by the distancing of subject domains from the information professions that have been forced, so as to preserve their budgets, to align with government policy and agendas, such as social inclusion and justice, to the detriment of their function as trusted places of deposit of the archive. This is not to say that those agendas are unimportant in a plural democracy; but they cannot be pursued exclusively. For the archive to be secured for the future, the disciplines need to communicate more effectively about the complex changes that are taking place in the information landscape that can neither be understood nor addressed from one perspective alone. Resolution will be expensive and may well require the painful restructuring of institutions that were taken for granted in a liberal economy. What is certain is that the internet has radically changed, if not revolutionized, modalities of resource distribution and discovery, the relationship between public and private spheres and the way research is conducted, but at a price.

ACKNOWLEDGEMENTS

The author would like to thank James Currall, Ruth Frendo, Norman Gray, and Susan Stuart for their advice and assistance.

REFERENCES

Battelle, J. (2005) *The Search: How Google and Its Rivals Rewrote the Rules of Business and Transformed Our Culture*, Boston and London: Nicholas Brealey.

Benjamin, W. (1935/6) *The Work of Art in the Age of Mechanical Reproduction*, New York: Schocken Books, reprinted 1968.

Bishop, A., House, N.V. and Buttenfield, B. (eds) (2003) *Digital Library Use: Social Practice in Design and Evaluation*, Cambridge, MA: MIT Press.

Breivik, P.S. and Gee, E.G. (2006) *Higher Education in the Internet Age*, Westport, Connecticut and London: American Council on Education and Praeger Publishers.

British American Tobacco Documents Archive (2004), http://bat.library.ucsf.edu/ (March 2004).

Bryant, S.L., Forte, A. and Bruckman, A. (2005) 'Becoming Wikipedian: transformation of participation in a collaborative Online Encyclopedia', Atlanta: Georgia Institute of Technology, http://www-static.cc.gatech.edu/~aforte/Bryant ForteBruckBecomingWikipedian.pdf (March 2007).

Buckland, M. (1999) 'The landscape of information science: the American Society For Information Science at 62', *Journal of the American Society of Information Science*, 50(11): 970–74.

Burke, P. (2000) *A Social History of Knowledge from Gutenberg to Diderot*, Cambridge: Polity Press.

Callahan, D. (2004) *The Cheating Culture Why More Americans Are Doing Wrong to Get Ahead*, New York: Harcourt.

Citizendium, 'Citizendium's Statement of Fundamental Policies' (2007) http://www.citizendium.org/index.html (March 2007).

Currall, J., Moss, M. and Stuart, S. (2006) 'Privileging information is inevitable', *Archives and Manuscripts - Journal of the Australian Society of Archivists*, 34(1): 98–122.

Derrida, J. (1996) *Archive Fever: A Freudian Impression*, translated by Eric Prenowitz, Chicago: University of Chicago Press.

Drury, S.B. (1997) *Leo Strauss and the American Right*, New York: St. Martin's Press.

Electronic Records (2001) 'Clinton Administration's management of Executive Office of the President's e-mail system', Washington, DC: US General Accounting Office; Executive Office President, http://www.gao.gov/new.items/d01446.pdf (March 2007).

FDA vs. Brown & Williamson Tobacco Corp. (98–1152) 529 U.S. 120 (2000) 153 F.3d 155, http://supreme.justia.com/us/529/120/case.html (February 2008)

Featherstone, M. (2006) 'Archive', *Theory, Culture & Society*, 23(2–3): 591–6.

Flickr (2007) 'About Flickr', http://www.flickr.com/about/ (March).

Ford Standards of Corporate Conduct (2007) available at http://www.ford.com/en/company/corporate Governance/governancePolicies.htm (February).

Foucault, M. (1977) *Discipline and Punish: The Birth of the Prison*, translated by Alan Sheridan, New York: Vintage Books.

Frendo, R. (2007) 'Archival and social structuring: the impact of the Internet', University of Glasgow IMP unpublished MSc dissertation.

Geisler, G., Giersch, S., McArthur, D. and McClelland, M. (2002) 'Creating virtual collections in digital libraries:

benefits and implementation issues', *Proceedings of the Second ACM/IEEE-CS Joint Conference on Digital Libraries*, New York: ACM Press.

Gibbons, M., Limoges, C., Nowotny, H., Schwartzman, S., Scott, P. and Trow, M. (1994) *The New Production of Knowledge : The Dynamics of Science and Research in Contemporary Societies*, London and Thousand Oaks, CA: Sage Publications.

Green, E. and Moss, M. (1987) *A Business of National Importance: The Royal Mail Shipping Group, 1903–1937*, London: Methuen.

Hargittai, E. (2007a) 'The social, political, economic, and cultural dimensions of search engines: an introduction', *Journal of Computer-Mediated Communication*, 12(3), available at http://jcmc.indiana.edu/vol12/issue3/hargittai.html. (October).

Hargittai, E. (2007b) 'A framework for studying differences in people's digital media uses' in Kutscher, Nadia, and Hans-Uwe, Otto (eds), *Cyberworld Unlimited*, (Wiesbaden, VS Verlag für Sozialwissenschaften/GWV Fachverlage GmbH) 121–137, available at http://www.eszter.com/research/pubs/hargittai-digitalmediausesframework.pdf (October).

Harris, V. (2001) 'Seeing (in) blindness: South Africa, archives and passion for justice', http://www.caldeson.com/RIMOS/harris01.html (February 2007).

Harris, V. (2002) 'The archival sliver: power, memory, and archives in South Africa', *Archival Science*, 2(1–2): 63–86.

HM Treasury (2004) *The Orange Book Management of Risk - Principles and Concepts*, Norwich: HM Stationary Office, http://www.hm-treasury.gov.uk/media/FE6/60/FE66035B-BCDC-D4B3-11057A7707D2521F.pdf (March 2007).

Hutton, L. (2004) *Report of the Inquiry into The Circumstances Surrounding the Death Of Dr David Kelly*, London: Stationary Office: HC 247.

Internet Archive (2007) http://www.archive.org/index.php (February).

ITConversations with Brewster Khale (2004) http://www.itconversations.com/shows/detail400.html (February 2007).

Jenkinson, Sir H. (1980) *Selected Writings of Sir Hilary Jenkinson*, Robert Ellis and Peter Walne (eds), Gloucester: Alan Sutton.

Langley, M. (2003) *Tearing Down the Walls: How Sandy Weill Fought His Way to the Top of the Financial World…and Then Nearly Lost It All*, New York: Simon and Schuster.

Larnier, J. (2006) 'Digital Maoism: the hazards of the new online collectivism', *Edge: The Third Culture*, http://www.edge.org/3rd_culture/lanier06/lanier06_index.html (March 2007).

Latour, B. (1987) *Science in Action*, Milton Keynes: Open University Press.

Lagoze, C. and Fielding, D. (1998) 'Defining collections in distributed digital libraries', *D-Lib Magazine*, Corporation for National Research Initiatives, November issue.

Leadbetter, C. (2006) *We Think: Why Mass Creativity is the Next Best Thing*, http://www.wethinkthebook.net/cms/site/docs/charles%20full%20draft.pdf (February 2007).

Lee H.-L. (2000) 'What is a Collection?', *Journal of the American Society for Information Science*, 51(12): 1106–13.

Levy, D.M. (2003) 'Documents and libraries: a sociotechnical perspective', in Bishop, Ann, House, Nancy Van, and Buttenfield, Barbara (eds) (2003), *Digital Library Use: Social Practice in Design and Evaluation*, Cambridge, MA: MIT Press.

LOCKSS (2007) http://www.lockss.org/lockss/Home (February).

Lynch, C.A. (2003) 'Colliding with the real world: heresies and unexplored questions about audience, economics, and control of digital libraries', in Ann Bishop, Barbara Butterfield, and Nancy Van House (eds), *Digital Library Use: Social Practice in Design and Evaluation*, Cambridge, MA: The MIT Press, pp.191–218.

McKemmish, S. (1998) 'The Smoking Gun: Recordkeeping and accountability', Dunedin, http://www.sims.monash.edu.au/research/rcrg/publications/recordscontinuum/smoking.html (March 2007).

McLaughlin, A. (2006) 'Social network sites – an SME business opportunity', *British Computing Society Communications*, November 2006, available at http://www.bcs.org/server.php?show=ConWebDoc.8451 (October 2007).

McLuhan, M. (1962) *The Gutenberg Galaxy: The Making of Typographic Man*, Toronto: University of Toronto Press.

Menne-Haritz, A. (2004a) *Business Processes. An Archival Science Approach to Collaborative Decision Making, Records, and Knowledge Management*, Dordrecht: Kluwer.

Menne-Haritz, A. (2004b) 'Knowledge management and administrative records', available at http://www.staff.uni-arburg.de/~mennehar/publikationen/kmar.pdf (March 2007).

Miksa, F.L. and Doty, P. (1994) 'Intellectual realities and the digital library', *Digital Libraries*, http://www.csdl.tamu.edu/DL94/paper/miksa.html (March 2007).

Miller, D. (1998) 'A theory of virtualism', in D. Miller and J. Carrier (eds), *Conclusion: Virtualism: A New Political Economy*, Oxford: Oxford University Press, pp. 187–216.

Moss, M. (2005) 'The Hutton inquiry, the President of Nigeria and what the Butler hoped to see?', *English Historical Review*, CXX, 487: 577–92.

Moss, M. (2006) 'The function of the archives', in Tough, Alistair and Moss, Michael (eds), *Record Keeping in a Hybrid Evironment: Managing the Creation, Use, Preservation and Disposal of Unique Information Objects in Context*, Oxford: Chandos, pp. 227–43.

MySpace (2007) http://www.myspace.com/Modules/Common/Pages/AboutUs.aspx (February 2007).

Nicholas, D., Huntington P., Jamali, H.R. and Dobrowolski, T. (2007) 'Characterizing and evaluating information seeking behaviour in a digital environment: spotlight on the "bouncer"', *Information Processing and Management*, 43(4): 1085–102.

Nowotny, H. (2004) ' "Mode 2" revisited: the new production of knowledge', *Minerva*, 41(3): 179–94.

O'Neill, O. (2004) 'Accuracy, independence and trust', in W.G. Runciman (ed.), *Hutton and Butler, Lifting the Lid on the Workings of Power*, Oxford and New York: Oxford University Press for the British Academy, pp. 87–109.

Orlow, U. and Maclennan, R. (2005) *Re: The Archive, The Image, and the Very Dead Sheep*, London: The National Archives and the School of Advanced Studies.

Phillips M.E. (2003) Collecting Australian Online Publications, Canberra: National Library of Australia, http://pandora.nla.gov.au/selectionguidelinesall-partners.html (March 2007).

Power, M. (1994) *The Audit Explosion*, London: Demos.

Power, M. (1997) *Audit Society: Rituals and Verification*, Oxford: Oxford University Press.

Raymond, E. (1999) *The Cathedral and the Bazaar: Musings on Linux and Open Source by an Accidental Revolutionary,* Beijing and Cambridge, MA: O'Reilly.

Ross, S. (2006) 'Approaching digital preservation holistically', in Tough, Alistair and Moss, Michael (eds), *Record Keeping in a Hybrid Evironment: Managing the Creation, Use, Preservation and Disposal of Unique Information Objects in Context*, Oxford: Chandos, pp. 115–53.

Sawchuk, K. and Johnson, S. (2001) 'Editorial/Introduction', *Canadian Journal of Communication*, 26 (2), available at http://www.cjc-online.ca/viewarticle.php?id=636&layout=html, (August 2007).

Securities and Exchange Commission (2003) against – Henry McKelvey Blodget, http://www.sec.gov/litigation/complaints/comp18115b.htm (March).

Shore, C. and Wright, S. (2000) 'Coercive accountability', in Marilyn Strathern (ed.), *Audit Cultures: Anthropological Studies in Accountability, Ethics and the Academy*, London: Routledge, 57–89.

Spivak, G.C. (1987) 'Explanation and culture: marginalia', (1979) in *In Other Worlds: Essays in Cultural Politics*, (London: Methuen), pp. 103–17.

Strathern, M. (1997) 'Improving ratings: audit in the British university system', *European Review*, 5: 305–21.

Strathern, M. (2000) 'Abstraction and decontextualisation: an anthropological comment or: e for ethnography', available at http://virtualsociety.sbs.ox.ac.uk/GRpapers/strathern.htm (February 2007).

Strathern, M. (2004) *Commons and Borderlands: Working Papers on Interdisciplinarity, Accountability and the Flow of Knowledge*, Wantage: Sean Kingston Publishing.

Time Magazine (2006) 'Time Person of the Year: You', 25 December, 168 (26) http://www.time.com/time/magazine/article/0,9171,1569514,00.html (February 2008).

Tough, A. and Moss, M. (2003) 'Metadata, controlled vocabulary and directories: electronic document management and standards for records management', *Records Management Journal*, 13(1): 24–31.

USA Patriot Act and Intellectual Freedom (2007) Chicago: American Library Association, http://www.ala.org/ala/oif/ifissues/usapatriotact.htm (March).

Viégas, F.B., Wattenberg, M., Kriss, J. and Ham, F. van (2006) 'Talk before you type: coordination in Wikipedia', *Visual Communication Lab*, IBM Research, http://www.research.ibm.com/visual/papers/wikipedia_coordination_final.pdf (March 2007).

Wesch, M. (2007) 'YouTube R/evolution', available at http://www.youtube.com/watch?v=-4CV05HyAbM (October).

Wigand, J. (2005) 'Inside the mind of a tobacco whistle-blower: Jeffrey Wigand on the risks and rewards of telling the truth', 2 June, available at http://www.msnbc.msn.com/id/8077025/ (February 2007).

Winston, B. (2006) 'A future scenario of education as a result of the digital age', in Michael Beaudoin (ed.), *Perspectives on Higher Education in the Digital Age*, New York: Nova Science Publishers, Inc., pp. 277–92.

Yakel, E. and Torres, D.A. (2003) 'AI: archival intelligence and user expertise', *American Archivist*, 44 (1) (Spring, Summer): 51–78.

Yates, J. (1989) *Control Through Communication: The Rise of System in American Management*, Baltimore: Johns Hopkins University Press.

YouTube (2007) http://www.youtube.com/t/about (February).

24

Studying Processes in and Around Organizations

Ann Langley

This chapter examines a research strategy that takes the dynamics of evolving processes rather than the systems of relationships among variables as its primary focus. I begin with a discussion of what this means, and why it is important, and then examine some overarching choices and dilemmas raised by the approach, relating this to my own experience and to examples of published process research. Throughout, I draw on my previous writing (Langley, 1999, 2007) as well as that of others who have discussed process research methods for studying organizations (Van de Ven, 1992; Van de Ven and Poole, 2005; Pettigrew, 1990; Poole, Van de Ven, Dooley and Holmes, 2000; Tsoukas and Chia, 2002).

The nature of process research

Process research addresses dynamic questions about temporally evolving phenomena. Beyond this elementary idea, the definition of precisely what process research is or is not can sometimes seem rather muddy. I will not attempt to resolve all the ambiguity, as I believe that too much clarity would misrepresent the richness, eclecticism, and variety of research practice. However, I review here various taxonomies that try to establish the distinctive meaning and importance of studying process.

It was Mohr (1982) who introduced the distinction between 'variance' and 'process' theories. While variance theories provide explanations in terms of relationships among dependent and independent variables, process theories provide explanations in terms of patterns in events, activities, and choices over time. Thus, process theories look very different from the nomothetic variable-based conceptual frameworks that still dominate our journals. Unlike variance theories, process theories take sequence and ordering to be critical. An outcome is explained in terms of diachronic patterns in who does what when and what happens next, rather than in terms of the synchronic presence of higher or lower levels of specific attributes. Thus, according to Mohr (1982), process theories emphasize necessary causality rather than necessary and sufficient causality, because the impact of any event will depend on what precedes it and what follows it. In practice, process theories may take the form of deterministic phase sequences, but a variety of other forms are possible, including models with parallel paths, feedback loops, nondeterministic branch points, interactions and reversals. As Van de Ven (1992) notes, to warrant the label 'theory' a process conceptualization also needs to be grounded in some kind of underlying logic or generative mechanism that produces the temporal patterns described.

Beyond the variance/process theory distinction, the social science literature provides other conceptualizations of theoretical forms that are related to but not perfectly isomorphic to those proposed by Mohr (1982). For example, Bruner (1990, 1991) and Polkinghorne (1988) distinguished between 'narrative', and 'logico-scientific' or 'paradigmatic' forms of knowing. Paradigmatic knowing is driven by the norms of formal scientific and logical reasoning where generalizations are made about causal influences among variables (implying variance theory). Narrative knowing, on the other hand, incorporates temporal linkages between events over time, and is a form of knowing that is used to give meaning to particular events drawing on culturally embedded narrative structures (e.g., the comedy, the tragedy, the fairy story, the joke, the moral fable, or any kind of recognizable story that reveals an underlying message, plot, or point). Thus, Bruner (1990, 1991) and Polkinghorne (1988) take a more subjectivist and interpretive approach to temporally arranged explanations, something absent in Mohr's (1982) notion of process theory, where a largely positivist and realist understanding of process remains dominant.

Definitional issues about what process theory really means are also complicated by distinctions between those who adopt what has been called a 'weak' process view, where emphasis is placed on the change and development of existing entities, and a 'strong' process ontology grounded in the thinking of process philosophers such as Bergson (1946) and James (1996) where

things are considered to be subordinated to and constituted by processes (Chia and Langley, 2004; Van de Ven and Poole, 2005). For example, while adherents of the weak process view might look at organizational change in terms of movement from one state to another, a strong view would look at change in terms of the ongoing microprocesses that contribute to constituting and reproducing the organization as a stable entity (Tsoukas and Chia, 2002). My own empirical work would mostly be classified as of the first type. However, the second approach offers intriguing possibilities to which I will return.

Thus, the conceptual definition of process theory is sometimes contested. In addition, as I rediscovered in reflecting on my own work and in my reading to prepare this chapter, the practice of process research does not always fit the neat distinctions suggested by theorists and philosophers. For example, while Mohr (1982) insisted on the necessity of keeping process and variance understandings separate, empirical researchers often exhibit varying degrees of hybridity (see Deetz, Chapter 2 this volume). In particular, many excellent studies begin by collecting process-oriented data about temporally evolving phenomena, but end by generating variance-based theoretical formulations (Eisenhardt, 1989a; Ferlie et al., 2005; Maitlis, 2005). While the data may be longitudinal, the theorizing derived from it may not always be processual in the sense of deriving temporally ordered explanations.

A final ambiguity surrounds the degree to which quantitative causal models incorporating data collected at different points in time do or do not qualify as 'processual'. The denser and longer the chain of intermediary variables arranged over time, the closer this kind of variance model might come to representing sequential and dynamic processes. However, such models still have difficulty capturing alternate paths, probabilistic interactions, mutual influence, and feedback loops. Quantitative agent-based simulations and event-history models have a greater capability for dealing explicitly with these phenomena. However, the conceptual entities used in these models usually represent coarse-grained outcroppings of underlying processes that strip away rich narrative detail in order to make events directly comparable and amenable to statistical methods. The use of event-history methods in population ecology studies is considered elsewhere in this volume (Carroll et al., Chapter 13) and suggestions for studying quantitative event sequences and histories are provided by Monge (1990), Abbott (1990), and Poole et al. (2000). While recognizing the value of this type of work, my preference is to delve more deeply into the processes themselves rather than skimming over their surface.

The examples of process research in this chapter will, therefore, be drawn mainly from studies that aim to examine temporally evolving phenomena directly and in richer detail. This usually means qualitative methods. Specifically, data sources for the examples of process research described here involve some or all of the 'big three' of qualitative research: observation (participant or nonparticipant), interviewing (retrospective or real-time; individual or group) and archival documents (internal or external; public or private). These methods are known to have complementary strengths and weaknesses (Patton, 2002). From a temporal perspective, observations are embedded in the present, documents are embedded in the past, and interviews are temporally versatile in that respondents can draw on their memories and link phenomena across time. In terms of specific content, observations are useful for understanding evolving patterns of interaction and behaviour, documents are an important source of data on key event chronologies (and they often provide records of arguments and justifications), and interviews are again versatile – but their unique strength lies in the capacity to access the internal life of participants; interpretations, feelings, and beliefs. Finally, each source has its limitations. Observations are localized and ephemeral, and depend critically on the observer as instrument. Documents emphasize the 'official' truth, and tend to gloss over conflict and complexity. Interviews are artificial interactions that can be influenced by lapses of memory, impression management, the moods of the participants, and the quality of the rapport between interviewer and interviewee. However, they can be multiplied easily, providing different perspectives on temporally embedded phenomena.

In practice, most process research involves combinations of sources to access different dimensions and to ensure that limitations of one source are compensated for by the strengths of others. The important thing in process research is that the data somehow enable the incorporation of time and the capture of temporal evolution (Dawson, 1997). I will discuss later in more detail the specific choices associated with temporal orientation.

The need for process research

The next question concerns why one would be interested in process research. The simple answer is that, since time is an inescapable reality, process conceptualizations that take time into account offer an essential contribution to our understanding of the world that is unavailable from variance-based generalizations that tend to either ignore time completely, compress it into variables (describing decision making as fast or slow, or environments as dynamic or stable), or reduce its role to what Pettigrew et al. (2001) called 'comparative statics' (re-evaluating quantitative relationships at successive times).

In addition, process knowledge is also relevant to practice. Many of the field's established variance theories that relate practices or organizational characteristics to performance are not as easily actionable as they appear, precisely because they assume static equilibrium conditions and ignore temporal dynamics (March and Sutton, 1997; Meyer et al., 2005). For example, findings that firms with characteristic B generally perform better than those with characteristic A say nothing about how to go about moving from A to B. Moreover, substantial organizational changes aimed at moving towards B and capturing its predicted benefits generally take time and involve costs that are not and indeed cannot be easily included in cross-sectional models. Finally, action under complexity interacts with its context to generate reactions, with unexpected ramifications that are absent from static models.

At a more micro level of analysis, an interesting editor's forum in *Academy of Management Journal* discusses why established 'evidence-based' human resources (HR) management knowledge is not adopted by practitioners (Rynes, 2007a and b). The research findings discussed in the forum were almost all variance-based, and considerable commentary was devoted to strategies for improving their uptake. However, relatively little attention was devoted to process issues. Yet as Rynes (2007b: 1048) indicated in her concluding comments, 'The real world of HR managers is messy, complex and filled with human drama, making it unlikely that it can be completely understood using 'hands-off' methodologies such as surveys and archival analyses'. Process research that examines how changes in practices are implemented, and how their influence spreads and interacts with existing organizational contexts, offers to move closer towards a dynamic understanding of how to improve them. To achieve this, however, researchers need to get beyond a perspective that sees variance-based generalizations as the only legitimate basis for scientific advance and for practical prescription. This is not to suggest that variance-based research is not useful. On the contrary, the two approaches are complementary – even orthogonal in their contributions. Variance-based research helps us understand what works – on average – across large samples, something that process research cannot provide. And yet, without knowledge of process, variance knowledge is very hard to use: the how is missing.

In other words, more process studies are needed. Excellent process research is also attractive to readers, as suggested by its strong representation in the 'most interesting article in management' list in the *Academy of Management Journal* (Bartunek et al., 2006). However, process research and theorizing can be challenging to do well. In the next section, I explore some of its choices and challenges drawing on my own experience as well as published work. Given space limitations, I have avoided nitty-gritty issues of design, data collection, and analysis for which several other sources are available. For example, Langley (1999) describes seven strategies for process theorizing that are summarized in this chapter. Pettigrew (1990) offers advice on developing longitudinal case studies. Van de Ven and Poole (1990) describe a method for quantifying event data. Dawson (1997) offers advice on modes of data collection. *Organization Science* (1990, vol. 1, nos. 3 and 4) reports a special forum on longitudinal research methods. The *Scandinavian Journal of Management* (1997, vol. 13, no. 4) focuses on process research methods.

Here, I have chosen three key sets of issues that have caused me to reflect on my own research practice and that might find resonance with others. These issues – temporal orientation, conceptual product, and researcher perspective – concern choices that affect the nature of the knowledge that emerging from the research. In other words, they have epistemological implications. I begin the discussion with a brief review of my own process research experience, and then situate this with respect to other examples of process work.

Choices and challenges of process research

Most of my own research has focused on organizational-level processes, often extending over several years. For example, I have worked with Jean-Louis Denis, Lise Lamothe, Linda Rouleau, and others on a series of in-depth longitudinal studies of forms of strategic and organizational change in the health care sector (Denis et al., 1996, 2000, 2001, 2006; Rodriguez et al., 2007). This work continues, as we examine the implementation of network forms of organization. Previous studies focused on strategic decision making (Langley, 1989), the implementation of management tools (Lozeau et al., 2002), and innovation processes (Langley and Truax, 1994; Denis et al., 2002). In all cases, we collected empirical data on processes evolving through time. Many (though not all) of our resulting conceptual contributions explicitly incorporate temporal dynamics into their formulations, generating process theory more than variance theory. For example, our comparative study of five organizational change processes in hospitals led us to propose a process theory of the dynamics of collective leadership and strategic change in pluralistic settings. We argued that, while collective leadership is important for achieving change in such settings, it is fragile. We showed how the difficulties of simultaneously maintaining coupling between the leadership team and its organizational base, between the team and its environment, and between the members of the team themselves, leads to sporadic and cyclical change processes driven by the effects of leaders' actions on their political positions (Denis et al., 2001).

Time is ubiquitous, however, and process research may contribute at any level of analysis or to any type of temporally evolving phenomenon relevant to organizations. The study of professional identity construction among medical residents by Pratt et al. (2006) is a good example of research at the individual level, as is Isabella's (1990) award-winning interpretive study of the phases of sensemaking about change. Gersick's (1988, 1989) work on group processes is a classic example of a process study at the group-level. At an intermediary level, Feldman's (2000, 2004) ethnographic work contributed to the development of a dynamic conceptualization of the nature and role of organizational routines. At the organizational level, the long term research by Burgelman (1991, 1994, 2002; Burgelman and Grove, 2007) on the strategic evolution of Intel revealed the interaction between top-down and bottom-up strategy making. Finally, recent examples of process research at the inter-organizational or field level include Jacobides' (2005) study of the process of vertical disintegration among mortgage banks, and the prize-winning work by Greenwood and Suddaby (2006) on the process of institutional entrepreneurship in the accounting industry. The appropriate temporal windows for process studies may also vary from a few days, weeks, or months, as in the groups studied by Gersick (1988) to very long periods of time, as in Burgelman's seventeen year study of the ups and downs of Intel. At first sight, processes at more macrolevels of analysis, such as in the studies by Greenwood and Suddaby (2006) and Jacobides (2005), seem likely to demand longer windows than the study of microprocesses at group or individual levels. But this will depend on the natural rhythm of the phenomenon studied. For example, the individual-level study of identity among medical residents (Pratt et al., 2006) traced evolution over several years in consonance with the training cycle.

Process research can thus be relevant to a wide range of different topics and temporal horizons. Drawing on these and other examples, I now explore three sets of choices and challenges. A first critical but ubiquitous choice concerns temporal orientation.

Temporal orientation: Past, present, or future

Process researchers may study their phenomenon by tracing it backward into the past (historical, retrospective studies), by following it forward into the future (ethnography, longitudinal case studies), by examining how it is constituted, or by doing all of these at the same time. As Leonard-Barton (1990) indicates, these options generate important trade-offs.

Tracing back

One advantage of excavating the past is that the outcome is known in advance, and the researcher has an idea about what a process model will have to explain. This focuses the data collection effort onto precisely those elements that seem directly linked to the outcome. Indeed, the outcome may well be an important motive for the research. For example, spectacular unique events such as the space shuttle catastrophes (Vaughan, 1996; Starbuck and Farjoun, 2005), or the Enron debacle (Boje and Rosile, 2003; Stein, 2007; Fleming and Zyglidopoulos, 2007) demand explanations of a process or narrative kind.

However, outcomes may also be a source of inspiration at a more general level. For example, Jacobides (2005) was interested in how vertical disintegration and the creation of new markets occurred over time, and he therefore needed to start with an industry where this had happened. Similarly, Repenning and Sterman (2002) were interested in understanding the process patterns that differentiated successful from unsuccessful improvement projects. They followed Pettigrew's (1990) and Eisenhardt's (1989b) recommendations to sample polar types of projects that differentiated themselves in terms of outcomes.

Studying processes retrospectively also means economy in data collection. Real-time observation is time-consuming, both in terms of person-hours spent in the field as well as in terms of elapsed time (especially when the processes spread out over many years). As long as accurate temporal chronologies can be reconstructed from archival data and extensive interviewing, retrospective studies can be an efficient and effective approach. Indeed, some interesting process analyses of change have emerged from studies that were largely retrospective. For example, Isabella's (1990) study of how managers construe critical organizational events as they evolve is based on retrospective interviews, and the process study of the interaction among image, identity, and action at the New York Port Authority by Dutton and Dukerich (1991, another prize-winning paper) is based on archival data and retrospective interviewing. In a more recent example, a study of the emergence of an 'accidental' radical change in a mission church by Plowman et al. (2007) was based on twenty-two retrospective interviews and archival data. All these studies generated attractive dynamic models – a phase model of interpretation in the case of Isabella (1990), a model of the relationship between image and identity in the case of Dutton and Dukerich (1991), and a rare empirical illustration of complexity dynamics

from Plowman et al. (2007). In my own work, retrospective analysis has also played an important role. The relatively modest time investment required is also helpful in enabling replication across comparative cases.

Following forward

And yet, there is nothing quite like being there in real time. Observing processes in action and wondering what will happen next is a very different experience from sifting through archival traces and second-hand narratives that have become immutable and fixed. With real-time data, there is an immeasurable gain in the richness of temporal recording, particularly so when it comes to studying interactions among people, and to recording people's perceptions and understandings at different points in time. Retrospective accounts, especially of cognitions, are subject to important limitations of memory and rationalization (making event chains seem more logical than they were at the time: Schwenk, 1985; Golden, 1992). Moreover, there are occasions when following forward in real time is a natural choice. Rather than starting with known outcomes, the researcher has access to a major change initiative that is just beginning. Here is a golden opportunity to understand how the change will interact with its context and penetrate the organization. This is the motive that has driven much of my own research on organizational change.

Although real time analysis may be desirable, it can pose problems when the object of analysis is the organization as a whole, or a physically dispersed process that is hard to capture completely. The open-ended nature of longitudinal research can generate uncertainty, frustration, or a sense of there being considerable dross among the richness (see Leonard-Barton, 1990). Balogun et al. (2003) and Balogun and Johnson (2004) identify ways to overcome such data collection dilemmas in dispersed sites, including the innovative use of management diaries and regular focus groups.

Although the nature of real-time data may be richer and more detailed, most longitudinal process researchers have generally taken a perspective quite similar to that of retrospective researchers in analyzing their data; they have looked at it as a whole, and attempted to theorize about how the processes examined evolved up to the point where they left the field. Thus, while data collection is prospective, analysis tends to be retrospective.

Yet, research in real time may also enable researchers to see events in a way that is closer to that experienced by the participants on the scene, that is sensitive to uncertainty, to activity in the present, and to the very arbitrariness of the notion of 'outcome', where endings and beginnings often flow into each other (Weick, 1999). Researchers have perhaps not taken sufficient advantage of this opportunity. In doing longitudinal research, one might see shifts not only in the way other people construe situations, but also shifts in one's own theoretical interpretation as events unfold. Burgelman's (1991, 1994, 2002) successive studies of Intel are interesting, in part because they show how the author himself learned and enriched his process interpretations over time as his cumulative knowledge of the firm developed. Looking at data prospectively in a systematic way would require more continuous researcher documentation, not only of site data, but also of personal theorizing over the length of a project, preferably with successive outputs generated over time (placed in a sealed envelope for future consultation?) and reviewed as they change. In this vein, Bitektine (2008) has recently proposed prospective case studies as a systematic research approach.

Reconstituting the evolving present

These comments bring me back to an earlier ontological distinction between process research that considers evolution over time, and process research that views things being dynamically and continually reconstituted by ongoing processes. The second approach is labelled a 'strong' process view (Chia and Langley, 2004) and is related to the notion of 'becoming' (Tsoukas and Chia, 2002). Research that emphasizes the activities of people, and how these activities contribute to the creation of stable categories, comes

closest to reflecting this view. Examples include Feldman's (2000, 2004) studies of the recursive yet dynamic nature of organizational routines, and Barley's (1986, 1990) classic work on how structure is regenerated through ongoing interactions surrounding technology (in this case, through the conversations between radiologists and radiation technologists in examining rooms). Such studies involve real-time ethnographic research following processes forward over a fairly long period. Yet, because of the focus on reproduction and recursiveness inspired by structuration theory (Giddens, 1984), the heading 'reconstituting the evolving present' better reflects their overall temporal orientation.

Indeed, some intriguing ideas are emerging from research that takes categories and concepts that are usually considered as stable, and questioning their underlying stability. For example, 'identity' is one apparently stable concept that has been problematized in recent work (Gioia et al., 2000). The term 'identity work' has been coined to show how individuals discursively and interactively construct their identities (Pratt et al., 2006; Maguire and Hardy, 2005). Like Weick's (1979) call for greater emphasis on verbs, adding the word 'work' to any apparently static and structural concept is an interesting device for making it more dynamic, and for forcing consideration of how human agency might operate on it. For example, Lawrence and Suddaby (2006) introduce the term 'institutional work' to describe activities involved in creating, sustaining, and changing institutions. In this case, institutions that are usually taken to embed and constrain organizations and individuals, become objects of agency whose evolution is then described processually (Maguire et al., 2004; Greenwood and Suddaby, 2006).

Temporal orientation is thus one critical choice with pragmatic and conceptual implications. Retrospective studies can generate sharp process conceptualizations and may be particularly useful when researchers wish to compare cases, or when the level of analysis is so broad as to render real-time analysis difficult. Real-time process research is more challenging, but likely to lead to more precise temporal data and richer understandings. Finally, work that adopts a strong process ontology concerned with understanding how the stable categories of organization such as structure, culture, and strategy are constituted through activity, offers attractive opportunities for rethinking organizational theory in more dynamic terms.

Conceptual products: Patterns, mechanisms, or meanings

A range of strategies is available to assist in making sense of process data (Langley, 1999). These include composing case narratives, quantification of incidents, using alternate theoretical templates, grounded theorizing, visual mapping, temporal decomposition, and case comparisons. These are summarized in Table 24.1. The first two strategies lie at opposite poles of a continuum. The 'narrative' strategy involves the reconstitution of events into an extended verbal account or 'thick description' and is associated with ethnography (Van Maanen, 1988) or organizational history (Chandler, 1964). In contrast, in the 'quantification' strategy, processes are decomposed into microincidents that are coded into a limited number of categories which can then be analyzed using statistical methods (Van de Ven and Poole, 1990). The other strategies lie between these extremes. For example, the 'alternate templates' strategy involves the 'top-down' application of multiple a priori theoretical frames or lenses to the same process data base. In contrast, in the 'grounded theory' strategy, theory is derived by inductive bottom-up coding from the data rather than through top-down deduction based on a priori theory (Locke, 1997). The 'visual mapping' strategy involves the representation of processes using diagrams, tables, and other kinds of visual display (Miles and Huberman, 1994). Sensemaking can also be stimulated by various forms of comparison. For example, the 'temporal bracketing' strategy involves the generation of comparative units of analysis in the form of distinct time periods, as in Barley's (1986) study of structuring in radiology departments. The 'synthetic strategy' involves

the comparison of processes as wholes across different cases.

My purpose in this section is not, however, to elaborate on these strategies, but to focus on the different types of conceptual products which these and other approaches may generate.

Patterns

Process analysis often seeks to identify repetitive temporal patterns among activities and events. How are events ordered? What is the typical sequence of phases? Are there different paths and cycles through the phases? What are the branch points where different paths may diverge? How are phases and activities interconnected? Examples of process research focusing on temporal patterns include the classic studies of decision making that plot phases and subroutines (Mintzberg et al., 1976; Nutt, 1984). My work with Jean Truax on technology adoption that involved detailed flow charting (Langley and Truax, 1994) also focused on common patterns in the evolution of events, illustrating the use of visual mapping for pattern detection. More recent work presenting process patterns includes James and Wooten's (2006) study of how firms handle discrimination lawsuits where a series of sequential paths are identified and associated with different forms of discrimination.

Gersick's (1988) study of group processes provides another classic example, as the task groups she studied all followed a common process pattern. At the temporal mid-point of their discussions, they all underwent a radical shift, moving from an initial stable template of behaviour in their task approach to a new template that carried them through to the end. Gersick's initial study with eight naturally occurring groups was subsequently replicated on eight experimental laboratory groups generating similar findings (Gersick, 1989). Here was a robust empirical process pattern that forms the foundation for an interesting and novel contribution to knowledge about group processes.

And yet, as Gersick (1992) notes in a refreshingly reflexive piece on the initial

Table 24.1 Seven strategies for sensemaking from process data (Adapted from Langley, 1999)

Strategy	Description	Exemplars	Strengths	Weaknesses	Specific data needs	Conceptual products
Narrative strategy	Reconstitution of events into an extended verbal account or 'thick description'.	Chandler (1964); Pettigrew (1985); Dawson (2004)	Enables accounts that reflect ambiguity and nuance. Offers insight based on sense of familiarity. Often useful as an initial step in analysis.	Narratives may read as descriptive, particularistic and hard to generalize. Not always easy to generate a clear conceptual contribution.	One or a few rich cases. Can be helped by comparison.	Meanings Mechanisms
Quantification strategy	Coding of events into quantitative categories analyzed using statistical methods.	Garud and Van de Ven (1992); Van de Ven and Poole (1990)	Enables testing of relationships among temporal phenomena to produce general models.	Forces simplification of complex data into the abstract categories needed to allow statistical treatment. Loss of richness.	Needs many similar events for statistical analysis: one or a few dense cases is best.	Patterns Mechanisms
Alternate templates strategy	Confronting data with several theoretical frames to produce multiple narratives or test alternate theories.	Allison (1971); Lapointe and Rivard (2005)	Different lenses may generate different insights providing a more complete explanation. Or, multiple lenses may enable the rejection of less accurate theories.	It may be difficult to integrate the insights from different theoretical lenses without loss of parsimony.	One case is enough. Degrees of freedom come from multiple templates.	Mechanisms Meanings
Grounded theory strategy	Deriving theoretical insight from detailed coding of incidents and relationships among emerging categories.	Isabella (1990); Gersick (1988); Pratt et al. (2006)	Generates theory that is closely and deeply connected to concrete observed phenomena.	A bottom-up process that can result in a very locally valid theory. Sometimes one may miss the forest through detailed focus on the trees.	Needs detail on many similar incidences; different processes or individual-level analysis of one case.	Meanings Patterns Mechanisms
Visual mapping strategy	Representation of processes using diagrams, tables and other visual displays.	Langley & Truax (1994); James and Wooten (2006)	Deals well with time, relationships. Enables the representation of large amounts of data parsimoniously while retaining some richness.	Cannot capture certain types of data well (emotions, subtle ambiguous phenomena). Attends to surface patterns more than deep explanations.	Needs several cases in moderate level of detail to begin generating patterns (5–10 or more).	Patterns
Temporal bracketing strategy	Generating units of analysis in the form of time periods or phases for which data are compared.	Barley (1986); Denis et al. (1996)	Enables study of structuration processes in which actions from one period contribute to modifying the structures affecting actions in future.	Determining transition points in temporal evolution is critical to using this strategy. Clear temporal breakpoints may not always exist.	One or two detailed cases are sufficient if processes have several phases used for replication.	Mechanisms
Synthetic strategy	Comparing processes as wholes across cases to detect similarities and differences.	Eisenhardt (1989); Maitlis (2005)	A useful strategy for detecting common features in processes and for understanding differences and their antecedents or consequences.	Needs clear process boundaries. Tends to compress processes into variables. May result in variance theory, not process theory.	Needs enough cases (5+) to generate convincing relationships. Moderate level of detail needed.	Patterns Predictions (variance models)

study that formed the basis for her doctoral thesis, something is missing in this picture. Her thesis supervisor was dissatisfied when she presented her preliminary results. The first version of her award-winning paper was rejected by a major journal. The process patterns that she discovered did not have a strong theoretical grounding, a mechanism that would explain their extraordinary empirical regularity. She then found an appropriate frame in punctuated equilibrium theory, and developed an integrative theoretical paper showing how that perspective explains phenomena at a variety of different levels (Gersick, 1991).

In doing process research, detecting patterns is useful step, but it may not be enough. An empirically observed temporal pattern has a similar status to an empirically observed correlation. Without explanation, it is incomplete. The pattern needs some underlying logic that enables the reader to understand why progression through phases would occur in precisely this way. This is where 'mechanisms' complement process patterns.

Mechanisms

Based on an exhaustive survey of research on development and change in a variety of disciplines, Van de Ven and Poole (1995) identified four basic generative mechanisms that they suggest cover the range of theoretical motors used to explain change, either alone or in combination. These motors are labelled life cycle mechanisms (based on the idea of genetic predetermination), teleological mechanisms (based on goal driven behaviours and learning), dialectical mechanisms (based on cycles of confrontation and resolution among opposing forces), and evolutionary mechanisms (based on the processes of variation, selection, and retention). The idea of generative motors or mechanisms derives from a realist ontology in which it is believed that underlying causal mechanisms that cannot be directly observed interact to produce empirically observed phenomena (Tsoukas, 1989; Hedström and Swedberg, 1998; Reed, Chapter 25, and Ackroyd, chapter 31 this volume).

The motors identified by Van de Ven and Poole (1995) offer promising templates for generating process understandings about change. As illustrated by Gersick's (1991) review of the punctuated equilibrium model, there are often commonalities in how processes at different levels of analysis reveal the action of similar mechanisms. In the examples discussed here, contradiction is often identified as a motor for change, suggesting the action of a dialectical mechanism. Our studies of the dynamics of collective leadership in hospitals focused on tensions between demands from the organization and the environment in generating cyclical change processes (Denis et al., 2001). In the study of identity construction among medical students, at the individual level, by Pratt et al. (2006), the discrepancy between work activities and identity (work-identity integrity assessments) is shown to stimulate adaptation. Finally, contradiction also plays an important role in stimulating change in the study by Greenwood and Suddaby (2006) of institutional entrepreneurship in mature fields (Seo and Creed, 2002).

While the four mechanisms suggested by Van de Ven and Poole (1995) provide a useful starting point, it is hard to see them as exhaustive, despite the claims of the authors. I think of them as sensitizing devices, among others, that can be tried out in attempting to understand empirical processes. Other sensitizing devices, that may or may not be reducible to the four motors, include more integrated metatheoretical frames that are inherently processual, such as structuration theory (Giddens, 1984), actor-network theory (Latour, 2005), activity theory (Engeström, 1987), sensemaking theory (Weick, 1995), and complexity theory (Stacey, 1999). In a book intended for novice researchers, Abbott (2004) proposes a set of 'heuristics' for generating theoretical ideas, drawing on the work of philosophers including Aristotle, Kant, and Burke, and exploring a variety of devices for stimulating theoretical creativity. Feldman (1995, 2004) describes four strategies based on ethnomethodology, semiotics, dramaturgy, and deconstruction that she uses to help see her data in new ways. The conceptual paradigms proposed by grounded theorists (Locke, 1997) constitute yet another set of heuristic sensitizing tools. One of these paradigms is more specifically oriented towards process formulations (Strauss and Corbin, 1990; Goulding, Chapter 22 this volume.

These ideas draw attention to the nature of the conceptual work of process researchers who are not in the business of hypothesis-testing (deduction), but who aim to reach beyond the detection of common surface patterns (induction) to develop plausible explanations for temporal dynamics. This is a partly creative process that is hard to pin down, although it can be assisted by the sensitizing devices described in the previous paragraph or by the heuristic use of the analytic strategies that I proposed previously (Langley, 1999). Following the work of Charles Pierce, Locke et al. (2008) refer to this process as abduction and offer some conditioning principles that might help stimulate it. These include amplifying engagement with the phenomenon, permissively exploring possibilities (where sensitizing concepts and theorizing strategies may assist), and selecting and shaping emerging ideas.

The most impressive process research delights the reader, both by the clarity and insightfulness of its theoretical explanation, and by the degree to which its empirical grounding is convincing. A good deal of systematic analysis and verification usually lies behind such work. And yet, paradoxically, generating process theory is a creative bridging process between data and theory that is hard to programme fully according to a set of formal procedures. In excellent articles, we admire the elegant way in which theoretical and empirical stories are constructed and inter-connected (Golden-Biddle and Locke, 2006), and yet the process of arriving at those connections remains mysterious. The notion of 'mechanism' captures the elements of explanation that process theorists mobilize, and yet the word does not necessarily reflect the interpretive and creative nature of

what they are doing as they construct their accounts, however plausible. It is notable that Golden-Biddle and Locke (2006) use the term 'story' to refer to the elements of qualitative articles. This brings us to another way of considering the potential conceptual contributions of process research.

Meanings

There are several ways in which the products of process research can reflect meanings instead of, or as well as, patterns or mechanisms. At one level, many process studies take the meanings or interpretations of individuals as both their raw material and their primary object. Isabella's (1990) study of how individuals construe change events as they evolve is a typical example. The author is not interested in the objective features of these events but in what they meant to people and how this changed over time. Similarly, in their studies of identity, Dutton and Dukerich (1991) and Pratt et al. (2006), are interested in how cognitive categories such as identity evolve and how they are affected by issues and actions. Their theorizations reflect the interpretations of the people they interviewed, although the researchers' own interpretations of process patterns and mechanisms driving change are also evident.

Another way in which the products of process research can emphasize meanings is when researchers give room to multiple and competing narratives of processes. Buchanan and Dawson (2007) suggest four different ways of managing conflicting narratives in process research: normative process theory (eliminating all but a single prescriptive management story), interpretive process theory (revealing multiple stories), critical process theory (giving voice to the silenced), and dialogic process theory (emphasizing fragmentation and incoherence). Their arguments suggest a need for more intensive use of narrative methods in which individuals' or groups' stories are recognized and become the object of analysis (see also Pentland, 1999; Rhodes and Brown, 2005). My assessment is that many process researchers do incorporate the divergent understandings of different groups (Balogun and Johnson, 2004; Denis et al., 2001; Feldman, 2004), but that they usually integrate these observations into a single researcher-based interpretation that encapsulates conflict of various kinds into its theoretical apparatus.

An alternative route is for process researchers to recognize explicitly the contestable nature of their interpretations, and to consider the possibility of multiple narratives or explanations – the 'alternate templates' strategy (Table 24.1). Allison's (1971) study of the Cuban missile crisis, in which he generated three different narratives for the events based on three different theories of decision making (rational actor, organizational process, and political), is an instructive classic that has rarely been repeated so successfully. However, there are other interesting attempts. For example, Lapointe and Rivard (2007) examined the distinctive contributions of three theoretical perspectives on resistance to new information technology adoption in hospitals. Mahring et al. (2004) used actor-network and escalation theories to generate two different narratives of an information technology failure at the Denver International Airport. Sloan (2005) mobilized four different theories of strategic management to develop four parallel narratives of strategy development in high technology manufacturing.

Using narrative theory directly, Boje and Rosile (2003) critically examine alternative published interpretations and explanations of the Enron meltdown. They show how the Enron story has usually been constructed as a 'tragedy' – a narrative with a particular plot structure that places 'key central agents and victims in situations in which their fortune is reversed and spectators get a cathartic lesson' (Boje and Rosile, 2003: 89). Based on Aristotelian definitions, the tragic narrative follows a simple storyline that is tightly coherent and ignores secondary elements to move the plot forward. The authors contrast the structure of this story with an 'epic' narrative of the Enron case, which has a more scattered structure involving a plurality of interacting plots and no central coherence (see Brown and Humphreys, 2003). Through this comparison, they show how the tragic narrative tends to constrain inquiry, absolving observers from blame but scapegoating the protagonists, while the epic narrative opens it up, leading in many directions and bringing in contextual elements that are connected in imprecise, chaotic and nonconvergent ways. The critical dramaturgical analysis of Boje and Rosile (2003) is a form of process theorizing that emphasizes meaning rather than patterns or mechanisms. Its value lies in showing how the narratives developed to explain particular phenomena can have political implications. The theoretical products of researchers could also be subject to this kind of story-based analysis. Indeed, the story metaphor that Golden-Biddle and Locke (2006) advocate for qualitative writing invites more attention to the structure and latent meanings of researchers' stories.

In summary, the contributions of process researchers take a variety of different forms. At the most basic level, process research often involves the search for empirical regularities or patterns in event sequences. However, descriptive surface patterns do not generally provide rich understanding on their own. Thus, researchers will look for underlying mechanisms or combinations of mechanisms that make process sequences more understandable. Sensitizing concepts may come from a variety of sources, but the abductive process of connecting data and theory often requires creative insight. Finally, the contributions of process research can also be viewed as meanings, sometimes reflecting the interpretations of respondents, or alternatively recognizing the researcher's own interpretive processes.

Researcher perspective: Site relationships and academic careers

This section moves away from the rather detached analysis of the previous sections to focus on two different but more personal and relational issues of doing process research. First, I consider relationships with research sites. Then, I consider issues of integrating process research into a viable academic career.

Site relationships: Access, ethics, neutrality, and engagement

Process research often requires researchers to collect rich data *in situ*. This raises pragmatic and ethical questions that are not always addressed in published articles. What kinds of arrangements are made with research sites to enable the research to proceed? How does the positioning of the researcher within the site affect the nature of the data obtained and the interpretations presented? How are questions of confidentiality and consent managed when publishing results?

In approaching organizations, a range of espoused researcher roles are conceivable, ranging from neutral scientist to action researcher or consultant. In our work, we attempt to position ourselves as empathetic but nonparticipant observers in a belief that more direct involvement might be problematic for the integrity of the data and our interpretation of it. We hope that our research will prove stimulating and useful for those who participate in it, and we welcome the opportunity to provide feedback, but we resist offering direct advice or assistance. This stance is viable for us, in part because most of our work is financed by research agencies, not the participating organizations, and because our public sector sites are generally open to research and welcome the opportunities for reflection it provides. Nevertheless, we regularly encounter dilemmas surrounding this positioning. Should a member of the team accept an invitation to be on a panel at a local professional conference where the research site is being discussed? Should a researcher accept an invitation to conduct a training seminar in the organization on a different topic? How does a researcher's involvement as a Board member of another local organization affect the research? Such issues involve the research team in constant reflection and discussion.

Clearly, access to process data usually requires some form of reciprocity between the organization and the research team (Pettigrew, 1990, 1992; Feldman et al., 2003) as well as a degree of trust. In some contexts, host organizations may require more substantive

contributions than those we offer, especially when there is some financial investment on the part of the organization. Reciprocally, for some researchers, the benefits that can be returned to the organization are not simply a price of access, but also an important responsibility given the time and effort required from organization members and the relevance of the knowledge base that academics may have acquired in previous research and consulting. For example, Bate et al. (2000) actively assisted a host organization manage a cultural change they studied and used their own interventions as a basis for generating knowledge in a form of action research. This is a different stance from ours, and closer to organization development.

Others have argued that research should ideally be collaborative; that neither researchers nor organization members have a monopoly on the development of knowledge and that, in some areas, practitioners have a clear advantage (Balogun et al., 2003; Reason, 1994). From this perspective, better and more relevant research will be done when both work together. Such a stance promotes access but allows organization members a more important role in defining and answering research questions. It may also mean that direct application rather than broader knowledge production is the more important objective of the team. Finally, in an interesting hybrid form of action research, Huxham and Vangen (2003) have drawn on data that they collected in the context of consulting and training mandates to theorize about different issues (e.g., the dynamics of inter-organizational partnerships).

Trade-offs between the quality of access and researcher independence underlie these choices. A researcher who is rigidly 'neutral' may miss out on important information that could be obtained by more active involvement. On the other hand, close participation may make the researcher more vulnerable to issues of reactivity (changing what happens on the research site), 'going native', and political alignment. In their study of strategy making processes in a university, Gioia and Chittipeddi (1991) used an interesting 'insider-outsider' approach to manage this trade-off; while one of the researchers was employed as a junior member of the strategy making team with exceptional real-time access to strategic management processes, the other was not involved directly and participated in a more neutral way. The combination of perspectives contributes to the credibility of this research.

Relationships with research sites in process studies also raise important ethical issues. Some of the data may be sensitive, and research participants may be identifiable by others in their organization, even if the research report anonymizes organizational and individual names. To obtain access, researchers must provide a degree of confidentiality and protection to their respondents. And yet, as researchers, their duty is also to report on what they see to the extent that it can improve learning about the phenomenon studied. This issue is rarely openly discussed, but it is inevitable that reporting is affected by the need for confidentiality, and most importantly by the commitment to avoid harm to people who willingly and trustingly gave their time to the researchers. Thus, there are things that a process researcher may want to say in an article or a report that they cannot easily reveal. Strategies to assist in these dilemmas may include inviting comment from research participants, fictionalizing contexts, disguising authorship of quotations, presenting data from multiple organizations so that the source cannot be traced, and avoiding sensitive topics. Researchers can only do their best to provide faithful interpretations while respecting those who contributed to them.

In summary, the delicate choices that process researchers need to make concerning how they relate to research sites are perhaps more important than is often recognized for the nature of the process knowledge that is produced.

Academic careers: Start early, accumulate, and collaborate

At first sight, it may seem that process research does not fit well with the standard academic career path that is usually organized around short-term projects entrained to tenure milestones and granting agency schedules. In this section, I reflect on how developing a career around a process research perspective can nevertheless work, arguing that starting early from a solid base, accumulating data and ideas over time, and building on collaborative relationships with fellow researchers and students can be enabling factors that also generate interesting research.

In conferences, doctoral consortia and other forums, I have often seen faculty members advise doctoral students not to consider investing in qualitative studies for their doctoral theses (and in particular in process research) because of the time investment required, as well as the supposed difficulty in publication. The message often is: you can do that later, preferably when you are tenured. Yet my own experience is that it was during my doctoral studies when I did not have a myriad other commitments that I felt myself most able to master everything needed to do quality work alone. Moreover, I see many strong examples of published process research emerging from doctoral theses, and very few people moving into it after tenure!

The time to start is early. Senior scholars need to encourage junior colleagues and students to become involved in process research, while providing the training and support needed to do it well. The pragmatics are not unmanageable. As I noted, retrospective studies or studies of microprocesses may not require long-term investment. Moreover, faculty with longitudinal research programmes can integrate students into them, sharing data if necessary. Students can also begin their empirical research earlier than usual in their doctoral programmes. For example, Quy Huy from INSEAD began collecting data for his thesis on emotions and strategic change almost the day he entered the doctoral programme at McGill University. As shown by the number of excellent published process studies based on doctoral theses, process research is not incompatible with early publication and a successful career (Gersick, 1988; Corley and Gioia, 2004; Howard-Grenville, 2005). Then, once the ball is rolling, process research and process research careers can be cumulative. Indeed, there is a lot to be said for not thinking too strongly in terms of distinct 'projects,' but looking at what one does as a researcher as programmatic – as a stream of data collection, analysis and insights, punctuated by research outputs, but where learning is cumulative and continuous, and where theoretical ideas and cumulated research materials on similar issues can feed off one another in synergistic and indeed sometimes unexpected ways.

One way this may happen is by combining data from successive research initiatives to generate stronger contributions that would not have been possible otherwise. Such replication may be planned or opportunistic. For example, Daniel Lozeau, Jean-Louis Denis and I accumulated data from four studies at different points in time (including my 1987 doctoral thesis) to look at the dynamics of penetration of two different management tools in the same organizational context several years apart (Lozeau et al., 2002). Ravasi and Schultz (2006) discovered that they had each separately acquired data from three identity change initiatives at Bang and Olufsen, a Danish producer of audiovisual systems, at different times and were able to pool these to develop a longitudinal perspective on identity change that neither could have accomplished alone.

Accumulation might also simply mean considering how a theoretical frame from one domain of research might be adapted to another. For example, the dialectic theoretical concepts we used in the study of managerial tools were partly inspired by the models we had investigated for an entirely different topic – the integration of a new leader (Denis et al., 2000). Reciprocally, accumulation means considering how different conceptual or empirical angles might be relevant to the same context, generating different research outputs at different points in time as more data emerge. Thus, in work that is still continuing, we have been viewing different facets of data on hospital mergers using frameworks related to decision making, to group identity, to the management of paradox,

and to management fashions. Sally Maitlis and colleagues considered her data on decision making in three British symphony orchestras in several different ways, focusing on the dynamics of strategy failure in one study (Maitlis and Lawrence, 2003), on toxic decision making in a second (Maitlis and Ozcelik, 2004), and on sensemaking (Maitlis, 2005) and sensegiving (Maitlis and Lawrence, 2007) in two others.

A number of conditions are necessary for an accumulative approach to work well as a long term career strategy, however. The first requirement is always to collect rich data. Qualitative data are to some extent multivocal; if looked at from a different angle, they may speak to a range of theoretical issues beyond those that inspired their collection, but for this to be possible they must provide deep coverage of the focal situation. A second requirement is that one's research should have a degree of thematic unity. I have essentially focused on four broad types of inter-related substantive topics in my career; decision making, the use of management tools, strategic change, and innovation. Much of this work has occurred in the healthcare context, although other types of organizations have been involved too. There are several sources of longitudinal continuity and possible inter-site comparisons.

Finally, another requirement is that the researcher be exposed to constant sources of variety and renewal that stimulate new modes of thinking about the same and different data – these may include conferences, reading, students, practitioners, and research colleagues. This emphasizes another key enabling factor for a successful long-term career doing process research, collaboration, and teamwork. This becomes necessary as the demands of intensive fieldwork become harder to fit into a busy faculty member's schedule. However, working with colleagues and students is another kind of enrichment that enables transition to the next generation, completing the cycle. Framing career patterns in this way helps to make process research a more attractive alternative while potentially contributing to better research.

Trustworthiness of process research

I have reviewed several choices and challenges of process research. Before closing I would like to address an important issue that underlies all these choices; the validity or trustworthiness of process research accounts. The preceding discussion has raised several potential problems. For example, research that involves tracing back or analyzing past processes raises issues of hindsight bias (Golden, 1992). Moreover, the debate between viewing conceptual products as patterns, mechanisms, or meanings raises the possibility that the same events may give rise to multiple accounts – how then can each be judged? Finally, the discussion of researcher perspective clearly reveals the dilemmas associated with direct involvement in processes, raising issues of reactivity and completeness in reporting. Beyond these potential biases, the impossibility of presenting more than a limited amount of the data in an article-length contribution enhances the challenge of credibility. Indeed, book-length accounts such as those of Pettigrew (1985) and Dawson (2003) on change, Allison (1971) on the Cuban missile crisis, and Vaughan (1996) on the Challenger disaster may provide a more satisfactory option for communicating process research.

Nevertheless, the best process-based articles succeed in generating strong and believable accounts. At least four elements contribute to communicating credibility and trustworthiness. A first requirement is that researchers do everything they can in terms of methodological rigour to ensure that their accounts are accurate and that their interpretations are reasonable. Thus, the use of multiple researchers, the determined pursuit of relevant data, triangulation of multiple sources, the validation of interpretations with members of the research site, the systematic organization of a research database, the recording of all steps of analysis, and the explicit recognition of any biases, will all be helpful. Moreover, the explicit documentation of methodological procedures will in itself contribute to the credibility and trustworthiness of the research (Golden-Biddle and Locke, 1993).

A second strategy that can enhance trustworthiness in research articles involves the inclusion of large amounts of original textual data, offering corroborative detail for the proposed conceptualization as well as particularistic stories that convince the reader that the authors had close access to research sites, something that Golden-Biddle and Locke (1993) refer to as a sense of 'authenticity'. An example of this attention to detail is Corley and Gioia's (2004) study of identity evolution after a spinoff. The paper includes a particularly dense tabular display that includes interview quotations supporting all the theoretical points derived from multiple sources. Another display illustrates the data coding procedure. Finally, extensive quotations support the argument in the text of the paper itself. Interestingly, there seems to be no duplication between the quotations in the text and the tabular displays. The reader comes away convinced. Most of the process-based papers published in the major journals incorporate extensive amounts of original data presented in tabular displays, and papers also tend to be rather long.

A complementary strategy involves finding reliable ways to classify processes using quantitative or categorical codes, perhaps including graphical representations to reduce the data and pin down process patterns. For example, Barley (1986) counted the frequency of different types of scripts surrounding radiology examinations and this enabled him to render his process account credible, despite the fact that he included only relatively small snippets of the original field notes in his text. This approach economizes and systematizes data presentation. Ideally, this type of coding will have been subjected to validation by multiple researchers. There is, however, an interesting trade-off between this and the previous strategy. Process studies that lose too much richness may be less credible.

A fourth approach – not available to all, and thus of secondary importance in most cases – is to reference extensively sources as in a historical account. There are distinct advantages in terms of verifiability and replicability of being able to do this. For example, the study of the interaction between innovations and institutions by Hargadon and Douglas (2001) drew largely on public sources, enabling other researchers to replicate their analysis. A somewhat less open strategy would be to name research sites even though some of the data might be private. In their study of the emergence of the Nouvelle Cuisine movement in France, Rao et al. (2003) documented the names of chefs and the dates of interviews with them in their paper alongside quotations from the interviews. Again, such in-depth documentation is difficult given confidentiality considerations, but it is something that might be more widely considered given its potential advantages.

CONCLUSION

This chapter has reviewed a research strategy that focuses on processes rather than variables. Key choices associated with this strategy were examined and their potential impact on the nature of process knowledge was discussed. Interested readers are invited to pursue their exploration of this topic by consulting the many other resources available in the literature (Barley, 1990; Langley, 1999; Van de Ven, 1992; Poole et al., 2000; Pettigrew, 1990, 1992; Pentland, 1999), as well as to review the cited exemplars of process research. I hope that I have provided a flavour of what process research means and why it is important. Organization theory needs to become more dynamic because organizations are dynamic. We cannot hope to act on them successfully equipped only with static theories.

ACKNOWLEDGEMENTS

I would like to thank the editors of this volume as well as Royston Greenwood and Patrick Dawson for their helpful comments during the preparation of this paper. I am also grateful to the Social Sciences and Humanities Research Council of Canada and the Fonds québécois de recherché sur la société et la culture for their support of this research.

REFERENCES

Abbott, A. (1990) 'A primer on sequence methods', *Organization Science*, 1(4): 375–92.

Abbott, A. (2004) *Methods of Discovery*, New York: W.W. Norton and Company.

Allison, G.T. (1971) *Essence of Decision*, Boston, MA: Little-Brown.

Balogun, J. and Johnson, G. (2004) 'Organizational restructuring and middle manager sensemaking', *Academy of Management Journal*, 47(4): 523–49.

Balogun, J., Huff, A. and P. Johnson, P. (2003) 'Three responses to the methodological challenges of studying strategizing', *Journal of Management Studies*, 40(1): 197–224.

Barley, S.R. (1986) 'Technology as an occasion for structuring: evidence from observations of CT scanners and the social order of radiology departments', *Administrative Science Quarterly*, 31: 78–108.

Barley, S. (1990) 'Images of imaging: notes on doing longitudinal fieldwork', *Organization Science*, 1(2): 220–47.

Bartunek, J.M., Rynes, S. and Ireland, R.D. (2006) 'What makes management research interesting, and why does it matter?', *Academy of Management Journal*, 49(1): 9–15.

Bate S.P, Khan R and Pye A. (2000) 'Towards a culturally sensitive approach to organisation structuring: where organisation design meets organisation development', *Organization Science*, 11(2): 197–211.

Bergson, H. (1946) *The Creative Mind*, New York: Carol Publishing Group.

Bitektine, A. (2008) 'Prospective case study design: qualitative method for deductive theory testing', *Organizational Research Methods*, 11(1): 160–80.

Boje, D. and Rosile, G.A. (2003) 'Life imitates art: Enron's epic and tragic narration', *Management Communication Quarterly*, 17(1): 85–125.

Brown, A.D. and Humphreys, M. (2003) 'Epic and tragic tales: making sense of change', *Journal of Applied Behavioral Science*, 39(2): 121–44.

Bruner, J. (1990) *Acts of Meaning*, Cambridge, MA: Harvard University Press.

Bruner, J. (1991) 'The narrative construction of reality', *Critical Thinking*, 18: 1–21.

Buchanan, D. and Dawson, P. (2007) 'Discourse and audience: organizational change as a multi-story process', *Journal of Management Studies*, 44(5): 669–86.

Burgelman, R.A. (1991) 'Intraorganizational ecology of strategy making and organizational adaptation: theory and field research', *Organization Science*, 2(3): 239–42.

Burgelman, R.A. (1994) 'Fading memories: a process theory of strategic business exit in dynamic environments', *Administrative Science Quarterly*, 39(1): 24–56.

Burgelman, R.A. (2002) 'Strategy as vector and the inertia of coevolutionary lock-in', *Administrative Science Quarterly*, 47(2): 325–57.

Burgelman, R.A. and Grove, A.S. (2007) 'Let chaos reign, then rein in chaos – repeatedly: managing strategic dynamics for corporate longevity', *Strategic Management Journal*, 28(10): 965–80.

Chandler, A.D. (1964) *Strategy and Structure*, Cambridge, MA: MIT Press.

Chia, R. and Langley, A. (2004) 'The First Organization Studies summer workshop: theorizing process in organizational research (call for papers)', *Organization Studies*, 25(8): 1486.

Corley, K.G. and Gioia, D.A. (2004) 'Identity ambiguity and change in the wake of a corporate spin-off', *Administrative Science Quarterly*, 49(2): 173–208.

Dawson, P. (1997) 'In at the deep end: conducting processual research on organizational change', *Scandinavian Journal of Management*, 13(4): 389–405.

Dawson, P. (2003) *Reshaping Change: A Processual Approach*, London: Routledge.

Denis, J.-L., Hébert, Y., Langley, A., Lozeau, D. and Trottier, L.-H. (2002) 'Explaining diffusion patterns for complex health care innovations', *Health Care Management Review*, 27(3): 60–73.

Denis, J.-L., Langley, A. and Cazale, L. (1996) 'Leadership and strategic change under ambiguity', *Organization Studies*, 17(4): 673–99.

Denis, J.-L., Langley, A. and Pineault, M. (2000) 'Becoming a leader in a complex organization', *Journal of Management Studies*, 37(8): 1063–99.

Denis, J.-L., Lamothe, L. and Langley, A. (2001) 'The dynamics of collective leadership and strategic change in pluralistic organizations', *Academy of Management Journal*, 44(4): 809–37.

Denis, J.-L., Langley, A., Rouleau, L. (2006) 'The power of numbers in strategizing', *Strategic Organization*, 4(4): 349–377.

Doolin, B. (2003) 'Narratives of change: discourse, technology and organization', *Organization*, 10(4): 751–70.

Dutton, J.E. and Dukerich, J.M. (1991) 'Keeping an eye on the mirror: image and identity in organizational adaptation', *Academy of Management Journal*, 34(3), 517–54.

Eisenhardt, K.M. (1989a) 'Making fast strategic decisions in high velocity environments', *Academy of Management Journal*, 31(4): 543–76.

Eisenhardt, K.M. (1989b) 'Building theories from case study research', *Academy of Management Review*, 14(4): 532–50.

Engeström, Y. (1987) *Learning by Expanding: An Activity Theoretical Approach to Developmental Research*, Helsinki: Orienta-Konsultit.

Feldman, M.S. (1995) *Strategies for Interpreting Qualitative Data*, Sage: Thousand Oaks.

Feldman, M.S. (2000) 'Organizational routines as a source of continuous change', *Organization Science*, 11(6): 611–29.

Feldman, M.S., Bell, J. and Berger, M.T. (2003) *Gaining Access*, Walnut Creek, CA: Altamira Press.

Feldman, M.S. (2004) 'Resources in emerging structures and processes of change', *Organization Science*, 15(3): 295–309.

Ferlie, E., Fitzgerald, L., Wood, M. and Hawkins, C. (2005) 'The nonspread of innovations: The mediating role of professionals', *Academy of Management Journal*, 48(1): 117–34.

Fleming, P.J. and Zyglidopoulos, S.C. (2007) The escalation of deception in organizations. *Journal of Business Ethics*, (published on line 24 August 2007: http://www.springerlink.com/content/71241t2535418667/.

Garud, R. and Van de Ven, A.H. (1992) 'An empirical evaluation of the internal corporate venturing process', *Strategic Management Journal*, 13 (special issue): 93–109.

Gersick, C.J.G. (1988) 'Time and transition in work teams: toward a new model of group development', *Academy of Management Journal*, 31(1): 9–41.

Gersick, C.J.G. (1989) 'Marking time: predictable transitions in work groups', *Academy of Management Journal*, 32(2): 274–309.

Gersick, C.J.G. (1991) 'Revolutionary change theories: a multilevel exploration of the punctuated equilibrium paradigm', *Academy of Management Review*, 16(1): 10–35.

Gersick, C.J.G. (1992) 'Journey 2: time and transition in my work on teams: looking back on a new model of group development', in P.J. Frost and R. Stablein (eds), *Doing Exemplary Research*, Newbury Park: Sage, pp. 52–76.

Giddens, A. (1984) *The Constitution of Society*, Berkeley, CA: University of California Press.

Gioia, D.A. and Chittipeddi, K. (1991) 'Sensemaking and sensegiving in strategic change initiation', *Strategic Management Journal*, 12: 433–448.

Gioia, D., Schultz, M. and Corley, K.G. (2000) 'Organizational Identity, Image and Instability',

Academy of Management Review, 25(1): 63–81.

Golden, B.R. (1992) 'The past is the past – or is it? the use of retrospective accounts as indicators of past strategy', *Academy of Management Journal*, 35(4): 848–60.

Golden-Biddle, K. and Locke, K. (1993) 'Appealing work: an investigation of how ethnographic texts convince', *Organization Science*, 4(4): 595–616.

Golden-Biddle, K. and Locke, K. (2006) *Composing Qualitative Research*, Thousand Oaks, CA: Sage.

Greenwood, R. and Suddaby, R. (2006) 'Institutional entrepreneurship in mature fields: the big five accounting firms', *Academy of Management Journal*, 49(1): 27–48.

Hargadon, A. and Douglas, Y. (2001) 'When innovations meet institutions: Edison and the design of the electric light', *Administrative Science Quarterly*, 46: 476–501.

Hedström, P. and Swedberg, R. (1998) *Social Mechanisms*, Cambridge: Cambridge University Press.

Howard-Grenville, J.A. (2005) 'The persistence of flexible organizational routines: the role of agency and organizational context', *Organization Science*, 16(6): 618–36.

Huxham C. and Vangen S. (2003) 'Researching organizational practice through action research', *Organizational Research Methods*, 6(3): 383–403.

Isabella, L.A. (1990) 'Evolving interpretations as change unfolds: How managers construe key organizational events', *Academy of Management Journal*, 33(1): 7–41.

Jacobides, M.G. (2005) 'Industry change through vertical disintegration: How and why markets emerged in mortgage banking', *Academy of Management Journal*, 48(3): 465–98.

James, W. (1909/1996) *A Pluralistic Universe*, Lincoln, NE: University of Nebraska Press.

James, E.H. and Wooten, L.P. (2006) 'Diversity crises: How firms manage discrimination lawsuits', *Academy of Management Journal*, 49(6): 1103–18.

Langley, A. (1989) 'In search of rationality: the purposes behind the use of formal analysis in organizations', *Administrative Science Quarterly*, 34(4): 598–631.

Langley, A. (1999) 'Strategies for theorizing from process data', *Academy of Management Review*, 24(4): 691–710.

Langley, A. (2007) 'Process thinking in strategic organization', *Strategic Organization*, 5(3): 271–82.

Langley, A. and Truax, J. (1994) 'A process study of new technology adoption in smaller manufacturing firms', *Journal of Management Studies*, 31(5): 619–52.

Lapointe, L. and Rivard, S. (2007) 'A triple take on information systems implementation', *Organization Science*, 18(1): 89–107.

Latour, B. (2005) *Reassembling the Social*, Oxford: Oxford University Press.

Lawrence, T.B. and Suddaby, R. (2006) 'Institutions and institutional Work', in S.R. Clegg, C. Hardy, T.B. Lawrence and W.R. Nord (eds), *The Sage Handbook of Organization Studies* (second edn.), London: Sage. pp. 215–54.

Leonard-Barton, D. (1990) 'A dual methodology for case studies: synergistic use of a longitudinal single site with replicated multiple sites', *Organization Science*, 1(3): 248–66.

Locke, K. (1997) *Grounded Theory in Management Research*, Thousand Oaks, CA: Sage.

Locke, K., Golden-Biddle, K. and Feldman, M.S. (2004) 'Imaginative theorizing in interpretive qualitative research', *Academy of Management Best Paper Proceedings*, RM: B1–B6.

Locke, K., Golden-Biddle, K. and Feldman, M.S. (2008) 'Making doubt generative: rethinking the role of doubt in the research process', *Organization Science*, 19(6): 907–18.

Lozeau, D., Langley, A. and Denis, J-L. (2002) 'The corruption of managerial techniques by organizations', *Human Relations*, 55(5): 537–64.

Maguire, S. and Hardy, C. (2005) 'Identity and collaborative strategy in the Canadian HIV/AIDS treatment domain', *Strategic Organization*, 3(1): 11–46.

Maguire, S., Hardy, C. and Lawrence, T.B. (2004) 'Institutional entrepreneurship in emerging fields: HIV/AIDS treatment advocacy in Canada', *Academy of Management Journal*, 47(3): 657–79.

Mahring, M., Holmström, J., Keil, M. and Montealegre, R. (2004) 'Trojan actor-networks and swift translation: bringing actor-network theory to IT project escalation studies', *Information Technology and People*, 17(2): 210–38.

Maitlis, S. and Lawrence, T. (2003) 'Orchestral manoeuvres in the dark: understanding failures in organizational strategizing', *Journal of Management Studies*, 40 (1): 109–40.

Maitlis, S. (2004) 'Toxic decision processes: a study of emotion and organizational decision making', *Organization Science*, 15(4): 375–93.

Maitlis, S. (2005) 'The social processes of organizational sensemaking', *Academy of Management Journal*, 48(1): 21–49.

Maitlis, S. and Lawrence, T.B. (2007) 'Triggers and enablers of sensegiving in organizations', *Academy of Management Journal*, 50(1): 57–84.

March, J.G. and Sutton, R.I. (1997) 'Organizational performance as a dependent variable', *Organization Science*, 8(6): 698–706.

Meyer, A.D., Gaba, V. and Colwell, K. (2005) 'Organizing far from equilibrium: nonlinear change in organizational forms', *Organization Science*, 16(5): 456–73.

Miles, M.B. and Huberman, A.M. (1994) *Qualitative Data Analysis*, Thousand Oaks, CA: Sage publications.

Mintzberg, H., Raisinghani, D. and Théorêt, A. (1976) 'The structure of unstructured decision processes', *Administrative Science Quarterly*, 21(2): 246–75.

Mohr, L.B. (1982) *Explaining Organizational Behavior: The Limits and Possibilities of Theory and Research*, San Francisco: Jossey-Bass.

Monge, P.R. (1990) 'Theoretical and analytical issues in studying organizational processes', *Organization Science*, 1(4): 406–30.

Nutt, P.C. (1984) 'Types of organizational decision processes', *Administrative Science Quarterly*, 29(3): 414–50.

Patton, M.Q. (2002) *Qualitative Research and Evaluation Methods*, (third edn.), Newbury Park: Sage.

Pentland, B.T. (1999) 'Building process theory with narrative: From description to explanation', *Academy of Management Review*, 24(4): 711–24.

Pettigrew, A.M. (1985) *The Awakening Giant*, Oxford: Basil Blackwell.

Pettigrew, A.M. (1990) 'Longitudinal field research on change: Theory and practice', *Organization Science*, 1(3): 267–92.

Pettigrew, A.M. (1992) 'The character and significance of strategy process research', *Strategic Management Journal*, 13(winter special issue): 5–16.

Pettigrew, A.M., Woodman R.W. and Cameron K.S. (2001) 'Studying organizational change and development: Challenges for future research', *Academy of Management Journal*, 44(4): 697-713.

Plowman, D.A., Baker, L.T., Beck, T.E., Kulkarni, M., Solansky, S.T. and Travis, D.V. (2007) 'Radical change accidentally: The emergence and amplification of small change', *Academy of Management Journal*, 50(3): 515–43.

Polkinghorne, D.E. (1988) *Narrative Knowing and the Human Sciences*, Albany: State University of New York Press.

Poole, M.S., Van de Ven, A.H., Dooley, K. and Holmes, M. (2000) *Organizational Change and Innovation Processes: Theory and Methods for Research*, Oxford: Oxford University Press.

Pratt, M.G., Rockmann, K.W. and Kaufmann, J.B. (2006) 'Constructing professional identity: the role of work and identity learning cycles in the customization of identity among medical residents', *Academy of Management Journal*, 49(2): 235–62.

Rao, H. Monin P. and Durand, R. (2003) 'Institutional change in Toque Ville: Nouvelle Cuisine as an identity movement in French gastronomy', *American Journal of Sociology* 108(4): 795–843.

Ravasi, D. and Schultz, M. (2006) 'Reponding to organization identity threats: Exploring the role of organizational culture', *Academy of Management Journal*, 49(3): 433–58.

Reason, P. (ed.) (1994) *Participation in Human Inquiry*, London: Sage Publications.

Repenning, N.P. and Sterman, J.D. (2002) 'Capability traps and self-confirming attribution errors in the dynamics of process improvement', *Administrative Science Quarterly*, 47(2): 265–95.

Rhodes, C. and Brown, A.D. (2005) 'Narrative, organizations and research', *International Journal of Management Reviews*, 7(3): 167–88.

Rodriguez, R., Langley, A., Béland, F. and Denis, J-L. (2007) 'Governance, power and mandated collaboration in an inter-organizational network', *Administration and Society*, 39(2): 150–93.

Rynes, S.L. (2007a) 'Editor's foreword: tackling the "great divide" between research production and dissemination in human resource management', *Academy of Management Journal*, 50(3): 985–6.

Rynes, S.L. (2007b) 'Editor's afterword – Let's create a tipping point: What academics and practitioners can do, alone and together', *Academy of Management Journal*, 50(3): 1046–54.

Schwenk, C. (1985) 'The use of participant recollection in the modeling of organizational processes', *Academy of Management Review*, 10(3): 496–503.

Seo, M.-G. and Creed, W.E.D. (2002) 'Institutional contradictions, praxis, and institutional change: a dialectical perspective', *Academy of Management Review*, 27(2): 222–47.

Sloan, P. (2005) 'Strategy as Synthesis: Andrews Revisited', Unpublished doctoral dissertation, HEC Montréal.

Stacey, R.D. (1995) 'The science of complexity: an alternative perspective for strategic change processes', *Strategic Management Journal*, 16(6): 477–95.

Starbuck,W.H. and Farjoun, M. (eds) (2005) *Organization at the Limit: Lessons from the Columbia Disaster*, Malden, MA: Blackwell Publishing.

Stein, M. (2007) 'Oedipus Rex at Enron: leadership, oedipal struggles and organizational collapse', *Human Relations*, 60(6): 1387–410.

Strauss, A. and Corbin, J. (1990) *Basics of Qualitative Research*, Newbury Park: Sage.

Tsoukas, H. (1989) 'The validity of idiographic research explanations', *Academy of Management Review*, 14(4): 551–61.

Tsoukas, H. and Chia, R. (2002) 'On organizational becoming: rethinking organizational change', *Organization Science*, 13(5): 567–82.

Van de Ven, A.H. (1992) 'Suggestions for studying strategy process: a research note', *Strategic Management Journal*, 13 (summer special issue): 169–88.

Van de Ven, A.H. and Poole, M.S. (1990) 'Methods for studying innovation development in the Minnesota Innovation Research Program', *Organization Science*, 1(3): 313–35.

Van de Ven, A.H. and Poole, M.S. (1995) 'Explaining development and change in organizations', *Academy of Management Review*, 20(3): 510–40.

Van de Ven, A.H. and Poole, M.S. (2005) 'Alternative approaches for studying organizational change', *Organization Studies*, 26(9): 1377–404.

Van Maanen, J. (1988) *Tales of the Field*, Chicago: University of Chicago Press.

Vaughan, D. (1996) *The Challenger Launch Decision: Risky Technology, Culture and Deviance at NASA*, Chicago: University of Chicago Press.

Weick, K. (1979) *The Social Psychology of Organizing*, Reading, MA: Addison-Wesley.

Weick, K. (1995) *Sensemaking in Organizations*, Thousand Oaks, CA: Sage.

Weick, K.E. (1999) 'That's moving: theories that matter', *Journal of Management Inquiry*, 8(2): 134–42.

25

Critical Realism: Philosophy, Method, or Philosophy in Search of a Method?

Michael I. Reed

INTRODUCTION

The purpose of this chapter is to identify the key features of critical realism (CR) as a philosophy of social science and its implications for the formulation and implementation of research strategy and design in organizational analysis. It explores the implications of CR, as a metatheory or philosophy of social science, for the formulation of research questions, and identifies the *distinctive methodological strategies and practices* through which they are to be pursued in the study of organizations.

As the editors emphasize, contemporary organizational research and analysis is diverse and eclectic, both in relation to philosophical paradigms and methodological predilections. Increasing interest in, if not commitment to, CR as a 'third way' approach to both scientific positivism and social constructionism, as the dominant philosophical paradigms that have shaped organizational research over the last three decades or more, is a manifestation of this increasing intellectual ferment. But

it also expresses an overlapping set of meta-theoretical concerns and their impact on the practice and evaluation of organizational research. While researchers may not share a common agenda in relation to research priorities and the tools appropriate to their realization, they do participate in a set of overlapping theoretical and methodological traditions that frame the evolving 'lines of inquiry' that give the field of organization studies some intellectual shape, significance, and continuity (Reed, 2006). The relatively recent emergence of CR, and the direct challenge that it poses to the dominant philosophical paradigms that have shaped the field's intellectual development over the last 30 years, has to be interpreted as part of an evolving dialogue concerning what organizational research is about and why it matters.

This chapter covers a range of themes central to the understanding and appreciation of CR as a distinctive philosophy that rejects both the current philosophical orthodoxies in the field of organization studies and offers a coherent alternative with clear implications for research strategy and design. It opens with a general overview of the major features of CR and their impact on the study of organizations. The chapter then identifies the distinctive social ontology on which CR rests and the relevance of this ontology for the specification of causal explanation in organizational research and analysis. It also unpacks the implications of this CR-based conception of ontology, causality, and explanation for the specification of the particular research focus that it recommends – that is, on the 'intermediate zone' of 'organizational position-practices and their relations over time and place' (Parker, 2000).

The chapter argues that organizational research and analysis, conceived in CR terms, is most appropriately understood as an applied historical sociology of dynamic organizational forms and practices focused on the complex 'points of intersection' between history, geography, and social structure. Engagement in such an intellectual enterprise is directed to the construction and evaluation of analytical histories of organizational emergence, elaboration, and transition in which the endemic tensions and contradictions between 'structure' and 'agency' become the focal point for description, understanding, and explanation. It is also argued that this form of intellectual engagement will require a 'retroductive' research strategy and an 'intensive' research design in which composite studies of organizational reproduction and change, drawing on rich combinations of historical, structural and discursive research methods, are formulated and assessed. A selective sample of recent research illustrating this broad strategy 'in action' is briefly reviewed. The penultimate section considers the inherent limitations of CR-based explanatory theories and research methodologies in organizational research.

Critical realism

CR possesses a number of distinctive principles or 'domain assumptions' (Gouldner, 1971) that set it apart from other philosophies of social science. First, its commitment to *a stratified and differentiated social ontology* distinguishes it from both positivist and constructionist philosophies of science (Baert, 2005). Second, its support for *a generative, rather than a successionist, model of causality* demonstrates its particular approach to social explanation. Third, its engagement in *retroductive analysis* provides CR with an identifiable 'take' on questions relating to research methodology and procedure. Fourth, its preference for *intensive, rather than extensive, research strategy, and design* gives CR a distinct position in relation to the emergence, formulation, and development of research questions and agendas. Fifth, the *transformative model of social action* that underpins the ontological, epistemological, and methodological positioning of CR, establishes a coherent conception of the 'structure/agency' issue or dilemma that has played key role in shaping sociopolitical theorizing and analysis (Reed, 2003). Finally, the commitment to the *concept of explanatory critique* (Danermark et al., 2002) gives CR a particular approach to the relationship between social analysis and social criticism in social science.

Each of these domain assumptions is discussed in detail in subsequent sections. Here, an outline of these components and their necessary interrelation is provided.

CR is grounded in a layered social ontology consisting of differentiated and stratified levels of reality that possess their own features and characteristics that are inherently resistant to being collapsed or reduced into each other. Each layer or level has distinctive objects and mechanisms with its own particular powers, capabilities and tendencies that come into a highly complex interaction with each other to produce certain outcomes rather than others. In this respect, CR is ontologically committed to the concept of 'emergence' – that is, the belief that new entities and powers emerge from the complex interplay between mechanisms and entities located and operating at different and irreducible levels of reality.

Danermark et al. (2002: 62–3) summarize this argument:

> Concrete phenomena are complexly composed of powers and mechanisms, which affect, reinforce, weaken, and sometimes neutralize the effects of one another. The question of which mechanisms are most significant for the object under study can, therefore, only be decided from case to case, through empirical studies and in relation to the problem we address.

Once this antireductionist/determinist ontology is in place, CR is allowed to develop a model of causality in which the identification and mapping of 'generative mechanisms' becomes central to the logic and practice of social explanation. Generative mechanisms consist of structures, powers, and capacities that, literally 'make things happen in the world' (Danermark et al., 2002: 206); they are structures, powers and capabilities that underlay the surface level of experienced events and which indelibly shape how the latter emerge and develop. They operate at different and stratified levels of reality within complex open systems that are inherently resistant to 'ontological closure'; that is, generative mechanisms are embedded and operate within different levels of reality that range from the more abstract and complex to the more concrete and immediate. This might range from the 'international division of labour', to a 'labour market', to an 'organization structure' to a 'workgroup sub-culture' to a 'psychological profile'; in this sense, generative mechanisms have to be identified and interrelated through a complex process of conceptual abstraction, model building, and testing that 'make it possible to describe how and under what circumstances exactly these mechanisms exist, and how they interact in exactly these circumstances' (Danermark et al., 2002: 69).

Retroductive analysis is a methodological procedure through which generative mechanisms, and their interplay in specific sociohistorical situations are identified and assessed. This form of analysis is also concerned with identifying the sociomaterial conditions under which certain forms of collective or corporate agency become more likely or feasible and the potential impact that the latter have on longer-term institutional outcomes (Clark, 2000). Retroduction is a form of description and analysis, involving conceptual abstraction, and theoretical model building and evaluation, geared to understanding and explaining concrete phenomena by reconstructing the conditions (generative mechanisms) under which they emerge and become the entities that they are. Thus, the explanatory aim of retroductive analysis is to provide systematic knowledge about the underlying mechanisms that generate concrete events and outcomes. Those mechanisms cannot be directly observed or experienced as they operate at an ontological level that cannot be accessed through direct sense-experience, but must be inferred through conceptual abstraction and interpretation. In this view, the objects of scientific investigation and analysis are not empirical regularities or tendencies but the structures and mechanisms that underlie, reproduce, and transform them.

This commitment to retroductive analysis is complemented by an intensive research strategy in which the inherent complexity and relative autonomy of generative mechanisms operating at different levels of reality and theoretical abstraction can be properly accommodated and appreciated. Consequently, intensive research strategy combines a range of conceptual, theoretical, and empirical procedures and practices focused on the operation and outcome of generative mechanisms in specific contexts. This requires probing the complex interplay between the generative mechanisms that produce a particular social phenomenon that cannot be accommodated within an extensive research strategy focused on general empirical regularities or patterns across a population of objects. Indeed, these are often taken as the initial focus of attention for CR researchers, but are followed by much deeper, more intensive, investigations into the mechanisms and conditions that generate and reproduce them.

This sustained focus on context-specific mechanisms and conditions is also legitimated by the 'transformative model of social action'

(Bhaskar, 1989; Archer, 1995). This model is based on the idea that 'structure' and 'agency' are ontologically and analytically distinct, but interact and combine in complex ways to generate the dynamics that have the potential to transform social situations and the manner in which they are institutionally structured and reproduced. It is based on the belief that social action or agency always possesses the inherent capacity to transform social situations. But whether or not the inherent 'transformative potential' of agency is actualized in any specific sociotemporal context depends on the conditions under which it operates and the complex conjunction between the generative mechanisms that indelibly shape its emergence and development. Agency always operates within a social and temporal context that is structured by constraining conditions that have developed over long periods of historical accretion and sedimentation. It can overcome these constraints and change the conditions and outcomes that prevail in specific social situations. But the inherent 'transformative power or capacity' of agency requires particular conditions under which it has a realistic chance to emerge and be sustained (Stones, 2005).

The identification of these constraints and an evaluation of their 'limiting effects' on the power of collective or corporate agency to change social situations also provides a vital component of the 'critical' element in CR. This insists that there are always powers or capacities that lie behind courses of events and the outcomes that they produce and sustain. By identifying and analysing the social structures that differentially equip social groups and corporate agents with the capabilities to reshape social outcomes, critical realists believe that they can pinpoint the conditions that reproduce social inequality. This means that CR is *inherently critical* to the extent that it necessarily subjects extant social conditions to critique. In this respect, CR insists that the selection of research questions or issues, the manner in which they are researched, and the production and dissemination of knowledge about these questions can never

be totally divorced from normative considerations (Sayer, 2000).

With this broad overview of the distinguishing features of CR, we can now explore in more detail their significance for organizational research.

Social ontology

Critical realists take ontology seriously, arguing that the way in which we define the world and the how it works has profound implications for how we acquire knowledge about it (Danermark, et al., 2002; Sayer, 2000; Trigg, 2001; Reed, 2005). Ontology is that set of presuppositions that we make about the nature of the phenomena that we are studying, and what that entails for how we study them. In this respect, ontological assumptions are unavoidable; we cannot study anything without them, and they are of fundamental importance to the extent that they provide a set of foundational orientations that shape the ways in which that study will be undertaken. Consequently, critical realists insist that ontology and epistemology are clearly distinguished in a way that avoids reducing or collapsing one into the other. The way that the world *is* cannot be determined by the principles and tools through which we come to understand and explain it; ontology cannot be collapsed into epistemology. Indeed, for critical realists, ontology has priority over epistemology to the extent that it legislates the terms under which the search for knowledge is to be undertaken and how the intellectual resources that it requires are to be deployed. As such, ontology exercises a powerful and pervasive influence on the specification of the intellectual goals that researchers set for themselves – that is, what it means to 'describe', 'understand', and 'explain' – and the intellectual means required for their realization.

Critical realist ontology differs in fundamental ways from positivist and constructionist ontology. Positivist ontology reduces the world to a series of discrete events or occurrences that can only be identified through the sense experiences of individuals and represented in the form of empirical regularities. As Blaikie (2000: 102–3) observes, positivism:

> ...entails ontological assumptions about an ordered universe made up of discrete and observable events. It assumes that this order can be represented by universal propositions, i.e., by generalizations about the relationships between concepts. Only that which can be observed, that is experienced by the senses, can be regarded as real and therefore worthy of the attention of science.

Constructionist ontology, on the other hand, presupposes that social reality is constituted through language or discourse as the ontological axiom that frames the study of that reality. It rejects positivism's commitment to an 'event-dependent' ontology that only deals in empirical regularities generated through systematic observation and experimental or quasi-experimental analysis. Instead, constructionist ontology goes to the other extreme of presupposing that social reality is necessarily constituted by and relative to the linguistic tools through which we come to know 'it', or more accurately, 'them'. For the social constructionist, there are only ever 'social realities' that can only be accessed, described, and understood through the linguistic traditions and discursive communities by means of which they are constituted (Gergen, 1994; Burkitt, 1998; Westwood and Linstead, 2001). Thus, social reality is regarded as the creation of social actors; it has no distinctive or 'objective' ontological status or meaning independent of the sociolinguistic practices through which it is inter-subjectively made possible as a continually developing 'work in progress'.

Once this ontological position is accepted, then the socially constructed mutual knowledge through which 'social reality' is meaningfully defined and communicated, by and between interdependent social actors, becomes the focal point for research. Social scientific research and the knowledge that engagement in such a social practice produces will, necessarily, be dependent on and derived from the socially constructed

meanings that social actors generate through their engagement in particular social situations. Social constructionist ontology thus legitimates a social epistemology in which a preinterpreted and constituted 'social reality' is subjected to somewhat more systematic redescription and reinterpretation by the social scientist through detailed and painstaking reconstruction and deconstruction of the actors' 'subjective worlds' (Blaikie, 2000: 114–19).

Critical realist ontology tries to navigate a 'middle course' through the extremes of positivist and constructionist ontologies, thereby providing an alternative conception of the intellectual goals that drive social research and the intellectual tools most appropriate to their realization. As previously indicated, critical realist ontology presupposes an independently existing social reality that cannot be reduced to a discrete set of observable events or a discursively manufactured inter-subjective construct. Critical realists accept that knowledge of social reality is always mediated through reflective and creative mobilization of existing stocks of knowledge – concepts, models, theories, discourses – accumulated through previous generations' attempts to describe, understand and explain 'what the world is and how it works'. But they reject the social constructionist inference that the necessarily mediated character of social reality entails that its ontological status and significance are circumscribed by the inter-subjectively constituted meanings and interpretations through which we understand it. For critical realists, social reality *consists of much more* than the linguistic, symbolic, and discursive resources and practices through which we come to describe, understand, and reflect on it; it also consists of entities, processes, relations, and mechanisms that are constituted and structured in particular ways, with fateful consequences for how we must try to identify and explain them.

As already indicated, critical realists are committed to a stratified social ontology consisting of different levels or domains of material and ideal entities, interconnected through complex links, relations, and processes that cannot be reduced or collapsed into each other (Sayer, 1992, 2000; Layder, 1994, 1997; Searle, 1995; Archer et al., 1998; Smith, 1998; Trigg, 2001; Reed, 2005a and b). Following Bhaskar's formulation (Bhaskar, 1975, 1979, 1986, 1989), this stratified ontology consists of three separable but interrelated levels or domains: 'the empirical', consisting of sense-experiences and perceptions; 'the actual', consisting of observable events and activities; and 'the real', consisting of unobservable structures and powers of objects. The interplay between each of these levels is characterized by a dynamic and open-ended conjunction that generates 'emergent' or new phenomena that exhibit properties and tendencies that are irreducible to those entities from which they originated. Over time, these emergent entities may become sufficiently stabilized and durable to exhibit long-term continuity and tractability of a kind characteristic of social structures, institutions, and organizations. This stratified ontology also directs critical realist researchers towards an explanatory focus on the real, underlying, and unobservable mechanisms that generate certain observable phenomena at the level of the actual and empirical. In turn (Blaikie, 2000: 108) this predisposes them towards a social epistemology that is:

> ...based on the building of models of mechanisms such that, if they were to exist and act in the postulated way, they would account for the phenomena being examined. These models constitute hypothetical descriptions that, it is hoped, will reveal the underlying mechanisms.

Social causality

This ontological position raises important questions about the nature of social causality and explanation. Given that a critical realist social ontology gives overriding emphasis to the real, generative mechanisms that produce and reproduce observable events and processes – such as strikes, recessions, ceremonies, and bureaucratization, professionalization, and democratization – then this predisposition has a major impact on the conception of social causality that critical realist researchers adopt, and how this feeds their explanatory logic.

Critical realists offer an alternative to the 'successionist' conception of causality (Sayer, 2000) that emerges from positivist ontology and the 'rejectionist' position on causality that comes out of constructionist ontology. While the former defines causality in terms of the regular succession of events that can be subsumed under – and explained and predicted by – a universal covering law, the latter insists that interpretive modes of inquiry abjure any concern with causal processes and relations. Again, critical realism offers a 'third way' between these rather dogmatic views of social causality. It advocates a conception of causal processes and relations redefined as powers or tendencies that inhere in particular social entities, such as social structures, movements, and organizations, and which work their way through, over time and place, with particular effects in specific sociohistorical contexts. Consequently, causal analysis, from a critical realist perspective, is focussed around the *elucidation of the processes and mechanisms* that generate the objects, events, and actions they are seeking to explain, rather than around the identification of empirical regularities that can be subsumed within linear universal 'causal chains' (Ekstrom, 1992). Social causality has to be analysed in terms of inherent tendencies or powers that are never found in their purity but operate in complex 'dialectical interaction' with each other within and across dynamic sociohistorical contexts. Motives, intentions, reasons, and practices, the 'bread and butter' of constructionist ontology and epistemology, are also regarded as central causal mechanisms in social-scientific research insofar as they provide insight into the ever more complex 'internal relations and conversations' that shape human agency and social action (Archer, 2000, 2003; Mutch, 2006).

As Sayer (2000) notes, a generative conception of causality predisposes critical realist researchers towards 'counterfactual' rather than 'associational' modes of thinking and analysis. While the latter is concerned with what is associated with what, and in what ways, in order to account for how empirical regularities come to exhibit the pattern that they do, the former is concerned with whether the postulated associations could have been different, and if so, why this could be the case. This counterfactual mode of analysis becomes even more crucial when we remember that, in contrast with constructionist ontology and epistemology, 'social actors may have little or no awareness of the mechanisms, and, in particular, the structures, which are involved in the production of the regularities in their social activities (Blaikie, 2000: 111). As a result, critical realists are often trying to explore the many interacting mechanisms and structures that are potential 'prime candidates or suspects' for assigning causal primacy in accounting for a specific set of events, processes, and outcomes. Trying to assign what Sayer (2000: 16) labels 'causal responsibility' – that is, identifying a prime causal mechanism that, in complex interaction with many other mechanisms under a range of contextual conditions, seems to best account for a particular phenomenon – is difficult, time-consuming and resource-intensive. This form of causal analysis also calls for the continuous interplay between conceptualization/model-building/theory development and contextualization/narrative reconstruction/theory testing that enables the critical realist to build robust 'analytical histories of emergence' (Parker, 2000; Stones, 2005).

Social explanation

The generative conception of social causality that emerges from a critical realist social ontology has implications for the explanatory focus, form, and function that critical realist research follows. First, the explanatory focus is directed towards the underlying generative mechanisms that account for surface level relations, processes and events. But these generative mechanisms never operate in isolation; they interact with a complex configuration of additional mechanisms that are contextually embedded within socially and temporally dynamic situations. Second, generative mechanisms are operative at different levels of analysis with differential 'causal powers or influences' triggered under variable contextual conditions. So, some generative mechanisms, such as modes of production, class structures, labour markets, gender regimes, and surveillance systems, will be highly abstract, broad-ranging and structurally constraining in their 'causal powers and effects'. Other generative mechanisms, such as neighbourhood networks, peer group subcultures and household support systems, are more localized, and limited in their impact on the range and viability of strategic 'intervention options' available to social actors. Third, the dynamic interplay, over time and place, between generative mechanisms can only be understood through a combination of conceptual abstraction and model building and contextual embedding and interpretation (Manicas, 2006).

This conception of generative mechanisms is central to the critical realist mode or logic of explanation. If the explanatory focus is on the identification of the complex interplay between various generative mechanisms as the latter shapes and reshapes the process of 'structuration' – that is, the process of generating social structures with fateful consequences for social actors (Parker, 2000; Stones, 2006) – *then the mode or logic of explanation that flows from this position must be equipped to accommodate an account of the genesis of those mechanisms and how they become combined or interwoven in ways that produce certain outcomes rather than others.* In other words, critical realist research combines historical, structural, and interpretive forms of analysis in order to describe, understand, and explain concrete events or outcomes and the complex structuration processes and relations through which they are produced, elaborated, and transformed.

Finally, this explanatory logic implies a distinctive contribution for critical realist research. It suggests that the analysis of the generative mechanisms that frame structuration processes *has to engage with the endemic contradictions and tensions between 'structure' and 'agency' as they work their way through various temporal sequences and situational contexts.* Thus, the contribution of critical realist research lies in the intellectual capacity to construct the analytical narratives that identify the conditions under which the endemic contradictions and tensions between structure and agency *are translated into 'live' forms of discontent that have the potential to change the situation in which agents are operating.*

In turn, this approach requires a detailed analysis of the power relations and dynamics within and between various social groups (elites, managers and workers) and their potential to facilitate or block the opportunities for social change released by the interplay between generative mechanisms operating in the sociohistorical situation under investigation (Archer, 1995; Lukes, 2005 and 2006; Manicas, 2006). This analysis opens up the possibility of understanding the unfolding strategic options considered by various social groups or corporate agents, embedded within and constrained by existing power structures, and their relative inclinations, skills, and capacities to exploit the opportunities that intensifying contradictions and tensions between 'the past' (structural inheritance), 'the present' (structural status quo), and 'the future' (structural alternatives) make available.

It also suggests that critical realist researchers should pay greater explanatory attention to the relationship between 'structure' and 'agency' as this is mediated through the strategic deliberations and reflections in which social actors routinely engage (Emirbayer and Mische, 1998; Hay, 2001; Archer, 2000 and 2003; Reed, 2003; Mutch, 2006). These strategic actors' reflections and deliberations may, in part, be habitual, informal, and intuitive, or they may take on a more explicit, formal, calculating, and rational character. But they indicate that the selective evaluations of social actors concerning their prospects for achieving change are the outcome of a complex interplay between the 'densely structured and highly contoured' (Hay, 2001) sociotemporal configurations in which they are located and the cognitive templates and discursive narratives through which they come to understand and assess the shifting balance between 'constraint' and 'opportunity' over time and place. Critical realist research must make a serious and sustained effort to access, describe and reinterpret the processes whereby social actors come to understand the contexts in which they operate and of the extent to which these emerging cognitive and discursive formulations may come to reinforce, facilitate, weaken, or block the potential for change opened up by intensifying structural contradictions and tensions (Stones, 2005).

Again, this takes us back to the critical realist ontological presupposition that social reality is differentiated into levels of structuration that correspond to the differentially distributed capacities, that is the power, of social groups, as corporate agents, to shape the contexts and conditions under which other corporate agents have to operate. These differentially distributed powers and capacities are not fixed or predetermined across time and space; they are contextually specific and temporally variable. But they are unlikely to change quickly or be easy to change from the viewpoint of those groups who may be relatively disadvantaged in terms of the material and cultural allocation mechanisms that existing power/authority structures legitimate. Thus, for the critical realist researcher (Parker, 2000: 117–19):

> Structures are real constraining conditions of action, which cannot be grasped adequately by regarding them simply as effects of systems of representation or 'discourse' … Institutional and distributional positioning conditions agency by defining interests and access to resources. This means that the stringency of constraint and the powers of agency vary from case to case … Explaining structuration in these terms demands facing the complexities of each historical case.

Research strategy and design

Critical realism presupposes that ontology precedes epistemology; ontology is prior to epistemology, because it tells us where to look and what to look for. We have to make ontological choices, whether we like it or not; sometimes, these choices are systematically articulated and supported, sometimes they are inferred from the substantive claims that researchers make and the ways in which these knowledge claims are justified. But for critical realists, ontological dilemmas cannot be resolved through empirical procedures; our social ontology necessarily sensitizes us to the nature of the world of which we are a part, and dealing with it predisposes us to look for the generative mechanisms that lie beneath the events and sense experiences that characterize our everyday lives. This search for the generative mechanisms that shape and reshape events, experiences, and outcomes is difficult, because it requires that we engage in an in-depth understanding and analysis of the historical contexts, structural conditions, and interpretive schemes that, in their interplay, shape our lives and the opportunities that are made available to us.

What sort of research strategy and design is most likely to sensitize and equip us with the intellectual resources required to identify those 'points of intersection' at which the contradictions and tensions between pre-existing structural constraints and actors' deliberations/interventions become so intense and deep-seated that they trigger potential institutional change and transformation? Possible answers to these questions raise a set of additional questions that revolve around the meaning and significance of the 'critical' appendage of critical realist research.

Critical realist researchers favour a *retroductive*, as opposed to an inductive, deductive, or abductive, research strategy, and an *intensive*, rather than extensive, research design (Blaikie, 1993 and 2000; Lawson, 1997; Smith, 1998; Sayer, 2000; Danermark et al., 2002). Previous discussion has indicated that critical realist researchers direct their explanatory focus on the underlying mechanisms which consist of necessary and enduring relationships (e.g. between employer and employee, landlord and tenant, lawyers and clients, and teachers and students) that reproduce patterns of social interaction and the associated social practices that link and mediate between different cycles of institutional elaboration, reproduction, and transformation. A retroductive strategy involves the construction and application of theoretical models that uncover the real and unobservable mechanisms or structures that are assumed to be causing actual events and experiences. This requires the creative, but disciplined, invention and application of plausible theoretical analogues in order to uncover the operation of underlying generative mechanisms and to identify their empirical consequences.

A retroductive research strategy logically involves 'working back' from the identification of certain phenomena, to theoretically postulated mechanisms or structures that are offered as explanatory candidates accounting for the phenomena being the way that they are, and exercising the powers, effects, and tendencies that they exhibit, to examining and adjudicating between these competing theoretical explanations in the light of empirical evidence. This leads to further rounds of creative model building whereby the improved understanding emerging from previous rounds, through the application of disciplined imagination and empirical investigation and analysis, are incorporated into the next round of theoretical abstraction and elaboration. Considered in this way, retroduction emphasizes the continuously accretive nature of theory building in social science research, which is seen as, 'an organic entity which is continuously developing and re-formulating itself as a result of the interchange and dialogue between emergent (data-embedded) theory and prior theory (models, concepts, frameworks)' (Layder, 1998: 156).

It should also be noted that the kind of knowledge that emerges from this retroductive strategy is always context-specific, and does not permit the formulation and testing of predictive laws or hypotheses. A retroductive strategy rejects the presupposition that explanation and prediction are synonymous, because it 'works back' from known phenomena located within specified sociohistorical contexts, that are inherently open and dynamic in nature, to the postulation and construction of theoretical models that identify and represent the operation of causal mechanisms or structures that interact in complex and unpredictable ways with other causal mechanisms or structures. The best that the social scientist can do in this perspective is to construct possible explanations of why certain phenomena are the way they are, and produce the outcomes that they produce, generated through an intellectual process in which creative and disciplined model-building has been combined with in-depth empirical investigation and analysis that remain attuned to the vicissitudes of social existence.

This retroductive strategy contrasts with the inductive, deductive, and abductive research strategies that have enjoyed greater intellectual recognition and legitimacy in both natural and social science (Smith, 1998; Blaikie, 2000). Inductive and deductive strategies are normally associated with variants of positivism that prioritize epistemology over ontology, and direct social research to the search for quasi-universal covering laws that are confirmed or rejected through a process of hypothesis construction and empirical testing in which statistical generalization is regarded as the key to reliable and valid scientific knowledge. An abductive research strategy focuses attention on producing systematic and inclusive redescriptions and understandings of the motives and accounts of the actors directly and intimately involved in particular social situations, and the complex ways in which these inter-subjectively meaningful motives and accounts inform social interaction. Technical concepts and theoretical interpretations are derived and legitimated from actors' concepts and 'theories-in-use', rather than from a pre-existing body of abstract theory that is externally imposed on the actors' understandings and meanings, as

they inform and shape unfolding patterns of social interaction and the wider institutional orders that they facilitate and legitimate (Smith, 2005).

None of these strategies involves the search for deep or hidden generative mechanisms that produce observable phenomena. Nevertheless, the retroductive strategy does emphasize an 'intensive' research design (Sayer, 2000; Danermark, et al., 2002) that starts with the attempt to produce an in-depth, ethnographic understanding of how the social actors in a specific context 'see' the constraints and opportunities that it embodies. But this is only *the starting point* for critical realist research and analysis that is likely to involve 'going beyond' the actors' understandings and discourses in ways that challenge their accounts of the situation and the potentialities that the latter embodies by invoking abstract theoretical models and interpretations that highlight the operation of mechanisms of which the actors may have little or no awareness. Thus, the role of critical realist ethnography is twofold (Porter, 2002: 65):

> First, it is used as a method to uncover the manifest interactions of the social world, which are then subjected to the transcendental process of theory generation to infer the structural conditioning of those interactions. Second, it is used to subsequently test the veracity of theories concerning the nature and effects of the structures pertaining ... Rather than confining its focus to individual experience, or rejecting the notion of knowledge altogether, critical realism is able to use ethnographic data to illuminate structured relations, and beyond that, to show how these relations may be oppressive, and to point to the sort of actions required to make them less oppressive.

An intensive research design has a number of central features. First, research questions are always context-specific, focusing on the detailed understanding of how underlying generative mechanisms 'work their way through' in a particular case or a limited number of cases. They usually ask why a certain change, rather than any other, was produced in a particular situation, and with what consequences for the agents involved. Second, attempting to answer these types of questions requires the generation and combination of ethnographic, textual, historical, and structural data that facilitate a deeper and wider understanding of the substantive relations or connections that shape social action and the outcomes that it produces. Third, this combination and recombination of phenomenological, discursive, interpretive, and material data facilitates the identification of concrete patterns and substantive relations and the underlying generative mechanisms that produced them. Fourth, there must be repeated movement between concrete and abstract, between empirical detail and theoretical analysis, throughout all phases of the research process. Finally, this constant iteration between specific cases and general theory establishes the basis for the formulation and corroboration of causal explanations that account for observed outcomes in terms of the generative mechanisms that produced them. Sayer (2000: 21–3) summarizes the intensive research process as follows:

> Intensive research is strong on causal explanation and interpretive meanings in context, but tends to be very time-consuming, so that one can normally only deal with a small number of cases … The research therefore aims to identify and explain various combinations of contexts, mechanisms and outcomes, and given the openness and complexity of social systems, the list of possibilities is likely to be long. No mechanism or set of mechanism … is to be taken as a 'black box'. Their identification is not a matter of finding more specific regularities, clusters or statistical associations, for to do so would not explain the mechanisms but merely redefine the problem. Explanation requires mainly interpretive and qualitative research to discover actors' reasoning and circumstances in specific contexts – not in abstraction from them.

Critical realist research in action

Critical realist thinking is relatively new in organizational research and analysis. Consequently, the cumulative body of research literature is limited when compared to well-established positivist and constructivist-inspired research work across this field.

Many of the modern classics in organizational research (Selznick, 1949;

Gouldner, 1954; Blau, 1955; Crozier 1964) exhibit strong implicit elements of realist thinking (Layder, 1993; Reed, 2005, and 2009, forthcoming). However, three distinctive, but closely interrelated, contemporary streams of realist-inspired research can be identified. First, a stream of work focused on detailed organizational ethnographies that identify the micropolitical power relations and processes that act as generative mechanisms in particular institutional contexts and organizational settings (Porter, 1993 and 2002; Delbridge, 1998 and 2004; Taylor and Bain, 2004; Kennedy and Kennedy, 2004). Second, another stream is concerned with the construction of analytical histories of 'organizational emergence' and implications for power relations and their impact on the changing design repertoires and control strategies available to organizational elites in post-Fordist political economies (Clark, 2000 and 2003; Mutch, 2006). A third research stream has recently emerged seeking to understand the complex and shifting 'organizational discourses and ideologies' through which contemporary organizational change is interpreted, mediated, and legitimated (Fairclough, 2005; Hesketh and Brown, 2004; Hesketh and Fleetwood, 2006; Reed 1998, 2001 and 2004).

The recurring theme in these three streams of research is the desire to formulate a richer understanding of the process of structuration and a better explanation of how it generates certain forms of organizational outcomes rather than others (Sibeon, 2004; Stones, 2005; Manicas, 2006). They also stand testimony to Stones' (2005: 81–2) axiom that:

> …any attempt to investigate the process of structuration at the substantive level will have to engage, at least at a minimal level, with a combination of hermeneutics and structural diagnostics … A pragmatic implication of needing to combine an investigation both of structures and of hermeneutics is that the detail implied by this will necessarily limit the scope and scale of studies that can be given the structuration treatment … the proper domain of study of students of the interplay between structure and agency … is the

'intermediate temporality of historical processes'. This is a scale of temporality within which one could specify both relations between specific events and agency, and relations between events themselves.

This axiom also commits critical realist researchers operating within and across each of these three research streams or domains – the ethnographic, the historical, and the discursive – to a sustained focus on the intermediate zone of position-practices, and the relatively durable and resilient structures that are embedded within it. These structures are routinely drawn upon by collective actors or corporate agents, but with varying degrees of power and control, as material and ideational resources through which they pursue their political and ideological interests in competition with and collaboration between other actors. In this way, critical realist thinking provides a set of sensitizing concepts that guide substantive research and a contextualizing framework within which the latter can be undertaken and justified.

The organizational ethnography stream has been driven by an interest in the particular combinations of structural influences that shape the processes through which everyday organizational life is reproduced and transformed. In this respect, critical realist ethnography is focused on mapping the fine detail of what Bhaskar (1989) has called the 'transformational model of social action'. This is the case insofar as the latter rejects the constant conjunction conception of causality as the ontological bedrock of positivistic research and offers an alternative in which complex combinations of generative structures operating in multilayered social situations and producing emergent phenomena with creative and innovative potential become the focal point for research. While critical realist ethnography retains many of the core features of ethnographic research in general (Hammersley, 1992; Hammersley and Atkinson, 1995; Silverman, 2000), its concern to produce 'thick descriptions' of how social actors, 'working with materials at hand' (Manicas, 2006: 4) and to understand

and describe their everyday social worlds, *is merely the starting point*. As Manicas (2006: 4) reflects:

> …an ethnographic (and hermeneutic) moment is essential to grasping a social mechanism, but as Weber had long since noted, it was but the first step in social scientific inquiry. That is, while we need to understand the social world as its members understand it, we need to go beyond this and to consider the adequacy of their understanding of the world. Since social process is the product of our activity, and since members may well *mis*understand their world, social science is potentially emancipatory.

Thus Porter's (1993 and 2002) ethnographic research on the interplay between 'latent racism' and 'professional ideology', as a combination of generative mechanisms reproducing hierarchical power structures and relations in British hospitals, moves beyond the actors' level of understanding to engage in abstract theoretical work in order to provide a critical realist *explanation* of how this combination of mechanisms operates and the effects that it has in specific locations. In this respect, it is representative of critical realist ethnography in its concern to provide in-depth understanding of the way in which social actors see their worlds operating – what Archer (2003) calls 'the internal conversation' embedded within its appropriate sociohistorical context – as a necessary precondition for explaining the actors' understandings and actions in relation to the structural mechanisms that generated them.

Critical realist research on 'organizational emergence' – on the structuration processes through which organizations are produced, elaborated, and transformed – has been directed at the changing repertoires of social practices through which different forms of organization are assembled and their longer-term implications for the transition between different forms. As Clark (2000 and 2003) has emphasized in a series of studies drawing on critical realist ontology and method, this stream of research has produced a more dynamic, complex, iterative, and political conception of organizing and organization in which a 'neo-modern global political economy' begins to take definite shape and form. His work has led to a more intensive and sustained focus on the antecedent, pre-existing cycles of structuration, in both organizations and contexts, that shape the 'zones of manoeuvre' or 'finite and emergent capacities' that elites have available to them in their strategic attempts to reproduce or transform existing design repertoires and the organizational forms that emerge from them. Clark (2000: 277) has striven to combine historical, structural, and discursive forms of research in order to 'pinpoint the processes guiding action in a particular direction and to explain the specific configuration that arises'. The overall conclusion emerging from this work is that pre-existing power distributions within and between elite groups and the antecedent design capabilities of the specialist groups of knowledge workers serving strategic elites combine to exert a dramatic restraining impact on the extent to which emerging 'zones of manoeuvrability' were exploited in ways that led to radical innovation and change in organizational forms. Thus, for Clark (2000: 292–4), critical realist research redirects 'organizational analysis to a more robust understanding of the futures of organizations':

> Robust analysis acknowledges the pre-existing, the unfolding and the future configuration of events … The realist turn gives sustenance to some of the dynamic elements linking the future with the present and past, thereby escaping the temporal conflation and extended present that besets so much of organizational analysis.

Finally, recent work on organizational discourses and ideologies has deepened the contribution of critical realist research to organizational analysis. Fairclough (2001: 124) argues that critical realist research should focus on the 'orders of discourse that emerge from the social structuring of semiotic difference' and their strategic role in generating and sustaining new forms of economic, social, and political dominance. Research,

Fairclough continues, needs to concentrate on the emergence of innovative discursive orders and technologies, such as 'enterprise culture' or 'new public management' or 'transformational leadership', and their longer-term impact on pre-existing discursive orders and technologies as they 'drill their way down' into everyday organizational practices and identities. In particular, the differentially distributed capacity of these innovative discursive orders and technologies to generate and mediate new forms of what Archer (2000) calls 'corporate agency' – that is, collective actors with the necessary organizational machinery and cultural capability to make themselves heard in an increasingly complex and contested decision-making arena – that colonize a widening range of institutional fields and organizational settings becomes a major area of research activity in critical realist discourse analysis.

A recent classic example of research on the process by which new corporate agencies are created by innovative discursive orders is the new, customer-led, bureaucratic discourses and technologies that are emerging in British local government under the auspices of 'best value' audit regimes and the 'new public management' discourses through which they are legitimated. Miller's (2005) research combines anthropological, historical and discourse forms of analysis to provide a penetrating account of how these new 'anti-bureaucratic', customer-focused ideologies generate organizational forms and practices that are the antithesis of that which they were supposed to produce – that is, customer-led systems of performance evaluation and resource allocation.

Organizational discourse research conducted in the critical realist tradition is likely to combine the mainstream techniques of discourse analysis, such as rhetorical analysis, textual analysis, conversational analysis, and narrative analysis (Gabriel, 1997; Grant et al., 1998; Westwood and Linstead 2001; Grant et al., 2004; Brown, 2004), with the more historically and structurally-oriented practices favoured by critical realists (Fairclough, 2002, 2003, 2005).

Problems and limitations

Although critical realism is a relatively new metatheoretical approach in organizational research (Ackroyd and Fleetwood, 2000; Fleetwood and Ackroyd, 2004; Reed, 2005), it has attracted a considerable amount of critical attention. Criticism has crystallized around four issues; the extent to which it unavoidably 'flirts' with a form of structural-cum-historical determinism that regards 'structure' as the driving force for explaining social and organizational change (Baert, 1998; Contu and Willmott, 2005); that it consequently dilutes the ontological status and explanatory significance of 'agency' to such an extent that the latter becomes redundant as a key analytical and substantive component of social scientific analysis (Stones, 2005); that it promotes an excessively complex research approach that makes clear and precise explanation of social phenomena almost impossible or, conversely, that it is so methodologically eclectic that it legitimates an anarchic 'anything goes' approach to research that is inconsistent with its commitment to 'science' (Blaikie, 2000); that it lacks reflexivity in relation to the problems that arise over the complex relationship between 'researcher' and 'researched' in a way that promotes an outmoded and unviable 'spectator theory of knowledge' (Baert, 2005).

The social ontology of critical realism is fundamentally antideterminist and antireductionist and, especially in its explanatory intent (Archer, 1995; Sayer, 2000; Boal et al., 2003; Manicas, 2006). It gives overriding emphasis to the *inherently* open, dynamic, and emergent nature of social phenomena, such as organizations, and the need for research methodologies and explanatory theories that are sensitive to the complex interplay between 'structure' and 'agency' over time and place as it shapes and reshapes structural and cultural outcomes (Ackroyd, 2004; Reed, 2003 and 2005; Mutch et al., 2006). Relocated in this context, the ontological status and explanatory role of 'agency' in critical realism can be further explored. A number of researchers sympathetic to a critical realist approach in social

theory and organizational analysis maintain that the concept of 'agency' and its ontological and explanatory significance require further elaboration. The 'relational sociology' of Emirbayer and Mische (1998) and more recent contributions from Sibeon (2004) and Stones (2006), provide an ontologically robust and analytically sharp conception of 'agency' in which its temporal, practical, and evaluative components are combined to form a rich and multilayered understanding of structured social interaction.

Given this relational understanding of 'agency' and its contextualization by structure, it is possible to consider the problems of 'over-complexity' and 'semi-anarchy' in research approach and explanatory logic. Baert (2005), among others, argued that there is a chronic lack of 'synchrony' between deep-level generative mechanisms ('the real') and surface-level events and experiences ('the actual' and 'the empirical') that critical realist research strategy ('retroduction') and design ('intensive research design') cannot overcome. No matter how extended retroductive analysis becomes, and no matter how multifaceted intensive research is, Baert (2005: 102–3) contends they cannot facilitate:

> ...access to the deeper level in the way in which critical realists claim that they can, for references to the empirical realm would be contaminated by the interferences of various mechanisms or powers. Likewise, the critical realist reliance on demi-regularities and stylized facts seems odd given their insistence on the lack of synchrony between the observable and the deep.

Baert seems to suggest that the inherent lack of synchrony between generative mechanisms and structural and cultural outcomes vitiates the causal model of explanation on which the critical realists' commitment to retroducive strategy and intensive design is based. If generative mechanisms and substantive outcomes are so 'out of sync' with each other – temporally, relationally, and practically – then it is difficult, if not impossible, to establish the type of complex causal linkages to which retroduction and intensive research aspire.

Additionally, if generative mechanisms are as complex and interwoven as critical realists claim, then it becomes doubly difficult to specify – that is, to separate them out – and to combine – that is, to relate them – with any degree of analytical precision or empirical confidence.

There are a number of responses to this criticism. The first is to draw an analytical distinction between the concept of 'generative mechanism', as a general conceptual tool, and as a defined sociohistorical reality. While the former operates in the domain of general model building and theoretical development, the latter is always recognized as inherently historical, contextual, and local (Pawson and Tilley, 1997; Blaikie, 2000). Consequently, the specific operation and impact of particular generative mechanisms in given sociohistorical contexts is inherently contingent in relation to the conditions under which they emerge and exert their influence over substantive outcomes at the level of social interaction.

The second response to Baert's critique is that the realist historical sociology of changing organizational forms and practices that is advocated here assumes that *causality is inherent in social interaction*. The latter necessarily contains certain productive powers and tendencies which bring about certain kinds of social structures and material conditions that substantially limit and constrain, but do not predetermine, present and future phases of structural elaboration and change (Manicas, 2006). The basic explanatory task for such a realist historical sociology of changing organizational forms is *to identify, trace, and map the complex ensembles of causes that emerged from the interaction between generative mechanisms, contextual conditions, and agents' strategies and to link these to outcomes that are inherently interesting, perplexing, and significant for us and, possibly, for future generations.*

This takes us to the final putative limitation of critical realism, that is its reluctant but expedient commitment to a 'spectator theory of knowledge', and the extent to which this legitimates 'imperialistic claims' to universal, objective truth (Baert, 2005; Contu and Willmott, 2005). This criticism suggests that critical realist researchers lack sensitivity and reflexivity concerning the extent to which they are directly implicated in and play a significant role in shaping their 'subject matter' and the knowledge that they generate as a result of 'researching it'. At the very worst, it is argued, critical realists presume to be able to achieve an external, objective, representational understanding and explanation of the social world that resonates strongly with the imperialistic knowledge claims typical of positivistic social science and the powerful ideological role that they played in legitimating organizational analysis as a 'policy science'. Thus, critical realists appear to be guilty of underestimating, if not ignoring, the significance of the 'double hermeneutic' in social scientific research – that social scientists interpret a preinterpreted 'social reality' of which they, and their knowledge claims, are constituent components – and of imposing a 'copying' or 'representational' theory of knowledge on their subject matter in such a way that 'scientific imperialism' can be smuggled in through the back door.

While critical realist research certainly aspires to provide a level of explanatory insight and understanding that goes beyond, and often challenges, actors' interpretations by offering a more explanatory powerful analysis, this does not legitimate a simple representational or 'mirror' theory of knowledge and the 'scientistic imperialism' flowing from it. This ambition is based on the belief that critical realist research can generate explanatory theories that are broader in their empirical scope and deeper in their analytical penetration than those produced by either positivist or constructionist-based theories. As Mutch et al. (2006: 611) reflect:

> What one notes in the critical realist position is a much more tentative approach to issues of truth and reality than suggested by some critics. The focus is on ways of understanding and explaining the world whose results are always avowedly provisional and corrigible, but which are presented as outcomes subject to further adjudication and

debate … What is central to critical realism, then, is not a claim to privileged access to the truth, but a genuine attempt to formulate better means of understanding … We cannot have any direct and unmediated access to this world, but we have not to tangle up our conceptions of the world with the existence of the world.

CONCLUSIONS

This chapter has provided an overview of critical realism, as a general philosophy of social science, and its implications for research strategy and design in organizational analysis. It has argued a case for critical realism to be seen as a 'third way' alternative to positivist and constructionist philosophies that have dominated organizational research for much of the second half of the twentieth century.

Critical realism thus resonates with many of the sensibilities and themes that shaped C. Wright Mills's (1959) critique of sociology in the 1950s. Mills identified two extreme philosophical tendencies and ideological positions in sociology. One was 'abstracted empiricism', with its emphasis on technical problem solving bereft of any kind of overarching intellectual rationale or purpose. The other was 'grand theory', with its combination of formalistic and formulaic sets of concepts and propositions, endlessly reformulated and rearranged, and high-level theoretical generalizations that seemed to bear little or no relationship to real social practices and actors in particular social situations. Neither of these extremes, Mills argued, was imbued with the 'sociological imagination', with a sensibility and a practice equipped to understand and explain the complex interconnections between 'personal troubles of milieu' and 'the public issues of the social structure' (Mills 1959: x). Whereas 'personal troubles' are embedded in localized streams of social interaction characteristic of particular communities and contexts, 'structural issues' transcend local environments of, in Archer's terms, 'primary agents' and are linked to the institutional structures of societies and the ongoing power

struggles between corporate agents located in the systems of position/practices that such structures generate and legitimate. The interconnections between the two, Mills concluded, are most likely to be revealed through a form of sociological research and analysis that focuses on the substantive problems faced by corporate agents working in structural contexts that endow them with unequal powers and skills to 'work these problems through', with fateful consequences for themselves, and for those with whom they struggle and collaborate for control over 'the past', 'the present', and 'the future'.

This is exactly the focus that drives critical realist organizational research and analysis, the desire to understand and explain the complex interplay between 'structure' and 'agency' as it works its way through the collective power struggles in which corporate agents are engaged and the longer-term impact of these struggles on institutional and practical outcomes. In this way, we may be better placed, as researchers and as social actors, to provide a hopeful response to Blaikie's (2000: 153) lament that:

> In spite of the fact that it is now forty years since Mills expressed these concerns, what he had to say can still be applied to a great deal of social research. The techniques may have become more sophisticated, and there may be more effort to avoid the appellation of being a-theoretical, but methodological inhibition is still rampant. With the advent of postmodernism, 'methodological paralysis' has taken over.

Critical realism can offer organizational researchers the required intellectual framework and tools that they need to rediscover the sense of intellectual challenge and excitement that Mills identified at the core of the 'sociological imagination', and to resist the theoretical stasis and methodological sterility of a positivistic organizational science and the theoretical paralysis and methodological anarchy of a postmodern organizational discourse.

REFERENCES

Ackroyd, S. (2004) 'Methodology for management and organization studies: some implications of critical realism', in S. Fleetwood and S. Ackroyd (eds), *Critical Realist Applications in Organization and Management Studies*, London: Sage, pp.137–63.

Ackroyd, S. and Fleetwood, S. (eds) (2000) *Realist Perspectives on Management and Organizations*, London: Routledge.

Archer, M. (1995) *Realist Social Theory: The Morphogenetic Approach*, Cambridge: Cambridge University Press.

Archer, M. (2000) *Being Human: The Problem of Agency*, Cambridge: Cambridge University Press.

Archer, M. (2003) *Structure, Agency and the Internal Conversation*, Cambridge: Cambridge University Press.

Archer, M., Bhaskar, R., Collier, A., Lawson, T. and Norrie, A. (eds) (1998) *Critical Realism: Essential Readings*, London: Routledge.

Baert, P. (1998) *Social Theory in the Twentieth Century*, Oxford: Polity Press.

Baert, P. (2005) *Philosophy of the Social Sciences: Towards Pragmatism*, Oxford: Polity Press.

Bhaskar, R. (1978) *A Realist Theory of Science*, (second edn.), Brighton: Harvester, (first edn. 1975).

Bhaskar, R. (1986) *Scientific Realism and Human Emancipation*, London: Verso.

Bhaskar, R. (1989) *The Possibility of Naturalism: A Philosophical Critique of the Contemporary Human Sciences*, Brighton: Harvester Press.

Blaikie, N. (1993) *Approaches to Social Enquiry*, Oxford: Polity Press.

Blaikie, N. (2000) *Designing Social Research*, Oxford: Polity Press.

Blau, P. (1955) *The Dynamics of Bureaucracy*, (first edn.), Chicago: University Of Chicago Press (Revised Edition 1963).

Boal, K., Hunt, J. and Jaros, S. (2004) 'Order is free: on the ontological status of organizations', in R. Westwood and S. Clegg (eds), *Debating Organization: Point-Counterpoint in Organization Studies*, Oxford: Blackwell, pp. 84–97.

Brown, A. (2004) 'Authoritative sense-making in a public inquiry report', *Organization Studies*, 25(1): 95–112.

Burkitt, I. (1998) 'Relations, communication and power', in I. Velody and R. Williams (eds), *The Politics of Constructionism*, London: Sage, pp. 121–31.

Clark, P. (2000), *Organizations in Action: Competition between Contexts*, London: Routledge.

Clark, P. (2003) *Organizational Innovations*, London: Sage.

Contu, A. and Willmott, H. (2005) 'You Spin me Around: The Realist Turn in Organization and Management Studies', *Journal of Management Studies*, 42(8): 1645–62.

Crozier, M. (1964) *The Bureaucratic Phenomenon*, Chicago: University of Chicago Press.

Danermark, B., Ekstrom, M., Jakobsen, L. and Karlsson, J. (2002) *Explaining Society: Critical Realism in the Social Sciences*, London: Routledge.

Delbridge, R. (1998) *Life on the Line in Contemporary Manufacturing*, Oxford: Oxford University Press.

Delbridge, R. (2004) 'Working in teams: ethnographic evidence from two high performance workplaces', in S. Fleetwood and S. Ackroyd (eds), *Critical Realist Applications in Organization and Management Studies*, London: Routledge, pp. 257–73.

Ekstrom, M. (1992) 'Causal explanation of social action: the contribution of Max Weber and of critical realism to a generative view of causal explanation in social science', *Acta Sociologica: Journal of the Scandinavian Sociological Association*, 35: 107–22.

Emirbayer, M. and Mische, A. (1998) 'What is agency?', *American Journal of Sociology*, 103(4): 962–1023.

Fairclough, N. (2003) *Analysing Discourse: Textual Analysis for Social Research*, London: Routledge.

Fairclough, N. (2005) 'Discourse Analysis in Organization Studies', *Organization Studies,* 26(6): 915–39.

Fairclough, N., Jessop, B. and Sayer, A. (2002) 'Critical realism and semiosis', Journal of Critical Realism, 5(1): 2–10.

Fleetwood, S. and Ackroyd, S. (eds) (2004) 'Critical realist applications in organization and management studies', London: Routledge.

Gabriel, Y. (1997) 'The use of stories in organizational research', in D. Symon and N. Cassell (eds), *Qualitative Methods in Organizational Research*, London: Sage, pp. 60–74.

Gergen, K. (1994) *Realities and Relationships: Soundings in Social Construction*, Cambridge, MA: Harvard University Press.

Gouldner, A. (1954) *Patterns of Industrial Bureaucracy*, New York: Collier Macmillan.

Gouldner, A. (1971) *The Coming Crisis of Western Sociology*, London: Heinemann.

Grant, D., Keenoy, T. and Oswick, C. (eds) (1998) *Discourse and Organization*, London: Sage.

Grant, D., Hardy, C., Oswick, C. and Putnam, L. (2004) *The Sage Handbook of Organizational Discourse*, London: Sage.

Hammersley, M. (1992) *What's Wrong with Ethnography?*, London: Routledge.

Hammersley, M. and Atkinson, P. (1995) *Ethnography: Principles in Practice*, (Second edn.), London: Routledge.

Hay, C. (2001) 'What place for ideas in the structure-agency debate?: globalization as a process without a subject', *Writing in the Critical Social Sciences*, London: First Press.

Hesketh, A. and Brown, P. (2004) 'I say Tomato, you say Tamato: putting critical realism to work in the knowledge worker recruitment process', in S. Fleetwood and S. Ackroyd (eds), *Critical Realist Applications in Organization and Management Studies*, London: Routledge, pp. 337–355.

Hesketh, A. and Fleetwood, S. (2006) 'Beyond measuring the human resources management-organizational performance link: applying critical realist meta-theory', *Organization*, 13(5): 677–99.

Kennedy, C. and Kennedy, P. (2004) 'The moral management of nursing labour power: conceptualizing control and reistance', in S. Fleetwood and S. Ackroyd (eds), *Critical Realist Applications in Organization and Management Studies*, London: Routledge, pp. 321–36.

Layder, D. (1994) *Understanding Social Theory*, London: Sage.

Layder, D. (1997) *Modern Social Theory*, London: UCL Press.

Layder, D. (1998), *Sociological Practice: Linking Theory and Social Research*, London: Sage.

Lopez, J. and Potter, G. (eds) (2001) *After Postmodernism: An Introduction to Critical Realism*, London: The Althone Press.

Lukes, S. (2005) *Power: A Radical View*, (Second edn.), Basingstoke: Palgrave Macmillan.

Lukes, S. (2006) 'Reply to Comments', *Political Studies Review*, Review Symposium on Steven Lukes', Power: A Radical View, (Second edn.), 4 (2): 164–173.

Manicas, P. (2006) *A Realist Philosophy of Social Science: Explanation and Understanding*, Cambridge: Cambridge University Press.

Miller, D. (2005) 'What is best value?: bureaucracy, virtualism and local governance', in P. Du Gay (ed.), *The Values of Bureaucracy*, Oxford: Oxford University Press, pp. 233–54.

Mills, C. W. (1959) 'The sociological imagination', New York: Oxford University Press.

Mutch, A. (2006) *Strategic and Organizational Change: From Production to Retailing in UK Brewing 1950–1990*, London: Routledge.

Mutch, A., Delbridge, R. and Ventresca, M. (2006) 'Situating organizational action: the relational sociology of organizations', *organization*, Special Issue – 'Situating Institutional Analysis of Organization', 13(5): 607–25.

Parker, J. (2000) *Structuration*, Buckingham: Open University Press.

Pawson, R. and Tilley, N. (1997) *Realistic Evaluation*, London: Sage.

Porter, S. (1993) 'Critical realist ethnography: the case of racism and professionalism in a medical setting', *Sociology*, 27(4): 591–609.

Porter, S. (2002) 'Critical realist ethnography', in T. May (ed), *Qualitative Research in Action*, London: Sage, pp. 53–72.

Reed, M. (1997) 'In praise of duality and dualism: rethinking structure and agency in organizational analysis', *Organization Studies*, 18(1): 21–42.

Reed, M. (1998) 'Organizational analysis as discourse analysis: a critique', in D. Grant, T. Keenoy, and C. Oswick (eds), *Discourse and Organization*, London: Sage, pp.193–213.

Reed, M. (2001) 'Organization, trust and control: a realist analysis', *Organization Studies*, 22(2): 201–23.

Reed, M. (2003) 'The agency/structure dilemma in organization theory: open doors and brick walls', in H. Tsoukas and C. Knudsen (eds), *The Oxford Handbook of Organization Theory: Meta-Theoretical Perspectives*, Oxford: Oxford University Press, pp. 289–309.

Reed, M. (2004) 'Getting real about organizational discourse', in D. Grant, C. Hardy, C. Oswick and L. Putnam (eds), *The Sage Handbook of Organizational Discourse*, London: Sage, pp. 413–20.

Reed, M. (2005a) 'Reflections on the realist turn in organization and management studies', *Journal of Management Studies*, 42(8): 1621–44.

Reed, M. (2005b) 'Beyond the iron cage?: bureaucracy and democracy in the knowledge economy and society', in P. Du Gay (ed.), *The Values of Bureaucracy*, Oxford: Oxford University Press, pp. 115–40.

Reed, M. (2006) 'Organizational theorizing: a historically contested terrain', in S. Clegg, C. Hardy, T. Lawrence and W. Nord (eds), *The Sage Handbook of Organization Studies*, Second Edition, London: Sage, pp. 19–54.

Reed, M. (forthcoming, 2009) 'Bureaucratic theory and the intellectual renewal of contemporary organization studies', in P. Adler (ed.), *Sociology Classics and Organization Studies*, Oxford: Oxford University Press.

Sayer, A. (1992) *Method in Social Science*, London: Routledge.

Sayer, A. (2000) *Realism and Social Science*, London: Sage.

Searle, J. (1995) *The Construction of Social Reality*, Harmondsworth: Penguin.

Selznick, P. (1949) *TVA and the Grass Roots* (Second edn. 1966), New York: Harper.

Sibeon, R. (2004) *Rethinking Social Theory*, London: Sage.

Silverman, D. (2000) *Doing Qualitative Research: A Practical Handbook*, London: Sage.

Smith, D. (2005) *Institutional Ethnography: A Sociology for People*, New York: Rowman and Littlefield.

Stones, R. (2005) *Structuration Theory*, London: Palgrave Macmillan.

Taylor, P. and Bain, P. (2004) 'Humour and subversion in two call centres', in S. Fleetwood and S. Ackroyd (eds), *Critical Realist Applications in Organization and Management Studies*, London: Routledge, pp. 274–97.

Trigg, R. (2001) *Understanding Social Science*, Second Edition, Oxford: Blackwell.

Westwood, R. and Linstead, S. (eds) (2001) *The Language of Organization*, London: Sage.

PART IV

Methods: Data Collection in Organizational Research

Focusing on methods of data collection in organizational research, demonstrating the inventiveness and innovation that now characterizes this field, and the widening range of possibilities concerning the development of data collection tools

26

Response Rates and Sample Representativeness: Identifying Contextual Response Drivers

Timothy R. Hinkin and Brooks C. Holtom

Whether assessing employee attitudes for organizational purposes or collecting data for an academic study, the primary objective of organizational surveys is to obtain high-quality data that are reliable and valid and that accurately reflect the beliefs and attitudes of the target population. There are two primary threats to achieving this objective. The first deals with the measures themselves and the second with the survey administration techniques.

With respect to measures, items must adequately sample the domain of interest, yet scales should be parsimonious and surveys not excessively lengthy to avoid creating respondent fatigue. They must demonstrate adequate psychometric properties such as stable factor structure and high internal consistency reliability. Items must be worded properly and in a manner that is easily understood by respondents. The measures must generate adequate variance and relate to other constructs as expected. Many articles that offer assistance in the development of sound measures have been published in the past (e.g., Hinkin, 1998; Bagozzi et al., 1991) and issues related to scale development are also discussed in Chapters 20 and 37 of this Handbook.

The second threat to obtaining quality data deals with survey administration procedures. Respondents must understand the language used, be motivated to participate, and have adequate time and opportunity to complete the survey. Obtaining a high response rate to surveys is important to ensure quality of the data and generalizability of results.

The purpose of this chapter is twofold. First, we examine contextual factors that may impact a potential respondent's willingness to participate in an employee opinion survey. Second, we offer suggestions for survey administration that will result in higher rates of respondent participation.

Importance of response rate

In order for researchers to appropriately support or reject their hypotheses, the data obtained from their samples must be comprehensive and representative (Baruch, 1999). When responses are obtained from only a portion of the sample, such responses may not represent the full sample and can thus introduce bias (Viswesvaran et al., 1993). Researchers have cause for concern when the sample of respondents differs from the population in terms of the variables of interest and such differences result in distortion of the 'true' effect (Schalm and Kelloway, 2001). To the extent that survey responses are affected by certain respondent characteristics, there is also a high probability of biased results and subsequent interpretations (Tomaskovic-Devey et al., 1994). Another reason high response rates are important to organizational researchers is more pragmatic. Response bias poses a threat to the generalizability of the findings and the weight they are given by organizational constituents. Though there are a variety of potential causes for nonresponse, the result is a serious concern about the external validity of the entire research project (Roth and BeVier, 1998).

To foster academic credibility, integrity, and professionalism, we use norms for response rates to establish what is publishable (Baruch, 1999). While the norm advocated by Baruch (60% +/−20% for general populations of employees, managers, or professionals) is only likely to be known to academics, its use as a benchmark can aid in practitioner understanding of survey response rates. When researchers use convenience samples as the majority do (Ludbrook and Dudley, 1998) and experience low response rates, the research importance will likely be diminished in the eyes of practitioners, because it lacks a critical element of credibility. Thus, when trying to mobilize change in an organization based on research, practitioners would be much more confident with a high response rate than with a low response rate. In sum, increasing response rate is one of the safest strategies for reducing nonsampling errors (Simsek and Veiga, 2000) and increasing the impact of organizational research.

A number of studies have been published indicating that response rate is not necessarily related to sample representativeness or the effect sizes between variables and that representativeness of research samples is much more important than the response rate (Cook et al., 2000; Krosnick, 1999; Schalm and Kelloway, 2001). It is not necessarily true that representativeness increases monotonically with increasing response rate (Krosnick, 1999). However, *in general,* increasing response rate leads to a higher *probability* of response from individuals who are representative of the overall sample, while at the same time increasing statistical power to identify significant effects. All other things being equal, a higher response rate is preferable to a lower response rate to increase statistical power, minimize the possibility of obtaining biased data, maximize the generalizability of the study, and increase the utility of the study for organizational purposes.

Given wide agreement that high response rates are desirable, why do so many researchers struggle to attain them? One prominent explanation is a general survey fatigue or what Baruch (1999) calls 'market saturation.' Organizations and people are bombarded with surveys and questionnaires from many sources. Given the increasing popularity of opinion polls, emergence of online survey tools, and fondness of organizational managers for insight into the attitudes and beliefs of their stakeholders, oversurveying has worsened the situation (Weiner and Dalessio, 2006). Consequently, people become increasingly selective in their attention to surveys. This undoubtedly contributes to the general decline in survey response rates that have been observed in organizational research (Baruch, 1999).

Survey administration techniques may also influence willingness to respond to surveys. (Singer, Van Hoewyk and Maher, 2000; Goldstein and Jennings, 2002). For nearly three decades, researchers have followed Dillman's (1978) 'total design method' (now called the 'tailored design method') to increase mailed survey response rates.

The tailored design method (Dillman, 2000) consists of five elements: (1) a respondent-friendly questionnaire, (2) up to five contacts with the questionnaire recipient, (3) inclusion of stamped return envelopes, (4) personalized correspondence, and (5) a token financial incentive that is sent with the survey request.

Over the years, scholars have tested these and other methods. Many meta-analyses of this work are available (Church, 1993; Roth and BeVier, 1998; Yammarino, Skinner and Childers, 1991; Yu and Cooper, 1983). The findings indicate that response rates from employees, customers, and the general public can be increased by: (1) providing advance notice, (2) following up with potential respondents, (3) offering gifts or monetary incentives, and (4) personalizing the cover letter or address. Among these techniques, Roth and BeVier's meta-analysis (1998) demonstrated that advance notice was the most effective at increasing return rates.

There has also been a recent increase in research examining the use of electronic channels such as e-mail or the internet in conducting organizational surveys. While earlier studies suggested that web-based studies suffer from lower response rates (Mavis and Brocato, 1998; Cook et al., 2000), recent research clearly shows that among articles published in the past seven years, the response rate for electronic surveys exceeds the response rate for traditional mail surveys (Baruch and Holtom, 2007).

While this research is interesting to researchers in general, it has not directly addressed theory-based reasons why people are resistant to responding to organizational surveys. Stated succinctly, ...despite the large volume of research, we know little about the attitudes and personalities of actual nonrespondents to an organizational survey' (Rogelberg et al., 2003: 1104). There has also been no examination of the impact of organization context on willingness to participate in a survey. For example, consider the possibility that conditions exist in an organization that inhibit responses of a certain group of employees. If the survey is trying to assess job satisfaction or organizational commitment (two of the most

studied variables in organizational research) and if this group of employees does not respond at the same rate as other groups, it is unlikely that the overall organizational levels of satisfaction or commitment will be accurately reported. Subsequent analysis will likely also be influenced, as will the prescriptions for change within the organization. In sum, it is critical to understand the context when conducting organizational research (Johns, 2006).

We believe that as researchers cooperate with managers to study their organizations, the researchers will also gain insight into the contextual factors that will increase the probability of obtaining a high response rate from the individuals within that organization. Many of those inhibiting factors are beyond the control of the researcher. Thus, without the assistance of managers, response rates could be negatively affected, resulting in potentially biased data. In other words, these cooperative activities form the foundation of knowledge and trust that will facilitate effective organizational research.

Individual level response rates

In this section we will discuss reasons why individuals would resist compliance with a request to complete an employee opinion survey. In most research settings, Human Subjects Committee standards require that potential respondents have the option to decline to participate in a survey for academic research. The key question is why they would or would not participate. We will first discuss existing literature examining survey nonresponse and then present a framework of response drivers.

Existing literature

Overall, there are relatively few published research articles specifically exploring organizational survey noncompliance. In one study, Rogelberg et al. (2000) examined possible reasons for noncompliance and found that it was related to intentions to quit, reduced satisfaction with one's supervisor and organizational commitment, and negative beliefs about what the organization might do with the survey results. They argue that reciprocity and a psychological contract may have an impact on willingness to comply, but they did not empirically examine this. Rogelberg et al. (2003) differentiated between active versus passive nonrespondents. The reasons they offered for passive nonresponse included losing the survey, forgetting, and missing the deadline. In contrast, active nonresponders make a conscious decision not to respond to the survey. Rogelberg et al. (2003) conducted a study using undergraduate students' responses to a survey administered by a university and found that those students who were more satisfied with the university and were more conscientious and agreeable, were more likely to complete the survey. They 'speculate that dissatisfaction with the survey-sponsoring entity is one of a number of drivers that independently and interactively led to an individual actively withholding his or her participation' (p. 1111). They then suggest that there are factors other than satisfaction and personality that will impact willingness to participate and discuss other potential issues such as skepticism about survey research, concerns for privacy, and trust. From this research, we have learned that positive affect toward the organization and personality are related to increased willingness to participate in an organizational survey. It is also very likely that potential respondents consider other factors when deciding whether to participate. There is still much to learn about the underlying causes of individual noncompliance.

In examining the factors that would impact response rates for surveys seeking organization-level data, Tomaskovic-Dvey et al. (1994), developed a theory of non-response. They identified key organizational characteristics that can affect response rates. Specifically, they stated that ...the likelihood that an organizational respondent will respond to a survey request to be a function of their authority to respond, capacity to respond, and motive to respond.' (p. 440). Authority refers to the formal or informal authority granted by the organization to respond to such a survey request. Capacity refers to ability and opportunity to respond to survey requests.

Motive refers to the organizational and individual desire to disclose information about the organization. They then go on to examine macrolevel factors that may affect response rates but do little to examine nonresponse at the individual level. They suggest that responding to surveys would not be covered in most job descriptions and that those whose personal goals are in alignment with those of the organization would be more likely to respond. To extend this framework to the individual level, we build on the 'capacity' and 'motive' dimensions by conceptualizing them as 'ability' and 'willingness' to respond.

Ability

We assume that any organizationally sanctioned survey would both implicitly and explicitly give respondents the authority to complete it. Thus, ability to respond in this context addresses primarily the availability of time to complete the survey, questionnaire characteristics, and administration practices that affect ease of responding. Clearly, if respondents are not provided ample opportunity to complete a survey, response rates will be affected. Passive nonresponse (Rogelberg, et al., 2003) would fall in to this category as individuals just do not seem to get around to completing the survey. It may also include language issues, as many organizations are comprised of individuals for whom English is not their first language. Respondents also must have the intellectual ability to read and understand the survey questions. There has been a plethora of research conducted on survey design studying such factors as item wording, response scaling, and survey length that may affect ability to respond (e.g., Hinkin 1995, 1998; Yu and Cooper, 1983; Roth and BeVier, 1998). The more complex and lengthy the survey, the greater the chance lack of ability would have a negative impact on response rates.

Willingness

The focus of the following section will be on six largely unexamined response drivers that could affect the willingness of an individual to respond to an organizational survey. We will present a framework and then integrate the material discussed in the preceding section and other relevant theory to explain why we believe these factors are important in affecting response rates.

We propose that the six response drivers could create a psychological predisposition, or willingness, to participate in an organizational survey (salience, significance, trust, fairness, coworker influence, and management support). These differ from attitudes toward the organization or personality variables studied in previous research (e.g., Rogelberg et al., 2000, 2003) in that they address the context of the actual survey administration. Context is defined as ... factors associated with units of analysis above those expressly under investigation' (Cappelli and Sherer, 1991: 56). Contextual factors include, but are not limited to, organizational climate, culture, norms, values, and relationships with managers and peers (Rousseau and Fried, 2001). Context can influence attitudes and behavior in organizational settings and result in biased responses if it is unrecognized by researchers (Johns, 2006). We believe that contextual factors may also impact survey response rates.

To broaden the research lens, we consulted literature that examines individuals' willingness to participate in any activity. It has been shown that the attractiveness or unattractiveness of the inherent features of an activity will determine if people will comply with a request to participate in that activity. These features may include personal relevance, interest value, and time and resources required to perform the activity. Cialdini (1988) argued that there are also social or psychological factors that affect willingness to comply with a request and proposed six basic compliance principles. Groves et al. (1992) extended this framework and used the principles to explain why individuals participate in telephone surveys. Similar to Rogelberg et al. (2003) the authors conceptualized a survey response as a helping behavior, and suggested that people are more likely to participate if they believe that doing so would have a positive impact.

These compliance principles are also applicable to organizational surveys (Tourangeau, 2004). The first principle is reciprocity or participating due to a sense of obligation, similar to the propositions put forth by Rogelberg et al. (2000). Second is consistency; once someone commits to a position, s/he should be more willing to comply with requests for behaviors that are consistent with that position. Third is social validation or compliance due to the fact that others perceived as similar to oneself are doing so. Fourth is authority; compliance is more likely if the request comes from a legitimate authority. Fifth is scarcity; the emphasis here is that there is an opportunity for the individual's opinion to be heard. Sixth is liking; an individual would be more positively inclined to comply with the requests of someone they like. Groves et al. (1992) also found that emotional state can impact helping behavior and proposed that anger would have a negative impact on compliance with a survey request while happiness enhances the desire to help. They did not discuss the targets of or causes for the emotions. We will draw on these principles to develop six response drivers for participation in organizational surveys.

Integrating and expanding upon the literatures discussed in the foregoing section leads us to describe the contextual response drivers as salience of the issue being examined, significance of respondent participation, organizational fairness, coworker influence, management support, and trust in the organization. We will briefly discuss each dimension and explain why we believe they could impact response rates. Further, in Table 26.1, we provide examples of organizational manifestations that suggest a contextual factor needs to be addressed by the researcher or the organization.

Salience of the survey

First, if an issue is salient to an individual he or she will be much more likely to be engaged in it (Cialdini, 2006). The consistency principle discussed previously suggests that involvement in an issue would likely increase participation in a survey that addresses that issue. This has shown to be true in telephone surveys

Table 26.1   Conceptual response drivers and organizational manifestations

Contextual response drivers	Organizational manifestations
WILLINGNESS	
Salience of survey	Organizational priorities have been clearly communicated by management and they do not include this survey. The survey examines issues that are unimportant to employees.
Significance of response	Nothing has been done following prior surveys.
Organizational fairness	Relations between employees and management are currently strained.
Coworker influence	Pre-existing culture of only completing any task that comes directly from internal management. Peers are resistant to survey participation.
Management support	There is a lack of expressed management commitment for surveys in general or for this one in particular.
Trust in the organization	There were negative consequences for employees following results of a prior survey.
ABILITY	
Survey characteristics/ administration/channel	Internal organizational distribution channels are unreliable. Employees have a mother tongue that is different from that used in the survey or do not understand parts or all of the survey for other reasons.
Time constraints	Employees are feeling overwhelmed with other work.

(Groves et al., 2004, 1992). Issue salience has also been associated with higher response rates in consumer populations (Roth and BeVier, 1998). Studies examining consumer surveys suggests that response rates can be increased by numerous contacts with respondents (Yammarino et al., 1991; Cook et al., 2000). This contact, in essence, increases the salience of the issue. It is, therefore, likely that surveys that deal with issues that employees feel are important and/or affect them would elicit a higher rate of response.

Significance of response

Significance can be thought of in two ways. First, 'Is my response to the survey going to make a difference?' This is an application of the scarcity principle discussed previously, as it has been shown that if respondents feel that their opinion will count they will be more likely to complete a telephone survey (Groves et al., 1992). Research examining university alumni response to a survey found that those who felt their response would make a difference were much more likely to respond than those who did not (Lundquist et al., 1994). If a respondent feels that her/his opinion will make a difference, they will be more likely to participate. A second question tapping into significance is, 'Will anything be done with the results of the survey?' Groves et al. (1992) suggest that survey participation may increase if respondents feel that results of the survey will lead to positive outcomes. This is analogous to the 'task significance' psychological state that impacts motivation (Hackman and Oldham, 1980). An individual feels that a task is significant to the extent that it has a substantial impact on the lives or work of other organizational members. If individuals feel that the results of the survey will be acted upon, they will be more likely to participate. There is also a historical aspect to this dimension. When previous survey results have not been acted upon, respondents are less likely to participate.

Organizational fairness

Perceived organizational fairness could significantly impact response rates. The reciprocity principle discussed previously is applicable here as people feel obligated to respond positively in return for receiving positive outcomes (Groves et al., 1992). Studies of leader-member exchange and organization citizenship behaviors have found that subordinates will reciprocate implied obligations with supervisors by expanding their roles beyond what is normally expected of them (Podsakoff et al., 2000).

Both distributive and procedural justice have a major impact on perceptions of fairness (Folger and Cropanzano, 1998). If people feel that they receive rewards that equal or exceed their contributions to the organizations, they will be more likely to participate. Similarly, if the procedures and systems utilized by the organization are consistent over time and across individuals, there will most likely be increased willingness to participate. Equity theory (Adams, 1965) suggests that individuals seek equilibrium between their inputs and the outcomes they receive from organizations. If there is an unfavorable imbalance, it is likely that the potential respondents will not be willing to exert any extra effort. Respondents may not complete a survey, because they perceive it as outside of their normal job responsibilities and an extra burden (Tomaskovic-Dvey et al., 1994). The study of perceived fairness in the service literature has found that when individuals feel as if they have been treated unfairly they may be driven to get even with the organization (Seiders and Berry, 1998). It is possible that respondents might be motivated to fill out a survey if they felt it was a way to 'get back' at the organization that is perceived to be treating the individual unfairly. In general, however, we would expect that if respondents feel they have not been treated fairly, they would be less likely to complete a survey if doing so was viewed as helping the organization.

Coworker influence
Coworker pressure could either increase or decrease one's willingness to respond to a survey for a number of reasons. The social validation principle discussed earlier states that people often decide how to act by observing how similar others act (Groves et al., 1992; Latané and Darley, 1970). An individual would be more likely to complete a survey if coworkers do so. There are strong normative pressures exerted by groups (Hackman, 1992). Opinions could be influenced significantly if there existed informal groups with strong norms to either participate or not. Another principle, liking another person (e.g., the researcher or the

supervisor providing the survey) or wanting to be liked by others could also impact participation (Tomaskovic-Dvey et al., 1994).

Management support
Management commitment and support for survey participation should have a strong positive impact on response rate. The authority principle states that compliance to a request is more likely if it comes from a legitimate source (Groves et al., 1992). There is an abundance of literature emphasizing the importance of top-management commitment to the success of a variety of programs or interventions (e.g., Bass and Avolio, 1994; Deming, 2000; Yukl, 2002). Immediate supervisors have been shown to have a large influence on the attitudes of their subordinates (Feldman, 1981; Tepper, 1995). Without the encouragement of both upper management and immediate supervisors, response rates are likely to be negatively affected.

Trust in the organization
Although it is not based on the principles presented by Cialdini (1988) or Groves et al. (1992) we propose that trust in the organization and/or researchers is an important contextual factor. Trust is believed to influence interpersonal behavior more than any other single variable (Kets de Vries, 1999; Golembiewski and McConkie, 1975) and a lack of trust could certainly have a negative impact on response rates. Rogelberg et al. (2003) stated that privacy and trust will impact willingness to participate in a survey. If individuals fear that their responses may be revealed, they would be much less likely to participate for fear of punishment. Also, there may be a fear that if one's manager receives bad news from the results of the survey, the work group will be punished. Even if individual responses are kept confidential, a manager may respond negatively toward his/her subordinates as a whole.

We have extended the concept of 'nonresponse drivers' proposed by Rogelberg, et al. (2003) and presented six contextual response drivers. We recognize that this list is not exhaustive but it has been developed based on existing theory and research.

More work is clearly needed on the issue. As discussed by Johns (2006), context may serve as an unmeasured moderator of relationships or have a main effect on organizational behavior. We have taken the position that the identified response drivers comprise a portion of the organizational context related to survey administration. As such, the response decision may be either open to influence via organizational intervention to encourage participation and overcome 'survey fatigue' or, at a minimum, more easily understood using the organizational context as a frame of reference. We further suggest that cooperation between academic researchers and organizations may offer both a window into a greater understanding of the context in which surveys are administered and opportunities to influence that context through organizational intervention in order to maximize response rates. Calls for contextualization are increasing and response rates are declining. One major reaction to this has been repeated exhortations for more academic-practitioner interaction in organizations to improve the quality of both research and teaching (Pfeffer and Fong, 2002; Mintzberg, 2004; Bennis and O'Toole, 2005; Rousseau and Fried, 2001). We will now introduce a prescriptive model for academic-organizational cooperation that offers ideas about how to influence response rates and thus external validity. We will then integrate the model with the previous discussion of contextual response drivers.

Academic/organization cooperation

To guide this section, we adopt the following definition of cooperation: 'acting together, in a coordinated way at work, leisure, or in social relationships, in the pursuit of shared goals, the enjoyment of the joint activity, or simply furthering the relationship' (Argyle, 1991: 4). According to Argyle (1991) there are three possible sources of motivation for cooperative behavior: external rewards, enjoyment of shared activities, and/or pre-existing valued relationships. The definition adopted here acknowledges that cooperative relationships

may be developed for the purposes of mutual material benefits.

In order to provide examples of the forms of cooperative involvement by organizations in academic survey research, we identified articles reporting organizational survey results in the *Academy of Management Journal* and *Journal of Applied Psychology* between 2002 and 2005. Following Baruch's advice (1999), we distinguished between surveys targeting individual employees and those targeting representative samples within organizations. For the purposes of this chapter, only the latter will be referred to as organizational surveys. We read the introduction, methods, discussion, and results sections of each paper. There were 48 studies using organizational surveys published in the *Journal of Applied Psychology* between 2002 and 2005. Twenty-four of these articles either explicitly described cooperative behavior between the researcher and the organization or described the research process in sufficient detail to demonstrate evidence that cooperative activity must have taken place. For example, Simons and Roberson (2003) do not discuss cooperative activities but note that the surveys were distributed during company time at employee meetings. The authors must, at minimum, have received consent from the organization to administer the surveys in this fashion. Forty-three studies using organizational surveys were found in the *Academy of Management Journal* between 2002 and 2005, of which 33 provided information on cooperative behavior. Once a list of all cooperative activities reported in the publications was generated, items were categorized (See Appendix 1).

We do not presume that all organizational survey research involves organizational cooperation. For example, academic researchers may identify employees from an organization at a conference or through an available list and simply send the survey directly to these employees through standard delivery vehicles such as regular mail, email, or telephone. In this case, the researcher may not be privy to elements of the pre-existing organizational context except through information that is publicly available. This seems to have been the case, for example, in Barling et al. (2002) in which a sample of employees working in fast-food restaurants appear to have been approached individually.

At a low level of involvement, organizational members assist academic researchers in the administration of the survey by approving requests from the academic researcher. However, the cooperation is passive, responding to requests from the researcher to gain access to the organization or granting approval to undertake various components of the study. It is assumed that the researcher initiates the research, and the only role the organization plays is one of approving aspects of the survey administration and/or design. For example, the researcher may ask a senior manager for permission to survey the organization's employees, and the manager may grant this permission. An example of this kind of cooperation may be found in Van Vianen et al. (2004) in which banks allowed organizational surveys to be sent through their intra-firm electronic network. This may have increased the salience of the survey as well as perceptions of management support of the survey. We posit that such approvals—even in the absence of any other participation from the organization—may assist researchers in increasing response rates.

In many cases, however, the organization's cooperation becomes more active. The researcher *or* the organization may initiate the study. For example, Kostova and Roth (2002) provide a detailed discussion of organizational involvement in their study, noting that the survey instrument was developed 'with the active participation of the target MNC's corporate quality department ...' (p. 22). Another example with active organizational cooperation is by Ostroff et al. (2002), who reported that management informed employees of the survey, encouraged participation, and allowed its completion on company time. These steps may have affected perceptions by employees of management support as well as survey salience and significance. This study resulted in responses from 75% of the entire employee population.

In the ideal case, the organization becomes a partner in the design, administration, and data analysis phases of the survey. Organization members may provide input in all phases of the study, contribute insights into key issues that may affect research design and administration and provide extensive organizational data that can enhance the survey's usefulness. The relationship is more likely, given the time commitment required by the organization, to be one in which the organization intends to reap direct benefits from the study. Amabile, Patterson, Mueller, Wojcik, Odomirok, Marsh and Kramer (2001) introduce the concept of academic/practitioner cooperation as a form of cross-professional relationship. Of the many important findings from their case study, one was the critical role of the practitioner in the data-collection process. They note that the 75% response rate they achieved was far above that of the average organizational survey.

It was difficult to determine from our review the extent of possible cooperation, as many articles did not discuss the nature of the relationship between the researcher and the organization. Two notable exceptions were found. A study by Green et al. (2003) notes that '... questionnaires were developed through a year-long joint effort of academic and R&D personnel.' In this study, R&D personnel from the organization studied were highly involved with design and administration stages of the survey. The response rate was 91%. Bachrach, Bamberger and Sonnenstuhl (2002) noted that the researchers spent 18 months inside of an organization collecting ethnographic data, for which they had received organizational support. They state, 'By the time the survey process began, most workers were aware of the nature of the study and its importance to them as union members' (p. 643). This could have increased factors such as salience, significance, and perceptions of management support of the survey.

We acknowledge that the absence of information on cooperative behavior in a published study does not necessarily imply that there was none and that information provided on organizational cooperation may not be complete. This list of cooperative activities cannot, therefore, be construed as necessarily exhaustive or representative of all organizational survey research publications. We do not attempt to correlate response rates and cooperation behavior given the significant variation in other factors affecting response rates that may have occurred across studies and that may not have been discussed in the publication. That said, additional commentary by study authors to develop a more complete portrait of the context in which surveys were completed could facilitate such an analysis and benefit readers.

We believe that two aspects of the academic/organization relationship beyond the study itself merit discussion as they may impact the likelihood that employees will respond to surveys. The first is whether or not the survey is part of a formal research program within the organization. As many academics are aware, there are a variety of formal programs for sponsored research (Cyert and Goodman, 1997). Examples of institutions that support organizational research include the Alfred P. Sloan Foundation, the Ford Foundation, the National Science Foundation, as well as others. There may be effects on employee willingness and ability to respond if they are aware of these programs, if the programs are based on topics that the organization has established as important, if there is a certain level of trust in the process associated with these programs, and/or if employees have had prior experience with them. None of the identified studies mentioned formal research programs. The second important aspect is the one-time versus ongoing nature of the cooperative relationships. The inter-organization cooperation literature proposes that longer-term relationships are more likely result in greater mutual trust, exposure to information, and mutual learning (Osborn and Hagedoom, 1997; Saxton, 1997). We would add that there may be a familiarity and trust developed over time between researchers and employees as well and this may affect employee willingness to respond. Lam et al. (2002) was the only study identified that made note of the previous participation of the organization in other

research studies. Their study had an 80% response rate.

Cooperation and employee response rates

Earlier we presented and discussed six response drivers that we suggest are part of the organizational context during survey administration. We will now integrate the concepts discussed in the preceding section and provide examples of how cooperation could affect those drivers, resulting in higher response rates or, at minimum, lead to a richer explanation of response rates. Table 26.2 presents response drivers and examples of cooperative activities to improve response rates.

As an example of how to apply the recommendations in Table 26.2, we look at 'Trust in the Organization' as a response driver. If negative outcomes followed a previous survey (e.g., specific employees were targeted for special attention on the basis of their ostensibly 'anonymous' responses to a survey) this may affect perceptions of trust in management. If in a subsequent survey administration the response rate is 20%, this contextual factor is important to the interpretation of results and may explain why a similar survey in other organizations may have had a higher response rate. Table 26.2 also lists examples of cooperative activities on the part of the organization that could logically impact the context. If trust between labor and management is affected at the time of the study, communications between management and the researchers may provide valuable insights that can guide design and/or administration modifications to increase survey response rates; otherwise the results of the study may be flawed.

The above examples of how organizational cooperation could affect or shed light on contextual factors influencing the individual survey response decision, may seem logical and even obvious. However, we could find no theoretical or empirical examination of academic/researcher cooperation with respect to understanding or affecting response rates. There have been calls for more research on the processes and effects of academic/researcher collaboration in academic research (Amabile et al., 2001; Rynes et al., 2001; Mohrman

Table 26.2 Contextual response drivers and cooperative activities to address them

Contextual response drivers	Cooperative activities to address nonresponse
WILLINGNESS	
Salience of survey	Management communication of importance that accompanies or precedes survey distribution. Management integrates the survey participation into job/task requirements for employees. Usefulness and expected use of survey results is integrated into multiple core management formal and/or informal communications Management is directly involved in explaining the study to employees.
Significance of response	Management communication linking the importance of responding with organizational goals and planned follow-up action.
Organizational fairness	Insights from management on existing climate to allow for design and/or administration adjustments.
Coworker influence	Management allows time and place for onsite administration Management helps create awareness and a culture of support for / perceived importance of the study throughout the organization (or among relevant groups).
Management support	Management provides cover letter of support.
Trust in the organization	Joint management/researcher communication committing to confidentiality.
ABILITY	
Survey characteristics/ administration/channel	Management allows face-to-face distribution and pick-up during working hours. Management allows researchers to introduce and explain study directly to employees.
Time constraints	Management allocates time for employees to complete the survey.

et al., 2001). There have also been repeated scholarly concerns about insufficient academic/researcher collaboration in academic research studies, citing barriers such as the inherent tension between research and practice orientations and goals, lack of incentives in the world of academic research to work with practitioners, and skepticism of practitioners with regard to the relevance of academic research (Huff, 2000; Bennis and O'Toole, 2005; Starkey and Madden, 2001). However, despite recent heightened calls for more collaborative research and for more studies on its processes and effects, there has been little mention to date on the particular effects of researcher/organization cooperation on response rates and on producing meaningful results. We hope that the framework developed here will provide a starting place for future research and discussion of the topic.

Discussion and conclusion

Organizational scholars have repeatedly called for appreciation for and report of the effects of context on organizational behavior (see Cappelli and Sherer, 1991; Johns, 2006; Rousseau, 1997; Rousseau and Fried, 2001). Individual participation in organizational surveys is in and of itself an organizational behavior subject to the influence of social and structural contextual factors within the organization. Yet context has rarely been considered in the general response rate literature or even in the more limited body of research on techniques to increase organizational survey response rates (Cycyota and Harrison, 2002; Roth and BeVier, 1998) and rarely are these factors discussed in the methods sections of published organizational survey research. We examined three years of two highly rated peer-reviewed academic journals and learned that the context in which a survey is administered often goes unmentioned.

We have identified six response drivers, acknowledging that this list is not exhaustive. We believe that they are part of the context in which organizational surveys are administered and that their presence may affect response rates. If there is a lack of trust about what will happen to individual responses, it is likely the results of a survey will not accurately reflect the views of the majority of the population. If a survey addresses issues perceived as unimportant, response rate will likely be negatively affected. If management and coworkers are not supportive of the data collection, individuals will be less likely to participate. Participation in a survey is seen as a helping behavior (Groves et al., 1992; Rogelberg et al., 2000, 2003) and respondents want to see positive action taken following the survey. At the least, the purpose of the survey should be clarified, along with an explanation of what will be done with the results.

In summary, we have presented a list of possible cooperative activities between academics and practitioners as well as specific recommendations for addressing response drivers. These tools serve three important purposes: first, to broaden the discussion of possibilities for fruitful organizational participation in academic surveys inclusive of but not limited to cooperative relationships conceived for mutual material gain; second, to stimulate more explicit and standardized discussion of organizational involvement in academic research in publications; and third, to encourage future empirical examination of potential links between levels and forms of involvement and survey response rates. Cooperation with an organization can lead to a greater understanding of the organizational context in which employees are being asked to respond and may offer opportunities to influence factors that may affect their decisions to respond. If researchers work cooperatively with organizations to understand some of these factors, a more robust interpretation of response rates and findings may be possible.

APPENDIX 1

List of Cooperative Activities for use in Academic Survey Research

Passive Cooperation
Approvals

- Approval to survey employees
- Allowing for observation from the inside
- Allowing for relationship building between researchers and employees prior to survey administration
- Allowing for pretesting among employees
- Allowing for meetings with employees to explain the study and to distribute surveys during work hours
- Allowing use of internal communication vehicles to distribute survey

Active Cooperation

Provision of contextual data

- Providing organizational data, lists, or employee coordinates
- Providing verbal insights into organizational context

Employee Participation Encouragement

- Formal endorsement of study to employees
- Management assurances of confidentiality

Feedback on aspects of the survey design and/or administration

- Feedback on content
- Feedback on survey language
- Feedback on survey distribution methods

Distribution Assistance

- Distribution by organizational staff or through organizational channels (e.g., intranet)

Assistance in follow-up with employees to maximize response rates

- Organizational staff follow-up with employees to request survey completion

Survey Design and/or Administration Collaboration

- Joint administration of the survey
- Joint development of the survey

REFERENCES

Adams, J.S. (1965) 'Inequity in social exchange', in L. Berkowitz (ed.), *Advances in Experimental and Social Psychology* (Vol. 2), New York: Academic Press. pp. 267–99.

Amabile, T.M., Patterson, C., Mueller, J., Wojcik, T., Odomirok, P.W., Marsh, M. and Kramer, S.J. (2001) 'Academic-practitioner collaboration in management research: a case of cross-profession collaboration', *Academy of Management Journal*, 44: 418–31.

Argyle, M. (1991) *Cooperation: The Basis of Sociability*, London: Routledge.

Bachrach, S.B., Bamberger, P.A. and Sonnenstuhl, W.J. (2002) 'Driven to drink: managerial control, work-related risk factors, and employee problem drinking', *Academy of Management Journal*, 45: 637–58.

Bagozzi, R.P., Yi, Y. and Phillips, L.W. (1991) 'Assessing construct validity in organizational research', *Administrative Science Quarterly*, 36: 421–58.

Barling, J., Loughlin, C., Kelloway, E.K. (2002) 'Development and test of a model linking safety-specific transformational leadership and occupational safety', *Journal of Applied Psychology*, 87: 488–96.

Baruch, Y. (1999) 'Response rate in academic studies—a comparative analysis', *Human Relations*, 52: 421–438.

Baruch, Y. and Holtom, B.C. (2007) 'Survey response rate levels and trends in organizational research', Working paper.

Bass, B.M. and Avolio, B.J. (1994) *Improving organizational effectiveness through transformational leadership*, Thousand Oaks, CA: Sage.

Bennis, W.G. and O'Toole, J. (2005) 'How business schools lost their way', *Harvard Business Review*, May, 96–104.

Cappelli, P. and Sherer, P.D. (1991) 'The missing role of context in OB: the need for a meso-level approach', *Research in Organizational Behavior*, 13: 55–110.

Church, A.H. (1993) 'Estimating the effect of incentives on mail survey response rates: a meta-analysis', *Public Opinion Quarterly*, 57: 62–79.

Cialdini, R.B. (1988) *Influence: Science and Practice*, Blenville, IL: Scott, Foresman.

Cialdini, R.B. (2006) *Influence: The Psychology of Persuasion*, New York: William Morrow.

Cook, C., Heath, F and Thompson, R.L. (2000) 'A meta-analysis of response rates in web—or Internet—based surveys, *Educational and Psychological Measurement*, 6: 821–36.

Cycyota, C.S. and Harrison, D.A. (2002) 'Enhancing survey response rates at the executive level: are employee- or consumer-level techniques effective? *Journal of Management*, 28: 151–76.

Cyert, R.M. and Goodman, P.S. (1997) 'Creating effective university-industry alliances: an organizational learning perspective', *Organizational Dynamics*, 25: 45–57.

Deming, W.E. (2000) *Out of the crisis*, Cambridge, MA: The MIT Press.

Dillman, D.A. (1978) *Mail and Telephone Surveys: The Total Design Method*, New York: Wiley.

Dillman, D.A. (2000) *Mail and Internet Surveys: The Tailored Design Method*, New York: Wiley.

Feldman, D.C. (1981) The multiple socialization of organization members, *Academy of Management Review*, 6: 309–318.

Folger, R. and Cropanzano, R. (1998) *Organizational Justice and Human Resource Management*, Thousand Oaks, CA: Sage.

Goldstein, K.M. and Jennings, M.K. (2002) 'The effect of advance letters on cooperation in a list sample telephone survey', *Public Opinion Quarterly*, 66: 608–17.

Golembiewski, R.T. and McConkie (1975) 'The centrality of interpersonal trust in group process', in C.. Cooper (ed.), *Theories of group process*, New York: John Wiley & Sons.

Green, S.G., Welsh, M.A. and Dehler, G.E. (2003) 'Advocacy, performance, and threshold influences on decisions to terminate new product development', *Academy of Management Journal*, 46: 419–34.

Groves, R.M., Cialdini, R.B. and Couper, M. P. (1992) 'Understanding the decision to participate in a survey', *Public Opinion Quarterly*, 56: 475–95.

Groves, R.M., Presser, S. and Dipko, S. (2004) 'The role of topic interest in survey participation decisions', *Public Opinion Quarterly*, 68: 2–31.

Hackman, J.R. and Oldham, G.R. (1980) *Work Redesign*, Reading, MA: Addison-Wesley.

Hackman, J.R. (1992) 'Group influences on individuals in organizations', in M.D. Dunette and I.M. Hough (eds) *Handbook of industrial and organizational psychology* (second ed.) (Vol. 3), Palo Alto, CA: Consulting Psychologists Press, pp. 199–268.

Hinkin, T.R. (1995) 'A review of scale development in the study of behavior in organizations', *Journal of Management*, 967–88.

Hinkin, T.R. (1998) 'A brief tutorial on the development of measures for use in survey Questionnaires', *Organizational Research Methods*, 1: 104–121.

Huff, A.S. (ed.) (2000) 'Citigroup's John Reed and Stanford's James March on management research and practice', *Academy of Management Executive*, 14: 52–64.

Johns, G. (2006) 'The essential impact of context on organizational behavior', *Academy of Management Review*, 31: 386–408.

Kets de Vries, M.F.R. (1999) 'High performance teams: lessons from the pygmies', *Organizational Dynamics*, Winter: 66–77.

Kostova, T. and Roth, K. (2002) 'Adoption of an organizational practice by subsidiaries of multinational corporations: institutional and relational effects', *Academy of Management Journal*, 45: 215–33.

Krosnick, J. (1999) 'Survey research', *Annual review of Psychology*, 50: 537–67.

Lam, S.S.K., Yik, M.S.M. and Schaubroeck, J. (2002) 'Responses to formal performance appraisal feedback: the role of negative affectivity', *Journal of Applied Psychology*, 87: 192–201.

Latane', B. and Darley, J.M. (1970) *The unresponsive bystander: why doesn't he help?*, New York: Appleton-Crofts.

Ludbrook, J. and Dudley, H. (1998) 'Why permutation tests are superior to *t* and *F* tests in medical research', *The American Statistician*, 52: 127–32.

Lundquist, J.L., Westcott, S.W. and Fleming, D.B. (1994) 'A strategy for improving response rates for annual surveys', Clemson University, Office of Institutional Research.

Mavis, B. E. and Brocato, J.J. (1998) 'Postal surveys versus electronic mail surveys: the tortoise and the hare revisited', *Evaluation & the Health Professions*, 21: 395–408.

Mintzberg, H. (2004) *Managers Not MBAs: A Hard Look at the Soft Practice of Managing and Management Development*, San Francisco: Berrett-Koehler Publishers.

Mohrman, S.A., Gibson, C.B. and Mohrman Jr., A.M. (2001) 'Doing research that is useful for practice: a model and empirical exploration', *Academy of Management Journal*, 44: 357–75.

Osborn, R.N. and Hagedoom, J. (1997) 'The institutionalization and evolutionary dynamics of interorganizational alliances and networks', *Academy of Management Journal*, 40: 261–78.

Ostroff, C., Kinicki, A.J. and Clark, M.A. (2002) 'Substantive and operational issues of response bias across levels of analysis: an example of climate-satisfaction relationships', *Journal of Applied Psychology*, 87: 355–68.

Pfeffer, J. and Fong, C.T. (2002) 'The end of business schools? less success than meets the eye', *Academy of Management Learning and Education*, 1: 78–95.

Podsakoff, P.M., MacKenzie, S.B., Paine, J.B. and Bachrach, D.G. (2000) 'Organizational citizenship behaviors: a critical review of the theoretical and empirical literature and suggestions for future research', *Journal of Management*, 26: 513–563.

Rogelberg, S.G., Luong, A., Sederburg, M.E. and Cristol, D.S. (2000) 'Employee attitude surveys: examining the attitudes of noncompliant employees', *Journal of Applied Psychology*, 85: 284–93.

Rogelberg, S.G., Conway, J.M., Sederburg, M.E., Spitzmuller, C., Aziz, S. and Knight, W.E. (2003) 'Profiling active and passive nonrespondents to an organizational survey', *Journal of Applied Psychology*, 88: 1104–14.

Rousseau, D.M. (1997) 'Organizational behavior in the new organizational era', Annual Review of Psychology, 48: 515–46.

Rousseau, D.M. and Fried, Y. (2001) 'Location, location, location: contextualizing organizational research', *Journal of Organizational Behavior*, 22: 1–13.

Roth, P.L. and BeVier, C.A. (1998) 'Response rates in HRM/OB survey research: norms and correlates, 1990–1994', *Journal of Management*, 24: 97–117.

Rynes, S.L., Bartunek, J.M. and Daft, R.L. (2001) 'Across the great divide: knowledge creation and transfer between practitioners and academics', *Academy of Management Journal*, 44: 340–55.

Saxton, T. (1997) 'The effects of partner and relationship characteristics on alliance outcomes', *Academy of Management Journal*, 40: 443–60.

Schalm, R.L. and Kelloway, E.K. (2001) 'The relationship between response rate and effect size in occupational health psychology research', *Journal of Occupational Health psychology*, 6: 160–3.

Seiders, K. and Berry, L.L. (1998) 'Service fairness: what it is and why it matters', *Academy of Management Executive*, 12: 8–20.

Simons, T. and Roberson, Q. (2003) 'Why managers should care about fairness: the effects of aggregate justice perceptions on organizational outcomes', *Journal of Applied Psychology*, 88: 432–43.

Simsek, Z. and Veiga, J.F. (2000) 'The electronic survey technique: an integration and assessment', *Organizational Research Methods*, 3: 93–115.

Singer, E., Van Hoewyk, J. and Maher. M.P. (2000) 'Experiments with incentives in telephone surveys', *Public Opinion Quarterly*, 64: 171–88.

Starkey, K. and Madden, P. (2001) 'Bridging the relevance gap: aligning stakeholders in the future of management research', *British Journal of Management*, 12: S3–S26.

Tepper, B.J. (1995) 'Upward maintenance tactics in supervisory mentoring and nonmentoring relationships', *Academy of Management Journal*, 58: 1171–205.

Tomaskovic-Devey, D., Leiter, J. and Thompson, S. (1994) 'Organizational survey nonresponse', *Administrative Science Quarterly*, 39: 439–57.

Tourangeau, R. (2004) 'Survey research and societal change', *Annual Review of Psychology*, 55: 775–801.

Van Vianen, A.E.M., De Pater, I.E. and Kristof-Brown, A.L. (2004) 'Fitting in: surface- and deep-level cultural differences and expatriates' adjustment', *Academy of Management Journal*, 47: 697–709.

Viswesvaran, C., Barrick, M.B. and Ones, D.S. (1993) 'How definitive are conclusions based on survey data: estimating robustness to nonresponse', *Personnel Psychology*, 46: 551–67.

Weiner, S.P. and Dalessio, A.T. (2006) 'Oversurveying: causes, consequences, and cures', in A.I. Kraut (ed.), *Getting Action from Organizational Surveys: New Concepts, Methods and Applications*, San Francisco: Jossey-Bass, pp. 294–311.

Yammarino, F.J., Skinner, S.J. and Childers, T.L. (1991) 'Understanding mail survey response behavior: a meta-analysis', *Public Opinion Quarterly*, 55: 614–39.

Yu, J. and Cooper, H. (1983) 'A quantitative review of research design effects on response rates to questionnaires', *Journal of Marketing Research*, 20: 36–44.

Yukl, G. (2002) *Leadership in Organizations* (second edn.), Upper Saddle River, NJ: Prentice-Hall.

27

Comparative Case Study Designs: Their Utility and Development in Organizational Research

Louise Fitzgerald and Sue Dopson

ORIENTATION AND INTRODUCTION

This chapter explores the use and design of comparative case studies as an approach to research in organization studies. The origins of case-study design lie mainly in the social sciences, in sociology and social anthropology, in psychology, and interestingly in specific forms in medicine for the presentation of individual cases. The early work of the Chicago School in the USA (Whyte, 1941; Whyte, 1943; Van Maanen, 1995) made a substantial impact and led the development of case-study design. This early impact meant that the utility of case-study designs was explored in other arenas (Yablonsky, 1988; Huberman and Miles, 1984; Pettigrew, 1985). Here we consider specifically how case-study designs have developed from their use within the social sciences into the field of organizational research. From their origins, the historical focus has been on single

individuals (as in psychology and medicine) and then on single units, events, groups, or organizations. This has led to a somewhat restrictive approach to case-study design and to widespread criticisms of their lack of generalizability (Kennedy, 1976), and a failure to contribute to theory construction despite the fact that research on single organizational cases has been demonstrably influential (Pettigrew, 1985; Child and Smith, 1987; Weick, 1993).

We commence from the premise that a case study in organizational research involves the collection of empirical data from multiple sources to explore an identified unit of analysis, such as an organization, part of an organization, or a division or group, and the characteristics of its context. The case unit of analysis can also be an incident, an event, or an event sequence, such as Weick's (1993) analysis of the Mann Gulch smokejumpers disaster, and the study of 'accidental' radical change in Mission Church over a prolonged period by Plowman et al. (2007). In the following sections, we expand on our justification for this definition.

If one examines the development of research approaches specifically within the field of organization studies, one can detect a varied range of designs. With no accepted paradigm, as in the physical sciences, research approaches have evolved from embryonic beginnings and in a more fragmented way. We wish to set out the epistemological framework for our chapter in which we adopt an interpretive, or constructionist approach to case-study design. As the chapter progresses, we explain and develop our thinking. In general, it is evident that one strand of the development of research in organization studies has been researchers drawing on the traditions of social science research and basing their approach on an interpretive paradigm. The interpretive paradigm is interested in the study of meanings that social actors attach to their actions. For example, what shapes the pattern of interactions between managers and staff? It is also more interested in understanding subjective experience than 'objective' data, and proponents would argue that such numerical data are themselves the product of processes of social construction. Interpretive methods are particularly indicated where the task is the description, interpretation, and explanation of a phenomenon rather than estimation of its prevalence (Lee, 1999). Case-study designs can clearly fall within this interpretive paradigm and can offer a powerful and useful approach to research on organizations. Case studies lend themselves well to the relatively uncontrolled and dynamic conditions of organizations.

One initial point of confusion is that case studies are sometimes labelled as a research method, and sometimes as a research design, which involves the deployment of multiple methods. As long as one recognizes that the case is the unit of analysis, whether based on a whole or part of an organization, some aspects of this confusion are mitigated. Each case must be constructed, whether the researcher is working on single or multiple case designs.

Whilst it is the overall design of the case study (or multiple case studies) which provides the framework of the research design, it is the individual elements in the construction of each case that constitute a research method and, as we have stated, each case involves the collection of empirical data from multiple sources in one form or another.

Within the social sciences, in a similar manner to case studies, ethnography has also been used as a research design which can provide in-depth and multifaceted data around a research question (Hammersley and Atkinson, 1995). Ethnography is an approach which is concerned with the description of social patterns, and the predominant method of data collection is through participant observation. However, ethnography as a research design has key differences in terms of the role of the researcher and the nature of the approach and research planning, when compared to case studies. In ethnography, researchers seek to immerse themselves within the research setting. They become part of the scene. Whilst their main method of data collection is observation, they may use other methods such as interviews. On the other hand, a researcher working on a case study does not seek to become part of the site, but to remain apart, if not neutral. A case-study researcher works to a planned and agreed protocol. This begins to illustrate the differences in approach and planning. An ethnographer must respond to and follow unpredicted activities and events, as they occur naturally. Thus, much of the substance of their observation is unanticipated and their recording of it unplanned. Interviews are spontaneous, free flowing conversations, not guided, as they would be within a case study. The approach to the construction of a case study is much more planned and preorganized. Data collection will include the formal collection of factual data on 'the case', as well as other potential methods, such as interviews and surveys.

Ethnography as a research approach in organizations has a number of major challenges. It requires the researcher to have extensive knowledge of the research context and to employ adequate means to document observations. As a result, it is expensive in resources and in time. This may be part of the explanation as to why ethnography is less frequently featured in organization studies (but see Fine et al., Chapter 35, this volume). As an alternative approach, Yin (2003) and Gummesson (2000) suggest case studies can be utilized as interpretivist, qualitative research designs. Yin positions case study designs as a research strategy which can answer the 'how' and 'why' questions. So, case studies, it is suggested, provide depth, but have less intrusive attributes than ethnography and are, therefore, potentially more acceptable to sponsors in the sense of reducing the potential disruption of the organization. In addition, one might offer the argument that case studies raise fewer ethical issues of respondents' consent and confidentiality than ethnography. Unlike ethnography, case-study research uses a blend of qualitative methods and can employ more quantitative approaches, for example the survey method. In this sense, the case study challenges the rather sterile debate that positions quantitative and qualitative research methods as either/or choices for the researcher.

Within our more specific focus of organization research, it may be argued that the evidence remains that case-study designs are undervalued (Bryman and Bell, 2003; Saunders, et al 2003; Silverman, 2004a). Despite these books having a focus on either research methods for business students or qualitative research on organizations, most of them devote little attention or discussion to case studies. Whilst Saunders et al. and Silverman provide only passing mention of case studies, Bryman and Bell offer insights into the design of case studies and comparative and multiple case-study design. Nevertheless, the construction of case studies is not featured in the detailed methods section. In contemplating the potential of case-study designs in organization studies, one needs to focus on the nature of the organization and the organization field. By their nature, organizations are dynamic; the aspects for study in an organization cannot be controlled. So, from the researcher's

viewpoint, experimental research designs are not feasible, since normally there is no means by which control can be exercised over such research variables. This is at one and the same time, an exciting challenge for the researcher and a limit on the appropriate research designs. A major value of case-study designs within this field, therefore, is that they can 'cope' with this dynamism and still offer flexibility and scope in the design of research. This stated, there remain critical questions concerning the scope and scale of the case-study design. Such questions relate to the quality of case-study design and the issue of depth versus breadth in the methods to be employed in data collection within a case.

Interestingly, across the research fields and especially if one concentrates on current US perspectives on research design and research methods teaching, one can perceive the predominant influence over thinking of the scientific and medical traditions in research. Despite the founding traditions of the Chicago school, the precedence given to case-study designs and the acceptance of theory generated from cases is relatively low. A useful, recent article (Eisenhardt and Graebner, 2007) highlights the significant role played by theory built from single or multiple cases and suggests such papers are among the most highly cited pieces in the *Academy of Management Journal*. Despite this and the historical antecedents, theory building from cases is described as one of the best bridges from rich, qualitative evidence 'to mainstream research' (Eisenhardt and Graebner, 2007: 25). Here we take issue with the subtle interpretation of the term 'mainstream'. We seek to argue vigorously that case-study design is a thriving and evolving part of the 'mainstream' of organization studies and that it should not be either denigrated or given lower precedence and/or ignored (Salkind, 2006).

We suggest that the uses and types of case-study designs are under continuous development and that in the field of organization studies, there has been fairly substantial experimentation and development with comparative case-study designs. Yin's

(2003) examples of descriptive and explanatory cases are helpful, but the current realities of organizational research mean that these designs need to be developed and improved in innovative ways. Here, we develop these ideas and delineate the logic and the justifications for the development of high quality, comparative case-study designs. Clearly, any research needs to take account of the substance and form of the research question, so the development of comparative case-study designs reflects the needs of the field of organization studies.

If case studies are a strategy for empirical research and a design which is particularly suited to organization studies, what are the facets of the design which underpin this suitability? In our judgement, these include:

- The study of the organization is embedded in complex contexts.
- A historical perspective on the 'case' is relevant.
- The case can be holistic.
- Case studies provide depth, rather than breadth.
- Cases lend themselves to a multistakeholder analysis.
- Within a case study, the elements of the design are flexible, but case studies must involve multimethods.
- They can be longitudinal and therefore more appropriate to the study of processes over time.
- Because they are easier to accomplish than ethnography and use multimethods, this makes them more attractive to sponsors and the audiences of research.
- Whilst ethical issues exist, they are comparatively easier to deal with.

The foundations of comparative case-study design: the constituents of case-study construction

In order to move to our specific orientation and focus on comparative case-study designs, this section discusses the essential building blocks of any such design, namely, the constituents from which a case is constructed. This provides an essential foundation from which to explore comparative case-study designs.

As Yin (2003) has noted, there are still many contested questions in relation to case studies. For example, do case studies preclude the use of quantitative data? Are single and multiple case studies 'in reality but two variants of case-study designs' as Yin (2003: 14) suggests? Here we first consider a generic definition of a case study and argue that each case has a number of critical components which it is essential to understand. We argue therefore, that in organization studies, a case consists of:

- Factual data on the context of the case; this might include archival data, as well as data specifically collected for the research. Contextual data ought whenever possible to have an historical dimension.
- Data, in one of a number of potential forms, from a range of stakeholders in the organization.
- Triangulation of data from several sources. Thus, data collected from interviews might be partially validated by observations, archival data, or survey data.
- Analysis of data should be multifactorial and should be triangulated.

Before discussing each of these elements, one needs to stress that it is essential to consider the unit of analysis at the outset. This may not be self evident. In many instances, a case study will be built around the whole organization, or some identifiable subunit. However, in an 'embedded' case study, one may wish to study a comparison of two units within a single, larger organization, such as two production units in a multinational company, one based in Europe and one based in Asia. (Later in this chapter, example 27.3 provides an example of an 'embedded' case-study design). The identification and clarification of the unit of analysis has to relate to the overall study design, its logic, and its focus.

In considering the constituent parts of a case study, we place considerable importance on the undervalued element of 'context'. The definition of 'context' is in itself not incontrovertible and many debates remain. In organization studies, the simplest definitions of 'context' revolve around the notion of the organizational boundary being the divider between the inner and outer context of the organization (Pettigrew, 1987; Pettigrew et al., 1992). Thus, it can be proposed that the organization is influenced by its 'outer' context, such as aspects of its position in a sector and in an economic and social system and also by its 'inner' context which includes its history, its competitive strategy, and position (in a 'for profits' organization) or its relative importance to the policy agenda (in a public sector organization). But 'context' as an element of a case is frequently 'taken for granted'. It is assumed, or a mere statement of the nature and purpose of the organization is considered adequate. This is far from the truth. If an organizational case may be justified because it is holistic, then clearly data on the context must form a constituent part of the analysis. In many instances, the factual attributes of a case, the purpose, strategy, size, scope, and performance of the organization are already documented and available. These characteristics may be supplemented by data on a broader range of factors that take some account of nonmeasurable criteria, such as trends in staff attitude surveys. One neglected element of context is the role of history in comprehending, for example, current strategy, commercial choices, and levels of institutionalization. (Because of the importance of this dimension, we refer the reader to the later discussion under data-collection methods on operationalizing these aspects.)

Another focus of the design is eliciting multiple stakeholders' perspectives. And the sheer flexibility of potential methods of data collection is one of the most positive attributes of a case-study design. In considering options, the researcher must always return to the research question. One favoured option is to use interviews, either structured, semistructured, or unstructured within a case study. Interviews enable researchers to develop both depth and breadth of data, as appropriate. Critically, however, the design has to consider carefully the selection of stakeholders and how these are justified in relation to the research question. Thus, the selection of interview respondents,

in terms of numbers and of roles/positions, needs to be transparent and the logic justified. One criticism which may be levelled at many organization researchers concerns the use of 'convenience' as a design justification. This tends to generate shoddy designs and justifiable criticism. Whilst interviews may be a common approach to data collection, this is an arena in which creativity can be employed. There have, for example, been some illuminating examples of visual methods (Buchanan 2001; Buchanan and Huczynski, 2004; and see Warren, Chapter 33, this volume).

Next, we move to the issues in triangulation and the forms of data triangulation. The simplest form of triangulation is using archival data to support and partially verify interview data. Alternatives would include using observation of interactions to verify interview data. Both of these may be useful in varied ways. Archival data allows recollections of events and decisions post hoc to be compared and verified against more formal committee minutes or reports (but see Moss, Chapter 23, this volume). Observation has the advantage of enabling the researcher to access the interactions of organizational members directly, rather than solely by report through an interview with individuals (albeit through different individuals).

Survey data can also be used to further illustrate and illuminate patterns or indeed highlight differences. A simple survey administered before the 'in depth' interviewing phase can be helpful in shaping interview schedules or observation. Equally, a survey following the use of interviews or observation and derived from these data can aid the researcher to establish patterns and confidence in findings.

Finally, analysis of data needs to be multifactorial. This can be a difficult and daunting process with the sheer volume of data generated from qualitative methods of data collection. There is limited guidance on alternative approaches to analysis. Essentially, researchers will need to make choices between a framed or themed analytic approach by which researchers code data against a pre-prepared template or a wholly grounded theory approach, by which codes are generated from the data (see Goulding, Chapter 22, this volume), or various combinations in between. In many instances, an iterative process of data analysis may be required.

Building quality in comparative case study designs

Here, we reach the core of our chapter, comparative case-study designs and before discussing the nature of such designs in depth, we address the question of quality in case-study design. We have argued that interpretive methods are particularly indicated where the task is the description, interpretation, and explanation of a phenomenon rather than estimation of its prevalence (Lee, 1999). However, such research methods also require appropriate standards for judging quality. The question of what might constitute indicators of 'rigour' within qualitative research which might parallel those used in scientific research in the physical sciences or medicine is more complex, and it is not possible to produce an analogous set of acknowledged and established standards. But the question: 'What does good quality qualitative research look like?' is an increasingly important one.

Yin (2003) proposes that as case-study designs are one form of empirical social research, then the four commonly used tests of quality should be applied to them too. These he states are:

- Construct validity: establishing correct operational measures for the concepts being studied.
- Internal validity: (not used in descriptive or exploratory studies) establishing a causal relationship, whereby certain conditions are shown to lead to other conditions.
- External validity: establishing the domain to which a study's findings can be generalized.
- Reliability: demonstrating that the operations of the study such as data collection procedures can be repeated, with the same results.

In various ways, three of these criteria, internal and external validity and reliability,

all present problems which we will discuss in the context of case-study research designs.

An alternative approach is adopted by Mays et al. (2001) who compared the assessment frameworks developed by three qualitative health services research groups (Blaxter, 1996; Mays and Pope, 2000; Popay et al, 1998) and who present a more modest set of quality criteria. All three groups suggested the following common criteria of quality:

- Consideration of the appropriateness of the methods used for the question and subject matter and why it was that qualitative methods were appropriate.
- Adequacy of sampling which is as much an issue in qualitative as quantitative research, and clear explanation of the sampling strategy.
- The rigour of data analysis – was it conducted in a systematic way, and did it succeed in incorporating all the observations and dealing with variation?
- The reflexivity of the account – 'sensitivity to the ways in which the researcher and research process have shaped the data collected' (Mays and Pope, 2000: 96) and the provision of sufficient information about the research process to enable readers to judge this.
- Adequacy of presentation of findings – is it clear how the analysis flows from the data, and are sufficient data presented to justify conclusions?
- Worth and relevance of that research.

Considering the issues raised by these differing quality frameworks, it is evident that both sets of criteria include the need to have effective construct validity, though Mays et al. avoid the use of the term 'measures' in discussing operationalization. Using internal validity as a criterion for quality, as suggested by Yin (2003), does raise important issues. However, in discussing and expanding on the 'tactics' to be used in establishing internal validity, Yin proposes pattern matching; explanation building; addressing rival explanations; and using logic models. It is evident from this that in relation to case studies in organization studies, the probability of relationships may be established and replace the standards of 'proof' of causal relationships applied to quantitative data. So, it may be suggested that one applies adapted approaches to internal validity in case studies.

The issues in applying the criterion of external validity to case-study research are complex and fraught. Yin (1999), in a discussion on the methodological quality of case studies within health services research, noted that the difficulty of generalizing from cases has been seen as a major shortcoming of the method. One way in which external validity can be increased is through theory building. Yin argues that each case study, as a unit, can be considered as a single experiment; a multiple case study can be considered as multiple experiments. Yin also suggests that an appropriate response to the need to build external validity through theory is not to select cases through a sampling logic, but through theoretical replication logic:

> ...the needed replication logic can be derived only from hypotheses or theories about the cases. In other words, a theory about what is being studied – and about whether a single case is a 'critical' exemplar of that theory or about why some multiple cases might be expected to be replications and others might not – is essential to case study design and analysis' (Yin, 1999: 1213).

We suggest that there is no need and little point for the social sciences and organization studies to mimic the physical or natural sciences. Organizations are not necessarily standardized or identical units, and this can be an accepted phenomenon. In contrast to the concept of statistical generalization to a population when analysing multiple cases, it may be more appropriate to consider the concept of analytical generalization to theory (see Tsoukas, Chapter 17, this volume). Thus, patterns can be detected, built upon, and verified, and lead to theory development.

In this chapter, we make a similar, but adapted argument for logic in the design of multiple case studies. We acknowledge that one logic for the selection of single cases is a theory-based exemplar of a 'critical' case. We argue that in multiple case-studies designs another optional design logic is based on replication, whilst other logics may be based in comparative differences, especially

of extremes. These design logics may be applied either in exploratory designs or in theory-based designs.

Finally, let us consider the criterion of reliability. Yin defines this as the operations being repeatable *with the same results*. Mays et al. (2001) on the other hand propose the rigour of data analysis and the need for analysis to be conducted systematically. Here we argue that the quality criteria of rigour of analysis and transparency are necessary and would enable the operations and procedures to be repeated. However, this might only lead to similar, rather than the same results. No two organizations will be identical, nor will they be static. So, to achieve the *same results*, one would have to conduct the research in the same organizations, with the same people and at the same time.

Given that there are issues in developing the quality of case-study research, what are the incentives for working towards the development of sounder designs and multiple case-study designs? Here we argue that there are several justifications for comparative case-study designs in organization studies.

Theoretical justification

Both Eisenhardt (1989) and Langley (1999) have explored the justification for developing research designs which contain multiple, comparative cases. Eisenhardt proposes that such a comparative case-study design can be used to facilitate the construction of a large-scale database with both internal and external validity. Langley explores a range of strategies for the analysis of 'process' data in order to generate patterns and develop theory (see Langley, Chapter 24, this volume). Both these authors argue that with sets of eight to ten cases, one can generate low-level patterns and develop generalizations.

Developmental justification

As with all research methods, there is a strong case for the development of the methods themselves. Extending the use of case studies into the field of organization studies brings with it new challenges and new demands.

The questions to be addressed within the arena of organization studies include many that are comparative in nature. For example, inter-sectoral comparisons of the impact of employment practices on public, private, and not-for-profit organizations.

International justification

One of the strongest justifications for the development of comparative case-study designs is the increasing evidence through time that many aspects of organizational life have to be understood within a global rather than a national context. There is tremendous interest in exploring, examining, and comparing the functioning of organizations within and between differing countries and cultures. Whilst international comparisons are a fruitful means of learning and a potential growth area, they are not simple to achieve. There are enormous pragmatic difficulties, such as language differences and contrasting research funding regimes. Comparative case-study designs offer one route forward which is achievable and viable and can yield substantial benefits.

Impact on policy and strategy

Whereas policy makers are likely to dismiss single case studies on the grounds that they do not offer sufficient foundation for policy change, more extensive comparative case-study designs cannot be dismissed in this manner. (As an aside, we note that despite this, there are many examples of national policies in health care and law enforcement being dramatically changed by single cases.) Moreover, for the policy maker, good quality case studies frequently have high face validity. Participants and actors in the field under study can identify with the analysis, and case studies provide illustrative vignettes, which can aid the engagement of key people.

Knowledge transfer and the development of multidisciplinary networks

From the perspective of knowledge transfer, comparative case-study designs increase the likelihood of research partnerships with multiple members and so facilitate the possibility of contributions from different disciplines and the development of new relationships (if the partnerships work).

Building comparative designs

So, the design of case studies for organization research is a field under scrutiny and development. The range of case-study research designs has not been codified. Yin (2003: 20) has explored what he describes as 'a basic set of research designs for doing single- and multiple-case studies'. Here we aspire to developing this basic set further.

Yin describes multiple case-study designs in terms of two types – embedded case-study designs and replicated case-study designs. We would argue that there are at least four forms of multiple case-study design, each of which is based in a different design logic. The commonest forms currently in evidence are:

(1) Matching or replication, to explore or verify ideas.
(2) Comparison of difference, such as cases selected for their different characteristics (as in example 27.2) to aid analysis of relationships.
(3) Outliers; comparison of extremes, to delineate key factors and the shape of a field.
(4) Embedded; to identify similarities /differences within contexts.

Each of these design approaches merits some discussion.

Matching or replication of multiple cases

In some respects, the logic of replicating cases draws on the modes of scientific research and is analogous to that used in multiple experiments. Replication of cases in organization studies may be based on either literal replication or theoretical replication. In the case of the former, it should be noted that it is extremely unlikely that a perfect 'replica' will be found. As a result, it might be more appropriate to describe this research design as 'matching' cases. The logic behind these designs is to take the single case design and extend its power through the use of multiple cases. The terms 'replication' or 'matching' refer to the process by which cases are selected by carefully delineating selection criteria, which will relate to the research focus, and then selecting cases. In the case of literal replication, because of the variable nature of organizations, it is unlikely that identical cases will be found, so researchers will select the closest matches and transparently highlight differences. In the case of theoretical replication, cases are selected to produce contrasting results, for theoretically predictable reasons.

Example 27.1 offers a prime illustration of a rich research design, which has several dimensions of interest. The example features a study of US multinational corporations, which are operating in Britain. As the detailed example demonstrates, this study can be perceived as a comparative study design at two levels of analysis. First, this is an interesting example of a case-study design which allows comparison of cases of multinationals within the British economy. In addition, the research team has collaborated with other teams in Spain, Germany, and Ireland, who, by adopting the same design, have extended the study by matching and replication into other societal cultures. Thus, the overall study has yielded comparative case analysis within Britain, and then comparative case analysis across four countries. This approach has proved to be highly productive (Almond et al., 2005; Edwards et al., 2005; Tempel et al., 2007; Almond and Ferner, 2006).

Example 27.1: The 'country-of-origin effect' in the cross-national management of human resources and industrial relations: the case of United States multinationals.

Research objectives and questions

The objectives of this study were to contribute to theory and practice by:

- Understanding the logic underlying the distinctive characteristics of US multinationals in the UK,

for example how far such characteristics can be explained by reference to distinctive features of the US business system within which these companies are embedded.
- Exploring the mechanisms whereby distinctive characteristics are transmitted from the parent company and are reproduced in the subsidiary.
- Teasing out and explaining patterns of variation in behaviour among different kinds of US multinational.
- Focusing on US multinationals as a source of innovation in human resources and industrial relations in the UK business system – in what areas, and by what means, do innovations occur?
- Investigating, by means of an international comparative element, whether there is a common core to US 'distinctiveness' across different host country business systems?

Methodology

Comparative focus: The research was comparative in focus. First, previous research provided a basis for systematic comparison of national differences; as far as was practicable, comparable case-study enterprises were chosen. Second, the research in Britain was paralleled by comparable projects in other European countries. The comparator countries were chosen in order to provide a mix of deregulated (Britain and Ireland) and regulated (Germany and Spain) environments, each with significantly different business cultures. This permitted the research to examine whether apparently distinctive features of US multinationals survive transplantation to different host countries, or whether they manifest themselves in different national 'variants' according to changing environmental constraints. Although each team was responsible for its own funding, they all closely followed the approach of the British project. Each team was responsible for research in its own country. 'Cross-interviewing' and data pooling were used to increase consistency, and joint meetings were held to discuss findings and output.

Research methods: The research relied primarily on multiple detailed case studies (eight to ten) in order to widen generality of theoretical constructs (Eisenhardt, 1989); for example, to see how far some notion of

'Americanness' was common across different sectors and kinds of company. Cases were chosen on the basis of 'theoretical' rather than 'statistical' sampling (Yin, 2003; Glaser and Strauss, 1967), i.e., for their potential contribution to theory building rather than statistical analysis. The case studies covered key theoretically important variations – union/nonunion, greenfield/brownfield, and manufacturing/services. Sectors were chosen to reflect US multinationals' major spheres of operation in the UK (i.e., from among chemicals, food, drink, and tobacco, electrical and nonelectrical engineering, and vehicles) as well as varying degrees of international integration of production, and covered the increasingly internationalized service sector (e.g., distribution, leisure, healthcare, and business services). The research was also sensitive to other potentially important cleavages, such as east-coast/west-coast provenance.

Data collection: Case studies used a mixture of qualitative and quantitative methods. Though survey work is appropriate for identifying broad cross-national differences, it is less useful for exploring complex chains of causality (e.g., the sometimes subtle ways in which nationality informs multinational behaviour), and it misses significant differences in behaviour that can be only be appreciated through in-depth case-study work (e.g., the significance of different varieties of nonunionism; Ferner and Varul, 1998). A qualitative approach was, therefore, most likely to get at more subtle modes of transmission and influence.

The qualitative aspect leant heavily on in-depth, semistructured interviews at both corporate (or divisional) headquarters and subsidiary levels. Interviews – around 10 to 15 in each company – were conducted with senior personnel managers and with key managers in other relevant functions, such as finance and production. Data were also collected through site visits, document analysis, and, where possible, observation. Comparisons could be made with returns reported by US-owned establishments in the survey by Cully et al. (1999), including several hundred employee questionnaires.

Comparison of difference

The logic of this design is that purposeful sampling will aid the process of analysis by facilitating the researcher to focus on differences and that such differences will aid the detection of interrelationships between variables and factors in the context. The criteria for the purposeful sampling of cases must relate to the core research question. Example 27.2 illustrates a design based in the comparison of purposefully selected difference (Ferlie et al., 2000; Ferlie et al., 2005; Fitzgerald et al., 2002). This design has also proved to be useful and effective.

Example 2: The diffusion of innovations in healthcare settings

Research objectives and questions

The aim of this research was to address the question, *what makes a clinical professional decide to adopt an innovation and use it in their clinical practice?*

Methodology

The selected methodology was comparative and longitudinal case studies of innovation careers, with purposeful case selection. The comparative design facilitated pattern recognition across the cases in order to generate generic, as well as issue-specific learning.

The underlying logic behind this research was to explore the extent to which 'strong' scientific evidence supporting an innovation would or would not aid the process of innovation adoption. Much of the literature concerning the movement towards evidence-based health care presumed or was based on the premise that strong scientific evidence when presented to professionals would lead them to change their clinical practices. So, in order to answer this question, the researchers planned to trace the relative uptake of four innovations across a geographic health region and to establish the pattern of diffusion. However, to assist analysis, the innovations

Table 27.1   The innovations in the 2 × 2 matrix design

	Strong scientific evidence	Weak scientific evidence
Largely uni-professional	Use of aspirin for prevention of secondary cardiac incidents	Use of HRT for prevention of osteoporosis
Multiprofessional	Treatment of diabetes following St Vincent Declaration	Direct employment of physiotherapist in GP practices

were purposefully selected with the aid of a scientific steering committee of medical experts in the relevant fields. Two innovations were selected, because it was agreed that there was strong scientific evidence to support their uptake, and two were selected because the evidence supporting their efficacy was weak. This resulted in a design built on the following two by two matrix.

Data collection: Data collection consisted of two phases. In the first phase, interviews were conducted across four health authority areas on the diffusion of innovation in primary care in general, with additional, innovation-specific questions. Data collection commenced with opinion leaders in key professional groups in the health authorities and used a snowball technique to identify other informants. In addition, general practitioners (GPs – local doctors) were selected at random from the GP lists supplied by the health authorities.

The second phase concentrated on the microprocesses of the diffusion of a single innovation in a specific clinical setting. In-depth interviews were conducted with a range of involved practitioners within one core practice in each health authority area, on each innovation. Core practices were picked at random from GP lists. The sole criterion for selection was that the practice had to have staff involved in delivering the specified care/intervention in order for the researcher to be able to study the detailed processes of innovation.

All interviews used a semistructured questionnaire, lasting between 50 to 90 minutes, with a common spine of questions, followed by innovation-specific questions. The questionnaires were designed for the study and piloted before use. Interviewees were approached individually, by letter, for agreement. None of the interviewees were previously known to the researchers and confidentiality was guaranteed. All the interviews were one-to-one, at the time and place chosen by the informant. Two experienced interviewers conducted the interviews, which were recorded and transcribed. In total, 113 interviews were conducted.

Data analysis: Content analysis (Glaser and Strauss, 1967; Eisenhardt, 1989; Langley, 1999) was conducted on the macro phase data initially, and then reviewed and revised when the micro phase interviews were completed. Transcripts were exchanged for double blind analysis.

Comparison of outliers or extremes

A modification of the previous design based on comparison of identified differences is to purposefully select cases which are at the extremes of the field under of study. This design can only be effectively implemented when there is a sufficient basis of knowledge of the field. This means that the study arena has to be reasonably well defined, so that the 'average' organization in the sector can be delineated and one can map the field with some degree of accuracy. One well-known application of this logic is demonstrated in the study by Pettigrew and Whipp (1991) of the factors influencing competitive success. In this study, comparison is made of firms in a range of sectors, and within each sector, firms were carefully selected for inclusion against a basket of performance criteria, so that a higher and a lower performer were compared in each sector. This design enables comparisons to be made both within the sector, between the higher and lower performers, and across sectors, across all the cases of higher and all the cases of lower performers, as well as across the full set of cases. Another such example, would be working on a topic in the field of higher vocational education in the UK where a national database exists of all colleges of higher education.

Embedded case studies

Embedded, multiple case-study designs are based on comparing several units within a given context and/or comparing several units within several comparable contexts. This design lends itself well to a variety of complex organizational situations. For example, it would be relevant in the study of labour turnover, within a given sector, such as food retailing (supermarkets). Some of the problems in the study of labour turnover include the identification of why employees stay as well as leave, and the balance between internal factors, which 'push' staff from the organization and external labour market factors which 'pull' staff towards alternative employment. Embedded case studies enable one to study several units within an organization, all embedded in the same context, but in the case of our retail supermarkets operating in different parts of the UK and with different managements. Again, this design is based in a particular logic. Here the embedded units all have the same organizational context, and nominally are operating under similar norms, rules, and hierarchies. This more readily enables closer examination of the factors that differ between the embedded units. Example 27.3 illustrates an embedded case study design.

Example 27.3: Strategic approaches to support workers in the British National Health Service (NHS)

Research objectives and question

This project focuses on the nature and consequences of support worker roles in acute hospitals. There are four key objectives:

(1) An assessment of the strategic intent underpinning the development of support roles.
(2) An exploration of the personal characteristics and backgrounds of support workers and their workplace activities.

(3) An evaluation of the consequences of the support worker role for different stakeholders.
(4) An analysis of the variation in the background, use and consequences of support workers' roles.

Methodology

Support workers providing assistance to professionals and patients have assumed a high public policy profile in recent years. They have been seen by the government to contribute to the provision of patient centred services, the standards agenda, and the adequate supply of labour. However, there have been few structured attempts to consider why they are used, who fill these roles, and how roles affect other stakeholders. Most striking has been the absence of explanations as to how and with what consequences, support workers are used in the NHS. This project aims to provide a more detailed understanding of the use of support workers' roles in hospitals from the perspective of different stakeholders: the support workers themselves, the professionals they work with, and the patients they care for. For each of these stakeholders, the role holds the possibility of both positive and negative outcomes. The study will explore these outcomes, paying particular attention to whether they vary between and within hospitals, between different departments, and by different supporting roles.

Data collection: This research is under way at the time of writing, and will be implemented over thirty months, in stages. It will focus on comparative case studies in three acute hospitals, and on the roles of ward housekeepers and healthcare assistants, who are typically found at levels 2 and 3 of the NHS Career Framework. It aims to generate both qualitative and quantitative data. In the first stage, interviews will be carried out with trust leaders and key national stakeholders on strategic intent and policy development. Analysis of the national staff datasets will take place to provide a benchmark for the evaluation of local trust level data. Next, three acute hospitals have been selected, drawn from three different strategic health authorities covering different labour markets. Within each of the comparative cases, there will be two units of analysis – a medical and a surgical ward. The 'embedded' cases within each trust will provide a detailed understanding of how support workers are used and ensure that departmental differences in the nature of the roles are captured.

For each comparative case, fifty interviews will be undertaken across the medical and surgical wards, covering support workers, professionals, managers, and patients. There will also be stakeholder surveys and focus groups of patients. These methods will be supplemented with documentary analysis of job descriptions, and pay and appraisal systems. Finally, there will be ward observation of shifts of selected support workers.

Data analysis: The qualitative data from the interviews, focus groups, and observation will be analysed using content analysis techniques and NVivo software. The survey data will be subject to a range of statistical tests. Patterns will be sought across the data points, and issues of difference debated by the group. Contextual analysis will be done on each setting to consider how contextual issues mediate the data.

Having described the use of logic in the design process and presented design examples of the approaches to comparative case study design, it may now be apparent that the effective production of several of these designs requires preparatory field work in order to complete the design. For example, the purposeful selection of comparators means that larger ranges of potential cases have to be surveyed and the data relevant to selection must be collected and inspected. Thus, this preparatory work favours researchers with prior knowledge of and familiarity with the field.

A second point which follows from the logic of these designs is that this logic also applies to the process of analysis. There is therefore a flow of logic from design to data collection and into analysis. The comparators which have been established within the design form at least a starting point for the analytic process and also aid that process. The utility

of this cannot be underestimated, as all qualitative researchers will be aware of facing the problem of massive volumes of data. Despite this, the researcher must also search for disconfirming data and seek to interrogate the empirical data, once collected, for other significant themes.

Data collection methods

One of the major advantages of a case-study design is that the potential range of data collection methods is highly flexible. It is clearly imperative to consider not only which methods of data collection will be employed within each case, but also how these data will be analysed, and especially how those data produced through a variety of means will be combined.

Before referring to a selective range of possible data collection methods, let us remind the reader of several key issues which will influence the selection of methods for data collection.

One essential constituent of case studies is data on the context of the case. Whilst some data are frequently available from published sources, such as data on trends, one core element which is less readily available is data on the history of the organization. One data collection method which can be adopted to accomplish the development of a broader, outline picture of the history of an organization is to interview a small range of stakeholders, deliberately selecting those with longer service and to include several 'lead' questions such as: 'What do you see as the critical events which have occurred in the organization over the last five to ten years?'. Gummesson (2000) offers further ideas on the processes, which can be utilized to build historical analysis into cases, particularly with a focus on organizational change.

An essential step in moving from the overall design of the comparative case studies and into the specification and implementation of data collection methods is to reflect carefully on how the stakeholders will be selected in order to ensure a comprehensive and representative picture. It is crucial to document the logic and rationale for selection. Whilst the selection of a sample in a survey design would almost automatically be subject to scrutiny and selected on the basis of established statistical conventions, such 'rules' are less well established within case-study methodology. But the selection of data sources, including individuals and groups, is critical.

The issue of triangulation has been high-lighted previously, and it is important to note that more data is not automatically better. The collection of large quantities of data, especially if those data are in differing forms, presents serious analytic issues. For example, individually transcribed interview data may follow a loose pathway, based on the interview questions, whether structured or semistructured, but how will these data be combined with fieldwork notes from observations of meetings which may be recorded in an entirely different structure? The approach to analysis forms a critical part of the study design and cannot be left to an 'afterthought'.

In considering the potential methods of data collection within a case study, the list of already established methods includes:

- Interviews; both structured and semi-structured
- Critical incident technique
- Surveys
- Observation
- Focus groups

Here, we will briefly consider each of these methods in turn. Whilst space precludes the detailed exposition of procedures for the planning, skilled operation, and implementation of each method, the reader will be referred to texts, which offer fuller explanations. In addition to these established methods of data collection, there is considerable potential for the development of novel methods, such as visual and remote methods of data collection and capture, and for combined or mixed methods (see Bryman, Chapter 30, this volume).

Interviews, structured and semistructured

Interviews are one of the most widely used of all the methods of qualitative research. They are a flexible method of obtaining information, face to face with the respondent (Silverman, 2004a&b; Saunders et al, 2003; Foddy, 1993). Interviews are frequently the method of choice, because they enable the researcher to achieve multiple objectives. These objectives may include gaining insight into the respondents' subjective experiences; contextualizing those experiences; recognizing the interwoven, interacting strands of experience; and capturing the dynamic nature of experience and the time dimension.

Interviews may differ substantially across a range according to their *degree of structure.* So, interviews may be structured (like a spoken questionnaire), semistructured or unstructured, and in-depth. As one moves from structured to unstructured, the differences in the data produced are substantial. Structured interviews will produce more standardized data, which is shorter and focussed. Indeed, an interview, which uses 'prompt' cards, might be perceived as a spoken questionnaire, with similar strengths and weaknesses. By contrast, an unstructured interview will be more in the nature of a gently guided conversation. It will produce detail, and a selection of material, which the respondent thinks is important. So structuring in an interview is about focus and control, as well as about depth. One notes too that the nature of the data has major implications for the process of analysis. The more standardized the form of the data, the easier it is to analyse. From the researcher's viewpoint, it is a question of whether it is better to invest more time in preparation or in analysis.

Interviews will also vary depending on *the kind and number of respondents.* Interviews may be either individual (face-to-face or telephone) or group interviews. Individual interviews are the most favourable medium for generating in-depth and/or confidential data. They allow the interviewer to develop a degree of rapport with the respondent, which can create a 'safe' environment in which to talk. One specific aspect to which attention is drawn is the vital need to consider ethical issues as part of the preparation. Serious attention needs to be paid to the issues of consent and confidentiality, and this may be critical in obtaining access.

Critical incident technique

This is 'a procedure for gathering certain important facts concerning behaviour in defined situations', and was developed by Flanagan (1954: 335). The technique yields in-depth material, which is grounded in concrete experience, in a natural setting; presents a holistic picture, and gives rich detail. A critical incident is a concrete example of the behaviour or situation in which the researcher is interested. For example, the researcher might ask, 'Think of incidents when', or 'Tell me about an incident in which'. Instead of asking a person's opinions about a topic, the researcher collects data on the concrete accounts of the events as recalled by those who have experienced them. Thus, the respondent is a storyteller, recounting their experience as perceived by them.

Surveys

Surveys require very careful design, admin-istration, and analysis (Oppenheimer, 1992; Rossi et al., 1988). The response rate for surveys is typically low, and a 50 percent response would be a good result. Justifications for their use in a case-study context might include enabling the collection of information that helps scope interview, observation, and other methods design; checking and adding validity to interview findings if administered after interview data collection; and offering another triangulated source of data.

Observation

Observational techniques are based on the idea of a systematic process of observing, noting, and later categorizing the observed activities (Lofland, 1995). Since observation in organizational settings frequently includes the observation of interactions between sev-eral individuals, this is not a simple process. Anyone who has ever tried to observe and record a meeting will know that it

is difficult to produce an accurate record. Observation, which centres on the activities of an individual, is the simplest form of research in this mode, but will nevertheless require a framework for recording contacts. The key art in observation is to record words, activities or events without judging them.

Some forms of observation will be based on a structure, which may itself be founded in a theoretical or conceptual idea or be based on prior research. Two such examples of these structures or frameworks are the work of Belbin (2003) on teams and team roles, and the earlier work of Bales (1950) on group process and interactions. Each of these research programmes produced a framework which could be adopted by other researchers to examine and analyse aspects of team functioning. These methods may require a high level of resourcing from the researcher.

Focus groups

Focus groups offer a process which is based on group interviews. Focus groups are useful for discovering new information or consolidating old information; obtaining a number of different perspectives on the same topic in the participants own words; and gaining information on participants' views, attitudes, beliefs, responses, or motivations on a topic, including their shared understandings of everyday life. Additionally, focus groups may be a better method for exploring controversial issues and complex or sensitive topics (Litosseliti, 2003).

Analysis processes

The analysis of multiple cases based on qualitative data inevitably involves the han-dling of large quantities of such data. As critical elements in the research design, it is essential that both the processes of analysis and the management of the data set are planned carefully. As stated, there is no uniform set of rules for qualitative analysis, and there is limited guidance on alternative approaches (Dey, 1993; Diamantopoulos and

Schlegelmilch, 1997; Silverman, 2004b). The approach to data analysis that we advocate here is consistent with the interpretative paradigm and our approach to case-study design.

It is crucial to remember that it *is* qualitative data and to resist the temptation to deal with volume by attempts at quantification. Rightfully, Eisenhardt and Graebner (2007) draw attention to the problems of presenting rich qualitative data, and we would agree that this is indeed a major challenge. However, they propose the use of 'extensive tables' and advocate a separate table to summarize the evidence for each theoretical construct. We would suggest caution may need to be exercised here, as there is a danger of mimicking the presentation of quantitative data and stifling creativity if the use of tables becomes the norm or the sole method for data presentation. This is not to suggest that such modes of presentation should not be explored. There have been excellent examples of the tabular presentation of qualitative data (e.g., Denis et al., 2002: 67), but the issues of the richness of the data and the transparency of the sources need addressing. Moreover, it may not be possible or wise to present tables based on separate constructs, as advocated, since the analysis may invoke the merging of constructs to promote understanding.

The analysis of comparative case studies is inevitably an iterative process, whatever be the original starting point. The process of analysing from raw data needs to move through a series of key stages, but with recaps and reiterations as necessary. These stages include familiarization, reflection, conceptualization, cataloguing concepts, recoding, linking, and re-evaluation.

The first issue with the handling of masses of data is familiarization. This is a much greater problem than may be immediately apparent. First, there is no software, which can aid the researcher in the process of familiarization. The software packages available for qualitative data can aid the later stages of the analytic process, the compiling and handling of comparisons between case studies, and the evolution of evidence on

thematic streams. However, researchers need to develop familiarity in order to be able to interpret, to select and extract novel findings, and to assess what is novel over what is already known. Second, working in a team means that the load of analytic work can be shared and crosschecked. But, it also means that more people have to work on the task of familiarization so that the debates can be knowledgeably shared.

Reflection follows familiarization, and here it is useful to debate with others, and also to test out ideas with case participants in the field. So, feedback workshops to site collaborators offer an opportunity to confirm early analysis, and to 'road test' some embryonic formulations. In an exploratory case study, this might be a set of ideas about what has been observed, whilst in an explanatory case study, it may be an initial explanation of links.

One of the early questions concerning the design of the analysis is whether to adopt a framework for analysis or to adopt a purely grounded approach. Adopting a framework or template for analysis requires the researcher to apply an initial analytic frame within which to interrogate the data. Minimally, this frame might be built on the original research question or it might utilize the spine of interview questions employed for data gathering. Either way, the researcher will need to develop and justify a template customized to the research objectives. Similarly, theoretically informed case selection leads to a theoretically informed analytic process, and provides a framework, at least in the first instance. Prior research may have raised some core questions, and it therefore makes logical sense to start the analysis by interrogating the data around these. However, even if there are some focused questions upon which to base initial scans of the data, there will also, again inevitably, be a need to rescan and search for disaffirming information. Adopting an initial framework for analysis requires that the researcher should be able to provide a transparent trail from the frame of analysis through the data to the resulting themes. A purely inductive, grounded content analysis commences from an open-minded stance towards the data and will require scanning and rescanning of the data for emerging themes.

IN CONCLUSION

It is our contention that case study research is a valuable and developing research design with significant potential to contribute to organizational studies and to the formation and implementation of policy. As a design, it particularly lends itself to the exploration of complex 'how' and 'why' questions, as well as improving our understanding of organizational behaviour embedded in the social context of which 'it' is a part.

We have argued that case-study designs have been undervalued in the field of organizational studies, and we have taken issue with the argument of Eisenhardt and Graebner (2007) that case studies are not mainstream in organizational studies. Far from being a bridge to the mainstream, it is our judgement that, both historically and currently, case studies are a fruitful part of the mainstream and are generating theory that is shaping the field. We acknowledge, however, that the mainstream argument may currently be easier to sustain when considering organizational studies scholarship in Europe, compared to the US. However, definitions of the 'mainstream' need to be inclusive; not all research questions can be appropriately answered by measures of covariation. And as Eisenhardt and Graebner (2007: 25) state, 'inductive and deductive logics are mirrors of one another, with inductive theory building from cases producing new theory from data and deductive theory testing completing the cycle by using data to test theory'.

We do concede that comparative case-study designs are an approach within organizational studies which remains under development and therefore scrutiny. Whilst we have many examples of robust designs that have been tested and have delivered excellent scholarly outcomes and policy contributions, there is still much to do to harvest the potential of comparative case studies for the field of organizational studies. It would therefore seem unproductive to marginalize or to stifle creativity and innovation in this arena. We need more studies that not only draw on the research design but also purposefully reflect in a detailed way on the lessons learnt from innovations in case design and implementation. We hope this chapter stimulates and provokes research communities and researchers into action to this effect.

ACKNOWLEDGMENTS

We would like to thank A. Ferner, T. Colling, and I. Clark for use of example 27.1. With acknowledgement and thanks to L. Fitzgerald, E. Ferlie, C. Hawkins, and M. Wood (2005) for the use of example 27.2. And with acknowledgement and thanks to I. Kessler; S. Dopson, and P. Heron for the use of example 27.3, which is based on research that is ongoing at the time of writing.

REFERENCES

Almond, P. and Ferner, A. (eds) (2006) *American Multinationals in Europe: Managing Employment Relations Across National Borders*, Oxford: Oxford University Press.

Almond, P., Edwards, P., Colling, T., Ferner, A., Gunnigle, P., Muller-Camen, M., Quintanilla, J. and Wächter, H. (2005) 'Unravelling home and host country effects: an investigation of the HR policies of an American multinational in four European countries', *Industrial Relations*, 44(2): 276–306.

Bales, R.F. (1950) *Interaction Process Analysis*, Cambridge, MA: Addison Wesley Press.

Belbin, R.M. (2003) *Management Teams: Why They Succeed or Fail*, London: Butterworth Heinemann.

Blaxter, M. (1996) 'on behalf of the BSA Medical Sociology Group "Criteria for the Evaluation of Qualitative Research" ', *Medical Sociology News*, 22: 68–71.

Bryman, A. and Bell, E. (2003) *Business Research Methods*, Oxford: Oxford University Press.

Buchanan, D., (2001) 'The role of photography in organization research: a re-engineering case illustration', *Journal of Management Inquiry*, 10(2): 151–64.

Buchanan, D. and Huczynski, A., (2004) 'Images of influence: Twelve Angry Men and Thirteen Days', *Journal of Management Inquiry*, 13(4): 312–23.

Child, J. and Smith, C. (1987) 'The context and process of organizational transformation – Cadbury limited in its sector', *Journal of Management Studies*, 24(6): 565–93.

Cully, M., Woodland, S., O'Reilly, A. and Dix, G. (1999) *Britain at Work: 4th Workplace Industrial Relations Survey*, London: Routledge.

Denzin, N.K. and Lincoln, Y.S. (2000) *Handbook of Qualitative Research*, (second edn.), London: Sage.

Denis, J-L., Hebert, Y., Langley, A., Lozeau, D. and Trottier, L-H. (2002) 'Explaining Diffusion patterns for complex health care innovations', *Health Care Management Review*, 27(3): 60–73.

Dey, I. (1993) *Qualitative Data Analysis*, Routledge: London.

Diamantopoulos, A. and Schlegelmilch, B.G. (1997) *Taking the Fear out of Data Analysis*, London: Dryden Press/Harcourt, Brace and Co.

Edwards, T., Almond, P., Clark, I., Colling, T. and Ferner, A. (2005) 'Reverse diffusion in US Multinationals: barriers from the American business system', *Journal of Management Studies*, 42(6): 1261–86.

Eisenhardt, K. (1989) 'Building theories from case research', *Academy of Management Review*, 14(4): 532–50.

Eisenhardt, K. and Graebner, M. (2007) 'Theory building from cases: opportunities and challenges', *Academy of Management Journal*, 50(1): 25–32.

Ferlie, E.; Fitzgerald, L. and Wood, M. (2000) 'Getting evidence into clinical practice: an organisational behaviour perspective', *Journal of Health Services Research and Policy*, 5(1): 1–7.

Ferlie, E.; Fitzgerald, L.; Wood, M. and Hawkins, C. (2005) 'The non spread of innovations: the mediating role of professionals', *Academy of Management Journal*, 48(1): 117–34.

Ferner, A. and Varul, M. Z. (1999) *The German Way? German Multinationals and the Management of Human Resources in Their UK Subsidiaries*, London: Anglo-German Foundation for the Study of Industrial Society.

Fitzgerald, L. and Ferlie, E. (2002) 'Interlocking interactions, the diffusion of innovations in health care', *Human Relations*, 55(12): 1429–49.

Flanagan, J.C. (1954) 'The critical incident technique', *Psychological Bulletin*, 51(4): 327–58.

Foddy, W. (1993) *Constructing Questions for Interviews and Questionnaires*, Cambridge: Cambridge University Press.

Glaser, B. and Strauss, A. (1967) *The Discovery of Grounded Theory: Strategies for Qualitative Research*, Chicago: Aldine.

Gummesson, E. (2000) *Qualitative Research in Management*, Thousand Oaks/London: Sage.

Hammersley, M., Atkinson, P. (1995) *Ethnography: Principles in Practice*, (second edn.), London: Routledge.

Huberman, A. and Miles, M. (1984) *Innovation Up Close: How School Improvement Works*, New York: Plenum Press.

Kennedy, M.M. (1976) 'Generalizing from single case studies', *Evaluation Quarterly*, 3: 661–78.

Langley, A. (1999) 'Strategies for theorizing from process data', *Academy of Management Review*, 24(4): 691–710.

Lee, T.S. (1999) *Using Qualitative Methods in Organizational Research*, Thousand Oaks, CA: Sage.

Litosseliti, L. (2003) *Using Focus Groups in Research*, London: Continuum.

Lofland, J. (1995) *Analyzing Social Settings: A Guide to Qualitative Observation and Analysis*, London: Wadsworth.

Mays, N. and Pope, C. (2000) 'Quality in qualitative research', in C. Pope, and N. Mays, (eds), *Qualitative Research in Health Care*, (second edn.), London: BMJ Books, pp. 89–101.

Mays, N., Roberts, E. and Popay, J. (2001) 'Synthesising research evidence', in N. Fulop, P. Allen, A. Clarke and N. Black (eds), *Studying the Organization and Delivery of Health Services: Research Methods*, London: Routledge, pp. 188–220.

Miles, M.B. (1979) 'Qualitative data as an attractive nuisance: the problem of analysis', *Administrative Science Quarterly*, 24: 590–601.

Oppenheimer, A.N. (1992) *Questionnaire Design, Interviewing and Attitude Measurement*, London: Cassell.

Pettigrew, A.M. (1985) *The Awakening Giant*, London, Blackwell.

Pettigrew, A.M. (1987) 'Context and action in the transformation of the firm', *Journal of Management Studies*, 24(6): 649–70.

Pettigrew, A.M. and Whipp, R. (1991) *Managing for Competitive Success*, Oxford: Basil Blackwell.

Pettigrew, A.M., Ferlie, E. and McKee, L. (1992) *Shaping Strategic Change: Making Change in Large Organizations – The Case of the National Health Service*, London: Sage.

Plowman, D.A., Baker, L.T., Beck, T.E., Kulkarni, M., Solansky, S.T. and Travis, D.V.T. (2007) 'Radical change accidentally: the emergence and amplification of small change', *Academy of Management Journal*, 50(3): 515–43.

Popay J., Rogers, A. and William, G. (1998) 'Rationale and standards for the systematic review of qualitative literature in health services research', *Qualitative Health Research*, 8: 341–51.

Rossi, P. Wright, J. and Anderson, A. (1988) *Handbook of Survey Research*, Oxford: Oxford University Press.

Salkind, N.J. (2006) *Exploring Research*, (sixth edn.), New Jersey: Pearson.

Saunders, M.Lewis, P. and Thornhill, A. (2003) *Research Methods for Business Students*, (fourth edn.), Harlow: Pearson.

Silverman, D. (2004a) *Qualitative Research: Theory, Method and Practice*, (second edn.), London: Sage.

Silverman, D (2004b) *Doing Qualitative Research: A Practical Handbook*, (second edn.), London: Sage.

Tempel, A., Edwards, T., Ferner, A. Müller-Carmen, M. and Walgenbach, P. (2007) 'Subsidiary responses to institutional duality: collective representation practices of US multinationals in Britain and Germany', *Human Relations*, Special issue, 59(11): 1543–70.

Weick, K.E. (1993) 'The collapse of sensemaking in organizations: the Mann Gulch disaster', *Administrative Science Quarterly*, 38(4): 628–52.

Van Maanen, J. (1995) 'An end to innocence: the ethnography of ethnography', in J. Van Maanen (ed.) *Representation in Ethnography*, London: Sage.

Whyte, W.F. (1943/1955) *Street Corner Society: The Social Structure of An Italian Slum*, Chicago: University of Chicago Press.

Yablonsky, L. (1988) *The Violent Gang*, New York: Wiley.

Yin, R.K. (1999) 'Enhancing the quality of case studies in health services research', *Health Services Research*, 34(5): 1209–24.

Yin, R.K. (2003) *Case Study Research: Design and Methods*, Thousand Oaks, CA: Sage Publications (second edn.).

28

Conversation Analysis in Organization Research

David Greatbatch

INTRODUCTION

Talk is a pervasive feature of organizational life and is at the heart of the accomplishment of key administrative activities, such as planning, selling, interviewing, chairing meetings, negotiating, presenting, and the like. Despite this, talk in organizational settings has attracted relatively little attention in the field of Organizational Studies (OS). Until recently, it was either overlooked, treated as epiphenomenal, or considered in the context of studies of 'communication skill', which pay little, if any, attention to the details of naturally occurring talk in organizations (Samra-Fredericks, 1998). However, in the last few years, an increasing number of researchers have begun to consider how various approaches to the analysis of talk, developed in a range of disciplines, can shed new light on the practical accomplishment of administrative activities and core themes and issues in OS (e.g. Boden, 1994; Cooren and Fairhurst, 2004; Forray and Woodilla, 2002; Fairhurst, 2004; Greatbatch and Clark, 2003, 2005; Llewellyn, 2004, 2006; Putnam, 2003; Samra-Fredericks, 2003, 2004; Silverman, 1997; Woodilla, 1999; Hindmarsh and Pilnick, forthcoming).

In this chapter, I introduce Conversation Analysis (CA), an approach which has attracted considerable interest in OS, and illustrate how it can be used to respecify core concepts and themes in OS. CA emerged in the 1960s as part of the broader sociological research initiative of ethnomethodology, which developed from Harold Garfinkel's (1967) seminal studies of the social organization underlying the production and intelligibility of everyday social actions and activities. Drawing on this initiative, Harvey Sacks and his colleagues, Emanuel Schegloff and Gail Jefferson, launched a radically distinct programme of research which recognized that the analysis of tape recordings of naturally occurring talk-in-interaction provided the possibility of developing a 'naturalistic observation discipline which could deal with the details of social action(s) rigorously, empirically, and formally' (Schegloff and Sacks, 1974: 233). Their groundbreaking research has inspired a substantial body of empirical studies of the social organization of a wide range of social actions and activities in an array of settings.

In the following section, I introduce some key methodological issues in CA and outline the scope of studies which have adopted this approach. I then draw on a study of management guru oratory (Greatbatch and Clark, 2003, 2005) to illustrate how CA can be used to explicate the ways in which administrative tasks and activities, in this case presenting, are accomplished as they emerge in real-time interactions and to 'respecify' key concepts and themes in OS.

Conversation analysis

Methodological considerations

CA involves fine-grained analysis of audio and visual recordings of naturally occurring talk in interaction. As Greatbatch, Heath, Luff, and Campion (1995: 202) observe:

> For the analysis of social interaction, these data offer a number of advantages over more traditional modes of inquiry such as field notes, interviews or the responses to questionnaires. They provide the researcher with access to the richness and complexity of social action, allowing particular events to be scrutinized repeatedly and subjected to detailed inspection. In contrast, for example, to field notes, they provide raw data to which a range of analytic interests can be applied, unconstrained by the concerns of a particular research study. Moreover, audio and video recordings enable other researchers within the scientific community to evaluate the strength of particular analyses with respect to the original data and thereby provide an important constraint on the quality and rigour of findings. Audio and video recordings provide repeatable access to specific details of real world actions, activities, and events; a microscope with which to study human life.

Thus, as Atkinson and Heritage (1984: 4) suggest:

> In sum, the use of recorded data serves as a control on the limitations and fallibilities of intuition and recollection; it exposes the observer to a wide range of interactional materials and circumstances and also provides some guarantee that analytic considerations will not arise as artefacts of intuitive idiosyncrasy, selective attention or recollection, or experimental design.

CA is not concerned with language per se. Its interest in language derives from the fact that talk is a primary vehicle for the accomplishment of social actions (Austin, 1962; Searle, 1969; Wittgenstein, 1974). CA focuses on the resources that members of society use and rely upon for the production and recognition of intelligible social actions (and activities) in talk-in-interaction. In contrast to some theories of language use and linguistic analysis (e.g. speech act theory), CA recognizes that that utterances and the actions they accomplish are inseparable from the context in which they occur. This is because each utterance/action is produced with respect to the immediately preceding utterances/actions, whilst simultaneously contributing to the framework to which subsequent utterances/actions will be addressed; in other words each utterance/action is both 'context shaped and context renewing' (Heritage, 1984: 242). In consequence, the character and organization of an utterance/action can only be determined with reference to the local configuration of conduct in which it is produced and rendered intelligible. As Schegloff and Sacks observe:

> ...a pervasively relevant issue (for participants) about utterances in conversation is 'why that now', a question whose [...] analysis may also be relevant to find what 'that' is. That is to say, some utterances may derive their character as actions entirely from placement considerations. (Schegloff and Sacks, 1974: 241).

CA, therefore, involves the detailed analysis of the sequential organization of utterances in talk-in-interaction. The core aim of CA research is to derive generalizable descriptions of the practices through which specific actions (and activities) are systematically accomplished in talk-in-interaction. Thus, in contrast to cognitive perspectives (in the fields of psycholinguistics, cognitive psychology, cognitive anthropology, etc.) which explain face-to-face interaction in terms of the participants' cognitive states (their plans, intentions, goals, etc.) and/or which treat talk as a passive medium through which information is transmitted from one mind to another, CA provides a methodological framework that renders the interactional practices through which social actions are accomplished in talk in interaction both visible and analysable.

CA places rigorous constraints on the use of 'wider' contexts to explain features of talk in interaction. Participants in talk-in-interaction can be accurately categorized in terms of numerous social identities, including those related to age, race, sex, social class, occupation, and organizational setting (Sacks, 1992). This poses the question of how professional analysts can determine which, if any, of the array of social identities that can be applied to participants are relevant to understanding their conduct at any point in time (Schegloff, 1991, 1992). Some approaches to the analysis of talk solve this problem by warranting the invocation of wider social identities on statistical or theoretical grounds, which are external to the speakers' own orientations. By contrast, CA restricts its focus to the endogenous orientations of the participants, as displayed in the specifiable details of their interactional conduct: it describes how the participants themselves orient to and make relevant specific social identities within their interactions on a moment-by-moment basis (Schegloff, 1987, 1992, 1997).

In doing this, CA distinguishes between discourse identities, such as 'questioner-answerer' and 'inviter-invitee', which are intrinsic to talk-in-interaction and larger social/organizational identities (Goodwin, 1987), such as sex, ethnicity, and occupational role, which derive from wider societal and institutional formations and thus reach beyond the talk itself. Some CA studies restrict their focus to discourse identities, explicating sequentially organized domains of talk-in-interaction, which are relatively autonomous of other aspects of social organization. However, others explore how participants make larger social identities relevant within their talk and how the invocation of such identities can constitute both a constraint on and a resource for the accomplishment of the activities in which the participants are engaged. Thus, for example, Goodwin (1987) shows how a speaker at a family gathering

makes relevant his spousal relationship with a coparticipant by producing a display of uncertainty about household affairs which positions the latter as a 'knowing recipient' and the other participants as 'unknowing recipients'. Similarly, research on the news interview shows how discourse identities (and the activities in which they are embedded) invoke the institutional identities news interviewer and news interviewee by positioning the broadcast journalists as 'neutralistic report elicitors', the guests as report producers, and the audience as primary recipients of the talk (Clayman and Heritage, 2003; Heritage and Greatbatch, 1991). Thus, rather than viewing context as 'external' to social interaction, CA focuses on those aspects of context that can be shown to be relevant to the participants themselves as their interactions unfold.

Analytic procedures/Modes of analysis

CA research does not involve the formulation and empirical testing of *a priori* hypotheses. Instead, it identifies patterns of verbal and/or nonverbal interaction through the use of the procedures of analytic induction. Heritage (1995: 399) describes the mode of analysis as follows:

> As competent language users, analysts develop more or less conceptually informed hunches about the uses and organizational properties of particular conversational practices. At this point, the work normally begins with an inductive search for instances of the practice under investigation using as wide a range of data as possible [...] Once possessed of a set of cases that appear to embody a conversational practice or procedure, the detailed work of specifying the scope and limits of the practice begins. A major component of this involves 'deviant case analysis'. This involves examining cases where the general pattern is departed from and examining whether, and in what ways, the participants orient to such departures. Used in this way, deviant case analysis is an important resource for determining whether the basic pattern simply embodies an empirical regularity that happens to occur, or whether it involves something that is oriented to as a normative interactional procedure.

In undertaking this form of 'pattern and deviant case' analysis (Heritage, 1995: 399), CA researchers repeatedly replay audio or video recordings of naturally occurring interaction, carefully transcribing the events. The transcripts capture not only what is said, but also a variety of details of speech production, such as overlapping talk, pauses within and between utterances, stress, pitch, and volume. They may also track visual conduct such as gaze direction and gesture. These transcripts facilitate the fine-grained analysis of the recordings, enabling researchers to reveal and analyse tacit, 'seen but unnoticed' aspects of human conduct, which would otherwise be unavailable for systematic study. Moreover, extracts from the transcripts are included in research reports as exemplars of interactional phenomena under investigation. For introductions to CA, see Heritage (1984, 1995, 1997), Hutchby and Woofitt (1998), Psthas (1995), ten Have (1999), Woofitt (2005) and Zimmerman 1988).

Talk and organizations

Although CA began from the study of ordinary conversations, as indicated in the preceding section, its approach and findings have been widely used to analyse 'interaction in institutional settings where more or less official or formal task- or role-based activities are undertaken' (Heritage, 1997: 406). Thus, for example, CA studies have focussed on interactions in medical consultations, broadcast interviews, telephone calls for emergency assistance, business meetings, classroom lessons, divorce mediation sessions, small claims courts, and psychiatric intake interviews (see, for example, Atkinson and Heritage, 1984; Boden, 1994; Button and Lee, 1987; Boden and Zimmerman, 1991; Drew and Heritage, 1992). These studies examine how social institutions are evoked and managed in interaction. Specifically, they show how participants make particular institutions and their associated identities relevant within their talk, and how this constitutes both a constraint on and a resource for the activities in which the participants are engaged. This generally involves analysts describing how

participants adapt a limited number of the full range of generic speaking practices, which are available to them to manage organizational roles, tasks and constraints that are indigenous to particular institutional settings.

The development of CA studies of institutional/organizational talk has led a number of influential figures to advocate bringing CA into OS, (e.g. Boden, 1994; Silverman, 1997; Llewellyn and Hindmarsh, forthcoming), and recently this has been carried through by a number of researchers, including Samra Fredericks (2003, 2004), Greatbatch and Clark (2003, 2005), Llewellyn, 2004, and Clifton, 2006. Nonetheless, the implications of CA studies of institutional talk for OS remain largely unexplored, as most CA research has addressed topics that are of marginal interest to OS. Next, I illustrate the potential of CA in the context of OS by drawing on a programme of CA-based research on management guru oratory, which sheds light on the key administrative task of presenting.

An example: A CA study of management guru oratory

The study focused on an elite group of management speakers/thought-leaders, who are often referred to as management gurus. Management gurus are purveyors of influential management ideas such as Excellence, Culture Change, Learning Organization, and Business Process Reengineering and, in the case of Daniel Goleman, Emotional Intelligence. In addition to writing best-selling management books, they disseminate their ideas in live presentations on the international management lecture circuit (Huczynski, 1993; Jackson, 1996). As perhaps the highest profile group of management speakers in the world, they use their lectures to build their personal reputations with audiences of managers. Many gain reputations as powerful orators and subsequently market recordings of their talks as parts of audio- and video-based management training packages.

The data for our study comprised video recordings of the gurus' public lectures, which were drawn from commercially produced training packages. The videos analysed in the study featured Tom Peters, Rosabeth Moss Kanter, Gary Hamel, and Peter Senge. The videos involving Peters and Moss Kanter combine footage of the two gurus lecturing with case studies and interviews concerning organizations that are mentioned in the gurus' lectures. The videos involving Senge and Hamel include complete performances. The twenty hours of video material contain approximately fifteen hours of the gurus lecturing to audiences of managers and consultants.

Initial viewings of the recordings revealed that these lectures are not episodes of one-way communication in which the speaker sends a message and the audience passively receive it. Rather the members of the audience actively participate in the proceedings. While the lectures do not contain any disaffiliative responses such as booing and heckling, the audience members do regularly produce displays of affiliation with the gurus by, inter alia, clapping, laughing supportively, nodding their heads, and smiling. In some cases, these affiliative responses are produced by one or two individuals. In others, however, they involve numerous audience members acting in concert with each other. When audience members collectively display their affiliation with the gurus, they do so predominantly by laughing in response to purportedly humorous messages. We, therefore, decided to focus on the occurrence of audience laughter.

Initial analysis of the guru tapes

We began by identifying and transcribing the segments of the lectures within which the eighty-eight cases of collective audience laughter were embedded. We then repeatedly viewed the video recordings of these episodes in order to establish how these occurrences of laughter were organized. To facilitate the analysis we used and refined detailed transcripts, using CA notation (see Appendix), which captured each laughter episode and the surrounding talk.

Analysis of the video recordings of laughter episodes (and transcripts thereof) revealed two key insights. The first of these concerned the positioning of the onset of collective laughter in relation to the gurus' talk, and built on the findings of previous CA studies of public speaking (largely political oratory), which demonstrate that collective audience responses, such as applause and laughter, are not simply spontaneous reactions to the messages which evoke them (e.g., Atkinson, 1984a,b; Clayman, 1993; Heritage and Greatbatch, 1986). As collective actions, their production is underpinned by the basic sociological principle that people prefer to act like those around them so as to avoid social isolation (Asch, 1951). Thus, for example, while individual audience members may wish to clap in response to public speakers' remarks, they will generally wish to do so in situations in which they are assured that other audience members will do the same. If this is not the case they may be found to be isolated in indicating their response to the speaker's foregoing remarks and socially embarrassed as a consequence. Thus, a key issue for audience members is to gauge when and how to appropriately respond.

According to Clayman (1993: 111–113), collective responses may be facilitated by two methods – independent decision-making and mutual monitoring. Independent decision-making involves audience members reacting independently of one another, but nonetheless managing to respond in concert. In this respect, audience members gravitate to those parts of the speech that stand out conspicuously from other parts of the talk. Where audience members can anticipate the completion of such a message then 'its completion may serve as a common reference point around which individual response decisions are coordinated' (Clayman, 1993: 112). In contrast, mutual monitoring involves individual response decisions being 'guided, at least in part, by reference to the [aural or, less commonly, visual] behaviour of other audience members' (Clayman, 1993: 112). Thus, for example, individual audience members may decide to respond after they observe others either doing likewise or acting in ways that suggest that they are about to do so (e.g., preparing to clap, murmuring approval, and nodding). As Clayman observes these two scenarios lead to different types of responses:

> Responses organised primarily by independent decision-making should begin with a 'burst' that quickly builds to maximum intensity as many audience members begin to respond in concert. Mutual monitoring, by contrast, should result in a 'staggered' onset as the initial reactions of a few audience members prompt others to respond. These scenarios are not mutually exclusive – a response episode may begin with a "burst" involving many independent starters, which subsequently encourages others to join in, Indeed, an initial "burst" should be most effective in prompting others because it *decisively* establishes the relevance of a response and *decisively* counteracts concerns about isolation. (Clayman, 1993: 112)

Our review of the video recordings of the management guru lectures revealed that independent decision-making plays a predominant role in the genesis of (the) audience laughter, with 83 (94%) cases of laughter beginning with a burst, either just before or immediately after message completion. This means that the speakers must supply the messages, which precipitate collective laughter with emphasis and clearly projectable completion points around which audience members can coordinate their actions.

The second insight was that the gurus (with only three exceptions) also signalled their humorous intent. Thus, the gurus rarely rely on audience members to recognize that collective laughter is relevant on the basis of the content of their messages alone. Rather, they also establish the relevance of audience laughter through the use of a range of verbal and nonverbal actions during the delivery, and/or following the completion, of their messages. These include: (1) announcing that they are about to say something humorous, (2) smiling or laughing and/or (3) using 'comedic' facial expressions, gestures and prosody. The latter involve, for example, displays of disgust, disbelief, anger, horror, amazement, or some other emotional reaction by themselves or others to the actions, practices, or issues that are being discussed. This is not to say that these nonverbal actions are inherently 'comedic'. Their possible status as such derives from their use with particular verbal messages and devices, whose 'comedic' status in turn derives in part from their use with such nonverbal actions. In other words, the speakers' verbal and nonverbal actions are reflexively related – the comedic status of each resting in part on their use in conjunction with the other.

The following data extract from a speech by the management guru Tom Peters, which is drawn from Greatbatch and Clark (2003, 2005) contains relatively straightforward examples of these phenomena. In this extract, Peters supports his argument that organizations should adopt 'flat and fluid' structures by quoting Ross Perot. The quotation praises one company, Electronic Data Systems (EDS) for purportedly adopting a 'flat and fluid' structure, and disparages another company, General Motors (GM), for purportedly retaining a cumbersome bureaucratic structure. Both the commendation of EDS and the criticism of GM are followed by audience laughter.

Extract 1

```
1 TP:          My favourite Perroism of all was his description, right before
2              leaving GM, of what he sa:w as the difference between
3              Electronic Data Systems and GM. (0.6) He said,
4              ['At EDS (.) WHEN YOU SEE A SNAKE (.) YOU KILL IT'.
5              [Leans forward, glares, uses angry tone of voice
6 Audience:--> [LLLLLLLLLL LLLLLLLLLL LLLLLL-L-L[-L
7              [Turns and walks          [
```

```
 9 Peters:                        [He said, 'At GM when
10                 you see a snake, [you search the world for the top
11                                 [ Leans forward/smile face
12                 consultant on snakes'.
13 Audience:-->   LLLLLLLLLL LLLLLLLLLL
14 Peters:        Then you appoint a committee on snakes and you study
15                snakes for the next two years. (1.0) <Flat (.) fluid (.) and get on with it (.)
16                that':s the creature
```

Peters provides the messages that evoke laughter with both emphasis and clearly projectable completion points by, inter alia, using a puzzle-solution format (Atkinson, 1984 a,b; Heritage and Greatbatch, 1986). Thus, he begins by establishing a puzzle in the minds of the audience members (lines 1–3): what did Ross Perot see as the difference between EDS and GM? He then offers a two-part solution, which is formed as a contrast (lines 3–4 and 8–11). In this way, he highlights the contents of the messages against a background of surrounding speech materials. He also provides the audience members with resources to anticipate the completion of the two messages, for they can match each part of the emerging solution to the puzzle in order to infer what it will take for it to be complete. In the case of the second part of the solution/contrast, they can also match it against the first part. In both instances, Peters confirms the relevance of laughter by ceding the floor until the audience's laughter ends and then, when he resumes speaking, neither asserting nor otherwise indicating that the audience's laughter was inappropriate or unexpected (lines 13–15).

Peters does not solely rely on the 'humourous' content of his remarks to establish the relevance of audience laughter; he also 'invites' audience laughter through the use of a range of nonverbal techniques. In the first case of laughter (line 6), which follows Peters's depiction of Perot's commendation of EDS, Peters uses comedic gestures, facial expressions, and prosody. As he quotes Perot on EDS (lines 4–5), he suddenly leans forward, glares at a section of the audience and speaks louder as he adopts a 'mock angry' tone. Then, as he completes the quotation ('you kill it'), he bares his teeth

as he 'spits' out the words. Together with Perot's incongruous metaphorical imagery – seeing and killing snakes in a corporate context – Peters's nonverbal actions establish the possible relevance of audience laughter. In the second case of audience laughter (line 12), which follows Peters's depiction of Perot's disparagement of GM (lines 8–11), Peters, reverting to a 'low key' form of speech delivery, establishes the possible relevance of laughter by leaning forward and smiling at the audience as he completes the quotation. Thus, Peters does not solely rely on the content of his message to indicate to the audience members that his message is humorous and that laughter is an appropriate response.

A review of the handful of incongruous/deviant cases in which the practices illustrated in this extract were absent, served to underline our thesis that the projection of clear message completion points and the signalling of humorous intent are key to understanding the evocation of collective audience laughter. Thus, for example, the importance of signalling humorous intent to audience members is underscored by the fact that, in all but one of the five cases in which the onset of audience laughter is 'staggered' – i.e. does not begin with an immediate 'burst' – the gurus rely on audience members to recognize on the basis of the content of their messages alone that laughter is a relevant, if not an expected, response. Consider Extract 2 in which Rosabeth Moss Kanter evokes audience laughter after she describes the purported reactions of a number of giant American corporations to a new packaging technology. After Kanter's description (line 1–13) one or two audience members start to laugh (line 15).

Extract 2

```
''Committee to study it'' [GCBA 1: 00.21.15]

 1 RMK:      They were the first producer of fruit and vegetable juice in the
 2           United State (.) to put their product in the cute little paper
 3           bottle.=The ( ) packaging. (0.7) A Well known packaging
 4           technology all over Europe not used in the United States. I
 5           mean again it just shows we're scouting the world (0.5) for technology
 6           including things like packaging can make a huge difference. (.) Anyhow
 7           they were not known in the United States. In the early eighties the
 8           European manufacturers came over (.) to make presentations to (0.2) to
 9           all the food companies to see if they could interest them in the
10           packaging. (.) So they make presentations to all of the giants, Coca Cola,
11           (.) Proctor and Gamble etcetera and one of the gia:nts (0.5) was
12           sufficiently interested in this that they immediately set up a committee to
13           study it.
14           (.)
15 Audience: L-L[-L-L -L- L- L- L     [LLLLLL--L-L-L-L-[L
16             [Expansive smile [                    [
17 RMK:                              [Right (.) uhm [
18 RMK:                                            [ Ocean Spra::y heard
19           the same presentation (0.8) committed the next da:y, (0.5)
20           signed a deal by the end of the week, (0.4) and got an eighteen month
21           exclusive license
```

The absence of an immediate burst of laughter may index, in part, uncertainty on the part of audience members as to whether collective laughter is relevant at this particular juncture. Kanter presents her message in a relatively straightforward way, with the result that the potential relevance of laughter rests largely, if not solely, on the content of her remarks. Subsequently, Kanter confirms that laughter is relevant by not only falling silent but also smiling (line 16). However, the audience members' audible response remains limited to isolated laughter (line 15). In the face of this, Kanter stops smiling and, walking away from the audience, resumes speaking (line 17: 'Right'). As she does so, however, additional audience members start to laugh – possibly in response not only to the preceding isolated laughter but also to Kanter's expansive smile. Kanter hesitates momentarily and then, as the laughter dissolves, goes on to praise the actions of a smaller company called Ocean Spray, which, she claims, is not weighed down by bureaucracy (lines 18–21). Examples like this perhaps underline the importance of the cues that gurus routinely use to signal their humorous intent to audience members.

In summary, we found that collective audience laughter is not simply a spontaneous reaction to messages whose content is self-evidently humorous. Usually, audience laughter is 'invited' by the gurus through the use of a range of verbal and non-verbal practices, which supply their messages with emphasis and clearly projectable completion points and signal humorous intent.

Conveying messages//content

Having identified a number of generic techniques through which audience laughter is invited and coordinated during the gurus' lectures, we turned to the relationship between the messages which evoke audience laughter and the gurus' core ideas and visions. We found that there were only three cases in which the gurus offer(ed) audience members opportunities to express through laughter unvarnished support for the values that are embedded in their core management ideas and visions. One of these is the foregoing Extract 2 in which Moss Kanter evokes laughter in response to her depiction of the reactions of a large corporation to an innovative packaging technology. To a large extent the humour of her remarks, which are produced 'straight-faced' with no humorous elaboration, derives from acceptance of her espoused view that most organizations are too bureaucratic, too conservative, too cautious when they encounter innovatory practices and products. Consequently, given the absence of other potential sources of humour, the audience's laughter may be interpreted as expressing support for her point of view concerning organizational practice in general.

In the vast majority of cases, however, the gurus do *not* construct and deliver their messages so as to invite audiences to produce, through laughter, unvarnished expressions of support for values that derive from their core ideas and visions. Thus, for example, the gurus frequently invest their messages with multiple sources of humour. This is starkly illustrated by comparing Moss Kanter's critique of bureaucratic organizations in Extract 2 with that of Tom Peters in Extract 1. In Extract 1, Peters evokes laughter in response to his (and Perot's) praise of the supposedly rapid reaction of one organization, and criticism of the purportedly slow reactions of another. In so doing, Peters conveys a critique of big, 'bureaucratic' organizations that closely resembles the stance taken by Kanter in Extract 2. However, in this instance, there are

several other potential sources of humour in addition to the critique per se. These include Perot's metaphorical imagery and style of speaking, and Peters's mimicry of these. Consequently, individual audience members may be displaying their appreciation of the humour in these features, as opposed to (or in addition to) Perot's evaluation of the corporations' actions and, by extension, Peters's core ideas. This means that while audience members' engage in collective displays of affiliation with Peters, their laughter does not represent *unvarnished* expressions of support for the position he is using the Perot quotation to substantiate. Thus, by offering multiple sources of humour, speakers are able to invest their remarks with considerable affiliative potential by permitting participants to hold multiple understandings of the situation but display these as a unified response.

As Extracts 3 and 4 illustrate, the gurus also frequently invite audience members to laugh at the by-products of the organizational practices they are recommending or criticizing, rather than at the practices themselves. Thus, for example, in Extract 3 described next, the target of Kanter's humour is the name of a product developed by a zoo that is purportedly adopting the practices she is advocating.

Extract 3

```
[MC: 00.06.19]

 1 RMK:      Now if it had been in New England (.) that person would
 2           ne(h)ver ha(h)d dar(h)ed speak up, but because it was California they
 3           are:
 4           (0.7) making their animals a profit centre.=Like the Toronto Zoo by the
 5           way that has been packaging fertiliser that they sell which has been
 6           contributed by the animals at the Toronto Zoo. (.) The Bronx Zoo also
 7           has one like this on the market I hate to say this out loud in front of
 8           several thousand people but they do have it on the market (.) under the
 9           brand na:me (.) [Zoo Doo.
10                          [RMK purses lips and widens eyes.
11 Audience: LLLLLLLLLL LL[LLL (1.5)
12 RMK:                   [Well you'll see my point in a minute, I'm no(h)t
13           ju(h)st try(h)ing to entertain you. (.) Because one more round
14           of the elephant,=I then thought…((Continues))
```

Similarly, the target of Gary Hamel's humour in Extract 4 in the following section is a purportedly surprising aspect of the success of a coffee shop chain strategy (construction workers lining up to buy a latte) that has apparently adopted his ideas by recreating the market for coffee. In contrast to the speakers in Extracts 1, 2, and 3 in the preceding sections, Hamel does not cede the floor whilst the audience members laugh. Having overlapped the onset of their laughter (line 9: 'Right'), he starts a new sentence and talks across the remainder of the audiences' response ('And if- and if I'm...'), as he initiates a spate of talk which assesses the implications of Starbucks' apparent success in the 'coffee business' for it's competitor Nestlé. By doing this, Hamel raises the possibility that he may not in fact have invited audience members to laugh and that their laughter was therefore a spontaneous, 'unexpected', 'unlooked for' response.

Consequently, although audience members exhibit that they share Kanters's perspective regarding the humour of the product name used by the zoo and Hamel's views concerning the popularity of a product amongst a particular occupational group, their laughter clearly does not represent an unvarnished expression of support for the gurus' core, underlying management ideas.

In summary, the gurus routinely invest their messages with multiple sources of humour and/or invite displays of affiliation with values that do not derive directly from their core management ideas and visions. The fact that the gurus routinely 'play safe' by inviting audience laughter, which is *not* open to interpretation as an unvarnished expression of support for their core positions is perhaps not surprising. The gurus often recommend/praise practices that audience members are unlikely to be using and criticize practices that audience members are likely to be using (Greatbatch and Clark, 2002). Although managers may welcome exposure to ideas that question what they do, it does not follow that they will wish to affiliate publicly with them. By inviting audience laughter that is not open to interpretation as an unvarnished expression of support for their core ideas, the gurus may, amongst other things, increase their chances of generating affiliative exchanges with audience members, even if these conditions apply. This enables them to elicit collective displays of affiliation, irrespective of whether audience members agree with their core ideas and visions.

The role of humour and laughter

The next stage of the analysis was to consider the theoretical implications of the findings.

Extract 4

```
[LinL: 0:38:30]

 1 GH:       Now this is not only in kind of high tech products and it's not
 2            only things about the internet.=Let me give you some very (.) mundane
 3            examples for a moment. (0.4) take something that certainly in the United
 4            States we all know as a company Starbucks.=Now beginning to go
 5            interna:tional. (0.7) Who would have predicted here that you could get
 6            construction workers to line up three deep to pay two and a half bucks
 7            for a latte after all.
 8 Audience: L[L L L L[L L L L L L L L L
 9 GH:        [Right. [And if- and if I'm sitting there inside Nestlé running
10            you know the world's largest coffee brand Nescafe (0.5) how do I feel
11            when in less than ten years somebody can build a coffee brand (0.6) that
12            in the largest mar:ket er: coffee drinking market in the world is a
13            demonstrably more valuable bra::nd (0.5) than my decades old coffee
14            brand. (0.5) Does it matter that er Nestlé grabs a little bit of market share
15            from P and G: in the (. ) isles of your local supermarket if most of the
16            new wealth in the coffee business is being created here.
```

This led us to recognize that the presentational devices identified in our analysis play an important role in the gurus' communication of their ideas and visions concerning organizations and the nature of the management role. Previous research into the functions of humour in organizational contexts suggest that it can promote the emergence and maintenance of group cohesiveness by, inter alia, clarifying and reinforcing shared values and social norms; disciplining those who violate the rules of a social group, and unifying other group members against them; and dividing group members from other groups (those who would be expected to adopt a different perspective; e.g., see Meyer, 2000). It is unclear whether the gurus and their audiences can be classified as members of distinctive social groups. Indeed, part of the management gurus' mission is to recruit managers to such groups, whose boundaries are defined by reference to their members' affiliation with the gurus' theories. Nonetheless, by evoking and producing laughter, the gurus and their audience members engage in public displays of consensus and 'like-mindedness' (Glenn, 1989) and thereby *constitute* themselves as 'in-groups' that share a common perspective in relation to the circumstances and events that the gurus describe. When gurus attack/disparage others (e.g., Extract 2), as opposed to emphasizing the positive qualities of a supposedly unusual situation (e.g., Extract 4), the gurus and those audience members who laugh also publicly differentiate themselves from individuals or groups who purportedly do not share the values or perspectives they are expressing. In these cases, then, humour and laughter delineate group boundaries by acting as both a unifier and divider (Meyer, 2000).

Whether these publicly displayed group affiliations actually reflect audience members' commitment to the gurus' views and thus may extend beyond the lifetime of the gurus' lectures is, of course, open to question. Nonetheless, even those cases of laughter that are not open to interpretation as unvarnished expressions of support for the gurus' core ideas indicate a shared perspective and – like affiliative interactional practices in general

(Goffman, 1983; Heritage, 1984) – contribute to a sense of cohesion and intimacy, which might make audiences more receptive to the gurus' recommendations.

SUMMARY

In summary, our exemplar study used the approach and findings of CA to examine how management ideas are disseminated and received in real-time speaker/audience interaction during management guru presentations. Having identified collective audience laughter as a feature of the lectures, our analysis revealed how the evocation of collective audience laughter rests, not merely upon the content of messages which precipitate the laughter, but also on the gurus' use of:

- Linguistic structures, together with paralinguistic and visual cues, that project clear message completion points around which audience members can coordinate their responses.
- Paralinguistic and visual cues that imbue messages, which precipitate collective audience laughter with a humorous tone.
- Discursive techniques which distinguish the values embodied within humorous messages from those which underpin the gurus' core management ideas and thus render audience laughter as ambiguous in relation to whether or not it comprises a display of affiliation with the latter.

The explication of these features depended not merely on repeated scrutiny of video recordings of the management gurus' presentations but also on our use of a methodological framework that:

- Treats talk as a primary vehicle for the accomplishment of social actions.
- Directs analytic attention to the sequential organization of social actions accomplished in and through naturally occurring talk.
- Seeks to explicate the resources that members of society use and rely upon for the production and recognition of intelligible social actions in talk-in-interaction.
- Treats *all* linguistic, paralinguistic, and visual actions as potentially relevant to the analysis of talk-in-interaction.

- Grounds social scientific analysis in the moment-to-moment understandings that participants negotiate and display during their interactions.

We concluded by exploring the implications of our findings for research on the communication of ideas by management gurus and, in so doing, drew on, and contributed to, the literature on group cohesiveness in organizational settings

CONCLUSION

Although talk is a pervasive feature of organizational life, the literature on organizations and organizational behaviour contains relatively few detailed studies of naturally occurring talk-in-interaction. This is unfortunate because such studies can, by drawing on CA, provide important insights into work and occupational life by explicating the ways in which personnel in organizational settings accomplish specialized administrative tasks and activities in and through interaction with colleagues and others. As our exemplar analysis shows, by shifting the focus of OS research to the social interactional foundations of tasks and activities in organizational settings, CA provides a distinctive perspective on core themes/topics within OS and provides opportunities for extending and respecifying key concepts in this field of scholarly enquiry. Thus, our analysis of management guru oratory contributed to the OS literature in at least two important respects. First, in contrast to previous research into so-called management gurus, it identified the presentational techniques that gurus use during their public lectures to communicate their ideas and visions concerning organizations, and showed how these techniques operate to maximize audience displays of consensus and to minimize audience displays of disagreement, regardless of whether audience members actually agree or disagree with the gurus' ideas.

Second, our analysis showed how studies of the real time accomplishment of administrative activities, such as presenting, can provide important insights into key themes in OS, such

as humour and group cohesiveness. Thus, while previous OS studies of humour adopt a variety of theoretical and methodological perspectives, none of them consider in detail the interactional practices through which humour-related actions – such as jokes, quips, laughter and smiling – are produced and rendered intelligible in real time interaction in organizational settings. Similarly, studies of group cohesiveness have not considered how displays of unity are evoked and coordinated in real-time interaction. Consequently, while the OS literature on these topics provides rich insights into organizational life, it does not consider what they consist of in ordinary organizational action and activities. As noted earlier, the same situation applies throughout OS research, with the result that until recently the practical accomplishment of work has not featured in theories of organization (Barley and Kunda, 2001; Llewellyn and Hindmarsh, forthcoming).

One apparent limitation of CA in the context of OS is that some administrative activities are not primarily accomplished through talk-in-interaction. However, in recent years a range of video-based studies of naturalistic work and interaction has emerged which, whilst drawing on CA, adopt a broader focus than those discussed in this paper (Heath, Luff, and Knoblauch, 2004). Whereas the latter studies (including our exemplar analysis) are primarily interested in the role of 'talk' in the accomplishment of social activities, these studies also analyse the use of tools, texts, and technologies. The objective is to explicate the informal, 'taken-for-granted' practices and reasoning which personnel rely upon in accomplishing and coordinating workplace activities, not only through talk-in-interaction but also through the use of various artefacts. Video-based studies which have drawn from CA in order to investigate the social organization of work, interaction, and the use of new technology have been conducted in a broad range of settings, including offices (Suchman, 1987, 1992), airport operation rooms (Goodwin and Goodwin, 1996), urban transport control rooms (Heath and Luff 2000), City trading rooms (Heath et al., 2000), and emergency dispatch centres (Whalen, 1995). In contrast to more traditional CA research, these video-based analyses of workplace activities often rely on information gathered through observation and interviews. This has proved necessary, because the patterns of interaction, and the organization of activities, in complex work settings often cannot be discerned or understood solely from analysis of video recordings. The use of such 'ethnographic' information remains highly contentious, because it may be used to warrant claims, which are not grounded in the understandings and orientations that interactants display to each other in situ (Hopper, 1991; Maynard and Clayman, 1995). Nonetheless, this body of research has demonstrated that, although the approach of CA cannot be simply 'applied' to activities in such settings, since those activities are rarely accomplished wholly through talk, it nonetheless provides the foundation for the explication of the social interactional organization of work, interaction, and technology (Luff, Heath, and Greatbatch, 1994).

In summary, CA comprises a data-driven methodology (Clayman and Maynard, 1995) which seeks to ground theoretical and analytic claims in the moment-to-moment understandings of their circumstances that participants unavoidably display to one another during their interactions. In contrast to many of those methodologies that involve quantification and/or experimental techniques, CA does not begin with *prior hypotheses*, which are then subjected to empirical testing. Rather, as our exemplar analysis illustrates, CA uses inductive search procedures in order to locate recurring patterns of action and interaction, focusing on aspects of linguistic, paralinguistic, and visual conduct which can only be systematically examined through repeated scrutiny of audio and video recordings of naturally occurring encounters.

While the fundamental aim of CA is to explicate the interactional practices through which people manage their interactions in an orderly, intelligible fashion, some CA researchers also examine the relationships between these practices and wider social and institutional formations. Others adopt a still broader focus by considering how various artefacts feature in everyday social action and interaction. Together these strands of research demonstrate how the analysis of audio and audio-visual recordings of naturally occurring social activities can reveal tacit 'seen-but-unnoticed background features' (Garfinkel, 1967: 36) of social and organizational settings which remain largely, if not wholly, unavailable to researchers who rely solely on data generated through observation, interviews, or questionnaires.

APPENDIX

Glossary of transcription symbols

The transcription symbols are drawn from the transcription notation developed by Gail Jefferson. For details on this notation, see Atkinson and Heritage (1984).

[	A left bracket indicates the point at which overlapping talk begins.
]	A right bracket indicates the point at which overlapping talk ends.
=	Equals signs indicate that different speakers' utterances are 'latched'. They also link continuous talk by a single speaker that has been distributed across nonadjacent because of another speaker's overlapping utterance.
(0.5)	Numbers in parentheses indicate the length of silences in tenths of a second.
(.)	A dot in parentheses indicates a gap of less than two-tenths of a second.
—	A dash indicates a cutoff sound like a guttural stop.
<u>Word</u>	Underlining indicates some form of stress via pitch and/or amplitude.
WORD	Capital letters indicate talk that is spoken louder than the surrounding talk.

Wo::rd	indicate prolongation of the
Colons	immediately preceding sound.
. , ?	Periods, commas, and question marks are used respectively to indicate falling, nonterminal, and rising intonation.
(Word)	Parenthesized words indicate that the transcriber was not sure of what was said.
( )	Empty parentheses indicate that the transcriber could not hear what was said.
(( ))	Double parentheses contain transcriber's comments and/or descriptions.
.hhh	hs preceded by a period represent discernible inhalations.
hhhh	hs without a preceding period represent discernible aspiration.
LLLL	A string of l's are used to indicate laughter
L-L-L	Spasmodic laughter is indicated by a chain punctuated by dashes.
xxxxx	A string of x's are used to indicate applause.

REFERENCES

Asch, S.E. (1951) 'Effects of group pressure on the modification and distortion of judgements', in J. Guetzhow (ed.), *Groups, Leadership, and Men*, Pittsburgh: Carnegie Press, pp. 177–90.

Atkinson, M. (1984a) *Our Masters' Voices: The Language and Body Language of Politics*, London: Routledge.

Atkinson, J.M. (1984b) 'Public speaking and audience response: some techniques for inviting applause', in Atkinson, J.M. and Heritage, J. (eds), *Structures of Social Action: Studies in Conversation Analysis*, Cambridge: Cambridge University Press, pp. 370–409.

Atkinson, J.M. and Heritage, J. (1984) *Structures of Social Action: Studies in Conversation Analysis*, Cambridge: Cambridge University Press.

Austin, J.L. (1962) *How to Do Things with Words*, Oxford: Oxford University Press.

Barley, S. and Kunda, G. (2001) 'Bringing the work back in', *Organization Science*, 12(1): 76–95.

Boden, D. (1994) 'The business of talk: organizations in action', Cambridge: CUP.

Boden, D. and Zimmerman, D.H. (1991) 'Talk and social structure: studies in ethnomethodology and conversation analysis', Cambridge: Polity Press.

Button, G. and Lee, J.R.E (eds) (1987) *Talk and Social Organization*, Clevedon and Philadelphia: Multilingual Matters.

Clayman, S.E. (1992) 'Caveat orator: audience disaffiliation in the 1988 presidential debates', *Quarterly Journal of Speech*, 78: 33–60.

Clayman, S.E. (1993) 'Booing: the anatomy of a disaffiliative response', *American Sociological Review*, 58: 110–30.

Clayman, S. and Heritage, J. (2003) *The News Interview: Journalists and Public Figures on the Air*, Cambridge: CUP.

Clayman, S. and Maynard, D. (1995) 'Ethnomethodology and conversation analysis', in P.ten Have and G.Psthas (eds) *Situated Order: Studies in the Social organization of Talk and Embodied activities*, Washington: University press America, 1–30.

Clifton, J. (2006) 'A conversation analytical approach to business communication', *Journal of Business Communication* 43(3): 202–19.

Cooren, F. (2006) 'Arguments for in-depth studies of organizational interactions: a rejoinder to McPhee, Myers and Trethewey', *Management Communication Quarterly*, 19(3): 327–40.

Cooren, F. and Fairhurst, G.T. (2004) 'Speech timing and spacing: the phenomenon of organizational closure', *Organization*, 11(6): 793–824.

Drew, P. and Heritage, J. (1992) *Talk at Work: Interaction in Institutional Settings*, Cambridge: CUP.

Fairhurst, G.T. (2004) 'Textuality and agency in interaction analysis', *Organization*, 11(3): 335–53.

Forray, J.M. and Woodilla, J. (2002) 'Temporal spans in talk: doing consistency to construct fair organization', *Organization Studies*, 22(6): 899–917.

Forray, J.M. and Woodilla, J. (2002) 'Temporal spans in talk: doing consistency to construct fair organization', *Organization Studies* 23(6): 553–81.

Garfinkel, H. (1967) *Studies in Ethnomethodology*, Cambridge: Polity Press.

Glenn, P.J. (1989) 'Initiating shared laughter in multi-party conversations', *Western Journal of Speech Communication*, 53: 127–49.

Goffman, E. (1983 'The interaction order', *American Sociological review*, 48(1): 1–17.

Goodwin, C. and Goodwin, M. (1996) 'Seeing as a situated activity: formulating planes', in Y.Engestrom and D.Middleton (eds), *Cognition and Communication at Work*, Cambridge: Cambridge University press, pp.61–95.

Greatbach, D. and Clark, T. (2002) 'Laughing with the Gurus', *Business Strategy Review*, 13(3): 10–18.

Greatbatch, D. (2006) 'Prescriptions and prescribing: coordinating talk-and text-based activities', in Heritage, J. and Maynard, D. (eds), *Practicing Medicine: Structure and Process in Primary Care Encounters*, Cambridge: Cambridge University Press, pp. 313–39.

Greatbatch, D. and Clark, T. (2003) 'Displaying group cohesiveness: humour and laughter in the public lectures of management gurus', *Human Relations*, 56(12): 1515–44.

Greatbatch, D. and Clark, T. (2005) *Management Speak: Why We Listen to What Management Gurus Tell Us*, London: Routledge.

Greatbatch, D. and Clark, T. (forthcoming 2008) 'The situated production of stories', To appear in Llewellyn, N. and Hindmarsh, J. (eds) *Organizations, Interaction and Practice: Studies in Real Time Work and Organising*, Cambridge: Cambridge University Press.

Greatbatch, D., Heath, C.C., Luff, P. and Campion, P. (1995) 'Conversation analysis: human-computer interaction and the general practice consultation'. Monk, A. and Gilbert, N. (eds.), *Perspectives on Human-Computer Interaction*, London: Academic Press, pp.199–222.

Goodwin, C. (1987) 'Forgetfulness as an interactive resource', *Social Psychology Quarterly*, 50: 115–30.

Heath, C., Jirotka, M, Luff, P and Hindmarsh, J. (1994–5) 'Unpacking collaboration: the interactional organisation of trading in a city dealing room', *CSCW*, 3(2): 147–65.

Heath, C. and Luff, P. (1993) 'Explicating face-to-face Interaction', in N.Gilbert (ed.), *Researching Social Life*, London: Sage, pp. 306–26.

Heath, C. and Luff, P. (2000) *Technology in Action*, Cambridge: Cambridge University Press.

Heath, C., Luff, P. and Knoblauch, H. (2004) 'Tools, technologies and organizational interaction: The emergence of workplace studies', in D. Grant, C. Hardy, C. Oswick and L. Putnam (eds), *Organizational Discourses*, London: Sage. 337–58.

Heritage, J. (1984) *Garfinkel and Ethnomethodology*, Cambridge: Polity Press.

Heritage, J. (1995) 'Conversation analysis: methodological aspects', in U.M. Quasthoff (ed.), *Aspects of Oral Communication*, Berlin: De Gruyter, pp. 391–418.

Heritage, J. (1997) 'Conversation analysis and institutional talk: analysing data', in D.Silverman (ed.) *Qualitative Research: Theory, Method and Practice*, London and Thousand Oaks, CA: Sage.

Heritage, J. and Greatbatch, D. (1991) 'On the institutional character of institutional talk: the case of news interviews', in Schegloff, E.A (1991) 'Reflections on Talk and social structure', in D. Boden and D.H. Zimmerman (eds), *Talk and Social structure: Studies in Ethnomethodology and Conversation Analysis*, Cambridge: Polity Press, pp. 93–137.

Heritage, J. and Greatbatch, D. (1986) 'Generating applause: a study of rhetoric and response at party political conferences', *American Journal of Sociology*, 92: 110–57.

Heritage, J. and Maynard, D. (eds) (2006) *Practicing Medicine: Structure and Process in Primary Care Encounters*, Cambridge: Cambridge University Press, pp. 313–39.

Hindmarsh, J. and Pilnick, A. (forthcoming) 'Knowing bodies at work: embodiment and ephemeral teamwork in anaesthesia, *Organizational Studies*.

Hopper, R. (ed.) (1991) *Conversation Analysis and Ethnography*, Special Issue of *Research on Language and Social Interaction*.

Huczynski, A. (1993) *Management Gurus: What Makes Them and How to Become One*, London: Routledge.

Hutchby, I. and Woofitt, R. (1998) *Conversation Analysis: Principles, Practices and Applications*, Oxford:Polity Press.

Jackson, B.G. (1996) 'Re-engineering the sense of self: the manager and the management guru', *Journal of Management Studies*, 33(5): 571–90.

Llewellyn, N. (2004) 'In search of modernization: the negotiation of social identity in organizational reform', *Organization Studies* 25(6): 947–68.

Llewellyn, N. (forthcoming) 'Identifying with the audience: a study of community police work', *International Journal of Public Administration*.

Llewellyn, N. and Hindmarsh, J. (eds) (forthcoming) *Organizations, Interaction and Practice: Studies in Real Time Work and Organising*, Cambridge: Cambridge University Press.

Luff, P., Heath, C.C. and Greatbatch, D. (1994) 'Work, interaction and technology: the naturalistic analysis of human conduct and requirements analysis', in Jirotka, M. and Goguen, J. (eds) *Requirements Engineering: Social and Technical Issues*, London: Academic press, pp. 259–88.

Meyer, J.C. (2000) 'Humor as a double-edged sword: four functions of humor in communication', *Communication Theory*, 10(3): 310–31.

Psathas, G. (1995) *Conversation Analysis: The Study of Talk-in-Interaction*, Thousand Oaks, CA: Sage.

Putnam, L. (2003). 'Dialectical tensions and rhetorical tropes in negotiations', *Organization Studies*, 25(1): 35–53.

Sacks, H. (1992) *Lectures on Conversation*, Oxford: Blackwell.

Samra-Fredericks, D. (1998) 'Conversation analysis', in Gillian Symon and Catherine Cassell (eds), *Qualitative*

Methods and Analysis in Organizational Research, London and Thousand Oaks, CA: Sage.

Samra-Fredericks, D. (2000) 'An analysis of the behavioural dynamics of corporate governance – a talk-based ethnography of a U.K. manufacturing "board-in-action"', *Corporate Governance*, 8(4): 311–26.

Samra-Fredericks, D. (2003) 'Strategizing as lived experience and strategists' everyday efforts to shape strategic decisions', *Journal of Management Studies*, 40(1): 141–74.

Samra-Fredericks, D. (2004) 'Managerial elites making rheotorical and linguistic "moves" for a moving (emotional) display', *Human relations*, 57(9): 1103–43.

Schegloff, E.A (1987) 'Between macro and micro: contexts and other connections', in J.C. Alexander, B. Giesen, R. Munch and N.J. Smelser (eds) *The Micro-Macro Link*, Berkeley, CA: University of California press, pp. 207–36.

Schegloff, E.A (1991) 'Reflections on talk and social structure', in D. Boden and D. H. Zimmerman (eds), *Talk and Social structure: Studies in Ethnomethodology and Conversation Analysis*, Cambridge: Polity Press, pp. 44–70.

Schegloff, E.A (1997) 'Whose text? whose context?', *Discourse and Society*, 8: 165–87.

Schegloff, E.A. and Sacks, H. (1974) 'Opening up closings', *Semiotica*, 7: 289–327.

Searle,J.R. (1969) *Speech Acts*, Cambridge: Cambridge University Press.

Silverman, D. (1997) 'Studying organizational interaction: ethomethodology's contribution to the "new institutionalism"', *Administrative Theory & Praxis*, 19(2): 178–95.

Suchman, L. (1987) *Plans and Situated Actions*, Cambridge: Cambridge University Press.

Suchman, L. (1992) 'Technologies of accountability: on lizards and aeroplanes', in Button, G. (ed.), *Technology in Working Order*, London: Routledge, pp.113–126.

ten have, O. (1999) *Doing Conversation Analysis: A Practical Guide*, London and Thousand Oaks, CA: Sage.

Wittgenstein, L. (1974) *Philosophical Investigations*. Oxford: Blackwell.

Woofitt, R. (2005) *Conversation Analysis and Discourse Analysis: A Comparative and Critical Introduction*, London: Sage.

Whalen, J. (1995) 'A technology of order production: computer aided dispatch in public safety communications', in P. ten Have and G. Psthas (eds) *Situated Order: Studies in the Social organization of Talk and Embodied Activities*, Washington: University Press America, pp.187–230.

Zimmerman, D.H. (1988) 'On conversation: the conversation analytic perspective', in J. Anderson (ed.), *Communication Yearbook* 11, Beverley Hills, CA: Sage.

29

Interviews in Organizational Research

Catherine Cassell

The interview is perhaps the most ubiquitous of all data collection techniques. It comes in many shapes and sizes and has had a long history within organizational research. Used in a variety of epistemological traditions with the potential to generate both quantitative and qualitative data, its popularity and enduring nature ensure that it has a place in any textbook on organizational research methods.

In understanding the role of the interview in social research, a key contextual factor is the extensive nature of its usage. Indeed a number of authors (e.g. Fontana and Frey, 2005; Kvale, 2006) link the prevalence of the interview to developments in mass culture. For example, Kvale (2006) argues that the pervasiveness of the interview can be traced to the development of the market economy, in which it is 'paramount' to investigate the meanings that products have for consumers (2006: 494). Authors have outlined how the move to an 'interview society' (Atkinson and Silverman, 1997) means that those who are participants in social research have familiar expectations about what agreeing to take part in an interview will involve. This shared understanding of the meaning of the interview by interviewees is only one reason for

the enthusiasm for the interview amongst social researchers. Atkinson and Silverman (1997: 304) highlight why the interview is so attractive to a wide range of researchers:

> For survey researchers, the interview can be a reliable instrument giving valid data on facts and attitudes. For the qualitatively minded researcher, the open-ended interview offers the opportunity for an authentic gaze into the soul of another, or even for a politically correct dialogue where researcher and researched offer mutual understanding and support.

As they suggest, one of the reasons for the widespread popularity and usage of the interview as a form of social research is that it can be used in numerous different ways, in a variety of epistemological stances. The term itself covers a multitude of research encounters, ranging from a structured schedule of questions where the aim is to standardize data collection, to the unstructured conversations that characterize some discourse-analysis approaches. This has led some authors such as Platt (2002), for example, to argue that it is difficult to make meaningful generalizations about the interview, when it can be understood as a number of different procedures.

Despite the prevalence of the interview and the role it has in mass culture, apart from the occasional article (e.g. Alvesson, 2003), surprisingly little has been written about its role in organizational research. For example, a review of the articles published in *Organization Research Methods*, the American Academy of Management journal that focuses on methodological developments in the organizational and management field, identified that, since the inception of the journal in 1998, only one of the articles published focused on developments in interviewing (Bourne and Jenkins, 2005). Similar literature searches of other journals in the field (e.g. *Organization Studies*, *Organization*, and *Journal of Management Studies*) identify that interviews are only mentioned in abstracts and key words when they have been one of the methods of data collection in reported empirical research. Although occasionally authors may have critiqued various aspects of the interview as part of a reflective or reflexive process (e.g. Alvesson, 2003; Bryman and Cassell, 2006; Learmonth, 2006), beyond that there has been little consideration of the role of the interview in organizational research. Similarly, although there are numerous investigations within the field that rely on the use of interview data, it would seem that few organizational researchers have been explicitly trained in interviewing skills (Cassell et al., 2009).

This chapter aims to highlight the contribution that the interview as a methodological tool has made to organizational research, and identify some of the challenges faced by those researchers aiming to use interviews in the future. It begins with an overview of the history of the interview in organizational research and traces its development from the seminal Hawthorne studies in the 1920s. As part of that history, the extent to which the interview in organizational research is different from other types of interviews in social research is considered. The diversity in organizational research interviews along a number of dimensions is then discussed. These include practical considerations such as medium and location; the level of structure in

an interview; and underlying epistemological assumptions. The final section of the chapter highlights some of the key issues associated with the interview in contemporary organizational research. These include issues of reflexivity and power, together with the impact of the increased globalization of organizational research for the development of the interview.

History of the interview in organizational research

The interview has had a long history within the field of organizational research. Fontana and Frey (2005: 699) suggest that the development of interviewing in the twentieth century emerged from two major trends within the social sciences. The first was the need to gain 'quality of responses' in the areas of counselling and clinical diagnosis, and the second from the increased concern with using interviews as the basis for psychological testing and management, a trend that emerged during the First World War. Perhaps the first classic study within the organizational field to rely on interviews was the Hawthorne Studies. Hollway (1991) suggests that interviewing as a qualitative data collection technique became prevalent around the same time as the human relations movement. At this time, within organization behaviour, there was a move away from Taylorist approaches where the worker was seen as cog in a machine, to the focus on the worker as an emotional human being. Interviews were seen as a valid way of collecting reliable and objective measurement data about the subjective aspects of worker experience, previously unacknowledged in the research of the time. The Second World War again saw an increase in the use of interviews both underpinning the development of psychological measurement (Hollway, 1991), and the documentation of the mental and emotional lives of soldiers (Fontana and Frey, 2005). During this period there was also a considerable increase in the use of survey methods in fields related to organizational research, a trend that was to lead to the domination of such approaches by the 1950s which still applies in the organizational field today.

Interviews were also components of some of the classic ethnographic studies that underpinned the development of the field. For example Jahoda, Lazarfeld and Ziesel's in-depth study of the impact of unemployment on the Austrian community, *Marienthal*, first published in 1933, drew on a range of innovative techniques to document the negative effects of unemployment. These included family meal records and children's school essays on the theme of 'What I want most of all'. Included also in the study were the detailed life histories of 32 men and 30 women. At that time, the authors noted the importance of using life history as an interview technique:

> When these people came to speak of the periods of unemployment, their narrative was already under way. They found it therefore, easier to give expression to the experience of being unemployed, since by then they had reported on that part of their life that offered a basis for comparison. Had we inquired directly about their present condition the result would probably have been embarrassed silence or empty phrases. (Jahoda, Lazarsfeld and Ziesel, 1972: 4)

Similarly, in Melville Dalton's classic work on *Men who manage*, where his explicit intention was to 'give academicians and industrialists a sharper picture of each other through the device of *unguarded* managerial plain talk and professorial analysis' (Dalton, 1953: vii), formal interviews were used as a form of data collection along side participant observation and work diaries. Likewise, *Working for Ford* (Benyon, 1973) drew upon interview data as well as other techniques such as participant observation.

By the 1970s interviews had become commonplace in social science research, and were evident in published work in the organizational field. Increasingly the use of interviews was becoming more formalized, and techniques for the analysis of data becoming more structured. For example, the publication of Glaser and Strauss's *The discovery of grounded theory* in 1967 paved

the way for qualitative researchers to seek credibility for their analytic processes through the use of structured procedures for dealing with the subjective data that interviews produced. Denzin and Lincoln (2005: 17) describe this period as 'the golden age of rigorous qualitative analysis' that charac-terized the modernist phase in qualitative research.

Within organizational research, by the 1980s interviews were in common usage. As Kvale (2006: 481) highlights, by this time:

> ...qualitative interviews ... were often regarded as a progressive dialogical form of research that provided a personal alternative to the objectifying positivist quantification of questionnaires and harsh manipulation of behaviourist experiments.

By way of contrast, interviewers were seen to have 'authentic personal relationships' with their subjects, which led to the production of insightful data. However, the increasing focus on new paradigms, and not least the linguistic turn that emerged through the 1980s, led to a range of new critiques of the interview and how it was used in organizational research. A particular challenge emerged from the critique that the interview was an 'active' process (e.g. Holstein and Gubrium, 1995), and could not be seen as a context-free occurrence or an isolated one-off event. The impact of such challenges will be returned to later.

The interview is used extensively in organizational research today, though in a plethora of different guises. Although there are some texts that provide advice specifically for organizational researchers conducting interviews (e.g. King, 2004; Bryman and Bell, 2007), the interview is primarily a method that has extensive usage throughout the social sciences, rather than being a distinctive tool for organizational analysis. Certainly, the key issues that concern the interviewer, as found in many of the texts available (e.g. Gubrium and Holstein, 2001) would apply equally to organizational researchers. In the sections that follow, however, the interview is considered specifically within the context of organizational research, starting with an examination of the characteristics of the organizational research interview.

Characteristics of the organizational interview

In line with the extensive usage of interviews, a number of authors have identified the different types of interviews that can occur in organizational research (e.g. Bryman and Bell, 2007; King, 2004; Lee, 1999). Interviews in organizational research can be differentiated in a number of ways. Of particular significance is the extent to which they are designed to gather data for quantification, or to access qualitative data. In this section, I focus upon some of the key criteria upon which they are differentiated, namely practical considerations such as who is interviewed and where; the medium of the interview; interview structure; and the underlying epistemological assumptions of the research study. Although the purpose of an interview is also important, it is assumed here that the focus is the research interview.

There are a number of practical considerations to be taken into account when conducting an organizational interview. These are examined in detail in some of the texts that provide advice for organizational researchers who wish to use the technique (e.g. Bryman and Bell, 2007; King, 2004), and are briefly considered next.

Structure

The key characteristic on which interviews have been differentiated within the organizational literature is that of structure, and the extent to which the interviewer determines the progression of the interview according to their pre-existing ideas and research questions. The structure of an interview is inextricably linked to its purpose. Typically, the more structured formats are associated with the quantification of the data generated. Indeed the aim of producing a standardized interview schedule is that accurate data can be generated from a range of individuals who are all submitted to the same questions. King (2004)

highlights how qualitative interviews differ from this approach in that their key aim is to access the interviewees' understanding and views of a particular research topic rather than seeking to standardize responses. In qualitative approaches, typically interviews are semistructured, or unstructured, encouraging the interviewee to talk at length around a subject, and shape the direction of the interview as necessary. Therefore, as King (2004) suggests, one of the key things that differentiates the various approaches to interviews is the relationship between the interviewer and the interviewee. In highly structured interviews, the aim is to minimize any bias that may occur from the role of the interviewer, hence the standardization of the questions and format. Within more qualitative, unstructured approaches, however, it is recognized that the interviewee takes an active role in constructing the nature of the interview, and can direct it as appropriate.

The distinction between different levels of structure in questioning is not as straightforward as it initially seems. For example, there are a number of different ways of structuring qualitative interviews designed to generate open-ended data in a particular format. For example, the repertory grid technique devised by Kelly (1955) has been used by some organizational researchers to investigate questions such as how organizational performance is defined (Parker et al., 1994; Cassell and Walsh, 2004). Located within a particular theoretical framework (Kelly's personal construct theory) and a specific epistemological position, it enables the interviewer to structure an individual's personal constructs through using a grid. Other examples of alternative formats are the life history interview (Musson, 2004) where the interview focuses on asking an individual to tell their life story, and then draws on various aspects of that story to make an interpretation about social phenomena; and critical incident technique (e.g. Flanagan, 1954; Chell, 2004) where the structure of the interview questions is built around particular incidents that the individual has experienced in relation to the research area of interest.

Both these techniques are widely used in organizational research.

A further point about structure with regard to qualitative interviews is that more structured interviews are easier to analyse using qualitative analytic techniques. So, for example, if the researcher has chosen to analyse the data thematically, using a template for example (King, 2004), then the interview questions can form the basis of a template constructed a priori, or before the data analysis process begins. Therefore, the coding process with a highly structured interview may be relatively standardized.

Medium, location, and interviewee selection

A further key consideration is the medium of the interview. Typically, interviews are conducted face-to-face or by telephone, though more recently there has been the development of online or electronic interviewing strategies (e.g. Morgan and Symon, 2004). Although the most common form of interview takes place face-to-face, within the organizational field, telephone interviews have been used in numerous studies in a wide variety of areas and there is a particular tradition within the marketing field. Research considering the quality of the output from different types of interviews strategies (e.g. Quinn et al., 1980) has found few differences between the two modes, though Sturges and Hanrahan (2004: 107) suggest: most of the 'mode comparison literature' has focused on comparing structured face-to-face interviews with telephone interviews rather than comparing the more qualitative types. Although the quality of output may be similar, clearly the processes are different. Additionally, something rarely reported in the literature that will have an impact on the quality of the output is the extent to which the interviewer is actually an organizational researcher. In some large studies, telephone interviews may be contracted out to market research companies, where the interviewer may not have a grasp of the theoretical foundation or the research questions underpinning the study. This is not to say that they will not be conducted

appropriately, but rather that the researcher may not actually be conducting them. The standardization of questions and structure is an important criterion for quality in these situations. Within the mode comparison literature, emphasis is put upon the subtle nuances that occur in face-to-face interviews that may be lost in telephone interviews. For example, Stephens (2007: 211) reflects how when interviewing elites (in this case macroeconomists) he realized that a qualitative face-to-face interview 'affords the interviewer the opportunity to continually re-mould the interaction to their [the interviewer's] needs and interests through visual cues and small utterances'. Therefore, it is in these more subtle aspects of the interaction that the differences between the two modes can be identified.

Selection of interviewees is also an important issue for consideration. Clearly, this is influenced by the research questions of the study, and the sampling strategy. It is also important to consider the purpose of the interview in regard to the type of information sought. Within organizational research, we may choose to interview people for a variety of different reasons. Some interviewees may be selected on the basis that they are informants in that they are providing details of aspects of their organization, such as its culture, structure, or whatever. Other interviewees, however, may be chosen as respondents, in that they are there to answer questions about themselves. In practice, there may also be some overlap between the different purposes and some interviewees will be asked to cover both.

A further practical issue to challenge organizational researchers is the location of the interview. Clearly, locations are not neutral. Indeed Herzog (2005: 25) argues that 'the choice of interview location (who chooses and what place is chosen) is not just a technical matter of convenience and comfort'. Rather it should be analysed as part of the overall social context of the study, and be considered as having a role in both the interaction and knowledge produced. Some organizational researchers have made explicit reference to the interview location and the impact this has had on the interview itself. Cassell (2005: 174) tells the story of interviewing workers on a night shift in a bed manufacturing company, where the only place to interview was the showroom, 'a darkened room that contained 20 beautifully made up double beds'. She uses the example to highlight how the salience of the interviewer's and interviewee's roles meant that any consideration of the potentially inappropriate nature of the location was suspended. Both knew what to expect of an interview setting. Being familiar with the wider location of the interview may also be useful. For example Burns (2004: 166) talks about how being given a tour of a chemical manufacturing site enabled him to gain insight into the organizational processes discussed in the interview, particularly terms that were in common usage but were specific to that company.

Other practical issues regarding the conduct of interviews have been mentioned in the accounts of organizational researchers. For example, Hayes and Mattimoe (2004) raise some of the issues associated with the tape and digital recording of interviews in their discussion of the use of interviews in accounting research. These include the impact of the presence of the machine on the interviewee, and the mundane processes associated with transcription. They conclude that this is a complex issue often ignored in conventional research methodology textbooks.

Underlying epistemological assumptions

A further key factor that influences the nature of the research interview is the underlying epistemological approach of the research. For example, the standardized or more structured interview is likely to be informed by positivist epistemological commitments, where the emphasis is upon generating objective data, which represents some truth about the interviewee's world. As such, the intention will be to minimize any contamination that may occur as a result of the social or active nature of the interview. Qualitative research is, however, informed by a range of different epistemological assumptions (e.g. Prasad, 2005; Symon and Cassell, 2004) and therefore, the qualitative organizational interview will also potentially be informed by any one of those different traditions. For example, according to Prasad (2005: 173), those writing within a feminist epistemology show a 'marked preference' for methods such as in-depth interviews because of their commitment to understanding the experience of women in organizations as a way of balancing out what is seen as a male dominated discipline. Limerick and O'Leary (2006: 108) for instance, in their discussion of how feminist qualitative research can inform the management field, reflect upon their use of interviews in a study of women's careers as a way of giving women a 'voice' in the 'co-creation of knowledge claims'. Similarly Mirchandani (2003) describes how open-ended qualitative interviews in the context of an antiracist feminist theoretical approach enabled her to identify the use of emotion work by the interviewees, which was not the intention of the original research study.

Prasad (2005: 22) highlights how the organizational interview is also used in other epistemological and theoretical traditions; for example, from the perspective of symbolic interactionism the interviewer seeks to 'substantially explore issues of self-identity by asking subjects how they see themselves and others in different social situations'. Authors such as Ezzamel and Willmott (1998) have also used in-depth interviews within the labour process tradition. King (2004) differentiates between three sets of different epistemological assumptions underlying qualitative interviews: the realist, phenomenological and social constructionist. Within a realist approach, the interviewer is keen to access the interviewee's understanding of a particular organizational phenomenon that is seen to exist outside of the person and then compare their account with other interviewees. Within a phenomenological approach, the concern is with the researcher reflecting upon how their own presuppositions may impact upon the data being collected, as well as exploring the lifeworld of the interviewee. Within social constructionist approaches, the interview is seen as the coproduction of a text, rather than as an account of any real world phenomenon. These approaches, which are underpinned by poststructuralist or postmodern approaches, create a range of challenges for how we traditionally conceive of the interview as a data gathering encounter. For example, Alvesson and Sköldberg (2000) highlight that, from this position, how interviewees represent reality in the interview situation may have more to do with how they understand and construct the discursive context of the interview itself, rather than any reflection of an enduring, external reality. Therefore, the interview from this perspective is a very different encounter from how it is perceived from those working in other epistemological traditions such as positivism, for example.

In practice, the distinctions between different approaches to qualitative interviewing that arise from different epistemological underpinnings are not as precisely differentiated as this account might suggest. Rather the key point here is that the format and process of an interview will be influenced by the epistemological approach of the research overall, making this an important factor that influences the variety found in organizational interviews.

Finally, the tendency so far has been to treat the interview as a solitary event. However, in the majority of organizational research studies, this is not necessarily the case. When a researcher plans an interview schedule, they will do it as a result of some preunderstanding of the phenomenon they want to study. Insights from one interview may be taken into another interview and the questioning developed accordingly. Furthermore, a qualitative study will go beyond simply what interviewees have stated in interviews, and will be interpreted in the wider social context in which the research is taking place. Taking one of the most popular forms of research strategy within the organizational field the case study, it is apparent that case findings often result from an interweaving of interview findings with other sources of data from other data collection approaches. So, the interview

is not necessarily an isolated incident, but rather a component of a complex research context.

Key contemporary debates about the interview in organizational research

The foregoing discussion highlights that the interview is a multifaceted phenomenon extensively used in organizational research. In this section, I turn to some of the key contemporary debates that surround the use of the interview, and how we understand it as a process of data collection and as a social encounter. These include the active nature of the interview; reflexivity; power; 'real-life' accounts; technological developments; the increased impact of the globalization of methodologies; ethics; defining quality; and the consequences of the diversity in organizational interviews. It is fair to say that these debates tend to occur around the nature of qualitative interviews in organizational research rather than the more structured quantitative kind. However, there are particular issues that impact upon both, for example, the increased technological developments.

The active nature of the interview

As referred to earlier, there has been an increased focus on the interview as an interactive process where meaning is coconstructed (e.g. Holstein and Gubrium, 1995; Denzin, 2001). This approach has more resonance with some epistemological positions rather than others, most notably social constructionist approaches. Within this framework, the interview is seen as an arena where both interviewer and interviewee are actively constructing and interpreting the process, potentially in different ways. For example, Denzin suggests that 'Interviews are performance texts' (2001: 27). Organizational researchers working in a constructionist paradigm have embraced the active nature of the interview in a number of ways. One way has been to focus on the nature of the 'identity work' that both interviewers and interviewees perform as part of the interview process (e.g. Alvesson, 2003; Cassell, 2005; Collinson, 2006). Rapley (2001) suggests that there are a number of different issues that the analyst can assess in relation to identity work within the interview. For example, he argues that the accounting work of the interviewer and interviewees should be a 'central part of the analysis' (2001: 304). Additionally, he argues that there should be an awareness and analysis of the function of the interviewer's talk in 'producing both the form and the content of the interview' (2001: 304). In a similar vein, Ortiz (2005) highlights the high degree of emotion work that is sometimes done by the interviewer, and the implications of this for the interview itself.

Drawing attention to identity work highlights how contextual aspects of the interview are important. For example, those researchers who focus on organizational story telling (e.g. Boje, 1991; Gabriel and Griffiths, 2004) are interested in aspects of context that lead to the production of stories in interviews. Ylijoki (2003: 562), in her research on academic nostaligia, notes that 'an interview represents a special story-telling context' and outlines what the characteristics of that context may be. In particular, compared to stories gathered as part of day to day organizational occurrences, the interview enables a story teller to reflect on their account as they proceed, which, she agues, may enhance the quality of the stories recollected.

This interest in the performative nature of the interview has emerged within the context of the increased concern with reflexivity in organizational research. This is now considered.

Reflexivity

Reflexivity and reflexive processes have attracted considerable attention within the organizational literature during the last 10 years (e.g. Alvesson and Sköldberg, 2000; Johnson and Duberley, 2003; Cunliffe, 2003; Symon and Cassell, 2004; Weick, 2002, Bryman and Cassell, 2006). Although there are different definitions of reflexivity within the literature, Alvesson and Sköldberg

(2000: 5) point out that attention to reflexivity means that:

> ...serious attention is paid to the way different kinds of linguistic, social, political and theoretical elements are woven together in the process of knowledge development, during which empirical material is constructed, interpreted and written.

Interviewers working in this tradition have, therefore, turned their attention to various aspects of the interview process and produced informative accounts framed by reflexive critique. There are numerous examples within the organizational literature of this kind of approach. For example, writers such as Haynes (2006) have analysed the interviews they have conducted from a reflexive position, examining how gender has an impact in the organizational interviewing process. Bryman and Cassell (2006) produced a reflexive account of researcher interviews – where researchers interview other researchers – focusing upon how the sensemaking processes of both interviewer and interviewee are influenced by their assumed understanding of the purpose and aims of research interviews. Similarly, where interviewers have interviewed other academics they have reflected upon the dynamics of the process. For example Ylijoki (2003: 562) outlined how both interviewer and interviewee are 'inhabitants' of the same territory, which can lead to the assumption of shared tacit knowledge". Others such as Nadin and Cassell (2006) have investigated how research diaries can fruitfully aid reflexive practices. Johnson and Duberley (2003) argue that there are different types of reflexivity used within different epistemological traditions in organizational research. Whereas we would expect those working in a social constructionist tradition to consider the factors that impact upon how interview knowledge is produced, by their very definition those working in a positivist paradigm would be unconcerned with these issues, subscribing to a form of methodological reflexivity where the concern would be to minimize the impact of the interviewer on the interview data collected.

Therefore, the extent to which reflexive approaches to the interview are taken, and how such reflexivity is manifested, is influenced by the epistemological assumptions underlying the research.

Power

A concern that has also received increasing attention is the power dynamics in the interview situation. This is a key theme that is dissected in the reflexive accounts referred to in the preceding section, and the status of the interviewee has received increasing consideration in the organizational arena. The nature of the power relationship within the interview setting is one that continues to concern many social science researchers (e.g. Kvale, 2006; Denzin and Lincoln, 2005). In some of these accounts, particularly those from an emancipatory perspective, the qualitative interviewer is presented as being in a powerful position in the role of expert who may indeed exploit the interviewee by taking their knowledge and giving little back, similar to the processes of acquiring colonial knowledge at the expense of indigenous communities (e.g. Denzin and Lincoln, 2005: 1). Kvale (2006: 483) for example, argues that the interview is inevitably a hierarchical encounter and that the 'power dynamics in research interviews, and potential oppressive use of interview-produced knowledge, tend to be left out in literature on qualitative research'. It is interesting to speculate the extent to which this power relationship, which is assumed as unidirectional in much of the social sciences literature about interviewing, is actually manifested in organizational research. Although there is a literature on interviewing organizational elites, and the dilemmas that may be involved (e.g., Zuckerman, 1972; Kezar, 2003; Stephens, 2007, Conti and O'Neill, 2007), other organizational researchers have drawn attention to the issue that, particularly within management research, interviewees may be in a more powerful position than that of the researcher by virtue of their organizational position. Individual characteristics of the interviewer and the interviewee such as gender, age, etc. have also been

considered here (e.g. Cassell, 2005; Lawthom, 1998). Lawthom (1998) for example, discusses some of the power relationships at work in her interviews with managers in manufacturing industry and highlights that, as a relatively young woman interviewing older men, a number of metaphors characterized the interviews as she experienced them. These ranged from feeling that the interview was some kind of sexual liaison, to a form of parent child interaction, in each case with her being in the less powerful position. Furthermore, Tanggaard (2007: 162) outlines how, in her interviews with apprentices about their vocational learning, the interview could meaningfully be seen as a 'battlefield', where competing discourses about the value of vocational learning came into play. She argues that although the direct struggle for power may not always be evident within an interview setting, the ongoing negotiation of meaning is evidence of a power struggle, which may in itself encourage the interviewer to reflect more thoroughly on their own assumptions with regard to question asking.

'Real-life' accounts

Discussions of reflexivity and power dynamics all bring to the fore the notion that the interview in practice may not be as sanitized an experience as may be presented in some of the more standard textbooks on organizational research methods. Again, the last ten years have seen an increased number of accounts that consider some of the difficulties that may arise in conducting interviews. These build on the tradition of producing 'warts and all' accounts of organizational research, and thinking more critically about the processes that go into its production (e.g. Bryman, 1988). These accounts are not just appearing in textbooks, but also in collections of researchers' stories, and journal articles informed by reflexive approaches. For example, there are now more warnings to organizational researchers about the more complicated things they may come across in interviews and how these may be handled. King (2004: 18–19), in his chapter providing advice for organizational researchers about how to interview, covers a range of 'difficult interviews' including the uncommunicative interviewee; the over-communicative interviewee; the high-status interviewee; interviews on emotionally-charged subjects; and the would-be interviewer. There are also collections of 'real-life' accounts of conducting interviews that can be found in texts such as Humphrey and Lee's 'Real-life guide to accounting research'. These focus upon researchers' experiences of conducting qualitative research more generally.

It would seem that the reflexive turn has made it more legitimate for interviewers to admit to some of the problems they may face. For example Nairn, Munro and Smith (2005) outline the anatomy of a 'failed interview' as a form of 'uncomfortable reflexivity' (Pillow, 2003: 188). They suggest that in reflecting upon why the research team originally classified the interview as a failure in data collection terms, they learned a considerable amount about the 'tenuous' nature of knowledge production which informed the later design of their study. Increasingly there are also accounts that critique both the desirability and likelihood of the researcher sticking to traditional interview protocols. For example McCabe (2007: 248), in discussing his interviews in an automobile manufacturing plant, explicitly states that the research was 'emergent' and progressed in line with his intuition during the 'extensive period of interviewing'. Therefore, the idea of a predictable interview based on set procedures is seen as inappropriate in this kind of research. As Learmonth (2006: 94) suggests: 'With research interviews (as with other parts of our lives) there is always an undecidability that disables mastery'. By implication, the interviewer can never be fully prepared for what might arise. These accounts, therefore, seek to highlight that the interview in 'real life' may be somewhat different from how it is traditionally construed. Again, these types of accounts focus more on qualitative interviews rather than the more structured quantitative approaches, and serve to remind organizational researchers that the research

interview can be unpredictable, and some-times produce the unexpected.

Technological developments

The increase in access to email facilities and developments in computer software have led to the increased use of electronic interviews as a tool for organizational research. Fontana and Frey (2005) suggest that these forms of interviews are currently primarily used for quantitative research through the use of highly structured interview schedules. However, Morgan and Symon (2004: 23) outline how electronic interviews of a qualitative nature 'can be held online, in real time, using the Internet or company intranets, or can be off-line, in asynchronous mode; using email communications'. They suggest that little has been written about how electronic interviews have so far been used in the organizational field, but that they offer con-siderable potential. Their research suggests that this form of interview can be used where there are already existing technological communications within an organization, for example, through an email system or intranet. Other researchers who have used electronic interviews suggest that one of the advantages is that they allow busy people to take part in an interview when it suits them, which may lead to a wider sample of interviewees to access (e.g. James and Busher, 2006). It also means that it is somewhat easier to conduct internationally based interview research where the time constraints and costs associated with telephone interviews are no longer an issue. As with telephone interviews, the key question is the quality of the data that online interviews produce. An initial response may be that it is potentially difficult to replace the same level of interaction that occurs face-to-face. However, Morgan and Symon (2004) and James and Busher (2006) both suggest that the asynchronous nature of online interviewing means that both interviewee and interviewer have time to reflect upon their responses, and indeed their questioning. This in itself may generate rich reflection that cannot occur in real-time interviewing.

The increased globalization of interview research made possible through these technological developments also raises other issues for organizational researchers, not least the use of foreign languages for interviewing and issues associated with the translation of interviews. Welch and Piekkari (2006: 418), in the context of international business research, comment that despite the fact that much research today involves international data collection, methodological texts on qualitative interviewing are 'typically silent on the topic of foreign language use in interviewing'. Rather, the assumption is that the organizational environment is monolingual internationally. They argue that the foreign language in use needs to be problematized within the interview literature and that decisions made about the language in which to interview a respondent have an impact on issues such as the amount of rapport generated within the interview, and the quality of data generated. Horton, Macve, and Struyven (2004: 347), in their account of using 55 interviews in European accounting research, point to their experience that interviewees who have English as a second language had concerns about discussing complex, technical issues in English. They found that the interviewees felt much better when two interviewers did the interview where one was competent in French and the other German. They were more reassured that they would have help if they did encounter language difficulties. Therefore, as organizational research becomes increasingly global, language concerns become even more significant.

Ethical issues

The impact of the increasing significance of ethical regulation on the practice of organizational research has been noted by a number of authors in the field (e.g. Buchanan and Bryman, 2007; Bell and Bryman, 2007), and the majority of textbooks about interviewing focus on some of the ethical issues involved with the process. One of the key issues discussed in relation to interviewing more generally are those related to power differentials, which are highlighted in the preceding

section (e.g. Kvale, 2006), and the potential for abuse of the interviewee. When discussing this earlier, I argued that the power relationships may be somewhat different in relation to organizational research interviews, making it somewhat different from other social science disciplines. Bell and Bryman (2007) argue that, in the field of management, there may be particular contextual factors that make it different from other areas. One example of this is in relation to confidentiality. Organizational interviewers have access to confidential insights, the inappropriate disclosure of which may lead to negative personal consequences for the interviewee. Additionally, within the organizational field, interviewees may be disclosing information that has competitive currency and therefore may have a concern that the inappropriate disclosure of interview information may lead to competitive disadvantage. Therefore, the protection of the organization is also important.

Apart from concerns about the protection of the interviewee and their organization, there are also concerns regarding the interviewer. For example, Chell (2004), when discussing her work using critical incident technique with entrepreneurs, points out that organizational researchers sometimes interview individuals in their own homes, where issues of personal safety may rise to the fore. There are also new ethical concerns from the technological developments outlined before. James and Busher (2006) highlight some of the dilemmas that arise from the use of online interviewing. Interviewees in their research expressed concerns that the content of emails may inadvertently be passed onto other people by mistake. Indeed electronic networks are relatively open, and it may be harder to ensure anonymity when some email systems routinely list addresses in any form of correspondence. They also raise the issue of the authenticity of the data collected, given that interviewees have an amount of time to reflect upon their contribution and alter it as necessary. On the one hand, as suggested earlier, a more reflective response may be seen as preferable, but in other cases, the interviewer may believe that an initial response to a question is more interesting or useful.

Ethical issues have also been discussed in relation to the presentation of interview data. For example, Gabriel (2004: 124), when discussing the interpretation of organizational stories, cautions against assuming that stories, as presented are fact. He suggests that:

> Stories are especially pernicious because of their memorable qualities. As every journalist knows, through selective presentation, editing, highlighting and framing, a narrative may be put to work within virtually any overall story.

The impact of how the results of interview studies are presented is consequently also a source of ethical concern. This raises the more general issue of how interview data is interpreted and used. In this situation, the interviewer does have the power to decide how to interpret the text and how to use that interpretation. There are also other factors that influence interpretation. The epistemological framework for the research will impact upon how the interviewer makes sense of the data and the extent to which it is taken as a truthful and authentic account of an individual's reality, or as an account jointly constructed through the interview process. Similarly, the interpretation process leads to the interviewer making claims about their findings on the basis of that interpretation. The extent to which interviewers can make claims about complex and ambiguous issues such as leadership, culture, and identity after individual interviews that may not last that long, is another potential ethical concern. Within the field of sociology for example, interviewing has been critiqued as located within a romanticist view of sociology where as Strong and Dingwall (1989: 50) suggest, there has been a 'lust for experience over reflection, the elevation of the personal above the communal'. Silverman (1997) argues that, in selecting what data to present, the interviewer may focus upon what is immediately newsworthy, a temptation the researcher should seek to avoid. Interviews from this perspective could be construed as quick and dirty methods of gaining immediate insights. Such insights may be of lower quality and ethically dubious when compared to the insights that come from prolonged observation, for example. These temptations may also be exacerbated by the potential difficulties in obtaining ethical clearance for in-depth observation studies in today's ethical climate (see Bryman and Bell, 2007). The organizational interviewer, therefore, has a number of ethical questions to contend with.

Defining quality in interview research

In a number of the challenges outlined in the foregoing section, an underlining concern has been with conducting 'good interviews' that produce 'high quality' research data. Textbooks within the area provide guidance on how to conduct a 'good' interview within organizational research. Typically, the quality of the interview is linked to the quality of the data collected. There are also quality issues surrounding the interview process and novice interviewers are advised to seek rapport with their interviewees, ensuring that they feel sufficiently relaxed in an interview setting to disclose the key information required. As Alvesson (2003: 17) suggests, the effective use of the interview as defined in most texts on the subject is related to 'how to get the interview subject to talk a lot – openly, trustfully, honestly, clearly and freely – about what the researcher is interested in'. Defining the quality of interview research can, however, be problematic. Given the range of different traditions within which interview research is conducted, a range of criteria may be needed to fairly assess the contribution of a particular study. For example, Johnson et al. (2006) talk about the need for a 'contingent criteriology' when assessing the quality of qualitative research more generally. Learmonth (2006:84) also makes the point that discussions of quality somehow seem to downplay the interdependence between interviewer and interviewee. For example:

> Many accounts of how to do "good" interview research seem to me to be underpinned by a celebration of independence and individualism that

encourages a (managerialist) reliance on self, whilst downplaying recognition of our interdependence on one another. (Learmonth, 2006: 84)

Defining quality is, therefore, problematic. Similar to the debate that has gone on within the qualitative research literature more generally about the uses and abuses of quality criteria (e.g. Seale, 1999), definitions of interview quality are linked into the epistemological perspective taken by the researcher. Whereas the issue of interdependence is acknowledged and deconstructed in critical management approaches (e.g. Learmonth, 2006), so the notion of the interviewer influencing the data collection process would be an anathema to those working in a positivist position. Inevitably linked to definitions of quality and a further concern for the organizational researcher interested in using interviews, is the extent to which research based on interviews is seen to have status or credibility within the organizational field. The key question is – is an interview study on its own enough to warrant publication? Although Buchanan and Bryman (2007) suggest that the field is no longer constrained by positivist approaches, with their resultant emphasis on quantitative techniques, organizational researchers who wish to publish interview studies in the closely aligned management field will have difficulty finding outlets in the so-called 'top' American journals. Where interview research is published in these journals, it tends to be as part of a mixed methods study. Studies based on interviews alone are more likely to be found within the European based organization and management journals. This may serve to discourage novice researchers from being confident about conducting research based on interview studies alone.

The consequences of diversity

The diverse nature of interview types, practices and underlying epistemologies has led to some authors claiming that the term itself now has little meaning in social sciences research (e.g., Platt, 2002). Indeed, we could question the extent to which we can make any generalized comments at all about the organizational interview. This dilemma has led to some organizational researchers attempting to create innovative frameworks for making sense of the organizational research interview. Alvesson (2003: 13) made an important step in this direction by examining the metaphors that underlie the use of the interview in organizational research. In doing so, his aim was to 'critique dominating neopositivist and romantic views of the interview' and produce a series of metaphors that enabled the interview to be reconceptualized theoretically. Eight metaphors are provided and the implications of each are denied or acknowledged in the different epistemological positions he outlines: neopositivism, romanticism, and localism. The metaphors involve seeing interviewing as a local accomplishment where the participants have to master the complex interaction taking place; as the establishment or perpetuation of a story line; as identity work; as the application of a cultural script; as moral storytelling; political action; construction work; or the play of the powers of discourse. Alvesson (2003: 31) suggests that taking a reflexive approach to the organizational interview and incorporating the metaphors into how we think about interviewing, may 'encourage theorizing about one's own research practice and reconsideration of what one may use interview material for'. Certainly, it enables us to focus upon and manage more clearly the diversity that occurs in organizational interviews. Thinking about metaphors also offers us an innovative way in which to make sense of the interview from a plurality of perspectives. Indeed examining the researcher's assumptions about what the interview is, may present rich insights beyond the practicalities associated with issues such as the level of structure. Similarly, a focus on the sensemaking of interviewees in this context would be an interesting direction along which to progress.

CONCLUSIONS

This chapter has highlighted the rich diversity in the organizational interview, in terms of format and process. This diversity has extended over time, particularly with the development of more critical and constructivist paradigms of organizational research. It is clear that the interview is here to stay within organizational research, and there are no signs that its use is declining. Indeed recent technological developments have enabled the method to change with the times. The interview seems to offer everything to organizational researchers. The general currency that the term 'interview' has within nonacademic circles means that relatively little explanation of the process is required for the potential interviewee, and there is the opportunity to collect both structured and unstructured data and conduct research within a number of paradigmatic perspectives.

The future for the interview is not without its challenges however, not least around developments within the electronic interview. Additionally, radical developments in technology enable face-to-face interactions between individuals who may be thousands of miles apart. Such new styles of interviewing inevitably mean a refocus on how we understand the dynamics of interviewing as a social encounter. It may be that we need to think about interviewing differently in the future, as the interview as a methodological tool metamorphoses to suit the changing context in which organizational research is conducted.

REFERENCES

Alvesson, M. (2003) 'Beyond neopositivists, romantics, and localists: a reflexive approach to interviews in organizational research', *Academy of Management Review*, 28(1): 13–33.

Alvesson, M. and Sköldberg, K. (2000) *Reflexive Methodology: New Vistas for Qualitative Research*, London: Sage Publications.

Atkinson, P. and Silverman, D. (1997) 'Kundera's 'Immortality': the interview society and the invention of self. (Milan Kundera)', *Qualitative Inquiry*, 3(3): 304–26.

Bell, E. and Bryman, A. (2007) 'The ethics of management research: an exploratory content analysis', *British Journal of Management*, 18(1): 63–77.

Benyon, H. (1973) *Working for Ford*, Harmondsworth: Penguin Books.

Boje, D.M. (1991) 'The story-telling organization: a study of story performance in an office-supply firm', *Administrative Science Quarterly*, 36: 106–26.

Bourne, H.and Jenkins, M. (2005) 'Eliciting managers' personal values: an adaptation of the laddering interview method', *Organizational Research Methods*, 8(4): 410–28.

Bryman, A. (1988) *Doing Research in Organizations*, London:Routledge.

Bryman, A. and Bell, E. (2007) *Business Research Methods* (revised edition), Oxford: Oxford University Press.

Bryman, A. and Cassell, C.M. (2006) 'The researcher interview: a reflexive perspective', *Qualitative Research in Organizations and Management: An International Journal*, 1(1): 41–55.

Buchanan, D. and Bryman, A. (2007) 'Contextualizing methods choice in organizational research', *Organizational Research Methods*, 10(3): 483–501.

Burns, J. (2004) 'Confessions of a research assistant', in C. Humphrey and B. Lee (eds), *The Real Life Guide to Accounting Research. A Behind-the-Scenes View of Using Qualitative Research Methods*, Amsterdam: Elsevier, pp. 163–74.

Cassell, C.M. (2005) 'Creating the role of the interviewer: identity work in the management research process', *Qualitative Research*, 5(2): 167–79.

Cassell, C.M. and Walsh, S. (2004) 'Repertory grids', in C.M. Cassell and G. Symon (eds), *Essential Guide to Qualitative Methods in Organizational Research*, London: Sage, pp. 61–72.

Cassell, C.M., Bishop, V., Symon, G., Johnson, P. and Buehring, A, (2007) 'Learning to be a qualitative management researcher', *Management Learning*, In press.

Chell, E. (2004) 'Critical incident technique', in C.M. Cassell and G. Symon (eds), *Essential Guide to Qualitative Methods in Organizational Research*, London: Sage, pp. 45–60.

Collinson, J.A. (2006) 'Just 'non-academics'?: research and ministrators and contested occupational identity', *Work, employment and society*, 20(2): 267–88.

Conti, J.A. and O'Neill, M. (2007) 'Studying power: qualitative methods and the global elite', *Qualitative Research*, 7(1): 63–82.

Cunliffe, A. (2003) 'Reflexive inquiry in organizational research: questions and possibilities', *Human Relations*, 56(8): 983–1003.

Dalton, M. (1953) *Men Who Manage: Fusions of Feeling and Theory in Administration*, New York: John Wiley and Sons.

Denzin, N.K. (2001) 'The reflexive interview and a performative social science', *Qualitative Research*, 1(1): 23–46.

Denzin, N.K. and Lincoln, Y.S. (2005) 'Introduction: the discipline and practice of qualitative research', in N.K. Denzin and Y.S. Lincoln (eds), *The Sage Handbook of qualitative research (third edn.)* Thousand Oaks, CA: Sage, pp. 1–32.

Ezzamel, M. and Willmott, H. (1998) 'Accounting for teamwork: a critical study of group-based systems of organizational control', *Administrative Science Quarterly*, 43(June): 358–96.

Flanagan, J.C. (1954) 'The critical incident technique', *Psychological Bulletin*, 51(4): 327–58.

Fontana, A. and Frey, J.H. (2005) 'The interview: from neutral stance to political involvement', 'Introduction: the discipline and practice of qualitative research', in N.K. Denzin and Y.S. Lincoln (eds), *The Sage Handbook of qualitative research (third edn.)* Thousand Oaks: Sage, pp. 695–728.

Gabriel, Y. and Griffiths, D.S. (2004) 'Stories in organizational research', in C.M. Cassell and G. Symon (eds), *Essential Guide to Qualitative Methods in Organizational Research*, London: Sage, pp. 114–26.

Glaser, B., and Straüss, A. (1967) *The Discovery of Grounded Theory: Strategies for Qualitative Research*, Chicago: Aldine.

Gubrium, J. and Holstein, J. (2001) *Handbook of Interview Research: Context and Method*, Thousand Oaks, CA: Sage.

Hayes, T. and Mattimoe, R. (2004) 'To tape or not to tape: reflections on methods of data collection', in C. Humphrey and B. Lee (eds), *The Real Life Guide to Accounting Research. A Behind-the-Scenes View of Using Qualitative Research Methods,* Amsterdam: Elsevier, pp. 359–72.

Haynes, K. (2006) 'A therapeutic journey: reflections on the effects of research on researcher and participants', *Qualitative Research in Organizations and Management: An International Journal*, 1(3): 204.

Herzog, H. (2005) 'On home turf: interview location and its social meaning', *Qualitative Sociology*, 28(1): 25–47.

Hollway, W. (1991) *Work Psychology and Organizational Behaviour: Managing the Individual at Work*, London: Sage Publications.

Holstein, J. and Gubrium, J. (1995) *The Active Interview*, Thousand Oaks, CA: Sage.

Horton, J., Macve, R. and Struyven, G. (2004) 'Qualitative research: experiences in using semi-structured interviews', in C. Humphrey and B. Lee (eds), *The Real Life Guide to Accounting Research. A Behind-the-Scenes View of Using Qualitative Research Methods,* Amsterdam: Elsevier, pp. 339–58.

Humphrey, C. and Lee, B. (2004) *The Real Life Guide to Accounting Research. A Behind-the-Scenes View of Using Qualitative Research Methods*, Amsterdam: Elsevier.

Jahoda, M, Lazarfeld, P.F. and Ziesel, H. (1972) *Marienthal: The Sociography of An Unemployed Community*, London: Tavistock Publications.

James, N. and Busher, H. (2006) 'Credibility, authenticity and voice: dilemmas in online interviewing', *Qualitative Research*, 6: 403–20.

Johnson, P. and Duberley, J. (2003) 'Reflexivity in management research', *Journal of Management Studies*, 40(5): 1279–303.

Johnson, P., Buehring, A., Cassell, C.M. and Symon, G. (2006) 'Evaluating qualitative management research: towards a contingent criteriology', *International Journal of Management Reviews*, 8(3): 131–56.

Kezar, A. (2003) 'Transformational elite interviews: principles and problems', *Qualitative Inquiry*, 9(3): 395–415.

Kelly, G.A. (1955) *The Psychology of Personal Constructs: volumes 1 and 2*, New York: Norton.

King, N. (2004) 'Using interviews in qualitative research', in C.M. Cassell and G. Symon (eds), *Essential Guide to Qualitative Methods in Organizational Research*, London: Sage, pp. 11–22.

Kvale, S. (2006) 'Dominance through interviews and dialogues', *Qualitative Inquiry*, 12: 480–500.

Lawthom, R. (1998) 'What do I do? a feminist in non-feminist research', *Feminism and Psychology*, 7(4): 641–52.

Learmonth, M. (2006) 'Doing critical management research interviews after reading Derrida', *Qualitative Research in Organizations and Management: An International Journal*, 1(2): 83–97.

Lee, T.W. (1999) *Using Qualitative Methods in Organizational Research*, Thousand Oaks, CA: Sage.

Limerick, B. and O'Leary, J. (2006) 'Re-inventing or recycling? examples of feminist qualitative research informing the management field', *Qualitative Research in Organizations and Management: An International Journal*, 1(2):98–112.

McCabe, D. (2007) 'Individualization at work?: subjectivity, teamworking and anti-unionism', *Organization*, 14(2): 243–66.

Mirchandani, K. (2003) 'Challenging racial silences in studies of emotion work: contributions from anti-racist feminist theory', *Organization Studies*, 24(5): 721–42.

Morgan, S. and Symon, G. (2004) 'Electronic interviews in organizational research', in C.M. Cassell and G. Symon (eds), *Essential Guide to Qualitative Methods in Organizational Research*, London: Sage, pp. 23–33.

Musson, G. (2004) 'Life histories', in C.M. Cassell and G. Symon (eds), *Essential Guide to Qualitative Methods in Organizational Research*, London: Sage, pp. 34–44.

Nadin, S. and Cassell, C.M. (2006) 'The use of a research diary as a tool for reflexive practice: some reflections from management research', *Qualitative Research in Accounting and Management*, 3(3): 208–17.

Nairn, K., Munro, J. and Smith, A.B. (2005) 'A counter-narrative of a failed interview', *Qualitative Research*, 5(2): 221–44.

Ortiz, S.M. (2005) 'The ethnographic process of gender management: doing the "right" masculinity with wives of professional athletes', *Qualitative Inquiry*, 11: 265–89.

Parker, S.K. Mullarkey, S. and Jackson, P.R. (1994) 'Dimensions of performance effectivenessin high-involvement work organizations', *Human Resource Management Journal*, 4(3): 1–22.

Pillow, W. (2003) 'Confession, catharsis or cure? rethinking the uses of reflexivity as methodological power in qualitative research', *Qualitative Studies in Education*, 16(2): 175–96.

Platt, J. (2002) 'The history of the interview', in J. Gubrium and J. Holstein (eds), *Handbook of Interview Research: Context and Method*, Thousand Oaks, CA: Sage, pp. 33–54.

Prasad, P. (2005) *Crafting Qualitative Research: Working in the Postpositivist Traditions*, New York: M.E. Sharpe.

Quinn, R.P., Gutek, B.A. and Walsh, J.T. (1980) 'Telephone interviewing: a reappraisal and a field experiment', *Basic and Applied Social Psychology*, 1(2): 127–53.

Rapley, T.R. (2001) 'The art(fullness) of open-ended interviewing: some considerations on analysing interviews', *Qualitative Research*, 1(3): 303–23.

Seale, C. (1999) 'Quality in qualitative research', *Qualitative Inquiry*, 5(4): 465–78.

Silverman, D. (1997) 'Towards an aesthetics of research', in D. Silverman (ed.), *Qualitative Research: Theory, Method and Practice*, London: Sage pp. 239–53.

Stephens, N. (2007) 'Collecting data from elites and ultra elites: telephone and face-to-face interviews with macroeconomists', *Qualitative Research*, 7(2): 203–16.

Strong, P. and Dingwall, R. (1989) 'Romantics and stoics', in J.F. Gubrium and D. Silverman (eds) *The Politics of Field Research: Sociology Beyond Enlightenment*, London: Sage, pp. 46–69.

Sturges, J.E. and Hanrahan, K.J. (2004) 'Comparing telephone and face-to-face qualitative interviewing', *Qualitative Research*, 4(1): 107–18.

Symon, G. and Cassell, C.M. (2004) 'Promoting new practices in organizational research', in C.M. Cassell and G. Symon (eds), *Essential Guide to Qualitative Methods in Organizational Research*, London: Sage, pp. 1–10.

Tanggaard, L. (2007) 'The research interview as discourses crossing swords. the researcher and apprentice on crossing roads', *Qualitative Inquiry*, 13(1): 160–76.

Weick, E. (2002) 'Essai: real time reflexivity: prods to reflection', *Organization Studies*, 2(6): 892–8.

Welch, C. and Piekkari, R. (2006) 'Crossing language boundaries: qualitative interviewing in international business', *Management International Review*, 46(4): 417–37.

Ylijoki, O. (2005) 'Academic nostalgia: a narrative approach to academic work', *Human Relations*, 58(5): 555–76.

Zuckerman, H. (1972) 'Interviewing an ultra-elite', *The Public Opinion Quarterly*, 36(2): 159–75.

30

Mixed Methods in Organizational Research

Alan Bryman

INTRODUCTION: THE RISE OF MIXED METHODS RESEARCH

Mixed methods research is an approach to the research process that is in an ambiguous position. The ambiguity arises from several factors but two are worth mentioning at the outset. First, it is in an ambiguous position, because it is not always obvious what it denotes. There is a growing tendency for it to refer to research that combines quantitative and qualitative research methods. However, methods can be combined within both quantitative research and qualitative research, as well as between them. In spite of the fact that this is generally recognized, mixed methods research has come to denote a distinctive approach that entails various modes of bringing together quantitative and qualitative research (e.g. Brannen, 2008: 54). Indeed, it is increasingly depicted as a research strategy in its own right that sits alongside quantitative and qualitative research (Denscombe, 2008; Greene, 2008; Johnson and Onwuegbuzie, 2008). In this chapter, the convention of reserving the term 'mixed methods research' for research integrating

quantitative and qualitative research will be followed. Second, it is in an ambiguous position, because it is simultaneously an old and a new approach to organizational and social research. Old because it has been around in different forms for many years; new because interest in it has burgeoned in recent years. This burgeoning of interest can be discerned in such indicators as: the arrival of new journals dedicated to mixed methods research – the *Journal of Mixed Methods Research* and *International Journal of Multiple Research Approaches* (http://mra.e-contentmanagement.com/ – accessed on 14 April 2008); a handbook of mixed methods research (Tashakkori and Teddlie, 2003); a regular conference series organized by the Homerton School of Health Studies, UK, which attracts an international audience; special issues of established journals (e.g. *International Journal of Social Research Methodology*, 8(3), 2005; *Qualitative Research*, 6(1), 2006; *Research in the Schools*, 13(1), 2006); and a stream of books and edited collections dedicated to mixed methods research (Bergman, 2008; Bryman, 2006b; Creswell and Plano Clark, 2007;

Greene, 2007; Plano Clark and Creswell, 2008; Tashakkori and Teddlie, 1998).

Further evidence of the growing interest in mixed methods research is the fact that a content analysis of articles in the social sciences that had used a mixed methods approach (see Exhibit 30.1) revealed over three times as many articles in 2003 than in 1994 (Bryman, 2008a). This content analysis derived from a search of articles in the Social Sciences Citation Index. While the rise in the number of mixed methods articles almost certainly reflects the growth in the publishing of social science more generally, it is also possible if not likely that it is also to do with a real upsurge of work based on the approach. Of further interest to the organizational researcher is that, over the period in question, articles in the field of organization and management as the primary discipline made up the third largest group of articles by primary discipline (Bryman, 2006a). The percentages of all articles in each disciplinary area were: sociology (36%); social psychology (27%); management and organizational research (23%); geography (8%); and media and cultural studies (7%). Indeed, several other authors in this volume have drawn attention to the significance of mixed methods in the field (e.g. see Fitzgerald and Dopson, Chapter 27, this volume). However, some authors express disappointment at the lack of penetration of mixed methods in the field. Writing about management and organizational research, Currall and Towler (2003) have suggested that 'procedures for linking qualitative and quantitative techniques within a single study have received little attention' (p. 514) and argue that a 'perusal of the management literature over the past ten years suggests that a combination of methods is still rare' (p. 520).

Mixed methods research and the paradigm wars

One of the chief reasons for the relatively recent upsurge of interest in mixed methods research is the fact that it has only relatively recently come to be regarded as a legitimate approach. One of the main impediments to undertaking mixed methods research for many social scientists has been that combining quantitative and qualitative research has been seen as illegitimate on epistemological (and often ontological) grounds. Because of a tendency to see the methods associated with quantitative research as inherently or predominantly drenched with positivism and for the

EXHIBIT 30.1:   Conducting mixed methods research on mixed methods research.

At several points in this chapter, reference will be made to Bryman's (2006a, 2007a) research on mixed methods research. This was in fact a study that employed mixed methods research to examine mixed methods research. Two of the main objectives for doing this research were:

1   To gain an understanding of mixed methods research practice in terms of such issues as: kinds of research methods used, disciplinary area, whether the quantitative preceded the qualitative component or vice versa, etc.
2   To gain an understanding of the contingencies of mixed methods research practice in terms of such issues as: why mixed methods research was chosen, problems encountered, lessons learned, etc.

In order to realise the first objective, a content analysis of 232 mixed methods research articles was conducted to map the general characteristics of mixed methods research in terms of a variety of features. From semistructured interviews, I wanted to glean the perspectives of mixed methods researchers in their own terms. The content analysis was designed to give a sense of the public face of mixed methods research, while the interviews were an attempt to get inside the heads of its practitioners in order to tease out how and why they used mixed methods research and their reflections on their own and others' practices. As such, this study of mixed methods research employed both a quantitative method – traditional quantitative content analysis – and a qualitative method – semistructured interviews – to examine different aspects of mixed methods research.

methods associated with qualitative research as inherently or predominantly drenched with interpretivism (e.g. phenomenology), combining quantitative and qualitative research was viewed as impossible because of their incompatibility. To underline this, quantitative and qualitative research were often depicted as paradigms, following Kuhn, and as such were deemed to be *ipso facto* incommensurable. At best, if quantitative and qualitative research *were* combined in research, it was viewed as turning qualitative research into an adjunct of quantitative research and hence positivism. Even quite recently, mixed methods research has been described as 'positivism in drag' (Giddings, 2006). Thus, although there has been a rise in the use of mixed methods research, this should not be taken to signal that the paradigm wars have given way to paradigm peace. For one thing, concerns about the epistemological problems associated with combining quantitative and qualitative research have not gone away completely and sometimes resurface (as signalled by the recency of the 'positivism in drag' comment). Indeed, in the present volume, Yanow and Ybema (Chapter 3, this volume) make the point that the mere existence of mixed methods research does not signal that the epistemological issues have been resolved or surmounted. They argue that combining quantitative and qualitative research does not signal that the underlying epistemologies are being somehow combined, though this position presumes a necessary association between research methods and epistemological positions. This view can be disputed on the grounds that methods are not necessarily associated with particular epistemologies; it is the *use* that is made of them that is crucial. A questionnaire may lend itself to the kinds of research question that are often asked within a positivist frame of reference but that does not mean that it should solely be viewed in this way. The other reason for doubting that the paradigm wars have abated is that they can be viewed as resurfacing in a different guise. Developments such as the rise of systematic review (see Denyer and Tranfield, Chapter 39,

this volume) and of 'Bush science', as it is sometimes called in some quarters of the social sciences, are testament to lingering or new forms of the paradigm wars (Bryman, 2008a).

In place of the paradigm wars and their underlying philosophical principles, pragmatism has emerged as the foundational philosophy of much mixed methods research (e.g. Denscombe, 2008; Maxcy, 2003). As a philosophy, pragmatism is viewed as freeing the researcher to select whichever methods and data sources that might reasonably be used to explore a research problem in pursuit of rigorous and comprehensive findings. It is no coincidence that this stance has found particular favour among practitioners in applied fields like evaluation and educational research, where the over-riding emphasis tends to be on dealing with practical research problems. While organizational research *could* be construed as an applied field, it is striking that discussions in the pages of the *Academy of Management Journal* of the relevance of management studies generally imply that it is an area that is predominantly concerned with the solution of theoretical problems than with applied ones. Nonetheless, as previously noted, mixed methods research has a considerable following in organization studies.

The development of mixed methods research

It has been suggested that mixed methods research has proceeded through distinct phases. Creswell and Plano Clark (2007) have proposed that there have been four stages of development:

(1) A *formative period* associated with early explorations of ways of combining quantitative and qualitative research as well as discussions of the use of more than one quantitative research technique, usually within an explicit or implicit triangulation framework.

(2) A *paradigm debate period*, which explored the foundations of quantitative and qualitative research and whether it is feasible to combine them. These discussions have mainly

occurred in the 1970s and 1980s. My own work (Bryman, 1988) is situated in this period by the authors.

(3) A *procedural development period* that is mainly associated with exploring how mixed methods studies have been and can be designed. Debates about paradigms did not disappear but the emphasis changed to exploring the doing of mixed methods research. This work is mainly associated with the late 1980s through the start of the new millennium.

(4) An *advocacy as separate design period* associated with the new millennium whereby mixed methods researchers began to advocate it as a new and distinctive design in its own right.

In many ways, the third and fourth periods are likely to overlap considerably as not all practising researchers with an interest in mixed methods research will be inclined to treat it as a separate approach in its own right. Thus, we can expect that procedural development is likely to continue alongside the articulation of mixed methods research and its advocacy as a distinct design.

Classifying mixed methods research

There has undoubtedly been a greater preparedness to regard mixed methods research as a legitimate endeavour in the social sciences in recent years. However, the precise roles that quantitative and qualitative research are supposed to play in relation to each other are many. For one thing, mixed methods research subsumes a variety of research designs. Thus, it has become quite commonplace to distinguish mixed methods projects in terms of: *sequence* – whether the quantitative component precedes the qualitative or vice versa or whether they occur more or less concurrently; and *priority* – whether the quantitative component is more important than the qualitative component or *vice versa* or whether they have more or less equal weighting. A consideration of these two elements yields a typology whose component cells vary considerably in the frequency with which they are found in published research.

Indeed, following the early initiative of Morse (1991), writers on mixed methods have developed a distinctive notation to express the various possibilities offered by these considerations. Writers use 'quan' and 'qual' to refer to the different components of a mixed methods study and use upper or lower case to reflect the relative weighting of those components. They use arrows to signify which element precedes the other or a plus sign to express simultaneity. Thus, for example, QUAN + QUAL signifies a design in which the quantitative and qualitative are of equal weight and conducted concurrently, as in a triangulation design (see the following section). QUAN → qual signifies a design in which the quantitative component is the lead one and precedes the qualitative component. This might occur with a design emphasizing complementarity (see the following section) where the emphasis is on quantitative findings and the qualitative data are used to shed light on and explain them.

Considering where a particular mixed methods study falls in terms of these two dimensions is not without problems. First, there are issues of judgement involved – for example, deciding whether the quantitative and qualitative components differ in importance may not be easy to establish in many cases. Second, what is to count as mixed methods research can be difficult to resolve. For example, if a researcher conducts a survey that entails mainly a quantitative research orientation and if the questionnaire or interview schedule includes some open questions to which predominantly textual responses are given and these are analysed using a method of qualitative data analysis, does this count as mixed methods research (Bryman 1992)? Definitional issues bedevil methodological discussions and mixed methods research is obviously not immune to this tendency (Holmes, 2006).

Establishing typologies of mixed methods research along these lines has been particularly popular among North American writers. A somewhat different way of classifying mixed methods research has been to explore the various reasons or rationales for conducting it. This has been a feature of both North American writers (e.g. Greene et al., 1989; Creswell and Plano Clark, 2007) and European writers (e.g. Bryman, 1988, 2006a; Hammersley, 1996; Niglas, 2004; O'Cathain et al., 2007). The emphasis on rationales is highly compatible with the focus on priority and sequence and many writers express design types that reflect rationale in these terms.

The investigation of researchers' reasons for conducting mixed methods research is usually arrived at inductively from an examination of published research. In some cases, this investigation has been conducted through a relatively informal analysis of published research (e.g. Bryman, 1988; Hammersley, 1996). However, other students of mixed methods research have conducted more formal analyses. Such authors have content analysed mixed methods articles in order to establish the relative frequency with which different bases for conducting mixed methods research can be found.

The Greene et al. (1989) scheme has probably been one of the most frequently employed classifications for this purpose. This scheme identifies five justifications for combining quantitative and qualitative research:

(1) Triangulation. This is to do with establishing the convergence, corroboration, and/or correspondence of results from different methods. In the context of mixed methods research, triangulation is to do with seeking corroboration between quantitative and qualitative data.
(2) Complementarity. This occurs when the researcher 'seeks elaboration, enhancement, illustration, clarification of the results from one method with the results from another' (Greene et al., 1989: 259).
(3) Development. Entails seeking 'to use the results from one method to help develop or inform the other method, where development is broadly construed to include sampling and implementation, as well as measurement decisions' (Greene et al., 1989: 259).
(4) Initiation. Entails seeking 'the discovery of paradox and contradiction, new perspectives of [sic] frameworks, the recasting of questions or results from one method with questions or

results from the other method' (Greene et al., 1989: 259).
(5) Expansion. Entails seeking 'to extend the breadth and range of enquiry by using different methods for different inquiry components' (Greene et al., 1989: 259).

One of the chief advantages of this classification is that it is parsimonious and uses generic categories. Thus, the fact that the typology was developed in relation to the authors' field of interest – evaluation research – does not preclude its being employed in relation to other fields. Indeed, it was employed by both Bryman (2006a) and Niglas (2004) in connection with their content analyses of five social science fields and educational research respectively. When Greene et al. (1989) applied the scheme to content analyse evaluation studies, each article was coded in terms of a primary and a secondary rationale. Other classificatory schemes have been developed (see Creswell and Plano Clark, 2007, Table 4.1 for a useful overview). In his content analysis of mixed methods articles, Bryman (2006a) preferred an approach that draws finer distinctions between possible bases for doing mixed methods research.

A further distinction that has been suggested is between the stated intentions of doing mixed methods research and how it is used in practice. This distinction has been a focus of the work of both Greene et al. (1989) and Bryman (2006a), with the latter distinguishing between rationale and practice: the rationale refers to the reasons given for combining quantitative and qualitative research; practice is to do with 'the ways in which quantitative and qualitative research[es] were actually combined' (Bryman, 2006a: 104). When this distinction is drawn and mixed methods articles are content analysed in terms of both rationale and practice, it is found that the two are often out of phase with each other. In other words, it is not always possible to establish how mixed methods research is actually used from a knowledge of the rationale that authors provide; similarly, knowing how mixed methods research has been used may not relate well to the way

Table 30.1   Rationales for mixed methods research using the Greene et al. (1989) scheme

Category	Rationale %	Practice
Triangulation	7.8	12.5
Complementarity	28.9	44.8
Development	10.3	8.6
Initiation	0.4	1.3
Expansion	25.4	31.5
Not stated/other	27.2	1.3
All percentages are based on 232 cases – see Exhibit 30.1		

it is rationalized by researchers. Two factors seem to lie behind this finding. First, in around a quarter of mixed methods articles, no rationale was provided, but it is nearly always possible to divine how quantitative and qualitative research were combined (see Table 30.1). Second, researchers appear to find more uses of mixed methods research than an examination of the rationales that they provide would lead the reader to expect. It would seem that when confronted with the two sets of data, more and often different possibilities open up than had been envisaged. In many ways, this points to much of the excitement as well as the unpredictability of a great deal of mixed methods research.

Table 30.1 provides previously unpublished findings relating to the content analysis of social science articles referred to in Exhibit 30.1 for both rationale and practice. It shows the distribution of articles in terms of just the primary rationale using the Greene et al. scheme (see column for 'Rationale'). In just over a quarter respectively of all articles, no rationale was provided. Complementarity and expansion were the most frequently cited primary rationales with 29% and 25% respectively of all articles mentioning each of them as a primary rationale. Triangulation and development were less commonly mentioned, while initiation was extremely uncommon. The latter was also the case in Greene et al. (1989) but was even more so in the data reported here. Turning to the actual uses of the integration of quantitative and qualitative research, Table 30.1 (column for 'Practice') provides the primary use in terms of the Greene et al. scheme. All of the frequencies

are greater, because the category of 'not stated' virtually disappears. Most striking is that nearly half of all articles can be subsumed into the complementarity category. In terms of the Greene et al. scheme, this is by far the most prominent primary approach to the integration of quantitative and qualitative research.

When the data for the 'practice' column in Table 30.1 using the Greene et al. scheme are contrasted with comparable data from Greene et al. (1989) and Niglas (2004), we find that the pattern is closer to Niglas's examination of educational research articles than to the analysis of evaluation research articles by Greene et al. Similarly to Niglas, complementarity is the most common use of mixed methods research, followed by expansion. In the examination of evaluation research articles by Greene et al., it was the other way around, in that expansion was more common that complementarity. In the case of all three studies, then, these two uses of mixed methods research were the most common forms.

Table 30.2 takes the analysis of these data somewhat further with another previously unpublished analysis. This table presents

Table 30.2   Rationales for mixed methods management and organizational research using the Greene et al. (1989) scheme

Category	MOR %	Other
Rationale		
Triangulation	18.9	4.5
Complementarity	24.5	30.2
Development	17.0	8.4
Initiation	1.9	0.0
Expansion	20.8	26.8
Not stated/other	17.0	30.2
N=	53	179
Practice		
Triangulation	22.6	9.5
Complementarity	37.7	46.9
Development	13.2	7.3
Initiation	3.8	0.6
Expansion	20.8	34.6
Not stated/other	1.9	1.1
N=	53	179
All percentages are based on 232 cases – see Exhibit 30.1		
MOR = management and organizational research		

the proportion of articles falling within Greene et al.'s five categories for articles in the management and organizational research (MOR) field versus the rest. The table presents the analysis for both rationale and practice. This table does indeed highlight some differences between MOR and the rest of the social sciences. At the level of rationale, MOR practitioners are noticeably more likely than other social scientists to use mixed methods research for the purpose of triangulation and development and are also noticeably less prone to not stating the purpose of doing mixed methods research. At the level of practice, the findings for triangulation and development are repeated. The findings for rationale and practice suggest that MOR practitioners are somewhat less likely to use mixed methods research for purposes of complementarity and expansion. On the one hand, these findings point to the existence of disciplinary differences in the uses to which mixed methods research is put, but, on the other hand, they point to areas where MOR practitioners might seek to extend their thinking about the possibilities with respect to integrating quantitative and qualitative research.

A classification of rationales for mixed methods research

We will now return to the issue of rationales in mixed methods research and use some examples from organization studies to illustrate the five-fold classification used by Greene et al. (1989). The aim will be to explore how mixed methods research is being used in organizational research through the examination of illustrations of a mixed methods approach.

Triangulation

As previously noted, triangulation is one of the most frequently encountered terms employed in a mixed methods research context to the extent that it is sometimes employed in a manner that suggests that it is seen as more or less synonymous with the combining of quantitative and qualitative

research. However, Greene et al. employ the term appropriately to refer to exploring whether the results from two or more research methods converge (Webb et al., 1966). We can see the operation of triangulation in both Exhibits 30.2 and 30.3.

In Exhibit 30.2, Fey and Dennison (2003: 698–699) propose that the findings from the case studies 'supported' and 'mirror' the quantitative findings. In Exhibit 30.3, triangulation was also a feature but the picture is somewhat complex. At one of the case study firms (referred to as PC), Yauch and Steudel (2003) were able to use their quantitative data to reinforce their qualitative findings. However, at the other firm – BEC – the quantitative data were not able to identify cultural factors that impeded the introduction of cellular manufacturing. In part, this appears to have been due to a limitation of the quantitative measurement scale employed, which, the authors suggest, means that for some companies this scale may not be appropriate. Thus, in one of the firms, the quantitative data could be used to corroborate the qualitative findings but in the other firm, they could not. Nonetheless, the authors propose that using a mixed methods approach can help to give a study like theirs 'greater validity … through data triangulation' (2003: 479).

Complementarity

Evidence of complementarity can be discerned in both Exhibits 30.2 and 30.3. With regard to the former, Fey and Denison say at one point that the 'qualitative elaboration' stage helped them to 'see many interesting and unanticipated insights that were hiding behind [their] quantitative analyses' (2003: 702). This was especially the case with respect to uncovering some of the cultural factors that helped them to understand the data relating to quantitative patterns, suggesting departures from the American model with respect to their Russian organizations. As noted in Exhibit 30.3, Yauch and Steudel (2003) explicitly employed the Greene et al. classification and rationalized the use of a mixed methods approach largely in terms of triangulation (see previous

EXHIBIT 30.2:   Mixed methods research in a cross-national context.

Fey and Denison (2003) report the findings of a mixed methods study that explored the relationship between organizational culture and effectiveness in the context of whether theory and findings stemming from the US can be applied to Russia. This was one of the studies included in Bryman's (2006a) content analysis. Fey and Denison's investigation was guided by three research questions: whether the US model is applicable to Russia; what differences in findings can be discerned concerning the culture-effectiveness relationship between the two countries; and the meaning and applicability in Russia of the concepts developed for examining culture and effectiveness in the US. The first two research questions were explored with a quantitative study of 179 Russian firms; the third through four qualitative case studies. Denison had previously developed measures to study four cultural traits exhibited by effective organizations: involvement (empowerment); consistency (strong cultures); adaptability (responsive to customers); and mission (sense of direction). These scales and measures of effectiveness were employed in questionnaires by senior managers. While the model was broadly validated, some differences were found between the Russian and previous US findings, e.g. in Russia adaptability and involvement were the main correlates of effectiveness, whereas in the US it tended to be mission. Fey and Denison argue that there is a risk that the researcher could wrongly assume that the cultural traits mean the same things in Russia as they do in the US. To consider this possibility, they conducted semistructured interviews with managers in a subsample of four of the firms, which were purposively selected. The authors note that the qualitative case study findings confirmed the quantitative ones. They also suggest that the case studies 'served to ground the theoretical concepts in the realities of the Russian context' and helped to identify aspects of the findings that were consistent with the US model and also ones that 'were not fully anticipated by the model' (p. 701). In addition, they propose that the qualitative findings helped to 'illustrate' some of the model's constituent concepts. They conclude that the insights from both the quantitative and the qualitative findings 'enabled [them] to both validate the model and to provide a more complete understanding of the dynamics of organizational cultures in the Russian context' (p. 702).

EXHIBIT 30.3:   Mixed methods research and the introduction of cellular manufacturing.

Yauch and Steudel (2003) report the findings of a mixed methods study that, like Exibit 30.1, explores organizational culture and was also one of the articles in Bryman's (2006a) content analysis. The authors draw on the work of Greene et al. (1989), which is referred to in the main text, to make sense of their findings. The goal of the study 'was to identify key cultural factors that aided or hindered a company's ability to successfully implement manufacturing cells' (p. 467). The authors conducted two exploratory case studies to explore the cultural factors that contributed to or impeded the process of converting from traditional to cellular manufacturing processes. The two case-study firms (referred to as PC and BEC) were both new to cellular manufacturing. The case studies entailed participant observation, examination of documents, and group interviews with organizational members at a variety of levels. For the quantitative component of the investigation, an established scale – the Organizational Culture Inventory (OCI) – was employed in each company. The OCI was administered to a random sample of both managers and nonmanagerial employees. The authors drew up an assessment of the strengths and weaknesses of both sets of findings but of particular significance for this summary of the research is the authors' assessment of their mixed methods findings. Yauch and Steudel found that at PC, a factor that has an adverse effect on implementation was 'avoidance', which refers to a tendency not to take responsibility for one's actions so that one is not blamed. This cultural factor was uncovered through the qualitative research and then confirmed through the quantitative evidence. The qualitative findings revealed the beliefs and assumptions that lay behind avoidance while the quantitative findings are deemed to have provided greater precision in explaining it and also helped with naming it. At BEC, a cultural factor referred to as 'rigid group boundaries' was identified through the qualitative data as an impediment to implementation. This cultural trait was to do with a tendency for organizational members to form barriers between groups that made it difficult for them to interact. However, rigid group boundaries was not revealed through the administration of the OCI, because this inventory is not designed to measure it! Yauch and Steudel propose that they were able to triangulate their findings at PC but at BEC the OCI did not reveal a particular cultural style. However, in addition, the combination of quantitative and qualitative research allowed the researchers to explore different aspects, and to some extent levels, of organizational culture. As they put it: 'Although the quantitative analysis identified behavioral norms for the organization as a whole, the qualitative analysis was necessary to get at the underlying reasons for this behavior' (p. 477).

section) and complementarity. They write, for example:

> Using a combination of qualitative and quantitative techniques revealed different aspects of organizational culture. Although the quantitative analysis revealed behavioral norms for the organization as a whole, the qualitative analysis was necessary to get at the underlying reasons for this behavior. Thus, the use of mixed methods created a deeper understanding of the organization ... Defining key cultural factors at the artefact level fit within the quantitative research paradigm, whereas the qualitative paradigm was needed to investigate the lived experience of managers and employees within the organization at the level of values and underlying assumptions. (Yauch and Steudel, 2003: 477)

Development

An interesting slant on development is provided by Yauch and Steudel (2003) in connection with what they feel they *should* have done. As noted in Exhibit 30.3, at the firm referred to as BEC, a cultural factor described as 'rigid group boundaries' (a tendency for organizational members to form barriers between groups that made it difficult for them to interact) was identified through the qualitative data as impeding implementation. However, this cultural factor was not revealed through the administration of the quantitative instrument used to measure organizational culture, because this inventory is not designed to measure that particular factor. Yauch and Steudel make an interesting point when they write: 'If the primary goal is to increase validity, an instrument should be selected *or developed* that specifically asks about the cultural aspects of the organization that have been identified through the preliminary qualitative work' (2003: 476, emphasis added). Essentially, what these authors seem to be proposing is that from the point of view of seeking to triangulate quantitative and qualitative findings, the exercise might have worked better had the quantitative measure of organizational culture been one that had been developed out of prior qualitative findings. This kind of use of mixed methods research can be found in an article by Myers and Oetzel (2003)

which is both frequently referred to and reprinted in Creswell and Plano Clark (2007). In this study, the researchers conducted semistructured interviews with a variety of organizational participants to develop the concept of organizational assimilation. The interviews revealed six dimensions of assimilation: familiarity with others; acculturation; recognition; involvement with the organization; job competency; and adaptation and role negotiation. Myers and Oetzel then developed a questionnaire scale to reflect these six dimensions. The scale comprised 61 items. The six dimensions were validated when the questionnaire was administered to a sample and construct validity was established when several hypotheses concerning organizational assimilation were supported.

An element of development could also be discerned in Fey and Denison's (2003) research in that the choice of the four case-study firms was undertaken with reference to what was already known about them through the quantitative data that had been collected.

Initiation

As the findings described in Tables 30.1 and 30.2 suggest, initiation is not a common basis for doing mixed methods research at the level of either rationale or practice and, as is noted in the foregoing section, it is uncommon in a variety of areas. However, Exhibit 30.4 provides an interesting illustration of initiation in practice. While the example used in Exhibit 30.4 was clearly not planned in a manner consistent with what Greene et al. mean by initiation, that is how it turned out. The authors were forced to salvage their overall research project by rethinking the nature of their research questions by collecting qualitative data. Fortunately, they resisted the temptation to write up their research as a purely quantitative research study in which a negative relationship was hypothesized and then confirmed through their quantitative findings (Sutton and Rafaeli, 1992). Instead, they collected qualitative data to understand their quantitative data better.

EXHIBIT 30.4:   Using mixed methods research to rescue a quantitative research project.

This exhibit is a favourite exemplar of mixed methods research in the organizations field and one I have used before (Bryman and Bell, 2007). It is Sutton and Rafaeli's (1988) study of the relationship between the display of positive emotions and organizational effectiveness. While a fascinating example of a mixed methods study, it is also a saga of academic endurance. Sutton and Rafaeli were afforded the opportunity to examine the organizational impact of the display of positive emotions when they were given access to data collected by a convenience store chain from a sample of 576 of its stores. The data had been collected by observation as part of an evaluation of the courtesy of its clerks. Sutton and Rafaeli hypothesized that stores where there was a high incidence of the display of positive emotions (smiling, thanking, eye contact, etc.) would have higher levels of sales. The researchers found that there was indeed a relationship between emotional display and sales but it was *negative*. In other words, the display of positive emotions was associated with lower levels of store sales. Sutton and Rafaeli then conducted a qualitative investigation 'to help explain the unexpected negative relationship' (p. 471). Four stores were purposively sampled as case studies based on their levels of sales and on the display of positive emotions. Data were collected by observation, semistructured interview, brief periods of participant observation and other qualitative methods. The qualitative data confirmed that the relationship was a negative one, but that sales was an independent rather than a dependent variable. In other words, because they tended to be busier, check-out clerks in stores with high sales typically had less time for the display of positive emotions. The quantitative data were reanalysed and this inference was supported. The experience of doing this research led the authors to appreciate the virtues of using both quantitative and qualitative methods (Sutton and Rafaeli, 1992).

Expansion

Although not a study in the field of organizational research, Exhibit 30.1 provides an example of a study 'using different methods for different inquiry components' (Greene et al., 1989: 259). The traditional quantitative content analysis was employed in order to reveal the nature of published mixed methods studies. As such, it was concerned to uncover the formal characteristics of mixed methods research in terms of such features as: the research methods and research designs employed, the main disciplines, whether the quantitative or the qualitative component was primary, and the rationales for using mixed methods research. The goal of the qualitative interviews was to get at the nature of mixed methods practice from the perspective of practitioners, looking at such issues as the contingencies of doing mixed methods research and problems encountered in the course of its implementation.

Mixed methods research and the problem of integration

One issue that has preoccupied methodologists in recent times has been the degree to which the findings deriving from mixed methods findings are genuinely integrated. The term '*mixed* methods research' implies that the quantitative and qualitative components involved in a mixed methods investigation are brought together. For example, in an editorial for the *Journal of Mixed Methods Research*, the journal's editors proposed that one criterion of a good mixed methods article is that the quantitative and qualitative components should be linked:

> Mixed methods research is simply more than reporting two distinct 'strands' of quantitative and qualitative research; these studies must also integrate, link, or connect these 'strands' in some way … The expectation is that by the end of the manuscript, conclusions gleaned from the two strands are integrated to provide a fuller understanding of the phenomenon under study. (Creswell and Tashakkori, 2007: 108)

A study that asked social policy researchers about the quality criteria that should be applied to mixed methods research found that one of the most frequently mentioned criteria was whether the quantitative and qualitative findings are integrated (Bryman, Becker and Sempik, 2008), while O'Cathain et al. (2007)

propose that it is important for a mixed methods publication to be more than the sum of its constituent parts (see also Tashakkori and Teddlie, 2008: 106, on this point).

Although there is a view that the integration of the quantitative and qualitative findings of a mixed methods project is highly desirable, there is evidence that this does not always happen. Several reasons have been identified for the lack of integration of findings. Most of these were covered in the course of interviews with twenty British mixed methods social researchers (Bryman, 2007a see Exhibit 30.1). Many of the interviewees recognized that quantitative and qualitative findings were often not integrated and typically felt that they themselves were guilty of this. The following were the main factors identified as impeding integration:

- Writing for *different audiences*. Mixed methods researchers sometimes find that they end up writing up the quantitative and qualitative findings for different audiences. This may be associated with the researcher's judgement about the acceptability of certain styles of research or types of data for particular audiences.
- Researchers' *methodological preferences*. Researchers sometimes reveal a tendency to have greater confidence in some types of data than in others. This tendency often reflects being more comfortable with some kinds of data resulting from training.
- The different components of a mixed methods project may follow different *timelines*. As a result, the findings of one component may emerge at a considerably earlier stage than those associated with the other component.
- The *structure of research projects* may mean that it is difficult for integration to be achieved. This can arise when one component of the overall project occupies a much more central role than the other component. A typical example is when the quantitative component is both highly structured and occupies a much more pivotal position than the qualitative component, the style of qualitative data collection may be too constrained by the quantitative research.
- When a mixed methods project is conducted by a team whose members have different *methods skills*, a division of labour within the team may arise that makes it difficult for the skills specialists to work together.

- Sometimes, one set of data may emerge as more *intrinsically interesting* than the other set, with the result that the researcher tends to emphasize the more striking findings.
- Although mentioned by only one interviewee, the presence of an *ontological divide* between the quantitative and qualitative elements can prove a difficulty. This can arise when the qualitative component reflects a strong constructionist position that problematizes the nature and even the existence of the phenomenon being investigated. It can then be difficult to explore this problematized phenomenon with an objectivist research strategy that presumes its existence.
- *Publication issues* can also pose a problem for integrating findings. This can arise because of the preferences of some journals and editors for research approaches that are associated with either quantitative or qualitative research. In this context, it is striking that Currall and Towler (2003) called for a re-evaluation of journal editorial policies as a means of garnering greater acceptance of mixed methods studies.

It may also be that when mixed methods research is being conducted within a framework consistent with expansion in terms of the five-fold classification by Greene et al. (1989), integration may be difficult to achieve. This was certainly the case with the research referred to in Exhibit 30.1, where the quantitative and qualitative components were designed to explore distinct research questions to generate an overall view of the phenomenon of interest.

One further reason for the limited integration of quantitative and qualitative findings in many mixed methods articles may be that there are relatively few guidelines for the writing up of findings deriving from such research and relatively few well known exemplars to draw upon. To the extent that guidelines and exemplars exist in the social sciences, they tend to be identifiable in relation to *either* quantitative or qualitative research. In fact, it could be argued that the emphasis in writing about mixed methods research should shift slightly away from data collection and design and towards the interpretation and representation of findings.

Writing mixed methods research

As previously suggested, one of the issues that needs greater consideration is how mixed methods research should be written up. There are well-established formats for the writing up of quantitative and qualitative research but few guidelines regarding mixed methods research. Creswell and Plano Clark (2007) have offered some helpful suggestions in this connection. They propose the following guidelines:

(1) The writing should be structured so that it is tailored to the kind of mixed methods design employed. Thus, if the study's primary orientation is towards qualitative research, this should be reflected in the approach taken to writing up the findings.
(2) The writing up should 'help to educate the reader about this form of research' (Creswell and Plano Clark, 2007: 152). This implies that key mixed methods terms should be clearly defined and there should be clear references to the mixed methods literature. This suggestion could be linked to the notion that mixed methods research is currently in the throes of an advocacy period (see foregoing section).
(3) Researchers should use visual and other aids to display and help the reader to follow the components of a mixed methods study and their interconnections.
(4) The researcher should aim to generate a unified narrative for the findings. This recommendation reflects the preference among mixed methods researchers for publications that integrate the quantitative and qualitative findings.

In addition, the following additional considerations could be registered:

(1) Creswell and Tashakkori (2007: 108) have proposed that mixed methods articles 'need to be well-developed in both quantitative and qualitative components'. This means that not only should the research have been conducted according to the respective standards or quality criteria of quantitative and qualitative research, but it should also be written up in such a way that it establishes the probity of these components.
(2) Researchers might also consider framing their research at the outset with research questions that reflect a specific orientation to research questions. For example, Tashakkori and Creswell (2007) and Creswell and Plano Clark (2007) refer to 'mixed methods research questions' which explicitly deal with how the quantitative and qualitative components will be mixed. This feature is likely to need to be tailored to the nature of the mixed methods design (see first point in this list). Edmondson and McManus (2007: 1165) advocate employing a mixed methods approach in situations when 'the combination of qualitative data to help elaborate a phenomenon and quantitative data to provide preliminary tests of relationships can promote insight and rigor'. However, this approach to stipulating mixed methods research questions seems to restrict mixed methods research to a rather narrow range of issues.
(3) It should be clear why a mixed methods approach was employed. Researchers should guard against simply presuming that it is obvious why both quantitative and qualitative research were employed on the grounds that more is better. The case for using a mixed methods approach needs to be clearly articulated, not least because in the eyes of many mixed methods researchers, the approach should only be used when relevant to the research questions asked (Bryman, 2006b; Bryman et al., 2008).

One of the impediments to mixed methods writing is that there are few generally accepted exemplary studies. It may be that once these are established, the writing process will become less problematic for researchers than is currently the case. An example of the use of an exemplary mixed methods study to illustrate good practice in this connection, but from outside the field of organizational research, can be found in Bryman (2008b).

CONCLUSION

Mixed methods research generally and in the field of organizational research in particular is at something of a crossroads. On the one hand, there is no doubt that it is attracting a great deal of attention and its popularity continues to grow. Its legitimacy is questioned less frequently than was the case even ten years ago. Indeed, it has the characteristics of a distinct 'community of practice' (Denscombe, 2008). However, there are also countervailing factors that should not be forgotten. In this Conclusion, four are emphasized:

First, the ontological and epistemological issues that previously inhibited mixed methods work have not gone away; they have simply been sidelined in the pursuit of pragmatism. On a personal note, I am not averse to this. As I have said before, I have never believed that a research method necessarily implies a certain epistemological orientation; rather it is the use that is made of the research method that links it to wider issues of epistemology and ontology. The affordances of a research method may predispose its use in connection with particular epistemological or ontological positions, but ultimately it is the use made of the research method that is the principal issue.

Second, as a field, organizational research is still largely dominated by quantitative research, as Bazeley's (2008) informal inspection of recent issues of the *Administrative Science Quarterly* and *Academy of Management Journal* reveals. Bazeley's analysis implies that, in these journals, to the extent that mixed methods research is published, the role of the qualitative component is largely that of handmaiden to the quantitative component. This means that in essence, such journals are only likely to publish a restricted range of forms of mixed methods work and that its wider acceptance may not be as great as some of the more optimistic accounts of the rise of mixed methods research imply. It may also reinforce the previous point about lingering epistemological issues and concerns redolent of the paradigm wars (Bryman, 2008a).

Third, the connection between mixed methods research and research questions remains opaque. There are two aspects to this issue. First, whether there are types of research questions that require or at least imply a mixed methods approach is not entirely resolved.

The notion expressed earlier that a mixed methods research question is which stipulates how the quantitative and the qualitative components will be brought together is significant but that relates to the issue of integration. What is still not clear is whether there is a specific kind of research question (that is, over and above how components are to be combined) that implies a mixed methods approach. Second, some writers on and practitioners of mixed methods research seem to suggest that the approach will almost always be superior to monomethod research, whereas others suggest that it should only be used when the research question(s) imply that it should be used (Bryman, 2007b; Bryman et al., 2008). This implies some uncertainty about the status of mixed methods research that needs to be resolved.

Fourth, there are skills issues that have not been fully resolved. What are the necessary skills for being a mixed methods researcher? Most obviously, a mixed methods researcher needs to have skills in both quantitative and qualitative research or when specific skills are not present needs to build a team that can incorporate missing skills. The first of these is often inhibited by the tendency for many researchers either to be trained in either quantitative or qualitative research skills or to have acquired a preference at an early stage for one or the other. The team-building solution can cause problems of integrating the components as suggested before (see also Bryman, 2007a). However, in addition to these issues, the many discussions about the nature of mixed methods research and the various types of design that the term can subsume and about the contingencies of the approach (such as the issue of integration) suggest that a mixed methods skills set is beginning to emerge that is in addition to the abilities that are required for doing both quantitative and qualitative research. In turn, these reflections have implications for the teaching of and training in mixed methods research for future generations, an issue to which writers on research methods are beginning to turn their attention (Creswell et al., 2003).

To some extent, these considerations relate to how writers on and practitioners of mixed methods research want to position themselves and their craft. If the goal is to position mixed methods research as a paradigm that stands alongside quantitative and qualitative research, which certainly seems to be an objective according to several commentators (Denscombe, 2008), deliberation on these and several of the other issues raised in this chapter are pressing. However, in so doing they must be wary of turning mixed methods into a methodological cult. As the second issue raised in this Conclusion suggests, the credibility of mixed methods research is still not as widely accepted as is sometimes supposed, and it is here that there are battles still to be fought.

It could be argued that although just under a quarter of all the articles content analysed in the research described in Exhibit 30.1 are based on mixed methods research, given the large number of journals in the MOR field, it is somewhat surprising that there are not more. It may be that this is what prompted Currall and Towler (2003: 520) to remark that 'a combination of methods is still rare'. MOR would appear to be an ideal field for the proliferation of mixed methods research. Its practitioners are very sensitive to the advantages of applying different paradigmatic approaches and readings of organizational phenomena (as Buchanan and Bryman, Chapter 1; Deetz, Chapter 2; Yanow and Ybema, Chapter 3; Alvesson and Ashcraft, Chapter 4; and Prasad and Prasad Chapter 8, among others in this volume, make clear). Further, qualitative researchers often perceive the mainstream journals as preferring articles based on quantitative research, so it might be that a mixed methods approach would be attractive as a strategic means of getting published (see Buchanan and Bryman, Chapter 1, this volume, on this point). In addition, it may be that mixed methods research is especially suited to the kinds of research questions that are asked in MOR. The fact that organizations can be examined at a variety of levels (sectors, populations, inter-organizational relations, single organization, departments, work groups, etc.) may make a mixed methods approach especially suitable. Research questions may be asked that require an appreciation of macro and micro issues and mixed methods research would be well placed to address them. In addition, the fact that organizational phenomena include combinations of both highly measurable constructs (profitability, size, market share, etc.) and ones which are less directly measurable and hence amenable to both quantitative and qualitative approaches (organizational culture, organizational aesthetics, emotional labour, etc.) would seem to point to several advantages of adopting a mixed methods approach. Also, some areas of MOR are dominated by either a quantitative or a qualitative research approach. Thus, for example, as Bryman and Buchanan note (Chapter 41, this volume), areas like job satisfaction (see Rafferty and Griffin, Chapter 12, this volume) are largely dominated by quantitative research. Other fields like organizational aesthetics (Strati, Chapter 14, this volume) are largely dominated by qualitative research. Again, a mixed methods approach has the potential to increase the range of enquiry for such subfields and enhance the understanding of their respective phenomena. Mixed methods research would seem, then, to offer great potential to organizational researchers, suggesting that while it has been responsible for some important and significant contributions in the field, there is the potential for a great deal more.

REFERENCES

Bazeley, P. (2008) 'Mixed methods in management research', in R. Thorpe and R. Holt (eds), *The SAGE Dictionary of Qualitative Management Research*, London: Sage, pp.133–6.

Bergman, M.M. (ed.) (2008) *Advances in Mixed Methods Research*, London: Sage.

Brannen, J. (2008) 'The practice of a mixed methods research strategy: personal, professional and project considerations', in M.M. Bergman (ed.), *Advances in Mixed Methods Research*, London: Sage, pp.53–65.

Bryman, A. (1988) *Quantity and Quality in Social Research*, London: Unwin Hyman.

Bryman, A. (1992) 'Quantitative and qualitative research: further reflections on their integration', in J. Brannen (ed.), *Mixing Methods: Qualitative and Quantitative Research*, Aldershot: Ashgate, pp. 57–78.

Bryman, A. (2006a) 'Integrating quantitative and qualitative research: how is it done?', *Qualitative Research*, 6(1): 97–113.

Bryman, A. (2006b) *Mixed Methods*, Four-volume set, London: Sage.

Bryman, A. (2007a) 'Barriers to integrating quantitative and qualitative research', *Journal of Mixed Methods Research*, 1(1): 8–22.

Bryman, A. (2007b) 'The research question in social research: what is its role?', *International Journal of Social Research Methodology*, 10(1): 5–20.

Bryman, A. (2008a) 'The end of the paradigm wars?', in P. Alasuutari, L. Bickman, and J. Brannen (eds), *The SAGE Handbook of Social Research Methods*, London: Sage, pp.13–25.

Bryman, A. (2008b) *Social Research Methods* (third edn.), Oxford: Oxford University Press.

Bryman, A. and Bell, E. (2007) *Business Research Methods* (Revised edn.), Oxford: Oxford University Press.

Bryman, A., Becker, S. and Sempik, J. (2008) 'Quality criteria for quantitative, qualitative and mixed methods research: the view from social policy', *International Journal of Social Research Methodology*, 11(4), 261–76.

Creswell, J.W., and Plano Clark, V.L. (2007) *Designing and Conducting Mixed Methods Research*, Thousand Oaks, CA: Sage.

Creswell, J.W. and Tashakkori, A. (2007) 'Developing publishable mixed methods manuscripts', *Journal of Mixed Methods Research*, 1(2): 107–11.

Creswell, J.W., Tashakkori, A., Jensen, K.D. and Shapley, K.L. (2003) 'Teaching mixed methods research: practices, dilemmas, and challenges', in A. Tashakkori and C. Teddlie (eds), *Handbook of Mixed Methods in Social & Behavioral Research*, Thousand Oaks, CA: Sage, pp. 619–38.

Currall, S.C. and Towler, A.J. (2003) 'Research methods in management and organizational research: toward integration of qualitative and quantitative techniques', in A. Tashakkori and C. Teddlie (eds), *Handbook of Mixed Methods in Social & Behavioral Research*, Thousand Oaks, CA: Sage, pp.513–26.

Denscombe, M. (2008) 'Communities of practice: a research paradigm for the mixed methods approach', *Journal of Mixed Methods Research*, 2(3): 270–83.

Edmondson, A.C. and McManus, S.E. (2007) 'Methodological fit in management field research', *Academy of Management Review*, 32(4): 1155–79.

Fey, C.F. and Denison, D.R. (2003) 'Organizational culture and effectiveness: can American theory be applied in Russia?', *Organization Science*, 14(6): 686–706.

Giddings, L.S. (2006) 'Mixed-methods research: positivism dressed in drag?', *Journal of Research in Nursing*, 11(3): 195–203.

Greene, J.C. (2007) *Mixed Methods in Social Inquiry*, San Francisco, CA: Jossey-Bass.

Greene, J.C. (2008) 'Is mixed methods social inquiry a distinctive methodology?', *Journal of Mixed Methods Research*, 2(1): 7–22.

Greene. J.C., Caracelli, V.J. and Graham, W.F. (1989) 'Toward a conceptual framework for mixed-method evaluation designs', *Educational Evaluation and Policy Analysis*, 11: 255–74.

Hammersley, M. (1996) 'The relationship between qualitative and quantitative research: paradigm loyalty versus methodological eclecticism', in J.T.E. Richardson (ed.), *Handbook of Research Methods for Psychology and the Social Sciences*, Leicester: BPS Books.

Holmes, C.A. (2006) 'Mixed(up) methods, methodology and interpretive frameworks', Paper presented at the Homerton Mixed Methods Conference, Cambridge.

Johnson, R.B. and Onwuegbuzie, A.J. (2004) 'Mixed methods research: a research paradigm whose time has come', *Educational Researcher*, 33(7): 14–26.

Maxcy, S.J. (2003) Pragmatic threads in mixed methods research in the social sciences: the search for multiple modes of inquiry and the end of the philosophy of formalism. in A. Tashakkori and C. Teddlie (Eds.), *Handbook of Mixed Methods in Social and Behavioral Research* Thousand Oaks, CA: Sage, pp. 51–89.

Morgan, D.L. (1998) 'Practical strategies for combining qualitative and quantitative methods: applications for health research', *Qualitative Health Research*, 8(3): 362–76.

Morse, J.M. (1991) 'Approaches to qualitative-quantitative methodological triangulation', *Nursing Research*, 40(2): 120–3.

Myers, K.K. and Oetzel, J.G. (2003) 'Exploring the dimensions of organizational assimilation: creating and validating a measure', *Communication Quarterly*, 51(4): 438–57.

Niglas, K. (2004) *The Combined Use of Qualitative and Quantitative Methods in Educational Research*, Tallinn, Estonia: Tallinn Pedagogical University Dissertation on Social Sciences.

O'Cathain, A., Murphy, E. and Nicholl, J. (2007) 'Integration and publications as indicators of "yield" from mixed methods studies', *Journal of Mixed Methods Research*, 1(2): 147–63.

Plano Clark, V.L. and Creswell, J.W. (2008) *The Mixed Methods Reader*, Thousand Oaks, CA: Sage.

Sutton, R.I. and Rafaeli, A. (1988) 'Untangling the relationship between displayed emotions and organizational sales: the case of convenience stores', *Academy of Management Journal*, 31 (3): 461–87.

Sutton, R.I. and Rafaeli, A. (1992) 'How we untangled the relationship between displayed emotions and organizational sales: a tale of bickering and optimism', in P.J. Frost and R. Stablein (1992), *Doing Exemplary Research*, Newbury Park, CA: Sage, pp.115–28

Tashakkori, A. and Creswell, J.W. (2007) 'Exploring the nature of research questions in mixed methods research', *Journal of Mixed Methods Research*, 1(3): 207–11.

Tashakkori, A. and Teddlie, C. (1998) *Mixed Methodology: Combining Qualitative and Quantitative Approaches*, Thousand Oaks, CA: Sage.

Tashakkori, A. and Teddlie, C. (eds) (2003) *Handbook of Mixed Methods in Social and Behavioral Research*, Thousand Oaks, CA: Sage.

Tashakkori, A. and Teddlie, C. (2008) 'Quality of inferences in mixed methods research: calling for an integrative framework', in M.M. Bergman (ed.), *Advances in Mixed Methods Research*, London: Sage, pp.101–19.

Webb, E.J., Campbell, D.T., Schwartz, R.D. and Sechrest, L. (1966) *Unobtrusive Measures: Non-Reactive Research in the Social Sciences*, Chicago: Rand McNally.

Yauch, C.A. and Steudel, H.J. (2003) 'Complementary use of qualitative and quantitative cultural assessment methods', *Organizational Research Methods*, 6(4): 465–81.

31

Research Designs for Realist Research

Stephen Ackroyd

INTRODUCTION

This chapter gives an account of the research designs used by researchers working with realist philosophical ideas explicitly or implicitly in mind. It gives the rationale for the choice of the research designs discussed and, where applicable, it extends to the consideration of data collection and handling. Few general accounts of research from a realist standpoint attempt to give guidance on such matters. For all their importance in setting out the general methodological implications of realist philosophy, and for establishing in principle that realist research is a distinctive approach to social science, the standard introductions to realist research (Sayer, 1992, 2000; Layder, 1998; Danermark et al., 2002), including those works that are specifically concerned with organizational research (Ackroyd, 2004; Reed, Chapter 25, this volume), typically do not contain much detailed consideration of the types of research designs in frequent use and why. This lack of specific advice is disappointing, especially from the viewpoint of someone who has been persuaded by the fundamental ideas of realism and who is possibly planning a

research project. Once beyond the general idea of conducting research, the absence of guidance may lead some potential converts to question the attractiveness – if not the value itself – of realist-informed approaches to organizational research. This chapter sets out to remedy this deficiency, by identifying some research designs recommended for use in realist-informed research, and by giving a rationale for their relevance and value.

This account will still largely operate at the level of overall research design; that is, considering research in terms of its general methodology or approach. However, it will also give some more detailed information. In this account, seven general research designs are considered. The discussion covers the ways that realists have tended to use these research designs. A key point to note here is that the realist-informed researcher, unlike those approaching research within or informed by other metatheoretical systems, does not have much in the way of preferences for kinds of data; though there are clear preferences concerning the types of observable event that merit attention. Realist-influenced researchers may consider different empirical factors and indicators in the same project observing behaviour directly, recording the opinions of participants and collecting published data. In the event, some data they may collect turns out to have little interest to them; while other material may become much more important as a research project unfolds. The reason for this is that realists are interested in observable things only because of what they may reveal about the mechanisms that are the real or underlying causes of social processes. They make a distinction between different 'realms' – the realm of the empirical, the actual, and the real or 'deep' (Bhaskar, 1989; Ackroyd and Fleetwood, 2000). What is sought in research is, of course, knowledge of what causes what in the realm of the real, but instead, the researcher has to deal with what can be observed in the realm of the empirical.

The realist-informed researcher is guided by theoretically derived conjectures about the social mechanisms at work in the world, and considers, through data collection and investigation, the extent to which theoretical ideas explain chosen outcomes. Constructing a causal account of events is a process to which theory and empirical research both contribute and, in view of this, the data sought are different in every research project. Hence, research from this set of assumptions tends to be ongoing, changing tack in the kinds of observations made and the data collected as knowledge in a field develops. Nevertheless, there are some research designs that are consistently selected by realist-informed organizational researchers, who do tend to have preferences about how they work within these.

Preferred research designs for realist research

Research designs recurrently used by realist-inclined organizational researchers include case studies, comparative case studies, generative institutional analysis, studies involving large scale data sets, action research and comparative and general policy evaluation. This list specifically excludes experimental

research designs and attempted approximations to them using statistical techniques.

The question arises: why this collection of designs and not others? The answer is that some research designs meet the realists' requirements for explanation, while other designs do not. Realists have particular convictions about valid explanations and how they are constituted, and these obviously have to be considered at the outset. However, the key point is that the research designs mentioned meet the realist's requirements for explanation, albeit in some different ways. Other elements of realist doctrine – in ontology, epistemology, and causality – bear on why particular designs are commonly adopted, but they are not given extended treatment here. In this chapter, attention is given to how research findings explain events and, as a secondary consideration, how they illustrate and exemplify specific logics of scientific discovery.

For the realist, to explain a regularity is to see it in relation to a set of causal events (identified as a generative mechanism or process), working itself out in a given situation (the context). Thus, the explanation of regularity is a function of mechanism and context (Pawson and Tilley 1997, pp. 55–82). The critical observation here is that some of the designs utilized focus on, and pay more empirical attention to, the generative processes involved in any outcome as opposed to prioritizing the context. How different designs prioritize different aspects of explanation, and embody different logics of scientific discovery, are the key matters considered in this account.

In Table 31.1, the research designs listed in the foregoing section are differentiated along a continuum between 'intensive' or 'extensive'. A simple distinction between these characteristics originated in the work of Harré (1979). Since, the distinction between intensive and extensive research designs has been retained by realist commentators. Among those adopting this distinction are Sayer (1992: 243; 2004: 21) and Danermark et al. (2002: 165). In this account, the idea of a continuum of combinations between

Table 31.1   Seven research designs relevant to realist-informed research

Classification by Harré, Sayer, and Danemark:	intensive			extensive
distinctive research strategy:	what is the mechanism? (context as given)	how do context and mechanism (a) typically interact?	(b) historically intersect?	what is the context? (mechanism inferred)
research procedures:				
passive study	case studies (1)	comparative case studies (2)	generative institutional analysis (3)	research surveys and census data (4)
active intervention	action research (5)	comparative policy evaluation (6)	general policy evaluation and critique (7)	
dominant logic of discovery:	abduction	abduction	abduction/ retroduction	abduction/ retroduction

intensive and extensive research designs has been adopted. In organizational and management studies, the research commonly undertaken by realists is more varied than the dichotomy suggests. Between organizational case studies that are usually intensive and the use of large samples of quantitative data, are other designs. Comparative case study research and generative institutional analysis are two of them. What distinguishes them is not the amount or even the kind of data utilized, so much as the way in which the designs target different aspects of the requirements of explanation. Either the mechanism or the context is the primary object of concern.

Because of the realist's ontological convictions, the concern of realist-informed researchers is to undertake work that, potentially at least, might penetrate below the surface to identify underlying social mechanisms or generative processes. All realist research implicitly or explicitly envisages the existence of generative mechanisms like this. Indeed, once a mechanism or process is identified, generalization from case studies becomes possible if the same mechanism is recognizably operative in many similar situations. However, different research designs differ in the extent of the effort devoted to the empirical validation of (a) the character of the mechanisms or processes involved, or (b) the contribution of the context in which such mechanisms work themselves out. Thus, because of their potential to reveal the operation of mechanisms, research using case studies may be thought of as the primary research design in the realist cannon (Miles and Huberman, 1994; Easton, 2008).

Realist research employs two related but distinguishable logics of discovery as it moves between the identification of underlying mechanisms and understanding the conditions of these mechanisms existing. Once something of a generative mechanism is known, knowledge may be extended by studying the context in which it operates. The context tends to either reinforce or consolidate a mechanism; otherwise, it may alter or redirect it. Thus, we may compare the unitary case study, in which unearthing of generative mechanisms is the main objective, with studies that involve the comparison of situations in which similar mechanisms operate. When something is known of the generative mechanisms, comparative research can help pin down the character of the process and distinguish these from the effects of the context. In such studies, the focus of research is shifted to ways in which differences of context may shape the outcome of intraorganizational mechanisms, and give rise to interorganizational processes.

Table 31.1 implies an array of research strategies, to which the designs listed are related. First, there is case study research targeted on unearthing mechanisms or showing their operation. Second, research can seek to establish, through judiciously chosen comparative case studies, how context and mechanism interact to produce typical outcomes. Third, it is possible to consider the interaction of context and mechanism over a range of places and over time, and to examine how context and mechanisms have actually interacted to produce unique, historically specific outcomes. Finally, it is possible to envisage research that looks at the context, usually through the yield of large-scale surveys or data relating to populations. These describe the context in which organizational mechanisms work and organizational changes take place, and can be a useful way of appraising them.

Table 31.1 also features a distinction between research in which the researcher is passive in relation to subject matter, and where active intervention is undertaken in the process of research. The classic distinction is between involvement or detachment (Elias, 1956; 1987). The table also suggests realist organizational research may be detached or engaged; that is, interested in explaining things and events as they are, or interested in trying to induce change though intervention. The use by realists of this kind of research is restricted largely to the evaluation of attempts to change social organization initiated by others. Yet the possibility of engaged research, involving active intervention, remains an important potential mode of engagement for some realists.

Case study research design

Case studies entail sustained consideration of activities and behaviour in a particular location. With limited membership and distinct boundaries, organizations are often chosen as suitable initial sites. Thus, we find case studies presenting accounts of the activities and social processes found in particular organizations, for example: General Gypsum (Gouldner,

1954); Hammertown Boys' School (Willis, 1977); Allied Machine Shop (Burawoy, 1979). Despite some prejudicial views of cases, which are based on the assumptions of other philosophical approaches to research, a defensible basis has been developed by realists (Easton, 2008; see Fitzgerald and Dopson, Chapter 27, this volume). Let us begin by noting two modalities of case-study work undertaken by realists – extensive and intensive.

Types of case study

The extensive case study aims to produce a comprehensive account of an organization through sustained study. Such an account will never be complete or definitive, but major internal processes occurring in a complex organization can be described after sustained investigation. The studies undertaken by Selznick (1948), Blau (1955) and Gouldner (1954, 1955), widely regarded as foundational for organization studies as an academic field (Reed, 1985), were of this kind. Despite their overdeveloped functionalism, such studies are realist in their presuppositions. Their authors set out to show that organizations are entities of sufficient complexity that they are not fully known to the participants in them. What surfaces is the idea that the organization is an entity constituted by its social processes. Some of these processes are latent. But, when considered together, a conception of the organization as a whole with its own distinctive, emergent properties is realized. By contrast with this, secondly, there is the intensive study, which makes no claim to holism, and focuses on identifying particular, highly formative processes in a given context. This second type of study is much used by realists today.

The two types of investigation are distinguished by assumptions about the generative process they identify. The extensive study sets out to describe all major processes at work and their interactions. The intensive study focuses on particular generative mechanisms, and makes expedient use of the organizational context. The generative mechanisms considered in intensive case study are present not merely or mainly because of the particular roles and relationships which make up the organization in which they appear. In the conception of realists, organizations are embedded in, and influenced by, wider sets of relations – especially those constituting the economy and society. Thus, the interest of realists in intensive studies is because the organization under study is a place in which the effects of wider economic and social connections have effects.

An example

An example of realist case research is that of Burawoy in *Manufacturing Consent* (1979), a sustained observational study of a Chicago machine shop. In this celebrated study, Burawoy notices that pieceworkers engaged with their work as if it were a game. Workers approached their work as a challenge to 'make out' in their negotiations with work-study engineers and so gain marginal advantages in pay for each machining job; this would lead to increases in wages. Burawoy shows that the game-like qualities of the daily interactions with managers and rate setters induced rivalry between fellow workers. Individuals competed to achieve high earnings and, if successful, they also achieved high status in the group. Thus, as a result of this set of relationships, vertical antagonisms between workers and manager are displaced by horizontal rivalry between worker and worker. By noting the existence of these rivalries and the extent to which they preoccupy workers, Burawoy shifts debate about how workplace behaviour should be interpreted. He shows that relationships in the workplace can change: from relationships constituted by resistance of workers to managerial control, to the 'manufacture of consent' through the workers' willing participation in bargaining games.

This example explains regularities in the outcome of social processes. It identifies regularly reproduced social patterns, but they are not in institutionally expected forms. Thus, we have a factory with an administrative system that produces neither the disciplined

conformity expected by management, nor the class-conscious resistance expected by some theorists. More generally, although realist research often features organizations, and shows how they tend to work with predictable regularity, explanations are not reducible to the suggestion that human interactions simply adopt institutionalized forms and patterns. The explanation offered by Burawoy features: (a) *patterns of interaction* involving different groups with different motivations, and (b) the central role of *discretionary behaviour*, in (c) *constituting, reproducing, and changing* those patterns. Thus, the ability of people to make informed choices is a key part of the reason the mechanisms identified by researchers take the precise form they do, giving rise to both continuity and change. Finally, and most importantly, though these explanatory accounts were found in specific contexts, they are not unique to them. Before following up such issues, we need to consider how these explanatory accounts are produced from the observations undertaken and the data collected.

Research techniques

Realist commentators suggest ethnography is a favoured method for realist researchers (Miles and Huberman, 1994; Porter, 1993; Reed, Chapter 25, this volume). Typically, realist-informed researchers appropriate elements of ethnographic fieldwork, turning them to their purposes. Direct and close observation of people is a procedure taken from anthropology, but is greatly adapted in practice. An anthropologist usually undertakes years of fieldwork. Sustained observation of the groups in an organization is typically for a lesser period. Burawoy was in his machine shop for eleven months. The aim of observation is not simply to provide knowledge of the outlook of groups. It is done to clarify patterns of relationships between participants as well as studying the meanings they attribute to events. Realists undertake fieldwork for the variety of empirical material available from such studies, and their aim is to put them together so as to give an account of the generative processes or social mechanisms at work in the situations they study. As Layder (1993: 50) has said, 'a central feature of realism is its attempt to preserve a scientific attitude towards social analysis, at the same time as recognizing the importance of actors' meanings and incorporating them into research'. Realists, then, are mindful of the fact that, as actors with their own meanings, they nonetheless seek to recover the meanings attributed to situations by other actors, and to feature them in their account of the generative processes that are at work. To this extent, they are reflexive in their approach to the meanings attributed to events by their subjects and themselves.

At the outset realist researchers tend to be empirically precocious. Clues about generative mechanisms are given in the attitudes and behaviour of group members, the actions to which these give rise and emergent patterns of interaction between groups. Only following the sustained observation of behaviour, and through noting deviations from sanctioned beliefs and expected patterns of action, may recognition of the precise nature of the generative mechanisms be discerned, understanding of their nature be developed, and extent of their effects confirmed. Hence, as the research proceeds, special interest in particular kinds of data may develop. As his study progressed, for example, Burawoy became more interested in the rivalries between workers, and collected data about them. This lack of precise prior definition of, and changing concern for, particular kinds of data is a feature of realist research. It is also a source of difficulty for some researchers with different philosophical assumptions. The great benefit of the organization as the context of a case study is that the site for the investigation of the generative process is held substantially constant.

The logic of discovery in case study research

Explanations of events produced by realist case research are not achieved by deduction from premises. Still less are the inductions; that is, propositions that are generally true, because they are frequently observed.

Looking at case-study results in this way leads to a perception of likely error, because generalizations are apparently made on the basis of a very limited sample. On the contrary, however, the reason for thinking the discovery of a generative mechanism is significant is conceptual as much as it is empirical. Case investigations that lead to the identification of the operation of generative social mechanisms are theoretically guided, but the precise operation of mechanisms is the subject of empirical corroboration. The result is an account of a process that involves the mutual reinforcement of the conception and the empirical exemplification of a causal sequence. To the extent that such generative mechanisms are identifiably at work in other locations, they can be the basis for generalization. Thus, because it produces actual changes in the world, any such process has a claim to being substantively important. Although there were only a score or so of machinists in Burawoy's vicinity during fieldwork, there is no doubting the general relevancy of the interpretation of his findings. Although the individual subjects included in Burawoy's studies behaved in particular ways, any individual peculiarities in them do not alter the perception that the processes found are reproduced in many other locations.

The key point is that accounts of generative processes discovered in case studies involve the conceptual interpretation of causal sequences. Such work offers a new and unanticipated view of organizational processes: what was hitherto largely unobserved has become the basis of new understanding. Our view of the organization, its properties and character, are recast. Once having seen a familiar organization construed in a new way like this, it is often difficult to revert to the old way of seeing it. A well-executed realist study, therefore, involves a reconceptualization of the subject and how it works. To the extent that an account of generative processes establishes a new and different account of the subject, this is an abduction as defined by Danermark et al. (2002). Other research designs are reapplications or elaborations of this basic logic of discovery. For a systematic analysis of the abductive and or retroductive logics typically in use in realist research, and their differences from induction and deduction, see Table 31.2. Thus, there are two ways forward once the bridgehead of identifying a generative mechanism has been accomplished: these roughly correspond to synchronic and diachronic approaches to social science (see Langley, Chapter 24, this volume).

Comparative case study research

The research design

Case study research is obviously not confined to single cases, and knowledge is not built up from a large number of discrete studies. Comparative case studies greatly extend the range of case study research. Clearly, it is possible to look at several cases at the same time, to compare similarities and differences in them and to draw conclusions.

The limitation on justifiable generalization from case studies is theoretical rather than empirical. On the other hand, there will be variations in the way a generative mechanism works itself out. Comparative research will clarify both the nature of a mechanism more fully and the range of variation it shows. To the extent that there are variations of this kind, this indicates that there is some bias arising from the use of single cases. Comparative work is a way forward. By designing research programmes featuring a range of cases with significant variation, there is the possibility of developing better-founded knowledge. What is sought is a causal account of the typical patterns of action and interaction found.

One way of thinking about this design is that its aim is to clarify the extent to which outcomes are attributable to a mechanism or to its context. How mechanism and context interact can be tied down more precisely by comparative research. Any variation in outcomes can be clarified by looking at either how differences of underlying mechanisms

Table 31.2 Positivist and realist logics of discovery in research

	the conception of explanation: something is explained when it is	the process of discovery: theory is developed by	the process of knowledge construction: knowledge is improved by
Positivist logics – typically not centrally used in realist research			
inductive	a reliable generalization from well-attested data (a 'valid' sample is required)	systematic data collection and the use of inductive techniques to produce valid generalizations	searching for associations between variables and comparing with the probability of a chance outcome
deductive	a conclusion deduced from known premises or theoretical postulates	the production of law-like statements in an abstract form, from which further testable postulates are inferred	testing propositions deduced from theoretical postulates; trying to refute laws by showing predictions false
Realist logics – central to realist research			
abductive	an elemental account of a basic process or mechanism, or something that is seen as the product of such a mechanism	combining the ideas of participants, with recognition of the powers and tendencies of other entities, to describe a generative process	building accounts of how generative processes work themselves out in given contexts
retroductive	established as a distinctive process, and the conditions of its existence have been elaborated	answering the question, what are the conditions for the existence of this generative process ?	locating accounts of particular generative processes in a broad socio-economic context

work themselves out in similar contexts, or how what is basically the same mechanism works itself out in different contexts. The point is that, if features of an operative mechanism are partly identified, more general knowledge may be sought through a larger number of instances. Thus, there is relevance to theoretically informed extensive research by the realist and this is more salient once the existence of particular operative mechanisms is established. Again, a contrast can be drawn between research involving the intensive comparison of two or three cases studied in detail as opposed to less detailed extensive study of a relatively large number of cases.

Examples

There are numerous examples of realist influenced research involving comparative case studies (Edwards and Scullion, 1982; Burawoy, 1985; Thompson et al., 1996; Delbridge, 1998; Taylor and Bain, 2005; Kirkpatrick et al., 2004). These days, realist research in organizations usually involves multiple cases studies. The idea is to consider and compare a range of instances that are similar in some ways. For this to be effective, cases have to be selected, because they exhibit or are likely to exhibit variations in the mechanism under scrutiny – or of its context. Comparative work is more effective if something is known about the generative mechanism(s) involved. With intensive studies, it is assumed a generative mechanism is more formative in shaping outcomes than context. However, precise interaction between context and mechanism is often unknown, and fixing the relative contribution of these components is the object of enquiry. It is the purpose of this design to raise the level of precision in the causal priority attributable to the mechanism or the context.

Two examples of comparative work, one intensive and one extensive, are: Burawoy's study of the labour process in factories in America, Britain, and Hungary (Burawoy, 1985, 2007), and the studies by Edwards and Scullion (1982) of the conflict arising in different factory regimes in Britain. These studies both feature the labour process as

part of the generative mechanisms examined. Burawoy compares intensive studies of the labour process in a few locations. In *The Politics of Production* (1985), he makes sustained comparisons between his work on the American-based Allied Machine Shop, that of Lupton (1963) at Jay's, a British engineering firm, and that of Haraszti (1977) in a Hungarian tractor factory. Burawoy's principal finding is that, despite similarities in the labour process and factory regime, the political and economic context are relevant to why the experience of the workers, and the outcome of factory discipline, is so different. Thus, despite considerable similarities in the labour process found in factories in different countries, the broader institutional arrangements, including the political circumstances, are highly formative of outcomes. Thus, because of the broader political economy, despite the lack of unemployment in Hungary, workers were under much tighter managerial control than that was found in Burawoy's American research.

Edwards and Scullion undertake an eight firm comparison of the effects of the factory regime on the labour process and the implications of these differences on the degrees and kinds of conflict found. Here, there was no sustained ethnographic component in the research, though the investigators were sometimes in their factories for a period of months. Focused ethnographic research was not undertaken, nor was historically deep study. The researchers opted for a design which sought information about the behaviour of labour and management policies and procedures. Although they combined carefully defined measures of conflict, along with uncodified interview data, it was not part of the study to correlate variables. What makes their study realistic is their recognition that, although there are tendencies for causal links, close control of worker behaviour might produce more conflict, but did not invariably do so. Direct control in clothing factories had less consequence in creating conflict than in engineering shops. Thus, the comparative design pins down the precise causation of outcomes.

The logic of discovery in comparative case study research

There is a temptation to regard comparative research designs as naturally occurring experiments, in which circumstances serve up, by chance, cases where everything is the same except for one crucial aspect. The causal effect of such a factor can then be tested by comparing outcomes. Such a chance would, it is true, allow for a rigorous test of the causal properties of a factor. Unfortunately, such a happy chance would be an extreme rarity and most comparative case studies do not meet, and cannot be expected to meet, the criteria for experimental research designs (see Stone-Romero, Chapter 18, this volume). The cases used in comparative work differ from each other in multiple ways and are not to be thought of as approximations to experimental designs (Siggelkow, 2007).

In comparative designs, it is accepted that almost everything is subtly different between the cases. The point to make is not that there is much that is the same, as deductive logic indicates is necessary, only that there are some elements – featured in the generative mechanism – that are in essence the same. Given this, it is not a surprise to find that, even where there are opportunities for realist researchers to get comparable data from different sites, they may choose not to. Edwards and Scullion did not seek comparable quantitative measurements of attitudes in their different plants, for example. All that is similar, or held to be so, are features of generative processes. Generative processes are of interest, because they can be seen to be working themselves out in similar ways in circumstances that are otherwise quite different. Any deductive elements of explanations arising from comparative case explanations are thus limited or even possibly absent. In short, the logic of this research design is little different from that of the single case. There is a recasting of the understanding of the nature of the phenomenon under study, and the logic of the research design is abductive, as outlined in Table 31.2 (See Danermark et al., 2002: 79).

A note on model building and the construction of typologies

Early extensive case study work often led to the construction of idealized and coherent organizational models and sets of these in the production of organizational typologies. The influential case studies of Selznick (1948) and Blau (1955) are examples. The explicit functionalism in their later writings, however, has no counterpart in the work of realist-inspired researchers.

Even extensive organizational case studies, in the hands of realists, are unlikely to lead to the formulation of typologies. However, the intensive case studies undertaken by realists are likely to identify characteristic faults and dysfunctions in organizations. How these faults have effects is likely to be varied from context to context. Thus, in a realist view, there can be greater diversity of organizational processes than functionalist and institutionalist writers typically assume, and their main purpose is not to look for an idealized account of an organization *per se*. For them, the typification of organizational models and their characteristic internal processes are best understood as heuristics, rather than functional patterns supposedly applicable in many contexts. More generally, it can be argued that the interest of the realist is not in typology (the basis of which is mainly conceptual) but in taxonomy (the basis of which combines the conceptual with the empirical; see Bailey, 1994).

Generative institutional investigations

Research design

Comparative case studies undertaken by realists can be combined with general studies of the development of socioeconomic systems and comparisons of their characteristics made. Burawoy's work includes such material, as does Edwards'. The latter wrote a follow-up to *The Social Organization of Industrial Conflict* (1982) in a wider study, *Conflict at Work* (1986), much of which simply invokes broader aspects of context. However, this research also involves elements, which are a significant departure from the designs already reviewed.

Work of this other kind, which explores causal connections producing changes over time, is present in Edwards' later research (1986). Chapter 3, for example, explores temporal sequences in the development of capitalism. He considers the connection of change in the economy with forms of collective protest. This is a shift from looking for similarities and differences in the interaction of context and mechanism at roughly the same time (synchronically), to searching for causal sequences over time (diachronically). What is sought are causal connections, suggesting the typical way generative mechanisms and contexts have intersected historically to produce unique outcomes. Such research has to be historical and analytical, being forced to rely on secondary sources, or ideally on the interpretation of data in the documentary record. However, as in the other designs, this research is guided by ideas about generative mechanisms occurring in context. In these examples, movement takes the form of change in specific combinations of generative mechanisms and their contexts so that sequences of cause and effect can be seen to work over time. There are examples of intensive and extensive research of this kind also.

Examples

Though few, there are important studies of linked generative processes. As realist-informed research develops, more may be expected. In addition to the later work of Edwards, some other recent research may be cited: Smith and Meiksins (1995); Smith (2005); Clark (2000); Mutch (2007); Muzio et al. (2008). Clark (2000) has perhaps done most to set out ideas about the temporal links between generative processes. His work combines discussion of temporal and geographical sequences and connections, and is complex for this reason. In another example of extensive research Smith (2005) investigates three analytically distinct generative processes ('system', 'societal', and 'dominance'

effects), and considers evidence of all three working themselves out over time. Smith shows that reference to all three processes may be necessary to explain current strategies and practices of firms. Such extensive work is difficult to summarize succinctly.

However, to illustrate this sort of research, a focused study by Mutch (2007) will be considered. Mutch looks at the effects of the practices of an individual entrepreneur on the transformation of the management of public houses in nineteenth century Liverpool. Using concepts from Archer classifying forms of reflexivity, Mutch identifies A.B. Walker, later Sir A.B. Walker, a nineteenth century provincial businessman, as exhibiting the qualities of one of these forms – the autonomous-reflexive. Mutch argues that only in virtue of this businessman possessing autonomous reflexivity, which combines the capacity to monitor one's actions with business performance, but also allows the possessor to respect their own judgement and so to persist with behaviour even in the face of adverse opinions from others about the likelihood of business success. Fortuitous circumstances also aided the rise of this businessman, such as being the owner-manager of a brewery, and having earlier business experience in Scotland. The latter suggested to Walker the relevancy of introducing new practices in pub management in Liverpool. However, according to Mutch, a key factor allowing the successful introduction of new forms of management of tied public houses by Walker, was his possession of the autonomous-reflective self-identity. This, suggests Mutch, allowed him to emerge as one of the first brewers to diversify successfully into the retail trade. This secured the conditions for the profitability of his business, and provided a template later copied and adapted in other British businesses. This study is more modest in its objectives than other research of this genre; but, as a generative mechanism, the process of organizational development described by Mutch is of interest, because it shows the origin of what became a reproduced and influential business innovation.

The logic of discovery in generative institutional processes

These research designs do not centrally reconceptualize their subjects, though they trade on work that has done so. However, to the extent that it involves characterizing generative mechanisms, it is abductive, as has been suggested for other designs. But that is by no means all it is. This work is concerned with the examination of the conditions leading to the emergence of a given generative mechanism or its consequences. Clearly, this research may take accounts of generative processes as given, using such accounts as a platform for further enquiries. It investigates the manner in which developments followed each other so that one set of outcomes emerged historically and not others. This kind of research enquires as to what set of factors gave rise to historically observed outcomes and into the conditions of their existence. Research of this kind is also retroductive (Danermark et al. 2002: 80). To some extent, all the research designs considered here give rise to reflection on the conditions of existence of what is found in research, but this is the first example of a design in which such reflection is a necessary feature of the approach to research itself.

Designs employing large-scale quantitative data sets

Issues concerning quantitative research design

Many realists support the use of quantitative data (Sayer, 1992; Danermark et al., 2002; Layder, 1998), but most propose the use of surveys in particular with caution. The reasons for ambivalence are, first, realists are sceptical about measuring attitudes. Attitude measurement techniques tend to impose the categories of the questioner on respondents, whereas beliefs and attitudes are subtle, and how they link to behaviour is complex. Because the way respondents think and act is complex, realists tend to use close observation. Second, realists are sceptical of the applicability of experimental logic to human behaviour – it is difficult to apply and does not reflect the

processes it is designed to assess. However, much quantitative methodology in social science has been developed to deal with the difficulties of achieving experimental control. Quantitative social science is built around the use of inductive statistics to test the strength of associations between variables and so to attempt to match the rigour of experimental research designs. These methods are ruled out by realists on practical and ontological grounds.

Realists have a range of basic concerns about quantitative methods from surveys. These include the following areas: problems with data collection and recording (Pawson, 1989), data handling and analysis (Marsh, 1982, 1988), and the unsocial and unreflective basis of research practice (Bateson, 1984). The root of the problem is that complex, open systems studied in social science are not appropriately conceptualized by the positivist assumptions underpinning quantitative research. Resolving complex and dynamic social situations as sets of 'variables', contradicts realist ontology. Byrne (2002) pursues the criticism of traditional methods as far as proposing new ways of analyzing quantitative data relating to populations. He argues that population data can be appropriately analyzed by abandoning variable analysis and substituting 'multi-level modelling'. This procedure requires innovations in survey data recording, moving to the collection of information about the groups in which respondents are located in addition to recording their individual characteristics. Byrne is correct that standard research practices in survey work are profoundly individualistic and also that, if problems are effectively tackled, theoretically adequate procedures for quantitative modelling of populations can be developed. There is some way to go before these methods are readily applied in organizational studies. However, there are less demanding uses of statistics for whole populations.

Quantitative research designs

Because of their concern for the context of generative processes, realists are interested in the dimensions and attributes of populations. It is this that gives them an interest in descriptive statistics. The characteristics of populations can say a good deal about the likely extent of trends and processes. Responses to questionnaires relating to populations are useful if their limitations are understood, and if their primary use is descriptive. It is also permissible to use samples to estimate population characteristics; such techniques offer economical and reliable ways of estimating population values and parameters.

Quantitative data collected from representative samples or whole populations can be revelatory about contexts in ways that allow connections to be made with known or conjectured generative processes. If key features of a mechanism(s) have been postulated, further insights may arise from considering data describing the context of their operation. Such information allows reflection on the operative context of particular mechanisms and gives insight into the likely extent of their operation. A common feature of the quantitative research undertaken by realists is its interest in obtaining data on whole populations as the context for consideration of generative mechanisms. Thus, the design of realist quantitative research is a way of reframing organizational processes and reflecting on the conditions of their existence.

Examples of research using population characteristics

The design of several large-scale research projects has included collection of information on populations. An example is research into employment practices of transnational companies in Britain (Edwards et al., 1995), where the numbers of such companies was estimated. Another large, ongoing research project from mainstream British research, which accepts the importance of establishing population characteristics, are the Workforce Industrial Relations (WIRS) surveys. Focussed work using such population data is also possible. To illustrate the possibilities, the work of Ackroyd and Muzio into change and reorganization in the legal profession

in the last twenty years will be considered (Ackroyd and Muzio, 2007; Ackroyd and Muzio, 2008).

Solicitors' firms have been studied in Britain and elsewhere through small sample studies and single case studies using ethnography. The leading model of professional firms, the managed professional business (MPB), originated in relatively small-scale studies of law firms. Research had brought to light evidence of decline in working conditions and employment prospects of lawyers, leading some to argue for the deprofessionalization, even the proletarianization, of the occupation. On the other hand, it also seemed clear that solicitor firms had been growing in size and importance in Britain and America, with very large and highly profitable firms emerging. A feature that was thought to unite these two trends was the rise of professional management. A key feature of the MPB model was the suggestion that the management of law firms was a growing phenomenon somehow implicated in the pattern of change. By considering general trends provided by data relating to the legal profession in Britain, however, Ackroyd and Muzio were able to show little evidence of any rise of a managerial cadre. Population figures showed the decline of administrative employees and a sustained rise in the numbers of employed solicitors. Professional hierarchies were growing, with longer promotion intervals and a more complex professional division of labour. As a result, understanding the generative mechanism explaining change in the organization of the legal profession was greatly refined and developed, and an alternative model of solicitor firms, this time constructed around the idea of professional reorganization, was put forward (Ackroyd and Muzio, 2007).

The logic of discovery

Similar considerations apply here as in generative studies; this kind of research design does not simply involve reconceptualizing the subject of the research. To the extent that research, which sets generative mechanisms against measured features of context involves identifying and characterizing the latter, abduction is part of the contribution of the research. However, examination of the conditions constituting the existence of generative mechanism is also being undertaken here. This involves retroductive logic (Danermark et al., 2002).

Research designs involving and evaluating active intervention

Realists do not assume that detachment is essential for effective research practice, despite the fact that much realist research adopts this posture. Although realist researchers and scholars are usually scrupulous in their approach to data collection and evaluation, they think complete detachment in research or scholarship is unlikely. At the same time, use by realists of the alternative – engaged research – is limited (Crotty, 1998; Byrne, 2002). The most important research realists do in this area is to evaluate and critique the engagements of others – most obviously policy-makers (Pawson and Tilley, 1997).

However, realist ideas do not rule out direct engagement of researchers in trying to induce change as part of research activity, and this type of research has its advocates (Byrne, 2002, pp. 164–5). Realist social theory (Archer, 1995) suggests that the social world is constructed. Thus, all groups (small work teams, multinational corporations, and whole societies) are constructed and reconstructed by the people constituting them – though the outcome of interaction is not equally in the control of constituent groups. Because outcomes are affected by actions of participants, it is obvious that any research – being itself an intervention in social relationships – will influence what occurs in the situations under study and beyond. Such an acknowledgement goes well beyond the recognition of so-called 'experimenter effects', in which the act of research can affect its outcome. In small-scale research, especially where the investigator participates with the groups under investigation, there is a real likelihood that the act of investigation will influence – and

even significantly change – the situation being investigated. In realist informed research, this is not taken as detrimental to the research.

Indeed, it can be argued that a research project that merely interprets data will not effectively test the nature and strength of existing generative mechanisms. More to the point, it will not discover what is possible in redirecting and changing existing mechanisms. If so, the role of research need not be simply to interpret the meaning of data, and to set out what the likely outcomes of causal processes will be. Researchers may intervene in social processes and attempt actively to change the relationships and institutions to find out the limits of the powers of groups and the possibilities of inducing change through action.

Action research

Action research deliberately seeks change in the behaviour and practices of a group under study. It usually involves a group formulating a diagnosis of its own behavioural patterns, deciding (with an external researcher) what needs to be done to produce change and then undertaking the change. This approach to research, which utilizes self-diagnosis followed by intervention, has had some success as a technique for inducing organizational change and of workgroups achieving greater autonomy in the process. The research design was invented by Kurt Lewin (Cooke, 1999), and the techniques have been developed since (Cooke and Wolfram Cox, 2005). Today, versions of action research are particularly advocated for use in public sector organizations – sometimes by espoused realists (O' Hanlon, 1996; Winter and Munn-Giddings, 2001; Le May and Lathlean, 2001).

Experience shows that action research cannot easily prevail against the generative mechanisms already in operation in the workplace. There are considerable forces working against the possibilities of emancipatory workplace change. Although induced change using action research is theoretically possible, successful innovations are in fact extremely rare. Against this background, the career of action research as a research design and practice is interesting. From being perceived as a research design with radical possibilities in the nineteen forties and fifties, it has become increasingly viewed as a managerial technique for achieving more productivity from work groups. (Cooke argues that the left has been written out of action research, and though this is true, so is the proposition that the left have seldom accepted that direct action in the workplace is likely to be effective. From this viewpoint, that action research was ever thought likely to be effective as a means of producing radical change, is the most remarkable thing about it). Recent proposals for action research in the public sector (some of them claiming realist auspices) are best seen as defensive manoeuvring. Largely proposed by public-sector professionals or academics allied to such professionals, current interest in action research may reflect the embattled situation of public-sector employees caught between the competing demands of new public managers and an increasingly consumerist and litigious public. Certainly some of the exponents of action research in the public sector see its adoption as a tool of professional self-development rather than a means to emancipation.

Evaluation research and policy critique

Recently researchers influenced by critical realism have made significant advances in the area of evaluation research (Pawson and Tilley, 1997), principally by advancing a powerful critique of existing research into evaluation, which is dominated by positivistic, quasi-experimental designs. Pawson and Tilley also suggest that adequate evaluation of policy is likely to be developed on the basis of understanding of generative mechanisms, and the contexts in which they operate. This work is part of a broader movement to show the relevance of realist ideas about research to policy (Fleetwood and Ackroyd, 2004; Carter and New, 2004).

Pawson and Tilley (1997) have made a powerful case for the relevance of realism to evaluation research. They propose that existing policy-related research is handicapped by positivist design. It seeks to clarify which 'variables' are associated with (and so assumed to cause) the undesired behaviour or outcomes that policy seeks to correct (Campbell and Stanley, 1966). But the conception of why and how misbehaviour occurs is wrong. The procedure of looking for statistical associations between, say, the levels of reported crime and the policy interventions designed to curb it, will never properly interpret the connections involved. While the aim of research is to see how strongly correlated, say, the reduction of measured incidents of crime are following changes of policy intervention, there is little chance of noting the operation of generative mechanisms. In this way, Pawson and Tilley show that current evaluation research is grounded in a faulty analysis of social processes. They show there are substantial flaws in both the implicit theory of behaviour in the approach and the methodology used to study it. If, on the other hand, research is aimed at clarifying the mechanisms which produce outcomes, and to understanding the contingencies that may prevent the expected outcomes from occurring, this can yield better explanations of why, and in what circumstances, policies are likely to be effective.

Knowledge of causal processes and the way they work (or do not work) makes realism relevant to the critique of established policy and orthodox thinking. Realist ideas about social processes have more general applications than are currently envisaged. Pawson and Tilley have identified what is a potentially very large area of opportunity for the application of realist ideas to the criticism of policy and conventional thinking. Indeed, to use a graphic metaphor, what they are doing in the application of realism to evaluation research is starting a war by mounting an attack on a heavily defended part of an enemy coast. On the other hand, much existing policy and habitual action is based on 'received wisdom' and not on research findings of any kind. This is thinking without very much sophistication and little empirical support. The discourses of the powerful are often sustained mainly by spin and impression management (Fairclough, 2000). And yet, power is exercised on the assumption that those who do so really know what they are doing and have defensible policies. On the face of it, there is a large area of critical engagement with the discourses of the powerful for realists to open up, and this seems a more likely direction of effective and engaged activity by realists committed to change than some other types of research involving intervention.

CONCLUDING COMMENTS

It seems to be clear from this review that the applicability of realism to many areas of organization studies is obvious, and it has a large and growing following of researchers in the field. As this review also indicates, however, in the methodology field, realist practitioners are behind the game. Paradoxically, in view of the importance of realist doctrines and the achievements of realist social science in the past, the exponents of other paradigms have a much more developed rationale for the research they do. They also have convenient techniques for research that can be readily taken off the shelf for use in research projects. Since realist techniques are both scarce and underdeveloped, the accidental production of realist research is unlikely. Moreover, the entrenched position of other paradigms means that publishing realist research is more difficult than other kinds of work. As Mutch et al. (2007) observe in their editorial to a special issue of the journal *Organization*, several of the contributors to which were realists, there is a considerable problem for researchers working with approaches that are methodologically unorthodox. Reviewers tend not to recognize the assumptions, procedures, and conclusions of such research as valid, because they do not fall squarely into categories that they recognize. Hopefully, however, this chapter is a small contribution to developing the perception that there are standard procedures for the realist-inclined researcher to use, which have a clear rationale, and which allow insightful research to be undertaken.

This may be so even if, for the most part, the forgoing discussion was merely commenting on successful practices that are already routinely employed by researchers.

Finally, it is important to note that this overview is incomplete. This account excludes areas of research that might legitimately be included. There is much more in the organizational field – research that takes up the consideration of language and culture for example – actually or potentially the subjects for realist research that have been discussed here, but which nonetheless are legitimate areas of work for realist inspired researchers. This is perhaps unfortunate, but we have to start somewhere.

ACKNOWLEDGEMENTS

The author would like to thank the participants at the 10th Annual Conference of the Forum for Business Ethics and Business Culture of the German Philosophical Association for comments on some of the key propositions contained in this chapter, and especially Peter Koslowski and Peter Clark. Thanks also to the editors for helpful and constructive comments in the course of the writing. David Buchanan, in particular, was exemplary for his forbearance and humour throughout what turned out to be an unexpectedly difficult gestation. Finally, thanks are also due to Steve Fleetwood and Paul Thompson for comments on the completed chapter.

REFERENCES

Ackroyd, S. (2004) 'Methodology for management and organization studies: some implications of critical realism', in Fleetwood, S. and Ackroyd, S. (eds), *Critical Realist Applications in Organization and Management Studies*, London: Routledge, pp. 137–63.

Ackroyd, S., Batt, R., Tolbert, P. and Thompson, P. (2005) (eds) *The Oxford Handbook of Work and Organization*, Oxford: Oxford University Press.

Ackroyd, S. and Fleetwood, S. (2000) *Realist Perspectives on Management and Organization Studies*, London: Routledge.

Ackroyd, S. and Muzio, D. (2007) 'The reconstructed professional firm: explaining change in English legal practices', *Organization Studies*, 28(5): 729–47.

Ackroyd, S. and Muzio, D. (2008) 'Reasserting the reconstructed professional firm: a rejoinder to Brock', *Organization Studies*, 29(1): 151–6.

Archer, M. (1995) *Realist Social Theory: The Morphogenic Approach*. Cambridge: Cambridge University Press.

Archer, M., Bhaskar, R., Collier, A., Lawson, T. and Norrie, A. (1998) *Critical Realism: Essential Readings*, London: Routledge.

Bailey, K. (1994) *Typologies and Taxonomies: Applications in the Social Sciences*, London: Sage.

Bateson, N. (1984) *Data Construction in Social Surveys*, London: Allen and Unwin.

Bhaskar, R. (1978) 'A realist theory of science', Brighton: harvester, Sections Reprinted in Archer, M. et al., *Critical Realism: Essential Readings*, London: Routledge.

Bhaskar, R. (1989) *Reclaiming Reality*, London: Verso.

Blaikie, N. (2000) *Designing Social Research: The Logic of Anticipation*, Cambridge: Polity Press.

Blau, P. (1955) *The Dynamics of Bureaucracy*, Chicago: Univerity of Chicago Press.

Bryman, A. (1988) *Quantity and Quality in Social Research*, London: Routledge.

Burawoy, M. (1979) *Manufacturing Consent: Changes in the Labour Process Under Monopoly Capitalism*, Chicago: University of Chicago Press.

Burawoy, M. (1985) *The Politics of Production: Factory Regimes Under Capitalism and Socialism*, London: Verso.

Burawoy, M. (2007) 'Multi-case ethnography', Paper presented at Sociology Symposium, Newcastle University, September.

Byrne, D. (2002) *Interpreting Quantitative Data*, London: Sage.

Campbell, D.T. and Stanley, J.C. (1966) *Experimental and Quasi-Experimental Designs for Research*, Chicago: Rand McNally & Company.

Carter, B. and New, C. (2004) *Making Realism Work: Realist Social Theory and Empirical Research*, London: Routledge.

Clark, P. (2000) *Organizations in Action: Competition Between Contexts*, London: Routledge.

Cooke, B. (1999) 'Writing the Left out of management theory: the historiography of management change', *Organization*, 6(1): 81–105.

Cooke, B. and Wolfram-Cox, J. (2005) (eds) *Fundamentals of Action Research Volume I: The Acknowledged Founders*, London: Sage Publications.

Crotty, M. (1998) *Foundations of Social Research*, London: Sage Publications.

Danermark, B. Ekstrom, M. Jakobsen and J. Ch Karlsson, (2002) *Explaining Society: Critical Realism in the Social Sciences*, London: Routlege.

Delbridge, R. (1998) *Life on the Line in Contemporary Manufacturing*, Oxford: Oxford University Press.

Delbridge, R. (2004) 'Working in teams: ethnographic evidence from two "high performance" workplaces', in Fleetwood, S. and Ackroyd, S. (eds), *Critical Realist Applications in Organization and Management Studies*, London: Routledge, pp. 257–73.

Denzin, N. and Lincoln, Y. (1994) (eds) *Handbook of Qualitative Research*, London: Sage Publications.

Easton, G. (2008) 'Case study research: a critical realist approach', Department of Marketing working paper, Lancaster University.

Edwards, P. (1986) *Conflict at Work: A Materialist Analysis of Workplace Relations*, Oxford: Blackwell.

Edwards, P. and Scullion, H. (1982) *The Social Organization of Industrial Conflict: Control and Resistance in the Workplace*, Oxford: Blackwell.

Edwards, P., Marginson, P., Armstrong, P. and Purcell, J. (1995) 'Extending beyond borders: multinational companies and the international management of labour', *International Journal of Human Resource Management*, 6: 702–19.

Elias, N. (1956) 'Problems of involvement and detachment', *The British Journal of Sociology*, 7 (3): 226–52.

Elias, N. (1987) *Involvement and Detachment*, Oxford: Basil Blackwell.

Fairclough, N. (2000) *New labour, New Language*, London: Routlege.

Fleetwood, S. (2004) 'The ontology of organization and management studies', in Fleetwood, S. and Ackroyd, S. (eds), *Critical Realist Applications Organization and Management Studies*, London: Routledge.

Fleetwood, S. and Ackroyd, S. (eds) (2004) *Critical Realist Applications Organization and Management Studies*, London: Routledge.

Gouldner, A. (1954) *Wildcat Strike*, London: Routledge and Kegan Paul.

Gouldner, A. (1955) *Patterns of Industrial Bureaucracy*, Glencoe Ill: Free Press.

Haraszti, M. (1977) *A Worker in a Workers' State: Piece Rates in Hungary*, (trans M. Wright), Harmondsworth: Penguin.

Harré, R. (1972) *The Philosophies of Science*, Oxford: Oxford University Press.

Harré, R. (1979) *Social Being*, Oxford: Blackwell.

Harré, R. and Secord, P.F. (1972) *The Explanation of Social Behaviour*, Oxford: Blackwell.

Harrison, D. and Easton, G. (2002) 'Temporally embedded case comparison in industrial marketing research', in Fleetwood, S. and Ackroyd, S. (eds) *Realism in Action in Management and Organization Studies*, London: Routledge.

Keat, R. and Urry, J. (1975) *Social Theory as Science*, London: Routledge.

Kirkpatrick, I., Ackroyd, S. and Walker, R. (2004) *The New Managerialism and the Public Service Professions*, Basingstoke: Palgrave.

Layder, D. (1993) *New Strategies in Social Research*, Cambridge: Polity Press.

Layder, D. (1998) *Sociological Practice: Linking Theory and Social Research*, London: Sage Publications.

Le May A. and Lathlean, J. (2001) 'Action research: a design with potential', *Journal of Research in Nursing*, 6(1): 502–09.

Lupton, T. (1963) *On the Shop Floor*, Oxford: Pergamon.

May, T. (1997) *Social Research: Issues, Methods and Process*, Buckingham: Open University Press.

Marsh, C. (1982) *The Survey Method*, London: Allen and Unwin.

Marsh, C. (1988) *Exploring Data: An Introduction to Data Analysis for Social Scientists*, Cambridge: Polity Press.

Miles, M. and Huberman, A.M. (1994) *Qualitative Data Analysis*, Beverley Hills: Sage Publications.

Mutch, A. (2007) 'Reflexivity and the institutional entrepreneur: a historical exploration', *Organization Studies*, 28(7): 1123–40.

Mutch, A., Delbridge, R. and Ventresca, M. (2006) 'Situating organizational action: the relational sociology of organizations', *Organization*, 13(5): 607–25.

Muzio, D., Ackroyd, S. and Chanlat, J-F. (2008) *Redirections in the Study of Expert Labour*, Basingstoke: Palgrave.

O'Hanlon, D. (1996) *Action Research in Educational Settings*, London: Falmer Press.

Pawson, R. (1989) *A Measure for Measures*, London: Routledge.

Pawson, R. and Tilly N. (1997) *Realistic Evaluation*, London: Sage Publications.

Porter, S. (1993) 'Critical realist ethnography: the case of racism and professionalism in a medical setting', *Sociology*, 27(4): 591–609.

Reed, M. (1985) *Redirections in Organizational Analysis*, London: Tavistock.

Robson, C. (2002) *Real World Research: A Resource for Social Scientists and Practitioner-Researchers*, Oxford: Basil Blackwell.

Sayer, A. (1992) *Method in Social Science: A Realist Approach*, London: Routledge.

Sayer, A. (2000) *Realism and Social Science*, London: Sage Publications.

Sayer, A. (2004) 'Why critical realism?', in Fleetwood, S. and Ackroyd, S. (eds), *Critical Realist Applications Organization and Management Studies*, London Routledge, pp. 6–20.

Selznick, P. (1948) *TVA and the Grass Roots: A Study in the Sociology of Formal Organization*, Glencoe Ill: University of California Press.

Siggelkow, N. (2007) 'Persuasion with case studies', *Academy of Management Journal*, 50(1): 20–4.

Smith, C. (2005) 'Beyond convergence and divergence: explaining variations in organizational practices and forms', in Ackroyd, S., Batt, R., Tolbert, P. and Thompson, P. (2005) (eds), *The Oxford Handbook of Work and Organization*, Oxford: Oxford University Press, pp. 620–35.

Smith, C. and Meiksins, P. (1995) 'System, society and dominance effects in cross-national organizational analysis', *Work, Employment and Society*, 9(2): 241–68.

Taylor, P. and Bain, P. (2005) 'An assembly line in the head: the call centre labour process', *Industrial Relations Journal*, 30(2): 101–17.

Thompson, P. (1996) 'Redesigning production through teamworking', *International Journal of Operations and Production Management*, 16(2): 103–18.

Willis, P. (1977) *Learning to Labour*, Aldershot: Ashgate.

Winter, R. and Munn-Giddings, C. (2001) *A Handbook for Action Research in Health and Social Care*, London: Routledge.

32

Discourse Analysis in Organizational Research: Methods and Debates

Nelson Phillips and MariaLaura Di Domenico

INTRODUCTION

Discourse analysis is one of a number of approaches to the study of the social world that grew out of the linguistic turn in social science (e.g. Rorty, 1992; Alvesson and Kärreman, 2000a). From the perspective of the linguistic turn, language does not simply reflect a pre-existing reality, but is the key to understanding how social reality is itself constituted (Berger and Luckmann, 1966; Gergen, 1999). Language and its effects are not a problem to be managed as in positivism, but become the core concern of social science (Winch, 1958). As a result, linguistic methods of research, such as conversation analysis, narrative analysis and rhetorical analysis, become the social scientists' primary tools, and discourse analysis in particular becomes an important approach to the study of the constitution of the social world.

Although there are many approaches to discourse analysis, they all share a common interest in exploring how elements of social reality are constituted through talk and text.

As Hardy (2001: 25) argues, '[s]cholars are increasingly conceptualizing societies, institutions, and identities as discursively constructed', and discourse analysis provides tools for investigating this process of discursive construction. Discourse analysis not only involves 'practices of data collection and analysis, but also a set of metatheoretical and theoretical assumptions and a body of research claims and studies' (Wood and Kroger, 2000: x). It focuses on the production of texts as a fundamental part of the construction of social reality and provides a theoretical frame and methods of data identification, collection, and analysis.

In organization research, discourse analysis is an increasingly common theoretical and methodological framework for exploring the social production of organizational and interorganizational phenomena (e.g., Alvesson and Kärreman, 2000b; Phillips and Hardy, 2002). In addition to an ever-growing number of articles using discourse analysis, there are conferences dedicated to organizational discourse, handbooks on the subject (e.g., Grant, Hardy, Oswick, and Putnam, 2004), and several special issues have been published in various journals (e.g. *Organization Studies* 2004, Vol. 25, Issue 1). All in all, it is clear that '[d]iscourse analysis has become an increasingly popular method for examining the linguistic elements in the construction of social phenomena ... [and] has been increasingly adopted by organization and management scholars' (Vaara, Kleymann, and Seristo, 2004: 3).

In this chapter, we discuss discourse analysis as a research method in organizational research. We begin with a general discussion of discourse analysis as a method. We then present a range of examples of work that has been done in organization research from this perspective and summarize the steps involved in conducting a discourse study. We go on to discuss the opportunities and challenges that discourse analysis presents researchers interested in studying organizational phenomena. We conclude with some final comments regarding the future of discourse analysis in organizational research.

DISCOURSE ANALYSIS: AN OVERVIEW

If we are to define discourse analysis, we need to start with an understanding of what we mean by the term 'discourse'. Unfortunately, like many of the fundamental concepts in social science, the meaning of 'discourse' is highly contested and ambiguous. Van Dijk, in the first chapter of his two-volume introduction to discourse analysis, explains the situation as follows:

> It would be nice if we could squeeze all we know about discourse into a handy definition. Unfortunately, as is also the case for such related concepts as 'language', 'communication', 'interaction', 'society' and 'culture', the notion of discourse is essentially fuzzy. (van Dijk, 1997b: 1)

Our challenge in this section, then, is to develop an understanding of discourse at a fairly broad level, useful in understanding organizational discourse analysis.

Part of the complexity, of course, is that discourse is a term that is commonly used in everyday speech. When used in this way, it generally refers to some form of 'language in use'. The focus is generally on public speech, or on spoken language more generally, as when one says that something has become 'a part of common discourse'. Or when, as in the Merriam-Webster dictionary (2008) definition, discourse is understood as the 'verbal interchange of ideas'.

However, discourse is also used more broadly. In this second sense, it refers to sets of ideas and the ways of expressing them such as the 'discourse of environmentalism' or Descartes' use of the term in the title of his (1637)[1960] book 'Discourse on Method'. The focus here is not so much on the specifics of the language used, but more on the underlying concepts and ideas contained in a particular set of texts. Furthermore, when studying this sort of discourse the focus is often on written texts rather than talk, and on the cumulative meaning of a number of such texts.

Discourse analysts combine and extend these commonsense definitions. While they are interested in language in use (generally both talk and text), it is language in use *in a context* that interests them. And while they are interested in ideas, they are also interested in how these ideas come to be constructed in texts and how they affect the context in which they occur. The concept of discourse in this more technical sense, therefore, has three main dimensions: pieces of talk or text, the social context in which they occur, and the body of texts that gives them meaning. In other words, discourse in this sense includes pieces of talk or text as they affect and are affected by the social context in which they appear, and by the texts and ideas they draw on and influence in turn.

Discourse analysis

As we discussed in the foregoing section, discourse analysis shares the concern with the meaningfulness of social life that characterizes all qualitative approaches. Unlike more traditional qualitative methods, however, discourse analysis adopts a different but complementary focus. It does not take the social world as it is and seeks to understand the meaning of this world for participants like, for example, ethnography or narrative analysis. Instead, it tries to explore the ways in which the socially produced ideas and objects that populate the world came to be through discourse.

This focus on processes of social construction is the central contribution of discourse analysis. Where other qualitative methodologies work to understand or interpret social reality, discourse analysis endeavours to uncover the ways in which it was produced. It examines how language, broadly defined, constructs social phenomena, not how it reveals them. In other words, discourse analysis views discursive activity as *constitutive* of the social world, not a route to understanding it.

The process of discourse analysis begins with texts. Discourses are embodied and enacted in a variety of texts, but exist beyond the individual texts that compose them (Chalaby, 1996). Texts are thus both the building blocks of discourse and a material manifestation of it.

> Texts are the sites of the emergence of complexes of social meanings, produced in the particular history of the situation of production, that record in partial ways the histories of both the participants in the production of the text and of the institutions that are "invoked" or brought into play, indeed a partial history of the language and the social system. (Kress, 1995: 122)

Texts may take a variety of forms, including written texts, spoken words, pictures, symbols, artefacts, etc. (Grant et al., 1998). What is interesting from a discourse analysis perspective is how they are made meaningful – how they draw on other texts and other discourses, how and to whom they are disseminated, and the ways in which they are produced, received and consumed – and what effect collections of texts have on the social context in which they occur.

Nevertheless, the word 'discourse' is often used in another sense by discourse analysts. In addition to talking about discourse as a general category of phenomena, discourse analysts talk about 'the discourse' or 'a

discourse'. When used in this sense they are referring to a particular collection of texts. More specifically, when used in this sense, they mean an inter-related set of texts, and related practices of production, dissemination, and reception, that brings an object into being (Parker, 1992). The addition of this level of analysis is one of the important differences that differentiate discourse analysis from other forms of interpretive linguistic methods.

For example, the collection of texts of various kinds, and the related discursive practices, that make up the discourse of psychiatry brought the notion of an 'unconscious mind' into existence in the mid-nineteenth century (Foucault, 1965). Prior to the appearance of this discourse, there was no concept of the unconscious that could be used to understand and explain human mental processes. Since the appearance of this discourse it is widely taken for granted (in Western countries at least) that humans have something called an unconscious and our idea of how the human mind functions has, therefore, fundamentally changed. The discourse of psychiatry constituted a particular social object, the unconscious, and made it available as a resource for social action.

Discourse analysis, therefore, is the study of discourse and the collections of texts and contexts in which they occur. More formally, it is *the structured and systematic study of collections of interrelated texts, the processes of their production, dissemination and consumption, and their effects on the context in which they occur*. Discourse analysis, therefore, generally involves some form of textual analysis, some sort of structured investigation of the broader discourse of which the focal texts are a part, and an investigation of the social context in which the texts appear melded together to produce insights into the social world.

Mapping approaches to discourse analysis

While the above discussion hopefully provides the reader with a clearer understanding

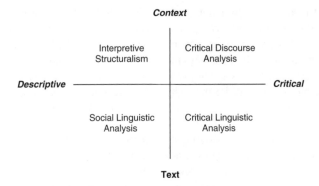

Figure 32.1   Different approaches to discourse analysis

of discourse analysis, it is intentionally broad. It is not surprising, then, that there are many different approaches that fit this definition and anyone interested in discourse analysis faces the challenge of making sense of the diversity of the field. Phillips and Hardy (2002) provide one frame and suggest that approaches to discourse analysis can be categorized along with two key theoretical dimensions. The first dimension concerns the relative importance of text versus context in the research. The second dimension concerns the degree to which the researcher focuses on power. Figure 32.1 combines these two dimensions to identify four main perspectives in discourse analysis.

The vertical axis shows the continuum between **text** and **context**. The need for a three-dimensional approach to discourse analysis means that researchers should include text *and* context in their studies, and consider discourse 'as a constitutive part of its local and global, social and cultural contexts' (Fairclough, 1995: 29). While this represents an important theoretical ideal, conducting empirical research is another matter, since researchers are forced to make choices about the data they select – no researcher can study everything. Consequently, empirical studies tend to focus either more closely either on the broad social context or on particular pieces of text (Burman and Parker, 1993; Keenoy et al., 1997; Alvesson and Kärreman, 2000b). Some studies will focus on the microanalysis of particular texts; others will conduct a broader sweep of the discursive elements of particular

contexts; and, since this is a continuum not a dichotomy, some studies combine some elements of both.

The horizontal axis reflects the choice between **critical** approaches, which include an explicit interest in the dynamics of power and ideology, and more **descriptive** approaches that focus on the explication of the way in which a particular social reality has been constructed. Critical studies are relatively common in discourse analysis, where the connection between discursive activity and the constitution of various sorts of knowledge has been the focus of a number of studies. This is largely due to the early influence of Foucault's work and the accessibility and practical utility of Fairclough's (1992) methodological prescriptions. The role of discourse theory in reinvigorating critical research agendas has also led to a substantial body of critically informed empirical work in organizational research.

Not all work is so explicitly interested in power, however, and many studies explore the constructive effects of discourse without explicitly considering the political dynamics. Important bodies of work in disciplines such as sociology (Gergen, 1991) or psychology (e.g., Harré, 1995; Parker, 1992, 2005; Potter and Wetherell, 1987; Wetherell, Taylor and Yates, 2001), as well as organizational research (e.g., Hirsch, 1986; Dunford and Jones, 2000), have produced a stream of research that is more focused on descriptions of constructive processes than power and politics per se. Rather than exploring who benefits or is disadvantaged by a socially constructed 'reality', these researchers are more interested in understanding the way in which discourses ensure that certain phenomena are created, reified, and taken for granted and come to constitute that 'reality'.

By combining the two axes, four major perspectives that are adopted in discourse analysis can be identified. They are social linguistic analysis, interpretive structuralism, critical discourse analysis, and critical linguistic analysis (for other useful categorizations see Putnam and Fairhurst, 2000 and Alvesson and Kärreman, 2000b). It is important to keep in mind that the dimensions of this framework are continua, not simple categories or dichotomies. The endpoints of the axis of the framework represent ideal types in the Weberian sense: not all research will necessarily fall neatly into a particular category. However, these four categories do allow us to identify and categorize quite different styles of empirical research.

ORGANIZATIONAL DISCOURSE: DOMINANT THEMES AND EMPIRICAL FOCI

Organization and management scholars have used discourse analysis to explore a wide range of empirical topics. We have chosen four topics – gender, identity, organizational change, and the natural environment – to discuss here. Our list is not intended to be exhaustive, nor is it meant to represent the 'best' studies. Rather it is indicative of the sorts of empirical studies that have been done and that can be done using this approach. This will, hopefully, provide the reader with an appreciation of how discourse analysis can be *done in practice* and the range of methodological tools that can be employed by researchers.

Gender

Discourse methods have been common in gender research since the mid 1970s (West,

Lazar and Kramarae, 1997; Spender, 1980). This rise in prominence was inspired, at least in part, by the upsurge of the women's movement and feminist sociopolitical rhetoric. However, just as gender research took sometime to take root in organization research, it was only quite recently that discourse as a method of study of gender issues developed within organization research.

The literature combining the interrelated areas of gender, discourse, and organization can be categorized into four broad areas, although these are not necessarily mutually exclusive and researchers may combine approaches or find their affiliation hard to categorize (Ashcraft, 2004). The first approach examines discourse as an expression or signifier of gender identity, defined in terms of what can be regarded as more fixed biological criteria or more socialized behaviours and norms. In other words, our gender shapes the texts we produce and research in this area examines the differences in, and the effects of, the interaction and speech patterns of members of the opposite sex and in particular how men and women use language differently (Tannen, 1990, 1994). Second, there is stream of research that involves the performance of gender identities in terms of the enactment of masculinities or femininities as purposeful or subversive acts. The organization is conceptualized as a stage (Goffman, 1959), one of many platforms in everyday life in which we enact our gendered constructions through discursive interactions and organizational routines (Kondo, 1990). The third approach goes even further by advocating that organizations are themselves gendered discursive constructions; their inherent make-up and logic are emblematic of undercurrents of power and structures of inequality which tend to disadvantage female participants (Acker and van Houten, 1974; Kanter, 1977). Finally, the fourth looks at how macrolevel societal discourse is manifest in organizations and how notions of both gender and organization are represented to actors in the wider society (Ashcraft and Flores, 2003). The broad societal discourses of gender and organization form the backdrop for more microorganizational activities, and the nature and effect of these wider societal discourses need to be understood.

As well as work that combines discourse analysis with the treatment of gender and organizations, some important research has also been more reflexive in examining the roots of gendered discourses within prevailing modes of academic enquiry and in the philosophical treatment of workplace subjects (Calás and Smircich, 1992; 1996; Mills and Tancred-Sheriff, 1992). For example, Runté and Mills (2006) critique the body of knowledge comprising theories of management and organization exploring issues of gender by arguing that gender tends to be addressed in ways that privilege masculinity and a distinctly masculinist project. They acknowledge four strands of research, which seek to embrace gender in management theory, namely gender and organizations; women in management; work-family conflict; and diversity management. Despite this, they put forward an account of a pervasive gendered discourse within the organizational literature, which can be traced back to 1950s discourses of family and work.

In terms of specific examples of discourse analysis, Garnsey and Rees (1996) examine the discourse surrounding a major initiative, the 'Opportunity 2000 campaign', a business-led campaign supported by the UK government to increase women's participation in the workforce and, in particular, in managerial roles. They were particularly interested in the part played by discourse in the *enactment* of identified inequality. Through an examination of particular policy texts, they show that the persistence of inequalities may, without apparent intention, be encoded in language. The specific texts chosen for analysis comprised four printed texts from three different sources, each representing a broad spectrum of ideological standpoints towards opportunities for women. One strongly supported the campaign, two provided a more balanced but critical treatment of it, and one was more challenging of it. Methodologically, they demonstrate how discourse analysis provides a tool for exposing the contradictions in the

way 'flexibility' is used, and the agendas behind what are purported to be neutral facades. They connect with wider social contexts of action by providing an empirical demonstration of how language on a micro level can perpetuate and embed ideology on a wider more macrolevel. Specific tools used included an initial content analysis, whereby the number of times specific discursive themes (e.g. 'family-friendly' policies, business reasons for the employment of women) arose within the texts was counted. Analysis using techniques from critical linguistics (Fowler, 1991) were also employed. These included close readings of texts to expose three linguistic techniques: transitivity, where the relationship between subject and object is conveyed or passed over through the use of, for example, the active or passive voice; lexical structure, a method exploring hierarchies of vocabulary which reinforce particular concepts; and modality, which reveals the stance or viewpoint of the writer(s).

Ainsworth (2002) also uses discourse analysis to examine the overlap of gender and age identity in the context of the older unemployed (defined as 45 years and over). She builds upon the tradition of critical discourse analysis and specifically work into 'discourses of difference' (Wodak, 1996). The texts analyzed are sourced from a public parliamentary inquiry, including the final report and texts leading to the production of the final report. The latter included newspaper advertisements, media releases, submissions, transcripts of public hearings, and parliamentary proceedings. Through an analysis of these texts, she shows how discourse analysis provided a means of studying processes of identity construction and argues in support of a fundamentally gendered view of age identity. Various levels of methodological analysis are used that look at broader and more microlevel phenomena.

The first stage of data analysis involved a pilot phase in which a sample of texts from the commencement and closure of the inquiry were examined using comparative textual analysis (Fairclough, 1995). The discourse-historical method (Gill, 1993a,

1993b; Wetherell and Potter, 1992) was used to look at textual patterns of similarity and difference in versions of identity and their link with context. Intertextual analysis (Fairclough, 1999) was used to investigate the links between different policy documents as inquiry texts. Techniques from critical linguistics (Fowler, 1996; Kress, 2001) were also employed in order to focus on microlevel language practice. For example, the researcher examined how texts can be constituted through the choices made concerning what is excluded/included, and foregrounded/backgrounded in terms of topics, actors and themes. These were also combined with conversation analysis, a method sometimes characterized as distinct from discourse analysis that focuses on the actual coordination of talk in interaction, and on microlevel language practice. Documents were used to show how the inquiry texts produce discursive outcomes whereby certain groups were discursively constructed in competition with other groups in the labour market, providing evidence of a hidden discursive struggle for recognition. The article demonstrates the discursive processes involved in these struggles and how argumentation strategies were used to promote what Ainsworth characterizes as male versions of older worker identity that are constructed as a 'disadvantaged group', and the consequent suppression of the feminine advantage (the 'flexible female').

In some ways, the article draws a similar point to the article by Garnsey and Rees (1996). The analytic lens allowed Ainsworth (2002) to theorize the repeated use of the term 'flexibility' and how it featured in this discursive shift which 'led to the naturalization of a lexical register in relation to employment that obscured its ideological basis ... Such condensation contributed to the reification of work structures and arrangements as the 'new reality' of the labour market' (p. 597).

Identity

There has been a significant body of work on identity in organizational research and research into identity has itself been subject to a linguistic turn in recent decades (Brown, 1997, 2001) with discourse analysis being applied to a range of subthemes in this area. These include social identity (e.g. Phillips and Hardy, 1997), organizational or corporate identity (e.g. Albert and Whetten, 1985; Salzer-Morling, 1998), national identity (e.g. Jack and Lorbiecki, 2007), and individual identity (e.g. Holmer-Nadeson, 1996; Phillips and Hardy, 1997). In line with shifts in approaches in areas such as gender studies, which often markedly overlap with questions and concerns of identity, research has moved from more static definitions of identity towards conceptualizations that embrace more fluid notions of identity that may be subject to change and reformulation in different contexts.

Understanding oneself as a part of a defined organizational setting, or of a prescribed occupational grouping, has a significant impact upon our self-constructions and our articulation of individual identity. This also affects our sense of shared or group belonging. Organizations often possess various collective identities that are shared, and sometimes resisted, by their members. Thus, the relation between the organizational sphere and other spheres of our everyday lives, such as home and leisure places/spaces, and identity can be understood from a discursive standpoint. Both individual and collective identities are the outcome of discursive linguistic practices, which frame social interactions.

If we consider the article by Phillips and Hardy (1997) in which they examine the UK refugee system, we can see the way in which there is a discursive struggle over the appropriation of individual identity reflecting a complex dynamic of power among different interest groups. Their empirical work uses discourse analysis to show that the purported discourse of an objectively rational process being used to frame the determination of refugees as 'genuine' or otherwise in fact conceals a more ill-defined discursive construction of multiple refugee 'identities'. They show that multiple organizations play a role in the determination of refugee status through their discursive practices. Different organizations were found to mobilize competing refugee identities. For instance, the government deployed categories of 'political' refugee fleeing persecution versus 'economic migrant' in search of better economic prospects, while refugee organizations such as the Refugee Forum discursively constructed refugees as willing and able individuals who could play an equal and dynamic part in British society. These various refugee identities thus exposed different organizational identities in terms of their interests and power effects.

Therefore, refugees are constituted through the discursive mechanisms of various relevant organizations. Building on this work, Phillips and Hardy (1999), in a study on the Canadian refugee system, expand this focus by elaborating upon the ways in which refugees' identities are not only produced by discourses occurring within the refugee system itself, but are also affected by broader discourses existing at a macrosocietal level. Therefore, broader societal discourses of human rights, sovereignty, paternalism, and empowerment are manifest as discursive struggles within the particular context. This illustrates the dynamic effect and interrelationship between specific sites and contexts and wider articulations of meaning and societal structures. Specifically, they critique the contextual links between broader sociopolitical discourses of immigration and the discursive practices and behaviours of individuals engaged in the system itself. A sample of cartoons was analyzed to show how the societal immigration discourse helps to constitute refugees. Political cartoons as caricatures of the social order are used, as they provide a narrative that taps into common perceptions and stereotypes. Their purpose is often to highlight certain events, claims, and contradictions to put across or ridicule political messages. The use of humour in this way provides a useful lens into discursive struggles and articulations. A total of 127 cartoons derived from Canadian newspapers on refugees and immigration during the years 1987, 1988, and 1989 were

examined. Their analysis involved looking at the objects represented (i.e. the refugee, the government, the immigration system, and the public) and analyzing how each cartoon constituted these objects according to one or more of 18 themes. This study shows that different textual practices, in this case cartoons, can provide useful avenues for discourse analytic research. The basis of both of these articles is a concern with power relations and the performativity of language and the way in which identity categories are discursively created and fostered.

There are many other important and interesting works to which we wish to direct readers who hold an interest in organizational discourse and identity. For example, Alvesson's (1994, 2002) research into advertising executives provide rich illustrations of the way in which work-based identity is discursively constructed. In addition, the work by Anderson-Gough et al. (1998, 2000) shows how language is used as a device to control, socialize, and discipline new trainee accountants into colleague-defined practices so that they go on to assume specific ideas about their professional make-up. Similarly, in her fascinating study of graduate trainees, Fournier (1998) highlights the way in which two different groups of graduate trainees at a large service sector organization used divergent identity tactics and discursive mechanisms. While one group embraced the organizationally espoused discourse of 'careering', another group used a militant register as a means of resisting this more managerialist discourse. For the latter group, this construction of a 'militant other' had the effect of sidelining their positional authority within the organizational hierarchy.

Organizational change

A significant amount of research has been carried out examining various aspects of organizational change (Johnson, 1987; Pettigrew, 1990; Pettigrew et al., 2001; Tsoukas and Chia, 2002), including work on changing organizational structures and the agency of organizational members in affecting change processes. Moreover, connecting discourse to an organizational change perspective highlights how action and communication influence the way in which organizational change occurs (Ford and Ford, 1994; Sackmann, 1989). It is not surprising then that a significant body of work, therefore, exists on using discourse perspectives with issues of organizational change (see, for example, Morgan and Sturdy, 2000; O'Connor, 1995, 2000; Sillince, 1999).

Fairclough (2005) argues for attention to be paid to the relationships between changes that take place as part of social interactions and the texts that exist therein and change in organizational structures. In his view, discourse analysis, in line with a realist perspective, should distinguish between agency and structure in organizational research in order to address their relationship and the tensions arising between them, rather than treating them in isolation. He argues that there are four research issues that should be the concern of those applying discourse analysis to concerns of organizational change encapsulating what he terms 'transdisciplinary research'. These are the problems of 'emergence, hegemony, recontextualization, and operationalization'. Identification of the emergence of new discourses, their properties and their similarity to, or reconstitution from, existing discourses should be a key focus, which takes a longitudinal perspective across organizational time and space.

Hegemonic discourses pertain to concerns with why particular discourses emerge rather than other competing discourses. He cites 'new public management' and 'total quality management' as examples of dominant discourses that are pervasive in certain organizations. Recontextualization involves the distribution of hegemonic discourses between organizations and institutional level structures such as across boundaries among those operating at local, national, or international scales. Therefore, external discourse properties colonize and influence organizations, which are in turn reconstituted within the internal setting of the organization itself.

The actual operationalization of discourse includes their organizational indoctrination and enactment.

The work by Heracleous and Barrett (2001) provides an interesting example of a discourse approach combining both action and structure. In this article, they look at discourses as dualities involving both action and structure and the role of discursive 'deep' structures in facilitating or hindering organizational change. They do so by exploring the characteristics of discourses of various stakeholder groups and the way in which these shape organizational change brought about by the introduction of electronic trading in the London Insurance Market over a five-year period. By deep structures, they refer to 'rhetorical enthymemes that guide actors' interpretations and actions. By virtue of this influence, they are thus central for gaining a deep understanding of the trajectory and success or otherwise of intended and actualized change processes' (p. 755).

Applying discourse analytic techniques to data collected as part of a longitudinal interpretative case study, they examined interview transcripts, media reports, market publications, memorandums and strategy plans, and transcribed ethnographic observations as texts. Their methods of discourse analysis included the exploration of texts for central themes and intertextual analysis. For the authors, intertextual analysis is applied not only within but also across texts 'arising from the hermeneutic concern of searching for emergent patterns through continual movement between part and whole' (p. 761).

Their approach to discourse draws upon the fields of rhetoric and hermeneutics to illustrate the importance of context and temporality in change processes. Their findings reveal discursive shifts at both the communicative action and deep structure levels. Different stakeholder groups engendered different discourses. For example, brokers and underwriters were found to resist the change initiative of electronic trading championed by the market leaders. Their research presents a view of organizations as comprising fragmented, competing discourses with complementary discourses arising only infrequently. This is reflected by discursive conflict between stakeholder groups concerning the change processes, where even when fragile agreement to the change was presented at the communicative action level, this did not yield results and meaningful cooperation as it was based on potentially conflicting deep structures.

The natural environment

In recent years, the field of management and organizational research has witnessed a significant growth in interest in environmental research (e.g. Andersson and Bateman, 2000; Banerjee, 2001, 2003; Banerjee, Iyer, and Kahyap, 2003; Bansal, 2003; Bansal and Clelland, 2004; Bansal and Roth, 2000; Epstein and Roy, 2003; McKay, 2001; Rojsek, 2001; Winn and Angell, 2000). This is notable, particularly as the natural environment previously held a position of comparative theoretical neglect. Indeed, this reflects a discursive 'mainstreaming' both in academic circles and in wider society.

However, when it comes to discourse methods, this is still an area that remains underrepresented in comparison to some of the other themes identified earlier. Despite this, there is some interesting research that examines the social and discursively constructed elements of the environment, nature, and the countryside (e.g. Macnaghten, 1993). Research has also tackled the issues of rhetoric in communicating messages of environmentalism to public audiences and stakeholder groups and the growing political clout of an explicit ecological repertoire as a moral discourse (Grove-White, 1993). There is debate over the most effective way for the environmental movement, governments, and other relevant bodies to put across their messages. There have also been arguments over whether environmental organizations manage to engage citizens effectively in meaningful and sustained dialogue and whether grassroots or the more supralevel professional advocacy efforts are the way forward for public engagement and buy-in. Voluntary or mandatory practices for public participation in a 'green' agenda is also a contested terrain of political debate. Interesting research also critiques the degree of 'spin' evident in processes of environmental organizing and the manipulation of opinion through sophisticated discursive practices and frames (Brulle and Jenkins, 2006).

Driscoll (2006) is a good example of work that deploys discourse analysis to examine different issues of environmental management and sustainability. Driscoll looks at the Canadian forest sector to examine organizational legitimacy and the use of legitimating mechanisms. She argues that the discourse being used in the sector often operates on a superficial (or 'mystifying') rather than a substantive level. Specific language was found to be purposefully deployed in an attempt to change definitions of legitimacy that are not in their interests and to enhance their external performance record of sustainable forest management practice.

An interesting example of a study that uses discourse methods is that of Prasad and Elmes (2005), who are interested in the emphasis upon pragmatic considerations in the field of environmental management. Applying critical discourse analysis, they explicate the hegemonic dimensions of this theme of pragmatism and show how three core messages emerged within the discourse of practicality, namely economic utilitarianism, compromise, and interorganizational collaboration. Broadly surveying what they refer to as the 'Mega-Discourse' of environmental management, they provide detailed comments and critique of the overall and collective emphases placed in writings derived from articles based in scholarly journals, practitioner-oriented periodicals, popular books on the subject, corporate and public policy reports, and speeches by government and business leaders. Rather than providing any kind of microlevel analysis, theirs is more of a macrolevel account of what they see as the prominent components of the environmental management discourse and the impact that the apparent emphasis upon practicality may have.

Summing up: A general guide to discourse analysis

In summary, discourse analysis can be applied to both traditional and emerging areas of study in organizational research and has been used in a range of empirical and substantive topics, as demonstrated by the examples we have explored in the preceding section. Furthermore, despite the important differences across studies, a number of general steps can be discerned in the process of designing and conducting a discourse analytic study: the development of a research question, selecting a site, collecting data, analyzing data, and writing up the study (Phillips and Hardy, 2002). We will outline these general steps here as a starting point for those wanting to carry out a study.

First, discourse analytic studies start with a research question. A good research study combines scientific methods and theoretical savvy with a creative turn that surprises and interests a community of scholars. As with any creative process, there is no one best way to approach this process. However, we have found that beginning with an explicit research question is often an effective first step. A good research question provides a frame for making decisions about data collection and analysis, explains the motivation behind the study, and provides guidance for writing it up. This is not to say that an explicit research question is always required before beginning a study. However, we have found a clear research question to be very helpful in designing and carrying out a study.

The nature of the research question will obviously vary from study to study as it depends on a range of factors that vary from researcher to researcher and topic to topic. In our experience, there are four factors that are important in shaping the research question and that should be explicitly included in the framing of the research question: the research philosophy of the researcher; the nature of the object of study; the particular body of theory on which the researcher is drawing; and the particular contribution that the researcher hopes to make. When framed to include these

issues, the resulting research question will provide motivation for the study, provide a clear measure for deciding when the study is complete (and if it has been successful), and function to orient readers of the resulting research.

Second, a research site must be selected. The choice of a research site is generally based on two sets of considerations: theoretical concerns related to the research question, and more practical concerns about access and timing. Developing a research question beforehand is, of course, very useful in guiding the subsequent choice of site. While we would certainly recommend this approach as an effective way to proceed, especially in the case of inexperienced researchers, such a linear process is a luxury not always available to researchers. It is a common experience to be presented with an interesting, opportunistic research site for which a researcher then must develop research questions. Moreover, even when one begins with a research question, unforeseen problems – or opportunities – can require plans to be changed. Fascinating research insights can still be gained from serendipitous access and, to capitalize on them, researchers need to be receptive to all eventualities and able to juggle both theoretical and practical constraints in selecting a research site should the need arise. What is important is that the site makes sense based on the research question, the researcher has good access, and the site is theoretically interesting.

Third, the research must collect and manage an appropriate corpus of data. While site selection assumes ready access to texts, deciding on which texts to use as data is not simple. One important question concerns which of the various sources of material constitutes data in the case of discourse analysis? Generally, 'naturally occurring' texts – in the sense that they appear in the normal day-to-day activities of the research subjects – are considered a better source of data for discourse analysis. For example, if the research question concerns the discursive construction of an organization, naturally occurring texts might include the different kinds of archival data that organizations store, such as e-mails, memos, internal reports, minutes of meetings, annual reports, as well as texts that accumulate outside the firm such as media articles, government reports, advertisements, etc. In addition, conversations and meetings among members of the organization and presentations by organizational members to outsiders, such as sales meetings, annual general meetings, presentations to customers, board meetings, etc. also represent talk that helps constitute the organization.

Another problem facing discourse researchers is choosing between texts. Given the myriad of ways in which an organization is constructed, the challenge is often not to find texts but deciding *which* texts to choose among given the myriad of texts that exist in most research contexts. The difficulty for discourse analysts, then, is how to identify a manageable, relatively limited corpus of texts that is helpful in exploring the construction of the object of analysis.

Fourth, the discourse researcher faces the challenge of analyzing the corpus of data that they have collected. This is a particularly difficult stage as the standardized methods that exist in more quantitative approaches are not available for discourse analysis. It is here then that the discourse analyst must be the most creative. While the freedom from such constraints provides considerable room for creativity, it does make the task of analysis somewhat daunting. It also means that discourse analysis regularly faces criticism concerning a lack of 'rigour'.

'Recipes' for successful data analysis are, therefore, hard to provide. The breadth of textual analysis techniques that could be used – from an emphasis on specific utterances to an analysis of a range of texts over time – and the diversity of the phenomena under investigation, mean that the form that analysis takes will vary greatly from study to study. As a result, researchers need to develop an approach that makes sense in the light of their particular study *and* establish a set of arguments to justify the particular approach they adopt. While this individualist approach to analysis undoubtedly causes difficulties,

particularly in convincing journal editors of the legitimacy of the analysis, it is in its contextual and interpretive sensitivities that the real benefits of discourse analysis lie.

Finally, the research study needs to be written up for publication. Like other forms of qualitative research, discourse analytic studies are as much about writing as they are about data collection or data analysis. And just as there is often a need to be creative in developing workable approaches to data analysis, there is also a need to develop innovative – and convincing – ways of presenting data, methods, and results. In addition, discourse analytic studies, like all qualitative studies, do not fit well within the conventional length restrictions of an academic paper. Researchers face the continual problem of trying to fit too much material into too little space. Explaining the research question, the research site, the method of data collection and analysis, and the findings generally requires more space than is available. The fact that there are few conventions for data collection and data analysis means that a convincing narrative must be developed to explain what was done and why. Researchers who have answered the questions posed in this chapter will, however, find themselves relatively well placed to construct an effective narrative.

DISCUSSION AND CONCLUSION

As we discussed in the foregoing section, discourse analysis is an increasingly popular research method, or set of methods, in organizational research. It allows researchers to gain important and novel insights into the social construction of organizational phenomena and shed new light on organizational processes. This is an important contribution given the growing acceptance of a social constructivist view of organizations among organizational researchers. We have looked at different approaches to discourse and how it has been applied to various organizational texts and contexts, exploring themes such as gender, identity, organizational change, and the natural environment. In so doing, we have dipped into a wide palette of discourse analytic tools and methods of engagement.

But, while a significant body of discourse studies has accumulated, many opportunities remain for further contributions to organizational research. We believe that there are four areas, in particular, where discourse analysis has obvious advantages. First, the potential of discourse analysis to explore the actual construction of organizations remains relatively unexplored. While the 'organizations as texts' perspective in organization research is well developed (e.g., Law, 1993), the actual processes through which organizations as social objects are produced and maintained through discourse has received little systematic attention. For example, how do entrepreneurs produce texts and draw intertextually and interdiscursively on other texts and discourses, to make their budding organizations 'real'? Similarly, how are organizations reconstructed in times of significant organizational change? In addition, how are two organizations reconstructed as one following mergers and acquisitions? The application of discourse analysis to these processes will provide a deeper understanding of these phenomena and over time coalesce into a theory of the discursive production of organizations.

Second, discourse analysis has much to contribute to institutional theory. While the roots of institutional theory lie in the social constructionism of Berger and Luckmann (1966), there has been little effort to study the processes of social construction that produce institutions. Understandably, much effort in institutional theory has been focused on the effects of institutions on organizations and organizational fields. However, this has left the question, of how institutions are socially constructed, under researched. As Zucker (1991: 105–106) observes:

Without a solid cognitive, microlevel foundation we risk treating institutionalization as a black box at the organizational level, focusing on content at the exclusion of developing a systematic explanatory theory of process, conflating institutionalization with resource dependency, and neglecting institutional variation and persistence.

Although important insights can be gained by examining the content of institutions, there is an ever present danger of making the neo-institutionalist enterprise a taxonomic rather than explanatory theory-building science. Institution theory is always in danger of forgetting that labeling a process or structure does not explain it.

There is an opportunity to apply discourse analysis to the microproduction of institutions and add an important additional perspective to institutional theory. As Phillips, Lawrence, and Hardy (2004: 635) argue, 'discourse analysis provides a coherent framework for the investigation of institutionalization'. Discourse analysis, therefore, has an important contribution to make in this area.

Third, while discourse analysis is being increasingly applied to the study of identity in organizations, there remains much work to be done in this area. The study of individual and organizational identity is a rapidly growing area in organizational research (e.g. Brown, 2001) and this rapid growth provides several new areas of potential contribution for discourse analysts. For example, the growing interest in processes of identification is an obvious place where discourse analysis could provide unique and much needed insight into the textual processes through which individual and organizational identity are constructed and how individuals come to identify, or not, with an organization. However, this is just one of a number of areas where discourse analysis can provide important insight into the actual processes through which identities of various kinds are socially constructed and through which they affect each other interdiscursively and intertextually.

Finally, there is an important opportunity for discourse analysis to contribute to strategy research. Strategy is, largely, textual and the process of strategy development and implementation can be usefully conceptualized as discursive. Some work in this area is beginning to show the potential of discourse analysis in understanding strategy processes. For example, Phillips, Sewell, and Jaynes (forthcoming) argue for the application of critical discourse analysis in strategy, arguing that it can draw together and extend several streams of research in the strategy literature. It is also clear that discourse analysis can contribute to the strategy as practice literature; one kind of practice that is central to strategy is discursive and discourse analysis provides a useful methodology for examining it.

It is important, however, not to understate the challenges that remain in adopting discourse analysis as a methodology in organization research. The approach is still new and it suffers from all of the opportunities and challenges that come with any new method. First and foremost, there are few standard and accepted approaches to data analysis. While there are exemplars (several of which we discussed in the preceding sections), these are by no means developed to the point where they can be applied in a standard way like other qualitative methods such as ethnography. Instead, they provide indications of how to proceed, but every study requires the development of a customized approach appropriate to the situation. Significant challenges continue to face researchers as they work to develop convincing and appropriate approaches to their chosen empirical context.

Finally, there is an additional issue facing discourse analysis in organizational research and that is the question of how to communicate and maintain the distinctiveness of discourse analysis in organizational research. This problem has two aspects. On the one hand, it seems helpful to us to differentiate between discourse analysis and other qualitative methods in organizational research. Where methods like rhetorical analysis and narrative analysis are very useful methods, their contribution is very different from that of discourse analysis: traditional qualitative methods explore the meaningfulness of the social world while discourse analysis is useful in investigating how it was socially constructed. These various methods are, therefore, complementary, not alternatives to one another. Moreover, this is even more confusing as methods of textual analysis like narrative and rhetoric

may play a role in discourse studies. For discourse analysis to fulfill its promise in organizational research, the term is best used for studies of social construction and not applied to general discussions and explorations of text.

To conclude, we hope we have shown that discourse analysis has already begun to make an interesting and significant contribution to organizational research. We also hope we have made a convincing case for the exciting opportunities that exist for further developing a discursive view of organizational phenomena. The increasing influence of social constructionism in organizational research makes the investigation of processes of social construction more and more important: discourse analysis provides the tools for that investigation. While much work needs to be done and significant challenges remain, we believe the future is bright for discourse analysis as an important approach to the empirical study of organizations.

REFERENCES

Acker, J. and van Houten, D.R. (1974) 'Differential recruitment and control: the sex structuring of organizations', *Administrative Science Quarterly*, 9(2): 152–63.

Ainsworth, S. (2002) 'The "feminine advantage": a discursive analysis of the invisibility of older women workers', *Gender, Work and Organization*, 9(5): 579–601.

Albert, S. and Whetten, D.A. (1985) 'Organizational identity', *Research in Organizational Behavior*, 7: 263–95.

Alvesson, M. (1994) 'Talking in organizations: managing identity and impressions in an advertising agency', *Organization Studies*, 15: 535–63.

Alvesson, M. (2002) 'Knowledge work: ambiguity, image and identity', *Human Relations*, 54(7): 863–86.

Alvesson, M. and Kärreman, D. (2000a) 'Taking the linguistic turn in organizational research: challenges, responses, consequences', *Journal of Applied Behavioural Science*, 36: 136–58.

Alvesson, M. and Kärreman, D. (2000b) 'Varieties of discourse: on the study of organizations through discourse analysis', *Human Relations*, 53(9): 125–49.

Anderson-Gough, F., Grey, C. and Robson, K. (1998) 'Work hard, play hard: an analysis of organizational cliché in two accountancy practices', *Organization*, 5(4): 565–92.

Anderson-Gough, F., Grey, C. and Robson, K. (2000) 'In the name of the client: the service ethic in two professional services firms', *Human Relations*, 53(9): 1151–74.

Andersson, L.M. and Bateman, T.S. (2000) 'Individual environmental initiative: championing natural environmental issues in U.S. business organizations', *Academy of Management Journal*, 43(4): 548–70.

Ashcraft, K.L. (2004) 'Gender discourse and organization: framing a shifting relationship', in D. Grant, C. Hardy and L. Putnam (eds), *The Sage Handbook of Organizational Discourse*, London: Sage, pp. 275–98.

Ashcraft, K.L. and Flores, L.A. (2003) "'Slaves with white collars": decoding a contemporary crisis of masculinity', *Text and Performance Quarterly*, 23: 1–29.

Banerjee, S.B. (2001) 'Managerial perceptions of corporate environmentalism: interpretations from industry and strategic implications for organizations', *Journal of Management Studies*, 38(4): 489–513.

Banerjee, S.B. (2003) 'Who sustains whose development? sustainable development and the reinvention of nature', *Organization Studies*, 24(1): 143–80.

Banerjee, S.B., Iyer, E.S. and Kahyap, R.K. (2003) 'Corporate environmentalism: antecedents and influence of industry type', *Journal of Marketing*, 67(2): 106–22.

Bansal, P. (2003) 'From issues to actions: The importance of individual concerns and organizational values in responding to natural environmental issues', *Organization Science*, 14(5): 510–27.

Bansal, P. and Clelland, I. (2004) 'Talking trash: legitimacy, impression management, and unsystematic risk in the context of the natural environment', *Academy of Management Journal*, 47(1): 93–103.

Bansal, P. and Roth, K. (2000) 'Why companies go green: a model of ecological responsiveness', *Academy of Management Journal*, 43(4): 717–36.

Berger, P. and Luckmann, T. (1966) *The Social Construction of Reality: A Treatise in the Sociology of Knowledge*, London: Penguin.

Brown, A.D. (1997) 'Narcissism, identity and legitimacy', *Academy of Management Review*, 22(3): 643–86.

Brown, A.D. (2001) 'Organization studies and identity: towards a research agenda', *Human Relations*, 54(1): 113–21.

Brulle, R. and Jenkins, J.C. (2006) 'Spinning our way to sustainability?', *Organization and Environment*, 19(1): 82–7.

Burman, E. and Parker, I. (1993) 'Against discursive imperialism, empiricism and constructionism: thirty-two problems with discourse analysis', in E. Burman and I. Parker (eds), *Discourse Analytic Research: Repertoires and Readings of Texts in Action*, London: New York, pp. 155–72.

Calás, M.B. and Smircich, L. (1992) 'Using the "F" word: Feminist theories and the social consequences of organizational research', in A. Mills and P. Tancred (eds), *Gendering Organizational Analysis*, London: Sage, pp. 222–34.

Calás, M.B. and Smircich, L. (1996) 'From the woman's point of view: Feminist approaches to organization studies', in S.Clegg, C. Hardy and W. Nord (eds), *Handbook of Organization Studies*, London: Sage, pp. 218–57.

Chalaby, J.K. (1996) 'Beyond the prison-house of language: discourse as a sociological concept',, *British Journal of Sociology*, 47(4): 684–98.

Descartes, R. (1637) L. J. Lafleur (Trans.) (1960) *Discourse on Method and Meditations,* New York: The Liberal Arts Press.

Driscoll, C. (2006) 'The not so clear-cut nature of organizational legitimating mechanisms in the Canadian forest sector', *Business and Society*, 45(3): 322–53.

Dunford, R. and Jones, D. (2000) 'Narrative in strategic change', *Human Relations*, 53(9): 1207–26

Epstein, M.J. and Roy, M.J. (2003) 'Making the business case for sustainability. linking social and environmental actions to financial performance', *Journal of Corporate Citizenship*, 9: 79–96.

Fairclough, N. (1992) *Discourse and Social Change*, Cambridge: Polity Press.

Fairclough, N. (1995) *Critical Discourse Analysis: The Critical Study of Language*, London: Longman.

Fairclough, N. (1999) 'Linguistic and intertextual analysis within discourse analysis', in A. Jaworski and N. Coupland (eds.), *The Discourse Reader*, London: Routledge, pp. 183–212.

Fairclough, N. (2005) 'Discourse analysis in organization studies: the case for critical realism', *Organization Studies*, 26(6): 915–39.

Ford, J. and Ford, L. (1994) 'The role of conversations in producing intentional change in organizations', *Academy of Management Review*, 20: 541–70.

Foucault, M. (1965) *Madness & Civilization: A History of Insanity in the Age of Reason*, New York: Vintage.

Fournier, V. (1998) 'Stories of development and exploitation: militant voices in enterprise culture', *Organization*, 5(1): 55–80.

Fowler, R. (1991) *Language in the News*, London: Routledge.

Fowler, R. (1996) 'On critical linguistics', in C.R. Caldas-Coulthard and M.Coulthard (eds), *Texts and Practices: Readings in Critical Dscourse Analysis*, London: Routledge, pp. 3–14.

Garnsey, E. and Rees, B. (1996) 'Discourse and enactment: gender inequality in text and context', *Human Relations*, 49(8): 1041–64.

Gergen, K.J. (1991) *The Saturated Self: Dilemmas of Identity in Contemporary Life*, New York: Basic Books.

Gergen, K.J. (1999) *An Invitation to Social Construction*, Thousand Oaks, CA: Sage.

Gill, R. (1993a) 'Justifying injustice: broadcasters' accounts of inequality in radio', in E. Burman and I. Parker (eds), *Discourse Analytic Research: Repertoires and Readings of Texts in Action*, London: Routledge, pp. 75–93.

Gill, R. (1993b) 'Ideology, gender and popular radio: a discourse analytic approach', *Innovation*, 6: 323–39.

Goffman, E. (1959) *The Presentation of Self in Everyday Life*, London: Penguin.

Grant, D., Keenoy, T. and Oswick, C. (1998) 'Introduction: organizational discourse: of diversity, dichotomy and multi-disciplinarity', in D. Grant, T. Keenoy and C. Oswick (eds), *Discourse and Organization*, London: Sage.

Grant, D., Hardy, C., Oswick, C. and Putnam, L. (2004) *Handbook of Organizational Discourse*, London: Sage.

Grove-White, R.B. (1993) 'Environmentalism: a new moral discourse for technological society?', in K. Milton (ed.), *Environmentalism: The View From Anthropology*, London: Routledge, pp. 18–30.

Hardy, C. (2001) 'Researching organizational discourse', *International Studies of Management and Organization*, 31(3): 25–47.

Hardy, C. and Phillips, N. (1999) 'No joking matter: discursive struggle in the Canadian refugee system', *Organization Studies*, 20(1): 1–24.

Harré, R. (1995) 'Discursive psychology', in J.A. Smith, R. Harré and L. van Langenhove (eds), *Rethinking Psychology*, Thousand Oaks, CA: Sage, pp. 143–59.

Heracleous, L. and Barrett, M. (2001) 'Organizational change as discourse: communicative actions and deep structures in the context of information technology implementation', *Academy of Management Journal*, 44(4): 755–78.

Hirsch, P.M. (1986) 'From ambushes to golden parachutes: corporate takeovers as an instance of cultural framing and institutional integration', *The American Journal of Sociology*, 91(4): 800–37.

Holmer-Nadeson, M. (1996) 'Organizational identity and space of action', *Organization Studies*, 17(1): 49–81.

Jack, G. and Lorbiecki, A. (2007) 'National identity, globalization and the discursive construction of organizational identity', *British Journal of Management*, 18(1): 79–94.

Johnson, G. (1987) *Strategic Change and the Management Process*, Oxford: Blackwell.

Kanter, R.M. (1977) *Men and Women of the Corporation*, New York: Basic Books.

Keenoy, T., Oswick, C. and Grant, D. (1997) 'Organizational discourses: text and context', *Organization*, 4: 147–57.

Kondo, D.K. (1990) *Crafting Selves: Power, Gender, and Discourses of Identity in a Japanese Workplace*, Chicago: University of Chicago Press.

Kress, G. (1995) 'The social production of language: History and structures of domination', in P. Fries and M. Gregory (eds), *Discourse in Society: Systemic Functional Perspectives*, Norwood, NJ: Ablex Publishing.

Kress, G. (2001) 'From Saussure to critical sociolinguistics: the turn towards a social view of language', in M. Wetherell, S. Taylor, and S.J. Yates (eds), *Discourse Theory and Practice: A Reader*, London: Sage, pp. 29–38.

Law, J. (1993) *Organizing Modernity*, London: Wiley.

Macnaghten, P. (1993) 'Discourses of nature: argumentation and power', in I. Parker and E. Burman (eds), *Discourse Analytic Research*, London: Routledge, pp. 52–72.

McKay, R.B. (2001) 'Organizational responses to an environmental Bill of Rights', *Organization Studies*, 22(4): 625–58.

Merriam-Webster dictionary (2008) Available Internet: http://www.merriam-webster.com/

Mills, A.J. and Tancred-Sheriff, P. (eds) (1992) *Gendering Organizational Analysis*, Newbury Park, CA: Sage.

Morgan, G. and Sturdy, A. (2000) *Beyond Organizational Change: Structure, Discourse and Power in UK Financial Services*, London: Macmillan.

O'Connor, E.S. (1995) 'Paradoxes of participation: textual analysis and organizational change', *Organization Studies*, 16(5): 769–803.

O'Connor, E.S. (2000) 'Plotting the organization: the embedded narrative as a construct for studying change', *Journal of Applied Behavioral Science*, 36(2): 174–92.

Parker, I. (1992) *Discourse Dynamics: Critical Analysis for Social and Individual Psychology*, London: Routledge.

Parker, I. (2005) 'Lacanian discourse analysis in psychology: seven theoretical elements', *Theory & Psychology*, 15(2): 163–82.

Pettigrew, A. (1990) 'Longitudinal field research on change: theory and practice', *Organization Science*, 1: 267–92.

Pettigrew, A., Woodman, R. and Cameron, K. (2001) 'Studying organizational change and development: challenges for future research', *Academy of Management Journal*, 44(4): 697–713.

Phillips, N. and Hardy, C. (1997) 'Managing multiple identities: discourse, legitimacy and resources in the UK refugee system', *Organization*, 4(2): 159–86.

Phillips, N. and Hardy, C. (1999) 'No joking matter: discursive struggle in the Canadian refugee system', *Organization Studies*, 20(1): 1–24.

Phillips, N. and Hardy, C. (2002) *Understanding Discourse Analysis*, Thousand Oaks, CA: Sage.

Phillips, N., Lawrence, T. and Hardy, C. (2004) 'Discourse and institutions', *Academy of Management Review*, 29: 635–52.

Phillips, N. Sewell, G. and Jaynes. S. (forthcoming) 'Applying critical discourse analysis in strategic management research', *Organizational Research Methods*.

Potter, J. and Wetherell, M. (1987) *Discourse and Social Psychology: Beyond Attitudes and Behaviour*, London: Sage.

Prasad, P. and Elmes, M. (2005) 'In the name of the practical: unearthing the hegemony of pragmatics in the discourse of environmental management', *Journal of Management Studies*, 42(2): 845–67.

Putnam, L.L. and Fairhurst, G.T. (2000) 'Discourse analysis in organizations: issues and concerns', in F.M. Jablin and L.L. Putnam (eds), *The New Handbook of Organizational Communication: Advances in Theory, Research and Methods*, Newbury Park, CA: Sage.

Rojsek, I. (2001) 'From red to green: towards the environmental management in the country in transition', *Journal of Business Ethics*, 33(1): 37–50.

Rorty, R. (1992) 'The linguistic turn: essays in philosophical method', Chicago, IL: University of Chicago Press.

Runte, M. and Mills, A. (2006) 'Cold War, chilly climate: exploring the roots of gendered discourse in organization and management theory', *Human Relations*, 59: 695–720.

Sackmann, S. (1989) 'The role of metaphors in organisation transformation', *Human Relations*, 42: 463–85.

Salzer-Morling, M. (1998) 'As God created the earth… a saga that makes sense?', in D. Grant, T. Keenoy and C. Oswick (eds), *Discourse and Organization*, London: Sage, pp. 114–18.

Sillince, J.A. (1999) 'The role of political language: forms and language coherence in the organizational change process', *Organization Studies*, 20(3): 485–518.

Spender, D. (1980) *Man-made Language*, London: Routledge & Kegan Paul.

Tannen, D. (1990) *You Just Don't Understand: Women and Men in Conversation*, New York: William Morrow.

Tannen, D. (1994) *Talking from 9 to 5. Women and men at Work: Language, Sex and Power*, Lancaster: Virago.

Tsoukas, H. and Chia, R. (2002) 'On organizational becoming: rethinking organizational change', *Organization Science*, 13(5): 567–85.

Vaara, E., Kleymann, B. and Seristo, H. (2004) 'Strategies as discursive constructions: the case of the airline alliances', *Journal of Management Studies*, 41: 1–35.

van Dijk, T.A. (1997b) 'The study of discourse', in T.A. van Dijk (ed.), *Discourse as Structure and Process* (Vol. 1), London: Sage, pp. 1–34.

Weedon, C. (1987) *Feminist Practice and Poststructuralist Theory*, Oxford: Blackwell.

West, C., Lazar, M. and Kramarae, C. (1997) 'Gender in discourse', in A. Teun and T.A. van Dijk (eds), *Discourse: A Multidisciplinary Introduction*, London: Sage, pp. 119–42.

Wetherell, M. and Potter, J. (1992) *Mapping the Language of Racism: Discourse and the Legitimation of Exploitation*, London: Harvester Wheatsheaf.

Wetherell, M., Taylor, S. and Yates, S. (2001) *Discourse Theory and Practice: A Reader*, London: Sage.

Winch, P. (1958) *The Idea of a Social Science*, London: Rouledge & Kegan Paul.

Winn, M.I. and Angell, L.C. (2000) 'Towards a process model of corporate greening', *Organization Studies*, 21(6): 1119–47.

Wodak, R. (1996) 'The genesis of racist discourse in Austria since 1989', in C.R. Caldas-Coulthard and M. Coulthard (eds), *Texts and Practices: Readings in Critical Discourse Analysis*, London: Routledge, pp. 107–28.

Wood, L.A. and Kroger, R.O. (2000) *Doing Discourse Analysis: Methods for Studying Action in Talk and Text*, Thousand Oaks, CA: Sage Publications.

Zucker, L. (1991) 'The role of institutionalization in cultural persistence', in W.W. Powell and P.J. DiMaggio (eds), *The New Institutionalism in Organizational Analysis*, Chicago: University of Chicago Press, pp. 83–107.

33

Visual Methods in Organizational Research

Samantha Warren

INTRODUCING VISUAL METHODS: SETTING THE SCENE

Visual methods are research practices that explicitly use images in various ways including drawing, photography, video, film, and Internet pages. The images are either regarded as a *source* of data in themselves, or as a way of *producing* data through their use, or a combination of the two. The point of departure for this chapter is that visual research methods in organization studies represent a nascent, flourishing, and *different* methodological field to that which has gone before. My aim is to explore what makes these techniques distinctive, with particular regard to their use in organizational settings.

Visual research is well established in anthropology (Banks and Morphy, 1997; Collier and Collier, 1986; Pink, 2006) and sociology (Emmison and Smith, 2000; Harper, 1998; Knowles and Sweetman, 2004), but is remarkably underused in organizational research. Although images have a (limited) history in sociological studies of work and labour, and in representations of organizational life by visual artists (Strangleman,

2004: 185–9; Cohen et al., 2006), studies explicitly using visual methods hardly featured in organization studies until the 1980s, their appearance coinciding with an explosion of interest in organizational symbolism with its inherently visual overtones (Dandridge et al., 1980).

This absence is particularly striking for a number of reasons. First, since organization studies is a branch of the social sciences, we might expect to see these methodological developments occurring there as in other social disciplines. Second, organizational life is rich with imagery and symbolism, offering the visual researcher fertile ground for study; for example, paying attention to artefacts and architecture can reveal much about corporations and 'their' lives (Gagliardi, 1990; Jones, 1996), and investigating organizational members' personal 'desk-clutter' can similarly open out a whole host of feelings, beliefs, stories, and meanings about working lives and professional selves (Tian and Belk, 2005; Warren, 2006). Furthermore, the phrase 'a picture is worth a thousand words' sums up the potential for visual methods to record or generate a range of rich data about organizational settings, enabling more sensually complete 'presentationally symbolic' dissemination than words alone allow (Langer, 1957). Third, organizations and their stakeholders (in the developed world, at least) exist in a mass-mediated, image-saturated society where aesthetic appeal is an increasingly important arbiter of economic value (Bohme, 2003). These cultural conditions mean that visual matters are likely to be significant to organizations, and to the lives of their members outside work. Organizational image and corporate identity are also key concerns under these conditions (Hatch and Schultz, 2000), resulting in a strategic focus on the visual dimension of goods, services, brands, and the 'aesthetics' of the organization more broadly – constructed through corporate livery, logos, staff uniforms, and so on (Hancock, 2003; Schroeder, 2002). Consequently, scholars need to pay attention to these visual elements of organizational life.

However, it would be wrong to assume that organization studies is bereft of visual investigations, and it is myopic to begin a chapter on visual methods in organization studies by claiming that none exist. The late 1990s and early 2000s have seen a steady growth in visual studies, linked to the development of affordable digital photographic apparatus, increased computer data storage, Internet bandwidth and connection speed – all of which greatly facilitate the collection and sharing of photographic images. Other technological developments that have occurred over a similar timeframe include desktop publishing and online journals where images can be more easily displayed than in print-based counterparts, and the proliferation of corporate imagery over the Internet and 3G mobile phones. Technologically, visual research is perhaps a methodology whose time has come.

Apart from these 'technology-push' explanations for the rise in interest in the visual, others have cited paradigmatic shifts in organization studies as facilitating the legitimacy and increased use of nontextual research methods. At the risk of caricaturing,

recent decades have seen moves away from positivist models of research, based on scientific method, towards more reflexive modes of knowing and interpretation (Denzin, 2001). The potential role of images in interpretive organizational research, with the emphasis on subjective meaning creation and qualitative data is considerable. Images evoke an immediacy of experience, tapping into levels of meaning that evade language and even consciousness (Meyer, 1991). Likewise, the production, consumption, and circulation of organizational images tells us much about the organizations that produce, consume, and circulate them.

It would be misleading to assert that organization studies have abandoned the rationalist imperative of positivism entirely; a considerable amount of influential 'mainstream' literature (especially that originating in America) still purports to be objective truth, presenting research findings as carefully calculated statistically robust models offered up for replication, used to predict workplace behaviours, and generalized as reasonably confident facts about organizational life. Such outlets have little place for visual images. Outside the academy, the legacy of positivism is perhaps even *more* prominent among managers who are products of MBA programmes taught by those same professors who cling to the scientific canon. This presents a credibility problem for the organizational researcher wishing to use visual methods. Ironically, as Bolton et al. (2001: 504) point out, 'it may be the very power and ready accessibility of visual images [and] the apparent transparency of their message, which leads us to dismiss their value as a serious source of data'.

The credibility of doing research using visual methods is just one challenge of employing them in organizational settings. Research in public, private, or even not-for-profit organizations, is complex and all organizational research takes place in contexts riddled with political and ethical conditions, against a backdrop of paradigmatic multiplicity (Buchanan and Bryman, 2007). Furthermore, the multiple, often competing stakeholders for evidence generated by organizational researchers muddy the water further. The driving force behind these nuances and difficulties is what I call the 'politics of profit', or safe custody of money in the case of public sector operations and donations in respect of charitable ones. An overarching desire for profit maximization and personal wealth creation colours every stage of the research process, including research in educational and healthcare organizations, given their increasingly quasi-marketized character.

For example, the likelihood of improving productivity governs the kinds of studies that are permissible and the people who can be involved (access), and of course, who pays the bill (funding). Concerns over commercial sensitivity and individual gains, such as career progression or fear of reprisals, often determine the information (data) that participants are prepared to offer. The use, to which results are put, and where they are disseminated, are also influenced by the financial gain that can be accrued; and significantly for my purposes here, the ways in which the research is carried out (method) must appear to support the rational, purposive, *profitable* business of doing business. Furthermore, as the unit of analysis in organization studies is often not one, unaccountable individual, these processes are multilayered, overlapping and repetitive. Put bluntly, while researchers are interested in designing research and utilizing methods that *tell* us as much as possible about organizational life – and are thus useful projects, in that they contribute to our stock of knowledge – managers' understanding of 'useful research' usually rests on what the outcomes of such projects can actually *do* for the organization regardless of their efficacy in generating new insights. While all organizational researchers undoubtedly face these barriers, those wishing to develop and/or employ new data gathering techniques are likely to encounter them more solidly.

Given the foregoing caveats and limitations, and whatever explanation for the rising interest in visual methods one prefers,

there is a need to think closely about the epistemological, methodological, and practical issues these techniques throw up, especially when used in organizational contexts. Just because we can use cheap digital technologies in our research practice does not mean that we should. Similarly, the prevalence of images in glossy company reports does not necessarily mean they are worthy of attention. Indeed, in an increasingly aestheticized age, where image comes to stand for reality and style takes precedence over substance (Welsch, 1997; Ritzer, 1999; Postrel, 2003; Warren and Rehn, 2006) researchers need to scrutinize their practice even more closely; are we in danger of aestheticizing our *own* practice through the use of images, and if we are, does this matter?

This chapter discusses a range of visual methods that have been used in organizational research, serving as a review of historical development and contemporary practice as well as a critical commentary on the opportunities and limitations of a visual approach. What this chapter does not do is offer a 'how to' guide to *using* image-based techniques. The studies referred to in this chapter can be consulted, and key approaches and exemplary studies are summarized in Table 33.1. The chapter is divided into two parts, corresponding with the division of visual methods into those that treat images as sources of data and those that employ images to generate data, respectively.

Images as data: looking at organizational life

Images used as sources of data are usually interrogated, either by the researcher or research participants, for their meaning and significance. There are two major forms. First, analysing existing images, for example in media and organizational literature. Second, the use of photography to document organizational processes, actions, and events. Both approaches assume that some kind of data is contained within the image; in the former, images can be 'read' for clues about the organization that produced them, and in the latter,

Table 33.1 Visual Methods, Foundations, Applications, and Assessment

Method	Conceptual foundations	Indicative applications	Benefits	Limitations
Analysis of existing images in organizational literature	Semiotics Content analysis Critical visual analysis	Williamson (1978) (advertising) Preston and Young (2000) (annual reports) Schroeder and Fillis (2006) (advertisements) Schroeder (2003) Kivinen (2006) (websites) Buchanan and Huczynski (2004) (film)	Images readily available Imbued with corporate meaning Allow historical/archival research Allows comparisons between different contexts	A-contextualized Relies on researcher interpretation Copyright issues
Documentary photography	Visual anthropology	Harper (1984) (work-study) Buchanan (2001) (process re-engineering)	'Removed fieldnotes' 'Cultural inventories' Potential to reveal unnoticed detail	Selective attention/emphasis Confidentiality and anonymity
Drawing: process mapping	Soft-systems methodology	Monk and Howard (1998) (work context)	Systematic No equipment needed	Works from within 'rational' paradigm
Drawing: freehand sketching	Psychoanalysis	Meyer (1978) (OD) Vince and Broussine (1996) (organizational change) Sievers and Beumer (2006) (role analysis)	Facilitates emotional expression Taps into unconscious	Credibility Reluctance to draw
Respondent-led photography Photo-voice	Interpretivism Critical theory	Wood and Ladkin (2007) (leadership) Cohen et al. (2006) (abjection) Warren (2002) (organizational aesthetics) Warren and Parker (2009) (professional identity)	Respondents' eye view Surface marginalized perspectives Enables collaboration Balances power dynamics Speeds rapport	Requires equipment Commercial sensitivity Anonymity/ethics

images may be assumed to correspond with the reality of the situation being researched and can help in communicating 'how it was' to others.

Analysing existing images

Analysis of organizationally produced images-as-data dates back most famously to Williamson's (1978) semiotic treatment of gendered meaning in advertisements. A highly structured approach to peeling back the layers of meaning imbued in a photograph, Williamson's precise analytical terminology set a benchmark for the rigorous study of what Rose (2007) refers to as 'found' images – images that already exist and are selected according to the researcher's investigative needs. Semiotic analysis involves identifying 'signs' contained in the picture, and determining what they signify. Importantly, what is signified in this process is culturally determined and consequently can tell us a lot about the ideologies and assumptions of both producer and audience. Williamson showed how dominant, gendered cultural ideologies were visually reproduced, and how audiences related to them as 'ideal' gender representations, with implications for men and women's perceptions of bodily and social normality.

There are several examples of quasi-semiotic approaches to 'found' visual images in organization studies, differing in analytical approach but all sharing the objective of discovering how images transmit and construct meaning in organizational literature. The ways in which graphs, diagrams, and photographic images are used to shape the meaning of annual reports has been studied in accounting research (e.g., Beattie and Jones, 1992; Dougherty and Kunda, 1990; Preston and Young, 2000). Davison (2007) uses Barthes' (1981) conceptual framework of the 'studium' and 'punctum' to explain how and why the charity Oxfam used various images in its annual review. Since charitable organizations are at a 'crossroads of activity between the corporate and the charitable, the developed and the developing worlds' (Davison, 2007: 153), Oxfam carefully craft the pictorial

dimension of their communications to manage a range of stakeholder perceptions. Hancock (2005) suggests a more holistic approach to analysing images in graduate recruitment brochures, arguing that the overall 'aesthetic' of the image is sometimes more than the deconstructed sum of its parts. Schroeder and Fillis (2006) also suggest a method for the 'critical visual analysis' of organizational images, moving away from the structural confines of semiotic analyses and based on ideas drawn from the genres of art history and criticism. For example, they apply conceptual understandings of the role and function of 'Dutch guild' group portrait painting to explore advertising images produced by Calvin Klein. Another example of interdisciplinary practice is exhibited by Guthey and Jackson (2005) who analyse the depiction of authenticity in Chief Executive Officer portraits using critical photographic theory. Similarly, Rose (2007) uses strategies from art criticism to assess compositional elements of images, although, by her own admission, these do little to investigate the socially embedded properties of images, assessing the formal characteristics for their own sake as works of art. As such, they are likely to be of limited interest to organizational researchers.

One application of this 'arts-based' approach is Doherty's (2006) study of paintings depicting workers during the depression era in America (1930 to 1941). Doherty dismisses the claim that descriptive analyses are of limited use in organization studies, asserting that it is precisely the rich description availed by art that is valuable in historical studies of organizational life, an argument also made by Parker (2009). Doherty's (2006) study did take account of the artistic influences and traditions of the various painters concerned, and this cultural contextualization aided the interpretation of their style and content.

Following Barrett (2005), Schroeder and Fillis (2006) also propose a framework for the systematic analysis of photographic images in relation to their observable features (simple description), subject matter, medium of presentation, aesthetic style, and relationship with other images used for similar purposes. They call for greater awareness of how different organizational stakeholders interpret images, how they are produced (encoded), and consumed (decoded), and how the meanings of images differ depending on their context and mobility. Audience studies attempt to do this in relation to film and television (Rose, 2007) and a distinct but related treatment of images-as-data is the analysis of organizational representations in television and film (Hassard and Holliday, 1998; see Hassard and Buchanan, Chapter 36, this volume). Although such popular culture texts are constructed to be sensationalizing and glamourizing discourses (Buchanan and Huczynski, 2004), one particular contribution to the edited collection by Hassard and Holliday observes how seemingly trivial 'entertainment' can function as pervasive amplifications of notions of gender identity and female success in organizations (Brewis, 1998), an argument also levelled at advertising in relation to women's body images, as in Williamson's study referred to in the preceding section (see Gill, 2006, for a contemporary excursion into these issues). One conclusion is that audience studies may have useful lessons for the organizational researcher, particularly with regard to the ways in which different social groupings decode and recode different organizational images, such as promotional literature and advertisements.

Websites are another important visual media ripe for investigation in this digital age. Schroeder (2003) studied the design of the web pages of banks to ascertain how these institutions conveyed the trustworthiness of their reputations. Traditionally, the imposing classical architecture of banking buildings connoted solidity, authority, and dependability. Schroeder was interested to see how this was transposed or adapted online. Likewise, Kivinen (2006) studied the design of energy companies' websites to explore how organizations (re)invent themselves on the seemingly blank slate of the Internet site, a space that has yet to be fully colonized by established norms of organizational communication.

Documentary photography

The idea that 'seeing is believing' is perhaps a good place to start in making sense of how photography has traditionally been used in the social sciences to document events and processes. Collier and Collier (1986, first published 1967) is widely cited as the first volume to explore photography as an anthropological research method, on the assumption that photographs faithfully record reality. They note that their book is about observation, and their interest in photography stems from the camera's 'sharp focus [that] might help us see with greater accuracy' (Collier and Collier, 1986: 5). They discuss the camera as a 'mirror with a memory' (p. 7), and the usefulness of photography in taking 'cultural inventories' of material life, such as the display and arrangements of personal effects on a dressing table (p. 45) or the spatial and temporal elements of social interaction (p. 77). As Buchanan (2001: 152) notes, the 'enhanced realism' that photography is presumed to bring has found a niche in the history of organization studies, including Gilbreth's time and motion studies and Hedges and Beynon's (1982) study of working life on the factory floor. As Rose (2007: 247) notes, photographs can effectively record the 'texture' of a scene. Collier and Colliers' (1986: 44–7) cultural inventories contain rich (and fascinating) detail that would not be conveyed in verbal accounts, which I have argued elsewhere (Warren, 2002, 2005, 2006).

The camera records light imprints of every object within the scope of its aperture. This indiscriminate property is especially useful for the organizational researcher who may have limited time to spend observing 'in the field'; photographs can function as 'removed field-notes' or aide-memoires for later analysis. Photographs are also useful in drawing attention to things that may have been missed or considered unimportant on first sight, revealing details that may be overlooked without the 'close observation' that photography enables. Another advantage, in common with all images, is photography's communicative power. From diagrammatic instructions to fine art, images describe, explain, depict, and reinforce all manner of knowledge, including emotions, feelings, and other 'intangibles' (Tufte, 1997; Warren, 2002; Whincup, 2004). Cognitive psychologists also claim that images are a more immediate form of communication, because the brain processes them 'intact' without the need to decode them (Meyer, 1991). Consequently, images, and especially photography, are potentially valuable in the dissemination of research accounts.

However, these properties – iconography, detail, and communicative power – are also problematic in organizational settings. The 'politics of profit' constrain what may be photographed and by whom. Commercial sensitivity and client confidentiality may limit what researchers are permitted to photograph. Organizations may also be reluctant to give inquisitive researchers access to spaces of power or conflict, such as boardrooms or executive meetings, a problem encountered by Betts (2006) in her study of boardroom art. Although access problems affect all organizational researchers, using a camera seems to exacerbate the situation (Prosser, 2005). Preserving organizational and individual anonymity is also challenging when photographing observable features such as buildings, corporate spaces, logos, staff in uniform, and so on, and informed consent is also difficult to ensure when subjects are moving in and out of the camera's 'gaze'. Finally, there is the issue of copyright; ownership of photographic images is contestable, and this is a concern where the researcher wishes to reproduce images in journal articles, books, and websites.

It is probably an intuitive point that images (particularly photography) bear striking resemblances to the reality the photographer is trying to capture, and this brings opportunities but also difficulties for the organizational researcher. The iconography of photography is paradoxically its strength, but also its weakness when used in organizational settings. After all, I would not show you a

photograph and say, 'this is a socio-technical constructed representation of the light reflecting from the objects on my desk'. I would simply say, 'this is my desk'. But, the apparent truth of the representation belies the fact that it is nonetheless a constructed image. Leaving aside the likelihood of my having arranged the objects on my desk to impart an effect, such as 'busy clutter', or 'tidy efficiency', and having chosen the composition and timing of the exposure to exclude, say, bypassers, we also need to realize that the scene has been selected from any number of possible scenes, lighting, perspective, camera angle, and framing, more or less consciously determined by the photographer, choices which in turn are conditioned by visual culture (Mirzoeff, 1999; see Warren, 2002, for a discussion of truth and representation in photographic images). Once these factors are taken into account, the 'realist tale' (Harper, 1998) of photography as a 'mirror with a memory' becomes dubious, and the status of image as documentary 'evidence' is shaken.

Furthermore, as soon as a camera is raised in readiness to take a picture, people usually do one of three things; they either hide or refuse to be photographed; they pose themselves, usually grinning or in a silly posture, or they demand to know why the picture is being taken. The last response constitutes a reasonable request, but any of these effects mean that it is unlikely that the scene depicted in the resulting photograph is a 'true' record documenting what was happening, even (especially?) if the subjects are told to 'act naturally' (see the respondents' accounts of photographs being taken in their organization in Wood and Ladkin, 2007). Nevertheless, as Buchanan (2001: 152) observes, we accept that interview data are subject to bias, researcher effects, and sociocultural construction, but these are not reasons to stop interviewing people. Instead, we recognize, and perhaps embrace, the influence, which these factors have on the construction and reporting of research findings, which we can also do in the case of images.

Images that produce data: I see what you mean

Images can also be used to *produce* data. Rather than assuming it is possible for images to capture data for analysis, the aim of using images as a method to generate data is explicitly collaborative, requiring cooperation between researcher and respondent over the production and/or viewing of images. It also leads us temporarily away from a fairly narrow focus on photographic images to include drawing as a visual technique to enable or to empower research participants in expressing sentiments and opinions about their organization and working lives. In this section, I also consider the importance of multiple interpretations of visual data and the context of production and meaning creation. So far, the visual methods discussed rely on the skills of the researcher as 'connoisseur' (Rusted, 2000) who is solely able to extract the 'correct' meaning from the image, either by structured semiotic analysis, or through techniques borrowed from the arts. In the following discussion, the importance of *contextualization* of images and the voices of stakeholders in the research process is fore-grounded. This is as much an ethical argument as one of data validity and integrity (Warren, 2005), and also means that images are no longer the sole source of data, but an *aid* to generating data. Here we can see the value of visual techniques in *multi-method* approaches as well as their standalone use in a solely visual project. The following remarks will thus be useful to researchers who wish to use visual methods to supplement more traditional forms of data generation.

Images used to produce data are those created specifically for the needs of the study – either by the researcher, participants, or both – and include drawings, paintings, still photography, and video or film, as a means of generating and communicating data, rather than as texts to be read and deconstructed for organizational clues. The importance of contextualizing images is a recurring theme in all studies that utilize photography as a research method. As noted earlier, this is

partly an ethical concern, aimed at allowing research participants greater control over how their realities are represented, but it is also tied to establishing the validity, or perhaps more accurately the plausibility, of visual research accounts. This is neatly summarized by Wagner (2005: 1481) who reminds us that:

> [T]he credibility and utility of photographs within empirical social inquiry rests not so much on whether they accurately reflect or arbitrarily invent the real world but on how those aspects of the real world they invent or reflect are related to questions we care about – to understand that we need something more than the photograph itself.

This means allowing research participants greater involvement in creating and interpreting images used in the study. This section discusses the main variants of this process, in depiction, freehand drawing, photo-elicitiation, and respondent-led photography.

Drawing as a research method: picturing data

There are two main types of drawing as research method – the use of depiction to map and/or to explain processes in a more or less systematic way, and 'freehand' variants where participants are asked to generate images that represent some facet of their experience. The first category is probably more familiar in organization studies, and I will not dwell on its use here, although it is worth noting that the *visuality* of process maps, schematics, and other depictions has largely been ignored. Although such techniques do not produce 'pictures' as such, they generate visualizations of *in*visible processes and can be regarded as a form of visual studies used in organizational research for some time. Visual means have long been used to construct explanatory models of processes and activities, the exemplar being the flowchart (Tufte, 1997; Meyer, 1991). Such images allow research participants to show the connections between elements of a process and perhaps where things are breaking down (Buchanan, 2001). The idea of pictures as forms of data about how things inter-relate and diverge is best known in soft-systems methodology, where 'rich pictures' are the cornerstone of participatory action research (Checkland, 2000), allowing researcher and participants to collaborate on generating, 'a cartoon-like representation that identifies all the stakeholders, their concerns and some of the structure underlying the work context' (Monk and Howard, 1998: 22). Soft-systems methodology was developed in recognition that organizations are in constant interdependent flux with their environments, but that these systems depend as much on tacit knowledge and human interpretation as things and processes – hence the qualifier 'soft', and the value of visual methods in transforming these intangibles into an analysable form (Checkland, 1981; Checkland and Scholes, 1990). 'Rich Pictures', therefore, rest on the premise that visual representation opens a mode of thinking, feeling, and knowing that is more direct than words or text.

The second use of drawing in research, 'freehand sketching' (Meyer, 1991: 224), is underpinned by Jungian psychoanalytic approaches to understanding the unconscious (Broussine, 2008; Rose, 2007: 110). The image in psychoanalytic thought is regarded as allegory or metaphor that gives symbolic form to unconscious 'inner objects' through imagination and dreams, and also though pictures and drawings. Ehrenzweig's (1975) theory of the deep and surface artistic mind underpins these ideas, suggesting that unconscious fears, desires, and repressed feelings bubble up through the mind to be given form in art, and particularly the visual arts.

Examples of uses of drawing in organization studies include Meyer's (1978) study of 22 hospital chief executives, Zuboff's (1988) study of the impact of information technology systems on work, the study of organizational change in the public sector by Vince and Broussine (1996), research on change in education by Kearney and Hyle (2004), and the analysis of organizational roles by Sievers and Beumer (2006). In these cases, participants were asked to depict personal perceptions of their organizations and working lives, with varying degrees of researcher direction

(Meyer asked his executives to depict their organizations as cars). In two studies – Vince and Broussine (1996), and Kearney and Hyle (2004) – the focus was on the emotional experiences of the research participants, and drawing was regarded as vehicle to enable such data to be 'accessed'. As Broussine (2008) notes, participant produced drawing also shares a heritage with the artistic genre of 'expressionism' whereby creative forms such as art, poetry, or drama are made for the purpose of allowing the artist an outlet for their emotions. Aesthetic theory has long been concerned with art's role as emotional expression (Morris-Jones, 1962), and organizational researchers wishing to ground the use of drawing as a research method in a rigorous conceptual framework will find firm footing in the arts (Warburton, 2003).

It is also interesting to note that Broussine (2008) locates expressionism as an explicitly political branch of the arts, originally concerned with social protest. It may be that drawing as a method couched in this tradition would be particularly useful for 'critical management' researchers, with an emphasis on marginalized voices and foregrounding alternative (nonmanagerialist) accounts of organizational life (Alvesson and Deetz, 2000; Grey and Willmott, 2005). I will return to this idea later, in the discussion of respondent-led photo interviewing, but it is salient to note that others have recognized the emancipatory potential of art as a form of organizational enquiry. For example, Gallhofer and Haslam (1996), and Carr (2003) suggest that we might borrow from surrealism to view organizations in unfamiliar ways, and in so doing, expose injustices and inequalities that are often hidden in more 'polished' organizational representations.

Kearney and Hyle (2004: 376–9) summarize their experiences of the benefits and limitations of using drawings in research, citing a faster 'path' to participants' emotional experiences as the main advantages, subject to the caveat that images need to be interpreted and explained by the participant themselves. However, they also caution that asking people to draw pictures in the name of research met with resistance, which contradicts the reported findings of others who have used similar methods. Usually, visual methods are held up as ways of establishing faster and greater rapport with research participants, facilitating more active engagement with the research agenda and process (Meyer, 1991; Warren, 2005). Kearney and Hyle reflected that, in their case, asking participants to draw pictures provoked anxiety for two reasons. First, because some participants perceived themselves to have poor artistic ability they were embarrassed. Second, participants indicated that they were afraid that they would not be able to 'control' the emotional outpouring which drawing pictures might trigger. Ironically, this hints at the primacy of visual imagery in relation to emotional control and self-identity.

These observations have important implications for organizational research. Organizations are typically regarded as serious, rational arenas where, although emotions are rife, they are normally suppressed and rarely expressed (Fineman, 1993 and 2000). Asking organizational members to engage in seemingly *non*-rational activities – such as drawing – in and about their workplace (on which their livelihood and career prospects depend) which might unleash messy emotions, is potentially damaging. Reluctance to draw is perhaps the legacy of a culture that prizes logico-scientific reasoning and modes of representation over 'aesthetico-intuitive' ones (Gagliardi, 1996) and, in so doing, marginalizes 'the arts' into elitist categories that deny 'ordinary creativity' as valuable and attainable by everyone.

This is an important ethical issue that other organizational methods have to contend with in a much less prominent way. It also points to the difficulties of using creative research approaches that appear to be at odds with the 'serious business of doing business', but which might be more effective routes to significant data (Taylor and Hansen, 2005). Ironically, such reactions also confirm the power of (in this case) creative visual methods to probe things differently and to generate fresh insights, but relatedly, using psychoanalytic techniques in organization studies is a dangerous business (Gilmore and Warren, 2007). It is impossible to predict, much less control, what may be 'unleashed' through drawing, dream-work, therapy, and other kinds of creative techniques aimed at tapping into the unconscious. Are researchers adequately equipped to deal with the unanticipated ethical dilemmas that may arise from using techniques intended for *therapeutic* purposes in clinical settings? Although Broussine (2008) carefully observes that techniques for using drawing in organizational research are not intended to be used for therapeutic purposes (this requires a two-year postgraduate diploma), the potential implications for participants and researcher should not be ignored.

With this in mind, the next section deals with the role of photography in research. On account of its technological bases and assumed relationship with reality, the photograph may be seen as a more credible research method than the use of drawing. Once again, since this section is concerned with the *generation* of data through images and not the analysis of images *as* data, the importance of contextualization is a continuing theme.

Photo-interviewing: talking pictures

Photo-interviews involve researcher and participant(s) discussing images that have been made (or selected) by the researcher, participant, or jointly. The important element in photo-interviewing is that the image itself is a starting point for the generation of data, incorporating dialogue and interpretation on the part of all parties involved. Hurworth's (2003) summary neatly maps variations on this theme.

Collier and Collier (1986) describe interviewing with images as 'photo-elicitation' whereby the photograph is used to elicit responses from the respondent, much like market researchers use flashcards of brands or packaging design to gauge consumer responses. Heisley and Levy (1991), working in the field of consumer behaviour, refer to 'auto-driving', which involves the researcher photographing an aspect of the participants' world(s) and eliciting their commentary about an appropriate selection of these images. Heisley and Levy note that asking participants to comment on photographs that had been taken of them by the researcher allowed them to view power relationships 'at a distance', and therefore reflect in a more considered way on the dynamics of the scene. This may be a useful technique to use in organizations given the power asymmetries at play in such contexts. It could be employed to record social interaction during meetings, visually document the spatial arrangements of workplaces or business processes, where the researcher's unfamiliarity with the setting might allow for probing of what organizational members take for granted (see Harper, 1984). Furthermore, commentary on what the researchers have *not* taken pictures of can also be instructive, as Buchanan (2001: 158) points out with regard to the use of photography to document the stages of the 'patient trail' in a hospital. He cites an instance where a medical secretary wanted to know why she had not been photographed pushing her heavy 'records trolley' – a significant physical undertaking, important to 'processing' patients through the system, which had become necessary due to financial cuts and loss of portering services. Attention to these sorts of visible details can, therefore, provide useful lenses through which to view political dimensions of organization (Warren and Fineman, 2007).

This form of photo-interview assumes that the data are to some extent contained 'within' the participant, with the photograph being a tool to extract it, which, according to Harper (1998), belies the collaborative nature of interviewing with images. Auto-driving also assumes that the researcher is best placed to select what is worthy of photographing for later analysis in the interview. While this may be appropriate in certain situations, as when participants' views are sought on specific events or organizational features, it does not engage participants in defining which aspects of their reality are significant to *them*, nor does this recognize the co-constructed nature of the

data resulting from discussions centring on the photographs taken.

Asking research participants to produce their own photographs is a technique well established in healthcare, social policy studies, educational research, and other branches of social science where the 'subjects' are socially disadvantaged, marginalized, or powerless. Wang and Burris (1994, 1997) refer to this as 'photo-voice' (www.photovoice.com) and connect the technique to a political agenda of empowering (giving voice) to those groups. We can trace parallels to applications in feminist, queer, black, and critical management studies, as noted in relation to art-based visual analysis, and perhaps to mainstream organization studies, where researchers are drawing attention to marginalized or silenced accounts of processes such as organizational change through the concept of polyvocality or polyphony (Buchanan and Dawson 2007; Wray-Bliss 2002; Warren 2005).

A recent development concerns applications of photo-voice in research into organizational aesthetics (Warren, 2002); leadership (Wood and Ladkin, 2007); fun at work (Warren and Fineman, 2007); immigrant workers' experiences (Gallo, 2002); facets of child employment (Bolton et al., 2001); organizational abjection (Cohen et al., 2006); and professional identity (Warren and Parker, 2007). These studies do not necessarily refer to photo-voice explicitly as a methodology, but what unites them is that research participants are provided with disposable or digital cameras and asked to compile a set of photographs of their choosing that are pertinent to the research agenda. These photographs are then discussed reflexively in subsequent interviews, with the resulting data being consciously co-constructed through a triad of image-participant-researcher (Schwartz, 1994). Photo-interviews need not be conducted with a single participant. Sievers (2007) discusses how viewing images in a 'social photo-matrix' can generate insights through free association centring on photographs shown to groups of participants. Buchanan (2001) invited participants to view photographs in groups, and Letiche (2001) used participant-produced videos in group settings to reveal the fragmented, contradictory nature of multiple interpretations, to highlight the potential of 'videocy' to contribute to postmodern organization studies.

Interviewing with images, individually or in groups, has several advantages for researchers working from within an interpretivist frame. First, this allows research participants to set the agenda for discussion in a more involved manner. This has various effects, including speedier rapport between parties, generation of unanticipated useful data (what Walker and Wiedel, 1985, call the 'can opener effect'), greater involvement of participants in the interpretive process, and corresponding adjustment in the power dynamics of the research process (Warren, 2002, 2005). Parker (2006) speculates that the role of the image as 'third party' has a depersonalizing effect, and participants self-disclose more readily, and 'open up' to a greater degree. Of course, this will not always be the case, and photo-interviews do not necessarily neutralize or reverse power differentials between researcher and researched, but this approach does appear to have a democratizing effect. Likewise, it is unrealistic to claim that the research agenda is entirely set by participants through their choice of images and accompanying explanations; as with any form of research, the focus of study is predetermined to a greater or lesser extent by the researcher, and the choice of data to include and exclude from analytical frameworks and resulting publications remains with the researcher, who thus imposes his own 'frame' on the findings.

Nonetheless, the inclusion of participants' own images can raise the 'voice' of those 'under study' by allowing their views (literally) of the world (as they construct it) to be communicated more forcefully (Warren, 2005). But it is not enough simply to include the images, either as data in their own right, or to stand alone as communicative media in research outputs. All the studies summarized in this section emphasize the *context* of images, the explanation by the participants that produced them, in the visual research process. Here again, we see a shift away from purely visual media towards a richer concept of visualization that also implicates language. Mitchell (1994) refers to this as 'image-text', noting that the relationship between images and text is uneasy and ambiguous – an argument eloquently developed by Scott (1999) in his thesis on the role of language in understanding photography (see Orobitg Canal, 2004, and Warren, 2002). A further strength of constructing image-texts through photo-interviewing is that diffuse, emotional, and intangible experiences can be expressed more readily through the multisensory character of visual iconography (Warren, 2002; Whincup, 2004). In other words, the photograph allows situations and experiences beyond the frame to be *imag*ined during discussion.

The future of visual methods in organizational research

This chapter has covered a range of visual and image-based techniques and their application in organization studies. The challenges of using visual methods in organizational contexts have been highlighted, and I hope to have conveyed what makes visual approaches useful and distinctive tools for organizational researchers. I will summarize these issues before speculating with regard to future developments in visual organizational research.

Visual research methods are well established in other social science disciplines. Correspondingly, we might expect to see similar developments in organization studies, particularly in the context of a shift towards interpretivist paradigms, meaning social changes driving the image-rich, aestheticized, and symbolic nature of much contemporary organizational life. However, visual studies of organization remain scarce, originating mainly from sociological and anthropological writers looking at work and organizations, rather than from organizational researchers themselves. This begs the question, 'what is so different or distinctive about organizational, business, and management research, that the use of the visual as a viable research approach appears to be precluded?' The answer perhaps lies with 'the politics of profit', including assumptions about what constitutes credible and/or valid business research and issues concerning commercial sensitivity and research ethics.

Organizations are still regarded as places of rational, cool-headed endeavour, where scientific techniques can be applied to any business problem; to many, there seems little scope for visual data to make a valid contribution to such a project. The visual researcher thus immediately faces the challenge of 'selling' these methods to those who control access to the organization, as valid ways to generate useful information about organizational life and its presenting problems, in a way that more traditional approaches do not require. However, visual studies of organization do exist, and this body of work is growing.

A second challenge, concerning ethics, arises once the 'credibility hurdle' has been cleared. The power of images, especially photographs, as assumed accurate representations of reality, raises issues of confidentiality and commercial sensitivity. The visual researcher needs to preserve the anonymity of the organization and its members if consent has not been gained to reveal their identities. This leads to the question, 'whose permission do we ask?', which in turn relates to the multilayered nature of organizations. As photographs can be useful records of events and places, these scenes will more than likely 'contain' people who were unaware that they were being photographed, rendering informed consent problematic.

This discussion may not seem to bode well for the future of visual researchers as institutional research boards and ethics committee scrutinize proposals ever more closely. However, it is important to remember that other disciplines are using visual methods, following codes of conduct and approved protocol, and this should not be an insurmountable problem for organizational researchers. Indeed, the issue of image ethics is generating significant debate (Prosser 2005; Ruby et al., 2003) which looks set to continue (see the International Visual Sociology Association's

discussion list at www.visualsociology.org). Furthermore, these considerations are not confined to visual methods; similar arguments arise with the field notes of participant observers, and the content of interviews. Do organizational members always know when they have been included in research findings, when others have spoken about them in interviews, or they have been observed unawares at work? These questions throw the ethical stance of traditional research methods into relief and highlight how important images are to our sense of self, truth and reality, which is perhaps good reason to pay attention to the visual world more closely.

Copyright is also a difficulty when conducting visual research, particularly in organization studies where many corporate images are trade-marked, or appear in copyright media. This extends to images displayed on webpages that are easily, but illegally, 'copied and pasted' although the concept of 'fair dealing' (through which it is permissible to reproduce images for the purposes of criticism rather than commercial gain) is likely to cover some circumstances (see www.dacs.org.uk). Indeed, the development of digital media has thrown up interesting copyright challenges in a range of settings, including the music and film industries. The notions of ownership, production, reproduction, sharing, sale, and permissions are all destabilized by technology, and image production, consumption and circulation is no different. There have been interesting developments in response to this: the creation of 'creative commons' licensing for publishing online books and articles has embraced the democratizing potential of the Internet through easy access to global information. Examples include include Dvalin Press (www.dvalin.com), Prickly Paradigm Press (www.prickly-paradigm.com), the journal *ephemera* (www.ephemeraweb.org), and the formation of institutional digital repositories (www.driver-community.eu). Furthermore, as Pink (2006: 105–28) observes, it is likely to be technology that continues to enable more 'sensually complete' visual research, through the Internet and hypermedia. In organization studies, online journals offering opportunities for multimedia dissemination of research include *Tamara, EJROT: the electronic journal of radical organization theory, ephemera: theory and politics in organizations*, and *m@n@gement*. As technology becomes more sophisticated, these types of publications are likely to increase in number and significance, transcending the limits of traditional 'hard copy' monochrome publications (Papson et al., 2007).

Against these challenges should be set the considerable benefits of visual methods, as self-contained techniques, and as a component of multimethod projects. The visual is of increasing importance in organizational life and spans many functions, including financial reporting, product design, promotion, service encounters, corporate culture, and architecture. The 'raw material' for visual organizational research is plentiful, and can be worked with in many of the ways explained in this chapter. Furthermore, processes including change management, leadership, role-taking, and identity-work can be understood in more nuanced terms using a visual approach, and visual techniques such as freehand drawing and respondent-led photography play a valuable role in a polysemic perspective on organizations, raising the involvement of research participants, and including multiple voices in research accounts. They can also act as a distancing mechanism through which to study power and politics, and these characteristics make visual methods particularly useful for researchers working in feminist, postcolonial, queer, and critical management studies traditions.

Developments in visual methods have been enabled, in part at least, by the development of digital imaging, and by the Internet as a mode of dissemination. Digital photography has overtaken traditional film, and the cost of cameras and printing has fallen. New visual technologies are being introduced apace; mobile camera-phones, video ipods, holographic technologies, and video sharing websites such as Youtube and Myspace demonstrate the ubiquity of visual modes of communication and narrative. These technologies sensitize us to the visual (Okabe and Ito, 2006), and may be reason enough for researchers to increase their visual literacy, especially as our social and organizational experience becomes more 'image-saturated'. As the visual becomes the *lingua franca* of new forms of communicative media, and images are an increasingly taken-for-granted part of (organizational) life, it becomes even more important to pay attention to the impact of the visual world.

REFERENCES

Alvesson, M. and Deetz, S. (2000) *Doing Critical Management Research*, London: Sage Publications.

Banks, M. and Morphy, H. (1997) *Rethinking Visual Anthropology*, London: Yale University Press

Barrett, T. (2005) *Criticizing Photographs: An Introduction to Understanding Images*, New York: McGraw Hill.

Barthes, R. (1981) *Camera Lucida*, London: Random House.

Beattie, V. and Jones, M. (1992) 'The use and abuse of graphs in annual reports: theoretical framework and empirical study', *Accounting and Business Research*, 22(88): 291–303.

Betts, J. (2006) 'Framing power: the case of the boardroom', *Consumption, Markets, Culture*, 9(2): 157–67.

Böhme, G. (2003) 'Contribution to the critique of the aesthetic economy', *Thesis Eleven*, 73(1): 71–82.

Bolton, A., Pole, C. and Mizen, P. (2001) 'Picture this: researching child workers', *Sociology*, 35(2):501–18.

Brewis, J. (1998) 'What is wrong with this picture?: sex and gender relations in *Disclosure*', in J. Hassard and R. Holliday (eds), *Organization/Representation: Work and Organizations in Popular Culture*, London: Sage Publications, pp. 83–99.

Broussine, M. (2008) *Creative Methods in Organizational Research*, London: Sage Publications.

Buchanan, D. (2001) 'The role of photography in organizational research: a reengineering case illustration', *Journal of Management Inquiry*, 10(2):151–64.

Buchanan, D. and Bryman, A. (2007) 'Contextualizing methods choice in organizational research', *Organizational Research Methods*, 10(3):483–501.

Buchanan, D. and Dawson, P. (2007) 'Discourse and audience: organizational change as multi-story process', *Journal of Management Studies*, 44(5):669–86.

Buchanan, D. and Huczynski, A. (2004) 'Images of influence: *Twelve Angry Men* and *Thirteen Days'*, *Journal of Management Inquiry*, 13(4): 312–23.

Carr, A. (2003) 'Art as a form of knowledge: the implications for critical management', in A. Carr and P. Hancock (eds), *Art and Aesthetics at Work*, London: Palgrave, pp. 7–37.

Checkland, P. (1981) *Systems Thinking, Systems Practice*, Chichester: John Wiley.

Checkland, P. (2000) 'Soft systems methodology: a thirty year retrospective', *Systems Research and Behavioral Science*, 17 (Nov 2000 supplement): 11–S58.

Checkland, P. and Scholes, J. (1990) *Soft Systems Methodology in Action*, Chichester: John Wiley.

Cohen, L., Hancock, P. and Tyler, M. (2006) 'Beyond the scope of the possible: art, photography and organizational abjection', *Culture and Organization*, 12(2): 109–25.

Collier, J. and Collier, M. (1986) *Visual Anthropology: Photography as Research Method*, Albequerque: University of New Mexico Press.

Czarniawska, B. (1999) *Writing Management: Organization Theory as a Literary Genre*, Oxford: Oxford University Press.

Dandridge, T., Mitroff, I. and Joyce, W. (1980) 'Organizational symbolism: a topic to expand organizational analysis', *Academy of Management Review*, 5(1): 77–82.

Davison, J. (2007) 'Photographs and accountability: cracking the codes of an NGO', *Accounting, Auditing and Accountability Journal*, 20(1): 133–58.

Denzin, N. (2001) *Interpretive Interactionism*, London: Sage Publications.

Doherty, E. (2006) 'Working historically through art: incorporating the visual arts into organization studies', *Journal of Management History*, 12(2): 137–53.

Dougherty, D. and Kunda, G. (1990) 'Photograph analysis: a method to capture organizational belief systems', in P. Gagliardi (ed.), *Symbols and Artefacts: Views of the Corporate Landscape*, New York: de Gruyter, pp. 185–206.

Ehrenzweig, A. (1975) *The Psychoanalysis of Artistic Vision and Hearing : An Introduction to a Theory of Unconscious Perception*, London: Sheldon Press.

Emmison, M. and Smith, P. (2000) *Researching the Visual: Images, Objects, Contexts and Interactions in Social and Cultural Inquiry*, London: Sage Publications.

Fineman, S. (ed.) (1993) *Emotion and Organizations*, London: Sage Pubications.

Fineman, S. (ed.) (2000) *Emotion in Organizations*, (second edn.), London: Sage Pubications.

Gagliardi, P. (1990) *Symbols and Artifacts: Views of the Corporate Landscape*, Berlin and New York: de Gruyter.

Gagliardi, P. (1996) 'Exploring the aesthetic side of organizational life', in S.R. Clegg, C. Hardy and W.R. Nord (eds), *Handbook of Organization Studies*, London: Sage Publications, pp. 565–80.

Gallo, M. (2002) 'Picture this: immigrant workers use photography for communication and change', *Journal of Workplace Learning*, 14(2): 49–57.

Gallhofer, S. and Haslam, J. (1996) 'Accounting/art and the emancipatory project: some reflections', *Accounting*, 9(5): 23–44.

Gill, R. (2006) *Gender and the Media*, Oxford: Polity Press.

Gilmore, S. and Warren, S. (2007) 'Unleashing the power of the creative unconscious within organizations: a case of craft, graft and disputed premises', *Tamara: The Journal of Critical Postmodern Organization Science*, 6(1–2): 106–22.

Grey, C. and Willmott, H. (2005) *Critical Management Studies: The Reader*, Oxford: Oxford University Press.

Guthey, E. and Jackson, B. (2005) 'CEO portraits and the authenticity paradox', *Journal of Management Studies*, 42(5): 1057–82.

Hancock, P. (2003) 'Aestheticizing the world of organization: creating beautiful untrue things', in A. Carr and P. Hancock (eds), *Art and Aesthetics at Work*, London: Palgrave pp. 174–94.

Hancock, P. (2005) 'Uncovering the semiotic in organizational aesthetics', *Organization*, 12(1): 29–50.

Harper, D. (1984) 'Meaning and work: a study in photo elicitation', *International Journal of Visual Sociology*, 2(1): 20–43.

Harper, D. (1998) 'An argument for visual sociology', in J. Prosser (ed.) *Image-Based Research: A Sourcebook for Qualitative Researchers*, London: Falmer Press, pp. 24–41.

Hassard, J. and Holliday, R. (eds) (1998) *Organization Representation: Work and Organization in Popular Culture*, London: Sage Publications.

Hatch, M-J. and Schultz, M. (2000) 'Scaling the tower of Babel: relational differences between identity, image and culture in organizations', in M. Schultz, M.J. Hatch and M. Larsen (eds), *The Expressive Organization: Linking Identity, Reputation and the Corporate Brand*, Oxford: Oxford University Press, pp. 11–35.

Hedges, N. and Beynon, H. (1982) *Born to Work: Images of Factory Life*, London: Pluto Press.

Heisley, D. Levy, S. (1991) 'Autodriving: a photoelicitation technique', *Journal of Consumer Research*, 18(3): 257–72.

Hurworth, R. (2003) 'Photo-interviewing for research', *Social Research Update*, 40, University of Surrey.

Jones, M. (1996) *Studying Organizational Symbolism: What, How, Why?*, London: Sage Publications.

Kearney, K. and Hyle, A. (2004) 'Drawing out emotions: the use of participant-produced drawings in qualitative inquiry', *Qualitative Research*, 4(3): 361–82.

Kivinen, N. (2006) *Entering Organizations: Essays on Image, Space and Difference*, Finland: Abo Akademi Turku.

Knowles, C. and Sweetman, P. (eds) (2004) *Picturing the Social Landscape: Visual Methods and Sociological Imagination*, London: Routledge.

Langer, S. (1957) *Philosophy in a New Key*, Milton Keynes: Open University Press.

Letiche, H. (2001) 'Video fractals: research as mass media', *Journal of Organizational Change Management*, 15(1): 63–80.

Linstead, S. (1994) 'Objectivity, reflexivity and fiction: humanity and inhumanity in the science of the social', *Human Relations*, 47(11): 1321–46.

Meyer, A. (1978) 'Management and strategy: the case of the voluntary hospital', in R.E. Miles, and C.C. Snow, *Organizational Strategy, Structure, and Process*, New York: McGraw-Hill, pp. 214–45.

Meyer, A.D. (1991) 'Visual data in organizational research', *Organization Science*, 2(2): 218–36.

Mirzoeff, N. (1999) *An Introduction to Visual Culture*, London: Routledge.

Mitchell, J. (1994) *Picture Theory*, Chicago: University of Chicago Press.

Monk, A. and Howard, S. (1998) 'Methods and tools: the rich picture, a tool for reasoning about work context', *Interactions*, 5(2): 21–30.

Morris-Jones, H. (1962) 'The language of feelings', *British Journal of Aesthetics*, 2(1):17–25.

Okabe, D. and Ito, M. (2006) 'Everyday contexts of camera phone use: steps towards technosocial ethnographic frameworks', in J. Höflich and M. Hartmann (eds), *Mobile Communication in Everyday Life: An Ethnographic View*, Berlin: Frank and Timme, pp. 79–102.

Orobitg Canal, G. (2004) 'Photography in the field: word and image in ethnographic research' in S. Pink, L. Kurti and Afonso, A.I. (eds), *Working Images: Visual Research and Representation in Ethnography*, London: Routledge, pp. 31–46.

Papson, S., Goldman, R. and Kersey, N. (2007) 'Website design: the precarious blend of narrative, aesthetics, and social theory', in G. Stanczak (ed.), *Visual Research Methods: Image, Society and Representation*, London: Sage Publications, pp. 307–44.

Parker, L. (2006) 'Photo-elicitation: an ethno-historical accounting and management research prospect', Paper presented to the *Interdisciplinary Perspectives on Accounting Conference*, Cardiff, Wales.

Parker, L. (2009) 'Photo-elicitation: an ethno-historical accounting and management research prospect' *Accounting, Auditing and Accountability Journal*, forthcoming.

Pink, S. (2006) *Doing Visual Ethnography*, London: Sage Publications.

Postrel, V. (2003) *The Substance of Style: How the Rise of Aesthetic Value is Remaking Commerce, Culture and* Consciousness, New York: Harper Collins.

Preston, A. and Young, J. (2000) 'Constructing the global corporation and corporate constructions of the global: a picture essay', *Accounting, Organizations and Society*, 25(4–5): 427–49.

Prosser, J. (ed.) (1998) *Image-Based Research: A Sourcebook for Qualitative Researchers*, London: Falmer Press.

Prosser, J. (2005) 'The moral maze of image ethics', in K. Sheehy, M. Nind, J. Rix and K. Simmons (eds), *Ethics and Research in Inclusive Education: Values into Practice*, London: RoutledgeFalmer, pp. 133–49.

Ritzer, G. (1999) *Enchanting a Disenchanted World: Revolutionizing the Means of Consumption*, California: Pine Forge Press.

Rose, G. (2007) *Visual Methodologies: An Introduction to the Interpretation of Visual Materials*, London: Sage Publications.

Ruby, J., Gras, L. and Katz, J. (2003) *Image Ethics in the Digital Age*, Minneapolis, MN: University of Minnesota Press.

Rusted, B. (2000) 'Cutting a show: grounded aesthetics and entertainment', in S. Linstead and H. Höpfl (eds), *The Aesthetics of Organizing*, London: Sage Publications, pp. 111–29.

Schroeder, J. (2002) *Visual Consumption*, London: Routledge.

Schroeder, J. (2003) 'Building brands: architectural expression in the electronic age', in L. Scott and R. Batra (eds), *Persuasive Imagery: A Consumer Response Perspective*, New Jersey: Lawrence Erlbaum, pp. 349–82.

Schroeder, J. and Fillis, I. (2006) 'Aesthetics and management: a view from marketing', Paper presented to the *Art of Management Conference*, Krakow, Poland.

Schwartz, D. (1994), 'Visual ethnography: using photographs in qualitative research', *Qualitative Sociology*, 12(2): 119–54.

Scott, C. (1999) *The Spoken Image: Photography and Language*, London: Reaktion Books.

Sievers, B. (2007) 'Pictures from below the surface of the university: the social photo-matrix as a method for understanding organizations in depth', in M. Reynolds and R. Vince (eds), *Experiential Learning and Management Education*, Oxford: Oxford University Press, pp. 241–57.

Sievers, B. and Beumer, U. (2006) 'Organizational role analysis and consultation: the organization as inner object', in J. Newton, S. Long and B. Sievers (eds), *Coaching in Depth: The Organizational Role Analysis Approach,* London: Karnac, pp. 65–81.

Strangleman, T. (2004) 'Ways of (not) seeing: the visual as a blind spot in WES?', *Work, Employment and Society*, 18(1): 179–92.

Taylor, S. and Hansen, H. (2005) 'Finding form: looking at the field of organizational aesthetics', *Journal of Management Studies*, 42(6): 1211–30.

Tian, K. and Belk, R. (2005) 'Extended self and possessions in the workplace', *Journal of Consumer Research*, 32(2): 297–310.

Tufte, E. (1997) *Visual Explanations*, Conneticut: Graphics Press.

Vince, R. and Broussine, M. (1996) 'Paradox, defense and attachment: accessing and working with emotions and relations underlying organizational change', *Organization Studies*, 17(1): 1–21.

Walker, R. and Wiedel, J. (1985) 'Using photographs in a discipline of words' in R. Burgess (ed.), *Field Methods in the Study of Education*, London: Falmer Press, pp. 191–216.

Wagner, J. (2005) 'What's new visually?', in N. Denzin and Y. Lincoln (eds), *Handbook of Qualitative Research*, London: Sage Publications, pp. 747–62.

Wang, C. and Burris, M.A. (1994) 'Empowerment through photo novella: portraits of participation', *Health Education Quarterly*, 21(2): 171–86.

Wang, C. and Burris, M.A. (1997), 'Photovoice: concept, methodology and use for participatory needs assessment', *Health and Behaviour*, 24(3): 369–87.

Warburton, N. (2003) *The Art Question*, London: Routledge.

Warren, S. (2002) 'Show me how it feels to work here: using photography to research organizational aesthetics', *ephemera: theory and politics in organizations*, 2(3): 224–45.

Warren, S. (2005) 'Photography and voice in critical qualitative management research', *Accounting, Auditing and Accountability Journal*, 18(6): 861–82.

Warren, S. (2006) 'Hot-nesting: a visual exploration of the personalisation of space in a hot-desking environment', in P. Case, S. Lilley and T. Owen (eds), *The Speed of Organization*, Copenhagen: Copenhagen Business School Press, pp. 119–46.

Warren, S. and Fineman, S. (2007) 'Don't get me wrong, it's fun here but: ambivalence and paradox in a 'fun' work environment', in R. Westwood and C. Rhodes (eds), *Humour, Work and Organization*, pp. 92–112.

Warren, S. and Parker, L. (2007) 'Bean counters or bright young things?: introduction to a visual study of identity construction among newly qualified professional accountants', Paper presented to the 25th *Standing Conference on Organizational Symbolism*, Ljubljana, Slovenia.

Warren, S. and L. Parker (2009) 'Bean counters or bright young things?: introduction to a visual study of identity construction among newly qualified professional accountants', *Qualitative Research in Management and Accounting*, forthcoming.

Warren, S. and Rehn, A. (2006) 'Oppression, art and aesthetics', *Consumption, Markets, Culture*, 9(2): 81–5.

Welsch, W. (1997) *Undoing Aesthetics*, London: Sage Publications.

Whincup, T. (2004) 'Imaging the intangible', in C. Knowles and P. Sweetman (eds), *Picturing the Social Landscape: Visual Methods and Sociological Imagination*, London: Routledge, pp. 79–92.

Williamson, J. (1978) *Decoding Advertisements: Ideology and Meaning in Advertising*, London: Boyars.

Wood, M. and Ladkin, D. (2007) 'The event's the thing: encounters with the leaderful moment', Paper presented to 25th *Standing Conference on Organizational Symbolism*, Ljubljana, Slovenia.

Wray-Bliss, E. (2002) 'Interpretation–appropriation: (making) an example of labour process theory', *Organizational Research Methods*, 5(1): 80–103.

Zuboff, S. (1988) *In the Age of the Smart Machine: The Future of Work and Power*, Oxford: Heinemann Professional Publishing.

34

Narrative and Stories in Organizational Research: An Exploration of Gendered Politics in Research Methodology

Carl Rhodes and Alison Pullen

Science it would seem is not sexless; he is a man, a father and infected too (Virginia Woolf, in Harding, 1986: 135)

Within organizational research it is increasingly common to find work that draws on notions of narrative and stories to inform its methodology. Such research has investigated a broad range of organizational phenomena, stretching from sensemaking, to communication, to politics and power, to learning and change, and to identity and identification (see Rhodes and Brown, 2005a). There have also been attempts to elucidate and explain the theoretical and methodological bases on which narrative and stories can be justified as valid practices to investigate and to investigate with (e.g. Boje, 1995; Czarniawska, 1998, 2004; Gabriel, 2000). It has even been claimed that there is a general tendency

towards a 'narrativization of organizational theory' (Gabriel, 2004: 63) and that narrative approaches to knowledge are an 'heir apparent' to organizational research after the broad ranging influence of 'postmodernism' in the 1980s and 1990s (Calás and Smircich, 1999).

In this chapter, we tell a story about this 'narrative turn' as it has been taken up in organizational research. In embarking on such a task, we are immediately drawing on one of the foundational distinctions in narratology—that between story and narrative discourse. If at its most basic level a narrative can be defined as 'the representation of an event or series of events' (Abbott, 2002: 12), then narrative immediately appears to consist of two components—the series of events themselves (the story), and the mode through which they are represented (the narrative discourse) (ibid.). Using such a distinction we can say, for example, that the same story can be told in numerous different ways and with different effects. This suggests a 'double logic' where stories emplot events that are assumed to exist prior to their narration, yet concurrently events can only be made significant and apparent in that they are narrated in a meaningful manner (Culler, 1981). In other words, story and narrative discourse depend on each other. This means that as we write about narrative and organizational research we invoke the convention that we are telling you about something that has already happened in this field. Simultaneously, however, our endeavors seek to determine those events and their significance through our writing.

The story we tell provides a critical introduction and discussion of the ways that narrative research methods have been deployed and developed in the study of management and organizations. What we bring to the narration of this story is a particular concern with the methodological contestation over the well worn and culturally established border between science and narration (Czarniawska, 1995; Rhodes and Brown, 2005a). This distinction is between narrative as being 'planted in an arts tradition emphasizing literary discourse, elegance of philosophical debate and historical analysis' and science as emphasizing 'observation, experimentation and systematic theory-building accompanied by a belief in ahistorical universal laws as the ultimate benchmark for success' (Butler, 1997: 928–9). In the structures of modern science, this has been understood as an impermeable boundary—after all, modern western sciences 'are not supposed to have any politically charged conceptual frameworks or narrative structures' instead positioning themselves as being 'transparent to the world they represent' (Harding, 2006: 4).

Our contention is that the struggle for narrative to take its place in organizational research is part of a broader methodological gender politics that associates science, rationality, and knowledge with masculinity (see Oakley, 2000), and where the feminine political struggle is to 'find an alternative to

objective scientific rigour' in research (Pullen, 2006a: 278). As Harding (1986) argues:

> Once we begin to theorize gender—to define gender as an analytical category within which humans think about and organize their social activity rather than as a natural consequence of sex difference, or even merely as a social variable assigned to individual people [...] we begin to appreciate the extent to which gender meanings have suffused our belief systems, institutions, and even such apparently gender-free phenomena as our architecture and urban planning (p. 17).

Following Harding's point, our task is to 'identify the trace of gender-codified normative values' (Keller, 1988: 244) in organizational research that does not explicitly account for itself as gendered, to offer a critique of those values and associated practices, and to draw attention to ways of knowing and writing that respond to such a critique. We do this with reference to narrative research and how its development has created legitimate options for organizational research and writing that are increasingly distanced from the rational traditions of scientism and positivism.

Science, and the reign of rationality that it promises, are genealogically entangled with the meaning of masculinity, both generally (Lloyd, 1993), and in the study of organizations (Ross-Smith and Kornberger, 2004). Masculinity and rationality are indelibly associated with the 'cognitive authority granted to scientific authority and its practices' (Laslett et al., 1996: 1) where in science 'objectivity, rationality, and good method are persistently linked to certain models of [dominant Western] masculinity' (Harding, 2006: 83). In this rational-masculine tradition, nonscientific knowledge such as that embodied in narrative discourse has been dismissed as being 'trivial compared to the real stuff heirs to logical positivism produce' (Adkins, 2002: 215) such that the ideals associated with rational knowledge are coterminous with 'character ideals associated with maleness' (Lloyd, 1993: 18).

What we have here is a deeply ingrained tradition in western culture, traceable back to ancient Greece, where rational-scientific discourse is associated with the masculine and narrative discourse being feminine other. In this powerful discourse, science qua rationality is seen as a transcendence of the feminine, with the image of the scientist being that of the 'man of reason' (Lloyd, 1993) who eschews narrative as part of a premodern and unenlightened legacy (Gabriel, 1998a). As Lloyd (1993) puts it:

> Rational knowledge has been constructed as a transcending, transformation or control of natural forces; and the feminine has been associated with what rational knowledge transcends, dominates of simply leaves behind (p. 1).

Despite the culturally sedimented assumptions about the valour and value of science qua masculine reason, as we shall see, the development and influence or narrative methodologies in organizational research has deeply contested the presumption of triviality of narrative discourse as a rightful part of research methodology. It is the nature and meanings of this contestation that we explore in this chapter. We examine the different ways that narrative research has been deployed in organizational research and how this reflects the seam lines of power that are at play in what is regarded as legitimate and permissible within this field.

DISTRIBUTING THE SENSIBLE

In telling this story of narrative research, our thinking is informed and inspired by Paul Rancière's (2004) notion of the 'distribution of the sensible,' a term he uses to describe the culturally acceptable ways of thinking that establish what a particular community includes and excludes as being obvious or self-evident. This distribution determines 'what is seen and what can be said about it [...] who has the ability to see and the talent to speak' (p. 13); it provides a legitimatory hierarchy around what is considered valid and invalid in terms of 'sense.' So inspired, we deploy the notion of the distribution

of the sensible in terms of the forms of discourse regarded as being 'sensible' to organizational research based on the socially 'necessary connections between a type of subject matter and a form of expression' (Rancière, 2004: 53).

Within the distribution of the sensible, Rancière identifies three historical 'regimes' that distinguish art from nonart—the ethical regime, the representative regime, and the aesthetic regime. We use these analogously for understanding the political distribution of capacities and entitlements within our research community and its modes of inquiry and expression. We also suggest that each of the regimes reflects a different position on the gendered relation between science and narrative. While the remainder of the paper focused on explicating and exemplifying the history and workings of these regimes in organizational research, we can summarize in advance.

In the ethical regime, narrative is understood as inferior to science and therefore best unacknowledged, disregarded, or purged. In this regime, artistic simulacra, in our case, narrative discourse, is dangerous in its corrupting effect on a community's devotion to the truth. Narrative is feminized and seen as a dangerous force that threatens the masculine rational order. In this regime, there is a relation of gender ignorance in that, while the privileging of masculine rationality is present, it is not explicit. Masculine knowledge is valorized as being ethically superior by suppressing and ignoring narrative as its feminine other such that the masculine norms of science achieve power by being considered universal and gender-free. Given the active suppression of gender in this regime, within it we find no ways that narrative is explicitly deployed as a research method.

In the representative regime the relationship between science and its scientific 'other' is re-evaluated so as to partially redeem the value of narrative. Narrative works are seen as being of value providing they adhere to what are defined as their 'proper' forms and usages. The gender ignorance of the ethical regime is loosened with narrative beginning to take a legitimate place in organizational research. This legitimacy, however, is bounded—narrative is something that is at the service of rational discourse such that it can be analyzed or explicated and, in a sense, 'tamed.' The feminine, although accounted for, is marginalized and subservient to proper scientific inquiry. In this regime, we locate three main methods that have been developed—narrative positivism, social constructionist approaches to analyzing narratives, and the theorization of organizations as 'storytelling systems.'

In the aesthetic regime, the hierarchies of distribution are destabilized. The division between narrative and science is no longer firm and the dualistic distinction between these two forms of knowledge collapses so as to create new hybridic forms. Narrative starts to free itself from the yoke of rationality and the boundaries between the masculine and feminine in methodology begin to be transgressed. This is achieved in research that openly values and deploys narrative discourse as a legitimate mode of knowledge. In the representative regime, narrative has been deployed in methodological stances that see all research as a form of storytelling, that report research in the form of 'tales from

the field,' and research that tells 'stories about stories.'

Using this threefold categorization, what follows is a review of the ways that narrative has been used in organizational research, as well as a critical account of the politics of these developments in relation to gendered methodology.

Narrative research in the ethical regime

The logic of the ethical regime is one which separates 'the world of artistic imitations from the world of vital concerns and politico-social grandeur' (Rancière, 2004: 17). Here works of imitation and representation as practiced by poets, painters, and playwrights are understood as a dangerous force that corrupts the proper pursuit of truth and knowledge. Rancière specifically links this regime to the ancient Greek philosopher Plato, especially his book *The Republic*. For Plato, the danger of poetic works emanate from the way that, in them it is not possible to distinguish between the author's speech and that of the characters. In poetic discourse, language is released from the 'control of those who use it' to such an extent that 'it is a threat to the community and the

Table 34.1   Narrative in organizational research

Regime	Relation Between Science and Narrative	Narrative Research Methods	Gendered Methodology
Ethical	Narrative is inferior to science and should be avoided or purged from it	• None	*Gender ignorance* – masculine norms are assumed universal, the feminine is absent, and gender neutrality and blindness prevail.
Representative	Narrative is other to science	• Narrative positivism • Narrative as social construction • Organizations as 'storytelling systems'	*Gender marginalization*—the coexistence yet hierarchical differentiation of the feminine text where the feminine is present but marginalized.
Aesthetic	The boundaries between science and narrative are blurred	• Research as storytelling • 'Tales from the field' • 'Stories about stories'	*Gender transgression*—contestation of the gendered boundaries between narrative and science.

political order' (Bell, 2004: 128). The poetic work is untrustworthy because 'it proffers imitations of imitations, when life's purpose is to seek eternal truth; poetry stirs up refractory emotions, challenging reason's rule, making men woman-ish' (Edmundson, 1995: 1).

The ethical distinction in this regime is between 'forms of knowledge based on the imitation of a model with precise ends, and artistic simulacra that imitate simple appearances' (Rancière, 2004: 21). Those who produce the latter are condemned for the 'falsity and the pernicious nature of the images [they] present' (p. 42). The key distinction is that reason and the search for truth should rule over emotion and the devotion to images—the former being understood specifically as masculine, and the latter as feminine (Lloyd, 1993). The gendered hierarchy between science and narrative is already established, such that the feminine is seen as 'inherently dangerous' on account of its presumed alterity and inferiority to reason and its association with subjectivity, desire, and passion (Rose, 1994: 7). For Plato (1974), 'story-tellers are in error in matters of the greatest human importance' (p. 148) and 'have no serious claim to truth' (p. 439). Such epistemological matters are better resolved by rationality coupled with 'calculations of number, measurement and weight' (p. 432).

Within organization studies, the traditional conception of narrative very much follows the tenets of the ethical regime. The dominant has been 'science should keep to facts and logic and stories to literature, this being the sediment of premodern time and societies' (Czarniawska, 1997b: 7). As is the case in both the natural and social sciences, the 'production and dissemination of knowledge [...was...] governed by largely scientific or quasi-scientific modes of inquiry and discourse, by non-storied forms of investigation and reportage' (Kreiswirth, 2000: 295). This history thinly veils the desire for organizational researchers to be seen as 'men of reason' (Lloyd, 1993) and, like Plato, to ignore, banish or disparage narrative—a tendency that is exacerbated in the modern era with the decline in the tradition of oral storytelling (Benjamin, 1936/68). Gabriel (1998a) describes this tendency as 'narrative de-skilling' where storytelling became dismissed as a form of communication and understood in an oppositional and inferior relation to fact and science.

In a microcosmic reflection of Plato's *Republic,* in the ethical regime narrative is excluded from the proper domain of organizational research on account of its presumed inferiority, irrationality, its implied femininity, and it potential for corruption. At best, narrative discourse might make research more enjoyable to read, but it is not part of its real value—the latter being reserved for 'rigorous method' (Eisenhardt, 1991: 621). In the 'contested discursive terrain' (Westwood and Clegg, 2003: 2) of organizational research, the powerful discursive force of 'normal science' is deemed as a desired (male) orthodoxy (Pfeffer, 1993) whereas nonscientific approaches such as narrative are relegated to the status of one of many idiosyncrasies—a problem to be resolved (McKelvey, 1997).

Dismissing narrative as a dimension of a proper science of organization is informed by the idea that 'real men don't collect soft data' (Gherardi and Turner, 1987) and that 'soft scientists are storytellers' (Churchman, 1968, in Mitroff and Kilmann, 1976: 190). This echoes a cultural distinction that regards science as being hard, and narrative/mythology as being soft and therefore inferior (Mitroff and Kilmann, 1976). The ethical regime prizes masculinist research values, yet this masculinism does not announce itself by name; it is ignorant of the gendered norms that sustain it. Research should be hard, rigorous, firm, logical, rational, conclusive, systematic, and so forth. Moreover, 'the focus on quantitative measures, variable analysis, impersonal and excessively abstract conceptual schemas is both a distinctly masculine tendency and one that serves to hide its own gendered character' (Harding, 1986: 105). These values privilege the masculine even though this gender bias is disguised through the 'neutrality' and 'objectivity' of science. While in its substantive areas of inquiry organizational research has historically been blind and deaf to gender (Wilson, 1996; Linstead, 2000), this sensory deprivation is also present at a methodological level. The obsession with purity and mastery manifests a 'science of erection' that must not be contaminated by the feminine, thus keeping it alien (Höpfl 2000: 104). Here, the opposition between scientific and narrative forms as genres of organizational research (Czarniawska, 1999a), like other forms of genre distinction, are related to the 'sexual difference between the feminine and masculine genre/gender' (Derrida, 1980: 74).

In organizational research under the ethical regime, the methodological masculine norm is presented as being gender neutral such that the feminine is abject, repressed and/or ignored—in this regard, organizational research follows the more general history of science as being dominated by men and by masculine norms (Rose, 1994) while at the same time blinding itself to the gendered character of knowledge by considering research only as an intellectual process rather than as a social and political one (Laslett et al., 1996). Narrative forms of knowing in the ethical regime are sublimated, because they are related to feminine emotion rather than masculine reason; they are improper to science (Golinski, 2002). If it is the case that we all do gender when we do research (Gherardi, 1995; Gherardi et al., 2003; Pullen, 2006a) then under the ethical regime the only gender that can be done (by men or women) is the masculine. With this suppression, narrative is explicitly absent as a research method in the ethical regime.

Narrative research in the representative regime

The Platonic legacy of the ethical regime establishes an explicitly gendered division whereby masculine reason (qua science) is established as the road to truth and knowledge, yet where feminine emotion (qua art and

storytelling) is considered frivolous and inferior. But, while Plato wanted to banish the poets from his ideal state because of their dangerous influence, his one time student Aristotle saw things differently, and it is in the thinking of Aristotle that Rancière (2004) identifies the representative regime.

Aristotle agreed with Plato that poetry, drama and comedy are to be classified as 'imitations' (mimesis). But while Plato saw them as an impoverished feminized imitation of reality, Aristotle saw them as an 'imitation of action' (Ricoeur, 1984)—a developed form of imitation that is quite naturally human and that, in its proper forms, can be used to understand and 'manage' the experience of emotion. Aristotle was particularly fond of tragedy, which he describes approvingly as 'an imitation of action that is admirable, complete and possesses magnitude' (Aristotle, 1996: 10) that tends to 'express universals' (p. 16) rather than just representing particular historical individuals. Poetics is valued because through it people can 'come to understand and work out what each thing is' (p. 7).

Taking his lead from Aristotle, in Rancière's representative regime the substance and value of art lies in 'the fabrication of a plot arranging actions that represent the activities of men' (Rancière, 2004: 21). Narrative is here not excluded from what is to be regarded as 'sensible' but takes a special place within it. No longer castigated as being a 'mere' imitation, poetics provides a means through which artistic representations can be assessed as proper and valuable—as long as they are kept in their place within the rational male order. Representations are seen as being 'good' providing that they contain particular qualities that differentiate them from the low arts. For Aristotle, this included the idea that art provided its spectators with access to knowledge and the discharging of emotions (Edmundson, 1995)—a point again expressing the gendered nature of these divisions, given the long association of emotion with femininity and the need for its repression and control to maintain masculine identity (Golinski, 2002).

Just as Rancière notes the historical emergence of the representative regime, in the smaller history of organizational research a similar emergence can be identified. In the late 1970s, organizational research came under significant scrutiny in the name of what was to be called the 'paradigm wars.' With the uptake of Burrell and Morgan's (1979) *Sociological Paradigms and Organizational Analysis*, there was a growing dissent towards the dominance of positivist methodologies and an active resistance to the 'hegemony of systems' (Hassard, 1993) that had hitherto dominated research as a masculine norm (Ross-Smith and Kornberger, 2004). The result was a significant pluralization of what was regarded as methodologically legitimate (Weaver and Gioia, 1994). The ethical regime that prized science and rationality exclusively was severely disrupted. While this ethical regime did not die and attempts to police it continued (see, for example, Donaldson, 1996; Pfeffer, 1993), things were changing. As part of these more general changes narrative methodologies started to develop in organizational research—a turn away from science towards the humanities for methodological inspiration and guidance (Zald, 1993). As Gabriel (2004) proposes 'twenty years ago, it was not uncommon for researchers to complain that narratives and stories were not taken seriously in organizational research [...] the climate of opinion has changed' (p. 72).

In the 1980s, there was an increasing interest in using narratives as a source of data. Such narratives could be 'treated analytically by field researchers' (Czarniawska, 1998: 15) and used as an 'overlooked yet valuable source of data for research in organizations' (Rhodes and Brown, 2005a: 169). The value of 'stories as data' was that they were thought to 'open valuable windows into the emotional and symbolic lives of organizations' (Gabriel, 1998b: 135)—a point that resonated with the growing substantive interest in researching organizational culture (Boyce, 1996), as well as the questioning of male rationality as the privileged methodological order. With stories the researcher's task is to collect, listen to and compare stories told in organizations and investigate and analyze how people construct narratives around particular events so as to gain 'access to deeper organizational realities, closely linked to members' experiences' (Gabriel, 1998b: 136). In this regime, narratives are legitimized as being valuable to research and no longer dismissed as 'soft' and feminine. This value has been realized in three primary forms: narrative positivism, narrative as social construction, and organizations as storytelling systems— each of these are discussed next.

Narrative positivism

In its most tame incarnation, narrative in research takes the form of what Abbott (1992) has called 'narrative positivism.' As the name suggests, this form of research retains the masculine-rational assumptions of positivism, incorporating narrative merely as a source of information about events that have transpired. While the methods and assumptions of positivist methodology remain intact—what is added is that 'narrative provides a wealth of information that is available and codable using familiar techniques' (Pentland, 1999: 716). Such coding reduces narrative to story— the 'hard facts' that are assumed to lurk behind their narrated mode of communication. Even though narrative positivism has not been extensively developed and deployed in organizational research, it has been of significant influence on 'process theories' or organizational change (Van de Ven and Poole, 1995) with its purveyors claiming that owe a 'great debt' to the 'inspiration of Abbott's work' (Poole et al., 2000: vii).

Following Pentland's (1999) critical commentary the achievement of narrative positivism is to reduce narrative data to their 'lowest common denominator: sequences of objectively coded events' by systematically excluding their narrative qualities, and hence their explanatory potential (p. 714). In reducing narratives to the events they describe, narrative positivism remains aligned with conventional methodology as summarized in the table below:

In narrative positivism, the contribution of narrative is its explicit incorporation

Table 34.2   Relationship of narrative properties to organizational theory (from Pentland, 1999: 713)

Narrative Property	Indicator For
Sequence	Patterns of events
Focal actor(s)	Role, social network, and demographics
Voice	Point of view, social relationships, and power
Moral context	Cultural values and assumptions
Other indicators	Other aspects of context

of temporality. Where 'normal' methods focus on 'fixed entities with variable qualities' and 'variables-hypostatized social characteristics,' narrative analysis focuses on 'process conceptions: that attribute causality to agents and social actors' (Abbot, 1992: 428). Pentland identifies Sabherwal and Robey's (1993) study of software development projects as an exemplar of narrative positivism in organizational research. While this study does not itself foreground narrativity in its methodological position, it acknowledges that it deploys a process model focused on the 'progression of events over time' and 'theoretical explanations about sequences of events'; the goal of which is to 'classify the sequence of activities within organizations that produce outcomes of social and technical change' (p. 550). The analytical strategy deployed was to gather stories from respondents, code those stories into types of events, and then to analyze the sequences of these events. The result is a generalized taxonomy of six 'archetypal' processes for software implementation (Pentland, 1999).

Narrative positivism assesses the causal relationship between organizational events to ascertain the replicable and generalizable rules that govern those events, such that the validity of the results is a core goal (Stevenson and Greenberg, 1998). Establishing the accurate story is central to narrative positivism—researchers must 'get the story "right" by correctly identifying the causal mechanisms that are actually operating in a world that exists independent of narratives' (Howlett and Rayner, 2006: 4). Retained from positivism

is the belief that 'an objective social world exists outside of our own perceptions of it, and we can discover lawful "reasonable stable relationships" (Huberman and Miles, 1994: 428) between social phenomena' (Stevenson and Greenberg, 1998: 744). Although narrative is included it is over-shadowed by the super-ordination of science and the gendered character of the ethical regime is barely disturbed.

Narrative as social construction

Although narrative positivism illustrates how narrative temporality can be used to augment the dimensions of analysis conducted within a positivist framework, there have also been uses of narrative informed by social constructivism that do not locate themselves in relation to positivism. Such approaches offer a step forward from the scientific masculinism of narrative positivism in that narratives are valued more on there own terms rather that being distilled into rational categories. An early example is Mitroff and Kilmann's (1976, 1978) narrative study of managerial preferences for organizational design. They used narratives as:

> Devices with which to peer into human desires, wishes, hopes and fears [… where..] the best stories are those which stir people's minds, hearts and souls and by doing so give them new insights into themselves, their problems and their human condition. The challenge is to develop a human science that more fully serves this aim (p. 93).

Under such auspices narrative discourse provides researchers with access to systems of meaning in organizations that are not available through other methods. As Hansen and Kahnweiler (1993) suggested, 'stories can be used to study the often unstated and perhaps unconscious codes for resolving conflicts, approaching decision making, determining perceptions of positive and negative organizational forces, and guiding role behaviour' (p. 1391). Narrative is now a way that organizational members individually and collectively make sense of their experiences. Moreover, that sense making reflects the culture of an organization. The link is created between social construction, narrative and organization in that narratives facilitate socialization and the generation of commitment and adaptation; they are a vehicle for organizational control, and they consciously and unconsciously develop meaning (Boyce, 1996: 7). Thus, narratives told and repeated in organizations can be gathered and analyzed for convergent and divergent themes and plots which reflect the dominant and contested structures of meaning that inform working life, organizational conduct, and political structures in organizations.

As Currie and Brown (2003) suggest, the methodological position for a social constructivist narratology is one where:

> Organizations are socially constructed phenomena, sustained by means of social, symbolic and political processes. In a sense organizations literally are the narratives that people author in networks of conversations, the intertextuality of which sustains an accumulation of continuous and (sufficiently) consistent story lines that in turn maintain and objectify 'reality' [...]. A narratological approach is particularly valuable for the light it sheds on aspects of individual and group sense-making; sense-making being understood to refer to those processes of interpretation and meaning production whereby people reflect on and interpret phenomena and produce inter-subjective accounts (p. 563).

From such a standpoint, the role of the researcher is that of 'story analyst' (Prichard et al., 2004) in that s/he gathers and interprets stories told by people in organizations to discern the cultural meaning structures that operate therein. Here organizational reality exists in its narration (Weick, 1995).

Organizations as storytelling systems

As well as narratives being used as data, within the representative regime, narrative also takes on a broader ambit in that researchers also consider organizations as a whole as 'storytelling systems.' With such 'interpretive approaches,' the researcher 'conceptualizes organizational life as story making and organizational theory as story reading' (Czarniawska, 1998:

14) where 'the organization is a multidiscursive and precarious effect or product' (Law, 1994: 250). Rather than narrative being subjected and reduced to masculine-rational analysis, the whole idea of narrative becomes a conceptual scaffolding on which to theorize organizations.

This approach has been developed comprehensively by Boje (1991, 1994, 1995) in relation to what he calls the 'storytelling organization.' Even though narratives are still gathered and analyzed as data (see Boje, 1991), their meanings are understood in relation to the 'whole' of an organization through their functioning as both shared and divergent meaning making systems (Boje, 1991) and their capacity to embody and transmit individual accounts of experience and common organizational myths (Gabriel, 1991). This is theorized by Boje (1994, 1995) using a Hollywood play called Tamara as a metaphor for 'collective storytelling' (1994: 435). In Tamara, rather than sitting in fixed positions the audience move around though the action with the play being set across many different rooms or stages simultaneously. Audience members decide which rooms to watch the action in and which actors and plot-lines to follow. While each member of the audience has seen the same play, each one has seen quite different plays. From this metaphor, organizations too are conceived of as simultaneously occurring narrative similarity and narrative difference, instead of being a singularity that can be captured and analyzed by an all-seeing observer.

This approach is also used in Barry and Elmes' (1997) narrative view of strategic discourse. For them, strategy is understood as standing 'somewhere between theatrical dream, the historical novel, futurist fantasy, and autobiography' (p. 432). The narrative quality of strategy is that it is a form of future oriented temporal action that is dramatically emplotted and contains prescribed 'parts' for the organizational actors involved. Strategic management relies on narrative devices in order to establish its credibility—in particular materiality, voice, perspective, ordering, setting, and reader-ship targeting. Barry and Elmes identify four distinct genres in which strategies are developed—the epic, where strategy is an epic journey of 'navigating toward opportunities and away from threats' (p. 440); technofutur-ist, where strategy involves detailed imagin-ings of the future state of the organization; purist, where organizations seek to emulate archetypes of strategy; and polyphonic, where strategy is borne out of having listened to and incorporated many different points of view.

As we have seen, in the representative regime narratives are regarded as proper and legitimate phenomena for researchers to analyze and theorize. In this regime, however, storytelling is still largely understood as a qualitatively different activity from that undertaken by researchers and the gendered distinction between narrative and science remains intact—put simply, research subjects tell stories, researchers do analysis. Although narrative discourse takes a place in research, the gendered division between subjective (feminine) and objective (masculine) is retained, as is the privileging of the latter over the former (Oakley, 2000). The cultural distinction between masculine and feminine knowledge and representation is retained, each having its own distinct value (although narrative still remains subservient to rational-ity qua science). The methodological stance in this regime can thus be characterized as one of gender subordination in that, while gendered difference can be identified, the feminine (i.e. narrative) is still marginalized as something to be subjected to, and penetrated by, proper analysis. It is within Rancière's third regime, the aesthetic regime, that these distinctions finally begin to be eroded and the gendered hierarchies disrupted.

Narrative research in the aesthetic regime

In Rancière's aesthetic regime, art is freed from old hierarchical rules and the distinction between art and non-art is destroyed. In this democratic regime, art is no longer evaluated on the basis of its imitative or representative status, but instead each work is apprehended in its own singularity and particularity. The hierarchies that operate under the two other regimes break down, such that distinctions between 'fine art' and other forms of art are no longer tenable. This third regime is where 'testimony and fiction come under the same regime of meaning' (p. 37) such that the division between story and history is revoked. Forms of representation associated with the 'real' and associated with the 'fictional' are both now located in the 'blurred border between the logic of facts and the logic of fiction' (p. 38). Consistent with the organizing principle of this regime, the traditional hierarchies which render the world sensible are redistributed, as are their gendered relations.

In organizational research, we can identify work that collapses the artificial division between science and narrative (Czarniawska, 1997a). In what has been called 'fiction science' (Watson, 2000), research activity is seen to involve the coproduction of narratives by researchers, organizations, and the people in them (Rhodes, 2000). In overcoming the dualism between science and narrative, researchers no longer feel 'embarrassment' about seeing truth in artistic forms and realize that 'art and science are not in opposition' (Butler, 1997: 945). In this regime narrative discourse approaches being freed from the yoke of the masculine-rational scientific as its defining and oppressive other.

While from the perspective of positivistic science the inclusion of literary concerns in research is regarded as an 'aberration,' because it blurs the distinction between research/truth and literature/fiction, such work can still be regarded as 'exemplary' (Smircich, 1992), creative and affirmative (Rhodes and Pitsis, 2008: 6). Much research that has been done capitalizes on this 'third space' between science and narrative. Three approaches to this are (1) 'research as storytelling' when research is re-evaluated as an implicit narrative practice, (2) 'tales from the field,' where research is theorized explicitly as a storytelling activity and

(3) 'stories about stories,' where narrative forms from literature and popular culture are revalued as valid forms of knowledge about organizations.

Research as storytelling

There have been numerous contributions to the organizational research literature that have re-evaluated the relationship between research and narrative and concluded that researchers have been telling stories all along. Although not necessarily explicit, research is itself understood as an inherently narrative practice—'people who write about organizations tell stories' (Rhodes, 2001a: 3) and in so doing 'we are constantly creating, recreating and representing the lives of others' (Pullen, 2006a: 281). This suggests that 'narrative has always played an important part in the production and distribution of human knowledge. Although not a trademark of scientific texts, the narrative is already present' (Czarniawska, 1999a: 64) and the ability to tell a good story has long been a foundation of sociology and organization studies (Clegg, 1993). It has thus been said that 'our functionalist models of organizations with their rationalistic management are nothing more that stories, dreams, adventures full of heroism and horrors' (Czarniawska and de Monthoux, 1994: 12). It seems that the feminine, although muted and repressed, was always present in the work of the 'man of reason.'

Hatch (1996) argues that those who write research adopt a 'narrative position' in relation to their written work. She identifies four such positions: (1) the researcher being the main character who tells the story, (2) the researcher narrating from the perspective of a minor character within the story, (3) the researcher as an analytical or omniscient narrator, and (4) the researcher as a narrator who tells the story as an objective observer. It is the final two of these that Hatch argues are the dominant narrative positions in organizational research. Rather than being innocent differences in writing style, the different narrative positions reflect different epistemological perspectives—'different ways of knowing are constructed within and through different narrative perspectives' (p. 369). Moreover 'for the individual researcher seeking the experience of fresh epistemological perspective, the technique of learning to write using forms of narrative not previously mastered is recommended' (p. 371).

Jeffcut (1994) also takes issue with the relationship between researchers' narratives and the meaning of research by analyzing the 'representational style' deployed in research into organizational culture. For Jeffcut, the dominant styles are the epic narrative (where the researcher is positioned as a hero in search of the true meaning of the organization), and the romantic narrative (where the researcher revels in the creation of organizational unity and harmony). Jeffcut's point is that by inadvertently adopting these styles, research in organizational culture had marginalized experiences and realities better characterized by ironic or tragic styles. What both Hatch and Jeffcut's commentaries suggest is not only that organizational research has an unacknowledged narrative quality, but also that the dominance of particular narrative styles and positions limits that which is knowable in the field. More critically, this acknowledges that while there is a desire for researchers to position themselves in heroic and superior ways in relation to their mastery of knowledge and practice, 'the "truths" offered by scientific research are subject to the limitations and intricacies of narrative (re)presentation and do not stand as "accurate" representations' (Rhodes, 2001a: 28). This is an important interruption by the aesthetic regime because researchers themselves now become understood as storytellers whose own work cannot stand erectly on the pedestal of masculine 'science.' This blurs the boundary between the gendered positions of science and narrative in the reflexive moment where academic knowledge becomes equalized in form with that previously relegated as belonging solely to the domain of those to be researched. At this point that ' "science" is closer to "narrative" than one might think' (Czarniawska, 1997a: 7) and that research was always inherently multigendered.

Tales from the field

Although it might be the case that organizational research can be, post hoc, analyzed as a form of narration, there are other researchers who are all too willing to admit to their practice as storytellers from the outset. Daft (1983) proposed that when we consider research as a form of 'craft' the scientific method itself is best viewed as a form of storytelling. For him, 'storytelling means explaining what the data mean, using data to describe how organizations work. Stories are theories [...] craftsmen [sic] in organization research use data to tell stories about behavior and processes within organizations' (p. 541). Theory here is explicitly understood in relation to narrative—that is theory as 'an account of a social process, with emphasis on empirical tests of plausibility of the narrative as well as careful attention to the scope of the account' (DiMaggio, 1995: 391).

Some of the best crafted narrative writing in organization studies has emerged from ethnographic studies, with notable examples being Rosen's (1985, 1988) studies of power, culture and symbolism in work settings and Kunda's (1992) writing on the every-day machinations of organizational culture. Indeed the turn to narrative has been most explicit within in organizational ethnography and the 'tales of the field' (Van Maanen, 1988) that are entailed in the practice of writing ethnography. These narratives stretch in style from the most conventional 'realist tales,' to the more researcher focused 'confessional tales', and the more dramatic 'impressionistic tales' (Van Maanen, 1988).

Numerous researchers have explicitly drawn on literary conventions in presenting their work, and in so doing irrevocably intervened in the gendered division between science and narrative. Phillips argues that while the writing practices of social scientists appear to be different from those of literary writers, they are also similar, because they both create order rather than disorder and seek to model the world (Phillips, 1995). This has meant that '[n]ew forms of analysis and representation have started to develop as the textual nature of the "object" of organizational

analysis has emerged' (Linstead, 2003: 4). Adding new forms of narrative writing to organizational analysis provides new ways to think about organizations that allow room for doubt, uncertainty, contradiction, and paradox (Phillips, 1995).

Brown and Kreps (1993) suggested that stories told in research interviews and gathered in observation can be legitimately (and creatively) combined to create composite narratives which 'blend the 'actual dialogue told in specific stories [...to create...] an impressionistic account of the concept under investigation' (p. 54). Similarly, Pacanowsky (1995) has promoted the use of narrative forms such as fiction, docudrama, journalism, and first-person confessionals for writing about the shape and texture of organizations and for helping others understand them. In such texts, 'facts' are used to generate productive scholarly discourse in the form of plausible narratives. This has meant that research has been written up within the borders of literary genres such as short stories (e.g. Jermier, 1985; Rhodes, 2001b) and plays (e.g. Steyaert and Hjorth, 2002; Starkey, 1999). Plato and his boys might well be turning in their graves (or in their beds).

Stories about stories

In the aesthetic regime, the connections between research and narrative have also been manifest in a renewed respect for the 'narrative arts' by researchers. Researchers have turned to narratives from literature and various forms of popular culture as exemplars of knowledge about organizations and management. There is a realization here that there are others outside of academic research who are much more practiced and skilled at telling stories about work and organizations.

Czarniawska and de Monthoux (1994) made a compelling case for bringing literature to the study of organizations, arguing that literature reclaimed the subjective and affective dimensions of work that had been expurgated by science. This suggests that fiction provides a potent and sensitive means to understand the facts of organizational life as they are lived (Rhodes and Brown, 2005b). Novels have been read by organizational researchers on the basis that they are inspired by a quest for insight, transmit tacit knowledge, and are culturally and historically sensitive (Czarniawska and de Monthoux, 1994). de Cock (2000) has both argued and demonstrated that literature provides an insight into the experience of work and organizing that, in its effectiveness, might even put organizational scholars to shame for their own limitations. As a result of such attractions to literary narratives, researchers have sought inspiration, for example, to learn methodology from detective novels (Czarniawska, 1999b), to understand organizational hierarchy by reading Charles Bukowski (Kornberger et al., 2006), to consider new modalities of worker resistance with Jaroslav Hašek (Fleming and Sewell, 2002), to rethink organizational interpretation and representation with Jorge Luis Borges (de Cock, 2000), to understand worker subjectivity with Herman Melville (ten Bos and Rhodes, 2003; Beverungen and Dunne, 2007), to consider workplace envy in Richard Russo's *Straight Man* (Patient et al., 2003), as well as using science fiction novels to consider organizational futures (Smith et al., 2001).

In addition to locating themselves in relation to the 'high' cultural space of the novel, organizational researchers have also examined narratives from popular culture. One reason for this, as Hassard and Holliday (1998) surmise, is that 'popular culture offers more dramatic, more intense, and more dynamic representations of organizations than management texts' (p. 1)—it can tell different or even better stories that research texts. Another reason is that, because a common cultural thread runs through cultural texts and cultures of organizations, reading organizations and reading cultural narratives might inform one another (Czarniawska and Rhodes, 2006). Further, popular culture might offer new forms of critical knowledge that is hidden in the masculine ideological commitments common to many organizational researchers (Rhodes and Westwood, 2008). Producing or

discussing a list of examples of how popular culture has been used in organization theory is too large a task to be undertaken here (see Rhodes and Westwood, 2008; Rhodes and Parker, 2008). It is worth noting, however, that researchers have drawn on a range of examples stretching from animated cartoons like *The Simpsons* (Rhodes, 2001b; Rhodes and Pullen, 2007), comic strips such as *Dilbert* (Kessler, 2001), Hollywood movies like *GI Jane* (Höpfl, 2003) and *Disclosure* (Brewis, 1998), music (Prichard et al., 2007) from rock (Rhodes, 2007) to rap (Rehn and Sköld, 2005), and both dramatic (e.g. O'Sullivan and Sheridan, 2005) and comedic (e.g. Tyler and Cohen, 2008) television programs.

In the aesthetic regime, the methodological stance as to what might count as research moves to a space between and beyond the rational traditions of science and the artistic traditions of narrative. This sees the gendered distinction between science and narrative losing its footing as the two begin to interact in different formations of hybridity. Methodologically, this can be regarded as a form of gender transgression, where those gendered forms that had hitherto been kept separate to preserve scientific purity, now become confused and/or conflated leaving neither the same as it was before.

CONCLUSIONS: SENSE AND NONSENSE IN ORGANIZATIONAL RESEARCH

In this chapter, we have identified three sets of gendered relations between scientific and narrative discourse in organizational research and discussed some examples of each. To recap, these are: the ethical regime where narrative discourse is positioned as being inferior to and irrelevant to science; the representative regime where narrative discourse is considered to be different to science, but still valuable on its own terms, especially as a form of data; and the aesthetic regime where the distinction between science and narrative discourse is blurred such that narrative is not only seen as valuable, but that researchers also are understood as particular types of storytellers. These distinctions demonstrate important issues about the political dimensions of methodology in organizational research, where masculinist assumptions that scientists 'have constructed scientific knowledge from positioned observations of privilege [...] cloaked in the guise of disinterested objectivity' (Laslett et al., 1996) have been shaken to their core in a practical response to the call that 'Western thought needs destabilization' (Harding, 1986: 245). In making this point, we note first that the distinction between rational discourse and narrative/poetic discourse is ancient, second that rational discourse has traditionally been considered super-ordinate, third that this distinction is gendered in character, and fourth that this distinction has given rise to significant contestation over the relative merits of each.

The growth of narrative methodologies in organizational research is part of a deep questioning of what constitutes appropriate models of inquiry and representation. This has involved resistance to the 'policing' (Rancière, 2004) efforts that seek to maintain masculine orthodoxy. If we accept this as a story about organizational research, the implications are serious. It is Rancière's contention that the aesthetic regime 'aims to effect a redistribution of the sensible to the extent that it promises both a new life for art and a new life for individuals and the community' (Bennett, 2007: 218). In organizational research, the political machinations that have marked the emergence of narrative based methodologies present the promise of new forms of life for research—a promise for organizational research to 'reinvigorate itself' (Czarniawska, 1998: 13).

Through the development of narrative methodologies and against the totalizing claims of science we can see that:

> ...there is another world hidden from the consciousness of science—the world of emotions, feelings, political values; of the individual and collective unconscious; or social and historical particularity explored by novels, drama, poetry,

music, and art—within which we live most of our waking hours under constant threat of its increasing infusion by scientific rationality (Harding, 1986: 245).

By way of concluding, we are not suggesting that the aesthetic regime in organizational research is a marker of the end of methodological politics or policing—narratives too can 'cut off and close meaning down, reining through it by means of a law of genre' (Kreiswirth, 2000: 311). As well as the generation of new rules for 'correct narratives' (Lyotard, 1984) and correct narrative forms, the acceptance of narrative in organizational research is by no means universal. The three regimes identified have not progressively replaced each other—they progressively coexist. Debate and contestation over narrative methodology and its gendered relationship with the scientific tradition, thus, becomes augmented and complexified rather than resolved.

The encroachment of narrative into the arena of legitimate organizational research reflects a gender politics that moves towards a partial subversion of masculine rational order and an emasculation of science. This does not, however, mark a form of feminine writing per se in organizational research (cf. Höpfl, 2000; Pullen, 2006a) and the location of narrative in relation to science and rationality does not qualify the research it produces as being a form of 'écriture féminine' (Cixous, 1981). Indeed with narrative, organizational research is defined in relation to masculine norms, even when that relation is oppositional or subversive. Narrative has admitted new forms of temporal, textual, and experiential ordering into the domain of organizational research, but it is still a form of gendered ordering—narrative questions the masculine logos of scientific rationality, but it does not do so by establishing a methodology that is independent of its relation to the masculine. If the politics of organizational research is to remain alive and well, there remains a need to disturb the 'cleansing effects' (Höpfl, 2007; Pullen and Rhodes, 2008) of research writing and the need for continuing dispute over orthodoxies newer and older.

If the desire is to disrupt the gendering of research texts, such an endeavor 'does not set itself the target of creating a new language, or a new genre, but of pursuing a new relation to language; one which might be called feminine, but even that category is likely to disappear in the journey's unfolding' (Pullen, 2006a: 294). The dualism between science and narrative that has informed the history of narrative methodology might no longer be productive, such that creation of ways of knowing need not be left in the shadow of masculine science and rationality. It is by destabilizing gendered meanings (see Linstead and Brewis, 2004; Pullen and Knights, 2007) rather than establishing new ones that the masculine can be dispersed (Höpfl, 2003; Linstead and Pullen, 2006). In the methodology of organizational research, while there are some indications of this destabilization, by and large, how it might be accomplished still remains an open question.

Historically, those dedicated to rational masculine discourse have perceived their own representations of the meaning of knowledge and of knowledge itself as far superior to those of the feminized versions of artists and storytellers. To reiterate, as is made so explicit in Plato, this is a gendered division (Lloyd, 1993)—rational discourse is masculine, and artistic or narrative discourse is its feminine other. For Plato, nonrational and poetic discourse is a 'bitch that growls and snarls at her master' (Plato, 1974: 438) just as narrative is often regarded as a bitch that growls at science. If we have come anywhere towards an ending to our story, it would be that in recent organizational research the bitch is still growling, and growling louder than before; perhaps even beginning to disrupt the boundaries of gender dichotomies. Plato quite rightly feared that the feminine can attack and challenge masculine mastery, but he underestimated the power of the bitch that bites. And this feminized power is not just about the assertion of the feminine, but also the dispersal of the masculine and of the rigid boundary between the two.

REFERENCES

Abbott, A. (1992) 'From causes to events: notes on narrative positivism', *Sociological Methods and Research*, 20: 428–55.

Abbott, P.A. (2002) *The Cambridge Introduction to Narrative*, Cambridge: Cambridge University Press.

Adkins, K.C. (2002) 'The real dirt: gossip and feminist epistemology', *Social Epistemology*, 16(3): 215–232.

Aristotle (1996) *Poetics*, (trans.), M. Heath, London: Penguin.

Barry, D. and Elmes, M. (1997) 'Strategy retold: towards a narrative view of strategic discourse', *Academy of Management Review*, 22: 429–52.

Bell, D.F. (2004) 'Writing, Movement/Space, Democracy: On Jacque Rancière's Literary History', *SubStance*, 33(1): 126–40.

Benjamin, W. (1936/1968) 'The storyteller: observations on the works of Nikolai Leskov', in H. Arendt (ed.), *Illuminations: Essays and Reflections*, London: Jonathon Cape, pp. 83–109.

Bennett, T. (2007) 'Habitus clivé: aesthetics and politics in the work of Pierre Bourdieu', *New Literary History*, 38: 201–28.

Beverungen, A. and Dunne, S. (2007) ' "I'd Prefer Not To". Bartleby and the Excesses of Interpretation', *Culture and Organization*, 13(2): 171–83.

Boje, D.M. (1991) 'The storytelling organization: a study of story performance in an office-supply firm', *Administrative Science Quarterly*, 36: 106–26.

Boje, D.M. (1994) Organizational storytelling: struggles of pre-modern, modern and postmodern organizational learning discourses, *Management Learning*, 25: 433–61.

Boje, D.M. (1995) 'Stories of the storytelling organization: a postmodern analysis of Disney as "Tamara-Land"', *Academy of Management Review*, 38(4): 997–1035.

Boje, D.M. (2001) *Narrative Methods for Organizational and Communication Research*, Thousand Oaks, CA: Sage.

Boyce, M.E. (1996) 'Organization story and storytelling: a critical review', *Journal of Organizational Change Management*, 9(5): 5–26.

Brewis, J. (1998) 'What is wrong with this picture? sex and gender relations in *disclosure*', in J. Hassard and R. Holliday (eds) *Organization Representation: Work and Organization in Popular Culture*, London: Sage, pp. 83–100.

Brown, A. (2006) 'A narrative approach to collective identities', *Journal of Management Studies*, 43(4): 731–53.

Brown, M.H. and Kreps, G.L. (1993) 'Narrative analysis and organizational development', in S.L. Herndon and G.L. Kreps (eds), *Qualitative Research: Applications in Organizational Communication*, Creskill, NJ: Hampton Press, pp. 47–62.

Burrell, G. and Morgan, G. (1979) *Sociological Paradigms and Organizational Analysis*, Aldershot: Gower.

Butler, R. (1997) 'Stories and experiments in social inquiry', *Organization Studies*, 18(6): 927–48.

Calás, M. and Smircich, L. (1999) 'Past postmodernism? reflections and tentative direction', *Academy of Management Review*, 24(4): 649–71.

Churchamn, C.W. (1968) *Challenge to Reason*, New York: McGraw-Hill.

Cixous, H. (1981) 'The laugh of Medusa', in E. Marks and I. de Courtivron (eds), *New French Feminisms: An Anthology*, New York: Schocken, pp. 245–64.

Clegg, S.R. (1993) 'Narrative, power and social theory', in D.K. Mumby (ed.), *Narrative and Social Control: Critical Perspectives*, Newbury Park: Sage, pp. 16–45.

Culler, J. (1981) *The Pursuit of Signs: Semiotics, Literature, Deconstruction*, Ithaca, NY: Cornell University Press.

Currie, G. and Brown, A.D. (2003) 'A narratological approach to understanding processes of organizing in a UK hospital', *Human Relations*, 56(5): 563–586.

Czarniawska, B. (1997a) 'A four times told tale: combining narrative and scientific knowledge in organization studies', *Organization*, 4(1): 7–30.

Czarniawska, B. (1997b) *Narrating the Organization: Dramas of Institutional Identity*, Chicago: Chicago University Press.

Czarniawska, B. (1999a) *Writing Management: Organization Studies as a Literary Genre*, Oxford: Oxford University Press.

Czarniawska, B. (1999b) 'Management she wrote: organization studies and detective stories', *Culture and Organization*, 5(1): 13–41.

Czarniawska, B. (2004) *Narratives in Social Science Research*, London: Sage.

Czarniawska, B. and Rhodes, C. (2006) 'Strong plots: the relationship between popular culture and management theory and practice', in P. Gagliardi and B. Czarniawska (eds), *Management and Humanities*, Edward Elgar: London, pp. 195–218.

Czarniawska-Joerges, B. (1995) 'Narration or science? collapsing the division in organization studies', *Organization*, 2(1): 11–33.

Czarniawska-Joerges, B. (1998) *A Narrative Approach to Organization Studies*, Thousand Oaks, CA: Sage.

Czarniawska-Joerges, B. and de Monthoux, P. (eds) (1994) *Good Novels, Better Management*: *Reading Organizational Realities*, Reading, MA: Harwood.

Daft, R.L. (1983) 'Learning the craft of organizational research', *Academy of Management Review*, 8: 539–47.

De Cock, C. (2000) 'Reflections on fiction, representation, and organization studies: an essay with special reference to the work of Jorge Luis Borges', *Organization Studies*, 21(3): 589–609.

Derrida, Jacques (1980) 'The law of genre', *Critical Inquiry*, 7: 55–82.

Di Maggio, P.J. (1995) 'Comments on "what theory is not?"', *Administrative Science Quarterly*, 40: 391–97.

Donaldson, L. (1996) *For Positivist Organization Theory: Proving the Hard Core*, London: Sage.

Edmundson, (1995) *Literature Against Philosophy, Plato to Derrida: A Defence of Poetry*, Cambridge: Cambridge University Press.

Eisenhardt, K.M. (1991) 'Better stories and better constructs: the case for rigour and comparative logic', *Academy of Management Review*, 16: 620–7.

Fleming, P. and Sewell, G. (2002) 'Looking for the good soldier, svejk alternative modalities of resistance in the contemporary workplace', *Sociology*, 36(4): 857–73.

Gabriel, Y. (1991) 'Turning facts into stories and stories into facts: a hermeneutic exploration of organizational folklore', *Human Relations*, 44(8): 857–75.

Gabriel, Y. (1998a) 'Same old story or changing stories? folkloric, modern and postmodern mutations', in D. Grant, T. Keenoy and C. Oswick (eds), *Discourse and Organization*, London: Sage, pp. 84–103.

Gabriel, Y. (1998b) 'The use of stories', in G. Symon and C, Cassell (eds), *Qualitative Methods and Analysis in Organizational Research*, London: Sage. pp. 135–60.

Gabriel, Y. (2000) *Storytelling in Organizations: Facts, Fictions, and Fantasies*, Oxford: Oxford University Press.

Gabriel, Y. (2004) 'Narratives, stories and texts', in D. Grant, C. Hardy, C. Oswick and L. Putnam (eds), *The Sage Handbook of Organizational Discourse*, London: Sage, pp. 61–78.

Gherardi, S. (1995) *Gender, Symbolism and Organizational Cultures*, London: Sage.

Gherardi, S. and Turner, B. (1987) *Real Men Don't Collect Soft Data*, Quaderni del Dipartimento di Politica Sociale13, Dipartimento di Politicia Sociale, Università di Trento.

Gherardi, S., Marshall, J. and Mills, A. (2003) 'Gender and identity', in R. Westwood and S.R. Clegg (eds), *Debating Organizations: Point-Counterpoint in Organization Studies*, Oxford: Blackwell, pp. 325–38.

Golinski, J. (2002) 'The care of the self and the masculine birth of science', *History of Science*, 40: 125–45.

Hansen, C.D. and Kahnweiler, W.H. (1993) 'Storytelling: an instrument for understanding the dynamics of corporate relationships', *Human Relations*, 46(12): 1391–410.

Harding, S. (1986) *The Science Question in Feminism*, Milton Keynes: Open University Press.

Harding, S. (2006) *Science and Social Inequality*, Chicago: University of Illinois Press.

Hassard, J. (1993) *Sociology and Organization Theory: Positivism, Paradigms and Postmodernity*, Cambridge: Cambridge University Press.

Hassard, J. and Holliday, R. (eds) (1998) *Organization - Representation: Work and Organization in Popular Culture*, London: Sage.

Hatch, M.J. (1996) 'The role of the researcher: an analysis of narrative position in organizational theory', *Journal of Management Inquiry*, 5(4): 359–74.

Höpfl, H. (2000) 'The suffering mother and the miserable son, organizing women and organizing women's writing', *Gender, Work and Organization*, 7(2): 98–105.

Höpfl, H. (2003) 'Becoming a (virile) member: women and the military body', *Body and Society*, 9(4): 13–30.

Höpfl, H. (2007) 'The codex, the codicil and the codpiece: some thoughts on diminution and elaboration in identity formation', *Gender, Work and Organization*, 14(6): 619–32.

Howlett, M. and Rayner, J. (2006) 'Understanding the historical turn in policy sciences: a critique of stochastic, narrative, path dependency and process-sequencing models of policy making over time', *Policy Sciences*, 39: 1–18.

Huberman, A.M. and Miles, M.B. (1994) 'Data management and analytical methods', in N.K. Denzin and Y.S. Lincoln (eds), *Handbook of Qualitative Research*, Thousand Oaks: Sage, pp. 428–44.

Jeffcut, P. (1994) 'From interpretation to representation in organizational analysis: postmodernism, ethnography and organizational symbolism', *Organization Studies*, 15(2): 241–74.

Jermier, J. (1985) ' "When the sleeper wakes": a short story extending themes in radical organization theory', *Journal of Management*, 11(2): 67–80.

Keller, E.F. (1988) 'Feminist perspectives on science studies', *Science, Technology and Human Values*, 13(3/4): 235–49.

Kessler, E.H. (2001) 'The idols of organizational theory: from francis bacon to the Dilbert principle', *Journal of Management Inquiry*, 10(4): 285–97.

Kornberger, M., Rhodes, C. and ten Bos, R. (2006) 'The others of hierarchy: rhizomatics of organizing', in M. Fugslang and B. Sorensen (eds), *Gilles Deleuze and the Multiplicity of the Social—Towards a New Social Analytic*, Edinburgh: Edinburgh University Press, pp. 58–74.

Kreiswirth, M. (2000) 'Merely telling stories? narrative knowledge in the human sciences', *Poetics Today*, 21(2): 295–318.

Kunda, G. (1992) *Engineering Culture: Control and Commitment in a High-Tech Corporation*, Philadelphia: Temple University Press.

Laslett, B., Kohlstedt. S.M., Longing, H. and Hammonds, E. (1996) 'Introduction', in B. Laslett, S.M. Kohlstedt, H. Longing and E. Hammonds (eds), *Gender and Scientific Authority*, Chicago: University of Chicago Press, pp. 1–17.

Law, J. (1994) 'Organization, narrative and strategy', in J. Hassard and M. Parker (eds), *Towards a New Theory of Organizations*, London: Routledge. pp. 249–68.

Linstead, S.A. (2000) 'Gender blindness or gender suppression? a comment on Fiona Wilson's research note', *Organization Studies*, 21(1): 297–303.

Linstead, S.A. (2003) *Text/Work: Representing Organization and Organizing Representation*, London: Routledge.

Linstead, A. and Brewis, J. (2004) 'Introduction', in Linstead, A. and Brewis, J. (eds), Beyond boundaries: towards fluidity in theorising and practice, Special Issue of the journal *Gender, Work and Organization*, 11(4): 335–62.

Linstead, S.A. and Pullen, A. (2006) 'Gender as multiplicity: desire, difference and dispersion', *Human Relations*, 59(9): 1287–310.

Lloyd, G. (1993) *The Man of Reason: 'Male' and 'Female' in Western Philosophy* (second edn.), London: Routledge.

Lyotard, J-F. (1984) *The Postmodern Condition: A Report on Knowledge*, Minneapolis: University of Minnesota Press.

McKelvey, B. (1997) 'Quasi-natural Organization Science', *Organization Science*, 8(4): 352–80.

Mitroff, I.I. and Kilmann, R.H. (1976) 'On organizational stories: an approach to the design and analysis of organizations through myths and stories', in R.H. Kilmann, L.R. Pondy and D.P. Slevin (eds), *The Management of Organizational Design* (vol. 1), New York: North-Holland, pp. 189–207.

Mitroff, I.I. and Kilmann, R.H. (1978) *Methodological Approaches to Social Science*, London: Jossey-Bass.

Oakley, A. (2000) *Experiments in Knowing: Gender and Method in the Social Sciences*, New York: The New Press.

O'Sullivan, J. and Sheridan, J. (2005) 'The King is dead, long live the King: tall tales of new men and new management', in *The Bill, Gender, Work and Organization*, 12(4): 299–318.

Pacanowsky, M. (1995) 'Creating and narrating organizational realities', in B. Dervin, L. Grossberg, B.J. O'Keefe and E. Wartella (eds), *Rethinking Communication: Volume 2 Paradigm Exemplars*, Newbury Park: Sage, pp. 250–8.

Patient, D., Lawrence, T.B. and Maitlis, S. (2003) 'Understanding workplace envy through narrative fiction', *Organization Studies*, 24(7): 1015–44.

Pentland, B.T. (1999) 'Building process theory with narrative', *Academy of Management Review*, 24(4): 711–24.

Pfeffer, J. (1993) 'Barriers to the advance of organizational science: paradigm development as a dependent variable', *Academy of Management Review*, 18: 599–620.

Phillips, N. (1995) 'Telling organizational tales: on the role of narrative fiction in the study of organizations', *Organization Studies*, 16: 625–49.

Plato (1974) *The Republic*, trans. D. Lee, London: Penguin.

Poole, M.S., Van de Ven, A.H., Dooley, K. and Holmes, M.E. (2000) *Organizational Change and Innovation Processes*, Oxford: Oxford University Press.

Prichard C., Jones, D. and Stablein, R. (2004) 'Doing research in organizational discourse—the importance of researcher context', in D. Grant, C. Hardy, C. Oswick and L. Putnam (eds), *The Sage Handbook of Organizational Discourse*, Sage Publications, pp. 213–36.

Prichard, C., Korczynski, M. and Lemes, C. (2007) 'Music at work', *Group and Organization Management*, 32(1): 4–21.

Pullen, A. (2006a) 'Gendering the research self: social practice and corporeal multiplicity in the writing of organizational research', *Gender, Work and Organization*, 13(3): 277–98.

Pullen, A. (2006b) *Managing Identity*, Basingstoke: Palgrave.

Pullen, A. and Knights, D. (2007) 'Undoing gender: organizing and disorganizing performance', *Gender, Work and Organization,* 14(6): 505–11.

Pullen, A. and Rhodes, C. (2008) 'Dirty writing', *Culture and Organization*, 14(3): 241–59.

Rancière, J. (2004) *The Politics of Aesthetics*, London: Continuum.

Rehn, A. and Sköld, D. (2005) ' "I love the dough": rap lyrics as a minor economic literature', *Culture and Organization*, 11(1): 17–31.

Rhodes, C. (2000) 'Reading and writing organizational lives', *Organization*, 7(1): 7–29.

Rhodes, C. (2001a) *Writing Organization: Representation and Control in Narratives at Work*, Amsterdam: Benjamins.

Rhodes, C. (2001b) 'D'Oh: The Simpsons, popular culture and the organizational carnival', *Journal of Management Inquiry*, 10: 374–83.

Rhodes, C. (2007) 'Outside the gates of Eden: Utopia and work in rock music', *Group and Organization Management*, 32(1): 22–49.

Rhodes, C. and Brown, A. (2005a) 'Narrative, organizations and research', *International Journal of Management Reviews*, 7(3): 167–88.

Rhodes, C. and Brown, A. (2005b) 'Writing responsibly: narrative fiction and organization studies', *Organization*, 12(4): 467–91.

Rhodes, C. and Parker, M. (2008) 'Images of organizing in popular culture', Special Issues of *Organization*, 15(5).

Rhodes, C. and Pitsis, A. (2008) 'Organization and mimetic excess: magic, critique and style', *Group and Organization Management*, 38(1): 72–92.

Rhodes, C. and Pullen, A. (2007) 'Humour, work and the grotesque body: Mr. Burns and The Simpsons Cartoon Carnival', in R. Westwood, and C. Rhodes, (eds), *Humour, Organizations and Work*, London: RoutledgeFalmer, pp. 161–79.

Rhodes, C. and Westwood, R. (2008) *Critical Representations of Organizations in Popular Culture*, London: Routledge.

Ricoeur, P. (1984) *Time and Narrative* (Vol. 1), (trans.) K. McLaughlin and D. Pellauer, Chicago: University of Chicago Press

Rose, H. (1994) *Love, Power and Knowledge: Towards a Feminist Transformation of the Sciences*, Cambridge: Polity.

Rosen, M. (1985) 'Breakfast at Spiros': dramaturgy and dominance', *Journal of Management*, 11(2): 31–48.

Rosen, M. (1988) 'You asked for it: Christmas at the bosses' expense', *Journal of Management Studies*, 25(5): 463–80.

Ross-Smith, A. and Kornberger, M. (2004) 'Gendered rationality? a genealogical exploration of the philosophical and sociological conceptions of rationality, masculinity and organization', *Gender, Work and Organization*, 11(3): 280–305.

Sabherwal, R. and Robey, D. (1993) 'An empirical taxonomy of implementation processes based on sequences of events in information system development', *Organization Science*, 4(4): 548–76.

Smircich, L. (1992) 'Stories of Mike Armstrong and the Idea of Exemplary Research', in P. Frost and R. Stablein (eds), *Doing Exemplary Research*, Newbury Park: Sage, pp. 227–32.

Smith, W., Higgins, M., Lightfoot, G. and Parker, M. (eds) (2001) *Science Fiction and Organization*, London: Routledge.

Starkey, K. (1999) 'Eleven characters in search of an ethic, or the spirit of capitalism revisited', *Studies in Cultures, Organizations and Societies*, 5: 179–94.

Stevenson, W.M. and Greenberg, D.N. (1998) 'The formal analysis of narratives of organizational change', *Journal of Management*, 24(6): 741–62.

Steyaert, C. and Hjorth, D. (2002) 'Thou art a scholar, speak to it ...'—on spaces of speech: a script', Human Relations, 55(7): 767–97.

Taussig, M. (1993) *Mimesis and Alterity: A Particular History of the Senses*, New York: Routledge.

ten Bos, R. and Rhodes, C. (2003) 'The game of exemplarity: subjectivity, work and the impossible politics of purity', *Scandinavian Journal of Management*, 19(4): 403–23.

Tyler, M. and Cohen, L. (2008) 'Management in/as comic relief: queer theory and gender performativity in the office', *Gender, Work and Organization*, 15(2): 113–32.

Van de Ven, A.H. and Poole, M.S. (1995) 'Explaining development and change in organizations', *Academy of Management Review*, 20: 510–40.

Van Maanen, J. (1988) *Tales of the Field: On Writing Ethnography*, Chicago: University of Chicago Press.

Watson, T.J. (2000) 'Making sense of managerial work and organizational research processes with Caroline and Terry', *Organization*, 7(3): 489–510.

Weaver, G.R. and Gioia, D.A. (1994) 'Paradigms lost: incommensurability vs. structurationist inquiry', Organization Studies, 15(4): 565–89.

Weick, K. (1995) *Sensemaking in Organizations*, Thousand Oaks, CA: Sage.

Westwood, R. and Clegg, S.R. (2003) 'The discourse of organization studies: dissensus, politics and paradigms', in R. Westwood and S. R. Clegg (eds), *Debating Organizations: Point-Counterpoint in Organization Studies*, Oxford: Blackwell. pp. 1–42.

Wilson, F. (1996) 'Organizational Theory: Blind and Deaf to Gender?', *Organization Studies*, 17(5): 825–42.

Zald, M.N. (1993) 'Organization studies as a scientific and humanistic enterprise: towards a reconceptualization of the foundations of the field', *Organization Science*, 4(4): 513–28.

35

Ethnography in Organizational Settings

Gary Alan Fine, Calvin Morrill, and
Sharmi Surianarain

ETHNOGRAPHIC TURNS

Despite the oft-remarked dominance of quantitative methodology during much of the twentieth century, qualitative analysis was the primary means by which research was conducted in the early decades of that century. This is particularly true in organizational studies, which until the 1960s was largely wedded to a case-study approach. Statistical analysis was, in fact, a scholarly latecomer. From the writings of Frederick Taylor onward, much early analysis consisted of detailed descriptions of a company or introspective renditions of personal experience. Since the seminal shop floor ethnographies of the 1950s, ethnographers have explored power, politics, informal relations, and resistance in organizations, producing insights unavailable to scholars using other research methods. The resurgence of ethnography in organizational sociology, while innovative, is thus also a return to tradition. Organizational life has long been amenable to qualitative analysis. Our goal in this chapter is to describe the role that ethnography has played in organization studies, its current position in the field,

and some hints for ethnography as it may develop.

The qualitative analysis of organizations has typically received acclaim for its ability to provide creative insights into the field. In 2004, the Academy of Management surveyed its editorial board on which management and organization science articles they considered important, competently executed, and particularly interesting (Bartunek et al., 2006). The results revealed that six of the top seven papers employed qualitative field methods of some kind (e.g. Barley, 1986; Dutton and Dukerich, 1991; Eisenhardt, 1989; Uzzi, 1997). For a field that is oriented towards quantitative empirical research, qualitative methods—notably, although not exclusively, ethnography—occupy a surprisingly important position.

In this chapter, we rely on a variety of exemplars to illustrate the contributions ethnography has made to organization studies, focusing on six substantive areas of inquiry: (1) the elaboration of informal relations, (2) organizations as systems of meaning, (3) organizations and their environments, (4) organizational change, (5) ethics and normative behavior, and (6) power, politics, and control. Although the early tradition was to focus on industrial contexts, later studies from the 1950s on have examined white-collar occupations as much as blue-collar. We attempt to examine the wide range of ethnography, recognizing that shop floors have received the bulk of attention from ethnographers.

We characterize ethnography as, 'sustained, explicit, methodical observation and para-phrasing of social situations in relation to their naturally occurring contexts' (Weick, 1985: 568). While recognizing the numerous definitions of qualitative methods, field methods, and ethnography, we use the terms inter-changeably in this chapter. The distinctions are often subtle and vary from writer to writer. None of these terms has a fully determined meaning. Moreover, ethnography can aid critical interventions into organizations or even coexist in blurred genres as in some forms of action research (Eden and Huxham, 2001). This characterization casts a wide net over a host of fieldwork studies that often employ a number of coordinated techniques, including participant and nonparticipant observation, unstructured and semistructured interviews, and the analysis of artifacts produced by those being studied. However, our focus excludes qualitative fieldwork in which the fieldworker does not remain in the field (for months or even years) to become 'saturated' with first-hand knowledge of the setting (Glaser and Strauss, 1967). It also excludes field studies, where the primary goal is not to describe and interpret the experiences of organizational members, but to produce critical interventions into organizational functioning. By specifying ethnography in this way, we highlight the methodological distinctiveness of a particular style of research (typically practiced by sociologists and anthropologists) to demonstrate how it has contributed to substantive knowledge in organizational studies.

We contend that ethnographic methods allow for a deeper understanding of the topic studied, in addition to providing multiple perspectives and an opportunity to examine process. However, ethnographers often face the charge that they lack control over what they study, in addition to the possibilities of researcher bias and generalizability. We will engage with each of these issues, to unpack fully the trade-offs and contributions of ethnographic methods in organizational research. We begin by locating the contributions of organizational ethnography in the six substantive areas listed in the preceding paragraphs. We then examine three claims that ethnographers typically make: that it provides for depth, multiple perspectives, and process. These claims permit its unique contributions, but also create trade-offs in terms of control, bias, and generalizability. We conclude by suggesting implications of the resurgent interest in organizational ethnography for its systematic practice and the development of standards to evaluate its cross-disciplinary usage.

The contributions of organizational ethnography

The discovery and elaboration of informal relations

In the 1920s and 1930s, the empirical studies of shop floor behavior at Western Electric's Hawthorne Plant first revealed the presence of an 'underside' of work—those hidden, informal arrangements by which organizational life operates in practice (Roethlisberger and Dickson, 1947). From the researchers' perspectives, informal relations operate in stark contrast to organizational rules and become the source of 'irrational' uncooperation with 'rational' managerial directives. Although the Hawthorne studies had quantitative components, they linked the power of narrative to rich, descriptive accounts of informal employee interaction. Much of the employee interaction observed at Hawthorne occurred in the context of management concerns about worker productivity and experimentally modified work spaces to investigate forces that affect productivity. As such, the Hawthorne narratives derive from a managerial rather than a worker perspective.

In the 1940s and 1950s, many observational studies of organizational behavior adopted an ethnographic slant as researchers took jobs as workers and managers. Such research posed practical issues of access and ethical issues to the extent that coworkers were unaware that they were being studied, but the richness of the observations were thought to trump such problems, even though such projects, lacking informed consent, would likely not pass muster today (see Bell and Wray-Bliss, Chapter 5, this volume). Ethnographers first turned to the shop floor and then to the managerial suite to analyze informal relations in organizations. These studies recast informal relations from an image of irrational uncooperation to one of rational adaptation. Whyte (1948), for example, worked in a hotel restaurant kitchen and found that informal status systems differed markedly from the formal lines of authority. Such alternative status systems adjusted the skeletal, formal chain of command by distributing various levels of trust, fealty, and interpersonal control among workers and supervisors. To an even greater degree, Roy's ethnographic studies of life in an industrial machine shop underscored the adaptive functions of informal relations in the workplace. Roy (1952, 1954, 1959–1960) demonstrated that factory workers could create autonomy in the face of an oppressive management regime. His analysis—counter to Taylor's scientific management principles evident in the Hawthorne studies, and counter to the beliefs of critics of corporate capitalism—depended upon an ethnographic investigation: in this case, a study in which Roy labored in the factory. Roy's analysis proved highly influential, notably in Burawoy's (1979) ethnography of the same factory a quarter of a century later.

Around the same time, Dalton (1959) published *Men Who Manage*. Dalton sought 'to get as close as possible to the world of managers and to interpret this world and its problems from the inside, as they are seen and felt at various points and levels' (Dalton, 1959: 1). He witnessed the political and social world of white-collar work while employed

as a manager in two of the three Midwestern organizations he studied. Just as there was an underside for blue-collar work, so for white-collar work. Dalton discovered that gaps between official and unofficial managerial practice, and the conflict between groups vying for power, were not momentary departures from Weberian 'rational bureaucracy' or Barnard's (1938) 'cooperative system' in his *The Functions of the Executive*. Nor did informal relations only act against the official structure. They served many ends, even buttressing official procedures by distributing rewards supporting organizational goals and punishing violators of official normative standards (Dalton, 1959: 222).

Dalton found that what managers claimed about their behavior and decision-making was inconsistent with their behavior. His findings could only have arisen from a method capable of discovering subtleties in both meaning and behavior as they unfold *in situ*. Such issues were difficult to study by other means, such as questionnaires or experiments, because those methods remove actors from their natural contexts, and introduce a layer of interpretation due to self-reports and retrospective statements. Dalton's attention to tacit understandings, multiple expectations, and taboos in managerial practice informed students of organizational culture in subsequent decades (Fine, 1996; Kunda, 1992; Morrill, 1995). As influential as his insights were, however, Dalton did not develop a distinctive theoretical perspective that could be applied systematically. The study of organizations as systems of meaning and, later, as social and communication networks, emerged from two traditions: symbolic interactionists who studied organizations ethnographically in the 1950s and 1960s, and ethnographers who began to study organizational environments in the 1970s.

Organizations as systems of meaning

Seeing organizations as meaning systems emerged from the tradition of symbolic interactionism in the 1950s, primarily at the University of Chicago. Interactionists, with their emphasis on embedded meanings, encouraged the study of organizations 'close up,' to observe how actors interpret their interactions in and across organizations. A series of team ethnographies, inspired by Hughes and led by Strauss, provided empirical grounding for what came to be known as the 'negotiated order' approach to organizations (Strauss et al., 1963 and 1964). Based on research in a psychiatric hospital, Strauss and his colleagues captured how diverse occupational groups (doctors, nurses, patients, and lay workers) 'negotiate' the meanings, routines, and tacit agreements of work against the backdrop of beliefs about the 'proper' goals and methods of psychiatry. Although Strauss's findings detail how actors negotiate, he was not merely interested in relationships among individuals. He came to view group interaction and negotiation, especially across status levels, as a core aspect of organizational life. Yet, such determinations depended on the inside observation that ethnography provides.

Working under Warner, Goffman completed his dissertation research as a participant observer in the Shetland Islands off the Scottish coast. Although never published as a stand-alone work, the Shetland observations (together with other materials from a variety of organizational settings) formed the empirical core of *The Presentation of Self in Everyday Life*, first published in 1956. Now regarded as a classic in the social psychology of interpersonal relations, Goffman intended *Presentation* as a 'handbook' for understanding organizational behavior, particularly that 'within the physical confines of a building or plant' (Goffman, 1956: xi). Goffman's observations and discussions of 'impression management,' 'back stage regions,' and 'front stage regions' created an image of organizations woven together through 'performances.' He argued that, while impression management is often viewed at the interpersonal level, it is also a 'team' phenomenon and has profound implications for understanding organizations. Goffman also did fieldwork in mental hospitals, first making brief observations at several mental wards during the mid-1950s, and then working for a year as an assistant to the

athletic director in a federal mental hospital. This fieldwork yielded *Asylums* (Goffman, 1961), which evokes the grit of organizational 'underlife' and its informal relations. On one level, *Asylums* is a ringing indictment of the treatment of the mentally ill. On another, it presents a set of sensitizing concepts and a theoretical rationale for analyzing the formation and maintenance of the self in organizations from both an 'institutional' and an 'individual' perspective.

By focusing on the sometimes smooth, often complex negotiations over meaning and purpose in organizations, Strauss and Goffman reinforced the ethnographic tradition of revealing unintended consequences of intended managerial decisions, as well as the divergences between back stage and front stage organizational behaviors. This tradition cuts across many organizational ethnographies that count symbolic interactionism as a theoretical point of departure (e.g. Barley, 1983; Becker, et al.,1968; Salaman, 1974).

Kolb's (1983) study of two industrial dispute mediation agencies is another example of the negotiated order turn in organizational ethnography. Mediation involves the intervention of a 'neutral' third party into disputes in order to facilitate discussion, negotiation, and resolution. The front stage of mediation underscores the creativity and flexibility of practitioners—mediation as art. The ideology of the agencies she studied reinforces this public posture by emphasizing the idiosyncratic nature of mediators and the work they do. Each dispute presents different challenges and a competent practitioner is one who can diagnose the issues of a conflict and fit his or her style to the case. The back stage behavior and interpretation of mediation practice is quite different. As Kolb (1983: 149) argues, 'the process appears to be more one of pattern and routine than it is of creativity and innovation.'

Perhaps the best recent exemplar of this work—and evocative of Goffman's analysis of the unintended effects of producing institutional 'selves'—is Kunda's (1992) study of 'culture control' in a high-tech firm. Kunda addresses many of the same issues posed by Strauss and Goffman, but targets 'corporate culture.' The concept of culture dominated managerial consciousness during the 1980s as organizations sought new ways to merge individual and organizational interests without explicit social control. Kunda's ethnography of the daily interactions, rituals, and material ideological productions (e.g. posters, handbills, and e-mails) experienced by 'Techies' (his label for those who worked at 'High Tech Firm'), suggests the potential tensions of 'strong' organizational cultures for individuals and organizations. The ideal Techie is driven by strong emotional attachments and a sense of moral obligation to serve the corporate interest. Consistent with Strauss and Goffman, Kunda found Techies active users, rather than passive recipients, of culture. It is through such active participation that each Techie's self becomes submerged and defined by organizational ideology. Paradoxically, the longer one stays and the higher one climbs the corporate ladder, the less likely Techies view the emotional attachments and moral obligations to Tech life as being authentic. The end result is 'unstable selves' (1992: 213–6) in which the processes of commitment unintentionally breed cynicism about firm structures and strategies. The very processes put into play to create strong work cultures eventually undermine their existence.

Organizational ethnographies using feminist perspectives have also been concerned with the friction between institutional and negotiated constructions of self. One such classic study is *Men and Women of the Corporation*, in which Kanter (1977) examined how organizations construct gender roles, images, and ethics associated with particular bureaucratic statuses. Ashcraft (1999) traced how one organization's response to and experience with a female chief executive who took maternity leave reflects changes in employee perspectives of CEO's initial 'feminine' leadership style, affording a critical perspective on 'gendered interaction styles' and 'women's ways of managing' (1999: 275). Given the changing nature of work, the increased numbers of women at top levels

of management, and the pressures on work-family balance, Ashcraft's study provides a rich set of insights that depend on her close observations.

Organizations and environments

Ethnographers have also studied the constraining and enabling relationships between organizations and their environments, crossing the boundaries of the organizations on which they focus. Concern for the world 'outside' organizations, whether called an environment, a field, or a network, is a critical task of organizational ethnography. Strauss claimed that the proper level of analysis for negotiated order analysis is the 'meso' level: the domain in which interaction among groups is shaped by structural constraints such as resources, authority structures, and broader institutional arrangements (Maines, 1982; Strauss, 1982). Kling and Gerson (1977) provide a compelling example of this approach to external, environmental constraints from the world of computing. They examined the relationship between organizational innovation and environmental conditions and discovered that each institutional segment is biased in favor of innovations that move from suppliers to customers (ultimately requiring new purchases). As innovations are processed, changes originally designed to produce more flexibility become increasingly constrained.

Observational research by Farberman (1975) on the 'criminogenic market structure' of used car dealerships illustrates how decisions outside of the interactional system affect internal choices, even seemingly unethical decisions. Farberman's ethnographic research suggests that actors in 'deviant' markets behave as they do, not from moral lapses, but because the structure of the market encourages them to act to survive. That automobile manufacturers push dealers to achieve high volume and low unit profit sets in motion a downward spiral of illegal and quasi-illegal actions: (a) leading to fraudulent service operations, (b) generating a kickback system allowing used-car managers of new-car dealerships to demand graft from independent used-car wholesalers, and (c) forcing the latter to generate cash from illegal 'short sales,' unrecorded in company books. Ethnographic research permits the examination of how decisions and policies made at one level of the market affects other levels, particularly those with less power, and those who are more resource-dependent.

Fine's (1996) work on the restaurant industry represents an explicit attempt to demonstrate how life in restaurant kitchens results from decisions and choices made outside that setting, including how the market niche of the restaurant and the costs of labor and foodstuffs, filtered through the decisions of managers and the responses of workers, affect what is served. Patterns of kitchen interaction derive from management choices, which are, in turn, a function of market typification.

Organizational ethnographers have paid increasing attention to how organizations or subunits work with each other, shedding light on how organizational boundaries are established and maintained. Carlile's (2002) ethnography of a design and manufacturing firm for auto fuel systems develops a sophisticated understanding of how knowledge is used at the boundaries of cross-functional teams, suggesting that different mechanisms must be employed to achieve knowledge integration across units. This study provides important insights on how knowledge at organizational boundaries is transformed to suit new ends and develops a nuanced understanding of the characteristics of boundary objects.

These projects illustrate through careful observation how external relations constrain internal decisions. In the late 1970s and 1980s, ethnographers also examined the multifunctional roles of external relations. Burawoy (1979) demonstrated that through a set of wider institutional arrangements, negotiated implicitly and explicitly by labor and management, workers were able to— and were implicitly expected to—carve out autonomy for themselves in the labor process. These arrangements enable management to gain what it most desires: a docile and stable labor force that ostensibly accepts

managerial control. External relations both constrain and enable workers and management as they pursue their collective interests.

In his essay on the legal and welfare policies encountered by divorcing couples, Simpson (2001: 113) suggests that ethnographies of 'organizations' need not be restricted to the spatial and bureaucratic existence that formally constitute organizations, but can also account for organizational 'effects,' including the rules, values, ideologies, and objectives that are enacted in practice on a daily basis. Perlow's (1997) ethnography of product development engineers at Ditto, a Fortune 500 company specializing in developing printers, illustrates this approach. She explores how organizations construct and utilize time, finding that decisions about time use at work significantly influence how time is conceptualized in nonwork contexts. Moreover, organizations often expect employees to privilege work over family time. At Ditto, excessive work demands resulted in a crisis-mode culture that intensified employee stress and morale, carrying implications for lives outside the workplace. By problematizing how time is constructed and used at work, Perlow suggests that, in addition to analyses of the environment as enabling or constraining, studies of the wider impact of organizations on their members can provide critical perspectives on issues such as work-family balance and leisure activities.

Powell's (1985) comparative fieldwork in an academic and a trade publishing house illustrates yet another variant of ethnography that explicitly focuses on organizations and their environments. Powell echoes Whyte's (1948) and Dalton's (1959) earlier insights concerning the role of social networks 'filling in the gaps of formal structure' (1985: xix) to address analytic concerns about managerial decision making. Powell finds that publishing houses are a central node in a network of relations that link a variety of constituents: authors, libraries, bookstores, the reading public, unions, banks, and parent corporations. Each of these sets of network ties both constrains and enables editorial decisions. In all of these contexts, editors use their network positions strategically to pursue career advancement, organizational goals, and aesthetic visions of 'good,' marketable books.

Change

In perhaps no other substantive area is ethnography more suitable as a method than in studying the dynamics of organizational change. Familiarity with the context enables the ethnographer to uncover subtle differences in the organization over time; and immersion in the process of change allows the researcher to capture nuances that may be barely discernible to scholars employing other methods. For instance, a cross-sectional view may blur the distinction between gradual, incremental changes and the discontinuous events that signal a more rapid, instantaneous change in the organization. Ethnographies allow scholars to probe the questions of what exactly constitutes change—for instance, at what point do multiple changes constitute a pattern of continuity, or whether change emanates from within or from the environment. Given the contentiousness surrounding the very definitions of change, it is not surprising that research on organizational change is fraught with contradiction (Barley, 1986). While ethnographers cannot magically produce order in this area, they offer sustained, empirical studies and theoretical insights that address key interpretive problems.

If the negotiated order perspective has taught nothing else, it is that incremental shifts and repositioning are the rule, not the exception in organizational life. Individuals and groups constantly adapt, which in turn produces slight shifts in the footing of actors and variation in the performance of routines. Change can occur through the 'selective retention' of such performances in everyday social interaction (Feldman and Pentland, 2003: 113). However, organizational change can strike well beyond incremental shifts or the selective retention of routine performances to reach quickly and deeply into organizational structures and strategies. Radical, rapid alterations in organizational components are relatively rare, but dramatic and analytically challenging when they occur.

Pettigrew's (1985) extensive study reveals the power of ethnography to capture the 'change patterns' in one of the world's largest multinationals, ICI. Pettigrew enjoyed access to the firm as both a consultant and a trainer, completed over one hundred depth interviews of personnel from the middle to the top levels of the firm, and collected nearly twenty-five years of documentation by the firm, and sixty years of secondary documentation produced about the firm. The changes Pettigrew documents are multidimensional and multilevel, involving production, diversification, marketing, and administration. By embedding his observations in a longer historical context, Pettigrew establishes that change occurs in rhythmic patterns: long incremental waves, punctuated by rapid, dramatic upheavals. He links these patterns to interest politics, internal and external, reflecting the constant give and take of organizational struggles. Interest groups emerge around issues of whether to grow or not to grow, diversify or centralize, to bring in new technology or not.

Barley (1986) offers an equally useful ethnographic vision of organizational change in his study of two radiology laboratories by addressing paradoxical findings about the relationship between technological innovation and organizational change. Social scientific and popular views have long held that technological innovation determines organizational change. However, empirical research is inconclusive, revealing contradictory findings in which the introduction of the same technologies can either produce different organizational structures or maintain the same structures (Barley, 1986). Couching his observations in negotiated order (Strauss, 1982) and structuration (Giddens, 1979) frameworks, Barley demonstrates the impact of new x-ray scanners in the radiology labs is an 'occasion' for redefining ('structuring') roles and role-relations by and among lab technicians and other personnel. Few of the outcomes were fully intended by management or the actors involved.

Ethnographic methods are particularly well-suited to understand the processual aspects of change. Bate's (2000) 'action ethnography' of a hospital in England, for example, documents how organizational change involves nonlinear processes as policies are translated and reconstructed among multiple constituencies. Bate also demonstrates how the 'end' result of organization change—in the hospital, trying to create a 'networked community' rather than a bureaucracy—is itself a process that requires continual achievement with respect to interpersonal interaction and sense making. Without ethnographic study in the organization, understanding the complexities of the cultural dynamics of change would have been difficult, if not impossible, which, in turn, would have created increased difficulties as Bate and his team turned to intervention in the organizational development portion of the project.

Ethnographies of organizational change often underscore its unintended effects, yet less often incorporate cross-case comparisons to aid in its analysis. A notable exception is Vallas's (2003) multisite ethnography of four manufacturing plants that attempted to implement team-based participatory practices among shop floor workers in the 1990s. Management's focus on scientific and technical rationality during the change led to the development of an expert-centered initiative that eventually stood at odds with the notion of worker participation. Where plant executives were more flexible (and less expert-centered) with respect to their approach to change, worker participation schemes were more likely to succeed.

Normative behavior and ethics

Ethnographic studies of normative behavior and ethics can be divided into two categories according to their organizational contexts. The first category comprises studies that focus on the dynamics of 'deviance,' systems of morality, and grievances, conflicts, and disputes in 'legitimate' organizations such as corporations, retail establishments, and government bureaucracies (Heimer and Staffen, 1995; Tucker, 1993; Vaughan, 1996). A second category comprises studies

of organizations considered 'deviant' from conventional normative or legal standards, such as organized crime families, drug dealers, and gangs (Adler, 1993; Bourgois, 1995; Decker and Van Winkle, 1996).

Ethnographers studying normative behavior in legitimate organizations discovered that boundaries between 'deviance' and 'normality,' as well as 'harmony' and 'conflict' are habitually blurred, questioning the absolutist and rationalist underpinnings of conventional understandings of normative behavior. Dalton (1959) demonstrated that conflict was endemic in organizations despite the pretence that it does not exist. Many of the social control mechanisms in organizations flow through informal rather than formal channels. Conflict is embedded in daily routines and is often handled behind the scenes, and not always by those with formal authority to settle disputes. These studies also reveal that seemingly irrational and individualistic conflict management actions have logics grounded in the social and cultural contexts in which they occur (Kolb and Bartunek, 1992; Morrill, 1995). Jackall's (1988) five-year ethnography of managerial decision-making in three corporations underscores the relativist nature of 'business ethics' in the corporate world. Jackall found that corporate managers follow a 'bureaucratic ethic' that situates moral choices in the 'rules-in-use' of particular organizational contexts.

If ethnographers of 'normal' or 'legal' organizations have often demonstrated their 'deviant' or 'conflictive' sides, ethnographers of 'deviant' organizations typically illuminate their 'normal' or 'harmonious' sides. Becker's (1963) ethnographic observations of 'deviant occupations' revealed the utility of applying the career concept to how people operate in deviant organizations. Adler's (1993) account of an upper-level drug dealing community demonstrates that drug dealers have business-like orientations to their occupations, are motivated by profit, and rationally organize their businesses, much as entrepreneurs in 'legitimate' organizations. Their commitment to drug dealing, however, originates in their choice of a deviant lifestyle. Finally, both Venkatesh (2006) and Sanchez Jankowski's (1991) ethnographies of gangs portray the gang as a quasi-rationalized business organization, in which the entrepreneurial spirit is the driving motivation, not motivations such as excitement, risk, or violence.

Power, politics, and control

Since the classic shop floor ethnographies of Roy (1959–1960) and Burawoy (1979), ethnographers have explored power and politics in organizations, drawing attention to phenomena that may have eluded scholars using other methods. Such studies often focused on the significance of informal relations among subordinates for contesting formal authority, coercion, and abuse exercised by supervisors and other overseers (Morrill et al., 2003). Contemporary ethnographic works on resistance investigate how its meanings and functions emerge from subordinates' knowledge of and encounters with organizational power and control (Ewick and Silbey, 2003).

Prasad and Prasad (2000) ethnographically examined the discursive practices through which resistance emerged during the implementation of a new computer system among health maintenance organization employees. They suggest that formal status influences how actors label and understand resistance, including managers who facilitate the emergence and persistence of resistance among nonmanagerial employees. Weeks' (2004) ethnography of a British bank goes one step further by illuminating how ritualized forms of resistance and complaint became woven into the very premises of the organizational culture. Roscigno and Hodson (2004), in their meta-analysis of 82 workplace ethnographies, confirm the linkage between different kinds of contestation, informal relations, and formal authority structures. Workplaces characterized by persistent managerial-worker conflict, strong union presence, and bureaucracy are more likely to experience collective contestation (such as strikes) than workplaces characterized by weak union presence and authority structures, which are likely to spawn individualized forms of resistance (such as sabotage and theft).

Ethnographers have not only examined resistance, but have also investigated the inverse—how authority and control are constituted through interactions among superiors and subordinates. Much of this work resonates with earlier work in the negotiated order and culture control traditions by carving out key roles for sense-making and identity in the exercise of authority and control. Through an in-depth ethnography of partners and staff in the Big Six (now five) accounting firms, Covaleski et al. (1998) argue that formal bureaucratic structures and professional socialization function as interrelated control systems that also create opportunities for resistance. They draw on Foucault's (1977) work on discipline to analyze how bureaucratic incentive and mentoring programs in those firms attempt to remake accountants as 'objects' of production that 'map' on to organizational goals. Such programs ultimately create crises in accountants' personal and professional identities and can lead to resistance or exit from firms. Pratt's (2000) multisite ethnography of Amway distributors suggests how organizational socialization can remake members' identities via sense-making activities. However, not all such activities lead to strong attachments to the organization. Pratt identifies the conditions under which such activities lead to identities congruent and incongruent with organizational goals. Hallett (2007) goes perhaps the furthest in pushing the negotiated order approach by investigating how symbolic power is generated via interaction rituals of deference and demeanor during administrators' attempts to change the institutional order of an elementary school. Deference, he finds, is a kind of 'credit' that administrators use to frame actions and events, thus inducing compliance and reshaping the underlying social order of an organization. Finally, ethnographers have noted explicitly and implicitly the importance of meaning and identity for control systems in alternative organizations that privilege democratic decision making (Rothschild-Whitt, 1979; Warhurst, 1998). Even more so than in traditional bureaucracies, control and authority reside in members' identifications with their organizational goals, especially their interactionally sustained definitions of themselves as participants in alternative organizations.

Methodological claims and trade-offs

The previous sections illustrate the theoretical and empirical payoffs of organizational ethnographies. We now describe the methodological claims and trade-offs of ethnographic research. On the positive side, ethnographic research provides depth, multiple perspectives, and process.

Depth

Ethnographers routinely justify their methodology by claiming that this approach permits a deeper and more nuanced understanding of an organization. If occasionally an illusion, the belief is deeply held. As we have argued, ethnographic data are often richer than those collected by quantitative measures are. Situational particulars add verisimilitude to narrative accounts. Whereas experimental data and survey research mesh cases, ethnographic research depends on the power of the extracted example. This emphasis on in-depth analysis permits researchers to examine the details of expressive culture.

Multiple perspectives

A second claim is that ethnography addresses how participants view their social world. The perspective is subjective and based on multiple points of view. To explore multiple perspectives, ethnographers typically use purposive sampling to select informants and contexts. Such strategies include maximum variation sampling (in which all of the relevant actors or contexts are sampled in an organization), extreme or deviant case sampling (in which information is gathered on exceptional or idiosyncratic actors or contexts), snowball sampling (which uses social network logic whereby one informant is asked to help the researcher find other informants), and theoretical sampling (in which the ethnographer seeks data relevant to emerging hypotheses).

The ethnographer typically is interested in what Gould et al. (1974) call 'perspectives in action' and 'perspectives of action.' Perspectives in action consist of talk that occurs during naturally occurring interaction in an ongoing social context. Perspectives of action, by contrast, consist of communications intended to make a context or situation meaningful to an outsider, such as when an informant responds to a question by a researcher. The longer the ethnographer stays in a social setting, the more important perspectives in action become as they learn about the lived experience of informants.

Process

The third distinguishing claim of ethnographic research is its ability to examine how organizations operate as ongoing concerns. Ethnographers have explored the how—daily social interaction, routines, and rituals—rather than the ends themselves. This processual strategy has many benefits. First, it provides an empirical foundation for examining, perhaps reassessing, the traditional relationship between means and ends in organizational behavior. What ethnographers demonstrate via their attention to process is that means and ends can have blurred boundaries and may not always occur in conventional chronological sequence (organizational actors can discover the ends they are pursuing by engaging in particular courses of action). Second, ethnographic attention to process enables the identification of mechanisms through which organizational behavior occurs, which can aid both ethnographers and other researchers in advancing stronger statements about how and why organizational behavior occurs. For instance, scholars employ ethnographic methods to examine not only the effects of corporate culture, but also how culture and its effects are achieved and/or subverted on a daily basis. Third, the focus on process (coupled with staying in the field for long periods) means that organizational ethnography has a built-in longitudinal component; ethnographers can observe how work sequences and change attempts unfold over time.

Ethnographic methods also entail trade-offs: issues of 'control,' 'researcher bias,' and 'generalizability.' While none of these trade-offs are fatal obstacles to the development of a meaningful organizational ethnography, they warrant discussion.

Control

Because ethnographers focus on obtaining the perspectives of participants as they enact their 'natural' routines, they have methodological strictures against playing too great a role in defining and organizing the setting. As such, ethnographers renounce a set of seemingly 'objective' rules, instead emphasizing situational choices. The behavior studied should be that of the participants, not that of the researcher. The traditional model for ethnographic research is for the participant observer to remain passive, observing the scene as might 'a fly on the wall' (Fine, 1993). This lack of control is a virtue as it demonstrates that the behaviors that are observed are 'real.' Yet, in being real they may not address the analytic concerns of the researcher; the content of the observations are haphazard and not entirely focused on the researcher's concerns, compromising the focus or the generalizability of the observations. As a consequence, many argue that ethnography must be inductive, rather than deductive: making a virtue of necessity.

This does not mean that ethnographic research proceeds haphazardly. The classic ethnographic research design situates a lone participant observer at a single site or several sites chosen to represent a particular organizational process. Leidner's (1993) ethnography of bureaucratic routinization at a McDonald's franchise, and in an insurance company, involved a careful consideration of appropriate research roles, field sites, and observational strategies. Ethnographers may also conduct multiple types of observation (e.g., moving from participant to nonparticipant) as another form of control. In Kleinman's (1996) study of a holistic healing

center, she volunteered for fundraising events, but also observed organizational members as a nonparticipant at meetings and retreats. Ethnographers sometimes adopt multiple researcher roles the longer they stay in the field, to maximize their perspectives as observers. Van Maanen initiated his (1973) classic study of a police department in the training academy as a police recruit. After graduating, he became a quasi-participant observer as a police officer 'reserve' riding with police patrols. Morrill's (1995) comparative study of conflict management among corporate executives in thirteen organizations provides a systematic approach to sampling and site selection using both interviews and direct observation. He first interviewed informants; question topics were laid out in advance, but pursued flexibly. Data from the interviews guided his observations at field sites chosen to represent types of organizational structures.

Researcher bias

Just as ethnographic research emphasizes the choices of the participants, it also privileges the judgments of the researcher more than other methodologies. The formal 'methodological rules' that one finds in quantitative research are largely absent in ethnography; the qualitative researcher is left to produce insight by whatever creative means. Countless essays (e.g. Fine, 1993; Van Maanen, 1979) demonstrate that the choices of ethnographers matter; one's research decisions interact with those of participants to create the ethnographic reality of organizational life.

Two common strategies by which ethnographers attempt to manage bias are member checks and triangulation. With member checks, research participants are asked to assess the plausibility of the ethnographer's interpretations. The recognition that an ethnographer's conclusions are plausible reconstructions of participants' own experiences enhances the authenticity of an ethnography and helps minimize research bias. Member checks typically occur at the end of data collection. Morrill (1995) used both informal member checks in his study of corporate executive conflict management, and formal 'exit' member checks when leaving the field. As useful as the member check is, their results must be situated in the rapport that exists between informants and researchers. There is always the possibility that informants share common myths, or a 'front,' which could affect what a researcher 'should' or 'should not' uncover (Douglas, 1976). Triangulation involves checking data gathered from one source against other sources. Typically, ethnographers triangulate data gathered from multiple informants with organizational documentation, secondary published material, and outsider perspectives. Less often, ethnographers address research bias by triangulating researchers' perspectives and data gathering efforts via 'team ethnography' (Douglas, 1976; Snow and Anderson, 1993; Snow et al., 1986). Prus and Irini (1980) worked part-time as bartenders, desk clerks, doormen, and waiters over five years to study an urban 'hotel community' of fifty hotels and bars catering to prostitutes and their clients. They triangulated their data gathering techniques, lessening the bias of their perspectives or role-relations in the hotel community.

Generalizability

The aim of science, it is frequently argued, is generalizability. Yet, the idiographic nature of ethnography seems to preclude the generalizability of findings. These contradicatory observations raise the question of what generalizability means. Most social scientists mean 'enumerative' generalizability; that is, the ability of a finding to represent some social process or state in a larger population from which a random sample was drawn. By these criteria, ethnography involves a trade-off— depth and perspective for generalizability. However, the relationship between ethnography and generalizability can be expanded in at least three ways. First, ethnographic studies on similar phenomena or in similar contexts can be used in qualitative 'meta-analyses,' with attention given to the quality of the data in each study, to form broader empirical understandings of phenomena (Yin, 1984). Such analyses can also translate findings

across contexts because of the added depth that each ethnography provides. Second, ethnography typically has more relevance to 'theoretical' generalization, which involves 'suggesting new interpretations and concepts or re-examining earlier concepts or interpretations in new and innovative ways' (Orum et al., 1991: 13). Third, ethnography contributes to the 'naturalistic' generalizability of findings (Stake, 1978); conclusions generalize when they resonate with a reader's empirical, often tacit, experiences. An ethnographic text need not agree with common belief; the issue is whether the account is plausible, even when it challenges existing frameworks (Lincoln and Guba, 1985: 119).

The resurgence of ethnography: sociology and organization studies

The previous section illustrated some methodological issues ethnographers have explicitly addressed. As ethnography has moved outside the social sciences into other domains, such as management, with a more applied focus, coupled with a strong tradition of quantitative research, the development of methodological standards for cross-disciplinary practice has increased in importance. This issue becomes particularly central when training novices. How can business students (or sociology graduate students, for that matter) be trained to observe organizations? Are guidelines possible?

Sufficiency and immersion

Sutton (1987) provides an intriguing answer. In his analysis of the process of organizational death, he presents tables that express the extent to which his theoretical conclusions are supported by ethnographic data. This form of data presentation has been alien to sociological ethnographers, who establish the credibility of their work through narrative. Even though letters replace numbers—with precision and exactitude lost—the model remains intact. Letters take on levels of support for the hypotheses in the model; C = strong evidence from initial contact; c = modest evidence from initial contact; I = strong evidence from interviews; i = modest evidence from interviews. This approach implies that a certain amount of data will suffice for presentation. It also argues that ethnography can be made 'rigorous' in the image of quantitative techniques, preventing methodological challenges to its legitimacy.

This model of data collection is one of sufficiency; how much data are sufficient to make a claim plausible? It stands in contrast to the standard ethnographic criterion of immersion; at what point will the researchers feel that they have enough insight into the scene that the data collected are redundant? The latter view asks whether the researcher knows enough that they could pass as a full member. Fine (1983) knew that it was time to discontinue his examination of fantasy role-playing games when participants began asking him for advice on the rules of the game. From being the pilgrim, he became the arbiter.

The issue of systematic analysis and standards is particularly relevant in organization studies, which often demand timely findings coupled with claims that give others the confidence to act. Research should be more than an expression of personal beliefs, swathed in memorable 'anecdotes.' If qualitative research does not, in this model, become a science, it can be a tool capable of being objectified and judged by others. It needs sufficient credibility that change agents should be able to utilize the results to demonstrate what changes might improve organizational functioning (Eccles, 1985).

How much is enough?

Ethnography in sociology and management is grounded upon different traditions. While the overlap is real, both in methodological dicta and in cited literatures, the research traditions are not identical. The goal in much sociological ethnography is to gain as full an interpretation of a social scene as possible. One collects data until one can act 'as a native' (Adler and Adler, 1987). A strong correlation is assumed between length of time in the field and quality of research. Further, this model suggests that not only

will the ethnographer wish to examine the scene for an extended period, but that during the research, the observations will be more intense, involving more hours per week. As many of our exemplars illustrate, the research often includes extensive in-depth interviews, archival data collection, and the compilation of detailed field notes. Given that many sociological research studies are explicitly inductive, the researcher is constrained to have few preconceptions before entering the field. This means that the first task of the researcher is to gain a sense of this unfamiliar, unexplored land. Once achieved, one can then, through grounded theory or analytic induction, explore the core conceptual and theoretical insights gained from patterns of interaction. The setting represents an empirical world from which one can generalize naturalistically, theoretically, and sometimes with enough cases, enumeratively. Glaser and Strauss (1967) make this explicit in their depiction of the 'constant comparative method.' One's research site is to be compared to other sites to discover the domain to which one can generalize one's findings linked to generic social processes (Couch, 1982; Prus, 1987).

At the risk of overgeneralization, demands are different in management-based organization research. Much management ethnography has an explicit applied link, sometimes even funded or supported by the organization(s) being studied (Eccles and Crane, 1988; Kanter, 1983 and 1992). Indeed, more than is true for sociologists, management ethnographers have 'their' organizations or industries, in which repeated observations are possible. Whereas the sociological investigator can spend years in the research setting, and often additional years writing up the analysis, this is unacceptable in situations in which the target organization expects or demands results. To the extent to which a research bargain exists that requires the investigator to provide information to the organization, the leisurely investigations of the sociologist are impossible. Even when no quid pro quo is involved, the model for research in organizational studies is linked to evaluation. Consequently, research in this style tends to be more tightly focused than the more general analysis preferred by many sociologists. Extensive data may be less necessary for addressing more focused questions.

Obviously, no simple or objective answers exist to the question of how much and what kind of data are necessary or how much time should be spent in the field. The answers to these questions depend upon what one hopes to gain. Efficiency is a value that should not be lightly dismissed. For every research project, a point of diminishing returns exists; a truth that all ethnographer learn when they attempt to tape record interaction in a field setting. Tapes keep running, participants keep talking, and eventually the unsuspecting researcher discovers mounds of data to be processed and digested—or ignored! A point exists at which there is too much data, either because little use can be made of the material, or because it redundantly exemplifies a point. In any ethnographic report, only a few fieldnote extracts are necessary to substantiate a claim. To be sure, one may not know until the final draft which examples are the most compelling, but a time comes when routine transactions do not add to ethnographic insight.

Students are often instructed that, in the early stages of research, fieldnotes should incorporate an array of topics, since it is often uncertain which will eventually prove central to analysis (Emerson et al., 1995; Lofland et al., 2006). Fieldnotes become progressively more targeted, and in time only the richest, most compelling, and most relevant examples are inscribed. This progression is akin to the more focused world of management or corporate ethnography. While the moment of analytic saturation may arrive earlier, and the scope of observations may be more limited, the process by which one learns that enough material has been collected is similar. In all perspectives, the reality is that the materials that are collected and the amount of time that one stays in the field are limited by occupational and organizational constraints. The driving need for generating compelling

conclusions also affects the amount of data to be collected. Different research goals, coupled with distinct standards of evaluation, determine what constitutes a competent research report. Given this, those with a more sociological approach may scorn the less intensive analysis of those in management programs, while those in management may define sociological work as too heavily theoretical, published in an untimely fashion and of less direct relevance.

Ultimately, those who conduct organizational ethnographies belong to the same intellectual community, even if we recognize that projects place different demands on researchers. Those who hope to conduct a detailed examination of an organization (however defined or embodied) have an extensive task; a large organization is not a small group. To study an organization is to accept the challenge of simultaneously examining many groups; most organizations are segmented and reticulated. The task is not simply one of examining a regularly interacting group, but of examining a network. We need to see the problem of 'how much data' not simply in terms of ethnography in general, but in light of the specific problems that come from examining organizational life.

Several features define how much data suffice. First, there is the problem of *disciplinary practice*. Inevitably, the standards of one's colleagues and disciplinary gatekeepers affect the choices of individual researchers. Second, the *structure of the organizational locale(s)* affects the style of research. Types of organization influence how complete a research project can hope to be. When management researchers examine large-scale organizations or those whose boundaries are difficult to define, the goal of completeness is less possible. Third, different projects have distinct *intended outcomes*. A research program that is narrowly focused will be less extensive than one broadly focused on the totality of organizational life. Related is the *model of theoretical development* that stands behind the research. Research that investigates a narrow range of hypotheses or set of assumptions may require less immersion than one that proceeds inductively or that seeks to modify existing theory.

No reason exists why any methodology demands one standard operating procedure. Nowhere is this more evident than in ethnographic research, whose flexibility is its sine qua non. While complete immersion can be justified, this benefit must be weighed against the efficiency and timeliness of briefer and more focused projects. Some research projects benefit from a more in-depth investigation. Yet, simultaneously, the extensive research projects, characteristic of working ethnographers in sociology may be needless luxuries, as the time involved in writing up the results may prevent the research from having impact.

CONCLUSIONS: MOBILE AND VIRTUAL ETHNOGRAPHY

Ethnographers have produced penetrating analyses of informal relations in orga-nizations, organizational meaning systems and culture, organizations and environments, organizational change, ethics and normative behaviors, and power relations. Organiza-tional ethnographers have confronted ques-tions that link organizational sociology to the larger discipline and other social sciences: agency and structure, rationality, and subjec-tive experience. Negotiated orders in which individual actors and groups act purposively, socially, and with some measure of agency exist within and between organizations and their environments. As we understand mem-bers' subjective meanings of organizational processes, restrictive notions of rationality become less tenable. What emerges is a more humane, less atomistic rationality that takes into account the social and cultural contexts that frame decision making.

The research addressed in this chapter reflects a snapshot of what scholars, given current definitions of what is important, have chosen to examine. Ethnography will surely change as the questions that are central to organizational studies change. Questions of performance, authenticity, the effects of localism and globalism are ripe for qualitative research. Recent shifts in technology and labor markets may prompt fundamental shifts in how organizational ethnographers ply their trade. Czarniawska (2004) maintains that organizational scholars must refocus on 'orga-nizing,' following Weick's (1979) dictum that organizations are not reified structures, but dynamic, ongoing accomplishments. In today's world, so Czarniawska argues, organi-zations are 'action nets' that involve complex interactions and rapid movements of people across time and region. As such, ethnogra-phers must develop triangulated techniques of 'mobile ethnology'; 'shadowing' people through multiple workdays across time zones and geographic regions; 'observant participa-tion' through which informants are trained in the arts of collecting systematic descriptions of their days; and 'narrative interviews' that yield chronological depictions of events from informants' perspectives. Czarniawska posits that traditional ethnography may be more appropriate for studying groups and communities situated in particular places, yet becomes difficult when organizations take the form of far-flung networks, virtual communi-ties, or constantly changing alliances. Barley and Kunda (2004) use similar techniques, cast in a team ethnographic approach, in their study of high-skilled contractors who circulate around the world. Such research might be considered virtual ethnographies, as physical presence is not always essential in a wired world.

Through its virtues, the various strains of field research contribute to our knowledge of structure and lived experience in the work-place. Ultimately, ethnography demonstrates the promise that the world in its nuance, as it is lived, can be comprehended through many lenses if we only look.

REFERENCES

Note: Portions of this chapter are based on material first published in Calvin Morrill and Gary Alan Fine, 'Ethnographic contributions to organizational sociology', *Sociological Methods and Research*, 25 (1997): 424–51.

Adler, P.A. (1993) *Wheeling and Dealing: An Ethnography of an Upper-Level Drug Dealing and Smuggling Community*, (second edn.), New York: Columbia University Press.

Adler, P.A. and Adler, P. (1987) *Membership Roles in Field Research*, Newbury Park, CA: Sage Publications.

Ashcraft, K.L. (1999) 'Managing maternity leave: a qualitative analysis of temporary executive succession', *Administrative Science Quarterly*, 44(2): 240–80.

Barley, S.R. (1983) 'Semiotics and the study of occupational and organizational culture', *Administrative Science Quarterly*, 28: 393–413.

Barley, S.R. (1986) 'Technology as an occasion for structuring: evidence from observations of CT scanners and the social order of radiology departments', *Administrative Science Quarterly*, 33: 24–60.

Barley, S.R. and Kunda, G. (2004) *Gurus, Hired Guns, and Warm Bodies: Itinerant Experts in a Knowledge Economy*, Princeton, NJ: Princeton University Press.

Barnard, C. (1938) 'The functions of the executive', in *The Theory and Structure of Formal Organizations*, Boston MA: Harvard University Press, pp. 65–114.

Bartunek, J.M., Rynes, S.L. and Ireland, R.D. (2006) 'What makes management research interesting, and why does it matter?', *Academy of Management Journal*, 49(1): 9–15.

Bate, P. (2000) 'Changing the culture of a hospital: from hierarchy to networked community', *Public Administration*, 78(3): 485–512.

Becker, H.S. (1963) *Outsiders: Studies in the Sociology of Deviance*, New York: Free Press.

Becker, H., Geer, B., Riesman, D. and Weiss, R.S. (1968) *Institutions and the Person*, Chicago: Aldine.

Bourgois, P.I. (1995) *In Search of Respect: Selling Crack in El Barrio*, Cambridge and New York: Cambridge University Press.

Burawoy, M. (1979) *Manufacturing Consent: Changes in the Labor Process Under Monopoly Capitalism*, Chicago: University of Chicago Press.

Carlile, P.R. (2002) 'A pragmatic view of knowledge and boundaries: boundary objects in new product development', *Organization Science*, 13(4): 442–55.

Couch, C.J. (1982) 'Toward a formal theory of social processes', *Symbolic Interaction*, 15: 117–34.

Covaleski, M.A., Dirsmith, M.W., Heian, J.B. and Samuel, S. (1998) 'The calculated and the avowed: techniques of discipline and struggles over identity in Big Six public accounting firms', *Administrative Science Quarterly*, 43(2): 293–327.

Czarniawska, B. (2004) 'On time, space, and action nets', *Organization*, 11(6): 773–91.

Dalton, M. (1959) *Men Who Manage: Fusions of Feeling and Theory in Administration*, New York: Wiley.

Decker, S.H. and Van Winkle, B. (1996) *Life in the Gang: Family, Friends and Violence*, Cambridge and New York: Cambridge University Press.

Douglas, J.D. (1976) *Investigative Social Research: Individual and Team Field Research*, Beverly Hills: Sage Publications.

Dutton, J. E. and Dukerich, J. M. (1991) 'Keeping an eye on the mirror: image and identity in organizational adaptation', *Academy of Management Review*, 34: 517–54.

Eccles, R.G. (1985) *The Transfer Pricing Problem: A Theory for Practice*, Lexington, MA: Lexington Books.

Eccles, R.G. and Crane, D.B. (1988) *Doing Deals: Investment Banks at Work*, Boston, MA: Harvard Business School Press.

Eden, C. and Huxham, C. (2001) 'Action research for the study of organizations', in S. Clegg, C. Hardy, and W.R. Nord (eds), *Handbook of Organization Studies*, London: Sage Publications, pp. 526–42.

Eisenhardt, K.M. (1989) 'Making fast strategic decisions in high-velocity environments', *Academy of Management Journal*, 32: 543–76.

Emerson, R.M., Fretz, R.I. and Shaw, L.L. (1995) *Writing Ethnographic Fieldnotes*, Chicago: University of Chicago Press.

Ewick, P. and Silbey, S. (2003) 'Narrating social structure: stories of resistance to legal authority', *American Journal of Sociology*, 108(6): 1328–72.

Farberman, H.A. (1975) A criminogenic market structure: the automobile industry. *Sociological Quarterly*, 16(4): 438–57.

Feldman, M.S. and Pentland, B.T. (2003) 'Reconceptualizing organizational routines as a source of flexibility and change', *Administrative Science Quarterly*, 48(1): 94–118.

Fine, G.A. (1983) 'Negotiated orders and organizational cultures', *Annual Review of Sociology*, 10: 239–62.

Fine, G.A. (1993) 'The sad demise, mysterious disappearance, and glorious triumph of symbolic interactionism', *Annual Review of Sociology*, 19(1): 61–87.

Fine, G.A. (1996) *Kitchens: The Culture of Restaurant Work*, Berkeley: University of California Press.

Foucault, M. (1977) *Discipline and Punish: The Birth of the Prison*, New York: Pantheon Books.

Giddens, A. (1979) *Central Problems in Social Theory*, Berkeley, CA: University of California Press.

Glaser, B.G. and Strauss, A.L. (1967) *The Discovery of Grounded Theory: Strategies for Qualitative Research*, Chicago: Aldine Publishing Company.

Goffman, E. (1956) *The Presentation of Self in Everyday Life*, New York: Anchor.

Goffman, E. (1961) *Asylums: Essays on the Social Situation of Mental Patients and Other Inmates*, New York: Doubleday.

Gould, L., Walker, A.L., Crane, L.E. and Lidz, C.W. (1974) *Connections: Notes From the Heroin World*, New Haven, CT: Yale University Press.

Hallet, T. (2007) 'Between deference and distinction: interaction ritual through symbolic power in an educational institution,' *Social Psychology Quarterly*, 70: 148–71.

Heimer, C.A. and Staffen, L.R. (1995) 'Interdependence and reintegrative social control: labeling and reforming 'inappropriate' parents in neonatal intensive care units', *American Sociological Review*, 60(5): 635–54.

Jackall, R. (1988) *Moral Mazes: The World of Corporate Managers*, New York: Oxford University Press.

Jankowski, M.S. (1991) *Islands in the Street: Gangs and American Urban Society*, Berkeley: University of California Press.

Kanter, R.M. (1977) *Men and Women of the Corporation*, New York: Basic Books.

Kanter, R.M. (1983) *The Change Masters: Innovations for Productivity in the American Corporation*, New York: Simon and Schuster.

Kanter, R.M. (1992) *The Challenge of Organizational Change: How Companies Experience it and Leaders Guide it*, New York: Free Press.

Kleinman, S. (1996) *Opposing Ambitions: Gender and Identity in an Alternative Organization*, Chicago, Ill: University of Chicago Press.

Kling, R. and Gerson, E. (1977) 'The social dynamics of technical innovations in the computing world', *Symbolic Interaction*, 1: 132–46.

Kolb, D.M. (1983) *The Mediators*, Cambridge, MA: MIT Press.

Kolb, D.M. and Bartunek, J. (1992) *Hidden Conflict in Organizations: Uuncovering Behind-the-Scenes Disputes*, Newbury Park, CA: Sage Publications.

Kunda, G. (1992) *Engineering Culture: Control and Commitment in a High-Tech Corporation*, Philadelphia, PA: Temple University Press.

Leidner, R. (1993) *Fast Food, Fast Talk: Service Work and the Routinization of Everyday Life*, Berkeley: University of California Press.

Lincoln, Y.S. and Guba, E.G. (1985) *Naturalistic Inquiry*, Beverly Hills, CA: Sage Publications.

Lofland, J., Snow, D.A., Anderson, L. and Lofland, L.H. (2006) *Analyzing Social Settings: A Guide to Qualitative Observation and Analysis*, Belmont, CA: Wadsworth (third edn.).

Maines, D. (1982) 'In search of mesostructure', *Urban Life*, 11: 267–79.

Morrill, C. (1995) *The Executive Way: Conflict Management in Corporations*, Chicago: University of Chicago Press.

Morrill, C., Zald, M.N. and Rao, H. (2003) 'Covert political conflict in organizations: challenges from below', *Annual Review of Sociology*, 29(1): 391–415.

Orum, A.M., Feagin, J.R. and Sjoberg, G. (1991). 'Introduction: the nature of the case study', in A.M. Orum, J.R. Feagin and G. Sjoberg (eds), *A Case for the Case Study*, Chapel Hill: University of North Carolina Press, pp. 1–26.

Perlow, L.A. (1997) *Finding Time: How Corporations, Individuals, and Families can Benefit from New Work Practices*, Ithaca, NY: ILR Press.

Pettigrew, A. (1985) *The Awakening Giant: Continuity and Change in ICI*, Oxford: Basil Blackwell.

Powell, W.W. (1985) *Getting Into Print: The Decision-Making Process in Scholarly Publishing*, Chicago: University of Chicago Press.

Prasad, P. and Prasad, A. (2000) 'Stretching the iron cage: the constitution and implications of routine workplace resistance', *Organization Science*, 11(4): 387–403.

Pratt, M.G. (2000) 'The good, the bad, and the ambivalent: managing identification among amway distributors', *Administrative Science Quarterly*, 45(3): 456–93.

Prus, R.C. (1987) 'Generic social processes: maximizing conceptual development in ethnographic research', *Journal of Contemporary Ethnography*, 16: 250–93.

Prus, R.C. and Irini, S. (1980) *Hookers, Rounders, and Desk Clerks: The Social Organization of the Hotel Community*, Toronto: Gage Publishing.

Roethlisberger, F.J. and Dickson, W.J. (1947) *Management and the Worker*, Cambridge, MA: Harvard University Press.

Roscigno, V.J. and Hodson, R. (2004) 'The organizational and social foundations of worker resistance', *American Sociological Review*, 69(1): 14–39.

Rothschild-Whitt, J. (1979) 'The collectivist organization: an alternative to rational-bureaucratic models', *American Sociological Review*, 44(4): 509–27.

Roy, D.F. (1952) 'Quota restriction and goldbricking in a machine shop', *American Journal of Sociology*, 57: 427–42.

Roy, D.F. (1954) 'Efficiency and the fix: informal intergroup relations in a piecework machine shop', *American Journal of Sociology*, 60: 255–66.

Roy, D.F. (1959–1960) 'Banana time: job satisfaction and informal interaction', *Human Organization*, 18: 158–68.

Salaman, G. (1974) *Community and Occupation*, London: Cambridge University Press.

Sánchez-Jankowski, Martín. (1991) *Islands in the Street: Gangs and American Urban Society*, Berkeley: University of California Press.

Simpson, B. (2001) 'Swords into ploughshares: manipulating metaphor in the divorce process', in D.N. Gellner and E. Hirsch (eds), *Inside Organizations: Anthropologists at Work* (pp. xi, 271), Oxford: Berg.

Snow, D.A. and Anderson, L. (1993) *Down on Their: Luck: A Study of Homeless Street People*, Berkeley, University of California Press.

Snow, D.A., Benford, R.D. and Anderson, L. (1986) 'Fieldwork roles and informational yield: a comparison of alternative settings and roles', *Urban Life*, 15: 377–408.

Stake, R. (1978) 'The case study method in social inquiry', *Educational Researcher*, 7: 5–8.

Strauss, A.L. (1964) *Psychiatric Ideologies and Institutions*, Glance, IL: Free Press.

Strauss, A.L. (1982) 'Interorganizational negotiation', *Urban Life*, 11: 350–67.

Sutton, R.I. (1987) 'The process of organizational death: disbanding and reconnecting', *Administrative Science Quarterly*, 32: 542–69.

Strauss, A.L., Schatzman, L., Erlich, D., Bucher, R. and Sabshin, M. (1963) 'The hospital and its negotiated order', in E. Friedson (ed), *The Hospital in Modern Society*, New York: Free Press, pp. 149–69.

Strauss, A.L., Schatzman, L., Erlich, D., Bucher, R. and Sabshin, M. (1964) *Psychiatric Ideologies and Institutions*, Glencoe, IL: Free Press.

Tucker, J. (1993) 'Everyday forms of employee resistance', *Sociological Forum*, 8(1): 25.

Uzzi, B. (1997) 'Social structure and competition in interfirm networks: the paradox of embeddedness', *Administrative Science Quarterly*, 42: 35–67.

Vallas, S.P. (2003) 'Why teamwork fails: obstacles to workplace change in four manufacturing plants', *American Sociological Review*, 68(2): 223–50.

Van Maanen, J. (1973) 'Observations on the making of policemen', *Human Organization*, 32(4): 407.

Van Maanen, J. (1979) 'The fact of fiction of organizational ethnography', *Administrative Science Quarterly*, 24: 539–50.

Vaughan, D. (1996) *The Challenger Launch Decision: Risky Technology, Culture, and Deviance at NASA*, Chicago, Ill: University of Chicago Press.

Venkatesh, S. (2006) *Off the Boioks: The Underground Economy of the Urban Poor*, Cambridge, MA: Harvard University Press.

Warhurst, C. (1998) 'Recognizing the possible: the organization and control of a socialist labor process', *Administrative Science Quarterly*, 43(2): 470–97.

Weeks, J. (2004) *Unpopular Culture: The Ritual of Complaint in a British Bank*, Chicago: The University of Chicago Press.

Weick, K.E. (1979) *The Social Psychology of Organizing*, Reading, MA: Addison-Wesley.

Weick, K.E. (1985) 'Systematic observational methods', in G. Lindzey and E. Aronson (eds), *The Handbook of Social Psychology* (third edn.), Hillsdale, NJ: Random House, pp. 567–634.

Whyte, W.F. (1948) *Human Relations in the Restaurant Industry*, New York: McGraw-Hill Book Company.

Yin, R.K. (1984) *Case Study Research: Design and Methods*, Beverly Hills, CA: Sage Publications.

36

From *Modern Times* to *Syriana*: Feature Films as Research Data

John S. Hassard and David A. Buchanan

INTRODUCTION

This chapter explores how feature films can be analyzed as research data in the form of process narratives, 'proxy documentaries', and case studies, to inform our understanding of organizational behaviour and to develop theory. For example, one of the last silent movies of the early twentieth century, *Modern Times* (1936, director Charles Chaplin), can be viewed as a case study of the dehumanizing effects of early American capitalism and the Detroit production system. *Syriana* (2006, director Stephen Gaghan) can be read as a documentary on the nature and implications of twenty-first century globalization (Zaniello, 2007), depicting collusion and corruption in the relationships between the oil industry and national politics. Those movies, produced seventy years apart, both cast organizations and managers in a negative light. Film representations of work often portray demeaning aspects of manual and white-collar labour, and managers as stereotypical villains; the company president in *Modern Times* turns from

his jigsaw and his newspaper 'funny pages' to order increases in the speed of Charlie Chaplin's assembly line. This viewpoint is seen in 'real' documentaries such as *Roger and Me* (1989, director Michael Moore), *The Corporation* (2003, directors Mark Achbar and Jennifer Abbott), and *Enron: The Smartest Guys in the Room* (2005, director Alex Gibney) (see Hassard, Chapter 16, this volume for an analysis of documentary film). Film is thus of considerable interest to researchers as a source of interpretations and illustrations of organizational behaviour. As a source of ideas and evidence for theory development and testing, however, film has much greater potential.

Beyond entertainment

[This text] adds excitement and relevance to organizational behaviour topics through selected film scenes from popular film releases. Film provides your students a visual portrayal of abstract management concepts and provides inexperienced students a greater feeling of reality and connection to the topic. Further, there are many unique aspects of film such as editing, sound, framing, and focusing techniques that make it a powerful communication device that often goes beyond what we can experience in reality (from the publisher's website for *Our Feature Presentation: Organizational Behaviour*, Champoux, 2005: www.thomsonedu.com).

The use of movies in teaching organization studies is well established. Champoux (1999, 2001a, 2001b, 2005, 2007) identifies numerous film clips illustrating concepts and theories spanning the organization studies agenda; other instructors have documented their uses of film to introduce specific themes (Serey, 1992; Baker, 1993; Willer, 1995; Comer and Cooper, 1998; Comer, 2000; Roth, 2001; Hunt, 2001; Shaw, 2004; Huczynski and Buchanan, 2005; Champoux, 2006). Novels have also been dissected in search of organizational topics (Knights and Willmott, 1999). However, films are popular because they can present topics in ways that are more graphic, engaging, motivating, and memorable than conventional classroom methods or novels can. While they may be attractive to students (watching a movie is easier than reading a book), Hobbs (1998) cautions that films are symbolic representations with their own 'language' and 'grammar', and an untrained passive viewing discourages a questioning and critical approach, leaving audiences vulnerable to manipulation. Nevertheless, film narratives can bring to life abstract ideas and perspectives, highlighting the role of context, complexity, ambiguity, and chance. Portraying 'what it's really like', giving 'the insider's view', films often depict emotional aspects of experience such as ambition, dedication, enthusiasm, envy, fear, humour, love, lust, struggle, and sacrifice (Phillips, 1995; Cortazzi, 2001). Narratives based on themes of power, conflict, resistance, and violence create opportunities for a critical reading of management (Hassard and Holliday, 1998). The relationship between these issues and 'reality' has been explored in texts working at the interface of organization theory and cultural studies (Rhodes and Westwood, 2007; Bell, 2008). Observing that films allow us to see events through the eyes of multiple stakeholders, and not just with a managerial

or research view, Sloane (2002: 8) argues that fictional accounts paint a more complete and 'elegant' picture of the organizational landscape:

> Here we have an opportunity to observe, under widely differing conditions and in varying perspectives, a 'whole' situation, one in which politics (or policy) and administration are joined by an act of artistic synthesis rather than separated by an act of scientific analysis.

Despite (or because of?) the pedagogical value of film, few researchers regard movies as empirical evidence equivalent in status to interviews and survey data. However, as Ulmer (1989) observes, the ability to interpret visual imagery – 'videocy' – is now as significant to the development of our understanding as literacy, and related disciplines have embraced visual methods more readily. Ball and Smith (2001) note, however, that the visual research traditions in sociology and ethnography are different. While sociologists have used still photographs, ethnographers have made extensive use of film, shot usually by researchers, but occasionally by the subjects of their research. Robert Flaherty's film of Eskimo life, *Nanook of the North* (made in 1922) is an iconic example of the former; the use of video diaries is a recent example of the latter (Holliday, 2004). The realist concern of ethnography, to capture the authentic nature of other cultures, is rooted in the documentary tradition in photography and film, which emerged in the late nineteenth century. Some early documentaries and photojournalism projects influenced reform movements and legislation by exposing the effects of industrial working conditions and economic depression. The social realist classic *Cathy Come Home* (1966, director Ken Loach) a film-length television play about the nature and impact of homelessness, shaped British government policy and led to the creation of the charity 'Shelter'. While Loach's film is often cited as a documentary, based on research and actual experience, the main characters were actors, and the scenes were staged (Zaniello, 2003: 15). Reflecting on his television work,

Loach said, 'we were very anxious for our plays not to be considered dramas but as continuations of the news' (Collins, 2008: 19).

Documentary (real, serious) is often distinguished from fiction (imagined, frivolous), but these categories are blurred. Documentaries give a point of view, designed to influence audiences to accept perspectives, to adopt attitudes. The realist project intends to persuade: 'John Grierson, the Scottish film-maker who is widely regarded as a pivotal figure in the development of British and North American documentary film in the 1930s and 1940s, considered cinema as a modernist pulpit. His approach was to exploit the potential of film in order to construct a picture of reality that would realize cinema's destiny as a social commentator and source of inspiration for social change' (Ball and Smith, 2001: 304). In his guide to 350 films about work, labour activism, and labour history, Zaniello (2003) notes that some documentaries are presented as dramatic investigative journalism, using actors, and many feature films strive for social realism and are intercut with film from actual events.

The ideological potential of film was recognized early. In the 1920s, Dziga Vertov's *Kinopravda* (film truth) in the Soviet Union used film for propaganda purposes; Leni Riefenstahl's documentary of the 1934 Nazi Party rally, *Triumph of Will*, was a propaganda vehicle. When the US entered the Second World War, the Walt Disney Studio was effectively commandeered by the US Army, and for the duration of the conflict, Mickey Mouse, Donald Duck and friends were enlisted in the war effort. The ensuing propaganda represented the majority of the studio's production activity, and a within a year of the commencement of US involvement in the war, the studio was in receipt of contracts totalling US$2.6 million (Bryman, 1995: 10; Holliss and Sibley, 1988: 47). Recognizing their power to persuade, Hollywood movies in the 1950s were constrained by the proceedings of the House Committee on Un-American Actitivies which, with the help of the Los Angeles FBI field office, produced a 'motion picture blacklist' of films showing 'subversive propaganda', including 'negative portrayals of the wealthy, bankers, big business or industrialists' (Spector, 2008, forthcoming). Actors, directors, writers, and technicians had to sign a loyalty oath, and those who refused to account for their political affiliations were denied employment. The FBI blacklisted *It's a Wonderful Life* (1946, director Frank Capra) in which honest George Bailey (played by James Stewart), whose small business is in trouble, confronts the ruthless 'fat cat' banker, Mr Potter (Lionel Barrymore). Are there links between government and the movies today? The Center for Responsive Politics reports (www.opensecrets.org) that the film industry in America since 1990 has given seven times more in political party donations to the Democrats (left wing liberals) than to the Republicans (right wing conservatives).

In his classic sociological/structuralist analysis of American western movies from 1930 to 1972, Wright (1975) argues that films are narrative vehicles depicting social myths and concerns. This may be one of the first treatments of 'movie as training programme', offering the audience guidance on how to behave: 'When the story is a myth and the characters represent social types or principles in a structure of oppositions, then the narrative structure offers a model of social action by presenting identifiable social types and showing how they interact. The receivers of the myth learn how to act by recognizing their own situation in it and observing how it is resolved' (Wright, 1975: 186). While movies can be interpreted 'as if' they were documentaries, the directors of many features deliberately present their work as provocative and controversial social commentaries. *Disclosure* (1994, director Barry Levinson) generated considerable debate by arguing that women are capable of sexually harassing and raping men. *The Constant Gardner* (2005, director Fernando Meirelles) documented the corruption and greed of a pharmaceutical company exploiting innocent Kenyans; the novel by John le Carré on which this movie is based was banned in Kenya for its portrayal of corrupt government officials. While the points of view of other movies are perhaps less contentious, they can still be interpreted from an ethnographic standpoint, as 'proxy documentaries' which articulate significant social, cultural, and organizational themes. Gabbard and Gabbard (1999) argue that the implicit ideology of American films endorses self help, the role of the individual as the source of and solution to life's problems, and the values of deferred gratification, hard work, and perseverance, which explain personal success.

The growth of large corporations in the decade following the end of the Second World War (in 1945) created a new professional executive class. What did they do for a living? Spector (2008) observes that popular culture answered this question by going through the closed doors of the executive suite to provide complex accounts of emotions, aspirations, motives, and power plays. In his analysis of over 220 'executive career' movies made between 1945 and 2001, Boozer (2002: 38) discusses these films as though they were 'native documentaries' describing the nature of corporate structures and career success:

> The fact that internal information on corporate operations was not readily accessible to the American public also gave these films a special educational place in popular culture. They had a contemporary relevance that most other genres – which looked to nostalgic or inaccessible worlds of the past, present, or future – did not. [...] The classical corporate executive film, therefore, in ways both manifest and latent, played a special role in creating a success mythology based on personal/family accommodation to an expanding corporate culture.

The career movies of the 1950s (*Executive Suite*, 1954, director Robert Wise; *The Man in the Grey Flannel Suit*, 1956, director Nunally Johnson) 'presumed to offer realistic boardroom and bedroom revelations of those in the mysterious upper echelons of the new corporate elite' (Boozer, 2002: 21). Nevertheless, just how accurate was the image of the rising corporate star, combining selfless ambition and moral concern for

family and the wider society? The early films that Boozer discusses, 'all insist or imply that ultimately what is good for the company will be good for the nation as well as for most families' (p.22). This model loses credibility in career movies from the 1960s onwards, as business goals come to be seen as controversial, and as the corporate executive comes to be viewed with suspicion. The early career movies, Boozer (2002: 5) observes, offered a causal model of upward mobility and success determined by individual ambition, initiative, and enterprise. They also portrayed the ethical, legal, domestic, and personal compromises that 'success' might involve, along with the contradictions between managerial work and domestic responsibility, between ethical behaviour and social responsibility. In the two versions of *Death of a Salesman* (1951, director Laslo Benedek; 1985, director Volker Schlörndorff), Boozer (2002: 7) sees 'America's most well known cultural investigation into the mythic force of the traditional success dream for its time', with the first version emphasizing 'the personal anguish that can result from an overdependence on a public success image' (Boozer, 2002: 7).

Fictional narratives, of course, are designed to influence an audience. We organize our understanding of the world, in part, through the stories, which we use to report, evaluate, and make sense of our experiences, and to share them with others (Weick, 1995). In addition, narrators do not simply tell stories; they present versions of events, coloured by their perspective and judgement concerning the relevance and meaning of what happened. As we tell stories about things, which are significant to both the teller and to the audience, an analysis of the topics, content, style, and context of stories can give researchers access to culturally significant themes as well as to narrators' understandings of issues, characters, and events. Telling a story is also a performance, through which meaning is coconstructed and jointly interpreted along with others. Cortazzi (2001: 388) argues that, in addition to providing information and entertainment, narratives can have several other functions:

- Give novices examples in a training context
- Enable audiences to diagnose a problem and clarify a situation
- Help a group to define an issue or determine a collective stance
- Establish rapport and solidarity, convey collective values, ratify group membership
- Provide a way of looking at and evaluating the past
- Convey a sense of history and progress
- Exercise social and moral control by provoking analogical reflexive thinking
- Serve as a substitute for argument, in order to persuade and to confer credibility
- Contribute to self-understanding and the formation of professional and occupational identity, making sense of who we are and who we wish to be
- Interpret events in terms of causality

Film is a potent and pervasive mode of communication. For most of the twentieth century, unless one worked in the industry, owning a copy of a movie would have been unthinkable. Now, most of us probably own several (Monaco, 2000). The narratives that we see on the screen variously invite us to admire, applaud, avoid, conform, criticize, desire, imitate, purchase, and to be repelled, shocked, titillated, or traumatized. The argument that an understanding of our social and organizational world is shaped at least in part by the images and narratives of film and television is difficult to challenge.

The intent of writers, producers, and directors can of course be subverted by audiences whose passive compliance is not guaranteed, and whose active interpretation of what they see and hear can differ markedly from that of the authors – and of other interpreters. Taking recourse to epistemology, we can doubt, for example, that the production of narrative consensus is achievable given the status of knowledge practices. Such practices are not stable and coherent, but continuously in the making; they shape and are shaped by power relations and competing discourses; they infer a process in which knowledge is at the same time produced and consumed; and they view knowledge as a set of cultural practices situated in and inextricably linked to the material and social circumstances in which it is produced and consumed (Foucault, 1980; Lyotard, 1997). As sociomaterial practice, knowledge is processual and provisional; its production relies on resources disembodied from their original content and made available through their transformation, legitimization, and institutionalization (Gherardi and Nicolini, 2000). Knowledge consumption is ensured through processes of social participation in a community of practice – a means of 'being in the world', not simply 'knowing the world' (Bourdieu, 1990). So, do movies reflect or shape social and organizational norms and values? Clearly, they have the potential to do both.

However, films are not regarded as 'serious' research data first, because they are fictitious and unrealistic (social science deals with fact; even movies based on real characters and events are 'fictionalized'), and second, because they are unrepresentative (many researchers prioritize statistical generalizability). To be commercially successful, films often have to exaggerate, sensationalize, and glamourize; surface not depth, form not substance. As cultural products, movies are made in order to make money, not to provide researchers with data. Consequently, films are 'unscientific, 'fluffy', and not rigorous or testable', and are often produced specifically, because they are idiosyncratic (Phillips, 1995: 644).

Both of those criticisms are easily dismissed. First, following the 'narrative turn' in social science (Czarniawska, 1998; 1999), the boundaries between fiction and science have been blurred. Theories are stories about the ways in which things happen, while narratives similarly offer accounts or hypotheses linking antecedents to consequences in particular contexts (Sutton and Staw, 1995; Richardson, 2000). Arguing that there can be no distinction between descriptive and explanatory narratives, Wright (1975: 128) observes that, 'a narrative is not just possibly an explanation; it is inevitably an explanation. It explains how a certain situation came about from a prior situation'. Science discovers, fiction makes things up; social scientists observe reality, writers create alternative realities; social scientists use method, writers use illusion and deception. However, as Phillips (1995) argues, social scientists also create as well as discover, focus on the unique as well as on the general, and often use illusion and rhetoric to make their case. Writers test ideas against evidence, generalize, pose questions about the social world, and attempt to remain faithful to the details of experience. In short, these are not 'two solitudes' but two communities, with a shared goal to 'model the world', but separated by the 'conventionalized understandings of their respective activities' (Phillips, 1995: 629). Narratives must be plausible if they are to work, and through the rich depiction of context and complexity, films can construct accounts of characters, settings, and events that are more realistic than the contents of sanitized textbooks and the data generated by conventional research methods (Hassard and Holliday, 1998; Burrell, 1998).

Second, the discounting of the single case as unrepresentative is based on a misunderstanding of the distinction between statistical, naturalistic, and analytical generalization. Cases in organization studies are not the statistician's single observation, but are often richly contextualized accounts working across different levels of analysis over extended periods. *Statistical* generalization of findings to a population on the basis of a single case may be inappropriate. *Naturalistic* generalization involves the application of conclusions to personal experience or to a comparable setting (Stake, 1994). This is the mode in which Willer (1995) uses the movie *Nine to Five* (1980, director Colin Higgins) as a teaching case study, based on one example. Willer also dismisses the criticism that this is an idiosyncratic account of sexual harassment, observing that the story is realistic, and encourages viewers to consider what they would do in similar circumstances.

Analytical generalization relates findings, even from a single case, to theory. Researchers are often advised to select cases, precisely because they represent extreme situations, critical incidents, or 'outliers', as the potential to learn from deviant examples can be high (Pettigrew, 1990). As this chapter was being drafted in August 2007, *The Leadership Quarterly* journal issued a call for papers exploring 'leadership in extreme contexts', defined as dangerous, unusual, and dynamic situations and crises, where leadership can either avoid or generate catastrophic physical, financial, and psychological consequences. The rationale for this focus is that we do not always learn much from research, which suggests how to deal with typical, average, regular settings. There is now a substantial literature on the epistemology of the singular (Mitchell, 1983; Dyer and Wilkins, 1991; Butler, 1997; Buchanan, 1999; Buchanan et al., 2007; Siggelkow, 2007). Tsoukas (1989 and Chapter 17, this volume) argues that single cases can clarify structural aspects of social configurations, the associated generative mechanisms and contingent factors leading to observed outcomes. Rueschemeyer (2003) argues that 'least likely' cases have significant theoretical implications when observations contradict expectations; for example, how many black swans does one have to observe before one's belief in the theory that 'all swans are white' is shaken? Hassard and Holliday (1998: 1) argue that film, 'offers more dramatic, more intense and more dynamic representations of organization than management texts', asking 'are such glimpses and insights perhaps the very focus, the heart of organizational life, too long ignored by mainstream theory?' Feature films, chosen with care, seem to fit well the category of extreme, idiosyncratic, critical, deviant, least likely, or 'outlier' cases that can challenge conventional assumptions.

Bad company

Once asked why real gangsters sounded so much like their movie counterparts, George Raft replied that it was because gangster movies (his in particular, he noted) taught gangsters how to talk (McCarty, 2004: 241).

Voyeurism is a facet of our experience of cinema; we watch others dealing with their circumstances, their relationships, their problems. Films can thus influence attitudes and behaviours by telling us what is 'OK', desirable, acceptable, and what is not, by presenting role models which suggest, literally, how we should act. The people that we see on the screen are often people like us, or people we would want to be, as well as those whom we would not wish to emulate. We are also, therefore, cast in a judgemental role; was that behaviour effective, appropriate, and one that I could use in similar circumstances? As well as being entertaining, informative, and persuasive, film also offers the viewer a vicarious experience which can be used in a number of related ways. First, it is common for the audience to consider how the settings, strategies, and behaviours seen on the screen could be relevant to them (naturalistic generalization). Second, vicarious experience is an invitation safely to explore unrealized possibilities; 'what would it be like to do this/to live like that?' Third, film can be inspirational; 'if I could do that'. As mentioned earlier, fictional narratives can contribute to our self-understanding and sense of identity.

While it can be argued that such influential narrative knowledge is produced through the interaction of symbolic and material conditions, we can argue also that it is 'reproduced' only when singled out for attention by those who find it meaningful (Knights, 1997). For Munro (1998), narrative knowledge is never meaningful in its own right – to become meaningful, it has to 'exteriorize' itself. Narrative knowledge is usually mediated/exteriorized through linguistic practices in which actions and interactions are made accountable to oneself and to the 'other' (Gherardi and Nicolini, 2000). Such practices are acts of consumption, serving purposes as diverse as expressing one's identity, marking attachment to social groups, exhibiting social distinction

or ensuring social participation in various activities (Edgell et al., 1996). The ways in which people, professions, occupational groups, events, and organizations are portrayed in films, and also what is omitted from those representations, are therefore significant.

While film studies have not traditionally considered movies from this perspective, two professions which have attracted attention are psychiatrists and gangsters. Given the ethical and legal problems of using live subjects in the classroom, film is increasingly used as a medium for teaching psychiatry. For some personality disorders (paranoia, obsessive compulsive disorder, and psychopathy), it is difficult to find subjects to interview, and film can provide graphic illustrations. Jack Nicolson plays an obsessive writer in *As Good as it Gets* (1997, director James L. Brooks). Russel Crowe plays John Nash the schizophrenic mathematician in *A Beautiful Mind* (2001, director Ron Howard). But how is the profession of psychiatry itself represented in films? From their analysis of 450 Hollywood movies portraying mental health professionals, Gabbard and Gabbard (1999) identify three stereotypes: *Dr Dippy* (from a 1906 comedy), *Dr Evil*, and *Dr Wonderful*. Psychiatry, they argue, is exploited by the film industry in the interests of entertainment and profit, and the stylized depiction of the profession is driven by the needs of the medium, with respect to character, motive, relationships, and plot. They also note that, in terms of prestige, psychiatry is portrayed across the spectrum, sometimes high, sometimes low, often idealized, occasionally devalued, but with few departures from narrow conventions and clichés.

Exploring the film representation of quite a different occupational group, McCarty (2004) argues that Hollywood gangster movies are heirs to the Western movie genre. The reticent cowboy forced into a showdown has simply been replaced by the bad guy grasping for power and position. As with the portrayal of psychiatry, McCarty identifies three recurring gangster stereotypes; the 'murderously covetous', the 'psychopath hooked on violence', and the 'doomed loner'. McCarty's analysis of over a thousand movies has two interesting conclusions with regard to what they reveal about the culture in which they were produced. First, he suggests that, in common with traditional Westerns, gangster movies confirm 'the American odyssey' in terms of preferred values, arguing that the appeal of these movies probably lies with the liberating implications of anarchic characters who ignore rules and regulations. Second, and reflected in the opening comment from George Raft, the gangster movie as a communications medium works in two directions. Many of the early leading actors in this genre – Edward G. Robinson, James Cagney, George Raft – based their dress, mannerisms, and actions (including nervous 'tics') on the gangster personalities of their era. However, those gangsters responded by emulating their screen images:

[T]he movie screen is a mirror with two sides, and gangsters, like children, are not immune from the desire to want to walk, talk, and be like their screen icons flickering back at them from the big screen' (McCarty, 2004: 242).

In other words, 'reel life and real life' overlap (McCarty, 2004: 215). While gangster movies were based on research, the fictions on the screen became 'facts' when members of the mob copied what they saw. Observing that a clear distinction between the Mafia and 'legitimate' business is difficult to sustain, Parker (2006) also notes that the boundary between fiction and reality is blurred, drawing examples from *The Godfather* movies (1972, 1974 and 1990, director Francis Ford Coppola) and the award-winning television series, *The Sopranos* (1999 to 2007). Mario Puzo, author of the novels on which *The Godfather* movies were based, allegedly modelled the character of Don Vito Corleone (played by Marlon Brando) on two real life New York mobsters, Frank Costello and Vito Genovese (but the word 'mafia' was not used in the screenplay). Observing that 'the audience' and

'the Mafia members' are also overlapping categories, Parker (2006: 2) claims that:

It seems to me that cowboys, outlaws, pirates, bank robbers, smugglers, Robin Hood and (of course) the Mafia, are examples of the cultural construction of boundaries around the edges of economy and organization. These are archetypes that are both fascinating and frightening, perhaps that map out domains of legitimacy, just as they illuminate the fascinations of the forbidden. Perfect material, I would argue, for understanding something about the historical and political construction of the subject matter of the Management School.

Tony Soprano can, therefore, be seen as a management role model, demonstrating leadership techniques for effectively managing people, resolving conflict, and negotiating (Schneider, 2004). Probably the first paperless business, and one that has been successful (in competition with various nation states) for well over a century, Parker (2006) argues that *The Godfather* and Tony Soprano have much to tell us about organization, management, business ethics, partnerships, networks, and the nature of capitalism.

Managers in movies, like mobsters, are invariably cast as the bad guys, working for large, faceless, exploitative corporations: *Modern Times*, *Syriana*, *The Constant Gardner, Nine to Five*. *Wall Street* (1989, director Oliver Stone) famously has Gordon Gekko (played by Michael Douglas) explain his ruthless management philosophy that 'greed is good'. In *The Manchurian Candidate* (2004, director Jonathan Demme), the multinational conglomerate Manchurian Global (a company whose revenues exceed that of the European Union) plots to put its own presidential candidate into the American White House. Foreman and Thatchenkery (1996) show how *Rising Sun* (1993, director Philip Kaufman) can be viewed as a case study of organizational power politics, displayed in the symbolic use of architecture, the exploitation of friendships, the use of surveillance technology, the role of golfing relationships, and the corrupt links with national politics exposed in the blackmail and manipulation of an American Senator for commercial ends. It is more difficult to find contemporary movies that portray management and organizations in a positive light; exceptions include *Schindler's List* (1993, director Steven Spielberg), *Pretty Woman* (1990, director Garry Marshall), and *Spotswood* (1992, director Mark Joffe).

The film portrayal of women in management is more complex. Observing that, since 1944, there have been as many movies about female as male managers, Boozer (2002: 97) notes the emergence of 'the entrepreneurial femme fatale' who embodies, 'the lust for money and sex, and the sense of prestige and power that are attached to both'. These women are a danger to men, as well as a threat to corporate values. Boozer traces how women's film roles have changed since the 1940s, initially nonviolent, then increasingly predatory and destructive, 'choosing instead to apply her sexuality to homicidal plots in the service of commercial power' (p.124). Where 'success' for women in earlier career movies involved the effective accommodation of family and job demands, by the 1990s, 'women's acceptance at the highest levels of the business and professional workforce transforms the contemporary seductress into a literal figure of abstracted image power', and 'the deadly dame's narrative positioning has continued to unfold as a barometer first of women's economic repression and desire, then of her victimization as unconscious repository of capitalist greed, and finally of her embodiment of the process of consumer reification and fetishism' (p.124). This shift in role is reflected in *Basic Instinct* (1992), *Disclosure* (1995), and *To Die For* (1995). *To Die For* was based on a true story concerning an aspiring television newsreader (played by Nicole Kidman) who arranges the death of her husband because he is interfering with her career.

While the senior female manager in *Disclosure* ruthlessly exploits (in one interpretation) a junior male colleague, Cate Blanchett as *Elizabeth* (1998, director Shekhar Kapur) achieves a successful 'corporate turnaround' of a failing nation state (England in the sixteenth century) by developing leadership skills and behaviours, including the ability to deal with enemies ruthlessly in order to maintain power. Shekhar Kapur also directed *Bandit Queen* (Hindi, with subtitles, 1994), based on the life of Phoolan Devi (played by Seema Biswas), a violently abused, exploited, and outlawed Indian woman persecuted and imprisoned in the early 1980s. She achieved celebrity status for her challenge to authority (the Indian police) through the actions of her ruthless bandit group. (Devi was assassinated in July 2001, in New Delhi, at the age of 38.) In *The Devil Wears Prada* (2006, director David Frankel), Miranda Priestly (played by Meryl Streep) is editor of the fashion magazine *Runway*. Her management style is intimidating, cruel, demanding, and merciless. However, her magazine is successful, people want to work for her, and her confrontational approach encourages others to excel. Drawing on more conventional research methods, she is an accurate fictional role model for Kramer's (2006) 'great intimidators'.

Developing the theme of 'the evil corporation', Sloane (2002) argues that the stories in feature films are a form of 'administrative fiction', case studies which help us to understand and resolve the conflicts between personal aspirations and organizational goals. Movies reveal what Sloane calls 'the legend of the dysfunctional system', which is 'the legend of the organization that may be working just fine, given the ends that it pursues, and not working at all, given the ends that satisfy the human needs of its members' (Sloane, 2002: 5). Films set in organizational contexts, thus, often expose the benefits and costs of organizational membership, and illustrate the probable consequences of particular lines of action.

Sloane identifies several categories of individual-organization conflict and movies that illustrate those problems. *Network* (1976, director Sidney Lumet) demonstrates the fragile nature of organizational consensus. *Twelve O'Clock High* (1949, director Henry King) illustrates the tragic personal consequences of the pursuit of multiple goals and concealed compassion. *Lost in America* (1985, director Albert Brooks) addresses the problems of role conflict and the consequences of unchecked ambition. *Patton* (1970, director Franklin J. Schaffner) demonstrates problems arising from organization hierarchy. To illustrate models of competence and incompetence, Sloane cites *The Caine Mutiny* (1954, director Edward Dmytryk) based on the story of the mentally unstable Captain Queeg (played by Humphrey Bogart). A more recent example is *Contact* (1997, director Robert Zemeckis) in which the successful but naive project leader Ellie Arroway (played by Jodie Foster) is repeatedly sidelined by her politically skilled adversary, David Drumlin (Tom Skerritt), highlighting the consequences of political incompetence.

While those are not the only themes portrayed in these movies, and while different audiences will potentially reach different interpretations and understandings, Sloane's main point is that feature films do not just depict the problems, but also identify solutions in the form of 'survival skills and coping mechanisms', including conformity (make the best of it by linking individual values to organizational goals), rejection (be a 'creative rebel' and change the problem setting), and separation (leave). In other words, this is a perspective that treats movies as personal education. Sloane presents film as a tool of self-discovery, challenging and shaping identity, exposing conflicts between what we *do*, and who we *are*.

So are movies attitude-forming? Do gangster movies stimulate some sneaking admiration for a wealthy and lawless lifestyle? Must practising psychiatrists and managers routinely confront negative stereotypes of their profession? Have 'bad company' and 'evil corporation' movies helped to fuel the antiglobalization movement? Do we really learn how to speak and dress by watching movies, which also help us to define our identities and establish desirable lifestyles? Do films raise our awareness of critical debates, and affect our points of view and subsequent actions? Are our perceptions of and attitudes towards other occupations and professions shaped by the actions of characters on the screen? Do negative images of organization affect our choices of work

and career? Can we learn how to act more effectively by observing the successful and unsuccessful strategies of actors in fictional accounts? These sound like exaggerated claims for an entertainment product, and it is important to remember that our experiences, in turn, affect the ways in which we view and interpret films, particularly with regard to the plausibility of contexts, narratives, and characters. From his analysis of 'career movies', Boozer (2002: 149) argues that:

> It is not enough that the stories of business films suggest the quest for success, but that the individual human and commodity models meant to signify success begin to run together, to collapse into evocations of character types, behavioural and dress styles, work and home and transportation scenarios, and finally to seepage into public attitudes, buying patterns, and values.

Finally, de Certeau (1984) reminds us that the consumption of knowledge should not be limited to a secondary role, for its social and intellectual significance is profound. However, film is an influential and pervasive communications medium with global reach. The messages that films code tend to be broadly consistent and often repeated. Passive viewing leaves us open to covert persuasion. So, it is perhaps remarkable that, from an organization studies perspective, these issues have attracted relatively little research interest.

Reading film as thesis

Viewed as case studies and documentaries which are sources of social commentary, role models, survival skills, and coping mechanisms, feature films can potentially:

- Reveal the interests, preoccupations, and dominant ideology of a culture
- Help to establish and reinforce social norms and values
- Raise critical awareness of key issues and debates
- Trigger controversy by challenging accepted norms and assumptions
- Reinforce stereotypes of occupations, professions, and organizations
- Offer vicarious experience that can be insightful, inspirational, and instructive

Films tell stories and, in doing so, they also offer explanations, concerning how and why things happen. As an event sequence implies causality, narratives are intrinsically theory-laden, and several commentators have argued that narratives are a significant but overlooked source of understanding in their own right (Butler, 1997; Czarniawska, 1998 and 1999; Boje, 1991 and 2001; Gabriel, 1998 and 2000). Putnam et al. (1996: 386–7) note that:

> Narratives are ubiquitous symbols that are prevalent in all organizations. Also referred to as stories, scripts, myths, legends and sagas, narratives are accounts of events, usually developed chronologically and sequentially to indicate causality. [...] They are the vehicles through which organizational values and beliefs are produced, reproduced, and transformed. They shape organizational meanings through functioning as retrospective sensemaking, serving as premises of arguments and persuasive appeals, acting as implicit mechanisms of social control, and constituting frames of reference for interpreting organizational actions.

Rather than dispute the distinction between stories and narratives, the latter term is better regarded as a category label (Buchanan and Dawson, 2007); stories, scripts, anecdotes, legends, sagas, histories, myths, reports, and other discursive accounts, including feature films, are thus categorically narratives. As quantitative data can be analyzed to identify correlations, film narratives can also be interrogated to develop and test explanations, or theses. Pentland (1999: 712), thus distinguishes between the surface structure of narratives (descriptions and illustrations) and deep structure (explanations of event sequences). While the explanation offered by many (especially Hollywood) movies is simply that 'the good guys always win', or that 'the course of true love never runs smooth', some films develop more interesting and controversial arguments, which can be a source of debatable, explorable, testable propositions, perhaps using other research methods. Table 36.1 lists a number

Table 36.1 Film as narrative as theory

Movie	Date and director	Outline of dominant thesis
Twelve O'Clock High	1949, Henry King	Leadership effectiveness depends on choice of style to fit organizational context and on the supportive behaviours of followers.
Twelve Angry Men	1957, Sidney Lumet	Group decisions are influenced by processual, contextual, social, emotional, temporal, and behavioural factors, as well as by evidence.
Dirty Rotten Scoundrels	1988, Frank Oz	Influence attempts depend on careful target selection and on simple verbal and nonverbal behaviour patterns that are consistent with timing and context.
Dead Poets Society	1989, Peter Weir	The process of diffusing innovative ideas between organizational settings faces individual, cultural, and institutional barriers, and a politically inept innovator is ineffective and damaging.
Contact	1997, Robert Zemeckis	Integrity loses, deceit wins. Political skills are as important for the project leader as technical knowledge and expertise.
Elizabeth	1998, Shekhar Kapur	To maintain their power base in a hostile organization context, (female) leaders must impression manage their public image and be ruthless with enemies.
American Beauty	1999, Sam Mendes	Society deals harshly with noncompliance with so-called normal values. Dissatisfying, demotivating work has a corrosive effect on identity, family, and wider relationships.
eXistenZ	1999, David Cronenberg	There is no objective social reality. What we perceive as reality is illusory. Reality, ultimately, is what we perceive reality to be.
Thirteen Days	2001, Roger Donaldson	Strategic decisions are shaped by interacting processual, contextual, social, emotional, temporal, political, and behavioural factors, as well as by a rational consideration of evidence.
Black Book	2006, Paul Verhoeven	In a crisis, we are all willing and able to exploit and to betray others in the interests of self preservation.

of movies and their potentially dominant theses (Huczynski and Buchanan, 2004). It is important to recognize, first, that this table presents only one set of interpretations that may not be shared by other audiences, and second, that many movies potentially offer a series of more intricate subplots and related hypotheses. *Elizabeth* (the movie character) perhaps did not want to be a 'ruthless leader', supporting an ethical humanist ideology, and is there a plausible alternative theory leadership of success developed here, based on the accidental acquisition of a coalition of 'truly' ruthless colleagues and advisers (in this case Lord Walsingham)?

Because the narratives in films typically relate antecedents to consequences through sequences of events in context over time, they are more useful for developing process theories than variance theories (Mohr, 1982; Langley, Chapter 24, this volume). Process theories try to understand ill-defined flows of action, demonstrating how outcomes are shaped by the interaction and combination of multiple influences at different levels of analysis over time in a particular context, or category of context. Variance theories rely on the observation and measurement of stable universal relationships between clearly operationalized variables. Langley (1999) identifies a range of inductive strategies for analyzing and interpreting process data, and Pentland (1999) explores how written narratives can generate data as the basis for developing process theory, but his arguments apply equally to stories in films.

Some movies offer focused theoretical perspectives applicable to narrowly defined contexts, such as illustrations and explanations of successful and unsuccessful social behaviours, strategies, and tactics. For example, in a two-minute scene in a railway dining car, Freddy Benson (played by Steve Martin) in *Dirty Rotten Scoundrels* (1988, director Frank Oz) demonstrates a theory of interpersonal influence which involves careful target selection, an internally consistent package of mundane but contextually appropriate behaviours, concluding with a single brief confirmation before acting

immediately on the target's compliance. Some movies, in contrast, theorize the nature of complex processes unfolding over extended timeframes involving multiple influences on outcomes at different levels of analysis. *Thirteen Days* (2001, director Roger Donaldson) can be read as a case study in strategic decision making (based on actual events), explaining how decisions, sequences, and outcomes are shaped by the multilayered interaction of contextual, temporal, processual, social, political, and emotional factors (Buchanan and Huczynski, 2004).

As well as presenting us with 'ready made' theories, Phillips (1995) suggests that film can also be used to *test* theoretical propositions, observing also that some fictional accounts resemble hypotheses. To be successful, if it is to 'work', a story must be credible, plausible, and realistic. In other words, if the narrative is plausible, then the argument that it expresses may be plausible, too. If Cate Blanchett as the fictional (or 'fictionalized') queen *Elizabeth* has to be ruthless with those who oppose her, including her friends, in order to maintain her leadership position and power, then is it unreasonable to assume that a female leader in a similarly challenging organizational context may be advised to act in a comparable manner? Boozer (2002) discusses *Robocop* (1987, director Paul Verhoeven) as if it were testing a hypothesis concerning the privatization of policing, based on the company OCP in Detroit. This 'experiment' reveals that the company is as corrupt as the city it is paid to protect, and that the main threat to Robocop comes from corrupt executives and not from the criminals on the streets. *Citizen Kane* (1941, director Orson Welles) was based on the life of William Randolph Hearst, demonstrating the dangers of allowing individuals with strong ideological agendas to control the media. If Meryl Streep, as the magazine editor Miranda Priestly in *The Devil Wears Prada*, is successful with her cruel and merciless treatment of subordinates, does this not suggest that such a management style could be successful in other contexts?

The next reel

Taking the use of movies beyond entertaining classroom applications, this chapter has argued that feature films can be viewed as theoretical narratives, case studies, and proxy documentaries, and as a source of primary data which can be useful with regard to theory development and testing. Film narratives have three advantages in this respect. First, they often tend to portray the extreme, the unusual, the idiosyncratic, and the inaccessible, rather than the typical or average (and more readily studied). Second, by exploring how antecedents lead to consequences in different contexts, films can help us to develop process theories of organizational phenomena. Third, the vicarious experience of film provides us with role models, and with examples of effective and ineffective strategies and solutions, which we can generalize to our own personal and organizational circumstances.

Developing a similar argument, Phillips (1995) emphasizes that narrative methods cannot displace conventional research tools, but provide a set of complementary practices, an argument echoed by Foreman and Thatchenkery (1996). Hobbs (1998) observes that, while films can be seen as *mirrors* reflecting social reality, and as *windows* on otherwise unobserved phenomena, they are also manufactured commercial *products*. Film narratives are highly selective. Some stories are told, and are told in a particular way, because they are more likely to make money. Other less popular themes, and narratives with material that company owners, shareholders, advisers, and others might find offensive, are more likely to be excluded. As with any source of evidence, feature films as research data have significant limitations. Similar problems of selectivity apply to the 'purist' products of ethnographic documentary. In contrast to the early philosophies of Vertov and Grierson, a key argument of recent sociological writing is to regard the truth claims of the genre as in some way 'fictional' (see Hassard, Chapter 16, this volume). In contrast to the early assumptions of 'film-truth', sociological assessments of ethnographic documentary suggest that its products are as fictional as those of feature films (Nicholls, 1991; Hassard and Holliday, 1998; Bell, 2008). Both present the viewer with cultural images and dilemmas, build heightened tensions and dramatic conflicts, and terminate with resolution and closure. In short, such documentaries operate with reference to a reality that is, above all, the product of signifying systems.

Feature films can be analyzed as research data, as novel sources of ideas, insight, and inspiration, combined with the potential for theory development and testing. As with any other research method and source of data, films have strengths and advantages, as well as limitations and drawbacks. While for presentational purposes this chapter has assumed that films can be analyzed on their own, significant contributions may lie in combination with other perspectives. In terms of future developments, the main complementarities may lie with the development of critical management perspectives (Alvesson and Ashcraft, Chapter 4, this volume), feminist perspectives in organization studies (Calas and Smircich, Chapter 15), process theory (Langley, Chapter 24), visual methods (Warren, Chapter 33) and narrative (Rhodes and Pullen, Chapter 34, this volume). As films also provide access to the past and to socio-cultural trends (Wright, 1975; Boozer, 2002), there may also be creative complementarities with archive methods (Moss, Chapter 23).

ACKNOWLEDGEMENTS

We would like to thank Richard Badham, Emma Bell, Alan Bryman, and Martin Parker for their insightful comments and criticisms relating to earlier drafts of this chapter, but the gaps and flaws that remain are wholly the authors' responsibility.

REFERENCES

Baker, H.E. (1993) 'Wax on-wax off: French and Raven at the movies', *Journal of Management Education*, 17: 517–9.

Ball, M. and Smith, G. (2001) 'Technologies of realism?: ethnographic uses of photography and film', in Paul Atkinson, Amanda Coffey, Sara Delamont, John Lofland and Lyn Lofland (eds), *Handbook of Ethnography*. London: Sage Publications. pp. 302–19.

Bell, E. (2008) *Reading Management and Organization in Film*, London: Palgrave Macmillan.

Boje, D.M. (1991) 'The storytelling organization: a study of story performance in an office-supply firm', *Administrative Science Quarterly*, 36(1): 106–26.

Boje, D.M. (2001) *Narrative Methods for Organizational and Communication Research*, London: Sage Publications.

Boozer, J. (2002) *Career Movies: American Business and the Success Mystique*, Austin, TX: University of Texas Press.

Bourdieu, P. (1990) *The Logic of Practice*, Cambridge: Polity Press.

Bryman, A. (1995) *Disney and his Worlds*, London: Routledge.

Buchanan, D.A. (1999) 'The logic of political action: an experiment with the epistemology of the particular', *British Journal of Management*, 10 (special conference issue): 73–88.

Buchanan, D.A. and Dawson, P. (2007) 'Discourse and audience: organizational change as multi-story process', *Journal of Management Studies*, 44(5): 669–86.

Buchanan, D.A. and Huczynski, A. (2004) 'Images of influence: twelve angry men and thirteen days', *Journal of Management Inquiry*, 13(4): 312–23.

Buchanan, D.A., Addicott, R., Fitzgerald, L., Ferlie, E. and Baeza, J. (2007) 'Nobody in charge: distributed change agency in healthcare', *Human Relations*, 60(7): 1065–90.

Burrell, G. (1998) *Pandemonium: Towards a Retro-Theory of Organizations*, London: Sage Publications.

Butler, R. (1997) 'Stories and experiments in social inquiry', *Organization Studies*, 12(6): 927–48.

Champoux, J.E. (1999) 'Film as a teaching resource', *Journal of Management Inquiry*, 8(2): 206–17.

Champoux, J.E. (2001a) *Management: Using Film to Visualize Principles and Practices*, Cincinnati, OH: South-Western College Publishing/Thomson Learning.

Champoux, J.E. (2001b) *Organizational Behaviour: Using Film to Visualize Principles and Practices*, Cincinnati, OH: South-Western College Publishing/Thomson Learning.

Champoux, J.E. (2005) *Our Feature Presentation: Organizational Behaviour*.

Champoux, J.E. (2006) 'At the cinema: aspiring to a higher ethical standard', *Academy of Management Learning and Education*, 5(3): 386–90.

Champoux, J.E. (2007) *Our Feature Presentation: Human Resource Management*, Mason, OH: Thomson South-Western.

Collins, M. (2008) 'White noise', *RSA Journal*, CLIV(5533): 16–21.

Comer, D.R. (2000) 'Not just a Mickey Mouse exercise: using Disney's "The Lion King" to teach leadership', *Journal of Management Education*, 25(4): 430–36.

Comer, D.R. and Cooper, E.A. (1998) 'Michael Crichton's "Disclosure" as a teaching tool', *Journal of Management Education*, 22(2): 227–41.

Cortazzi, M. (2001) 'Narrative analysis in ethnography', in P. Atkinson, A. Coffey, S. Delamont, J. Lofland and L. Lofland (eds), *Handbook of Ethnography*, London: Sage Publications. pp. 384–94.

Czarniawska, B. (1998) *A Narrative Approach to Organization Studies*, Thousand Oaks, CA: Sage Publications.

Czarniawska, B. (1999) *Writing Management: Organization Theory as a Literary Genre*, Oxford: Oxford University Press.

de Certeau, M. (1984) *The Practice of Everyday Life*, California: University of California Press.

Dyer, W.G. and Wilkins, A.L. (1991) 'Better stories, not better constructs, to generate a better theory: a rejoinder to Eisenhardt', *Academy of Management Review*, 16: 613–19.

Edgell, S., Hetherington, K. and Warde, A. (eds) (1997) *Consumption Matters*, Oxford: Blackwell.

Foreman, J. and Thatchenkery, T.J. (1996) 'Filmic representations for organizational analysis: the characterization of a transplant organization in the film Rising Sun', *Journal of Organizational Change Management*, 9(3): 44–61.

Foucault, M. (1980) *Power/Knowledge*, New York: Pantheon.

Gabbard, K. and Gabbard, G.O. (1999) *Psychiatry and the Cinema* (second edn.), Washington, DC/London: American Psychiatric Press Inc.

Gabriel, Y. (1998) 'The use of stories', in G. Symon and C. Cassell (eds), *Qualitative Methods and Analysis in Organizational Research: A Practical Guide*, London: Sage Publications, pp. 135–60.

Gabriel, Y. (2000) *Storytelling in Organizations: Facts, Fictions and Fantasies*, Oxford: Oxford University Press.

Gherardi, S. and Nicolini, D. (2000) 'To transfer is to transform', *Organization* 7(2): 329–48.

Hassard, J. and Holliday, R. (eds) (1998) *Organization Representation: Work and Organization in Popular Culture*, London: Sage Publications.

Hobbs, R. (1998) 'Teaching with and about film and television', *Journal of Management Development*, 17(4): 259–72.

Holliday, R. (2004) 'Filming "The Closet": the role of video diaries in researching sexualities', *American Behavioral Scientist*, 47(12): 1597–616.

Holliss, R. and Sibley, B. (1988) *The Disney Studio Story*, New York: Crown.

Huczynski, A. and Buchanan, D. (2004) 'Theory from fiction: a narrative process perspective on the pedagogical use of feature film', *Journal of Management Education*, 28(6): 707–26.

Huczynski, A. and Buchanan, D. (2005) 'Feature films in management education: beyond illustration and entertainment', *Journal of Organizational Behaviour Education*, 1(1): 73–94.

Hunt, C.S. (2001) 'Must see TV: the timeliness of television as a teaching tool', *Journal of Management Education*, 25(6): 631–47.

Knights, D. (1997) 'Organization theory in the age of deconstruction', *Organization Studies*, 18(10): 1–19.

Knights, D. and Willmott, H. (1999) *Management Lives: Power and Identity in Work Organizations*, London: Sage Publications.

Kramer, R.M. (2006) 'The great intimidators', *Harvard Business Review*, 84(2): 88–96.

Langley, A. (1999) 'Strategies for theorizing from process data', *Academy of Management Review*, 24(4): 691–710.

Lyotard, J.-F. (1997) *The Postmodern Condition: A Report on Knowledge*, Minneapolis, MN: University of Minnesota Press.

McCarty, J. (2004) *Bullets Over Hollywood: The American Gangster Picture from the Silents to 'The Sopranos'*, Cambridge, MA: Da Capo Press.

Mitchell, J.C. (1983) 'Case and situational analysis', *Sociological Review*, 31(2): 187–211.

Mohr, L.B. (1982) *Explaining Organizational Behaviour: The Limits and Possibilities of Theory and Research*, San Francisco: Jossey-Bass Publishers.

Monaco, J. (2000) *How to Read a Film: The World of Movies, Media, and Multimedia* (third edn.), New York and Oxford: Oxford University Press.

Munro, R. (1998) 'Belonging on the move', *Sociological Review*, 46(2): 208–43.

Nicholls, B. (1991) *Representing Reality: Issues and Concepts in Documentary*, Bloomington, IN: Indiana University Press.

Parker, M. (2006) 'Violence incorporated: the Mafia and organizational excellence', Leicester: University of Leicester, Inaugural Lecture.

Pentland, B.T. (1999) 'Building process theory with narrative: from description to explanation', *Academy of Management Review*, 24(4): 711–24.

Pettigrew, A.M. (1990) 'Longitudinal field research on change: theory and practice', *Organization Science*, 1(3): 267–92.

Phillips, N. (1995) 'Telling organizational tales: on the role of narrative fiction in the study of organization', *Organization Studies*, 16(4): 625.

Putnam, L.L., Phillips, N. and Chapman, P. (1996) 'Metaphors of communication and organization', in Stewart R. Clegg, Cynthia Hardy and Walter R. Nord (eds), *Handbook of Organization Studies*, London: Sage Publications, pp. 375–408.

Rhodes, C. and Westwood, R. (2007) *Critical Representations of Work and Organization in Popular Culture*, London: Routledge.

Richardson, L. (2000) 'Writing: a method of inquiry', in Norman K. Denzin and Yvonna S. Lincoln (eds), *Handbook of Qualitative Research* (second edn.), Thousand Oaks: Sage Publications, pp. 923–48.

Roth, L. (2001) 'Introducing students to the "Big Picture"', *Journal of Management Education*, 25(1): 21–31.

Rueschemeyer, D. (2003) 'Can one or a few cases yield theoretical gains?', in James Mahoney and Dietrich Rueschemeyer (eds), *Comparative Historical Analysis in the Social Sciences*, Cambridge: Cambridge University Press, pp. 305–36.

Schneider, A. (2004) *Tony Soprano on Management: Leadership Lessons Inspired by America's Favourite Mobster*, New York: Berkley Books.

Serey, T.T. (1992) 'Carpe diem: lessons about organization and management from "Dead Poets Society"', *Journal of Management Education*, 16(3): 374–81.

Shaw, B. (2004) 'Hollywood ethics: developing ethical issues Hollywood style', *Journal of Business Ethics*, 49(2): 167–77.

Siggelkow, N. (2007) 'Persuasion with case studies', *Academy of Management Journal*, 50(1): 20–24.

Sloane, S.B. (2002) *Organizations in the Movies: The Legend of the Dysfunctional System*, Lanham, Maryland: University Press of America, Inc.

Spector, B. (2008) 'The man in the gray flannel suit in the executive suite: American corporate movies in the 1950s', *Journal of Management History*, 14.

Stake, R.E. (1994) 'Case Studies', in Norman K. Denzin and Yvonna S. Lincoln (eds), *Handbook of Qualitative Research*, Thousand Oaks, CA: Sage Publications, pp. 236–47.

Sutton, R.I. and Staw, B.M. (1995) 'What theory is *not*', *Administrative Science Quarterly*, 40(3): 371–84.

Tsoukas, H. (1989) 'The validity of idiographic research explanations', *Academy of Management Review*, 14: 551–61.

Ulmer, G. (1989) *Teletheory: Grammatology in the Age of Video*, London: Routledge.

Weick, K.E. (1995) *Sensemaking in Organizations*, Thousand Oaks, CA/London: Sage Publications.

Willer, L.R. (1995) 'Working 9 to 5: the use of film/video analysis as an adaptation of the case study method in teaching organizational behaviour', *The International Journal of Organizational Analysis*, 3(2): 198–204.

Wright, W. (1975) *Sixguns and Society: A Structural Study of the Western*, Berkely, CA: University of California Press.

Zaniello, T. (2003) *Working Stiffs, Union Maids, Reds, and Riffraff: An Expanded Guide to Films About Labor*, Ithaca and London: ILR Press/Cornell University Press.

Zaniello, T. (2007) *The Cinema of Globalization: A Guide to Films About The New Economic Order*, Ithaca and London: ILR Press/Cornell University Press.

37

Measurement in the Organizational Sciences: Conceptual and Technological Advances

Charles A. Scherbaum and
Adam W. Meade

INTRODUCTION

Measurement is at the heart of any field of scientific inquiry. In order to understand, predict, and change the phenomena we study, we must be able to observe and to describe them. As Thorndike (1918: 16) noted, '[W]hatever exists at all exists in some amount. To know it thoroughly involves knowing its quantity as well as its quality'. In the most basic sense, measurement is a system for conceptualizing, observing, and describing the quality and quantity of the phenomena we study (Klimoski and Zukin, 2003). These systems are intricately related to the development and advancement of our theories (Judd and McClelland, 1998) and the use of the findings from our research (Aguinis et al., 2002). The theories and research of the organizational sciences have little value without a solid measurement foundation (Aguinis et al., 2002).

Despite the widely acknowledged importance of measurement for the progress of the organizational sciences, attention to measurement issues is often less than it could be (Scandura and Williams, 2000; Schriesheim et al., 1993), modern developments are infrequently utilized, and there several areas where the best and actual practices are not aligned (Hinkin, 1995). This state of affairs is potentially problematic as opportunities to further advance science and practice may have been missed. We believe that this situation stems in part from the deceptively simple nature of measurement, and from the rapid conceptual and technological developments that are only beginning to become widely accessible to organizational researchers. The purpose of this chapter is to help bridge these gaps by providing a resource for organizational researchers as they navigate the measurement aspects of their research.

In this chapter, we provide an overview and introduction to many of the conceptual aspects of measurement and the array of choices that researchers must contend with in organizational research. We address the nature of measurement and measurement theory, the techniques available for measuring organizationally relevant phenomena, and approaches to evaluating the quality of these measures. We give particular attention to modern measurement developments and areas where there has been continued debate. Less attention is given to creating measures as there are many good resources for guidance on these issues (e.g., Hinkin, 1998).

What is measurement?

Measurement is a system for conceptualizing, observing, and describing the quality and quantity of the phenomena we study (Klimoski and Zukin, 2003). Although measurement has been defined by many authors (e.g., Guilford, 1954; Nunnally, 1978; Pedhazur and Schmelkin, 1991), most definitions are based on Stevens' (1968) classic description of measurement as the assignment of numbers to properties or attributes of objects, events, or people according to a set of rules. Several principles are common to most definitions of measurement. First, measurement has a purpose. Although the specific purpose varies between situations, the general purpose is to allow for description, explanation, or prediction (Pedhazur and Schmelkin, 1991). Second, measurement is concerned with properties and attributes of objects, events, and people as opposed to the objects, events, and people themselves. For example, measurement focuses on the strength and direction of an employee attitude, not the actual attitude.

Third, measurement entails a system of rules that should produce consistent descriptions or representations of a given property or attribute. Fourth, measurement is typically based on numerical descriptions or representations. That is, numbers are used to represent the properties or attributes (e.g., 5 = strongly agree). Fifth, measurement

systems must represent observable and meaningful properties and attributes (Dawes and Smith, 1985). An infinite set of rules and numbers can be applied to a given property or attribute, but not all rules and numbers provide meaningful description, explanation, or prediction.

Why is measurement important?

Although the notion that measurement is important is generally recognized, the specific reasons for why it is important are often more difficult to articulate. We recognize at least six reasons that measurement is important in organizational research. First, measurement can provide a level of objectivity in the observation of properties or attributes. Measurement involves standardization, which minimizes subjective judgments and error in the observation process (Aguinis et al., 2002). The objectivity achieved through measurement allows for independent replications of an observation and facilitates agreement about an observation among scientists (Guilford, 1954; Nunnally, 1978).

Second, measurement involves quantification. Quantification allows for more detailed, less ambiguous, and more consistent descriptions of the properties of objects, events or people than verbal accounts (Nunnally, 1978; Pedhazur and Schmelkin, 1991). Also, quantification allows for the use of statistical and mathematical methods for description and prediction as well as an assessment of the quality of measurement. Third, measurement improves communication. It provides a shared language among scientists for understanding the phenomena they study and comparing research findings (Aguinis et al., 2002; Nunnally, 1978). Fourth, measurement improves the efficiency with which properties and attributes can be observed. The standardization inherent in measurement allows researchers to assess more quickly and cheaply the properties or attributes of objects, events, or people (Nunnally, 1978). Fifth, measurement can provide relevant, consistent, and accurate information on which decisions can be made (Aguinis et al., 2002).

Sixth, measurement requires a close link to theory. For measurement to be of value, the attributes and properties assessed must be meaningful (Dawes and Smith, 1985). Only theory can indicate what should be measured and how it should be measured (Pedhazur and Schmelkin, 1991). Only measurement can provide the basis for empirical tests of theoretical hypotheses (Judd and McClelland, 1998).

Measurement in the organizational sciences

In the organizational sciences, little attention has been given to measurement (Scandura and Williams, 2000; Schoenfeldt, 1984; Schriesheim et al., 1993). In fact, Scandura and Williams (2000) present some evidence that the attention to measurement actually decreased from the 1980s to the 1990s. They found that researchers often do not present evidence of the consistency, accuracy, or theoretical adequacy of the scores on their measures. This evidence echoes the findings of many other organizational scholars (e.g., Podsakoff and Dalton, 1987). The potential consequence is that organizational theories and research may have limited interpretability (Schriesheim et al., 1993) and value (Aguinis et al., 2002). For example, the area of leadership has seen reports of both substantial measurement concerns (Schriesheim et al., 1993) and theories estimated to have mixed or low scientific validity (Miner, 2003). The potential consequences of limited attention to measurement are unreliable and invalid measures, which can lead to rejecting scientific hypotheses that may have merit while erroneously finding support for poor theories.

While we applaud attention to established measurement principles, the over-reliance on a few 'best practices' that have developed over the past hundred years have given measurement a recipe-like quality, in which researchers believe that if certain steps are followed, high quality measurement is assured. If the recipe never changes and produces the desired result, there is little reason to give measurement much attention. We believe that this thinking has led to organizational researchers to get stuck in a measurement rut. Researchers have primarily used the same techniques (e.g., Likert-type scales and Cronbach's alpha) over and over again. Developments in measurement theory, technology, and techniques have dramatically expanded the possibilities over the past twenty years. Staying current with these developments is a constant challenge all researchers face and is difficult as advances often come from other fields (e.g., item response theory models and multilevel models). Despite efforts to help organizational researchers monitor these developments (e.g., the journal *Organizational Research Methods*; Drasgow and Schmidt, 2002), researchers have not taken full advantage of the techniques available to them. Some techniques have been widely adopted (e.g., covariance structure analyses), but others have not (e.g., item response theory). This chapter will focus on several techniques that have the potential to improve measurement in the organizational sciences, but have only begun to be adopted by organizational researchers.

Measurement techniques

Currently, organizational researchers have a variety of techniques available to them to assess attributes and properties of interest. Organizational researchers may utilize direct observation, ratings provided by individuals about themselves (i.e., self-report), rating provided by others, archival records (e.g., company records), physiological measures, or trace measures (i.e., by-products of behaviour: usage, electronic monitoring of computers). Each measurement technique has its advantages and disadvantages and none is universally appropriate. More recently, 'implicit' techniques based on mental processes that are not consciously accessed are increasing in use (Fazio and Olson, 2003; James, 1998). These techniques are considered in more detail in the subsequent sections. Despite the variety of techniques available, researchers continue to rely almost exclusively on Likert-type self-report measures (Hinkin, 1995). Given their frequency of use, we explore some of the conceptual issues around the use of this technique.

Self-report measures typically provide a statement or question and instruct the respondent to select from a set of response options or to construct a response. There are a number of approaches to constructing the statements and response options (e.g., Coombs, 1964; Thurstone, 1931) with the most common approach drawing on the work of Likert (1932). In Likert's approach, the respondent is presented with a statement and asked to evaluate that statement using ordered response categories (e.g., strongly agree to strongly disagree). The popularity of this approach stems, in part, from the ease of constructing these items, and plentiful guidance that currently exists on how to create these types of measures (e.g., Hinkin, 1998). The measurement challenge that is often overlooked is an understanding of the cognitive and psychological processes underlying the responses to these items (Schwartz, 1999).

When constructing items, attention is typically focused on rules that may make an item readable or interpretable (e.g., avoid double negatives). Much less attention is given to how respondents will make sense of the item and response options, and how the items interact with basic human information processing systems (e.g., memory and judgment). A number of researchers have found that aspects of the items, response options, and context, can have profound effects on response behaviour (see Krosnick, 1999; Rivers et al., in press; or Schwartz, 1999, for reviews). For example, self-report items may elicit construct irrelevant response patterns (e.g., socially desirable or extreme responding). Although techniques have been developed for addressing these concerns (e.g., reverse scoring and pilot testing), there are no definitive solutions at this point.

The anchor labels and range of response options can also have an impact on response behaviour. For example, Schwartz et al. (1991) found that respondents provide substantially different answers when a response scale ranges from -5 to $+5$ than when it ranges from 0 to 10. The use of numbers and the placement of the zero serve as cues that inform respondents of the meaning of the item. In addition, the ordering of the items can impact response behaviour (Rivers et al., in press). The degree to which verbal anchors versus numerical anchors are used to label response options can influence response behaviour, and ultimately reliability and validity (Krosnick and Berent, 1993). In many cases, the numbers carry no substantive meaning. Organizational researchers are well advised to use verbal labels for all response options and to avoid the use of numerical labels unless they are consistent with and support the verbal labels (Krosnick, 1999).

Evaluating the quality of measures

Given the latent nature of the constructs that are often assessed in the organizational sciences, researchers need approaches for estimating how well they are measuring a latent construct. The quality of a measure can be defined as whether a measure accurately and consistently assesses what it is supposed to assess. In other words, the quality of measurement is typically viewed from the lenses of reliability and validity. Reliability is concerned with consistency or freedom from error (Feldt and Brennan, 1989), while validity is concerned with the accuracy of the inferences drawn from the scores on a measure (Messick, 1989). A variety of techniques can be used to evaluate the reliability and validity of scores (see Feldt and Brennan, 1989; Messick, 1989). Although validity is the ultimate criterion for evaluating a measure, we will focus here on the classical and modern techniques for evaluating reliability, as validity is conceptually and mathematically bound by reliability (Nunnally, 1978).

Reliability is concerned with the quantification of error that exists in any score or observation that is taken as part of measurement. A given score or observation can be said to be reliable to the extent to which it is free from error. The dominant model of reliability partitions observed scores into 'true' scores of individuals on the given construct and error. The error can be random (e.g., mood) or systematic (e.g., bias). There are three major approaches for evaluating reliability and other properties of measurement: classical measurement theory, generalizability theory, and item response theory. Each is described in the following section. However, we will focus primarily on item response theory, as most of the recent measurement advances are based on it.

Classical measurement theory

Classical measurement theory, also know as the 'true score' model, is based on the notion that an observed score on a measure is composed solely of true score and random error. Based on classical measurement theory, a variety of techniques have been developed that allow researchers to assess the reliability of scores and the measurement properties of items. These techniques are familiar to many organizational researchers (e.g., test-retest reliability and Cronbach's coefficient alpha), and therefore, are only briefly considered here.

The evaluation of the measurement properties in the classical approach begins with an item analysis. In an item analysis, the researcher examines the items' means and standard deviations to understand the location of the items on the continuum for that construct and the variability in that location. On some measures, one may want items to be located in the middle of the continuum, but at the extremes for other measures. The item analysis will also consist of an examination of the item discrimination. Item discrimination reflects how well an item differentiates between individuals with different scores. The item-total correlation (with the focal item removed from the total score) is one index for item discrimination. Ideally, one wants items that are highly correlated with the total score. Other indices include the difference in the percentage 'correct' on an item between the top 25 percent and bottom 25 percent

of test scorers. Larger differences indicate better discrimination. Researchers may also examine the factor structure of the measure using exploratory and confirmatory factor analytic techniques. The reliability of the scores on a measure can be evaluated using several different approaches depending on the data available (internal consistency, test-retest, and alternate forms). Ellis and Mead (2002) provide a detailed example of the item analysis process.

Classical techniques remain extremely useful for evaluating the quality of the measurement properties of scores and are by far the predominant method in organizational research. Building on the classical measurement model, these techniques have become increasingly sophisticated (e.g., confirmatory factor analysis). Nevertheless, techniques based on classical measurement theory have well-known limitations. Classical indices of test quality are sample dependent, at the measure or test (as opposed to the item) level of analysis, and assume that measurement error is constant for all respondents (see Hambleton et al., 1991 for a review of the limitations). These limitations are not fatal, but they can shape the nature of the conclusions that one may draw from scores on a measure and the questions that one may ask. Modern measurement theories of generalizability theory and item response theory offer several approaches that overcome many of the limitations of classical measurement theory.

Generalizability theory

Generalizability theory is a major extension of the assumptions about measurement error in classical measurement theory (Cronbach et al., 1972). Specifically, generalizability theory conceptualizes measurement error much more broadly. In generalizability theory, error can be decomposed into the random and systematic factors such as rater characteristics, characteristics of the target of observation, characteristics of the observation context, and other factors (Murphy and DeShon, 2000). For example, assessment centre ratings can include estimates of error due to ratees, raters, and exercises, as well as the interactions between these factors.

The decomposition of the sources of error allows researchers to understand how observed scores generalize across these different sources of error. In contrast, classical methods typically limit researchers to examining generalizability across one source of error such as items (e.g., internal consistency) or time (e.g., test-retest). These methods do not support generalization across the other sources of error that are simultaneously impacting an observed score (DeShon, 2003). Using the generalizability theory approach, one computes a generalizability coefficient as an index of the generalizability of the scores on a measure across the specified sources of error. These coefficients are interpreted in the same way as traditional reliability coefficients (see Brennan, 1992 or Shavelson and Webb, 1991 for the calculations).

A major advantage of generalizability theory is that it requires a clear articulation of the sources of error that impact the scores on a measure. The major disadvantages include the complexity of the terminology, and accurately estimating the coefficients for the type of data (incomplete, unbalanced) that organizational researchers often encounter (DeShon, 2003). A detailed treatment of generalizability is beyond the scope of this chapter and the reader is referred to Brennan (1992) or Shavelson and Webb (1991) for an introduction to generalizability theory.

Item response theory

Item response theory (IRT) is a set of techniques for understanding the properties of measures and relationships between properties of the measures and the individuals completing those measures. These techniques are the most recently developed and are not widely used in the organizational sciences, though IRT has been used to advance our understanding in a few domains of organizational research (e.g., dishonest responding on personality inventories; Zickar and Robie, 1999).

IRT is a model-based (i.e., mathematical) approach to understanding the relationships between individual characteristics (e.g., ability and traits), item characteristics (e.g., discrimination), and particular response patterns (Embretson and Reise, 2000). Classical techniques rely on total scores, means, and correlations as observed parameters of the item and person characteristics. IRT, on the other hand, estimates latent parameters for the persons (i.e., the characteristic underlying the total scores) and items using the responses from the sample of data. The relationship between the latent person and item parameters in IRT is probabilistic, such that one can estimate the probability of an individual with a particular level of the latent characteristic selecting a particular response option.

These probabilistic relationships can be demonstrated graphically using an item characteristic curve (ICC). ICCs graph the relationship between the latent characteristic (called *theta* and labeled θ) underlying the responses to an item and the conditional probability of particular response to an item given theta (labeled $P(\theta)$). Many ICCs take an S-shaped curve (e.g., logistic or cumulative normal distribution), but the exact shape is determined by the IRT model used and the item parameters included in the model. Figure 37.1 presents a generic representation of an ICC from an IRT model called the three-parameter logistic model, which is used with dichotomous data. For example, consider an item about commitment to one's organization where the response options are yes or no (no = 0, yes = 1). In the figure, the latent characteristic, θ, is depicted along the x-axis and the probability of a particular response, $P(\theta)$, is depicted along the y-axis. The values of θ are normally distributed and typically expressed as standardized scores. For example, an individual with $\theta = 1$ has a value of organizational commitment that is one standard deviation above the mean. Using Figure 37.1, we see that, as the level of commitment increases (i.e., moves to the right), the probability of selecting the option scored 'yes' increases. For any level of θ, we can determine $P(\theta)$, the probability of responding 'yes', by finding the height of the curve at that particular value of θ.

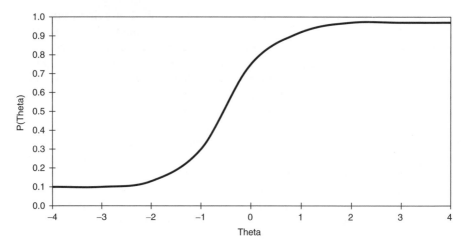

Figure 37.1 Item characteristic curve

IRT is best seen as a family of different models. Although not an exhaustive taxonomy, these models can be classified based on the type of data used, the number of parameters estimated, the dimensionality of the data, and the nature of the underlying psychological response process (see van der Linden and Hambleton, 1997, for additional classifications). Next, we briefly describe logistic and graded response models, which are the most frequently used models in organizational research.

Logistic models

Logistic models are used with data that are dichotomously scored (e.g., 0 or 1 for 'yes' or 'no' or for 'correct' and 'incorrect' test items). The most common logistic model involves estimation of three item parameters. The first is an item location parameter, which is the point on the scale for the latent characteristic, θ, where the probability of selecting the response coded as '1' is 0.50 when there is no guessing. When there is guessing, the probability associated with this parameter will be greater than 0.50. That is, the location parameter reflects the level of the characteristic that is needed for a 0.50 percent chance of selecting the option coded as '1' for the item. The value of the location parameter determines the horizontal location (i.e., left to right) of the ICC on

the x-axis (see Figure 37.1). Positive values indicate that above average levels of the latent characteristic are needed to select the option coded as '1' and negative values indicate that lower levels are needed. The value of this parameter typically ranges between -2.0 and $+2.0$ (Hambleton et al., 1991).

Logistic models can also contain an item discrimination parameter, which represents how well an item discriminates between individuals with different, but similar levels of the latent characteristic. Larger values indicate that the item is better able to discriminate between individuals with different levels of the characteristic. Put differently, discrimination is the index of the magnitude of the relationship between the latent characteristic and the observed item response. The numerical values of the discrimination parameter typically range from 0.5 to 1.5.

On some measures, such as multiple choice test items, it is unlikely that the probability of a correct response is zero for individuals with very low levels of the latent characteristic because of random or chance responding. The third parameter is the pseudo-guessing parameter. It sets the nonzero lower bound of the ICC. The value of this parameter tends to be near 1 divided by the number of response options (i.e., chance guessing).

Models that contain all three item parameters are called the three-parameter logistic model (3-PL). The 3-PL model is expressed as:

$$P_i(\theta) = c_i + (1 - c_i)\frac{e^{Da_i(\theta-b_i)}}{1 + e^{Da_i(\theta-b_i)}} \qquad (1)$$

where $P_i(\theta)$ is the probability of an examinee with a given level of θ (i.e., latent characteristic) selecting the response coded '1' on item i, b_i is the item location parameter, a_i is the item discrimination parameter, c_i is the pseudo-guessing parameter, and D is a scaling constant equal to 1.702.

Models that include only the discrimination and location parameter are called the two-parameter logistic model (2-PL). The 2-PL is derived by setting the 'c' parameter to zero. Models that include only the location parameter are called the one-parameter logistic (1-PL) or Rasch model. The 1-PL is derived by setting the 'c' parameter to zero and holding the 'a' parameter constant across items or setting it to a value of 1.0.

Graded response models

The data in organizational research are usually not dichotomous. Typically, there are three or more response options that can be ordered (i.e., graded) such that higher ordered options reflect greater levels of the latent construct (e.g., Likert-type response options). There are several models that are appropriate with graded response data (see van der Linden and Hambleton, 1997). The most commonly used model in the organizational sciences is Samejima's (1969) graded response model (GRM), in which two types of parameters associated with the items are estimated. The first is a series of option location parameters, referred to as the 'threshold' parameter. This parameter reflects the probability of an individual with a given level of the latent characteristic selecting a given option (e.g., neutral) *or* any of the subsequent higher ordered options (e.g., agree and strongly agree). Specifically, this parameter is the point on the scale for the latent characteristic where there is a 0.50 probability that a given option or a higher ordered option will be selected (i.e., $P(\theta) = 0.5$). The second parameter

is an item discrimination parameter. This parameter represents how well an option discriminates between individuals at different levels, but similar of the latent characteristic. In Samejima's (1969) GRM, this parameter is held constant across response options within an item.

Samejima's GRM is called an indirect model, because it requires multiple computations to estimate the probabilities associated with particular response options. First, boundary response functions are estimated. Boundary response functions are the cumulative probability of selecting a response option equal to or higher than the current response option. There are $m_i - 1$ boundary response functions where m_i equals the number of response options. Mathematically, the boundary response function is expressed as:

$$P_{ik}^*(\theta) = \frac{e^{Da_i(\theta-b_{ik})}}{1 + e^{Da_i(\theta-b_{ik})}} \qquad (2)$$

where $P^*_{ik}(\theta)$ is the probability of a respondent at a particular level of the latent characteristic responding to option k or any of the other higher ordered options on item i, b_{ik} is the option location parameter, a_i is the discrimination parameter, and D is a scaling constant equal to 1.702. The probability of selecting option k is a function of the level of the latent characteristic, the location of the option, and the discrimination.

From the boundary response functions, the probability of selecting each response option is computed (see Embretson and Reise, 2000 for the equations) and the relationship between the estimate of the latent characteristic and the probability of selecting a particular option can be presented graphically with an option characteristic curve (OCC). An example OCC for an organizational commitment item is presented in Figure 37.2. This item is rated on a six-point scale with the anchors of 'strongly disagree' and 'strongly agree'. In the figure, theta is presented along the x-axis and the probability of selecting a particular response option at a given level of theta appears along the y-axis. Using the first

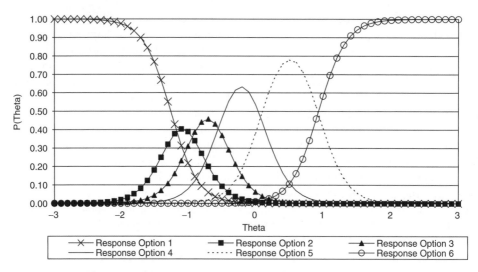

Figure 37.2 Option characteristic curve

response option (i.e., 'strongly disagree') as an example, the probability of selecting this option is greatest for individuals with low commitment ($\theta < 0.0$) and the probability becomes smaller as commitment increases. The sixth response option (i.e., 'strongly agree') demonstrates the reverse pattern, in which the probability of selecting the option is small for individuals with low levels of commitment and the probability increases as the level of commitment increases.

The IRT models presented in this chapter require that the model fits the data (see Chernyshenko et al., 2001, for a discussion of IRT model fit) and local independence. Local independence is the degree that the latent characteristic specified in the IRT model accounts for the relationship between the items (i.e., unidimensionality). That is, responses to the items are unrelated after controlling for the latent characteristic.

The IRT approach for examining properties of measures is more complex than the classical approach. However, this complexity is associated with substantially more information about the properties of a measure and other advantages (see Embretson and Reise, 2000 for all IRT advantages). First, the estimated person and item parameters in IRT are invariant (i.e., independent). Therefore, the item parameters are not needed to interpret the person parameters and vice versa. With classical techniques, this is not the case, as the person parameters (e.g., percent correct scores) or item parameters (e.g., percentage of sample getting an item correct) cannot be understood out of the context of the other. The implication is that IRT can provide unbiased estimates of the item parameters from unrepresentative samples (Embretson and Reise, 2000). Organizational research is frequently conducted using samples that may not be representative of the populations to which generalizations are desired (Scandura and Williams, 2000).

Second, the items and persons are on the same metric (e.g., z-scores). Therefore, the level of a characteristic that an individual possesses can be compared to the level of the characteristic required by the item. With classical methods, individuals can only be compared to other individuals (e.g., normative data) or to an external standard. This feature, in combination with the invariance property, allows for tailored testing (e.g., computer adaptive testing) which presents items for which the difficulty is matched to the level of ability of the respondent (see Wainer, 2000), and is a much more efficient testing approach (Embretson and Reise, 2000).

Third, IRT allows one to determine the amount of information an item provides about the latent characteristic for every level of the characteristic using item information functions. The item information function indicates the quality and appropriateness of an item for different levels of the latent characteristic. It may be the case that a measure of teamwork, for example, contains several items that provide a substantial amount of information about the quality of the teamwork, and other items may provide very little information. Item information plays a central role in test and scale development in IRT and varies across different levels of the latent characteristic.

Lastly, the IRT approach does not assume equal standard error of measurement for all respondents (Embretson and Reise, 2000). In IRT, the standard error measurement is the inverse of the test information function. The standard error of measurement is an indication of how well a characteristic is assessed by a measure. IRT makes explicit that persons with different levels of the characteristic may be measured with different levels of precision. For example, an extroversion measure may be more precise for individuals with average levels than for individuals with extreme levels of extroversion. With IRT, the standard error of measurement differs across levels of the latent characteristic. One major implication of the last two advantages is that the classical measurement approach to reliability does not apply to IRT. Classical techniques examine reliability as a function of an entire measure. In IRT, reliability is examined at the item level via the information function (which is inversely related to the standard error). Thus, there is no single reliability estimate.

Although IRT has many advantages, it is not without limitations. A primary limitation, especially for organizational research, is the sample size requirements. IRT requires sample sizes for many of the models that often exceed what is typically seen in some areas of organizational research (e.g., research on executives). The simplest models (e.g., 1-PL) can require sample sizes in excess of 150 respondents, and more complex models can require substantially more respondents when estimating both person and item parameters.

Another limitation involves the additional assumptions required by IRT models. As noted in the foregoing section, IRT carries several assumptions that are not required by classical techniques. The confidence in the results from an IRT analysis will, in part, depend on the degree to which the assumptions are met. Although IRT models are robust to modest violations of these assumptions, explicit tests of these assumptions are required. Additionally, the complexity of performing IRT analyses can be a limitation. Training in IRT is not widespread in the organizational sciences, and some of the IRT literature can be quite technical. These analyses require special software, and often several different programmes are needed to perform the analyses and tests of the assumptions. Most IRT software was DOS-based until recently, and the current software remains less user-friendly than most mainstream data analysis software. However, as the technology continues to develop and training in using these methods becomes more widespread, these limitations will become less of a concern.

Revising existing measures

Researchers are often discouraged from creating new measures and encouraged to use previously published measures. In many situations, this is good advice as creating new measures carries a number of risks associated with the unknown measurement properties of the new measure. However, revising existing measures to meet the needs of a particular study is a common challenge faced by organizational researchers. Researchers may need to modify a measure, because the reading level is well above the sample in their study, there are too many or too few items, the language is out of date or biased, the specific topic of study is different from the topic used with the original measure, or there are concerns about the reactions or response behaviour of those completing the measure.

Modifications to existing measures are common in organizational research (Keller and Dansereau, 2001), but the impact of these modifications to the measurement properties are not well understood (Rivers et al., in press). For example, adding or removing items can change the factor structure of the measure, decrease reliability and validity, introduce additional constructs into the measure, or change the meaning of a construct. The impact of these types of changes is not trivial. Keller and Dansereau (2001) found that adding items to LMX measures (based on leader-member exchange theory) can reduce the predictive validity for other items already included in the measure.

There are several strategies for defensibly revising measures (see Stanton et al., 2002 for a review of the best practices). The typical practice in organizational research is to retain items that maximize internal consistency. The resultant measure will have narrow content, the items will be redundant, the factor structure may change, and validity can decrease. Some of the most promising alternatives are based on IRT. For example, an IRT analysis can indicate if and how the item properties have changed as a function of any revisions to a measure (e.g., Rivers et al., in press). Because item parameters are not completely sample dependent in IRT, organizational researchers can use different samples to compare how IRT parameters of modified measures compare to the IRT parameters of the original measures. In addition, using the item and test information functions, one could identify which existing items are unnecessary, and therefore shorten the measure without sacrificing the usefulness of the entire measure. With classical methods, it is not possible to identify truly the contribution of a single item. The item parameters, test and item information functions, as well as the standard error of measurement, provide a set of tools for organizational researchers to examine empirically the impact of modifying existing measures. However, the blind use of IRT or any statistic is not advisable. Content is the most important criterion when revising a measure. Ensuring that the entire content domain is adequately sampled should be as or more important than relying on statistical indicators to revise items.

Alternative measurement techniques

Nearly all measurement in organizational research can be characterized as measures of *explicit social cognitions* (Greenwald and Banaji, 1995). Such cognitions are conscious and underlie the use of self-report surveys, interviews, and other explicit measurement techniques. The psychological processes underlying explicit measurement techniques is thought to involve four unique stages; interpreting the question, retrieving relevant information from memory, forming a judgment, and mapping the judgment to the response options (Tourangeau and Rasinski, 1988). While parts of the process occur without conscious awareness, any response from the participant is ultimately the result of a conscious decision to choose a given option in response to a question or item.

Conversely, *implicit social cognitions* are by definition cognitions that affect mental processes but are not consciously available. Implicit cognitions such as attitudes are thought to stem from past experiences (Greenwald and Banaji, 1995), are thought to be more sensitive to affective experiences than are explicit attitudes (Rudman, 2004), and may be more reflective of the general cultural environment in which one lives than explicit attitudes (Nosek et al., 2002).

Two recent developments in measurement hold potential for organizational researchers in need of measures of implicit cognitions. One is the Implicit Association Test (IAT; Greenwald et al., 1998) which has received considerable attention in the popular press, yet has been utilized little by organizational researchers. Conversely, well known organizational researcher Larry James and colleagues have developed the Conditional Reasoning Test (CRT).

Implicit association test

The IAT grew out of research on social cognition as researchers looked for a way of assessing attitudes that are prone to self-presentation effects. For example, much of the early IAT work focused on implicit attitudes regarding stereotypes of race and gender (e.g., Fazio et al., 1995; Rudman and Glick, 2001), and has only more recently moved towards more commonly assessed organizational phenomena such as personality assessment (e.g., Asendorpf et al., 2002; Egloff and Schmukle, 2002).

Typically, IATs are computer-based tests that assess response latency to a series of paired response trials. As an illustration, an IAT created to assess attitudes about race would typically include several series of trials. After a few learning trials, response latency is assessed for a condition in which either positive words (e.g., 'pleasant') or White faces are presented and demand a response from the left hand, while negative words or Black faces are responded to with the right hand. This is then compared with another trial in which response latency is recorded for Black faces and positive words paired together and White faces and negative words are paired (Greenwald et al., 1998).

The initial work on the measurement properties of the IAT is promising (Greenwald and Nosek, 2001). For instance, test-retest coefficients of 0.61 over six weeks were reported by Cunningham et al. (2001), and split-half internal consistency measures above 0.75 have been observed (Asendorf et al., 2002; Cunningham et al., 2001). Convergent validity with explicit measures is often present (Greenwald et al., 1998), despite a potential theoretical rationale for finding no such relationship. Predictive validity for the IAT has been demonstrated for both behavioural criteria (e.g., Asendorpf et al., 2002; Ziegert and Hanges, 2005), and physiological criteria (e.g., Egloff and Schmukle, 2002). Despite promising early work, there are some limitations (see Greenwald, 2004 for a summary). IATs are more resistant to response manipulation than explicit measures, but it is still possible with repeated exposure to the same IAT (Haines and Sumner, 2006). Presentation order and context effects have also been shown to affect IAT scores (Greenwald, 2004; Karpinski and Hilton, 2001).

IATs have been infrequently used in organizational research despite calls to do so

(e.g., Haines and Sumner, 2006). A few studies have been reported that used the IAT to examine racial discrimination (Ziegert and Hanges, 2005) and job satisfaction (Haines and Sumner, 2006). Haines and Sumner (2006) suggest that other areas of organizational research may be amenable to measurement via the IAT, such as more organizationally relevant stereotypes and organizational commitment.

Conditional reasoning test

In contrast to IATs, CRTs were developed as implicit measure of stable personality-based traits, rather than attitudes, and were intended for organizational use from the outset. CRTs appear on the surface as standard cognitive ability-style multiple-choice tests of logical reasoning. However, the choice of some response options on a CRT is thought to be conditioned upon the person's standing on the trait of interest (hence the name CRT). As an example, James et al. (2004), ask respondents which of four response options was the 'biggest problem with the "eye for an eye" plan?'. The response option, 'people have to wait until they are attacked before they can strike', is given as indicative of an implicit motivation towards aggressive tendencies. As of yet, two CRTs of implicit tendencies have been developed and reported in published organizational research; aggressive tendencies (CRT-A; James et al., 2005), and achievement motivation (CRT-AM; James, 1998).

James (1998) posited that because individuals are motivated to justify behaviours as reasonable, they would rely on justification mechanisms to infer the logic of behaviours consistent with their own, such as aggressive tendencies. CRTs, therefore, are meant to assess differences in reasoning (i.e., question framing, analysis, and inference) due to the use of justification mechanisms by respondents with certain inclinations (James et al., 2004). Underlying the response process of a CRT is an elaborate theoretical framework in which (a) individuals realize that they behave in certain ways, (b) they are motivated to justify such behaviour as logical and consistent, (c) they rely on these justification mechanisms when framing and evaluating a CRT item, and (d) they are therefore more likely to choose the response indicative of the trait measured by the CRT than are other participants.

The initial evidence for CRTs is generally supportive. James et al. (2004) reported an internal consistency KR-20 value of 0.76 for the CRT-A. James et al. (2005) reported predictive validity of several counterproductive behaviours at an average of 0.44. CRTs have also been found to predict grade point average (James, 1998), assessment-centre performance (Bing et al., 2001), and supervisor's ratings of performance among patrol officers (James et al., 2004).

CRTs, however, are not without limitations. First, existing CRT measures were designed to be proprietary instruments and only a few example items are available for review. An implication is that the existing CRTs are not widely available for investigation by researchers not affiliated with the developers. Second, the construct validity of CRTs is rooted in an extremely complex theoretical framework in which past actions lead to justification mechanisms, which in turn affects the CRT item response process. This, combined with the proprietary nature of the instruments, means that potential users of the existing CRTs must place a great deal of trust in the developers and in the validity of the instrument. Given the theoretical complexity underlying CRTs, it is extremely difficult and time consuming to develop additional CRT measures. As with IATs, CRTs are new, innovative, and potentially promising measurement methods for organizational research.

Advances in evaluation techniques

Measurement invariance

Recent years have seen an increase in the number of studies involving measurement invariance (Vandenberg, 2002). Measurement invariance (MI) can be considered to be the degree to which measurements conducted under different conditions exhibit identical measurement properties (Drasgow, 1984). Such conditions include measures over time (e.g., Chan, 1998), across different populations (e.g., cultures, Riordan and Vandenberg, 1994), or over different mediums of administration (e.g., Ployhart et al., 2003). Measurement invariance must be ensured before making group-level comparisons of observed scores such as group means (Millsap, 1995; Raju et al., 2002).

There are two commonly used approaches to assessing measurement invariance; confirmatory factor analysis (CFA) and IRT. These methods share the common purpose of providing assessments of the equivalence of the measurement properties of the instruments in question; however, they approach the task somewhat differently, and provide somewhat different information (Meade and Lautenschlager, 2004; Raju et al., 2002; Stark et al., 2006).

The CFA approach to invariance tests involves the comparison of multiple factor analytic models, under a variety of model constraints, to determine which parts of a factor model differ across groups. In the most common application, components of the model are estimated independently across samples (e.g., men and women) using a multigroup CFA model. Fit statistics are then gathered for the multigroup CFA model in which both samples are analyzed concurrently yet model parameters (e.g., factor loadings) are allowed to differ across the two groups. Once adequate model fit is established, a series of more constrained models are analyzed in which various model parameters are constrained to be equal across the two groups (see Vandenberg and Lance, 2000, for a review).

There are several IRT methods available to assess measurement invariance. One of the more common IRT-based approaches to assessing measurement invariance is the differential functioning of items and tests (DFIT) technique (Raju et al., 1995). DFIT assesses both item and test-level invariance by first estimating item parameters and persons' scores separately in two groups. Once these parameters are placed onto a common metric via a linking procedure, one group's person scores are estimated using both the item parameters estimated for that group and also the item parameters of the other group. The differences in these estimated person scores are then compared to determine differential functioning of items and the test as a whole.

Although some measurement invariance approaches in CFA and IRT are comparable (Stark et al., 2006), there are some differences between the information provided by CFA and IRT. Perhaps most notable, CFA uses a linear response model to relate item responses to the latent trait, whereas IRT uses a nonlinear model (Raju et al., 2002). Second, for polytomous data, most commonly used IRT models provide several additional item parameters per item than does CFA. As such, it is possible that some types of subtle group differences in the properties of items can be readily detected via IRT methods, but not with the CFA approach (Meade and Lautenschlager, 2004). Third, IRT approaches assume unidimensionality and therefore only assess the invariance of the relationships between items and latent traits for one scale at a time. Conversely, CFA affords the comparisons of the relationships among latent traits across groups.

Recent IRT models

We highlight two classes of IRT models, more recently developed, that have the potential to provide richer data on common organizational measures; mixed measurement models, and unfolding models. Mixed measurement models (Rost, 1991) can also examine questions of measurement invariance. These models are a combination of item response theory and latent class/profile analysis. Traditional measurement invariance analyses require that manifest classes (e.g., culture and race) be identified and differences between the manifest classes are examined in the analyses. In mixed measurement models, manifest classes are not identified a priori. The analyses attempt to identify the latent classes that may exist in the data and simultaneously estimate IRT item parameters. Currently, there are only a few examples of organizational researchers using these models (e.g., dishonest responding on personality inventories – Zickar et al., 2004; use of the middle category on organizational surveys – Hernández et al., 2004).

Most IRT models assume that a monotonic function represents the relationship between the selection of response options and the level of the latent characteristic. Conversely, unfolding IRT models specify that there is an 'ideal point' for each individual on the continuum of a latent characteristic and individuals will endorse items that are close their ideal point on the attitude continuum. In other words, the relationship between the selection of response options and the level of the latent characteristic is nonmonotonic (Roberts et al., 2000). This notion is based on the research of Coombs (1964) and Thurstone (1931) on ideal point response processes. In the organizational sciences, these models have recently been applied to personality (e.g., Stark et al., 2006) and leadership data (Scherbaum et al., 2006).

CONCLUSIONS

There have been many methodological advances with respect to measurement in the past two decades. However, organizational research continues to lag substantially behind these advances, and continues to rely largely on the same classical measurement methods as it has for the past decades. This situation is unfortunate as theory testing and refinement is limited by the quality and sophistication of the measures employed to operationalize the substantive relationships (Judd and McClelland, 1998). While overview guides to scale development in the organizational sciences have been extremely helpful in ensuring that novice methodologists are following established best practices, it is important that organizational researchers are aware that common methods, such as Likert-type scales, are but one of a number of potential methods. Moreover, many of these alternative methods of measurement have substantial advantages over commonly used measures. In other words, it is important that organizational researchers are not hamstrung by their own 'best practices' recommendations.

The question then is, how should organizational researchers approach measurement? We recommend that researchers start by developing a sound measurement theory and fully explicating the nature of the construct they want to assess. How is the construct defined? What types of attributes and behaviours does the construct include? What attributes and behaviours does the construct *not* include? Such questions are imperative for adequately defining the construct domain. Once the construct space is thoroughly defined, researchers should give serious consideration to the types of measures that would afford adequate measurement of that construct domain. Are explicit or implicit measures most appropriate? If explicit, what types of items would be best suited for the construct (e.g., Likert or Thurstone scale items)? Next, any set of items generated should adequately sample the theoretical domain of the construct. Researchers should use optimal techniques to assess the quality of the resultant measure, whether those techniques be IRT or classical in nature. Finally, we emphasize that researchers should not blindly rely on statistics in refining their measures. Some techniques (e.g., internal consistency) can produce highly redundant items with construct deficiency. Sound judgment and measurement theory should be a part of any measurement effort.

REFERENCES

Aguinis, H., Henle, C.A. and Ostroff, C. (2002) 'Measurement in work and organizational psychology', in N. Anderson and D.S. Ones (eds), *Handbook of Industrial, Work and Organizational Psychology, Volume 1: Personnel psychology*, London, England: Sage, pp. 27–50.

Asendorpf, J.B., Banse, R. and Mucke, D. (2002) 'Double dissociation between implicit and explicit personality self-concept: the case of shy behavior', *Journal of Personality and Social Psychology*, 83: 380–93.

Bing, M.N., LeBreton, J.M., Davison, H.K., Migetz, D.Z. and James, L.R. (2007) 'Integrating implicit and explicit social cognitions for enhanced personality assessment: a general framework for choosing measurement and statistical methods', *Organizational Research Methods*, 10: 346–89.

Bing, M.N., LeBreton, J.M., Migetz, D.Z., Vermillion, D.B., Davison, H.K. and James, L.R. (2001, April) 'The integrative model of personality assessment for achievement motivation and fear of failure: Implications for the prediction of effort, attribution, and performance', in J. LeBreton and J. Binning, *Recent issues and innovations in personality assessment*, Symposium at the 16th annual conference of the Society for Industrial and Organizational Psychology, San Diego, CA.

Brennan, R.L. (1992) 'An NCME instructional module on generalizability theory', *Educational Measurement: Issues and Practice*, 11: 27–34.

Chan, D. (1998) 'The conceptualization and analysis of change over time: an integrative approach incorporating longitudinal mean and covariance structures analysis (LMACS) and multiple indicator latent growth modeling (MLGM)', *Organizational Research Methods*, 1: 421–83.

Chernyshenko, O.S., Stark, S., Chan, K.-Y., Drasgow, F. and Williams, B. (2001) 'Fitting item response theory models to two personality inventories: issues and insights', *Multivariate Behavioral Research*, 36: 523–62.

Coombs, C.H. (1964) *A Theory of Data*, New York: John Wiley and Sons.

Crocker, L. and Algina, J. (1986) *Introduction to Classical and Modern Test Theory*, New York: Holt, Rinehart, and Winston.

Cronbach, L.J., Gleser, G.C. Nanda, H. and Rajaratnam, N. (1972) *The Dependability of Behavioral Measurements: Theory of Generalizability of Scores and Profiles*, New York: Wiley.

Cunningham, W.A., Preacher, K.J. and Banaji, M.R. (2001) 'Implicit attitude measures: consistency, stability, and convergent validity', *Psychological Science*, 12: 163–70.

Dawes, R.M. and Smith, T.L. (1985) 'Attitude and opinion measurement', in G. Lindzey and E. Aronson (eds), *The Handbook of Social Psychology* (third edn.) (Vol. 1), New York: Random House, pp, 509–66.

DeShon, R.P. (2003) 'Generalizability theory', in F. Drasgow and N. Schmidt (eds), *Measuring and Analyzing Behavior in Organizations: Advances in Measurement and Data Analysis*, San Francisco, CA: Jossey-Bass, pp. 189–220.

Drasgow, F. (1984) 'Scrutinizing psychological tests: measurement equivalence and equivalent relations with external variables are the central issues', *Psychological Bulletin*, 95: 134–5.

Drasgow, F. and Schmidt, N. (2002) *Measuring and analyzing behavior in organizations: advances in measurement and data analysis*, San Francisco, CA: Jossey-Bass.

Egloff, B. and Schmukle, S.C. (2002) 'Predictive validity of an implicit association test for assessing anxiety', *Journal of Personality and Social Psychology*, 83: 1441–55.

Ellis, B.B. and Mead, A.D. (2002) 'Item analysis: theory and practice using classical and modern test theory', in S.G. Rogelberg (ed.), *Handbook of Research Methods in Industrial and Organizational Psychology*, Malden, MA: Blackwell Publishers, pp. 324–43.

Embretson, S.E. and Reise, S.P. (2000) *Item Response Theory for Psychologists*, Mahwah, NJ: Lawrence Erlbaum.

Fazio, R.H., Jackson, J.R., Dunton, B.C. and Williams, C.J. (1995) 'Variability in automatic activation as an unobstrusive measure of racial attitudes: a bona fide pipeline?', *Journal of Personality and Social Psychology*, 69: 1013–27.

Fazio, R.H. and Olson, M.A. (2003) 'Implicit measures in social cognition research: their meaning and use', *Annual Review of Psychology*, 54: 297–327.

Feldt, L.S. and Brennan, R.L. (1989) 'Reliability', in R.L. Linn (ed.), *Educational Measurement* (third ed.), Washington, DC: American Council on Education, pp. 105–46.

Greenwald, A.G. (2004) January) 'Revised top 10 list of things wrong with the IAT', Paper presented at the Attitudes Preconference of the fifth annual meeting of the Society of Personality and Social Psychology, Austin, TX.

Greenwald, A.G. and Banaji, M.R. (1995) 'Implicit social cognition: attitudes, self-esteem, and stereotypes', *Psychological Review*, 102: 4–27.

Greenwald, A.G., McGhee, D.E. and Schwartz, J.L.K. (1998) 'Measuring individual differences in implicit cognition: the implicit association test', *Journal of Personality and Social Psychology*, 74: 1464–80.

Greenwald, A.G. and Nosek, B.A. (2001) 'Health of the implicit association test at age 3', *Zeitschrift fur Experimentelle Psychologie*, 48: 85–93.

Guilford, J.P. (1954) *Psychometric Methods* (second edn.), New York: McGraw-Hill.

Haines, E.L. and Sumner, K.E. (2006) 'Implicit measurement of attitudes, stereotypes, and self-concepts in organizations: teaching old dogmas new tricks', *Organizational Research Methods*, 9: 536–53.

Hambleton, R.K., Swaminathan, H. and Rogers, H.J. (1991) *Fundamentals of Item Response Theory*, Newbury Park, CA: Sage.

Hernández, A., Drasgow, F. and González-Romá, V. (2004) 'Investigating the functioning of a middle category by means of a mixed-measurement model', *Journal of Applied Psychology*, 89: 687–99.

Hinkin, T.R. (1995) 'A review of scale development practices in the study of organizations', *Journal of Management*, 21: 967–88.

Hinkin, T.R. (1998) 'A brief tutorial on the development of measures for use in survey questionnaires', *Organizational Research Methods*, 1: 104–21.

James, L.R. (1998) 'Measurement of personality via conditional reasoning', *Organizational Research Methods*, 1: 131–63.

James, L.R., McIntyre, M.D., Glisson, C.A., Bowler, J.L. and Mitchell, T.R. (2004) 'The conditional reasoning measurement system for aggression: an overview', *Human Performance*, 17: 271–95.

James, L.R., McIntyre, M.D., Glisson, C.A., Green, P.D., Patton, T.W., LeBreton, J.M. (2005) 'A conditional reasoning measure for aggression', *Organizational Research Methods*, 8: 69–99.

Judd, C.M. and McClelland, G.H. (1998) 'Measurement', in D.T. Gilbert and S.T. Fiske (eds), *The Handbook of Social Psychology* (fourth edn., Vol. 1), New York: McGraw-Hill, pp. 180–232.

Karpinski, A. and Hilton, J.L. (2001) 'Attitudes and the implicit association test', *Journal of Personality and Social Psychology*, 81: 774–88.

Keller, T. and Dansereau, F. (2001) 'The effect of adding items to scales: an illustrative case of LMX', *Organizational Research Methods*, 4: 131–43.

Klimoski, R.J. and Zukin, L.B. (2003) 'Psychological assessment in industrial/organizational settings', in J.R. Graham and J.A. Naglieri (eds), *Handbook of Psychology: Assessment Psychology* (Vol. 10), Hoboken, NJ: John Wiley and Sons, pp. 317–43.

Krosnick, J.A. (1999) 'Survey research', *Annual Review of Psychology*, 50: 537–67.

Krosnick J.A. and Berent, M.K. (1993) 'Comparisons of party identification and policy preferences: the impact of survey question format', *American Journal of Political Science*, 37: 941–64.

Likert, R. (1932) 'A technique for the measurement of attitudes', *Archives of Psychology*, 22(140): 5–53.

Meade, A.W. and Lautenschlager, G.J. (2004) 'A comparison of item response theory and confirmatory factor analytic methodologies for establishing measurement equivalence/invariance', *Organizational Research Methods*, 7: 361–88.

Messick, S. (1989) 'Validity', in R.L. Linn (ed.), *Educational Measurement* (third edn.), Washington, D.C.: American Council on Education, pp. 221–62.

Millsap, R.E. (1995) 'Measurement invariance, predictive invariance, and the duality paradox', *Multivariate Behavioral Research*, 30: 577–605.

Miner, J.B. (2003) 'The rated importance, scientific validity, and practical usefulness of organizational behavior theories: a quantitative review', *Academy of Management Learning and Education*, 2: 250–68.

Murphy, K.R. and DeShon, R. (2000) 'Interrater correlations do not estimate the reliability of job performance ratings', *Personnel Psychology*, 53: 873–900.

Nosek, B.A., Banaji, M. and Greenwald, A.G. (2002) 'Harvesting implicit group attitudes and beliefs from a demonstration web site', *Group Dynamics: Theory, Research, and Practice*, 6: 101–15.

Nunnally, J.C (1978) *Psychometric Theory* (second edn.), New York: McGraw-Hill.

Pedhazur, E.J. and Pedhazur-Schmelkin, L. (1991) *Measurement, Design, and Analysis*, Hillsdale, NJ: Lawrence Erlbaum.

Ployhart, R.E., Weekley, J.A., Holtz, B.C. and Kemp, C. (2003) 'Web-based and paper-and-pencil testing of applicants in a proctored setting: are personality, biodata and situational judgment tests comparable?', *Personnel Psychology*, 56: 733–52.

Podsakoff, P.M. and Dalton, D.R. (1987) 'Research methodology in organizational studies', *Journal of Management*, 13: 419–41.

Raju, N.S., Laffitte, L.J. and Byrne, B.M. (2002) 'Measurement equivalence: a comparison of methods based on confirmatory factor analysis and item response theory', *Journal of Applied Psychology*, 87: 517–29.

Raju, N.S., van der Linden, W.J. and Fleer, P.F. (1995) 'IRT-based internal measures of differential functioning of items and tests', *Applied Psychological Measurement*, 19: 353–68.

Riordan, C.M. and Vandenberg, R.J. (1994) 'A central question in cross-cultural research: do employees of different cultures interpret work-related measures in an equivalent manner?', *Journal of Management*, 20: 643–71.

Rivers, D., Meade, A. and Fuller, W. (in dpress) 'Examining question and context effects in organization survey data using item response theory', *Organizational Research Methods*.

Roberts, J.S., Donoghue, J.R. and Laughlin, J.E. (2000) 'A general item response theory model for unfolding unidimensional polytomous responses', *Applied Psychological Measurement*, 24: 3–32.

Rost, J. (1991) 'A logistic mixture distribution model for polychotomous item responses', *British Journal of Mathematical and Statistical Psychology*, 44: 75–92.

Rudman, L.A. (2004) 'Sources of implicit attitudes', *Current Directions in Psychological Science*, 13(2): 79–82.

Rudman, L.A. and Glick, P. (2001) 'Prescriptive gender stereotypes and backlash toward agentic women', *Journal of Social Issues*, 57: 743–62.

Samejima, F. (1969) 'Estimation of latent ability using a response pattern of graded scores', *Psychometrika*, 34: 1–100.

Scandura, T.A. and Williams, E.A. (2000) 'Research methodology in management: current practices, trends, and implications for future research', *Academy of Management Journal*, 43: 1248–64.

Scherbaum, C.A., Finlinson, S., Barden, K. and Tamanini, K. (2006) 'Applications of item response theory to measurement issues in leadership research', *Leadership Quarterly*, 17: 366–86.

Schoenfeldt, L.F. (1984) 'Psychometric properties of organizational research instruments', in T. Bateman and G. Ferris (eds), *Method and analysis in organizational research*, Reston, VA: Reston Publishing Company, pp.68–80.

Schriesheim, C.A., Powers, K.J., Scandura, T.A. and Gardiner, C.C. (1993) 'Improving construct measurement in management research: comments and a quantitative approach for assessing the theoretical content adequacy of paper-and-pencil survey-type instruments', *Journal of Management*, 19: 385–417.

Schwarz, N. (1999) Self-reports: 'How the questions shape the answers', *American Psychologist*, 54: 93–105.

Schwarz, N., Knauper, B., Hippler, H.J., Noelle-Neumann, E. and Clark, F. (1991) 'Rating scales: numeric values may change the meaning of scale labels', *Public Opinion Quarterly*, 55: 570–82.

Shavelson, R.J. and Webb, N.M. (1991) *Generalizability Theory: A Primer*, Newbury Park, CA: Sage.

Stanton, J.M., Sinar, E.F., Balzer, W.K. and Smith, P.C. (2002) 'Issues and strategies for reducing the length of self-report scales', *Personnel Psychology*, 55: 167–94.

Stark, S., Chernyshenko, O.S. and Drasgow, F. (2006) 'Detecting differential item functioning with confirmatory factor analysis and item response theory: toward a unified strategy', *Journal of Applied Psychology*, 91: 1292–306.

Stark, S., Chernyshenko, O.S., Drasgow, F. and Williams, B.A. (2006) 'Examining assumptions about item responding in personality assessment: should ideal point methods be considered for scale development and scoring?', *Journal of Applied Psychology*, 91: 25–39.

Stevens S.S. (1968) 'Measurement, statistics, and schemapiric view', *Science*, 56; 849–56.

Thorndike, E. (1918) 'The nature, purposes, and general methods of measurements of educational products', in G.M. Whipple (ed.), *The Seventeenth Yearbook of the National Society for Study of Education* (Vol. 17), Bloomington, IL: Public School Publishing Co. pp. 2: 16.

Thurstone, L.L. (1931) 'The measurement of social attitudes', *Abnormal and Social Psychology*, 26: 249–69.

Tourangeau, R. and Rasinski, K.A. (1988) 'Cognitive processes underlying context effects in attitude measurement', *Psychological Bulletin*, 103: 299–314.

van der Linden, W.J. and Hambleton, R.K. (eds) (1997) *Handbook of Modern Item Response Theory*, New York: Springer.

Vandenberg, R.J. (2002) 'Toward a further understanding of an improvement in measurement invariance methods and procedures', *Organizational Research Methods*, 5: 139–58.

Vandenberg, R.J. and Lance, C.E. (2000) 'A review and synthesis of the measurement invariance literature: suggestions, practices, and recommendations for organizational research', *Organizational Research Methods*, 3: 4–69.

Wainer, H. (2000) *Computer adaptive testing: a primer* (second edn.), Mahwah, NJ: Lawrence Erlbaum Associates.

Zickar, M.J. and Robie, C. (1999) 'Modeling faking good on personality items: an item-level analysis', *Journal of Applied Psychology*, 84: 551–63.

Zickar, M.J., Gibby, R.E. and Robie, C. (2004) 'Uncovering faking samples in applicant, incumbent, and experimental data sets: an application of mixed-model item response theory', *Organizational Research Methods*, 7: 168–90.

Ziegert, J.C. and Hanges, P.J. (2005) 'Employment Discrimination: the role of implicit attitudes, motivation, and a climate for racial bias', *Journal of Applied Psychology*, 90: 553–62.

38

Making Visible the Hidden: Researching Off-The-Books Work

Colin C. Williams and Monder Ram

INTRODUCTION

This chapter critically reviews the research methods used to investigate a form of work organization concealed from the state for tax, social security, and labour law purposes but often very much in plain sight in everyday life, namely off-the-books work. At first glance, it might appear that, given the illegitimate character of off-the-books working practices, detecting such work will be not only a difficult task but probably doomed to failure. Yet, for some decades now, researchers have been seeking to hone a range of indirect and direct research methods to understand better the extent and character of this clandestine work. In this chapter, therefore, the intention is to evaluate critically these methods for detecting this mode of work organization. A key theme is that visibility and access is not always to be equated with interest and significance. Within the field of 'mainstream' organization studies, a number of important populations are either excluded from the research agenda, or appear rarely; and their voices, roles, and influence are consequently silenced and overlooked. This observation applies, for example, to managerial elites. For instance, in corporate ethnographies, access to the highest echelons of organizations can be problematic (Dalton, 1959; Kunda, 1992). Kunda (1992: 236) discovered that access was inversely related to hierarchical level; his 'interactions with the pinnacle of power were limited'. Dalton (1959) operated covertly in his study of industrial managers, because he suspected that chief executives would limit the enquiry to specific areas if he had adopted an open approach. Groups that appear in the present chapter – employees, working family members, and members of ethnic minorities – are even less likely to attract the interest of organizational scholars. Researchers face a number of barriers, including the perceived difficulties of securing access, the 'marginal' nature of these groups, and language and cultural norms. However, such challenges can be exaggerated. We argue that, appropriately conducted, research on 'cash-in-hand work' can open up new terrain for organizational researchers and be theoretically rewarding. Studies focusing on informal work have helped to form the empirical basis of a new model of employment relations in small firms (Edwards and Ram, 2006), shed light on the impact of regulations (Jones et al., 2006; Ram et al., 2007), and the integration of migrant populations (Sepulveda and Syrett, 2007).

To do this, first, we will provide a review of the various indirect methods that have been employed to detect such work; second, we will review the range of direct survey methods, third, we will evaluate the current controversies and methodological debates in this field of enquiry and fourth and finally, based on informed speculation, draw some conclusions about likely trends and developments in the near future, along with signposts regarding future developments. A notable feature of extant studies is the preoccupation with the extent of off-the-books work rather than about other aspects of it, such as how it is experienced and why people do it. This may reflect the policy consequences of ignoring informal economic activity, which include increased tax burdens, increased cost of regulatory compliance and a general lack of trust in government (Leonard, 1998). Nonetheless, the dynamics of off-the-books work has been a feature of recent studies (Jones et al., 2006; Ram et al., 2007; Sepulveda and Syrett, 2007).

It is first necessary to define off-the-books work, or what has alternatively been called the 'cash-in-hand', 'informal', 'black', 'underground', 'hidden' and 'shadow' economy/sector (Williams, 2004). Despite the diverse array of terms and competing views of its relationship to formal modes of work organization, a strong consensus has emerged regarding what types of endeavour should be included and excluded when discussing this form of work. Off-the-books work is widely accepted as involving only the production and sale of goods and services that are licit in all respects, besides the fact that they are unregistered by or hidden from the state for tax, benefit and/or labour law purposes (European Commission, 1998; Feige, 1999; Portes, 1994;

Renooy et al., 2004; Thomas, 1992; Williams, 2006a; Williams and Windebank, 1998). Where goods and services are provided that are themselves illicit (e.g., drug-trafficking), these have been normally excluded from the scope of what is considered off-the-books work, as have noncash exchanges and subsistence production that is not exchanged. Blurred edges, nevertheless, do remain. For example, depending on the tax regime, in some countries gift giving is included and in others excluded.

Indirect methods for detecting off-the-books work

Indirect methods seek evidence of off-the-books working practices in macroeconomic data collected and/or constructed for other purposes. These indirect methods have been of three broad types. First, there are those seeking statistical traces of off-the-books work in nonmonetary indicators; second, those employing monetary proxy indicators; and third, those analyzing discrepancies between income and expenditure levels. Each of these three broad categories involves a range of techniques.

Indirect non-monetary methods

The most common methods using nonmonetary surrogate indicators are, first, those that seek traces in formal labour force statistics; second, those that use very small enterprises as a proxy; and third, those that use electricity demand as a surrogate.

Those that seek traces of off-the-books work in formal *labour force statistics* are of two varieties. The first method examines unaccountable increases in the numbers in various types of employment (e.g., self-employment and second-job holding) as a proxy indicator of the level of off-the-books work (Alden, 1982; Crnkovic-Pozaic, 1999; Del Boca and Forte, 1982; Hellberger and Schwarze, 1986). However, the notion that off-the-books work prevails in these categories of employment is an assumption, rather than a finding, and there is no way of knowing the degree to which it is off-the-books work, rather than other factors, that has led to such an increase. Second-job holding, for example, is not always a direct result of off-the-books work except if such job holding is illegal per se. It is also the result of broader economic and cultural restructuring processes such as the demise of the 'breadwinner wage' and the proliferation of part-time work. To identify the proportion of growth in multiple-job holding attributable to such processes and the share attributable to off-the-books work is thus a difficult if not impossible task. The second technique, using labour force statistics, seeks discrepancies in the results of different official surveys, such as the population census and firm surveys (Denison, 1982; Lobo, 1990; Mattera, 1985; US Congress Joint Economic Committee, 1983). This method, however, erroneously assumes that individuals are either legitimate or off-the-books workers.

A second method uses *very small enterprises* (VSEs) as a nonmonetary proxy indicator of off-the-books work (ILO, 2002; Portes and Sassen-Koob, 1987; Sassen and Smith, 1992; US General Accounting Office, 1989). As an indicator of off-the-books work, however, the VSE approach is subject to two contradictory assumptions. On the one hand, not all VSEs engage in off-the-books practices, which could lead to an overestimate. On the other hand, fully off-the-books VSEs will escape government record keeping that could lead to an underestimate (Portes, 1994). It also totally ignores more individualized forms of off-the-books work conducted by people on a one-to-one basis to meet final demand.

A third and final nonmonetary method uses *electricity demand* as a surrogate indicator of off-the-books work (Friedman et al., 2000; Kaufmann and Kaliberda, 1996; Lacko, 1999). Economic activity and electricity consumption are claimed to move in step with each other with an electricity-to-GDP elasticity of close to one, meaning that the growth of total electricity consumption is a fairly reliable indicator for the growth of overall (formal and off-the-books) GDP.

By using this measure and subtracting the official GDP, these analysts derive an estimate of unofficial GDP. The problems are that not all types of off-the-books work require a considerable amount of electricity (e.g., personal services) and other energy sources can be used (e.g., gas, oil, and coal) and that using this to measure temporal changes in off-the-books work does not take into account either increases in energy efficiency or how alterations in the elasticity of electricity-to-GDP vary across countries and over time.

Indirect monetary methods

Other indirect methods use monetary rather than nonmonetary proxy indicators. Three principal proxies have been used; large denomination notes, the cash-deposit ratio, and money transactions, although a more recent method uses multiple indicators.

For those using the *large denomination notes* approach, the belief is that off-the-books workers use exclusively cash in their transactions and that large sums are involved with high denomination notes exchanged (Bartlett, 1998; Carter, 1984; Freud, 1979; Henry, 1976; Matthews, 1982). This approach suffers from a multitude of problems; it cannot separate the proportion of large denomination notes used for crime from their use in off-the-books work (Bartlett, 1998); many off-the-books transactions are for relatively small amounts of money (Cornuel and Duriez, 1985; Evason and Woods, 1995; Tanzi, 1982); and a multitude of other factors resulting from changes in mode of payments (e.g., credit cards and store cards) influence the use of large denomination bank notes.

A second common monetary proxy is the ratio of currency in circulation to demand deposits, otherwise known as the *cash-deposit ratio approach*. Assuming that, in order to conceal income, illegitimate transactions will occur in cash, this method estimates the currency in circulation required by legitimate activities and subtracts this from the actual money in circulation. The difference, multiplied by the velocity of money, is taken as the currency in circulation due to off-the-books work. The ratio of this figure to the observed GNP measures the proportion of the national economy represented by off-the-books work. This was pioneered by Gutmann (1977, 1978) in America and subsequently widely adopted (Atkins, 1999; Caridi and Passerini, 2001; Cocco and Santos, 1984; Matthews, 1983; Matthews and Rastogi, 1985; Meadows and Pihera, 1981; Santos, 1983; Tanzi, 1980). It again suffers from major problems; cash is not always the medium of exchange for off-the-books transactions (Contini, 1982; Smith, 1985); it cannot distinguish the share of illegitimate cash circulation due to off-the-books work and the proportion due to crime, nor how it is changing over time; the choice of the cash-deposit ratio as a proxy is arbitrary and not derived from economic theory (Trundle, 1982); the cash-deposit ratio is influenced by a myriad of tendencies besides off-the-books work (e.g., changing methods of payment, financial exclusion), often working in opposite directions to one another; the choice of a base period when off-the-books work supposedly did not exist is problematic, especially given the sensitivity of the results to which base year is chosen (O'Higgins, 1981; Thomas, 1988); it assumes the same velocity of cash circulation in the off-the-books and formal spheres when there is no evidence that this is the case (Frey and Weck, 1983), and it is impossible to determine how much of the currency of a country is held domestically and how much abroad.

Recognizing that cheques as well as cash are used in off-the-books transactions, a third approach estimates the extent to which the total quantity of *monetary transactions* exceeds what would be predicted in the absence of off-the-books work (Feige, 1979). As evidence that cheques as well as cash are used in off-the-books transactions in America, Feige (1990) quotes a study by the Internal Revenue Service showing that between a quarter and third of unreported income was paid by cheque rather than currency. In Norway, Isachsen et al. (1982) found that, in 1980, about 20 percent of off-the-books services were paid for by cheque, while in Detroit, Smith (1985) provides a higher

estimate in the realm of informal home repair, displaying that bills were settled roughly equally in cheques and cash. This approach, however, suffers the same problems as the cash-deposit approach. The only problem it overcomes is acceptance that cheques can be used in off-the-books transactions. Consequently, the above criticisms are not repeated. Instead, attention turns towards another monetary proxy approach believed by its advocates to be far more sophisticated.

The *MIMIC* (Multiple Indicators Multiple Causes) approach seeks to overcome some of the problems of the aforementioned methods by considering multiple indicators and multiple causes (Schneider, 2001; Schneider and Enste, 2002). Schneider (2001), for example, views the causes (and indicators) of off-the-books work as: the burden of direct and indirect taxation, both actual and perceived; the burden of regulation; and tax morality (citizens' attitudes towards paying taxes). However, it is not only possible to challenge all of these supposed causes (and indicators), but there also seems little recognition that it is not these factors per se but, how they combine with a multitude of other factors that produce high or low levels of off-the-books work. This approach, nevertheless, has grown in popularity (Bajada and Schneider, 2003; Chatterjee et al., 2002; Giles, 1999a and b; Giles and Tedds, 2002). Although adherents promote this approach as more sophisticated, the important point to consider is whether there is a 'gigo' effect (garbage in-garbage out). It is by no evident that the causes and indicators used in this model always and everywhere lead to the existence and growth of off-the-books working practices. For this reason, a cautious approach is urged.

Income/expenditure discrepancies

This approach evaluates differences in expenditure and income, either at the aggregate national level, or through detailed microeconomic studies of different types of individuals or households, premised on the assumption that even if off-the-books workers can conceal their incomes, they cannot hide their expenditures. An assessment of income/expenditure discrepancies thus supposedly reveals the extent of off-the-books work and who does it.

On the one hand, therefore, there have been aggregate level studies that analyze the discrepancy between national expenditure and income to estimate the size of off-the-books work. Such studies have been conducted in Germany (Langfelt, 1989), Sweden (Apel, 1994; Hansson, 1982, 1984; Park, 1979; Tengblad, 1994), Britain (O'Higgins, 1981), and America (Macafee, 1980; Paglin, 1994). On the other hand, others study income/expenditure discrepancies at the household level. In Britain, the Family Expenditure Survey (FES) has been analyzed (Dilnot and Morris, 1981; Macafee, 1980; O'Higgins, 1981).

Although this method has advantages over other indirect monetary methods, not least its reliance on relatively direct and statistically representative survey data, its problems remain manifold (Thomas, 1988, 1992; Smith, 1986). For the discrepancy to represent a reasonable measure of off-the-books work, one has to make a number of assumptions about the accuracy of the income and expenditure data. On the expenditure side, estimates depend on the accurate declaration of expenditure. Mattera (1985) suggests that it is somewhat naive to assume that this is the case. Equally convincing is the criticism that, for most people, spending is either over- or under-estimated during a survey, because records are kept by few members of the population compared with income, which for employees comes in regular recorded uniform instalments.

On the income side, these studies cannot decipher whether the income derives from criminal or off-the-books activities, or even whether it derives from wealth accumulated earlier, such as savings. In addition, and so far as studies such as the FES are concerned, there are problems of nonresponse as well as underreporting (Thomas, 1992). Consequently, the accuracy of this method is doubtful. Weck-Hannemann and Frey (1985) clearly display this when reporting that the

national income in Switzerland is larger than expenditure. According to this, Swiss off-the-books work is negative, which is nonsensical, and reveals that the discrepancy does not display the level of off-the-books work but is due to other factors.

Direct methods for detecting off-the-books work

Rather than use proxy indicators to evaluate the magnitude and/or character of off-the-books work, a parallel stream of research has directly investigated participation in this mode of work organization. Direct surveys involving mailshots and various forms of interview techniques have been used in Belgium (Pestieau, 1983, 1985; Kesteloot and Meert, 1999), Canada (Fortin et al., 1996), Germany (Frey et al., 1982), Italy (Bàculo, 2001; Censis, 1976), Norway (Isachsen and Strom, 1985), the Netherlands (van Eck and Kazemier, 1985; Renooy, 1990), Britain (Leonard, 1994; Pahl, 1984; Ram, 2002a and b; Williams, 2004), Sweden (Jönsson, 2001) and America (Ross, 1978; Jensen et al., 1995; Nelson and Smith, 1999; Tickamyer and Wood, 1998). Here we review the range of direct survey methods used by analyzing how they differ with regard to some key survey design issues.

Defining off-the-books work

Reviewing the reports of surveys, few explicitly communicate their definition of off-the-books work to respondents when asking them about their off-the-books transactions (an exception is Pedersen, 1998 and 2003). Instead, the norm has been to leave it to respondents to determine whether a task received or supplied has been conducted on an 'off-the-books' basis. The resultant problem is that one has no way of knowing whether respondents define off-the-books in the same manner as each other, or in the manner intended by the researchers. This is particularly a problem when investigating different populations who may have different views of what constitutes off-the-books work, such as people living in different nations or different immigrant groups living in the same nation.

Whether to use an explicit definition or whether to leave it to respondents to decide is a difficult choice. An explicit definition might help respondents to report activities which they otherwise might not have defined as off-the-books work, such as paid favours conducted for kin and acquaintances, or selling homemade products (in countries where these types of activities must be declared to authorities). On the other hand, an explicit definition might deter some from either participating in the interview, or from admitting to off-the-books work, since it highlights the unlawful character of the activities which they are reporting. The magnitude of this effect is likely to depend in part on the degree to which off-the-books work is deemed morally acceptable in the respondent's environment and on the interview situation itself. However, an important advantage of an explicit definition is that it allows for a clear distinction at the analysis stage between those facets which were covered and those which were not covered by the survey. In surveys not clearly defining the subject a priori, it is difficult to know which facets respondents had in mind when answering the questions.

However, it is important to enter the caveat that the definition of off-the-books work is, in part, a socially constructed phenomenon, where moral issues and limits of acceptability are judged differently by different individuals and groups in different contexts. For instance, the Asian restaurateurs interviewed by Ram et al. (2007) routinely evaded employment regulations, justifying this practice by arguing that it was a feature of the 'trade'.

Unit of analysis

To survey off-the-books work, studies can take either households or businesses as the unit of analysis. In practice, most take the household as the unit of analysis and request information from respondents, both as suppliers and purchasers of off-the-books work (e.g., Leonard, 1994; Pahl, 1984; Warde,

1990). Fewer have used the enterprise as a unit of analysis (for exceptions, see Fries et al., 2003; Ram et al., 2001, 2002a and b, 2003; Williams, 2006b), especially when asking questions about off-the-books work supplied.

Direct versus gradual approach

Another key decision is whether to approach this sensitive topic in a relatively direct manner or in a more gradual way. If approached in a direct manner, then questions on off-the-books work might be asked immediately after a general introductory section (e.g. on sociodemographic questions), or other more general questions. An advantage of this approach might be a certain 'overwhelming effect' on respondents (they might answer honestly, because they are unprepared for such questions on illicit activities and therefore have no time to prepare evasive answers). If approached in a more gradual manner, the subject is raised more slowly by first asking respondents about issues which are related to the subject, but which are not particularly sensitive (household activities, ways of organizing the maintenance of the home, general opinions on off-the-books transactions, etc.). Such 'warm-up' questions may help to establish a certain interest in the topic and create an atmosphere of confidence between interviewer and interviewee. The more sensitive 'core' questions about off-the-books work, such as whether and to what extent the respondent has either sold or bought services or goods on an off-the-books basis, might then be answered more openly when raised.

Reviewing previous survey designs, nearly all adopt a gradual approach. In some, for example, questions are first asked about their knowledge of and opinions on off-the-books work before asking about their own participation. In others, totally different topics are investigated, such as do-it-yourself activity, before moving onto questions on off-the-books work (Pedersen, 1998). In yet others, questions on off-the-books work are embedded in discussions of their overall household work practices. Thus, respondents are asked who last undertook specific domestic service tasks and whether self-provisioning was used and, if not, whether somebody outside the household conducted the work and, if so, whether they were paid or not. If they were paid, they are then asked whether they were paid 'off-the-books' or formally (Pahl, 1984; Leonard, 1994; Williams, 2004).

Data collection methodology

Data can be collected, moreover, through either mail-shot questionnaires (Fortin et al., 1996), telephone interviews (Jönsson, 2001) or face-to-face interviews of the unstructured (Bàculo, 2001; Howe, 1988) or structured variety (Williams, 2004), using either mostly open- or closed-ended questions. Most have used face-to-face interviews given the relatively sensitive nature of the topic. Reflecting the lack of data generally available, most have then employed relatively quantitative approaches composed largely of closed-ended questions, and then frequently employed a variety of more open-ended questions and/or qualitative methods for in-depth exploration of particular aspects (Leonard, 1994; Pahl, 1984). Even studies relying primarily on ethnography, such as Howe (1988), conduct some interviews as a quantitative precursor for their ethnographic material. Pahl (1984) in Britain, and Jönsson (2001) in Sweden, use follow-up in-depth interviews with a limited number of households to explore specific issues. Until now, online questionnaires have not been used so far as is known, except in mass media flash surveys. For example, visitors to a German real estate online portal were asked to complete a short online questionnaire asking for their opinion about informal work from a buyer's perspective.

In a study comparing the implications of different techniques, the finding was that different methods resulted in varying levels of off-the-books work being identified. In 1983 and 1984 in the Netherlands, Kazemier and van Eck (1992) compared the outcomes of direct and gradual approaches in combination with several data collection methodologies (face-to-face, mail, and telephone). With structured face-to-face interviews and a gradual approach, much higher rates of participation in informal work and higher average off-the-books incomes were identified than when a direct approach was employed. Among the eight different variants tested, face-to-face data collection with a gradual approach produced the highest levels of off-the-books work reported. Yet, in the case of mail and telephone surveys, the gradual approach did not produce higher results compared with the direct approach.

Supply- and/or demand-side?

A further issue when designing direct surveys is whether to ask respondents questions about off-the-books work solely from their position as customers and/or suppliers. Examining the surveys carried out in the past two decades, those examining the household have tended to ask about both the demand and supply side (Fortin et al., 1996; Isachsen et al., 1982; Lemieux et al., 1994; Williams, 2004), although some examine respondents only as purchasers (McCrohan et al., 1991; Smith, 1985). Most asking both supply- and demand-side questions, moreover, have tended first to pose questions about the demand-side, and then turn to the supply-side (Pahl, 1984; Williams, 2004). This is because the demand-side is widely viewed as more acceptable to discuss with respondents, and these questions thus serve as a kind of 'warm up' to questions regarding their supply of off-the-books work. Surveys using businesses as the unit of analysis, however, have so far tended to avoid asking questions about businesses as suppliers (Williams, 2006b).

Relationship between buyers and sellers

In recent years, greater interest has been taken in the relationship between the clients and providers of off-the-books work. This has been stimulated by a growing number of studies revealing that a large proportion of off-the-books work is conducted by and for kin, friends, and neighbours (Cornuel and Duriez, 1985; Jensen et al., 1995; Williams, 2004). The outcome is that Hanousek and Palda (2003), for instance, ask respondents whether the sale and purchase of off-the-books goods and services were for/by the following types of client; family members, friends, neighbours, colleagues from current or former job, own current or former employees, own current or former bosses – and others. Williams (2004) similarly distinguishes between whether work was conducted by/for kin, friends, neighbours, self-employed people previously known to them, and self-employed people or businesses not previously known to them. When such questions about the social relations involved between the supplier and customer are combined with questions regarding their reasons for engaging in such work, both as customers and suppliers, this distinction enables the social relations and motives underpinning off-the-books work to be investigated in much greater depth (Howe, 1990; Leonard, 1994; Williams, 2004).

Definition of the survey population

A further issue to be addressed is who is to be interviewed. Although direct surveys could be carried out on either national, regional, or local population samples, in most instances they have been applied to particular localities (Barthe, 1985; Fortin et al., 1996; Leonard, 1994; Pahl, 1984; Renooy, 1990; Warde, 1990; Williams, 2004), socioeconomic groups such as home-workers (Phizacklea and Wolkowitz, 1995) or industrial sectors such as garment manufacturing (Lin, 1995). Few nationally representative direct surveys have been conducted (an exception is Williams, 2006b), and even fewer cross-national comparative surveys (a notable exception is Pedersen, 2003).

Socio-demographic background information

Nearly all social surveys collect socio-demographic background information on their respondents to enable cross-tabulations to be produced regarding the socio-demographic structure. Direct surveys of off-the-books work are no different. An analysis of previous off-the-books surveys shows that there is a core set of socio-demographic variables

used in the majority of the studies: gender, age (at least in rough age groups), ethnicity, marital status, composition of the household (number of children and total household size), level of education, occupational status, income – usually for both the chosen individual and his/her household, and characteristics of the respondent's place of residence (e.g., urban or rural).

The reference period

A time limit is often put when asking questions about participation in off-the-books work, the most common being the past 12 months. In some surveys, the current year is the reference period. Some also ask questions about off-the-books work without imposing a time limit, which obviously leads to higher results. Hanousek and Palda (2003) ask about engagement in off-the-books activities in three reference years (2000, 1999, 1995) to obtain longitudinal data, and then refer all other questions to informal work conducted in the year 2000.

Net sample size

This depends on whether qualitative or quantitative methods are used. For the more extensive quantitative surveys, there are wide variations in terms of the number of interviews finally achieved (net sample size). Some surveys are based on only a few hundred interviews. Others are based on more than 20,000. The majority of the larger surveys, however, are in the range of about 1,000 to 2,000 net interviews. Considering the fact that in most countries only a relatively small minority of respondents will be engaged in off-the-books activities, this can be considered as an absolute minimum for any survey aimed at identifying the specific characteristics of those involved in off-the-books work.

Direct approaches in action

In this section, we illuminate the discussion on direct approaches to researching 'off the books' work by considering recent studies of employment relations in small firms (Jones et al., 2006; Ram et al., 2007).

Comparatively little is known of the internal workings of firms operating informally in the manner described earlier. The vast and eclectic literature on informal employment has shed light on a variety of issues, including measurement of the phenomenon; cross-national comparisons; the role of the state; spatial dynamics; alternative economic spaces (for example, local exchange trading schemes); differential impact on men and women; and evaluations of policy initiatives. For present purposes – particularly in relation to the objective of 'making visible the hidden' – a number of pertinent gaps remain. First, the particular ways in which informal firms are 'connected' to the wider economy is not readily understood. For example, in Britain, how does the informal economy continue to reproduce itself despite the presence of a raft of employment regulations aiming to encourage greater formality? Second, the precise ways in which employers operating 'informally' determine pay and working hours have rarely been marked out for particular attention. Some studies of 'informal' employers (Kloosterman et al., 1999; Bailey, 1987) identify practices such as the prevalence of long hours and low pay; workers tolerate these conditions because of an absence of labour market choice and a sense of obligation often rooted in paternalist management arrangements. Reinforcing this paternalistic binding of workers to bosses are various compensatory nonmonetary rewards, including relatively lax work discipline, individual negotiating leverage, and free food and transport (Ram et al., 2001a). Third, outside America, the participation of ethnic minorities in informal employment has rarely been documented. Indeed, the European literature on informal employment has been described as 'racially blind' (Williams and Windebank, 1998: 6).

Ram et al. (2007; see also Jones et al., 2006) addressed these gaps by taking a major labour market innovation, the introduction of the National Minimum Wage (NMW) in Britain in 1999, to explore the interplay between employment regulation and informal economic activity. They examined how ethnic minority employers (and workers) in the clothing and restaurant sector evaded it. In explaining the persistence of evasion, despite the arrival of the NMW, the authors found that pay practices were more likely to be determined by established norms in those trades than by official diktat. Firms using informal employment practices existed long before the arrival of the NMW, a single measure that was hardly likely to overturn deeply embedded practices. The most important considerations were market conditions, 'ability to pay', negative perceptions of state interference, and the absence of compelling pressures for wage increases from employees. The latter factor itself reflects the paternalistic bargain prevailing in such firms (often reinforced by coethnic ties and an absence of labour market choice). This informal status quo was further reinforced by the absence of any effective external deterrent from the state.

The methods adopted by Ram et al. (2007) are worth reflecting upon, not least for the implications that they have for conducting research in a particularly sensitive context. Perhaps surprisingly, concern about access and ethics are rarely evident in qualitatively oriented investigations of informal work. This may be due to the fact that those undertaking informal economic activities are not reluctant to share their experiences with researchers (Williams, 2004). For example, Leonard (1998) reports few problems in her study, based in Northern Ireland, of women operating in the informal economy. The self-employed workers interviewed by MacDonald (1994) were equally willing to reveal the 'fiddles' that were a routine part of their entrepreneurial activities. Snyder's (2003) study of 'autonomous' informal economy workers in a New York village suggests little reticence on the part of its respondents.

Yet, the study by Ram et al. clearly fell within the domain of 'sensitive' research, defined by Lee (1993: 2) as 'research which potentially poses a substantial threat to those who have been involved in it'. Lee specifies three elements to this threat. First, there is a *political* dimension. Many of the workers in the study were illegal immigrants. At the time of the study, illegal immigration (conflated in the public mind with asylum seeking) helped set the tone of an exceedingly negative British parliamentary election campaign pervaded by the politics of fear. Though certainly stoked by emotive media coverage, this mood also stemmed from conditions which are not, as Cohen (1995: 163) puts it, 'purely mythical'. Concern is justified by the fact that much undocumented migration is orchestrated via the global criminal economy, with people trafficking now bigger than drug trafficking (*The Economist*, 24 June 2000). An industry with £20 billion annual global turnover, by the late 1990s, it was already smuggling over 30 million migrants a year across international frontiers, with 400,000 of these making their way into the European Union (*The Economist*, 16 October, 1999).

The second potential threat of sensitive research relates to the study of *deviance and social control* and involves information that may be revealed which is stigmatizing or incriminating in some way. The central concern of Ram et al. was to understand why small business owners, and workers, were not complying with NMW legislation. In some cases, it was clear that these discussions were undertaken with individuals who were in the country illegally. During the course of the study, it was clear that labour market options were limited, confirming that Asian workers in these two sectors were effectively constrained, sometimes by their illegal status, poor qualifications, and lack of self-confidence, occasionally by language barriers, and also by the benefits trap. Moreover, self-imposed psychological barriers often reinforce entrapment, as one worker explained: 'Some are used to this job, environment and culture, it's all they know ... I stick to what I know ... I am too afraid to take the risk' [of moving to another employer]. Whatever its origins, the presence of this captive labour force was one of the major factors holding down wages and conditions in these restaurants and clothing firms.

The final source of threat was the potentially *intrusive* nature of the study; Ram et al. wanted to understand how respondents evaded employment regulations. The underdeclaration of earnings was a key factor, as one owner explained:

> We pay people a weekly wage, but we do not declare the whole amount as it is not beneficial for me or the staff as they will not be able to get maximum working tax credit. The lower the wages declared, the lower the turnover can be declared by the owners. Accountants who work for restaurant owners know how the system operates and they are basically our point of contact and how to manage the NMW. Everyone in this trade will, if they are honest, give you similar answers; some may be afraid of the consequences.

Ram et al. were able to minimize the three threats identified by Lee (1993) in two ways. First, they adopted the principle of informed consent; the subjects of the research were informed that they were being researched and also told about the nature of the research. Second, a 'chain referral', or network sampling, approach was adopted to securing research participants. Such an approach can be advantageous when studying vulnerable groups. As Lee (1993: 67) observes, 'Security features are built into the method, because the intermediaries who form the links of the referral chain are known to the potential respondents and trusted by them. They are thus able to vouch for the researcher's bona fides. Ram et al. enlisted the services of industry insiders who were fluent in the relevant languages. These intermediaries were fully apprised of the aims of the research, the types of employers and workers required, and the critical importance of confidentiality. The intermediaries' 'practical understanding' (Van Maanen, 1991) of the exigencies of small firms operating in the informal economy was, therefore, of vital importance in expediting the research.

This example highlights that, providing the political context of research is sensitively handled, research on excluded groups is feasible and capable of casting light on important academic and policy issues. Many of the problems associated with this kind of research – its perceived bias, marginality, and limited theoretical importance – can be countered. Appropriate contextualization, theoretically informed recruitment of research participants, and analytically oriented generalizations are key to responding to such challenges (see Penrod et al., 2003, for discussion of systematic approaches to researching hard to reach groups). This opens a means of incorporating excluded groups within the 'mainstream' of organization studies as, for example, Tomlinson (2005) has recently done in the case of 'partnership working' in agencies working with refugees.

Current controversies and trends

Today, as has been continuously the case for some three decades, the major controversy in this field concerns whether indirect or direct approaches are the more appropriate means of detecting off-the-books work.

Those advocating direct methods criticize the proxies of the indirect methods for being not only unreliable and inaccurate but also for providing very little information on the characteristics of this endeavour. They argue that these indirect methods are driven by crude assumptions concerning its nature that are far from proven (Thomas, 1992; Williams, 2004; Williams and Windebank, 1998). Indeed, indirect methods are increasingly argued to be redundant. In previous decades, when little empirical data was directly collected, such methods played an important role in highlighting the existence of this form of work organization. Today, however, the growing number of direct surveys suggests that indirect methods are no longer necessary (Williams, 2006a).

The major criticism that advocates of indirect approaches target at users of direct survey methods is that they naively assume that people will reveal to them, or even know, the character and magnitude of off-the-books work. It is intimated, on the one hand, that purchasers may not even know if such work is being offered on an off-the-books basis, and on the other hand, that sellers will be reticent about disclosing the nature and extent of their off-the-books working.

The former point might well be valid. For example, if purchasers have their external windows cleaned or buy goods from a market stall, they might assume that these exchanges are not being declared by the sellers when this is not necessarily the case, or vice versa. In other words, although consumers may often assume that goods and services bought in certain contexts are purchased on an off-the-books basis, while in other contexts they are not, their assumptions might not be correct. Goods acquired in formal retail outlets, for example, may not only have been produced on an off-the-books basis but may even be sold in such a manner (e.g., in illegally inhabited shop premises) without the knowledge of the consumer. Not all those dealing in cash, meanwhile, may necessarily be working on an off-the-books basis (e.g., they may not have confidence in the purchaser's cheques), just as some accepting cheques may be tax evaders. On the whole, therefore, although people who purchase goods and services may be more willing to reveal whether they think it has been bought on an off-the-books basis, they cannot necessarily be sure whether this is indeed the case unless the supplier tells them so.

However, it is not necessarily the case that those supplying off-the-books work will be untruthful in their dealings with researchers. Indeed, such a criticism has been refuted many times although it continues to be raised. As Bàculo (2001: 2) states regarding her face-to-face interviews, 'they were curious and flattered that university researchers were interested in their problems', and were more than willing to share their experiences. Pahl (1984) found that when the results from individuals as suppliers and purchasers were compared, the same level of off-the-books work was discovered. The implication, therefore, is that individuals are not secretive about the off-the-books work they supply. Just because it is activity hidden from or unregistered by the state for tax, social security, and/or labour law purposes does not mean that people will hide it from each other or even from academic researchers.

Similar conclusions have been reached about the openness of research participants in Canada (Fortin et al., 1996) and Britain (Evason and Woods, 1995; Leonard, 1994; MacDonald, 1994). As MacDonald (1994) reveals in his study of off-the-books work among the unemployed in a deprived region of Britain, 'fiddly work' was not a provocative subject from their perspective. They happily talked about it in the same breath as discussing, for instance, their experiences of starting up in self-employment or of voluntary work. This willingness of people to talk about their off-the-books work was also identified in Belfast (Leonard, 1994). Indeed, there are no grounds for assuming that businesses will not report their participation in off-the-books working practices. In one of the few direct surveys that asks businesses about the extent of their off-the-books practices, the 2002 EBRD/World Bank Business Environment and Enterprise Performance Survey, implemented in 26 countries of central and eastern Europe and the Commonwealth of Independent States (CIS), Fries et al. (2003) identify that it is wholly possible to collect such data. There have also been several qualitative surveys revealing the willingness of employers and employees to talk openly about their participation in off-the-books work (Jones et al., 2004; Ram et al., 2001, 2002a and b, 2003).

Turning to current trends, there is little doubt that the trajectory is towards the use of direct surveys. A consensus has emerged that carefully designed direct methods are the most appropriate means of investigating off-the-books work. This is the conclusion of OECD (2002) experts in their handbook on measurement methods, and the most recent European Commission report on undeclared work (Renooy et al., 2004), as well as a host of evaluations by national governments (e.g., ONS, 2005). For the moment, therefore, the popularity of indirect methods is in abeyance. Indeed, this is reflected in the fact that the European Commission have commissioned an evaluation of the feasibility of conducting a direct survey of undeclared work across the European Union, along with a pilot study (European Commission, 2005), as have national ministries, including Her Majesty's Revenue and Customs in Britain (HMRC, 2005).

Future trends and developments

This trajectory towards the use of direct methods does not mean, however, that the long-standing indirect methods are coming to an end. Instead, what appears to be happening is that the previous antagonisms between adherents to direct and indirect methods are being resolved as those who previously used indirect methods seek to identify ways of combining the two. Given the years of open conflict between these two methodologies, this is a significant move.

Two examples of how this is occurring are, first, the Brooking Institute's Urban Markets Initiative that is bringing together proponents of both the direct and indirect approaches to understand off-the-books work in American cities by combining direct and indirect methods (Brookings Institute, 2007), and second, an initiative by Social Compact, a group of American business leaders interested in investment opportunities in deprived urban neighbourhoods, who again wish to understand the size and character of the off-the-books economy to determine whether there are greater opportunities than so far estimated. The intention in both cases is to use the results of direct surveys to identify better proxy indicators of the off-the-books economy. Here, in consequence, direct survey methods are being used to improve indirect methods.

It should not be assumed, however, that this integrative approach is the likely future. It might be the case, as seems likely in Europe, that direct methods will simply replace indirect methods. Another alternative is that indirect and direct methods might be used separately but alongside each other with indirect methods used to measure the magnitude of the off-the-books economy (given the costs of direct surveys), while smaller direct surveys will be employed to unravel its character in terms of who does it and their motives. Indeed, in practice, this seems to be what is occurring. Indirect methods appear to be increasingly confining themselves to discussing the overall magnitude of the off-the-books economy and to say little on its character (Schneider and Enste, 2002), while direct methods are largely focusing upon the character of off-the-books work and saying little about its overall size (Ram et al., 2002a and b; Williams, 2004).

There also seems to be growing recognition of the need for more surveys that adopt businesses as the primary unit of analysis. The principal barrier, however, remains the continuing perception that businesses will be unwilling to discuss their participation in off-the-books work. Although this has been overcome in relation to households, this perception remains strong in relation to businesses. Where surveys have attempted to explore this issue, however, it has been revealed that, although businesses hide such endeavour from the state, they are often willing to discuss such issues with researchers (Fries et al., 2003; Ram et al., 2002a and b). In future, therefore, one may see a growing trend towards the wider use of business surveys, which ask them about their engagement in off-the-books transactions.

CONCLUSIONS

This chapter has provided a critical review of the research methods used to make visible a hidden form of work organization, namely off-the-books working practices. To do this, it has displayed the range of indirect methods that use proxy indicators and/or statistical traces of off-the-books work in data collected for other purposes, as well as how survey methods have attempted to directly investigate this issue, along with the problems involved in each method.

Reviewing the indirect methods that range from those using nonmonetary or monetary indicators, to analyses of income/expenditure discrepancies to determine the magnitude of off-the-books work, as well as the variety of direct survey methods that have been employed, it has been revealed that in recent years, there has been a growing rejection of

the validity of using indirect methods and a shift towards direct surveys in order to understand the extent and character of this form of work organization. The result is that the long-standing antagonism between adherents to indirect and direct approaches has started to decay as advocates of indirect methods have begun using direct methods to enhance their understanding of the variables to be used in their indirect models (see Bryman, Chapter 30, on mixed methods, this volume). Whether this marks a new direction for research in this field, however, is doubtful. It is more a reaction by those previously using indirect methods to the fact that their methods are in abeyance. It is more likely that there will be a continuing growth in the use of direct surveys, at first in the form of cross-national extensive quantitative surveys, as witnessed at a European level, followed by a renewed growth in in-depth qualitative surveys to explore the meanings and motives underpinning off-the-books work.

The challenges of researching informal work are of degree not kind. Researchers attuned to the political context of excluded groups have a genuine opportunity to pursue important theoretical and policy-related questions that cast light on the workings of the modern economy. The interdependency of 'formal' and 'informal' modes of organizing, the racialization of work, and the meaning of integration for newcomer populations, are key questions for future research. Organizational researchers have fertile terrain on which to apply their insights.

REFERENCES

Alden, J. (1982) 'A comparative analysis of moonlighting in Great Britain and the USA', *Industrial Relations Journal*, 13(1): 21–31.

Apel, M. (1994) *An Expenditure-Based Estimate of Tax Evasion in Sweden*, Stockholm: RSV Tax Reform Evaluation Report No.1.

Atkins F.J. (1999) 'Macroeconomic time series and the monetary aggregates approach to estimating the underground economy', *Applied Economics Letters*, 6(9): 609–11.

Bàculo, L. (2001) 'The shadow economy in Italy: results from field studies', Paper presented at the European Scientific Workshop on The Shadow economy: empirical evidence and new policy issues at the European level, Ragusa, Sicily, September 20–21.

Bailey, T. (1987) *Immigrant and Native Workers*, Boulder: Westview Press.

Bajada, C. and Schneider, F. (2003) *The Size and Development of the Shadow Economies in the Asia Pacific*, Linz: University of Linz Department of Economics discussion paper.

Barthe, M.A. (1985) 'Chômage, travail au noir et entraide familial', *Consommation*, 3(1): 23–42.

Bartlett, B. (1998) *The Underground Economy, National Center for Policy Analysis*, http://www.ncpa.org/ba/ba273.html.

Brookings Institute (2007) *Urban Markets Initiative: The Informal Economy*, http://www.brookings.edu/metro/umi/collaboratory/informaleconomy.htm (last accessed 21 February 2007).

Caridi, P. and Passerini, P. (2001) 'The underground economy, the demand for currency approach and the analysis of discrepancies: some recent European experience', *The Review of Income and Wealth*, 47(2): 239–50.

Carter, M. (1984) 'Issues in the hidden economy: a survey', *Economic Record*, 60(170): 209–21.

Censis (1976) 'L'occupazione occultra-carratteristiche della partecipazione al lavoro in Italia', cited in B.S. Frey and W.W. Pommerehne (1984), 'The hidden economy: state and prospects for measurement', *Review of Income and Wealth*, 30(1): 1–23.

Chatterjee, S., Chaudhury, K. and Schneider, F. (2002) *The Size and Development of the Indian Shadow Economy and a Comparison with 18 Asian countries: An Empirical Investigation*, Linz: University of Linz Department of Economics Discussion Paper.

Cocco, M.R. and Santos, E. (1984) 'A economia subterranea: contributos para a sua analisee quanticacao no caso Portugues', *Buletin Trimestral do Banco de Portugal*, 6(1): 5–15.

Cohen, R. (1995) 'International migration and the future of the nation state', *New Community*, 22: 139–64.

Contini, B. (1982) 'The second economy in Italy', in V.V. Tanzi (ed.), *The Underground Economy in the United States and Abroad*, Lexington, MA: Lexington Books.

Cornuel, D. and Duriez, B. (1985) 'Local exchange and state intervention', in N. Redclift and E. Mingione (eds), *Beyond Employment: Household, Gender and Subsistence*, Oxford: Basil Blackwell.

Crnkovic-Pozaic, S. (1999) 'Measuring employment in the unofficial economy by using labor market data', in E.L. Feige and K. Ott (eds), *Underground Economies in Transition: Unrecorded Activity, Tax Evasion, Corruption and Organized Crime*, Aldershot: Ashgate.

Dalton, M. (1959) *Men Who Manage*, New York: Wiley.

Del Boca, D. and Forte, F. (1982) 'Recent empirical surveys and theoretical interpretations of the parallel economy', in V. Tanzi (ed.), *The Underground Economy in the United States and Abroad*, Lexington, MA: Lexington Books.

Denison, E. (1982) 'Is US growth understated because of the underground economy?: employment ratios suggest not', *Review of Income and Wealth*, 28(1): 1–16.

Dilnot, A. and Morris, C.N. (1981) 'What do we know about the black economy?', *Fiscal Studies*, 2(1): 58–73.

Edwards, P. and Ram, M. (2006) 'Still living on the edge: marginal small firms, negotiated orders and the dynamics of the modern economy', *Journal of Management Studies*, 43(4): 895–916.

European Commission (1998) *Communication of the Commission on Undeclared Work*, http://europa.eu.int/comm/employment_social/empl_esf/docs/com98-219_en.pdf.

European Commission (2005) *Feasibility of a Direct Survey and Pilot Study of Undeclared Work in the European Union*, Brussels: European Commission.

Evason, E. and Woods, R. (1995) 'Poverty, deregulation of the labour market and benefit fraud', *Social Policy and Administration*, 29(1): 40–55.

Feige, E.L. (1979) 'How big is the irregular economy?', *Challenge*, November/December: 5–13.

Feige, E.L. (1990) 'Defining and estimating underground and informal economies', *World Development*, 18(7): 989–1002.

Feige, E.L. (1999) 'Underground economies in transition: non-compliance and institutional change', in E.L. Feige and K. Ott (eds), *Underground Economies in Transition: Unrecorded Activity, Tax Evasion, Corruption and Organized Crime*, Aldershot: Ashgate.

Fortin, B., Garneau, G., Lacroix, G., Lemieux, T. and Montmarquette, C. (1996) *L'Economie Souterraine au Quebec: Mythes et Realites*, Laval: Presses de l'Universite Laval.

Freud, D. (1979) 'A guide to underground economics', *Financial Times*, 9 April, 16.

Frey, B.S. and H. Weck (1983) 'What produces a hidden economy? an international cross-section analysis', *Southern Economic Journal*, 49(4): 822–32.

Frey, B.S., Weck, H. and Pommerhne, W.W. (1982) 'Has the shadow economy grown in Germany? an exploratory study', *Weltwirtschaftliches Archiv*, 118: 499–524.

Friedman, E., Johnson, S., Kaufmann, D. and Zoido, P. (2000) 'Dodging the grabbing hand: the determinants of unofficial activity in 69 countries', *Journal of Public Economics*, 76(3): 459–93.

Fries, S., Lysenko, T. and Polanec, S. (2003) *The 2002 Business Environment and Enterprise Performance Survey: Results from a Survey of 6,100 Firms*, EBRD Working Paper no. 84, www.ebrd.com/pubs/find/index.html.

Giles, D. (1999a) 'Measuring the hidden economy: implications for econometric modelling', *The Economic Journal*, 109(456): 370–80.

Giles, D. (1999b) *Modelling the hidden economy in the tax gap in New Zealand*. Victoria: Department of Economics, University of Victoria.

Giles, D. and Tedds, L. (2002) *Taxes and the Canadian Underground Economy*, Canadian Tax Paper No.106. Toronto: Canadian Tax Foundation.

Gutmann, P.M. (1977) 'The subterranean economy', *Financial Analysts Journal*, 34(11): 26–7.

Gutmann, P.M. (1978) 'Are the unemployed, unemployed?', *Financial Analysts Journal*, 34(1): 26–9.

Hanousek, J. and Palda, F. (2003) 'Why people evade taxes in the Czech and Slovak Republics: a tale of twins', in B. Belev (ed.), *The Informal Economy in the EU Accession Countries*, Sofia: Center for the Study of Democracy.

Hansson, I. (1982) 'The underground economy in Sweden', in V. Tanzi (ed.), *The Underground Economy in the United States and Abroad*, Massachusetts: Lexington Books.

Hansson, I. (1984) *Sveriges Svarta Sector. Berakning av Skatteundandragandet I Sverige*. Stockholm: RSV.

Hellberger, C. and Schwarze, J. (1986) Umfang und struktur der nebenerwerbstatigkeit in der Bundesrepublik Deutschland. Berlin: Mitteilungen aus der Arbeits-market- und Berufsforschung.

Henry, J. (1976) 'Calling in the big bills', *Washington Monthly*, 5: 6.

HMRC (2005) *The Design and Piloting of a Direct Survey of the Hidden Economy*, London: Her Majesty's Revenue and Customs.

Howe, L. (1990) *Being Unemployed in Northern Ireland: An Ethnographic Study*, Cambridge: Cambridge University Press.

Howe, L. (1988) 'Unemployment, doing the double and local labour markets in Belfast', in C. Cartin and T. Wilson (eds), *Ireland From Below: Social Change and Local Communities in Modern Ireland*, Dublin: Gill and Macmillan.

International Labour Office (2002) *Decent Work and the Informal Economy*, Geneva: International Labour Office.

Isachsen, A.J. and Strom, S. (1985) 'The size and growth of the hidden economy in Norway', *Review of Income and Wealth*, 31(1): 21–38.

Isachsen, A.J., Klovland, J.T. and Strom, S. (1982) 'The hidden economy in Norway', in V. Tanzi (ed.), *The Underground Economy in the United Sates and Abroad*, Lexington, KY: D.C. Heath.

Jensen, L., Cornwell, G.T. and Findeis, J.L. (1995) 'Informal work in nonmetropolitan Pennsylvania', *Rural Sociology*, 60(1): 91–107.

Jones, T., Ram, M. and Edwards, P. (2004) 'Illegal immigrants and the informal economy: worker and employer experiences in the Asian underground economy', *International Journal of Economic Development*, 6(1): 92–106.

Jones, T., Ram, M. and Edwards, P. (2006) 'Shades of grey in the informal economy', *International Journal of Sociology and Social Policy*, 26,9/10: 357–73.

Jönsson, H. (2001) 'Undeclared work in Sweden: results and recommendations', Paper presented at the European Scientific Workshop on The Shadow economy: empirical evidence and new policy issues at the European level, Ragusa, Sicily, September 20–21.

Kaufmann, D. and Kaliberda, A. (1996) 'Integrating the unofficial economy into the dynamics of post-socialist economies: a framework for analyses and evidence', in B. Kaminski (ed.), *Economic Transition in Russia and the New States of Eurasia*, London: M.E. Sharpe.

Kazemier, B. and van Eck, R. (1992) *Survey Investigations of the Hidden Economy: Some Empirical and Methodological Results*, Brussels: Economic Commission for Europe Statistical Division.

Kesteloot, C. and Meert, H. (1999) 'Informal spaces: the geography of informal economic activities in Brussels', *International Journal of Urban and Regional Research*, 23(2): 232–51.

Kloosterman, R., van der Leun, J. and Rath, J. (1999) 'Mixed embeddedness: (in)formal economic activities and immigrant businesses in the Netherlands', *International Journal of Urban and Regional Research*, 23: 252–66.

Kunda, G. (1992) *Engineering Culture*, Philadelphia: Temple University Press.

Lacko, M. (1999) 'Electricity intensity and the unrecorded economy in post-socialist countries', in E.L. Feige and K. Ott (eds), *Underground Economies in Transition: Unrecorded Activity, Tax Evasion, Corruption and Organized Crime*, Aldershot: Ashgate.

Langfelt, E. (1989) 'The underground economy in the Federal republic of Germany: a preliminary assessment', in E.L. Feige (ed.), *The Underground Economies: Tax Evasion and Information Distortion*, Cambridge: Cambridge University Press.

Lemieux, T., Fortin, B. and Frechette, P. (1994) 'The effect of taxes on labor supply in the underground economy', *American Economic Review*, 84(1): 231–54.

Leonard, M. (1994) *Informal Economic Activity in Belfast*, Aldershot: Avebury.

Leonard, M. (1998) *Invisible Work, Invisible Workers: The Informal Economy in Europe and the US*, London: Macmillan.

Lee, R. (1993) *Doing Research on Sensitive Topics*, London: Sage

Lin, J. (1995) 'Polarized development and urban change in New York's Chinatown', *Urban Affairs Review*, 30(3): 332–54.

Lobo, F.M. (1990) 'Irregular work in Portugal', in *Underground Economy and Irregular Forms of Employment, Final Synthesis Report*, Brussels: Office for Official Publications of the European Communities.

Macafee, K. (1980) 'A glimpse of the hidden economy in the national accounts', *Economic Trends*, 2(1): 81–7.

MacDonald, R. (1994) 'Fiddly jobs, undeclared working and the something for nothing society', *Work, Employment and Society*, 8(4): 507–30.

Mattera, P. (1985) *Off the Books: The Rise of the Underground Economy*, New York: St Martin's Press.

Matthews, K. (1982) 'The demand for currency and the black economy in the UK', *Journal of Economic Studies*, 9(2): 3–22.

Matthews, K. (1983) 'National income and the black economy', *Journal of Economic Affairs*, 3(4): 261–7.

Matthews, K. and Rastogi, A. (1985) 'Little mo and the moonlighters: another look at the black economy', *Quarterly Economic Bulletin*, 6(1): 21–4.

McCrohan, K., Smith, J.D. and Adams, T.K. (1991) 'Consumer purchases in informal markets: estimates for the 1980s, prospects for the 1990s', *Journal of Retailing*, 67(1): 22–50.

Meadows, T.C. and Pihera, J.A. (1981) 'A regional perspective on the underground economy', *Review of Regional Studies*, 11(1): 83–91.

Nelson, M.K. and Smith, J. (1999) *Working Hard and Making Do: Surviving in Small Town America*, Los Angeles: University of California Press.

O'Higgins, M. (1981) 'Tax evasion and the self-employed', *British Tax Review*, 26: 367–78.

OECD (2002) *Measuring the Non-Observed Economy*, Paris: OECD.

ONS (2005) *Identifying Sources on Entrepreneurship and the Informal Economy*, London: Office of National Statistics.

Paglin, M. (1994) 'The underground economy: new estimates from household income and expenditure surveys', *The Yale Law Journal*, 103(8): 2239–57.

Pahl, R.E. (1984) *Divisions of Labour*, Oxford: Blackwell.

Park, T. (1979) *Reconciliation Between Personal Income and Taxable Income (1947–1977)*, Washington, DC: Bureau of Economic Analysis.

Pedersen, S. (1998) *The Shadow Economy in Western Europe: Measurement and Results for Selected Countries: Study no.5*, Copenhagen: Rockwool Foundation Research Unit.

Pedersen, S. (2003) *The Shadow Economy in Germany, Great Britain and Scandinavia: A Measurement Based on Questionnaire Surveys*, Copenhagen: The Rockwool Foundation Research Unit.

Penrod, J., Preston, D., Cain, R. and Starks, M. (2003) 'A discussion of chain referral as a method of sampling hard-to-reach populations', *Journal of Transcultural Nursing*, 14(2): 100–7.

Pestieau, P. (1983) 'Belgium's irregular economy', paper presented to the *International Conference on the Economics of the Shadow Economy*, University of Bielefeld, West Germany, October 10–14.

Pestieau, P. (1985) 'Belgium's irregular economy', in W. Gaeartner and A. Wenig (eds), *The Economics of the Shadow Economy*, Berlin: Springer Verlag.

Phizacklea, A. and Wolkowitz, C. (1995) *Homeworking Women: Gender, Racism and Class at Work*, London: Sage Publications.

Portes, A. (1994) 'The informal economy and its paradoxes', in N.J. Smelser and R. Swedberg (eds), *The Handbook of Economic Sociology*, Princeton: Princeton University Press.

Portes, A. and Sassen-Koob, S. (1987) 'Making it underground: comparative material on the informal sector in Western market economies', *American Journal of Sociology*, 93(1): 30–61.

Ram, M., Edwards, P., Gilman, M. and Arrowsmith, J. (2001) 'The dynamics of informality: employment relations in small firms and the effects of regulatory change', *Work, Employment and Society*, 15(4): 845–61.

Ram, M., Edwards, P. and Jones, T. (2002a) *Employers and Illegal Migrant Workers in the Clothing and Restaurant Sectors*, London: DTI Central Unit Research.

Ram, M., Jones, T., Abbas, T. and Sanghera, B. (2002b) 'Ethnic minority enterprise in its urban context: South Asian restaurants in Birmingham', *International Journal of Urban and Regional Research*, 26(1): 24–40.

Ram, M., Gilman, M., Arrowsmith, J. and Edwards, P. (2003) 'Once more into the sunset?: Asian clothing firms after the National Minimum Wage', *Environment and Planning C: Government and Policy*, 71(3): 238–61.

Ram, M., Edwards, P. and Jones, T. (2007) 'Staying underground: informal work, small firms and employment regulation in the UK', *Work and Occupations*, 34(3): 318–44.

Renooy, P. (1990) *The Informal Economy: Meaning, Measurement and Social Significance*, Amsterdam: Netherlands Geographical Studies no.115.

Renooy, P., Ivarsson, S., van der Wusten-Gritsai, O. and Meijer, R. (2004) *Undeclared Work in an Enlarged Union: An Analysis of Shadow Work – An In-Depth Study of Specific Items*, Brussels: European Commission.

Ross, I. (1978) 'Why the underground economy is booming', *Fortune*, October: 92–8.

Santos, J.A. (1983) *A Economia Subterranea*. Lisbon: Minietrio do trabalho e seguranca social, Coleccao estudos, serie A, no.4.

Sassen, S. and Smith, R.C. (1992) 'Post-industrial growth and economic reorganisation: their impact on immigrant employment', in J. Bustamante, C.W. Reynolds and R.A. Hinojosa (eds), *US-Mexico Relations: Labour Markets Interdependence*, Stanford, CA: Stanford University Press.

Schneider F. (2001) 'What do we know about the shadow economy? Evidence from 21 OECD countries', *World Economics*, 2(4): 19–32.

Schneider, F. and Enste, D.H. (2002) *The Shadow Economy: An International Survey*, Cambridge: Cambridge University Press.

Sepulveda, L. and Syrett, S. (2007) 'Out of the shadows? formalisation approaches to informal economic activity', *Policy and Politics*, 35(1): 87–104

Smith, J.D. (1985) 'Market motives in the informal economy', in W. Gaertner and A. Wenig (eds), *The Economics of the Shadow Economy*, Berlin: Springer-Verlag.

Smith, S. (1986) *Britain's Shadow Economy*, Oxford: Clarendon.

Snyder, K. (2003) 'Working "off the books": patterns of informal market participation within New York's East Village',. *Socological Inquiry*, 73: 284–308.

Social Compact (2007) *Hidden in Plain Sight*, available at http://www.socialcompact.org/research.htm (last accessed 21 February 2007).

Tanzi, V. (1980) 'The underground economy in the United States: estimates and implications', *Banco Nazionale del Lavoro*, 135: 427–53.

Tanzi, V. (1982) (ed.) *The Underground Economy in the United States and Abroad*, Massachusetts: Lexington books.

Tengblad, A. (1994) *Berakning av svart ekonomi och skatteundandragandet I Sverige 1980–1991*, Stockholm: Arhundradets Skattereform.

Thomas, J.J. (1988) 'The politics of the black economy', *Work, Employment and Society*, 2(2): 169–90.

Thomas, J.J. (1992) *Informal Economic Activity*, Hemel Hempstead: Harvester Wheatsheaf.

Tickamyer, A.R. and Wood, T.A. (1998) 'Identifying participation in the informal economy using survey research methods', *Rural Sociology*, 63(2): 323–39.

Tomlinson, F. (2005) 'Idealistic and pragmatic versions of the discourse of partnership', *Organization Studies*, 26(2): 1169–88.

Trundle, J.M. (1982) 'Recent changes in the use of cash', *Bank of England Quarterly Bulletin*, 22: 519–29.

US Congress Joint Economic Committee (1983) *Growth of the Underground Economy 1950–81*, Washington, DC: Government Printing Office.

US General Accounting Office (1989) *Sweatshops in New York City: A Local Example of a Nationwide Problem*, Washington, DC: US General Accounting Office.

Van Eck, R. and Kazemeier, B. (1985) *Swarte Inkomsten uit Arbeid: resultaten van in 1983 gehouden experimentele*, Den Haag: CBS–Statistische Katernen nr 3, Central Bureau of Statistics.

Van Maanen, J. (1991) 'Playing back the tape: early days in the field', in W.B. Shaffir and R.A. Stebbins, (eds), *Experiencing Fieldwork*, Thousand Oaks, CA: Sage Publications.

Warde, A. (1990) 'Household work strategies and forms of labour: conceptual and empirical issues', *Work, Employment and Society*, 4(4): 495–515.

Weck-Hanneman, H. and Frey, B.S. (1985) 'Measuring the shadow economy: the case of Switzerland', in W. Gaertner and A. Wenig (eds), *The Economics of the Shadow Economy*, Berlin: Springer-Verlag.

Williams, C.C. (2004) *Cash-in-Hand Work: The Underground Sector and the Hidden Economy of Favours*, Basingstoke: Palgrave Macmillan.

Williams, C.C. (2006a) *The Hidden Enterprise Culture: Entrepreneurship in the Underground Economy*, Cheltenham: Edward Elgar.

Williams, C.C. (2006b) 'Evaluating the magnitude of the shadow economy: a direct survey approach', *Journal of Economic Studies*, 33(5): 369–85.

Williams, C.C. and Windebank, J. (1998) *Informal Employment in the Advanced Economies: Implications for Work and Welfare*, London: Routledge.

39

Producing a Systematic Review

David Denyer and David Tranfield

INTRODUCTION

The aim of this chapter is to provide guidance to scholars, practitioners, and policy makers who are engaged in producing, commissioning, or using reviews of research evidence in the field of management and organization studies. In contrast with many other natural and social science fields, inexperienced researchers, particularly doctoral students in management and organization studies, often receive relatively little training in conducting research reviews. Compared to the wealth of texts on philosophical approaches to social science research and methods for empirical investigation, there are few instructional texts on literature reviewing. This is surprising given the critical role that literature reviews play in doctoral theses and journal publications, and the potential role that they could play in creating and building bodies of knowledge and informing policy and practice (Tranfield et al., 2003). We argue that researchers in management and organization studies have a significant opportunity to evaluate and learn from many other fields that have developed an evidence-based approach using systematic review as a

key technique. However, different academic fields have idiosyncratic characteristics and as a result require the development of bespoke approaches specifically tailored to serve their particular purposes, forms, and applications.

Systematic review is a specific methodology that locates existing studies, selects and evaluates contributions, analyses and synthesizes data, and reports the evidence in such a way that allows reasonably clear conclusions to be reached about what is and is not known. A systematic review should not be regarded as a literature review in the traditional sense, but as a self-contained research project in itself that explores a clearly specified question, usually derived from a policy or practice problem, using existing studies. Additionally, systematic review also differs from other review methods because of its distinct and exacting principles. For example, in a systematic review, the researcher is required to set prespecified relevance and quality criteria for the selection/inclusion of studies and to make such criteria transparent to readers. Extensive searches are conducted to incorporate both published and unpublished studies. In terms of outcome, where studies provide consistent results, systematic reviews might be expected to provide solid and dependable evidence that is robust and has potential for transfer across different contexts. On the other hand, if the review identifies knowledge gaps or incongruent findings, then this signifies a research need and raises questions for future research.

Major improvements in review techniques over the last fifteen years or so have helped to raise the profile of systematic review as an important research methodology. Applications of systematic review in medical science have led the way and are often considered to reflect the most advanced thinking. A 'standard' approach to systematic review was developed initially in the medical field by the Cochrane Collaboration (2008), and has been followed later by other consortia dedicated to commissioning and disseminating systematic reviews.

A Systematic review has been argued to bring replicable, scientific, and transparent approach, which seeks to minimize bias (NHS Centre for Reviews and Dissemination, 2001) and requires reviewers to summarize all existing information about a phenomenon in a thorough and unbiased manner. More widely, systematic reviews have been argued also to have value in collating and synthesizing existing evidence across a wide range of settings (including the social sciences) and empirical methods (Petticrew, 2001).

On the otherhand the use of systematic review, particularly its traditional form, has been criticized when applied to the social sciences (Hammersley, 2001). Usually, these criticisms have centred on uncritical mimetic application encouraging the simple transfer of the medical model of systematic review, exemplified by the Cochrane Collaboration (2008), into other fields. Critics have placed four sets of arguments at the centre of this debate concerning:

- Competing ontological and epistemological positions related to the traditions of different disciplines.
- Different perspectives on the systematic review methodology regarding the types of study to be included in a review.

- The extent to which systematic review methods can or should be proceduralized and the extent to which bias can be reduced or mitigated.
- The validity and reliability of synthesized evidence produced by systematic reviews, and how such evidence is used subsequently to inform policy, practice, and future research.

Other critics have suggested that evidence-based management is overtly managerialist (Learmonth and Harding, 2006) and fails to take into account situated judgement and ethics (Morrell, 2008). They also express a concern that evidence-based management and systematic review privileges certain types of research and other forms, such as critical theory, are precluded.

We appreciate many of these concerns and challenges and take the view that it is unwise to adopt, in an uncritical fashion, that which has proved useful in other fields. Consequently, out purpose in this Chapter is to explain how and in what ways the notion of evidence-based management might benefit the field through improved quality and rigour, by defining a bespoke and fit for purpose format for review. Differences in context are vital, for example, in medicine, there has been a general consensus regarding what constitutes an appropriate methodology to be used for evaluating evidence from primary studies to be included (Evans, 2003). In fields where the value of quantitative, qualitative, and theoretical contributions are equally respected (such as management and organization studies), reviewers are likely to need more inclusive and comprehensive quality criteria and novel approaches to research synthesis. Such inherent epistemological diversity necessitates an alternative to 'Cochrane-style' systematic reviews. Therefore, we argue for the development of a bespoke and fit for purposed methodology, which can cope with the variety and richness of research designs, purposes, and potential end uses of management and organization studies reviews.

Despite these differences our point of departure is that systematic review methodology has proved demonstrably worthwhile in many natural and social science fields, and that would be wise to consider the lessons researchers in management and organization studies already learned. Consequently, this chapter first outlines the principles of systematic review developed elsewhere and evaluates their relevance for the field of management and organization studies. We discuss both the origins of systematic review and its roots in evidence-based policy and practice and also examine the methodological challenges to developing an evidence base in management and organization studies. We note that some of the key principles of systematic review that are manifest in fields such as medicine, often remain elusive and perhaps undesirable for the field of management and organization studies. Second, and on the basis of this considered reflection, we offer a revised and (to an extent) alternative framework and set of principles for developing transparent, inclusive, explanatory and heuristic reviews for use in our field. Finally, we explore how the output from systematic reviews might be used to inform policy, practice and further research. In doing so, we argue that the methods of review should be selected according to the purpose and the nature and characteristics of the field of study (e.g. degree of fragmentation, plurality of methods, etc) and the nature of the evidence available. We argue the case for combining the many facets of systematic review with aspects of realist synthesis (Pawson, 2006). Harnessing the strength of both of these approaches offers an important methodology for management and organization studies that has the potential to inform policy, practice, and future research.

The origins and principles of systematic review

The idea of reviewing existing research studies for the purpose of informing policy, practice, and research is not new. However, over recent years, there has been a proliferation of formal approaches and systematic methods for locating, selecting, appraising, synthesizing, and reporting evidence. This can be seen as a response to the increasing demands to organize knowledge into a format that is rigorous and reliable as well as make a difference to practice. Evidence-based practice requires decision making and action to be informed by the best and robust evidence produced by high-quality research studies. In addition to the traditional approach of conducting new empirical studies, many natural and social science fields have turned to reviews of existing primary studies reported in the literature to address important and pressing questions. In this demanding context, systematic review increasingly has become a standard method for locating, selecting, and appraising research and transferring the synthesized findings not only to researchers and academics but also to practitioners and policymakers in a digestible format to inform action.

Evidence-based policy and practice (EBPP) constitutes a movement that can be traced to the early 1970s (Cochrane, 1972). EBPP in medicine can be defined as the 'conscientious, explicit and judicious use of current best evidence in making decisions' about the care of individual patients (Sackett et al., 1996: 1). Since the early 1980s, researchers in health care have been engaged in a programme of systematic reviews on the effectiveness of interventions. The Cochrane Collaboration was formed in 1992 to gather, evaluate, and disseminate research evidence and developed a sophisticated and substantial set of guidelines for conducting systematic reviews. Since then, researchers have developed and refined the systematic review methodology with the aim of improving both the rigour and reliability of the review process, and organizing knowledge into a useable format. The results of systematic reviews have become well established as legitimate evidence on which to base policy and practice. Websites, such as the Cochrane database (2008b), now offer clinicians a practical solution to the problem of staying up to date with the latest research.

Given the relative success of evidence-based approaches in medicine, the core principles, processes, and practices of systematic review have been adopted elsewhere. As Petticrew (2001: 99) argues:

> ...systematic review is an efficient technique for hypothesis testing, for summarizing the results of existing studies, and for assessing the consistency among previous studies; these tasks are clearly not unique to medicine.

Following this line of thinking, the Campbell Collaboration was formed in 1999 to establish the systematic review process in the broader public policy arena (Campbell Collaboration, 2008). The Evidence for Policy and Practice Information and Co-ordinating Centre (EPPI-Centre) conducts systematic reviews in many fields, including education and social care, and has developed an approach for addressing a broad range of review questions and incorporating both quantitative and qualitative evidence.

In general terms most fields using, systematic review prescribe that studies are expected to conform to a set of principles as well as adopting specific methods to identify, select, and critically appraise relevant primary research, before it is appropriate to extract and analyse data from the studies that are included in the review (NHS Centre for Reviews and Dissemination, 2001).

In the following section, we outline the four core principles traditionally applied to a standard systematic review template. Reviews are expected to be: replicable, exclusive, aggregative, and algorithmic. We then contrast these with a suggested set of principles for systematic reviews in management and organization studies.

Replicable

A first key principle suggests that the general methodological characteristics of systematic review reflect an epistemology stipulating that knowledge should be acquired through a 'scientific', objective using an unbiased process. Systematic reviews, particularly those associated with the Cochrane Collaboration, attempt to avoid or to mitigate bias. As such, 'systematic reviews have been developed to synthesize research according to an explicit and reproducible methodology' (Greenhalgh, 1997). As in any scientific endeavour, the methods to be used are required to be established beforehand (Light and Pillemer, 1984). Consquently, prior to a systematic review being undertaken, a protocol is produced to detail precisely how the review will be conducted. The protocol is analogous to and as crucial as a research design for an empirical study (Antman et al., 1992; Cook et al., 1997). In medicine and other fields, review protocols must be developed and approved before the systematic review can commence. Reviewers are encouraged to publish their draft protocols (sometimes on these websites) allowing interested parties to provide feedback. While the intention should be that a review will adhere to the published protocol, it is acknowledged that the review protocol may need to be changed during the course of the review. If modifications are made to the protocol, they must be documented explicitly and explained (Higgins and Green, 2006).

Systematic reviews have a clearly defined methods section with each step of the systematic review rigorously reported. Justifications are given for all decisions taken by the reviewer. The aim is to mitigate the preformed opinions that can bias his/her assessments of both the relevance and validity of articles in a review (Cooper and Hedges, 1994). Only studies that meet the inclusion and exclusion criteria are included in the review. The reviewer also needs to discuss whether or not all relevant studies were identified, whether or not all relevant data could be obtained, and whether or not the methods used (for example, searching, study selection, data extraction, and analysis and reporting) could have introduced bias. The aim is for systematic reviews to:

> ...bring the same level of rigour to reviewing research evidence as should be used in producing that research evidence in the first place (Davies and Crombie, 2001: 1).

The use of explicit, systematic methods in reviews has been argued both to help produce

more reliable results upon which to draw conclusions and make decisions (Antman et al.,
1992). Cooper and Hedges (1994: ix) also
argue that the 'intended result is a research
synthesis that can be replicated by others'.

However, within a review of social science
literature, it is generally recognized that
professional judgment and interpretation play
an important role and cannot be eliminated or
replaced by proceduralization. Hammersley
(2001: 6) argues that:

> ...insisting that people follow a set of procedures
> rigidly can be a hindrance. Literally, it may rule out
> any reflection on issues that actually need attention,
> encouraging a rather pragmatic orientation. And
> this is especially likely where the time available for
> producing a review is very limited. As Polanyi points
> out, science, like many other activities, relies on
> skilled judgement, the capacity for which is built up
> through experience; and skilled judgement means
> taking account of particulars, and will often involve
> apparently breaking the rules.

Exclusive

A second key principle requires that if
systematic reviews are to inform policy,
practice, and future research, they should
synthesize the best evidence available (Slavin,
1986). In systematic reviews, the validity of
a study is governed by the extent to which
its design and conduct are likely to prevent
systematic errors, or bias (Moher et al., 1995).
A review:

> ...should always focus on the best available
> evidence: that is, studies to be included in a
> review should use methods that provide the least
> biased answer to the question asked (Counsell,
> 1997: 380).

The Cochrane Reviewers' Handbook
(Higgins and Green, 2006) and the NHS
Centre for Reviews and Dissemination
guidelines (2001) both suggest that quality
relates to the extent to which the study
minimizes bias and maximizes internal
and external validity. Relevant studies are
critically evaluated to assess their quality
using checklists that are included in the
protocol along with details of how the
checklist was used in the study.

**Table 39.1   The hierarchy of evidence in
medical science (Davies, Nutley and Smith,
1999: 11)**

I-I	Systematic review and meta-analysis of two or more double blind randomized controlled trials.
I-2	One or more large double-blind randomized controlled trials.
II-1	One or more well-conducted cohort studies.
II-2	One or more well-conducted case-control studies.
II-3	A dramatic uncontrolled experiment.
III	Expert committee sitting in review; peer leader opinion.
IV	Personal experience.

Typically, systematic reviews in medicine
adopt a hierarchy of evidence (Table 39.1)
that ranks research designs according to
their internal and external validity. Studies
are selected on the basis of relevance for
inclusion (ideally assessed by two reviewers).
In the medical field, randomized controlled
trials are regarded as the 'gold standard'
for judging 'what works' (Evans, 2003).
For example, Oakley (2000: 318, quoting
Macdonald, 1996: 21) claims that anything
except randomized controlled trials 'is a
"disservice to vulnerable people"'.

Whilst most evidence in medicine is made
available in quantitative form, a number of
systematic reviews include evidence from
qualitative studies. Consequently, a set of
quality standards for qualitative research
have been developed (see, for example,
Harden et al., 1999; Oliver et al., 2005;
Popay et al., 1998) although the matter
of what constitutes appropriate standards to
apply to qualitative research still remains
contested. More usually, evidence from
qualitative studies is rarely included in the
actual synthesis process, and is more usually
descriptively summarized in the systematic
review report. Whilst efforts have been
made to incorporate qualitative evidence in
medical science, there remains a privileging of
quantitative over qualitative research (Dixon-
Woods et al., 2005).

In the field of management and organization
studies, there is a plurality of accepted
methods and approaches. Whilst this variety is
often regarded as a weakness, it also provides

diversity and richness which are a major strengths considering that:

> Organizations are fuzzy, ambiguous, complex socially constructed systems that cannot be well understood from a single perspective (Denyer et al., 2008).

However, there is no doubt that there is little agreement over what represents high quality evidence across this field (Tranfield and Starkey, 1998) and certainly there is robust opposition to prioritizing one research method over another.

Aggregative

The third key principle suggests that alongside systematic review, statistical meta-analysis has become the preferred approach to research synthesis in many domains. A meta-analysis extracts and aggregates data from separate studies to increase the effective sample size, in order to calculate an overall effect size for an intervention. In order to perform a meta-analysis, it is important to identify whether or not results from studies are consistent one with another (i.e. homogeneous) or inconsistent (e.g. heterogeneous). Data from individual studies are extracted and tabulated in systematic review reports to display the impact of potential sources of heterogeneity, e.g., study type, study quality, and sample size.

If the data extracted from these studies meet certain requirements (the most important being a high level of homogeneity of effect measures across studies) then they can be aggregated. Pooling data provides a larger sample, increasing the possibility of detecting real effects that individual smaller studies are unable to ascertain. However, aggregating studies can also cause problems if the researcher fails to account for subtle differences in study design and study context, since it is possible to reveal minor biases as well as true effects.

Therefore, a key problem with aggregative synthesis is that primary studies are rarely entirely homogeneous. However, there are strong arguments that studies can be pooled despite subtle differences in effects or lack of correspondence in the populations or study contexts such as variation in form of implementation, measured outcomes, or contextual factors that influence observed effects (Rousseau et al., 2008). Yet, the danger remains that unless primary studies carefully report implementation processes and context, aggregative syntheses can mask the mechanisms underlying effects (Pawson, 2002). Advocates of meta-analysis (Rauch and Frese, 2006; Shadish and Sweeney, 1991) argue that heterogeneity can be dealt with by including mediators and moderator variables into statistical techniques. A mediator is an intermediate variable that links an intervention with an outcome. A moderator accounts for contextual differences, either in terms of the population or the circumstances. A host of demographic and contextual factors can be specified and accounted for in the analysis. The problem with this technique is that each of the likely mediators and moderators must be identified at the outset of the review, and it is likely that in a managerial and organizational context the list of variables could be extensive. Further, each of the studies included in the review must have comparable mediators and moderators, thus severely limiting the number of studies on any specific topic that are amenable to aggregative synthesis.

Additionally, despite advances in meta analytical techniques, many questions are not amenable to aggregative approaches. In complex systems comprised of a large variety of dynamically interacting variables such as can be found in management and organizational studies, the value of statistical synthesis adopted as a single point solution is often questionable. Many systematic reviews, even in medicine, do not contain a meta-analysis. Dixon-Woods et al. (2006) assert that alternative approaches to synthesis, including qualitative techniques, can be incorporated into systematic reviews.

Algorithmic

In health care, systematic reviews tend to focus on questions relating to the effectiveness of interventions. A large number of reviews provide a comparison of two or more alternative treatments to identify which is the most effective. Systematic reviews in medical science tend to address specific questions structured according to three features; the population, the intervention, and the outcomes. A review may focus on very specific population groups by addressing factors such as the age and sex of the patients or the severity of their illness. Reviews may also specify a particular setting of interest such as whether people are living in the community or are hospitalized (NHS Centre for Reviews and Dissemination, 2001). The interventions are often the treatments given to the populations of interest, which are usually a particular therapy, prevention, diagnosis, or screening (Higgins and Green, 2006). The resulting outcomes are specific, measurable clinical and economic factors that are used for comparison. In some instances, the study designs to be included in the review are also specified. An example of a well-formatted review question is provided in the Cochrane Handbook (Higgins and Green, 2006: 62):

> ...whether a particular antiplatelet agent, such as aspirin, [intervention] is effective in decreasing the risks of a particular thrombotic event, stroke, [outcome] in elderly persons with a previous history of stroke.

Such algorithmic guidelines provide a procedure (a finite set of well-defined instructions) for overcoming a condition and accomplishing a defined outcome. Algorithmic rules require limited redesign for use in practice (van Aken, 2005). The problem with this approach is that it seeks to identify what works without sufficient knowledge of why an intervention works or the particular conditions of success (Pawson, 2006). To achieve richer understanding often requires practitioners to integrate evidence with their knowledge of local circumstances and the preferences of the end user. Therefore, it is usually thought wise for mature users of systematic reviews to decide how appropriate the evidence is to their

particular circumstances in order to obtain optimum benefit.

Methodological challenges

A review of the literature in the field of management and organization studies is typically the first step in the process of doing scientific research, and is usually presented as either a brief introduction to an empirical study or as an extensive detailed account of a body of literature (see *Academy of Management Review* or the *International Journal of Management Reviews* for examples). Reviewing in management and organization studies is particularly challenging due to the fragmented nature of the field (Whitley, 1984) and also its transdisciplinarity (Tranfield et al., 2003). It is a field in which many separate sub fields can generate idiosyncratic questions, hypotheses, methodologies, and conclusions (Baligh et al., 1996). Subfield academic communities easily detach from identification with the whole and can often engage in their research unaware of work in associated areas:

> The complicated state of MOS (Management and Organization Studies) research makes it tough to know what we know, especially as specialization spawns research communities that often don't and sometimes can't talk with each other. Organizational researchers commonly adopt positions regarding management practices and organizational decisions for which no accumulation of evidence exists, or where at least some of the evidence is at odds (Rousseau et al., 2008: 477).

Tranfield et al. (2003) argue that management research is a nascent field still developing in terms of agenda and focus. In contrast with more mature fields, such as medicine or engineering, management research does not enjoy consensus on research methods and convergence on research questions. Accordingly, researchers tend to ask and to address a steady flow of questions rather than integrate and build coherent knowledge stocks or seek further understanding of particular phenomena. Vastly increasing volumes of management research, coupled with the potential of information technologies, has meant recently that synthesizing diverse literatures and accumulating a knowledge base serving both the research and practitioner communities, has become an increasingly topical challenge.

In addition to informing the research community, a review of existing research evidence has the potential to guide practitioners by providing ideas, information, examples, and recommendations for practice. So why have practicing managers so far rarely used systematic review to improve their performance? First, practicing managers rarely have access to academic journals or posses the skills required to interpret and appraise research evidence. Second, many reviews have been framed to answer theoretical questions for academics and do not address the problems that managers face in their work roles. The aim of academic reviews is to position an empirical study within an established body of knowledge. According to Wallace and Wray (2006) such reviews relate to one or more explicit or, more typically, implicit review questions that may be substantive (about some aspect of the social world), theoretical (about concepts, perspectives, theories, or models that relate to some aspect of the social world), or methodological (about the approach to conducting an empirical or theoretical enquiry). A traditional review seeks an understanding of the nature of the field, the major issues and debates about the topic, how the field has been structured and organized, the key theories, concepts and ideas, and the ways in which the field has been researched to date (Hart, 1998). Such reviews usually tackle knowledge problems and focus on analysis and explanation, and on problems and their causes (Denyer et al., 2008). Such research 'criticizes everyday accounts and practices ... but does not seek to transform them except in the general sense of demonstrating their incorrectness' (Whitley, 1984: 372).

Denyer et al. (2008) argue that, if the product of a review is intended to be used by practitioners and policy makers, then it should address field problems, that is the problems faced by professionals such as clinicians, engineers, lawyers, and managers in their work roles, rather than focusing on pure knowledge problems. In so doing, they argue that systematic reviews in management and organization studies can produce knowledge of use to managers in providing insight or designing solutions to field problems.

Revised principles for management and organization studies?

A number of authors have argued that the field of management and organization studies might benefit from the adoption of systematic review methods (Briner, 2000; Pittaway et al., 2004; Tranfield et al., 2003). However, Tranfield et al. (2003) voice a concern that the adoption of Cochrane-style systematic review is questionable and potentially undesirable for use in the field of management and organization studies, arguing that a revised and fit for-purpose systematic review methodology might be more appropriate. However, it has remained unclear precisely which elements of the standard systematic review template should remain unaltered, which facets require amendment, what should be refuted, and what needs to be added for effective use in the field of management and organization studies. Reviews in medical science, we have noted, are based on four core principles, but all of them have limitations when applied to management and organization studies. Consquently, we now offer, four alternative principles for systematic reviews for use in management and organization studies. We suggest reviews be tested for their transparency, inclusivity, explanatory, and heuristic nature.

Transparency

Concerning our first key principle, we contend that the reasons for documenting the review methods is not to achieve replication or eradication of bias, as in a Cochrane-style review, but rather to aid transparency (Tranfield et al., 2003). We believe that there are three aspects to transparency in a systematic review.

First, reviewers must be open and explicit about the processes and methods employed in the review. This enables readers to determine precisely its scope and boundaries. Throughout the review, the steps undertaken need to be specified, applied, recorded, and monitored (Tranfield et al., 2003). For example, the practice of making the review methods explicit before the review commences is a constructive exercise. Producing a review protocol enables the reviewer to gain feedback on the proposed methods and highlight any obvious errors or omissions so that they can be amended or rectified. Including a methodology section in the systematic review report enables readers to determine precisely the scope and boundaries of the review. It also provides an audit trail and enables the review to be updated and appraised in the future. A systematic review protocol does not mean that the predetermined methods are set in stone. It is important that the protocol does not restrict the review and it is quite normal for reviewers to alter the protocol during the course of conducting the review. A reviewer may, for example, find a body of work that they had not foreseen or alternatively for which they may wish to alter the selection criteria as their understanding of the field develops. In such circumstances, the protocol can be used to document and justify these changes. In the final systematic review methodology section, it is customary to produce an overview of the main changes between the original and final protocols.

The second expression of transparency concerns the presentation of the findings of the review in such a way that there are clear links between the evidence found and the reviewers' conclusions and recommendations. As noted by Slavin (1986: 17):

> No review procedure can make errors impossible or eliminate any chance that reviewers' biases will affect the conclusions drawn. However, applications of best-evidence synthesis should at least make review procedures clear to the reader and should provide the reader with enough information about the primary research on which the review is based to reach independent conclusions.

A clear audit trail is required linking the claims made by the authors of the review with the existing evidence. According to Pawson (2006: 79):

> ...other researchers, decision makers and other stakeholders can look behind an existing review, to assure themselves of its rigour and validity, reliability and verifiability of its findings and conclusions.

The third element to transparency necessitates the reviewer making clear the assumptions underpinning the review and engaging in a mindful questioning of a priori beliefs regarding the scope and implications of relevant research. In conducting a review, particularly problem specification, study selection and synthesis, the reviewer necessarily falls back on their values, prejudices, and beliefs. Wallace and Wray (2006: 88) argue that the 'authors' explicit or implicit values about some aspect of the social world, their theorizing, research methodology, and methods may affect their focus and the nature of the knowledge claims that they make'.

In particular, the reviewer's prior knowledge of the literature may influence the review. At worst, 'a reviewer may simply build a case in support of their personal beliefs, selectively citing studies along the way' (Davies and Crombie, 2001: 2). As such, it is important that reviewers make explicit their value stance towards the aspect of the social world they are studying (Wallace and Wray, 2006).

Inclusivity

Our second key principle emphasizes that systematic reviewers in the field of organization and management are likely to encounter difficulties when appraising the quality of information sources. Authors of articles, even those published in some of the highest impact journals, sometimes fail to report on the methods of data collection and analysis in sufficient detail, rendering impossible attempts to assess study quality. Within management and organization studies, there is also little uniformity in methods of data collection and analysis. Studies rarely address identical questions and samples vary in terms of the populations, sizes, study context, and the data reported.

Boaz and Ashby (2003: 4) suggest that rather than a hierarchy of evidence, the selection of articles can be based on the criterion 'fit for purpose'; this, 'helps us to get away from the technocratic preoccupation with elegant research designs and allows for notions of appropriateness to be added into the appraisal of research'. Pawson (2006) also argues that the researcher should simply ask whether or not the literature retrieved adds anything new to our understanding of the intervention. Pawson's approach has no hierarchy of evidence. The worth of the study can only be determined through the synthesis by evaluating each study's contribution to theory building, prioritizing the vital evidence from primary studies as the original researchers' interpretations and explanations, not just the results. Hence, Pawson encourages the scope of the review to include a wide range of studies, research types and data forms to promote a full understanding of the phenomenon of interest.

Salipante et al. (1982) have also argued that the inclusion of a broad variety of sources in a review can compensate for researcher value judgments and uncontrolled validity threats. Heterogeneity also makes possible the investigation of contextual factors influencing the study's design and its findings. They argue that the more heterogeneous the distribution of uncontrolled validity threats in a set of similar findings, the greater the validity of the findings from the set. Following this logic, we suggest that reviewers in management and organization studies should beware of excluding studies solely on the basis of adherence to the pursuit of absolute epistemological standards. In particular, reviewers are best advised to guard against using proxies for research quality such as the quality rating of journals as a basis for exclusion. We do, however, agree that systematic reviewers in management and organization studies devise quality checklist(s) appropriate to

the subfield(s) involved, justify the reasons for inclusion/exclusion of studies, apply the criteria to all relevant studies, and communicate the warrants underpinning their claims (Wallace and Wray, 2006).

Explanatory

Our third key principle addresses the vexing question of synthesis. The evidence-based community in the UK (see for example the Evidence Network website: http://www. evidencenetwork.org/) has been working hard to develop several alternative approaches to meta-analysis as a mode of synthesis. Particularly, progress has been made in narrative reviewing (see Popay et al., 2006; Greenhalgh et al., 2005) and the use of the metaethnographic approach of Noblit and Hare (1982; see Campbell et al., 2003). Evidence syntheses using these approaches are tasked with the construction of larger narratives and more generalizable theory (Estabrooks et al., 1994; Sandelowski et al., 1997). Interpretive and explanatory synthesis extracts descriptive data and exemplars from individual studies, building them into a mosaic or map (Hammersley, 2004). The reviewer is involved in juxtaposing the evidence, which can be quantitative, qualitative, or theoretical, from one study with that of another.

Unlike aggregative synthesis which seeks to avoid or mitigate bias, interpretive and explanatory syntheses are 'active' and 'creative' methods (Pawson, 2006) that go beyond a descriptive reporting of the evidence. The process is one of conceptual innovation and reinterpretation (Campbell et al., 2003), while attempting to preserve the original study's integrity or wholeness (Pawson, 2006). As such, the synthesis provides a feasible explanation of the study findings rather than a replicable explanation (Noblit and Hare, 1988). Therefore, synthesis involves the process of bringing the pieces from individual texts together to make a whole that should be more than the sum of the parts.

Pawson (2006) has introduced the notion of realist synthesis by using existing primary studies to build a nascent theory of how an intervention may work. This will include 'conjectures on the generative mechanisms that change behaviour, ideas on the contexts that influence its operation, and hunches about the different outcome patterns that ensue' (Pawson, 2006: 73). The texts that are to be included in the synthesis are 'regarded as case studies, whose purpose is to test, revise and refine the preliminary theory' (Pawson, 2006: 74). The review entails the systematic organization of the data into formats that allow summary. This body of evidence is then probed, sifted, coded, and cross tabulated in numerous ways. Each relevant published article is described and discussed in terms of its contribution to the emerging theory (Pawson, 2002: 345):

> ...the reviewer's basic task is to sift through the mixed fortunes of a programme attempting to discover those contexts (C+) that have produced solid and successful outcomes (O) from those contexts (C) that induce failure (O-). The review process is then repeated across a number of additional studies featuring the same underlying mechanism (M), with the aim of gathering together the various permutations of success and failure ... the aim is to differentiate and accumulate evidence of positive and negative CMO configurations.

Generalization is sought not in terms of the associations among variables but in terms of the role and impact of generative mechanisms that play out in different ways over time.

Heuristic

The output of a systematic review in management will allude to what works, and to why or how the relation occurs and in what circumstances, but is likely to be relatively abstract and is best regarded by the practitioner as a 'design exemplar' (van Aken, 2005). Given the complexity of organizational settings, such outputs are likely to be heuristic. A heuristic rule may help in solving a problem, but is not guaranteed to provide a detailed solution. Outputs of systematic review in management and organization studies are likely to be rules, suggestions, guides, or prototype protocols that may be useful in making progress toward a solution of a problem rather

than providing a detailed solution to a specific problem. Heuristic rules will almost always require the application of informal judgment or experience to contextualise action. Denyer et al. (2008) suggest that systematic reviews of the existing published science base in management and organization studies can develop knowledge that managers can use to design solutions to problems in their field. In management research, rather than presenting the truth, in the form of 'valid evidence', managers may be presented with some 'clues/ideas', 'tools', and 'methods' that may help to guide design for effective implementation. Deciding the degree to which the findings presented in any particular review can inform practice is therefore a matter of judgment for the practitioner.

Applying the new principles

Step 1: Question formulation

As with any research, the primary decision in preparing a review is to establish its focus (Light and Pillemar, 1984). This is done most effectively by asking clearly framed questions (Cooper and Hedges, 1994). By clearly formulating the question, criteria for primary study inclusion in the review become clear:

> A good systematic review is based on a well-formulated, answerable question. The question guides the review by defining which studies will be included, what the search strategy to identify the relevant primary studies should be, and which data need to be extracted from each study. Ask a poor question and you will get a poor review' (Counsell, 1997: 381).

In order to clarify review questions, inform the review process and improve the utilization of findings from systematic reviews, it is best to involve a broad range of stakeholders in the development of review questions and procedures (Tranfield et al., 2004). Petticrew (2001: 100) argues that,

> 'potential users of systematic reviews, such as consumers and policy makers, can be involved in the process. This can help to ensure that reviews

are well focused, ask relevant questions, and are disseminated effectively to appropriate audiences'.

Advisory groups can assist with defining the broad topic area to be investigated and identifying the specific areas within that topic that would be most useful to scrutinize in depth. Involving experts is particularly important when the literature is sparse. The review panel best includes people with academic knowledge and practical expertise in the subject area such as librarians and information scientists and systematic review specialists, who may be consulted individually or as a group at key points throughout the review.

In the first instance, the review question may be free-form, written in natural language. The free-form question can then be structured into a reviewable question. In management and organization studies, it is sometimes difficult to define and measure constructs of interest. There is usually an emphasis on the requirement to understand the impact of study context on the study results. In a complex social world, it is often difficult to predict with any surety a uniform link between intervention and desirable outcome. Therefore, research in complex social systems (such as organizations) must always take into account the crucial role of context. As noted by Pawson and Tilley (1997), interventions in such systems will be affected by at least four contextual layers – the individual, interpersonal relationships, institutional setting, and wider infrastructural system. Pawson and Tilley also highlight the role of generative mechanisms, which help to explain the ephemeral relationship between the intervention and outcome. Generative mechanisms are the nucleus of explanation in realist synthesis (Pawson, 2006) and typically, for any process, there will be at least one mechanism operating (see Reed, Chapter 25, this volume). More likely, in complex social situations, there will be many mechanisms working concurrently (Denyer et al., 2008). The generative mechanism is a theory that helps to explain causal relations by 'describing powers inherent in the system' (Pawson, 2006: 2). Pawson (2006: 24) provides an

interesting example of how organizational forms are constrained by context:

> Bureaucracies organize work routines in certain ways and provide tightly specified employment functions for their workforces, but whether any of this happens depends on the availability of work, and ultimately, on the overall economic heath of the nation. The efficacy of bureaucratic management is also contingent on the type of work carried out. In sectors that thrive on innovation and entrepreneurial activity, the applicability of fixed duties to fixed roles is likely to flop.

In social science fields such as organization and management studies, it is not enough to know what works but also to ascertain why or how the relation occurs and in what circumstances. Pawson's (2006) realist approach requires the reviewer to determine (or infer) context, mechanism, and outcome configurations through comparing and contrasting interventions in different contexts. Such an approach has the advantage of including different types of information, such as case studies, so long as they provide some insight into what works, why, where, and when. Denyer et al. (2008) develop this argument using the acronym CIMO (Context, Intervention, Mechanism, and Outcome) – an acronym that can be used to specify the four critical parts of a well-built systematic review question (see Figure 39.1).

In management and organization studies, a practitioner question may be framed as follows: how can project team performance be optimized through leadership behaviours? This may be structured into a series of reviewable questions such as: under what conditions (C) does leadership style (I) influence the performance of project teams? What mechanisms operate in the influence of leadership style (I) on project team performance (O)?

In reviewing these questions, there are multiple perspectives with regard to the meaning of key constructs. Team performance, for example, may be measured in terms of project outcomes such as time, cost, and quality. However, from team members' perspective, performance may be interpreted

Component	Questions to ask
Context (C)	Who are the individuals of interest?
	• Employees, customers, shareholders, etc.
	• Sex, age, etc.
	• Role, position in organization, etc.
	Which interpersonal relationships are of interest?
	• Teams, group dynamics, structure of social networks, etc.
	Which aspects of the institutional setting are of interest?
	• Politics, power, technical system, complexity, interdependencies, etc.
	Which aspects of the wider infrastructural system are of interest?
	• Degree of competition, stability, etc.
Interventions (I)	What is the intervention of interest?
	• Leadership style, planning and control systems, training, performance management, etc.
Mechanisms (M)	What are the mechanisms of interest?
	What is it about interventions acting in a context that leads to the outcome?
	Why are mechanisms activated or not activated?
Outcomes (O)	What are the relevant outcomes?
	What outcomes would be important to the individuals involved?
	How will the outcomes be measured?
	What is the primary outcome and what are the secondary outcomes?
	• Performance improvement, cost reduction, low error rates, etc.

Figure 39.1 Constructing review questions using the CIMO logic.

in terms of internal dynamics and their experience of being a team member. It is, therefore, essential to define key terms during the question formulation phase. Since definitions and concepts are value laden, different perspectives and beliefs need to be made transparent. Although the review questions are specified a priori, a certain flexibility and modification of questions may be necessary as the reviewer gains a fuller understanding of the problem.

Until a very precise question(s) for a systematic review is specified, detailed work on a systematic review is best not started. It is impractical and unfair for novice researchers to begin a systematic review without a significant grounding in their field. Tranfield et al. (2003) suggest that prior to a systematic review, novices and less experienced researchers are best advised to produce a scoping study of the field. Scoping studies are exploratory reviews, since what to include and exclude is not self-evident. The purpose of the scoping study is to make clear the existing basis for the researcher's work and specify where and how the proposed systematic review fits into the current body of knowledge. The scoping study should help to define concepts and determine the review questions to be addressed.

Step 2: Locating studies

Systematic reviews aim to locate, select, and appraise as much as possible of the research relevant to the particular review question(s). The methods used to find studies (database searches, searches of specialist bibliographies, hand-searching of likely journals, and attempts to track down unpublished research) need to be reported in some detail.

Exhaustive literature searches of published and unpublished studies are conducted to ensure that the review results have taken into account all the available evidence and are based on best quality contributions. The people of the search is to identify all relevant studies and can cover a range of different types of information (academic articles, books, practitioner materials, working papers, and the Internet). It sounds trite to say so, but the searches need to be aligned tightly with the review questions.

The search generally commences with an investigation of citation databases using search strings, grouping keywords, and applying search conventions.

- Simple operators include:

  - Truncation characters – '*', '?'; e.g. team? – searches for documents which contain the term team, teams, teamwork, teamworking, etc.
  - Word association – 'w' or 'near'; e.g. high(w)reliability; high(near)reliability
  - Exact phrase – ' ', ' '; e.g. 'high reliability'; 'high reliability'

- Boolean Logic includes:

  - OR, e.g. team* OR group* searches for either term in a document
  - AND, e.g. 'high reliability' AND organi*ation searches for both terms in a document
  - AND NOT, e.g. team* AND NOT virtual* searches for documents which contain the term team, teams, teamwork, teamworking but not virtual

- By combining Boolean operators with parentheses complex searches can be constructed:

  - 'high reliability' AND (team* OR group*) AND NOT virtual

It is often wise to spend significant time on constructing the search strings, for this investment can improve the efficiency of the search. It is important to note that different citation databases use different search conventions.

There is a common misconception that systematic reviews only involve electronic database searches. However, Greenhalgh and Peacock (2005) have shown that, in systematic reviews addressing complex questions, database searching can often account for as little as 30 percent of the total number of relevant articles. Therefore, a systematic search can be expected to use several methods, including; searching electronic databases, hand searching known journals, recommendations from experts, and cross-referencing. In addition to academic papers, articles in nonpeer reviewed journals, books, databases, websites, conference papers, seminars, workshops, technical reports and discussion papers and other 'grey literature' are all important. The decision whether or not to search specific data sources is dependent on the field and on the evidence available. For example, in nascent and fast moving fields, much of the evidence might reside in working papers. As with other aspects of the review, explicit and transparent choices must be made by the reviewer.

The output of the search is a comprehensive listing of articles and papers (core contributions) which helps to address the review questions. To aid information management, citation management software packages, such as Endnote or Refworks, can be used to store information accurately.

Step 3: Study selection and evaluation

Following the requirement for transparency of process, systematic reviews use a set of explicit selection criteria to assess the relevance of each study found to see if it actually does address the review question. Detailed decisions are recorded specifying precisely the basis on which information sources have been included and excluded. The aim of being explicit about the selection criteria is to make the reviewer's decisions available for scrutiny and evaluation. Selection criteria also facilitate the updating of systematic reviews. One simple method for constructing selection criteria is to undertake a small number of some pilot searches in a citation database and then make a list of the reasons for the inclusion and exclusion of articles. If the search is well focused then within a short time it is usually possible to produce an exhaustive list of reasons for inclusion and exclusion. The reasons for inclusion and exclusion then form the selection criteria.

General quality checklists, such as those produced by the Critical Appraisal Skills Programme (2008), may be used to help evaluate studies. Different subfields of management have different perspectives on research quality and so it is also important to take this into consideration. For example, some journals produce comprehensive guidance on appraising research evidence, such as the *Journal of Occupational and Organizational Psychology*'s guidance on qualitative studies. By combining general quality criteria and guidance from key journals in the field, it is possible to create a bespoke and practical quality appraisal tool. The purpose of the tool is not to exclude papers that are deemed to be low quality, but to evaluate and report on the study and its limitations. However, if studies are excluded on the basis of quality, it is crucial for the reviewer to document and justify the reasons for this exclusion.

Step 4: Analysis and synthesis

After assembling the appropriate collection of relevant sources, the data analysis and synthesis commences. The aim of the analysis is to break down individual studies into constituent parts and describe how each relates to the other. On the other hand, the aim of synthesis is to make associations between the parts identified in individual studies. A synthesis needs to go beyond mere description by recasting the information into a new or different arrangement and developing knowledge that is not apparent from reading the individual studies in isolation.

The first step of analysis is to extract and store information on data extraction forms for every study included in the review. The data extraction forms generally address a series of interrelated questions, but the specific data collected may vary from study to study. The following questions were adapted from

Wallace and Wray (2006) and Solesbury (2001):

(1) What are the general details of the study – author, title, journal, date, language?
(2) What are you seeking to understand or decide by reading this?
(3) What type of study is this (philosophical/discursive/conceptual, literature review, survey, case study, evaluation, experiment/quasi experiment, etc.)?
(4) What are the authors trying to achieve in writing this? What are the broad aims of the study? What are the study research questions and/or hypotheses?
(5) How is the study informed by, or linked to, an existing body of empirical and/or theoretical research?
(6) In which contexts (country, sector and setting, etc.) and which people (age, sex, ethnicity, occupation, role, etc.) or organizations was the study conducted?
(7) What are the methodology, research design, sample, and methods of data collection and analysis?
(8) What are the key findings?
(9) How relevant is this to what we are seeking to understand or decide?
(10) How reliable/convincing is it – how well-founded theoretically/empirically is this (regardless of method)?
(11) How representative is this of the population/context that concerns us?
(12) In conclusion, what use can I make of this?

The extraction form may also include the details of the reviewer (particularly if there are multiple extractors) and the date of the review. At the end of a systematic review, a full tabulation of all the included studies is displayed, providing a comprehensive summary representation of the field of study. By cross tabulating the studies, key issues can be identified. For example, in the column that lists the existing body of empirical and/or theoretical research that studies refer to, it will be possible to see whether the field has a single theoretical foundation or contending or complementary theories.

Many systematic reviews employ two or more independent reviewers to extract data from studies. When the interpretations and findings of reviewers are compared, it is possible to minimize errors, resolve any differences, and produce a more robust data set. The aim of using data extraction forms is to provide an audit trail from the claims made in the review to the underlying evidence.

As noted in the foregoing section, reviews in management and organization studies are in general more likely to be interpretive or explanatory rather than aggregative. Harmonizing synthesis with the purpose of the review therefore is critical. In all cases, the resulting body of evidence is then explored, cross-tabulated and analyzed while engaging in rigorous reflection on any values, beliefs, and perspectives that might impact the interpretation. In a quantitative synthesis, the reviewer might highlight both the regularities and discrepancies in the data, whereas, in a qualitative synthesis, the reviewer could explore analogous and different meanings of respondents across the studies. Where multiple forms of evidence are available, it may be possible to attempt triangulation of the data/findings.

Step 5: Reporting and using the results

A systematic review is structured in a similar manner to a report of empirical research. The introduction section provides a statement of the problem and the review questions. The methodology section provides precise details of how the review was conducted – the search strategy, the selection criteria, and the analysis and synthesis criteria. The findings and discussion section contains a summary of all the studies in terms of the data extracted from the studies such as the percentage of studies in the field that are philosophical/discursive/conceptual, literature reviews, surveys, case studies, evaluations, or experiments/quasi experiments. The findings and discussion section also specifies precisely what is known and unknown about the questions addressed in the review. The conclusion section provides a summary of the review, the limitations of the study, recommendations for policy and practice, and future research needs.

In Cochrane-style reviews, reviewers are encouraged to think about whether or not there is sufficient evidence to provide clear guidelines for practice by asking three questions:

(1) Will the practice improve outcomes?
(2) Should the practice be abandoned in light of the available evidence?
(3) Are there trade-offs between known benefits and known adverse effects?

If the review provides insufficient evidence to provide clear guidelines for practice, three further questions are raised:

(1) Is the practice promising but requires further evaluation?
(2) Does a practice that has been shown not to have the effects expected from it require further attention?
(3) Is there reasonable evidence that practice is not effective?

Reviewers in management and organization studies may make similar claims. However, since recommendations from reviews in our field are likely to be heuristic rather than algorithmic, it is essential that systematic review reports should provide considerable detail from the original studies so that any users of the review can, if necessary, interpret the results and judge for themselves the strength of the findings.

CONCLUSION

Despite common misconceptions in the press and popular media, evidence-based practice has never sought to provide 'answers' or to replace judgment and experience, but instead attempts to inform decision making and action (Sackett et al., 1996). The Cochrane Handbook (Higgins and Green, 2006: 175) is careful to point out that:

> ...the primary purpose of the review should be to present information, rather than offer advice, the discussion and conclusions should be to help people to understand the implications of the evidence in relationship to practical decisions.

Academic evidence is only one input into the decision making process even in more developed fields such as medical science, for 'clinicians reason about individual patients on the basis of analogy, experience, heuristics, and theory, as well as evidence' (Cook et al., 1997: 380). Therefore, the terms 'evidence informed' or even 'evidence aware', rather than 'evidence based' may be more appropriate in management and organization studies (Tranfield, et al., 2003). Hammersley (2004: 4) argues, that:

> …sometimes it will simply not be sensible to engage in elaborate explication of goals, to consider all possible alternatives, to engage in a search for information about the relative effectiveness of various strategies as against relying on judgements about this, or to try to measure outcomes. The linear rational model tends to underplay the extent to which in many circumstances the only option is trial and error, or even 'muddling through'.

However, any assumption that practitioners are unlikely to use evidence that has been produced by a systematic and rigorous process solely because they do not have the necessary time and appropriate skills, fails to question the desirability of such an outcome and draws attention to the training and development needs of managers. It is true that managers have at present rarely been trained to evaluate research but it is patronizing in the extreme to suggest that their efforts could not, or worst still should not be informed by the very best available evidence. For academic evidence to be used by managers it needs to be rendered accessible, palatable, relevant and useful. The linking of science base with practice remains a key challenge for management and organization studies. Therefore, in this chapter, we have identified alternative principles and outlined a methodology designed to further enhance and strengthen both management practice and management research. The methodology offers the potential to couple the best available academic evidence with the judgement and experience of practitioners in the true tradition of evidence-based practice.

REFERENCES

Antman, E.M., Lau, J., Kupelnick, B., Mosteller, F. and Chalmers, T.C. (1992) 'A comparison of results of meta-analyses of randomized control trials and recommendations of clinical experts. treatments for myocardial infarction', *JAMA*, 268(2): 240–8.

Baligh, H.H., Burton, R.M. and Obel, B. (1996) 'Organizational consultant: creating a useable theory for organizational design', *Management Science*, 42(12): 1648–62.

Boaz, A. and Ashby, D. (2003) *Fit for Purpose? Assessing Research Quality for Evidence Based Policy and Practice*, Queen Mary: University of London, London.

Briner, R. (2000) 'Evidence-based human resource management', in L. Trinder and S. Reynolds (eds), *Evidence-Based Practice: A Critical Appraisal*, Blackwell Publishing, pp. 184.

Campbell Collaboration (2008) http://www.campbell collaboration.org/ [Accessed 22 June 2008].

Campbell, R., Pound, P., Pope, C. and Britten, N. (2003) 'Evaluating meta-ethnography: a synthesis of qualitative research on lay experiences of diabetes and diabetes care', *Social science and medicine*, 56(4): 671.

Cassell, C. *Criteria for Evaluating Papers Using Qualitative Research Methods* [Homepage of Journal of Occupational and Organizational Psychology], [Online]. Available: http://www.bps.org.uk/publications/journals/joop/qualitative-guidelines.cfm [February 2008].

Cochrane, A. (1972) *Effectiveness And Efficiency: Random Reflections on Health Services*, (first edn.), London, Nuffield Provincial Hospitals Trust.

Cochrane Collaboration (2008a) http://www.cochrane.org/ [Accessed 22 June 2008].

Cochrane Collaboration (2008b) http://www.cochrane.org/reviews/ [Accessed 22 June 2008].

Cook, D.J., Mulrow, C.D. and Haynes, R.B. (1997) 'Systematic reviews: synthesis of best evidence for clinical decisions', *Annals of Internal Medicine*, 126(5): 376–80.

Cooper, H.M. and Hedges, L.V. (1994) *The Handbook of Research Synthesis*, Russell: Sage Foundation.

Counsell, C. (1997) 'Formulating questions and locating primary studies for inclusion in systematic reviews', *Annals of Internal Medicine*, 127(5): 380–7.

Critical Appraisal Skills Programme. (2008) *Home* [Homepage of Public Health Resource Unit (PHRU)], [Online]. Available: http://www.phru.nhs.uk/Pages/PHD/CASP.htm [February 2008].

Davies, H.T.O., Nutley, S.M. and Smith, P.C. (1999) 'Editorial: what works? the role of evidence in public sector policy and practice', *Public Money and Management*, 19(1): 3–5.

Davies, H.T. and Crombie, I.K. (2001) *What is a Systematic Review?*, Hayward Medical Communications.

Denyer, D., Tranfield, D. and van Aken, J.E. (2008) 'Developing design propositions through research synthesis', *Organization Studies*, 29(3): 393–415.

Dixon-Woods, M., Agarwall, S., Young, B., Jones, D. and Sutton, A. (2006) *Integrative Approaches to Qualitative and Quantitative Evidence*, London. Health Development Agency.

Dixon-Woods, M., Agarwal, S., Jones, D., Young, B. and Sutton, A. (2005) 'Synthesising qualitative and quantitative evidence: a review of possible methods', *Journal of Health Services Research and Policy*, 10(1): 45–53.

Estabrooks, C.A., Field, P.A. and Morse, J.M. (1994) 'Aggregating qualitative findings: an approach to theory development', *Qualitative Health Research*, 4(4): 503–11.

Evans, D. (2003) 'Hierarchy of evidence: a framework for ranking evidence evaluating healthcare interventions', *Journal of Clinical Nursing*, 12(1): 77–84.

Greenhalgh, T. and Peacock, R. (2005) 'Effectiveness and efficiency of search methods in systematic reviews of complex evidence: audit of primary sources', *British Medical Journal*, 331: 1064–65.

Greenhalgh, T. (1997) 'Papers that summarise other papers (systematic reviews and meta-analyses)', *BMJ (Clinical research ed.)*, 315(7109): 672–5.

Greenhalgh, T., Robert, G., Bate, P., Kyriakidou, O. and MacFarlane, F. (2005) *Diffusion of Innovations in Health Service Organizations: A Systematic Literature Review*, BMJ Books.

Hammersley, M. (2001) 'On "systematic" reviews of research literatures: a "narrative" response to Evans and Benefield', *British Educational Research Journal*, 27(5): 543–54.

Hammersley, M. (2004) 'Some questions about evidence-based practice in education', in G. Thomas and R. Pring (eds), *Evidence-Based Practice in Education*, Maidenhead: Open University Press, pp. 133–49.

Harden, A., Peersman, G., Oliver, S., Mauthner, M. and Oakley, A. (1999) 'A systematic review of the effectiveness of health promotion interventions in the workplace', *Occupational medicine (Oxford, England)*, 49(8): 540–8.

Hart, C. (1998) *Doing a Literature Review: Releasing the Social Science Research Imagination*, London: Sage Publications.

Higgins, J.P.T. and Green, S. (updated September 2006) 'Cochrane Handbook for Systematic Reviews of Interventions', *The Cochrane Library*, 4.2. 6.

Learmonth, M. and Harding, N.(2006) 'Evidence-based management: the very idea', *Public Administration*, 84(2): 245–66.

Light, R.J. and Pillemer, D.B. (1984) *Summing Up: The Science of Reviewing Research*, Harvard, MA: Harvard University Press.

Macdonald, G. (1996) 'Ice therapy: why we need randomised controlled trials', *What Works*, pp. 16–32.

Moher, D., Jadad, A.R., Nichol, G., Penman, M., Tugwell, P. and Walsh, S. (1995) 'Assessing the quality of randomized controlled trials: an annotated bibliography of scales and checklists', *Controlled clinical trials*, 16(1): 62–73.

Morrell, K. (2008) 'The narrative of "evidence based" management: a polemic', *Journal of Management Studies*, 45(3): 613–35.

NHS Centre for Reviews and Dissemination. (2001) *Undertaking systematic reviews of research on effectiveness: CRD's guidance for those carrying out or commissioning reviews*, NHS Centre for Reviews and Dissemination.

Noblit, G. and Hare, R. (1988) *Meta-Ethnography: Synthesizing Qualitative Studies*, London: Sage.

Oakley, A. (2000) *Experiments in Knowing: Gender and Method in the Social Sciences*, Cambridge: Polity Press.

Oliver, S., Harden, A., Rees, R., Shepherd, J., Brunton, G., Garcia, J. and Oakley, A. (2005) 'An emerging framework for including different types of evidence in systematic reviews for public policy', *Evaluation*, 11(4): 428.

Pawson, R. (2002) 'Evidence based policy: the promise of 'Realist Synthesis'', *Evaluation*, 8(3): 340–58.

Pawson, R. (2006) *Evidence-Based Policy: A Realist Perspective*, London: Sage Publications.

Pawson, R. and Tilley, N. (1997) *Realistic Evaluation*, London: Sage.

Petticrew, M. (2001) 'Systematic reviews from astronomy to zoology: myths and misconceptions', *British Medical Journal*, 322(7278): 98–101.

Pittaway, L., Robertson, M., Munir, K., Denyer, D. and Neely, A. (2004) 'Networking and innovation: a systematic review of the evidence', *International Journal of Management Reviews*, 5(3–4): 137–68.

Popay, J., Roberts, H., Sowden, A., Petticrew, M., Arai, L., Rodgers, M. and Britten, N. (2006) *Guidance on the Conduct of Narrative Synthesis in Systematic Reviews*, A Product from the ESRC Methods Programme, http://www.conted.ox.ac.uk/cpd/healthsciences/courses/short_courses/qsr/NSguidanceV1-JNoyes.pdf.

Popay, J., Rogers, A. and Williams, G. (1998) 'Rationale and standards for the systematic review of qualitative literature in health services research', *Qualitative health research*, 8(3): 341–51.

Rauch, A. and Frese, M. (2006) 'Meta-analysis as a tool for developing entrepreneurship research and theory', *Entrepreneurship: Frameworks and Empirical Investigations from Forthcoming Leaders of European Research.*

Rousseau, D.M., Manning, J. and Denyer, D. (2008) 'Evidence in management and organizational science: assembling the field's full weight of scientific knowledge through syntheses', *Annals of the Academy of Management,* 2(1): 475–515.

Sackett, D.L., Rosenberg, W.M., Gray, J.A., Haynes, R.B. and Richardson, W.S. (1996) 'Evidence based medicine: what it is and what it isn't', *BMJ (Clinical research ed.),* 312(7023): 71–2.

Salipante, P., Notz, W. and Bigelow, J. (1982) 'A matrix approach to literature reviews', *Research in Organizational Behavior,* 4: 321–48.

Sandelowski, M., Docherty, S., and Emden, C. (1997) 'Qualitative metasynthesis: issues and techniques', *Research in Nursing and Health,* 20(4): 365–71.

Shadish, W.R. and Sweeney, R.B. (1991) 'Mediators and moderators in meta-analysis: there's a reason we don't let dodo birds tell us which psychotherapies should have prizes', *Journal of consulting and clinical psychology,* 59(6): 883–93.

Slavin, R.E. (1986) 'Best-evidence synthesis: an alternative to meta-analytic and traditional reviews', *Educational Researcher,* 15(9): 5–11.

Solesbury, W. (2001) *Evidence Based Policy: Whence it Came and where It's Going.* ESRC UK Centre for Evidence Based Policy and Practice, UK.

The Campbell Collaboration , *Home.* Available: http://www.campbellcollaboration.org/ [February 2008].

The Cochrane Collaboration , *Homepage* [Homepage of The Cochrane Collaboration], [Online]. Available: http://www.cochrane.org/ [February 2008].

The Evidence for Policy and Practice Information and Co-ordinating Centre (EPPI-Centre) , *Home* [Homepage of EPPI Centre], [Online]. Available: http://eppi.ioe.ac.uk/cms/ [February 2008].

Tranfield, D., Denyer, D., Marcos, J. and Burr, M. (2004) 'Co-producing management knowledge', *Management Decision,* 42(3/4): 375.

Tranfield, D., Denyer, D. and Smart, P. (2003) 'Towards a methodology for developing evidence-informed management knowledge by means of systematic review', *British Journal of Management,* 14(3): 207.

Tranfield, D. and Starkey, K. (1998) 'The nature, social organization and promotion of management research: Towards policy', *British Journal of Management,* 9(4): 341.

van Aken, J.E. (2005) 'Management research as a design science: articulating the research products of mode 2 knowledge production in management', *British Journal of Management,* 16(1): 19.

Wallace, M. and Wray, A. (2006) *Critical Reading and Writing for Postgraduates,* London: Sage Publications.

Whitley, R. (1984) 'The fragmented state of management studies: reasons and consequences', *The Journal of Management Studies,* 21(3): 331.

40

Organizational Autoethnography

Ken Parry and Maree Boyle

There is nothing more theoretical than a good story
(Bochner, 1997: 435)

Prior to the 1960s, organizational sociology relied heavily on case study fieldwork as a methodology. Dalton's *Men Who Manage* (1959) is one prominent ethnographic example from this golden era of organizational sociology. However, coinciding with the advent of widely-available computing technology, ethnography went in to decline as a method for organizational research. In recent years, it has once again become an increasingly popular research approach within organizational studies. Many scholars, particularly in the United Kingdom rather than North America, would argue that this increase in popularity has been in response to the 'reflexive turn' within organizational research more generally. The reflexive turn represents the broad move toward reflexivity as a characteristic of sound research. Of course, other scholars (e.g. Watson, 1994) used an interpretive style of ethnography without consciously being part of any reflexive turn. Either way, due to

the dominance of postpositivist and realist approaches within organizational studies, this may be one of the last academic fields to acknowledge ethnographic methods as an acceptable methodological approach.

However, there are many types of organizational ethnographies, and many ways of 'doing' ethnography. Within this chapter, we outline one of those approaches, which is called organizational autoethnography. We acknowledge that there is no one clear definition of what autoethnography is. However, in relation to the study of organizations, we have identified writing genres and approaches within the autoethnographic tradition that are a good fit between the objectivist tradition popular within organizational studies, and the hyperreflexive nature of autoethnographic writing more generally. Therefore, autoethnography offers a great potential contribution to organizational research. Within this chapter, we will address four key issues. First, we briefly identify the key components of organizational ethnography. Second, we discuss how autoethnography is differentiated from ethnography, whether in the organizational domain or not. Third, we discuss how the autoethnographic approach can enhance our understanding of the twenty-first century organization. Fourth, we discuss the major methodological, ethical and personal challenges that confront autoethnographers who might be engaged in organizational research.

Sparkes (2000: 21) says that autoethnographies 'are highly personalized accounts that draw upon the experience of the author/researcher for the purposes of extending sociological understanding'. Moreover, Richardson states that autoethnographies are highly personalized, revealing texts in which authors tell stories about their own lived experience by relating the personal to the cultural. In telling the story, the writer can call upon fiction-writing techniques. Through these techniques, the writing constructs a sequence of events, asking the reader to emotionally 'relive' the events with the writer (Richardson, 2000: 11).

As explained by Boyle and Parry (2007), the intensely reflexive nature of autoethnography as an autobiographical form of research, allows the organizational researcher to connect intimately the personal to the cultural through a 'peeling back' of multiple layers of consciousness, thoughts, feelings and beliefs. Consequently, we believe that autoethnography provides some of the richest and most original data available to organizational researchers.

Similarly, autoethnography can expose the reader to stories that would otherwise be 'shrouded in secrecy' (Ellis and Bochner, 1996: 25). Hence, organizational autoethnographies can provide first-hand accounts of taboo topics such as sexual harassment and bullying (Vickers, 2007), motherhood at work (Riad, 2007), various moral dilemmas, and highly-charged emotional situations in the workplace. These are situations that otherwise remain shrouded in secrecy, or possibly considered 'untouchable' by serious organizational researchers. Consequently, autoethnography can open the door to these fascinating and hugely important organizational phenomena. In so doing, autoethnography raises great opportunities for organizational researchers.

Our aim for this chapter is to begin a long and hopefully fruitful conversation about how and why autoethnography can help make valuable contributions to organizational studies. We contend that the prime role of an organizational autoethnographic study is to illuminate the relationship between the individual and the organization. Indeed, the ethnographic process has always been an essential way of studying culture, especially culture as it is practiced and understood within institutional and organizational settings. We contend that, in the spirit of Carolyn Ellis' (1997) work on introspective and retrospective forays into the self, the study of organizations and culture can be significantly enhanced by the inclusion of work conducted and located within the autoethnographic genre.

ORGANIZATIONAL ETHNOGRAPHY

Initial forays into ethnography by organizational researchers were informed by the classical anthropological tradition led by Malinowski (1922). Ethnography, in the traditional sense, provides accounts of the culture of human populations (Atkinson et al., 2001), which involve a very dense but accurate description of a culture other than one's own that is based on the 'native's perspective' (Werner and Shoepfle, 1987). Traditional ethnographic studies have utilized fieldwork methods such as participant observation through researcher immersion within the culture being studied. Ethnographic studies within the classical anthropological tradition can be characterized by their non-reflexive, objective approach. The principal data collection tool for ethnographers has always been the various forms of participant observation, where the ethnographer would be become, in varying degrees, immersed within the culture she/he was studying. This, combined with methodical and regular note-taking, formed the first stage in the writing of an ethnography through the transformation of the 'raw' field notes into ethnographic text. However, field notes rarely were placed within the published text in a raw or untreated form. In particular, personal insights into one's own behaviour or feeling states were usually omitted from the final version of the text so as not to contaminate the scientific value of the ethnographic text.

Therefore, although anthropologists often did collect autoethnographic data, they were restricted in their ability to present their findings reflexively so as to uphold the tradition of anthropology as scientific endeavour. The objectivism and arms-length scientism of ethnography has always been attractive to organizational scholars.

With the arrival of the alleged 'crisis of representation' in the social sciences in the 1980s, more organizational scholars made forays into ethnography. Van Maanen's special issue of *Administrative Science Quarterly* in 1979, Stephen Barley and Gideon Kunda's (2004) work in Silicon Valley, and Collinson's (1992) work on shop-floor culture, all became well cited fresh perspectives on key organizational issues such as power, control, technology, and leadership. However, published organizational ethnographies within major academic refereed journals are still rare. For example, between 1975 and 1994, only 36 out of a possible 548 articles published in *Administrative Science Quarterly* used participant observation as a data collection tool. In recent years, journals such as *Organization* and other journals have become more open to ethnographic work. Humphreys, Brown, and Hatch (2003) used the metaphor of jazz music to understand the challenges of undertaking organizational ethnography. Watson (2000) used 'ethnographic fiction science' to study and to narrative organizational phenomena ethnographically. Only very recently, Neyland (2008) has condensed the literature on organizational ethnography. Despite this, organizational ethnographers still have difficulty publishing their work in well respected and high ranking journals, certainly in 'business' or 'management' organization journals. This probably explains why ethnographers tend to shy away from journal publication and move towards other forms of publication, often as chapters or monographs.

Although still comparatively rare in contemporary writing, ethnography has a rich history in organizational scholarship. Apart from the works already mentioned, it has been strengthened by work conducted under the rubrics of narrative and discourse analysis. The narrative approach to organizational research has been led by Czarniawska (1997) and Boje (2001). Barry and Elmes (1997) examined organizational strategy via the narrative lens. Gabriel (2000) and Mitroff and Kilmann (1975) have made a rich contribution to organizational ethnography through storytelling as data and as method. Dawson (for example, in Buchanan and Dawson, 2007) has researched organizational change via ethnographic studies of major corporations in the UK.

Discourse analysis and the use of discursive data in organizational research has been brought together by Grant et al. (2004) as well as Keenoy and others (Oswick et al., 2002). Linstead and Höpfl (2000) have led the drive to examine the aesthetic nature of organizations. This work also is ethnographic in nature. Even though the issue of reflexivity is dealt with at length by these scholars, research is still conducted invariably with an arm's length objectivity. Hyperreflexivity and self-ethnography have seldom been undertaken. The lens through which organizational behaviour has been studied has rarely been turned inward.

Even when organizational ethnographers do successfully publish their work, much of their reflexive comment and their role in the narrative has been either written out or sanitized in order to conform to scientific standards. Within many organizational ethnographies, without such reflexive content, it is often difficult to ascertain who actually was present during fieldwork. There are no references to cite here. After all, one cannot cite something that was not published. Once a work is published, there is no record of what the author originally intended. All we have to cite are informal conversations with colleagues who have had a common experience.

From ethnography to autoethnography

The initial anthropological definition of autoethnography is quite different from the definition used today. As Hayano (1979) states, autoethnography is a type of ethnography that is conducted within one's own cultural milieu, or the conduct of a hyper-reflexive study by an indigenous member of a particular group or culture. In other words, anthropologists who did fieldwork within their own culture were conducting an auto study, in the sense that they were not behaving as the true participant observer or outsider, but rather as an insider who was also attempting to simultaneously adopt the outsider role. It was not until the 1970s that anthropologists such as Lewis (1973) questioned the insider/outsider dimension as simply a dichotomous phenomenon. Instead, Lewis argued that these roles can be adopted simultaneously, and it is the degree to which a fieldworker adopts one or the other that is the important issue.

Thus, for traditional ethnographers, the practice of autoethnography meant the fieldworker gained intimacy with a social group, culture or subculture for which the fieldworker had attained insider membership. It was characterized by a descriptive narrative and the focus of the study was often centred on the fieldworker's positionality. The growth of autoethnography within anthropology drew resistance from within the field as nonscientific and overly subjective. For instance, Yang (1972) asserted that an anthropologist should work more like a scientist than a sentimentalist, which was in keeping with the long held belief in traditional anthropology that the fieldworker needed to practice objectivity and neutrality, especially in relation to expression of the ethnographer's personal feelings about the culture in which he or she was conducting fieldwork. Thus, in order to be a proper and scientific anthropologist, one needed to follow the canons of objective research procedures, and practice detachment and noninvolvement, rather than be guided by an intense personal interest in the object of the study. Such an argument has traditionally been attractive to organizational researchers.

Despite the appearance of the reflexive turn in social science, published autoethnographic accounts are still rare in the world of social enquiry. The level of emotional intensity and occasional personal risk means that autoethnographies are very difficult to write well, and even more difficult to justify as trustworthy. As autoethnographies try to bridge the gap between art and science, they are often left swinging between the two, not being recognized in either camp.

Ellis's key forays into the world of autoethnography illustrates how this approach can cloud the postpositivist distinction between science and literature, the organization and the individual, the self and the other, and most of all, between research and subject (Ellis, 2001). Ellis' approach has a strong focus on emotion-driven knowledge in addition to cognitive perceptions. For Ellis however, such emotional knowledge emanates from an exhausting and rigorous process of self analysis and critique. What Ellis is proposing is not just a realist style of self-report of how the autoethnographer 'felt' during fieldwork, but rather the conduct of a study within a study, which includes a depth of self disclosure and analysis that is not reported within the majority of ethnographies. Therefore, she makes a clear distinction between 'being reflexive' and 'doing' autoethnography.

Thus, knowledge is gained through the direct observation of the interplay between observer and observed, which involves both reflection inward together with observation outwards (Jackson 1989; Ellis and Bochner 1996). Ellis also highlights the tendency for autoethnographers to write epiphany narratives that emerge out of accounts of personal loss, grief, or tragedy. Denzin (1989) agrees that the process of storytelling has the effect of making sense of epiphanies, and that this can only be achieved through the blending of art and science. Humphreys (2005) is a strong and persuasive advocate of the use of vignettes in autoethnography to enhance reflexivity and identity development.

An example of where this potential can be realized is in the area of identity research within organizational contexts. The methodology of autoethnography has a rich history in identity research within the discipline of sociology. This is particularly so with studies on race, gender, and social conflict (Jovanovic, 2003; Olson, 2004; Rambo, 2005). Indeed, it has also been used in mental health nursing research (Foster et al., 2006). However, there is very little literature about identity in 'organizational' studies of identity using autoethnography. One possible exception could be Keefe's (2006) autoethnographic account of her career development as an academic from an early age. A second is Rhodes' (2001) text on representation and control in work narratives. Rhodes' work on narrative features in another chapter in this handbook (Rhodes and Pullen, Chapter 34, this volume). A third might be Jago's (2002) experience of dealing with depression in an organizational context, although the emphasis is on 'depression' rather than on 'organizational'. Another example of organizational autoethnography is Parry's (2008) account of leadership identity construction in organizational settings. There appears to be great potential for autoethnography to make a contribution to research about identity within organizational settings.

Ellis identifies three autoethnographic approaches – storytelling, *co-constructed narratives*, and *interactive interviewing*. Regardless of the type of approach taken, the autoethnographic text is characterized by an emotional, multivocal and interactive nature, which will evoke the readers' emotional linkages to the topic. However, in the case of Ellis' own work, the relationship between her dying partner and herself, she clearly indicates that she needed to exercise the scientific discipline and rigour of fieldwork methods by writing consistent, regular, and ordered notes about her personal experience of dying and grief. Her intention was to speak 'therapeutically' to a nonacademic audience

and 'sociologically' to an academic one (Ellis, 1995).

The separation between researcher and subject through writing about the self and one's personal connections with the group or culture provides considerable challenges to the traditional ideas of generalizability. In contrast to other types of qualitative approaches, the autoethnography is less like a snapshot and more like a continual and systematic unfolding of episodes through systematic introspection (Ellis 1991). Coconstructed narratives are essentially autoethnographic narratives written in a group of two or more. They provide the opportunity to blend together the emotive subjectivity of the insider with the traditional objectivity of the observer. This form of data triangulation provides great potential for enhancing the validity and reliability of organizational autoethnography.

The opportunity arises for a *pseudonymous autoethnography*. The pseudonym will probably be the subject of the autoethnography, except that the narrative is written in the third person. The use of a pseudonym enables the usual level of subjectivity and emotion to be integrated into the research. It also allows for a more objective appraisal of the emerging theory than might otherwise be the case with an autoethnography. It is an attempt to integrate third person anonymity into what is otherwise a very onymous genre of research. Because of the inherent subjectivity and first-person style of autoethnography, and because the author and subject of the research are essentially one and the same person, the subject of the research would otherwise have 'nowhere to hide'.

Interactive interviewing, while similar to other types of qualitative interviews, has great potential for use in any ethnographic research. It requires the interview to probe and encourage the interview to explore the emotional experience of what the topic is (Healy, 1997). These interviews are rarely 'one off' and may be held over a number of months, even years. The other unique aspect of this kind of interviewing is that the interviewer's voice is also present and clearly marked as an actor within the story. Thus, the multilayered and multivocal nature of this kind of interview adds layers of rich and textured data that other methods have previously not been able to access through 'snapshot' interviews or even diaries.

Toward organizational autoethnography

We identify three key elements of the autoethnographic method that allow for a more insightful and culturally richer understanding of organizational life. First, this approach has the ability to connect the micro and everyday and mundane aspects of organizational life with broader political and strategic organizational agendas and practices. An ethnographic example is Kempster's (2006) reflexive data gathering about leadership development. This work linked the experience of the self with the dynamics of organizational life in a rich narrative. However, it lacked some of the enthralling 'grab' that an autoethnographic examination of the same phenomenon might have produced. Humphrey's (2006) autoethnographic account of his parallel existences as learner and as teacher in a business school provided more of this self-reflexive lure for the reader.

Second, we propose that autobiographical and retrospective approaches are more likely to uncover and illuminate the tacit and subaltern aspects of organization, such as how actions which lead to negative or positive organizational outcomes actually play out. For example, a good piece of autoethnographic writing will always engage readers to the point where they will develop a clearer understanding of things like emotional ambivalence, organizational deadlocks and roadblocks, and the ongoing and variable nature of organizational relationships. To this extent, vicarious learning by the reader is enhanced through the use of autoethnography.

Third, we acknowledge that there is no perfect methodology, and autoethnography does have its problems. Morse (2002) identified ethical problems, wherein the identity of other participants might not be concealed. She also noted that the voice of the author/subject of an autoethnography might overshadow the voices of other participants in the autoethnographic narrative. Apart from the risk of narcissism, self-absorption, exaggeration, and self-indulgence from the author/subject, we also admit that exposing the vulnerable self through autobiographical processes can be fraught with personal and professional risk, and, in some instances, can be considered the most dangerous fieldwork of all (Holt, 2003; Kleinman and Copp, 1993; Lee, 1995; Rose, 1990). However, we do challenge critics of this method by suggesting that we may need to move beyond triangulation as the only way of determining validity in qualitative research. We suggest an extension of Richardson's (2000) work where she suggests that the imagery of the crystal is more useful than one of the triangle, especially for interpretive work. The autoethnographic approach is one that younger researchers may view as a more acceptable form of social enquiry, especially one that is used to a world of blogging, myspace, reality TV, personal websites as ways of communicating about the self.

At first glance, it is often difficult to comprehend how intensely personal and sometimes harrowing accounts of organizational life could provide a better understanding of the link between individual lived experience and the more rarefied and objective meta aspects of organization. By its very nature, autoethnography is characterized by personal experience narratives (Denzin, 1989), narrative ethnography (Goodall, 2004), auto-observation (Adler and Adler, 1994), personal ethnography (Crawford, 1996), lived experience (van Maanen, 1990), self-ethnography, (van Maanen, 1995), reflexive ethnography (Ellis and Bochner, 1996), ethno-biography, (Lejeune, 1989), emotionalism (Gubrium and Holstein, 1997), experiential texts, (Denzin, 1997), and autobiographical ethnography (Reed-Danahay, 1997). Thus, autoethnographic accounts are characterized by the move from a broad lens approach on a person's situatedness within the cultural and social aspects of their experience to a focus on the inner, vulnerable, and often resistant self. In an organizational autoethnographic account, the lens moves from cultural and social situatedness to the inner self and then back again to the situated individual. Therefore, such an ethnography does not end at the personal, as there are constant reminders throughout the text of how the individual self interacts with, resists, cajoles, and shapes the organizational and institutional context in which he/she is situated.

A central feature of autoethnography is the use of an aesthetic style of text, which may take a variety of forms – personal essays, poetry, short stories, journals, stream of consciousness, detailed unstructured interview narratives, and other forms of fragmented writing. For example, Blenkinsopp (2007) wrote the story of the 'double-bind' or Catch-22, wherein the victim could not escape the consequences of the situation. The text was evocative and ironic. Vickers (2007) used diary entries and historiographic reflection to present an anguished narrative about bullying in one organization. Yarborough and Lowe (2007) use the analogy of a movie script to bring home to the reader the emotive impact of learning about leadership. Apart from irony, anguish, and reflection, other forms of autoethnographic text can evoke aesthetic impacts upon readers that are comic, sublime, inspiring, and even grotesque, ugly or creepy.

Through these usually first-person accounts, the multiple and fragmented leading self is revealed and delayered via stories of action, dialogue, linking of embodiment and emotion, fragmented thought, and different uses of language. An increasing use of the first person in the write-up of management research indicates heightened acceptance of the self-narrative as a form of sense-making within organizational life. Although using the genre of fiction, Banks and Banks (1998) highlight the enriching value of narrative and storytelling for research. However, we acknowledge that the commonalities between organizational ethnography and organizational autoethnography include

the need for an aesthetic element – in other words, it needs to read well, and the researcher needs to be able to write well and write truthfully. Therefore, organizational autoethnography would be classed as nonfiction. Fiction writing merely serves to enhance the narrative and aesthetic style of the nonfictional autoethnography. Having said that, there is a valid concern that the 'permission' to use first person narratives might invite careless writing and sloppy reasoning on occasion. However, the forms of writing indicated in this chapter suggest a rather more consciously disciplined and structured analytical approach.

Because ethnographies are ostensibly concerned with the nature of relational interactions between humans in groups and cultures, autoethnographers will take this one step further and focus intensely on their positionality within these relationships over a period of time. This is quite different to that of realist ethnographies, whereby ethnographers would provide a 'real' or 'true' account that would focus outwards on group or organizational behaviour, and less inwards on their own reaction to such behaviour. Thus, autoethnography is the connection between personal observation and public account. Neuman (2000) describes this as both simultaneously gazing inwards and outwards for an accurate account of the self.

The challenges and risks for twenty-first century organizational autoethnographers

We see a number of logistical and methodological challenges for organizational autoethnographers to overcome. We also see several risks, and usually they involve personal risk, that need to be avoided. We shall examine the methodological challenges first.

Challenges

The first challenge relates to the criteria of reliability and the generation of sense-making within the mind of the audience for the autoethnography. One might read the write-up of a worldwide survey where $n = 20,000$ and the findings are generalizable. By contrast, one might read an autoethnography where n = 1, and the findings are substantive to the experience of just one person. Either way, we suggest that, irrespective of the methodology that is employed, it is the reporting of the findings that will influence the impact of the original piece of research. In other words, the impact is no more and no less than the reading of the manuscript by each individual reader. While the first research report might have an impact due to its cognitive nature, so too would the autoethnography due to its emotional and evocative nature. Indeed, the emotional and evocative write-up might well have the greater impact. Because of this strong impact, the reader can make up her or his mind about the generalizability of the findings. We would suggest that the critical 'n' factor in much organizational research is the number of people who read the research, rather than the number of people who are the subjects of the research.

Ellis and Bochner (1996, 2000) have reminded us that autoethnography expresses how we struggle to make sense of our experiences. This is usually achieved via encouraging compassion and promoting dialogue. Therefore, autoethnography is about the author's sensemaking. Part of the challenge for organizational researchers is to communicate that sense-making to the 'organizational' audience. Some authors (Vickers, 2007; Duarte and Hodge, 2007; Blenkinsopp, 2007) have identified this dual sensemaking role within the autoethnographic method. In one sense, all organizational research helps the reader to make sense of the phenomenon under investigation. However, sensemaking is more than just the outcome of research in terms of generating plausible theory. The cognitive impacts of the research, in combination with the affective or emotive impacts, are essential elements of this genre of organizational research. With organizational autoethnography, the reader can do more than sympathize with the author – the reader can actually empathize with the author. Perhaps, in an ideal world, every organizational research project would include

a hyper-reflexive component, which could take an autoethnographic form.

Critics of autoethnographic approaches could argue that a researcher as research instrument and source of data has little control, in a positivist sense, over the research process. These critics might also contend that the researcher needs to be in total control of the research process, and hence, be able to take the research where it needs to go. In contrast, we argue that the process of conducting autoethnography throws down a challenge to this notion of researcher as controller. The process of creating an autoethnographic account involves, in a sense, an acknowledgement that there is no guarantee that there is a correlation between the degree of control a researcher exercises over the research process, and the end result. As with much ethnography, the data might lead the researcher in a certain direction. This direction might not be predetermined by the researcher. For example, Duarte and Hodge (2007) changed the direction of their research entirely as a result of the changing direction of the emerging data. They significantly changed the epistemological and methodological approach to their research. The research was initially conceived within a positivist and psychometric framework to investigate urban sustainability in Brazil. Instead, the researchers found a complex social reality and they found that subjectivity can be an asset. Ultimately, the research was written up as a meta-autoethnography of the research process itself. The final product was not conceived at the start of the project.

If the research is funded by private sources and the researcher intends to include a highly reflexive, autobiographical component within a research paper or report, there need to be negotiations well before the final write up of the report. This negotiation is in addition to all the standard negotiation that is conducted to gain support for and access to an organization for research purposes. Such recognition is further support for Ellis and Bochner's (2000) claim that the writing of an autoethnography is a time consuming and lengthy process. Having said that, we recognize that autoethnography is a relatively inexpensive form of research, financially at least.

The narrative that is organizational autoethnography is an explanation of what has happened in the past. It is not a prediction about what will happen in the future to other people in similar situations. Much organizational research presumes to be able to predict the future as a result of the findings of the research. This is especially so of 'business' related research which purports to be able to get the most out of employees or to positively 'impact' the bottom line. However, Fleetwood and Hesketh (2006) provide a persuasive argument that much organizational research can only explain the past and cannot predict the future, in spite of many claims to the contrary. It is still the responsibility of individual readers to make up their minds about the predictive validity of what they read in scholarly journals about the experiences of others. In this sense, organizational autoethnography has no less predictive validity than any other organizational research. In fact, the emotive power of this research makes it a more powerful explanation of phenomena. Therefore, this impact alone might make organizational autoethnography a more powerful research genre than most mainstream organizational research.

We would agree with Fleetwood and Hesketh that the research domain is not the closed system that many researchers would like to think it is. The number and influence of variables is so many and so great that organizational research simply cannot be constrained to a closed loop system. In a sense, organizational autoethnography recognizes this dilemma. By researching the phenomenon in its entirety, the problems associated with attempting to 'close' an 'open-loop' system are avoided.

Because organizational autoethnography is oriented so strongly toward the past, we cannot use the criterion of historical bias to detract from the validity of the research. In fact, we would advocate that the historical dimension is the strength of organizational autoethnography. In retrospect, and in the cold hard light of day, and with all the emotionality drained from the narrative, the reader can appraise the validity of the contribution to theory more clearly.

Brevity and parsimony have a place in organizational autoethnographic research. The author is engaging in a narrative. It must be an engaging narrative. The story-line need not be compromised by or congested with too many references to 'standing by the coffee machine' or 'opening the door as he entered the room'. The author can benefit from the skill of the wordsmith and the story-teller. After all, the autoethnography is more like the screenplay for a historical documentary than the verbatim transcript of an interview. If the autoethnography reads too much like the latter, the impact on the reader (the audience) will be compromised. Organizational reader-ships have high expectations with regard to the brevity and parsimony of the narrative.

Duncan criticized evocative personal writing that relies on a direct emotional response from a reader rather than offering analysis, grounding in theory, and methodological rigour. She advocated 'more experimental forms of autoethnography in which the boundaries of scholarship are merged with artistic expression as a way of challenging the limitations of what is normally accepted as knowledge in academic contexts' (Duncan, 2004: 11).

We also acknowledge that the strength of organizational autoethnography is demonstrated through its ability to weave the extant literature into the narrative that the author presents. To do so is normally proscribed in mainstream organizational research methodologies. However, in organizational autoethnography, it is a strength. At present, it is difficult to find published examples of organizational autoethnography, where the narrative is woven through the extant organizational literature. An exception might be Edgar Schein's (2006) fascinating travel through his career, which could fall within this category. He uses the metaphor of the drama and music as the integrating theme as he takes the reader on this journey. At one time, he is able to bring together autoethnography with aesthetic method and leadership development. To be sure, the majority of the literature that he cites is his own, and we would propose that organizational autoethnography needs to cite extant theory and make a contribution to organizational theory. Vickers (2007), Riad (2007), and Yarborough and Lowe (2007) have been able to do this successfully, and present role models for how this might be done in future.

Risks

To embark on an organizational autoethnography often constitutes a significant personal and professional risk for scholars often located within politically and socially conservative business schools. The risk is probably even greater for women, people of colour, and junior faculty; anyone from a potentially minority group against whom the deep power structures of the organization might be weighed.

Because of the perennial tension between individual disclosure and organizational protection, there exists a covertness about the process of 'doing' an autoethnography as a member of an organization. Although the majority of ethnographers would not set out to deliberately adopt such a hidden membership role, nevertheless the nature of autoethnography is such that one cannot continually alert other organizational members that one is engaging in such an activity, especially if one is currently an active member of the organization.

Organizational autoethnographers face difficult decisions about what narrative of the self will be told, especially narratives that reveal intensely personal information that may create emotional discomfort amongst colleagues. Organizational ethnography is not just *about* intensely emotive experiences. The *writing* of an autoethnography is an intensely emotive experience. The conduct of an organizational ethnography, let alone an organizational *auto*ethnography, can be fraught with danger for both the ethnographer and the organizational members with which he or she has contact. In contrast with a biographical account of a part of one's life, or

of a personal relationship, an organizational ethnography can make reference to persons other than the ethnographer. As with much ethnography, personal disclosure may involve reference to others in close proximity or friends. This can then lead to difficult and often painful decisions about how to report personal accounts, narratives, and opinions, particularly where the author's organizational location is possibly identifiable. Thus, description of organizational mores, subcultures, conflicts, and problems can leave both the ethnographer and the organization vulnerable in terms of professional reputation and sometimes legal responsibility. The autoethnography of Vickers (2007) highlights these potential risks. It is an autoethnography of being bullied at work. Another person was the bully, and that person was breaking the law. Maintaining the anonymity of that person and of the organization within the context of an autoethnography was difficult. Keeping the subject free from potential liability for a case of slander was challenging. One can appreciate readily how an autoethnography will elevate these risks to an entirely new level of vulnerability. We do not see this as a reason not to engage in organizational autoethnography, nor do we see it as a limitation. Rather, it is yet another challenge to be overcome by organizational researchers, while remaining ethical and courageous concurrently.

Publication outlets may be limited and those available may be nonacademic, so decisions need to be made about outlets before the write-up. Time needs to be spent entering into dialogue with editors who are open to potential work in this area. If a researcher relies on solely autoethnographic publications for tenure, they may find themselves having to provide more justification than those who have not embarked on this path.

CONCLUSION – NOT AN END, BUT A NEW BEGINNING

Autoethnography is not a solution to our organizational research problems. Rather, it is but one more piece in a fascinating research jigsaw. We contend that autoethnography can produce rigorous and fruitful contributions to organizational theory. By adding autoethnography to our repertoire, we can all generate marvellous research insights in to our organizations.

REFERENCES

Adler, P.A. and Adler, P. (1994) 'Observational techniques', in N.K. Denzin and Y.S. Lincoln (eds), *Handbook of Qualitative Research*, Thousand Oaks, CA: Sage

Atkinson, P., Coffey, A., Delamont, S., Lofland, J. and Lofland, L. (eds) (2001) *Handbook of Ethnography*, Thousand Oaks, CA: Sage Publications.

Banks, A. and Banks, S.P. (eds) (1998) *Fiction and Social Research: By Ice or Fire*, Walnut Creek, CA: AltaMira Press.

Barley, S. and Kunda, G. (2004) *Gurus, Hired Guns, and Warm Bodies: Itinerant Experts in a Knowledge Economy*, Princeton, New Jersey: Princeton University Press.

Barry, D. and Elmes, M. (1997) 'Strategy retold: Toward a narrative view of strategic discourse', *Academy of Management Review*, 22(2): 429–52.

Blenkinsopp, J. (2007) 'The ties that bind us: Career, emotion and narrative coping in difficult working relationships', *Culture & Organization*, 13(3): 251–66.

Bochner, A. P. (1997) 'It's About Time: Narrative and the Divided Self', *Qualitative Inquiry*, 3: 418–438.

Bochner, A.P. (2001) 'Narrative's virtues', *Qualitative Inquiry*, 7(2): 131–57.

Boje, D.M. (2001) *Narrative Methods for Organizational and Communication Research*, Thousand Oaks, CA: Sage.

Boyle, M. and Parry, K.W. (2007) 'Telling the whole story: the case for organizational autoethnography', *Culture & Organization*, September, 13(3): 185–90.

Buchanan, D. and Dawson, P. (2007) 'Discourse and audience: organizational change as multi-story process', *Journal of Management Studies*, 44 (5): 669–86.

Collinson, D.L. (1992) 'Managing the shopfloor: subjectivity, masculinity and workplace culture. Hawthorne', HY: De Gruyter.

Crawford, L.C. (1996) 'Personal ethnography', *Communication Monographs*, 63: 158–70.

Czarniawska, Barbara (1997) *A Narrative Approach to Organization Studies*, Thousand Oaks, CA: Sage Publications.

Dalton, M. (1959) *Men Who Manage*, New York: Wiley.

Denzin, N. (1989) *Interpretive Interactionism*, Newbury Park, CA: Sage.

Denzin, N.K. (1997) *Interpretive Ethnography: Ethnographic Practices for the 21st Century*, Thousand Oaks, CA: Sage.

Duarte, F. and Hodge, B. (2007) 'Crossing paradigms: A meta-autoethnography of a fieldwork trip to Brazil', *Culture & Organization*, 13(3): 191–203.

Duncan, M. (2004) 'Autoethnography: Critical appreciation of an emerging art', *International Journal of Qualitative Methods*, 3(4): Article 3. Retrieved June 28, 2005, from http://www.ualberta.ca/~iiqm/backissues/3_4/pdf/duncan.pdf

Ellis, C. (1991) 'Sociological introspection and emotional experience', *Symbolic Interaction*, 14(1): 23–50.

Ellis, C. (1995) *Final Negotiations: A Story of Love, Loss, and Chronic Illness*, Philadelphia: Temple University Press.

Ellis, C. (1997) 'Evocative autoethnography', in: W.G. Tierney and Y.S. Lincoln (eds), *Representation and the Text*, New York, State University of New York Press.

Ellis, C. (2000) Creating criteria: an ethnographic short story, *Qualitative Inquiry*, 6(2): 273–7.

Ellis, C. (2001) 'With mother/with child: a true story', *Qualitative Inquiry*, 7(5): 598–616.

Ellis, C. and Bochner, A. (1996) *Composing Ethnography: Alternative Forms of Qualitative Writing*, Walnut Creek, CA: Sage.

Ellis, C. and Bochner, A.P. (2000) 'Autoethnography, personal narrative, reflexivity', in N.K. Denzin and Y.S. Lincoln (eds), *Handbook of Qualitative Research* (second edn.), Thousand Oaks, CA: Sage, pp.733–768.

Ellis, C., Kiesinger, C. and Tillman-Healy, L. (1997) 'Interactive Interviewing: talking about emotional experience', in R. Hertz (ed.) *Reflexivity and Voice*, Newbury Park, CA: Sage, pp. 119–49.

Fleetwood, S. and Hesketh, A. (2006) 'Prediction in social science: the case of research on the human resource management-organizational performance link', *Journal of Critical Realism*, 5(2): 228–50.

Foster, K., McAllister, M. and O'Brien, L. (2006) 'Extending the boundaries: autoethnography as an emergent method in mental health nursing research', *International Journal of Mental Health Nursing*, 15: 44–53.

Gabriel, Y. (2000) *Storytelling in Organizations*, London: Oxford.

Goodall, H.L. (2004) 'Narrative ethnography as applied communication research', *Journal of Applied Communication Research*, 32(3): 185–94.

Grant, D., Hardy, C., Oswick, C. and Putnam, L. (eds) (2004) *The Sage Handbook of Organizational Discourse*, London: Sage.

Gubrium, J.F. and Holstein, J.A. (1997) 'Emotionalism', in J.F. Gubrium and J.A. Holstein (eds) *The New Language of Qualitative Method*, New York: Oxford University Press.

Hayano, D.M. (1979) 'Auto-ethnography: paradigms, problems, and prospects', *Human Organization*, 38: 113–120.

Holt, N. (2003) 'Representation, legitimation, and autoethnography: an autoethnographic writing story', *International Journal of Qualitative Methods*, 2: 1–22.

Humphreys, M. (2005) 'Getting personal: reflexivity and autoethnographic vignettes', *Qualitative Inquiry*, 11(6): 840–60.

Humphreys, M. (2006) 'Teaching qualitative research methods: I'm beginning to see the light', *Qualitative Research in Organizations and Management: An International Journal*, 1(3): 173–88.

Humphreys, M., Brown, A.D. and Hatch, M.J. (2003) 'Is Ethnography Jazz?', *Organization*, 10(1): 5–31.

Jackson, M. (1989) *Paths Towards a Clearing: Radical Empiricism and Ethnographic Inquiry*, Bloomington IN: Indiana University Press.

Jago, B.J. (2002) 'Chronicling an academic depression', *Journal of Contemporary Ethnography*, 13(6): 729–57.

Jovanovic, S. (2003) 'Difficult conversations as moral imperative: negotiating ethnic identities during war', *Communication Quarterly*, 51(1): 57–72.

Keefe, K.C. (2006) 'Degrees of separation: an ourstory about working-class and poverty-class academic identity', *Qualitative Inquiry* journal, 12(6): 1180–97.

Kempster, S. (2006) 'Leadership learning through lived experience', *Journal of Management & Organization*, 12(1): 4–22.

Kleinman, S. and Copp, M.A. (1993) *Emotions and Fieldwork*, Newbury Park, CA: Sage.

Lee, R.M. (1995) *Dangerous Fieldwork*, Newbury Park, CA: Sage.

Lejeune, P. (1989) *On Autobiography*, Minneapolis, MN: University of Minnesota Press

Lewis, D.K. (1973) 'Anthropology and colonialism', *Current Anthropology*, 14(5): 581–602.

Linstead, S. and Höpfl, H. (eds) (2000) *The Aesthetics of Organization*, London: Sage.

Malinowski, B. (1922) *Argonauts of the Western Pacific*, London: Routledge.

Mitroff, I. and Kilmann, R. (1975) 'Stories managers tell: a new tool for organizational problem solving', *Management Review*, 67(7): 18–28.

Morse, J. (2002) 'Writing my own experience', *Qualitative Health Research*, 12(9):1159–60.

Neuman, W.L. (2000) *Social Research Methods: Qualitative and Quantitative Approaches* (fourth edn.), Needham Heights, MA: Allyn and Bacon.

Neyland, D. (2008) *Organizational Ethnography*, London: Sage.

Olson, L.N. (2004) 'The role of voice in the (re)construction of a battered woman's identity: an autoethnography of one woman's experience of abuse', *Women's Studies in Communication*, 27(1): 1–33.

Oswick, C., Keenoy, T. and Grant, D. (2002) 'Metaphors and analogical reasoning in organization theory: beyond orthodoxy', *Academy of Management Review*, 27(2): 294–303.

Parry, K.W. (2008) 'Viewing the leadership narrative through alternate lenses: an autoethnographic investigation', *Management Revue: The International Review of Management Studies*, 19(2): 126–47.

Rambo, C. (2005) 'Impressions of grandmother: an autoethnographic portrait', *Journal of Contemporary Ethnography*, 34(5): 561–86.

Reed-Danahay, D.E. (1997) *Auto/Ethnography: Rewriting the self and the social*, Oxford: Berg.

Rhodes, C. (2001) *Writing Organization: (Re)presentation and Control in Narratives at Work*, Advances in Organization Studies 7, Amsterdam/Philadelphia: John Benjamins Publishing Company.

Riad, S. (2007) 'Under the desk: on becoming a mother in the workplace', *Culture & Organization*, 13(3): 205–22.

Richardson, L. (2000) 'New writing practices in qualitative research', *Sociology of Sport Journal*, 17: 5–20.

Rose, D. (1990) *Living the Ethnographic Life*, Newbury Park, CA: Sage.

Schein, E.H. (2006) 'From brainwashing to organizational therapy: a conceptual and empirical journey in search of 'systemic' health and a general model of change dynamics. a drama in five sets', *Organization Studies*, 27(2): 287–301.

Sparkes, A.C. (2000) 'Autoethnography and narratives of self: reflections on criteria in action', *Sociology of Sport Journal*, 17: 21–43.

Van Maanen, J. (1979) 'The fact of fiction in organizational ethnography', *Administrative Science Quarterly*, 24(4): 539–50.

Van Maanen, J. (1995) 'Style as theory', *Organizational Science*, 6:133–43.

Van Maanen, M. (1990) *Researching Lived Experience: Human Science for an Action Sensitive Pedagogy*, Ontario, Canada: The University of Western Ontario Press.

Vickers, M. (2007) 'Autoethnography as sensemaking: a story of bullying', *Culture & Organization*, 13(3): 223–37.

Vidich, A.J. and Lyman, S.M. (2000) 'Qualitative methods: their history in sociology and anthropology', in N.K. Denzin and Y.S. Lincoln (eds), *Handbook of Qualitative Research* (second edn.), Thousand Oaks, CA: Sage, pp.37–84.

Watson, T.J. (1994) *In Search of Management: Culture, Chaos and Control in Managerial Work*, London, Routledge.

Watson, T.J. (2000) 'Ethnographic fiction science: making sense of managerial work and organisational research processes with Caroline and Terry', *Organization*, 7(3): 31–38.

Werner, O. and Shoepfle, G.M. (1987) 'Systematic fieldwork: foundations of ethnography and interviewing', Newbury Park: Sage Publications.

Yang M. M. (1972) 'How *a chinese village* was written', in S. Kimball and J. Watson (eds), *Crossing Cultural Boundaries: The Anthropological Experience*, San Francisco: Chandler, pp 63–73.

Yarborough, J.P. and Lowe, K.B. (2007) 'Unlocking foreclosed beliefs: an autoethnographic study about a family business leadership dilemma', *Culture & Organization*, 13(3): 239–49.

PART V

Conclusion: The Future of Organizational Research

41

The Present and Futures of Organizational Research

Alan Bryman and David A. Buchanan

INNOVATION AND ITS ENEMIES

As argued in Chapter 1, the field of organizational research methods has been extraordinarily inventive with respect to the development of new ways to capture data. Novice researchers, and those who teach research methods, now have ground to cover that extends well beyond the conduct of interviews and the design of survey questionnaires. Continuing innovation can be interpreted as a sign of a healthy field (e.g., Broussine, 2008; Fielding et al., 2008). One possible future, therefore, concerns the development of further fresh insights based on increasingly creative combinations of traditional and novel research methods.

That optimistic view is under attack from at least three directions, concerning the overarching regulatory context of research, increasing ethical scrutiny, and (perhaps paradoxically) the development of an evidence-based management movement.

The regulatory context

The concept of academic freedom, particularly with regard to the issue of who frames the research agenda, has been diluted significantly by the 'research assessment' process and its attendant priorities, at least in Britain. The 'pursuit of knowledge' as the answer to questions concerning 'the role of research' today sounds quaint, as priorities have shifted to issues of journal rankings, impact factors, publications grade point averages, citations, research income generation, and departmental profile – all of which contribute to personal and institutional reputations and funding. Research that does not contribute to those metrics, which in turn drive funding, is less likely to be supported or undertaken. Surely, publications in top-ranking journals are still contributing to knowledge. That may be the case, but researchers are pushed to publish results more rapidly, rather than to delay while ideas develop. Moreover, publications that appeared prior to the start date of the current window of assessment are not merely devalued; they have become valueless in the contemporary research economy. Consequently, to the extent that innovative and creative research implies higher risks with regard to research funding and publication, then innovation and creativity are likely to be discouraged.

Ethical scrutiny

This century has witnessed the growing power in America of Institutional Review Boards (IRBs), and in Britain (particularly in healthcare, but applying to organization studies) of Local and Multi-centre Research Ethics Committees (LRECs and MRECs; see Emma Bell and Edward Wray-Bliss, Chapter 5). These boards and committees tend to be populated with members for whom 'research' implies a positivist biomedical model involving double-blind randomized control trials (RCTs), which are of necessity designed with detailed precision before they begin. On the grounds that a poorly designed study is by definition unethical, these bodies routinely extend their reach beyond the traditional themes of informed consent and confidentiality into aspects of research method. They can be particularly critical of studies that rely on constructivist ontology and qualitative methods (with both of which they are unlikely to be familiar), and where the research design incorporates a degree of flexibility, which of course means that methods cannot be prespecified, but will be adapted as the researchers' understanding of the organizational context and the data being gathered develop during the project. As ethical approval is a precondition of funding (and, for some journals, a prerequisite for publication), researchers are encouraged to adopt traditional, familiar, 'safe' methods when designing studies, and to avoid using perspectives and techniques that are more likely to be rejected on 'ethical' grounds.

Evidence-based management

Faced with perennial complaints concerning the lack of practical relevance of research output in organization and management studies, the development of an evidence-based management movement, drawing from experience with evidence-based medicine, appears at last to address those concerns (Pfeffer and Sutton, 2006). Following extensive commentary in the American *Academy of Management Journal*, and other sources, The British Academy of Management in 2008 launched its annual conference with the strapline, 'The Academy Goes Relevant' (as though its members never were), adding that, 'relevance to practice is now being taken seriously by government and research councils', highlighting the need for research to meet the 'double hurdle of rigour and relevance' (conference flyer). However, as Mark Learmonth observes (Chapter 6), evidence-based management can be seen as an academic hoax perpetrated in the interests of securing research funding, and studies that fail in their aims and methods to promise directly to inform practice are less likely to find support. The range of organizational problems that are amenable, as in aspects of medicine, to exploration and understanding using a positivist ontology and variance-based theoretical perspective is limited (see Ann Langley, Chapter 24), and such an approach encourages the use of conventional research designs and methods. We will consider shortly some further complications in this domain, concerning the social role of research, the nature of 'evidence', and how management in any sense is an activity that can be 'based' on the findings of organizational research.

While one reading of recent trends predicts an innovative future for organizational research methods, the mutually reinforcing implications of institutional regulation, ethical scrutiny, and evidence-based management suggest instead a retreat to tradition, and the suspicion if not rejection of new (i.e., perceived risky) methods. 'Innovation' in organizational research methods may become confined to lone, small-scale, unfunded, 'maverick' projects, which struggle to secure 'high value' publications.

THE BALKANIZATION OF ORGANIZATIONAL RESEARCH

Another contemporary feature concerns what might be described as the Balkanization of organizational research methods. The field appears to have fragmented, geographically, epistemologically, and methodologically, into communities which scarcely recognize or cite each others' work. Stanley Deetz (Chapter 2) addresses the multiparadigmatic nature of our field, observing that while researchers borrow each others' orientations and preferences, we are not all multilingual, and that good quality research conducted with a single frame remains valuable. Similarly, Antonio Strati (Chapter 14) notes the coexistence of a variety of approaches to the aesthetic understanding of organizational life. Dvora Yanow and Sierk Ybema (Chapter 3) point to a deep and enduring transatlantic divide between (broadly) positivist America and constructivist Europe, arguing that the latter (unlike the former) can mostly speak both 'languages'. In his research on quality criteria among qualitative researchers, Pratt (2008: 495) found that many of his respondents felt that there are differences between North American and European management journals. In particular, it was felt that European journals place less emphasis on encouraging qualitative researchers to conform to 'more positivistic standards' when publishing their work. Similarly, Savall et al. (2008: 536) propose that their content analysis of referees' reviews of qualitative research articles submitted to the European management journal *Sciences de Gestion-Management Sciences-Ciencias de Gestión*, most likely revealed a different pattern of findings from those that would be arrived at in a North American journal, because qualitative research is 'probably better established and more widespread than in the United States'. Deetz also refers to the nonreflexive style of neopositivist researchers, in contrast with their interpretive and critical colleagues. The 'paradigm wars' of the 1970s and 1980s at least required researchers in different trenches to engage with and to speak to each other (Bryman, 2008). That dialogue appears today to be much more muted. As Yanow and Ybema observe, this has perhaps become a 'cold war' with little energy or dynamism.

Collating and editing this volume, we have been struck repeatedly by reviewers' comments concerning the absence of acknowledgement in individual chapters to relevant work in a particular subject area, carried out in another (usually the reviewer's) country, from another perspective. Even an acrimonious exchange implies that one takes the work of others seriously enough to be worth reading, understanding, and criticizing. Simply ignoring the work of others who are ostensibly working in the same field sends other signals. To the extent that we have here different researchers working on different kinds of organizational problems from appropriately differentiated perspectives, such insularity may not be problematic. However, to the extent that studying issues from multiple perspectives can generate greater enlightenment than single approaches alone can achieve and that dialogue around the strengths and limitations of each others' perspectives can benefit all, regardless of their orientation, the Balkanization of the field may cause widespread damage. The dangers of a lack of appreciation of work in different areas are illustrated in the comments of Paul Spector and Michael Brannick on common method variance (Chapter 20). They show that the impact of common method variance, which is supposed to undermine studies that demonstrate relationships between variables that derive from the same questionnaire instrument, can be and often is exaggerated. They argue that the presence of measurement biases are likely to be more damaging than common method variance. However, it is widely assumed that common method variance is damaging and that it casts doubt on many questionnaire-based studies (Bryman, 1989). The commentary by Spector and Brannick thus points to the need to be fully conversant with the methodological issues thrown up by a wide variety of traditions and not to Balkanize research approaches.

A further element is that Balkanization can reveal itself in a lack of or insufficient attention to cultural difference at the national level. This can be seen in the discussion by Pushkala Prasad and Anshuman Prasad on organizational culture (Chapter 8). They argue that researchers have paid insufficient attention to cultural difference, and that in particular they have been slow to develop research approaches that capture or reflect globalization. It is for this reason that they argue strenuously for multi-sited ethnographies of organizational culture that are capable of capturing global cultural flows.

CAUSALITY AND ORGANIZATIONAL PHENOMENA

Continuing the theme of Balkanization, organizational researchers differ markedly in their approaches to understanding causality and disagree, also as to whether the search for causality is indeed a significant research goal in the first place. Qualitative researchers, for example, often seek to understand meaning, interpretations, power inequalities, polyphony, and silenced voices and are not necessarily concerned with causality at all. Eugene Stone-Romero (Chapter 18) takes a traditional and uncompromising positivist stance, which regards rigorous experimental design as the only adequate model of proof of causal relationships. This means that for researchers like Stone-Romero, it is unwarranted to draw definitive causal conclusions from something like a cross-sectional design. When a study is not truly experimental, the most that can be done is to infer causality, something that experimentalists see as potentially misleading. Thus, when Pushkala Prasad and Anshuman Prasad (Chapter 8) ask whether organizational culture should be operationalized as either an independent or a dependent variable, it is likely that Stone-Romero would doubt the legitimacy of viewing culture in these terms as they imply a causal attribution. In areas like the study of job satisfaction, as Alannah Rafferty and Mark Griffin (Chapter 12) suggest, cross-sectional, quasi-experimental, and experimental designs coexist, though the last of the three occurs least frequently. Roy Suddaby and Royston Greenwood (Chapter 11) note this tendency to explore causality in positivist terms in relation to institutional analyses, observing that 'multivariate analyses of institutional change *infer* the causality between dependent and independent variables' (their emphasis). In contrast, Ann Langley (Chapter 24) argues that synchronic variance theories of the

kind which Stone-Romero elevates (exploring covariance between dependent and independent variables) are inadequate for explaining dynamic organizational phenomena, and that diachronic process theories (focusing on the flow and combination of events over time) are necessary instead. As Suddaby and Greenwood observe, processual perspectives are also a feature of many, if not most, historical accounts of institutional and organizational change. Stewart Clegg (Chapter 9) further argues for an understanding of the operation of power that entails an appreciation of how it is constituted over time in our organizations and its contextual bases.

That distinction between variance and process theory (not necessarily wholly aligned with positivist and constructivist, quantitative and qualitative) does not capture the range of explanatory perspectives currently in use and/or under construction. Robert David and Alex Bitektine (Chapter 10) observe how institutional theory has flexed from explaining stability to explaining change, a theme developed further by Roy Suddaby and Royston Greenwood (Chapter 11). Mike Reed (Chapter 25) describes how a critical realist perspective bases generative causal explanations of social and organizational phenomena on interactions between the empirical, the actual, and the real. Stephen Ackroyd (Chapter 31), focusing on methods appropriate to realist research, also contrasts the logic of explanation in deductive, inductive, retroductive, and abductive perspectives.

Although they may often be presented and discussed in such terms, these divisions are not mere technical disagreements. They have deep ontological, epistemological, and ideological foundations. With whose causality, for instance, should researchers be primarily concerned in organizational research? Mats Alvesson and Karen Ashcraft (Chapter 4) note that critical management studies adopts the position of the weak and powerless in organizational settings; David Denyer and David Tranfield (Chapter 39) describe the development of the technique of systematic review, one aim of which is to inform management practice more effectively. This is perhaps another set of issues where the current 'cold war' in organization studies is not being fought as the respective brigades simply do not recognize each other's existence.

Howard Becker (1967) once famously asked sociologists 'whose side are we on?' Becker argued that, in areas like the sociology of deviance, sociologists are often in a position in which they are examining groups in hierarchical relationships, and that in the process of studying them, researchers feel compelled to take sides. Very often, Becker argued, it is the 'underdog' in the relationship whose perspective is taken. Becker's position did not go uncriticized (Gouldner, 1968), but there is an interesting parallel here with organizational research; while critical management studies researchers often take the perspective of the weak and powerless in organizations, advocates of evidence-based management invite the researcher to improve management decision-making. So, whose side are we on? Must we take sides? Should we take sides? These considerations arise in several chapters here; the development of feminist organization studies (Marta Calás and Linda Smircich, Chapter 15); collaborative research designs (Jean-Louis Denis and Pascal Lehoux, Chapter 21), ensuring that we do not neglect less visible groups and activities (Colin Williams and Monder Ram, Chapter 38) and the relevance of organizational research to practice (Mark Learmonth, Chapter 6). At a time when there is a growing interest in the relevance of management and organizational research (Rynes et al., 2001; Rynes, 2007), these issues have a particular resonance, which is likely to be sustained for some time. This issue of the relevance of management and organizational research resurfaces in the next section. However, the issue of partisanship affects the questions which are researched, the mode in which explanations are cast, the audiences to which outputs are addressed, and the framing of resultant advice or guidelines for action.

The issue of sides surfaces in relation to the Positive Organizational Scholarship (POS) approach that has gained in popularity in recent years. POS elevates 'virtuousness'

among organizations and their members as a positive force that provides values that can act as anchors in turbulent times. POS promotes the benefits of ethical behaviour, but also of positive attitudes and actions. However, virtuousness is valued not solely because of its intrinsic qualities, but also because it has positive outcomes for organizations as well as their members. As one of the movement's advocates observes, 'Virtuousness pays dividends. Doing good helps organizations to do well' (Cameron, 2006: 321). In this perspective, therefore, we do not have to take sides; what is good for members of organizations is good for their organizations too. However, we might ask what we should infer if such a happy positive relationship between virtuousness and organizational performance had *not* materialized, if in fact virtuousness was *negatively* associated with organizational performance. Organizational scholars might want to promote virtuousness, because it is regarded as an ethical imperative, but writing from a managerial perspective they may be inclined to adopt the position of a chief executive, quoted by Cameron (2006: 320); 'Virtuousness may be fine as a discussion topic at a late night coffee bar, but it's too soft and syrupy to be taken seriously in my world of competitive positioning, customer demands, and shareholder performance pressure'. In this context, taking sides would be difficult to avoid, and would also raise questions about the relevance of organizational research – relevance for whom? Such considerations point to the ideologically charged nature of much organizational research and the need to be sensitive to this dimension of our work.

It may thus be possible to argue that innovations in organizational research methods have been paralleled by innovations in modes of explanation for organizational phenomena. Disputes about causality, however, have implications beyond the research community. The potential end-users of organizational research are likely to be less concerned with academic disputes over logics of explanation, and more interested in 'what works'. Lay perceptions of cause and effect are still more likely to be closest to a positivist, variance, biomedical model (take pill and cure headache). Approaches to causality rooted in other perspectives are difficult to explain to lay audiences, who, not surprisingly, find these difficult to understand, and thus confusing. If interpretivists, positivists, institutional theorists, discourse analysts, critical management theorists, process theorists, and critical realists have difficulty in sharing these issues with each other, what chance does the lay reader have?

ORGANIZATIONAL RESEARCH INTO PRACTICE?

What is the role of organizational research? The many answers to this simple question range from developing understanding, through contributions to organization and management practice, to social and organizational reform, along with the continued employment and entertainment of relevant sections of the academic community, and the reputation and funding of their employing institutions. Many organizational researchers have no desire to see practical application of their work, and certainly not in the service of managers to exploit and manipulate less powerful organizational members. However, as suggested earlier, the evidence-based management movement has brought these issues onto centre stage, with potentially significant consequences for the organizational research themes and questions that are pursued, the methods through which these are addressed, and for the funding of such studies in comparison with those which promise no (or more distant) links to practice.

The concept of a 'link to practice' from organizational research appears now to have three broad strands. One lies with the long-established tradition of action research, which has developed into a range of collaborative designs, as Jean-Louis Denis and Pascale Lehoux explain (Chapter 21). The aim of recruiting participants as co-researchers is to increase the probability that research will deliver both theoretical and practically

useful outcomes, and Denis and Lehoux emphasize the 'transformative potential' of collaborative designs in organizational settings. A second strand lies, perhaps paradoxically, with critical management studies (CMS; Mats Alvesson and Karen Ashcraft, Chapter 4), which seeks to expose power inequalities and management exploitation, and to undermine what are regarded as damaging and unacceptable aspects of contemporary organizational practice. The feminist organization studies explored by Marta Calás and Linda Smircich (Chapter 15) adopt a similar critical agenda concerning the transformation of unequal gender and power relations, putting social justice ahead of 'the business case'. CMS and feminist perspectives share a concern with the 'transformative redefinition' of current arrangements, in other words helping to establish and to develop practical and positive agendas for change. Similarly, in the hands of Carl Rhodes and Alison Pullen (Chapter 34), narrative analysis becomes a lens through which gendered relations in organizations may be critically appraised. The dialectical approach referred to by Roy Suddaby and Royston Greenwood (Chapter 11) is also more or less synonymous with CMS. Nelson Phillips and MariaLaura Di Domenico (Chapter 32) show how an approach to discourse analysis exhibits an 'explicit interest in the dynamics of power and ideology', and as such represents a critical dimension and provides one of a number of methodological foundations for CMS.

A third strand lies with the more recent emergence of evidence-based management (ebm; Mark Learmonth, Chapter 6) and the related technique of systematic review (which has also developed from a positivist-oriented biomedical model; David Denyer and David Tranfield, Chapter 39). Effectively debunking ebm, Learmonth's discussion concentrates on supply-side considerations (how should I, as researcher, function in this new environment?) and largely overlooks the demand side (how should I, as manager, use the outputs of organizational research?). He exposes the simplistic, positivistic, decontextualized, managerially-oriented, and ideologically-biased characteristics of ebm, which from his standpoint adopts out-dated, narrow, and unrealistic concepts of 'evidence', overlooks the paradoxical nature of 'management', and simplifies the bases of management decisions and actions, which are far from dependent on 'evidence' (however defined) on its own. Denyer and Tranfield recognize the multifaceted nature of manage-ment decisions, suggesting that terms such as 'evidence-informed' and 'evidence-aware' are more appropriate than 'evidence-based'.

The tragedy, therefore, is that ebm, in its cur-rent guise, may actually *understate* the poten-tial contributions of organizational research to practice, which can be achieved through:

- Developing fresh conceptualizations and frame-works
- Suggesting transformative redefinitions of current arrangements
- Confronting and correcting social and organiza-tional injustices
- Encouraging creative new ways to see and to understand
- Highlighting issues, events, and processes that are particularly significant
- Surfacing issues that might otherwise remain concealed
- Broadcasting voices that might otherwise remain silenced
- Revealing the importance of process, context, and contingency
- Developing narrative understanding to replace misleading variance theories
- Providing practical exemplars, positive and negative, as sources of ideas
- Demonstrating the potential consequences of particular lines of action
- Illustrating the value of different ways of knowing and thinking

This list is indicative, not definitive. If funded and published research were to be constrained to organization and management problems that can be expressed in variance terms, and where findings can be translated into prescriptions in the form, 'take pill, cure headache', then organizational research would be substantially impoverished. That is

surely one future for this field to which few readers of this volume would subscribe.

THE NATURE AND ROLE OF THE CASE STUDY

The case study has long been a popular research design in organizational research (Yin, 2003). However, its popularity waned in the 1960s and 1970s as studies based on cross-sectional designs using variable analysis (Blumer, 1956), exemplified by the Aston Studies (Pugh and Hickson, 1976; Pugh and Hinings, 1976; Pugh and Payne, 1977), gained in popularity. By then, former advocates of the case study were making the case for studying multiple organizations (Blau, 1965). One factor behind the decline in the status of case studies was the perceived problem that, while samples of organizations could yield generalizable findings (in the statistical sense), a case study could not, because it would be unlikely that the researcher could find a representative organization.

However, while the case study declined in popularity, it did not disappear from the research scene altogether, and has staged something of a comeback in recent years. One of the chief reasons for its resurgence is the growing recognition of the advantages of multiple case study designs. Eisenhardt (1989) developed a compelling argument for the use of such designs, highlighting their advantages with respect to the generation of theory. The rationale for the use of multiple case studies in terms of theory development in large part is underpinned by grounded theory, an approach to qualitative data analysis (see Christina Goulding, Chapter 22). Louise Fitzgerald and Sue Dopson (Chapter 27) argue strongly for multiple case studies (which they call comparative case studies) arguing that one of the main advantages is the 'flexibility and scope in the design of research'. In other words, in addition to the generation of theory, multiple case studies offer an approach that can be changed in the course of fieldwork and allow the researcher to explore the pervasiveness of the phenomena of interest. Not everyone agrees. Eisenhardt (1989) was criticized in a subsequent issue of the *Academy of Management Review*, where it was suggested that the problem with her argument was that it led to the neglect of context and resulted in an excessive emphasis on what was comparable between cases rather than what is unique to them (Dyer and Wilkins, 1991). This concern is evident in Haridimos Tsoukas's argument (Chapter 17), which emphasizes the value of the particular and the unique, as opportunities for broadening our theoretical conceptualizations of the general through analytical refinement or heuristic generalization.

To some, it may be important not to overstate the distinction between single cases and multiple case study research. Williams (2000) argues that case study researchers frequently engage in *moderatum generalizations*, that is, inferences drawn about the wider relevance or applicability of findings by relating them to research done by others on similar or comparable cases. This suggests that case study researchers are at least able to engage in limited generalizations. However, given that it implies that single case study researchers draw attention to links between their own and others' findings, the approach has affinities with doing multiple case study research, as much as the study of a single instance. This point is made very cogently by Haridimos Tsoukas (Chapter 17) in his discussion of 'family resemblances' between cases and the importance these have for theory development.

Further issues relate to just what a case is, and to what a case study is. Fitzgerald and Dopson (Chapter 27) acknowledge this when they note the lack of consensus over whether the case study is a research method or a research design. The case study is often referred to as a research method but some writers, such as Bryman and Bell (2007), prefer to treat it as a research design equivalent to experiments and cross-sectional designs as distinctive structures within which data are collected to answer research questions. This issue of the nature of the case study was also evident when one of our reviewers noted that too often social scientists 'mix up

"case studies" with "field studies", and "sites" with "cases"'. The presence of terminological ambiguities is by no means uncommon in discussions of research methods, but the case study seems to be particularly prone to uncertainties about its nature and purposes. Given the tradition of case-study research in organization studies, this is surprising and may also point to an area of methodological discussion requiring further development. In conversation analysis, as David Greatbatch (Chapter 28) shows, the case may be a very short sequence of language in use subjected to fine-grained analysis in order to reveal an underlying social organization.

A further issue concerns the role of theory in relation to case study research. There is a tendency for the case study to be associated with theory generation, as previously noted. This is certainly the prevalent notion of its role in relation to qualitative research and grounded theory, as Goulding (Chapter 22) suggests. However, Suddaby and Greenwood (Chapter 11) point to a further relationship between the case study and theory, drawing attention to Burawoy's (1998) account of the 'extended case method'. They see this design as distinctive, because its role is not to generate theory, as in the grounded theory approach, but to extend existing theories. Some commentators take this argument further, observing that single cases can be used to test theory (Phillips, 1995; Rueschemeyer, 2003), as John Hassard and David Buchanan (Chapter 36) argue with regard to the potential contributions of feature films viewed as case studies.

The main contrast that is often made between case studies and surveys is that the latter are more likely to be based on a 'representative sample', thus (ostensibly) permitting more confident generalizations to a wider population. However, in organization studies, even a large sample may not be 'representative' as organizations differ in so many ways, internal and contextual, for which it is difficult to control unless the sample size is extremely large indeed. As Glenn Carroll, Mi Feng, Gaël Le Mens and David McKendrick (Chapter 13) observe, in studying population ecology, the strategy of focusing on organizations that occupy a similar niche in terms of products or services, and which therefore face similar environments, reduces the need for such elaborate controls. However, that research design is not always available, or appropriate, depending on the topic of investigation. The point is that large samples do not necessarily overcome 'the problem' with single cases or small-N studies, and this criticism of surveys and sampling can be found both within and outside the positivist perspective.

Case studies thus appear to have multiple applications in organizational research with regard to data collection, conceptual insight, theory building, and theory testing, not confined to particular topics or questions. Whether a case study is defined as a research design or a research method, it appears to be a matter of personal preference or style rather than technical debate. Moreover, as Fitzgerald and Dopson observe, this is a flexible and valuable mode of research which is probably subject to further creative development. Contrary to the view expressed recently by Eisenhardt and Graebner (2007), case studies, at least in the hands of some researchers, are very much in the 'mainstream' of organizational research methods.

MIXED METHODS AND EPISTEMOLOGIES

One of the most enduring debates about research methods is the degree to which they are suffused with epistemological and ontological assumptions. Related to this is the fact that the protagonists in the 'paradigm wars' were unsympathetic to the notion that methods associated with quantitative and qualitative research could be mixed. Their reservations were mainly to do with the suggestion that, because quantitative and qualitative methods pertained to divergent epistemological assumptions, they were inevitably incompatible. As Alan Bryman notes (Chapter 30), this viewpoint has given way to pragmatism as the basis for discussing the possibility of mixing methods. Indeed,

mixed methods research has to a significant degree become a distinctive approach in its own right, viewed as sitting alongside quantitative and qualitative research. The fact that the paradigm wars are no longer as fiercely fought as they have been should not be taken to imply that the epistemological issues are somehow seen as resolved. As Stanley Deetz (Chapter 2) and Dvora Yanow and Sierk Ybema (Chapter 3) observe, at the paradigm level, there are still intractable epistemological issues that coexist with the lessening of hostilities between quantitative and qualitative research. Roy Suddaby and Royston Greenwood (Chapter 11) also note the continuing significance, and to a certain extent the continuing intractability, of epistemological issues when they advocate a mixed methods approach, while simultaneously giving their 'apologies to those who advocate hard epistemological boundaries between paradigms'.

A further issue is the nature of the role that the quantitative and the qualitative components of a mixed methods investigation should play in relation to each other. Several writers draw attention to the restrictive influence of journals for both qualitative and mixed methods researchers. For example, Suddaby and Greenwood (Chapter 11) note that, 'it is highly unusual for a management journal to publish an article that employs multiple or mixed methods. Mixing qualitative and quantitative elements in a single manuscript would violate highly institutionalized norms of presentation'. They also refer to the 'pragmatic problems of presenting complex methodologies in the restrictive format of a journal article'. Given such restrictive attitudes among journal editors and reviewers, there is always the risk that the typically favoured quantitative component of a mixed methods project is emphasized and the role of the qualitative component ends up being suppressed (Sutton, 1997). It is all too easy for the qualitative component of a mixed methods study to end up in what Bryman calls (Chapter 30) the 'handmaiden' role. This typically takes the form of the qualitative component acting as a source of research questions or providing illustrative material to tack onto the bare bones of the quantitative findings. The chief problem with such a role is that it does not allow the true strengths of qualitative findings to emerge. It may also hamper the extent to which mixed methods researchers integrate their quantitative and qualitative findings (Bryman, 2007).

Equally, there are areas where a mixed methods approach is barely in evidence. Mats Alvesson and Karen Lee Ashcraft (Chapter 4) note that quantitative research (and by implication mixed methods research) is rare in critical management studies. Indeed, they encourage practitioners of the approach to consider quantitative studies, provided they are mindful of the wider political and ethical allegiances of the perspective. By contrast, one of the insights from job satisfaction research offered by Alannah Rafferty and Mark Griffin (Chapter 12) is that this is an area where qualitative methods have made very little impact, in spite of the widespread use of such methods in the study of work and jobs (Smith, 2001). The study of population ecology (Glenn Carroll, Mi Feng, Gaël Le Mens and David McKendrick, Chapter 13) is more or less exclusively driven by quantitative research. It is interesting to compare this situation with the institutional approach, which is sometimes viewed as a competing perspective (Oliver, 1991). As Robert David and Alex Bitektine (Chapter 10) and Roy Suddaby and Royston Greenwood (Chapter 11) show, while researchers working within this tradition have tended to use quantitative research, there is a growing use of qualitative and mixed methods research. And of course, as Suddaby and Greenwood note, early institutional research made considerable use of qualitative case studies (Selznick, 1949). Michael Mumford, Tamara Friedrich, Jay Caughron, and Alison Antes (Chapter 7) characterize leadership research as a field in which a variety of different research approaches coexist and indeed in which mixed methods studies are coming increasingly to the fore.

It should be remembered that, while the idea of mixing methods is nowadays often associated almost exclusively with the mixing of quantitative and qualitative research, methods of different kinds may be, and frequently are, mixed. Colin Williams and Monder Ram (Chapter 38) discuss how combinations of direct and indirect methods for studying 'off the books' work have become more commonplace. Suddaby and Greenwood (Chapter 11) also draw attention to the mixing of different approaches within institutional analyses of organizations. In their overview, they identify studies that combine historical analysis with either a quantitative approach using multivariate analysis or an interpretive case study. Moreover, they argue that the multilevel nature of institutional research, which shifts between wider belief systems and individual interpretation, may actually require a mixed methods approach that combines quantitative and qualitative research components within an overall project. Bryman (Chapter 30) also observes that the nature of organizations and the kinds of issue that interest organizational researchers may also be especially suited to a mixed methods approach. Also, as Gary Alan Fine, Calvin Morrill and Sharmi Surianarain (Chapter 35) indicate, an approach to data collection like ethnography is almost inherently mixed method in style in that it invariably incorporates such activities as participant observation, interviewing, nonparticipant observation, and the examination of documents. Christina Goulding (Chapter 22) points out that the process of constant comparison that is a feature of grounded theory frequently includes an element of comparison of different kinds of data. Thus, what is and what is not mixed methods research is at least partially contested terrain, quite aside from its entanglements with epistemological and ontological issues and debates. It is also worth adding that the issue of the level of analysis is especially pronounced in cross-cultural research, as Mark Peterson (Chapter 19) observes. It is not surprising, therefore, that mixed methods research is beginning to make inroads into cross-cultural studies and indeed one of Bryman's 'exhibits' (Chapter 30) has a cross-cultural component to it.

WRITING

An issue arising in some chapters is how organizational research should be written up. While Golden-Biddle and Locke (2006) and Watson (2000) have given this issue some attention, albeit with a specific focus on qualitative research, it has not attracted much commentary. Suddaby and Greenwood (Chapter 10) note the restrictions that some academic journals present for mixed methods researchers. Catherine Cassell (Chapter 29) notes that qualitative researchers still have difficulty placing articles in the 'top' American journals. One route open to qualitative and mixed methods researchers is to write up research in a manner that it is likely to be acceptable to a traditional audience that is imbued with a positivist proclivity. In this context, it is interesting that Alvesson and Ashcraft (Chapter 4) draw attention to a writing issue when they note (with a sense of disappointment?) that critical management studies scholars 'continue to write in voices of decided analytic distance'. It may be that this tendency is at least in part a response to the preference of mainstream journal editors and reviewers for the 'scientific article' style in which most quantitative research is written.

Equally, however, Christina Goulding (Chapter 22) takes note of the criticisms that are often levelled at qualitative researchers using a grounded theory approach (for example, that it is not the presentation of raw data; Suddaby, 2006) to explore how grounded theory should be written up in a way that is more likely to be acceptable to a variety of readers. Nelson Phillips and MariaLaura Di Domenico (Chapter 32) note the challenges of writing up research based on discourse analysis because 'the standards of proof required to justify publication remain unclear'. However, they suggest that this problem may ease as more discourse studies are published and standards therefore become clearer.

Quality issues

These issues are to a significant extent intertwined with the assessment of quality in research. Here again, epistemological issues raise their collective heads, as quality criteria are saturated with epistemological assumptions. One of the key developments in recent commentary on research methods in organization and management, and in social research, is recognition of the need for different quality criteria for quantitative and qualitative research. Quantitative research has traditionally been judged according to the criteria of reliability and validity. We see this in the opening remark by Timothy Hinkin and Brooks Holtom (Chapter 26); 'the primary objective of organizational surveys is to obtain high-quality data that are reliable and valid'. It is becoming increasingly accepted that qualitative research should not be judged by the same criteria, although it is interesting that Pratt's (2008) research shows that qualitative researchers seeking to publish in top-tier North American management journals often feel that their papers are judged by inappropriate quantitative research criteria. However, there is a lack of agreement on which criteria should be applied to qualitative research, as Louise Fitzgerald and Sue Dopson (Chapter 27) observe (see also Bryman, 2006; Savall et al., 2008). As David Denyer and David Tranfield (Chapter 39) note, this lack of agreement poses particular problems for the systematic review process when a field of research includes both quantitative and qualitative research findings. One response to the lack of agreement over quality criteria for qualitative research has been to compile different criteria to form a compendium of quality benchmarks (Spencer et al., 2003). The quality criteria developed by Lincoln and Guba (1985) are probably the most commonly used, but their acceptance is by no means universal. Further, given the growing use of mixed methods research, it is likely that quality criteria will become significant in that respect too, going beyond the tentative steps that have been taken thus far (Bryman, 2006; Bryman et al., 2008; Sale and Brazil, 2004). Jean-Louis Denis and Pascale Lehoux (Chapter 20) suggest that, for collaborative research, further considerations will be involved in assessments of quality, such as participation and practical outcomes, as well as conventional criteria such as transparency. Ann Langley (Chapter 24) outlines strategies for strengthening the credibility and trustworthiness of process research, which is often predominantly qualitative.

Reflexivity

A further issue that rears its head in relation to writing, and which arises at various points in some chapters, is the significance of reflexivity. Mats Alvesson and Karen Ashcraft (Chapter 4) helpfully observe that, 'As a methodological construct, reflexivity references many things, such as examining the broader social and political context of knowledge production, interrogating the role of the researcher and the relation of researcher and "researched", challenging one's preferred perspective and language through deployment of alternative viewpoints and vocabularies, and so on'. As Alvesson and Ashcraft note, reflexivity is a particular concern in critical management studies, but this tradition does not hold a monopoly of reflexive stances. They then examine some of the dilemmas of reflexive practices. Samantha Warren (Chapter 33) notes that there has been a shift towards greater reflexivity in organizational research, and employs her own and the work of others using photo-elicitation as an illustration of the way in which research participants are encouraged to reflect on photographs that they have taken. Catherine Cassell (Chapter 29) explores reflexive practices in relation to different types of interview, noting that these are influenced by epistemological considerations. Ken Parry and Maree Boyle (Chapter 40) describe organizational autoethnography as hyper-reflexive, while Jean-Louis Denis and Pascale Lehoux (Chapter 21) view reflexivity in the form of learning from practice as an important consideration in collaborative research. The examination of such issues is clearly valuable and consistent with a greater awareness of the limitations of the notion of the researcher as neutral and detached observer. However, reflexivity remains a slippery construct, and attention in future is

likely to emphasize its diverse meanings and their respective implications, as Alvesson, Hardy and Harley (2008) have done. It is also worth noting that most of the discussion of reflexivity occurs in relation to qualitative research and there is a need for greater consideration of its significance in relation to quantitative research.

BLEAK OR BRIGHT: THE FUTURES OF ORGANIZATIONAL RESEARCH METHODS

Finally, it may be helpful, in the light of the contributions to this volume, to outline two scenarios for the future of our field. The reality, of course, is likely to lie on the continuum between these extremes, but this leaves open the question of emphasis with regard to the way in which the field responds to current pressures, demands, and opportunities. So that we can end on a positive note, let's explore first the negative scenario.

The future's bleak

As indicated earlier in this chapter, there are several pressures, encouraging in organizational research a methodological conservatism rooted in traditional positivist epistemology. This is reinforced, first, by a regulatory environment that legislates a narrow construct of 'research excellence', in which journals that publish work that is based on traditional positivist perspectives and methods are the most highly rated. Ethical scrutiny that is suspicious of unconventional research designs and methods (qualitative, responsive, collaborative, observation based, case study based, using visual methods and film, and small-n), where the details of the research process cannot be predetermined, further encourages the use of traditional and familiar approaches. A third and more recent factor concerns the rise of the evidence-based management movement, narrowing the research field to studies that are more amenable to variance-based (rather than processual) explanations, and that are of particular value to a management audience (potentially overlooking the interests of other organizational stakeholders).

This is a future in which qualitative methods and mixed methods are considered as aberrations, where 'innovation' in method is more likely to be considered 'eccentric', where reflexivity has no role in a neutral, objective scientific enterprise, and where 'non-conformist' modes of academic writing are not to be found in those top ranking journals. The cold warriors are still not communicating or debating with each other, and the current geographical epistemological schism (crudely, between the United States and most of the rest of the planet) persists and strengthens. Some contributors to this volume clearly regard paradigm plurality as a sign of dynamism, a symbol of a healthy field. Pfeffer (1993) thought otherwise, and it appears that the consensus that he advocated may now be driven by institutional forces beyond the direct control of the organizational research community.

The future's bright

In an alternative future, the field retains its multiparadigmatic character, methodological inventiveness continues, and the cold warriors engage with each other once again, in the interests of generating debate, ideas, discourse, and new lines of enquiry. The regulatory environment accepts a pluralist notion of 'excellence' in research, which is no longer dominated by any particular perspective, epistemology, geography, or select group of journals. A contingent model of research ethics (Bell and Wray-Bliss, Chapter 5) holds sway, and research ethics committees and institutional review boards open their membership to those with knowledge and expertise across a range of epistemologies and methods and how these are used in different research fields and subjects. The evidence-based management movement develops beyond its apparently narrow base to advocate a significantly more diversified, socially constructed, and ideologically coloured understanding of the nature of 'evidence' and the multiple ways in which evidence can inform practice in relation to the many users of, or stakeholders in, the findings of organizational research.

This is a future in which mixed and qualitative methods and further innovations are regarded as routine, with the 'balance of power' between qualitative and quantitative depending on the subject of the investigation, and not on a journal editor's preference. Reflexivity is an expectation, not an aberration, and creative modes of writing research sit comfortably alongside traditional styles of scientific communication. The paradigm wars resume, but are fought on different terrain; the engagement is not focused on 'winning', but on creative and mutually informative dialogue, overriding the parochial focus on domestic colleagues, recognizing and exploiting the global nature of the field and its research community.

Bleak or bright? Which of these futures for organization studies and research methods is the more desirable, and which in the light of current trends is the more likely?

REFERENCES

Alvesson, M., Hardy, C. and Harley, B. (2008) 'Reflecting on reflexivity: reflexive textual practices in organization and management theory', *Journal of Management Studies*, 45(3): 480–501.

Becker, H.S. (1967) 'Whose side are we on?', *Social Problems*, 14(3): 239–47.

Blau, P.M. (1965) 'The comparative study of organizations', *Industrial and Labor Relations Review*, 18(3): 323–38.

Blumer, H. (1956) 'Sociological analysis and the "variable"', *American Sociological Review*, 21(6): 683–90.

Broussine, M. (2008) *Creative Methods in Organizational Research*, London: Sage Publications.

Bryman, A. (1989) *Research Methods and Organization Studies*, London: Unwin Hyman.

Bryman, A. (2006) 'Paradigm peace and the implications for quality', *International Journal of Social Research Methodology*, 9(2): 111–26.

Bryman, A. (2007) 'Barriers to integrating quantitative and qualitative research', *Journal of Mixed Methods Research*, 1(1): 8–22.

Bryman, A. (2008) 'The end of the paradigm wars?', in Pertti Alasuutari, Leonard Bickman and Julia Brannen (eds), *The Sage Handbook of Social Research Methods*, London: Sage Publications, pp. 13–25.

Bryman, A. and Bell, E. (2007) *Business Research Methods*, (revised edition), Oxford: Oxford University Press.

Bryman, A., Becker, S. and Sempik, J. (2008) 'Quality criteria for quantitative, qualitative and mixed methods research: the view from social policy', *International Journal of Social Research Methodology*, 11.

Burawoy, M. (1998) 'The extended case method', *Sociological Theory*, 16: 4–33.

Cameron, K. (2006) 'Good or not bad: standards and ethics in managing change', *Academy of Management Learning and Education*, 5(3): 317–23.

Dyer, W.G. and Wilkins, A.L. (1991) 'Better stories, not better constructs, to generate a better theory: a rejoinder to Eisenhardt', *Academy of Management Review*, 16: 613–19.

Eisenhardt, K.M. (1989) 'Building theories from case study research', *Academy of Management Review*, 14(4): 532–50.

Eisenhardt, K.M. and Graebner, M.E. (2007) 'Theory building from cases: opportunities and challenges', *Academy of Management Journal*, 50(1): 25–32.

Fielding, N., Lee, R.M. and Blank, G. (eds) (2008) *The Sage Handbook of Online Research Methods*, London: Sage Publications.

Golden-Biddle, K. and Locke, K.D. (2006) *Composing Qualitative Research*, Thousand Oaks, CA: Sage Publications. (Second edn.)

Gouldner, A. (1968) 'The sociologist as partisan: sociology and the welfare state', *American Sociologist*, 3: 103–16.

Lincoln, Y.S. and Guba, E. (1985) *Naturalistic Inquiry*, Beverly Hills, CA: Sage Publications.

Oliver, C. (1991) 'Strategic responses to institutional processes', *Academy of Management Review*, 16: 145–79.

Pfeffer, J. (1993) 'Barriers to the advance of organizational science: paradigm development as a dependent variable', *Academy of Management Review*, 18(4): 599–620.

Pfeffer, J. and Sutton, R.I. (2006) *Hard Facts, Dangerous Half-Truths, and Total Nonsense: Profiting from Evidence-Based Management*, Boston, MA: Harvard Business School Press.

Phillips, N. (1995) 'Telling organizational tales: on the role of narrative fiction in the study of organization', *Organization Studies*, 16(4): 625–49.

Pratt, M.G. (2008) 'Fitting oval pegs into round holes: tensions in evaluating and publishing qualitative research in top-tier North American journals', *Organizational Research Methods*, 11(3): 481–509.

Pugh, D.S. and Hickson, D.J. (1976) *Organization Structure in its Context: The Aston Programme 1*, Farnborough: Gower.

Pugh, D.S. and Hinings, C.R. (1976) *Organizational Structure: Extensions and Replications, The Aston Programme II*, Farnborough: Gower.

Pugh, D.S. and Payne, R.L. (1977) *Organizational Structure in its Context: The Aston Programme III*, Farnborough: Gower.

Rueschemeyer, D. (2003) 'Can one or a few cases yield theoretical gains?', in James Mahoney and Dietrich Rueschemeyer (eds), *Comparative Historical Analysis in the Social Sciences*, Cambridge: Cambridge University Press, pp. 305–36.

Rynes, S.L. (2007) 'Let's create a tipping point: what academics and practitioners can do, alone and together', *Academy of Management Journal*, 50(5): 1046–54.

Rynes, S.L., Bartunek, J.M. and Daft, R.L. (2001) 'Across the great divide: knowledge creation and transfer between practitioners and academics', *Academy of Management Journal*, 44 (2): 340–55.

Sale, J.E.M. and Brazil, K. (2004) 'A strategy to identify critical appraisal criteria for primary mixed-methods studies', *Quality and Quantity*, 38: 351–65.

Savall, H., Zardet, V., Bonnet, M. and Péron, M. (2008) 'The emergence of implicit criteria actually used by reviewers of qualitative research articles: case of a European journal', *Organizational Research Methods*, 11(3): 510–40.

Selznick, P. (1949) *TVA and the Grass Roots*, Berkeley, CA: University of California Press.

Smith, V. (2001) 'Ethnographies of work and the work of ethnographers', in P. Atkinson, A. Coffey, S. Delamont, J. Lofland and L. Lofland (eds), *Handbook of Ethnography*, London: Sage, pp. 220–33.

Spencer, L., Ritchie, J., Lewis, J. and Dillon, L. (2003) *Quality in Qualitative Evaluation: A Framework for Assessing Research Evidence*, London: Government Chief Social Researcher's Office.

Suddaby, R. (2006) 'From the editors: what grounded theory is not,' *Academy of Management Journal*, 49(4): 633–42.

Sutton, R.I. (1997) 'The virtues of closet qualitative research', *Organization Science*, 8(1): 97–106.

Watson, T.J. (2000) 'Ethnographic fiction science: making sense of managerial work and organizational research processes with Caroline and Terry', *Organization*, 7(3): 489–510.

Williams, M. (2000) 'Interpretivism and generalization', *Sociology*, 34(2): 209–24.

Yin, R.K. (2003) *Case Study Research: Design and Methods*, Thousand Oaks, CA: Sage Publications. (third edn.)

Author Index

Subject Index

Figures in **Bold**, Tables in *italics*